Webster's Spanish-English Dictionary

Created in Cooperation with
the Editors of
MERRIAM-WEBSTER

A Division of Merriam-Webster, Incorporated
Springfield, Massachusetts

Federal Street Press is a trademark of
Federal Street Press,
a division of Merriam-Webster, Incorporated.

This 2008 edition published by
Federal Street Press,
A Division of Merriam-Webster, Incorporated
P.O. Box 281
Springfield, MA 01102

Federal Street Press books are available for bulk purchase for sales promotion and premium use. For details write the manager of special sales, Federal Street Press, P.O. Box 281, Springfield, MA 01102

ISBN 978-1-59695-040-5

Printed in the United States of America

08 09 10 11 12 5 4 3 2

Contents

Preface

This Spanish-English Dictionary is a concise reference to the core vocabulary of Spanish and English. Its 40,000 entries and over 50,000 translations provide up-to-date coverage of the basic vocabulary and idioms in both languages. In addition, the book includes many specifically Latin-American words and phrases.

IPA (International Phonetic Alphabet) pronunciations are given for all English words. Included as well are tables of irregular verbs in both languages and the most common Spanish and English abbreviations.

This book shares many details of presentation with larger Spanish-English Dictionaries, but for reasons of conciseness it also has a number of features uniquely its own. Users need to be familiar with the following major features of this dictionary.

Main entries follow one another in strict alphabetical order, without regard to intervening spaces or hyphens. The Spanish letter combinations *ch* and *ll* are alphabetized within the letters *C* and *L*; however, the Spanish letter *ñ* is alphabetized separately between *N* and *O*.

Homographs (words spelled the same but having different meanings or parts of speech) are run on at a single main entry if they are closely related. Run-on homograph entries are replaced in the text by a boldfaced swung dash (as **haber** . . . *v aux* . . . — **~** *nm* . . .). Homographs of distinctly different origin (as **date**[1] and **date**[2]) are given separate entries.

Run-on entries for related words that are not homographs may also follow the main entry. Thus we have the main entry **calcular** *vt* followed by run-on entries for — **calculador, -dora** *adj* . . . — **calculadora** *nf* . . . and — **cálculo** *nm*. However, if a related word falls later in the alphabet than a following unrelated main entry, it will be entered at its own place; **ear** and its run-on — **eardrum** precede the main entry **earl** which is followed by the main entry **earlobe**.

Variant spellings appear at the main entry separated by *or* (as **judgment** *or* **judgement, paralyze** *or Brit* **paralyse,** and **cacahuate** *or* **cacahuete**).

Inflected forms of English verbs, adjectives, adverbs, and nouns are shown when they are irregular (as **wage** . . . **waged; waging; ride** . . . **rode; ridden; good** . . . **better, best;** and **fly** . . . *n, pl* **flies**) or when there might be doubt about their spelling (as **ego** . . . *n, pl* **egos**). Inflected forms of Spanish irregular verbs are shown in the section Conjugation of Spanish Verbs on page 6a; numerical references to this table are included at the main entry (as **poseer** {20} *vt*). Irregular plurals of Spanish nouns or adjectives are shown at the main entry (as **ladrón, -drona** *n, mpl* **-drones**).

Cross-references are provided to lead the user to the appropriate main entry (as **mice → mouse** and **sobrestimar → sobreestimar**).

Pronunciation information is either given explicitly or implied for all English words. Pronunciation of Spanish words is assumed to be regular and is generally omitted; it is included, however, for certain foreign borrowings (as **pizza** [ˈpitsa, ˈpisa]). A full list of the pronunciation symbols used appears on page 24a.

The grammatical function of entry words is indicated by an italic **functional label** (as *vt, adj,* and *nm*). Italic **usage labels** may be added at the entry or sense as well (as **timbre** *nm* . . . **4** *Lat* **:** postage stamp, **center** *or Brit* **centre** . . . *n* . . ., or **garra** *nf* . . . **2** *fam* **:** hand, paw). These labels are also included in the translations (**bag** *n* . . . **2** HANDBAG **:** bolso *m,* cartera *f Lat*).

Usage notes are occasionally placed before a translation to clarify meaning or use (as **que** *conj* . . . **2** (*in comparisons*) **:** than).

Synonyms may appear before the translation word(s) in order to provide context for the meaning of an entry word or sense (as **sitio** *nm* . . . **2** ESPACIO **:** room, space; or **meet** . . . *vt* . . . **2** SATISFY **:** satisfacer).

Bold notes are sometimes used before a translation to introduce a plural sense or a common phrase using the main entry word (as **mueble** *nm* . . . **2 ∼s** *nmpl* **:** furniture, furnishings, or **call** . . . vt . . . **2 ∼ off :** cancelar). Note that when an entry word is repeated in a bold note, it is replaced by a swung dash.

Conjugation of Spanish Verbs

Simple Tenses

Tense	Regular Verbs Ending in -AR hablar	
PRESENT INDICATIVE	hablo hablas habla	hablamos habláis hablan
PRESENT SUBJUNCTIVE	hable hables hable	hablemos habléis hablen
PRETERIT INDICATIVE	hablé hablaste habló	hablamos hablasteis hablaron
IMPERFECT INDICATIVE	hablaba hablabas hablaba	hablábamos hablabais hablaban
IMPERFECT SUBJUNCTIVE	hablara hablaras hablara *or* hablase hablases hablase	habláramos hablarais hablaran hablásemos hablaseis hablasen
FUTURE INDICATIVE	hablaré hablarás hablará	hablaremos hablaréis hablarán
FUTURE SUBJUNCTIVE	hablare hablares hablare	habláremos hablareis hablaren
CONDITIONAL	hablaría hablarías hablaría	hablaríamos hablaríais hablarían
IMPERATIVE	 habla hable	hablemos hablad hablen
PRESENT PARTICIPLE (GERUND)	hablando	
PAST PARTICIPLE	hablado	

Regular Verbs Ending in -ER comer		**Regular Verbs Ending in -IR** vivir	
como comes come	comemos coméis comen	vivo vives vive	vivimos vivís viven
coma comas coma	comamos comáis coman	viva vivas viva	vivamos viváis vivan
comí comiste comió	comimos comisteis comieron	viví viviste vivió	vivimos vivisteis vivieron
comía comías comía	comíamos comíais comían	vivía vivías vivía	vivíamos vivíais vivían
comiera comieras comiera	comiéramos comierais comieran	viviera vivieras viviera	viviéramos vivierais vivieran
or		*or*	
comiese comieses comiese	comiésemos comieseis comiesen	viviese vivieses viviese	viviésemos vivieseis viviesen
comeré comerás comerá	comeremos comeréis comerán	viviré vivirás vivirá	viviremos viviréis vivirán
comiere comieres comiere	comiéremos comiereis comieren	viviere vivieres viviere	viviéremos viviereis vivieren
comería comerías comería	comeríamos comeríais comerían	viviría vivirías viviría	viviríamos viviríais vivirían
 come coma	comamos comed coman	 vive viva	vivamos vivid vivan
comiendo		viviendo	
comido		vivido	

Compound Tenses

1. Perfect Tenses

The perfect tenses are formed with *haber* and the past participle:

PRESENT PERFECT

he hablado, etc. (*indicative*);
haya hablado, etc. (*subjunctive*)

PAST PERFECT

había hablado, etc. (*indicative*);
hubiera hablado, etc. (*subjunctive*)
or
hubiese hablado, etc. (*subjunctive*)

PRETERIT PERFECT

hube hablado, etc. (*indicative*)

FUTURE PERFECT

habré hablado, etc. (*indicative*)

CONDITIONAL PERFECT

habría hablado, etc. (*indicative*)

2. Progressive Tenses

The progressive tenses are formed with *estar* and the present participle:

PRESENT PROGRESSIVE

estoy llamando, etc. (*indicative*);
esté llamando, etc. (*subjunctive*)

IMPERFECT PROGRESSIVE

estaba llamando, etc. (*indicative*);
estuviera llamando, etc. (*subjunctive*)
or
estuviese llamando, etc. (*subjunctive*)

PRETERIT PROGRESSIVE

estuve llamando, etc. (*indicative*)

FUTURE PROGRESSIVE

estaré llamando, etc. (*indicative*)

CONDITIONAL PROGRESSIVE

estaría llamando, etc. (*indicative*)

PRESENT PERFECT PROGRESSIVE

he estado llamando, etc. (*indicative*);
haya estado llamando, etc. (*subjunctive*)

PAST PERFECT PROGRESSIVE

había estado llamando, etc. (*indicative*);
hubiera estado llamando, etc. (*subjunctive*)
or
hubiese estado llamando, etc. (*subjunctive*)

Irregular Verbs

The *imperfect subjunctive*, the *future subjunctive*, the *conditional*, and most forms of the *imperative* are not included in the model conjugations, but can be derived as follows:

The *imperfect subjunctive* and the *future subjunctive* are formed from the third person plural form of the preterit tense by removing the last syllable (*-ron*) and adding the appropriate suffix:

PRETERIT INDICATIVE, THIRD PERSON PLURAL (querer)	quisieron
IMPERFECT SUBJUNCTIVE (querer)	quisiera, quisieras, etc. *or* quisiese, quisieses, etc.
FUTURE SUBJUNCTIVE (querer)	quisiere, quisieres, etc.

The conditional uses the same stem as the future indicative:

FUTURE INDICATIVE (poner)	pondré, pondrás, etc.
CONDITIONAL (poner)	pondría, pondrías, etc.

The third person singular, first person plural, and third person plural forms of the *imperative* are the same as the corresponding forms of the present subjunctive.

The second person singular form of the *imperative* is generally the same as the third person singular of the present indicative. Exceptions are noted in the model conjugations list.

The second person plural *(vosotros)* form of the *imperative* is formed by removing the final *-r* of the infinitive form and adding a *-d* (ex.: *oír* → *oíd*).

Model Conjugations of Irregular Verbs

The model conjugations below include the following simple tenses: the *present indicative* (*IND*), the *present subjunctive* (*SUBJ*), the *preterit indicative* (*PRET*), the *imperfect indicative* (*IMPF*), the *future indicative* (*FUT*), the second person singular form of the *imperative* (*IMPER*) when it differs from the third person singular of the present indicative, the *gerund* or *present participle* (*PRP*), and the *past participle* (*PP*). Each set of conjugations is preceded by the corresponding infinitive form of the verb, shown in bold type. Only tenses containing irregularities are listed, and the irregular verb forms within each tense are displayed in bold type.

Each irregular verb entry in the Spanish-English section of this dictionary is cross-referenced by number to one of the following model conjugations. These cross-reference numbers are shown in curly braces { } immediately following the entry's functional label.

1 **abolir** *(defective verb)* : *IND* abolimos, abolís *(other forms not used); SUBJ (not used); IMPER (only second person plural is used)*

2 **abrir** : *PP* abierto

3 **actuar** : *IND* **actúo, actúas, actúa**, actuamos, actuáis, **actúan;** *SUBJ* **actúe, actúes, actúe,** actuemos, actuéis, **actúen;** *IMPER* **actúa**

4 **adquirir** : *IND* **adquiero, adquieres, adquiere,** adquirimos, adquirís, **adquieren;** *SUBJ* **adquiera, adquieras, adquiera,** adquiramos, adquiráis, **adquieran;** *IMPER* **adquiere**

5 **airar** : *IND* **aíro, aíras, aíra,** airamos, airáis, **aíran;** *SUBJ* **aíre, aíres, aíre,** airemos, airéis, **aíren;** *IMPER* **aíra**

6 **andar** : *PRET* **anduve, anduviste, anduvo, anduvimos, anduvisteis, anduvieron**

7 **asir** : *IND* **asgo,** ases, ase, asimos, asís, asen; *SUBJ* **asga, asgas, asga, asgamos, asgáis, asgan**

8 **aunar** : *IND* **aúno, aúnas, aúna,** aunamos, aunáis, **aúnan;** *SUBJ* **aúne, aúnes, aúne,** aunemos, aunéis, **aúnen;** *IMPER* **aúna**

9 **avergonzar** : *IND* **avergüenzo, avergüenzas, avergüenza,** avergonzamos, avergonzáis, **avergüenzan;** *SUBJ* **avergüence, avergüences, avergüence, avergoncemos, avergoncéis, avergüencen;** *PRET* **avergoncé;** *IMPER* **avergüenza**

10 **averiguar** : *SUBJ* **averigüe, averigües, averigüe, averigüemos, averigüéis, averigüen**; *PRET* **averigüé**, averiguaste, averiguó, averiguamos, averiguasteis, averiguaron

11 **bendecir** : *IND* **bendigo, bendices, bendice**, bendecimos, bendecís, **bendicen**; *SUBJ* **bendiga, bendigas, bendiga, bendigamos, bendigáis, bendigan**; *PRET* **bendije, bendijiste, bendijo, bendijimos, bendijisteis, bendijeron**; *IMPER* **bendice**

12 **caber** : *IND* **quepo**, cabes, cabe, cabemos, cabéis, caben; *SUBJ* **quepa, quepas, quepa, quepamos, quepáis, quepan**; *PRET* **cupe, cupiste, cupo, cupimos, cupisteis, cupieron**; *FUT* **cabré, cabrás, cabrá, cabremos, cabréis, cabrán**

13 **caer** : *IND* **caigo**, caes, cae, caemos, caéis, caen; *SUBJ* **caiga, caigas, caiga, caigamos, caigáis, caigan**; *PRET* caí, **caíste, cayó, caímos, caísteis, cayeron**; *PRP* **cayendo**; *PP* **caído**

14 **cocer** : *IND* **cuezo, cueces, cuece**, cocemos, cocéis, **cuecen**; *SUBJ* **cueza, cuezas, cueza, cozamos, cozáis, cuezan**; *IMPER* **cuece**

15 **coger** : *IND* **cojo**, coges, coge, cogemos, cogéis, cogen; *SUBJ* **coja, cojas, coja, cojamos, cojáis, cojan**

16 **colgar** : *IND* **cuelgo, cuelgas, cuelga**, colgamos, colgáis, **cuelgan**; *SUBJ* **cuelgue, cuelgues, cuelgue, colguemos, colguéis, cuelguen**; *PRET* **colgué**, colgaste, colgó, colgamos, colgasteis, colgaron; *IMPER* **cuelga**

17 **concernir** *(defective verb; used only in the third person singular and plural of the present indicative, present subjunctive, and imperfect subjunctive) see* 25 **discernir**

18 **conocer** : *IND* **conozco**, conoces, conoce, conocemos, conocéis, conocen; *SUBJ* **conozca, conozcas, conozca, conozcamos, conozcáis, conozcan**

19 **contar** : *IND* **cuento, cuentas, cuenta**, contamos, contáis, **cuentan**; *SUBJ* **cuente, cuentes, cuente**, contemos, contéis, **cuenten**; *IMPER* **cuenta**

20 **creer** : *PRET* creí, **creíste, creyó, creímos, creísteis, creyeron**; *PRP* **creyendo**; *PP* **creído**

21 **cruzar** : *SUBJ* **cruce, cruces, cruce, crucemos, crucéis, crucen**; *PRET* **crucé**, cruzaste, cruzó, cruzamos, cruzasteis, cruzaron

22 **dar** : IND **doy,** das, da, damos, **dais,** dan; SUBJ **dé,** des, **dé,** demos, **deis,** den; PRET **di, diste, dio, dimos, disteis, dieron**

23 **decir** : IND **digo, dices, dice,** decimos, decís, **dicen;** SUBJ **diga, digas, diga, digamos, digáis, digan;** PRET **dije, dijiste, dijo, dijimos, dijisteis, dijeron;** FUT **diré, dirás, dirá, diremos, diréis, dirán;** IMPER **di;** PRP **diciendo;** PP **dicho**

24 **delinquir** : IND **delinco,** delinques, delinque, delinquimos, delinquís, delinquen; SUBJ **delinca, delincas, delinca, delincamos, delincáis, delincan**

25 **discernir** : IND **discierno, disciernes, discierne,** discernimos, discernís, **disciernen;** SUBJ **discierna, disciernas, discierna,** discernamos, discernáis, **disciernan;** IMPER **discierne**

26 **distinguir** : IND **distingo,** distingues, distingue, distinguimos, distinguís, distinguen; SUBJ **distinga, distingas, distinga, distingamos, distingáis, distingan**

27 **dormir** : IND **duermo, duermes, duerme,** dormimos, dormís, **duermen;** SUBJ **duerma, duermas, duerma, durmamos, durmáis, duerman;** PRET dormí, dormiste, **durmió,** dormimos, dormisteis, **durmieron;** IMPER **duerme;** PRP **durmiendo**

28 **elegir** : IND **elijo, eliges, elige,** elegimos, elegís, **eligen;** SUBJ **elija, elijas, elija, elijamos, elijáis, elijan;** PRET elegí, elegiste, **eligió,** elegimos, elegisteis, **eligieron;** IMPER **elige;** PRP **eligiendo**

29 **empezar** : IND **empiezo, empiezas, empieza,** empezamos, empezáis, **empiezan;** SUBJ **empiece, empieces, empiece, empecemos, empecéis, empiecen;** PRET **empecé,** empezaste, empezó, empezamos, empezasteis, empezaron; IMPER **empieza**

30 **enraizar** : IND **enraízo, enraízas, enraíza,** enraizamos, enraizáis, **enraízan;** SUBJ **enraíce, enraíces, enraíce, enraicemos, enraicéis, enraícen;** PRET **enraicé,** enraizaste, enraizó, enraizamos, enraizasteis, enraizaron; IMPER **enraíza**

31 **erguir** : IND **irgo** *or* **yergo, irgues** *or* **yergues, irgue** *or* **yergue,** erguimos, erguís, **irguen** *or* **yerguen;** SUBJ **irga** *or* **yerga, irgas** *or* **yergas, irga** *or* **yerga, irgamos, irgáis, irgan** *or* **yergan;** PRET erguí, erguiste, **irguió,** erguimos, erguisteis, **irguieron;** IMPER **irgue** *or* **yergue;** PRP **irguiendo**

32 **errar** : IND **yerro, yerras, yerra,** erramos, erráis, **yerran;** SUBJ **yerre, yerres, yerre,** erremos, erréis, **yerren;** IMPER **yerra**

33 **escribir** : PP **escrito**

34 **estar** : *IND* **estoy, estás, está**, estamos, estáis, **están**; *SUBJ* **esté, estés, esté**, estemos, estéis, **estén**; *PRET* **estuve, estuviste, estuvo, estuvimos, estuvisteis, estuvieron**; *IMPER* **está**

35 **exigir** : *IND* **exijo**, exiges, exige, exigimos, exigís, exigen; *SUBJ* **exija, exijas, exija, exijamos, exijáis, exijan**

36 **forzar** : *IND* **fuerzo, fuerzas, fuerza**, forzamos, forzáis, **fuerzan**; *SUBJ* **fuerce, fuerces, fuerce, forcemos, forcéis, fuercen**; *PRET* **forcé**, forzaste, forzó, forzamos, forzasteis, forzaron; *IMPER* **fuerza**

37 **freír** : *IND* **frío, fríes, fríe, freímos**, freís, **fríen**; *SUBJ* **fría, frías, fría, friamos, friáis, frían**; *PRET* freí, **freíste, frió, freímos, freísteis, frieron**; *IMPER* **fríe**; *PRP* **friendo**; *PP* **frito**

38 **gruñir** : *PRET* gruñí, gruñiste, **gruñó**, gruñimos, gruñisteis, **gruñeron**; *PRP* **gruñendo**

39 **haber** : *IND* **he, has, ha, hemos**, habéis, **han**; *SUBJ* **haya, hayas, haya, hayamos, hayáis, hayan**; *PRET* **hube, hubiste, hubo, hubimos, hubisteis, hubieron**; *FUT* **habré, habrás, habrá, habremos, habréis, habrán**; *IMPER* **he**

40 **hacer** : *IND* **hago**, haces, hace, hacemos, hacéis, hacen; *SUBJ* **haga, hagas, haga, hagamos, hagáis, hagan**; *PRET* **hice, hiciste, hizo, hicimos, hicisteis, hicieron**; *FUT* **haré, harás, hará, haremos, haréis, harán**; *IMPER* **haz**; *PP* **hecho**

41 **huir** : *IND* **huyo, huyes, huye**, huimos, huís, **huyen**; *SUBJ* **huya, huyas, huya, huyamos, huyáis, huyan**; *PRET* huí, huiste, **huyó**, huimos, huisteis, **huyeron**; *IMPER* **huye**; *PRP* **huyendo**

42 **imprimir** : *PP* **impreso**

43 **ir** : *IND* **voy, vas, va, vamos, vais, van**; *SUBJ* **vaya, vayas, vaya, vayamos, vayáis, vayan**; *PRET* **fui, fuiste, fue, fuimos, fuisteis, fueron**; *IMPF* **iba, ibas, iba, íbamos, ibais, iban**; *IMPER* **ve**; *PRP* **yendo**; *PP* **ido**

44 **jugar** : *IND* **juego, juegas, juega**, jugamos, jugáis, **juegan**; *SUBJ* **juegue, juegues, juegue, juguemos, juguéis, jueguen**; *PRET* **jugué**, jugaste, jugó, jugamos, jugasteis, jugaron; *IMPER* **juega**

45 **lucir** : *IND* **luzco**, luces, luce, lucimos, lucís, lucen; *SUBJ* **luzca, luzcas, luzca, luzcamos, luzcáis, luzcan**

46 **morir** : *IND* **muero, mueres, muere**, morimos, morís,

mueren; *SUBJ* **muera, mueras, muera, muramos, muráis, mueran**; *PRET* morí, moriste, **murió**, morimos, moristeis, **murieron**; *IMPER* **muere**; *PRP* **muriendo**; *PP* **muerto**

47 **mover** : *IND* **muevo, mueves, mueve,** movemos, movéis, **mueven**; *SUBJ* **mueva, muevas, mueva,** movamos, mováis, **muevan**; *IMPER* **mueve**

48 **nacer** : *IND* **nazco,** naces, nace, nacemos, nacéis, nacen; *SUBJ* **nazca, nazcas, nazca, nazcamos, nazcáis, nazcan**

49 **negar** : *IND* **niego, niegas, niega,** negamos, negáis, **niegan**; *SUBJ* **niegue, niegues, niegue, neguemos, neguéis, nieguen**; *PRET* **negué,** negaste, negó, negamos, negasteis, negaron; *IMPER* **niega**

50 **oír** : *IND* **oigo, oyes, oye, oímos,** oís, **oyen**; *SUBJ* **oiga, oigas, oiga, oigamos, oigáis, oigan**; *PRET* oí, **oíste, oyó, oímos, oísteis, oyeron**; *IMPER* **oye**; *PRP* **oyendo**; *PP* **oído**

51 **oler** : *IND* **huelo, hueles, huele,** olemos, oléis, **huelen**; *SUBJ* **huela, huelas, huela,** olamos, oláis, **huelan**; *IMPER* **huele**

52 **pagar** : *SUBJ* **pague, pagues, pague, paguemos, paguéis, paguen**; *PRET* **pagué,** pagaste, pagó, pagamos, pagasteis, pagaron

53 **parecer** : *IND* **parezco,** pareces, parece, parecemos, parecéis, parecen; *SUBJ* **parezca, parezcas, parezca, parezcamos, parezcáis, parezcan**

54 **pedir** : *IND* **pido, pides, pide,** pedimos, pedís, **piden**; *SUBJ* **pida, pidas, pida, pidamos, pidáis, pidan**; *PRET* pedí, pediste, **pidió,** pedimos, pedisteis, **pidieron**; *IMPER* **pide**; *PRP* **pidiendo**

55 **pensar** : *IND* **pienso, piensas, piensa,** pensamos, pensáis, **piensan**; *SUBJ* **piense, pienses, piense,** pensemos, penséis, **piensen**; *IMPER* **piensa**

56 **perder** : *IND* **pierdo, pierdes, pierde,** perdemos, perdéis, **pierden**; *SUBJ* **pierda, pierdas, pierda,** perdamos, perdáis, **pierdan**; *IMPER* **pierde**

57 **placer** : *IND* **plazco,** places, place, placemos, placéis, placen; *SUBJ* **plazca, plazcas, plazca, plazcamos, plazcáis, plazcan**; *PRET* plací, placiste, plació *or* **plugo,** placimos, placisteis, placieron *or* **pluguieron**

58 **poder** : *IND* **puedo, puedes, puede,** podemos, podéis, **pueden**; *SUBJ* **pueda, puedas, pueda,** podamos, podáis, **puedan**; *PRET*

pude, pudiste, pudo, pudimos, pudisteis, pudieron; *FUT* **podré, podrás, podrá, podremos, podréis, podrán;** *IMPER* **puede;** *PRP* **pudiendo**

59 **podrir** *or* **pudrir :** *PP* **podrido** *(all other forms based on* pudrir*)*

60 **poner :** *IND* **pongo,** pones, pone, ponemos, ponéis, ponen; *SUBJ* **ponga, pongas, ponga, pongamos, pongáis, pongan;** *PRET* **puse, pusiste, puso, pusimos, pusisteis, pusieron;** *FUT* **pondré, pondrás, pondrá, pondremos, pondréis, pondrán;** *IMPER* **pon;** *PP* **puesto**

61 **producir :** *IND* **produzco,** produces, produce, producimos, producís, producen; *SUBJ* **produzca, produzcas, produzca, produzcamos, produzcáis, produzcan;** *PRET* **produje, produjiste, produjo, produjimos, produjisteis, produjeron**

62 **prohibir :** *IND* **prohíbo, prohíbes, prohíbe,** prohibimos, prohibís, **prohíben;** *SUBJ* **prohíba, prohíbas, prohíba,** prohibamos, prohibáis, **prohíban;** *IMPER* **prohíbe**

63 **proveer :** *PRET* proveí, **proveíste, proveyó, proveímos, proveísteis, proveyeron;** *PRP* **proveyendo;** *PP* **provisto**

64 **querer :** *IND* **quiero, quieres, quiere,** queremos, queréis, **quieren;** *SUBJ* **quiera, quieras, quiera,** queramos, queráis, **quieran;** *PRET* **quise, quisiste, quiso, quisimos, quisisteis, quisieron;** *FUT* **querré, querrás, querrá, querremos, querréis, querrán;** *IMPER* **quiere**

65 **raer :** *IND* rao *or* **raigo** *or* **rayo,** raes, rae, raemos, raéis, raen; *SUBJ* **raiga** *or* **raya, raigas** *or* **rayas, raiga** *or* **raya, raigamos** *or* **rayamos, raigáis** *or* **rayáis, raigan** *or* **rayan;** *PRET* **raí, raíste, rayó, raímos, raísteis, rayeron;** *PRP* **rayendo;** *PP* **raído**

66 **reír :** *IND* **río, ríes, ríe, reímos,** reís, **ríen;** *SUBJ* **ría, rías, ría, riamos, riáis, rían;** *PRET* reí, **reíste, rió, reímos, reísteis, rieron;** *IMPER* **ríe;** *PRP* **riendo;** *PP* **reído**

67 **reñir :** *IND* **riño, riñes, riñe,** reñimos, reñís, **riñen;** *SUBJ* **riña, riñas, riña, riñamos, riñáis, riñan;** *PRET* reñí, reñiste, **riñó,** reñimos, reñisteis, **riñeron;** *PRP* **riñendo**

68 **reunir :** *IND* **reúno, reúnes, reúne,** reunimos, reunís, **reúnen;** *SUBJ* **reúna, reúnas, reúna,** reunamos, reunáis, **reúnan;** *IMPER* **reúne**

69 **roer :** *IND* roo *or* **roigo** *or* **royo,** roes, roe, roemos, roéis, roen;

SUBJ roa *or* **roiga** *or* **roya,** roas *or* **roigas** *or* **royas,** roa *or* **roiga** *or* **roya,** roamos *or* **roigamos** *or* **royamos,** roáis *or* **roigáis** *or* **royáis,** roan *or* **roigan** *or* **royan;** *PRET* roí, **roíste, royó, roímos, roísteis, royeron;** *PRP* **royendo;** *PP* **roído**

70 **romper :** *PP* **roto**

71 **saber :** *IND* **sé,** sabes, sabe, sabemos, sabéis, saben; *SUBJ* **sepa, sepas, sepa, sepamos, sepáis, sepan;** *PRET* **supe, supiste, supo, supimos, supisteis, supieron;** *FUT* **sabré, sabrás, sabrá, sabremos, sabréis, sabrán**

72 **sacar :** *SUBJ* **saque, saques, saque, saquemos, saquéis, saquen;** *PRET* **saqué,** sacaste, sacó, sacamos, sacasteis, sacaron

73 **salir :** *IND* **salgo,** sales, sale, salimos, salís, salen; *SUBJ* **salga, salgas, salga, salgamos, salgáis, salgan;** *FUT* **saldré, saldrás, saldrá, saldremos, saldréis, saldrán;** *IMPER* **sal**

74 **satisfacer :** *IND* **satisfago,** satisfaces, satisface, satisfacemos, satisfacéis, satisfacen; *SUBJ* **satisfaga, satisfagas, satisfaga, satisfagamos, satisfagáis, satisfagan;** *PRET* **satisfice, satisficiste, satisfizo, satisficimos, satificisteis, satisficieron;** *FUT* **satisfaré, satisfarás, satisfará, satisfaremos, satisfaréis, satisfarán;** *IMPER* **satisfaz** *or* **satisface;** *PP* **satisfecho**

75 **seguir :** *IND* **sigo, sigues, sigue,** seguimos, seguís, **siguen;** *SUBJ* **siga, sigas, siga, sigamos, sigáis, sigan;** *PRET* seguí, seguiste, **siguió,** seguimos, seguisteis, **siguieron;** *IMPER* **sigue;** *PRP* **siguiendo**

76 **sentir :** *IND* **siento, sientes, siente,** sentimos, sentís, **sienten;** *SUBJ* **sienta, sientas, sienta, sintamos, sintáis, sientan;** *PRET* sentí, sentiste, **sintió,** sentimos, sentisteis, **sintieron;** *IMPER* **siente;** *PRP* **sintiendo**

77 **ser :** *IND* **soy, eres, es, somos, sois, son;** *SUBJ* **sea, seas, sea, seamos, seáis, sean;** *PRET* **fui, fuiste, fue, fuimos, fuisteis, fueron;** *IMPF* **era, eras, era, éramos, erais, eran;** *IMPER* **sé;** *PRP* **siendo;** *PP* **sido**

78 **soler** *(defective verb; used only in the present, preterit, and imperfect indicative, and the present and imperfect subjunctive)* *see* 47 **mover**

79 **tañer :** *PRET* tañí, tañiste, **tañó,** tañimos, tañisteis, **tañeron;** *PRP* **tañendo**

80 **tener :** *IND* **tengo, tienes, tiene,** tenemos, tenéis, **tienen;** *SUBJ* **tenga, tengas, tenga, tengamos, tengáis, tengan;** *PRET* **tuve,**

tuviste, tuvo, tuvimos, tuvisteis, tuvieron; *FUT* **tendré, tendrás, tendrá, tendremos, tendréis, tendrán;** *IMPER* **ten**

81 **traer :** *IND* **traigo,** traes, trae, traemos, traéis, traen; *SUBJ* **traiga, traigas, traiga, traigamos, traigáis, traigan;** *PRET* **traje, trajiste, trajo, trajimos, trajisteis, trajeron;** *PRP* **trayendo;** *PP* **traído**

82 **trocar :** *IND* **trueco, truecas, trueca,** trocamos, trocáis, **truecan;** *SUBJ* **trueque, trueques, trueque, troquemos, troquéis, truequen;** *PRET* **troqué,** trocaste, trocó, trocamos, trocasteis, trocaron; *IMPER* **trueca**

83 **uncir :** *IND* **unzo,** unces, unce, uncimos, uncís, uncen; *SUBJ* **unza, unzas, unza, unzamos, unzáis, unzan**

84 **valer :** *IND* **valgo,** vales, vale, valemos, valéis, valen; *SUBJ* **valga, valgas, valga, valgamos, valgáis, valgan;** *FUT* **valdré, valdrás, valdrá, valdremos, valdréis, valdrán**

85 **variar :** *IND* **varío, varías, varía,** variamos, variáis, **varían;** *SUBJ* **varíe, varíes, varíe,** variemos, variéis, **varíen;** *IMPER* **varía**

86 **vencer :** *IND* **venzo,** vences, vence, vencemos, vencéis, vencen; *SUBJ* **venza, venzas, venza, venzamos, venzáis, venzan**

87 **venir :** *IND* **vengo, vienes, viene,** venimos, venís, **vienen;** *SUBJ* **venga, vengas, venga, vengamos, vengáis, vengan;** *PRET* **vine, viniste, vino, vinimos, vinisteis, vinieron;** *FUT* **vendré, vendrás, vendrá, vendremos, vendréis, vendrán;** *IMPER* **ven;** *PRP* **viniendo**

88 **ver :** *IND* veo, **ves, ve, vemos, veis, ven;** *PRET* **vi, viste, vio, vimos, visteis, vieron;** *IMPER* **ve;** *PRP* **viendo;** *PP* **visto**

89 **volver :** *IND* **vuelvo, vuelves, vuelve,** volvemos, volvéis, **vuelven;** *SUBJ* **vuelva, vuelvas, vuelva,** volvamos, volváis, **vuelvan;** *IMPER* **vuelve;** *PP* **vuelto**

90 **yacer :** *IND* **yazco** *or* **yazgo** *or* **yago,** yaces, yace, yacemos, yacéis, yacen; *SUBJ* **yazca** *or* **yazga** *or* **yaga, yazcas** *or* **yazgas** *or* **yagas, yazca** *or* **yazga** *or* **yaga, yazcamos** *or* **yazgamos** *or* **yagamos, yazcáis** *or* **yazgáis** *or* **yagáis, yazcan** *or* **yazgan** *or* **yagan;** *IMPER* yace *or* **yaz**

Irregular English Verbs

INFINITIVE	PAST	PAST PARTICIPLE
arise	arose	arisen
awake	awoke	awoken *or* awaked
be	was, were	been
bear	bore	borne
beat	beat	beaten *or* beat
become	became	become
befall	befell	befallen
begin	began	begun
behold	beheld	beheld
bend	bent	bent
beseech	beseeched *or* besought	beseeched *or* besought
beset	beset	beset
bet	bet	bet
bid	bade *or* bid	bidden *or* bid
bind	bound	bound
bite	bit	bitten
bleed	bled	bled
blow	blew	blown
break	broke	broken
breed	bred	bred
bring	brought	brought
build	built	built
burn	burned *or* burnt	burned *or* burnt
burst	burst	burst
buy	bought	bought
can	could	—
cast	cast	cast
catch	caught	caught
choose	chose	chosen
cling	clung	clung
come	came	come
cost	cost	cost
creep	crept	crept
cut	cut	cut
deal	dealt	dealt
dig	dug	dug
do	did	done
draw	drew	drawn

INFINITIVE	PAST	PAST PARTICIPLE
dream	dreamed *or* dreamt	dreamed *or* dreamt
drink	drank	drunk *or* drank
drive	drove	driven
dwell	dwelled *or* dwelt	dwelled *or* dwelt
eat	ate	eaten
fall	fell	fallen
feed	fed	fed
feel	felt	felt
fight	fought	fought
find	found	found
flee	fled	fled
fling	flung	flung
fly	flew	flown
forbid	forbade	forbidden
forecast	forecast	forecast
forego	forewent	foregone
foresee	foresaw	foreseen
foretell	foretold	foretold
forget	forgot	forgotten *or* forgot
forgive	forgave	forgiven
forsake	forsook	forsaken
freeze	froze	frozen
get	got	got *or* gotten
give	gave	given
go	went	gone
grind	ground	ground
grow	grew	grown
hang	hung	hung
have	had	had
hear	heard	heard
hide	hid	hidden *or* hid
hit	hit	hit
hold	held	held
hurt	hurt	hurt
keep	kept	kept
kneel	knelt *or* kneeled	knelt *or* kneeled
know	knew	known
lay	laid	laid
lead	led	led
lean	leaned	leaned
leap	leaped *or* leapt	leaped *or* leapt
learn	learned	learned

INFINITIVE	PAST	PAST PARTICIPLE
leave	left	left
lend	lent	lent
let	let	let
lie	lay	lain
light	lit *or* lighted	lit *or* lighted
lose	lost	lost
make	made	made
may	might	—
mean	meant	meant
meet	met	met
mow	mowed	mowed *or* mown
pay	paid	paid
put	put	put
quit	quit	quit
read	read	read
rend	rent	rent
rid	rid	rid
ride	rode	ridden
ring	rang	rung
rise	rose	risen
run	ran	run
saw	sawed	sawed *or* sawn
say	said	said
see	saw	seen
seek	sought	sought
sell	sold	sold
send	sent	sent
set	set	set
shake	shook	shaken
shall	should	—
shear	sheared	sheared *or* shorn
shed	shed	shed
shine	shone *or* shined	shone *or* shined
shoot	shot	shot
show	showed	shown *or* showed
shrink	shrank *or* shrunk	shrunk *or* shrunken
shut	shut	shut
sing	sang *or* sung	sung
sink	sank *or* sunk	sunk
sit	sat	sat
slay	slew	slain
sleep	slept	slept

INFINITIVE	PAST	PAST PARTICIPLE
slide	slid	slid
sling	slung	slung
smell	smelled *or* smelt	smelled *or* smelt
sow	sowed	sown *or* sowed
speak	spoke	spoken
speed	sped *or* speeded	sped *or* speeded
spell	spelled	spelled
spend	spent	spent
spill	spilled	spilled
spin	spun	spun
spit	spit *or* spat	spit *or* spat
split	split	split
spoil	spoiled	spoiled
spread	spread	spread
spring	sprang *or* sprung	sprung
stand	stood	stood
steal	stole	stolen
stick	stuck	stuck
sting	stung	stung
stink	stank *or* stunk	stunk
stride	strode	stridden
strike	struck	struck
swear	swore	sworn
sweep	swept	swept
swell	swelled	swelled *or* swollen
swim	swam	swum
swing	swung	swung
take	took	taken
teach	taught	taught
tear	tore	torn
tell	told	told
think	thought	thought
throw	threw	thrown
thrust	thrust	thrust
tread	trod	trodden *or* trod
wake	woke	woken *or* waked
waylay	waylaid	waylaid
wear	wore	worn
weave	wove *or* weaved	woven *or* weaved
wed	wedded	wedded
weep	wept	wept
will	would	—

INFINITIVE	PAST	PAST PARTICIPLE
win	won	won
wind	wound	wound
withdraw	withdrew	withdrawn
withhold	withheld	withheld
withstand	withstood	withstood
wring	wrung	wrung
write	wrote	written

Abbreviations in this Work

adj	adjective
adv	adverb
adv	adverbial phrase
algn	alguien (someone)
art	article
Brit	Great Britain
conj	conjunction
conj phr	conjunctive phrase
esp	especially
etc	et cetera
f	feminine
fam	familiar or colloquial
fpl	feminine plural
interj	interjection
Lat	Latin America
m	masculine
mf	masculine or feminine
mpl	masculine plural
n	noun
nf	feminine noun
nfpl	feminine plural noun
nfs & pl	invariable singular or plural feminine noun
nm	masculine noun
nmf	masculine or feminine noun
nmfpl	plural noun invariable for gender
nmfs & pl	noun invariable for both gender and number
nmpl	masculine plural noun
nms & pl	invariable singular or plural masculine noun
npl	plural noun
ns & pl	noun invariable for plural
pl	plural
pp	past participle
prep	preposition
prep phr	prepositional phrase
pron	pronoun
s.o.	someone
sth	something
usu	usually
v	verb
v aux	auxiliary verb
vi	intransitive verb
v impers	impersonal verb
vr	reflexive verb
vt	transitive verb

Pronunciation Symbols

VOWELS

æ **ask**, **bat**, **glad**
ɑ **cot**, **bomb**
a *New England* **aunt**, *British* **ask**, **glass**, *Spanish* **casa**
ɛ **egg**, **bet**, **fed**
ə **about**, **javelin**, **Alabama**
ə when italicized as in *ə*l, *ə*m, *ə*n, indicates a syllabic pronunciation of the consonant as in bot**tle**, pris**m**, butt**on**
i ver**y**, an**y**, thirt**y**, *Spanish* piñ**a**
iː **ea**t, b**ea**d, b**ee**
ɪ **i**d, b**i**d, p**i**t
o **O**hi**o**, yell**o**wer, potat**o**, *Spanish* **ó**valo
oː **oa**ts, **ow**n, z**o**ne, bl**ow**
ɔ **aw**l, m**au**l, c**au**ght, p**aw**
ʊ s**u**re, sh**ou**ld, c**ou**ld
uː b**oo**t, f**ew**, c**oo**
ʌ **u**nder, p**u**tt, b**u**d
eɪ **ei**ght, w**a**de, b**ay**
aɪ **i**ce, b**i**te, t**ie**
aʊ **ou**t, g**ow**n, pl**ow**
ɔɪ **oy**ster, c**oi**l, b**oy**
ː indicates that the preceding vowel is long. Long vowels are almost always diphthongs in English, but not in Spanish.

STRESS MARKS

ˈ high stress **pen**manship
ˌ low stress penman**ship**

CONSONANTS

b **b**a**b**y, la**b**or, ca**b**
d **d**ay, rea**d**y, ki**d**
dʒ **j**ust, ba**dg**er, fu**dg**e
ð **th**en, ei**th**er, ba**th**e
f **f**oe, tou**gh**, bu**ff**
g **g**o, bi**gg**er, ba**g**
h **h**ot, a**h**a
j **y**es, vine**y**ard
k **c**at, **k**eep, la**cqu**er, flo**ck**
l **l**aw, ho**ll**ow, boi**l**
m **m**at, he**m**p, ha**mm**er, ri**m**
n **n**ew, te**n**t, te**n**or, ru**n**
ŋ ru**ng**, ha**ng**, swi**ng**er
p **p**ay, la**p**se, to**p**
r **r**ope, bu**r**n, ta**r**
s **s**ad, mi**s**t, ki**ss**
ʃ **sh**oe, mi**ss**ion, slu**sh**
t **t**oe, bu**tt**on, ma**t**
ţ indicates that some speakers of English pronounce this sound as a voiced alveolar flap [ɾ], as in la**t**er, ca**tt**y, ba**tt**le
tʃ **ch**oose, ba**tch**
θ **th**in, e**th**er, ba**th**
v **v**at, ne**v**er, ca**v**e
w **w**et, soft**w**are
z **z**oo, ea**s**y, bu**zz**
ʒ a**z**ure, bei**g**e
h, *k*, *p*, *t* when italicized indicate sounds which are present in the pronunciation of some speakers of English but absent in the pronunciation of others, so that *whence* [ˈ*h*wɛn*t*s] can be pronounced as [ˈhwɛns], [ˈhwɛnts], [ˈwɛnts], or [ˈwɛns]

Spanish-English Dictionary

A

a[1] *nf* : a, first letter of the Spanish alphabet

a[2] *prep* **1** : to **2 ~ las dos** : at two o'clock **3 al día siguiente** : (on) the following day **4 ~ pied** : on foot **5 de lunes ~ viernes** : from Monday until Friday **6 tres veces ~ la semana** : three times per week **7 ~ la** : in the manner of, like

abadía *nf* : abbey

abajo *adv* **1** : down, below, downstairs **2 ~ de** *Lat* : under, beneath **3 de ~** : (at the) bottom **4 hacia ~** : downwards

abalanzarse {21} *vr* : hurl oneself, rush

abandonar *vt* **1** : abandon, leave **2** RENUNCIAR A : give up — **abandonarse** *vr* **1** : neglect oneself **2 ~ a** : give oneself over to — **abandonado, -da** *adj* **1** : abandoned, deserted **2** DESCUIDADO : neglected **3** DESALIÑADO : slovenly — **abandono** *nm* **1** : abandonment, neglect **2 por ~** : by default

abanico *nm* : fan — **abanicar** {72} *vt* : fan

abaratar *vt* : lower the price of — **abaratarse** *vr* : become cheaper

abarcar {72} *vt* **1** : cover, embrace **2** *Lat* : monopolize

abarrotar *vt* : pack, cram — **abarrotes** *nmpl Lat* **1** : groceries **2 tienda de ~** : grocery store

abastecer {53} *vt* : supply, stock — **abastecimiento** *nm* : supply, provisions — **abasto** *nm* **1** : supply **2 no dar ~ a** : be unable to cope with

abatir *vt* **1** : knock down, shoot down **2** DEPRIMIR : depress — **abatirse** *vr* **1** : get depressed **2 ~ sobre** : swoop down on — **abatido, -da** *adj* : dejected, depressed — **abatimiento** *nm* : depression, dejection

abdicar {72} *v* : abdicate — **abdicación** *nf, pl* **-ciones** : abdication

abdomen *nm, pl* **-dómenes** : abdomen — **abdominal** *adj* : abdominal

abecé *nm* : ABC — **abecedario** *nm* : alphabet

abedul *nm* : birch

abeja *nf* : bee — **abejorro** *nm* : bumblebee

aberración *nf, pl* **-ciones** : aberration

abertura *nf* : opening

abeto *nm* : fir (tree)

abierto, -ta *adj* : open

abigarrado, -da *adj* : multicolored

abismo *nm* : abyss, chasm — **abismal** *adj* : vast, enormous

abjurar *vi* **~ de** : abjure

ablandar *vt* : soften (up) — **ablandarse** *vr* : soften

abnegarse {49} *vr* : deny oneself — **abnegado, -da** *adj* : self-sacrificing — **abnegación** *nf, pl* **-ciones** : self-denial

abochornar *vt* : embarrass — **abochornarse** *vr* : get embarrassed

abofetear *vt* : slap

abogado, -da *n* : lawyer — **abogacía** *nf* : legal profession — **abogar** {52} *vi* **~ por** : plead for, defend

abolengo *nm* : lineage

abolir {1} *vt* : abolish — **abolición** *nf, pl* **-ciones** : abolition

abollar *vt* : dent — **abolladura** *nf* : dent

abominar *vt* : abominate — **abominable** *adj* : abominable — **abominación** *nf, pl* **-ciones** : abomination

abonar *vt* **1** : pay (a bill, etc.) **2** : fertilize (the soil) — **abonarse** *vr* : subscribe — **abonado, -da** *n* : subscriber — **abono** *nm* **1** : payment, installment **2** FERTILIZANTE : fertilizer **3** : season ticket (to the theater, etc.)

abordar *vt* **1** : tackle (a problem) **2** : accost, approach (a person) **3** *Lat* : board — **abordaje** *nm* : boarding

aborigen *nmf, pl* **-rígenes** : aborigine — **~** *adj* : aboriginal, native

aborrecer {53} *vt* : abhor, detest — **aborrecible** *adj* : hateful — **aborrecimiento** *nm* : loathing

abortar *vi* : have a miscarriage — *vt* : abort — **aborto** *nm* : abortion, miscarriage

abotonar *vt* : button — **abotonarse** *vr* : button up

abovedado, -da *adj* : vaulted

abrasar *vt* : burn, scorch — **abrasarse** *vr* : burn up — **abrasador, -dora** *adj* : burning

abrasivo, -va *adj* : abrasive — **abrasivo** *nm* : abrasive

abrazar {21} *vt* : hug, embrace — **abrazarse** *vr* : embrace — **abraza-**

dera *nf* : clamp — **abrazo** *nm* : hug, embrace

abrebotellas *nms & pl* : bottle opener — **abrelatas** *nms & pl* : can opener

abrevadero *nm* : watering trough

abreviar *vt* **1** : shorten, abridge **2** : abbreviate (a word) — **abreviación** *nf, pl* **-ciones** : shortening — **abreviatura** *nf* : abbreviation

abridor *nm* : bottle opener, can opener

abrigar {52} *vt* **1** : wrap up (in clothing) **2** ALBERGAR : cherish, harbor — **abrigarse** *vr* : dress warmly — **abrigado, -da** *adj* **1** : sheltered **2** : warm, wrapped up (of persons) — **abrigo** *nm* **1** : coat, overcoat **2** REFUGIO : shelter, refuge

abril *nm* : April

abrillantar *vt* : polish, shine

abrir {2} *vt* **1** : open **2** : unlock, undo — *vi* : open up — **abrirse** *vr* **1** : open up **2** : clear up (of weather)

abrochar *vt* : button, fasten — **abrocharse** *vr* : fasten, do up

abrogar {52} *vt* : annul, repeal

abrumar *vt* : overwhelm — **abrumador, -dora** *adj* : overwhelming, oppressive

abrupto, -ta *adj* **1** ESCARPADO : steep **2** ÁSPERO : rugged, harsh **3** REPENTINO : abrupt

absceso *nm* : abscess

absolución *nf, pl* **-ciones 1** : absolution **2** : acquittal (in law)

absoluto, -ta *adj* **1** : absolute, unconditional **2 en absoluto** : not at all — **absolutamente** *adv* : absolutely

absolver {89} *vt* **1** : absolve **2** : acquit (in law)

absorber *vt* **1** : absorb **2** : take up (time, energy, etc.) — **absorbente** *adj* **1** : absorbent **2** INTERESANTE : absorbing — **absorción** *nf, pl* **-ciones** : absorption — **absorto, -ta** *adj* : absorbed, engrossed

abstemio, -mia *adj* : abstemious — **~** *n* : teetotaler

abstenerse {80} *vr* : abstain, refrain — **abstención** *nf, pl* **-ciones** : abstention — **abstinencia** *nf* : abstinence

abstracción *nf, pl* **-ciones** : abstraction — **abstracto, -ta** *adj* : abstract — **abstraer** {81} *vt* : abstract — **abstraerse** *vr* : lose oneself in thought — **abstraído, -da** *adj* : preoccupied

absurdo, -da *adj* : absurd, ridiculous — **absurdo** *nm* : absurdity

abuchear *vt* : boo, jeer — **abucheo** *nm* : booing

abuelo, -la *n* **1** : grandfather, grandmother **2 abuelos** *nmpl* : grandparents

abulia *nf* : apathy, lethargy

abultar *vi* : bulge, be bulky — *vt* : enlarge, expand — **abultado, -da** *adj* : bulky

abundar *vi* : abound, be plentiful — **abundancia** *nf* : abundance — **abundante** *adj* : abundant

aburrir *vt* : bore — **aburrirse** *vr* : get bored — **aburrido, -da** *adj* **1** : bored **2** TEDIOSO : boring — **aburrimiento** *nm* : boredom

abusar *vi* **1** : go too far **2 ~ de** : abuse — **abusivo, -va** *adj* : outrageous, excessive — **abuso** *nm* : abuse

abyecto, -ta *adj* : abject, wretched

acá *adv* : here, over here

acabar *vi* **1** : finish, end **2 ~ de** : have just (done something) **3 ~ con** : put an end to **4 ~ por** : end up (doing sth) — *vt* : finish — **acabarse** *vr* : come to an end — **acabado, -da** *adj* **1** : finished, perfect **2** AGOTADO : old, worn-out — **acabado** *nm* : finish

academia *nf* : academy — **académico, -ca** *adj* : academic

acaecer {53} *vi* : happen, occur

acallar *vt* : quiet, silence

acalorar *vt* : stir up, excite — **acalorarse** *vr* : get worked up — **acalorado, -da** *adj* : emotional, heated

acampar *vi* : camp — **acampada** *nf* **ir de ~** : go camping

acanalado, -da *adj* **1** : grooved **2** : corrugated (of iron, etc.)

acantilado *nm* : cliff

acaparar *vt* **1** : hoard **2** MONOPOLIZAR : monopolize

acápite *nm Lat* : paragraph

acariciar *vt* **1** : caress **2** : cherish (hopes, ideas, etc.)

ácaro *nm* : mite

acarrear *vt* **1** : haul, carry **2** OCASIONAR : give rise to — **acarreo** *nm* : transport

acaso *adv* **1** : perhaps, maybe **2 por si ~** : just in case

acatar *vt* : comply with, respect — **acatamiento** *nm* : compliance, respect

acatarrarse *vr* : catch a cold

acaudalado, -da *adj* : wealthy, rich

acaudillar *vt* : lead

acceder *vi* **1** : agree **2 ~ a** : gain access to, enter

acceso *nm* **1** : access **2** ENTRADA : entrance **3** : attack, bout (of an illness) — **accesible** *adj* : accessible

accesorio *nm* : accessory — **accesorio, -ria** *adj* : incidental

accidentado, -da *adj* **1** : eventful, turbulent **2** : rough, uneven (of land, etc.) **3** HERIDO : injured — **~** *n* : accident victim
accidental *adj* : accidental — **accidentarse** *vr* : have an accident — **accidente** *nm* **1** : accident **2** : unevenness (of land)
acción *nf, pl* **-ciones 1** : action **2** ACTO : act, deed **3** : share, stock (in finance) — **accionar** *vt* : activate — *vi* : gesticulate — **accionista** *nmf* : stockholder
acebo *nm* : holly
acechar *vt* : watch, stalk — **acecho** *nm* **estar al ~ por** : be on the lookout for
aceite *nm* : oil — **aceitar** *vt* : oil — **aceitera** *nf* **1** : oilcan **2** : cruet (in cookery) **3** *Lat* : oil refinery — **aceitoso, -sa** *adj* : oily
aceituna *nf* : olive
acelerar *v* : accelerate — **acelerarse** *vr* : hurry up — **aceleración** *nf, pl* **-ciones** : acceleration — **acelerador** *nm* : accelerator
acelga *nf* : (Swiss) chard
acentuar {3} *vt* **1** : accent **2** ENFATIZAR : emphasize, stress — **acentuarse** *vr* : stand out — **acento** *nm* **1** : accent **2** ÉNFASIS : stress, emphasis
acepción *nf, pl* **-ciones** : sense, meaning
aceptar *vt* : accept — **aceptable** *adj* : acceptable — **aceptación** *nf, pl* **-ciones 1** : acceptance **2** ÉXITO : success
acequia *nf* : irrigation ditch
acera *nf* : sidewalk
acerbo, -ba *adj* : harsh, caustic
acerca *prep* **~ de** : about, concerning
acercar {72} *vt* : bring near or closer — **acercarse** *vr* : approach, draw near
acero *nm* **1** : steel **2 ~ inoxidable** : stainless steel
acérrimo, -ma *adj* **1** : staunch, steadfast **2** : bitter (of an enemy)
acertar {55} *vt* : guess correctly — *vi* **1** ATINAR : be accurate **2 ~ a** : manage to — **acertado, -da** *adj* : correct, accurate
acertijo *nm* : riddle
acervo *nm* : heritage
acetona *nf* : acetone, nail-polish remover
achacar {72} *vt* : attribute, impute
achacoso, -sa *adj* : sickly
achaparrado, -da *adj* : squat, stocky
achaque *nm* : aches and pains
achatar *vt* : flatten
achicar {72} *vt* **1** : make smaller **2** ACOBARDAR : intimidate **3** : bail out (water) — **achicarse** *vr* : become intimidated
achicharrar *vt* : scorch, burn to a crisp
achicoria *nf* : chicory
aciago, -ga *adj* : fateful, unlucky
acicalar *vt* : dress up, adorn — **acicalarse** *vr* : get dressed up
acicate *nm* **1** : spur **2** INCENTIVO : incentive
ácido, -da *adj* : acid, sour — **acidez** *nf, pl* **-deces** : acidity — **ácido** *nm* : acid
acierto *nm* **1** : correct answer **2** HABILIDAD : skill, sound judgment
aclamar *vt* : acclaim — **aclamación** *nf, pl* **-ciones** : acclaim, applause
aclarar *vt* **1** CLARIFICAR : clarify, explain **2** : rinse (clothing) **3 ~ la voz** : clear one's throat — *vi* : clear up — **aclararse** *vr* : become clear — **aclaración** *nf, pl* **-ciones** : explanation — **aclaratorio, -ria** *adj* : explanatory
aclimatar *vt* : acclimatize — **aclimatarse** *vr* **~ a** : get used to — **aclimatación** *nf, pl* **-ciones** : acclimatization
acné *nm* : acne
acobardar *vt* : intimidate — **acobardarse** *vr* : become frightened
acodarse *vr* **~ en** : lean (one's elbows) on
acoger {15} *vt* **1** REFUGIAR : shelter **2** RECIBIR : receive, welcome — **acogerse** *vr* **1** : take refuge **2 ~ a** : resort to — **acogedor, -dora** *adj* : cozy, welcoming — **acogida** *nf* **1** : welcome **2** REFUGIO : refuge
acolchar *vt* : pad
acólito *nm* MONAGUILLO : altar boy
acometer *vt* **1** : attack **2** EMPRENDER : undertake — *vi* **~ contra** : rush against — **acometida** *nf* : attack, assault
acomodar *vt* **1** ADAPTAR : adjust **2** COLOCAR : put, make a place for — **acomodarse** *vr* **1** : settle in **2 ~ a** : adapt to — **acomodado, -da** *adj* : well-to-do — **acomodaticio, -cia** *adj* : accommodating, obliging — **acomodo** *nm* : job, position
acompañar *vt* **1** : accompany **2** ADJUNTAR : enclose — **acompañamiento** *nm* : accompaniment — **acompañante** *nmf* **1** COMPAÑERO : companion **2** : accompanist (in music)
acompasado, -da *adj* : rhythmic, measured
acondicionar *vt* : fit out, equip — **acondicionado, -da** *adj* : equipped
acongojar *vt* : distress, upset — **acongojarse** *vr* : get upset

aconsejar *vt* : advise — **aconsejable** *adj* : advisable
acontecer {53} *vi* : occur, happen — **acontecimiento** *nm* : event
acopiar *vt* : gather, collect — **acopio** *nm* : collection, stock
acoplar *vt* : couple, connect — **acoplarse** *vr* : fit together — **acoplamiento** *nm* : connection, coupling
acorazado, -da *adj* : armored — **acorazado** *nm* : battleship
acordar {19} *vt* **1** : agree (on) **2** *Lat* : award — **acordarse** *vr* : remember
acorde *adj* **1** : in agreement **2 ~ con** : in keeping with — **~** *nm* : chord (in music)
acordeón *nm, pl* **-deones** : accordion
acordonar *vt* **1** : cordon off **2** : lace up (shoes)
acorralar *vt* : corner, corral
acortar *vt* : shorten, cut short — **acortarse** *vr* : get shorter
acosar *vt* : hound, harass — **acoso** *nm* : harassment
acostar {19} *vt* : put to bed — **acostarse** *vr* **1** : go to bed **2** TUMBARSE : lie down
acostumbrar *vt* : accustom — *vi* **~ a** : be in the habit of — **acostumbrarse** *vr* **~ a** : get used to — **acostumbrado, -da** *adj* **1** HABITUADO : accustomed **2** HABITUAL : usual
acotar *vt* **1** ANOTAR : annotate **2** DELIMITAR : mark off (land) — **acotación** *nf, pl* **-ciones** : marginal note — **acotado, -da** *adj* : enclosed
acre *adj* **1** : pungent **2** MORDAZ : harsh, biting
acrecentar {55} *vt* : increase — **acrecentamiento** *nm* : growth, increase
acreditar *vt* **1** : accredit, authorize **2** PROBAR : prove — **acreditarse** *vr* : prove oneself — **acreditado, -da** *adj* **1** : reputable **2** : accredited (in politics, etc.)
acreedor, -dora *adj* : worthy — **~** *n* : creditor
acribillar *vt* **1** : riddle, pepper **2 ~ a** : harass with
acrílico *nm* : acrylic
acrimonia *nf or* **acritud** *nf* **1** : pungency **2** RESENTIMIENTO : bitterness, acrimony
acrobacia *nf* : acrobatics — **acróbata** *nmf* : acrobat — **acrobático, -ca** *adj* : acrobatic
acta *nf* **1** : certificate **2** : minutes *pl* (of a meeting)
actitud *nf* **1** : attitude **2** POSTURA : posture, position
activar *vt* **1** : activate **2** ESTIMULAR : stimulate, speed up — **actividad** *nf* : activity — **activo, -va** *adj* : active — **activo** *nm* : assets *pl*
acto *nm* **1** ACCIÓN : act, deed **2** : act (in theater) **3 en el ~** : right away
actor *nm* : actor — **actriz** *nf, pl* **-trices** : actress
actual *adj* : present, current — **actualidad** *nf* **1** : present time **2 ~es** *nfpl* : current affairs — **actualizar** {21} *vt* : modernize — **actualización** *nf, pl* **-ciones** : modernization — **actualmente** *adv* : at present, nowadays
actuar {3} *vi* **1** : act, perform **2 ~ de** : act as
acuarela *nf* : watercolor
acuario *nm* : aquarium
acuartelar *vt* : quarter (troops)
acuático, -ca *adj* : aquatic, water
acuchillar *vt* : knife, stab
acudir *vi* **1** : go, come **2 ~ a** : be present at, attend **3 ~ a** : turn to
acueducto *nm* : aqueduct
acuerdo *nm* **1** : agreement **2 de ~** : OK, all right **3 de ~ con** : in accordance with **4 estar de ~** : agree
acumular *vt* : accumulate — **acumularse** *vr* : pile up — **acumulación** *nf, pl* **-ciones** : accumulation — **acumulador** *nm* : storage battery — **acumulativo, -va** *adj* : cumulative
acunar *vt* : rock
acuñar *vt* **1** : mint (money) **2** : coin (a word)
acuoso, -sa *adj* : watery
acupuntura *nf* : acupuncture
acurrucarse {72} *vr* : curl up, nestle
acusar *vt* **1** : accuse **2** MOSTRAR : reveal, show — **acusación** *nf, pl* **-ciones** : accusation, charge — **acusado, -da** *adj* : prominent, marked — **~** *n* : defendant
acuse *nm* **~ de recibo** : acknowledgment of receipt
acústica *nf* : acoustics — **acústico, -ca** *adj* : acoustic
adagio *nm* **1** REFRÁN : adage, proverb **2** : adagio (in music)
adaptar *vt* **1** : adapt **2** AJUSTAR : adjust, fit — **adaptarse** *vr* **~ a** : adapt to — **adaptable** *adj* : adaptable — **adaptación** *nf, pl* **-ciones** : adaptation — **adaptador** *nm* : adapter (in electricity)
adecuar {8} *vt* : adapt, make suitable — **adecuarse** *vr* **~ a** : be appropriate

for — **adecuado, -da** *adj* : suitable, appropriate
adelantar *vt* **1** : advance, move forward **2** PASAR : overtake **3** : pay in advance — **adelantarse** *vr* **1** : move forward, get ahead **2** : be fast (of a clock) — **adelantado, -da** *adj* **1** : advanced, ahead **2** : fast (of a clock) **3 por ~** : in advance — **adelante** *adv* **1** : ahead, forward **2 ¡~!** : come in! **3 más ~** : later on, further on — **adelanto** *nm* **1** : advance **2** *or* **~ de dinero** : advance payment
adelgazar {21} *vt* : make thin — *vi* : lose weight
ademán *nm, pl* **-manes 1** GESTO : gesture **2 ~es** *nmpl* : manners **3 en ~ de** : as if to
además *adv* **1** : besides, furthermore **2 ~ de** : in addition to, as well as
adentro *adv* : inside, within — **adentrarse** *vr* **~ en** : go into, get inside of
adepto, -ta *n* : follower, supporter
aderezar {21} *vt* : season, dress — **aderezo** *nm* : dressing, seasoning
adeudar *vt* **1** : debit **2** DEBER : owe — **adeudo** *nm* **1** DÉBITO : debit **2** *Lat* : debt
adherirse {76} *vr* : adhere, stick — **adherencia** *nf* : adherence — **adhesión** *nf, pl* **-siones 1** : adhesion **2** APOYO : support — **adhesivo, -va** *adj* : adhesive — **adhesivo** *nm* : adhesive
adición *nf, pl* **-ciones** : addition — **adicional** *adj* : additional
adicto, -ta *adj* : addicted — **~** *n* : addict
adiestrar *vt* : train
adinerado, -da *adj* : wealthy
adiós *nm, pl* **adioses 1** : farewell **2 ¡~!** : good-bye!
aditamento *nm* : attachment, accessory
aditivo *nm* : additive
adivinar *vt* **1** : guess **2** PREDECIR : foretell — **adivinación** *nf, pl* **-ciones** : guessing, prediction — **adivinanza** *nf* : riddle — **adivino, -na** *n* : fortune-teller
adjetivo *nm* : adjective
adjudicar {72} *vt* : award — **adjudicarse** *vr* : appropriate — **adjudicación** *nf, pl* **-ciones** : awarding
adjuntar *vt* : enclose (with a letter, etc.) — **adjunto, -ta** *adj* : enclosed, attached — **~** *n* : assistant
administración *nf, pl* **-ciones 1** : administration **2** : administering (of a drug, etc.) **3** DIRECCIÓN : management — **administrador, -dora** *n* : administrator, manager — **administrar** *vt* **1** : manage, run **2** : administer (a drug, etc.) — **administrativo, -va** *adj* : administrative
admirar *vt* : admire — **admirarse** *vr* : be amazed — **admirable** *adj* : admirable — **admiración** *nf, pl* **-ciones 1** : admiration **2** ASOMBRO : amazement — **admirador, -dora** *n* : admirer
admitir *vt* **1** : admit **2** ACEPTAR : accept — **admisible** *adj* : admissible, acceptable — **admisión** *nf, pl* **-siones 1** : admission **2** ACEPTACIÓN : acceptance
ADN *nm* : DNA
adobe *nm* : adobe
adobo *nm* : marinade
adoctrinar *vt* : indoctrinate — **adoctrinamiento** *nm* : indoctrination
adolecer {53} *vi* **~ de** : suffer from
adolescente *adj & nmf* : adolescent — **adolescencia** *nf* : adolescence
adonde *conj* : where
adónde *adv* : where
adoptar *vt* : adopt (a child), take (a decision) — **adopción** *nf, pl* **-ciones** : adoption — **adoptivo, -va** *adj* : adopted, adoptive
adoquín *nm, pl* **-quines** : cobblestone
adorar *vt* : adore, worship — **adorable** *adj* : adorable — **adoración** *nf, pl* **-ciones** : adoration, worship
adormecer {53} *vt* **1** : make sleepy **2** ENTUMECER : numb — **adormecerse** *vr* : doze off — **adormecimiento** *nm* : drowsiness — **adormilarse** *vr* : doze
adornar *vt* : decorate, adorn — **adorno** *nm* : ornament, decoration
adquirir {4} *vt* **1** : acquire **2** COMPRAR : purchase — **adquisición** *nf, pl* **-ciones 1** : acquisition **2** COMPRA : purchase
adrede *adv* : intentionally, on purpose
adscribir {33} *vt* : assign, appoint
aduana *nf* : customs (office) — **aduanero, -ra** *adj* : customs — **~** *n* : customs officer
aducir {61} *vt* : cite, put forward
adueñarse *vr* **~ de** : take possession of
adular *vt* : flatter — **adulación** *nf, pl* **-ciones** : adulation, flattery — **adulador, -dora** *adj* : flattering — **~** *n* : flatterer
adulterar *vt* : adulterate
adulterio *nm* : adultery — **adúltero, -ra** *n* : adulterer
adulto, -ta *adj & n* : adult
adusto, -ta *adj* : stern, severe
advenedizo, -za *n* : upstart
advenimiento *nm* : advent, arrival
adverbio *nm* : adverb — **adverbial** *adj* : adverbial
adversario, -ria *n* : adversary, opponent — **adverso, -sa** *adj* : adverse — **adversidad** *nf* : adversity

advertir {76} *vt* **1** AVISAR : warn **2** NOTAR : notice — **advertencia** *nf* : warning
adviento *nm* : Advent
adyacente *adj* : adjacent
aéreo, -rea *adj* : aerial, air
aerobic *nm* : aerobics *pl*
aerodinámico, -ca *adj* : aerodynamic
aeródromo *nm* : airfield
aerolínea *nf* : airline
aeromozo, -za *n* : flight attendant, steward *m*, stewardess *f*
aeronave *nf* : aircraft
aeropuerto *nm* : airport
aerosol *nm* : aerosol, spray
afable *adj* : affable — **afabilidad** *nf* : affability
afán *nm, pl* **afanes 1** ANHELO : eagerness **2** EMPEÑO : effort, hard work — **afanarse** *vr* : toil — **afanosamente** *adv* : industriously, busily — **afanoso, -sa** *adj* **1** : eager **2** TRABAJOSO : arduous
afear *vt* : make ugly, disfigure
afección *nf, pl* **-ciones** : ailment, complaint
afectar *vt* : affect — **afectación** *nf, pl* **-ciones** : affectation — **afectado, -da** *adj* : affected
afectivo, -va *adj* : emotional
afecto *nm* : affection — **afecto, -ta** *adj* **~ a** : fond of — **afectuoso, -sa** *adj* : affectionate, caring
afeitar *vt* : shave — **afeitarse** *vr* : shave — **afeitada** *nf* : shave
afeminado, -da *adj* : effeminate
aferrarse {55} *vr* : cling, hold on
afianzar {21} *vt* : secure, strengthen — **afianzarse** *vr* : become established
afiche *nm Lat* : poster
afición *nf, pl* **-ciones 1** : penchant, fondness **2** PASATIEMPO : hobby — **aficionado, -da** *n* **1** ENTUSIASTA : enthusiast, fan **2** AMATEUR : amateur — **aficionarse** *vr* **~ a** : become interested in
afilar *vt* : sharpen — **afilado, -da** *adj* : sharp — **afilador** *nm* : sharpener
afiliarse *vr* **~ a** : join, become a member of — **afiliación** *nf, pl* **-ciones** : affiliation — **afiliado, -da** *adj* : affiliated
afín *adj, pl* **afines** : related, similar — **afinidad** *nf* : affinity, similarity
afinar *vt* **1** : tune **2** PULIR : perfect, refine
afirmar *vt* **1** : state, affirm **2** REFORZAR : strengthen — **afirmación** *nf, pl* **-ciones** : statement, affirmation — **afirmativo, -va** *adj* : affirmative
afligir {35} *vt* **1** : afflict **2** APENAR : distress — **afligirse** *vr* : grieve — **aflicción** *nf, pl* **-ciones** : grief, sorrow — **afligido -da** *adj* : sorrowful, distressed
aflojar *vt* : loosen, slacken — *vi* : ease up — **aflojarse** *vr* : become loose, slacken
aflorar *vi* : come to the surface, emerge — **afloramiento** *nm* : outcrop
afluencia *nf* : influx — **afluente** *nm* : tributary
afortunado, -da *adj* : fortunate, lucky — **afortunadamente** *adv* : fortunately
afrentar *vt* : insult — **afrenta** *nf* : affront, insult
africano, -na *adj* : African
afrontar *vt* : confront, face
afuera *adv* **1** : out **2** : outside, outdoors — **afueras** *nfpl* : outskirts
agachar *vt* : lower — **agacharse** *vr* : crouch, stoop
agalla *nf* **1** BRANQUIA : gill **2 tener ~s** *fam* : have guts
agarrar *vt* **1** ASIR : grasp **2** *Lat* : catch — **agarrarse** *vr* : hold on, cling — **agarradera** *nf Lat* : handle — **agarrado, -da** *adj fam* : stingy — **agarre** *nm* : grip, grasp — **agarrón** *nm, pl* **-rones** : tug, pull
agasajar *vt* : fête, wine and dine — **agasajo** *nm* : lavish attention
agave *nm* : agave
agazaparse *vr* : crouch down
agencia *nf* : agency, office — **agente** *nmf* : agent, officer
agenda *nf* **1** : agenda **2** LIBRETA : notebook
ágil *adj* : agile — **agilidad** *nf* : agility
agitar *vt* **1** : agitate, shake **2** : wave, flap (wings, etc.) **3** PERTURBAR : stir up — **agitarse** *vr* **1** : toss about **2** INQUIETARSE : get upset — **agitación** *nf, pl* **-ciones 1** : agitation, shaking **2** INTRANQUILIDAD : restlessness — **agitado, -da** *adj* **1** : agitated, excited **2** : choppy, rough (of the sea)
aglomerar *vt* : amass — **aglomerarse** *vr* : crowd together
agnóstico, -ca *adj & n* : agnostic
agobiar *vt* **1** : oppress **2** ABRUMAR : overwhelm — **agobiado, -da** *adj* : weary, weighed down — **agobiante** *adj* : oppressing, oppressive
agonizar {21} *vi* : be dying — **agonía** *nf* **1** : death throes **2** PENA : agony — **agonizante** *adj* : dying
agorero, -ra *adj* : ominous
agostar *vt* : wither
agosto *nm* : August
agotar *vt* **1** : deplete, use up **2** CANSAR : exhaust, weary — **agotarse** *vr* **1**

: run out, give out **2** CANSARSE : get tired — **agotado, -da** *adj* **1** CANSADO : exhausted **2** : sold out — **agotador, -dora** *adj* : exhausting — **agotamiento** *nm* : exhaustion

agraciado, -da *adj* **1** : attractive **2** AFORTUNADO : fortunate

agradar *vi* : be pleasing — **agradable** *adj* : pleasant, agreeable — **agrado** *nm* **1** : taste, liking **2** **con ~** : with pleasure

agradecer {53} *vt* : be grateful for, thank — **agradecido, -da** *adj* : grateful — **agradecimiento** *nm* : gratitude

agrandar *vt* : enlarge — **agrandarse** *vr* : grow larger

agrario, -ria *adj* : agrarian, agricultural

agravar *vt* **1** : make heavier **2** EMPEORAR : aggravate, worsen — **agravarse** *vr* : get worse

agraviar *vt* : insult — **agravio** *nm* : insult

agredir {1} *vt* : attack

agregar {52} *vt* : add, attach — **agregado, -da** *n* : attaché — **agregado** *nm* : aggregate

agresión *nf, pl* **-siones** : aggression, attack — **agresividad** *nf* : aggressiveness — **agresivo, -va** *adj* : aggressive — **agresor, -sora** *n* : aggressor, attacker

agreste *adj* : rugged, wild

agriar *vt* : sour — **agriarse** *vr* **1** : turn sour (of milk, etc.) **2** : become embittered

agrícola *adj* : agricultural — **agricultura** *nf* : agriculture, farming — **agricultor, -tora** *n* : farmer

agridulce *adj* **1** : bittersweet **2** : sweet-and-sour (in cooking)

agrietar *vt* : crack — **agrietarse** *vr* **1** : crack **2** : chap

agrimensor, -sora *n* : surveyor

agrio, agria *adj* : sour

agrupar *vt* : group together — **agruparse** *vr* : form a group — **agrupación** *nf, pl* **-ciones** : group, association — **agrupamiento** *nm* : grouping

agua *nf* **1** : water **2** **~ oxigenada** : hydrogen peroxide **3** **~s negras** *or* **~s residuales** : sewage

aguacate *nm* : avocado

aguacero *nm* : downpour

aguado, -da *adj* **1** : watery **2** *Lat fam* : soft, flabby — **aguar** {10} *vt* **1** : water down, dilute **2** **~ la fiesta** *fam* : spoil the party

aguafuerte *nm* : etching

aguanieve *nf* : sleet

aguantar *vt* **1** SOPORTAR : bear, withstand **2** SOSTENER : hold — *vi* : hold out, last — **aguantarse** *vr* **1** : resign oneself **2** CONTENERSE : restrain oneself — **aguante** *nm* **1** : patience **2** RESISTENCIA : endurance

aguardar *vt* : await

aguardiente *nm* : clear brandy

aguarrás *nm* : turpentine

agudo, -da *adj* **1** : acute, sharp **2** : shrill, high-pitched (in music) — **agudeza** *nf* **1** : sharpness **2** : witticism

agüero *nm* : augury, omen

aguijón *nm, pl* **-jones** **1** : stinger (of an insect) **2** ESTÍMULO : goad, stimulus — **aguijonear** *vt* : goad

águila *nf* : eagle

aguja *nf* **1** : needle **2** : hand (of a clock) **3** : spire (of a church)

agujero *nm* : hole

agujeta *nf* **1** *Lat* : shoelace **2** **~s** *nfpl* : (muscular) stiffness

aguzar {21} *vt* **1** : sharpen **2** **~ el oído** : prick up one's ears

ahí *adv* **1** : there **2** **por ~** : somewhere, thereabouts

ahijado, -da *n* : godchild, godson *m*, goddaughter *f*

ahínco *nm* : eagerness, zeal

ahogar {52} *vt* **1** : drown **2** ASFIXIAR : smother — **ahogarse** *vr* : drown — **ahogo** *nm* : breathlessness

ahondar *vt* : deepen — *vi* : elaborate, go into detail

ahora *adv* **1** : now **2** **~ mismo** : right now

ahorcar {72} *vt* : hang, kill by hanging — **ahorcarse** *vr* : hang oneself

ahorita *adv Lat fam* : right now

ahorrar *vt* : save, spare — *vi* : save up — **ahorrarse** *vr* : spare oneself — **ahorro** *nm* : saving

ahuecar {72} *vt* **1** : hollow out **2** : cup (one's hands)

ahumar {8} *vt* : smoke, cure — **ahumado, -da** *adj* : smoked

ahuyentar *vt* : scare away, chase away

airado, -da *adj* : irate, angry

aire *nm* **1** : air **2** **~ acondicionado** : air-conditioning **3** **al ~ libre** : in the open air, outdoors — **airear** *vt* : air, air out

aislar {5} *vt* **1** : isolate **2** : insulate (in electricity) — **aislamiento** *nm* **1** : isolation **2** : (electrical) insulation

ajar *vt* **1** : crumple, wrinkle **2** ESTROPEAR : spoil

ajedrez *nm* : chess

ajeno, -na *adj* **1** : someone else's **2** EXTRAÑO : alien **3** **~ a** : foreign to

ajetreado, -da *adj* : hectic, busy —

ajetrearse *vr* : bustle about — **ajetreo** *nm* : hustle and bustle
ají *nm, pl* **ajíes** *Lat* : chili pepper
ajo *nm* : garlic
ajustar *vt* **1** : adjust, adapt **2** ACORDAR : agree on **3** SALDAR : settle — **ajustarse** *vr* : fit, conform — **ajustable** *adj* : adjustable — **ajustado, -da** *adj* **1** : close, tight **2** CEÑIDO : tight-fitting — **ajuste** *nm* : adjustment
ajusticiar *vt* : execute, put to death
al (*contraction of* **a** *and* **el**) → **a**[2]
ala *nf* **1** : wing **2** : brim (of a hat)
alabanza *nf* : praise — **alabar** *vt* : praise
alacena *nf* : cupboard, larder
alacrán *nm, pl* **-cranes** : scorpion
alado, -da *adj* : winged
alambre *nm* : wire
alameda *nf* **1** : poplar grove **2** : tree-lined avenue — **álamo** *nm* : poplar
alarde *nm* : show, display — **alardear** *vi* : boast
alargar {52} *vt* **1** : extend, lengthen **2** PROLONGAR : prolong — **alargarse** *vr* : become longer — **alargador** *nm* : extension cord
alarido *nm* : howl, shriek
alarmar *vt* : alarm — **alarma** *nf* : alarm — **alarmante** *adj* : alarming
alba *nf* : dawn
albahaca *nf* : basil
albañil *nm* : bricklayer, mason
albaricoque *nm* : apricot
albedrío *nm* **libre ~** : free will
alberca *nf* **1** : reservoir, tank **2** *Lat* : swimming pool
albergar {52} *vt* : house, lodge — **albergue** *nm* **1** : lodging **2** REFUGIO : shelter **3 ~ juvenil** : youth hostel
albóndiga *nf* : meatball
alborear *v impers* : dawn — **albor** *nm* : dawning — **alborada** *nf* : dawn
alborotar *vt* : excite, stir up — *vi* : make a racket — **alborotarse** *vr* : get excited — **alborotado, -da** *adj* : excited, agitated — **alborotador, -dora** *n* : agitator, rioter — **alboroto** *nm* : ruckus
alborozar {21} *vt* : gladden — **alborozo** *nm* : joy
álbum *nm* : album
alcachofa *nf* : artichoke
alcalde, -desa *n* : mayor
alcance *nm* **1** : reach **2** ÁMBITO : range, scope
alcancía *nf* : money box
alcantarilla *nf* : sewer, drain
alcanzar {21} *vt* **1** : reach **2** LLEGAR A : catch up with **3** LOGRAR : achieve, attain — *vi* **1** : suffice, be enough **2 ~ a** : manage to
alcaparra *nf* : caper
alcázar *nm* : fortress, castle
alce *nm* : moose, European elk
alcoba *nf* : bedroom
alcohol *nm* : alcohol — **alcohólico, -ca** *adj & n* : alcoholic — **alcoholismo** *nm* : alcoholism
aldaba *nf* : door knocker
aldea *nf* : village — **aldeano, -na** *n* : villager
aleación *nf, pl* **-ciones** : alloy
aleatorio, -ria *adj* : random
aleccionar *vt* : instruct, teach
aledaño, -ña *adj* : bordering — **aledaños** *nmpl* : outskirts
alegar {52} *vt* : assert, allege — *vi Lat* : argue — **alegato** *nm* **1** : allegation (in law) **2** *Lat* : argument
alegoría *nf* : allegory — **alegórico, -ca** *adj* : allegorical
alegrar *vt* : make happy, cheer up — **alegrarse** *vr* : be glad — **alegre** *adj* **1** CONTENTO : glad, happy **2** : colorful, bright — **alegremente** *adv* : happily — **alegría** *nf* : joy, cheer
alejar *vt* **1** : remove, move away **2** ENAJENAR : estrange — **alejarse** *vr* : move away, drift apart — **alejado, -da** *adj* : remote — **alejamiento** *nm* **1** : removal **2** : estrangement (of persons)
alemán, -mana *adj, mpl* **-manes** : German — **alemán** *nm* : German (language)
alentar {55} *vt* : encourage — **alentador, -dora** *adj* : encouraging
alergia *nf* : allergy — **alérgico, -ca** *adj* : allergic
alero *nm* : eaves *pl*
alertar *vt* : alert — **alerta** *adv* : on the alert — **alerta** *adj & nf* : alert
aleta *nf* **1** : fin, flipper **2** : small wing
alevosía *nf* : treachery — **alevoso, -sa** *adj* : treacherous
alfabeto *nm* : alphabet — **alfabético, -ca** *adj* : alphabetical — **alfabetismo** *nm* : literacy — **alfabetizar** {21} *vt* **1** : teach literacy **2** : alphabetize
alfalfa *nf* : alfalfa
alfarería *nf* : pottery
alféizar *nm* : sill, windowsill
alfil *nm* : bishop (in chess)
alfiler *nm* **1** : pin **2** BROCHE : brooch — **alfiletero** *nm* : pincushion
alfombra *nf* : carpet, rug — **alfombrilla** *nf* : small rug, mat
alga *nf* : seaweed
álgebra *nf* : algebra

algo *pron* **1** : something **2 ~ de** : some, a little — **~** *adv* : somewhat, rather
algodón *nm, pl* **-dones** : cotton
alguacil *nm* : constable, bailiff
alguien *pron* : somebody, someone
alguno, -na *adj* (**algún** *before masculine singular nouns*) **1** : some, any **2** (*in negative constructions*) : not any, not at all **3 algunas veces** : sometimes — **~** *pron* **1** : one, someone, somebody **2 algunos, -nas** *pron pl* : some, a few
alhaja *nf* : jewel
alharaca *nf* : fuss
aliado, -da *n* : ally — **~** *adj* : allied — **alianza** *nf* : alliance — **aliarse** {85} *vr* : form an alliance
alias *adv & nm* : alias
alicaído, -da *adj* : depressed
alicates *nmpl* : pliers
aliciente *nm* **1** : incentive **2** : attraction (to a place)
alienar *vt* : alienate — **alienación** *nf, pl* **-ciones** : alienation
aliento *nm* **1** : breath **2** ÁNIMO : encouragement, strength
aligerar *vt* **1** : lighten **2** APRESURAR : hasten, quicken
alimaña *nf* : pest, vermin
alimentar *vt* : feed, nourish — **alimentarse** *vr* **~ con** : live on — **alimentación** *nf, pl* **-ciones 1** : feeding **2** NUTRICIÓN : nourishment — **alimenticio, -cia** *adj* : nourishing — **alimento** *nm* : food, nourishment
alinear *vt* : align, line up — **alinearse** *vr* **~ con** : align oneself with — **alineación** *nf, pl* **-ciones 1** : alignment **2** : lineup (in sports)
aliño *nm* : dressing, seasoning — **aliñar** *vt* : season, dress
alisar *vt* : smooth
alistarse *vr* : join up, enlist — **alistamiento** *nm* : enlistment
aliviar *vt* : relieve, soothe — **aliviarse** *vr* : recover, get better — **alivio** *nm* : relief
aljibe *nm* : cistern, tank
allá *adv* **1** : there, over there **2 más ~** : farther away **3 más ~ de** : beyond
allanar *vt* **1** : smooth, level out **2** *Spain* : break into (a house) **3** *Lat* : raid — **allanamiento** *nm* **1** *Spain* : breaking and entering **2** *Lat* : raid
allegado, -da *n* : close friend, relation
allí *adv* : there, over there
alma *nf* : soul
almacén *nm, pl* **-cenes 1** : warehouse **2** *Lat* : shop, store **3 grandes almacenes** : department store — **almacenamiento** *or* **almacenaje** *nm* : storage — **almacenar** *vt* : store
almádena *nf* : sledgehammer
almanaque *nm* : almanac
almeja *nf* : clam
almendra *nf* **1** : almond **2** : kernel (of nuts, fruit, etc.)
almiar *nm* : haystack
almíbar *nm* : syrup
almidón *nm, pl* **-dones** : starch — **almidonar** *vt* : starch
almirante *nm* : admiral
almohada *nf* : pillow — **almohadilla** *nf* : small pillow, pad — **almohadón** *nm, pl* **-dones** : bolster, large cushion
almorranas *nfpl* : hemorrhoids, piles
almorzar {36} *vi* : have lunch — *vt* : have for lunch — **almuerzo** *nm* : lunch
alocado, -da *adj* : crazy, wild
áloe *or* **aloe** *nm* : aloe
alojar *vt* : house, lodge — **alojarse** *vr* : lodge, room — **alojamiento** *nm* : lodging, accommodations *pl*
alondra *nf* : lark
alpaca *nf* : alpaca
alpinismo *nm* : mountain climbing — **alpinista** *nmf* : mountain climber
alpiste *nm* : birdseed
alquilar *vt* : rent, lease — **alquilarse** *vr* : be for rent — **alquiler** *nm* : rent, rental
alquitrán *nm, pl* **-tranes** : tar
alrededor *adv* **1** : around, about **2 ~ de** : approximately — **alrededor de** *prep phr* : around — **alrededores** *nmpl* : outskirts
alta *nf* : discharge (of a patient)
altanería *nf* : haughtiness — **altanero, -ra** *adj* : haughty
altar *nm* : altar
altavoz *nm, pl* **-voces** : loudspeaker
alterar *vt* **1** : alter, modify **2** PERTURBAR : disturb — **alterarse** *vr* : get upset — **alteración** *nf, pl* **-ciones 1** : alteration **2** ALBOROTO : disturbance — **alterado, -da** *adj* : upset
altercado *nm* : altercation, argument
alternar *vi* **1** : alternate **2 ~ con** : socialize with — *vt* : alternate — **alternarse** *vr* : take turns — **alternativa** *nf* : alternative — **alternativo, -va** *adj* : alternating, alternative — **alterno, -na** *adj* : alternate
Alteza *nf* : Highness
altiplano *nm* : high plateau
altitud *nf* : altitude
altivez *nf, pl* **-veces** : haughtiness — **altivo, -va** *adj* : haughty
alto, -ta *adj* **1** : tall, high **2** RUIDOSO

: loud — **alto** *adv* **1** ARRIBA : high **2** : loud, loudly — **~** *nm* **1** ALTURA : height, elevation **2** : stop, halt — **~** *interj* : halt!, stop! — **altoparlante** *nm Lat* : loudspeaker
altruista *adj* : altruistic — **altruismo** *nm* : altruism
altura *nf* **1** : height **2** ALTITUD : altitude **3 a la ~ de** : near, up by
alubia *nf* : kidney bean
alucinar *vi* : hallucinate — **alucinación** *nf, pl* **-ciones** : hallucination
alud *nm* : avalanche
aludir *vi* : allude, refer — **aludido, -da** *adj* **darse por ~** : take it personally
alumbrar *vt* **1** : light, illuminate **2** PARIR : give birth to — **alumbrado** *nm* : (electric) lighting — **alumbramiento** *nm* : childbirth
aluminio *nm* : aluminum
alumno, -na *n* : pupil, student
alusión *nf, pl* **-siones** : allusion
aluvión *nm, pl* **-viones** : flood, barrage
alzar {21} *vt* : lift, raise — **alzarse** *vr* : rise (up) — **alza** *nf* : rise — **alzamiento** *nm* : uprising
ama → **amo**
amabilidad *nf* : kindness — **amable** *adj* : kind, nice
amaestrar *vt* : train
amagar {52} *vt* **1** : show signs of **2** AMENAZAR : threaten — *vi* : be imminent — **amago** *nm* **1** INDICIO : sign **2** AMENAZA : threat
amainar *vi* : abate
amamantar *v* : breast-feed, nurse
amanecer {53}*v impers* : dawn — *vi* : wake up — **~** *nm* : dawn, daybreak
amanerado *adj* : affected, mannered
amansar *vt* **1** : tame **2** APACIGUAR : soothe — **amansarse** *vr* : calm down
amante *adj* **~ de** : fond of — **~** *nmf* : lover
amañar *vt* : rig, tamper with
amapola *nf* : poppy
amar *vt* : love
amargar {52} *vt* : make bitter — **amargado, -da** *adj* : embittered — **amargo, -ga** *adj* : bitter — **amargo** *nm* : bitterness — **amargura** *nf* : bitterness, grief
amarillo, -lla *adj* : yellow — **amarillo** *nm* : yellow
amarrar *vt* **1** : moor **2** ATAR : tie up
amasar *vt* **1** : knead **2** : amass (a fortune, etc.)
amateur *adj & nmf* : amateur
amatista *nf* : amethyst
ambages *nmpl* **sin ~** : without hesitation, straight to the point
ámbar *nm* : amber
ambición *nf, pl* **-ciones** : ambition — **ambicionar** *vt* : aspire to — **ambicioso, -sa** *adj* : ambitious
ambiente *nm* **1** AIRE : atmosphere **2** MEDIO : environment, surroundings *pl* — **ambiental** *adj* : environmental
ambigüedad *nf* : ambiguity — **ambiguo, -gua** *adj* : ambiguous
ámbito *nm* : domain, sphere
ambos, -bas *adj & pron* : both
ambulancia *nf* : ambulance
ambulante *adj* : traveling, itinerant
ameba *nf* : amoeba
amedrentar *vt* : intimidate
amén *nm* **1** : amen **2 ~ de** : in addition to
amenazar {21} *vt* : threaten — **amenaza** *nf* : threat, menace
amenizar {21} *vt* : make pleasant, enliven — **ameno, -na** *adj* : pleasant
americano, -na *adj* : American
ameritar *vt Lat* : deserve
ametralladora *nf* : machine gun
amianto *nm* : asbestos
amiba → **ameba**
amígdala *nf* : tonsil — **amigdalitis** *nf* : tonsilitis
amigo, -ga *adj* : friendly, close — **~** *n* : friend — **amigable** *adj* : friendly
amilanar *vt* : daunt — **amilanarse** *vr* : lose heart
aminorar *vt* : diminish
amistad *nf* : friendship — **amistoso, -sa** *adj* : friendly
amnesia *nf* : amnesia
amnistía *nf* : amnesty
amo, ama *n* **1** : master *m*, mistress *f* **2 ama de casa** : homemaker, housewife **3 ama de llaves** : housekeeper
amodorrado, -da *adj* : drowsy
amolar {19} *vt* **1** : grind, sharpen **2** MOLESTAR : annoy
amoldar *vt* : adapt, adjust — **amoldarse** *vr* **~ a** : adapt to
amonestar *vt* : admonish, warn — **amonestación** *nf, pl* **-ciones** : admonition, warning
amoníaco *or* **amoniaco** *nm* : ammonia
amontonar *vt* : pile up — **amontonarse** *vr* : pile up (of things), form a crowd (of persons)
amor *nm* : love
amordazar {21} *vt* : gag
amorío *nm* : love affair — **amoroso, -sa** *adj* **1** : loving **2** *Lat* : sweet, lovable
amortado, -da *adj* : black-and-blue
amortiguar {10} *vt* : muffle, soften, tone down — **amortiguador** *nm* : shock absorber

amortizar {21} *vt* : pay off — **amortización** *nf* : repayment
amotinar *vt* : incite (to riot) — **amotinarse** *vr* : riot, rebel
amparar *vt* : shelter, protect — **ampararse** *vr* **1** ~ **de** : take shelter from **2** ~ **en** : have recourse to — **amparo** *nm* : refuge, protection
ampliar {85} *vt* **1** : expand **2** : enlarge (a photograph) — **ampliación** *nf, pl* **-ciones 1** : expansion, enlargement **2** : extension (of a building)
amplificar {72} *vt* : amplify — **amplificador** *nm* : amplifier
amplio, -plia *adj* : broad, wide, ample — **amplitud** *nf* **1** : breadth, extent **2** ESPACIOSIDAD : spaciousness
ampolla *nf* **1** : blister **2** : vial, ampoule — **ampollarse** *vr* : blister
ampuloso, -sa *adj* : pompous
amputar *vt* : amputate — **amputación** *nf, pl* **-ciones** : amputation
amueblar *vt* : furnish (a house, etc.)
amurallar *vt* : wall in
anacardo *nm* : cashew nut
anaconda *nf* : anaconda
anacrónico, -ca *adj* : anachronistic — **anacronismo** *nm* : anachronism
ánade *nmf* : duck
anagrama *nm* : anagram
anales *nmpl* : annals
analfabeto, -ta *adj & n* : illiterate — **analfabetismo** *nm* : illiteracy
analgésico *nm* : painkiller, analgesic
analizar {21} *vt* : analyze — **análisis** *nm* : analysis — **analítico, -ca** *adj* : analytical, analytic
analogía *nf* : analogy — **análogo, -ga** *adj* : analogous
ananá *or* **ananás** *nm, pl* **-nás** : pineapple
anaquel *nm* : shelf
anaranjado, -da *adj* : orange-colored
anarquía *nf* : anarchy — **anarquista** *adj & nmf* : anarchist
anatomía *nf* : anatomy — **anatómico, -ca** *adj* : anatomic, anatomical
anca *nf* **1** : haunch **2** ~**s de rana** : frogs' legs
ancestral *adj* : ancestral
ancho, -cha *adj* : wide, broad, ample — **ancho** *nm* : width
anchoa *nf* : anchovy
anchura *nf* : width, breadth
anciano, -na *adj* : aged, elderly — ~ *n* : elderly person
ancla *nf* : anchor — **anclar** *v* : anchor
andadas *nfpl* **1** : tracks **2 volver a las** ~ : go back to one's old ways
andadura *nf* : walking, journey
andaluz, -luza *adj & n, mpl* **-luces** : Andalusian
andamio *nm* : scaffold
andanada *nf* **1** : volley **2 soltar una** ~ : reprimand
andanzas *nfpl* : adventures
andar {6} *vi* **1** CAMINAR : walk **2** IR : go, travel **3** FUNCIONAR : run, work **4** ~ **en** : rummage around in **5** ~ **por** : be approximately — *vt* : cover, travel — ~ *nm* : gait, walk
andén *nm, pl* **-denes 1** : (train) platform **2** *Lat* : sidewalk
andino, -na *adj* : Andean
andorrano, -na *adj* : Andorran
andrajos *nmpl* : tatters — **andrajoso, -sa** *adj* : ragged
anécdota *nf* : anecdote
anegar {52} *vt* : flood — **anegarse** *vr* **1** : be flooded **2** AHOGARSE : drown
anemia *nf* : anemia — **anémico, -ca** *adj* : anemic
anestesia *nf* : anesthesia — **anestésico, -ca** *adj* : anesthetic — **anestésico** *nm* : anesthetic
anexar *vt* : annex, attach — **anexo, -xa** *adj* : attached — **anexo** *nm* : annex
anfibio, -bia *adj* : amphibious — **anfibio** *nm* : amphibian
anfiteatro *nm* : amphitheater
anfitrión, -triona *n, mpl* **-triones** : host, hostess *f*
ángel *nm* : angel — **angelical** *adj* : angelic, angelical
angloparlante *adj* : English-speaking
anglosajón, -jona *adj, mpl* **-jones** : Anglo-Saxon
angosto, -ta *adj* : narrow
anguila *nf* : eel
ángulo *nm* **1** : angle **2** ESQUINA : corner — **angular** *adj* : angular — **anguloso, -sa** *adj* : angular
angustiar *vt* **1** : anguish, distress **2** INQUIETAR : worry — **angustiarse** *vr* : get upset — **angustia** *nf* **1** : anguish **2** INQUIETUD : worry — **angustioso, -sa** *adj* **1** : anguished **2** INQUIETANTE : distressing
anhelar *vt* : yearn for, crave — **anhelante** *adj* : yearning, longing — **anhelo** *nm* : longing
anidar *vi* : nest
anillo *nm* : ring
ánima *n* : soul
animación *nf, pl* **-ciones 1** VIVEZA : liveliness **2** BULLICIO : hustle and bustle — **animado, -da** *adj* : cheerful, animated — **animador, -dora** *n* **1** : (television) host **2** : cheerleader

animadversión *nf, pl* **-siones** : animosity
animal *nm* : animal — **~** *nmf* : brute, beast — **~** *adj* : brutish
animar *vt* **1** ALENTAR : encourage **2** ALEGAR : cheer up — **animarse** *vr* **1** : liven up **2** **~ a** : get up the nerve to
ánimo *nm* **1** : spirit, soul **2** HUMOR : mood, spirits *pl* **3** ALIENTO : encouragement
animosidad *nf* : animosity, ill will
animoso, -sa *adj* : spirited, brave
aniquilar *vt* : annihilate — **aniquilación** *n, pl* **-ciones** : annihilation
anís *nm* : anise
aniversario *nm* : anniversary
ano *nm* : anus
anoche *adv* : last night
anochecer {53} *vi* : get dark — **~** *nm* : dusk, nightfall
anodino, -na *adj* : insipid, dull
anomalía *nf* : anomaly
anonadado, -da *adj* : dumbfounded
anónimo, -ma *adj* : anonymous — **anonimato** *nm* : anonymity
anorexia *nf* : anorexia
anormal *adj* : abnormal — **anormalidad** *nf* : abnormality
anotar *vt* **1** : annotate **2** APUNTAR : jot down — **anotación** *nf, pl* **-ciones** : annotation, note
anquilosarse *vr* **1** : become paralyzed **2** ESTANCARSE : stagnate — **anquilosamiento** *nm* **1** : paralysis **2** ESTANCAMIENTO : stagnation
ansiar {85} *vt* : long for — **ansia** *nf* **1** INQUIETUD : uneasiness **2** ANGUSTIA : anguish **3** ANHELO : longing — **ansiedad** *nf* : anxiety — **ansioso, -sa** *adj* **1** : anxious **2** DESEOSO : eager
antagónico, -ca *adj* : antagonistic — **antagonismo** *nm* : antagonism — **antagonista** *nmf* : antagonist
antaño *adv* : yesteryear, long ago
antártico, -ca *adj* : antarctic
ante[1] *nm* **1** : elk, moose **2** GAMUZA : suede
ante[2] *prep* **1** : before, in front of **2** : in view of **3** **~ todo** : above all
anteanoche *adv* : the night before last
anteayer *adv* : the day before yesterday
antebrazo *nm* : forearm
anteceder *vt* : precede — **antecedente** *adj* : previous, prior — **~** *nm* : precedent — **antecesor, -sora** *n* **1** : ancestor **2** PREDECESOR : predecessor
antedicho, -cha *adj* : aforesaid
antelación *nf, pl* **-ciones** **1** : advance notice **2** **con ~** : in advance
antemano *adv* **de ~** : beforehand
antena *nf* : antenna
antenoche → **anteanoche**
anteojos *nmpl* **1** : glasses, eyeglasses **2** **~ bifocales** : bifocals
antepasado, -da *n* : ancestor
antepecho *nm* : ledge
antepenúltimo, -ma *adj* : third from last
anteponer {60} *vt* **1** : place before **2** PREFERIR : prefer
anterior *adj* **1** : previous, earlier **2** DELANTERO : front — **anterioridad** *nf* **con ~** : beforehand, in advance — **anteriormente** *adv* : previously
antes *adv* **1** : before, earlier **2** ANTERIORMENTE : previously **3** PRIMERO : first **4** MEJOR : rather **5** **~ de** : before, previous to **6** **~ que** : before
antesala *nf* : waiting room
antiaéreo, -rea *adj* : antiaircraft
antibiótico *nm* : antibiotic
anticipar *vt* **1** : move up (a date, etc.) **2** : pay in advance — **anticiparse** *vr* **1** : be early **2** ADELANTARSE : get ahead — **anticipación** *nf, pl* **-ciones** **1** : anticipation **2** **con ~** : in advance — **anticipado, -da** *adj* **1** : advance, early **2** **por ~** : in advance — **anticipo** *nm* **1** : advance (payment) **2** : foretaste
anticoncepción *nf, pl* **-ciones** : contraception — **anticonceptivo, -va** *adj* : contraceptive — **anticonceptivo** *nm* : contraceptive
anticongelante *nm* : antifreeze
anticuado, -da *adj* : antiquated, outdated
anticuario, -ria *n* : antique dealer — **anticuario** *nm* : antique shop
anticuerpo *nm* : antibody
antídoto *nm* : antidote
antier → **anteayer**
antiestético, -ca *adj* : unsightly
antifaz *nm, pl* **-faces** : mask
antífona *nf* : anthem
antigualla *nf* : relic, old thing
antiguo, -gua *adj* **1** : ancient, old **2** ANTERIOR : former **3** ANTICUADO : old-fashioned **4** **muebles antiguos** : antique furniture — **antiguamente** *adv* **1** : long ago **2** ANTES : formerly — **antigüedad** *nf* **1** : antiquity **2** : seniority (in the workplace) **3** **~es** *nfpl* : antiques
antihigiénico, -ca *adj* : unsanitary
antihistamínico *nm* : antihistamine
antiinflamatorio, -ria *adj* : anti-inflammatory
antílope *nm* : antelope
antinatural *adj* : unnatural

antipatía *nf* : aversion, dislike — **antipático, -ca** *adj* : unpleasant
antirreglamentario, -ria *adj* : unlawful
antirrobo, -ba *adj* : antitheft
antisemita *adj* : anti-Semitic — **antisemitismo** *nm* : anti-Semitism
antiséptico, -ca *adj* : antiseptic — **antiséptico** *nm* : antiseptic
antisocial *adj* : antisocial
antítesis *nf* : antithesis
antojarse *vr* **1** APETECER : crave **2** PARECER : seem, appear — **antojadizo, -za** *adj* : capricious — **antojo** *nm* : whim, craving
antología *nf* : anthology
antorcha *nf* : torch
antro *nm* : dive, den
antropófago, -ga *nmf* : cannibal
antropología *nf* : anthropology
anual *adj* : annual, yearly — **anualidad** *nf* : annuity — **anuario** *nm* : yearbook, annual
anudar *vt* : knot — **anudarse** *vr* : tie, knot
anular *vt* : annul, cancel — **anulación** *nf, pl* **-ciones** : annulment, cancellation
anunciar *vt* **1** : announce **2** : advertise (products) — **anunciante** *nmf* : advertiser — **anuncio** *nm* **1** : announcement **2** *or* **~ publicitario** : advertisement
anzuelo *nm* **1** : fishhook **2 morder el ~** : take the bait
añadir *vt* : add — **añadidura** *nf* **1** : additive, addition **2 por ~** : in addition, furthermore
añejo, -ja *adj* : aged, vintage
añicos *nmpl* **hacer(se) ~** : smash to pieces
añil *adj & nm* : indigo (color)
año *nm* **1** : year **2 Año Nuevo** : New Year
añorar *vt* : long for, miss — **añoranza** *nf* : nostalgia
añoso, -sa *adj* : aged, old
aorta *nf* : aorta
apabullar *vt* : overwhelm
apacentar {55} *vt* : pasture, graze
apachurrar *vt Lat* : crush
apacible *adj* : gentle, mild
apaciguar {10} *vt* : appease, pacify — **apaciguarse** *vr* : calm down
apadrinar *vt* **1** : be a godparent to **2** : sponsor (an artist, etc.)
apagar {52} *vt* **1** : turn or switch off **2** EXTINGUIR : extinguish, put out — **apagarse** *vr* **1** EXTINGUIRSE : go out **2** : die down — **apagado, -da** *adj* **1** : off, out **2** : dull, subdued (of colors, sounds, etc.) — **apagador** *nm Lat* : (light) switch — **apagón** *nm, pl* **-gones** : blackout
apalancar {72} *vt* **1** LEVANTAR : jack up **2** ABRIR : pry open — **apalancamiento** *nm* : leverage
apalear *vt* : beat up, thrash
aparador *nm* **1** : sideboard **2** *Lat* : shop window
aparato *nm* **1** : machine, appliance, apparatus **2** : system (in anatomy) **3** OSTENTACIÓN : ostentation — **aparatoso, -sa** *adj* **1** : ostentatious **2** ESPECTACULAR : spectacular
aparcar {72} *v Spain* : park — **aparcamiento** *nm Spain* **1** : parking **2** : parking lot
aparcero, -ra *n* : sharecropper
aparear *vt* : mate, pair up — **aparearse** *vr* : mate
aparecer {53} *vi* **1** : appear **2** PRESENTARSE : show up — **aparecerse** *vr* : appear
aparejar *vt* **1** : rig (a ship) **2** : harness (an animal) — **aparejado, -da** *adj* **llevar ~** : entail — **aparejo** *nm* **1** : equipment, gear **2** : harness (for an animal) **3** : rigging (for a ship)
aparentar *vt* **1** : seem **2** FINGIR : feign — **aparente** *adj* : apparent, seeming
aparición *nf, pl* **-ciones 1** : appearance **2** FANTASMA : apparition — **apariencia** *nf* **1** : appearance, look **2 en ~** : apparently
apartado *nm* **1** : section, paragraph **2 ~ postal** : post office box
apartamento *nm* : apartment
apartar *vt* **1** ALEJAR : move away **2** SEPARAR : set aside, separate — **apartarse** *vr* **1** : move away **2** DESVIARSE : stray — **aparte** *adv* **1** : apart, separately **2** ADEMÁS : besides
apasionar *vt* : excite, fascinate — **apasionarse** *vr* : get excited — **apasionado, -da** *adj* : passionate, excited — **apasionante** *adj* : exciting
apatía *nf* : apathy — **apático, -ca** *adj* : apathetic
apearse *vr* **1** : dismount **2** : get out of or off (a vehicle)
apedrear *vt* : stone
apegarse {52} *vr* **~ a** : become attached to, grow fond of — **apegado, -da** *adj* : devoted — **apego** *nm* : fondness
apelar *vi* **1** : appeal **2 ~ a** : resort to — **apelación** *nf, pl* **-ciones** : appeal
apellido *nm* : last name, surname — **apellidarse** *vr* : have for a last name
apenar *vt* : sadden — **apenarse** *vr* **1** : grieve **2** *Lat* : become embarrassed

apenas *adv* : hardly, scarcely — ~ *conj* : as soon as
apéndice *nm* : appendix — **apendicitis** *nf* : appendicitis
apercibir *vt* **1** : warn **2** *Lat* : notice — **apercibirse** *vr* ~ **de** : notice — **apercibimiento** *nm* : warning
aperitivo *nm* **1** : appetizer **2** : aperitif
apero *nm* : tool, implement
apertura *nf* : opening
apesadumbrar *vt* : sadden — **apesadumbrarse** *vr* : be weighed down
apestar *vi* : stink — **apestoso, -sa** *adj* : stinking, foul
apetecer {53} *vt* : crave, long for — **apetecible** *adj* : appealing
apetito *nm* : appetite — **apetitoso, -sa** *adj* : appetizing
ápice *nm* **1** : apex, summit **2** PIZCA : bit, smidgen
apilar *vt* : pile up — **apilarse** *vr* : pile up
apiñar *vt* : pack, cram — **apiñarse** *vr* : crowd together
apio *nm* : celery
apisonadora *nf* : steamroller
aplacar {72} *vt* : appease, placate — **aplacarse** *vr* : calm down
aplanar *vt* : flatten, level
aplastar *vt* : crush — **aplastante** *adj* : overwhelming
aplaudir *v* : applaud — **aplauso** *nm* **1** : applause **2** : acclaim
aplazar {21} *vt* : postpone, defer — **aplazamiento** *nm* : postponement
aplicar {72} *vt* : apply — **aplicarse** *vr* : apply oneself — **aplicable** *adj* : applicable — **aplicación** *nf, pl* **-ciones** : application — **aplicado, -da** *adj* : diligent
aplomo *nm* : aplomb
apocarse {72} *vr* : belittle oneself — **apocado, -da** *adj* : timid — **apocamiento** *nm* : timidity
apodar *vt* : nickname
apoderar *vt* : empower — **apoderarse** *vr* ~ **de** : seize — **apoderado, -da** *n* : agent, proxy
apodo *nm* : nickname
apogeo *nm* : peak, height
apología *nf* : defense, apology
apoplegía *nf* : stroke, apoplexy
aporrear *vt* : bang on, beat
aportar *vt* : contribute — **aportación** *nf, pl* **-ciones** : contribution
apostar[1] {19} *v* : bet, wager
apostar[2] *vt* : station, post
apostillar *vt* : annotate — **apostilla** *nf* : note
apóstol *nm* : apostle
apóstrofo *nm* : apostrophe
apostura *nf* : elegance, grace
apoyar *vt* **1** : support **2** INCLINAR : lean, rest — **apoyarse** *vr* ~ **en** : lean on, rest on — **apoyo** *nm* : support
apreciar *vt* **1** ESTIMAR : appreciate **2** EVALUAR : appraise — **apreciable** *adj* : considerable — **apreciación** *nf, pl* **-ciones** **1** : appreciation **2** VALORACIÓN : appraisal — **aprecio** *nm* **1** : appraisal **2** ESTIMA : esteem
aprehender *vt* : apprehend — **aprehensión** *nf, pl* **-siones** : apprehension, capture
apremiar *vt* : urge — *vi* : be urgent — **apremiante** *adj* : pressing, urgent — **apremio** *nm* : urgency
aprender *v* : learn — **aprenderse** *vr* : memorize
aprendiz, -diza *n, mpl* **-dices** : apprentice, trainee — **aprendizaje** *nm* : apprenticeship
aprensión *nf, pl* **-siones** : apprehension, dread — **aprensivo, -va** *adj* : apprehensive
apresar *vt* : capture, seize — **apresamiento** *nm* : seizure, capture
aprestar *vt* : make ready — **aprestarse** *vr* : get ready
apresurar *vt* : speed up — **apresurarse** *vr* : hurry — **apresuradamente** *adv* : hurriedly, hastily — **apresurado, -da** *adj* : in a rush
apretar {55} *vt* **1** : press, push (a button) **2** : tighten (a knot, etc.) **3** ESTRECHAR : squeeze — *vi* **1** : press (down) **2** : fit too tightly — **apretón** *nm, pl* **-tones** **1** : squeeze **2** ~ **de manos** : handshake — **apretado, -da** *adj* **1** : tight **2** *fam* : tightfisted
aprieto *nm* : predicament, jam
aprisa *adv* : quickly
aprisionar *vt* : imprison
aprobar {19} *vt* **1** : approve of **2** : pass (an exam, etc.) — *vi* : pass — **aprobación** *nf, pl* **-ciones** : approval
apropiarse *vr* ~ **de** : take possession of, appropriate — **apropiación** *nf, pl* **-ciones** : appropriation — **apropiado, -da** *adj* : appropriate
aprovechar *vt* : take advantage of, make good use of — *vi* : be of use — **aprovecharse** *vr* ~ **de** : take advantage of — **aprovechado, -da** *adj* **1** : diligent **2** OPORTUNISTA : opportunistic
aproximar *vt* : bring closer — **aproximarse** *vr* : approach — **aproximación** *nf, pl* **-ciones** : approximation — **aproximadamente** *adv*

: approximately — **aproximado, -da** *adj* : approximate
apto, -ta *adj* **1** : suitable **2** CAPAZ : capable — **aptitud** *nf* : aptitude, capability
apuesta *nf* : bet, wager
apuesto, -ta *adj* : elegant, good-looking
apuntalar *vt* : prop up, shore up
apuntar *vt* **1** : aim, point **2** ANOTAR : jot down **3** SEÑALAR : point at **4** : prompt (in theater) — **apuntarse** *vr* **1** : sign up **2** : score, chalk up (a victory, etc.) — **apunte** *nm* : note
apuñalar *vt* : stab
apurar *vt* **1** : hurry, rush **2** AGOTAR : use up **3** PREOCUPAR : trouble — **apurarse** *vr* **1** : worry **2** *Lat* : hurry up — **apuradamente** *adv* : with difficulty — **apurado, -da** *adj* **1** : needy **2** DIFÍCIL : difficult **3** *Lat* : rushed — **apuro** *nm* **1** : predicament, jam **2** *Lat* : hurry
aquejar *vt* : afflict
aquel, aquella *adj, mpl* **aquellos** : that, those
aquél, aquélla *pron, mpl* **aquéllos 1** : that (one), those (ones) **2** : the former
aquello *pron* : that, that matter
aquí *adv* **1** : here **2** AHORA : now **3 por ~** : hereabouts
aquietar *vt* : calm — **aquietarse** *vr* : calm down
ara *nf* **1** : altar **2 en ~s de** : for the sake of
árabe *adj* : Arab, Arabic — **~** *nm* : Arabic (language)
arado *nm* : plow
arancel *nm* : tariff
arándano *nm* : blueberry
araña *nf* **1** : spider **2** LÁMPARA : chandelier
arañar *v* : scratch, claw — **arañazo** *nm* : scratch
arar *v* : plow
arbitrar *v* **1** : arbitrate **2** : referee, umpire (in sports) — **arbitraje** *nm* : arbitration — **arbitrario, -ria** *adj* : arbitrary — **arbitrio** *nm* **1** : (free) will **2** JUICIO : judgment — **árbitro, -tra** *n* **1** : arbitrator **2** : referee, umpire (in sports)
árbol *nm* : tree — **arboleda** *nf* : grove
arbusto *nm* : shrub, bush
arca *nf* **1** : ark **2** COFRE : chest
arcada *nf* **1** : arcade **2 ~s** *nfpl* : retching
arcaico, -ca *adj* : archaic
arcano, -na *adj* : arcane, secret
arce *nm* : maple tree
archipiélago *nm* : archipelago
archivar *vt* : file — **archivador** *nm* : filing cabinet — **archivo** *nm* **1** : file **2** : archives *pl*
arcilla *nf* : clay
arco *nm* **1** : arch **2** : bow (in sports, music, etc.) **3** : arc (in geometry) **4 ~ iris** : rainbow
arder *vi* : burn
ardid *nm* : scheme, ruse
ardiente *adj* **1** : burning **2** FOGOSO : ardent
ardilla *nf* **1** : squirrel **2 ~ listada** : chipmunk
ardor *nm* **1** : burning **2** ENTUSIASMO : passion, ardor
arduo, -dua *adj* : arduous
área *nf* : area
arena *nf* **1** : sand **2** PALESTRA : arena — **arenoso, -sa** *adj* : sandy, gritty
arenque *nm* : herring
arete *nm Lat* : earring
argamasa *nf* : mortar
argentino, -na *adj* : Argentinian, Argentine
argolla *nf* : hoop, ring
argot *nm* : slang
argüir {41} *vt* **1** : argue **2** DEMOSTRAR : prove, show — *vi* : argue
argumentar *vt* : argue, contend — **argumentación** *nf, pl* **-ciones** : (line of) argument — **argumento** *nm* **1** : argument, reasoning **2** TRAMA : plot, story line
árido, -da *adj* : dry, arid — **aridez** *nf, pl* **-deces** : aridity
arisco, -ca *adj* : surly
aristocracia *nf* : aristocracy — **aristócrata** *nmf* : aristocrat — **aristocrático, -ca** *adj* : aristocratic
aritmética *nf* : arithmetic — **aritmético, -ca** *adj* : arithmetic, arithmetical
armar *vt* **1** : arm **2** MONTAR : assemble — **arma** *nf* **1** : arm, weapon **2 ~ de fuego** : firearm — **armada** *nf* : navy — **armado, -da** *adj* : armed — **armadura** *nf* **1** : armor **2** ARMAZÓN : framework — **armamento** *nm* : armament, arms *pl*
armario *nm* **1** : (clothes) closet **2** : cupboard, cabinet
armazón *nmf, pl* **-zones** : frame, framework
armisticio *nm* : armistice
armonizar {21} *vt* **1** : harmonize **2** : reconcile (differences, etc.) — *vi* : harmonize, go together — **armonía** *nf* : harmony — **armónica** *nf* : harmonica — **armónico, -ca** *adj* : harmonic — **armonioso, -sa** *adj* : harmonious
arnés *nm, pl* **-neses** : harness

aro *nm* **1** : hoop, ring **2** *Lat* : earring
aroma *nm* : aroma, scent — **aromático, -ca** *adj* : aromatic
arpa *nf* : harp
arpón *nm, pl* **-pones** : harpoon
arquear *vt* : arch, bend — **arquearse** *vr* : bend, bow
arqueología *nf* : archaeology — **arqueológico, -ca** *adj* : archaeological — **arqueólogo, -ga** *n* : archaeologist
arquero, -ra *n* **1** : archer **2** PORTERO : goalkeeper, goalie
arquetipo *nm* : archetype
arquitectura *nf* : architecture — **arquitecto, -ta** *n* : architect — **arquitectónico, -ca** *adj* : architectural
arrabal *nm* **1** : slum **2** **~es** *nmpl* : outskirts
arracimarse *vr* : cluster together
arraigar {52} *vi* : take root, become established — **arraigarse** *vr* : settle down — **arraigado, -da** *adj* : deeply rooted, well established — **arraigo** *nm* : roots *pl*
arrancar {72} *vt* **1** : pull out, tear off **2** : start (an engine), boot (a computer) — *vi* **1** : start an engine **2** : get going — **arranque** *nm* **1** : starter (of a car) **2** ARREBATO : outburst **3** **punto de ~** : starting point
arrasar *vt* **1** : destroy, devastate **2** LLENAR : fill to the brim
arrastrar *vt* **1** : drag **2** ATRAER : draw, attract — *vi* : hang down, trail — **arrastrarse** *vr* **1** : crawl, creep **2** HUMILLARSE : grovel — **arrastre** *nm* **1** : dragging **2** : trawling (for fish)
arrear *vt* : urge on
arrebatar *vt* **1** : snatch, seize **2** CAUTIVAR : captivate — **arrebatarse** *vr* : get carried away — **arrebatado, -da** *adj* : hotheaded, rash — **arrebato** *nm* : outburst
arreciar *vi* : intensify, worsen
arrecife *nm* : reef
arreglar *vt* **1** COMPONER : fix **2** ORDENAR : tidy up **3** SOLUCIONAR : solve, work out — **arreglarse** *vr* **1** : get dressed (up) **2** **arreglárselas** *fam* : get by, manage — **arreglado, -da** *adj* **1** : fixed, repaired **2** ORDENADO : tidy **3** SOLUCIONADO : settled, sorted out **4** ATAVIADO : smart, dressed-up — **arreglo** *nm* **1** : arrangement **2** REPARACIÓN : repair **3** ACUERDO : agreement
arremangarse {52} *vr* : roll up one's sleeves
arremeter *vi* : attack, charge — **arremetida** *nf* : attack, onslaught
arremolinarse *vr* **1** : crowd around, mill about **2** : swirl (about)
arrendar {55} *vt* : rent, lease — **arrendador, -dora** *n* : landlord, landlady *f* — **arrendamiento** *nm* : rent, rental — **arrendatario, -ria** *n* : tenant, renter
arrepentirse {76} *vr* **1** : regret, be sorry **2** : repent (for one's sins) — **arrepentido, -da** *adj* : repentant — **arrepentimiento** *nm* : regret, repentance
arrestar *vt* : arrest, detain — **arresto** *nm* : arrest
arriar *vt* : lower
arriba *adv* **1** (*indicating position*) : above, overhead **2** (*indicating direction*) : up, upwards **3** : upstairs (of a house) **4** **~ de** : more than **5** **de ~ abajo** : from top to bottom
arribar *vi* **1** : arrive **2** : dock, put into port — **arribista** *nmf* : parvenu, upstart — **arribo** *nm* : arrival
arriendo → **arrendimiento**
arriesgar {52} *vt* : risk, venture — **arriesgarse** *vr* : take a chance — **arriesgado, -da** *adj* : risky
arrimar *vt* : bring closer, draw near — **arrimarse** *vr* : approach
arrinconar *vt* **1** : corner, box in **2** ABANDONAR : push aside
arrobar *vt* : entrance — **arrobarse** *vr* : be enraptured — **arrobamiento** *nm* : rapture, ecstasy
arrodillarse *vr* : kneel (down)
arrogancia *nf* : arrogance — **arrogante** *adj* : arrogant
arrojar *vt* **1** : hurl, cast **2** EMITIR : give off, spew out **3** PRODUCIR : yield — **arrojarse** *vr* : throw oneself — **arrojado, -da** *adj* : daring — **arrojo** *nm* : boldness, courage
arrollar *vt* **1** : sweep away **2** DERROTAR : crush, overwhelm **3** : run over (with a vehicle) — **arrollador, -dora** *adj* : overwhelming
arropar *vt* : clothe, cover (up) — **arroparse** *vr* : wrap oneself up
arroyo *nm* **1** RIACHUELO : stream **2** : gutter (in a street)
arroz *nm, pl* **arroces** : rice
arrugar {52} *vt* : wrinkle, crease — **arrugarse** *vr* : get wrinkled — **arruga** *nf* : wrinkle, crease
arruinar *vt* : ruin, wreck — **arruinarse** *vr* **1** : be ruined **2** EMPOBRECERSE : go bankrupt
arrullar *vt* : lull to sleep — *vi* : coo — **arrullo** *nm* **1** : lullaby **2** : cooing (of doves)
arrumbar *vt* : lay aside
arsenal *nm* : arsenal

arsénico *nm* : arsenic
arte *nmf* (*usually m in singular, f in plural*) **1** : art **2** HABILIDAD : skill **3** ASTUCIA : cunning, cleverness **4** → **bello**
artefacto *nm* : artifact, device
arteria *nf* : artery
artesanía *nm* **1** : craftsmanship **2** : handicrafts *pl* — **artesanal** *adj* : handmade — **artesano, -na** *n* : artisan, craftsman
ártico, -ca *adj* : arctic
articular *vt* : articulate — **articulación** *nf, pl* **-ciones 1** : articulation, pronunciation **2** COYUNTURA : joint
artículo *nm* **1** : article **2 ~s de primera necesidad** : essentials **3 ~s de tocador** : toiletries
artífice *nmf* : artisan, craftsman
artificial *adj* : artificial
artificio *nm* **1** HABILIDAD : skill **2** APARATO : device **3** ARDID : artifice, ruse — **artificioso, -sa** *adj* : cunning, deceptive
artillería *nf* : artillery
artilugio *nm* : gadget
artimaña *nf* : ruse, trick
artista *nmf* **1** : artist **2** ACTOR : actor, actress *f* — **artístico, -ca** *adj* : artistic
artritis *nms & pl* : arthritis — **artrítico, -ca** *adj* : arthritic
arveja *nf Lat* : pea
arzobispo *nm* : archbishop
as *nm* : ace
asa *nf* : handle
asado, -da *adj* : roasted, grilled — **asado** *nm* : roast — **asador** *nm* : spit — **asaduras** *nfpl* : offal, entrails
asalariado, -da *n* : wage earner — **~** *adj* : salaried
asaltar *vt* **1** : assault **2** ROBAR : mug, rob — **asaltante** *nmf* **1** : assailant **2** ATRACADOR : mugger, robber — **asalto** *nm* **1** : assault **2** ROBO : mugging, robbery
asamblea *nf* : assembly, meeting
asar *vt* : roast, grill — **asarse** *vr fam* : roast, feel the heat
asbesto *nm* : asbestos
ascender {56} *vi* **1** : ascend, rise up **2** : be promoted (in a job) **3 ~ a** : amount to — *vt* : promote — **ascendencia** *nf* : ancestry, descent — **ascendiente** *nmf* : ancestor — **~** *nm* : influence — **ascensión** *nf, pl* **-siones** : ascent — **ascenso** *nm* **1** : ascent, rise **2** : promotion (in a job) — **ascensor** *nm* : elevator
asco *nm* **1** : disgust **2 hacer ~s de** : turn up one's nose at **3 me da ~** : it makes me sick
ascua *nf* **1** : ember **2 estar en ~s** *fam* : be on edge
asear *vt* : clean, tidy up — **asearse** *vr* : get cleaned up — **aseado, -da** *adj* : clean, tidy
asediar *vt* **1** : besiege **2** ACOSAR : harass — **asedio** *nm* **1** : siege **2** ACOSO : harassment
asegurar *vt* **1** : assure **2** FIJAR : secure **3** : insure (a car, house, etc.) — **asegurarse** *vr* : make sure
asemejarse *vr* **1** : be similar **2 ~ a** : look like, resemble
asentar {55} *vt* **1** : set down **2** INSTALAR : set up, establish **3** *Lat* : state — **asentarse** *vr* **1** : settle **2** ESTABLECERSE : settle down — **asentado, -da** *adj* : settled, established
asentir {76} *vi* : assent, agree — **asentimiento** *nm* : assent
aseo *nm* : cleanliness
asequible *adj* : accessible, attainable
aserrar {55} *vt* : saw — **aserradero** *nm* : sawmill — **aserrín** *nm, pl* **-rrines** : sawdust
asesinar *vt* **1** : murder **2** : assassinate — **asesinato** *nm* **1** : murder **2** : assassination — **asesino, -na** *n* **1** : murderer, killer **2** : assassin
asesorar *vt* : advise, counsel — **asesorarse** *vr* **~ de** : consult — **asesor, -sora** *n* : advisor, consultant — **asesoramiento** *nm* : advice, counsel
asestar {55} *vt* **1** : aim (a weapon) **2** : deal (a blow)
aseverar *vt* : assert — **aseveración** *nf, pl* **-ciones** : assertion
asfalto *nm* : asphalt
asfixiar *vt* : asphyxiate, suffocate — **asfixiarse** *vr* : suffocate — **asfixia** *nf* : asphyxiation, suffocation
así *adv* **1** : like this, like that, thus **2 ~ de** : so, that (much) **3 ~ que** : so, therefore **4 ~ que** : as soon as **5 ~ como** : as well as — **~** *adj* : such, like that — **~** *conj* AUNQUE : even though
asiático, -ca *adj* : Asian, Asiatic
asidero *nm* : handle
asiduo, -dua *adj* : frequent, regular
asiento *nm* : seat
asignar *vt* **1** : assign, allocate **2** DESTINAR : appoint — **asignación** *nf, pl* **-ciones 1** : assignment **2** SUELDO : salary, pay — **asignatura** *nf* : subject, course
asilo *nm* **1** : asylum, home **2** REFUGIO : refuge, shelter — **asilado, -da** *n* : inmate
asimilar *vt* : assimilate — **asimilarse** *vr* **~ a** : resemble

asimismo *adv* **1** : similarly, likewise **2** TAMBIÉN : as well, also

asir {7} *vt* : seize, grasp — **asirse** *vr* **~ a** : cling to

asistir *vi* **~ a** : attend, be present at — *vt* : assist — **asistencia** *nf* **1** : attendance **2** AYUDA : assistance — **asistente** *nmf* **1** : assistant **2 los ~s** : those present

asma *nf* : asthma — **asmático, -ca** *adj* : asthmatic

asno *nm* : ass, donkey

asociar *vt* : associate — **asociarse** *vr* **1** : form a partnership **2 ~ a** : join, become a member of — **asociación** *nf, pl* **-ciones** : association — **asociado, -da** *adj* : associate, associated — **~** *n* : associate, partner

asolar {19} *vt* : devastate

asomar *vt* : show, stick out — *vi* : appear, show — **asomarse** *vr* **1** : appear **2** : stick one's head out (of a window)

asombrar *vt* : amaze, astonish — **asombrarse** *vr* : be amazed — **asombro** *nm* : amazement, astonishment — **asombroso, -sa** *adj* : amazing, astonishing

asomo *nm* **1** : hint, trace **2 ni por ~** : by no means

aspaviento *nm* : exaggerated gestures, fuss

aspecto *nm* **1** : aspect **2** APARIENCIA : appearance, look

áspero, -ra *adj* : rough, harsh — **aspereza** *nf* : roughness, harshness

aspersión *nf, pl* **-siones** : sprinkling — **aspersor** *nm* : sprinkler

aspiración *nf, pl* **-ciones 1** : breathing in **2** ANHELO : aspiration

aspiradora *nf* : vacuum cleaner

aspirar *vi* **~ a** : aspire to — *vt* : inhale, breathe in — **aspirante** *nmf* : applicant, candidate

aspirina *nf* : aspirin

asquear *vt* : sicken, disgust

asquerosidad *nf* : filth, foulness — **asqueroso, -sa** *adj* : disgusting, sickening

asta *nf* **1** : flagpole **2** CUERNO : antler, horn **3** : shaft (of a spear) — **astado, -da** *adj* : horned

asterisco *nm* : asterisk

asteroide *nm* : asteroid

astigmatismo *nm* : astigmatism

astillar *vt* : splinter — **astilla** *nf* : splinter, chip

astillero *nm* : shipyard

astral *adj* : astral

astringente *adj & nm* : astringent

astro *nm* **1** : heavenly body **2** : star (of movies, etc.)

astrología *nf* : astrology

astronauta *nmf* : astronaut — **astronáutica** *nf* : astronautics

astronave *nf* : spaceship

astronomía *nf* : astronomy — **astronómico, -ca** *adj* : astronomical — **astrónomo, -ma** *n* : astronomer

astucia *nf* **1** : astuteness **2** ARDID : cunning, guile — **astuto, -ta** *adj* **1** : astute **2** TAIMADO : crafty

asueto *nm* : time off, break

asumir *vt* : assume — **asunción** *nf, pl* **-ciones** : assumption

asunto *nm* **1** : matter, affair **2** NEGOCIO : business

asustar *vt* : scare, frighten — **asustarse** *vr* **~ de** : be frightened of — **asustadizo, -za** *adj* : jumpy, skittish — **asustado, -da** *adj* : frightened, afraid

atacar {72} *v* : attack — **atacante** *nmf* : attacker

atado *nm* : bundle

atadura *nf* : tie, bond

atajar *vt* : block, cut off — *vi* **~ por** : take a shortcut through — **atajo** *nm* : shortcut

atañer {79} *vi* **~ a** : concern, have to do with

ataque *nm* **1** : attack, assault **2** ACCESO : fit **3 ~ de nervios** : nervous breakdown

atar *vt* : tie up, tie down — **atarse** *vr* : tie (up)

atardecer {53} *v impers* : get dark — **~** *nm* : late afternoon, dusk

atareado, -da *adj* : busy

atascar {72} *vt* **1** : block, clog **2** ESTORBAR : hinder — **atascarse** *vr* **1** OBSTRUIRSE : become obstructed **2** : get bogged down — **atasco** *nm* **1** : blockage **2** EMBOTELLAMIENTO : traffic jam

ataúd *nm* : coffin

ataviar {85} *vt* : dress (up) — **ataviarse** *vr* : dress up — **atavío** *nm* : attire

atemorizar {21} *vt* : frighten — **atemorizarse** *vr* : get scared

atención *nf, pl* **-ciones 1** : attention **2 prestar ~** : pay attention **3 llamar la ~** : attract attention — **~** *interj* : attention!, watch out!

atender {56 } *vt* **1** : attend to **2** CUIDAR : look after **3** : heed (advice, etc.) — *vi* : pay attention

atenerse {80} *vr* **~ a** : abide by

atentamente *adv* **1** : attentively **2 le saluda ~** : sincerely yours

atentar {55} *vi* **~ contra** : make an attempt on — **atentado** *nm* : attack
atento, -ta *adj* **1** : attentive, mindful **2** CORTÉS : courteous
atenuar {3} *vt* **1** : dim (lights), tone down (colors, etc.) **2** DISMINUIR : lessen — **atenuante** *nmf* : extenuating circumstances
ateo, atea *adj* : atheistic — **~** *n* : atheist
aterciopelado, -da *adj* : velvety, downy
aterido, -da *adj* : frozen stiff
aterrar {55} *vt* : terrify — **aterrador, -dora** *adj* : terrifying
aterrizar {21} *vi* : land — **aterrizaje** *nm* : landing
aterrorizar {21} *vt* : terrify
atesorar *vt* : hoard, amass
atestar {55} *vt* **1** : crowd, pack **2** : testify to (in law) — **atestado, -da** *adj* : stuffed, packed
atestiguar {10} *vt* : testify to
atiborrar *vt* : stuff, cram — **atiborrarse** *vr* : stuff oneself
ático *nm* **1** : penthouse **2** DESVÁN : attic
atildado, -da *adj* : smart, neat
atinar *vi* : be on target
atípico, -ca *adj* : atypical
atirantar *vt* : tighten
atisbar *vt* **1** : spy on **2** VISLUMBRAR : catch a glimpse of — **atisbo** *nm* : sign, hint
atizar {21} *vt* **1** : poke (a fire) **2** : rouse, stir up (passions, etc.) — **atizador** *nm* : poker
atlántico, -ca *adj* : Atlantic
atlas *nm* : atlas
atleta *nmf* : athlete — **atlético, -ca** *adj* : athletic — **atletismo** *nm* : athletics
atmósfera *nf* : atmosphere — **atmosférico, -ca** *adj* : atmospheric
atolondrado, -da *adj* **1** : scatterbrained **2** ATURDIDO : bewildered, dazed
átomo *nm* : atom — **atómico, -ca** *adj* : atomic — **atomizador** *nm* : atomizer
atónito, -ta *adj* : astonished, amazed
atontar *vt* : stun, daze
atorar *vt* : block — **atorarse** *vr* : get stuck
atormentar *vt* : torment, torture — **atormentarse** *vr* : torment oneself, agonize — **atormentador, -dora** *n* : tormenter
atornillar *vt* : screw
atorrante *nmf Lat* : bum, loafer
atosigar {52} *vt* : harass, annoy
atracar {72} *vi* : dock, land — *vt* : hold up, mug — **atracarse** *vr fam* **~ de** : gorge oneself with — **atracadero** *nm* : dock, pier — **atracador, -dora** *n* : robber, mugger
atracción *nf, pl* **-ciones** : attraction
atraco *nm* : holdup, robbery
atractivo, -va *adj* : attractive — **atractivo** *nm* : attraction, appeal
atraer {81} *vt* : attract
atragantarse *vr* : choke
atrancar {72} *vt* : block, bar — **atrancarse** *vr* : get blocked, get stuck
atrapar *vt* : trap, capture
atrás *adv* **1** DETRÁS : back, behind **2** ANTES : before, earlier **3 para ~** *or* **hacia ~** : backwards
atrasar *vt* **1** : put back (a clock) **2** DEMORAR : delay — *vi* : lose time — **atrasarse** *vr* : fall behind — **atrasado, -da** *adj* **1** : late, overdue **2** : backward (of countries, etc.) **3** : slow (of a clock) — **atraso** *nm* **1** RETRASO : delay **2** : backwardness **3 ~s** *nmpl* : arrears
atravesar {55} *vt* **1** CRUZAR : cross **2** TRASPASAR : pierce **3** : lay across (a road, etc.) **4** : go through (a situation) — **atravesarse** *vr* : be in the way
atrayente *adj* : attractive
atreverse *vr* : dare — **atrevido, -da** *adj* **1** : bold **2** INSOLENTE : insolent — **atrevimiento** *nm* **1** : boldness **2** DESCARO : insolence
atribuir {41} *vt* **1** : attribute **2** : confer (powers, etc.) — **atribuirse** *vr* : take credit for
atribular *vt* : afflict, trouble
atributo *nm* : attribute
atrincherar *vt* : entrench — **atrincherarse** *vr* : dig oneself in
atrocidad *nf* : atrocity
atronador, -dora *adj* : thunderous
atropellar *vt* **1** : run over **2** : violate, abuse (a person) — **atropellarse** *vr* : rush — **atropellado, -da** *adj* : hasty — **atropello** *nm* : abuse, outrage
atroz *adj, pl* **atroces** : atrocious
atuendo *nm* : attire
atufar *vt* : vex — **atufarse** *vr* : get angry
atún *nm, pl* **atunes** : tuna
aturdir *vt* **1** : stun, shock **2** CONFUNDIR : bewilder — **aturdido, -da** *adj* : dazed, bewildered
audaz *adj, pl* **-daces** : bold, daring — **audacia** *nf* : boldness, audacity
audible *adj* : audible
audición *nf, pl* **-ciones** **1** : hearing **2** : audition (in theater, etc.)
audiencia *nf* : audience
audífono *nm* **1** : hearing aid **2 ~s** *nmpl Lat* : headphones, earphones
audiovisual *adj* : audiovisual

auditar *vt* : audit — **auditor, -tora** *n* : auditor
auditorio *nm* **1** : auditorium **2** PÚBLICO : audience
auge *nm* **1** : peak **2** : (economic) boom
augurar *vt* : predict, foretell — **augurio** *nm* : omen
augusto, -ta *adj* : august
aula *nf* : classroom
aullar {8} *vi* : howl — **aullido** *nm* : howl
aumentar *vt* : increase, raise — *vi* : increase, grow — **aumento** *nm* : increase, rise
aun *adv* **1** : even **2** ~ **así** : even so
aún *adv* **1** : still, yet **2 más** ~ : furthermore
aunar {8} *vt* : join, combine — **aunarse** *vr* : unite
aunque *conj* **1** : though, although, even if **2** ~ **sea** : at least
aureola *nf* **1** : halo **2** FAMA : aura
auricular *nm* **1** : telephone receiver **2** ~**es** *nmpl* : headphones
aurora *nf* : dawn
ausentarse *vr* : leave, go away — **ausencia** *nf* : absence — **ausente** *adj* : absent — ~ *nmf* **1** : absentee **2** : missing person (in law)
auspicios *nmpl* : sponsorship, auspices
austero, -ra *adj* : austere — **austeridad** *nf* : austerity
austral *adj* : southern
australiano, -na *adj* : Australian
austriaco *or* **austríaco, -ca** *adj* : Austrian
auténtico, -ca *adj* : authentic, genuine — **autenticidad** *nf* : authenticity
auto *nm* : auto, car
autoayuda *nf* : self-help
autobiografía *nf* : autobiography — **autobiográfico, -ca** *adj* : autobiographical
autobús *nm, pl* **-buses** : bus
autocompasión *nf* : self-pity
autocontrol *nm* : self-control
autocracia *nf* : autocracy
autóctono, -na *adj* : indigenous, native
autodefensa *nf* : self-defense
autodidacta *adj* : self-taught
autodisciplina *nf* : self-discipline
autoestop → **autostop**
autografiar *vt* : autograph — **autógrafo** *nm* : autograph
autómata *nm* : automaton
automático, -ca *adj* : automatic — **automatización** *nf, pl* **-ciones** : automation — **automatizar** {21} *vt* : automate
automotor, -triz *adj, fpl* **-trices** : self-propelled
automóvil *nm* : automobile — **automovilista** *nmf* : motorist — **automovilístico, -ca** *adj* : automobile, car
autonomía *nf* : autonomy — **autónomo, -ma** *adj* : autonomous
autopista *nf* : expressway, highway
autopropulsado, -da *adj* : self-propelled
autopsia *nf* : autopsy
autor, -tora *n* **1** : author **2** : perpetrator (of a crime)
autoridad *nf* : authority — **autoritario, -ria** *adj* : authoritarian
autorizar {21} *vt* : authorize, approve — **autorización** *nf, pl* **-ciones** : authorization — **autorizado, -da** *adj* **1** PERMITIDO : authorized **2** : authoritative
autorretrato *nm* : self-portrait
autoservicio *nm* **1** : self-service restaurant **2** SUPERMERCADO : supermarket
autostop *nm* **1** : hitchhiking **2 hacer** ~ : hitchhike — **autostopista** *nmf* : hitchhiker
autosuficiente *adj* : self-sufficient
auxiliar *vt* : aid, assist — ~ *adj* : auxiliary — ~ *nmf* **1** : assistant, helper **2** ~ **de vuelo** : flight attendant — **auxilio** *nm* **1** : aid, assistance **2 primeros** ~**s** : first aid
avalancha *nf* : avalanche
avalar *vt* : guarantee, endorse — **aval** *nm* : guarantee, endorsement
avanzar {21} *v* : advance, move forward — **avance** *nm* : advance — **avanzado, -da** *adj* : advanced
avaricia *nf* : greed, avarice — **avaricioso, -sa** *adj* : avaricious, greedy — **avaro, -ra** *adj* : miserly — ~ *n* : miser
avasallar *vt* : overpower, subjugate — **avasallador, -dora** *adj* : overwhelming
ave *nf* : bird
avecinarse *vr* : approach
avecindarse *vr* : settle, take up residence
avellana *nf* : hazelnut
avena *nf* **1** : oats *pl* **2** *or* **harina de** ~ : oatmeal
avenida *nf* : avenue
avenir {87} *vt* : reconcile, harmonize — **avenirse** *vr* : agree, come to terms
aventajar *vt* : be ahead of, surpass
aventar {55} *vt* **1** : fan **2** : winnow (grain) **3** *Lat* : throw, toss
aventurar *vt* : venture, risk — **aventurarse** *vr* : take a risk — **aventura** *nf* **1** : adventure **2** RIESGO : risk **3** AMORÍO : love affair — **aventurado, -da** *adj*

: risky — **aventurero, -ra** *adj* : adventurous — ~ *n* : adventurer
avergonzar {9} *vt* : shame, embarrass — **avergonzarse** *vr* : be ashamed, be embarrassed
averiar {85} *vt* : damage — **averiarse** *vr* : break down — **avería** *nf* **1** : damage **2** : breakdown (of an automobile) — **averiado, -da** *adj* **1** : damaged, faulty **2** : broken down (of an automobile)
averiguar {10} *vt* **1** : find out **2** INVESTIGAR : investigate — **averiguación** *nf, pl* **-ciones** : investigation, inquiry
aversión *nf, pl* **-siones** : aversion, dislike
avestruz *nm, pl* **-truces** : ostrich
aviación *nf, pl* **-ciones** : aviation — **aviador, -dora** *n* : aviator
aviar {85} *vt* : prepare, make ready
ávido, -da *adj* : eager, avid — **avidez** *nf, pl* **-deces** : eagerness
avío *nm* **1** : preparation, provision **2** **~s** *nmpl* : gear, equipment
avión *nm, pl* **aviones** : airplane — **avioneta** *nf* : light airplane
avisar *vt* **1** : notify **2** ADVERTIR : warn — **aviso** *nm* **1** : notice **2** ADVERTENCIA : warning **3** *Lat* : advertisement, ad **4** **estar sobre ~** : be on the alert
avispa *nf* : wasp — **avispón** *nm, pl* **-pones** : hornet
avispado, -da *adj fam* : clever, sharp
avistar *vt* : catch sight of
avivar *vt* **1** : enliven, brighten **2** : arouse (desire, etc.) **3** : intensify (pain)
axila *nf* : underarm, armpit
axioma *nm* : axiom
ay *interj* **1** : oh! **2** : ouch!, ow!
ayer *adv* : yesterday — **~** *nm* : yesteryear, days gone by
ayote *nm Lat* : pumpkin
ayudar *vt* : help, assist — **ayudarse** *vr* **~ de** : make use of — **ayuda** *nf* : help, assistance — **ayudante** *nmf* : helper, assistant
ayunar *vi* : fast — **ayunas** *nfpl* **en ~** : fasting — **ayuno** *nm* : fast
ayuntamiento *nm* **1** : town hall, city hall (building) **2** : town or city council
azabache *nm* : jet
azada *nf* : hoe — **azadonar** *vt* : hoe
azafata *nf* : stewardess *f*
azafrán *nm, pl* **-franes** : saffron
azalea *nf* : azalea
azar *nm* **1** : chance **2** **al ~** : at random — **azaroso, -sa** *adj* : hazardous (of a journey, etc.), eventful (of a life)
azorar *vt* **1** : alarm **2** DESCONCERTAR : embarrass — **azorarse** *vr* : get embarrassed
azotar *vt* : beat, whip — **azote** *nm* **1** LÁTIGO : whip, lash **2** CALAMIDAD : scourge
azotea *nf* : flat or terraced roof
azteca *adj* : Aztec
azúcar *nmf* : sugar — **azucarado, -da** *adj* : sugary — **azucarera** *nf* : sugar bowl — **azucarero, -ra** *adj* : sugar
azufre *nm* : sulphur
azul *adj & nm* : blue — **azulado, -da** *adj* : bluish
azulejo *nm* **1** : ceramic tile **2** *Lat* : bluebird
azur *n* : azure, sky blue
azuzar {21} *vt* : incite, urge on

B

b *nf* : b, second letter of the Spanish alphabet
babear *vi* : drool, slobber — **baba** *nf* : saliva, drool
babel *nmf* : bedlam
babero *nm* : bib
babor *nm* : port (side)
babosa *nf* : slug — **baboso, -sa** *adj* **1** : slimy **2** *Lat fam* : silly
babucha *nf* : slipper
babuino *nm* : baboon
bacalao *nm* : cod
bache *nm* **1** : pothole, rut **2** DIFICULTADES : bad time
bachiller *nmf* : high school graduate — **bachillerato** *nm* : high school diploma
bacon *nm Spain* : bacon
bacteria *nf* : bacterium
bagaje *nm* : baggage, luggage
bagatela *nf* : trinket
bagre *nm* : catfish
bahía *nf* : bay
bailar *v* : dance — **bailarín, -rina** *n, mpl* **-rines** : dancer — **baile** *nm* **1** : dance **2** FIESTA : dance party, ball
bajar *vt* **1** : bring down, lower **2** DESCENDER : go down, come down — *vi* : descend, drop — **bajarse** *vr* **~ de** : get out of, get off — **baja** *nf* **1** : fall, drop **2** CESE : dismissal **3** PERMISO : sick leave **4** : (military) casualty — **bajada** *nf* **1** : descent, drop **2** PENDIENTE : slope

bajeza *nf* : lowness, meanness
bajío *nm* : sandbank, shoal
bajo, -ja *adj* **1** : low, lower **2** : short (in stature) **3** : soft, faint (of sounds) **4** VIL : base, vile — **bajo** *adv* **1** : low **2** **habla más ~** : speak more softly — **~** *nm* **1** : ground floor **2** DOBLADILLO : hem **3** : bass (in music) — **~** *prep* : under, below — **bajón** *nm, pl* **-jones** : sharp drop, slump
bala *nf* **1** : bullet **2** : bale (of cotton, etc.)
balada *nf* : ballad
balancear *vt* **1** : balance **2** : swing (one's arms, etc.), rock (a boat) — **balancearse** *vr* : swing, sway — **balance** *nm* **1** : balance **2** : balance sheet — **balanceo** *nm* : swaying, rocking
balancín *nm, pl* **-cines 1** : seesaw **2** MECEDORA : rocking chair
balanza *nf* : scales *pl,* balance
balar *vi* : bleat
balaustrada *nf* : balustrade, banister
balazo *nm* **1** DISPARO : shot **2** : bullet wound
balbucear *vi* **1** : stammer, stutter **2** : babble (of a baby) — **balbuceo** *nm* : stammering, muttering, babbling
balcón *nm, pl* **-cones** : balcony
balde *nm* **1** : bucket, pail **2 en ~** : in vain
baldío, -día *adj* **1** : uncultivated **2** INÚTIL : useless — **baldío** *nm* : wasteland
baldosa *nf* : floor tile
balear *vt Lat* : shoot (at) — **baleo** *nm Lat* : shot, shooting
balido *nm* : bleat
balín *nm, pl* **-lines** : pellet
balística *nf* : ballistics — **balístico, -ca** *adj* : ballistic
baliza *nf* **1** : buoy **2** : beacon (for aircraft)
ballena *nf* : whale
ballesta *nf* **1** : crossbow **2** : spring (of an automobile)
ballet *nm* : ballet
balneario *nm* : spa
balompié *nm* : soccer
balón *nm, pl* **-lones** : ball — **baloncesto** *nm* : basketball — **balonvolea** *nm* : volleyball
balsa *nf* **1** : raft **2** ESTANQUE : pond, pool
bálsamo *nm* : balsam, balm — **balsámico, -ca** *adj* : soothing
baluarte *nm* : bulwark, bastion
bambolear *vi* : sway, swing — **bambolearse** *vr* : sway, rock
bambú *nm, pl* **-búes** *or* **-bús** : bamboo
banal *adj* : banal
banana *nf Lat* : banana — **banano** *nm Lat* : banana
banca *nf* **1** : banking **2** BANCO : bench — **bancario, -ria** *adj* : bank, banking — **bancarrota** *nf* : bankruptcy — **banco** *nm* **1** : bank **2** BANCA : stool, bench, pew **3** : school (of fish)
banda *nf* **1** : band, strip **2** : band (in music) **3** PANDILLA : gang **4** : flock (of birds) **5 ~ sonora** : sound track — **bandada** *nf* : flock (of birds), school (of fish)
bandazo *nm* : lurch
bandeja *nf* : tray, platter
bandera *nf* : flag, banner
banderilla *nf* : banderilla
banderín *nm, pl* **-rines** : pennant, small flag
bandido, -da *n* : bandit
bando *nm* **1** : proclamation, edict **2** PARTIDO : faction, side
bandolero, -ra *n* : bandit
banjo *nm* : banjo
banquero, -ra *n* : banker
banqueta *nf* **1** : stool, footstool **2** *Lat* : sidewalk
banquete *nm* : banquet
bañar *vt* **1** : bathe, wash **2** SUMERGIR : immerse **3** CUBRIR : coat, cover — **bañarse** *vr* **1** : take a bath **2** : go swimming — **bañera** *nf* : bathtub — **bañista** *nmf* : bather — **baño** *nm* **1** : bath, swim **2** BAÑERA : bathtub **3** **¿donde está el ~?** : where is the bathroom? **4 ~ María** : double boiler
baqueta *nf* **1** : ramrod **2 ~s** *nfpl* : drumsticks
bar *nm* : bar, tavern
barajar *vt* **1** : shuffle (cards) **2** CONSIDERAR : consider — **baraja** *nf* : deck of cards
baranda *nf* : rail, railing — **barandal** *nm* : handrail, banister
barato, -ta *adj* : cheap — **barato** *adv* : cheap, cheaply — **barata** *nf Lat* : sale, bargain — **baratija** *nf* : trinket — **baratillo** *nm* : secondhand store, flea market
barba *nf* **1** : beard, stubble **2** BARBILLA : chin
barbacoa *nf* : barbecue
barbaridad *nf* **1** : barbarity, cruelty **2** **¡qué ~!** : that's outrageous! — **barbarie** *nf* : barbarism, savagery — **bárbaro, -ra** *adj* : barbaric
barbecho *nm* : fallow land
barbero, -ra *n* : barber — **barbería** *nf* : barbershop
barbilla *nf* : chin
barbudo, -da *adj* : bearded
barca *nf* **1** : boat **2 ~ de pasaje** : ferryboat — **barcaza** *nf* : barge — **barco** *nm* : boat, ship
barítono *nm* : baritone

barman *nm* : bartender
barnizar {21} *vt* **1** : varnish **2** : glaze (ceramics) — **barniz** *nm, pl* **-nices 1** : varnish **2** : glaze (on ceramics)
barómetro *nm* : barometer
barón *nm, pl* **-rones** : baron — **baronesa** *nf* : baroness
barquero *nm* : boatman
barquillo *nm* : wafer, cone
barra *nf* **1** : bar, rod, stick **2** : counter (of a bar, etc.)
barraca *nf* **1** : hut, cabin **2** CASETA : booth, stall
barranco *nm or* **barranca** *nf* : ravine, gorge, gully
barredera *nf* : street-sweeping machine
barrenar *vt* : drill — **barrena** *nf* : drill, auger
barrer *v* : sweep
barrera *nf* : barrier
barreta *nf* : crowbar
barriada *nf* : district, quarter
barrica *nf* : cask, keg
barricada *nf* : barricade
barrido *nm* : sweep, sweeping
barriga *nf* : belly
barril *nm* **1** : barrel, keg **2 de ~** : draft
barrio *nm* **1** : neighborhood **2 ~ bajo** : slums *pl*
barro *nm* **1** : mud **2** ARCILLA : clay **3** GRANO : pimple, blackhead — **barroso, -sa** *adj* : muddy
barrote *nm* : bar (on a window)
barrunto *nm* **1** : suspicion **2** INDICIO : sign, indication
bártulos *nmpl* : things, belongings
barullo *nm* : racket, ruckus
basa *nf* : base, pedestal — **basar** *vt* : base — **basarse** *vr* **~ en** : be based on
báscula *nf* : scales *pl*
base *nf* **1** : base **2** FUNDAMENTO : basis, foundation **3 ~ de datos** : database — **básico, -ca** *adj* : basic
basquetbol *or* **básquetbol** *nm Lat* : basketball
bastar *vi* : be enough, suffice — **bastante** *adv* **1** : fairly, rather **2** SUFICIENTE : enough — **~** *adj* : enough, sufficient — **~** *pron* : enough
bastardo, -da *adj & n* : bastard
bastidor *nm* **1** : frame **2** : wing (in theater) **3 entre ~es** : behind the scenes, backstage
bastilla *nf* : hem
bastión *nf, pl* **-tiones** : bastion, stronghold
basto, -ta *adj* : coarse, rough
bastón *nm, pl* **-tones 1** : cane, walking stick **2** : baton (in parades)
basura *nf* : garbage, rubbish — **basurero, -ra** *n* : garbage collector
bata *nf* **1** : bathrobe, housecoat **2** : smock (of a doctor, laboratory worker, etc.)
batallar *vi* : battle, fight — **batalla** *nf* **1** : battle, fight, struggle **2 de ~** : ordinary, everyday — **batallón** *nm, pl* **-llones** : battalion
batata *nf* : yam, sweet potato
batear *v* : bat, hit — **bate** *nm* : baseball bat — **bateador, -dora** *n* : batter, hitter
batería *nf* **1** : battery **2** : drums *pl* **3 ~ de cocina** : kitchen utensils *pl*
batir *vt* **1** : beat, whip **2** DERRIBAR : knock down — **batirse** *vr* : fight — **batido** *nm* : milk shake — **batidor** *nm* : eggbeater, whisk — **batidora** *nf* : electric mixer
batuta *nf* : baton
baúl *nm* : trunk, chest
bautismo *nm* : baptism — **bautismal** *adj* : baptismal — **bautizar** {21} *vt* : baptize — **bautizo** *nm* : baptism, christening
baya *nf* : berry
bayeta *nf* : cleaning cloth
bayoneta *nf* : bayonet
bazar *nm* : bazaar
bazo *nm* : spleen
bazofia *nf fam* : rubbish, hogwash
beato, -ta *adj* : blessed
bebé *nm* : baby
beber *v* : drink — **bebedero** *nm* : watering trough — **bebedor, -dora** *n* : (heavy) drinker — **bebida** *nf* : drink, beverage — **bebido, -da** *adj* : drunk
beca *nf* : grant, scholarship
becerro, -rra *n* : calf
befa *nf* : jeer, taunt
beige *adj & nm* : beige
beisbol *or* **béisbol** *nm* : baseball — **beisbolista** *nmf* : baseball player
beldad *nf* : beauty
belén *nf, pl* **-lenes** : Nativity scene
belga *adj* : Belgian
beliceño, -ña *adj* : Belizean
bélico, -ca *adj* : military, war — **belicoso, -sa** *adj* : warlike
beligerancia *nf* : belligerence — **beligerante** *adj & nmf* : belligerent
belleza *nf* : beauty — **bello, -lla** *adj* **1** : beautiful **2 bellas artes** : fine arts
bellota *nf* : acorn
bemol *adj & nm* : flat (in music)
bendecir {11} *vt* **1** : bless **2 ~ la mesa** : say grace — **bendición** *nf, pl* **-ciones** : benediction, blessing — **bendito, -ta** *adj* **1** : blessed, holy **2** DI-

CHOSO : fortunate **3 ¡bendito sea Dios!** : thank goodness!
benefactor, -tora *n* : benefactor
beneficiar *vt* : benefit, assist — **beneficiarse** *vr* : benefit, profit — **beneficiario, -ria** *n* : beneficiary — **beneficio** *nm* **1** : gain, profit **2** BIEN : benefit — **beneficioso, -sa** *adj* : beneficial — **benéfico, -ca** *adj* : charitable
benemérito, -ta *adj* : worthy
beneplácito *nm* : approval, consent
benévolo, -la *adj* : benevolent, kind — **benevolencia** *nf* : benevolence, kindness
bengala *nf or* **luz de ~** : flare
benigno, -na *adj* **1** : mild **2** : benign (in medicine) — **benignidad** *nf* : mildness, kindness
benjamín, -mina *n, mpl* **-mines** : youngest child
beodo, -da *adj & n* : drunk
berenjena *nf* : eggplant
berrear *vi* **1** : bellow, low **2** : bawl, howl (of a person) — **berrido** *nm* **1** : bellowing **2** : howl, scream (of a person)
berro *nm* : watercress
berza *nf* : cabbage
besar *vt* : kiss — **besarse** *vr* : kiss (each other) — **beso** *nm* : kiss
bestia *nf* : beast, animal — **bestial** *adj* : bestial, brutal — **bestialidad** *nf* : brutality
betabel *nm Lat* : beet
betún *nm, pl* **-tunes** : shoe polish
bianual *adj* : biannual
biberón *nm, pl* **-rones** : baby's bottle
Biblia *nf* : Bible — **bíblico, -ca** *adj* : biblical
bibliografía *nf* : bibliography — **bibliográfico, -ca** *adj* : bibliographic, bibliographical
biblioteca *nf* : library — **bibliotecario, -ria** *n* : librarian
bicarbonato *nm* **~ de soda** : baking soda
bicentenario *nm* : bicentennial
bíceps *nms & pl* : biceps
bicho *nm* : small animal, bug
bicicleta *nf* : bicycle — **bici** *nf fam* : bike
bicolor *adj* : two-tone
bidón *nm, pl* **-dones** : large can, drum
bien *adv* **1** : well, good **2** CORRECTAMENTE : correctly, right **3** MUY : very, quite **4** DE BUENA GANA : willingly **5 ~ que** : although **6 más ~** : rather — **bien** *adj* **1** : all right, well **2** AGRADABLE : pleasant, nice **3** SATISFACTORIO : satisfactory **4** CORRECTO : correct, right — **bien** *nm* **1** : good **2 ~es** *nmpl* : property, goods
bienal *adj & nf* : biennial
bienaventurado, -da *adj* : blessed, fortunate
bienestar *nm* : welfare, well-being
bienhechor, -chora *n* : benefactor
bienintencionado, -da *adj* : well-meaning
bienvenido, -da *adj* : welcome — **bienvenida** *nf* **1** : welcome **2 dar la ~ a** : welcome (s.o.)
bife *nm Lat* : steak
bifocales *nmpl* : bifocals
bifurcarse {72} *vr* : fork — **bifurcación** *nf, pl* **-ciones** : fork, branch
bigamia *nf* : bigamy
bigote *nm* **1** : mustache **2 ~s** *nmpl* : whiskers (of an animal)
bikini *nm* : bikini
bilingüe *adj* : bilingual
bilis *nf* : bile
billar *nm* : pool, billiards
billete *nm* **1** : bill, banknote **2** BOLETO : ticket — **billetera** *nf* : billfold, wallet
billón *nm, pl* **-llones** : trillion
bimensual, -suale *adj* : twice a month — **bimestral** *adj* : bimonthly
binario, -ria *adj* : binary
bingo *nm* : bingo
binoculares *nmpl* : binoculars
biodegradable *adj* : biodegradable
biofísica *nf* : biophysics
biografía *nf* : biography — **biográfico, -ca** *adj* : biographical — **biógrafo, -fa** *n* : biographer
biología *nf* : biology — **biológico, -ca** *adj* : biological, biologic — **biólogo, -ga** *n* : biologist
biombo *nm* : folding screen
biomecánica *nf* : biomechanics
biopsia *nf* : biopsy
bioquímica *nf* : biochemistry — **bioquímico, -ca** *adj* : biochemical
biotecnología *nf* : biotechnology
bipartidista *adj* : bipartisan
bípedo *nm* : biped
biquini → **bikini**
birlar *vt fam* : swipe, pinch
bis *adv* **1** : twice (in music) **2** : A (in an address) — **~** *nm* : encore
bisabuelo, -la *n* : great-grandfather *m*, great-grandmother *f*
bisagra *nf* : hinge
bisecar {72} *vt* : bisect
biselar *vt* : bevel
bisexual *adj* : bisexual
bisiesto *adj* **año ~** : leap year
bisnieto, -ta *n* : great-grandson *m*, great-granddaughter *f*
bisonte *nm* : bison, buffalo
bisoño, -ña *n* : novice

bistec *nm* : steak
bisturí *nm* : scalpel
bisutería *nf* : costume jewelry
bit *nm* : bit (unit of information)
bizco, -ca *adj* : cross-eyed
bizcocho *nm* : sponge cake
bizquear *vi* : squint — **bizquera** *nf* : squint
blanco, -ca *adj* : white — **blanco, -ca** *n* : white person — **blanco** *nm* **1** : white **2** DIANA : target, bull's-eye **3** : blank (space) — **blancura** *nf* : whiteness
blandir {1} *vt* : wave, brandish
blando, -da *adj* **1** : soft, tender **2** DÉBIL : weak-willed **3** INDULGENTE : lenient — **blandura** *nf* **1** : softness, tenderness **2** DEBILIDAD : weakness **3** INDULGENCIA : leniency
blanquear *vt* **1** : whiten, bleach **2** : launder (money) — *vi* : turn white — **blanqueador** *nm Lat* : bleach
blasfemar *vi* : blaspheme — **blasfemia** *nf* : blasphemy — **blasfemo, -ma** *adj* : blasphemous
bledo *nm* **no me importa un ~** *fam* : I couldn't care less
blindaje *nm* : armor, armor plating — **blindado, -da** *adj* : armored
bloc *nm, pl* **blocs** : (writing) pad
bloquear *vt* **1** OBSTRUIR : block, obstruct **2** : blockade — **bloque** *nm* **1** : block **2** : bloc (in politics) — **bloqueo** *nm* **1** OBSTRUCCIÓN : blockage **2** : blockade
blusa *nf* : blouse — **blusón** *nm, pl* **-sones** : smock
boato *nm* : showiness
bobina *nf* : bobbin, reel
bobo, -ba *adj* : silly, stupid — **~** *n* : fool, simpleton
boca *nf* **1** : mouth **2** ENTRADA : entrance **3 ~ arriba** : faceup **4 ~ abajo** : facedown, prone **5 ~ de riego** : hydrant
bocacalle *nf* : entrance (to a street)
bocado *nm* **1** : bite, mouthful **2** : bit (of a bridle) — **bocadillo** *nm Spain* : sandwich
bocajarro *nm* **a ~** : point-blank
bocallave *nf* : keyhole
bocanada *nf* **1** : swallow, swig **2** : puff, gust (of smoke, wind, etc.)
boceto *nm* : sketch, outline
bochorno *nm* **1** VERGÜENZA : embarrassment **2** : muggy weather — **bochornoso, -sa** *adj* **1** VERGONZOSO : embarrassing **2** : muggy, sultry
bocina *nf* **1** : horn **2** : mouthpiece (of a telephone) — **bocinazo** *nm* : honk, toot
boda *nf* : wedding
bodega *nf* **1** : wine cellar **2** : warehouse **3** : hold (of a ship or airplane) **4** *Lat* : grocery store
bofetear *vt* : slap — **bofetada** *nf or* **bofetón** *nm* : slap (in the face)
boga *nf* : fashion, vogue
bohemio, -mia *adj & n* : bohemian
boicotear *vt* : boycott — **boicot** *nm, pl* **-cots** : boycott
boina *nf* : beret
bola *nf* **1** : ball **2** *fam* : fib
bolera *nf* : bowling alley
boleta *nf Lat* : ticket — **boletería** *nf Lat* : ticket office
boletín *nm, pl* **-tines 1** : bulletin **2 ~ de noticias** : news release
boleto *nm* : ticket
boliche *nm* **1** : bowling **2** BOLERA : bowling alley
bolígrafo *nm* : ballpoint pen
bolillo *nm* : bobbin
boliviano, -na *adj* : Bolivian
bollo *nm* : bun, sweet roll
bolo *nm* **1** : bowling pin **2 ~s** *nmpl* : bowling
bolsa *nf* **1** : bag **2** *Lat* : pocketbook, purse **3 la Bolsa** : the stock market — **bolsillo** *nm* : pocket — **bolso** *nm Spain* : pocketbook, handbag
bomba *nf* **1** : bomb **2 ~ de gasolina** : gas pump
bombachos *nmpl* : baggy trousers
bombardear *vt* : bomb, bombard — **bombardeo** *nm* : bombing, bombardment — **bombardero** *nm* : bomber (airplane)
bombear *vt* : pump — **bombero, -ra** *n* : firefighter
bombilla *nf* : lightbulb — **bombillo** *nm Lat* : lightbulb
bombo *nm* **1** : bass drum **2 a ~s y platillos** : with a great fanfare
bombón *nm, pl* **-bones** : candy, chocolate
bonachón, -chona *adj, mpl* **-chones** *fam* : good-natured
bonanza *nf* **1** : fair weather (at sea) **2** PROSPERIDAD : prosperity
bondad *nf* : goodness, kindness — **bondadoso, -sa** *adj* : kind, good
boniato *nm* : sweet potato
bonificación *nf, pl* **-ciones 1** : bonus, extra **2** DESCUENTO : discount
bonito, -ta *adj* : pretty, lovely
bono *nm* **1** : bond **2** VALE : voucher
boquear *vi* : gasp — **boqueada** *nf* : gasp
boquerón *nm, pl* **-rones** : anchovy
boquete *nm* : gap, opening
boquiabierto, -ta *adj* : open-mouthed, speechless

boquilla *nf* : mouthpiece (of a musical instrument)
borbollar *vi* : bubble
borbotar *or* **borbotear** *vi* : boil, bubble, gurgle — **borbotón** *nm, pl* **-tones** **1** : spurt **2 salir a borbotones** : gush out
bordar *v* : embroider — **bordado** *nm* : embroidery, needlework
borde *nm* **1** : border, edge **2 al ~ de** : on the verge of — **bordear** *vt* : border — **bordillo** *nm* : curb
bordo *nm* **a ~** : aboard, on board
borla *nf* **1** : pom-pom, tassel **2** : powder puff
borracho, -cha *adj & n* : drunk — **borrachera** *nf* : drunkenness
borrar *vt* : erase, blot out — **borrador** *nm* **1** : rough draft **2** : eraser (for a blackboard)
borrascoso, -sa *adj* : stormy
borrego, -ga *n* : lamb, sheep — **borrego** *nm Lat* : false rumor, hoax
borrón *nm, pl* **-rrones** **1** : smudge, blot **2 ~ y cuenta nueva** : let's forget about it — **borroso, -sa** *adj* **1** : blurry, smudgy **2** INDISTINTO : vague, hazy
bosque *nm* : woods, forest — **boscoso, -sa** *adj* : wooded
bosquejar *vt* : sketch (out) — **bosquejo** *nm* : outline, sketch
bostezar {21} *vi* : yawn — **bostezo** *nm* : yawn
bota *nf* : boot
botánica *nf* : botany — **botánico, -ca** *adj* : botanical
botar *vt* **1** : throw, hurl **2** *Lat* : throw away **3** : launch (a ship) — *vi* : bounce
bote *nm* **1** : small boat **2** *Spain* : can **3** TARRO : jar **4** SALTO : bounce, jump
botella *nf* : bottle
botín *nm, pl* **-tines** **1** : ankle boot **2** DESPOJOS : booty, plunder
botiquín *nm, pl* **-quines** **1** : medicine cabinet **2** : first-aid kit
botón *nm, pl* **-tones** **1** : button **2** YEMA : bud — **botones** *nmfs & pl* : bellhop
botulismo *nm* : botulism
boutique *nf* : boutique
bóveda *nf* : vault
boxear *vi* : box — **boxeador, -dora** *n* : boxer — **boxeo** *nm* : boxing
boya *nf* : buoy — **boyante** *adj* **1** : buoyant **2** PRÓSPERO : prosperous, thriving
bozal *nm* **1** : muzzle **2** : halter (for a horse)
bracear *vi* **1** : wave one's arms **2** NADAR : swim, crawl
bracero, -ra *n* : day laborer
bragas *nf Spain* : panties
bragueta *nf* : fly, pants zipper
braille *adj & nm* : braille
bramante *nm* : twine, string
bramar *vi* **1** : bellow, roar **2** : howl (of the wind) — **bramido** *nm* : bellow, roar
brandy *nm* : brandy
branquia *nf* : gill
brasa *nf* : ember
brasier *nm Lat* : brassiere
brasileño, -ña *adj* : Brazilian
bravata *nf* **1** : boast, bravado **2** AMENAZO : threat
bravo, -va *adj* **1** : fierce, savage **2** : rough (of the sea) **3** *Lat* : angry — **~** *interj* : bravo!, well done! — **bravura** *nf* **1** FEROCIDAD : fierceness **2** VALENTÍA : bravery
braza *nf* **1** : breaststroke **2** : fathom (measurement) — **brazada** *nf* : stroke (in swimming)
brazalete *nm* **1** : bracelet **2** : (cloth) armband
brazo *nm* **1** : arm **2** : branch (of a river, etc.) **3 ~ derecho** : right-hand man **4 ~s** *nmpl* : hands, laborers
brea *nf* : tar
brebaje *nm* : concoction
brecha *nf* : breach, gap
brécol *nm* : broccoli
bregar {52} *vi* **1** LUCHAR : struggle **2** TRABAJAR : work hard — **brega** *nf* **andar a la ~** : struggle
breña *nf or* **breñal** *nm* : scrubland, brush
breve *adj* **1** : brief, short **2 en ~** : shortly, in short — **brevedad** *nf* : brevity, shortness — **brevemente** *adv* : briefly
brezal *nm* : moor, heath — **brezo** *nm* : heather
bricolaje *or* **bricolage** *nm* : do-it-yourself
brida *nf* : bridle
brigada *nf* **1** : brigade **2** EQUIPO : gang, team, squad
brillar *vi* : shine, sparkle — **brillante** *adj* : brilliant, shiny — **~** *nm* : diamond — **brillantez** *nf* : brilliance — **brillo** *nm* **1** : luster, shine **2** ESPLENDOR : splendor — **brilloso, -sa** *adj* : shiny
brincar {72} *vi* : jump about, frolic — **brinco** *nm* : jump, skip
brindar *vi* : drink a toast — *vt* : offer, provide — **brindarse** *vr* : offer one's assistance — **brindis** *nm* : drink, toast
brío *nm* **1** : force, determination **2** ÁNIMO : spirit, verve — **brioso, -sa** *adj* : spirited, lively
brisa *nf* : breeze

británico, -ca *adj* : British
brizna *nf* **1** : strand, thread **2** : blade (of grass)
brocado *nm* : brocade
brocha *nf* : paintbrush
broche *nm* **1** : fastener, clasp **2** ALFILER : brooch
brocheta *nf* : skewer
brócoli *nm* : broccoli
bromear *vi* : joke, fool around — **broma** *nf* : joke, prank — **bromista** *adj* : fun-loving, joking — ~ *nmf* : joker, prankster
bronca *nf fam* : fight, row
bronce *nm* : bronze — **bronceado, -da** *adj* : suntanned — **bronceado** *nm* : tan — **broncearse** *vr* : get a suntan
bronco, -ca *adj* **1** : harsh, rough **2** : untamed, wild (of a horse)
bronquitis *nf* : bronchitis
broqueta *nf* : skewer
brotar *vi* **1** : bud, sprout **2** : stream, gush (of a river, tears, etc.) **3** : arise (of feelings, etc.) **4** : break out (in medicine) — **brote** *nm* **1** : outbreak **2** : sprout, bud, shoot (of plants)
brujería *nf* : witchcraft — **bruja** *nf* **1** : witch **2** *fam* : old hag — **brujo** *nm* : warlock, sorcerer — **brujo, -ja** *adj* : bewitching
brújula *nf* : compass
bruma *nf* : haze, mist — **brumoso, -sa** *adj* : hazy, misty
bruñir {38} *vt* : burnish, polish
brusco, -ca *adj* **1** SÚBITO : sudden, abrupt **2** TOSCO : brusque, rough — **brusquedad** *nf* : abruptness, brusqueness
brutal *adj* : brutal — **brutalidad** *nf* : brutality
bruto, -ta *adj* **1** : brutish, stupid **2** : crude (of petroleum, etc.), uncut (of diamonds) **3 peso** ~ : gross weight — ~ *n* : brute
bucal *adj* : oral
bucear *vi* **1** : dive, swim underwater **2** ~ **en** : delve into — **buceo** *nm* : (underwater) diving
bucle *nm* : curl
budín *nm, pl* **-dines** : pudding
budismo *nm* : Buddhism — **budista** *adj & nmf* : Buddhist
buenamente *adv* **1** : easily **2** VOLUNTARIAMENTE : willingly
buenaventura *nf* **1** : good luck **2 decir la** ~ **a uno** : tell s.o.'s fortune
bueno, -na *adj* (**buen** *before masculine singular nouns*) **1** : good **2** AMABLE : kind **3** APROPIADO : appropriate **4** SALUDABLE : well, healthy **5** : nice, fine (of weather) **6 buenos días** : hello, good day **7 buenas noches** : good night **8 buenas tardes** : good afternoon, good evening — **bueno** *interj* : OK!, all right!
buey *nm* : ox, steer
búfalo *nm* : buffalo
bufanda *nf* : scarf
bufar *vi* : snort — **bufido** *nm* : snort
bufet *or* **bufé** *nm* : buffet-style meal
bufete *nm* **1** : law practice **2** MESA : writing desk
bufo, -fa *adj* : comic — **bufón, -fona** *n, mpl* **-fones** : buffoon, jester — **bufonada** *nf* : wisecrack
buhardilla *nf* : attic, garret
búho *nm* : owl
buitre *nm* : vulture
bujía *nf* : spark plug
bulbo *nm* : bulb (of a plant)
bulevar *nm* : boulevard
búlgaro, -ra *adj* : Bulgarian
bulla *nf* : uproar, racket
bulldozer *nm* : bulldozer
bullicio *nm* **1** : uproar **2** AJETREO : hustle and bustle — **bullicioso, -sa** *adj* : noisy, boisterous
bullir {38} *vi* **1** : boil **2** AJETREARSE : bustle, stir
bulto *nm* **1** : package, bundle **2** VOLUMEN : bulk, size **3** FORMA : form, shape **4** PROTUBERANCIA : lump, swelling
bumerán *nm, pl* **-ranes** : boomerang
buñuelo *nm* : fried pastry
buque *nm* : ship
burbujear *vi* : bubble — **burbuja** *nf* : bubble
burdel *nm* : brothel
burdo, -da *adj* : coarse, rough
burgués, -guesa *adj & n, mpl* **-gueses** : bourgeois — **burguesía** *nf* : bourgeoisie
burlar *vt* : trick, deceive — **burlarse** *vr* ~ **de** : make fun of — **burla** *nf* **1** MOFA : mockery, ridicule **2** BROMA : joke, trick
burlesco, -ca *adj* : comic, funny
burlón, -lona *adj, mpl* **-lones** : mocking
burocracia *nf* : bureaucracy — **burócrata** *nmf* : bureaucrat — **burocrático, -ca** *adj* : bureaucratic
burro, -rra *n* **1** : donkey **2** *fam* : dunce — ~ *adj* : stupid — **burro** *nm* **1** : sawhorse **2** *Lat* : stepladder
bus *nm* : bus
buscar {72} *vt* **1** : look for, seek **2 ir a** ~ **a uno** : fetch s.o. — *vi* : search — **busca** *nf* : search — **búsqueda** *nf* : search

busto *nm* : bust (in sculpture)
butaca *nf* **1** : armchair **2** : (theater) seat
butano *nm* : butane
buzo *nm* : diver
buzón *nm, pl* **-zones** : mailbox
byte ['bait] *nm* : byte

C

c *nf* : c, third letter of the Spanish alphabet
cabal *adj* **1** : exact **2** COMPLETO : complete — **cabales** *nmpl* **no estar en sus ~** : not be in one's right mind
cabalgar {52} *vi* : ride — **cabalgata** *nf* : cavalcade
caballa *nf* : mackerel
caballería *nf* **1** : cavalry **2** CABALLO : horse, mount — **caballeriza** *nf* : stable
caballero *nm* **1** : gentleman **2** : knight (rank) — **caballerosidad** *nf* : chivalry — **caballeroso, -sa** *adj* : chivalrous
caballete *nm* **1** : ridge (of a roof) **2** : easel (for a canvas) **3** : bridge (of the nose)
caballito *nm* **1** : rocking horse **2 ~s** *nmpl* : merry-go-round
caballo *nm* **1** : horse **2** : knight (in chess) **3 ~ de fuerza** : horsepower
cabaña *nf* : cabin, hut
cabaret *nm, pl* **-rets** : nightclub, cabaret
cabecear *vi* **1** : shake one's head, nod **2** : pitch, lurch (of a boat)
cabecera *nf* **1** : head (of a bed, etc.) **2** : heading (in a text) **3 médico de ~** : family doctor
cabecilla *nmf* : ringleader
cabello *nm* : hair — **cabelludo, -da** *adj* : hairy
caber {12} *vi* **1** : fit, go (into) **2 no cabe duda** : there's no doubt
cabestro *nm* : halter
cabeza *nf* **1** : head **2 de ~** : head first — **cabezada** *nf* **1** : butt (of the head) **2 dar ~s** : nod off
cabezal *nm* : bolster, headrest
cabida *nf* **1** : room, capacity **2 dar ~ a** : accomodate, find room for
cabina *nf* **1** : booth **2** : cab (of a truck, etc.) **3** : cabin, cockpit (of an airplane)
cabizbajo, -ja *adj* : downcast
cable *nm* : cable
cabo *nm* **1** : end, stub **2** TROZO : bit **3** : corporal (in the military) **4** : cape (in geography) **5 al fin y al ~** : after all **6 llevar a ~** : carry out, do
cabra *nf* : goat
cabriola *nf* **1** : leap, skip **2 hacer ~s** : prance around
cabrito *nm* : kid (goat)
cacahuate *or* **cacahuete** *nm* : peanut
cacao *nm* **1** : cacao (tree) **2** : cocoa (drink)
cacarear *vi* : crow, cackle — *vt fam* : boast about
cacería *nf* : hunt
cacerola *nf* : pan, saucepan
cacharro *nm* **1** *fam* : thing, piece of junk **2** *fam* : jalopy **3 ~s** *nmpl* : pots and pans
cachear *vt* : search, frisk
cachemir *nm or* **cachemira** *nf* : cashmere
cachete *nm Lat* : cheek — **cachetada** *nf Lat* : slap
cacho *nm* **1** *fam* : piece, bit **2** *Lat* : horn
cachorro, -rra *n* **1** : cub **2** PERRITO : puppy
cactus *or* **cacto** *nm* : cactus
cada *adj* : each, every
cadalso *nm* : scaffold
cadáver *nm* : corpse
cadena *nf* **1** : chain **2** : (television) channel **3 ~ de montaje** : assembly line
cadencia *nf* : cadence
cadera *nf* : hip
cadete *nmf* : cadet
caducar {72} *vi* : expire — **caducidad** *nf* : expiration
caer {13} *vi* **1** : fall, drop **2 ~ bien a uno** : be to one's liking **3 dejar ~** : drop **4 me cae bien** : I like her, I like him — **caerse** *vr* : drop, fall (down)
café *nm* **1** : coffee **2** : café — **~** *adj Lat* : brown — **cafetera** *nf* : coffeepot — **cafetería** *nf* : coffee shop, cafeteria — **cafeína** *nf* : caffeine
caída *nf* **1** : fall, drop **2** PENDIENTE : slope
caimán *nm, pl* **-manes** : alligator
caja *nf* **1** : box, case **2** : checkout counter, cashier's desk (in a store) **3 ~ fuerte** : safe **4 ~ registradora** : cash register — **cajero, -ra** *n* **1** : cashier **2** : (bank) teller — **cajetilla** *nf* : pack (of cigarettes) — **cajón** *nm, pl* **-jones 1**

: drawer (in furniture) **2** : large box, crate
cajuela *nf Lat* : trunk (of a car)
cal *nf* : lime
cala *nf* : cove
calabaza *nf* **1** : pumpkin, squash, gourd **2 dar ~s a** *fam* : give the brush-off to — **calabacín** *nm, pl* **-cines** *or* **calabacita** *nf Lat* : zucchini
calabozo *nm* **1** : prison **2** CELDA : cell
calamar *nm* : squid
calambre *nm* **1** ESPASMO : cramp **2** : (electric) shock
calamidad *nf* : calamity
calar *vt* **1** : soak (through) **2** PERFORAR : pierce — **calarse** *vr* : get drenched
calavera *nf* : skull
calcar {72} *vt* **1** : trace **2** IMITAR : copy, imitate
calcetín *nm, pl* **-tines** : sock
calcinar *vt* : char
calcio *nm* : calcium
calcomanía *nf* : decal
calcular *vt* : calculate, estimate — **calculador, -dora** *adj* : calculating — **calculadora** *nf* : calculator — **cálculo** *nm* **1** : calculation **2** : calculus (in mathematics and medicine) **3 ~ biliar** : gallstone
caldera *nf* **1** : cauldron **2** : boiler (for heating, etc.) — **caldo** *nm* : broth, stock
calefacción *nf, pl* **-ciones** : heating, heat
calendario *nm* : calendar
calentar {55} *vt* : heat (up), warm (up) — **calentarse** *vr* : get warm, heat up — **calentador** *nm* : heater — **calentura** *nf* : temperature, fever
calibre *nm* **1** : caliber **2** DIÁMETRO : bore, diameter — **calibrar** *vt* : calibrate
calidad *nf* **1** : quality **2 en ~ de** : as, in the capacity of
cálido, -da *adj* : hot, warm
calidoscopio *nm* : kaleidoscope
caliente *adj* **1** : hot **2** ACALORADO : heated, fiery
calificar {72} *vt* **1** : qualify **2** EVALUAR : rate **3** : grade (an exam, etc.) — **calificación** *nf, pl* **-ciones 1** : qualification **2** EVALUACIÓN : rating **3** NOTA : grade — **calificativo, -va** *adj* : qualifying — **calificativo** *nm* : qualifier, epithet
caligrafía *nf* : penmanship
calistenia *nf* : calisthenics
cáliz *nm, pl* **-lices** : chalice
caliza *nf* : limestone
callar *vi* : keep quiet, be silent — *vt* **1** : silence, hush **2** OCULTAR : keep secret — **callarse** *vr* : remain silent — **callado, -da** *adj* : quiet, silent
calle *nf* : street, road — **callejear** *vi* : wander about the streets — **callejero, -ra** *adj* **1** : street **2 perro callejero** : stray dog — **callejón** *nm, pl* **-jones 1** : alley **2 ~ sin salida** : dead-end street
callo *nm* : callus, corn
calma *nf* : calm, quiet — **calmante** *adj* : soothing — **~** *nm* : tranquilizer — **calmar** *vt* : calm, soothe — **calmarse** *vr* : calm down — **calmo, -ma** *adj Lat* : calm — **calmoso, -sa** *adj* **1** : calm **2** LENTO : slow
calor *nm* **1** : heat, warmth **2 tener ~** : be hot — **caloría** *nf* : calorie
calumnia *nf* : slander, libel — **calumniar** *vt* : slander, libel
caluroso, -sa *adj* **1** : hot **2** : warm, enthusiastic (of applause, etc.)
calvo, -va *adj* : bald — **calvicie** *nf* : baldness
calza *nf* : wedge
calzada *nf* : roadway
calzado *nm* : footwear — **calzar** {21} *vt* **1** : wear (shoes) **2** : put shoes on (s.o.)
calzones *nmpl Lat* : panties — **calzoncillos** *nmpl* : underpants, briefs
cama *nf* : bed
camada *nf* : litter, brood
camafeo *nm* : cameo
cámara *nf* **1** : chamber **2** *or* **~ fotográfica** : camera **3** : house (in government)
camarada *nmf* : comrade — **camaradería** *nf* : camaraderie
camarero, -ra *n* **1** : waiter, waitress *f* **2** : steward *m*, stewardess *f* (on a ship, etc.) — **camarera** *nf* : chambermaid *f*
camarón *nm, pl* **-rones** : shrimp
camarote *nm* : cabin, stateroom
cambiar *vt* **1** : change **2** CANJEAR : exchange — *vi* **1** : change **2** : shift gears (of an automobile) — **cambiarse** *vr* **1** : change (clothing) **2** : move (to a new address) — **cambiable** *adj* : changeable — **cambio** *nm* **1** : change **2** CANJE : exchange **3 en ~** : on the other hand
camello *nm* : camel
camilla *nf* : stretcher — **camillero** *nm* : orderly (in a hospital)
caminar *vi* : walk — *vt* : cover (a distance) — **caminata** *nf* : hike
camino *nm* **1** : road, path **2** RUTA : way **3 a medio ~** : halfway (there) **4 ponerse en ~** : set out
camión *nm, pl* **-miones 1** : truck **2** *Lat*

: bus — **camionero, -ra** *n* **1** : truck driver **2** *Lat* : bus driver — **camioneta** *nm* : light truck, van
camisa *nf* **1** : shirt **2 ~ de fuerza** : straitjacket — **camiseta** *nf* : T-shirt, undershirt — **camisón** *nm, pl* **-sones** : nightshirt, nightgown
camorra *nf fam* : fight, trouble
camote *nm Lat* : sweet potato
campamento *nm* : camp
campana *nf* : bell — **campanada** *nf* : stroke (of a bell), peal — **campanario** *nm* : bell tower — **campanilla** *nf* : (small) bell
campaña *nf* **1** : countryside **2** : (military or political) campaign
campeón, -peona *n, mpl* **-peones** : champion — **campeonato** *nm* : championship
campesino, -na *n* : peasant, farm laborer — **campestre** *adj* : rural, rustic
camping *nm* **1** : campsite **2 hacer ~** : go camping
campiña *nf* : countryside
campo *nm* **1** : field **2** CAMPIÑA : countryside, country **3** CAMPAMENTO : camp
camuflaje *nm* : camouflage — **camuflar** *vt* : camouflage
cana *nf* : gray hair
canadiense *adj* : Canadian
canal *nm* **1** : canal **2** MEDIO : channel **3** : (radio or television) channel — **canalizar** {21} *vt* : channel
canalete *nm* : paddle (of a canoe)
canalla *nf* : rabble — **~** *nmf fam* : swine, bastard
canapé *nm* **1** : canapé **2** SOFÁ : sofa, couch
canario *nm* : canary
canasta *nf* : basket — **canasto** *nm* : large basket
cancelar *vt* **1** : cancel **2** : pay off, settle (a debt) — **cancelación** *nf, pl* **-ciones** **1** : cancellation **2** : payment in full (of a debt)
cáncer *nm* : cancer — **canceroso, -sa** *adj* : cancerous
cancha *nf* : court, field (for sports)
canciller *nm* : chancellor
canción *nf, pl* **-ciones** **1** : song **2 ~ de cuna** : lullaby — **cancionero** *nm* : songbook
candado *nm* : padlock
candela *nf* : candle — **candelabro** *nm* : candelabra — **candelero** *nm* **1** : candlestick **2 estar en el ~** : be in the limelight
candente *adj* : red-hot
candidato, -ta *n* : candidate — **candidatura** *nf* : candidacy
cándido, -da *adj* : naïve — **candidez** *nf* **1** : simplicity **2** INGENUIDAD : naïveté
candil *nm* : oil lamp — **candilejas** *nfpl* : footlights
candor *nm* : naïveté, innocence
canela *nf* : cinnamon
cangrejo *nm* : crab
canguro *nm* : kangaroo
caníbal *nmf* : cannibal — **canibalismo** *nm* : cannibalism
canicas *nfpl* : (game of) marbles
canino, -na *adj* : canine — **canino** *nm* : canine (tooth)
canjear *vt* : exchange — **canje** *nm* : exchange, trade
cano, -na *adj* : gray, gray-haired
canoa *nf* : canoe
canon *nm, pl* **cánones** : canon
canonizar {21} *vt* : canonize
canoso, -sa *adj* : gray, gray-haired
cansar *vt* : tire (out) — *vi* : be tiring — **cansarse** *vr* : get tired — **cansado, -da** *adj* **1** : tired **2** PESADO : tiresome — **cansancio** *nm* : fatigue, weariness
cantalupo *nm* : cantaloupe
cantar *v* : sing — **~** *nm* : song — **cantante** *nmf* : singer
cántaro *nm* **1** : pitcher, jug **2 llover a ~s** *fam* : rain cats and dogs
cantera *nf* : quarry (excavation)
cantidad *nf* **1** : quantity, amount **2 una ~ de** : lots of
cantimplora *nf* : canteen, water bottle
cantina *nf* **1** : canteen, cafeteria **2** *Lat* : tavern, bar
canto *nm* **1** : singing, song **2** BORDE, LADO : edge **3 de ~** : on end, sideways **4 ~ rodado** : boulder — **cantor, -tora** *adj* **1** : singing **2 pájaro ~** : songbird — **~** *n* : singer
caña *nf* **1** : cane, reed **2 ~ de pescar** : fishing pole
cáñamo *nm* : hemp
cañería *nf* : pipes, piping — **caño** *nm* **1** : pipe **2** : spout (of a fountain) — **cañón** *nm, pl* **-ñones** **1** : cannon **2** : barrel (of a gun) **3** : canyon (in geography)
caoba *nf* : mahogany
caos *nm* : chaos — **caótico, -ca** *adj* : chaotic
capa *nf* **1** : cape, cloak **2** : coat (of paint, etc.), coating (in cooking) **3** ESTRATO : layer, stratum **4** : (social) class
capacidad *nf* **1** : capacity **2** APTITUD : ability
capacitar *vt* : train, qualify — **capacitación** *nf, pl* **-ciones** : training

caparazón *nm, pl* **-zones** : shell
capataz *nmf, pl* **-taces** : foreman
capaz *adj, pl* **-paces 1** : capable, able **2** ESPACIOSO : spacious
capellán *nm, pl* **-llanes** : chaplain
capilla *nf* : chapel
capital *adj* **1** : capital **2** PRINCIPAL : chief, principal — **~** *nm* : capital (assets) — **~** *nf* : capital (city) — **capitalismo** *nm* : capitalism — **capitalista** *adj & nmf* : capitalist, capitalistic — **capitalizar** {21} *vt* : capitalize
capitán, -tana *n, mpl* **-tanes** : captain
capitolio *nm* : capitol
capitular *vi* : capitulate, surrender — **capitulación** *nf, pl* **-ciones** : surrender
capítulo *nm* : chapter
capó *nm* : hood (of a car)
capote *nm* : cloak, cape
capricho *nm* : whim, caprice — **caprichoso, -sa** *adj* : whimsical, capricious
cápsula *nf* : capsule
captar *vt* **1** : grasp **2** ATRAER : gain, attract (interest, etc.) **3** : harness (waters)
capturar *vt* : capture, seize — **captura** *nf* : capture, seizure
capucha *nf* : hood (of clothing)
capullo *nm* **1** : cocoon **2** : (flower) bud
caqui *adj & nm* : khaki
cara *nf* **1** : face **2** ASPECTO : appearance **3** *fam* : nerve, gall **4 ~ a** *or* **de ~ a** : facing
carabina *nf* : carbine
caracol *nm* **1** : snail **2** *Lat* : conch **3** RIZO : curl
carácter *nm, pl* **-racteres 1** : character **2** ÍNDOLE : nature — **característica** *nf* : characteristic — **característico, -ca** *adj* : characteristic — **caracterizar** {21} *vt* : characterize
caramba *interj* : oh my!, good grief!
carámbano *nm* : icicle
caramelo *nm* **1** : caramel **2** DULCE : candy
carátula *nf* **1** CARETA : mask **2** : jacket (of a record, etc.) **3** *Lat* : face (of a watch)
caravana *nf* **1** : caravan **2** REMOLQUE : trailer
caray → **caramba**
carbohidrato *nm* : carbohydrate
carbón *nm, pl* **-bones 1** : coal **2** : charcoal (for drawing) — **carboncillo** *nm* : charcoal — **carbonero, -ra** *adj* : coal — **carbonizar** {21} *vt* : char — **carbono** *nm* : carbon — **carburador** *nm* : carburetor — **carburante** *nm* : fuel
carcajada *nf* : loud laugh, guffaw
cárcel *nf* : jail, prison — **carcelero, -ra** *n* : jailer
carcinógeno *nm* : carcinogen
carcomer *vt* : eat away at — **carcomido, -da** *adj* : worm-eaten
cardenal *nm* **1** : cardinal **2** CONTUSIÓN : bruise
cardíaco *or* **cardiaco, -ca** *adj* : cardiac, heart
cárdigan *nm, pl* **-gans** : cardigan
cardinal *adj* : cardinal
cardiólogo, -ga *n* : cardiologist
cardo *nm* : thistle
carear *vt* : bring face-to-face
carecer {53} *vi* **~ de** : lack — **carencia** *nf* : lack, want — **carente** *adj* **~ de** : lacking (in)
carestía *nf* **1** : high cost **2** ESCASEZ : dearth, scarcity
careta *nf* : mask
cargar {52} *vt* **1** : load **2** : charge (a battery, a purchase, etc.) **3** LLEVAR : carry **4 ~ de** : burden with — *vi* **1** : load **2 ~ con** : pick up, carry away — **carga** *nf* **1** : load **2** CARGAMENTO : freight, cargo **3** RESPONSABILIDAD : burden **4** : charge (in electricity, etc.) — **cargado, -da** *adj* **1** : loaded, burdened **2** PESADO : heavy, stuffy **3** : charged (of a battery) **4** FUERTE : strong, concentrated — **cargamento** *nm* : cargo, load — **cargo** *nm* **1** : charge **2** PUESTO : position, office
cariarse *vr* : decay (of teeth)
caribe *adj* : Caribbean
caricatura *nf* **1** : caricature **2** : (political) cartoon — **caricaturizar** *vt* : caricature
caricia *nf* : caress
caridad *nf* **1** : charity **2** LIMOSNA : alms *pl*
caries *nfs & pl* : cavity (in a tooth)
cariño *nm* : affection, love — **cariñoso, -sa** *adj* : affectionate, loving
carisma *nf* : charisma — **carismático, -ca** *adj* : charismatic
caritativo, -va *adj* : charitable
cariz *nm, pl* **-rices** : appearance, aspect
carmesí *adj & nm* : crimson
carmín *nm, pl* **-mines** *or* **~ de labios** : lipstick
carnada *nf* : bait
carnal *adj* **1** : carnal **2 primo ~** : first cousin
carnaval *nm* : carnival
carne *nf* **1** : meat **2** : flesh (of persons or fruits) **3 ~ de cerdo** : pork **4 ~ de gallina** : goose bumps **5 ~ de ternera** : veal
carné *nm* → **carnet**

carnero *nm* **1** : ram, sheep **2** : mutton (in cooking)
carnet *nm* **1 ~ de conducir** : driver's license **2 ~ de identidad** : identification card, ID
carnicería *nf* **1** : butcher shop **2** MATANZA : slaughter — **carnicero, -ra** *n* : butcher
carnívoro, -ra *adj* : carnivorous — **carnívoro** *nm* : carnivore
carnoso, -sa *adj* : fleshy
caro, -ra *adj* **1** : expensive **2** QUERIDO : dear — **caro** *adv* : dearly
carpa *nf* **1** : carp **2** TIENDA : tent
carpeta *nf* : folder
carpintería *nf* : carpentry — **carpintero, -ra** *n* : carpenter
carraspear *vi* : clear one's throat — **carraspera** *nf* **1** : hoarseness **2 tener ~** : have a frog in one's throat
carrera *nf* **1** : running, run **2** COMPETICIÓN : race **3** : course (of studies) **4** PROFESIÓN : career, profession
carreta *nf* : cart, wagon
carrete *nm* : reel, spool
carretera *nf* : highway, road
carretilla *nf* : wheelbarrow
carril *nm* **1** : lane (of a road) **2** : rail (for a railroad)
carrillo *nm* : cheek
carrito *nm* : cart, trolley
carrizo *nm* : reed
carro *nm* **1** : wagon, cart **2** *Lat* : automobile, car — **carrocería** *nf* : body (of an automobile)
carroña *nf* : carrion
carroza *nf* **1** : carriage **2** : float (in a parade)
carruaje *nm* : carriage
carrusel *nm* : merry-go-round, carousel
carta *nf* **1** : letter **2** NAIPE : playing card **3** : charter (of an organization, etc.) **4** MENÚ : menu **5** MAPA : map, chart
cartel *nm* : poster, bill — **cartelera** *nf* : billboard
cartera *nf* **1** : briefcase **2** BILLETERA : wallet **3** *Lat* : pocketbook, handbag — **carterista** *nmf* : pickpocket
cartero, -ra *nm* : mail carrier, mailman *m*
cartílago *nm* : cartilage
cartilla *nf* **1** : primer, reader **2** : booklet, record (of a savings account, etc.)
cartón *nm, pl* **-tones 1** : cardboard **2** : carton (of cigarettes, etc.)
cartucho *nm* : cartridge
casa *nf* **1** : house **2** HOGAR : home **3** EMPRESA : company, firm **4 ~ flotante** : houseboat
casar *vt* : marry — *vi* : go together, match up — **casarse** *vr* **1** : get married **2 ~ con** : marry — **casado, -da** *adj* : married — **casamiento** *nm* **1** : marriage **2** BODA : wedding
cascabel *nm* : small bell
cascada *nf* : waterfall
cascanueces *nms & pl* : nutcracker
cascar {72} *vt* : crack (a shell, etc.) — **cascarse** *vr* : crack, chip — **cáscara** *nf* : skin, peel, shell — **cascarón** *nm, pl* **-rones** : eggshell
casco *nm* **1** : helmet **2** : hull (of a boat) **3** : hoof (of a horse) **4** : fragment (of ceramics, etc.) **5** : center (of a town) **6** ENVASE : empty bottle
caserío *nm* **1** *Spain* : country house **2** POBLADO : hamlet
casero, -ra *adj* **1** : homemade **2** DOMÉSTICO : domestic, household — **~** *n* : landlord, landlady *f*
caseta *nf* : booth, stall
casete → **cassette**
casi *adv* **1** : almost, nearly **2** (*in negative phrases*) : hardly
casilla *nf* **1** : compartment, pigeonhole **2** CASETA : booth **3** : box (on a form)
casino *nm* **1** : casino **2** : (social) club
caso *nm* **1** : case **2 en ~ de** : in the event of **3 hacer ~** : pay attention **4 no venir al ~** : be beside the point
caspa *nf* : dandruff
cassette *nmf* : cassette
casta *nf* **1** : lineage, descent **2** : breed (of animals) **3** : caste (in India)
castaña *nf* : chestnut
castañetear *vi* : chatter (of teeth)
castaño, -ña *adj* : chestnut (color)
castañuela *nf* : castanet
castellano *nm* : Spanish, Castilian (language)
castidad *nf* : chastity
castigar {52} *vt* **1** : punish **2** : penalize (in sports) — **castigo** *nm* **1** : punishment **2** : penalty (in sports)
castillo *nm* : castle
casto, -ta *adj* : chaste, pure — **castizo, -za** *adj* : pure, traditional (in style)
castor *nm* : beaver
castrar *vt* : castrate
castrense *adj* : military
casual *adj* : chance, accidental — **casualidad** *nf* **1** : coincidence **2 por ~** *or* **de ~** : by chance — **casualmente** *adv* : by chance
cataclismo *nm* : cataclysm
catalán, -lana *adj, mpl* **-lanes** : Catalan — **catalán** *nm* : Catalan (language)
catalizador *nm* : catalyst
catalogar {52} *vt* : catalog, classify — **catálogo** *nm* : catalog

catapulta *nf* : catapult
catar *vt* : taste, sample
catarata *nf* **1** : waterfall **2** : cataract (in medicine)
catarro *nm* RESFRIADO : cold
catástrofe *nf* : catastrophe, disaster — **catastrófico, -ca** *adj* : catastrophic, disastrous
catecismo *nm* : catechism
cátedra *nf* : chair (at a university)
catedral *nf* : cathedral
catedrático, -ca *n* : professor
categoría *nf* **1** : category **2** RANGO : rank **3 de ~** : first-rate — **categórico, -ca** *adj* : categorical
católico, -ca *adj & n* : Catholic — **catolicismo** *nm* : Catholicism
catorce *adj & nm* : fourteen — **catorceavo** *nm* : fourteenth
catre *nm* : cot
cauce *nm* **1** : riverbed **2** VÍA : channel, means *pl*
caucho *nm* : rubber
caución *nf, pl* **-ciones** : security, guarantee
caudal *nm* **1** : volume of water, flow **2** RIQUEZA : wealth
caudillo *nm* : leader, commander
causar *vt* : cause, provoke — **causa** *nf* **1** : cause **2** RAZÓN : reason **3** : case (in law) **4 a ~ de** : because of
cáustico, -ca *adj* : caustic
cautela *nf* : caution — **cauteloso, -sa** *adj* : cautious — **cautelosamente** *adv* : cautiously, warily
cautivar *vt* **1** : capture **2** ENCANTAR : captivate — **cautiverio** *nm* : captivity — **cautivo, -va** *adj & n* : captive
cauto, -ta *adj* : cautious
cavar *v* : dig
caverna *nf* : cavern, cave
cavidad *nf* : cavity
cavilar *vi* : ponder
cayado *nm* : crook, staff
cazar {21} *vt* **1** : hunt **2** ATRAPAR : catch, bag — *vi* : go hunting — **caza** *nf* **1** : hunt, hunting **2** : game (animals) — **cazador, -dora** *n* : hunter
cazo *nm* **1** : saucepan **2** CUCHARÓN : ladle — **cazuela** *nf* : casserole
CD *nm* : CD, compact disc
cebada *nf* : barley
cebar *vt* **1** : bait **2** : feed, fatten (animals) **3** : prime (a firearm, etc.) — **cebo** *nm* **1** CARNADA : bait **2** : charge (of a firearm)
cebolla *nf* : onion — **cebolleta** *nf* : scallion, green onion — **cebollino** *nm* : chive
cebra *nf* : zebra
cecear *vi* : lisp — **ceceo** *nm* : lisp
cedazo *nm* : sieve
ceder *vi* **1** : yield, give way **2** DISMINUIR : diminish, abate — *vt* : cede, hand over
cedro *nm* : cedar
cédula *nf* : document, certificate
cegar {49} *vt* **1** : blind **2** TAPAR : block, stop up — *vi* : be blinded, go blind — **ceguera** *nf* : blindness
ceja *nf* : eyebrow
cejar *vi* : give in, back down
celada *nf* : trap, ambush
celador, -dora *n* : guard, warden
celda *nf* : cell (of a jail)
celebrar *vt* **1** : celebrate **2** : hold (a meeting), say (Mass) **3** ALEGRARSE DE : be happy about — **celebrarse** *vr* : take place — **celebración** *nf, pl* **-ciones** : celebration — **célebre** *adj* : famous, celebrated — **celebridad** *nf* : celebrity
celeridad *nf* : swiftness, speed
celeste *adj* **1** : celestial, heavenly **2** *or* **azul ~** : sky blue — **celestial** *adj* : celestial, heavenly
celibato *nm* : celibacy — **célibe** *adj* : celibate
celo *nm* **1** : zeal **2 en ~** : in heat **3 ~s** *nmpl* : jealousy **4 tener ~s** : be jealous
celofán *nm, pl* **-fanes** : cellophane
celoso, -sa *adj* **1** : jealous **2** DILIGENTE : zealous
célula *nf* : cell — **celular** *adj* : cellular
celulosa *nf* : cellulose
cementerio *nm* : cemetery
cemento *nm* **1** : cement **2 ~ armado** : reinforced concrete
cena *nf* : supper, dinner
cenagal *nm* : bog, quagmire — **cenagoso** *adj* : swampy
cenar *vi* : have dinner, have supper — *vt* : have for dinner or supper
cenicero *nm* : ashtray
cenit *nm* : zenith
ceniza *nf* : ash
censo *nm* : census
censurar *vt* **1** : censor **2** REPROBAR : censure, criticize — **censura** *nf* **1** : censorship **2** REPROBACIÓN : censure, criticism
centavo *nm* **1** : cent **2** : centavo (unit of currency)
centellear *vi* : sparkle, twinkle — **centella** *nf* **1** : flash **2** CHISPA : spark — **centelleo** *nm* : twinkling, sparkle
centenar *nm* : hundred — **centenario** *nm* : centennial
centeno *nm* : rye

centésimo, -ma *adj* : hundredth
centígrado *adj* : centigrade, Celsius
centigramo *nm* : centigram
centímetro *nm* : centimeter
centinela *nmf* : sentinel, sentry
central *adj* : central — **~** *nf* : main office, headquarters — **centralita** *nf* : switchboard — **centralizar** {21} *vt* : centralize
centrar *vt* : center — **centrarse** *vr* **~ en** : focus on — **céntrico, -ca** *adj* : central — **centro** *nm* **1** : center **2** : downtown (of a city) **3 ~ de mesa** : centerpiece
centroamericano, -na *adj* : Central American
ceñir {67} *vt* **1** : encircle **2** : fit (s.o.) tightly — **ceñirse** *vr* **~ a** : limit oneself to — **ceñido, -da** *adj* : tight
ceño *nm* **1** : frown **2 fruncir el ~** : knit one's brow, frown
cepillo *nm* **1** : brush **2** : (carpenter's) plane **3 ~ de dientes** : toothbrush — **cepillar** *vt* **1** : brush **2** : plane (wood)
cera *nf* **1** : wax, beeswax **2** : floor wax, furniture wax
cerámica *nf* **1** : ceramics *pl* **2** : (piece of) pottery
cerca[1] *nf* : fence — **cercado** *nm* : enclosure
cerca[2] *adv* **1** : close, near **2 ~ de** : near, close to **3 ~ de** : nearly, almost — **cercano, -na** *adj* : near, close — **cercanía** *nf* **1** : proximity **2 ~s** *nfpl* : outskirts
cercar {72} *vt* **1** : fence in **2** RODEAR : surround
cerciorarse *vr* **~ de** : make sure of
cerco *nm* **1** : circle, ring **2** ASEDIO : siege **3** *Lat* : fence
cerda *nf* : bristle
cerdo *nm* **1** : pig, hog **2 ~ macho** : boar
cereal *adj & nm* : cereal
cerebro *nm* : brain — **cerebral** *adj* : cerebral
ceremonia *nf* : ceremony — **ceremonial** *adj* : ceremonial — **ceremonioso, -sa** *adj* : ceremonious
cereza *nf* : cherry
cerilla *nf* : match — **cerillo** *nm Lat* : match
cerner{56} *or* **cernir** *vt* : sift — **cernerse** *vr* **1** : hover **2 ~ sobre** : loom over — **cernidor** *nm* : sieve
cero *nm* : zero
cerrar {55} *vt* **1** : close, shut **2** : turn off (a faucet, etc.) **3** : bring to an end — *vi* **1** : close up, lock up **2** : close down (a business, etc.) — **cerrarse** *vr* **1** : close, shut **2** TERMINAR : come to a close, end — **cerrado, -da** *adj* **1** : closed, shut, locked **2** : overcast (of weather) **3** : sharp (of a curve) **4** : thick, broad (of an accent) — **cerradura** *nf* : lock — **cerrajero, -ra** *n* : locksmith
cerro *nm* : hill
cerrojo *nm* : bolt, latch
certamen *nm, pl* **-támenes** : competition, contest
certero, -ra *adj* : accurate, precise
certeza *nf* : certainty — **certidumbre** *nf* : certainty
certificar {72} *vt* **1** : certify **2** : register (mail) — **certificado, -da** *adj* : certified, registered — **certificado** *nm* : certificate
cervato *nm* : fawn
cerveza *nf* **1** : beer **2 ~ de barril** : draft beer — **cervecería** *nf* **1** : brewery **2** BAR : beer hall, bar
cesar *vi* : cease, stop — *vt* : dismiss, lay off — **cesación** *nf, pl* **-ciones** : cessation, suspension — **cesante** *adj* **1** : laid off **2** *Lat* : unemployed — **cesantía** *nf Lat* : unemployment
cesárea *nf* : cesarean (section)
cese *nm* **1** : cessation, stop **2** DESTITUCIÓN : dismissal
césped *nm* : lawn, grass
cesta *nf* : basket — **cesto** *nm* **1** : (large) basket **2 ~ de basura** : wastebasket
cetro *nm* : scepter
chabacano *nm Lat* : apricot
chabola *nf Spain* : shack, shanty
chacal *nm* : jackal
cháchara *nf fam* : gabbing, chatter
chacra *nf Lat* : (small) farm
chafar *vt fam* : flatten, crush
chal *nm* : shawl
chaleco *nm* : vest
chalet *nm Spain* : house
chalupa *nf* **1** : small boat **2** *Lat* : small stuffed tortilla
chamarra *nf* : jacket
chamba *nf Lat fam* : job
champaña *or* **champán** *nm* : champagne
champiñón *nm, pl* **-ñones** : mushroom
champú *nm, pl* **-pús** *or* **-púes** : shampoo
chamuscar {72} *vt* : scorch
chance *nm Lat* : chance, opportunity
chancho *nm Lat* : pig
chanclos *nmpl* : galoshes
chantaje *nm* : blackmail — **chantajear** *vt* : blackmail
chanza *nf* : joke, jest
chapa *nf* **1** : sheet, plate **2** INSIGNIA : badge — **chapado, -da** *adj* **1** : plated

2 chapado a la antigua : old-fashioned
chaparrón *nm, pl* **-rrones** : downpour
chapotear *vi* : splash
chapucero, -ra *adj* : shoddy, sloppy — **chapuza** *nf* : botched job
chapuzón *nm, pl* **-zones** : dip, short swim
chaqueta *nf* : jacket
charca *nf* : pond — **charco** *nm* : puddle
charlar *vi* : chat — **charla** *nf* : chat, talk — **charlatán, -tana** *adj, mpl* **-tanes** : talkative — **~** *n* **1** : chatterbox **2** FARSANTE : charlatan
charol *nm* **1** : patent leather **2** BARNIZ : varnish
chasco *nm* **1** : trick, joke **2** DECEPCIÓN : disappointment
chasis *nms & pl* : chassis
chasquear *vt* **1** : click (the tongue), snap (one's fingers) **2** : crack (a whip) — **chasquido** *nm* **1** : click, snap **2** : crack (of a whip)
chatarra *nf* : scrap (metal)
chato, -ta *adj* **1** : pug-nosed **2** APLANADO : flat
chauvinismo *nm* : chauvinism — **chauvinista** *adj* : chauvinist, chauvinistic
chaval, -vala *n fam* : kid, boy *m*, girl *f*
checo, -ca *adj* : Czech — **checo** *nm* : Czech (language)
chef *nm* : chef
cheque *nm* : check — **chequera** *nf* : checkbook
chequear *vt Lat* **1** : check, inspect, verify **2** : check in (baggage) — **chequeo** *nm* **1** : (medical) checkup **2** *Lat* : check, inspection
chica → **chico**
chicano, -na *adj* : Chicano, Mexican-American
chícharo *nm Lat* : pea
chicharrón *nm, pl* **-rrones** : pork rind
chichón *nm, pl* **-chones** : bump
chicle *nm* : chewing gum
chico, -ca *adj* : little, small — **~** *n* : child, boy *m*, girl *f*
chiflar *vt* : whistle at, boo — *vi Lat* : whistle — **chiflado, -da** *adj fam* : crazy, nuts — **chiflido** *nm* : whistling
chile *nm* : chili pepper
chileno, -na *adj* : Chilean
chillar *vi* **1** : shriek, scream **2** CHIRRIAR : screech, squeal — **chillido** *nm* **1** : scream **2** CHIRRIDO : screech, squeal — **chillón, -llona** *adj, mpl* **-llones** : shrill, loud
chimenea *nf* **1** : chimney **2** HOGAR : fireplace
chimpancé *nm* : chimpanzee
chinche *nf* : bedbug
chino, -na *adj* : Chinese — **chino** *nm* : Chinese (language)
chiquillo, -lla *n* : kid, child
chiquito, -ta *adj* : tiny — **~** *n* : little child, tot
chiribita *nf* : spark
chiripa *nf* **1** : fluke **2 de ~** : by sheer luck
chirivía *nf* : parsnip
chirriar {85} *vi* **1** : squeak, creak **2** : screech (of brakes, etc.) — **chirrido** *nm* **1** : squeak, creak **2** : screech (of brakes)
chisme *nm* : (piece of) gossip — **chismear** *vi* : gossip — **chismoso, -sa** *adj* : gossipy — **~** *n* : gossip
chispear *vi* : spark — **chispa** *nf* : spark
chisporrotear *vi* : crackle, sizzle — **chisporroteo** *nm* : crackle
chiste *nm* : joke, funny story — **chistoso, -sa** *adj* : funny, witty
chivo, -va *n* : kid, young goat
chocar {72} *vi* **1** : crash, collide **2** ENFRENTARSE : clash — **chocante** *adj* **1** : striking, shocking **2** *Lat* : unpleasant, rude
choclo *nm Lat* : ear of corn, corncob
chocolate *nm* : chocolate
chofer *or* **chófer** *nm* **1** : chauffeur **2** CONDUCTOR : driver
choque *nm* **1** : shock **2** : crash, collision (of vehicles) **3** CONFLICTO : clash
chorizo *nm* : chorizo, sausage
chorrear *vi* **1** : drip **2** BROTAR : pour out, gush — **chorro** *nm* **1** : stream, jet **2** HILO : trickle
chovinismo → **chauvinismo**
choza *nf* : hut, shack
chubasco *nm* : downpour, squall
chuchería *nf* **1** : knickknack, trinket **2** DULCE : sweet
chueco, -ca *adj Lat* : crooked
chuleta *nf* : cutlet, chop
chulo, -la *adj fam* : cute, pretty
chupar *vt* **1** : suck **2** ABSORBER : absorb **3** *fam* : guzzle — *vi* : suckle — **chupada** *nf* : suck, sucking — **chupete** *nm* **1** : pacifier **2** *Lat* : lollipop
churro *nm* **1** : fried dough **2** *fam* : botch, mess
chusco, -ca *adj* : funny
chusma *nf* : riffraff, rabble
chutar *vi* : shoot (in soccer)
cianuro *nm* : cyanide
cicatriz *nf, pl* **-trices** : scar — **cicatrizar** {21} *vi* : form a scar, heal
cíclico, -ca *adj* : cyclical
ciclismo *nm* : cycling — **ciclista** *nmf* : cyclist

ciclo *nm* : cycle
ciclón *nm, pl* **-clones** : cyclone
ciego, -ga *adj* : blind — **ciegamente** *adv* : blindly
cielo *nm* **1** : sky **2** : heaven (in religion)
ciempiés *nms & pl* : centipede
cien *adj* : a hundred, hundred — **~** *nm* : one hundred
ciénaga *nf* : swamp, bog
ciencia *nf* **1** : science **2 a ~ cierta** : for a fact
cieno *nm* : mire, mud, silt
científico, -ca *adj* : scientific — **~** *n* : scientist
ciento *adj* (*used in compound numbers*) : one hundred — **~** *nm* **1** : hundred, group of a hundred **2 por ~** : percent
cierre *nm* **1** : closing, closure **2** BROCHE : fastener, clasp
cierto, -ta *adj* **1** : true **2** SEGURO : certain **3 por ~** : as a matter of fact
ciervo, -va *n* : deer, stag *m*, hind *f*
cifra *nf* **1** : number, figure **2** : sum (of money, etc.) **3** CLAVE : code, cipher — **cifrar** *vt* **1** : write in code **2 ~ la esperanza en** : pin all one's hopes on
cigarrillo *nm* : cigarrette — **cigarro** *nm* **1** : cigarette **2** PURO : cigar
cigüeña *nf* : stork
cilantro *nm* : cilantro, coriander
cilindro *nm* : cylinder — **cilíndrico, -ca** *adj* : cylindrical
cima *nf* : peak, summit
címbalo *nm* : cymbal
cimbrar *or* **cimbrear** *vt* : shake, rock — **cimbrarse** *or* **cimbrearse** *vr* : sway
cimentar {55} *vt* **1** : lay the foundation of **2** : cement, strengthen (relations, etc.) — **cimientos** *nmpl* : base, foundation(s)
cinc *nm* : zinc
cincel *nm* : chisel — **cincelar** *vt* : chisel
cinco *adj & nm* : five
cincuenta *adj & nm* : fifty — **cincuentavo, -va** *adj* : fiftieth — **cincuentavo** *nm* : fiftieth
cine *nm* : cinema, movies *pl* — **cinematográfico, -ca** *adj* : movie, film
cínico, -ca *adj* : cynical — **~** *n* : cynic — **cinismo** *nm* : cynicism
cinta *nf* **1** : ribbon, band **2 ~ adhesiva** : adhesive tape **3 ~ métrica** : tape measure **4 ~ magnetofónica** : magnetic tape
cinto *nm* : belt, girdle — **cintura** *nf* : waist — **cinturón** *nm, pl* **-rones 1** : belt **2 ~ de seguridad** : seat belt
ciprés *nm, pl* **-preses** : cypress
circo *nm* : circus
circuito *nm* : circuit
circulación *nf, pl* **-ciones 1** : circulation **2** TRÁFICO : traffic — **circular** *vi* **1** : circulate **2** : drive (a vehicle) — **~** *adj* : circular
círculo *nm* : circle
circuncidar *vt* : circumcise — **circuncisión** *nf, pl* **-siones** : circumcision
circundar *vt* : surround
circunferencia *nf* : circumference
circunscribir {33} *vt* : confine, limit — **circunscribirse** *vr* **~ a** : limit oneself to — **circunscripción** *nf, pl* **-ciones** : district, constituency
circunspecto, -ta *adj* : circumspect, cautious
circunstancia *nf* : circumstance — **circunstancial** *adj* : chance — **circunstante** *nmf* **1** : bystander **2 los ~s** : those present
circunvalación *nf, pl* **-ciones 1** : encircling **2 carretera de ~** : bypass
cirio *nm* : candle
ciruela *nf* **1** : plum **2 ~ pasa** : prune
cirugía *nf* : surgery — **cirujano, -na** *n* : surgeon
cisma *nf* : schism
cisne *nm* : swan
cisterna *nf* : cistern
cita *nf* **1** : appointment, date **2** REFERENCIA : quote, quotation — **citación** *nf, pl* **-ciones** : summons — **citar** *vt* **1** : quote, cite **2** CONVOCAR : make an appointment with **3** : summon (in law) — **citarse** *vr* **~ con** : arrange to meet
cítrico *nm* : citrus (fruit)
ciudad *nf* : city, town — **ciudadano, -na** *n* **1** : citizen **2** HABITANTE : resident — **ciudadanía** *nf* : citizenship
cívico, -ca *adj* : civic
civil *adj* : civil — **~** *nmf* : civilian — **civilidad** *nf* : civility — **civilización** *nf, pl* **-ciones** : civilization — **civilizar** {21} *vt* : civilize
cizaña *nf* : discord, rift
clamar *vi* : clamor, cry out — **clamor** *nm* : clamor, outcry — **clamoroso, -sa** *adj* : clamorous, loud
clan *nm* : clan
clandestino, -na *adj* : clandestine, secret
clara *nf* : egg white
claraboya *nf* : skylight
claramente *adv* : clearly
clarear *v impers* **1** : dawn **2** ACLARAR : clear up — *vi* : be transparent
claridad *nf* **1** : clarity, clearness **2** LUZ : light
clarificar {72} *vt* : clarify — **clarificación** *nf, pl* **-ciones** : clarification
clarín *nm, pl* **-rines** : bugle

clarinete *nm* : clarinet
clarividente *adj* **1** : clairvoyant **2** PERSPICAZ : perspicacious — **clarividencia** *nf* **1** : clairvoyance **2** PERSPICACIA : farsightedness
claro *adv* **1** : clearly **2** POR SUPUESTO : of course, surely — **~** *nm* **1** : clearing, glade **2 ~ de luna** : moonlight — **claro, -ra** *adj* **1** : clear, bright **2** : light (of colors) **3** EVIDENTE : clear, evident
clase *nf* **1** : class **2** TIPO : sort, kind
clásico, -ca *adj* : classic, classical — **clásico** *nm* : classic
clasificar {72} *vt* **1** : classify, sort out **2** : rate, rank (a hotel, a team, etc.) — **clasificarse** *vr* : qualify (in competitions) — **clasificación** *nf, pl* **-ciones** **1** : classification **2** : league (in sports)
claudicar {72} *vi* : back down
claustro *nm* : cloister
claustrofobia *nf* : claustrophobia — **claustrofóbico, -ca** *adj* : claustrophobic
cláusula *nf* : clause
clausurar *vt* : close (down) — **clausura** *nf* : closure, closing
clavado *nm Lat* : dive
clavar *vt* **1** : nail, hammer **2** HINCAR : drive in, plunge
clave *nf* **1** CIFRA : code **2** SOLUCIÓN : key **3** : clef (in music) — **~** *adj* : key
clavel *nm* : carnation
clavicémbalo *nm* : harpsichord
clavícula *nf* : collarbone
clavija *nf* **1** : peg, pin **2** : (electric) plug
clavo *nm* **1** : nail **2** : clove (spice)
claxon *nm, pl* **cláxones** : horn (of an automobile)
clemencia *nf* : clemency, mercy — **clemente** *adj* : merciful
clerical *adj* : clerical — **clérigo, -ga** *n* : clergyman, cleric — **clero** *nm* : clergy
cliché *nm* **1** : cliché **2** : negative (of a photograph)
cliente, -ta *n* : customer, client — **clientela** *nf* : clientele, customers *pl*
clima *nm* **1** : climate **2** AMBIENTE : atmosphere — **climático, -ca** *adj* : climatic
climatizar {21} *vt* : air-condition — **climatizado, -da** *adj* : air-conditioned
clímax *nm* : climax
clínica *nf* : clinic — **clínico, -ca** *adj* : clinical
clip *nm, pl* **clips** : (paper) clip
cloaca *nf* : sewer
cloquear *vi* : cluck — **cloqueo** *nm* : cluck, clucking
cloro *nm* : chlorine
clóset *nm Lat, pl* **clósets** : (built-in) closet, cupboard
club *nm* : club
coacción *nf, pl* **-ciones** : coercion — **coaccionar** *vt* : coerce
coagular *v* : clot, coagulate — **coagularse** *vr* : coagulate — **coágulo** *nm* : clot
coalición *nf, pl* **-ciones** : coalition
coartada *nf* : alibi
coartar *vt* : restrict, limit
cobarde *nmf* : coward — **~** *adj* : cowardly — **cobardía** *nf* : cowardice
cobaya *nf* : guinea pig
cobertizo *nm* : shelter, shed
cobertor *nm* : bedspread
cobertura *nf* **1** : cover **2** : coverage (of news, etc.)
cobijar *vt* : shelter — **cobijarse** *vr* : take shelter — **cobija** *nf Lat* : blanket — **cobijo** *nm* : shelter
cobra *nf* : cobra
cobrar *vt* **1** : charge, collect **2** : earn (a salary, etc.) **3** ADQUERIR : acquire, gain **4** : cash (a check) — *vi* : be paid — **cobrador, -dora** *n* **1** : collector **2** : conductor (of a bus, etc.)
cobre *nm* : copper
cobro *nm* : collection (of money), cashing (of a check)
cocaína *nf* : cocaine
cocción *nf, pl* **-ciones** : cooking
cocear *vi* : kick
cocer {14} *vt* **1** : cook **2** HERVIR : boil
coche *nm* **1** : car, automobile **2** : coach (of a train) **3** *or* **~ de caballos** : carriage **4 ~ fúnebre** : hearse — **cochecito** *nm* : baby carriage, stroller — **cochera** *nf* : garage, carport
cochino, -na *n* : pig, hog — **~** *adj fam* : dirty, filthy — **cochinada** *nf fam* : dirty thing — **cochinillo** *nm* : piglet
cocido, -da *adj* **1** : boiled, cooked **2 bien ~** : well-done — **cocido** *nm* : stew
cociente *nm* : quotient
cocina *nf* **1** : kitchen **2** : (kitchen) stove **3** : (art of) cooking, cuisine — **cocinar** *v* : cook — **cocinero, -ra** *n* : cook, chef
coco *nm* : coconut
cocodrilo *nm* : crocodile
coctel *or* **cóctel** *nm* **1** : cocktail **2** FIESTA : cocktail party
codazo *nm* **1** : nudge **2 dar un ~ a** : elbow, nudge
codicia *nf* : greed — **codiciar** *vt* : covet — **codicioso, -sa** *adj* : covetous, greedy

código *nm* **1** : code **2 ~ postal** : zip code **3 ~ morse** : Morse code
codo *nm* : elbow
codorniz *nf, pl* **-nices** : quail
coexistir *vi* : coexist
cofre *nm* : chest, coffer
coger {15} *vt* **1** : take (hold of) **2** ATRAPAR : catch **3** : pick up (from the ground) **4** : pick (fruit, etc.) — **cogerse** *vr* : hold on
cohechar *vt* : bribe — **cohecho** *nm* : bribe, bribery
coherencia *nf* : coherence — **coherente** *adj* : coherent — **cohesión** *nf, pl* **-siones** : cohesion
cohete *nm* : rocket
cohibir {62} *vt* **1** : restrict **2** : inhibit (a person) — **cohibirse** *vr* : feel inhibited — **cohibido, -da** *adj* : inhibited, shy
coincidir *vi* **1** : coincide **2 ~ con** : agree with — **coincidencia** *nf* : coincidence
cojear *vi* **1** : limp **2** : wobble (of furniture, etc.) — **cojera** *nf* : limp
cojín *nm, pl* **-jines** : cushion — **cojinete** *nm* **1** : pad, cushion **2** : bearing (of a machine)
cojo, -ja *adj* **1** : lame **2** : wobbly (of furniture) — **~** *n* : lame person
col *nf* **1** : cabbage **2 ~ de Bruselas** : Brussels sprout
cola *nf* **1** : tail **2** FILA : line (of people) **3** : end (of a line) **4** PEGAMENTO : glue **5 ~ de caballo** : ponytail
colaborar *vi* : collaborate — **colaboración** *nf, pl* **-ciones** : collaboration — **colaborador, -dora** *n* **1** : collaborator **2** : contributor (to a periodical)
colada *nf Spain* **1** : laundry **2 hacer la ~** : do the washing
colador *nm* : colander, strainer
colapso *nm* : collapse
colar {19} *vt* : strain, filter — **colarse** *vr* : sneak in, gate-crash
colcha *nf* : bedspread, quilt — **colchón** *nm, pl* **-chones** : mattress — **colchoneta** *nf* : mat
colear *vi* : wag its tail
colección *nf, pl* **-ciones** : collection — **coleccionar** *vt* : collect — **coleccionista** *nmf* : collector — **colecta** *nf* : collection (of donations)
colectividad *nf* : community — **colectivo, -va** *adj* : collective — **colectivo** *nm* **1** : collective **2** *Lat* : city bus
colector *nm* : sewer
colega *nmf* : colleague
colegio *nm* **1** : school **2** : (professional) college — **colegial, -giala** *n* : schoolboy *m*, schoolgirl *f*
colegir {28} *vt* : gather
cólera *nm* : cholera — **~** *nf* : anger, rage — **colérico, -ca** *adj* **1** : bad-tempered **2** FURIOSO : angry
colesterol *nm* : cholesterol
coleta *nf* : pigtail
colgar {16} *vt* **1** : hang **2** : hang up (a telephone) **3** : hang out (laundry) — *vi* : hang up — **colgante** *adj* : hanging — **~** *nm* : pendant
colibrí *nm* : hummingbird
cólico *nm* : colic
coliflor *nf* : cauliflower
colilla *nf* : (cigarette) butt
colina *nf* : hill
colindar *vi* **~ con** : be adjacent to — **colindante** *adj* : adjacent
coliseo *nm* : coliseum
colisión *nf, pl* **-siones** : collision — **colisionar** *vi* **~ contra** : collide with
collar *nm* **1** : necklace **2** : collar (for pets)
colmar *vt* **1** : fill to the brim **2** : fulfill (a wish, etc.) **3 ~ de** : shower with — **colmado, -da** *adj* : heaping
colmena *nf* : beehive
colmillo *nm* **1** : canine (tooth) **2** : fang (of a dog, etc.), tusk (of an elephant)
colmo *nm* **1** : height, limit **2 ¡eso es el ~!** : that's the last straw!
colocar {72} *vt* **1** PONER : place, put **2** : find a job for — **colocarse** *vr* **1** SITUARSE : position oneself **2** : get a job — **colocación** *nf, pl* **-ciones 1** : placement, placing **2** EMPLEO : position, job
colombiano, -na *adj* : Colombian
colon *nm* : (intestinal) colon
colonia *nf* **1** : colony **2** PERFUME : cologne **3** *Lat* : residential area — **colonial** *adj* : colonial — **colonizar** {21} *vt* : colonize — **colonización** *nf, pl* **-ciones** : colonization — **colono, -na** *n* : settler, colonist
coloquial *adj* : colloquial — **coloquio** *nm* **1** : talk, discussion **2** CONGRESO : conference
color *nm* : color — **colorado, -da** *adj* : red — **colorear** *vt* : color — **colorete** *nm* : rouge — **colorido** *nm* : colors *pl*, coloring
colosal *adj* : colossal
columna *nf* **1** : column **2 ~ vertebral** : spine, backbone — **columnista** *nmf* : columnist
columpiar *vt* : push (on a swing) — **columpiarse** *vr* : swing — **columpio** *nm* : swing
coma[1] *nm* : coma
coma[2] *nf* : comma
comadre *nf* **1** : godmother of one's child, mother of one's godchild **2** *fam*

: (female) friend — **comadrear** *vi fam* : gossip
comadreja *nf* : weasel
comadrona *nf* : midwife
comandancia *nf* : command headquarters, command — **comandante** *nmf* **1** : commander **2** : major (in the military) — **comando** *nm* **1** : commando **2** *Lat* : command
comarca *nf* : region, area
combar *vt* : bend, curve
combatir *vt* : combat, fight against — *vi* : fight — **combate** *nm* **1** : combat **2** : fight (in boxing) — **combatiente** *nmf* : combatant, fighter
combinar *vt* **1** : combine **2** : put together, match (colors, etc.) — **combinarse** *vr* : get together — **combinación** *nf, pl* **-ciones 1** : combination **2** : connection (in travel)
combustible *nm* : fuel — ~ *adj* : combustible — **combustión** *nf, pl* **-tiones** : combustion
comedia *nf* : comedy
comedido, -da *adj* : moderate
comedor *nm* : dining room
comensal *nmf* : diner, dinner guest
comentar *vt* **1** : comment on, discuss **2** MENCIONAR : mention — **comentario** *nm* **1** : comment, remark **2** ANÁLISIS : commentary — **comentarista** *nmf* : commentator
comenzar {29} *v* : begin, start
comer *vt* **1** : eat **2** *fam* : eat up, eat into — *vi* **1** : eat **2** CENAR : have a meal **3** **dar de** ~ : feed — **comerse** *vr* : eat up
comercio *nm* **1** : commerce, trade **2** NEGOCIO : business — **comercial** *adj* : commercial — **comercializar** {21} *vt* : market — **comerciante** *nmf* : merchant, dealer — **comerciar** *vi* : do business, trade
comestible *adj* : edible — **comestibles** *nmpl* : groceries, food
cometa *nm* : comet — ~ *nf* : kite
cometer *vt* **1** : commit **2** ~ **un error** : make a mistake — **cometido** *nm* : assignment, task
comezón *nf, pl* **-zones** : itchiness, itching
comicios *nmpl* : elections
cómico, -ca *adj* : comic, comical — ~ *n* : comic, comedian
comida *nf* **1** ALIMENTO : food **2** *Spain* : lunch **3** *Lat* : dinner **4** **tres ~s al día** : three meals a day
comienzo *nm* : beginning
comillas *nfpl* : quotation marks
comino *nm* : cumin
comisario, -ria *n* : commissioner — **comisaría** *nf* : police station
comisión *nf, pl* **-siones 1** : commission **2** COMITÉ : committee
comité *nm* : committee
como *conj* **1** : as, since **2** SI : if — ~ *prep* **1** : like, as **2** **así** ~ : as well as — ~ *adv* **1** : as **2** APROXIMADAMENTE : around, about
cómo *adv* **1** : how **2** ~ **no** : by all means **3** **¿~ te llamas?** : what's your name?
cómoda *nf* : chest of drawers
comodidad *nf* : comfort, convenience
comodín *nm, pl* **-dines** : joker (in playing cards)
cómodo, -da *adj* **1** : comfortable **2** ÚTIL : handy, convenient
comoquiera *adv* **1** : in any way **2** ~ **que** : however
compacto, -ta *adj* : compact
compadecer {53} *vt* : feel sorry for — **compadecerse** *vr* ~ **de** : take pity on
compadre *nm* **1** : godfather of one's child, father of one's godchild **2** *fam* : buddy
compañero, -ra *n* : companion, partner — **compañerismo** *nm* : companionship
compañía *nf* : company
comparar *vt* : compare — **comparable** *adj* : comparable — **comparación** *nf, pl* **-ciones** : comparison — **comparativo, -va** *adj* : comparative
comparecer *vt* : appear (before a court, etc.)
compartimiento *or* **compartimento** *nm* : compartment
compartir *vt* : share
compás *nm, pl* **-pases 1** : compass **2** : rhythm, time (in music)
compasión *nf, pl* **-siones** : compassion, pity — **compasivo, -va** *adj* : compassionate
compatible *adj* : compatible — **compatibilidad** *nf* : compatibility
compatriota *nmf* : compatriot, fellow countryman
compeler *vt* : compel
compendiar *vt* : summarize — **compendio** *nm* : summary
compensar *vt* : compensate for — **compensación** *nf, pl* **-ciones** : compensation
competir {54} *vi* : compete — **competencia** *nf* **1** : competition, rivalry **2** CAPACIDAD : competence — **competente** *adj* : competent — **competición** *nf, pl* **-ciones** : competition — **competidor, -dora** *n* : competitor

compilar *vt* : compile
compinche *nmf fam* : friend, chum
complacer {57} *vt* : please — **complacerse** *vr* ~ **en** : take pleasure in — **complaciente** *adj* : obliging, helpful
complejidad *nf* : complexity — **complejo, -ja** *adj* : complex — **complejo** *nm* : complex
complementar *vt* : complement — **complementario, -ria** *adj* : complementary — **complemento** *nm* **1** : complement **2** : object (in grammar)
completar *vt* : complete — **completo, -ta** *adj* **1** : complete **2** PERFECTO : perfect **3** LLENO : full — **completamente** *adv* : completely
complexión *nf, pl* **-xiones** : constitution, build
complicar {72} *vt* **1** : complicate **2** IMPLICAR : involve — **complicación** *nf, pl* **-ciones** : complication — **complicado, -da** *adj* : complicated, complex
cómplice *nmf* : accomplice — ~ *adj* : conspiratorial, knowing
complot *nm, pl* **-plots** : conspiracy, plot
componer {60} *vt* **1** : make up, compose **2** : compose, write (a song) **3** ARREGLAR : fix, repair — **componerse** *vr* ~ **de** : consist of — **componente** *adj & nm* : component, constituent
comportarse *vr* : behave — **comportamiento** *nm* : behavior
composición *nf, pl* **-ciones** : composition — **compositor, -tora** *n* : composer, songwriter
compostura *nf* **1** : composure **2** REPARACIÓN : repair
comprar *vt* : buy, purchase — **compra** *nf* **1** : purchase **2 ir de ~s** : go shopping — **comprador, -dora** *n* : buyer, shopper
comprender *vt* **1** : comprehend, understand **2** ABARCAR : cover, include — **comprensible** *adj* : understandable — **comprensión** *nf, pl* **-siones** : understanding — **comprensivo, -va** *adj* : understanding
compresa *nf* **1** : compress **2** *or* ~ **higiénica** : sanitary napkin
compresión *nf, pl* **-siones** : compression — **comprimido** *nm* : pill, tablet — **comprimir** *vt* : compress
comprobar {19} *vt* **1** VERIFICAR : check **2** DEMOSTRAR : prove — **comprobación** *nf, pl* **-ciones** : verification, check — **comprobante** *nm* **1** : proof **2** RECIBO : receipt, voucher
comprometer *vt* **1** : compromise **2** ARRIESGAR : jeopardize **3** OBLIGAR : commit, put under obligation — **comprometerse** *vr* **1** : commit oneself **2** ~ **con** : get engaged to — **comprometedor, -dora** *adj* : compromising — **comprometido, -da** *adj* **1** : compromising, awkward **2** : engaged (to be married) — **compromiso** *nm* **1** : obligation, commitment **2** : (marriage) engagement **3** ACUERDO : agreement **4** APURO : awkward situation
compuesto, -ta *adj* **1** : compound **2** ~ **de** : made up of, consisting of — **compuesto** *nm* : compound
compulsivo, -va *adj* : compelling, urgent
computar *vt* : compute, calculate — **computadora** *nf or* **computador** *nm* **1** : computer **2** ~ **portátil** : laptop computer — **cómputo** *nm* : calculation
comulgar {52} *vi* : receive Communion
común *adj, pl* **-munes 1** : common **2** ~ **y corriente** : ordinary **3 por lo ~** : generally
comuna *nf* : commune — **comunal** *adj* : communal
comunicar {72} *vt* : communicate — **comunicarse** *vr* **1** : communicate **2** ~ **con** : get in touch with — **comunicación** *nf, pl* **-ciones** : communication — **comunicado** *nm* : communiqué — **comunicativo, -va** *adj* : communicative
comunidad *nf* : community
comunión *nf, pl* **-niones** : communion, Communion
comunismo *nm* : Communism — **comunista** *adj & nmf* : Communist
con *prep* **1** : with **2** A PESAR DE : in spite of **3** (*before an infinitive*) : by **4** ~ **(tal) que** : so long as
cóncavo, -va *adj* : concave
concebir {54} *v* : conceive — **concebible** *adj* : conceivable
conceder *vt* **1** : grant, bestow **2** ADMITIR : concede
concejal, -jala *n* : councilman, alderman
concentrar *vt* : concentrate — **concentrarse** *vr* : concentrate — **concentración** *nf, pl* **-ciones** : concentration
concepción *nf, pl* **-ciones** : conception — **concepto** *nm* **1** : concept **2** OPINIÓN : opinion
concernir {17} *vi* ~ **a** : concern — **concerniente** *adj* ~ **a** : concerning
concertar {55} *vt* **1** : arrange, coordinate **2** (*used before an infinitive*) : agree **3** : harmonize (in music) — *vi* : be in harmony

concesión *nf, pl* **-siones 1 :** concession **2 :** awarding (of prizes, etc.)
concha *nf* **:** shell
conciencia *nf* **1 :** conscience **2** CONOCIMIENTO **:** consciousness, awareness — **concientizar** {21} *vt Lat* **:** make aware — **concientizarse** *vr Lat* **~ de :** realize
concienzudo, -da *adj* **:** conscientious
concierto *nm* **1 :** concert **2 :** concerto (musical composition)
conciliar *vt* **:** reconcile — **conciliación** *nf, pl* **-ciones :** reconciliation
concilio *nm* **:** council
conciso, -sa *adj* **:** concise
conciudadano, -na *n* **:** fellow citizen
concluir {41} *vt* **:** conclude — *vi* **:** come to an end — **conclusión** *nf, pl* **-siones :** conclusion — **concluyente** *adj* **:** conclusive
concordar {19} *vi* **:** agree — *vt* **:** reconcile — **concordancia** *nf* **:** agreement — **concordia** *nf* **:** harmony, concord
concretar *vt* **:** make concrete, specify — **concretarse** *vr* **:** become definite, take shape — **concreto, -ta** *adj* **1 :** concrete **2** DETERMINADO **:** specific **3 en ~ :** specifically — **concreto** *nm Lat* **:** concrete
concurrir *vi* **1 :** come together, meet **2 ~ a :** take part in — **concurrencia** *nf* **:** audience, turnout — **concurrido, -da** *adj* **:** busy, crowded
concursar *vi* **:** compete, participate — **concursante** *nmf* **:** competitor — **concurso** *nm* **1 :** competition **2** CONCURRENCIA **:** gathering **3** AYUDA **:** help, cooperation
condado *nm* **:** county
conde, -desa *n* **:** count *m*, countess *f*
condenar *vt* **1 :** condemn, damn **2 :** sentence (a criminal) — **condena** *nf* **1 :** condemnation **2** SENTENCIA **:** sentence — **condenación** *nf, pl* **-ciones :** condemnation, damnation
condensar *vt* **:** condense — **condensación** *nf, pl* **-ciones :** condensation
condesa *nf* → **conde**
condescender {56} *vi* **1 :** acquiesce, agree **2 ~ a :** condescend to — **condescendiente** *adj* **:** condescending
condición *nf, pl* **-ciones 1 :** condition, state **2** CALIDAD **:** capacity, position — **condicional** *adj* **:** conditional
condimento *nm* **:** condiment, seasoning
condolerse {47} *vr* **:** sympathize — **condolencia** *nf* **:** condolence
condominio *nm* **1 :** joint ownership **2** *Lat* **:** condominium
condón *nm, pl* **-dones :** condom
conducir {61} *vt* **1** DIRIGIR **:** direct, lead **2** MANEJAR **:** drive — *vi* **1 :** drive **2 ~ a :** lead to — **conducirse** *vr* **:** behave
conducta *nf* **:** behavior, conduct
conducto *nm* **:** conduit, duct
conductor, -tora *n* **:** driver
conectar *vt* **1 :** connect **2** ENCHUFAR **:** plug in — *vi* **:** connect
conejo, -ja *n* **:** rabbit — **conejera** *nf* **:** (rabbit) hutch
conexión *nf, pl* **-xiones :** connection — **conexo, -xa** *adj* **:** connected
confabularse *vr* **:** conspire, plot
confeccionar *vt* **:** make (up), prepare — **confección** *nf, pl* **-ciones 1 :** making, preparation **2 :** tailoring, dressmaking
confederación *nf, pl* **-ciones :** confederation
conferencia *nf* **1 :** lecture **2** REUNIÓN **:** conference
conferir {76} *vt* **:** confer, bestow
confesar {55} *v* **:** confess — **confesarse** *vr* **:** go to confession — **confesión** *nf, pl* **-siones 1 :** confession **2** CREDO **:** religion, creed
confeti *nm* **:** confetti
confiar {85} *vi* **:** trust — *vt* **:** entrust — **confiable** *adj* **:** trustworthy, reliable — **confiado, -da** *adj* **1 :** confident **2** CRÉDULO **:** trusting — **confianza** *nf* **1 :** trust **2 :** confidence (in oneself)
confidencia *nf* **:** confidence, secret — **confidencial** *adj* **:** confidential — **confidencialidad** *nf* **:** confidentiality — **confidente** *nmf* **1 :** confidant, confidante *f* **2 :** (police) informer
configuración *nf, pl* **-ciones :** configuration, shape
confín *nm, pl* **-fines :** boundary, limit — **confinar** *vt* **1 :** confine **2** DESTERRER **:** exile
confirmar *vt* **:** confirm — **confirmación** *nf, pl* **-ciones :** confirmation
confiscar {72} *vt* **:** confiscate
confitería *nm* **:** candy store
confitura *nf* **:** jam
conflagración *nf, pl* **-ciones 1 :** war, conflict **2** INCENDIO **:** fire
conflicto *nm* **:** conflict
confluencia *nf* **:** junction, confluence
conformar *vt* **:** shape, make up — **conformarse** *vr* **1** RESIGNARSE **:** resign oneself **2 ~ con :** content oneself with — **conforme** *adj* **1 :** content, satisfied **2 ~ a :** in accordance with — **~** *conj* **:** as — **conformidad** *nf* **1 :** agreement **2** RESIGNACIÓN **:** resignation

confortar *vt* : comfort — **confortable** *adj* : comfortable
confrontar *vt* **1** : confront **2** COMPARAR : compare — *vi* : border — **confrontarse** *vr* **~ con** : face up to — **confrontación** *nf, pl* **-ciones** : confrontation
confundir *vt* : confuse, mix up — **confundirse** *vr* : make a mistake, be confused — **confusión** *nf, pl* **-siones** : confusion — **confuso, -sa** *adj* **1** : confused **2** INDISTINTO : hazy, indistinct — **congelar** *vt* : freeze — **congelarse** *vr* : freeze — **congelación** *nf, pl* **-ciones** : freezing — **congelado, -da** *adj* : frozen — **congelador** *nm* : freezer
congeniar *vi* : get along
congestión *nf, pl* **-tiones** : congestion — **congestionado, -da** *adj* : congested
congoja *nf* : anguish, grief
congraciarse *vr* : ingratiate oneself
congratular *vt* : congratulate
congregar {52} *vt* : bring together — **congregarse** *vr* : congregate — **congregación** *nf, pl* **-ciones** : congregation, gathering
congreso *nm* : congress — **congresista** *nmf* : member of congress
conjeturar *vt* : guess, conjecture — **conjetura** *nf* : guess, conjecture
conjugar {52} *vt* : conjugate — **conjugación** *nf, pl* **-ciones** : conjugation
conjunción *nf, pl* **-ciones** : conjunction
conjunto, -ta *adj* : joint — **conjunto** *nm* **1** : collection **2** : outfit (of clothing) **3** GRUPO : band **4 en ~** : as a whole
conjurar *vt* : ward off — *vi* : conspire, plot
conllevar *vt* : entail
conmemorar *vt* : commemorate — **conmemoración** *nf, pl* **-ciones** : commemoration — **conmemorativo, -va** *adj* : commemorative
conmigo *pron* : with me
conminar *vt* : threaten
conmiseración *nf, pl* **-ciones** : pity, commiseration
conmocionar *vt* : shock — **conmoción** *nf, pl* **-ciones 1** : shock, upheaval **2** *or* **~ cerebral** : concussion
conmover {47} *vt* **1** : move, touch **2** SACUDIR : shake (up) — **conmoverse** *vr* : be moved — **conmovedor, -dora** *adj* : moving, touching
conmutador *nm* **1** : (electric) switch **2** *Lat* : switchboard
cono *nm* : cone
conocer {18} *vt* **1** : know **2** : meet (a person), get to know (a city, etc.) **3** RECONOCER : recognize — **conocerse** *vr* **1** : meet, get to know each other **2** : know oneself — **conocedor, -dora** *adj & n* : expert — **conocido, -da** *adj* : well-known — **~** *n* : acquaintance — **conocimiento** *nm* **1** : knowledge **2** SENTIDO : consciousness
conque *conj* : so
conquistar *vt* : conquer — **conquista** *nf* : conquest — **conquistador, -dora** *adj* : conquering — **conquistador** *nm* : conqueror
consabido, -da *adj* **1** : well-known **2** HABITUEL : usual
consagrar *vt* **1** : consecrate **2** DEDICAR : devote — **consagración** *nf, pl* **-ciones** : consecration
consciencia *nf* → **conciencia** — **consciente** *adj* : conscious, aware
consecución *nf, pl* **-ciones** : attainment
consecuencia *nf* **1** : consequence **2 en ~** : accordingly — **consecuente** *adj* : consistent
consecutivo, -va *adj* : consecutive
conseguir {75} *vt* **1** : get, obtain **2 ~ hacer algo** : manage to do sth
consejo *nm* **1** : advice, counsel **2** : council (assembly) — **consejero, -ra** *n* : adviser, counselor
consenso *nm* : consensus
consentir {76} *vt* **1** : allow, permit **2** MIMAR : pamper, spoil — *vi* : consent — **consentimiento** *nm* : consent, permission
conserje *nmf* : caretaker, janitor
conservar *vt* **1** : preserve **2** GUARDAR : keep, conserve — **conservarse** *vr* : keep — **conserva** *nf* **1** : preserve(s) **2 ~s** *nfpl* : canned goods — **conservación** *nf, pl* **-ciones** : conservation, preservation — **conservador, -dora** *adj & n* : conservative — **conservatorio** *nm* : conservatory
considerar *vt* **1** : consider **2** RESPETAR : respect — **considerable** *adj* : considerable — **consideración** *nf, pl* **-ciones 1** : consideration **2** RESPETO : respect — **considerado, -da** *adj* **1** : considerate **2** RESPETADO : respected
consigna *nf* **1** ESLOGAN : slogan **2** ORDEN : orders **3** : checkroom (for baggage)
consigo *pron* : with her, with him, with you, with oneself
consiguiente *adj* **1** : consequent **2 por ~** : consequently

consistir *vi* ~ **en 1** : consist of **2** : lie in, consist in — **consistencia** *nf* : consistency — **consistente** *adj* **1** : firm, solid **2** ~ **en** : consisting of
consolar {19} *vt* : console, comfort — **consolarse** *vr* : console oneself — **consolación** *nf, pl* **-ciones** : consolation
consolidar *vt* : consolidate — **consolidación** *nf, pl* **-ciones** : consolidation
consomé *nm* : consommé
consonante *adj* : consonant, harmonious — ~ *nf* : consonant
consorcio *nm* : consortium
conspirar *vi* : conspire, plot — **conspiración** *nf, pl* **-ciones** : conspiracy — **conspirador, -dora** *n* : conspirator
constancia *nf* **1** : record, evidence **2** PERSEVERANCIA : perseverance — **constante** *adj* : constant — **constantemente** *adv* : constantly, continually
constar *vi* **1** : be evident, be clear **2** ~ **de** : consist of
constatar *vt* **1** : verify **2** AFIRMAR : state, affirm
constelación *nf, pl* **-ciones** : constellation
consternación *nf, pl* **-ciones** : consternation
constipado, -da *adj* **estar** ~ : have a cold — **constipado** *nm* : cold — **constiparse** *vr* : catch a cold
constituir {41} *vt* **1** FORMAR : constitute, form **2** FUNDAR : establish, set up — **constituirse** *vr* ~ **en** : set oneself up as — **constitución** *nf, pl* **-ciones** : constitution — **constitucional** *adj* : constitutional — **constitutivo, -va** *adj* : constituent — **constituyente** *adj & nm* : constituent
constreñir {67} *vt* **1** : force, compel **2** RESTRINGIR : restrict, limit
construir {41} *vt* : build, construct — **construcción** *nf, pl* **-ciones** : construction, building — **constructivo, -va** *adj* : constructive — **constructor, -tora** *n* : builder
consuelo *nm* : consolation, comfort
consuetudinario, -ria *adj* : customary
cónsul *nmf* : consul — **consulado** *nm* : consulate
consultar *vt* : consult — **consulta** *nf* : consultation — **consultor, -tora** *n* : consultant — **consultorio** *nm* : office (of a doctor or dentist)
consumar *vt* **1** : consummate, complete **2** : commit (a crime)
consumir *vt* : consume — **consumirse** *vr* : waste away — **consumición** *nf, pl* **-ciones 1** : consumption **2** : drink (in a restaurant) — **consumido, -da** *adj* : thin, emaciated — **consumidor, -dora** *n* : consumer — **consumo** *nm* : consumption
contabilidad *nf* **1** : accounting, bookkeeping **2** : accountancy (profession) — **contable** *nmf Spain* : accountant, bookkeeper
contactar *vi* ~ **con** : get in touch with, contact — **contacto** *nm* : contact
contado, -da *adj* : numbered, few — **contado** *nm* **al** ~ : (in) cash
contador, -dora *n Lat* : accountant — **contador** *nm* : meter
contagiar *vt* **1** : infect **2** : transmit (a disease) — **contagiarse** *vr* **1** : be contagious **2** : become infected (with a disease) — **contagio** *nm* : contagion, infection — **contagioso, -sa** *adj* : contagious, infectious
contaminar *vt* : contaminate, pollute — **contaminación** *nf, pl* **-ciones** : contamination, pollution
contar {19} *vt* **1** : count **2** NARRAR : tell — *vi* **1** : count **2** ~ **con** : rely on, count on
contemplar *vt* **1** MIRAR : look at, behold **2** CONSIDERAR : contemplate — **contemplación** *nf, pl* **-ciones** : contemplation
contemporáneo, -nea *adj & n* : contemporary
contender {56} *vi* : contend, compete — **contendiente** *nmf* : competitor
contener {80} *vt* **1** : contain **2** RESTRINGIR : restrain, hold back — **contenerse** *vr* : restrain oneself — **contenedor** *nm* : container — **contenido, -da** *adj* : restrained — **contenido** *nm* : contents *pl*
contentar *vt* : please, make happy — **contentarse** *vr* ~ **con** : be satisfied with — **contento, -ta** *adj* : glad, happy, contented
contestar *vt* : answer — *vi* : reply, answer back — **contestación** *nf, pl* **-ciones** : answer, reply
contexto *nm* : context
contienda *nf* **1** COMBATE : dispute, fight **2** COMPETICIÓN : contest
contigo *pron* : with you
contiguo, -gua *adj* : adjacent
continente *nm* : continent — **continental** *adj* : continental
contingencia *nf* : contingency — **contingente** *adj & nm* : contingent
continuar {3} *v* : continue — **continuación** *nf, pl* **-ciones 1** : continuation **2 a** ~ : next, then — **continuidad** *nf* : continuity — **continuo, -nua** *adj* **1**

: continuous, steady **2** FRECUENTE : continual
contorno *nm* **1** : outline **2 ~s** *nmpl* : surrounding area
contorsión *nf, pl* **-siones** : contortion
contra *prep* **1** : against **2 en ~** : against — **~** *nm* **los pros y los ~s** : the pros and cons
contraatacar {72} *v* : counterattack — **contraataque** *nm* : counterattack
contrabajo *nm* : double bass
contrabalancear *vt* : counterbalance
contrabandista *nmf* : smuggler — **contrabando** *nm* **1** : smuggling **2** : contraband (goods)
contracción *nf, pl* **-ciones** : contraction
contrachapado *nm* : plywood
contradecir {11} *vt* : contradict — **contradicción** *nf, pl* **-ciones** : contradiction — **contradictorio, -ria** *adj* : contradictory
contraer {81} *vt* **1** : contract **2 ~ matrimonio** : get married — **contraerse** *vr* : contract, tighten up
contrafuerte *nm* : buttress
contragolpe *nm* : backlash
contralto *nmf* : contralto
contrapartida *nf* : compensation
contrapelo: **a ~** *adv phr* : the wrong way
contrapeso *nm* : counterbalance
contraponer {60} *vt* **1** : counter, oppose **2** COMPARAR : compare
contraproducente *adj* : counterproductive
contrariar {85} *vt* **1** : oppose **2** MOLESTAR : vex, annoy — **contrariedad** *nf* **1** : obstacle **2** DISGUSTO : annoyance — **contrario, -ria** *adj* **1** OPUESTO : opposite **2 al contrario** : on the contrary **3 ser ~ a** : be opposed to
contrarrestar *vt* : counteract
contrasentido *nm* : contradiction (in terms)
contraseña *nf* : password
contrastar *vt* **1** : check, verify **2** RESISTIR : resist — *vi* : contrast — **contraste** *nm* : contrast
contratar *vt* **1** : contract for **2** : hire, engage (workers)
contratiempo *nm* **1** : mishap **2** DIFICULTAD : setback
contrato *nm* : contract — **contratista** *nmf* : contractor
contraventana *nf* : shutter
contribuir {41} *vi* **1** : contribute **2** : pay taxes — **contribución** *nf, pl* **-ciones 1** : contribution **2** IMPUESTO : tax — **contribuyente** *nmf* **1** : contributor **2** : taxpayer
contrincante *nmf* : opponent
contrito, -ta *adj* : contrite
controlar *vt* **1** : control **2** COMPROBAR : monitor, check — **control** *nm* **1** : control **2** VERIFICACIÓN : inspection, check — **controlador, -dora** *n* : controller
controversia *nf* : controversy
contundente *adj* **1** : blunt **2** : forceful, convincing (of arguments, etc.)
contusión *nf, pl* **-siones** : bruise
convalecencia *nf* : convalescence — **convaleciente** *adj & nmf* : convalescent
convencer {86} *vt* : convince, persuade — **convencerse** *vr* : be convinced — **convencimiento** *nm* : conviction, belief
convención *nf, pl* **-ciones** : convention — **convencional** *adj* : conventional
convenir {87} *vi* **1** : be suitable, be advisable **2 ~ en** : agree on — **conveniencia** *nf* **1** : convenience **2** : suitability (of an action, etc.) — **conveniente** *adj* **1** : convenient **2** ACONSEJABLE : suitable, advisable **3** PROVECHOSO : useful — **convenio** *nm* : agreement, pact
convento *nm* : convent, monastery
converger {15} *or* **convergir** *vi* : converge
conversar *vi* : converse, talk — **conversación** *nf, pl* **-ciones** : conversation
conversión *nf, pl* **-siones** : conversion — **converso, -sa** *n* : convert
convertir {76} *vt* : convert — **convertirse** *vr* **~ en** : turn into — **convertible** *adj & nm* : convertible
convexo, -xa *adj* : convex
convicción *nf, pl* **-ciones** : conviction — **convicto, -ta** *adj* : convicted
convidar *vt* : invite — **convidado, -da** *n* : guest
convincente *adj* : convincing
convite *nm* **1** : invitation **2** : banquet
convivir *vi* : live together — **convivencia** *nf* : coexistence, living together
convocar {72} *vt* : convoke, call together
convulsión *nf, pl* **-siones 1** : convulsion **2** TRASTORNO : upheaval — **convulsivo, -va** *adj* : convulsive
conyugal *adj* : conjugal — **cónyuge** *nmf* : spouse, partner
coñac *nm* : cognac, brandy
cooperar *vi* : cooperate — **cooperación** *nf, pl* **-ciones** : cooperation — **cooperativa** *nf* : cooperative, coop — **cooperativo, -va** *adj* : cooperative

coordenada *nf* : coordinate
coordinar *vt* : coordinate — **coordinación** *nf, pl* **-ciones** : coordination — **coordinador, -dora** *n* : coordinator
copa *nf* **1** : glass, goblet **2** : cup (in sports) **3 tomar una ~** : have a drink
copia *nf* : copy — **copiar** *vt* : copy
copioso, -sa *adj* : copious, abundant
copla *nf* **1** : (popular) song **2** ESTROFA : verse, stanza
copo *nm* **1** : flake **2** *or* **~ de nieve** : snowflake
coquetear *vi* : flirt — **coqueteo** *nm* : flirting, flirtation — **coqueto, -ta** *adj* : flirtatious — **~** *n* : flirt
coraje *nm* **1** : valor, courage **2** IRA : anger
coral[1] *nm* : coral
coral[2] *adj* : choral — **~** *nf* : choir, chorale
Corán *nm* **el ~** : the Koran
coraza *nf* **1** : armor plating **2** : shell
corazón *nm, pl* **-zones 1** : heart **2** : core (of fruit) **3 mi ~** : my darling — **corazonada** *nf* **1** : hunch **2** IMPULSO : impulse
corbata *nf* : tie, necktie
corchete *nm* **1** : hook and eye, clasp **2** : square bracket (punctuation mark)
corcho *nm* : cork
cordel *nm* : cord, string
cordero *nm* : lamb
cordial *adj* : cordial — **cordialidad** *nf* : cordiality
cordillera *nf* : mountain range
córdoba *nf* : córdoba (Nicaraguan unit of currency)
cordón *nm, pl* **-dones 1** : cord **2 ~ policial** : (police) cordon **3 cordones** *nmpl* : shoelaces
cordura *nf* : sanity
corear *vt* : chant
coreografía *nf* : choreography
cornamenta *nf* : antlers *pl*
corneta *nf* : bugle
coro *nm* **1** : chorus **2** : (church) choir
corona *nf* **1** : crown **2** : wreath, garland (of flowers) — **coronación** *nf, pl* **-ciones** : coronation — **coronar** *vt* : crown
coronel *nm* : colonel
coronilla *nf* **1** : crown (of the head) **2 estar hasta la ~** : be fed up
corporación *nf, pl* **-ciones** : corporation
corporal *adj* : corporal, bodily
corporativo, -va *adj* : corporate
corpulento, -ta *adj* : stout
corral *nm* **1** : farmyard **2** : pen, corral (for animals) **3** *or* **corralito** : playpen
correa *nf* **1** : strap, belt **2** : leash (for a dog, etc.)
corrección *nf, pl* **-ciones 1** : correction **2** : correctness, propriety (of manners) — **correccional** *nm* : reformatory — **correctivo, -va** *adj* : corrective — **correcto, -ta** *adj* **1** : correct, right **2** CORTÉS : polite
corredizo, -za *adj* : sliding
corredor, -dora *n* **1** : runner, racer **2** AGENTE : agent, broker — **corredor** *nm* : corridor, hallway
corregir {28} *vt* : correct — **corregirse** *vr* : mend one's ways
correlación *nf, pl* **-ciones** : correlation
correo *nm* **1** : mail **2 ~ aéreo** : airmail
correr *vi* **1** : run, race **2** : flow (of a river, etc.) **3** : pass (of time) — *vt* **1** : run **2** RECORRER : travel over, cover **3** : draw (curtains) — **correrse** *vr* **1** : move along **2** : run (of colors)
corresponder *vi* **1** : correspond **2** PERTENECER : belong **3** ENCAJAR : fit **4 ~ a** : reciprocate, repay — **corresponderse** *vr* : write to each other — **correspondencia** *nf* **1** : correspondence **2** : connection (of a train, etc.) — **correspondiente** *adj* : corresponding, respective — **corresponsal** *nmf* : correspondent
corretear *vi* : run about, scamper
corrida *nf* **1** : run **2** *or* **~ de toros** : bullfight — **corrido, -da** *adj* **1** : straight, continuous **2** *fam* : worldly
corriente *adj* **1** : current **2** NORMAL : common, ordinary **3** : running (of water, etc.) — **~** *nf* **1** : current (of water, electricity, etc.), draft (of air) **2** TENDENCIA : tendency, trend — **~** *nm* **al ~ 1** : up-to-date **2** ENTERADO : aware, informed
corrillo *nm* : clique, circle — **corro** *nm* : ring, circle (of people)
corroborar *vt* : corroborate
corroer {69} *vt* **1** : corrode (of metals) **2** : erode, wear away — **corroerse** *vr* : corrode
corromper *vt* **1** : corrupt **2** PUDRIR : rot — **corrompido, -da** *adj* : corrupt
corrosión *nf, pl* **-siones** : corrosion — **corrosivo, -va** *adj* : corrosive
corrupción *nf, pl* **-ciones 1** : corruption **2** DESCOMPOSICIÓN : decay, rot — **corrupto, -ta** *adj* : corrupt
corsé *nm* : corset
cortar *vt* **1** : cut **2** RECORTAR : cut out **3** QUITAR : cut off — *vi* : cut — **cortarse** *vr* **1** : cut oneself **2** : be cut off (on the telephone) **3** : curdle (of milk) **4 ~ el pelo** : have one's hair cut — **cortada**

nf Lat : cut — **cortante** *adj* : cutting, sharp
cortauñas *nms & pl* : nail clippers
corte[1] *nm* **1** : cutting **2** ESTILO : cut, style **3 ~ de pelo** : haircut
corte[2] *nf* **1** : court **2 hacer la ~ a** : court, woo — **cortejar** *vt* : court, woo
cortejo *nm* **1** : entourage **2** NOVIAZGO : courtship **3 ~ fúnebre** : funeral procession
cortés *adj* : courteous, polite — **cortesía** *nf* : courtesy, politeness
corteza *nf* **1** : bark **2** : crust (of bread) **3** : rind, peel (of fruit)
cortina *nm* : curtain
corto, -ta *adj* **1** : short **2** ESCASO : scarce **3** *fam* : timid, shy **4 ~ de vista** : nearsighted — **cortocircuito** *nm* : short circuit
corvo, -va *adj* : curved, bent
cosa *nf* **1** : thing **2** ASUNTO : matter, affair **3 ~ de** : about **4 poca ~** : nothing much
cosechar *v* : harvest, reap — **cosecha** *nf* **1** : harvest, crop **2** : vintage (of wine)
coser *v* : sew
cosmético, -ca *adj* : cosmetic — **cosmético** *nm* : cosmetic
cósmico, -ca *adj* : cosmic
cosmopolita *adj* : cosmopolitan
cosmos *nm* : cosmos
cosquillas *nfpl* **1** : tickling **2 hacer ~** : tickle — **cosquilleo** *nm* : tickling sensation, tingle
costa *nf* **1** : coast, shore **2 a toda ~** : at any cost
costado *nm* **1** : side **2 al ~** : alongside
costar {19} *v* : cost
costarricense *or* **costarriqueño, -ña** *adj* : Costa Rican
coste *nm* → **costo** — **costear** *vt* : pay for
costero, -ra *adj* : coastal
costilla *nf* **1** : rib **2** CHULETA : chop, cutlet
costo *nm* : cost, price — **costoso, -sa** *adj* : costly
costra *nf* : scab
costumbre *nf* **1** : custom, habit **2 de ~** : usual
costura *nf* **1** : sewing, dressmaking **2** PUNTADAS : seam — **costurera** *nf* : dressmaker
cotejar *vt* : compare
cotidiano, -na *adj* : daily
cotizar {21} *vt* : quote, set a price on — **cotización** *nf, pl* **-ciones** : quotation, price — **cotizado, -da** *adj* : in demand
coto *nm* : enclosure, reserve
cotorra *nf* **1** : small parrot **2** *fam* : chatterbox — **cotorrear** *vi fam* : chatter, gab
coyote *nm* : coyote
coyuntura *nf* **1** : joint **2** SITUACIÓN : situation, moment
coz *nm, pl* **coces** : kick (of an animal)
cráneo *nf* : cranium, skull
cráter *nm* : crater
crear *vt* : create — **creación** *nf, pl* **-ciones** : creation — **creativo, -va** *adj* : creative — **creador, -dora** *n* : creator
crecer {53} *vi* **1** : grow **2** AUMENTAR : increase — **crecido, -da** *adj* **1** : full-grown **2** : large (of numbers) — **creciente** *adj* **1** : growing, increasing **2** : crescent (of the moon) — **crecimiento** *nm* **1** : growth **2** AUMENTO : increase
credenciales *nfpl* : credentials
credibilidad *nf* : credibility
crédito *nm* : credit
credo *nm* : creed
crédulo, -la *adj* : credulous, gullible
creer {20} *v* **1** : believe **2** SUPONER : suppose, think — **creerse** *vr* : regard oneself as — **creencia** *nf* : belief — **creíble** *adj* : believable, credible — **creído, -da** *adj fam* : conceited
crema *nf* : cream
cremación *nf, pl* **-ciones** : cremation
cremallera *nf* : zipper
cremoso, -sa *adj* : creamy
crepe *nmf* : crepe, pancake
crepitar *vi* : crackle
crepúsculo *nm* : twilight, dusk
crespo, -pa *adj* : curly, frizzy
crespón *nm, pl* **-pones** : crepe (fabric)
cresta *nf* **1** : crest **2** : comb (of a rooster)
cretino, -na *n* : cretin
creyente *nmf* : believer
criar {85} *vt* **1** : nurse (a baby) **2** EDUCAR : bring up, rear **3** : raise, breed (animals) — **cría** *nf* **1** : breeding, rearing **2** : young animal — **criadero** *nm* : farm, hatchery — **criado, -da** *n* : servant, maid *f* — **criador, -dora** *n* : breeder — **crianza** *nf* : upbringing, rearing
criatura *nf* **1** : creature **2** NIÑO : baby, child
crimen *nm, pl* **crímenes** : crime — **criminal** *adj & nmf* : criminal
críquet *nm* : cricket (game)
crin *nf* : mane
criollo, -lla *adj & n* : Creole
cripta *nf* : crypt
crisantemo *nm* : chrysanthemum

crisis *nf* **1** : crisis **2 ~ nerviosa** : nervous breakdown
crispar *vt* **1** : tense (muscles), clench (one's fist) **2** IRRITAR : irritate, set on edge — **crisparse** *vr* : tense up
cristal *nm* **1** : crystal **2** VIDRIO : glass, piece of glass — **cristalería** *nf* : glassware — **cristalino, -na** *adj* : crystalline — **cristalino** *nm* : lens (of the eye) — **cristalizar** {21} *vi* : crystallize
cristiano, -na *adj & n* : Christian — **cristianismo** *nm* : Christianity — **Cristo** *nm* : Christ
criterio *nm* **1** : criterion **2** JUICIO : judgment, opinion
criticar {72} *vt* : criticize — **crítica** *nf* **1** : criticism **2** RESEÑA : review, critique — **crítico, -ca** *adj* : critical — **~** *n* : critic, reviewer
croar *vi* : croak
cromo *nm* : chromium, chrome
cromosoma *nm* : chromosome
crónica *nf* **1** : chronicle **2** : (news) report
crónico, -ca *adj* : chronic
cronista *nmf* : reporter, newscaster
cronología *nf* : chronology — **cronológico, -ca** *adj* : chronological
cronometrar *vt* : time, clock — **cronómetro** *nm* : chronometer, stopwatch
croqueta *nf* : croquette
croquis *nms & pl* : (rough) sketch
cruce *nm* **1** : crossing **2** : crossroads, intersection **3 ~ peatonal** : crosswalk
crucero *nm* **1** : cruise **2** : cruiser (ship)
crucial *adj* : crucial
crucificar {72} *vt* : crucify — **crucifijo** *nm* : crucifix — **crucifixión** *nf, pl* **-fixiones** : crucifixion
crucigrama *nm* : crossword puzzle
crudo, -da *adj* **1** : harsh, crude **2** : raw (of food) — **crudo** *nm* : crude oil
cruel *adj* : cruel — **crueldad** *nf* : cruelty
crujir *vi* : rustle, creak, crackle, crunch — **crujido** *nm* : rustle, creak, crackle, crunch — **crujiente** *adj* : crunchy, crisp
cruzar {21} *vt* **1** : cross **2** : exchange (words) — **cruzarse** *vr* **1** : intersect **2** : pass each other — **cruz** *nf, pl* **cruces** : cross — **cruzada** *nf* : crusade — **cruzado, -da** *adj* : crossed — **cruzado** *nm* : crusader
cuaderno *nm* : notebook
cuadra *nf* **1** : stable **2** *Lat* : (city) block
cuadrado, -da *adj* : square — **cuadrado** *nm* : square
cuadragésimo, -ma *adj* : fortieth, forty- — **~** *n* : fortieth, forty- (in a series)
cuadrar *vi* **1** : conform, agree **2** : add up, tally (numbers) — *vt* : square — **cuadrarse** *vr* : stand at attention
cuadrilátero *nm* **1** : quadrilateral **2** : ring (in sports)
cuadrilla *nf* : gang, group
cuadro *nm* **1** : square **2** PINTURA : painting **3** DESCRIPCIÓN : picture, description **4** : staff, management (of an organization) **5** CUADRADO : check, square **6** : (baseball) diamond
cuadrúpedo *nm* : quadruped
cuadruple *adj* : quadruple — **cuadruplicar** {72} *vt* : quadruple
cuajar *vi* **1** : curdle **2** COAGULAR : clot, coagulate **3** : set (of pudding, etc.) **4** AFIANZARSE : catch on — *vt* **1** : curdle **2 ~ de** : fill with
cual *pron* **1 el ~, la ~, los ~es, las ~es** : who, whom, which **2 lo ~** : which **3 cada ~** : everyone, everybody — **~** *prep* : like, as
cuál *pron* : which (one), what (one) — **~** *adj* : which, what
cualidad *nf* : quality, trait
cualquiera (**cualquier** *before nouns*) *adj, pl* **cualesquiera** : any, whatever — **~** *pron, pl* **cualesquiera** : anyone, whatever
cuán *adv* : how
cuando *conj* **1** : when **2** SI : since, if **3 ~ más** : at the most **4 de vez en ~** : from time to time — **~** *prep* : during, at the time of
cuándo *adv* **1** : when **2 ¿desde ~?** : since when?
cuantía *nf* **1** : quantity, extent **2** IMPORTANCIA : importance — **cuantioso, -sa** *adj* : abundant, considerable
cuanto *adv* **1** : as much as **2 ~ antes** : as soon as possible **3 en ~** : as soon as **4 en ~ a** : as for, as regards — **cuanto, -ta** *adj* : as many, whatever — **~** *pron* **1** : as much as, all that, everything **2 unos cuantos, unas cuantas** : a few
cuánto *adv* : how much, how many — **cuánto, -ta** *adj* : how much, how many — **~** *pron* : how much, how many
cuarenta *adj & nm* : forty — **cuarentavo, -va** *adj* : fortieth — **cuarentavo** *nm* : fortieth
cuarentena *nf* : quarantine
Cuaresma *nf* : Lent
cuartear *vt* : quarter, divide up — **cuartearse** *vr* : crack, split
cuartel *nm* **1** : barracks *pl* **2 ~ general** : headquarters **3 no dar ~** : show no mercy

cuarteto *nm* : quartet
cuarto, -ta *adj* : fourth — ~ *n* : fourth (in a series) — **cuarto** *nm* **1** : quarter, fourth **2** HABITACIÓN : room
cuarzo *nm* : quartz
cuatro *adj & nm* : four — **cuatrocientos, -tas** *adj* : four hundred — **cuatrocientos** *nms & pl* : four hundred
cuba *nf* : cask, barrel
cubano, -na *adj* : Cuban
cubeta *nf* **1** : keg, cask **2** *Lat* : pail, bucket
cúbico, -ca *adj* : cubic, cubed — **cubículo** *nm* : cubicle
cubierta *nf* **1** : cover, covering **2** : (automobile) tire **3** : deck (of a ship) — **cubierto** *nm* **1** : cutlery, place setting **2 a ~** : under cover
cubo *nm* **1** : cube **2** *Spain* : pail, bucket **3** : hub (of a wheel)
cubrecama *nm* : bedspread
cubrir {2} *vt* : cover — **cubrirse** *vr* **1** : cover oneself **2** : cloud over
cucaracha *nf* : cockroach
cuchara *nf* : spoon — **cucharada** *nf* : spoonful — **cucharilla** *or* **cucharita** *nf* : teaspoon — **cucharón** *nm, pl* **-rones** : ladle
cuchichear *vi* : whisper — **cuchicheo** *nm* : whisper
cuchilla *nf* **1** : (kitchen) knife **2 ~ de afeitar** : razor blade — **cuchillada** *nf* : stab, knife wound — **cuchillo** *nm* : knife
cuclillas *nfpl* **en ~** : squatting, crouching
cuco *nm* : cuckoo — **cuco, -ca** *adj fam* : pretty, cute
cucurucho *nm* : ice-cream cone
cuello *nm* **1** : neck **2** : collar (of clothing)
cuenca *nf* **1** : river basin **2** : (eye) socket — **cuenco** *nm* **1** : bowl **2** CONCAVIDAD : hollow
cuenta *nf* **1** : calculation, count **2** : (bank) account **3** FACTURA : check, bill **4** : bead (for a necklace, etc.) **5 darse ~** : realize **6 tener en ~** : bear in mind
cuento *nm* **1** : story, tale **2 ~ de hadas** : fairy tale
cuerda *nf* **1** : cord, rope, string **2 ~s vocales** : vocal cords **3 dar ~ a** : wind up
cuerdo, -da *adj* : sane, sensible
cuerno *nm* **1** : horn **2** : antlers *pl* (of a deer)
cuero *nm* **1** : leather, hide **2 ~ cabelludo** : scalp
cuerpo *nm* **1** : body **2** : corps (in the military, etc.)
cuervo *nm* : crow
cuesta *nf* **1** : slope **2 a ~s** : on one's back **3 ~ abajo** : downhill **4 ~ arriba** : uphill
cuestión *nf, pl* **-tiones** : matter, affair — **cuestionar** *vt* : question — **cuestionario** *nm* **1** : questionnaire **2** : quiz (in school)
cueva *nf* : cave
cuidar *vt* **1** : take care of, look after **2** : pay attention to (details, etc.) — *vi* **1 ~ de** : look after **2 ~ de que** : make sure that — **cuidarse** *vr* : take care of oneself — **cuidado** *nm* **1** : care **2** PREOCUPACIÓN : worry, concern **3 tener ~** : be careful **4 ¡cuidado!** : watch out!, careful! — **cuidadoso, -sa** *adj* : careful — **cuidadosamente** *adv* : carefully
culata *nf* : butt (of a gun) — **culatazo** *nf* : kick, recoil
culebra *nf* : snake
culinario, -ria *adj* : culinary
culminar *vi* : culminate — **culminación** *nf, pl* **-ciones** : culmination
culo *nm fam* : backside, bottom
culpa *nf* **1** : fault, blame **2** PECADO : sin **3 echar la ~ a** : blame **4 tener la ~** : be at fault — **culpabilidad** *nf* : guilt — **culpable** *adj* : guilty — **~** *nmf* : culprit, guilty party — **culpar** *vt* : blame
cultivar *vt* : cultivate — **cultivo** *nm* **1** : farming, cultivation **2 ~s** : crops
culto, -ta *adj* : cultured, educated — **culto** *nm* **1** : worship **2** : (religious) cult — **cultura** *nf* : culture — **cultural** *adj* : cultural
cumbre *nf* : summit, top
cumpleaños *nms & pl* : birthday
cumplido, -da *adj* **1** : complete, full **2** CORTÉS : courteous — **cumplido** *nm* : compliment, courtesy
cumplimentar *vt* **1** : congratulate **2** CUMPLIR : carry out — **cumplimiento** *nm* : carrying out, performance
cumplir *vt* **1** : accomplish, carry out **2** : keep (a promise), observe (a law, etc.) **3** : reach (a given age) — *vi* **1** : expire, fall due **2 ~ con el deber** : do one's duty — **cumplirse** *vr* **1** : expire **2** REALIZARSE : come true
cúmulo *nm* **1** : heap, pile **2** : cumulus (cloud)
cuna *nf* **1** : cradle **2** ORIGEN : birthplace
cundir *vi* **1** PROPAGARSE : spread, propagate **2** : go a long way
cuneta *nf* : ditch (in a road), gutter (in a street)
cuña *nf* : wedge

cuñado, -da *n* : brother-in-law *m,* sister-in-law *f*
cuota *nf* **1** : fee, dues **2** CUPO : quota **3** *Lat* : installment, payment
cupo *nm* **1** : quota, share **2** *Lat* : capacity, room
cupón *nm, pl* **-pones** : coupon
cúpula *nf* : dome, cupola
cura *nf* : cure, treatment — ~ *nm* : priest — **curación** *nf, pl* **-ciones** : healing — **curar** *vt* **1** : cure **2** : dress (a wound) **3** CURTIR : tan (hides) — **curarse** *vr* : get well
curiosear *vi* **1** : snoop, pry **2** : browse (in a store) — *vt* : look over — **curiosidad** *nf* : curiosity — **curioso, -sa** *adj* **1** : curious, inquisitive **2** RARO : unusual, strange
currículum *nm, pl* **-lums** *or* **currículo** *nm* : résumé, curriculum vitae
cursar *vt* **1** : take (a course), study **2** ENVIAR : send, pass on
cursi *adj fam* : affected, pretentious
cursiva *nf* : italics *pl*
curso *nm* **1** : course **2** : (school) year **3** **en** ~ : under way **4** **en** ~ : current
curtir *vt* **1** : tan **2** : harden (skin, features, etc.) — **curtiduría** *nf* : tannery
curva *nf* **1** : curve, bend **2** ~ **de nivel** : contour — **curvo, -va** *adj* : curved, bent
cúspide *nf* : apex, peak
custodia *nf* : custody — **custodiar** *vt* : guard, look after — **custodio, -dia** *n* : guardian
cutáneo, -nea *adj* : skin
cutícula *nf* : cuticle
cutis *nms & pl* : skin, complexion
cuyo, -ya *adj* **1** : whose, of whom, of which **2** **en cuyo caso** : in which case

D

d *nf* : d, fourth letter of the Spanish alphabet
dádiva *nf* : gift, handout — **dadivoso, -sa** *adj* : generous
dado, -da *adj* **1** : given **2** **dado que** : provided that, since — **dados** *nmpl* : dice
daga *nf* : dagger
daltónico, -ca *adj* : color-blind
dama *nf* **1** : lady **2** ~**s** *nfpl* : checkers
damnificar {72} *vt* : damage, injure
danés, -nesa *adj* : Danish — **danés** *nm* : Danish (language)
danzar {21} *v* : dance — **danza** *nf* : dance, dancing
dañar *vt* : damage, harm — **dañarse** *vr* **1** : be damaged **2** : hurt oneself — **dañino, -na** *adj* : harmful — **daño** *nm* **1** : damage, harm **2** ~**s y perjuicios** : damages
dar {22} *vt* **1** : give **2** PRODUCIR : yield, produce **3** : strike (the hour) **4** MOSTRAR : show — *vi* **1** ~ **como** : consider, regard as **2** ~ **con** : run into, meet **3** ~ **contra** : knock against **4** ~ **para** : be enough for — **darse** *vr* **1** : happen **2** ~ **contra** : bump into **3** ~ **por** : consider oneself **4** **dárselas de** : pose as
dardo *nm* : dart
dársena *nf* : dock
datar *vt* : date — *vi* ~ **de** : date from
dátil *nm* : date (fruit)
dato *nm* **1** : fact **2** ~**s** *nmpl* : data
de *prep* **1** : of **2** ~ **Managua** : from Managua **3** ~ **niño** : as a child **4** ~ **noche** : at night **5** **las tres** ~ **la mañana** : three o'clock in the morning **6** **más** ~ **10** : more than 10
deambular *vi* : wander about, stroll
debajo *adv* **1** : underneath **2** ~ **de** : under, underneath **3** **por** ~ : below, beneath
debatir *vt* : debate — **debatirse** *vr* : struggle — **debate** *nm* : debate
deber *vt* : owe — *v aux* **1** : have to, should **2** (*expressing probability*) : must — **deberse** *vr* ~ **a** : be due to — ~ *nm* **1** : duty **2** ~**es** *nmpl* : homework — **debido, -da** *adj* ~ **a** : due to, owing to
débil *adj* : weak, feeble — **debilidad** *nf* : weakness — **debilitar** *vt* : weaken — **debilitarse** *vr* : get weak — **débilmente** *adv* : weakly, faintly
débito *nm* **1** : debit **2** DEUDA : debt
debutar *vi* : debut — **debut** *nm, pl* ~**s** : debut — **debutante** *nf* : debutante *f*
década *nf* : decade
decadencia *nf* : decadence — **decadente** *adj* : decadent
decaer {13} *vi* : decline, weaken
decano, -na *n* : dean
decapitar *vt* : behead
decena *nf* : ten, about ten
decencia *nf* : decency
decenio *nm* : decade
decente *adj* : decent

decepcionar *vt* : disappoint — **decepción** *nf, pl* **-ciones** : disappointment
decibelio *or* **decibel** *nm* : decibel
decidir *vt* : decide, determine — *vi* : decide — **decidirse** *vr* : make up one's mind — **decididamente** *adv* : definitely, decidedly — **decidido, -da** *adj* : determined, resolute
decimal *adj* : decimal
décimo, -ma *adj & n* : tenth
decimoctavo, -va *adj* : eighteenth — ~ *n* : eighteenth (in a series)
decimocuarto, -ta *adj* : fourteenth — ~ *n* : fourteenth (in a series)
decimonoveno, -na *or* **decimonono, -na** *adj* : nineteenth — ~ *n* : nineteenth (in a series)
decimoquinto, -ta *adj* : fifteenth — ~ *n* : fifteenth (in a series)
decimoséptimo, -ma *adj* : seventeenth — ~ *n* : seventeenth (in a series)
decimosexto, -ta *adj* : sixteenth — ~ *n* : sixteenth (in a series)
decimotercero, -ra *adj* : thirteenth — ~ *n* : thirteenth (in a series)
decir {23} *vt* **1** : say **2** CONTAR : tell **3 es ~** : that is to say **4 querer ~** : mean — **decirse** *vr* **1** : tell oneself **2 ¿cómo se dice...en español?** : how do you say...in Spanish? — ~ *nm* : saying, expression
decisión *nf, pl* **-siones** : decision — **decisivo, -va** *adj* : decisive
declarar *vt* : declare — *vi* : testify — **declararse** *vr* **1** : declare oneself **2** : break out (of a fire, an epidemic, etc.) — **declaración** *nf, pl* **-ciones** : statement
declinar *v* : decline
declive *nm* **1** : decline **2** PENDIENTE : slope
decolorar *vt* : bleach — **decolorarse** *vr* : fade
decoración *nf, pl* **-ciones** : decoration — **decorado** *nm* : stage set — **decorar** *vt* : decorate — **decorativo, -va** *adj* : decorative
decoro *nm* : decency, decorum — **decoroso, -sa** *adj* : decent, proper
decrecer {53} *vi* : decrease
decrépito, -ta *adj* : decrepit
decretar *vt* : decree — **decreto** *nm* : decree
dedal *nm* : thimble
dedicar {72} *vt* : dedicate — **dedicarse** *vr* **~ a** : devote oneself to — **dedicación** *nf, pl* **-ciones** : dedication — **dedicatoria** *nf* : dedication, inscription
dedo *nm* **1** : finger **2 ~ del pie** : toe
deducir {61} *vt* **1** INFERIR : deduce **2** DESCONTAR : deduct — **deducción** *nf, pl* **-ciones** : deduction
defecar {72} *vi* : defecate
defecto *nm* : defect — **defectuoso, -sa** *adj* : defective, faulty
defender {56} *vt* : defend — **defenderse** *vr* : defend oneself — **defensa** *nf* : defense — **defensiva** *nf* : defensive — **defensivo, -va** *adj* : defensive — **defensor, -sora** *n* **1** : defender **2** *or* **abogado defensor** : defense counsel
deferencia *nf* : deference — **deferente** *adj* : deferential
deficiencia *nf* : deficiency — **deficiente** *adj* : deficient
déficit *nm, pl* **-cits** : deficit
definir *vt* : define — **definición** *nf, pl* **-ciones** : definition — **definitivo, -va** *adj* **1** : definitive **2 en definitiva** : in short
deformar *vt* **1** : deform **2** : distort (the truth, etc.) — **deformación** *nf, pl* **-ciones** : distortion — **deforme** *adj* : deformed — **deformidad** *nf* : deformity
defraudar *vt* **1** : defraud **2** DECEPCIONAR : disappoint
degenerar *vi* : degenerate — **degenerado, -da** *adj* : degenerate
degradar *vt* **1** : degrade **2** : demote (in the military)
degustar *vt* : taste
dehesa *nf* : pasture
deidad *nf* : deity
dejar *vt* **1** : leave **2** ABANDONAR : abandon **3** PERMITIR : allow — *vi* **~ de** : quit — **dejado, -da** *adj* : slovenly, careless
dejo *nm* **1** : aftertaste **2** : (regional) accent
delantal *nm* : apron
delante *adv* **1** : ahead **2 ~ de** : in front of
delantera *nf* **1** : front **2 tomar la ~** : take the lead — **delantero, -ra** *adj* : front, forward — ~ *n* : forward (in sports)
delatar *vt* : denounce, inform against
delegar {52} *vt* : delegate — **delegación** *nf, pl* **-ciones** : delegation — **delegado, -da** *n* : delegate, representative
deleitar *vt* : delight, please — **deleite** *nm* : delight
deletrear *vi* : spell (out)
delfín *nm, pl* **-fines** : dolphin
delgado, -da *adj* : thin
deliberar *vi* : deliberate — **deliberación** *nf, pl* **-ciones** : deliberation

— **deliberado, -da** *adj* : deliberate, intentional
delicadeza *nf* **1** : delicacy, daintiness **2** SUAVIDAD : gentleness **3** TACTO : tact — **delicado, -da** *adj* **1** : delicate **2** SENSIBLE : sensible **3** DISCRETO : tactful
delicia *nf* : delight — **delicioso, -sa** *adj* **1** : delightful **2** RICO : delicious
delictivo, -va *adj* : criminal
delimitar *vt* : define, set the boundaries of
delincuencia *nf* : delinquency, crime — **delincuente** *adj & nmf* : delinquent, criminal — **delinquir** {24} *vi* : break the law
delirante *adj* : delirious — **delirar** *vi* **1** : be delirious **2** ~ **por** *fam* : rave about — **delirio** *nm* **1** : delirium **2** ~ **de grandeza** : delusions of grandeur
delito *nm* : crime
delta *nm* : delta
demacrado, -da *adj* : emaciated
demandar *vt* **1** : sue **2** PEDIR : demand **3** *Lat* : require — **demanda** *nf* **1** : lawsuit **2** PETICIÓN : request **3 la oferta y la** ~ : supply and demand — **demandante** *nmf* : plaintiff
demás *adj* : rest of the, other — ~ *pron* **1 lo (la, los, las)** ~ : the rest, others **2 por** ~ : extremely **3 por lo** ~ : otherwise **4 y** ~ : and so on
demasiado *adv* **1** : too **2** : too much — ~ *adj* : too much, too many
demencia *nf* : madness — **demente** *adj* : insane, mad
democracia *nf* : democracy — **demócrata** *nmf* : democrat — **democrático, -ca** *adj* : democratic
demoler {47} *vt* : demolish — **demolición** *nf, pl* **-ciones** : demolition
demonio *nm* : devil, demon
demorar *v* : delay — **demorarse** *vr* : take a long time — **demora** *nf* : delay
demostrar {19} *vt* **1** : demonstrate **2** MOSTRAR : show — **demostración** *nf, pl* **-ciones** : demonstration
demudar *vt* : change, alter
denegar {49} *vt* : deny, refuse — **denegación** *nf, pl* **-ciones** : denial, refusal
denigrar *vt* **1** : denigrate **2** INJURIAR : insult
denominador *nm* : denominator
denotar *vt* : denote, show
densidad *nf* : density — **denso, -sa** *adj* : dense
dental *adj* : dental — **dentado, -da** *adj* : toothed, notched — **dentadura** *nf* ~ **postiza** : dentures *pl* — **dentífrico** *nm* : toothpaste — **dentista** *nmf* : dentist
dentro *adv* **1** : in, inside **2** ~ **de poco** : soon, shortly **3 por** ~ : inside
denuedo *nm* : courage
denunciar *vt* **1** : denounce **2** : report (a crime) — **denuncia** *nf* **1** : accusation **2** : (police) report
departamento *nm* **1** : department **2** *Lat* : apartment
depender *vi* **1** : depend **2** ~ **de** : depend on — **dependencia** *nf* **1** : dependence, dependency **2** SUCURSAL : branch office — **dependiente** *adj* : dependent — **dependiente, -ta** *n* : clerk, salesperson
deplorar *vt* : deplore, regret
deponer {60} *vt* : remove from office, depose
deportar *vt* : deport — **deportación** *nf, pl* **-ciones** : deportation
deporte *nm* : sport, sports *pl* — **deportista** *nmf* : sportsman *m*, sportswoman *f* — **deportivo, -va** *adj* **1** : sporty **2 artículos deportivos** : sporting goods
depositar *vt* **1** : put, place **2** : deposit (in a bank, etc.) — **depósito** *nm* **1** : deposit **2** ALMACÉN : warehouse
depravado, -da *adj* : depraved
depreciarse *vr* : depreciate — **depreciación** *nf* : depreciation
depredador *nm* : predator
deprimir *vt* : depress — **deprimirse** *vr* : get depressed — **depresión** *nf, pl* **-siones** : depression
derecha *nf* **1** : right side **2** : right wing (in politics) — **derechista** *adj* : right-wing — **derecho** *nm* **1** : right **2** LEY : law — ~ *adv* : straight — **derecho, -cha** *adj* **1** : right, right-hand **2** VERTICAL : upright **3** RECTO : straight
deriva *nf* **1** : drift **2 a la** ~ : adrift — **derivación** *nf, pl* **-ciones** : derivation — **derivar** *vi* **1** : drift **2** ~ **de** : derive from
derramamiento *nm* ~ **de sangre** : bloodshed
derramar *vt* **1** : spill **2** : shed (tears, blood) — **derramarse** *vr* : overflow — **derrame** *nm* **1** : spilling **2** : discharge, hemorrhage
derrapar *vi* : skid — **derrape** *nm* : skid
derretir {54} *vt* : melt, thaw — **derretirse** *vr* **1** : melt, thaw **2** ~ **por** *fam* : be crazy about
derribar *vt* **1** : demolish **2** : bring down (a plane, a tree, etc.) **3** : overthrow (a government, etc.)
derrocar {72} *vt* : overthrow
derrochar *vt* : waste, squander — **der-**

rochador, -dora *n* : spendthrift — **derroche** *nm* : extravagance, waste
derrotar *vt* : defeat — **derrota** *nf* : defeat
derruir {41} *vt* : demolish, tear down
derrumbar *vt* : demolish, knock down — **derrumbarse** *vr* : collapse, break down — **derrumbamiento** *nm* : collapse — **derrumbe** *nm* : collapse
desabotonar *vt* : unbutton, undo
desabrido, -da *adj* : bland
desabrochar *vt* : unbutton, undo — **desabrocharse** *vr* : come undone
desacato *nm* **1** : disrespect **2** : contempt (of court) — **desacatar** *vt* : defy, disobey
desacertado, -da *adj* : mistaken, wrong — **desacertar** {55} *vi* : be mistaken — **desacierto** *nm* : mistake, error
desaconsejar *vt* : advise against — **desaconsejable** *adj* : inadvisable
desacreditar *vt* : discredit
desactivar *vt* : deactivate
desacuerdo *nm* : disagreement
desafiar {85} *vt* : defy, challenge — **desafiante** *adj* : defiant
desafilado, -da *adj* : blunt
desafinado, -da *adj* : out-of-tune, off-key
desafío *nm* : challenge, defiance
desafortunado, -da *adj* : unfortunate — **desafortunadamente** *adv* : unfortunately
desagradar *vt* : displease — **desagradable** *adj* : disagreeable, unpleasant
desagradecido, -da *adj* : ungrateful
desagrado *nm* **1** : displeasure **2 con ~** : reluctantly
desagravio *nm* : amends, reparation
desagregarse {52} *vr* : disintegrate
desaguar {10} *vi* : drain, empty — **desagüe** *nm* **1** : drainage **2** : drain (of a sink, etc.)
desahogar {52} *vt* **1** : relieve **2** : give vent to (anger, etc.) — **desahogarse** *vr* : let off steam, unburden oneself — **desahogado, -da** *adj* **1** : roomy **2** ADINERADO : comfortable, well-off — **desahogo** *nm* **1** : relief **2 con ~** : comfortably
desahuciar *vt* **1** : deprive of hope **2** DESALOJAR : evict — **desahucio** *nm* : eviction
desaire *nm* : snub, rebuff — **desairar** *vt* : snub, slight
desalentar {55} *vt* : discourage — **desaliento** *nm* : discouragement
desaliñado, -da *adj* : slovenly
desalmado, -da *adj* : heartless, cruel
desalojar *vt* **1** : evacuate **2** DESAHUCIAR : evict
desamparar *vt* : abandon — **desamparo** *nm* : abandonment, desertion
desamueblado, -da *adj* : unfurnished
desangrarse *vr* : lose blood, bleed to death
desanimar *vt* : discourage — **desanimarse** *vr* : get discouraged — **desanimado, -da** *adj* : downhearted, despondent — **desánimo** *nm* : discouragement
desanudar *vt* : untie
desaparecer {53} *vi* : disappear — **desaparecido, -da** *n* : missing person — **desaparición** *nf, pl* **-ciones** : disappearance
desapasionado, -da *adj* : dispassionate
desapego *nm* : indifference
desapercebido, -da *adj* : unnoticed
desaprobar {19} *vt* : disapprove of — **desaprobación** *nf, pl* **-ciones** : disapproval
desaprovechar *vt* : waste
desarmar *vt* **1** : disarm **2** DESMONTAR : dismantle, take apart — **desarme** *nm* : disarmament
desarraigar {52} *vt* : uproot, root out
desarreglar *vt* **1** : mess up **2** : disrupt (plans, etc.) — **desarreglado, -da** *adj* : disorganized — **desarreglo** *nm* : untidiness, disorder
desarrollar *vt* : develop — **desarrollarse** *vr* : take place — **desarrollo** *nm* : development
desarticular *vt* **1** : break up, dismantle **2** : dislocate (a bone)
desaseado, -da *adj* **1** : dirty **2** DESORDENADO : messy
desastre *nm* : disaster — **desastroso, -sa** *adj* : disastrous
desatar *vt* **1** : undo, untie **2** : unleash (passions) — **desatarse** *vr* **1** : come undone **2** DESENCADENARSE : break out, erupt
desatascar {72} *vt* : unclog
desatender {56} *vt* **1** : disregard **2** : neglect (an obligation, etc.) — **desatento, -ta** *adj* : inattentive
desatinado, -da *adj* : foolish, silly
desautorizado, -da *adj* : unauthorized
desavenencia *nf* : disagreement
desayunar *vi* : have breakfast — *vt* : have for breakfast — **desayuno** *nm* : breakfast
desbancar {72} *vt* : oust
desbarajuste *nm* : disorder, confusion
desbaratar *vt* : ruin, destroy — **desbaratarse** *vr* : fall apart

desbocarse {72} *vr* : run away, bolt
desbordar *vt* **1** : overflow **2** : exceed (limits) — **desbordarse** *vr* : overflow — **desbordamiento** *nm* : overflow
descabellado, -da *adj* : crazy
descafeinado, -da *adj* : decaffeinated
descalabrar *vt* : hit on the head — **descalabro** *nm* : misfortune, setback
descalificar {72} *vt* : disqualify — **descalificación** *nf, pl* **-ciones** : disqualification
descalzarse {21} *vr* : take off one's shoes — **descalzo, -za** *adj* : barefoot
descaminar *vt* : mislead, lead astray
descansar *v* : rest — **descanso** *nm* **1** : rest **2** : landing (of a staircase) **3** : intermission (in theater), halftime (in sports)
descapotable *adj & nm* : convertible
descarado, -da *adj* : insolent, shameless
descargar {52} *vt* **1** : unload **2** : discharge (a firearm, etc.) — **descarga** *nf* **1** : unloading **2** : discharge (of a firearm, of electricity, etc.) — **descargo** *nm* **1** : unloading **2** : discharge (of a duty, etc.) **3** : defense (in law)
descarnado, -da *adj* : scrawny, gaunt
descaro *nm* : insolence, nerve
descarrilar *vi* : derail — **descarrilarse** *vr* : be derailed
descartar *vt* : reject — **descartarse** *vr* : discard
descascarar *vt* : peel, shell, husk
descender {56} *vt* **1** : go down **2** BAJAR : lower — *vi* **1** : descend **2** ~ **de** : be descended from — **descendiencia** *nf* **1** : descendants *pl* **2** LINAJE : lineage, descent — **descendiente** *nmf* : descendant — **descenso** *nm* **1** : descent **2** : drop, fall (in level, in temperature, etc.)
descifrar *vt* : decipher, decode
descolgar {16} *vt* **1** : take down **2** : pick up, answer (the telephone)
descolorarse *vr* : fade — **descolorido, -da** *adj* : faded, discolored
descomponer {60} *vt* : break down — **descomponerse** *vr* **1** : rot, decompose **2** *Lat* : break down — **descompuesto, -ta** *adj Lat* : out of order
descomunal *adj* : enormous
desconcertar {55} *vt* : disconcert, confuse — **desconcertante** *adj* : confusing — **desconcierto** *nm* : confusion, bewilderment
desconectar *vt* : disconnect
desconfiar {85} *vi* ~ **de** : distrust — **desconfiado, -da** *adj* : distrustful — **desconfianza** *nf* : distrust
descongelar *vt* **1** : thaw, defrost **2** : unfreeze (assets)
descongestionante *nm* : decongestant
desconocer {18} *vt* : not know, fail to recognize — **desconocido, -da** *adj* : unknown — ~ *n* : stranger
desconsiderado, -da *adj* : inconsiderate
desconsolar *vt* : distress — **desconsolado, -da** *adj* : heartbroken — **desconsuelo** *nm* : grief, sorrow
descontar {19} *vt* : discount
descontento, -ta *adj* : dissatisfied — **descontento** *nm* : discontent
descontinuar *vt* : discontinue
descorazonado, -da *adj* : discouraged
descorrer *vt* : draw back
descortés *adj, pl* **-teses** : rude — **descortesía** *nf* : discourtesy, rudeness
descoyuntar *vt* : dislocate
descrédito *nm* : discredit
descremado, -da *adj* : nonfat, skim
describir {33} *vt* : describe — **descripción** *nf, pl* **-ciones** : description — **descriptivo, -va** *adj* : descriptive
descubierto, -ta *adj* **1** : exposed, uncovered **2 al descubierto** : in the open — **descubierto** *nm* : deficit, overdraft
descubrir {2} *vt* **1** : discover **2** REVELAR : reveal — **descubrimiento** *nm* : discovery
descuento *nm* : discount
descuidar *vt* : neglect — **descuidarse** *vr* **1** : be careless **2** ABANDONARSE : let oneself go — **descuidado, -da** *adj* **1** : careless, sloppy **2** DESATENDIDO : neglected — **descuido** *nm* : neglect, carelessness
desde *prep* **1** : from (a place), since (a time) **2** ~ **luego** : of course
desdén *nm* : scorn, disdain — **desdeñar** *vt* : scorn — **desdeñoso, -sa** *adj* : disdainful
desdicha *nf* **1** : misery **2** DESGRACIA : misfortune — **desdichado, -da** *adj* : unfortunate, unhappy
desear *vt* : wish, want — **deseable** *adj* : desirable
desecar *vt* : dry up
desechar *vt* **1** : throw away **2** RECHAZAR : reject — **desechable** *adj* : disposable — **desechos** *nmpl* : rubbish
desembarazarse {21} *vr* ~ **de** : get rid of
desembarcar {72} *vi* : disembark — *vt* : unload — **desembarcadero** *nm* : jetty, landing pier — **desembarco** *nm* : landing
desembocar {72} *vi* ~ **en 1** : flow

into **2** : lead to (a result) — **desembocadura** *nf* **1** : mouth (of a river) **2** : opening, end (of a street)
desembolsar *vt* : pay out — **desembolso** *nm* : payment, outlay
desembragar *vi* : disengage the clutch
desempacar {72} *v Lat* : unpack
desempate *nm* : tiebreaker
desempeñar *vt* **1** : play (a role) **2** : redeem (from a pawnshop) — **desempeñarse** *vr* : get out of debt
desempleo *nm* : unemployment — **desempleado, -da** *adj* : unemployed
desempolvar *vt* : dust
desencadenar *vt* **1** : unchain **2** : trigger, unleash (protests, crises, etc.) — **desencadenarse** *vr* : break loose
desencajar *vt* **1** : dislocate **2** DESCONECTAR : disconnect
desencanto *nm* : disillusionment
desenchufar *vt* : disconnect, unplug
desenfadado, -da *adj* : carefree, confident — **desenfado** *nm* : confidence, ease
desenfrenado, -da *adj* : unrestrained — **desenfreno** *nm* : abandon, lack of restraint
desenganchar *vt* : unhook
desengañar *vt* : disillusion — **desengaño** *nm* : disappointment
desenlace *nm* : ending, outcome
desenmarañar *vt* : disentangle
desenmascarar *vt* : unmask
desenredar *vt* : untangle — **desenredarse** *vr* **~ de** : extricate oneself from
desenrollar *vt* : unroll, unwind
desentenderse {56} *vr* **~ de** : want nothing to do with
desenterrar {55} *vt* : dig up, disinter
desentonar *vi* **1** : be out of tune **2** : clash (of colors, etc.)
desenvoltura *nf* : confidence, ease
desenvolver {89} *vt* : unfold, unwrap — **desenvolverse** *vr* : unfold, develop
desenvuelto, -ta *adj* : confident, self-assured
deseo *nm* : desire — **deseoso, -sa** *adj* : eager, anxious
desequilibrar *vt* : throw off balance — **desequilibrado, -da** *adj* : unbalanced — **desequilibrio** *nm* : imbalance
desertar *vt* : desert — **deserción** *nf, pl* **-ciones** : desertion — **desertor, -tora** *n* : deserter
desesperar *vt* : exasperate — *vi* : despair — **desesperarse** *vr* : become exasperated — **desesperación** *nf, pl* **-ciones** : desperation, despair — **desesperado, -da** *adj* : desperate, hopeless
desestimar *vt* : reject
desfalcar {72} *vt* : embezzle — **desfalco** *nm* : embezzlement
desfallecer {53} *vi* **1** : weaken **2** DESMAYARSE : faint
desfavorable *adj* : unfavorable
desfigurar *vt* **1** : disfigure, mar **2** : distort (the truth)
desfiladero *nm* : mountain pass, gorge
desfilar *vi* : march, parade — **desfile** *nm* : parade, procession
desfogar {52} *vt* : vent — **desfogarse** *vr* : let off steam
desgajar *vt* : tear off, break apart — **desgajarse** *vr* : come off
desgana *nf* **1** : lack of appetite **2** : lack of enthusiasm, reluctance
desgarbado, -da *adj* : gawky, ungainly
desgarrar *vt* : tear, rip — **desgarrador, -dora** *adj* : heartbreaking — **desgarro** *nm* : tear
desgastar *vt* : wear away, wear down — **desgaste** *nm* : deterioration, wear and tear
desgracia *nf* **1** : misfortune **2 caer en ~** : fall into disgrace **3 por ~** : unfortunately — **desgraciadamente** *adv* : unfortunately — **desgraciado, -da** *adj* : unfortunate
deshabitado, -da *adj* : uninhabited
deshacer {40} *vt* **1** : undo **2** DESTRUIR : destroy, ruin **3** DISOLVER : dissolve **4** : break (an agreement), cancel (plans, etc.) — **deshacerse** *vr* **1** : come undone **2 ~ de** : get rid of **3 ~ en** : lavish, heap (praise, etc.) — **deshecho, -cha** *adj* **1** : undone **2** DESTROZADO : destroyed, ruined
desheredar *vt* : disinherit
deshidratar *vt* : dehydrate
deshielo *nm* : thaw
deshilachar *vt* : unravel — **deshilacharse** *vr* : fray
deshonesto, -ta *adj* : dishonest
deshonrar *vt* : dishonor, disgrace — **deshonra** *nf* : dishonor — **deshonroso, -sa** *adj* : dishonorable
deshuesar *vt* **1** : pit (a fruit) **2** : bone, debone (meat)
desidia *nf* **1** : indolence **2** DESASEO : sloppiness
desierto, -ta *adj* : deserted, uninhabited — **desierto** *nm* : desert
designar *vt* : designate — **designación** *nf, pl* **-ciones** : appointment (to an office, etc.)
designio *nm* : plan
desigual *adj* **1** : unequal **2** DISPAREJO

: uneven — **desigualdad** *nf* : inequality
desilusionar *vt* : disappoint, disillusion — **desilusión** *nf, pl* **-siones** : disappointment, disillusionment
desinfectar *vt* : disinfect — **desinfectante** *adj & nm* : disinfectant
desinflar *vt* : deflate — **desinflarse** *vr* : deflate, go flat
desinhibido, -da *adj* : uninhibited
desintegrar *vt* : disintegrate — **desintegrarse** *vr* : disintegrate — **desintegración** *nf, pl* **-ciones** : disintegration
desinteresado, -da *adj* : unselfish, generous — **desinterés** *nm* : unselfishness
desistir *vi* ~ **de** : give up
desleal *adj* : disloyal — **deslealtad** *nf* : disloyalty
desleír {66} *vt* : dilute, dissolve
desligar {52} *vt* **1** : untie **2** SEPARAR : separate — **desligarse** *vr* : extricate oneself
desliz *nm, pl* **-lices** : slip, mistake — **deslizar** {21} *vt* : slide, slip — **deslizarse** *vr* : slide, glide
deslucido, -da *adj* : dingy, tarnished
deslumbrar *vt* : dazzle — **deslumbrante** *adj* : dazzling, blinding
deslustrar *vt* : tarnish, dull
desmán *nm, pl* **-manes** : outrage, excess
desmandarse *vr* : get out of hand
desmantelar *vt* : dismantle
desmañado, -da *adj* : clumsy
desmayar *vi* : lose heart — **desmayarse** *vr* : faint — **desmayo** *nm* : faint
desmedido, -da *adj* : excessive
desmejorar *vt* : impair — *vi* : deteriorate
desmemoriado, -da *adj* : forgetful
desmentir {76} *vt* : deny — **desmentido** *nm* : denial
desmenuzar {21} *vt* **1** : crumble **2** EXAMINAR : scrutinize — **desmenuzarse** *vr* : crumble
desmerecer {53} *vt* : be unworthy of — *vi* : decline in value
desmesurado, -da *adj* : excessive
desmigajar *vt* : crumble
desmontar *vt* **1** : dismantle, take apart **2** ALLANAR : level — *vi* : dismount
desmoralizar {21} *vt* : demoralize
desmoronarse *vr* : crumble
desnivel *nm* : unevenness
desnudar *vt* : undress, strip — **desnudarse** *vr* : get undressed — **desnudez** *nf, pl* **-deces** : nudity, nakedness — **desnudo, -da** *adj* : nude, naked — **desnudo** *nm* : nude
desnutrición *nf, pl* **-ciones** : malnutrition
desobedecer {53} *v* : disobey — **desobediencia** *nf* : disobedience — **desobediente** *adj* : disobedient
desocupar *vt* : empty, vacate — **desocupado, -da** *adj* **1** : vacant **2** DESEMPLEADO : unemployed
desodorante *adj & nm* : deodorant
desolado, -da *adj* **1** : desolate **2** DESCONSOLADO : devastated, distressed — **desolación** *nf, pl* **-ciones** : desolation
desorden *nm, pl* **desórdenes** : disorder, mess — **desordenado, -da** *adj* : untidy — **desordenadamente** *adv* : in a disorderly way
desorganizar {21} *vt* : disorganize — **desorganización** *nf, pl* **-ciones** : disorganization
desorientar *vt* : disorient, confuse — **desorientarse** *vr* : lose one's way
desovar *vi* : spawn
despachar *vt* **1** : deal with (a task, etc.) **2** ENVIAR : dispatch, send **3** : wait on, serve (customers) — **despacho** *nm* **1** : dispatch, shipment **2** OFICINA : office
despacio *adv* : slowly
desparramar *vt* : spill, scatter, spread
despavorido, -da *adj* : terrified
despecho *nm* **1** : spite **2 a ~ de** : despite, in spite of
despectivo, -va *adj* **1** : pejorative **2** DESPRECIATIVO : contemptuous
despedazar {21} *vt* : tear apart
despedir {54} *vt* **1** : see off **2** DESTITUIR : dismiss, fire **3** DESPRENDER : emit — **despedirse** *vr* : say good-bye — **despedida** *nf* : farewell, good-bye
despegar {52} *vt* : detach, unstick — *vi* : take off — **despegado, -da** *adj* : cold, distant — **despegue** *nm* : takeoff
despeinar *vt* : ruffle (hair) — **despeinado, -da** *adj* : disheveled, unkempt
despejar *vt* : clear, free — *vi* : clear up — **despejado, -da** *adj* **1** : clear, fair **2** LÚCIDO : clear-headed
despellejar *vt* : skin (an animal)
despensa *nf* : pantry, larder
despeñadero *nm* : precipice
desperdiciar *vt* : waste — **desperdicio** *nm* **1** : waste **2 ~s** *nmpl* : scraps
desperfecto *nm* : flaw, defect
despertar {55} *vi* : awaken, wake up — *vt* : wake, rouse — **despertador** *nm* : alarm clock
despiadado, -da *adj* : pitiless, merciless

despido *nm* : dismissal, layoff
despierto, -ta *adj* : awake
despilfarrar *vt* : squander — **despilfarrador, -dora** *n* : spendthrift — **despilfarro** *nm* : extravagance, wastefulness
despistar *vt* : throw off the track, confuse — **despistarse** *vr* : lose one's way — **despistado, -da** *adj* **1** : absentminded **2** DESORIENTADO : confused — **despiste** *nm* **1** : absentmindedness **2** ERROR : mistake
desplazar {21} *vt* : displace — **desplazarse** *vr* : travel
desplegar {49} *vt* : unfold, spread out — **despliegue** *nm* : display
desplomarse *vr* : collapse
desplumar *vt* **1** : pluck **2** *fam* : fleece
despoblado, -da *adj* : uninhabited, deserted — **despoblado** *nm* : deserted area
despojar *vt* : strip, deprive — **despojos** *nmpl* **1** : plunder **2** RESTOS : remains, scraps
desportillar *vt* : chip — **desportillarse** *vr* : chip — **desportilladura** *nf* : chip, nick
despota *nmf* : despot
despotricar *vi* : rant (and rave)
despreciar *vt* : despise, scorn — **despreciable** *adj* **1** : despicable **2 una cantidad ~** : a negligible amount — **desprecio** *nm* : disdain, scorn
desprender *vt* **1** : detach, remove **2** EMITIR : give off — **desprenderse** *vr* **1** : come off **2** DEDUCIRSE : be inferred, follow — **desprendimiento** *nm* **~ de tierras** : landslide
despreocupado, -da *adj* : carefree, unconcerned
desprestigiar *vt* : discredit — **desprestigiarse** *vr* : lose face
desprevenido, -da *adj* : unprepared
desproporcionado, -da : out of proportion
despropósito *nm* : (piece of) nonsense, absurdity
desprovisto, -ta *adj* **~ de** : lacking in
después *adv* **1** : afterward **2** ENTONCES : then, next **3 ~ de** : after **4 después (de) que** : after **5 ~ de todo** : after all
despuntado, -da *adj* : blunt, dull
desquiciar *vt* : drive crazy
desquitarse *vr* **1** : retaliate **2 ~ con** : take it out on, get back at — **desquite** *nm* : revenge
destacar {72} *vt* : emphasize — *vi* : stand out — **destacado, -da** *adj* : outstanding
destapar *vt* : open, uncover — **destapador** *nm Lat* : bottle opener
destartalado, -da *adj* : dilapidated
destellar *vi* : flash, sparkle — **destello** *nm* : sparkle, twinkle, flash
destemplado, -da *adj* **1** : out of tune **2** MAL : out of sorts **3** : unpleasant (of weather)
desteñir {67} *vt* : fade, bleach — *vi* : run, fade — **desteñirse** *vr* : fade
desterrar {55} *vt* : banish, exile — **desterrado, -da** *n* : exile
destetar *vt* : wean
destiempo *adv* **a ~** : at the wrong time
destierro *nm* : exile
destilar *vt* : distill — **destilería** *nf* : distillery
destinar *vt* **1** : assign, allocate **2** NOMBRAR : appoint — **destinado, -da** *adj* : destined — **destinatario, -ria** *n* : addressee — **destino** *nm* **1** : destiny **2** RUMBO : destination
destituir {41} *vt* : dismiss — **destitución** *nf, pl* **-ciones** : dismissal
destornillar *vt* : unscrew — **destornillador** *nm* : screwdriver
destreza *nf* : skill, dexterity
destrozar {21} *vt* : destroy, wreck — **destrozos** *nmpl* : damage, destruction
destrucción *nf, pl* **-ciones** : destruction — **destructivo, -va** *adj* : destructive — **destruir** {41} *vt* : destroy
desunir *vt* : split, divide
desusado, -da *adj* **1** : obsolete **2** INSÓLITO : unusual — **desuso** *nm* **caer en ~** : fall into disuse
desvaído, -da *adj* **1** : pale, washed-out **2** BORROSO : vague, blurred
desvalido, -da *adj* : destitute, needy
desvalijar *vt* : rob
desván *nm, pl* **-vanes** : attic
desvanecer {53} *vt* : make disappear — **desvanecerse** *vr* **1** : vanish **2** DESMAYARSE : faint
desvariar {85} *vi* : be delirious — **desvarío** *nm* : delirium
desvelar *vt* : keep awake — **desvelarse** *vr* : stay awake — **desvelo** *nm* **1** : sleeplessness **2 ~s** *nmpl* : efforts
desvencijado, -da *adj* : dilapidated, rickety
desventaja *nf* : disadvantage
desventura *nf* : misfortune
desvergonzado, -da *adj* : shameless — **desvergüenza** *nf* : shamelessness
desvestir {54} *vt* : undress — **desvestirse** *vr* : get undressed
desviación *nf, pl* **-ciones 1** : deviation **2** : detour (in a road) — **desviar** {85} *vt* : divert, deflect — **desviarse** *vr* **1** : branch off **2** APARTARSE : stray — **desvío** *nm* : diversion, detour

detallar *vt* : detail — **detallado, -da** *adj* : detailed, thorough — **detalle** *nm* **1** : detail **2 al ~** : retail — **detallista** *adj* : retail — **~** *nmf* : retailer
detectar *vt* : detect — **detective** *nmf* : detective
detener {80} *vt* **1** : arrest, detain **2** PARAR : stop **3** RETRASAR : delay — **detenerse** *vr* **1** : stop **2** DEMORARSE : linger — **detención** *nf, pl* **-ciones** : arrest, detention
detergente *nm* : detergent
deteriorar *vt* : damage — **deteriorarse** *vr* : wear out, deteriorate — **deteriorado, -da** *adj* : damaged, worn — **deterioro** *nm* : deterioration, damage
determinar *vt* **1** : determine **2** MOTIVAR : bring about **3** DECIDIR : decide — **determinarse** *vr* : decide — **determinación** *nf, pl* **-ciones 1** : determination **2 tomar una ~** : make a decision — **determinado, -da** *adj* **1** : determined **2** ESPECÍFICO : specific
detestar *vt* : detest
detonar *vi* : explode, detonate — **detonación** *nf, pl* **-ciones** : detonation
detrás *adv* **1** : behind **2 ~ de** : in back of **3 por ~** : from behind
detrimento *nm* **en ~ de** : to the detriment of
deuda *nf* : debt — **deudor, -dora** *n* : debtor
devaluar {3} *vt* : devalue — **devaluarse** *vr* : depreciate
devastar *vt* : devastate — **devastador, -dora** *adj* : devastating
devenir {87} *vi* **1** : come about **2 ~ en** : become, turn into
devoción *nf, pl* **-ciones** : devotion
devolución *nf, pl* **-ciones** : return
devolver {89} *vt* **1** RESTITUIR : give back **2** : refund, pay back — *vi* : vomit — **devolverse** *vr Lat* : return, come back
devorar *vt* : devour
devoto, -ta *adj* : devout — **~** *n* : devotee
día *nm* **1** : day **2** : daytime **3 al ~** : up-to-date **4 en pleno ~** : in broad daylight
diabetes *nf* : diabetes — **diabético, -ca** *adj & n* : diabetic
diablo *nm* : devil — **diablillo** *nm* : imp, rascal — **diablura** *nf* : prank — **diabólico, -ca** *adj* : diabolic, diabolical
diafragma *nm* : diaphragm
diagnosticar {72} *vt* : diagnose — **diagnóstico, -ca** *adj* : diagnostic — **diagnóstico** *nm* : diagnosis
diagonal *adj & nf* : diagonal
diagrama *nm* : diagram
dial *nm* : dial (of a radio, etc.)
dialecto *nm* : dialect
dialogar {52} *vi* : have a talk — **diálogo** *nm* : dialogue
diamante *nm* : diamond
diámetro *nm* : diameter
diana *nf* **1** : reveille **2** BLANCO : target, bull's-eye
diario, -ria *adj* : daily — **diario** *nm* **1** : diary **2** PERIÓDICO : newspaper — **diariamente** *adv* : daily
diarrea *nf* : diarrhea
dibujar *vt* **1** : draw **2** DESCRIBIR : portray — **dibujante** *nmf* : draftsman *m*, draftswoman *f* — **dibujo** *nm* **1** : drawing **2 ~s animados** : (animated) cartoons
diccionario *nm* : dictionary
dicha *nf* **1** ALEGRÍA : happiness **2** SUERTE : good luck — **dicho** *nm* : saying, proverb — **dichoso, -sa** *adj* **1** : happy **2** AFORTUNADO : lucky
diciembre *nm* : December
dictar *vt* **1** : dictate **2** : pronounce (a sentence), deliver (a speech) — **dictado** *nm* : dictation — **dictador, -dora** *n* : dictator — **dictadura** *nf* : dictatorship
diecinueve *adj & nm* : nineteen — **diecinueveavo, -va** *adj* : nineteenth
dieciocho *adj & nm* : eighteen — **dieciochoavo, -va** *or* **dieciochavo, -va** *adj* : eighteenth
dieciséis *adj & nm* : sixteen — **dieciseisavo, -va** *adj* : sixteenth
diecisiete *adj & nm* : seventeen — **diecisieteavo, -va** *adj* : seventeenth
diente *nm* **1** : tooth **2** : prong, tine (of a fork, etc.) **3 ~ de ajo** : clove of garlic **4 ~ de león** : dandelion
diesel ['disɛl] *adj & nm* : diesel
diestra *nf* : right hand — **diestro, -tra** *adj* **1** : right **2** HÁBIL : skillful
dieta *nf* : diet — **dietético, -ca** *adj* : dietetic, dietary
diez *adj & nm, pl* **dieces** : ten
difamar *vt* : slander, libel — **difamación** *nf, pl* **-ciones** : slander, libel
diferencia *nf* : difference — **diferenciar** *vt* : distinguish between — **diferenciarse** *vr* : differ — **diferente** *adj* : different
diferir {76} *vt* : postpone — *vi* : differ
difícil *adj* : difficult — **dificultad** *nf* : difficulty — **dificultar** *vt* : hinder, obstruct
difteria *nf* : diphtheria
difundir *vt* **1** : spread (out) **2** : broadcast (television, etc.)

difunto, -ta *adj & n* : deceased
difusión *nf, pl* **-siones** : spreading
digerir {76} *vt* : digest — **digerible** *adj* : digestible — **digestión** *nf, pl* **-tiones** : digestion — **digestivo, -va** *adj* : digestive
dígito *nm* : digit — **digital** *adj* : digital
dignarse *vr* ~ **a** : deign to
dignatario, -ria *n* : dignitary — **dignidad** *nf* : dignity — **digno, -na** *adj* : worthy
digresión *nf , pl* **-ciones** : digression
dilapidar *vt* : waste, squander
dilatar *vt* **1** : expand, dilate **2** PROLONGAR : prolong **3** POSPONER : postpone
dilema *nm* : dilemma
diligencia *nf* **1** : diligence **2** TRÁMITE : procedure, task — **diligente** *adj* : diligent
diluir {41} *vt* : dilute
diluvio *nm* **1** : flood **2** LLUVIA : downpour
dimensión *nf, pl* **-siones** : dimension
diminuto, -ta *adj* : minute, tiny
dimitir *vi* : resign — **dimisión** *nf, pl* **-siones** : resignation
dinámico, -ca *adj* : dynamic
dinamita *nf* : dynamite
dínamo *or* **dinamo** *nmf* : dynamo
dinastía *nf* : dynasty
dineral *nm* : large sum, fortune
dinero *nm* : money
dinosaurio *nm* : dinosaur
diócesis *nfs & pl* : diocese
dios, diosa *n* : god, goddess *f* — **Dios** *nm* : God
diploma *nm* : diploma — **diplomado, -da** *adj* : qualified, trained
diplomacia *nf* : diplomacy — **diplomático, -ca** *adj* : diplomatic — ~ *n* : diplomat
diputación *nf, pl* **-ciones** : delegation — **diputado, -da** *n* : delegate
dique *nm* : dike
dirección *nf, pl* **-ciones** **1** : address **2** SENTIDO : direction **3** GESTIÓN : management **4** : steering (of an automobile) — **direccional** *nf Lat* : turn signal, blinker — **directa** *nf* : high gear — **directiva** *nf* : board of directors — **directivo, -va** *adj* : managerial — ~ *n* : manager, director — **directo, -ta** *adj* **1** : direct **2** DERECHO : straight — **director, -tora** *n* **1** : director, manager **2** : conductor (of an orchestra) — **directorio** *nm* : directory — **directriz** *nf, pl* **-trices** : guideline
dirigencia *nf* : leaders *pl,* leadership — **dirigente** *nmf* : director, leader
dirigible *nm* : dirigible, blimp
dirigir {35} *vt* **1** : direct, lead **2** : address (a letter, etc.) **3** ENCAMINAR : aim **4** : conduct (music) — **dirigirse** *vr* **1** ~ **a** : go towards **2** ~ **a algn** : speak to s.o., write to s.o.
discernir {25} *vt* : discern, distinguish — **discernimiento** *nm* : discernment
disciplinar *vt* : discipline — **disciplina** *nf* : discipline
discípulo, -la *n* : disciple, follower
disco *nm* **1** : disc, disk **2** : discus (in sports) **3** ~ **compacto** : compact disc
discordante *adj* : discordant — **discordia** *nf* : discord
discoteca *nf* : disco, discotheque
discreción *nf, pl* **-ciones** : discretion
discrepancia *nf* **1** : discrepancy **2** DESACUERDO : disagreement — **discrepar** *vi* : differ, disagree
discreto, -ta *adj* : discreet
discriminar *vt* **1** : discriminate against **2** DISTINGUIR : distinguish — **discriminación** *nf, pl* **-ciones** : discrimination
disculpar *vt* : excuse, pardon — **disculparse** *vr* : apologize — **disculpa** *nf* **1** : apology **2** EXCUSA : excuse
discurrir *vi* **1** : pass, go by **2** REFLEXIONAR : ponder, reflect
discurso *nm* : speech, discourse
discutir *vt* **1** : discuss **2** CUESTIONAR : dispute — *vi* : argue — **discusión** *nf, pl* **-siones** **1** : discussion **2** DISPUTA : argument — **discutible** *adj* : debatable
disecar {72} *vt* : dissect — **disección** *nf, pl* **-ciones** : dissection
diseminar *vt* : disseminate, spread
disentería *nf* : dysentery
disentir {76} *vi* ~ **de** : disagree with — **disentimiento** *nm* : disagreement, dissent
diseñar *vt* : design — **diseñador, -dora** *n* : designer — **diseño** *nm* : design
disertación *nf, pl* **-ciones** **1** : lecture **2** : (written) dissertation
disfrazar {21} *vt* : disguise — **disfrazarse** *vr* ~ **de** : disguise oneself as — **disfraz** *nm, pl* **-fraces** **1** : disguise **2** : costume (for a party, etc.)
disfrutar *vt* : enjoy — *vi* : enjoy oneself
disgustar *vt* : upset, annoy — **disgustarse** *vr* **1** : get annoyed **2** ENEMISTARSE : fall out (with s.o.) — **disgusto** *nm* **1** : annoyance, displeasure **2** RIÑA : quarrel
disidente *adj & nmf* : dissident
disimular *vt* : conceal, hide — *vi* : pretend — **disimulo** *nm* : pretense
disipar *vt* **1** : dispel **2** DERROCHAR : squander

diskette [di'sket] *nm* : floppy disk, diskette
dislexia *nf* : dyslexia — **disléxico, -ca** *adj* : dyslexic
dislocar {72} *vt* : dislocate — **dislocarse** *vr* : become dislocated
disminuir {41} *vt* : reduce — *vi* : decrease, drop — **disminución** *nf, pl* **-ciones** : decrease
disociar *vt* : dissociate
disolver {89} *vt* : dissolve — **disolverse** *vr* : dissolve
disparar *vi* : shoot, fire — *vt* : shoot — **dispararse** *vr* : shoot up, skyrocket
disparatado, -da *adj* : absurd — **disparate** *nm* : nonsense, silly thing
disparejo, -ja *adj* : uneven — **disparidad** *nf* : difference, disparity
disparo *nm* : shot
dispensar *vt* **1** : dispense, distribute **2** DISCULPAR : excuse
dispersar *vt* : disperse, scatter — **dispersarse** *vr* : disperse — **dispersión** *nf, pl* **-siones** : scattering
disponer {60} *vt* **1** : arrange, lay out **2** ORDENAR : decide, stipulate — *vi* **~ de** : have at one's disposal — **disponerse** *vr* **~ a** : be ready to — **disponibilidad** *nf* : availability — **disponible** *adj* : available
disposición *nf, pl* **-ciones 1** : arrangement **2** APTITUD : aptitude **3** : order, provision (in law) **4 a ~ de** : at the disposal of
dispositivo *nm* : device, mechanism
dispuesto, -ta *adj* : prepared, ready
disputar *vi* **1** : argue **2** COMPETIR : compete — *vt* : dispute — **disputa** *nf* : dispute, argument
disquete → **diskette**
distanciar *vt* : space out — **distanciarse** *vr* : grow apart — **distancia** *nf* : distance — **distante** *adj* : distant
distinguir {26} *vt* : distinguish — **distinguirse** *vr* : distinguish oneself, stand out — **distinción** *nf, pl* **-ciones** : distinction — **distintivo, -va** *adj* : distinctive — **distinto, -ta** *adj* **1** : different **2** CLARO : distinct, clear
distorsión *nf, pl* **-siones** : distortion
distraer {81} *vt* **1** : distract **2** DIVERTIR : entertain — **distraerse** *vr* **1** : get distracted **2** ENTRETENERSE : amuse oneself — **distracción** *nf, pl* **-ciones 1** : amusement **2** DESPISTE : absentmindedness — **distraído, -da** *adj* : distracted, absentminded
distribuir {41} *vt* : distribute — **distribución** *nf, pl* **-ciones** : distribution — **distribuidor, -dora** *n* : distributor
distrito *nm* : district
disturbio *nm* : disturbance
disuadir *vt* : dissuade, discourage — **disuasivo, -va** *adj* : deterrent
diurno, -na *adj* : day, daytime
divagar {52} *vi* : digress
diván *nm, pl* **-vanes** : divan, couch
divergir {35} *vi* **1** : diverge **2 ~ en** : differ on
diversidad *nf* : diversity
diversificar {72} *vt* : diversify
diversión *nf, pl* **-siones** : fun, entertainment
diverso, -sa *adj* : diverse
divertir {76} *vt* : entertain — **divertirse** *vr* : enjoy oneself, have fun — **divertido, -da** *adj* : entertaining
dividendo *nm* : dividend
dividir *vt* **1** : divide **2** REPARTIR : distribute
divinidad *nf* : divinity — **divino, -na** *adj* : divine
divisa *nf* **1** : currency **2** EMBLEMA : emblem
divisar *vt* : discern, make out
división *nf, pl* **-siones** : division — **divisor** *nm* : denominator
divorciar *vt* : divorce — **divorciarse** *vr* : get a divorce — **divorciado, -da** *n* : divorcé *m,* divorcée *f* — **divorcio** *nm* : divorce
divulgar {52} *vt* **1** : divulge, reveal **2** PROPAGAR : spread, circulate
dizque *adv Lat* : supposedly, apparently
doblar *vt* **1** : double **2** PLEGAR : fold **3** : turn (a corner) **4** : dub (a film) — *vi* : turn — **doblarse** *vr* **1** : double over **2 ~ a** : give in to — **dobladillo** *nm* : hem — **doble** *adj & nm* : double — **~** *nmf* : stand-in, double — **doblemente** *adv* : doubly — **doblegar** {52} *vt* : force to yield — **doblegarse** *vr* : give in — **doblez** *nm, pl* **-bleces** : fold, crease
doce *adj & nm* : twelve — **doceavo, -va** *adj* : twelfth — **docena** *nf* : dozen
docente *adj* : teaching
dócil *adj* : docile
doctor, -tora *n* : doctor — **doctorado** *nm* : doctorate
doctrina *nf* : doctrine
documentar *vt* : document — **documentación** *nf, pl* **-ciones** : documentation — **documental** *adj & nm* : documentary — **documento** *nm* : document
dogma *nm* : dogma — **dogmático, -ca** *adj* : dogmatic
dólar *nm* : dollar

doler {47} *vi* **1** : hurt **2 me duelen los pies** : my feet hurt — **dolerse** *vr* **~ de** : complain about — **dolor** *nm* **1** : pain **2** PENA : grief **3 ~ de cabeza** : headache **4 ~ de estómago** : stomachache — **dolorido, -da 1** : sore **2** AFLIGIDO : hurt — **doloroso, -sa** *adj* : painful
domar *vt* : tame, break in
domesticar {72} *vt* : domesticate, tame — **doméstico, -ca** *adj* : domestic
domicilio *nm* : home, residence
dominar *vt* **1** : dominate, control **2** : master (a subject, a language, etc.) — **dominarse** *vr* : control oneself — **dominación** *nf, pl* **-ciones** : domination — **dominante** *adj* : dominant
domingo *nm* : Sunday — **dominical** *adj* **periódico ~** : Sunday newspaper
dominio *nm* **1** : authority **2** : mastery (of a subject) **3** TERRITORIO : domain
dominó *nm, pl* **-nós** : dominoes *pl* (game)
don[1] *nm* : courtesy title preceding a man's first name
don[2] *nm* **1** : gift **2** TALENTO : talent — **donación** *nf, pl* **-ciones** : donation — **donador, -dora** *n* : donor
donaire *nm* : grace, charm
donar *vt* : donate — **donante** *nmf* : donor — **donativo** *nm* : donation
donde *conj* : where — **~** *prep Lat* : over by
dónde *adv* **1** : where **2 ¿de ~ eres?** : where are you from? **3 ¿por ~?** : whereabouts?
dondequiera *adv* **1** : anywhere **2 ~ que** : wherever, everywhere
doña *nf* : courtesy title preceding a woman's first name
doquier *adv* **por ~** : everywhere
dorar *vt* **1** : gild **2** : brown (food) — **dorado, -da** *adj* : gold, golden
dormir {27} *vt* : put to sleep — *vi* : sleep — **dormirse** *vr* : fall asleep — **dormido, -da** *adj* **1** : asleep **2** ENTUMECIDO : numb — **dormilón, -lona** *n* : sleepyhead, late riser — **dormitar** *vi* : doze — **dormitorio** *nm* **1** : bedroom **2** : dormitory (in a college)
dorso *nm* : back
dos *adj & nm* : two — **doscientos, -tas** *adj* : two hundred — **doscientos** *nms & pl* : two hundred
dosel *nm* : canopy
dosis *nfs & pl* : dose, dosage
dotar *vt* **1** : provide, equip **2 ~ de** : endow with — **dotación** *nf, pl* **-ciones 1** : endowment, funding **2** PERSONAL : personnel — **dote** *nf* **1** : dowry **2 ~s** *nfpl* : gift, talent
dragar {52} *vt* : dredge — **draga** *nf* : dredge
dragón *nm, pl* **-gones** : dragon
drama *nm* : drama — **dramático, -ca** *adj* : dramatic — **dramatizar** {21} *vt* : dramatize — **dramaturgo, -ga** *n* : dramatist, playwright
drástico, -ca *adj* : drastic
drenar *vt* : drain — **drenaje** *nm* : drainage
droga *nf* : drug — **drogadicto, -ta** *n* : drug addict — **drogar** {52} *vt* : drug — **drogarse** *vr* : take drugs — **droguería** *nf* : drugstore
dromedario *nm* : dromedary
dual *adj* : dual
ducha *nf* : shower — **ducharse** *vr* : take a shower
ducho, -cha *adj* : experienced, skilled
duda *nf* : doubt — **dudar** *vt* : doubt — *vi* **~ en** : hesitate to — **dudoso, -sa** *adj* **1** : doubtful **2** SOSPECHOSO : questionable
duelo *nm* **1** : duel **2** LUTO : mourning
duende *nm* : elf, imp
dueño, -na *n* **1** : owner **2** : landlord, landlady *f*
dulce *adj* **1** : sweet **2** : fresh (of water) **3** SUAVE : mild, gentle — **~** *nm* : candy, sweet — **dulzura** *nf* : sweetness
duna *nf* : dune
dúo *nm* : duo, duet
duodécimo, -ma *adj* : twelfth — **~** *n* : twelfth (in a series)
dúplex *nms & pl* : duplex (apartment)
duplicar {72} *vt* **1** : double **2** : duplicate, copy (a document, etc.) — **duplicado, -da** *adj* : duplicate — **duplicado** *nm* : copy
duqe *nm* : duke — **duquesa** *nf* : duchess
durabilidad *nf* : durability
duración *nf, pl* **-ciones** : duration, length
duradero, -ra *adj* : durable, lasting
durante *prep* **1** : during **2 ~ una hora** : for an hour
durar *vi* : endure, last
durazno *nm Lat* : peach
duro *adv* : hard — **duro, -ra** *adj* **1** : hard **2** SEVERO : harsh — **dureza** *nf* **1** : hardness **2** SEVERIDAD : harshness

E

e[1] *nf* : e, fifth letter of the Spanish alphabet
e[2] *conj* (*used instead of* **y** *before words beginning with i or hi*) : and
ebanista *nmf* : cabinetmaker
ébano *nm* : ebony
ebrio, -bria *adj* : drunk
ebullición *nf, pl* **-ciones** : boiling
echar *vt* **1** : throw, cast **2** EXPULSAR : expel, dismiss **3** : give off, emit (smoke, sparks, etc.) **4** BROTAR : sprout **5** PONER : put (on) **6 ~ a perder** : spoil, ruin **7 ~ de menos** : miss — **echarse** *vr* **1** : throw oneself **2** ACOSTARSE : lie down **3 ~ a** : start (to)
eclesiástico, -ca *adj* : ecclesiastic — **~** *nm* : clergyman
eclipse *nm* : eclipse — **eclipsar** *vi* : eclipse
eco *nm* : echo
ecología *nf* : ecology — **ecológico, -ca** *adj* : ecological — **ecologista** *nmf* : ecologist
economía *nf* **1** : economy **2** : economics (science) — **economico, -ca** *adj* **1** : economic, economical **2** BARATO : inexpensive — **economista** *nmf* : economist — **economizar** {21} *v* : save
ecosistema *nm* : ecosystem
ecuación *nf, pl* **-ciones** : equation
ecuador *nm* : equator
ecuánime *adj* **1** : even-tempered **2** : impartial (in law)
ecuatoriano, -na *adj* : Ecuadorian, Ecuadorean, Ecuadoran
ecuestre *adj* : equestrian
edad *nf* **1** : age **2 Edad Media** : Middle Ages *pl* **3 ¿qué ~ tienes?** : how old are you?
edición *nf, pl* **-ciones 1** : publishing, publication **2** : edition (of a book, etc.)
edicto *nm* : edict
edificar {72} *vt* : build — **edificio** *nm* : building
editar *vt* **1** : publish **2** : edit (a film, a text, etc.) — **editor, -tora** *n* **1** : publisher **2** : editor — **editorial** *adj* : publishing — **~** *nm* : editorial — **~** *nf* : publishing house
edredón *nm, pl* **-dones** : (down) comforter, duvet
educar {72} *vt* **1** : educate **2** CRIAR : bring up, raise **3** : train (the body, the voice, etc.) — **educación** *nf, pl* **-ciones 1** : education **2** MODALES : (good) manners *pl* — **educado, -da** *adj* : polite — **educador, -dora** *n* : educator — **educativo, -va** *adj* : educational
efectivo, -va *adj* **1** : effective **2** REAL : real — **efectivo** *nm* : cash — **efectivamente** *adv* **1** : really **2** POR SUPUESTO : yes, indeed — **efecto** *nm* **1** : effect **2 en ~** : in fact **3 ~s** *nmpl* : goods, property — **efectuar** {3} *vt* : bring about, carry out
efervescente *adj* : effervescent — **efervescencia** *nf* : effervescence
eficaz *adj, pl* **-caces 1** : effective **2** EFICIENTE : efficient — **eficacia** *nf* **1** : effectiveness **2** EFICIENCIA : efficiency
eficiente *adj* : efficient — **eficiencia** *nf* : efficiency
efímero, -ra *adj* : ephemeral
efusivo, -va *adj* : effusive
egipcio, -cia *adj* : Egyptian
ego *nm* : ego — **egocéntrico, -ca** *adj* : egocentric — **egoísmo** *nm* : egoism — **egoísta** *adj* : egoistic — **~** *nmf* : egoist
egresar *vi* : graduate — **egresado, -da** *n* : graduate — **egreso** *nm* : graduation, commencement
eje *nm* **1** : axis **2** : axle (of a wheel, etc.)
ejecutar *vt* **1** : execute, put to death **2** REALIZAR : carry out — **ejecución** *nf, pl* **-ciones** : execution
ejecutivo, -va *adj & n* : executive
ejemplar *adj* : exemplary — **~** *nm* **1** : copy, issue **2** EJEMPLO : example — **ejemplificar** {72} *vt* : exemplify — **ejemplo** *nm* **1** : example **2 por ~** : for example
ejercer {86} *vt* **1** : practice (a profession) **2** : exercise (a right, etc.) — *vi* **~ de** : practice as, work as — **ejercicio** *nm* **1** : exercise **2** : practice (of a profession, etc.)
ejército *nm* : army
el, la *art, pl* **los, las** : the — **el** *pron* (*referring to masculine nouns*) **1** : the one **2 ~ que** : he who, whoever, the one that
él *pron* : he, him
elaborar *vt* **1** : manufacture, produce **2** : draw up (a plan, etc.)

elástico, -ca *adj* : elastic — **elástico** *nm* : elastic — **elasticidad** *nf* : elasticity
elección *nf, pl* **-ciones 1** : election **2** SELECCIÓN : choice — **elector, -tora** *n* : voter — **electorado** *nm* : electorate — **electoral** *adj* : electoral
electricidad *nf* : electricity — **eléctrico, -ca** *adj* : electric, electrical — **electricista** *nmf* : electrician — **electrificar** {72} *vt* : electrify — **electrizar** {21} *vt* : electrify, thrill — **electrocutar** *vt* : electrocute
electrodo *nm* : electrode
electrodoméstico *nm* : electric appliance
electromagnético, -ca *adj* : electromagnetic
electrón *nm, pl* **-trones** : electron — **electrónico, -ca** *adj* : electronic — **electrónica** *nf* : electronics
elefante, -ta *n* : elephant
elegante *adj* : elegant — **elegancia** *nf* : elegance
elegía *nf* : elegy
elegir {28} *vt* **1** : elect **2** ESCOGER : choose, select — **elegible** *adj* : eligible
elemento *nm* : element — **elemental** *adj* **1** : elementary, basic **2** ESENCIAL : fundamental
elenco *nm* : cast (of actors)
elevar *vt* **1** : raise, lift **2** ASCENDER : elevate (in a hierarchy), promote — **elevarse** *vr* : rise — **elevación** *nf, pl* **-ciones** : elevation — **elevador** *nm* **1** : hoist **2** *Lat* : elevator
eliminar *vt* : eliminate — **eliminación** *nf, pl* **-ciones** : elimination
elipse *nf* : ellipse — **elíptico, -ca** *adj* : elliptical, elliptic
elite *or* **élite** *nf* : elite
elixir *or* **elíxir** *nm* : elixir
ella *pron* : she, her — **ello** *pron* : it — **ellos, ellas** *pron pl* **1** : they, them **2 de ellos, de ellas** : theirs
elocuente *adj* : eloquent — **elocuencia** *nf* : eloquence
elogiar *vt* : praise — **elogio** *nm* : praise
eludir *vt* : avoid, elude
emanar *vi* **~ de** : emanate from
emancipar *vt* : emancipate — **emanciparse** *vr* : free oneself — **emancipación** *nf, pl* **-ciones** : emancipation
embadurnar *vt* : smear, daub
embajada *nf* : embassy — **embajador, -dora** *n* : ambassador
embalar *vt* : wrap up, pack — **embalaje** *nm* : packing
embaldosar *vt* : pave with tiles
embalsamar *vt* : embalm
embalse *nm* : dam, reservoir
embarazar {21} *vt* **1** : make pregnant **2** IMPEDIR : restrict, hamper — **embarazada** *adj* : pregnant — **embarazo** *nm* **1** : pregnancy **2** IMPEDIMENTO : hindrance, obstacle — **embarazoso, -sa** *adj* : embarrassing
embarcar {72} *vt* : load — **embarcarse** *vr* : embark, board — **embarcación** *nf, pl* **-ciones** : boat, craft — **embarcadero** *nm* : pier, jetty — **embarco** *nm* : embarkation
embargar {52} *vt* **1** : seize, impound **2** : overwhelm (with emotion, etc.) — **embargo** *nm* **1** : embargo **2** : seizure (in law) **3 sin ~** : nevertheless
embarque *nm* : loading (of goods), boarding (of passengers)
embarrancar {72} *vi* : run aground
embarullarse *vr fam* : get mixed up
embaucar {72} *vt* : trick, swindle — **embaucador, -dora** *n* : swindler
embeber *vt* : absorb — *vi* : shrink — **embeberse** *vr* : become absorbed
embelesar *vt* : enchant, delight — **embelesado, -da** *adj* : spellbound
embellecer {53} *vt* : embellish, beautify
embestir {54} *vt* : attack, charge at — *vi* : charge, attack — **embestida** *nf* **1** : attack **2** : charge (of a bull)
emblema *nm* : emblem
embobar *vt* : amaze, fascinate
embocadura *nf* **1** : mouth (of a river, etc.) **2** : mouthpiece (of an instrument)
émbolo *nm* : piston
embolsarse *vr* : put in one's pocket
emborracharse *vr* : get drunk
emborronar *vt* **1** : smudge, blot **2** GARABATEAR : scribble
emboscar {72} *vt* : ambush — **emboscada** *nf* : ambush
embotar *vt* : dull, blunt
embotellar *vt* : bottle (up) — **embotellamiento** *nm* : traffic jam
embrague *nm* : clutch — **embragar** {52} *vi* : engage the clutch
embriagarse {52} *vr* : get drunk — **embriagado, -da** *adj* : intoxicated, drunk — **embriagador, -dora** *adj* : intoxicating — **embriaguez** *nf* : drunkenness
embrión *nm, pl* **-briones** : embryo
embrollo *nm* : tangle, confusion
embrujar *vt* : bewitch — **embrujo** *nm* : spell, curse
embrutecer *vt* : brutalize
embudo *nm* : funnel

embuste *nm* : lie — **embustero, -ra** *adj* : lying — ~ *n* : liar, cheat
embutir *vt* : stuff — **embutido** *nm* : sausage, cold meat
emergencia *nf* : emergency
emerger {15} *vi* : emerge, appear
emigrar *vi* **1** : emigrate **2** : migrate (of animals) — **emigración** *nf, pl* **-ciones 1** : emigration **2** : migration (of animals) — **emigrante** *adj & nmf* : emigrant
eminente *adj* : eminent — **eminencia** *nf* : eminence
emitir *vt* **1** : emit **2** EXPRESAR : express (an opinion, etc.) **3** : broadcast (on radio or television) **4** : issue (money, stamps, etc.) — **emisión** *nf, pl* **-siones 1** : emission **2** : broadcast (on radio or television) **3** : issue (of money, etc.) — **emisora** *nf* : radio station
emoción *nf, pl* **-ciones** : emotion — **emocional** *adj* : emotional — **emocionante** *adj* **1** : moving, touching **2** APASIONANTE : exciting, thrilling — **emocionar** *vt* **1** : move, touch **2** APASIONAR : excite, thrill — **emocionarse** *vr* **1** : be moved **2** APASIONARSE : get excited — **emotivo, -va** *adj* **1** : emotional **2** CONMOVEDOR : moving
empacar {72} *vt Lat* : pack
empachar *vt* : give indigestion to — **empacharse** *vr* : get indigestion — **empacho** *nm* : indigestion
empadronarse *vr* : register to vote
empalagoso, -sa *adj* : excessively sweet, cloying
empalizada *nf* : palisade (fence)
empalmar *vt* : connect, link — *vi* : meet, converge — **empalme** *nm* **1** : connection, link **2** : junction (of a railroad, etc.)
empanada *nf* : pie, turnover — **empanadilla** *nf* : meat or seafood pie
empanar *vt* : bread (in cooking)
empantanar *vt* : flood — **empantanarse** *vr* **1** : become flooded **2** : get bogged down
empañar *vt* **1** : steam (up) **2** : tarnish (one's reputation, etc.) — **empañarse** *vr* : fog up
empapar *vt* : soak — **empaparse** *vr* : get soaking wet
empapelar *vt* : wallpaper
empaquetar *vt* : pack, package
emparedado, -da *adj* : walled in, confined — **emparedado** *nm* : sandwich
emparejar *vt* : match up, pair — **emparejarse** *vr* : pair off
emparentado, -da *adj* : related, kindred
empastar *vt* : fill (a tooth) — **empaste** *nm* : filling
empatar *vi* : result in a draw, be tied — **empate** *nm* : draw, tie
empedernido, -da *adj* : inveterate, hardened
empedrar {55} *vt* : pave (with stones) — **empedrado** *nm* : paving, pavement
empeine *nm* : instep
empeñar *vt* : pawn — **empeñarse** *vr* **1** : insist, persist **2** ENDEUDARSE : go into debt **3** ~ **en** : make an effort to — **empeñado, -da** *adj* **1** : determined, committed **2** ENDEUDADO : in debt — **empeño** *nm* **1** : determination, effort **2 casa de ~s** : pawnshop
empeorar *vi* : get worse — *vt* : make worse
empequeñecer {53} *vt* : diminish, make smaller
emperador *nm* : emperor — **emperatriz** *nf, pl* **-trices** : empress
empezar {29} *v* : start, begin
empinar *vt* : raise — **empinarse** *vr* : stand on tiptoe — **empinado, -da** *adj* : steep
empírico, -ca *adj* : empirical
emplasto *nm* : poultice
emplazar {21} *vt* **1** : summon, subpoena **2** SITUAR : place, locate — **emplazamiento** *nm* **1** : location, site **2** CITACIÓN : summons, subpoena
emplear *vt* **1** : employ **2** USAR : use — **emplearse** *vr* **1** : get a job **2** USARSE : be used — **empleado, -da** *n* : employee — **empleador, -dora** *n* : employer — **empleo** *nm* **1** : occupation, job **2** USO : use
empobrecer {53} *vt* : impoverish — **empobrecerse** *vr* : become poor
empollar *vi* : brood (eggs) — *vt* : incubate
empolvarse *vr* : powder one's face
empotrar *vt* : fit, build into — **empotrado, -da** *adj* : built-in
emprender *vt* : undertake, begin — **emprendedor, -dora** *adj* : enterprising
empresa *nf* **1** COMPAÑIA : company, firm **2** TAREA : undertaking — **empresarial** *adj* : business, managerial — **empresario, -ria** *n* **1** : businessman *m*, businesswoman *f* **2** : impresario (in theater), promoter (in sports)
empujar *v* : push — **empuje** *nm* : impetus, drive — **empujón** *nm, pl* **-jones** : push, shove
empuñar *vt* : grasp, take hold of
emular *vt* : emulate
en *prep* **1** : in **2** DENTRO DE : into, inside

(of) **3** SOBRE : on **4 ~ avión** : by plane **5 ~ casa** : at home
enajenar *vt* : alienate — **enajenación** *nf, pl* **-ciones** : alienation
enagua *nf* : slip, petticoat
enaltecer {53} *vt* : praise, extol
enamorar *vt* : win the love of — **enamorarse** *vr* : fall in love — **enamorado, -da** *adj* : in love — **~** *n* : lover, sweetheart
enano, -na *adj & n* : dwarf
enarbolar *vt* **1** : hoist, raise **2** : brandish (arms, etc.)
enardecer {53} *vt* : stir up, excite
encabezar {21} *vt* **1** : head, lead **2** : put a heading on (an article, a list, etc.) — **encabezamiento** *nm* **1** : heading **2** : headline (in a newspaper)
encabritarse *vr* : rear up
encadenar *vt* **1** : chain, tie (up) **2** ENLAZAR : connect, link
encajar *vt* : fit (together) — *vi* **1** : fit **2** CUADRAR : conform, tally — **encaje** *nm* : lace
encalar *vt* : whitewash
encallar *vi* : run aground
encaminar *vt* : direct, aim — **encaminarse** *vr* **~ a** : head for — **encaminado, -da** *adj* **~ a** : aimed at, designed to
encandilar *vt* : dazzle
encanecer {53} *vi* : turn gray
encantar *vt* : enchant, bewitch — *vi* **me encanta esta canción** : I love this song — **encantado, -da** *adj* **1** : delighted **2** HECHIZADO : bewitched — **encantador, -dora** *adj* : charming, delightful — **encantamiento** *nm* : enchantment, spell — **encanto** *nm* **1** : charm, fascination **2** HECHIZO : spell
encapotarse *vr* : cloud over — **encapotado, -da** *adj* : overcast
encapricharse *vr* **~ con** : be infatuated with
encapuchado, -da *adj* : hooded
encaramar *vt* : lift up — **encaramarse** *vr* **~ a** : climb up on
encarar *vt* : face, confront
encarcelar *vt* : imprison — **encarcelamiento** *nm* : imprisonment
encarecer {53} *vt* : increase, raise (price, value, etc.) — **encarecerse** *vr* : become more expensive
encargar {52} *vt* **1** : put in charge of **2** PEDIR : order — **encargarse** *vr* **~ de** : take charge of — **encargado, -da** *adj* : in charge — **~** *n* : manager, person in charge — **encargo** *nm* **1** : errand **2** TAREA : assignment, task **3** PEDIDO : order
encariñarse *vr* **~ con** : become fond of
encarnar *vt* : embody — **encarnación** *nf, pl* **-ciones** : embodiment — **encarnado, -da** *adj* **1** : incarnate **2** ROJO : red
encarnizarse {21} *vr* **~ con** : attack viciously — **encarnizado, -da** *adj* : bitter, bloody
encarrilar *vt* : put on the right track
encasillar *vt* : pigeonhole
encauzar {21} *vt* : channel
encender {56} *vt* **1** : light, set fire to **2** PRENDER : switch on, start **3** AVIVAR : arouse (passions, etc.) — **encenderse** *vr* **1** : get excited **2** RUBORIZARSE : blush — **encendedor** *nm* : lighter — **encendido, -da** *adj* : lit, on — **encendido** *nm* : ignition (switch)
encerar *vt* : wax, polish — **encerado, -da** *adj* : waxed — **encerado** *nm* : blackboard
encerrar {55} *vt* **1** : lock up, shut away **2** CONTENER : contain
encestar *vi* : score (in basketball)
enchilada *nf* : enchilada
enchufar *vt* : plug in, connect — **enchufe** *nm* : plug, socket
encía *nf* : gum (tissue)
encíclica *nf* : encyclical
enciclopedia *nf* : encyclopedia — **enciclopédico, -ca** *adj* : encyclopedic
encierro *nm* **1** : confinement **2** : sit-in (at a university, etc.)
encima *adv* **1** : on top **2** ADEMÁS : as well, besides **3 ~ de** : on, over, on top of **4 por ~ de** : above, beyond
encinta *adj* : pregnant
enclenque *adj* : weak, sickly
encoger {15} *v* : shrink — **encogerse** *vr* **1** : shrink **2** : cower, cringe **3 ~ de hombros** : shrug (one's shoulders) — **encogido, -da** *adj* **1** : shrunken **2** TÍMIDO : shy
encolar *vt* : glue, stick
encolerizar {21} *vt* : enrage, infuriate — **encolerizarse** *vr* : get angry
encomendar {55} *vt* : entrust
encomienda *nf* **1** : charge, mission **2** *Lat* : parcel
encono *nm* : rancor, animosity
encontrar {19} *vt* **1** : find **2** : meet, encounter (difficulties, etc.) — **encontrarse** *vr* **1** : meet **2** HALLARSE : find oneself, be — **encontrado, -da** *adj* : contrary, opposing
encorvar *vt* : bend, curve — **encorvarse** *vr* : bend over, stoop
encrespar *vt* **1** : curl **2** IRRITAR : irritate — **encresparse** *vr* **1** : curl one's hair

2 IRRITARSE : get annoyed **3** : become choppy (of the sea)
encrucijada *nf* : crossroads
encuadernar *vt* : bind (a book) — **encuadernación** *nf, pl* **-ciones** : bookbinding
encuadrar *vt* **1** : frame **2** ENCAJAR : fit **3** COMPRENDER : contain, include
encubrir {2} *vt* : conceal, cover (up) — **encubierto, -ta** *adj* : covert — **encubrimiento** *nm* : cover-up
encuentro *nm* : meeting, encounter
encuestar *vt* : poll, take a survey of — **encuesta** *nf* **1** : investigation, inquiry **2** SONDEO : survey — **encuestador, -dora** *n* : pollster
encumbrado, -da *adj* : eminent, distinguished
encurtir *vt* : pickle
endeble *adj* : weak, feeble — **endeblez** *nf* : weakness, frailty
endemoniado, -da *adj* : wicked
enderezar {21} *vt* **1** : straighten (out) **2** : put upright, stand on end
endeudarse *vr* : go into debt — **endeudado, -da** *adj* : indebted, in debt — **endeudamiento** *nm* : debt
endiablado, -da *adj* **1** : wicked, diabolical **2** : complicated, difficult
endibia *or* **endivia** *nf* : endive
endosar *vt* : endorse — **endoso** *nm* : endorsement
endulzar {21} *vt* **1** : sweeten **2** : soften, mellow (a tone, a response, etc.) — **endulzante** *nm* : sweetener
endurecer {53} *vt* : harden — **endurecerse** *vr* : become hardened
enema *nm* : enema
enemigo, -ga *adj* : hostile — **~** *n* : enemy — **enemistad** *nf* : enmity — **enemistar** *vt* : make enemies of — **enemistarse** *vr* **~ con** : fall out with
energía *nf* : energy — **enérgico, -ca** *adj* : energetic, vigorous, forceful
enero *nm* : January
enervar *vt* **1** : enervate, weaken **2** *fam* : get on one's nerves
enésimo, -ma *adj* **por enésima vez** : for the umpteenth time
enfadar *vt* : annoy, make angry — **enfadarse** *vr* : get annoyed — **enfado** *nm* : anger, annoyance — **enfadoso, -sa** *adj* : annoying
enfatizar {21} *vt* : emphasize — **énfasis** *nms & pl* : emphasis — **enfático, -ca** *adj* : emphatic
enfermar *vt* : make sick — *vi* : get sick — **enfermedad** *nf* : sickness, disease — **enfermería** *nf* : infirmary — **enfermero, -ra** *n* : nurse — **enfermizo, -za** *adj* : sickly — **enfermo, -ma** *adj* : sick — **~** *n* : sick person, patient
enflaquecer {53} *vi* : lose weight
enfocar {72} *vt* **1** : focus (on) **2** : consider (a problem, etc.) — **enfoque** *nm* : focus
enfrascarse {72} *vr* **~ en** : immerse oneself in, get caught up in
enfrentar *vt* **1** : confront, face **2** : bring face to face — **enfrentarse** *vr* **~ con** : confront, clash with — **enfrente** *adv* **1** : opposite **2 ~ de** : in front of
enfriar {85} *vt* : chill, cool — **enfriarse** *vr* **1** : get cold **2** RESFRIARSE : catch a cold — **enfriamiento** *nm* **1** : cooling off **2** CATARRO : cold
enfurecer {53} *vt* : infuriate — **enfurecerse** *vr* : fly into a rage
enfurruñarse *vr fam* : sulk
engalanar *vt* : decorate — **engalanarse** *vr* : dress up
enganchar *vt* : hook, snag, catch — **engancharse** *vr* **1** : get caught **2** ALISTARSE : enlist
engañar *vt* **1** EMBAUCAR : trick, deceive **2** : cheat on, be unfaithful to — **engañarse** *vr* **1** : deceive oneself **2** EQUIVOCARSE : be mistaken — **engaño** *nm* : deception, deceit — **engañoso, -sa** *adj* : deceptive, deceitful
engatusar *vt* : coax, cajole
engendrar *vt* **1** : beget **2** : engender, give rise to (suspicions, etc.)
englobar *vt* : include, embrace
engomar *vt* : glue
engordar *vt* : fatten — *vi* : gain weight
engorroso, -sa *adj* : bothersome
engranar *v* : mesh, engage — **engranaje** *nm* : gears *pl*
engrandecer {53} *vt* **1** : enlarge **2** ENALTECER : exalt
engrapar *vt Lat* : staple — **engrapadora** *nf Lat* : stapler
engrasar *vt* : lubricate, grease — **engrase** *nm* : lubrication
engreído, -da *adj* : conceited
engrosar {19} *vt* : swell — *vi* : gain weight
engrudo *nm* : paste
engullir {38} *vt* : gulp down, gobble up
enhebrar *vt* : thread
enhorabuena *nf* : congratulations *pl*
enigma *nm* : enigma — **enigmático, -ca** *adj* : enigmatic
enjabonar *vt* : soap (up), lather
enjaezar {21} *vt* : harness
enjalbegar {52} *vt* : whitewash
enjambrar *vi* : swarm — **enjambre** *nm* : swarm
enjaular *vt* **1** : cage **2** *fam* : jail

enjuagar {52} *vt* : rinse — **enjuague** *nm* **1** : rinse **2** ~ **bucal** : mouthwash

enjugar {52} *vt* **1** : wipe away (tears) **2** : wipe out (debt)

enjuiciar *vt* **1** : prosecute **2** JUZGAR : try

enjuto, -ta *adj* : gaunt, lean

enlace *nm* **1** : bond, link **2** : junction (of a highway, etc.)

enlatar *vt* : can

enlazar {21} *vt* : join, link — *vi* ~ **con** : link up with

enlistarse *vr Lat* : enlist

enlodar *vt* : cover with mud

enloquecer {53} *vt* : drive crazy — **enloquecerse** *vr* : go crazy

enlosar *vt* : pave, tile

enlutarse *vr* : go into mourning

enmarañar *vt* **1** : tangle **2** COMPLICAR : complicate **3** CONFUNDIR : confuse — **enmarañarse** *vr* **1** : get tangled up **2** CONFUNDIRSE : become confused

enmarcar {72} *vt* : frame

enmascarar *vt* : mask

enmendar {55} *vt* **1** : amend **2** CORREGIR : emend, correct — **enmendarse** *vr* : mend one's ways — **enmienda** *nf* **1** : amendment **2** CORRECCIÓN : correction

enmohecerse {53} *vr* **1** : become moldy **2** OXIDARSE : rust

enmudecer {53} *vt* : silence — *vi* : fall silent

ennegrecer {53} *vt* : blacken

ennoblecer {53} *vt* : ennoble, dignify

enojar *vt* **1** : anger **2** MOLESTAR : annoy — **enojarse** *vr* ~ **con** : get upset with — **enojo** *nm* **1** : anger **2** MOLESTIA : annoyance — **enojoso, -sa** *adj* : annoying

enorgullecer {53} *vt* : make proud — **enorgullecerse** *vr* ~ **de** : pride oneself on

enorme *adj* : enormous — **enormemente** *adv* : enormously, extremely — **enormidad** *nf* : enormity

enraizar {30} *vi* : take root

enredadera *nf* : climbing plant, vine

enredar *vt* **1** : tangle up, entangle **2** CONFUNDIR : confuse **3** IMPLICAR : involve — **enredarse** *vr* **1** : become entangled **2** ~ **en** : get mixed up in — **enredo** *nm* **1** : tangle **2** EMBROLLO : confusion, mess — **enredoso, -sa** *adj* : tangled up, complicated

enrejado *nm* **1** : railing **2** REJILLA : grating, grille **3** : trellis (for plants)

enrevesado, -da *adj* : complicated

enriquecer {53} *vt* : enrich — **enriquecerse** *vr* : get rich

enrojecer {53} *vt* : redden — **enrojecerse** *vr* : blush

enrolar *vt* : enlist — **enrolarse** *vr* ~ **en** : enlist in

enrollar *vt* : roll up, coil

enroscar {72} *vt* **1** : roll up **2** ATORNILLAR : screw in

ensalada *nf* : salad

ensalzar {21} *vt* : praise

ensamblar *vt* : assemble, fit together

ensanchar *vt* **1** : widen **2** AMPLIAR : expand — **ensanche** *nm* **1** : widening **2** : (urban) expansion, development

ensangrentado, -da *adj* : bloody, bloodstained

ensañarse *vr* : act cruelly

ensartar *vt* : string, thread

ensayar *vi* : rehearse — *vt* : try out, test — **ensayo** *nm* **1** : essay **2** PRUEBA : trial, test **3** : rehearsal (in theater, etc.)

enseguida *adv* : right away, immediately

ensenada *nf* : inlet, cove

enseñar *vt* **1** : teach **2** MOSTRAR : show — **enseñanza** *nf* **1** EDUCACIÓN : education **2** INSTRUCCIÓN : teaching

enseres *nmpl* **1** : equipment **2** ~ **domésticos** : household goods

ensillar *vt* : saddle (up)

ensimismarse *vr* : lose oneself in thought

ensombrecer {53} *vt* : cast a shadow over, darken

ensoñación *nf, pl* **-ciones** : fantasy, daydream

ensordecer {53} *vt* : deafen — *vi* : go deaf — **ensordecedor, -dora** *adj* : deafening

ensortijar *vt* : curl

ensuciar *vt* : soil — **ensuciarse** *vr* : get dirty

ensueño *nm* : daydream, fantasy

entablar *vt* : initiate, start

entallar *vt* : tailor, fit (clothing) — *vi* : fit

entarimado *nm* : floorboards, flooring

ente *nm* **1** : being **2** ORGANISMO : body, organization

entender {56} *vt* **1** : understand **2** OPINAR : think, believe — *vi* **1** : understand **2** ~ **de** : know about, be good at — **entenderse** *vr* **1** : understand each other **2** LLEVARSE BIEN : get along well — ~ *nm* **a mi** ~ : in my opinion — **entendido, -da** *adj* **1** : understood **2 eso se da por** ~ : that goes without saying **3 tener** ~ : be under the impression — **entendimiento** *nm* **1** : understanding **2** INTELIGENCIA : intellect

enterar *vt* : inform — **enterarse** *vr* : find out, learn — **enterado, -da** *adj* : well-informed
entereza *nf* **1** HONRADEZ : integrity **2** FORTALEZA : fortitude **3** FIRMEZA : resolve
enternecer {53} *vt* : move, touch
entero, -ra *adj* **1** : whole **2** TOTAL : absolute, total **3** INTACTO : intact — **entero** *nm* : integer, whole number
enterrar {55} *vt* : bury
entibiar *vt* : cool (down) — **entibiarse** *vr* : become lukewarm
entidad *nf* **1** : entity **2** ORGANIZACIÓN : body, organization
entierro *nm* **1** : burial **2** : funeral (ceremony)
entomología *nf* : entomology — **entomólogo, -ga** *n* : entomologist
entonar *vt* : sing, intone — *vi* : be in tune
entonces *adv* **1** : then **2 desde ~** : since then
entornado, -da *adj* : half-closed, ajar
entorno *nm* : surroundings *pl*, environment
entorpecer {53} *vt* **1** : hinder, obstruct **2** : numb, dull (wits, reactions, etc.)
entrada *nf* **1** : entrance, entry **2** BILLETE : ticket **3** COMIENZO : beginning **4** : inning (in baseball) **5 ~s** *nfpl* : income **6 tener ~s** : have a receding hairline
entraña *nf* **1** : core, heart **2 ~s** *nfpl* VÍSCERAS : entrails, innards — **entrañable** *adj* : close, intimate — **entrañar** *vt* : involve
entrar *vi* **1** : enter **2** EMPEZAR : begin — *vt* : introduce, bring in
entre *prep* **1** : between **2** : among
entreabrir {2} *vt* : leave ajar — **entreabierto, -ta** *adj* : half-open, ajar
entreacto *nm* : intermission
entrecejo *nm* **fruncir el ~** : knit one's brows, frown
entrecortado, -da *adj* : faltering (of the voice), labored (of breathing)
entrecruzar {21} *vi* : intertwine
entredicho *nm* : doubt, question
entregar {52} *vt* : deliver, hand over — **entregarse** *vr* : surrender — **entrega** *nf* **1** : delivery **2** DEDICACIÓN : dedication, devotion **3 ~ inicial** : down payment
entrelazar {21} *vt* : intertwine — **entrelazarse** *vr* : become intertwined
entremés *nm, pl* **-meses 1** : hors d'oeuvre **2** : short play (in theater)
entremeterse → **entrometerse**
entremezclar *vt* : mix (up)
entrenar *vt* : train, drill — **entrenarse** *vr* : train — **entrenador, -dora** *n* : trainer, coach — **entranamiento** *nm* : training
entrepierna *nf* : crotch
entresacar {72} *vt* : pick out, select
entresuelo *nm* : mezzanine
entretanto *adv* : meanwhile — **~** *nm* **en el ~** : in the meantime
entretener {80} *vt* **1** : entertain **2** DESPISTAR : distract **3** RETRASAR : delay, hold up — **entretenerse** *vr* **1** : amuse oneself **2** DEMORARSE : dawdle — **entretenido, -da** *adj* : entertaining — **entretenimiento** *nm* **1** : entertainment, amusement **2** PASATIEMPO : pastime
entrever {88} *vt* : catch a glimpse of, make out
entrevistar *vt* : interview — **entrevista** *nf* : interview — **entrevistador, -dora** *n* : interviewer
entristecer {53} *vt* : sadden
entrometerse *vr* : interfere — **entrometido, -da** *adj* : meddling, nosy — *n* : meddler
entroncar {72} *vi* : be related, be connected
entumecer {53} *vt* : make numb — **entumecerse** *vr* : go numb — **entumecido, -da** *adj* **1** : numb **2** : stiff (of muscles, etc.)
enturbiar *vt* : cloud — **enturbiarse** *vr* : become cloudy
entusiasmar *vt* : fill with enthusiasm — **entusiasmarse** *vr* : get excited — **entusiasmo** *nm* : enthusiasm — **entusiasta** *adj* : enthusiastic — **~** *nmf* : enthusiast
enumerar *vt* : enumerate, list — **enumeración** *nf, pl* **-ciones** : enumeration, count
enunciar *vt* : enunciate — **enunciación** *nf, pl* **-ciones** : enunciation
envalentonar *vt* : make bold, encourage — **envalentonarse** *vr* : be brave
envanecerse {53} *vr* : become vain
envasar *vt* **1** : package **2** : bottle, can — **envase** *nm* **1** : packaging **2** RECIPIENTE : container **3** : jar, bottle, can
envejecer {53} *v* : age — **envejecido, -da** *adj* : aged, old — **envejecimiento** *nm* : aging
envenenar *vt* : poison — **envenenamiento** *nm* : poisoning
envergadura *nf* **1** ALCANCE : scope **2** : span (of wings, etc.)
envés *nm, pl* **-veses** : reverse side
enviar {85} *vt* : send — **enviado, -da** *n* : envoy, correspondent
envidiar *vt* : envy — **envidia** *nf* : envy,

jealousy — **envidioso, -sa** *adj* : jealous, envious
envilecer {53} *vt* : degrade, debase — **envilecimiento** *nm* : degradation
envío *nm* **1** : sending, shipment **2** : remittance (of funds)
enviudar *vi* : be widowed
envolver {89} *vt* **1** : wrap **2** RODEAR : surround **3** IMPLICAR : involve — **envoltorio** *nm or* **envoltura** *nf* : wrapping, wrapper
enyesar *vt* **1** : plaster **2** ESCAYOLAR : put in a plaster cast
enzima *nf* : enzyme
épico, -ca *adj* : epic — **épica** *nf* : epic
epidemia *nf* : epidemic — **epidémico, -ca** *adj* : epidemic
epilepsia *nf* : epilepsy — **epiléptico, -ca** *adj & n* : epileptic
epílogo *nm* : epilogue
episodio *nm* : episode
epitafio *nm* : epitaph
epíteto *nm* : epithet
época *nf* **1** : epoch, period **2** ESTACIÓN : season
epopeya *nf* : epic poem
equidad *nf* : equity, justice
equilátero, -ra *adj* : equilateral
equilibrar *vt* : balance — **equilibrado, -da** *adj* : well-balanced — **equilibrio** *nm* **1** : balance, equilibrium **2** JUICIO : good sense
equinoccio *nm* : equinox
equipaje *nm* : baggage, luggage
equipar *vt* : equip
equiparar *vt* **1** IGUALAR : make equal **2** COMPARAR : compare — **equiparable** *adj* : comparable
equipo *nm* **1** : equipment **2** : team, crew (in sports, etc.)
equitación *nf, pl* **-ciones** : horseback riding
equitativo, -va *adj* : equitable, fair, just
equivaler {84} *vi* : be equivalent — **equivalencia** *nf* : equivalence — **equivalente** *adj & nm* : equivalent
equivocar {72} *vt* : mistake, confuse — **equivocarse** *vr* : make a mistake — **equivocación** *nf, pl* **-ciones** : error, mistake — **equivocado, -da** *adj* : mistaken, wrong
equívoco, -ca *adj* : ambiguous — **equívoco** *nm* : misunderstanding
era *nf* : era
erario *nm* : public treasury, funds *pl*
erección *nf, pl* **-ciones** : erection
erguir {31} *vt* : raise, lift — **erguirse** *vr* : rise (up) — **erguido, -da** *adj* : erect, upright
erigir {35} *vt* : build, erect — **erigirse** *vr* **~ en** : set oneself up as
erizarse {21} *vr* : bristle, stand on end — **erizado, -da** *adj* : bristly
erizo *nm* **1** : hedgehog **2 ~ de mar** : sea urchin
ermitaño, -ña *n* : hermit
erosionar *vt* : erode — **erosión** *nf, pl* **-siones** : erosion
erótico, -ca *adj* : erotic
erradicar {72} *vt* : eradicate
errar {32} *vt* : miss — *vi* **1** : be wrong, be mistaken **2** VAGAR : wander — **errado, -da** *adj Lat* : wrong, mistaken
errata *nf* : misprint
errático, -ca *adj* : erratic
error *nm* : error — **erróneo, -nea** *adj* : erroneous, mistaken
eructar *vi* : belch, burp — **eructo** *nm* : belch, burp
erudito, -ta *adj* : erudite, learned
erupción *nf, pl* **-ciones 1** : eruption **2** SARPULLIDO : rash
esa, ésa → ese, ése
esbelto, -ta *adj* : slender, slim
esbozar {21} *vt* : sketch, outline — **esbozo** *nm* : sketch, outline
escabechar *vt* : pickle — **escabeche** *nm* : brine (for pickling)
escabel *nm* : footstool
escabroso, -sa *adj* **1** : rugged, rough **2** ESPINOSO : thorny, difficult **3** ATREVIDO : shocking, risqué
escabullirse {38} *vr* : slip away, escape
escalar *vt* : climb, scale — *vi* : escalate — **escala** *nf* **1** : scale **2** ESCALERA : ladder **3** : stopover (of an airplane, etc.) — **escalada** *nf* : ascent, climb — **escalador, -dora** *n* ALPINISTA : mountain climber
escaldar *vt* : scald
escalera *nf* **1** : stairs *pl*, staircase **2** ESCALA : ladder **3 ~ mecánica** : escalator
escalfar *vt* : poach
escalinata *nf* : flight of stairs
escalofrío *nm* : shiver, chill — **escalofriante** *adj* : chilling, horrifying
escalonar *vt* **1** : stagger, spread out **2** : terrace (land) — **escalón** *nm, pl* **-lones** : step, rung
escama *nf* **1** : scale (of fish or reptiles) **2** : flake (of skin) — **escamoso, -sa** *adj* : scaly
escamotear *vt* **1** : conceal **2 ~ algo a algn** : rob s.o. of sth
escandalizar {21} *vt* : scandalize — **escandalizarse** *vr* : be shocked — **escándalo** *nm* **1** : scandal **2** ALBOROTO : scene, commotion — **escandaloso,**

-sa *adj* **1** : shocking, scandalous **2** RUIDOSO : noisy
escandinavo, -va *adj* : Scandinavian
escáner *nm* : scanner
escaño *nm* **1** : seat (in a legislative body) **2** BANCO : bench
escapar *vi* : escape, run away — **escaparse** *vr* **1** : escape **2** : leak out (of gas, water, etc.) — **escapada** *nf* : escape
escaparate *nm* : store window
escapatoria *nf* : loophole, way out
escape *nm* **1** : leak (of gas, water, etc.) **2** : exhaust (from a vehicle)
escarabajo *nm* : beetle
escarbar *vt* **1** : dig, scratch, poke **2** ~ **en** : pry into
escarcha *nf* : frost (on a surface)
escarlata *adj & nf* : scarlet — **escarlatina** *nf* : scarlet fever
escarmentar {55} *vi* : learn one's lesson — **escarmiento** *nm* : lesson, punishment
escarnecer {53} *vt* : ridicule, mock — **escarnio** *nm* : ridicule, mockery
escarola *nf* : escarole, endive
escarpa *nf* : steep slope — **escarpado, -da** *adj* : steep
escasear *vi* : be scarce — **escasez** *nf, pl* **-seces** : shortage, scarcity — **escaso, -sa** *adj* **1** : scarce **2** ~ **de** : short of
escatimar *vt* : be sparing with, skimp on
escayolar *vt* : put in a plaster cast — **escayola** *nf* **1** : plaster (for casts) **2** : plaster cast
escena *nf* **1** : scene **2** ESCENARIO : stage — **escenario** *nm* **1** : setting, scene **2** ESCENA : stage — **escénico, -ca** *adj* : scenic
escepticismo *nm* : skepticism — **escéptico, -ca** *adj* : skeptical — ~ *n* : skeptic
esclarecer {53} *vt* : shed light on, clarify
esclavo, -va *n* : slave — **esclavitud** *nf* : slavery — **esclavizar** {21} *vt* : enslave
esclerosis *nf* ~ **múltiple** : multiple sclerosis
esclusa *nf* : floodgate, lock (of a canal)
escoba *nf* : broom
escocer {14} *vi* : sting
escocés, -cesa *adj, mpl* **-ceses** **1** : Scottish **2** : tartan, plaid — **escocés** *nm, pl* **-ceses** : Scotch (whiskey)
escoger {15} *vt* : choose — **escogido, -da** *adj* : choice, select
escolar *adj* : school — ~ *nmf* : student, pupil
escolta *nmf* : escort — **escoltar** *vt* : escort, accompany
escombros *nmpl* : ruins, rubble
esconder *vt* : hide, conceal — **esconderse** *vr* : hide — **escondidas** *nfpl* **1** *Lat* : hide-and-seek **2** **a** ~ : secretly, in secret — **escondite** *nm* **1** : hiding place **2** : hide-and-seek (game) — **escondrijo** *nm* : hiding place
escopeta *nf* : shotgun
escoplo *nm* : chisel
escoria *nf* **1** : slag **2** : dregs *pl* (of society, etc.)
escorpión *nm, pl* **-piones** : scorpion
escote *nm* **1** : (low) neckline **2** **pagar a** ~ : go Dutch
escotilla *nf* : hatchway
escribir {33} *v* : write — **escribirse** *vr* **1** : write to one another, correspond **2** : be spelled — **escribiente** *nmf* : clerk — **escrito, -ta** *adj* : written — **escritos** *nmpl* : writings — **escritor, -tora** *n* : writer — **escritorio** *nm* : desk — **escritura** *nf* **1** : handwriting **2** : deed (in law)
escroto *nm* : scrotum
escrúpulo *nm* : scruple — **escrupuloso, -sa** *adj* : scrupulous
escrutar *vt* **1** : scrutinize **2** : count (votes) — **escrutinio** *nm* **1** : scrutiny **2** : count (of votes)
escuadra *nf* **1** : square (instrument) **2** : fleet (of ships), squad (in the military) — **escuadrón** *nm, pl* **-drones** : squadron
escuálido, -da *adj* **1** : skinny **2** SUCIO : squalid
escuchar *vt* **1** : listen to **2** *Lat* : hear — *vi* : listen
escudo *nm* **1** : shield **2** *or* ~ **de armas** : coat of arms
escudriñar *vt* : scrutinize, examine
escuela *nf* : school
escueto, -ta *adj* : plain, simple
esculpir *v* : sculpt — **escultor, -tora** *n* : sculptor — **escultura** *nf* : sculpture
escupir *v* : spit
escurrir *vt* **1** : drain **2** : wring out (clothes) — *vi* **1** : drain **2** : drip-dry (of clothes) — **escurrirse** *vr* **1** : drain **2** *fam* : slip away — **escurridizo, -da** *adj* : slippery, evasive — **escurridor** *nm* **1** : dish drainer **2** COLADOR : colander
ese, esa *adj, mpl* **esos** : that, those
ése, ésa *pron, mpl* **ésos** : that one, those ones *pl*
esencia *nf* : essence — **esencial** *adj* : essential

esfera *nf* **1** : sphere **2** : dial (of a watch) — **esférico, -ca** *adj* : spherical
esfinge *nf* : sphinx
esforzar {36} *vt* : strain — **esforzarse** *vr* : make an effort — **esfuerzo** *nm* : effort
esfumarse *vr* : fade away, vanish
esgrimir *vt* **1** : brandish, wield **2** : make use of (an argument, etc.) — **esgrima** *nf* **1** : fencing **2 hacer ~** : fence
esguince *nm* : sprain, strain
eslabonar *vt* : link, connect — **eslabón** *nm, pl* **-bones** : link
eslavo, -va *adj* : Slavic
eslogan *nm, pl* **-lóganes** : slogan
esmaltar *vt* : enamel — **esmalte** *nm* **1** : enamel **2 ~ de uñas** : nail polish
esmerado, -da *adj* : careful
esmeralda *nf* : emerald
esmerarse *vr* : take great care
esmeril *nm* : emery
esmoquin *nm, pl* **-móquines** : tuxedo
esnob *nmf, pl* **esnobs** : snob — **~** *adj* : snobbish
eso *pron* (*neuter*) **1** : that **2 ¡~ es!** : that's it!, that's right! **3 en ~** : at that point, then
esófago *nm* : esophagus
esos, ésos → **ese, ése**
espabilarse *vr* **1** : wake up **2** DARSE PRISA : get moving — **espabilado, -da** *adj* **1** : awake **2** LISTO : bright, clever
espaciar *vt* : space out, spread out — **espacial** *adj* : space — **espacio** *nm* **1** : space **2 ~ exterior** : outer space — **espacioso, -sa** *adj* : spacious
espada *nf* **1** : sword **2 ~s** *nfpl* : spades (in playing cards)
espagueti *nm or* **espaguetis** *nmpl* : spaghetti
espalda *nf* **1** : back **2 ~ s** *nfpl* : shoulders, back
espantar *vt* : scare, frighten — **espantarse** *vr* : become frightened — **espantajo** *nm or* **espantapájaros** *nms & pl* : scarecrow — **espanto** *nm* : fright, fear — **espantoso, -sa** *adj* **1** : frightening, horrific **2** TERRIBLE : awful, terrible
español, -ñola *adj* : Spanish — **español** *nm* : Spanish (language)
esparadrapo *nm* : adhesive bandage
esparcir {83} *vt* : scatter, spread — **esparcirse** *vr* **1** : be scattered, spread out **2** DIVERTIRSE : enjoy oneself
espárrago *nm* : asparagus
espasmo *nm* : spasm — **espasmódico, -ca** *adj* : spasmodic
espátula *nf* : spatula
especia *nf* : spice
especial *adj & nm* : special — **especialidad** *nf* : specialty — **especialista** *nmf* : specialist — **especializarse** {21} *vr* **~ en** : specialize in — **especialmente** *adv* : especially
especie *nf* **1** : species **2** CLASE : type, kind
especificar {72} *vt* : specify — **especificación** *nf, pl* **-ciones** : specification — **específico, -ca** *adj* : specific
espécimen *nm, pl* **especímenes** : specimen
espectáculo *nm* **1** : show, performance **2** VISIÓN : spectacle, view — **espectacular** *adj* : spectacular — **espectador, -dora** *n* : spectator
espectro *nm* **1** : spectrum **2** FANTASMA : ghost
especulación *nf, pl* **-ciones** : speculation
espejo *nm* : mirror — **espejismo** *nm* **1** : mirage **2** ILUSIÓN : illusion
espeluznante *adj* : terrifying, hair-raising
esperar *vt* **1** : wait for **2** CONTAR CON : expect **3 ~ que** : hope (that) — *vi* : wait — **espera** *nf* : wait — **esperanza** *nf* : hope, expectation — **esperanzado, -da** *adj* : hopeful — **esperanzar** {21} *vt* : give hope to
esperma *nmf* **1** : sperm **2 ~ de ballena** : blubber
esperpento *nm* : (grotesque) sight, fright
espesar *vt* : thicken — **espesarse** *vr* : thicken — **espeso, -sa** *adj* : thick, heavy — **espesor** *nm* : thickness, density — **espesura** *nf* **1** ESPESOR : thickness **2** : thicket
espetar *vt* : blurt (out)
espiar {85} *vt* : spy on — *vi* : spy — **espía** *nmf* : spy
espiga *nf* : ear (of wheat, etc.)
espina *nf* **1** : thorn **2** : (fish) bone **3 ~ dorsal** : spine, backbone
espinaca *nf* **1** : spinach (plant) **2 ~s** *nfpl* : spinach (food)
espinazo *nm* : spine, backbone
espinilla *nf* **1** : shin **2** GRANO : blackhead, pimple
espinoso, -sa *adj* **1** : prickly **2** : bony (of fish) **3** : difficult, thorny (of problems, etc.)
espionaje *nm* : espionage
espiral *adj & nf* : spiral
espirar *v* : breathe out, exhale
espíritu *nm* **1** : spirit **2 Espíritu Santo** : Holy Spirit — **espiritual** *adj* : spiritual — **espiritualidad** *nf* : spirituality
espita *nf* : spigot, faucet
espléndido, -da *adj* **1** : splendid **2** GE-

NEROSO : lavish — **esplendor** *nm* : splendor
espliego *nm* : lavender
espolear *vt* : spur on
espoleta *nf* : fuse
espolvorear *vt* : sprinkle, dust
esponja *nf* **1** : sponge **2 tirar la ~** : throw in the towel — **esponjoso, -sa** *adj* : spongy
espontaneidad *nf* : spontaneity — **espontáneo, -nea** *adj* : spontaneous
espora *nf* : spore
esporádico, -ca *adj* : sporadic
esposo, -sa *n* : spouse, wife *f*, husband *m* — **esposar** *vt* : handcuff — **esposas** *nfpl* : handcuffs
esprintar *vi* : sprint (in sports) — **esprint** *nm* : sprint
espuela *nf* : spur
espumar *vt* : skim — **espuma** *nf* **1** : foam, froth **2** : (soap) lather **3** : head (on beer) — **espumoso, -sa** *adj* **1** : foamy, frothy **2** : sparkling (of wine)
esqueleto *nm* : skeleton
esquema *nf* : outline, sketch
esquí *nm* **1** : ski **2** : skiing (sport) **3 ~ acuático** : waterskiing — **esquiador, -dora** *n* : skier — **esquiar** {85} *vi* : ski
esquilar *vt* : shear
esquimal *adj* : Eskimo
esquina *nf* : corner
esquirol *nm* : strikebreaker, scab
esquivar *vt* **1** : evade, dodge (a blow) **2** EVITAR : avoid — **esquivo, -va** *adj* : shy, elusive
esquizofrenia *nf* : schizophrenia — **esquizofrénico, -ca** *adj & n* : schizophrenic
esta, ésta → **este**[1], **éste**
estable *adj* : stable — **estabilidad** *nf* : stability — **estabilizar** {21} *vt* : stabilize
establecer {53} *vt* : establish — **establecerse** *vr* : establish oneself, settle — **establecimiento** *nm* : establishment
establo *nm* : stable
estaca *nf* : stake — **estacada** *nf* **1** : (picket) fence **2 dejar en la ~** : leave in a lurch
estación *nf, pl* **-ciones 1** : season **2 ~ de servicio** : gas station — **estacionar** *v* : park — **estacionamiento** *nm* : parking — **estacionario, -ria** *adj* : stationary
estadía *nf Lat* : stay
estadio *nm* **1** : stadium **2** FASE : phase, stage
estadista *nmf* : statesman
estadística *nf* : statistics — **estadístico, -ca** *adj* : statistical
estado *nm* **1** : state **2 ~ civil** : marital status
estadounidense *adj & nmf* : American (from the United States)
estafar *vt* : swindle, defraud — **estafa** *nf* : swindle, fraud — **estafador, -dora** *n* : cheat, swindler
estallar *vi* **1** : explode **2** : break out (of war, an epidemic, etc.) **3 ~ en llamas** : burst into flames — **estallido** *nm* **1** : explosion **2** : report (of a gun) **3** : outbreak (of war, etc.)
estampar *vt* : stamp, print — **estampa** *nf* **1** : print, illustration **2** ASPECTO : appearance — **estampado, -da** *adj* : printed
estampida *nf* : stampede
estampilla *nf* : stamp
estancarse {72} *vr* **1** : stagnate **2** : come to a halt — **estancado, -da** *adj* : stagnant
estancia *nf* **1** : stay **2** HABITACIÓN : (large) room **3** *Lat* : (cattle) ranch
estanco, -ca *adj* : watertight
estándar *adj & nm* : standard — **estandarizar** {21} *vt* : standardize
estandarte *nm* : standard, banner
estanque *nm* **1** : pool, pond **2** : reservoir (for irrigation)
estante *nm* : shelf — **estantería** *nf* : shelves *pl*, bookcase
estaño *nm* : tin
estar {34} *v aux* : be — *vi* **1** : be **2** : be at home **3** QUEDARSE : stay, remain **4 ¿cómo estás?** : how are you? **5 ~ a** : cost **6 ~ bien (mal)** : be well (sick) **7 ~ para** : be in the mood for **8 ~ por** : be in favor of **9 ~ por** : be about to — **estarse** *vr* : stay, remain
estarcir {83} *vt* : stencil
estárter *nm* : choke (of an automobile)
estatal *adj* : state, national
estático, -ca *adj* **1** : static **2** INMÓVIL : unmoving, still — **estática** *nf* : static
estatua *nf* : statue
estatura *nf* : height
estatus *nm* : status, prestige
estatuto *nm* : statute — **estatutario, -ria** *adj* : statutory
este[1], **esta** *adj, mpl* **estos** : this, these
este[2] *adj* : eastern, east — **este** *nm* **1** : east **2** : east wind **3 el Este** : the Orient
éste, ésta *pron, mpl* **éstos 1** : this one, these ones *pl* **2** : the latter
estela *nf* **1** : wake (of a ship) **2** : trail (of smoke, etc.)
estera *nf* : mat
estéreo *adj & nm* : stereo — **estereofónico, -ca** *adj* : stereophonic

estereotipo *nm* : stereotype
estéril *adj* **1** : sterile **2** : infertile — **esterilidad** *nf* **1** : sterility **2** : infertility — **esterilizar** {21} *vt* : sterilize
estética *nf* : aesthetics — **estético, -ca** *adj* : aesthetic
estiércol *nm* : dung, manure
estigma *nm* : stigma — **estigmatizar** {21} *vt* : stigmatize
estilarse {21} *vr* : be in fashion
estilo *nm* **1** : style **2** MANERA : fashion, manner — **estilista** *nmf* : stylist
estima *nf* : esteem, regard — **estimación** *nf, pl* **-ciones 1** : esteem **2** VALORACIÓN : estimate — **estimado, -da** *adj* **Estimado señor** : Dear Sir — **estimar** *vt* **1** : esteem, respect **2** VALORAR : value, estimate **3** CONSIDERAR : consider
estimular *vt* **1** : stimulate **2** ALENTAR : encourage — **estimulante** *adj* : stimulating — **~** *nm* : stimulant — **estímulo** *nm* : stimulus
estío *nm* : summertime
estipular *vt* : stipulate
estirar *vt* : stretch (out), extend — **estirado, -da** *adj* **1** : stretched, extended **2** ALTANERO : stuck-up, haughty — **estiramiento** *nm* **~ facial** : face-lift — **estirón** *nm, pl* **-rones** : pull, tug
estirpe *nf* : lineage, stock
estival *adj* : summer
esto *pron* (*neuter*) **1** : this **2 en ~** : at this point **3 por ~** : for this reason
estofa *nf* **1** : class, quality **2 de baja ~** : low-class
estofar *vt* : stew — **estofado** *nm* : stew
estoicismo *nm* : stoicism — **estoico, -ca** *adj* : stoic, stoical — **~** *n* : stoic
estómago *nm* : stomach — **estomacal** *adj* : stomach
estorbar *vt* : obstruct — *vi* : get in the way — **estorbo** *nm* **1** : obstacle **2** MOLESTIA : nuisance
estornino *nm* : starling
estornudar *vi* : sneeze — **estornudo** *nm* : sneeze
estos, éstos → **este, éste**
estrabismo *nm* : squint
estrado *nm* : platform, stage
estrafalario, -ria *adj* : eccentric, bizarre
estragar {52} *vt* : devastate — **estragos** *nmpl* **1** : ravages **2 hacer ~ en** *or* **causar ~ entre** : wreak havoc with
estragón *nm* : tarragon
estrangular *vt* : strangle — **estrangulación** *nf* : strangulation
estratagema *nf* : stratagem
estrategia *nf* : strategy — **estratégico, -ca** *adj* : strategic
estrato *nm* : stratum
estratosfera *nf* : stratosphere
estrechar *vt* **1** : narrow **2** : strengthen (a bond) **3** ABRAZAR : embrace **4 ~ la mano a uno** : shake s.o.'s hand — **estrecharse** *vr* : narrow — **estrechez** *nf, pl* **-checes 1** : narrowness **2 estrecheces** *nfpl* : financial problems — **estrecho, -cha** *adj* **1** : tight, narrow **2** ÍNTIMO : close — **estrecho** *nm* : strait
estrella *nf* **1** : star **2** DESTINO : destiny **3 ~ de mar** : starfish — **estrellado, -da** *adj* **1** : starry **2** : star-shaped
estrellar *v* : crash — **estrellarse** *vr* **~ contre** : smash into
estremecer {53} *vt* : cause to shudder — *vi* : tremble, shake — **estremecerse** *vr* : shudder, shiver (with emotion) — **estremecimiento** *nm* : shaking, shivering
estrenar *vt* **1** : use for the first time **2** : premiere, open (a film, etc.) — **estrenarse** *vr* : make one's debut — **estreno** *nm* : debut, premiere
estreñirse {67} *vr* : be constipated — **estreñimiento** *nm* : constipation
estrépito *nm* : clamor, din — **estrepitoso, -sa** *adj* : noisy, clamorous
estrés *nm, pl* **estreses** : stress — **estresante** *adj* : stressful — **estresar** *vt* : stress (out)
estría *nf* : groove
estribaciones *nfpl* : foothills
estribar *vi* **~ en** : stem from, lie in
estribillo *nm* : refrain, chorus
estribo *nm* **1** : stirrup **2** : running board (of a vehicle) **3** CONTRAFUERTE : buttress **4 perder los ~s** : lose one's temper
estribor *nm* : starboard
estricto, -ta *adj* : strict
estridente *adj* : strident, shrill
estrofa *nf* : stanza, verse
estropajo *nm* : scouring pad
estropear *vt* **1** : ruin, spoil **2** DAÑAR : damage — **estropearse** *vr* **1** : go bad **2** AVERIARSE : break down — **estropicio** *nm* : damage, havoc
estructura *nf* : structure — **estructural** *adj* : structural
estruendo *nm* : din, roar — **estruendoso, -sa** *adj* : thunderous
estrujar *vt* : squeeze
estuario *nm* : estuary
estuche *nm* : kit, case
estuco *nm* : stucco
estudiar *v* : study — **estudiante** *nmf* : student — **estudiantil** *adj* : student — **estudio** *nm* **1** : study **2** OFICINA

: studio, office 3 **~s** *nmpl* : studies, education — **estudioso, -sa** *adj* : studious

estufa *nf* : stove, heater

estupefaciente *adj & nm* : narcotic — **estupefacto, -ta** *adj* : astonished

estupendo, -da *adj* : stupendous, marvelous

estúpido, -da *adj* : stupid — **estupidez** *nf, pl* **-deces** : stupidity

estupor *nm* **1** : stupor **2** ASOMBRO : amazement

etapa *nf* : stage, phase

etcétera : et cetera, and so on

éter *nm* : ether

etéreo, -rea *adj* : ethereal

eterno, -na *adj* : eternal — **eternidad** *nf* : eternity — **eternizarse** {21} *vr* : take forever

ética *nf* : ethics — **ético, -ca** *adj* : ethical

etimología *nf* : etymology

etíope *adj* : Ethiopian

etiqueta *nf* **1** : tag, label **2** PROTOCOLO : etiquette **3 de ~** : formal, dressy — **etiquetar** *vt* : label

étnico, -ca *adj* : ethnic

eucalipto *nm* : eucalyptus

Eucaristía *nf* : Eucharist, communion

eufemismo *nm* : euphemism — **eufemístico, -ca** *adj* : euphemistic

euforia *nf* : euphoria — **eufórico, -ca** *adj* : euphoric

europeo, -pea *adj* : European

eutanasia *nf* : euthanasia

evacuar *vt* : evacuate, vacate — *vi* : have a bowel movement — **evacuación** *nf, pl* **-ciones** : evacuation

evadir *vt* : evade, avoid — **evadirse** *vr* : escape

evaluar {3} *vt* : evaluate — **evaluación** *nf, pl* **-ciones** : evaluation

evangelio *nm* : gospel — **evangélico, -ca** *adj* : evangelical — **evangelismo** *nm* : evangelism

evaporar *vt* : evaporate — **evaporarse** *vr* : evaporate, disappear — **evaporación** *nf, pl* **-ciones** : evaporation

evasión *nf, pl* **-siones 1** : evasion **2** FUGA : escape — **evasiva** *nf* : excuse, pretext — **evasivo, -va** *adj* : evasive

evento *nm* : event

eventual *adj* **1** : temporary **2** POSIBLE : possible — **eventualidad** *nf* : possibility, eventuality

evidencia *nf* **1** : evidence, proof **2 poner en ~** : demonstrate — **evidenciar** *vt* : demonstrate, show — **evidente** *adj* : evident — **evidentemente** *adj* : evidently, apparently

evitar *vt* **1** : avoid **2** IMPEDIR : prevent — **evitable** *adj* : avoidable

evocar {72} *vt* : evoke

evolución *nf, pl* **-ciones** : evolution — **evolucionar** *vi* : evolve

exacerbar *vt* **1** : exacerbate **2** IRRITAR : irritate

exacto, -ta *adj* : precise, exact — **exactamente** *adv* : exactly — **exactitud** *nf* : precision, accuracy

exagerar *v* : exaggerate — **exageración** *nf, pl* **-ciones** : exaggeration — **exagerado, -da** *adj* : exaggerated

exaltar *vt* **1** : exalt, extol **2** EXCITAR : excite, arouse — **exaltarse** *vr* : get worked-up — **exaltado, -da** *adj* : worked up, hotheaded

examen *nm, pl* **exámenes 1** : examination, test **2** ANÁLISIS : investigation — **examinar** *vt* **1** : examine **2** ESTUDIAR : study, inspect — **examinarse** *vr* : take an exam

exánime *adj* : lifeless

exasperar *vt* : exasperate, irritate — **exasperación** *nf, pl* **-ciones** : exasperation

excavar *v* : excavate — **excavación** *nf, pl* **-ciones** : excavation

exceder *vt* : exceed, surpass — **excederse** *vr* : go too far — **excedente** *adj & nm* : surplus, excess

excelente *adj* : excellent — **excelencia** *nf* **1** : excellence **2 Su Excelencia** : His/Her Excellency

excéntrico, -ca *adj & n* : eccentric — **excentricidad** *nf* : eccentricity

excepción *nf, pl* **-ciones** : exception — **excepcional** *adj* : exceptional

excepto *prep* : except (for) — **exceptuar** {3} *vt* : exclude, except

exceso *nm* **1** : excess **2 ~ de velocidad** : speeding — **excesivo, -va** *adj* : excessive

excitar *vt* : excite, arouse — **excitarse** *vr* : get excited — **excitable** *adj* : excitable — **excitación** *nf, pl* **-ciones** : excitement, agitation, arousal — **excitante** *adj* : exciting

exclamar *v* : exclaim — **exclamación** *nf, pl* **-ciones** : exclamation

excluir {41} *vt* : exclude — **exclusión** *nf, pl* **-siones** : exclusion — **exclusivo, -va** *adj* : exclusive

excomulgar {52} *vt* : excommunicate — **excomunión** *nf, pl* **-niones** : excommunication

excremento *nm* : excrement

exculpar *vt* : exonerate

excursión *nf, pl* **-siones** : excursion —

excursionista *nmf* **1 :** tourist, sightseer **2 :** hiker
excusar *vt* **1 :** excuse **2** EXIMIR **:** exempt — **excusarse** *vr* **:** apologize — **excusa** *nf* **1 :** excuse **2** DISCULPA **:** apology
exento, -ta *adj* **:** exempt
exequias *nfpl* **:** funeral rites
exhalar *vt* **1 :** exhale **2 :** give off (an odor, etc.)
exhaustivo, -va *adj* **:** exhaustive — **exhausto, -ta** *adj* **:** exhausted, worn-out
exhibir *vt* **:** exhibit, show — **exhibición** *nf, pl* **-ciones :** exhibition
exhortar *vt* **:** exhort, admonish
exigir {35} *vt* **:** demand, require — **exigencia** *nf* **:** demand, requirement — **exigente** *adj* **:** demanding
exiguo, -gua *adj* **:** meager
exiliar *vt* **:** exile — **exiliarse** *vr* **:** go into exile — **exiliado, -da** *adj* **:** exiled, in exile — **~** *n* **:** exile — **exilio** *nm* **:** exile
eximir *vt* **:** exempt
existir *vi* **:** exist — **existencia** *nf* **1 :** existence **2 ~s** *nfpl* MERCANCÍA **:** goods, stock — **existente** *adj* **:** existing
éxito *nm* **1 :** success, hit **2 tener ~ :** be successful — **exitoso, -sa** *adj Lat* **:** successful
éxodo *nm* **:** exodus
exorbitante *adj* **:** exorbitant
exorcizar {21} *vt* **:** exorcize — **exorcismo** *nm* **:** exorcism
exótico, -ca *adj* **:** exotic
expandir *vt* **:** expand — **expandirse** *vr* **:** spread — **expansión** *nf, pl* **-siones :** expansion — **expansivo, -va** *adj* **:** expansive
expatriarse {85} *vr* **1 :** emigrate **2** EXILIARSE **:** go into exile — **expatriado, -da** *adj & n* **:** expatriate
expectativa *nf* **1 :** expectation, hope **2 ~s** *nfpl* **:** prospects
expedición *nf, pl* **-ciones :** expedition
expediente *nm* **1 :** expedient **2** DOCUMENTOS **:** file, record **3** INVESTIGACIÓN **:** inquiry, proceedings
expedir {54} *vt* **1 :** issue **2** ENVIAR **:** dispatch — **expedito, -ta** *adj* **:** free, clear
expeler *vt* **:** expel, eject
expendedor, -dora *n* **:** dealer, seller
expensas *nfpl* **1 :** expenses **2 a ~ de :** at the expense of
experiencia *nf* **:** experience
experimentar *vi* **:** experiment — *vt* **1 :** experiment with, test out **2** SENTIR **:** experience, feel — **experimentado, -da** *adj* **:** experienced — **experimental** *adj* **:** experimental — **experimento** *nm* **:** experiment
experto, -ta *adj & n* **:** expert
expiar {85} *vt* **:** atone for
expirar *vi* **1 :** expire **2** MORIR **:** die
explayar *vt* **:** extend — **explayarse** *vr* **1 :** spread out **2** HABLAR **:** speak at length
explicar {72} *vt* **:** explain — **explicarse** *vr* **:** understand — **explicación** *nf, pl* **-ciones :** explanation — **explicativo, -va** *adj* **:** explanatory
explícito, -ta *adj* **:** explicit
explorar *vt* **:** explore — **exploración** *nf, pl* **-ciones :** exploration — **explorador, -dora** *n* **:** explorer, scout — **exploratorio, -ria** *adj* **:** exploratory
explosión *nf, pl* **-siones 1 :** explosion **2 :** outburst (of anger, laughter, etc.) — **explosivo, -va** *adj* **:** explosive — **explosivo** *nm* **:** explosive
explotar *vt* **1 :** exploit **2 :** operate, run (a factory, etc.), work (a mine) — *vi* **:** explode — **explotación** *nf, pl* **-ciones 1 :** exploitation **2 :** running (of a business), working (of a mine)
exponer {60} *vt* **1 :** expose **2 :** explain, set out (ideas, theories, etc.) **3** EXHIBIR **:** exhibit, display — *vi* **:** exhibit — **exponerse** *vr* **~ a :** expose oneself to
exportar *vt* **:** export — **exportaciones** *nfpl* **:** exports — **exportador, -dora** *n* **:** exporter
exposición *nf, pl* **-ciones 1 :** exposure **2 :** exhibition (of objects, art, etc.) **3 :** exposition, setting out (of ideas, etc.) — **expositor, -tora** *n* **1 :** exhibitor **2 :** exponent (of a theory, etc.)
exprés *nms & pl* **1 :** express (train) **2** *or* **café ~ :** espresso
expresamente *adv* **:** expressly, on purpose
expresar *vt* **:** express — **expresarse** *vr* **:** express oneself — **expresión** *nf, pl* **-siones :** expression — **expresivo, -va** *adj* **1 :** expressive **2** CARIÑOSO **:** affectionate
expreso, -sa *adj* **:** express — **expreso** *nm* **:** express train, express
exprimir *vt* **1 :** squeeze **2** EXPLOTAR **:** exploit — **exprimidor** *nm* **:** squeezer, juicer
expuesto, -ta *adj* **1 :** exposed **2** PELIGROSO **:** risky, dangerous
expulsar *vt* **:** expel, eject — **expulsión** *nf, pl* **-siones :** expulsion
exquisito, -ta *adj* **1 :** exquisite **2** RICO **:** delicious — **exquisitez** *nf* **1 :** exquisiteness **2 :** delicacy, special dish
éxtasis *nms & pl* **:** ecstasy — **extático, -ta** *adj* **:** ecstatic
extender {56} *vt* **1 :** spread out **2 :** draw up (a document), write out (a check)

— **extenderse** *vr* **1** : extend, spread **2** DURAR : last — **extendido, -da** *adj* **1** : widespread **2** : outstretched (of arms, wings, etc.)
extensamente *adv* : extensively
extensión *nf, pl* **-siones 1** : extension **2** AMPLITUD : expanse **3** ALCANCE : range, extent — **extenso, -sa** *adj* : extensive
extenuar {3} *vt* : exhaust, tire out
exterior *adj* **1** : exterior, external **2** EXTRANJERO : foreign — **~** *nm* **1** : outside **2 en el ~** : abroad — **exteriorizar** {21} *vt* : show, reveal — **exteriormente** *adv* : outwardly, externally
exterminar *vt* : exterminate — **exterminación** *nf, pl* **-ciones** : extermination — **exterminio** *nm* : extermination
externo, -na *adj* : external
extinguir {26} *vt* **1** : extinguish (a fire) **2** : put an end to, wipe out — **extinguirse** *vr* **1** : go out (of fire, light, etc.) **2** : become extinct — **extinción** *nf, pl* **-ciones** : extinction — **extinguidor** *nm Lat* : fire extinguisher — **extinto, -ta** *adj* : extinct — **extintor** *nm* : fire extinguisher
extirpar *vt* : remove, eradicate
extorsión *nf, pl* **-siones 1** : extortion **2** MOLESTIA : trouble
extra *adv* : extra — **~** *adj* **1** ADICIONAL : additional **2** : top-quality — **~** *nmf* : extra (in movies) — **~** *nm* : extra (expense)
extraditar *vt* : extradite
extraer {81} *vt* : extract — **extracción** *nf, pl* **-ciones** : extraction — **extracto** *nm* **1** : extract **2** RESUMEN : abstract, summary
extranjero, -ra *adj* : foreign — **~** *n* : foreigner — **extranjero** *nm* : foreign countries *pl*
extrañar *vt* : miss (someone) — **extrañarse** *vr* : be surprised — **extrañeza** *nf* : surprise — **extraño, -ña** *adj* **1** : foreign **2** RARO : strange, odd — **~** *n* : stranger
extraoficial *adj* : unofficial
extraordinario, -ria *adj* : extraordinary
extrasensorial *adj* : extrasensory
extraterrestre *adj & nmf* : extraterrestrial
extravagante *adj* : extravagant, outrageous — **extravagancia** *nf* : extravagance, outlandishness
extraviar {85} *vt* : lose, misplace — **extraviarse** *vr* : get lost — **extravío** *nm* : loss
extremar *vt* : carry to extremes — **extremarse** *vr* : do one's utmost — **extremadamente** *adv* : extremely — **extremado, -da** *adj* : extreme — **extremidad** *nf* **1** : tip, end **2 ~es** *nfpl* : extremities — **extremista** *adj & nmf* : extremist — **extremo, -ma** *adj* **1** : extreme **2 en caso ~** : as a last resort — **extremo** *nm* **1** : end **2 en ~** : in the extreme, extremely **3 en ultimo ~** : as a last resort
extrovertido -da *adj* : extroverted — **~** *n* : extrovert
exuberante *adj* : exuberant — **exuberancia** *nf* : exuberance
exudar *vt* : exude
eyacular *vi* : ejaculate — **eyaculación** *nf, pl* **-ciones** : ejaculation

F

f *nf* : f, sixth letter of the Spanish alphabet
fabricar {72} *vt* **1** : manufacture **2** CONSTRUIR : build, construct **3** INVENTAR : fabricate — **fábrica** *nf* : factory — **fabricación** *nf, pl* **-ciones** : manufacture — **fabricante** *nmf* : manufacturer
fábula *nf* **1** : fable **2** MENTIRA : story, lie
fabuloso, -sa *adj* : fabulous
facción *nf, pl* **-ciones 1** : faction **2 ~es** *nfpl* RASGOS : features
faceta *nf* : facet
facha *nf* : appearance, look
fachada *nf* : façade
facial *adj* : facial
fácil *adj* **1** : easy **2** PROBABLE : likely — **facilemente** *adv* : easily, readily —
facilidad *nf* **1** : facility, ease **2 ~es** *nfpl* : facilities, services — **facilitar** *vt* **1** : facilitate **2** PROPORCIONAR : provide, supply
facsímil *or* **facsímile** *nm* **1** COPIA : facsimile, copy **2** : fax
factible *adj* : feasible
factor *nm* : factor
factoría *nf* : factory
factura *nf* **1** : bill, invoice **2** HECHURA : making, manufacture — **facturar** *vt* **1** : bill for **2** : check in (baggage, etc.)
facultad *nf* **1** : faculty, ability **2** AUTORIDAD : authority **3** : school (of a university) — **facultativo, -va** *adj* : optional
faena *nf* **1** : task, job **2 ~s domésticas** : housework

fagot *nm* : bassoon
faisán *nm, pl* **-sanes** : pheasant
faja *nf* **1** : sash **2** : girdle, corset **3** : strip (of land)
fajo *nm* : bundle, sheaf
falda *nf* **1** : skirt **2** : side, slope (of a mountain)
falible *adj* : fallible
fálico, -ca *adj* : phallic
fallar *vi* : fail, go wrong — *vt* **1** : pronounce judgment on **2** ERRAR : miss — **falla** *nf* **1** : flaw, defect **2** : (geological) fault
fallecer {53} *vi* : pass away, die — **fallecimiento** *nm* : demise, death
fallido, -da *adj* : failed, unsuccessful
fallo *nm* **1** : error **2** SENTENCIA : sentence, verdict
falo *nm* : phallus, penis
falsear *vt* : falsify, distort — **falsedad** *nf* **1** : falseness **2** MENTIRA : falsehood, lie — **falsificación** *nf, pl* **-ciones** : forgery, fake — **falsificador, -dora** *n* : forger — **falsificar** {72} *vt* **1** : counterfeit, forge **2** ALTERAR : falsify — **falso, -sa** *adj* **1** : false, untrue **2** FALSIFICADO : counterfeit, forged
falta *nf* **1** CARENCIA : lack **2** DEFECTO : defect, fault, error **3** AUSENCIA : absence **4** : offense, misdemeanor (in law) **5** : foul (in sports) **6 hacer ~** : be lacking, be needed **7 sin ~** : without fail — **faltar** *vi* **1** : be lacking, be needed **2** : be missing **3** QUEDAR : remain, be left **4 ¡no faltaba más!** : don't mention it! — **falto, -ta** *adj* **~ de** : lacking (in)
fama *nf* **1** : fame **2** REPUTACIÓN : reputation
famélico, -ca *adj* : starving
familia *nf* : family — **familiar** *adj* **1** : familial, family **2** CONOCIDO : familiar **3** : informal (of language, etc.) — **~** *nmf* : relation, relative — **familiaridad** *nf* : familiarity — **familiarizarse** {21} *vr* **~ con** : familiarize oneself with
famoso, -sa *adj* : famous
fanático, -ca *adj* : fanatic, fanatical — **~** *n* : fanatic — **fanatismo** *nm* : fanaticism
fanfarria *nf* : fanfare
fanfarrón, -rrona *adj, mpl* **-rrones** *fam* : boastful — **~** *n fam* : braggart — **fanfarronear** *vi* : boast, brag
fango *nm* : mud, mire — **fangoso, -sa** *adj* : muddy
fantasear *vi* : fantasize, daydream — **fantasía** *nf* **1** : fantasy **2** IMAGINACIÓN : imagination
fantasma *nm* : ghost, phantom — **fantasmal** *adj* : ghostly
fantástico, -ca *adj* : fantastic
fardo *nm* : bundle
farfullar *v* : jabber, gabble
farmacéutico, -ca *adj* : pharmaceutical — **~** *n* : pharmacist — **farmacia** *nf* : drugstore, pharmacy
faro *nm* **1** : lighthouse **2** : headlight (of an automobile) — **farol** *nm* **1** LINTERNA : lantern **2** FAROLA : streetlight — **farola** *nf* **1** : lamppost **2** FAROL : streetlight
farsa *nf* : farce — **farsante** *nmf* : charlatan, fraud
fascículo *nm* : installment, part (of a publication)
fascinar *vt* : fascinate — **fascinación** *nf, pl* **-ciones** : fascination — **fascinante** *adj* : fascinating
fascismo *nm* : fascism — **fascista** *adj & nmf* : fascist
fase *nf* : phase
fastidiar *vt* : annoy, bother — *vi* : be annoying or bothersome — **fastidio** *nm* : annoyance — **fastidioso, -sa** *adj* : annoying, bothersome
fatal *adj* **1** : fateful **2** MORTAL : fatal **3** *fam* : awful, terrible — **fatalidad** *nf* **1** : fate, destiny **2** DESGRACIA : misfortune
fatídico, -ca *adj* : fateful, momentous
fatiga *nf* : fatigue — **fatigado, -da** *adj* : weary, tired — **fatigar** {52} *vt* : tire — **fatigarse** *vr* : get tired — **fatigoso, -sa** *adj* : fatiguing, tiring
fatuo, -tua *adj* **1** : fatuous **2** PRESUMIDO : conceited
fauna *nf* : fauna
favor *nm* **1** : favor **2 a ~ de** : in favor of **3 por ~** : please — **favorable** *adj* **1** : favorable **2 ser ~ a** : be in favor of — **favorecedor, -dora** *adj* : flattering — **favorecer** {53} *vt* **1** AYUDAR : favor **2** : look well on, suit — **favoritismo** *nm* : favoritism — **favorito, -ta** *adj & n* : favorite
fax *nm* : fax — **faxear** *vt* : fax
faz *nf, pl* **faces** : face, countenance
fe *nf* **1** : faith **2 dar ~ de** : bear witness to **3 de buena ~** : in good faith
fealdad *nf* : ugliness
febrero *nm* : February
febril *adj* : feverish
fecha *nf* **1** : date **2 ~ de caducidad** *or* **~ de vencimiento** : expiration date **3 ~ límite** : deadline — **fechar** *vt* : date, put a date on
fechoría *nf* : misdeed
fécula *nf* : starch (in food)
fecundar *vt* **1** : fertilize (an egg) **2** : make fertile — **fecundo, -da** *adj* : fertile

federación *nf, pl* **-ciones** : federation — **federal** *adj* : federal
felicidad *nf* **1** : happiness **2** **¡∼es!** : best wishes!, congratulations!, happy birthday! — **felicitación** *nf, pl* **-ciones** : congratulation — **felicitar** *vt* : congratulate — **felicitarse** *vr* **∼ de** : be glad about
feligrés, -gresa *n, mpl* **-greses** : parishioner
felino, -na *adj & n* : feline
feliz *adj, pl* **-lices** **1** : happy **2** AFORTUNADO : fortunate **3** **Feliz Navidad** : Merry Christmas
felpa *nf* **1** : plush **2** : terry cloth (for towels, etc.)
felpudo *nm* : doormat
femenino, -na *adj* **1** : feminine **2** : female (in biology) — **femenino** *nm* : feminine (in grammar) — **femineidad** *nf* : femininity — **feminismo** *nm* : feminism — **feminista** *adj & nmf* : feminist
fenómeno *nm* : phenomenon — **fenomenal** *adj* **1** : phenomenal **2** *fam* : fantastic, terrific
feo, fea *adj* **1** : ugly **2** DESAGRADABLE : unpleasant, nasty
féretro *nm* : coffin
feria *nf* **1** : fair, market **2** FIESTA : festival, holiday **3** *Lat fam* : small change — **feriado, -da** *adj* **día feriado** : public holiday
fermentar *v* : ferment — **fermentación** *nf, pl* **-ciones** : fermentation — **fermento** *nm* : ferment
feroz *adj, pl* **-roces** : ferocious, fierce — **ferocidad** *nf* : ferocity, fierceness
férreo, -rrea *adj* **1** : iron **2** **vía férrea** : railroad track
ferretería *nf* : hardware store
ferrocarril *nm* : railroad, railway — **ferroviario, -ria** *adj* : rail, railroad
ferry *nm, pl* **ferrys** : ferry
fértil *adj* : fertile, fruitful — **fertilidad** *nf* : fertility — **fertilizante** *nm* : fertilizer — **fertilizar** *vt* : fertilize
fervor *nm* : fervor, zeal — **ferviente** *adj* : fervent
festejar *vt* **1** : celebrate **2** AGASAJAR : entertain, wine and dine — **festejo** *nm* : celebration, festivity
festín *nm, pl* **-tines** : banquet, feast
festival *nm* : festival — **festividad** *nf* : festivity — **festivo, -va** *adj* **1** : festive **2** **día festivo** : holiday
fetiche *nm* : fetish
fétido, -da *adj* : foul-smelling, fetid
feto *nm* : fetus — **fetal** *adj* : fetal
feudal *adj* : feudal
fiable *adj* : reliable — **fiabilidad** *nf* : reliability
fiado, -da *adj* : on credit — **fiador, -dora** *n* : bondsman, guarantor
fiambres *nfpl* : cold cuts
fianza *nf* **1** : bail, bond **2** **dar ∼** : pay a deposit
fiar {85} *vt* **1** : guarantee **2** : sell on credit — *vi* **ser de ∼** : be trustworthy — **fiarse** *vr* **∼ de** : place trust in
fiasco *nm* : fiasco
fibra *nf* **1** : fiber **2** **∼ de vidrio** : fiberglass
ficción *nf, pl* **-ciones** : fiction
ficha *nf* **1** : token **2** TARJETA : index card **3** : counter, chip (in games) — **fichar** *vt* : file, index — **fichero** *nm* **1** : card file **2** : filing cabinet
ficticio, -cia *adj* : fictitious
fidedigno, -na *adj* : reliable, trustworthy
fidelidad *nf* : fidelity, faithfulness
fideo *nm* : noodle
fiebre *nf* **1** : fever **2** **∼ del heno** : hay fever **3** **∼ palúdica** : malaria
fiel *adj* **1** : faithful, loyal **2** PRECISO : accurate, reliable — **∼** *nm* **1** : pointer (of a scale) **2** **los ∼es** : the faithful — **fielmente** *adv* : faithfully
fieltro *nm* : felt
fiero, -ra *adj* : fierce, ferocious — **fiera** *nf* : wild animal, beast
fierro *nm Lat* : iron (bar)
fiesta *nf* **1** : party **2** DIA FESTIVO : holiday, feast day
figura *nf* **1** : figure **2** FORMA : shape, form — **figurar** *vi* **1** : figure (in), be included (among) **2** DESTACAR : stand out — *vt* : represent — **figurarse** *vr* : imagine
fijar *vt* **1** : fasten, affix **2** CONCRETAR : set, fix — **fijarse** *vr* **1** : settle **2** **∼ en** : notice, pay attention to — **fijo, -ja** *adj* **1** : fixed, firm **2** PERMANENTE : permanent
fila *nf* **1** : line, file, row **2** **ponerse en ∼** : line up
filantropía *nf* : philanthropy — **filantrópico, -ca** *adj* : philanthropic — **filántropo, -pa** *n* : philanthropist
filatelia *nf* : philately, stamp collecting
filete *nm* : fillet
filial *adj* : filial — **∼** *nf* : affiliate, subsidiary
filigrana *nf* **1** : filigree **2** : watermark (on paper)
filipino, -na *adj* : Filipino
filmar *vt* : film, shoot — **filme** *or* **film** *nm* : film, movie
filo *nm* **1** : edge **2** **dar ∼ a** : sharpen
filón *nm, pl* **-lones** **1** : vein (of minerals) **2** *fam* : gold mine
filoso, -sa *adj Lat* : sharp

filosofía *nf* : philosophy — **filosófico, -ca** *adj* : philosophical — **filósofo, -fa** *n* : philosopher
filtrar *v* : filter — **filtrarse** *vr* : leak out, seep through — **filtro** *nm* : filter
fin *nm* **1** : end **2** OBJETIVO : purpose, aim **3 en ~** : well, in short **4 ~ de semana** : weekend **5 por ~** : finally, at last
final *adj* : final — **~** *nm* : end, conclusion — **~** *nf* : final (in sports) — **finalidad** *nf* : purpose, aim — **finalista** *nmf* : finalist — **finalizar** {21} *v* : finish, end — **finalmente** *adv* : finally
financiar *vt* : finance, fund — **financiero, -ra** *adj* : financial — **~** *n* : financier — **finanzas** *nfpl* : finance
finca *nf* **1** : farm, ranch **2** *Lat* : country house
fingir {35} *v* : feign, pretend — **fingido, -da** *adj* : false, feigned
finito, -ta *adj* : finite
finlandés, -desa *adj* : Finnish
fino, -na *adj* **1** : fine **2** DELGADO : slender **3** REFINADO : refined **4** AGUDO : sharp, keen — **finura** *nf* **1** : fineness **2** REFINAMIENTO : refinement
firma *nf* **1** : signature **2** : (act of) signing **3** EMPRESA : firm, company
firmamento *nm* : firmament, sky
firmar *v* : sign
firme *adj* **1** : firm, resolute **2** ESTABLE : steady, stable — **firmeza** *nf* **1** : strength, resolve **2** ESTABILIDAD : firmness, stability
fiscal *adj* : fiscal — **~** *nmf* : district attorney — **fisco** *nm* : (national) treasury
fisgar {52} *vt* : pry into — *vi* : pry — **fisgón, -gona** *n, mpl* **-gones** : snoop, busybody
física *nf* : physics — **físico, -ca** *adj* : physical — **~** *n* : physicist — **físico** *nm* : physique
fisiología *nf* : physiology — **fisiológico, -ca** *adj* : physiological — **fisiólogo, -ga** *n* : physiologist
fisioterapia *nf* : physical therapy — **fisioterapeuta** *nmf* : physical therapist
fisonomía *nf* : features *pl,* appearance
fisura *nf* : fissure
fláccido, -da *or* **flácido, -da** *adj* : flaccid, flabby
flaco, -ca *adj* **1** : thin, skinny **2** DÉBIL : weak
flagrante *adj* : flagrant
flamante *adj* **1** : bright, brilliant **2** NUEVO : brand-new
flamenco, -ca *adj* **1** : flamenco (of music or dance) **2** : Flemish — **flamenco** *nm* **1** : flamingo **2** : flamenco (music or dance)
flaquear *vi* : weaken, flag — **flaqueza** *nf* **1** : thinness **2** DEBILIDAD : weakness
flash *nm* : flash
flatulencia *nf* : flatulence
flauta *nf* **1** : flute **2 ~ dulce** : recorder — **flautín** *nm, pl* **-tines** : piccolo — **flautista** *nmf* : flutist
flecha *nf* : arrow
fleco *nm* **1** : fringe **2** *Lat* : bangs *pl*
flema *nf* : phlegm — **flemático, -ca** *adj* : phlegmatic
flequillo *nm* : bangs *pl*
fletar *vt* **1** : charter, rent **2** *Lat* : transport — **flete** *nm* **1** : charter **2** : shipping (charges) **3** *Lat* : transport, freight
flexible *adj* : flexible — **flexibilidad** *nf* : flexibility
flirtear *vi* : flirt
flojo, -ja *adj* **1** SUELTO : loose, slack **2** DÉBIL : weak **3** PEREZOSO : lazy — **flojera** *nf fam* : lethargy
flor *nf* : flower — **flora** *nf* : flora — **floral** *adj* : floral — **floreado, -da** *adj* : flowered — **florear** *vi Lat* : flower, bloom — **florecer** {53} *vi* **1** : bloom, blossom **2** PROSPERAR : flourish — **floreciente** *adj* : flourishing — **florero** *nm* : vase — **florido, -da** *adj* : flowery — **florista** *nmf* : florist — **floritura** *nf* : frill, flourish
flota *nf* : fleet
flotar *vi* : float — **flotador** *nm* **1** : float **2** : life preserver (for a swimmer) — **flotante** *adj* : floating, buoyant — **flote: a ~** *adv phr* : afloat
flotilla *nf* : flotilla, fleet
fluctuar {3} *vi* : fluctuate — **fluctuación** *nf, pl* **-ciones** : fluctuation
fluir {41} *vi* : flow — **fluidez** *nf* **1** : fluidity **2** : fluency (of language, etc.) — **fluido, -da** *adj* **1** : fluid **2** : fluent (of language) — **fluido** *nm* : fluid — **flujo** *nm* : flow
fluorescente *adj* : fluorescent
fluoruro *nm* : fluoride
fluvial *adj* : river
fobia *nf* : phobia
foca *nf* : seal (animal)
foco *nm* **1** : focus **2** : spotlight, floodlight (in theater, etc.) **3** *Lat* : lightbulb
fofo, -fa *adj* : flabby
fogata *nf* : bonfire
fogón *nm, pl* **-gones** : burner
fogoso, -sa *adj* : ardent
folklore *nm* : folklore — **folklórico, -ca** *adj* : folk, traditional
follaje *nm* : foliage
folleto *nm* : pamphlet, leaflet

fomentar *vt* : promote, encourage — **fomento** *nm* : promotion, encouragement
fonda *nf* : boarding house
fondear *vt* : sound out, examine — *vi* : anchor
fondillos *nmpl* : seat (of pants, etc.)
fondo *nm* **1** : bottom **2** : rear, back, end **3** PROFUNDIDAD : depth **4** : background (of a painting, etc.) **5** *Lat* : slip, petticoat **6** **~s** *nmpl* : funds, resources **7 a ~** : thoroughly, in depth **8 en el ~** : deep down
fonético, -ca *adj* : phonetic — **fonética** *nf* : phonetics
fontanería *nf Spain* : plumbing — **fontanero, -ra** *n Spain* : plumber
footing ['fuˌtɪŋ] *nm* **1** : jogging **2 hacer ~** : jog
forajido, -da *n* : bandit, outlaw
foráneo, -nea *adj* : foreign, strange
forastero, -ra *n* : stranger, outsider
forcejear *vi* : struggle — **forcejeo** *nm* : struggle
forense *adj* : forensic
forja *nf* : forge — **forjar** *vt* **1** : forge **2** CREAR, FORMAR : build up, create
forma *nf* **1** : form, shape **2** MANERA : manner, way **3 en ~** : fit, healthy **4** **~s** *nfpl* : appearances, conventions — **formación** *nf, pl* **-ciones** **1** : formation **2** EDUCACIÓN : training
formal *adj* **1** : formal **2** SERIO : serious **3** FIABLE : dependable, reliable — **formalidad** *nf* **1** : formality **2** SERIEDAD : seriousness **3** FIABILIDAD : reliability
formar *vt* **1** : form, shape **2** CONSTITUIR : constitute **3** EDUCAR : train, educate — **formarse** *vr* **1** DESARROLLARSE : develop, take shape **2** EDUCARSE : be educated
formato *nm* : format
formidable *adj* **1** : tremendous **2** *fam* : fantastic, terrific
fórmula *nf* : formula
formular *vt* **1** : formulate, draw up **2** : make, lodge (a complaint, etc.)
formulario *nm* : form
fornido, -da *adj* : well-built, burly
foro *nm* : forum
forraje *nm* : forage, fodder — **forrajear** *vi* : forage
forrar *vt* **1** : line (a garment) **2** : cover (a book) — **forro** *nm* **1** : lining **2** CUBIERTA : book cover
fortalecer {53} *vt* : strengthen — **fortaleza** *nf* **1** : fortress **2** FUERZA : strength **3** : (moral) fortitude
fortificar {72} *vt* : fortify — **fortificación** *nf, pl* **-ciones** : fortification
fortuito, -ta *adj* : fortuitous, chance
fortuna *nf* **1** SUERTE : fortune, luck **2** RIQUEZA : wealth, fortune **3 por ~** : fortunately
forzar {36} *vt* **1** : force **2** : strain (one's eyes) — **forzosamente** *adv* : necessarily — **forzoso, -sa** *adj* : necessary, inevitable
fosa *nf* **1** : pit, ditch **2** TUMBA : grave **3** **~s nasales** : nostrils
fósforo *nm* **1** : phosphorus **2** CERILLA : match — **fosforescente** *adj* : phosphorescent
fósil *nm* : fossil
foso *nm* **1** : ditch **2** : pit (of a theater) **3** : moat (of a castle)
foto *nf* : photo
fotocopia *nf* : photocopy — **fotocopiadora** *nf* : photocopier — **fotocopiar** *vt* : photocopy
fotogénico, -ca *adj* : photogenic
fotografía *nf* **1** : photography **2** : photograph, picture — **fotografiar** {85} *vt* : photograph — **fotográfico, -ca** *adj* : photographic — **fotógrafo, -fa** *n* : photographer
fotosíntesis *nf* : photosynthesis
fracasar *vi* : fail — **fracaso** *nm* : failure
fracción *nf, pl* **-ciones** **1** : fraction **2** : faction (in politics) — **fraccionamiento** *nm Lat* : housing development
fractura *nf* : fracture — **fracturarse** *vr* : fracture, break (a bone)
fragancia *nf* : fragrance, scent — **fragante** *adj* : fragrant
fragata *nf* : frigate
frágil *adj* **1** : fragile **2** DÉBIL : frail, delicate — **fragilidad** *nf* **1** : fragility **2** DEBILIDAD : frailty
fragmento *nm* : fragment
fragor *nm* : clamor, din
fragoso, -sa *adj* : rough, rugged
fragua *nf* : forge — **fraguar** {10} *vt* **1** : forge **2** IDEAR : concoct — *vi* : harden, solidify
fraile *nm* : friar, monk
frambuesa *nf* : raspberry
francés, -cesa *adj, mpl* **-ceses** : French — **francés** *nm* : French (language)
franco, -ca *adj* **1** : frank, candid **2** : free (in commerce) — **franco** *nm* : franc
francotirador, -dora *n* : sniper
franela *nf* : flannel
franja *nf* **1** : stripe, band **2** FLECO : fringe
franquear *vt* **1** : clear (a path, etc.) **2** : cross over (a doorstep, etc.) **3** : pay postage on (mail) — **franqueo** *nm* : postage

franqueza *nf* : frankness
frasco *nm* : small bottle, vial, flask
frase *nf* **1** : phrase **2** ORACIÓN : sentence
fraternal *adj* : brotherly, fraternal — **fraternidad** *nf* : brotherhood, fraternity — **fraternizar** {21} *vi* : fraternize — **fraterno, -na** *adj* : brotherly, fraternal
fraude *nm* : fraud — **fraudulento, -ta** *adj* : fraudulent
fray *nm* (*used in titles*) : brother, friar
frazada *nf Lat* : blanket
frecuencia *nf* **1** : frequency **2 con ~** : often, frequently — **frecuentar** *vt* : frequent, haunt — **frecuente** *adj* : frequent
fregadero *nm* : kitchen sink
fregar {49} *vt* **1** : scrub, wash **2** *Lat fam* : annoy — *vi Lat fam* : be a pest
freír {37} *vt* : fry
fregona *nf Spain* : mop
frenar *vt* **1** : brake **2** RESTRINGIR : curb, check
frenesí *nm* : frenzy — **frenético, -ca** *adj* : frantic, frenzied
freno *nm* **1** : brake **2** : bit (of a bridle) **3** CONTROL : check, restraint
frente *nm* **1** : front **2** : facade (of a building) **3 al ~ de** : at the head of **4 ~ a** : opposite **5 de ~** : (facing) forward **6 hacer ~ a** : face up to, brave — **~** *nf* : forehead
fresa *nf* : strawberry
fresco, -ca *adj* **1** : fresh **2** FRÍO : cool **3** *fam* : insolent, nervy — **fresco** *nm* **1** : fresh air **2** FRESCOR : coolness **3** : fresco (art or painting) — **frescor** *nm* : coolness, cool air — **frescura** *nf* **1** : freshness **2** FRÍO : coolness **3** *fam* : nerve, insolence
fresno *nm* : ash (tree)
frialdad *nf* **1** : coldness **2** INDIFERENCIA : indifference
fricción *nf, pl* **-ciones 1** : friction **2** MASAJE : rubbing, massage — **friccionar** *vt* : rub
frigidez *nf* : frigidity
frigorífico *nm Spain* : refrigerator
frijol *nm Lat* : bean
frío, fría *adj* **1** : cold **2** INDIFERENTE : cool, indifferent — **frío** *nm* **1** : cold **2** INDIFERENCIA : coldness, indifference **3 hacer ~** : be cold (outside) **4 tener ~** : be cold, feel cold
frito, -ta *adj* **1** : fried **2** *fam* : fed up
frívolo, -la *adj* : frivolous — **frivolidad** *nf* : frivolity
fronda *nf* **1** : frond **2** *or* **~s** *nfpl* : foliage — **frondoso, -sa** *adj* : leafy
frontera *nf* : border, frontier — **fronterizo, -za** *adj* : border, on the border — **frontero, -ra** *adj* : facing, opposite
frotar *vt* : rub — **frotarse** *vr* **~ las manos** : rub one's hands
fructífero, -ra *adj* : fruitful
frugal *adj* : frugal, thrifty — **frugalidad** *adj* : frugality
fruncir {83} *vt* **1** : gather (in pleats) **2 ~ el ceño** : frown **3 ~ la boca** : purse one's lips
frustrar *vt* : frustrate — **frustrarse** *vr* : fail — **frustración** *nf, pl* **-ciones** : frustration — **frustrado, -da** *adj* **1** : frustrated **2** FRACASADO : failed, unsuccessful — **frustrante** *adj* : frustrating
fruta *nf* : fruit — **frutilla** *nf Lat* : strawberry — **fruto** *nm* **1** : fruit **2** RESULTADO : result, consequence
fucsia *adj & nm* : fuchsia
fuego *nm* **1** : fire **2** : flame, burner (on a stove) **3 ~s artificiales** *nmpl* : fireworks **4 ¿tienes fuego?** : have you got a light?
fuelle *nm* : bellows
fuente *nf* **1** : fountain **2** MANANTIAL : spring **3** ORIGEN : source **4** PLATO : platter, serving dish
fuera *adv* **1** : outside, out **2** : abroad, away **3 ~ de** : outside of, beyond **4 ~ de** : aside from, in addition to
fuerte *adj* **1** : strong **2** : bright (of colors), loud (of sounds) **3** EXTREMO : intense **4** DURO : hard — **~** *adv* **1** : strongly, hard **2** : loudly **3** MUCHO : abundantly, a lot — **~** *nm* **1** : fort **2** ESPECIALIDAD : strong point
fuerza *nf* **1** : strength **2** VIOLENCIA : force **3** PODER : power, might **4 ~s armadas** *nfpl* : armed forces **5 a ~ de** : by dint of **6 a la ~** : necessarily
fuga *nf* **1** : flight, escape **2** : fugue (in music) **3** ESCAPE : leak — **fugarse** {52} *vr* : flee, run away — **fugaz** *adj, pl* **-gaces** : fleeting — **fugitivo, -va** *adj & n* : fugitive
fulano, -na *n* : so-and-so, what's-his-name, what's-her-name
fulgor *nm* : brilliance, splendor
fulminar *vt* **1** : strike with lightning **2** : strike down (with an illness, etc.) — **fulminante** *adj* : devastating
fumar *v* : smoke — **fumarse** *vr* **1** : smoke **2** *fam* : squander — **fumador, -dora** *n* : smoker
funámbulo, -la *n* : tightrope walker
función *nf, pl* **-ciones 1** : function **2** TRABAJOS : duties *pl* **3** : performance, show (in theater) — **funcional** *adj* : functional — **funcionamiento** *nm* **1**

: functioning **2 en ~** : in operation — **funcionar** *vi* **1** : function, run, work **2 no funciona** : out of order — **funcionario, -ria** *n* : civil servant, official

funda *nf* **1** : cover, sheath **2** *or* **~ de almohada** : pillowcase

fundar *vt* **1** ESTABLECER : found, establish **2** BASAR : base — **fundarse** *vr* **~ en** : be based on — **fundación** *nf, pl* **-ciones** : foundation — **fundador, -dora** *n* : founder — **fundamental** *adj* : fundamental, basic — **fundamentalmente** *adv* : basically — **fundamentar** *vt* **1** : lay the foundations for **2** BASAR : base — **fundamento** *nm* **1** : foundation **2 ~s** *nmpl* : fundamentals

fundir *vt* **1** : melt down, smelt **2** FUSIONAR : fuse, merge — **fundirse** *vr* **1** : blend, merge **2** DERRETIRSE : melt **3** : burn out (of a lightbulb) — **fundición** *nf, pl* **-ciones 1** : smelting **2** : foundry

fúnebre *adj* **1** : funeral **2** LÚGUBRE : gloomy

funeral *adj* : funeral, funerary — **~** *nm* **1** : funeral **2 ~es** *nmpl* EXEQUIAS : funeral (rites) — **funeraria** *nf* : funeral home

funesto, ta *adj* : terrible, disastrous

fungir {35} *vi Lat* : act, function

furgón *nm, pl* **-gones 1** : van, truck **2** : freight car (of a train) **3 ~ de cola** : caboose — **furgoneta** *nf* : van

furia *nf* **1** CÓLERA : fury, rage **2** VIOLENCIA : violence — **furibundo, -da** *adj* : furious — **furioso, -sa** *adj* **1** : furious, irate **2** INTENSO : intense, violent — **furor** *nm* : fury

furtivo, -va *adj* : furtive

furúnculo *nm* : boil

fuselaje *nm* : fuselage

fusible *nm* : fuse

fusil *nm* : rifle — **fusilar** *vt* : shoot (by firing squad)

fusión *nf, pl* **-siones 1** : fusion **2** UNIÓN : union, merger — **fusionar** *vt* **1** : fuse **2** UNIR : merge — **fusionarse** *vr* : merge

futbol *or* **fútbol** *nm* **1** : soccer **2 ~ americano** : football — **futbolista** *nmf* : soccer player, football player

fútil *adj* : trifling, trivial

futuro, -ra *adj* : future — **futuro** *nm* : future

G

g *nf* : g, seventh letter of the Spanish alphabet

gabán *nm, pl* **-banes** : topcoat, overcoat

gabardina *nf* **1** : trench coat, raincoat **2** : gabardine (fabric)

gabinete *nm* **1** : cabinet (in government) **2** : (professional) office

gacela *nf* : gazelle

gaceta *nf* : gazette

gachas *nfpl* : porridge

gacho, -cha *adj* : drooping

gaélico, -ca *adj* : Gaelic

gafas *nfpl* **1** : eyeglasses **2 ~ de sol** : sunglasses

gaita *nf* : bagpipes *pl*

gajo *nm* : segment (of fruit)

gala *nf* **1** : gala **2 de ~** : formal **3 hacer ~ de** : display, show off **4 ~s** *nfpl* : finery

galáctico, -ca *adj* : galactic

galán *nm, pl* **-lanes 1** : leading man (in theater) **2** *fam* : boyfriend

galante *adj* : gallant — **galantear** *vt* : court, woo — **galantería** *nf* **1** : gallantry **2** CUMPLIDO : compliment

galápago *nm* : (aquatic) turtle

galardón *nm, pl* **-dones** : reward

galaxia *nf* : galaxy

galera *nf* : galley

galería *nf* **1** : corridor **2** : gallery, balcony (in a theater)

galés, -lesa *adj, mpl* **-leses** : Welsh

galgo *nm* : greyhound

galimatías *nms & pl* : gibberish

gallardía *nf* **1** : bravery **2** ELEGANCIA : elegance — **gallardo, -da** *adj* **1** : brave **2** APUESTO : elegant, good-looking

gallego, -ga *adj* : Galician

galleta *nf* **1** : (sweet) cookie **2** : (salted) cracker

gallina *nf* **1** : hen **2 ~ de Guinea** : guinea fowl — **gallinero** *nm* : henhouse, (chicken) coop — **gallo** *nm* : rooster, cock

galón *nm, pl* **-lones 1** : gallon **2** : stripe (military insignia)

galopar *vi* : gallop — **galope** *nm* : gallop

galvanizar {21} *vt* : galvanize

gama *nf* **1** : range, spectrum **2** : scale (in music)

gamba *nf* : large shrimp, prawn

gamuza *nf* **1** : chamois (animal) **2** : chamois (leather), suede
gana *nf* **1** : desire, wish **2** APETITO : appetite **3 de buena ~** : willingly, heartily **4 de mala ~** : unwillingly **5 no me da la ~** : I don't feel like it **6 tener ~s de** : feel like, be in the mood for
ganado *nm* **1** : cattle *pl*, livestock **2 ~ ovino** : sheep *pl* **3 ~ porcino** : swine *pl* — **ganadería** *nf* **1** : cattle raising **2** GANADO : livestock
ganador, -dora *adj* : winning — **~** *n* : winner
ganancia *nf* : profit
ganar *vt* **1** : earn **2** : win (in games, etc.) **3** CONSEGUIR : gain **4** ADQUERIR : get, obtain **5 ~ a algn** : win over s.o., beat s.o. — *vi* : win — **ganarse** *vr* **1** : win, gain **2 ~ la vida** : make a living
gancho *nm* **1** : hook **2** HORQUILLA : hairpin **3** *Lat* : (clothes) hanger
gandul, -dula *adj & n fam* : good-for-nothing — **gandul** *nm Lat* : pigeon pea
ganga *nf* : bargain
gangrena *nf* : gangrene
gángster *nmf* : gangster
ganso, -sa *n* : goose, gander *m* — **gansada** *nf* : silly thing, nonsense
gañir {38} *vi* : yelp — **gañido** *nm* : yelp
garabatear *v* : scribble — **garabato** *nm* : scribble
garaje *nm* : garage
garantizar {21} *vt* : guarantee — **garante** *nmf* : guarantor — **garantía** *nf* **1** : guarantee, warranty **2** FIANZA : surety
garapiñar *vt* : candy (fruits, etc.)
garbanzo *nm* : chickpea, garbanzo
garbo *nm* : grace, elegance — **garboso, -sa** *adj* : graceful, elegant
gardenia *nf* : gardenia
garfio *nm* : hook, gaff
garganta *nf* **1** : throat **2** CUELLO : neck **3** DESFILADERO : ravine, gorge — **gargantilla** *nf* : necklace
gárgara *nf* **1** : gargling, gargle **2 hacer ~s** : gargle
gárgola *nf* : gargoyle
garita *nf* **1** : sentry box **2** CABAÑA : cabin, hut
garito *nm* : gambling den
garra *nf* **1** : claw, talon **2** *fam* : hand, paw
garrafa *nf* : decanter, carafe — **garrafón** *nm, pl* **-fones** : large decanter or bottle
garrapata *nf* : tick
garrocha *nf* **1** : lance, pike **2** *Lat* : pole (in sports)
garrote *nm* : club, cudgel
garúa *nf Lat* : drizzle
garza *nf* : heron
gas *nm* **1** : gas **2 ~ lacrimógeno** : tear gas
gasa *nf* : gauze
gaseosa *nf* : soda, soft drink
gasolina *nf* : gasoline, gas — **gasoil** *or* **gasóleo** *nm* : diesel fuel — **gasolinera** *nf* : gas station, service station
gastar *vt* **1** : spend **2** CONSUMIR : consume, use up **3** DESPERDICIAR : squander, waste — **gastarse** *vr* **1** : spend **2** DETERIORARSE : wear out — **gastado, -da** *adj* **1** : spent **2** : worn-out (of clothing, etc.) — **gastador, -dora** *n* : spendthrift — **gasto** *nm* **1** : expense, expenditure **2 ~s generales** : overhead
gástrico, -ca *adj* : gastric
gastronomía *nf* : gastronomy — **gastrónomo, -ma** *n* : gourmet
gatas: a ~ *adv phr* : on all fours
gatear *vi* : crawl, creep
gatillo *nm* : trigger — **gatillero** *nm Mex* : gunman
gato, -ta *n* : cat — **gatito, -ta** *n* : kitten — **gato** *nm* : jack (for an automobile)
gaucho *nm* : gaucho
gaveta *nf* : drawer
gavilla *nf* **1** : sheaf **2** PANDILLA : gang
gaviota *nf* : gull, seagull
gay ['ge, 'gai] *adj* : gay (homosexual)
gaza *nf* : loop
gazpacho *nm* : gazpacho
géiser *nm* : geyser
gelatina *nf* : gelatin
gema *nf* : gem
gemelo, -la *adj & n* : twin — **gemelo** *nm* **1** : cuff link **2 ~s** *nmpl* : binoculars
gemir {54} *vi* : moan, groan, whine — **gemido** *nm* : moan, groan, whine
gen *or* **gene** *nm* : gene
genealogía *nf* : genealogy — **genealógico, -ca** *adj* : genealogical
generación *nf, pl* **-ciones** : generation
generador *nm* : generator
general *adj* **1** : general **2 en ~** *or* **por lo ~** : in general, generally — **~** *nmf* : general — **generalidad** *nf* **1** : generalization **2** MAYORÍA : majority — **generalizar** {21} *vi* : generalize — *vt* : spread (out) — **generalizarse** *vr* : become widespread — **generalmente** *adv* : usually, generally
generar *vt* : generate
género *nm* **1** : kind, sort **2** : gender (in

grammar) **3 ~ humano :** human race — **genérico, -ca** *adj* **:** generic
generoso, -sa *adj* **1 :** generous, unselfish **2 :** ample (in quantity) — **generosidad** *nf* **:** generosity
génesis *nfs & pl* **:** genesis
genética *nf* **:** genetics — **genético, -ca** *adj* **:** genetic
genial *adj* **1 :** brilliant **2** ESTUPENDO **:** great, terrific
genio *nm* **1 :** genius **2** CARÁCTER **:** temper, disposition **3 :** genie (in mythology)
genital *adj* **:** genital — **genitales** *nmpl* **:** genitals
genocidio *nm* **:** genocide
gente *nf* **1 :** people **2** *fam* **:** relatives *pl,* folks *pl* **3 ser buena ~ :** be nice, be kind
gentil *adj* **1** AMABLE **:** kind **2 :** gentile (in religion) — **gentileza** *nf* **:** kindness, courtesy
gentío *nm* **:** crowd, mob
gentuza *nf* **:** riffraff, rabble
genuflexión *nf, pl* **-xiones :** genuflection
genuino, -na *adj* **:** genuine
geografía *nf* **:** geography — **geográfico, -ca** *adj* **:** geographic, geographical
geología *nf* **:** geology — **geológico, -ca** *adj* **:** geologic, geological
geometría *nf* **:** geometry — **geométrico, -ca** *adj* **:** geometric, geometrical
geranio *nm* **:** geranium
gerencia *nf* **:** management — **gerente** *nmf* **:** manager
geriatría *nf* **:** geriatrics — **geriátrico, -ca** *adj* **:** geriatric
germen *nm, pl* **gérmenes :** germ
germinar *vi* **:** germinate, sprout
gestación *nf, pl* **-ciones :** gestation
gesticular *vi* **:** gesticulate, gesture — **gesticulación** *nf, pl* **-ciones :** gesticulation
gestión *nf, pl* **-tiones 1 :** procedure, step **2** ADMINISTRACIÓN **:** management — **gestionar** *vt* **1 :** negotiate, work towards **2** ADMINISTRAR **:** manage, handle
gesto *nm* **1 :** gesture **2 :** (facial) expression **3** MUECA **:** grimace
gigante *adj & nm* **:** giant — **gigantesco, -ca** *adj* **:** gigantic
gimnasia *nf* **:** gymnastics — **gimnasio** *nm* **:** gymnasium, gym — **gimnasta** *nmf* **:** gymnast
gimotear *vi* **:** whine, whimper
ginebra *nf* **:** gin
ginecología *nf* **:** gynecology — **ginecólogo, -ga** *n* **:** gynecologist
gira *nf* **:** tour
girar *vi* **:** turn (around), revolve — *vt* **1 :** turn, twist, rotate **2 :** draft (checks) **3 :** transfer (funds)
girasol *nm* **:** sunflower
giratorio, -ria *adj* **:** revolving
giro *nm* **1 :** turn, rotation **2** LOCUCIÓN **:** expression **3 ~ bancario :** bank draft **4 ~ postal :** money order
giroscopio *nm* **:** gyroscope
gis *nm Lat* **:** chalk
gitano, -na *adj & n* **:** Gypsy
glaciar *nm* **:** glacier — **glacial** *adj* **:** glacial, icy
gladiador *nm* **:** gladiator
glándula *nf* **:** gland
glasear *vt* **:** glaze, ice (cake, etc.) — **glaseado** *nm* **:** icing
glicerina *nf* **:** glycerin
globo *nm* **1 :** globe **2 :** balloon **3 ~ ocular :** eyeball — **global** *adj* **1 :** global **2** TOTAL **:** total, overall
glóbulo *nm* **:** blood cell, corpuscle
gloria *nf* **:** glory
glorieta *nf* **1 :** bower, arbor **2** *Spain* **:** rotary, traffic circle
glorificar {72} *vt* **:** glorify
glorioso, -sa *adj* **:** glorious
glosario *nm* **:** glossary
glotón, -tona *adj, mpl* **-tones :** gluttonous — **~** *n* **:** glutton — **glotonería** *nf* **:** gluttony
glucosa *nf* **:** glucose
gnomo ['nomo] *nm* **:** gnome
gobernar {55} *v* **1 :** govern, rule **2** DIRIGIR **:** direct, manage **3 :** steer (a boat, etc.) — **gobernación** *nf, pl* **-ciones :** governing, government — **gobernador, -dora** *n* **:** governor — **gobernante** *adj* **:** ruling, governing — **~** *n* **:** ruler, leader — **gobierno** *nm* **:** government
goce *nm* **:** enjoyment
gol *nm* **:** goal (in sports)
golf *nm* **:** golf — **golfista** *nmf* **:** golfer
golfo *nm* **:** gulf
golondrina *nf* **1 :** swallow **2 ~ de mar :** tern
golosina *nf* **:** sweet, candy — **goloso, -sa** *adj* **:** fond of sweets
golpe *nm* **1 :** blow **2** PUÑETAZO **:** punch **3 :** knock (on a door, etc.) **4 de ~ :** suddenly **5 de un ~ :** all at once **6 ~ de estado :** coup d'etat — **golpear** *vt* **1 :** hit, punch **2 :** slam, bang (a door, etc.) — *vi* **:** knock (at a door)
goma *nf* **1** CAUCHO **:** rubber **2** PEGAMENTO **:** glue **3** *or* **~ elástica :** rubber band **4 ~ de mascar :** chewing gum **5 ~ de borrar :** eraser
gong *nm* **:** gong

gordo, -da *adj* **1** : fat, plump **2** GRUESO : thick **3** : fatty (of meat) **4** *fam* : big, serious — **~** *n* : fat person — **gorda** *nf Lat* : thick corn tortilla — **gordo** *nm* **1** GRASA : fat **2** : jackpot (in a lottery) — **gordura** *nf* : fatness, flab
gorgotear *vi* : gurgle, bubble
gorila *nm* : gorilla
gorjear *vi* **1** : chirp, tweet **2** : gurgle (of a baby) — **gorjeo** *nm* : chirping
gorra *nf* **1** : cap, bonnet **2 de ~** *fam* : for free
gorrear *vt fam* : bum, scrounge
gorrión *nm, pl* **-rriones** : sparrow
gorro *nm* **1** : cap, bonnet **2 de ~** *fam* : for free
gota *nf* **1** : drop **2** : gout (in medicine) — **gotear** *vi* : drip, leak — **goteo** *nm* : drip, dripping — **gotera** *nf* : leak
gótico, -ca *adj* : Gothic
gozar {21} *vi* **1** : enjoy oneself **2 ~ de algo** : enjoy sth
gozne *nm* : hinge
gozo *nm* **1** : joy **2** PLACER : enjoyment, pleasure — **gozoso, -sa** *adj* : joyful, glad
grabar *vt* **1** : engrave **2** : record, tape — **grabación** *nf, pl* **-ciones** : recording — **grabado** *nm* : engraving — **grabadora** *nf* : tape recorder
gracia *nf* **1** : grace **2** FAVOR : favor, kindness **3** HUMOR : humor, wit **4 ~s** *nfpl* : thanks **5 ¡(muchas) ~s!** : thank you (very much)! — **gracioso, -sa** *adj* : funny, amusing
grada *nf* **1** : step, stair **2** : row (in a theater, etc.) **3 ~s** *nfpl* : bleachers, grandstand — **gradación** *nf, pl* **-ciones** : gradation, scale — **gradería** *nf* : rows *pl*, stands *pl* — **grado** *nm* **1** : degree **2** : grade (in school) **3 de buen ~** : willingly
graduar {3} *vt* **1** : regulate, adjust **2** MARCAR : calibrate **3** : confer a degree on (in education) — **graduarse** *vr* : graduate (from a school) — **graduación** *nf, pl* **-ciones 1** : graduation **2** : alcohol content, proof — **graduado, -da** *n* : graduate — **gradual** *adj* : gradual — **gradualmente** *adv* : little by little, gradually
gráfico, -ca *adj* : graphic — **gráfica** *nf* : graph — **gráfico** *nm* **1** : graph **2** : graphic (in computers)
gragea *nf* : pill, tablet
grajo *nm* : rook (bird)
gramática *nf* : grammar — **gramatical** *adj* : grammatical
gramo *nm* : gram
gran → **grande**
grana *nf* : scarlet
granada *nf* **1** : pomegranate **2** : grenade (in the military)
granate *nm* : garnet
grande *adj* (**gran** *before singular nouns*) **1** : large, big **2** ALTO : tall **3** : great (in quality, intensity, etc.) **4** *Lat* : grown-up — **grandeza** *nf* **1** : greatness **2** NOBLEZA : nobility — **grandiosidad** *nf* : grandeur — **grandioso, -sa** *adj* : grand, magnificent
granel: **a ~** *adv phr* **1** : in bulk **2** : in abundance
granero *nm* : barn, granary
granito *nm* : granite
granizar {21} *v impers* : hail — **granizada** *nf* : hailstorm — **granizado** *nm* : iced drink — **granizo** *nm* : hail
granja *nf* : farm — **granjero, -ra** *n* : farmer
grano *nm* **1** : grain **2** SEMILLA : seed **3** : (coffee) bean **4** BARRO : pimple
granuja *nmf* : rascal
grapa *nf* : staple — **grapadora** *nf* : stapler — **grapar** *vt* : staple
grasa *nf* **1** : grease **2** : fat (in cooking, etc.) — **grasiento, -ta** *adj* : greasy, oily — **graso, -sa** *adj* : fatty, greasy, oily — **grasoso, -sa** *adj Lat* : greasy, oily
gratificar {72} *vt* **1** : give a tip or bonus to **2** SATISFACER : gratify, satisfy — **gratificación** *nf, pl* **-ciones 1** : bonus, tip, reward **2** SATISFACCIÓN : gratification
gratis *adv & adj* : free
gratitud *nf* : gratitude
grato, -ta *adj* : pleasant, agreeable
gratuito, -ta *adj* **1** : gratuitous, unwarranted **2** GRATIS : free
grava *nf* : gravel
gravar *vt* **1** : tax **2** CARGAR : burden — **gravamen** *nm, pl* **-vámenes 1** : burden, obligation **2** IMPUESTO : tax
grave *adj* **1** : grave, serious **2** : deep, low (of a voice, etc.) — **gravedad** *nf* : gravity
gravilla *nf* : gravel
gravitar *vi* **1** : gravitate **2 ~ sobre** : weigh on — **gravitación** *nf, pl* **-ciones** : gravitation
gravoso, -sa *adj* : costly, burdensome
graznar *vi* : caw, quack, honk — **graznido** *nm* : caw, quack, honk
gregario, -ria *adj* : gregarious
gremio *nm* : guild, (trade) union
greñas *nfpl* : shaggy hair, mop
griego, -ga *adj* : Greek — **griego** *nm* : Greek (language)
grieta *nf* : crack, crevice

grifo *nm Spain* : faucet, tap
grillete *nm* : shackle
grillo *nm* **1** : cricket **2 ~s** *nmpl* : fetters, shackles
grima *nf* **dar ~** : annoy, irritate
gringo, -ga *adj & n Lat fam* : Yankee, gringo
gripe *nf or* **gripa** *nf Lat* : flu, influenza
gris *adj & nm* : gray
gritar *v* : shout, scream, cry — **grito** *nm* **1** : shout, scream, cry **2 dar ~s** : shout
grosella *nf* : currant
grosería *nf* **1** : vulgar remark **2** DESCORTESÍA : rudeness — **grosero, -ra** *adj* **1** : coarse, vulgar **2** DESCORTÉS : rude
grosor *nm* : thickness
grotesco, -ca *adj* : grotesque, hideous
grúa *nf* : crane, derrick
grueso, -sa *adj* **1** : thick **2** CORPULENTO : stout, heavy — **gruesa** *nf* : gross — **grueso** *nm* **1** GROSOR : thickness **2** : main body, mass **3 en ~** : wholesale
grulla *nf* : crane (bird)
grumo *nm* : lump, clot — **grumoso, -sa** *adj* : lumpy
gruñir {38} *vi* **1** : growl, grunt **2** *fam* : grumble — **gruñido** *nm* **1** : growl, grunt **2** *fam* : grumble — **gruñón, -ñona** *adj, mpl* **-ñones** *fam* : grumpy, grouchy — **~** *n fam* : grouch
grupa *nf* : rump, hindquarters *pl*
grupo *nm* : group
gruta *nf* : grotto
guacamayo *nm or* **guacamaya** *nf Lat* : macaw
guacamole *nm* : guacamole
guadaña *nf* : scythe
guagua *nf Lat* **1** : baby **2** AUTOBÚS : bus
guajalote, -ta *or* **guajolote, -ta** *n Lat* : turkey
guante *nm* : glove
guapo, -pa *adj* : handsome, good-looking
guaraní *nm* : Guarani (language of Paraguay)
guarda *nmf* **1** : keeper, custodian **2** GUARDIÁN : security guard — **guardabarros** *nms & pl* : fender — **guardabosque** *nmf* : forest ranger — **guardacostas** *nmfs & pl* : coast guard vessel — **guardaespaldas** *nmfs & pl* : bodyguard — **guardameta** *nmf* : goalkeeper — **guardapolvo** *nm* : overalls *pl* — **guardar** *vt* **1** : keep **2** PROTEGER : guard, protect **3** RESERVAR : save — **guardarse** *vr* **~ de 1** : refrain from **2** : guard against — **guardarropa** *nm* **1** : cloakroom, checkroom **2** ARMARIO : wardrobe
guardería *nf* : nursery, day-care center
guardia *nf* **1** : guard, vigilence **2** TURNO : duty, watch — **~** *nmf* **1** : guard **2** *or* **~ municipal** : police officer — **guardián, -diana** *n, mpl* **-dianes 1** : guardian, keeper **2** GUARDA : security guard
guarecer {53} *vt* : shelter, protect — **guarecerse** *vr* : take shelter
guarida *nf* **1** : den, lair (of animals) **2** : hideout (of persons)
guarnecer {53} *vt* **1** : adorn, garnish **2** : garrison (an area) — **guarnición** *nf, pl* **-ciones 1** : garnish, trimming **2** : (military) garrison
guasa *nf fam* **1** : joke **2 de ~** : in jest — **guasón, -sona** *adj, mpl* **-sones** *fam* : joking, witty — **~** *n fam* : joker
guatemalteco, -ca *adj* : Guatemalan
guayaba *nf* : guava
gubernamental *or* **gubernativo, -va** *adj* : governmental
guepardo *nm* : cheetah
güero, -ra *adj Lat* : blond, fair
guerra *nf* **1** : war, warfare **2** LUCHA : conflict, struggle — **guerrear** *vi* : wage war — **guerrero, -ra** *adj* **1** : war, fighting **2** BELICOSO : warlike — **~** *n* : warrior — **guerrilla** *nf* : guerrilla warfare — **guerrillero, -ra** *adj & n* : guerrilla
gueto *nm* : ghetto
guiar {85} *vt* **1** : guide, lead **2** ACONSEJAR : advise — **guiarse** *vr* : be guided by, go by — **guía** *nf* **1** : guidebook **2** ORIENTACIÓN : guidance — **~** *nmf* : guide, leader
guijarro *nm* : pebble
guillotina *nf* : guillotine
guinda *nf* : morello (cherry)
guiñar *vi* : wink — **guiño** *nm* : wink
guión *nm, pl* **guiones 1** : script, screenplay **2** : hyphen, dash (in punctuation) — **guionista** *nmf* : scriptwriter, screenwriter
guirnalda *nf* : garland
guisa *nf* **1** : manner, fashion **2 a ~ de** : by way of **3 de tal ~** : in such a way
guisado *nm* : stew
guisante *nm* : pea
guisar *vt* : cook — **guiso** *nm* : stew, casserole
guitarra *nf* : guitar — **guitarrista** *nmf* : guitarist
gula *nf* : gluttony
gusano *nm* **1** : worm **2** : maggot (larva)
gustar *vt* **1** : taste **2** *Lat* : like — *vi* **1** : be pleasing **2 como guste** : as you like **3**

me gustan los dulces : I like sweets — **gusto** *nm* **1** : taste **2** PLACER : pleasure, liking **3 a ~** : comfortable, at ease **4 al ~** : to taste **5 mucho ~** : pleased to meet you — **gustoso, -sa** *adj* **1** : tasty **2** AGRADABLE : pleasant **3 hacer algo ~** : do sth willingly

gutural *adj* : guttural

H

h *nf* : h, eighth letter of the Spanish alphabet

haba *nf* : broad bean

habanero, -ra *adj* : Havanan — **habano** *nm* : Havana cigar

haber {39} *v aux* **1** : have, has **2 ~ de** : must — *v impers* **1 hay** : there is, there are **2 hay que** : it is necessary (to) **3 ¿qué hay?** *or* **¿qué hubo?** : how's it going? — **~** *nm* **1** : assets *pl* **2** : credit side (in accounting) **3 ~es** *nmpl* : income, earnings

habichuela *nf* **1** : bean **2 ~ verde** : string bean

hábil *adj* **1** : able, skillful **2** LISTO : clever **3 horas ~es** : business hours — **habilidad** *nf* : ability, skill

habilitar *vt* **1** : equip, furnish **2** AUTORIZAR : authorize

habitar *vt* : inhabit — *vi* : reside, dwell — **habitable** *adj* : habitable, inhabitable — **habitación** *nf, pl* **-ciones 1** : room, bedroom **2** MORADA : dwelling, abode **3** : habitat (in biology) — **habitante** *nmf* : inhabitant, resident — **hábitat** *nm* : habitat

hábito *nm* : habit — **habitual** *adj* : habitual, usual — **habituar** {3} *vt* : accustom, habituate — **habituarse** *vr* **~ a** : get used to

hablar *vi* **1** : speak, talk **2 ~ de** : mention, talk about **3 ~ con** : talk to, speak with — *vt* **1** : speak (a language) **2** DISCUTIR : discuss — **hablarse** *vr* **1** : speak to each other **2 se habla inglés** : English spoken — **habla** *nf* **1** : speech **2** IDIOMA : language, dialect **3 de ~ inglesa** : English-speaking — **hablador, -dora** *adj* : talkative — **~** *n* : chatterbox — **habladuría** *nf* **1** : rumor **2 ~s** *nfpl* : gossip — **hablante** *nmf* : speaker

hacedor, -dora *n* : creator, maker

hacendado, -da *n* : landowner, rancher

hacer {40} *vt* **1** : do, perform **2** CONSTRUIR, CREAR : make **3** OBLIGAR : force, oblige — *vi* : act — *v impers* **1 ~ calor/viento** : be hot/be windy **2 ~ falta** : be necessary **3 hace mucho tiempo** : a long time ago **4 no lo hace** : it doesn't matter — **hacerse** *vr* **1** VOLVERSE : become **2** : pretend (to be) **3 ~ a** : get used to **4 se hace tarde** : it's getting late

hacha *nf* **1** : hatchet, ax **2** ANTORCHA : torch

hachís *nm* : hashish

hacia *prep* **1** : toward, towards **2** CERCA DE : near, around, about **3 ~ abajo** : downward **4 ~ adelante** : forward

hacienda *nf* **1** : estate, ranch **2** BIENES : property **3** *Lat* : livestock **4 Hacienda** : department of revenue

hacinar *vt* : stack

hada *nf* : fairy

hado *nm* : fate

halagar {52} *vt* : flatter — **halagador, -dora** *adj* : flattering — **halago** *nm* : flattery — **halagüeño, -ña** *adj* **1** : flattering **2** PROMETEDOR : promising

halcón *nm, pl* **-cones** : hawk, falcon

halibut *nm, pl* **-buts** : halibut

hálito *nm* : breath

hallar *vt* **1** : find **2** DESCUBRIR : discover, find out — **hallarse** *vr* : be, find oneself — **hallazgo** *nm* : discovery, find

halo *nm* : halo

hamaca *nf* : hammock

hambre *nf* **1** : hunger **2** INANICIÓN : starvation, famine **3 tener ~** : be hungry — **hambriento, -ta** *adj* : hungry, starving — **hambruna** *nf* : famine

hamburguesa *nf* : hamburger

hampa *nf* : underworld — **hampón, -pona** *n, mpl* **-pones** : criminal, thug

hámster *nm* : hamster

hándicap *nm* : handicap (in sports)

hangar *nm* : hangar

haragán, -gana *adj, mpl* **-ganes** : lazy, idle — **~** *n* : slacker, idler — **haraganear** : be lazy, loaf

harapiento, -ta *adj* : ragged, in rags — **harapos** *nmpl* : rags, tatters

harina *nf* : flour

hartar *vt* **1** : glut, satiate **2** FASTIDIAR : annoy — **hartarse** *vr* **1** : gorge oneself **2** CANSARSE : get fed up — **harto, -ta** *adj* **1** : full, satiated **2** CANSADO : tired, fed up — **harto** *adv* : extremely, very — **hartura** *nf* **1** : surfeit **2** ABUNDANCIA : abundance, plenty

hasta *prep* **1** : until, up until (in time) **2**

: as far as, up to (in space) **3 ¡~ luego!** : see you later! **4 ~ que** : until — ~ *adv* : even

hastiar {85} *vt* **1** : make weary, bore **2** ASQUEAR : sicken — **hastiarse** *vr* **~ de** : get tired of — **hastío** *nm* **1** : weariness, tedium **2** REPUGNANCIA : disgust

hato *nm* **1** : flock, herd **2** : bundle (of possessions)

haya *nf* : beech

haz *nm, pl* **haces 1** : bundle, sheaf **2** : beam (of light)

hazaña *nf* : feat, exploit

hazmerreír *nm fam* : laughingstock

he {39} *v impers* **~ aquí** : here is, here are, behold

hebilla *nf* : buckle

hebra *nf* : strand, thread

hebreo, -brea *adj* : Hebrew — **hebreo** *nm* : Hebrew (language)

hecatombe *nm* : disaster

hechizo *nm* **1** : spell **2** ENCANTO : charm, fascination — **hechicería** *nf* : sorcery, witchcraft — **hechicero, -ra** *n* : sorcerer, sorceress *f* — **hechizar** {21} *vt* **1** : bewitch **2** CAUTIVAR : charm

hecho, -cha *adj* **1** : made, done **2** : ready-to-wear (of clothing) **3 ~ y derecho** : full-fledged, mature — **hecho** *nm* **1** : fact **2** SUCESO : event **3** ACTO : act, deed **4 de ~** : in fact — **hechura** *nf* **1** : making, creation **2** FORMA : shape, form **3** : build (of the body) **4** ARTESANÍA : workmanship

heder {56} *vi* : stink, reek — **hediondez** *nf, pl* **-deces** : stench — **hediondo, -da** *adj* : stinking — **hedor** *nm* : stench

helar {55} *v* : freeze — **helarse** *vr* : freeze up, freeze over — **helado, -da** *adj* **1** : freezing cold **2** CONGELADO : frozen — **helada** *nf* : frost — **heladería** *nf* : ice-cream parlor — **helado** *nm* : ice cream — **heladora** *nf* : freezer

helecho *nm* : fern

hélice *nf* **1** : propeller **2** ESPIRAL : spiral, helix

helicóptero *nm* : helicopter

helio *nm* : helium

hembra *nf* **1** : female **2** MUJER : woman

hemisferio *nm* : hemisphere

hemorragia *nf* **1** : hemorrhage **2 ~ nasal** : nosebleed

hemorroides *nfpl* : hemorrhoids, piles

henchir {54} *vt* : stuff, fill

hender {56} *vt* : cleave, split — **hendidura** *nf* : crevice, fissure

henequén *nm, pl* **-quenes** : sisal

heno *nm* : hay

hepatitis *nf* : hepatitis

heraldo *nm* : herald

herbolario, -ria *n* : herbalist

heredar *vt* : inherit — **heredad** *nm* : rural property, estate — **heredero, -ra** *n* : heir, heiress *f* — **hereditario, -ria** *adj* : hereditary

hereje *nmf* : heretic — **herejía** *nf* : heresy

herencia *nf* **1** : inheritance **2** : heredity (in biology)

herir {76} *vt* **1** : injure, wound **2** : hurt (feelings, pride, etc.) — **herida** *nf* : injury, wound — **herido, -da** *adj* **1** : injured, wounded **2** : hurt (of feelings, pride, etc.) — ~ *n* : injured person, casualty

hermano, -na *n* : brother *m,* sister *f* — **hermanastro, -tra** *n* : half brother *m,* half sister *f* — **hermandad** *nf* : brotherhood

hermético, -ca *adj* : hermetic, watertight

hermoso, -sa *adj* : beautiful, lovely — **hermosura** *nf* : beauty

hernia *nf* : hernia

héroe *nm* : hero — **heroico, -ca** *adj* : heroic — **heroína** *nf* **1** : heroine **2** : heroin (narcotic) — **heroísmo** *nm* : heroism

herradura *nf* : horseshoe

herramienta *nf* : tool

herrero, -ra *n* : blacksmith

herrumbre *nf* : rust

hervir {76} *v* : boil — **hervidero** *nm* **1** : mass, swarm **2** : hotbed (of intrigue, etc.) — **hervidor** *nm* : kettle — **hervor** *nm* **1** : boiling **2** ENTUSIASMO : fervor, ardor

heterogéneo, -nea *adj* : heterogeneous

heterosexual *adj & nmf* : heterosexual

hexágono *nm* : hexagon — **hexagonal** *adj* : hexagonal

hez *nf, pl* **heces** : dregs *pl,* scum

hiato *nm* : hiatus

hibernar *vi* : hibernate — **hibernación** *nf, pl* **-ciones** : hibernation

híbrido, -da *adj* : hybrid — **híbrido** *nm* : hybrid

hidalgo, -ga *n* : nobleman *m,* noblewoman *f*

hidratante *adj* : moisturizing

hidrato *nm* **~ de carbono** : carbohydrate

hidráulico, -ca *adj* : hydraulic

hidroavión *nm, pl* **-aviones** : seaplane

hidroeléctrico, -ca *adj* : hydroelectric

hidrofobia *nf* : rabies

hidrógeno *nm* : hydrogen

hidroplano *nm* : hydroplane

hiedra *nf* **1** : ivy **2 ~ venenosa** : poison ivy
hiel *nm* **1** : bile **2** AMARGURA : bitterness
hielo *nm* **1** : ice **2** FRIALDAD : coldness **3 romper el ~** : break the ice
hiena *nf* : hyena
hierba *nf* **1** : herb **2** CÉSPED : grass **3 mala ~** : weed — **hierbabuena** *nf* : mint
hierro *nm* **1** : iron **2 ~ fundido** : cast iron
hígado *nm* : liver
higiene *nf* : hygiene — **higiénico, -ca** *adj* : hygienic
higo *nm* : fig
hijo, -ja *n* **1** : son *m*, daughter *f* **2 hijos** *nmpl* : children, offspring — **hijastro, -tra** *n* : stepson *m*, stepdaughter *f*
hilar *v* **1** : spin **2 ~ delgado** : split hairs — **hilado** *nm* : yarn, thread
hilaridad *nf* : hilarity
hilera *nf* : file, row
hilo *nm* **1** : thread **2** LINO : linen **3** ALAMBRE : wire **4** : trickle (of water, etc.) **5 ~ dental** : dental floss
hilvanar *vt* **1** : baste, tack **2** : put together (ideas, etc.)
himno *nm* **1** : hymn **2 ~ nacional** : national anthem
hincapié *nm* **hacer ~ en** : emphasize, stress
hincar {72} *vt* : drive in, plunge — **hincarse** *vr* **~ de rodillas** : kneel (down)
hinchar *vt Spain* : inflate, blow up — **hincharse** *vr* **1** : swell (up) **2** *Spain fam* : stuff oneself — **hinchado, -da** *adj* **1** : swollen **2** POMPOSO : pompous — **hinchazón** *nf*, *pl* **-zones** : swelling
hindú *adj & nmf* : Hindu — **hinduismo** *nm* : Hinduism
hinojo *nm* : fennel
hiperactivo, -va *adj* : hyperactive
hipersensible *adj* : oversensitive
hipertensión *nf*, *pl* **-siones** : hypertension, high blood pressure
hípico, -ca *adj* : equestrian, horse
hipil → **huipil**
hipnosis *nfs & pl* : hypnosis — **hipnótico, -ca** *adj* : hypnotic — **hipnotismo** *nm* : hypnotism — **hipnotizador, -dora** *n* : hypnotist — **hipnotizar** {21} *vt* : hypnotize
hipo *nm* **1** : hiccup, hiccups *pl* **2 tener ~** : have hiccups
hipocondríaco, -ca *adj* : hypochondriacal — **~** *n* : hypochondriac
hipocresía *nf* : hypocrisy — **hipócrita** *adj* : hypocritical — **~** *nmf* : hypocrite
hipodérmico, -ca *adj* : hypodermic
hipódromo *nm* : racetrack
hipopótamo *nm* : hippopotamus
hipoteca *nf* : mortgage — **hipotecar** {72} *vt* : mortgage
hipótesis *nfs & pl* : hypothesis — **hipotético, -ca** *adj* : hypothetical
hiriente *adj* : hurtful, offensive
hirsuto, -ta *adj* **1** : hairy **2** : bristly, wiry (of hair)
hirviente *adj* : boiling
hispano, -na *or* **hispánico, -ca** *adj & n* : Hispanic — **hispanoamericano, -na** *adj* : Latin-American — **~** *n* : Latin American — **hispanohablante** *or* **hispanoparlante** *adj* : Spanish-speaking
histeria *nf* : hysteria — **histérico, -ca** *adj* : hysterical — **histerismo** *nm* : hysteria
historia *nf* **1** : history **2** CUENTO : story — **historiador, -dora** *n* : historian — **historial** *nm* : record, background — **histórico, -ca** *adj* **1** : historical **2** IMPORTANTE : historic, important — **historieta** *nf* : comic strip
hito *nm* : milestone, landmark
hocico *nm* : snout, muzzle
hockey ['hɔke, -ki] *nm* : hockey
hogar *nm* **1** : home **2** CHIMENEA : hearth, fireplace — **hogareño, -ña** *adj* **1** : home-loving **2** DOMÉSTICO : home, domestic
hoguera *nf* : bonfire
hoja *nf* **1** : leaf **2** : sheet (of paper) **3 ~ de afeitar** : razor blade — **hojalata** *nf* : tinplate — **hojaldre** *nm* : puff pastry — **hojear** *vt* : leaf through — **hojuela** *nf Lat* : flake
hola *interj* : hello!, hi!
holandés, -desa *adj*, *mpl* **-deses** : Dutch
holgado, -da *adj* **1** : loose, baggy **2** : comfortable (of an economic situation, a victory, etc.) — **holgazán, -zana** *adj*, *mpl* **-zanes** : lazy — **~** *n* : slacker, idler — **holgazanear** *vi* : laze about, loaf — **holgura** *nf* **1** : looseness **2** BIENESTAR : comfort, ease
hollín *nm*, *pl* **-llines** : soot
holocausto *nm* : holocaust
hombre *nm* **1** : man **2 el ~** : mankind **3 ~ de estado** : statesman **4 ~ de negocios** : businessman
hombrera *nf* **1** : shoulder pad **2** : epaulet (of a uniform)
hombría *nf* : manliness
hombro *nm* : shoulder
hombruno, -na *adj* : mannish

homenaje *nm* **1** : homage **2 rendir ~ a** : pay tribute to
homeopatía *nf* : homeopathy
homicidio *nm* : homicide, murder — **homicida** *adj* : homicidal, murderous — **~** *nmf* : murderer
homogéneo, -nea *adj* : homogeneous
homólogo, -ga *adj* : equivalent — **~** *n* : counterpart
homosexual *adj & nmf* : homosexual — **homosexualidad** *nf* : homosexuality
hondo, -da *adj* : deep — **hondo** *adv* : deeply — **hondonada** *nf* : hollow — **hondura** *nf* : depth
hondureño, -ña *adj* : Honduran
honesto, -ta *adj* : decent, honorable — **honestidad** *nf* : honesty, integrity
hongo *nm* **1** : mushroom **2** : fungus (in botany and medicine)
honor *nm* : honor — **honorable** *adj* : honorable — **honorario, -ria** *adj* : honorary — **honorarios** *nmpl* : payment, fee — **honra** *nf* : honor — **honradez** *nf, pl* **-deces** : honesty, integrity — **honrado, -da** *adj* : honest, upright — **honrar** *vt* : honor — **honrarse** *vr* : be honored — **honroso, -sa** *adj* : honorable
hora *nf* **1** : hour **2** : (specific) time **3** CITA : appointment **4 a la última ~** : at the last minute **5 ~ punta** : rush hour **6 media ~** : half an hour **7 ¿qué ~ es?** : what time is it? **8 ~s de oficina** : office hours **9 ~s extraordinarias** : overtime
horario *nm* : schedule, timetable
horca *nf* **1** : gallows *pl* **2** : pitchfork (in agriculture)
horcajadas: **a ~** *adv phr* : astride
horda *nf* : horde
horizonte *nm* : horizon — **horizontal** *adj* : horizontal
horma *nf* **1** : form, mold, last **2** : shoe tree
hormiga *nf* : ant
hormigón *nm, pl* **-gones** : concrete
hormigueo *nm* : tingling, pins and needles
hormiguero *nm* **1** : anthill **2** : swarm (of people)
hormona *nf* : hormone
horno *nm* **1** : oven (for cooking) **2** : small furnace, kiln — **hornada** *nf* : batch — **hornear** *vt* : bake — **hornillo** *nf* : portable stove
horóscopo *nm* : horoscope
horquilla *nf* **1** : hairpin, bobby pin **2** HORCA : pitchfork
horrendo, -da *adj* : horrendous, awful — **horrible** *adj* : horrible — **horripilante** *adj* : horrifying — **horror** *nm* **1** : horror, dread **2** ATROCIDAD : atrocity — **horrorizar** {21} *vt* : horrify, terrify — **horrorizarse** *vr* : be horrified — **horroroso, -sa** *adj* : horrifying, dreadful
hortaliza *nf* : (garden) vegetable — **hortelano, -na** *n* : truck farmer — **horticultura** *nf* : horticulture
hosco, -ca *adj* : sullen, gloomy
hospedar *vt* : put up, lodge — **hospedarse** *vr* : stay, lodge — **hospedaje** *nm* : lodging
hospital *nm* : hospital — **hospitalario, -ria** *adj* : hospitable — **hospitalidad** *nf* : hospitality — **hospitalizar** {21} *vt* : hospitalize
hostería *nf* : small hotel, inn
hostia *nf* : host (in religion)
hostigar {52} *vt* **1** : whip **2** ACOSAR : harass, pester
hostil *adj* : hostile — **hostilidad** *nf* : hostility
hotel *nm* : hotel — **hotelero, -ra** *adj* : hotel — **~** *n* : hotel manager, hotelier
hoy *adv* **1** : today **2 de ~ en adelante** : from now on **3 ~ (en) día** : nowadays **4 ~ mismo** : this very day
hoyo *nm* : hole — **hoyuelo** *nm* : dimple
hoz *nf, pl* **hoces** : sickle
huarache *nm* : huarache (sandal)
hueco, -ca *adj* **1** : hollow, empty **2** ESPONJOSO : soft, spongy **3** RESONANTE : resonant — **hueco** *nm* **1** : hollow, cavity **2** : recess (in a wall, etc.) **3 ~ de escalera** : stairwell
huelga *nf* **1** : strike **2 declararse en ~** : go on strike — **huelguista** *nmf* : striker
huella *nf* **1** : footprint **2** VESTIGIO : track, mark **3 ~ digital** *or* **~ dactilar** : fingerprint
huérfano, -na *n* : orphan — **~** *adj* : orphaned
huerta *nf* : truck farm — **huerto** *nm* **1** : vegetable garden **2** : (fruit) orchard
hueso *nm* **1** : bone **2** : pit, stone (of a fruit)
huésped, -peda *n* : guest — **huésped** *nm* : host (organism)
huesudo, -da *adj* : bony
huevo *nm* **1** : egg **2 ~s estrellados** : fried eggs **3 ~s revueltos** : scrambled eggs — **hueva** *nf* : roe
huida *nf* : flight, escape — **huidizo, -za** *adj* **1** : shy **2** FUGAZ : fleeting
huipil *nm Lat* : traditional embroidered blouse or dress

huir {41} *vi* **1** : escape, flee **2 ~ de** : shun, avoid
hule *nm* **1** : oilcloth **2** *Lat* : rubber
humano, -na *adj* **1** : human **2** COMPASIVO : humane — **humano** *nm* : human (being) — **humanidad** *nf* **1** : humanity, mankind **2** BENEVOLENCIA : humaneness **3 ~es** *nfpl* : humanities — **humanismo** *nm* : humanism — **humanista** *nmf* : humanist — **humanitario, -ria** *adj & n* : humanitarian
humear *vi* : smoke, steam — **humareda** *nf* : cloud of smoke
humedad *nf* **1** : dampness **2** : humidity (in meteorology) — **humedecer** {53} *vt* : moisten, dampen — **humedecerse** *vr* : become moist — **húmedo, -da** *adj* **1** : moist, damp **2** : humid (in meteorology)
humildad *nf* : humility — **humilde** *adj* : humble — **humillación** *nf, pl* **-ciones** : humiliation — **humillante** *adj* : humiliating — **humillar** *vt* : humiliate — **humillarse** *vr* : humble oneself
humo *nm* **1** : smoke, steam, fumes **2 ~s** *nmpl* : airs, conceit
humor *nm* **1** : mood, temper **2** GRACIA : humor **3 de buen ~** : in a good mood — **humorismo** *nm* : humor, wit — **humorista** *nmf* : humorist, comedian — **humorístico, -ca** *adj* : humorous
hundir *vt* **1** : sink **2** : destroy, ruin (a building, plans, etc.) — **hundirse** *vr* **1** : sink **2** DERRUMBARSE : collapse — **hundido, -da** *adj* : sunken — **hundimiento** *nm* **1** : sinking **2** DERRUMBE : collapse
húngaro, -ra *adj* : Hungarian
huracán *nm, pl* **-canes** : hurricane
huraño, -ña *adj* : unsociable
hurgar {52} *vi* **~ en** : rummage around in
hurón *nm, pl* **-rones** : ferret
hurra *interj* : hurrah!, hooray!
hurtadillas: **a ~** *adv phr* : stealthily, on the sly
hurtar *vt* : steal — **hurto** *nm* **1** ROBO : theft **2** : stolen property
husmear *vt* : sniff out, pry into — *vi* : nose around
huy *interj* : ow!, ouch!

I

i *nf* : i, ninth letter of the Spanish alphabet
ibérico, -ca *adj* : Iberian — **ibero, -ra** *or* **íbero, -ra** *adj* : Iberian
iceberg *nm, pl* **-bergs** : iceberg
icono *nm* : icon
ictericia *nf* : jaundice
ida *nf* **1** : outward journey **2 ~ y vuelta** : round-trip **3 ~s y venidas** : comings and goings
idea *nf* **1** : idea **2** OPINIÓN : opinion
ideal *adj & nm* : ideal — **idealismo** *nm* : idealism — **idealista** *adj* : idealistic — **~** *nmf* : idealist — **idealizar** {21} *vt* : idealize
idear *vt* : devise, think up
ídem *nm* : the same, ditto
identidad *nf* : identity — **idéntico, -ca** *adj* : identical — **identificar** {72} *vt* : identify — **identificarse** *vr* **1** : identify oneself **2 ~ con** : identify with — **identificación** *nf, pl* **-ciones** : identification
ideología *nf* : ideology — **ideológico, -ca** *adj* : ideological
idílico, -ca *adj* : idyllic
idioma *nm* : language — **idiomático, -ca** *adj* : idiomatic
idiosincrasia *nf* : idiosyncrasy — **idiosincrásico, -ca** *adj* : idiosyncratic
idiota *adj* : idiotic — **~** *nmf* : idiot — **idiotez** *nf* : idiocy
ídolo *nm* : idol — **idolatrar** *vt* : idolize — **idolatría** *nf* : idolatry
idóneo, -nea *adj* : suitable, fitting — **idoneidad** *nf* : fitness, suitability
iglesia *nf* : church
iglú *nm* : igloo
ignición *nf, pl* **-ciones** : ignition
ignífugo, -ga *adj* : fire-resistant, fireproof
ignorar *vt* **1** : ignore **2** DESCONOCER : be unaware of — **ignorancia** *nf* : ignorance — **ignorante** *adj* : ignorant — **~** *nmf* : ignorant person
igual *adv* **1** : in the same way **2 por ~** : equally — **~** *adj* **1** : equal **2** IDÉNTICO : the same **3** LISO : smooth, even **4** SEMEJANTE : similar — **~** *nmf* : equal, peer — **igualar** *vt* **1** : make equal **2** : be equal to **3** NIVELAR : level (off) — **igualdad** *nf* **1** : equality **2** UNIFORMI-

DAD : uniformity — **igualmente** *adv* : likewise
iguana *nf* : iguana
ijada *nf* : flank
ilegal *adj* : illegal
ilegible *adj* : illegible
ilegítimo, -ma *adj* : illegitimate — **ilegitimidad** *nf* : illegitimacy
ileso, -sa *adj* : unharmed
ilícito, -ta *adj* : illicit
ilimitado, -da *adj* : unlimited
ilógico, -ca *adj* : illogical
iluminar *vt* : illuminate — **iluminarse** *vr* : light up — **iluminación** *nf, pl* **-ciones 1** : illumination **2** ALUMBRADO : lighting
ilusionar *vt* : excite — **ilusionarse** *vr* : get one's hopes up — **ilusión** *nf, pl* **-siones 1** : illusion **2** ESPERANZA : hope — **ilusionado, -da** *adj* : excited
iluso -sa *adj* : naïve, gullible — ~ *n* : dreamer, visionary — **ilusorio, -ria** *adj* : illusory
ilustrar *vt* **1** : illustrate **2** ACLARAR : explain — **ilustración** *nf, pl* **-ciones 1** : illustration **2** SABER : learning **3 la Ilustración** : the Enlightenment — **ilustrado, -da** *adj* **1** : illustrated **2** ERUDITO : learned — **ilustrador, -dora** *n* : illustrator
ilustre *adj* : illustrious
imagen *nf, pl* **imágenes** : image, picture
imaginar *vt* : imagine — **imaginarse** *vr* : imagine — **imaginación** *nf, pl* **-ciones** : imagination — **imaginario, -ria** *adj* : imaginary — **imaginativo, -va** *adj* : imaginative
imán *nm, pl* **imanes** : magnet — **imantar** *vt* : magnetize
imbécil *adj* : stupid, idiotic — ~ *nmf* : idiot
imborrable *adj* : indelible
imbuir {41} *vt* ~ **de** : imbue with
imitar *vt* **1** COPIAR : imitate, copy **2** : impersonate — **imitación** *nf, pl* **-ciones 1** COPIA : imitation, copy **2** : impersonation — **imitador, -dora** *n* : impersonator
impaciencia *nf* : impatience — **impacientar** *vt* : make impatient, exasperate — **impacientarse** *vr* : grow impatient — **impaciente** *adj* : impatient
impacto *nm* : impact
impar *adj* : odd — ~ *nm* : odd number
imparcial *adj* : impartial — **imparcialidad** *nf* : impartiality
impartir *vt* : impart, give
impasible *adj* : impassive
impasse *nm* : impasse
impávido, -da *adj* : fearless
impecable *adj* : impeccable, spotless
impedir {54} *vt* **1** : prevent **2** DIFICULTAR : impede, hinder — **impedido, -da** *adj* : disabled — **impedimento** *nm* : obstacle, impediment
impeler *vt* : drive, propel
impenetrable *adj* : impenetrable
impenitente *adj* : unrepentant
impensable *adj* : unthinkable — **impensado, -da** *adj* : unexpected
imperar *vi* **1** : reign, rule **2** PREDOMINAR : prevail — **imperante** *adj* : prevailing
imperativo, -va *adj* : imperative — **imperativo** *nm* : imperative
imperceptible *adj* : imperceptible
imperdible *nm* : safety pin
imperdonable *adj* : unforgivable
imperfección *nf, pl* **-ciones** : imperfection — **imperfecto, -ta** *adj* : imperfect — **imperfecto** *nm* : imperfect (tense)
imperial *adj* : imperial — **imperialismo** *nm* : imperialism — **imperialista** *adj & nmf* : imperialist
impericia *nf* : lack of skill
imperio *nm* **1** : empire **2** DOMINIO : rule — **imperioso, -sa** *adj* **1** : imperious **2** URGENTE : pressing, urgent
impermeable *adj* **1** : waterproof **2** ~ **a** : impervious to — ~ *nm* : raincoat
impersonal *adj* : impersonal
impertinente *adj* : impertinent — **impertinencia** *nf* : impertinence
ímpetu *nm* **1** : impetus **2** ENERGÍA : energy, vigor **3** VIOLENCIA : force — **impetuoso, -sa** *adj* : impetuous — **impetuosidad** *nf* : impetuosity
impío, -pía *adj* : impious, ungodly
implacable *adj* : implacable
implantar *vt* **1** : implant **2** ESTABLECER : establish, introduce
implemento *nm Lat* : implement, tool
implicar {72} *vt* **1** : involve, implicate **2** SIGNIFICAR : imply — **implicación** *nf, pl* **-ciones** : implication
implícito, -ta *adj* : implicit
implorar *vt* : implore
imponer {60} *vt* **1** : impose **2** : command (respect, etc.) — *vi* : be imposing — **imponerse** *vr* **1** : assert oneself, command respect **2** PREVALECER : prevail — **imponente** *adj* : imposing, impressive — **imponible** *adj* : taxable
impopular *adj* : unpopular — **impopularidad** *nf* : unpopularity
importación *nf, pl* **-ciones 1** : importation **2 importaciones** *nfpl* : imports — **importado, -da** *adj* : imported — **importador, -dora** *adj* : importing — ~ *n* : importer

importancia *nf* : importance — **importante** *adj* : important — **importar** *vi* **1** : matter, be important **2 no me importa** : I don't care — *vt* **1** : import **2** ASCENDER A : amount to, cost
importe *nm* **1** : price **2** CANTIDAD : sum, amount
importunar *vt* : bother — **importuno, -na** *adj* **1** : inopportune **2** MOLESTO : bothersome
imposible *adj* : impossible — **imposibilidad** *nf* : impossibility
imposición *nf, pl* **-ciones 1** : imposition **2** IMPUESTO : tax
impostor, -tora *n* : impostor
impotente *adj* : powerless, impotent — **impotencia** *nf* : impotence
impracticable *adj* **1** : impracticable **2** INTRANSITABLE : impassable
impreciso, -sa *adj* : vague, imprecise — **imprecisión** *nf, pl* **-siones 1** : vagueness **2** ERROR : inaccuracy
impredecible *adj* : unpredictable
impregnar *vt* : impregnate
imprenta *nf* **1** : printing **2** : printing shop, press
imprescindible *adj* : essential, indispensable
impresión *nf, pl* **-siones 1** : impression **2** IMPRENTA : printing — **impresionable** *adj* : impressionable — **impresionante** *adj* : impressive — **impresionar** *vt* **1** : impress **2** CONMOVER : affect, move — *vi* : make an impression — **impresionarse** *vr* **1** : be impressed **2** CONMOVERSE : be affected
impreso, -sa *adj* : printed — **impreso** *nm* **1** FORMULARIO : form **2 ~s** *nmpl* : printed matter — **impresor, -sora** *n* : printer — **impresora** *nf* : (computer) printer
imprevisible *adj* : unforeseeable — **imprevisto, -ta** *adj* : unexpected, unforeseen
imprimir {42} *vt* **1** : print **2** DAR : impart, give
improbable *adj* : improbable — **improbabilidad** *nf* : improbability
improcedente *adj* : inappropriate
improductivo, -va *adj* : unproductive
improperio *nm* : insult
impropio, -pia *adj* **1** : inappropriate **2** INCORRECTO : incorrect
improvisar *v* : improvise — **improvisado, -da** *adj* : improvised, impromptu — **improvisación** *nf, pl* **-ciones** : improvisation — **improviso**: **de ~** *adv phr* : suddenly
imprudente *adj* : imprudent, rash — **imprudencia** *nf* : imprudence, carelessness
impúdico, -ca *adj* : shameless, indecent
impuesto *nm* **1** : tax **2 ~ sobre la renta** : income tax
impugnar *vt* : challenge, contest
impulsar *vt* : propel, drive — **impulsividad** *nf* : impulsiveness — **impulsivo, -va** *adj* : impulsive — **impulso** *nm* **1** : drive, thrust **2** MOTIVACIÓN : impulse
impune *adj* : unpunished — **impunidad** *nf* : impunity
impuro, -ra *adj* : impure — **impureza** *nf* : impurity
imputar *vt* : impute, attribute
inacabable *adj* : interminable, endless
inaccesible *adj* : inaccessible
inaceptable *adj* : unacceptable
inactivo, -va *adj* : inactive — **inactividad** *nf* : inactivity
inadaptado, -da *adj* : maladjusted — **~** *n* : misfit
inadecuado, -da *adj* **1** : inadequate **2** INAPROPIADO : inappropriate
inadmisible *adj* : inadmissible
inadvertido, -da *adj* **1** : unnoticed **2** DISTRAÍDO : distracted — **inadvertencia** *nf* : oversight
inagotable *adj* : inexhaustible
inaguantable *adj* : unbearable
inalámbrico, -ca *adj* : wireless, cordless
inalcanzable *adj* : unreachable, unattainable
inalterable *adj* **1** : unchangeable **2** : impassive (of character) **3** : fast (of colors)
inanición *nf, pl* **-ciones** : starvation, famine
inanimado, -da *adj* : inanimate
inaplicable *adj* : inapplicable
inapreciable *adj* : imperceptible
inapropiado, -da *adj* : inappropriate
inarticulado, -da *adj* : inarticulate
inasequible *adj* : unattainable
inaudito, -ta *adj* : unheard-of, unprecedented
inaugurar *vt* : inaugurate — **inauguración** *nf, pl* **-ciones** : inauguration — **inaugural** *adj* : inaugural
inca *adj* : Inca, Incan
incalculable *adj* : incalculable
incandescencia *nf* : incandescence — **incandescente** *adj* : incandescent
incansable *adj* : tireless
incapacitar *vt* : incapacitate, disable — **incapacidad** *nf* : incapacity, inability — **incapaz** *adj, pl* **-paces** : incapable
incautar *vt* : confiscate, seize

incendiar *vt* : set fire to, burn (down) — **incendiarse** *vr* : catch fire — **incendiario, -ria** *adj* : incendiary — ~ *n* : arsonist — **incendio** *nm* **1** : fire **2** ~ **premeditado** : arson
incentivo *nm* : incentive
incertidumbre *nf* : uncertainty
incesante *adj* : incessant
incesto *nm* : incest — **incestuoso, -sa** *adj* : incestuous
incidencia *nf* **1** : impact **2** SUCESO : incident — **incidental** *adj* : incidental — **incidente** *nm* : incident
incidir *vi* ~ **en 1** : fall into (a habit, mistake, etc.) **2** INFLUIR EN : affect, influence
incienso *nm* : incense
incierto, -ta *adj* : uncertain
incinerar *vt* **1** : incinerate **2** : cremate (a corpse) — **incineración** *nf, pl* **-ciones 1** : incineration **2** : cremation (of a corpse) — **incinerador** *nm* : incinerator
incipiente *adj* : incipient
incisión *nf, pl* **-siones** : incision
incisivo, -va *adj* : incisive — **incisivo** *nm* : incisor
incitar *vt* : incite, rouse
incivilizado, -da *adj* : uncivilized
inclinar *vt* : tilt, lean — **inclinarse** *vr* **1** : lean (over) **2** ~ **a** : be inclined to — **inclinación** *nf, pl* **-ciones 1** : inclination **2** LADEAR : incline, tilt
incluir {41} *vt* **1** : include **2** ADJUNTAR : enclose — **inclusión** *nf, pl* **-siones** : inclusion — **inclusive** *adv* : up to and including — **inclusivo, -va** *adj* : inclusive — **incluso** *adv* : even, in fact — **incluso, -sa** *adj* : enclosed
incógnito, -ta *adj* **1** : unknown **2 de** ~ : incognito
incoherente *adj* : incoherent — **incoherencia** *nf* : incoherence
incoloro, -ra *adj* : colorless
incombustible *adj* : fireproof
incomible *adj* : inedible
incomodar *vt* **1** : inconvenience **2** ENFADAR : bother, annoy — **incomodarse** *vr* **1** : take the trouble **2** ENFADARSE : get annoyed — **incomodidad** *nf* : discomfort — **incómodo, -da** *adj* **1** : uncomfortable **2** INCONVENIENTE : inconvenient, awkward
incomparable *adj* : incomparable
incompatible *adj* : incompatible — **incompatibilidad** *nf* : incompatibility
incompetente *adj* : incompetent — **incompetencia** *nf* : incompetence
incompleto, -ta *adj* : incomplete
incomprendido, -da *adj* : misunderstood — **incomprensible** *adj* : incomprehensible — **incomprensión** *nf, pl* **-siones** : lack of understanding
incomunicado, -da *adj* **1** : isolated **2** : in solitary confinement
inconcebible *adj* : inconceivable
inconcluso, -sa *adj* : unfinished
incondicional *adj* : unconditional
inconformista *adj & nmf* : nonconformist
inconfundible *adj* : unmistakable
incongruente *adj* : incongruous
inconmensurable *adj* : vast, immeasurable
inconsciente *adj* **1** : unconscious, unaware **2** IRREFLEXIVO : reckless — ~ *nm* **el** ~ : the unconscious — **inconsciencia** *nf* **1** : unconsciousness **2** INSENSATEZ : thoughtlessness
inconsecuente *adj* : inconsistent — **inconsecuencia** *nf* : inconsistency
inconsiderado, -da *adj* : inconsiderate
inconsistente *adj* **1** : flimsy **2** : watery (of a sauce, etc.) **3** : inconsistent (of an argument) — **inconsistencia** *nf* : inconsistency
inconsolable *adj* : inconsolable
inconstante *adj* : changeable, unreliable — **inconstancia** *nf* : inconstancy
inconstitucional *adj* : unconstitutional
incontable *adj* : countless
incontenible *adj* : irrepressible
incontestable *adj* : indisputable
incontinente *adj* : incontinent — **incontinencia** *nf* : incontinence
inconveniente *adj* **1** : inconvenient **2** INAPROPIADO : inappropriate — ~ *nm* : obstacle, problem — **inconveniencia** *nf* **1** : inconvenience **2** : tactless remark
incorporar *vt* **1** AGREGAR : incorporate, add **2** : mix (in cooking) — **incorporarse** *vr* **1** : sit up **2** ~ **a** : join — **incorporación** *nf, pl* **-ciones** : incorporation
incorrecto, -ta *adj* **1** : incorrect **2** DESCORTÉS : impolite
incorregible *adj* : incorrigible
incrédulo, -la *adj* : incredulous — **incredulidad** *nf* : incredulity, disbelief
increíble *adj* : incredible, unbelievable
incrementar *vt* : increase — **incremento** *nm* : increase
incriminar *vt* **1** : incriminate **2** ACUSAR : accuse
incrustar *vt* : set, inlay — **incrustarse** *vr* : become embedded
incubar *vt* : incubate — **incubadora** *nf* : incubator

incuestionable *adj* : unquestionable
inculcar {72} *vt* : instill
inculpar *vt* : accuse, charge
inculto, -ta *adj* **1** : uneducated **2** : uncultivated (of land)
incumplimiento *nm* **1** : noncompliance **2 ~ de contrato** : breach of contract
incurable *adj* : incurable
incurrir *vi* **~ en 1** : incur (expenses, etc.) **2** : fall into, commit (crimes)
incursión *nf, pl* **-siones** : raid
indagar {52} *vt* : investigate — **indagación** *nf, pl* **-ciones** : investigation
indebido, -da *adj* : undue
indecente *adj* : indecent, obscene — **indecencia** *nf* : indecency, obscenity
indecible *adj* : inexpressible
indecisión *nf, pl* **-siones** : indecision — **indeciso, -sa** *adj* **1** : undecided **2** IRRESOLUTO : indecisive
indefenso, -sa *adj* : defenseless, helpless
indefinido, -da *adj* : indefinite — **indefinidamente** *adv* : indefinitely
indeleble *adj* : indelible
indemnizar {21} *vt* : indemnify, compensate — **indemnización** *nf, pl* **-ciones** : compensation
independiente *adj* : independent — **independencia** *nf* : independence — **independizarse** {21} *vr* : become independent
indescifrable *adj* : indecipherable
indescriptible *adj* : indescribable
indeseable *adj* : undesirable
indestructible *adj* : indestructible
indeterminado, -da *adj* : indeterminate
indicar {72} *vt* **1** : indicate **2** MOSTRAR : show — **indicación** *nf, pl* **-ciones 1** : sign, indication **2 indicaciones** *nfpl* : directions — **indicador** *nm* **1** : sign, signal **2** : gauge, dial, meter — **indicativo, -va** *adj* : indicative — **indicativo** *nm* : indicative (mood)
índice *nm* **1** : indication **2** : index (of a book, etc.) **3** : index finger **4 ~ de natalidad** : birth rate
indicio *nm* : indication, sign
indiferente *adj* **1** : indifferent **2 me es ~** : it doesn't matter to me — **indiferencia** *nf* : indifference
indígena *adj* : indigenous, native — **~** *nmf* : native
indigente *adj & nmf* : indigent — **indigencia** *nf* : poverty
indigestión *nf, pl* **-tiones** : indigestion — **indigesto, -ta** *adj* : indigestible
indignar *vt* : outrage, infuriate — **indignarse** *vr* : become indignant — **indignación** *nf, pl* **-ciones** : indignation — **indignado, -da** *adj* : indignant — **indignidad** *nf* : indignity — **indigno, -na** *adj* : unworthy
indio, -dia *adj* **1** : American Indian **2** : Indian (from India)
indirecta *nf* **1** : hint **2 lanzar una ~** : drop a hint — **indirecto, -ta** *adj* : indirect
indisciplina *nf* : lack of discipline — **indisciplinado, -da** *adj* : undisciplined
indiscreto, -ta *adj* : indiscreet — **indiscreción** *nf, pl* **-ciones 1** : indiscretion **2** : tactless remark
indiscriminado, -da *adj* : indiscriminate
indiscutible *adj* : indisputable
indispensable *adj* : indispensable
indisponer {60} *vt* **1** : upset, make ill **2** ENEMISTAR : set against, set at odds — **indisponerse** *vr* **1** : become ill **2 ~ con** : fall out with — **indisposición** *nf, pl* **-ciones** : indisposition, illness — **indispuesto, -ta** *adj* : unwell, indisposed
indistinto, -ta *adj* : indistinct
individual *adj* : individual — **individualidad** *nf* : individuality — **individualizar** {21} *vt* : individualize — **individuo** *nm* : individual
indivisible *adj* : indivisible
índole *nf* **1** : nature, character **2** TIPO : type, kind
indolente *adj* : indolent, lazy — **indolencia** *nf* : indolence, laziness
indoloro, -ra *adj* : painless
indómito, -ta *adj* : indomitable
indonesio, -sia *adj* : Indonesian
inducir {61} *vt* **1** : induce **2** DEDUCIR : infer
indudable *adj* : beyond doubt — **indudablemente** *adv* : undoubtedly
indulgente *adj* : indulgent — **indulgencia** *nf* : indulgence
indultar *vt* : pardon, reprieve — **indulto** *nm* : pardon, reprieve
industria *nf* : industry — **industrial** *adj* : industrial — **~** *nmf* : industrialist, manufacturer — **industrialización** *nf, pl* **-ciones** : industrialization — **industrializar** {21} *vt* : industrialize — **industrioso, -sa** *adj* : industrious
inédito, -ta *adj* : unpublished
inefable *adj* : inexpressible
ineficaz *adj, pl* **-caces 1** : ineffective **2** INEFICIENTE : inefficient
ineficiente *adj* : inefficient — **ineficiencia** *nf* : inefficiency
ineligible *adj* : ineligible

ineludible *adj* : unavoidable, inescapable
inepto, -ta *adj* : inept — **ineptitud** *nf* : ineptitude
inequívoco, -ca *adj* : unequivocal
inercia *nf* : inertia
inerme *adj* : unarmed, defenseless
inerte *adj* : inert
inesperado, -da *adj* : unexpected
inestable *adj* : unstable — **inestabilidad** *nf* : instability
inevitable *adj* : inevitable
inexacto, -ta *adj* **1** : inexact **2** INCORRECTO : incorrect, wrong
inexistente *adj* : nonexistent
inexorable *adj* : inexorable
inexperiencia *nf* : inexperience — **inexperto, -ta** *adj* : inexperienced, unskilled
inexplicable *adj* : inexplicable
infalible *adj* : infallible
infame *adj* **1** : infamous, vile **2** *fam* : horrible — **infamia** *nf* : infamy, disgrace
infancia *nf* : infancy — **infanta** *nf* : infanta, princess — **infante** *nm* **1** : infante, prince **2** : infantryman (in the military) — **infantería** *nf* : infantry — **infantil** *adj* **1** : child's, children's **2** INMADURO : childish
infarto *nm* : heart attack
infatigable *adj* : tireless
infectar *vt* : infect — **infectarse** *vr* : become infected — **infección** *nf, pl* **-ciones** : infection — **infeccioso, -sa** *adj* : infectious — **infecto, -ta** *adj* **1** : infected **2** : foul, sickening
infecundo, -da *adj* : infertile
infeliz *adj, pl* **-lices** : unhappy — **infelicidad** *nf* : unhappiness
inferior *adj & nmf* : inferior — **inferioridad** *nf* : inferiority
inferir {76} *vt* **1** DEDUCIR : infer **2** : cause (harm or injury)
infernal *adj* : infernal, hellish
infestar *vt* : infest
infiel *adj* : unfaithful — **infidelidad** *nf* : infidelity
infierno *nm* **1** : hell **2 el quinto ~** *fam* : the middle of nowhere
infiltrar *vt* : infiltrate — **infiltrarse** *vr* : infiltrate
infinidad *nf* **1** : infinity **2 una ~ de** : countless — **infinitivo** *nm* : infinitive — **infinito, -ta** *adj* : infinite — **infinito** *nm* : infinity
inflación *nf, pl* **-ciones** : inflation — **inflacionario, -ria** *or* **inflacionista** *adj* : inflationary
inflamar *vt* : inflame — **inflamable** *adj* : flammable, inflammable — **inflamación** *nf, pl* **-ciones** : inflammation — **inflamatorio, -ria** *adj* : inflammatory
inflar *vt* **1** : inflate **2** EXAGERAR : exaggerate — **inflarse** *vr* **~ de** : swell (up) with
inflexible *adj* : inflexible — **inflexión** *nf, pl* **-xiones** : inflection
infligir {35} *vt* : inflict
influencia *nf* : influence — **influenciar** → **influir**
influenza *nf* : influenza
influir {41} *vt* : influence — *vi* **~ en** *or* **~ sobre** : have an influence on — **influjo** *nm* : influence — **influyente** *adj* : influential
información *nf, pl* **-ciones 1** : information **2** NOTICIAS : news **3** : directory assistance (on the telephone)
informal *adj* **1** : informal **2** IRRESPONSABLE : unreliable
informar *v* : inform — **informarse** *vr* : get information, find out — **informante** *nmf* : informant — **informática** *nf* : information technology — **informativo, -va** *adj* : informative — **informatizar** {21} *vt* : computerize
informe *adj* : shapeless — **~** *nm* **1** : report **2 ~s** *nmpl* : information, data **3 ~s** *nmpl* : references (for employment)
infortunado, -da *adj* : unfortunate — **infortunio** *nm* : misfortune
infracción *nf, pl* **-ciones** : violation, infraction
infraestructura *nf* : infrastructure
infrahumano, -na *adj* : subhuman
infranqueable *adj* **1** : impassable **2** INSUPERABLE : insurmountable
infrarrojo, -ja *adj* : infrared
infrecuente *adj* : infrequent
infringir {35} *vt* : infringe
infructuoso, -sa *adj* : fruitless
infundado, -da *adj* : unfounded, baseless
infundir *vt* : instill, infuse — **infusión** *nf, pl* **-siones** : infusion
ingeniar *vt* : invent, think up
ingeniería *nf* : engineering — **ingeniero, -ra** *n* : engineer
ingenio *nm* **1** : ingenuity **2** AGUDEZA : wit **3** MÁQUINA : device, apparatus **4 ~ azucarero** *Lat* : sugar refinery — **ingenioso, -sa** *adj* **1** : ingenious **2** AGUDO : clever, witty — **ingeniosamente** *adv* : cleverly
ingenuidad *nf* : naïveté, ingenuousness — **ingenuo, -nua** *adj* : naive
ingerir {76} *vt* : ingest, consume

ingle *nf* : groin
inglés, -glesa *adj, mpl* **-gleses** : English — **inglés** *nm* : English (language)
ingrato, -ta *adj* **1** : ungrateful **2 un trabajo ingrato** : a thankless task — **ingratitud** *nf* : ingratitude
ingrediente *nm* : ingredient
ingresar *vt* : deposit — *vi* **~ en** : enter, be admitted into, join — **ingreso** *nm* **1** : entrance, entry **2** : admission (into a hospital, etc.) **3 ~s** *nmpl* : income, earnings
inhábil *adj* **1** : unskillful, clumsy **2 ~ para** : unsuited for — **inhabilidad** *nf* : unskillfulness
inhabitable *adj* : uninhabitable — **inhabitado, -da** *adj* : uninhabited
inhalar *vt* : inhale — **inhalación** *nf* : inhalation
inherente *adj* : inherent
inhibir *vt* : inhibit — **inhibición** *nf, pl* **-ciones** : inhibition
inhóspito, -ta *adj* : inhospitable
inhumano, -na *adj* : inhuman, inhumane — **inhumanidad** *nf* : inhumanity
iniciar *vt* : initiate, begin — **iniciación** *nf, pl* **-ciones 1** : initiation **2** COMIENZO : beginning — **inicial** *adj & nf* : initial — **iniciativa** *nf* : initiative — **inicio** *nm* : start, beginning
inigualado, -da *adj* : unequaled
ininterrumpido, -da *adj* : uninterrupted
injerirse {76} *vr* : interfere — **injerencia** *nf* : interference
injertar *vt* : graft — **injerto** *nm* : graft
injuriar *vt* : insult — **injuria** *nf* : insult — **injurioso, -sa** *adj* : insulting, abusive
injusticia *nf* : injustice, unfairness — **injusto, -ta** *adj* : unfair, unjust
inmaculado, -da *adj* : immaculate
inmaduro, -ra *adj* **1** : immature **2** : unripe (of fruit) — **inmadurez** *nf* : immaturity
inmediaciones *nfpl* : surrounding area
inmediato, -ta *adj* **1** : immediate **2** CONTIGUO : adjoining **3 de ~** : immediately, right away **4 ~ a** : next to, close to — **inmediatamente** *adv* : immediately
inmejorable *adj* : excellent
inmenso, -sa *adj* : immense, vast — **inmensidad** *nf* : immensity
inmerecido, -da *adj* : undeserved
inmersión *nf, pl* **-siones** : immersion
inmigrar *vi* : immigrate — **inmigración** *nf, pl* **-ciones** : immigration — **inmigrante** *adj & nmf* : immigrant
inminente *adj* : imminent, impending — **inminencia** *nf* : imminence
inmiscuirse {41} *vr* : interfere
inmobiliario, -ria *adj* : real estate, property
inmodesto, -ta *adj* : immodest
inmoral *adj* : immoral — **inmoralidad** *nf* : immorality
inmortal *adj & nmf* : immortal — **inmortalidad** *nf* : immortality
inmóvil *adj* : motionless, still — **inmovilizar** {21} *vt* : immobilize
inmueble *nm* : building, property
inmundicia *nf* : filth, trash — **inmundo, -da** *adj* : dirty, filthy
inmunizar {21} *vt* : immunize — **inmune** *adj* : immune — **inmunidad** *nf* : immunity — **inmunización** *nf, pl* **-ciones** : immunization
inmutable *adj* : unchangeable
innato, -ta *adj* : innate
innecesario, -ria *adj* : unnecessary, needless
innegable *adj* : undeniable
innoble *adj* : ignoble
innovar *vt* : introduce — *vi* : innovate — **innovación** *nf, pl* **-ciones** : innovation — **innovador, -dora** *adj* : innovative — **~** *n* : innovator
innumerable *adj* : innumerable
inocencia *nf* : innocence — **inocente** *adj & nmf* : innocent — **inocentón, -tona** *adj, mpl* **-tones** : naive — **~** *n* : simpleton, dupe
inocular *vt* : inoculate — **inoculación** *nf, pl* **-ciones** : inoculation
inocuo, -cua *adj* : innocuous
inodoro, -ra *adj* : odorless — **inodoro** *nm* : toilet
inofensivo, -va *adj* : inoffensive, harmless
inolvidable *adj* : unforgettable
inoperable *adj* : inoperable
inoperante *adj* : ineffective
inopinado, -da *adj* : unexpected
inoportuno, -na *adj* : untimely, inopportune
inorgánico, -ca *adj* : inorganic
inoxidable *adj* **1** : rustproof **2 acero ~** : stainless steel
inquebrantable *adj* : unwavering
inquietar *vt* : disturb, worry — **inquietarse** *vr* : worry — **inquietante** *adj* : disturbing, worrisome — **inquieto, -ta** *adj* : anxious, worried — **inquietud** *nf* : anxiety, worry
inquilino, -na *n* : tenant
inquirir {4} *vi* : make inquiries — *vt* : investigate
insaciable *adj* : insatiable
insalubre *adj* : unhealthy

insatisfecho, -cha *adj* **1** : unsatisfied **2** DESCONTENTO : dissatisfied
inscribir {33} *vt* **1** : enroll, register **2** GRABAR : inscribe, engrave — **inscribirse** *vr* : register — **inscripción** *nf, pl* **-ciones 1** : inscription **2** REGISTRO : registration
insecto *nm* : insect — **insecticida** *nm* : insecticide
inseguro, -ra *adj* **1** : insecure **2** PELIGROSO : unsafe **3** DUDOSO : uncertain — **inseguridad** *nf* **1** : insecurity **2** PELIGRO : lack of safety **3** DUDA : uncertainty
inseminar *vt* : inseminate — **inseminación** *nf, pl* **-ciones** : insemination
insensato, -ta *adj* : senseless, foolish — **insensatez** *nf* : foolishness, thoughtlessness
insensible *adj* **1** : insensitive, unfeeling **2** : numb (in medicine) **3** IMPERCEPTIBLE : imperceptible — **insensibilidad** *nf* : insensitivity
inseparable *adj* : inseparable
insertar *vt* : insert
insidia *nf* : snare, trap — **insidioso, -sa** *adj* : insidious
insigne *adj* : noted, famous
insignia *nf* **1** : insignia, badge **2** BANDERA : flag
insignificante *adj* : insignificant, negligible
insincero, -ra *adj* : insincere
insinuar {3} *vt* : insinuate — **insinuarse** *vr* **~ en** : worm one's way into — **insinuación** *nf, pl* **-ciones** : insinuation — **insinuante** *adj* : insinuating, suggestive
insípido, -da *adj* : insipid
insistir *v* : insist — **insistencia** *nf* : insistence — **insistente** *adj* : insistent
insociable *adj* : unsociable
insolación *nf, pl* **-ciones** : sunstroke
insolencia *nf* : insolence — **insolente** *adj* : insolent
insólito, -ta *adj* : rare, unusual
insoluble *adj* : insoluble
insolvencia *nf* : insolvency, bankruptcy — **insolvente** *adj* : insolvent, bankrupt
insomnio *nm* : insomnia — **insomne** *nmf* : insomniac
insondable *adj* : unfathomable
insonorizado, -da *adj* : soundproof
insoportable *adj* : unbearable
insospechado, -da *adj* : unexpected
insostenible *adj* : untenable
inspeccionar *vt* : inspect — **inspección** *nf, pl* **-ciones** : inspection — **inspector, -tora** *n* : inspector
inspirar *vt* : inspire — *vi* : inhale — **inspirarse** *vr* : be inspired — **inspiración** *nf, pl* **-ciones 1** : inspiration **2** RESPIRACIÓN : inhalation — **inspirador, -dora** *adj* : inspirational
instalar *vt* : install — **instalarse** *vr* : settle — **instalación** *nf, pl* **-ciones** : installation
instancia *nf* **1** : request **2 en última ~** : ultimately, as a last resort
instantáneo, -nea *adj* : instantaneous, instant — **instantánea** *nf* : snapshot — **instante** *nm* **1** : instant **2 a cada ~** : frequently, all the time **3 al ~** : immediately
instar *vt* : urge, press
instaurar *vt* : establish — **instauración** *nf, pl* **-ciones** : establishment
instigar {52} *vt* : incite, instigate — **instigador, -dora** *n* : instigator
instinto *nm* : instinct — **instintivo, -va** *adj* : instinctive
institución *nf, pl* **-ciones** : institution — **institucional** *adj* : institutional — **institucionalizar** {21} *vt* : institutionalize — **instituir** {41} *vt* : institute, establish — **instituto** *nm* : institute — **institutriz** *nf, pl* **-trices** : governess
instruir {41} *vt* : instruct — **instrucción** *nf, pl* **-ciones 1** : instruction **2 instrucciones** *nfpl* : instructions, directions — **instructivo, -va** *adj* : instructive — **instructor, -tora** *n* : instructor
instrumento *nm* : instrument — **instrumental** *adj* : instrumental
insubordinarse *vr* : rebel — **insubordinado, -da** *adj* : insubordinate — **insubordinación** *nf, pl* **-ciones** : insubordination
insuficiente *adj* : insufficient, inadequate — **insuficiencia** *nf* **1** : insufficiency, inadequacy **2 ~ cardíaca** : heart failure
insufrible *adj* : insufferable
insular *adj* : insular, island
insulina *nf* : insulin
insulso, -sa *adj* **1** : insipid, bland **2** SOSO : dull
insultar *vt* : insult — **insultante** *adj* : insulting — **insulto** *nm* : insult
insuperable *adj* : insurmountable
insurgente *adj & nmf* : insurgent
insurrección *nf, pl* **-ciones** : insurrection, uprising
intachable *adj* : irreproachable
intacto, -ta *adj* : intact
intangible *adj* : intangible
integrar *vt* : integrate — **integrarse** *vr* : become integrated — **integración**

nf, pl **-ciones** : integration — **integral** *adj* **1** : integral **2 pan ~** : whole grain bread — **íntegro, -gra** *adj* **1** : honest, upright **2** ENTERO : whole, complete — **integridad** *nf* **1** RECTITUD : integrity **2** TOTALIDAD : wholeness
intelecto *nm* : intellect — **intelectual** *adj & nmf* : intellectual
inteligencia *nf* : intelligence — **inteligente** *adj* : intelligent — **inteligible** *adj* : intelligible
intemperie *nf* **a la ~** : in the open air, outside
intempestivo, -va *adj* : untimely, inopportune
intención *nf, pl* **-ciones** : intention, intent — **intencionado, -da** *adj* **1** : intended **2 bien ~** : well-meaning **3 mal ~** : malicious — **intencional** *adj* : intentional
intensidad *nf* : intensity — **intensificar** {72} *vt* : intensify — **intensificarse** *vr* : intensify — **intensivo, -va** *adj* : intensive — **intenso, -sa** *adj* : intense
intentar *vt* : attempt, try — **intento** *nm* **1** : intention **2** TENTATIVA : attempt
interactuar {3} *vi* : interact — **interacción** *nf, pl* **-ciones** : interaction — **interactivo, -va** *adj* : interactive
intercalar *vt* : insert, intersperse
intercambio *nm* : exchange — **intercambiable** *adj* : interchangeable — **intercambiar** *vt* : exchange, trade
interceder *vi* : intercede
interceptar *vt* : intercept — **intercepción** *nf, pl* **-ciones** : interception
intercesión *nf, pl* **-siones** : intercession
interés *nm, pl* **-reses** : interest — **interesado, -da** *adj* **1** : interested **2** EGOISTA : selfish — **interesante** *adj* : interesting — **interesar** *vt* : interest — *vi* : be of interest — **interesarse** *vr* : take an interest
interfaz *nf, pl* **-faces** : interface
interferir {76} *vi* : interfere — *vt* : interfere with — **interferencia** *nf* : interference
interino, -na *adj* : temporary, interim — **interiormente** *adv* : inwardly
interior *adj* : interior, inner — **~** *nm* : interior, inside — **interiormente** *adv* : inwardly
interjección *nf, pl* **-ciones** : interjection
interlocutor, -tora *n* : speaker
intermediario, -ria *adj & n* : intermediary
intermedio, -dia *adj* : intermediate — **intermedio** *nm* : intermission
interminable *adj* : interminable, endless
intermisión *nf, pl* **-siones** : intermission, pause
intermitente *adj* : intermittent — **~** *nm* : blinker, turn signal
internacional *adj* : international
internar *vt* : commit, confine — **internarse** *vr* : penetrate — **internado** *nm* : boarding school — **interno, -na** *adj* : internal — **~** *n* **1** : boarder **2** : inmate (in a jail, etc.)
interponer {60} *vt* : interpose — **interponerse** *vr* : intervene
interpretar *vt* **1** : interpret **2** : play, perform (in theater, etc.) — **interpretación** *nf, pl* **-ciones** : interpretation — **intérprete** *nmf* **1** TRADUCTOR : interpreter **2** : performer (of music)
interrogar {52} *vt* : interrogate, question — **interrogación** *nf, pl* **-ciones 1** : interrogation **2 signo de ~** : question mark — **interrogativo, -va** *adj* : interrogative — **interrogatorio** *nm* : interrogation, questioning
interrumpir *v* : interrupt — **interrupción** *nf, pl* **-ciones** : interruption — **interruptor** *nm* : (electrical) switch
intersección *nf, pl* **-ciones** : intersection
intervalo *nm* : interval
intervenir {87} *vi* **1** : take part **2** MEDIAR : intervene — *vt* **1** : tap (a telephone) **2** INSPECCIONAR : audit **3** OPERAR : operate on — **intervención** *nf, pl* **-ciones 1** : intervention **2** : audit (in business) **3** *or* **~ quirúrgica** : operation — **interventor, -tora** *n* : inspector, auditor
intestino *nm* : intestine — **intestinal** *adj* : intestinal
intimar *vi* **~ con** : become friendly with — **intimidad** *nf* **1** : private life **2** AMISTAD : intimacy
intimidar *vt* : intimidate
íntimo, -ma *adj* **1** : intimate, close **2** PRIVADO : private
intolerable *adj* : intolerable — **intolerancia** *nf* : intolerance — **intolerante** *adj* : intolerant
intoxicar {72} *vt* : poison — **intoxicación** *nf, pl* **-ciones** : poisoning
intranquilizar {21} *vt* : make uneasy — **intranquilizarse** *vr* : be anxious — **intranquilidad** *nf* : uneasiness, anxiety — **intranquilo, -la** *adj* : uneasy, worried
intransigente *adj* : unyielding, intransigent
intransitable *adj* : impassable

intransitivo, -va *adj* : intransitive
intrascendente *adj* : unimportant, insignificant
intravenoso, -sa *adj* : intravenous
intrépido, -da *adj* : intrepid, fearless
intrigar {52} *v* : intrigue — **intriga** *nf* : intrigue — **intrigante** *adj* : intriguing
intrincado, -da *adj* : intricate, involved
intrínseco, -ca *adj* : intrinsic — **intrínsecament** *adv* : intrinsically, inherently
introducción *nf, pl* **-ciones** : introduction — **introducir** {61} *vt* **1** : introduce **2** METER : insert — **introducirse** *vr* **~ en** : penetrate, get into — **introductorio, -ria** *adj* : introductory
intromisión *nf, pl* **-siones** : interference
introvertido, -da *adj* : introverted — **~** *n* : introvert
intrusión *nf, pl* **-siones** : intrusion — **intruso, -sa** *adj* : intrusive — **~** *n* : intruder
intuir {41} *vt* : sense — **intuición** *nf, pl* **-ciones** : intuition — **intuitivo, -va** *adj* : intuitive
inundar *vt* : flood — **inundarse** *vr* **~ de** : be inundated with — **inundación** *nf, pl* **-ciones** : flood
inusitado, -da *adj* : unusual, uncommon
inútil *adj* **1** : useless **2** INVÁLIDO : disabled — **inutilidad** *nf* : uselessness — **inutilizar** {21} *vt* **1** : make useless **2** INCAPACITAR : disable
invadir *vt* : invade
invalidez *nf, pl* **-deces 1** : invalidity **2** : disability (in medicine) — **inválido, -da** *adj & n* : invalid
invalorable *adj Lat* : invaluable
invariable *adj* : invariable
invasión *nf, pl* **-siones** : invasion — **invasor, -sora** *adj* : invading — **~** *n* : invader
invencible *adj* : invincible
inventar *vt* **1** : invent **2** : fabricate, make up (a word, an excuse, etc.) — **invención** *nf, pl* **-ciones 1** : invention **2** MENTIRA : lie, fabrication
inventario *nm* : inventory
inventiva *nf* : inventiveness — **inventivo, -va** *adj* : inventive — **inventor, -tora** *n* : inventor
invernadero *nm* : greenhouse
invernal *adj* : winter
inverosímil *adj* : unlikely
inversión *nf, pl* **-siones 1** : inversion, reversal **2** : investment (of money, time, etc.)
inverso, -sa *adj* **1** : inverse **2** CONTRARIO : opposite **3 a la inversa** : the other way around, inversely
inversor, -sora *n* : investor
invertebrado, -da *adj* : invertebrate — **invertebrado** *nm* : invertebrate
invertir {76} *vt* **1** : invert, reverse **2** : invest (money, time, etc.) — *vi* : make an investment
investidura *nf* : investiture
investigar {52} *vt* **1** : investigate **2** ESTUDIAR : research — *vi* **~ sobre** : do research into — **investigación** *nf, pl* **-ciones 1** : investigation **2** ESTUDIO : research — **investigador, -dora** *n* : investigator, researcher
investir {54} *vt* : invest
inveterado, -da *adj* : deep-seated, inveterate
invicto, -ta *adj* : undefeated
invierno *nm* : winter
invisible *adj* : invisible — **invisibilidad** *nf* : invisibility
invitar *vt* : invite — **invitación** *nf, pl* **-ciones** : invitation — **invitado, -da** *n* : guest
invocar {72} *vt* : invoke — **invocación** *nf, pl* **-ciones** : invocation
involuntario, -ria *adj* : involuntary
invulnerable *adj* : invulnerable
inyectar *vt* : inject — **inyección** *nf, pl* **-ciones** : injection, shot — **inyectado, -da** *adj* **ojos inyectados** : bloodshot eyes
ion *nm* : ion — **ionizar** {21} *vt* : ionize
ir {43} *vi* **1** : go **2** FUNCIONAR : work, function **3** CONVENIR : suit **4 ¿cómo te va?** : how are you? **5 ~ con prisa** : be in a hurry **6 ~ por** : follow, go along **7 vamos** : let's go — *v aux* **1 ~ a** : be going to, be about to **2 ~ caminando** : take a walk **3 vamos a ver** : we shall see — **irse** *vr* : go away, be gone
ira *nf* : rage, anger — **iracundo, -da** *adj* : irate, angry
iraní *adj* : Iranian
iraquí *adj* : Iraqi
iris *nms & pl* **1** : iris (of the eye) **2 arco ~** : rainbow
irlandés, -desa *adj, mpl* **-deses** : Irish
ironía *nf* : irony — **irónico, -ca** *adj* : ironic, ironical
irracional *adj* : irrational
irradiar *vt* : radiate, irradiate
irrazonable *adj* : unreasonable
irreal *adj* : unreal
irreconciliable *adj* : irreconcilable
irreconocible *adj* : unrecognizable
irrecuperable *adj* : irretrievable

irreductible *adj* : unyielding
irreemplazable *adj* : irreplaceable
irreflexivo, -va *adj* : rash, unthinking
irrefutable *adj* : irrefutable
irregular *adj* : irregular — **irregularidad** *nf* : irregularity
irrelevante *adj* : irrelevant
irreparable *adj* : irreparable
irreprimible *adj* : irrepressible
irreprochable *adj* : irreproachable
irresistible *adj* : irresistible
irresoluto, -ta *adj* : indecisive, irresolute
irrespetuoso, -sa *adj* : disrespectful
irresponsable *adj* : irresponsible — **irresponsabilidad** *nf* : irresponsibility
irreverente *adj* : irreverent
irreversible *adj* : irreversible
irrevocable *adj* : irrevocable
irrigar {52} *vt* : irrigate — **irrigación** *nf, pl* **-ciones** : irrigation
irrisorio, -ria *adj* : laughable, ridiculous
irritar *vt* : irritate — **irritarse** *vr* : get annoyed — **irritable** *adj* : irritable — **irritación** *nf, pl* **-ciones** : irritation — **irritante** *adj* : irritating
irrompible *adj* : unbreakable
irrumpir *vi* **~ en** : burst into
isla *nf* : island
islámico, -ca *adj* : Islamic, Muslim
islandés, -desa *adj, mpl* **-deses** : Icelandic
isleño, -ña *n* : islander
israelí *adj* : Israeli
istmo *nm* : isthmus
italiano, -na *adj* : Italian — **italiano** *nm* : Italian (language)
itinerario *nm* : itinerary
izar {21} *vt* : hoist, raise
izquierda *nf* : left — **izquierdista** *adj & nmf* : leftist — **izquierdo, -da** *adj* : left

J

j *nf* : j, tenth letter of the Spanish alphabet
jabalí *nm, pl* **-líes** : wild boar
jabalina *nf* : javelin
jabón *nm, pl* **-bones** : soap — **jabonar** *vt* : soap (up) — **jabonera** *nf* : soap dish — **jabonoso, -sa** *adj* : soapy
jaca *nf* : pony
jacinto *nm* : hyacinth
jactarse *vr* : boast, brag — **jactancia** *nf* : boastfulness, bragging — **jactancioso, -sa** *adj* : boastful
jadear *vi* : pant, gasp — **jadeante** *adj* : panting, breathless — **jadeo** *nm* : gasp, panting
jaez *nm, pl* **jaeces 1** : harness **2 jaeces** *nmpl* : trappings
jaguar *nm* : jaguar
jaiba *nf Lat* : crab
jalapeño *nm Lat* : jalapeño pepper
jalar *v Lat* : pull, tug
jalea *nf* : jelly
jaleo *nm fam* **1** : uproar, racket **2 armar un ~** : raise a ruckus
jalón *nm, pl* **-lones** *Lat* : pull, tug
jamaicano, -na *or* **jamaiquino, -na** *adj* : Jamaican
jamás *adv* **1** : never **2 para siempre ~** : for ever and ever
jamelgo *nm* : nag (horse)
jamón *nm, pl* **-mones 1** : ham **2 ~ serrano** : cured ham
Januká *nmf* : Hanukkah
japonés, -nesa *adj, mpl* **-neses** : Japanese — **japonés** *nm* : Japanese (language)
jaque *nm* **1** : check (in chess) **2 ~ mate** : checkmate
jaqueca *nf* : headache, migraine
jarabe *nm* : syrup
jardín *nm, pl* **-dines 1** : garden **2 ~ infantil** *or* **~ de niños** *Lat* : kindergarten — **jardinería** *nf* : gardening — **jardinero, -ra** *n* : gardener
jarra *nf* : pitcher, jug — **jarro** *nm* : pitcher — **jarrón** *nm, pl* **-rrones** : vase
jaula *nf* : cage
jauría *nf* : pack of hounds
jazmín *nm, pl* **-mines** : jasmine
jazz ['jas, 'dʒas] *nm* : jazz
jeans ['jins, 'dʒins] *nmpl* : jeans
jefe, -fa *n* **1** : chief, leader **2** PATRÓN : boss **3 ~ de cocina** : chef — **jefatura** *nf* **1** : leadership **2** SEDE : headquarters
jengibre *nm* : ginger
jeque *nm* : sheikh, sheik
jerarquía *nf* **1** : hierarchy **2** RANGO : rank — **jerárquico, -ca** *adj* : hierarchical
jerez *nm, pl* **-reces** : sherry
jerga *nf* **1** : coarse cloth **2** ARGOT : jargon, slang
jerigonza *nf* **1** : jargon **2** GALIMATÍAS : gibberish

jeringa *or* **jeringuilla** *nf* : syringe — **jeringar** {52} *vt fam* : annoy, pester
jeroglífico *nm* : hieroglyphic
jersey *nm, pl* **-seys** : jersey
jesuita *adj & nm* : Jesuit
Jesús *nm* : Jesus
jilguero *nm* : goldfinch
jinete *nmf* : horseman, horsewoman *f,* rider
jirafa *nf* : giraffe
jirón *nm, pl* **-rones** : shred, tatter
jitomate *nm Lat* : tomato
jockey ['jɔki, 'dʒɔ-] *nmf, pl* **-keys** [-kis] : jockey
jocoso, -sa *adj* : humorous, jocular
jofaina *nf* : washbowl
jolgorio *nm* : merrymaking
jornada *nf* **1** : day's journey **2** : working day — **jornal** *nm* : day's pay — **jornalero, -ra** *n* : day laborer
joroba *nf* : hump — **jorobado, -da** *adj* : hunchbacked, humpbacked — ~ *n* : hunchback — **jorobar** *vt fam* : annoy
jota *nf* **1** : iota, jot **2 no veo ni ~** : I can't see a thing
joven *adj, pl* **jóvenes** : young — ~ *nmf* : young man *m,* young woman *f,* youth
jovial *adj* : jovial, cheerful
joya *nf* : jewel — **joyería** *nf* : jewelry store — **joyero, -ra** *n* : jeweler — **joyero** *nm* : jewelry box
juanete *nm* : bunion
jubilación *nf, pl* **-ciones** : retirement — **jubilado, -da** *adj* : retired — ~ *nmf* : retiree — **jubilar** *vt* : retire, pension off — **jubilarse** *vr* : retire — **jubileo** *nm* : jubilee
júbilo *nm* : joy, jubilation — **jubiloso, -sa** *adj* : joyous, jubilant
judaísmo *nm* : Judaism
judía *nf* **1** : bean **2** *or* **~ verde** : green bean, string bean
judicial *adj* : judicial
judío, -día *adj* : Jewish — ~ *n* : Jew
judo ['juðo, 'dʒu-] *nm* : judo
juego *nm* **1** : game **2** : playing (of children, etc.) **3** *or* **~s de azar** : gambling **4** CONJUNTO : set **5 estar en ~** : be at stake **6 fuera de ~** : offside (in sports) **7 hacer ~** : go together, match **8 ~ de manos** : conjuring trick **9 poner en ~** : bring into play
juerga *nf fam* : spree, binge
jueves *nms & pl* : Thursday
juez *nmf, pl* **jueces 1** : judge **2** ÁRBITRO : umpire, referee
jugar {44} *vi* **1** : play **2** : gamble (in a casino, etc.) **3** APOSTAR : bet **4 ~ (al) tenis** : play tennis — *vt* : play — **jugarse** *vr* : risk, gamble (away) — **jugada** *nf* **1** : play, move **2** TRETA : (dirty) trick — **jugador, -dora** *n* **1** : player **2** : gambler
juglar *nm* : minstrel
jugo *nm* **1** : juice **2** SUSTANCIA : substance, essence — **jugoso, -sa** *adj* **1** : juicy **2** SUSTANCIAL : substantial, important
juguete *nm* : toy — **juguetear** *vi* : play — **juguetería** *nf* : toy store — **juguetón, -tona** *adj, mpl* **-tones** : playful
juicio *nm* **1** : judgment **2** RAZÓN : reason, sense **3 a mi ~** : in my opinion — **juicioso, -sa** *adj* : wise, sensible
julio *nm* : July
junco *nm* : reed, rush
jungla *nf* : jungle
junio *nm* : June
juntar *vt* **1** UNIR : join, unite **2** REUNIR : collect — **juntarse** *vr* **1** : join (together) **2** REUNIRSE : meet, get together — **junta** *nf* **1** : board, committee **2** REUNIÓN : meeting **3** : (political) junta **4** : joint, gasket — **junto, -ta** *adj* **1** : joined **2** PRÓXIMO : close, adjacent **3** (*used adverbially*) : together **4 ~ a** : next to **5 ~ con** : together with — **juntura** *nf* : joint
Júpiter *nm* : Jupiter
jurar *v* **1** : swear **2 ~ en falso** : commit perjury — **jurado** *nm* **1** : jury **2** : juror, member of a jury — **juramento** *nm* : oath
jurídico, -ca *adj* : legal
jurisdicción *nf, pl* **-ciones** : jurisdiction
jurisprudencia *nf* : jurisprudence
justamente *adv* **1** : fairly, justly **2** PRECISAMENTE : precisely, exactly
justicia *nf* : justice, fairness
justificar {72} *vt* **1** : justify **2** DISCULPAR : excuse, vindicate — **justificación** *nf, pl* **-ciones** : justification
justo, -ta *adj* **1** : just, fair **2** EXACTO : exact **3** APRETADO : tight — **justo** *adv* **1** : just, exactly **2 ~ a tiempo** : just in time
juvenil *adj* : youthful — **juventud** *nf* **1** : youth **2** JÓVENES : young people
juzgar {52} *vt* **1** : try (a case in court) **2** ESTIMAR : judge, consider **3 a ~ por** : judging by — **juzgado** *nm* : court, tribunal

K

k *nf* : k, eleventh letter of the Spanish alphabet
kaki → **caqui**
karate *or* **kárate** *nm* : karate
kilo *nm* : kilo — **kilogramo** *nm* : kilogram
kilómetro *nm* : kilometer — **kilometraje** *nm* : distance in kilometers, mileage — **kilométrico, -ca** *adj fam* : endless
kilovatio *nm* : kilowatt
kiosco *nm* → **quiosco**

L

l *nf* : l, twelfth letter of the Spanish alphabet
la *pron* **1** : her, it **2** (*formal*) : you **3 ~ que** : the one who — **~** *art* → **el**
laberinto *nm* : labyrinth, maze
labia *nf fam* : gift of gab
labio *nm* : lip
labor *nf* **1** : work, labor **2** TAREA : task **3 ~es domésticas** : housework — **laborable** *adj* **día ~** : business day — **laborar** *vi* : work — **laboratorio** *nm* : laboratory, lab — **laborioso, -sa** *adj* : laborious
labrar *vt* **1** : cultivate, till **2** : work (metals), carve (stone, wood) **3** CAUSAR : cause, bring about — **labrado, -da** *adj* **1** : cultivated, tilled **2** : carved, wrought — **labrador, -dora** *n* : farmer — **labranza** *nf* : farming
laca *nf* **1** : lacquer **2** : hair spray
lacayo *nm* : lackey
lacerar *vt* : lacerate
lacio, -cia *adj* **1** : limp **2** : straight (of hair)
lacónico, -ca *adj* : laconic
lacra *nf* : scar
lacrar *vt* : seal — **lacre** *nm* : sealing wax
lacrimógeno, -na *adj* **gas lacrimógeno** : tear gas — **lacrimoso, -sa** *adj* : tearful
lácteo, -tea *adj* **1** : dairy **2 Vía Láctea** : Milky Way
ladear *vt* : tilt — **ladearse** *vr* : lean
ladera *nf* : slope, hillside
ladino, -na *adj* : crafty
lado *nm* **1** : side **2 al ~** : next door, nearby **3 al ~ de** : beside, next to **4 de ~** : sideways **5 por otro ~** : on the other hand **6 por todos ~s** : everywhere, all around
ladrar *vi* : bark — **ladrido** *nm* : bark
ladrillo *nm* : brick
ladrón, -drona *n, mpl* **-drones** : thief
lagarto *nm* : lizard — **lagartija** *nf* : (small) lizard
lago *nm* : lake
lágrima *nf* : tear
laguna *nf* **1** : lagoon **2** VACÍO : gap
laico, -ca *adj* : lay, secular — **~** *n* : layman *m*, layperson
lamentar *vt* **1** : regret, be sorry about **2 lo lamento** : I'm sorry — **lamentarse** *vr* : lament — **lamentable** *adj* **1** : deplorable **2** TRISTE : sad, pitiful — **lamento** *nm* : lament, moan
lamer *vt* **1** : lick **2** : lap (against) — **lamida** *nf* : lick
lámina *nf* **1** PLANCHA : sheet **2** DIBUJO : plate, illustration — **laminar** *vt* : laminate
lámpara *nf* : lamp
lampiño, -ña *adj* : beardless, hairless
lana *nf* **1** : wool **2 de ~** : woolen
lance *nm* **1** : event, incident **2** : throw (of dice, etc.) **3** RIÑA : quarrel
lanceta *nf* : lancet
lancha *nf* **1** : boat, launch **2 ~ motora** : motorboat
langosta *nf* **1** : lobster **2** : locust (insect) — **langostino** *nm* : prawn, crayfish
languidecer {53} *vi* : languish — **languidez** *nf, pl* **-deces** : languor — **lánguido, -da** *adj* : languid, listless
lanilla *nf* : nap (of fabric)
lanudo, -da *adj* : woolly
lanza *nf* : spear, lance
lanzar {21} *vt* **1** : throw **2** : shoot (a glance), give (a sigh, etc.) **3** : launch (a missile, a project) — **lanzarse** *vr* : throw oneself — **lanzamiento** *nm* : throwing, launching
lapicero *nm* : (mechanical) pencil
lápida *nf* : tombstone

lapidar *vt* : stone
lápiz *nm, pl* **-pices 1** : pencil **2 ~ de labios** : lipstick
lapso *nm* : lapse (of time) — **lapsus** *nms & pl* : lapse, slip (of the tongue)
largar {52} *vt* **1** AFLOJAR : loosen, slacken **2** *fam* : give — **largarse** *vr fam* : go away, beat it — **largo, -ga** *adj* **1** : long **2 a la larga** : in the long run **3 a lo largo** : lengthwise **4 a lo largo de** : along — **largo** *nm* : length — **largometraje** *nm* : feature film — **largueza** *nf* : generosity
laringe *nf* : larynx — **laringitis** *nfs & pl* : laryngitis
larva *nf* : larva
las → **el**
lascivo, -va *adj* : lascivious, lewd
láser *nm* : laser
lastimar *vt* : hurt — **lastimarse** *vr* : hurt oneself — **lástima** *nf* **1** : pity **2 dar ~** : be pitiful **3 me dan ~** : I feel sorry for them **4 ¡qué ~!** : what a shame! — **lastimero, -ra** *adj* : pitiful, wretched — **lastimoso, -sa** *adj* : pitiful, terrible
lastre *nm* : ballast
lata *nf* **1** : tinplate **2** : (tin) can **3** *fam* : nuisance, bore **4 dar (la) lata a** *fam* : bother, annoy
latente *adj* : latent
lateral *adj* : side, lateral
latido *nm* **1** : beat, throb **2 ~ del corazón** : heartbeat
latifundio *nm* : large estate
látigo *nm* : whip — **latigazo** *nm* : lash
latín *nm* : Latin (language)
latino, -na *adj* **1** : Latin **2** : Latin-American — **~** *n* : Latin American — **latinoamericano, -na** *adj* : Latin-American — **~** *n* : Latin American
latir *vi* : beat, throb
latitud *nf* : latitude
latón *nm, pl* **-tones** : brass
latoso, -sa *adj fam* : annoying
laúd *nm* : lute
laudable *adj* : laudable
laureado, -da *adj* : prize-winning
laurel *nm* **1** : laurel **2** : bay leaf (in cooking)
lava *nf* : lava
lavar *vt* : wash — **lavarse** *vr* **1** : wash oneself **2 ~ las manos** : wash one's hands — **lavable** *adj* : washable — **lavabo** *nm* **1** : sink **2** RETRETE : lavatory, toilet — **lavadero** *nm* : laundry room — **lavado** *nm* : wash, washing — **lavadora** *nf* : washing machine — **lavamanos** *nms & pl* : washbowl — **lavandería** *nf* : laundry (service) — **lavaplatos** *nms & pl* **1** : dishwasher **2** *Lat* : kitchen sink — **lavativa** *nf* : enema — **lavatorio** *nm* : lavatory, washroom — **lavavajillas** *nms & pl* : dishwasher
laxante *adj & nm* : laxative — **laxo, -xa** *adj* : loose
lazo *nm* **1** VÍNCULO : link, bond **2** LAZADA : bow **3** : lasso, lariat — **lazada** *nf* : bow, loop
le *pron* **1** : (to) her, (to) him, (to) it **2** (*formal*) : (to) you **3** (*as direct object*) : him, you
leal *adj* : loyal, faithful — **lealtad** *nf* : loyalty, allegiance
lebrel *nm* : hound
lección *nf, pl* **-ciones 1** : lesson **2** : lecture (in a classroom)
leche *nf* **1** : milk **2 ~ descremada** *or* **~ desnatada** : skim milk **3 ~ en polvo** : powdered milk — **lechera** *nf* : milk jug — **lechería** *nf* : dairy store — **lechero, -ra** *adj* : dairy — **~** *n* : milkman *m*, milk dealer
lecho *nm* : bed
lechón, -chona *n, mpl* **-chones** : suckling pig
lechoso, -sa *adj* : milky
lechuga *nf* : lettuce
lechuza *nf* : owl
lector, -tora *n* : reader — **lectura** *nf* **1** : reading **2** ESCRITOS : reading matter
leer {20} *v* : read
legación *nf, pl* **-ciones** : legation
legado *nm* **1** : legacy **2** ENVIADO : legate, emissary
legajo *nm* : dossier, file
legal *adj* : legal — **legalidad** *nf* : legality — **legalizar** {21} *vt* : legalize — **legalización** *nf, pl* **-ciones** : legalization
legar {52} *vt* : bequeath
legendario, -ria *adj* : legendary
legible *adj* : legible
legión *nf, pl* **-giones** : legion — **legionario, -ria** *n* : legionnaire
legislar *vi* : legislate — **legislación** *nf, pl* **-ciones** : legislation — **legislador, -dora** *n* : legislator — **legislatura** *nf* : legislature
legítimo, -ma *adj* **1** : legitimate **2** GENUINO : authentic — **legitimidad** *nf* : legitimacy
lego, -ga *adj* **1** : secular, lay **2** IGNORANTE : ignorant — **~** *n* : layman *m*, layperson
legua *nf* : league
legumbre *nf* : vegetable
leído, -da *adj* : well-read
lejano, -na *adj* : distant, far away — **lejanía** *nf* : distance
lejía *nf* : bleach

lejos *adv* **1** : far (away) **2 a lo ~** : in the distance **3 de ~** *or* **desde ~** : from afar **4 ~ de** : far from
lelo, -la *adj* : silly, stupid
lema *nm* : motto
lencería *nf* **1** : linen **2** : (women's) lingerie
lengua *nf* **1** : tongue **2** IDIOMA : language **3 morderse la ~** : hold one's tongue
lenguado *nm* : sole, flounder
lenguaje *nm* : language
lengüeta *nf* **1** : tongue (of a shoe) **2** : reed (of a musical instrument)
lengüetada *nf* **beber a ~s** : lap (up)
lente *nmf* **1** : lens **2 ~s** *nmpl* : eyeglasses **3 ~s de contacto** : contact lenses
lenteja *nf* : lentil — **lentejuela** *nf* : sequin
lento, -ta *adj* : slow — **lento** *adv* : slowly — **lentitud** *nf* : slowness
leña *nf* : firewood — **leñador, -dora** *n* : lumberjack, woodcutter — **leño** *nm* : log
león, -ona *n, mpl* **leones** : lion, lioness *f*
leopardo *nm* : leopard
leotardo *nm* : leotard, tights *pl*
lepra *nf* : leprosy — **leproso, -sa** *n* : leper
lerdo, -da *adj* **1** TORPE : clumsy **2** TONTO : slow-witted
les *pron* **1** : (to) them, (to) you **2** (*as direct object*) : them, you
lesbiano, -na *adj* : lesbian — **lesbiana** *nf* : lesbian — **lesbianismo** *nm* : lesbianism
lesión *nf, pl* **-siones** : lesion, wound — **lesionado, -da** *adj* : injured, wounded — **lesionar** *vt* **1** : injure, wound **2** DAÑAR : damage
letal *adj* : lethal
letanía *nf* : litany
letárgico, -ca *adj* : lethargic — **letargo** *nm* : lethargy
letra *nf* **1** : letter **2** ESCRITURA : handwriting **3** : lyrics *pl* (of a song) **4 ~ de cambio** : bill of exchange **5 ~s** *nfpl* : arts — **letrado, -da** *adj* : learned — **letrero** *nm* : sign, notice
letrina *nf* : latrine
leucemia *nf* : leukemia
levadizo, -za *adj* **puente levadizo** : drawbridge
levadura *nf* **1** : yeast **2 ~ en polvo** : baking powder
levantar *vt* **1** : lift, raise **2** RECOGER : pick up **3** CONSTRUIR : erect, put up **4** ENCENDER : rouse, stir up **5 ~ la mesa** *Lat* : clear the table — **levantarse** *vr* **1** : rise, stand up **2** : get out of bed **3** SUBLEVARSE : rise up — **levantamiento** *nm* **1** : raising, lifting **2** SUBLEVACIÓN : uprising
levante *nm* **1** : east **2** : east wind
levar *vt* **~ anclas** : weigh anchor
leve *adj* **1** : light, slight **2** : minor, trivial (of wounds, sins, etc.) — **levedad** *nf* : lightness — **levemente** *adv* : lightly, slightly
léxico *nm* : vocabulary, lexicon
ley *nf* **1** : law **2 de (buena) ~** : genuine, pure (of metals)
leyenda *nf* **1** : legend **2** : caption (of an illustration, etc.)
liar {85} *vt* **1** : bind, tie (up) **2** : roll (a cigarette) **3** CONFUNDIR : confuse, muddle — **liarse** *vr* : get mixed up
libanés, -nesa *adj, mpl* **-neses** : Lebanese
libelo *nm* **1** : libel **2** : petition (in court)
libélula *nf* : dragonfly
liberación *nf, pl* **-ciones** : liberation, deliverance
liberal *adj & nmf* : liberal — **liberalidad** *nf* : generosity, liberality
liberar *vt* : liberate, free — **libertad** *nf* **1** : freedom, liberty **2 ~ bajo fianza** : bail **3 ~ condicional** : parole **4 en ~** : free — **libertar** *vt* : set free
libertinaje *nm* : licentiousness — **libertino, -na** *n* : libertine
libido *nf* : libido
libio, -bia *adj* : Libyan
libra *nf* **1** : pound **2 ~ esterlina** : pound sterling
librar *vt* **1** : free, save **2** : wage, fight (a battle) **3** : draw, issue (a check, etc.) — **librarse** *vr* **~ de** : free oneself from, get rid of
libre *adj* **1** : free **2** : unoccupied (of space), spare (of time) **3 al aire ~** : in the open air **4 ~ de impuestos** : taxfree
librea *nf* : livery
libro *nm* **1** : book **2 ~ de bolsillo** : paperback — **librería** *nf* : bookstore — **librero, -ra** *n* : bookseller — **librero** *nm Lat* : bookcase — **libreta** *nf* : notebook
licencia *nf* **1** : license, permit **2** PERMISO : permission **3** : (military) leave — **licenciado, -da** *n* **1** : graduate **2** *Lat* : lawyer — **licenciar** *vt* : dismiss, discharge — **licenciarse** *vr* : graduate — **licenciatura** *nf* : degree
licencioso, -sa *adj* : licentious
liceo *nm* : high school
licitar *vt* : bid for

lícito, -ta *adj* **1** : lawful, legal **2** JUSTO : just, fair
licor *nm* **1** : liquor **2** : liqueur — **licorera** *nf* : decanter
licuadora *nf* : blender — **licuado** *nm* : milk shake — **licuar** {3} *vt* : liquefy
lid *nf* **1** : fight **2 en buena ~** : fair and square
líder *adj* : leading — **~** *nmf* : leader — **liderato** *or* **liderazgo** *nm* : leadership
lidia *nf* : bullfight — **lidiar** *v* : fight
liebre *nf* : hare
lienzo *nm* **1** : cotton or linen cloth **2** : canvas (for a painting) **3** PARED : wall
liga *nf* **1** : league **2** *Lat* : rubber band **3** : garter (for stockings) — **ligadura** *nf* **1** ATADURA : tie, bond **2** : ligature (in medicine or music) — **ligamento** *nm* : ligament — **ligar** {52} *vt* : bind, tie (up)
ligero, -ra *adj* **1** : light, lightweight **2** LEVE : slight **3** ÁGIL : agile **4** FRÍVOLO : lighthearted, superficial — **ligeramente** *adv* : lightly, slightly — **ligereza** *nf* **1** : lightness **2** : flippancy (of character), thoughtlessness (of actions) **3** AGILIDAD : agility
lija *nf* : sandpaper — **lijar** *vt* : sand
lila *nf* : lilac
lima *nf* **1** : file **2** : lime (fruit) **3 ~ para uñas** : nail file — **limar** *vt* : file
limbo *nm* : limbo
limitar *vt* : limit — *vi* **~ con** : border on — **limitación** *nf, pl* **-ciones** : limitation, limit — **límite** *nm* **1** : limit **2** CONFÍN : boundary, border **3 ~ de velocidad** : speed limit **4 fecha ~** : deadline — **limítrofe** *adj* : bordering
limo *nm* : slime, mud
limón *nm, pl* **-mones 1** : lemon **2 ~ verde** *Lat* : lime — **limonada** *nf* : lemonade
limosna *nf* **1** : alms **2 pedir ~** : beg — **limosnero, -ra** *n* : beggar
limpiabotas *nmfs & pl* : bootblack
limpiaparabrisas *nms & pl* : windshield wiper
limpiar *vt* **1** : clean, wipe (away) **2 ~ en seco** : dry-clean — **limpieza** *nf* **1** : cleanliness **2** : (act of) cleaning — **limpio** *adv* : cleanly, fairly — **limpio, -pia** *adj* **1** : clean, neat **2** HONRADO : honest **3** NETO : net, clear
limusina *nf* : limousine
linaje *nm* : lineage, ancestry
linaza *nf* : linseed
lince *nm* : lynx
linchar *vt* : lynch
lindar *vi* **~ con** : border on — **lindante** *adj* : bordering — **linde** *nmf or* **lindero** *nm*: boundary
lindo, -da *adj* **1** : pretty, lovely **2 de lo lindo** *fam* : a lot
línea *nf* **1** : line **2 ~ de conducta** : course of action **3 en ~** : on-line **4 guardar la ~** : watch one's figure — **lineal** *adj* : linear
lingote *nm* : ingot
lingüista *nmf* : linguist — **lingüística** *nf* : linguistics — **lingüístico, -ca** *adj* : linguistic
linimento *nm* : liniment
lino *nm* **1** : flax (plant) **2** : linen (fabric)
linóleo *nm* : linoleum
linterna *nf* **1** FAROL : lantern **2** : flashlight
lío *nm* **1** : bundle **2** *fam* : mess, trouble **3** *fam* : (love) affair
liofilizar {21} *vt* : freeze-dry
liquen *nm* : lichen
liquidar *vt* **1** : liquefy **2** : liquidate (merchandise, etc.) **3** : settle, pay off (a debt, etc.) — **liquidación** *nf, pl* **-ciones 1** : liquidation **2** REBAJA : clearance sale — **líquido, -da** *adj* **1** : liquid **2** NETO : net — **líquido** *nm* : liquid
lira *nf* : lyre
lírico, -ca *adj* : lyric, lyrical — **lírica** *nf* : lyric poetry
lirio *nm* : iris
lisiado, -da *adj* : disabled — **~** *n* : disabled person — **lisiar** *vt* : disable, cripple
liso, -sa *adj* **1** : smooth **2** PLANO : flat **3** SENCILLO : plain **4 pelo ~** : straight hair
lisonjear *vt* : flatter — **lisonja** *nf* : flattery
lista *nf* **1** : stripe **2** ENUMERACIÓN : list **3** : menu (in a restaurant) — **listado, -da** *adj* : striped
listo, -ta *adj* **1** : clever, smart **2** PREPARADO : ready
listón *nm, pl* **-tones 1** : ribbon **2** : strip (of wood)
lisura *nf* : smoothness
litera *nf* : bunk bed, berth
literal *adj* : literal
literatura *nf* : literature — **literario, -ria** *adj* : literary
litigar {52} *vi* : litigate — **litigio** *nm* **1** : litigation **2 en ~** : in dispute
litografía *nf* **1** : lithography **2** : lithograph (picture)
litoral *adj* : coastal — **~** *nm* : shore, seaboard
litro *nm* : liter

liturgia *nf* : liturgy — **litúrgico, -ca** *adj* : liturgical
liviano, -na *adj* **1** LIGERO : light **2** INCONSTANTE : fickle
lívido, -da *adj* : livid
llaga *nf* : sore, wound
llama *nf* **1** : flame **2** : llama (animal)
llamar *vt* **1** : call **2** : call up (on the telephone) — *vi* **1** : phone, call **2** : knock, ring (at the door) — **llamarse** *vr* **1** : be called **2 ¿cómo te llamas?** : what's your name? — **llamada** *nf* : call — **llamado, -da** *adj* : named, called — **llamamiento** *nm* : call, appeal
llamarada *nf* **1** : blaze **2** : flushing (of the face)
llamativo, -va *adj* : flashy, showy
llamear *vi* : flame, blaze
llano, -na *adj* **1** : flat **2** : straightforward (of a person, a message, etc.) **3** SENCILLO : plain, simple — **llano** *nm* : plain — **llaneza** *nf* : simplicity
llanta *nf* **1** : rim (of a wheel) **2** *Lat* : tire
llanto *nm* : crying, weeping
llanura *nf* : plain
llave *nf* **1** : key **2** *Lat* : faucet **3** INTERRUPTOR : switch **4 cerrar con ~** : lock **5 ~ inglesa** : monkey wrench — **llavero** *nm* : key chain
llegar {52} *vi* **1** : arrive, come **2** ALCANZAR : reach **3** BASTAR : be enough **4 ~ a** : manage to **5 ~ a ser** : become — **llegada** *nf* : arrival
llenar *vt* : fill (up), fill in — **lleno, -na** *adj* **1** : full **2 de lleno** : completely — **lleno** *nm* : full house
llevar *vt* **1** : take, carry **2** CONDUCIR : lead **3** : wear (clothing, etc.) **4** TENER : have **5 llevo una hora aquí** : I've been here for an hour — **llevarse** *vr* **1** : take (away) **2 ~ bien** : get along well — **llevadero, -ra** *adj* : bearable
llorar *vi* : cry, weep — **lloriquear** *vi* : whimper, whine — **lloro** *nm* : crying — **llorón, -rona** *n, mpl* **-rones** : crybaby, whiner — **lloroso, -sa** *adj* : tearful
llover {47} *v impers* : rain — **llovizna** *nf* : drizzle — **lloviznar** *v impers* : drizzle
lluvia *nf* : rain — **lluvioso, -sa** *adj* : rainy
lo *pron* **1** : him, it **2** (*formal, masculine*) : you **3 ~ que** : what, that which — **~** *art* **1** : the **2 ~ mejor** : the best (part) **3 sé ~ bueno que eres** : I know how good you are
loa *nf* : praise — **loable** *adj* : praiseworthy — **loar** *vt* : praise
lobo, -ba *n* : wolf
lóbrego, -ga *adj* : gloomy
lóbulo *nm* : lobe
local *adj* : local — **~** *nm* : premises *pl* — **localidad** *nf* : town, locality — **localizar** {21} *vt* **1** : localize **2** ENCONTRAR : locate — **localizarse** *vr* : be located
loción *nf, pl* **-ciones** : lotion
loco, -ca *adj* **1** : crazy, insane **2 a lo loco** : wildly, recklessly **3 volverse ~** : go mad — **~** *n* **1** : crazy person, lunatic **2 hacerse el loco** : act the fool
locomoción *nf, pl* **-ciones** : locomotion — **locomotora** *nf* : engine, locomotive
locuaz *adj, pl* **-cuaces** : talkative, loquacious
locución *nf, pl* **-ciones** : expression, phrase
locura *nf* **1** : insanity, madness **2** INSENSATEZ : crazy act, folly
locutor, -tora *n* : announcer
locutorio *nm* : phone booth
lodo *nm* : mud — **lodazal** *nm* : quagmire
logaritmo *nm* : logarithm
lógica *nf* : logic — **lógico, -ca** *adj* : logical — **logística** *nf* : logistics *pl*
logotipo *nm* : logo
lograr *vt* **1** : achieve, attain **2** CONSEGUIR : get, obtain **3 ~ hacer** : manage to do — **logro** *nm* : achievement, success
loma *nf* : hill, hillock
lombriz *nf, pl* **-brices** : worm
lomo *nm* **1** : back (of an animal) **2** : spine (of a book) **3 ~ de cerdo** : pork loin
lona *nf* : canvas
loncha *nf* : slice (of bacon, etc.)
lonche *nm Lat* : lunch — **lonchería** *nf Lat* : luncheonette
longaniza *nf* : sausage
longevidad *nf* : longevity — **longevo, -va** *adj* : long-lived
longitud *nf* **1** : longitude **2** LARGO : length
lonja → **loncha**
loro *nm* : parrot
los, las *pron* **1** : them **2** : you **3 los que, las que** : those who, the ones who — **los** *art* → **el**
losa *nf* **1** : flagstone **2** *or* **~ sepulcral** : tombstone
lote *nm* **1** : batch, lot **2** *Lat* : plot of land
lotería *nf* : lottery
loto *nm* : lotus
loza *nf* : crockery, earthenware
lozano, -na *adj* **1** : healthy-looking, vigorous **2** : luxuriant (of plants) — **lozanía** *nf* **1** : (youthful) vigor **2** : luxuriance (of plants)
lubricar {72} *vt* : lubricate — **lubri-**

cante *adj* : lubricating — **~** *nm* : lubricant
lucero *nm* : bright star
luchar *vi* **1** : fight, struggle **2** : wrestle (in sports) — **lucha** *nf* **1** : struggle, fight **2** : wrestling (sport) — **luchador, -dora** *n* : fighter, wrestler
lucidez *nf, pl* **-deces** : lucidity — **lúcido, -da** *adj* : lucid
lucido, -da *adj* : magnificent, splendid
luciérnaga *nf* : firefly, glowworm
lucir {45} *vi* **1** : shine **2** *Lat* : appear, seem — *vt* **1** : wear, sport **2** OSTENTAR : show off — **lucirse** *vr* **1** : shine, excel **2** PRESUMIR : show off — **lucimiento** *nm* **1** : brilliance **2** ÉXITO : brilliant performance, success
lucrativo, -va *adj* : lucrative — **lucro** *nm* : profit
luego *adv* **1** : then **2** : later (on) **3 desde ~** : of course **4 ¡hasta ~!** : see you later! **5 ~ que** : as soon as — **~** *conj* : therefore
lugar *nm* **1** : place **2** ESPACIO : space, room **3 dar ~ a** : give rise to **4 en ~ de** : instead of **5 tener ~** : take place
lugarteniente *nmf* : deputy
lúgubre *adj* : gloomy
lujo *nm* **1** : luxury **2 de ~** : deluxe — **lujoso, -sa** *adj* : luxurious
lujuria *nf* : lust
lumbre *nf* **1** : fire **2 poner en la ~** : put on the stove
luminoso, -sa *adj* : shining, luminous
luna *nf* **1** : moon **2** : (window) glass **3** ESPEJO : mirror **4 ~ de miel** : honeymoon — **lunar** *adj* : lunar — **~** *nm* : mole, beauty spot
lunes *nms & pl* : Monday
lupa *nf* : magnifying glass
lúpulo *nm* : hops
lustrar *vt* : shine, polish — **lustre** *nm* **1** BRILLO : luster, shine **2** ESPLENDOR : glory — **lustroso, -sa** *adj* : lustrous, shiny
luto *nm* **1** : mourning **2 estar de ~** : be in mourning
luxación *nf, pl* **-ciones** : dislocation
luz *nf, pl* **luces 1** : light **2** : lighting (in a room, etc.) **3** *fam* : electricity **4 a la ~ de** : in light of **5 dar a ~** : give birth **6 sacar a la ~** : bring to light

M

m *nf* : m, 13th letter of the Spanish alphabet
macabro, -bra *adj* : macabre
macarrón *nm, pl* **-rrones 1** : macaroon **2 macarrones** *nmpl* : macaroni
maceta *nf* : flowerpot
machacar {72} *vt* : crush, grind — *vi* **~ sobre** : go on about — **machacón, -cona** *adj, mpl* **-cones** : tiresome, boring
machete *nm* : machete — **machetear** *vt* : hack with a machete
macho *adj* **1** : male **2** *fam* : macho — **~** *nm* **1** : male **2** *fam* : he-man — **machista** *nm* : male chauvinist
machucar {72} *vt* **1** : beat, crush **2** : bruise (fruit)
macizo, -za *adj* : solid — **macizo** *nm* **~ de flores** : flower bed
mácula *nf* : stain
madeja *nf* : skein, hank
madera *nf* **1** : wood **2** : lumber (for construction) **3 ~ dura** : hardwood — **madero** *nm* : piece of lumber, plank
madre *nf* **1** : mother **2 ~ política** : mother-in-law — **madrastra** *nf* : stepmother
madreselva *nf* : honeysuckle
madriguera *nf* : burrow, den
madrileño, -ña *adj* : of or from Madrid
madrina *nf* **1** : godmother **2** : bridesmaid (at a wedding)
madrugada *nf* : dawn, daybreak — **madrugador, -dora** *n* : early riser
madurar *v* **1** : mature **2** : ripen (of fruit) — **madurez** *nf, pl* **-reces 1** : maturity **2** : ripeness (of fruit) — **maduro, -ra** *adj* **1** : mature **2** : ripe (of fruit)
maestría *nf* : mastery, skill — **maestro, -tra** *adj* : masterly, skilled — **~** *n* **1** : teacher (in grammar school) **2** EXPERTO : expert, master
Mafia *nf* : Mafia
magia *nf* : magic — **mágico, -ca** *adj* : magic, magical
magisterio *nm* : teachers *pl*, teaching profession
magistrado, -da *n* : magistrate, judge
magistral *adj* **1** : masterful **2** : magisterial (of an attitude, etc.)
magnánimo, -ma *adj* : magnanimous — **magnanimidad** *nf* : magnanimity
magnate *nmf* : magnate, tycoon
magnesia *nf* : magnesia — **magnesio** *nm* : magnesium
magnético, -ca *adj* : magnetic — **mag-**

netismo *nm* : magnetism — **magnetizar** {21} *vt* : magnetize
magnetófono *nm* : tape recorder
magnificencia *nf* : magnificence — **magnífico, -ca** *adj* : magnificent
magnitud *nf* : magnitude
magnolia *nf* : magnolia
mago, -ga *n* **1** : magician **2 los Reyes Magos** : the Magi
magro, -gra *adj* **1** : lean **2** MEZQUINO : poor, meager
magullar *vt* : bruise — **magulladura** *nf* : bruise
mahometano, -na *adj* : Islamic, Muslim — ~ *n* : Muslim
maicena *nf* : cornstarch
maíz *nm* : corn
maja *nf* : pestle
majadero, -ra *adj* : foolish, silly — ~ *n* : fool
majar *vt* : crush
majestad *nf* **1** : majesty **2 Su Majestad** : His/Her Majesty — **majestuoso, -sa** *adj* : majestic
majo, -ja *adj* **1** : nice **2** GUAPO : good-looking
mal *adv* **1** : badly, poorly **2** INCORRECTAMENTE : incorrectly **3** DIFÍCILMENTE : with difficulty, hardly **4 de ~ en peor** : from bad to worse **5 menos ~** : it's just as well — ~ *nm* **1** : evil **2** DAÑO : harm, damage **3** ENFERMEDAD : illness — ~ *adj* → **malo**
malabarismo *nm* : juggling — **malabarista** *nmf* : juggler
malacostumbrar *vt* : spoil, pamper — **malacostumbrado, -da** *adj* : spoiled
malaria *nf* : malaria
malasio, -sia *adj* : Malaysian
malaventura *nf* : misfortune — **malaventurado, -da** *adj* : unfortunate
malayo, -ya *adj* : Malay, Malayan
malcriado, -da *adj* : bad-mannered, spoiled
maldad *nf* **1** : evil **2** : evil deed
maldecir {11} *vt* : curse, damn — *vi* **1** : curse, swear **2 ~ de** : speak ill of — **maldición** *nf, pl* **-ciones** : curse — **maldito, -ta** *adj fam* : damned
maleable *adj* : malleable
maleante *nmf* : crook
malecón *nm, pl* **-cones** : jetty
maleducado, -da *adj* : rude
maleficio *nm* : curse — **maléfico, -ca** *adj* : evil, harmful
malentendido *nm* : misunderstanding
malestar *nm* **1** : discomfort **2** INQUIETUD : uneasiness
maleta *nf* **1** : suitcase **2 hacer la ~** : pack one's bags — **maletero, -ra** *n* : porter — **maletero** *nm* : trunk (of an automobile) — **maletín** *nm, pl* **-tines 1** PORTAFOLIO : briefcase **2** : overnight bag
malévolo, -la *adj* : malevolent — **malevolencia** *nf* : malevolence
maleza *nf* **1** : underbrush **2** MALAS HIERBAS : weeds *pl*
malgastar *vt* : waste, squander
malhablado, -da *adj* : foul-mouthed
malhechor, -chora *n* : criminal, delinquent
malhumorado, -da *adj* : bad-tempered, cross
malicia *nf* : malice — **malicioso, -sa** *adj* : malicious
maligno, -na *adj* **1** : malignant **2** PERNICIOSO : harmful, evil
malla *nf* **1** : mesh **2 ~s** *nfpl* : tights
malo, -la *adj* (**mal** *before masculine singular nouns*) **1** : bad **2** : poor (in quality) **3** ENFERMO : unwell **4 estar de malas** : be in a bad mood — ~ *n* : villain, bad guy (in movies, etc.)
malograr *vt* : waste — **malograrse** *vr* **1** FRACASAR : fail **2** : die young — **malogro** *nm* : failure
maloliente *adj* : smelly
malpensado, -da *adj* : malicious, nasty
malsano, -na *adj* : unhealthy
malsonante *adj* : rude
malta *nf* : malt
maltratar *vt* : mistreat
maltrecho, -cha *adj* : battered
malvado, -da *adj* : evil, wicked
malvavisco *nm* : marshmallow
malversar *vt* : embezzle — **malversación** *nf, pl* **-ciones** : embezzlement
mama *nf* : teat (of an animal), breast (of a woman)
mamá *nf fam* : mom, mama
mamar *vi* **1** : suckle **2 dar de ~ a** : breast-feed — *vt* **1** : suckle, nurse **2** : learn from childhood, grow up with — **mamario, -ria** *adj* : mammary
mamarracho *nm fam* : mess, sight
mambo *nm* : mambo
mamífero, -ra *adj* : mammalian — **mamífero** *nm* : mammal
mamografía *nf* : mammogram
mampara *nf* : screen, room divider
mampostería *nf* : masonry
manada *nf* **1** : flock, herd, pack **2 en ~** : in droves
manar *vi* **1** : flow **2 ~ en** : be rich in — **manantial** *nm* **1** : spring **2** ORIGEN : source
manchar *vt* **1** : stain, spot, mark **2** : tarnish (a reputation, etc.) — **mancharse** *vr* : get dirty — **mancha** *nf* : stain

mancillar *vt* : sully, stain
manco, -ca *adj* : one-armed, one-handed
mancomunar *vt* : combine, join — **mancomunarse** *vr* : unite — **mancomunidad** *nf* : union
mandar *vt* **1** : command, order **2** ENVIAR : send **3** *Lat* : hurl, throw — *vi* **1** : be in charge **2 ¿mande?** *Lat* : yes?, pardon? — **mandadero, -ra** *nm* : messenger — **mandado** *nm* : errand — **mandamiento** *nm* **1** : order, warrant **2** : commandment (in religion)
mandarina *nf* : mandarin orange, tangerine
mandato *nm* **1** : term of office **2** ORDEN : mandate — **mandatario, -ria** *n* **1** : leader (in politics) **2** : agent (in law)
mandíbula *nf* : jaw, jawbone
mandil *nm* : apron
mando *nm* **1** : command, leadership **2 al ~ de** : in charge of **3 ~ a distancia** : remote control
mandolina *nf* : mandolin
mandón, -dona *adj, mpl* **-dones** : bossy
manecilla *nf* : hand (of a clock), pointer
manejar *vt* **1** : handle, operate **2** : manage (a business, etc.) **3** : manipulate (a person) **4** *Lat* : drive (a car) — **manejarse** *vr* **1** : manage, get by **2** *Lat* : behave — **manejo** *nm* **1** : handling, use **2** : management (of a business, etc.)
manera *nf* **1** : way, manner **2 de ~ que** : so that **3 de ninguna ~** : by no means **4 de todas ~s** : anyway
manga *nf* **1** : sleeve **2** MANGUERA : hose
mango *nm* **1** : hilt, handle **2** : mango (fruit)
mangonear *vt fam* : boss around — *vi* **1** : be bossy **2** HOLGAZANEAR : loaf, fool around
manguera *nf* : hose
maní *nm, pl* **-níes** *Lat* : peanut
manía *nf* **1** : mania, obsession **2** MODA PASAJERA : craze, fad **3** ANTIPATÍA : dislike — **maníaco, -ca** *adj* : maniacal — **~** *n* : maniac
maniatar *vt* : tie the hands of
maniático, -ca *adj* : obsessive, fussy — **~** *n* : fussy person, fanatic
manicomio *nm* : insane asylum
manicura *nf* : manicure — **manicuro, -ra** *n* : manicurist
manido, -da *adj* : stale, hackneyed
manifestar {55} *vt* **1** : demonstrate, show **2** DECLARAR : express, declare — **manifestarse** *vr* **1** : become evident **2** : demonstrate (in politics) — **manifestación** *nf, pl* **-ciones 1** : manifestation, sign **2** : demonstration (in politics) — **manifestante** *nmf* : protester, demonstrator — **manifiesto, -ta** *adj* : manifest, evident — **manifiesto** *nm* : manifesto
manija *nf* : handle
manillar *nm* : handlebars *pl*
maniobra *nf* : maneuver — **maniobrar** *v* : maneuver
manipular *vt* **1** : manipulate **2** MANEJAR : handle — **manipulación** *nf, pl* **-ciones** : manipulation
maniquí *nmf, pl* **-quíes** : mannequin, model — **~** *nm* : mannequin, dummy
manirroto, -ta *adj* : extravagant — **~** *n* : spendthrift
manivela *nf* : crank
manjar *nm* : delicacy, special dish
mano *nf* **1** : hand **2** : coat (of paint, etc.) **3 a ~** *or* **a la ~** : at hand, nearby **4 dar la ~** : shake hands **5 de segunda ~** : secondhand **6 ~ de obra** : labor, manpower
manojo *nm* : bunch
manopla *nf* : mitten
manosear *vt* **1** : handle excessively **2** : fondle (a person)
manotazo *nm* : slap
mansalva: **a ~** *adv phr* : at close range, without risk
mansarda *nf* : attic
mansedumbre *nf* **1** : gentleness **2** : tameness (of an animal)
mansión *nf, pl* **-siones** : mansion
manso, -sa *adj* **1** : gentle **2** : tame (of an animal)
manta *nf* **1** : blanket **2** *Lat* : poncho
manteca *nf* : lard, fat — **mantecoso, -sa** *adj* : greasy
mantel *nm* : tablecloth — **mantelería** *nf* : table linen
mantener {80} *vt* **1** : support **2** CONSERVAR : preserve **3** : keep up, maintain (relations, correspondence, etc.) **4** AFIRMAR : affirm — **mantenerse** *vr* **1** : support oneself **2 ~ firme** : hold one's ground — **mantenimiento** *nm* **1** : maintenance **2** SUSTENTO : sustenance
mantequilla *nf* : butter — **mantequera** *nf* : churn — **mantequería** *nf* : dairy
mantilla *nf* : mantilla
manto *nm* : cloak
mantón *nm, pl* **-tones** : shawl
manual *adj* : manual — **~** *nm* : manual, handbook
manubrio *nm* **1** : handle, crank **2** *Lat* : handlebars *pl*

manufactura *nf* **1** : manufacture **2** FÁBRICA : factory

manuscrito *nm* : manuscript — **manuscrito, -ta** *adj* : handwritten

manutención *nf, pl* **-ciones** : maintenance

manzana *nf* **1** : apple **2** : (city) block — **manzanar** *nm* : apple orchard — **manzano** *nm* : apple tree

maña *nf* **1** : skill **2** ASTUCIA : cunning, guile

mañana *adv* : tomorrow — ~ *nm* **el** ~ : the future — ~ *nf* : morning

mañoso, -sa *adj* **1** : skillful **2** *Lat* : finicky

mapa *nm* : map — **mapamundi** *nm* : map of the world

mapache *nm* : raccoon

maqueta *nf* : model, mock-up

maquillaje *nm* : makeup — **maquillarse** *vr* : put on makeup

máquina *nf* **1** : machine **2** LOCOMOTORA : locomotive **3 a toda** ~ : at full speed **4** ~ **de escribir** : typewriter — **maquinación** *nf, pl* **-ciones** : machination — **maquinal** *adj* : mechanical — **maquinaria** *nf* **1** : machinery **2** : mechanism, works *pl* (of a watch, etc.) — **maquinilla** *nf* : small machine — **maquinista** *nmf* **1** : machinist **2** : (railroad) engineer

mar *nmf* **1** : sea **2 alta** ~ : high seas *pl*

maraca *nf* : maraca

maraña *nf* **1** : thicket **2** ENREDO : tangle, mess

maratón *nm, pl* **-tones** : marathon

maravilla *nf* **1** : wonder, marvel **2** : marigold (flower) — **maravillar** *vt* : astonish — **maravillarse** *vr* : be amazed — **maravilloso, -sa** *adj* : marvelous

marca *nf* **1** : mark **2** : brand (on livestock) **3** *or* ~ **de fábrica** : trademark **4** : record (in sports) — **marcado, -da** *adj* : marked — **marcador** *nm* **1** : scoreboard **2** *Lat* : marker, felt-tipped pen

marcapasos *nms & pl* : pacemaker

marcar {72} *vt* **1** : mark **2** : brand (livestock) **3** INDICAR : indicate, show **4** : dial (a telephone, etc.) **5** : score (in sports) — *vi* **1** : score **2** : dial (on the telephone, etc.)

marchar *vi* **1** : go **2** CAMINAR : walk **3** FUNCIONAR : work, run — **marcharse** *vr* : leave, go — **marcha** *nf* **1** : march **2** PASO : pace, speed **3** : gear (of an automobile) **4 poner en** ~ : put in motion

marchitarse *vr* : wither, wilt — **marchito, -ta** *adj* : withered

marcial *adj* : martial, military

marco *nm* **1** : frame **2** : goalposts *pl* (in sports) **3** ENTORNO : setting, framework

marea *nf* : tide — **marear** *vt* **1** : make nauseous or dizzy **2** CONFUNDIR : confuse — **marearse** *vr* **1** : become nauseated or dizzy **2** CONFUNDIRSE : get confused — **mareado, -da** *adj* **1** : sick, nauseous **2** ATURDIDO : dazed, dizzy

maremoto *nm* : tidal wave

mareo *nm* **1** : nausea, seasickness **2** VÉRTIGO : dizziness

marfil *nm* : ivory

margarina *nf* : margarine

margarita *nf* : daisy

margen *nm, pl* **márgenes 1** : edge, border **2** : margin (of a page, etc.) — **marginado, -da** *adj* **1** : alienated **2 clases marginadas** : underclass — ~ *n* : outcast — **marginal** *adj* : marginal — **marginar** *vt* : ostracize, exclude

mariachi *nm* : mariachi musician or band

maridaje *nm* : marriage, union — **marido** *nm* : husband

marihuana *or* **mariguana** *or* **marijuana** *nf* : marijuana

marimba *nf* : marimba

marina *nf* **1** : coast **2** *or* ~ **de guerra** : navy, fleet

marinada *nf* : marinade — **marinar** *vt* : marinate

marinero, -ra *adj* **1** : sea, marine **2** : seaworthy (of a ship) — **marinero** *nm* : sailor — **marino, -na** *adj* : marine — **marino** *nm* : seaman, sailor

marioneta *nf* : puppet, marionette

mariposa *nf* **1** : butterfly **2** ~ **nocturna** : moth

mariquita *nf* : ladybug

marisco *nm* **1** : shellfish **2** ~**s** *nmpl* : seafood

marisma *nf* : salt marsh

marítimo, -ma *adj* : maritime, shipping

mármol *nm* : marble

marmota *nf* ~ **de América** : groundhog

marquesina *nf* : marquee, (glass) canopy

marrano, -na *n* **1** : pig, hog **2** *fam* : slob

marrar *vt* : miss (a target) — *vi* : fail

marrón *adj & nm, pl* **-rrones** : brown

marroquí *adj* : Moroccan

marsopa *nf* : porpoise

marsupial *nm* : marsupial

Marte *nm* : Mars

martes *nms & pl* : Tuesday

martillo *nm* **1** : hammer **2** ~ **neumáti-**

co : jackhammer — **martillar** *or* **martillear** *v* : hammer
mártir *nmf* : martyr — **martirio** *nm* : martyrdom — **martirizar** {21} *vt* **1** : martyr **2** ATORMENTAR : torment
marxismo *nm* : Marxism — **marxista** *adj & nmf* : Marxist
marzo *nm* : March
mas *conj* : but
más *adv* **1** : more **2 el/la/lo ~** : (the) most **3** (*in negative constructions*) : (any) longer **4 ¡qué día ~ bonito!** : what a beautiful day! — **~** *adj* **1** : more **2** : most **3 ¿quién ~?** : who else? — **~** *prep* : plus — **~** *pron* **1 a lo ~** : at most **2 de ~** : extra, spare **3 ~ o menos** : more or less **4 ¿tienes ~?** : do you have more?
masa *nf* **1** : mass, volume **2** : dough (in cooking) **3 ~s** *nfpl* : people, masses
masacre *nf* : massacre
masaje *nm* : massage — **masajear** *vt* : massage
mascar {72} *v* : chew
máscara *nf* : mask — **mascarada** *nf* : masquerade — **mascarilla** *nf* : mask (in medecine, etc.)
mascota *nf* : mascot
masculino, -na *adj* **1** : masculine, male **2** VARONIL : manly **3** : masculine (in grammar) — **masculinidad** *nf* : masculinity
mascullar *v* : mumble
masilla *nf* : putty
masivo, -va *adj* : mass, large-scale
masón *nm, pl* **-sones** : Mason, Freemason — **masónico, -ca** *adj* : Masonic
masoquismo *nm* : masochism — **masoquista** *adj* : masochistic — **~** *nmf* : masochist
masticar {72} *v* : chew
mástil *nm* **1** : mast **2** ASTA : flagpole **3** : neck (of a stringed instrument)
mastín *nm, pl* **-tines** : mastiff
masturbarse *vr* : masturbate — **masturbación** *nf, pl* **-ciones** : masturbation
mata *nf* : bush, shrub
matadero *nm* : slaughterhouse
matador *nm* : matador, bullfighter
matamoscas *nms & pl* : flyswatter
matar *vt* **1** : kill **2** : slaughter (animals) — **matarse** *vr* **1** : be killed **2** SUICIDARSE : commit suicide — **matanza** *nf* : slaughter, killing
matasanos *nms & pl fam* : quack
matasellos *nms & pl* : postmark
mate *adj* : matte, dull — **~** *nm* **1** : maté **2 jaque ~** : checkmate
matemáticas *nfpl* : mathematics — **matemático, -ca** *adj* : mathematical — **~** *n* : mathematician
materia *nf* **1** ASUNTO : matter **2** MATERIAL : material — **material** *adj* **1** : material **2 daños ~es** : property damage — **~** *nm* **1** : material **2** EQUIPO : equipment, gear — **materialismo** *nm* : materialism — **materialista** *adj* : materialistic — **materializar** {21} *vt* : bring to fruition — **materializarse** *vr* : materialize — **materialmente** *adv* : absolutely
maternal *adj* : maternal — **maternidad** *nf* **1** : motherhood **2** : maternity hospital — **materno, -na** *adj* **1** : maternal **2 lengua materna** : mother tongue
matinal *adj* : morning
matinée *or* **matiné** *nf* : matinee
matiz *nm, pl* **-tices 1** : nuance **2** : hue, shade (of colors) — **matizar** {21} *vt* **1** : blend (colors) **2** : qualify (a statement, etc.) **3 ~ de** : tinge with
matón *nm, pl* **-tones 1** : bully **2** CRIMINAL : gangster, hoodlum
matorral *nm* : thicket
matraca *nf* **1** : rattle, noisemaker **2 dar la ~ a** : pester
matriarcado *nm* : matriarchy
matrícula *nf* **1** : list, roll, register **2** INSCRIPCIÓN : registration **3** : license plate (of an automobile) — **matricular** *vt* : register — **matricularse** *vr* : register, matriculate
matrimonio *nm* **1** : marriage **2** PAREJA : (married) couple — **matrimonial** *adj* : marital
matriz *nf, pl* **-trices 1** : matrix **2** : uterus, womb (in anatomy)
matrona *nf* : matron
matutino, -na *adj* : morning
maullar {8} *vi* : meow — **maullido** *nm* : meow
maxilar *nm* : jaw, jawbone
máxima *nf* : maxim
máxime *adv* : especially
máximo, -ma *adj* : maximum, highest — **máximo** *nm* **1** : maximum **2 al ~** : to the full
maya *adj*: Mayan
mayo *nm* : May
mayonesa *nf* : mayonnaise
mayor *adj* **1** (*comparative of* **grande**) : bigger, larger, greater, older **2** (*superlative of* **grande**) : biggest, largest, greatest, oldest **3 al por ~** : wholesale **4 ~ de edad** : of (legal) age — **~** *nmf* **1** : major (in the military) **2** ADULTO : adult **3 ~es** *nmfpl* : grownups — **mayoral** *nm* : foreman

mayordomo *nm* : butler
mayoreo *nm Lat* : wholesale
mayoría *nf* : majority
mayorista *adj* : wholesale — ~ *nmf* : wholesaler
mayormente *adv* : primarily
mayúscula *nf* : capital letter — **mayúsculo, -la** *adj* **1** : capital, uppercase **2 un fallo mayúsculo** : a terrible mistake
maza *nf* : mace (weapon)
mazapán *nm, pl* **-panes** : marzipan
mazmorra *nf* : dungeon
mazo *nm* **1** : mallet **2** MAJA : pestle
mazorca *nf* ~ **de maíz** : corncob
me *pron* **1** (*direct object*) : me **2** (*indirect object*) : to me, for me, from me **3** (*reflexive*) : myself, to myself, for myself, from myself
mecánica *nf* : mechanics — **mecánico, -ca** *adj* : mechanical — ~ *n* : mechanic
mecanismo *nm* : mechanism — **mecanización** *nf, pl* **-ciones** : mechanization — **mecanizar** {21} *vt* : mechanize
mecanografiar {85} *vt* : type — **mecanografía** *nf* : typing — **mecanógrafo, -fa** *n* : typist
mecate *nm Lat* : rope
mecedora *nf* : rocking chair
mecenas *nmfs & pl* : patron, sponsor — **mecenazgo** *nm* : patronage, sponsorship
mecer {86} *vt* **1** : rock **2** : push (on a swing) — **mecerse** *vr* : rock, swing
mecha *nf* **1** : fuse (of a bomb, etc.) **2** : wick (of a candle)
mechero *nm* **1** : burner **2** *Spain* : cigarette lighter
mechón *nm, pl* **-chones** : lock (of hair)
medalla *nf* : medal — **medallón** *nm, pl* **-llones 1** : medallion **2** : locket (jewelry)
media *nf* **1** : average **2** ~**s** *nfpl* : stockings **3 a** ~**s** : by halves, halfway
mediación *nf, pl* **-ciones** : mediation
mediado, -da *adj* **1** : half full, half empty, half over **2** : halfway through — **mediados** *nmpl* **a** ~ **de** : halfway through, in the middle of
mediador, -dora *n* : mediator
medialuna *nf* **1** : crescent **2** : croissant (pastry)
medianamente *adv* : fairly
medianero, -ra *adj* **pared medianera** : dividing wall
mediano, -na *adj* **1** : medium, average **2** MEDIOCRE : mediocre
medianoche *nf* : midnight
mediante *prep* : through, by means of
mediar *vi* **1** : be in the middle **2** INTERVENIR : mediate **3** ~ **entre** : be between
medicación *nf, pl* **-ciones** : medication — **medicamento** *nm* : medicine — **medicar** {72} *vt* : medicate — **medicarse** *vr* : take medicine — **medicina** *nf* : medicine — **medicinal** *adj* : medicinal
medición *nf, pl* **-ciones** : measurement
médico, -ca *adj* : medical — ~ *n* : doctor, physician
medida *nf* **1** : measurement, measure **2** MODERACIÓN : moderation **3** GRADO : extent, degree **4 tomar** ~**s** : take steps — **medidor** *nm Lat* : meter, gauge
medieval *adj* : medieval
medio, -dia *adj* **1** : half **2** MEDIANO : average **3 una media hora** : half an hour **4 la clase media** : the middle class — **medio** *adv* : half — ~ *nm* **1** : half **2** MANERA : means *pl,* way **3 en** ~ **de** : in the middle of **4** ~ **ambiente** : environment **5** ~**s** *nmpl* : means, resources
mediocre *adj* : mediocre, average — **mediocridad** *nf* : mediocrity
mediodía *nm* : noon, midday
medioevo *nm* : Middle Ages
medir {54} *vt* **1** : measure **2** CONSIDERAR : weigh, consider — **medirse** *vr* : be moderate
meditar *vi* : meditate, contemplate — *vt* **1** : think over, consider **2** PLANEAR : plan, work out — **meditación** *nf, pl* **-ciones** : meditation
mediterráneo, -nea *adj* : Mediterranean
medrar *vt* : flourish, thrive
medroso, -sa *adj* : fearful
médula *nf* **1** : marrow **2** ~ **espinal** : spinal cord
medusa *nf* : jellyfish
megabyte *nm* : megabyte
megáfono *nm* : megaphone
mejicano → **mexicano**
mejilla *nf* : cheek
mejillón *nm, pl* **-llones** : mussel
mejor *adv* **1** (*comparative*) : better **2** (*superlative*) : best **3 a lo** ~ : maybe, perhaps — ~ *adj* **1** (*comparative of* **bueno** *or* **bien**) : better **2** (*superlative of* **bueno** *or* **bien**) : best **3 lo** ~ : the best thing **4 tanto** ~ : so much the better — **mejora** *nf* : improvement
mejorana *nf* : marjoram
mejorar *vt* : improve — *vi* : improve, get better
mejunje *nm* : concoction, brew

melancolía *nf* : melancholy — **melancólico, -ca** *adj* : melancholic, melancholy
melaza *nf* : molasses
melena *nf* **1** : long hair **2** : mane (of a lion)
melindroso, -sa *adj* **1** : affected **2** *Lat* : finicky
mella *nf* : chip, nick — **mellado, -da** *adj* : chipped, jagged
mellizo, -za *adj & n* : twin
melocotón *nm, pl* **-tones** : peach
melodía *nf* : melody — **melódico, -ca** *adj* : melodic
melodrama *nm* : melodrama — **melodramático, -ca** *adj* : melodramatic
melón *nm, pl* **-lones** : melon
meloso, -sa *adj* **1** : sweet, honeyed **2** EMPALAGOSO : cloying
membrana *nf* : membrane
membrete *nm* : letterhead, heading
membrillo *nm* : quince
membrudo, -da *adj* : muscular, burly
memorable *adj* : memorable
memorándum *or* **memorando** *nm, pl* **-dums** *or* **-dos 1** : memorandum **2** AGENDA : notebook
memoria *nf* **1** : memory **2** RECUERDO : remembrance **3** INFORME : report **4 de ~** : by heart **5 ~s** *nfpl* : memoirs — **memorizar** {21} *vt* : memorize
mena *nf* : ore
menaje *nm* : household goods *pl,* furnishings *pl*
mencionar *vt* : mention, refer to — **mención** *nf, pl* **-ciones** : mention
mendaz *adj, pl* **-daces** : lying
mendigar {52} *vi* : beg — *vt* : beg for — **mendicidad** *nf* : begging — **mendigo, -ga** *n* : beggar
mendrugo *nm* : crust (of bread)
menear *vt* **1** : move, shake **2** : sway (one's hips) **3** : wag (a tail) — **menearse** *vr* **1** : sway, shake, move **2** *fam* : hurry up
menester *nm* **ser ~** : be necessary — **menestroso, -sa** *adj* : needy
menguar *vt* : diminish, lessen — *vi* **1** : decline, decrease **2** : wane (of the moon) — **mengua** *nf* : decrease, decline
menopausia *nf* : menopause
menor *adj* **1** (*comparative of* **pequeño**) : smaller, lesser, younger **2** (*superlative of* **pequeño**) : smallest, least, youngest **3** : minor (in music) **4 al por ~** : retail — **~** *nmf* : minor, juvenile
menos *adv* **1** (*comparative*) : less **2** (*superlative*) : least **3 ~ de** : fewer than — **~** *adj* **1** (*comparative*) : less, fewer **2** (*superlative*) : least, fewest — **~** *prep* **1** : minus **2** EXCEPTO : except — **~** *pron* **1** : less, fewer **2 al ~** *or* **por lo ~** : at least **3 a ~ que** : unless — **menoscabar** *vt* **1** : lessen **2** ESTROPEAR : harm, damage — **menospreciar** *vt* **1** DESPRECIAR : scorn **2** SUBESTIMAR : undervalue — **menosprecio** *nm* : contempt
mensaje *nm* : message — **mensajero, -ra** *n* : messenger
menso, -sa *adj Lat fam* : foolish, stupid
menstruar {3} *vi* : menstruate — **menstruación** *nf* : menstruation
mensual *adj* : monthly — **mensualidad** *nf* **1** : monthly payment **2** : monthly salary
mensurable *adj* : measurable
menta *nf* **1** : mint, peppermint **2 ~ verde** : spearmint
mental *adj* : mental — **mentalidad** *nf* : mentality
mentar {55} *vt* : mention, name
mente *nf* : mind
mentir {76} *vi* : lie — **mentira** *nf* : lie — **mentirilla** *nf* : fib — **mentiroso, -sa** *adj* : lying — **~** *n* : liar
mentís *nms & pl* : denial
mentol *nm* : menthol
mentón *nm, pl* **-tones** : chin
menú *nm, pl* **-nús** : menu
menudear *vi* : occur frequently — **menudeo** *nm Lat* : retail, retailing
menudillos *nmpl* : giblets
menudo, -da *adj* **1** : small, insignificant **2 a ~** : often
meñique *nm or* **dedo ~** : little finger, pinkie
meollo *nm* **1** : marrow **2** ESENCIA : essence, core
mercado *nm* **1** : market **2 ~ de valores** : stock market — **mercadería** *nf* : merchandise, goods *pl*
mercancía *nf* : merchandise, goods *pl* — **mercante** *nmf* : merchant, dealer — **mercantil** *adj* : commercial
mercenario, -ria *adj & n* : mercenary
mercería *nf* : notions store
mercurio *nm* : mercury
Mercurio *nm* : Mercury (planet)
merecer {53} *vt* : deserve — *vi* : be worthy — **merecedor, -dora** *adj* : deserving, worthy — **merecido** *nm* **recibir su ~** : get one's just deserts
merendar {55} *vi* : have an afternoon snack — *vt* : have as an afternoon snack — **merendero** *nm* **1** : snack bar **2** : picnic area
merengue *nm* **1** : meringue **2** : merengue (dance)

meridiano, -na *adj* **1** : midday **2** CLARO : crystal-clear — **meridiano** *nm* : meridian — **meridional** *adj* : southern
merienda *nf* : afternoon snack, tea
mérito *nm* : merit, worth — **meritorio, -ria** *adj* : deserving — ~ *n* : intern, trainee
mermar *vi* : decrease — *vt* : reduce, cut down — **merma** *nf* : decrease
mermelada *nf* : marmalade, jam
mero, -ra *adj* **1** : mere, simple **2** *Lat fam* (*used as an intensifier*) : very, real — **mero** *adv Lat fam* **1** : nearly, almost **2** **aquí** ~ : right here
merodear *vi* **1** : maraud **2** ~ **por** : prowl about (a place)
mes *nm* : month
mesa *nf* **1** : table **2** COMITÉ : committee, board
mesarse *vr* ~ **los cabellos** : tear one's hair
meseta *nf* : plateau
Mesías *nm* : Messiah
mesilla *nf* : small table
mesón *nm, pl* **-sones** : inn — **mesonero, -ra** *nm* : innkeeper
mestizo, -za *adj* **1** : of mixed ancestry **2** HÍBRIDO : hybrid — ~ *n* : person of mixed ancestry
mesura *nf* : moderation — **mesurado, -da** *adj* : moderate, restrained
meta *nf* : goal, objective
metabolismo *nm* : metabolism
metafísica *nf* : metaphysics — **metafísico, -ca** *adj* : metaphysical
metáfora *nf* : metaphor — **metafórico, -ca** *adj* : metaphoric, metaphorical
metal *nm* **1** : metal **2** : brass section (in an orchestra) — **metálico, -ca** *adj* : metallic, metal — **metalurgia** *nf* : metallurgy
metamorfosis *nfs & pl* : metamorphosis
metano *nm* : methane
metedura *nf* ~ **de pata** *fam* : blunder
meteoro *nm* : meteor — **meteórico, -ca** *adj* : meteoric — **meteorito** *nm* : meteorite — **meteorología** *nf* : meteorology — **meteorólogo, -ga** *adj* : meteorological, meteorologic — ~ *n* : meteorologist
meter *vt* **1** : put (in) **2** : place (in a job, etc.) **3** ENREDAR : involve **4** CAUSAR : make, cause **5** : spread (a rumor) **6** *Lat* : strike (a blow) — **meterse** *vr* **1** : get in, enter **2** ~ **en** : get involved in, meddle in **3** ~ **con** *fam* : pick a fight with
meticuloso, -sa *adj* : meticulous
método *nm* : method — **metódico, -ca** *adj* : methodical — **metodología** *nf* : methodology
metomentodo *nmf fam* : busybody
metralla *nf* : shrapnel — **metralleta** *nf* : submachine gun
métrico, -ca *adj* : metric, metrical
metro *nm* **1** : meter **2** : subway (train)
metrópoli *nf or* **metrópolis** *nfs & pl* : metropolis — **metropolitano, -na** *adj* : metropolitan
mexicano, -na *adj* : Mexican — **mexicoamericano, -na** *adj* : Mexican-American
mezcla *nf* **1** : mixture **2** ARGAMASA : mortar — **mezclar** *vt* **1** : mix, blend **2** CONFUNDIR : mix up, muddle **3** INVOLUCRAR : involve — **mezclarse** *vr* **1** : get mixed up **2** : mingle (socially) — **mezcolanza** *nf* : mixture
mezclilla *nf Lat* : denim
mezquino, -na *adj* **1** : mean, petty **2** ESCASO : meager — **mezquindad** *nf* : meanness, stinginess
mezquita *nf* : mosque
mezquite *nm* : mesquite
mi *adj* : my
mí *pron* **1** : me **2** *or* ~ **mismo,** ~ **misma** : myself **3 a** ~ **no me importa** : it doesn't matter to me
miajas → **migajas**
miau *nm* : meow
mica *nf* : mica
mico *nm* : (long-tailed) monkey
microbio *nm* : microbe, germ — **microbiología** *nf* : microbiology
microbús *nm, pl* **-buses** : minibus
microcosmos *nms & pl* : microcosm
microfilm *nm, pl* **-films** : microfilm
micrófono *nm* : microphone
microondas *nms & pl* : microwave (oven)
microorganismo *nm* : microorganism
microscopio *nm* : microscope — **microscópico, -ca** *adj* : microscopic
miedo *nm* **1** : fear **2 dar** ~ : be frightening — **miedoso, -sa** *adj* : fearful
miel *nf* : honey
miembro *nm* **1** : member **2** EXTREMIDAD : limb, extremity
mientras *adv or* ~ **tanto** : meanwhile, in the meantime — ~ *conj* **1** : while, as **2** ~ **que** : while, whereas **3** ~ **viva** : as long as I live
miércoles *nms & pl* : Wednesday
mies *nf* : (ripe) corn, grain
miga *nf* : crumb — **migajas** *nfpl* **1** : breadcrumbs **2** SOBRAS : leftovers
migración *nf, pl* **-ciones** : migration
migraña *nf* : migraine
migrar *vi* : migrate

mijo *nm* : millet
mil *adj & nm* : thousand
milagro *nm* : miracle — **milagroso, -sa** *adj* : miraculous
milenio *nm* : millennium
milésimo, -ma *adj* : thousandth
milicia *nf* **1** : militia **2** : military (service)
miligramo *nm* : milligram
mililitro *nm* : milliliter
milímetro *nm* : millimeter
militante *adj & nmf* : militant
militar *adj* : military — **~** *nmf* : soldier — **militarizar** {21} *vt* : militarize
milla *nf* : mile
millar *nm* : thousand
millón *nm, pl* **-llones 1** : million **2 mil millones** : billion — **millonario, -ria** *n* : millionaire — **millonésimo, -ma** *adj* : millionth
mimar *vt* : pamper, spoil
mimbre *nm* : wicker
mímica *nf* **1** : mime, sign language **2** IMITACIÓN : mimicry
mimo *nm* : pampering — **~** *nmf* : mime
mina *nf* **1** : mine **2** : lead (for pencils) — **minar** *vt* **1** : mine **2** DEBILITAR : undermine
mineral *adj* : mineral — **~** *nm* **1** : mineral **2** : ore (of a metal)
minería *nf* : mining — **minero, -ra** *adj* : mining — **~** *n* : miner
miniatura *nf* : miniature
minifalda *nf* : miniskirt
minifundio *nm* : small farm
minimizar {21} *vt* : minimize
mínimo, -ma *adj* **1** : minimum **2** MINÚSCULO : minute **3 en lo más ~** : in the slightest — **mínimo** *nm* : minimum
minino, -na *n fam* : pussycat
ministerio *nm* : ministry — **ministro, -tra** *n* **1** : minister, secretary **2 primer ministro** : prime minister
minoría *nf* : minority
minorista *adj* : retail — **~** *nmf* : retailer
minoritario, -ria *adj* : minority
minucia *nf* : trifle, small detail — **minucioso, -sa** *adj* **1** : detailed **2** METICULOSO : thorough
minué *nm* : minuet
minúsculo, -la *adj* : minuscule, tiny
minusvalía *nf* : handicap, disability — **minusválido, -da** *adj* : disabled
minuta *nf* **1** : bill, fee **2** BORRADOR : rough draft
minuto *nm* : minute — **minutero** *nm* : minute hand
mío, mía *adj* **1** : mine **2 una amiga mía** : a friend of mine — **~** *pron* **el mío, la mía** : mine, my own
miope *adj* : nearsighted
mirar *vt* **1** : look at **2** OBSERVAR : watch **3** CONSIDERAR : consider — *vi* **1** : look **2 ~ a** : face, overlook **3 ~ por** : look after — **mirarse** *vr* **1** : look at oneself **2** : look at each other — **mira** *nf* **1** : sight (of a firearm or instrument) **2** INTENCIÓN : aim, objective — **mirada** *nf* : look — **mirado, -da** *adj* **1** : careful **2** CONSIDERADO : considerate **3 bien ~** : well thought of — **mirador** *nm* **1** BALCÓN : balcony **2** : lookout, vantage point — **miramiento** *nm* : consideration
mirlo *nm* : blackbird
misa *nf* : Mass
miscelánea *nf* : miscellany
miserable *adj* **1** : poor **2** LASTIMOSO : miserable, wretched — **miseria** *nf* **1** : poverty **2** DESGRACIA : misfortune, misery
misericordia *nf* : mercy — **misericordioso, -sa** *adj* : merciful
mísero, -ra *adj* : wretched, miserable
misil *nm* : missile
misión *nf, pl* **-siones** : mission — **misionero, -ra** *adj & n* : missionary
mismo *adv* (*used for emphasis*) : right, exactly — **mismo, -ma** *adj* **1** : same **2** (*used for emphasis*) : very **3** : **-self 4 por lo ~** : for that reason
misoginia *nf* : misogyny — **misógino** *nm* : misogynist
misterio *nm* : mystery — **misterioso, -sa** *adj* : mysterious
mística *nf* : mysticism — **místico, -ca** *adj* : mystic, mystical — **~** *n* : mystic
mitad *nf* **1** : half **2** MEDIO : middle
mítico, -ca *adj* : mythical, mythic
mitigar {52} *vt* : mitigate
mitin *nm, pl* **mítines** : (political) meeting
mito *nm* : myth — **mitología** *nm* : mythology — **mitológico, -ca** *adj* : mythological
mixto, -ta *adj* **1** : mixed, joint **2** : coeducational (of a school)
mnemónico, -ca *adj* : mnemonic
mobiliario *nm* : furniture
mocasín *nm, pl* **-sines** : moccasin
mochila *nf* : backpack, knapsack
moción *nf, pl* **-ciones** : motion
moco *nm* **1** : mucus **2 limpiarse los ~s** : wipe one's nose — **mocoso, -sa** *n fam* : kid, brat
moda *nf* **1** : fashion, style **2 a la ~** *or* **de ~** : in style, fashionable **3 ~ pasajera** : fad — **modal** *adj* : modal — **modales** *nmpl* : manners — **modalidad** *nf* : type, kind

modelar *vt* : model, mold — **modelo** *adj* : model — **~** *nm* : model, pattern — **~** *nmf* : model, mannequin
módem *or* **modem** ['moðεm] *nm* : modem
moderar *vt* **1** : moderate **2** : reduce (speed, etc.) **3** PRESIDIR : chair (a meeting) — **moderarse** *vr* : restrain oneself — **moderación** *nf, pl* **-ciones** : moderation — **moderado, -da** *adj & n* : moderate — **moderador, -dora** *n* : moderator, chairperson
moderno, -na *adj* : modern — **modernismo** *nm* : modernism — **modernizar** {21} *vt* : modernize
modesto, -ta *adj* : modest — **modestia** *nf* : modesty
modificar {72} *vt* : modify, alter — **modificación** *nf, pl* **-ciones** : alteration
modismo *nm* : idiom
modista *nmf* **1** : dressmaker **2** : (fashion) designer
modo *nm* **1** : way, manner **2** : mood (in grammar) **3** : mode (in music) **4 a ~ de** : by way of **5 de ~ que** : so (that) **6 de todos ~s** : in any case, anyway
modorra *nf* : drowsiness
modular *vt* : modulate — **modulación** *nf, pl* **-ciones** : modulation
módulo *nm* : module, unit
mofa *nf* : ridicule, mockery — **mofarse** *vr* **~ de** : make fun of
mofeta *nf* : skunk
moflete *nm fam* : fat cheek — **mofletudo, -da** *adj fam* : fat-cheeked, chubby
mohín *nm, pl* **-hines** : grimace — **mohino, -na** *adj* : sulky
moho *nm* **1** : mold, mildew **2** ÓXIDO : rust — **mohoso, -sa** *adj* **1** : moldy **2** OXIDADO : rusty
moisés *nm, pl* **-seses** : bassinet, cradle
mojar *vt* **1** : wet, moisten **2** : dunk (food) — **mojarse** *vr* : get wet — **mojado, -da** *adj* : wet, damp
mojigato, -ta *adj* : prudish — **~** *n* : prude
mojón *nm, pl* **-jones** : boundary stone, marker
molar *nm* : molar
moldear *vt* : mold, shape — **molde** *nm* : mold, form — **moldura** *nf* : molding
mole[1] *nf* : mass, bulk
mole[2] *nm* **1** : Mexican chili sauce **2** : meat served with mole
molécula *nf* : molecule — **molecular** *adj* : molecular
moler {47} *vt* : grind, crush
molestar *vt* **1** : annoy, bother **2 no ~** : do not disturb — *vi* : be a nuisance — **molestarse** *vr* **1** : bother **2** OFENDERSE : take offense — **molestia** *nf* **1** : annoyance, nuisance **2** MALESTAR : discomfort — **molesto, -ta** *adj* **1** : annoyed **2** FASTIDIOSO : annoying **3** INCÓMODO : in discomfort — **molestoso, -sa** *adj* : bothersome, annoying
molido, -da *adj* **1** : ground (of meat, etc.) **2** *fam* : worn out, exhausted
molino *nm* **1** : mill **2 ~ de viento** : windmill — **molinero, -ra** *n* : miller — **molinillo** *nm* : grinder, mill
mollera *nf* **1** : crown (of the head) **2** *fam* : brains *pl*
molusco *nm* : mollusk
momento *nm* **1** : moment, instant **2** : (period of) time **3** : momentum (in physics) **4 de ~** : for the moment **5 de un ~ a otro** : any time now — **momentáneamente** *adv* : momentarily — **momentáneo, -nea** *adj* **1** : momentary **2** PASAJERO : temporary
momia *nf* : mummy
monaguillo *nm* : altar boy
monarca *nmf* : monarch — **monarquía** *nf* : monarchy
monasterio *nm* : monastery — **monástico, -ca** *adj* : monastic
mondadientes *nms & pl* : toothpick
mondar *vt* : peel
mondongo *nm* : innards *pl,* guts *pl*
moneda *nf* **1** : coin **2** : currency (of a country) — **monedero** *nm* : change purse
monetario, -ria *adj* : monetary
monitor *nm* : monitor
monja *nf* : nun — **monje** *nm* : monk
mono, -na *n* : monkey — **~** *adj fam* : lovely, cute
monogamia *nf* : monogamy — **monógamo -ma** *adj* : monogamous
monografía *nf* : monograph
monograma *nm* : monogram
monolingüe *adj* : monolingual
monólogo *nm* : monologue
monopatín *nm, pl* **-tines** : scooter, skateboard
monopolio *nm* : monopoly — **monopolizar** {21} *vt* : monopolize
monosílabo *nm* : monosyllable — **monosilábico, -ca** *adj* : monosyllabic
monoteísmo *nm* : monotheism — **monoteísta** *adj* : monotheistic
monotonía *nf* : monotony — **monótono, -na** *adj* : monotonous
monóxido *nm* **~ de carbono** : carbon monoxide
monstruo *nm* : monster — **monstruosidad** *nf* : monstrosity — **monstruoso, -sa** *adj* : monstrous

monta *nf* : importance, value
montaje *nm* **1** : assembly **2** : staging (in theater), editing (of films)
montaña *nf* **1** : mountain **2** ~ **rusa** : roller coaster — **montañero, -ra** *n* : mountain climber — **montañoso, -sa** *adj* : mountainous
montar *vt* **1** : mount **2** ESTABLECER : establish **3** ENSAMBLAR : assemble, put together **4** : stage (a performance) **5** : cock (a gun) — *vi* **1** ~ **a caballo** : ride horseback **2** ~ **en bicicleta** : get on a bicycle
monte *nm* **1** : mountain **2** BOSQUE : woodland **3** *or* ~ **bajo** : scrubland **4** ~ **de piedad** : pawnshop
montés *adj, pl* **-teses** : wild (of animals or plants)
montículo *nm* : mound, hillock
montón *nm, pl* **-tones 1** : heap, pile **2** **un** ~ **de** *fam* : lots of
montura *nf* **1** : mount (horse) **2** SILLA : saddle **3** : frame (of glasses)
monumento *nm* : monument — **monumental** *adj fam* : monumental, huge
monzón *nm, pl* **-zones** : monsoon
moño *nm* **1** : bun (of hair) **2** *Lat* : bow (knot)
mora *nf* **1** : mulberry **2** ZARZAMORA : blackberry
morada *nf* : residence, dwelling
morado, -da *adj* : purple — **morado** *nm* : purple
moral *adj* : moral — ~ *nf* **1** : ethics, morals *pl* **2** ÁNIMO : morale — **moraleja** *nf* : moral (of a story) — **moralidad** *nf* : morality — **moralista** *adj* : moralistic — ~ *nmf* : moralist
morar *vi* : live, reside
morboso, -sa *adj* : morbid
mordaz *adj* : caustic, scathing — **mordacidad** *nf* : bite, sharpness
mordaza *nf* : gag
morder {47} *v* : bite — **mordedura** *nf* : bite (of an animal)
mordisquear *vt* : nibble (on) — **mordisco** *nm* : nibble, bite
moreno, -na *adj* **1** : dark-haired, brunette **2** : dark-skinned — ~ *n* **1** : brunette **2** : dark-skinned person
moretón *nm, pl* **-tones** : bruise
morfina *nf* : morphine
morir {46} *vi* **1** : die **2** APAGARSE : die out, go out — **morirse** *vr* **1** ~ **de** : die of **2** ~ **por** : be dying for — **moribundo, -da** *adj* : dying
moro, -ra *adj* : Moorish — ~ *n* : Moor
moroso, -sa *adj* : delinquent, in arrears — **morosidad** *nf* : delinquency (in payment)
morral *nm* : backpack
morriña *nf* : homesickness
morro *nm* : snout
morsa *nf* : walrus
morse *nm* : Morse code
mortaja *nf* : shroud
mortal *adj* **1** : mortal **2** : deadly (of a wound, an enemy, etc.) — ~ *nmf* : mortal — **mortalidad** *nf* : mortality — **mortandad** *nf* : death toll
mortero *nm* : mortar
mortífero, -ra *adj* : deadly, lethal
mortificar {72} *vt* **1** : mortify **2** ATORMENTAR : torment — **mortificarse** *vr* : be distressed
mosaico *nm* : mosaic
mosca *nf* : fly
moscada *adj* → **nuez**
mosquearse *vr fam* **1** : become suspicious **2** ENFADARSE : get annoyed
mosquito *nm* : mosquito — **mosquitero** *nm* **1** : (window) screen **2** : mosquito net
mostachón *nm, pl* **-chones** : macaroon
mostaza *nf* : mustard
mostrador *nm* : counter (in a store)
mostrar {19} *vt* : show — **mostrarse** *vr* : show oneself, appear
mota *nf* : spot, speck — **moteado, -da** *adj* : speckled, spotted
mote *nm* : nickname
motel *nm* : motel
motín *nm, pl* **-tines 1** : riot, uprising **2** : mutiny (of troops)
motivo *nm* **1** : motive, cause **2** : motif (in art, music, etc.) — **motivación** *nf, pl* **-ciones** : motivation — **motivar** *vt* **1** : cause **2** IMPULSAR : motivate
moto *nf* : motorcycle, motorbike — **motocicleta** *nf* : motorcycle — **motociclista** *nmf* : motorcyclist
motor, -triz *or* **-tora** *adj* : motor — **motor** *nm* : motor, engine — **motorista** *nmf* **1** : motorcyclist **2** *Lat* : motorist
mover {47} *vt* **1** : move, shift **2** : shake (the head) **3** PROVOCAR : provoke — **moverse** *vr* **1** : move (over) **2** APRESURARSE : get a move on — **movedizo, -za** *adj* : movable, shifting — **movible** *adj* : movable
móvil *adj* : mobile — ~ *nm* **1** MOTIVO : motive **2** : mobile — **movilidad** *nf* : mobility — **movilizar** {21} *vt* : mobilize
movimiento *nm* **1** : movement, motion **2** ~ **sindicalista** : labor movement
mozo, -za *adj* : young — ~ *n* **1** : young man *m,* young woman *f* **2** *Lat* : waiter *m,* waitress *f*

muchacho, -cha *n* . kid, boy *m,* girl *f*
muchedumbre *nf* : crowd
mucho *adv* **1** : very much, a lot **2** : long, a long time — **mucho, -cha** *adj* **1** : a lot of, many, much **2 muchas veces** : often — ~ *pron* : a lot, many, much
mucosidad *nf* : mucus
muda *nf* **1** : molting (of animals) **2** : change (of clothing) — **mudanza** *nf* **1** : change **2** TRASLADO : move, change of residence — **mudar** *v* **1** : molt, shed **2** CAMBIAR : change — **mudarse** *vr* **1** : change (one's clothes) **2** TRASLADARSE : move (one's residence)
mudo, -da *adj* **1** : mute **2** SILENCIOSO : silent
mueble *nm* **1** : piece of furniture **2** ~**s** *nmpl* : furniture, furnishings
mueca *nf* **1** : grimace, face **2 hacer** ~**s** : makes faces
muela *nf* **1** : tooth, molar **2** ~ **de juicio** : wisdom tooth
muelle *adj* : soft — ~ *nm* **1** : wharf, jetty **2** RESORTE : spring
muérdago *nm* : mistletoe
muerte *nf* : death — **muerto, -ta** *adj* **1** : dead **2** : dull (of colors, etc.) — ~ *nm* : dead person, deceased
muesca *nf* : nick, notch
muestra *nf* **1** : sample **2** SEÑAL : sign, show
mugir {35} *vi* : moo, bellow — **mugido** *nm* : mooing, bellowing
mugre *nf* : grime, filth — **mugriento, -ta** *adj* : filthy, grimy
muguete *nm* : lily of the valley
mujer *nf* **1** : woman **2** ESPOSA : wife **3** ~ **de negocios** : businesswoman
mulato, -ta *adj & n* : mulatto
muleta *nf* **1** : crutch **2** APOYO : prop, support
mullido, -da *adj* : soft, spongy
mulo, -la *n* : mule
multa *nf* : fine — **multar** *vt* : fine
multicolor *adj* : multicolored
multicultural *adj* : multicultural
multimedia *adj* : multimedia
multinacional *adj* : multinational
multiplicar {72} *v* : multiply — **multiplicarse** *vr* : multiply, reproduce — **múltiple** *adj* : multiple — **multiplicación** *nf, pl* **-ciones** : multiplication — **múltiplo** *nm* : multiple
multitud *nf* : crowd, multitude
mundo *nm* **1** : world **2 todo el** ~ : everyone, everybody — **mundanal** *adj* : worldly — **mundano, -na** *adj* **1** : worldly, earthly **2 la vida mundana** : high society — **mundial** *adj* : world, worldwide
municiones *nfpl* : ammunition
municipal *adj* : municipal — **municipio** *nm* **1** : municipality **2** AYUNTAMIENTO : town council
muñeca *nf* **1** : doll **2** : wrist (in anatomy) — **muñeco** *nm* **1** : boy doll **2** MANIQUÍ : dummy, puppet
muñon *nm, pl* **-ñones** : stump (of an arm or leg)
mural *adj & nm* : mural — **muralla** *nf* : wall, rampart
murciélago *nm* : bat (animal)
murmullo *nm* **1** : murmur, murmuring **2** : rustling (of leaves, etc.)
murmurar *vi* **1** : murmur, whisper **2** CRITICAR : gossip
muro *nm* : wall
musa *nf* : muse
musaraña *nf* : shrew
músculo *nm* : muscle — **muscular** *adj* : muscular — **musculatura** *nf* : muscles *pl* — **musculoso, -sa** *adj* : muscular
muselina *nf* : muslin
museo *nm* : museum
musgo *nm* : moss — **musgoso, -sa** *adj* : mossy
música *nf* : music — **musical** *adj* : musical — **músico, -ca** *adj* : musical — ~ *n* : musician
musitar *vt* : mumble
muslo *nm* : thigh
musulmán, -mana *adj & n, mpl* **-manes** : Muslim
mutar *v* : mutate — **mutación** *nf, pl* **-ciones** : mutation — **mutante** *adj & nmf* : mutant
mutilar *vt* : mutilate — **mutilación** *nf, pl* **-ciones** : mutilation
mutuo, -tua *adj* : mutual
muy *adv* **1** : very, quite **2** DEMASIADO : too

N

n *nf* : n, 14th letter of the Spanish alphabet
nabo *nm* : turnip
nácar *nm* : mother-of-pearl
nacer {48} *vi* **1** : be born **2** : hatch (of an egg), sprout (of a plant) **3** SURGIR : arise, spring up — **nacido, -da** *adj & n* **recién** ~ : newborn — **naciente** *adj* **1** : new, growing **2** : rising (of the sun) — **nacimiento** *nm* **1** : birth **2** : source (of a river) **3** ORIGEN : beginning **4** BELÉN : Nativity scene
nación *nf, pl* **-ciones** : nation, country — **nacional** *adj* : national — ~ *nmf* : national, citizen — **nacionalidad** *nf* : nationality — **nacionalismo** *nm* : nationalism — **nacionalista** *adj & nmf* : nationalist — **nacionalizar** {21} *vt* **1** : nationalize **2** : naturalize (as a citizen) — **nacionalizarse** *vr* : become naturalized
nada *pron* **1** : nothing **2 de** ~ : you're welcome **3** ~ **más** : nothing else, nothing more — ~ *adv* : not at all — ~ *nf* **la** ~ : nothingness
nadar *v* : swim — **nadador, -dora** *n* : swimmer
nadería *nf* : small thing, trifle
nadie *pron* : nobody, no one
nado: **a** ~ *adv phr* : swimming
nafta *nf Lat* : gasoline
naipe *nm* : playing card
nalgas *nfpl* : buttocks, bottom
nana *nf* : lullaby
naranja *adj & nm* : orange (color) — ~ *nf* : orange (fruit) — **naranjal** *nm* : orange grove — **naranjo** *nm* : orange tree
narciso *nm* : narcissus, daffodil
narcótico, -ca *adj* : narcotic — **narcótico** *nm* : narcotic — **narcotizar** {21} *vt* : drug — **narcotraficante** *nmf* : drug trafficker — **narcotráfico** *nm* : drug trafficking
nariz *nf, pl* **-rices 1** : nose **2** OLFATO : sense of smell **3 narices** *nfpl* : nostrils
narrar *vt* : narrate, tell — **narración** *nf, pl* **-ciones** : narration — **narrador, -dora** *n* : narrator — **narrativa** *nf* : narrative, storytelling
nasal *adj* : nasal
nata *nf Spain* : cream
natación *nf, pl* **-ciones** : swimming
natal *adj* : native, birth — **natalicio** *nm* : birthday — **natalidad** *nf* : birthrate
natillas *nfpl* : custard
natividad *nf* : birth, nativity
nativo, -va *adj & n* : native
natural *adj* **1** : natural **2** NORMAL : normal **3** ~ **de** : native of, from — ~ *nm* **1** : temperament **2** NATIVO : native — **naturaleza** *nf* : nature — **naturalidad** *nf* : naturalness — **naturalista** *adj* : naturalistic — **naturalización** *nf, pl* **-ciones** : naturalization — **naturalizar** {21} *vt* : naturalize — **naturalizarse** *vr* : become naturalized — **naturalmente** *adv* **1** : naturally **2** POR SUPUESTO : of course
naufragar {52} *vi* **1** : be shipwrecked **2** FRACASAR : fail — **naufragio** *nm* : shipwreck — **náufrago, -ga** *adj* : shipwrecked — ~ *n* : castaway
náusea *nf* **1** : nausea **2 dar ~s** : nauseate **3 ~s matutinas** : morning sickness — **nauseabundo, -da** *adj* : nauseating
náutico, -ca *adj* : nautical
navaja *nf* : pocketknife, penknife
naval *adj* : naval
nave *nf* **1** : ship **2** : nave (of a church) **3** ~ **espacial** : spaceship
navegar {52} *v* : navigate, sail — **navegable** *adj* : navigable — **navegación** *nf, pl* **-ciones** : navigation — **navegante** *adj* : sailing, seafaring — ~ *nmf* : navigator
Navidad *nf* **1** : Christmas **2 feliz** ~ : Merry Christmas — **navideño, -ña** *adj* : Christmas
naviero, -ra *adj* : shipping
nazi *adj & nmf* : Nazi — **nazismo** *nm* : Nazism
neblina *nf* : mist
nebuloso, -sa *adj* **1** : hazy, misty, foggy **2** VAGO : vague, nebulous
necedad *nf* **1** : stupidity **2 decir ~es** : talk nonsense
necesario, -ria *adj* : necessary — **necesariamente** *adv* : necessarily — **necesidad** *nf* **1** : need, necessity **2** POBREZA : poverty **3 ~es** *nfpl* : hardships — **necesitado, -da** *adj* : needy — **necesitar** *vt* : need — *vi* ~ **de** : have need of

necio, -cia *adj* : silly, dumb
necrología *nf* : obituary
néctar *nm* : nectar
nectarina *nf* : nectarine
neerlandés, -desa *adj, mpl* **-deses** : Dutch — **neerlandés** *nm* : Dutch (language)
nefasto, -ta *adj* **1** : ill-fated **2** *fam* : terrible, awful
negar {49} *vt* **1** : deny **2** REHUSAR : refuse **3** : disown (a person) — **negarse** *vr* : refuse — **negación** *nf, pl* **-ciones** **1** : denial **2** : negative (in grammar) — **negativa** *nf* **1** : denial **2** RECHAZO : refusal — **negativo, -va** *adj* : negative — **negativo** *nm* : negative (of a photograph)
negligente *adj* : negligent — **negligencia** *nf* : negligence
negociar *vt* : negotiate — *vi* : deal, do business — **negociable** *adj* : negotiable — **negociación** *nf, pl* **-ciones** : negotiation — **negociante** *nmf* : businessman *m*, businesswoman *f* — **negocio** *nm* **1** : business **2** TRANSACCIÓN : deal **3** **~s** : business, commerce
negro, -gra *adj* : black, dark — **~** *n* : dark-skinned person — **negro** *nm* : black (color) — **negrura** *nf* : blackness — **negruzco, -ca** *adj* : blackish
nene, -na *n fam* : baby, small child
nenúfar *nm* : water lily
neón *nm* : neon
neoyorquino, -na *adj* : of or from New York
nepotismo *nm* : nepotism
Neptuno *nm* : Neptune
nervio *nm* **1** : nerve **2** : sinew (in meat) **3** VIGOR : vigor, energy **4** **tener ~s** : be nervous — **nerviosismo** *nf* : nervousness — **nervioso, -sa** *adj* **1** : nervous, anxious **2** **sistema nervioso** : nervous system
nervudo, -da *adj* : sinewy
neto, -ta *adj* **1** : clear, distinct **2** : net (of weight, salaries, etc.)
neumático *nm* : tire
neumonía *nf* : pneumonia
neurología *nf* : neurology — **neurológico, -ca** *adj* : neurological, neurologic — **neurólogo, -ga** *n* : neurologist
neurosis *nfs & pl* : neurosis — **neurótico, -ca** *adj & n* : neurotic
neutral *adj* : neutral — **neutralidad** *nf* : neutrality — **neutralizar** {21} *vt* : neutralize — **neutro, -tra** *adj* **1** : neutral **2** : neuter (in biology and grammar)
neutrón *nm, pl* **-trones** : neutron
nevar {55} *v impers* : snow — **nevada** *nf* : snowfall — **nevado, -da** *adj* **1** : snow-covered, snowy **2** : snow-white — **nevasca** *nf* : snowstorm
nevera *nf* : refrigerator
nevisca *nf* : light snowfall, flurry
nexo *nm* : link, connection
ni *conj* **1** : neither, nor **2** **~ que** : as if **3** **~ siquiera** : not even
nicaragüense *adj* : Nicaraguan
nicho *nm* : niche
nicotina *nf* : nicotine
nidada *nf* : brood (of chicks, etc.)
nido *nm* **1** : nest **2** GUARIDA : hiding place, den
niebla *nf* : fog, mist
nieto, -ta *n* **1** : grandson *m*, granddaughter *f* **2** **nietos** *nmpl* : grandchildren
nieve *nf* : snow
nigeriano, -na *adj* : Nigerian
nilón *or* **nilon** *nm, pl* **-lones** : nylon
nimio, -mia *adj* : insignificant, trivial — **nimiedad** *nf* **1** : trifle **2** INSIGNIFICANCIA : triviality
ninfa *nf* : nymph
ninguno, -na (**ningún** *before masculine singular nouns*) *adj* : no, not any — **~** *pron* **1** : neither, none **2** : no one, nobody
niña *nf* **1** : pupil (of the eye) **2** **la ~ de los ojos** : the apple of one's eye
niño, -ña *n* : child, boy *m*, girl *f* — **~** *adj* **1** : young **2** INFANTIL : immature, childish — **niñero, -ra** *n* : baby-sitter, nanny — **niñez** *nf, pl* **-ñeces** : childhood
nipón, -pona *adj* : Japanese
níquel *nm* : nickel
nítido, -da *adj* : clear, sharp — **nitidez** *nf, pl* **-deces** : clarity, sharpness
nitrato *nm* : nitrate
nitrógeno *nm* : nitrogen
nivel *nm* **1** : level, height **2** **~ de vida** : standard of living — **nivelar** *vt* : level (out)
no *adv* **1** : not **2** (*in answer to a question*) : no **3** **¡como ~!** : of course! **4** **~ bien** : as soon as **5** **~ fumador** : non-smoker — **~** *nm* : no
noble *adj & nmf* : noble — **nobleza** *nf* : nobility
noche *nf* **1** : night, evening **2** **buenas ~s** : good evening, good night **3** **de ~** *or* **por la ~** : at night **4** **hacerse de ~** : get dark — **Nochebuena** *nf* : Christmas Eve — **nochecita** *nf* : dusk — **Nochevieja** *nf* : New Year's Eve
noción *nf, pl* **-ciones** **1** : notion, concept **2** **nociones** *nfpl* : rudiments
nocivo, -va *adj* : harmful, noxious

nocturno, -na *adj* **1** : night **2** : nocturnal (of animals, etc.) — **nocturno** *nm* : nocturne
nogal *nm* **1** : walnut tree **2 ~ americano** : hickory
nómada *nmf* : nomad — **~** *adj* : nomadic
nomás *adv Lat* : only, just
nombrar *vt* **1** : appoint **2** CITAR : mention — **nombrado, -da** *adj* : famous, well-known — **nombramiento** *nm* : appointment, nomination — **nombre** *nm* **1** : name **2** SUSTANTIVO : noun **3** FAMA : fame, renown **4 ~ de pila** : first name
nómina *nf* : payroll
nominal *adj* : nominal
nominar *vt* : nominate — **nominación** *nf, pl* **-ciones** : nomination
nomo *nm* : gnome
non *adj* : odd, not even — **~** *nm* : odd number
nonagésimo, -ma *adj & n* : ninetieth
nopal *nm* : nopal, prickly pear
nordeste *or* **noreste** *adj* **1** : northeastern **2** : northeasterly (of wind, etc.) — **~** *nm* : northeast
nórdico, -ca *adj* : Scandinavian
noreste → **nordeste**
noria *nf* **1** : waterwheel **2** : Ferris wheel (at a fair, etc.)
norma *nf* : rule, norm, standard — **normal** *adj* **1** : normal **2 escuela ~** : teacher-training college — **normalidad** *nf* : normality — **normalizar** {21} *vt* **1** : normalize **2** ESTANDARIZAR : standardize — **normalizarse** *vr* : return to normal — **normalmente** *adv* : ordinarily, generally
noroeste *adj* **1** : northwestern **2** : northwesterly (of wind, etc.) — **~** *nm* : northwest
norte *adj* : north, northern — **~** *nm* **1** : north **2** : north wind
norteamericano, -na *adj* : North American
norteño, -ña *adj* : northern
noruego, -ga *adj* : Norwegian — **noruego** *nm* : Norwegian (language)
nos *pron* **1** (*direct object*) : us **2** (*indirect object*) : to us, for us, from us **3** (*reflexive*) : ourselves **4** : each other, one another
nosotros, -tras *pron* **1** (*subject*) : we **2** (*object*) : us **3** *or* **~ mismos** : ourselves
nostalgia *nf* **1** : nostalgia **2 sentir ~ por** : be homesick for — **nostálgico, -ca** *adj* : nostalgic
nota *nf* **1** : note **2** : grade, mark (in school) **3** CUENTA : bill, check — **notable** *adj* : noteworthy, notable — **notar** *vt* : notice — **notarse** *vr* : be evident, seem
notario, -ria *n* : notary (public)
noticia *nf* **1** : news item, piece of news **2 ~s** *nfpl* : news — **noticiario** *nm* : newscast — **noticiero** *nm Lat* : newscast
notificar {72} *vt* : notify — **notificación** *nf, pl* **-ciones** : notification
notorio, -ria *adj* **1** : obvious **2** CONOCIDO : well-known — **notoriedad** *nf* : fame, notoriety
novato, -ta *adj* : inexperienced — **~** *n* : beginner, novice
novecientos, -tas *adj* : nine hundred — **novecientos** *nms & pl* : nine hundred
novedad *nf* **1** : newness, innovation **2** NOTICIAS : news **3 ~es** : novelties, latest news — **novedoso, -sa** *adj* : original, novel
novela *nf* **1** : novel **2** : soap opera (on television) — **novelesco, -ca** *adj* **1** : fictional **2** FANTÁSTICO : fabulous — **novelista** *nmf* : novelist
noveno, -na *adj* : ninth — **noveno** *nm* : ninth
noventa *adj & nm* : ninety — **noventavo, -va** *adj* : ninetieth — **noventavo** *nm* : ninetieth
novia → **novio**
noviazgo *nm* : engagement
novicio, -cia *n* : novice
noviembre *nm* : November
novillo, -lla *n* : young bull *m,* heifer *f*
novio, -via *n* **1** : boyfriend *m,* girlfriend *f* **2** PROMETIDO : fiancé *m,* fiancée *f* **3** : bridegroom *m,* bride *f* (at a wedding)
novocaína *nf* : novocaine
nube *nf* : cloud — **nubarrón** *nm, pl* **-rrones** : storm cloud — **nublado, -da** *adj* **1** : cloudy **2** ENTURBIADO : clouded, dim — **nublado** *nm* : storm cloud — **nublar** *vt* **1** : cloud **2** OSCURECER : obscure — **nublarse** *vr* : get cloudy — **nuboso, -sa** *adj* : cloudy
nuca *nf* : nape, back of the neck
núcleo *nm* **1** : nucleus **2** CENTRO : center, core — **nuclear** *adj* : nuclear
nudillo *nm* : knuckle
nudismo *nm* : nudism — **nudista** *adj & nmf* : nudist
nudo *nm* **1** : knot **2** : crux, heart (of a problem, etc.) — **nudoso, -sa** *adj* : knotty, gnarled
nuera *nf* : daughter-in-law
nuestro, -tra *adj* : our — **~** *pron* (*with definite article*) : ours, our own
nuevamente *adv* : again, anew

nueve *adj & nm* : nine
nuevo, -va *adj* **1** : new **2 de nuevo** : again, once more
nuez *nf, pl* **nueces 1** : nut **2** *or* **~ de nogal** : walnut **3 ~ de Adán** : Adam's apple **4 ~ moscada** : nutmeg
nulo, -la *adj* **1** *or* **~ y sin efecto** : null and void **2** INCAPAZ : useless, inept — **nulidad** *nf* **1** : nullity **2 es una ~** *fam* : he's a total loss
numerar *vt* : number — **numeración** *nf, pl* **-ciones 1** : numbering **2** NÚMEROS : numbers *pl,* numerals *pl* — **numeral** *adj* : numeral — **número** *nm* **1** : number, numeral **2** : issue (of a publication) **3 sin ~** : countless — **numérico, -ca** *adj* : numerical — **numeroso, -sa** *adj* : numerous
nunca *adv* **1** : never, ever **2 ~ más** : never again **3 ~ jamás** : never ever
nupcial *adj* : nuptial, wedding — **nupcias** *nfpl* : nuptials, wedding
nutria *nf* : otter
nutrir *vt* **1** ALIMENTAR : feed, nourish **2** FOMENTAR : fuel, foster — **nutrición** *nf, pl* **-ciones** : nutrition — **nutrido, -da** *adj* **1** : nourished **2** ABUNDANTE : considerable, abundant — **nutriente** *nm* : nutrient — **nutritivo, -va** *adj* : nourishing, nutritious

O

o[1] *nf* : o, 16th letter of the Spanish alphabet
o[2] *conj* (**u** *before words beginning with o- or ho-*) **1** : or, either **2 ~ sea** : in other words
oasis *nms & pl* : oasis
obcecar {72} *vt* : blind (by emotions) — **obcecarse** *vr* : become stubborn
obedecer {53} *vt* : obey — *vi* **1** : obey **2 ~ a** : respond to **3 ~ a** : be due to — **obediencia** *nf* : obedience — **obediente** *adj* : obedient
obertura *nf* : overture
obeso, -sa *adj* : obese — **obesidad** *nf* : obesity
obispo *nm* : bishop
objetar *v* : object — **objeción** *nf, pl* **-ciones** : objection
objeto *nm* : object — **objetivo, -va** *adj* : objective — **objetivo** *nm* **1** : objective, goal **2** : lens (in photography, etc.)
objetor, -tora *n* **~ de conciencia** : conscientious objector
oblicuo, -cua *adj* : oblique
obligar {52} *vt* : require, oblige — **obligarse** *vr* : commit oneself (to do something) — **obligación** *nf, pl* **-ciones** : obligation — **obligado, -da** *adj* **1** : obliged **2** FORZOSO : obligatory — **obligatorio, -ria** *adj* : mandatory
oblongo, -ga *adj* : oblong
oboe *nm* : oboe — **~** *nmf* : oboist
obra *nf* **1** : work, deed **2** : work (of art, literature, etc.) **3** CONSTRUCCIÓN : construction work **4 ~ maestra** : masterpiece **5 ~s públicas** : public works — **obrar** *vt* : work, produce — *vi* : act, behave — **obrero, -ra** *adj* **la clase obrera** : the working class — **~** *n* : worker, laborer
obsceno, -na *adj* : obscene — **obscenidad** *nf* : obscenity
obsequiar *vt* : give, present — **obsequio** *nm* : gift, present
observar *vt* **1** : observe, watch **2** ADVERTIR : notice **3** ACATAR : observe, obey **4** COMENTAR : remark — **observación** *nf, pl* **-ciones** : observation — **observador, -dora** *adj* : observant — **~** *n* : observer — **observancia** *nf* : observance — **observatorio** *nm* : observatory
obsesionar *vt* : obsess — **obsesionarse** *vr* : be obsessed — **obsesión** *nf, pl* **-siones** : obsession — **obsesivo, -va** *adj* : obsessive — **obseso, -sa** *adj* : obsessed
obsoleto, -ta *adj* : obsolete
obstaculizar {21} *vt* : hinder — **obstáculo** *nm* : obstacle
obstante: **no ~** *conj phr* : nevertheless, however — **~** *prep phr* : in spite of, despite
obstar {21} *vi* **~ a** *or* **~ para** : stop, prevent
obstetricia *nf* : obstetrics — **obstetra** *nmf* : obstetrician
obstinarse *vr* : be stubborn — **obstinado, -da** *adj* **1** : obstinate, stubborn **2** TENAZ : persistent
obstruir {41} *vt* : obstruct — **obstrucción** *nf, pl* **-ciones** : obstruction
obtener {80} *vt* : obtain, get
obtuso, -sa *adj* : obtuse
obviar *vt* : get around, avoid
obvio, -via *adj* : obvious — **obviamente** *adv* : obviously, clearly
oca *nf* : goose
ocasión *nf, pl* **-siones 1** : occasion **2** OPORTUNIDAD : opportunity **3** GANGA

: bargain — **ocasional** *adj* **1** : occasional **2** ACCIDENTAL : accidental, chance — **ocasionar** *vt* : cause

ocaso *nm* **1** : sunset **2** DECADENCIA : decline

occidente *nm* **1** : west **2 el Occidente** : the West — **occidental** *adj* : western, Western

océano *nm* : ocean — **oceanografía** *nf* : oceanography

ochenta *adj & nm* : eighty

ocho *adj & nm* : eight — **ochocientos, -tas** *adj* : eight hundred — **ochocientos** *nms & pl* : eight hundred

ocio *nm* **1** : free time, leisure **2** INACTIVIDAD : idleness — **ociosidad** *nf* : idleness, inactivity — **ocioso, -sa** *adj* **1** : idle, inactive **2** INÚTIL : useless

ocre *adj & nm* : ocher

octágono *nm* : octagon — **octagonal** *adj* : octagonal

octava *nf* : octave

octavo, -va *adj & n* : eighth

octeto *nm* : byte

octogésimo, -ma *adj & n* : eightieth

octubre *nm* : October

ocular *adj* : ocular, eye — **oculista** *nmf* : ophthalmologist

ocultar *vt* : conceal, hide — **ocultarse** *vr* : hide — **oculto, -ta** *adj* : hidden, occult

ocupar *vt* **1** : occupy **2** : hold (a position, etc.) **3** : provide work for — **ocuparse** *vr* **1 ~ de** : concern oneself with **2 ~ de** : take care of (children, etc.) — **ocupación** *nf, pl* **-ciones 1** : occupation **2** EMPLEO : job — **ocupado, -da** *adj* **1** : busy **2** : occupied (of a place) **3 señal de occupado** : busy signal — **ocupante** *nmf* : occupant

ocurrir *vi* : occur, happen — **ocurrirse** *vr* **~ a** : occur to — **occurrencia** *nf* **1** : occurrence, event **2** SALIDA : witty remark, quip

oda *nf* : ode

odiar *vt* : hate — **odio** *nm* : hatred — **odioso, -sa** *adj* : hateful

odisea *nf* : odyssey

odontología *nf* : dentistry, dental surgery — **odontólogo, -ga** *n* : dentist, dental surgeon

oeste *adj* : west, western — **~** *nm* **1** : west **2 el Oeste** : the West

ofender *v* : offend — **ofenderse** *vr* : take offense — **ofensa** *nf* : offense, insult — **ofensiva** *nf* : offensive — **ofensivo, -va** *adj* : offensive

oferta *nf* **1** : offer **2 de ~** : on sale **3 ~ y demanda** : supply and demand

oficial *adj* : official — **~** *nmf* **1** : skilled worker **2** : officer (in the military)

oficina *nf* : office — **oficinista** *nmf* : office worker

oficio *nm* : trade, profession — **oficioso, -sa** *adj* : unofficial

ofrecer {53} *vt* **1** : offer **2** : provide, present (an opportunity, etc.) — **ofrecerse** *vr* : volunteer — **ofrecimiento** *nm* : offer

ofrenda *nf* : offering

oftalmología *nf* : ophthalmology — **oftalmólogo, -ga** *n* : ophthalmologist

ofuscar {72} *vt* **1** : blind, dazzle **2** CONFUNDIR : confuse — **ofuscarse** *vr* **~ con** : be blinded by — **ofuscación** *nf, pl* **-ciones 1** : blindness **2** CONFUSIÓN : confusion

ogro *nm* : ogre

oír {50} *vi* : hear — *vt* **1** : hear **2** ESCUCHAR : listen to **3 ¡oiga!** *or* **¡oye!** : excuse me!, listen! — **oídas: de ~** *adv phr* : by hearsay — **oído** *nm* **1** : ear **2** : (sense of) hearing **3 duro de ~** : hard of hearing

ojal *nm* : buttonhole

ojalá *interj* : I hope so!, if only!

ojear *vt* : eye, look at — **ojeada** *nf* : glimpse, glance

ojeriza *nf* **1** : ill will **2 tener ~ a** : have a grudge against

ojo *nm* **1** : eye **2** PERSPICACIA : shrewdness **3** : span (of a bridge) **4 ¡~!** : look out!, pay attention!

ola *nf* : wave — **oleada** *nf* : wave, surge — **oleaje** *nm* : swell (of the sea)

olé *interj* : bravo!

oleada *nf* : wave, swell — **oleaje** *nm* : waves *pl*, surf

óleo *nm* **1** : oil **2** CUADRO : oil painting — **oleoducto** *nm* : oil pipeline

oler {51} *vt* : smell — *vi* **1** : smell **2 ~ a** : smell of — **olerse** *vr fam* : have a hunch about

olfatear *vt* **1** : sniff **2** OLER : sense, sniff out — **olfato** *nm* **1** : sense of smell **2** PERSPICACIA : nose, instinct

Olimpiada *or* **Olimpíada** *nf* : Olympics *pl*, Olympic Games *pl* — **olímpico, -ca** *adj* : Olympic

oliva *nf* : olive — **olivo** *nm* : olive tree

olla *nf* **1** : pot **2 ~ podrida** : (Spanish) stew

olmo *nm* : elm

olor *nm* : smell — **oloroso, -sa** *adj* : fragrant

olvidar *vt* **1** : forget **2** DEJAR : leave (behind) — **olvidarse** *vr* : forget — **olvidadizo, -za** *adj* : forgetful — **olvido** *nm* **1** : forgetfulness **2** DESCUIDO : oversight

ombligo *nm* : navel

omelette *nmf Lat* : omelet

ominoso, -sa *adj* : ominous
omitir *vt* : omit — **omisión** *nf, pl* **-siones** : omission
ómnibus *nm, pl* **-bus** *or* **-buses** : bus
omnipotente *adj* : omnipotent
omóplato *or* **omoplato** *nm* : shoulder blade
once *adj & nm* : eleven — **onceavo, -va** *adj & n* : eleventh
onda *nf* : wave — **ondear** *vi* : ripple — **ondulación** *nf, pl* **-ciones** : undulation — **ondulado, -da** *adj* : wavy — **ondular** *vt* : wave (hair) — *vi* : undulate, ripple
ónice *nmf or* **ónix** *nm* : onyx
onza *nf* : ounce
opaco, -ca *adj* **1** : opaque **2** DESLUSTRADO : dull
ópalo *nm* : opal
opción *nf, pl* **-ciones** : option — **opcional** *adj* : optional
ópera *nf* : opera
operar *vt* **1** : operate on **2** *Lat* : operate, run (a machine) — *vi* **1** : operate **2** NEGOCIAR : deal, do business — **operarse** *vr* **1** : have an operation **2** OCURRIR : take place — **operación** *nf, pl* **-ciones 1** : operation **2** TRANSACCIÓN : transaction, deal — **operacional** *adj* : operational — **operador, -dora** *n* **1** : operator **2** : cameraman (for television, etc.)
opereta *nf* : operetta
opinar *vt* : think — *vi* : express an opinion — **opinión** *nf, pl* **-niones** : opinion
opio *nm* : opium
oponer {60} *vt* **1** : raise, put forward (arguments, etc.) **2** ~ **resistencia** : put up a fight — **oponerse** *vr* ~ **a** : oppose, be against — **oponente** *nmf* : opponent
oporto *nm* : port (wine)
oportunidad *nf* : opportunity — **oportunista** *nmf* : opportunist — **oportuno, -na** *adj* **1** : opportune, timely **2** APROPIADO : suitable
opositor, -tora *n* **1** : opponent **2** : candidate (for a position) — **oposición** *nf, pl* **-ciones** : opposition
oprimir *vt* **1** : press, squeeze **2** TIRANIZAR : oppress — **opresión** *nf, pl* **-siones 1** : oppression **2** ~ **de pecho** : tightness in the chest — **opresivo, -va** *adj* : oppressive — **opresor, -sora** *n* : oppressor
optar *vi* **1** ~ **a** : apply for **2** ~ **por** : choose, opt for
óptica *nf* **1** : optics **2** : optician's (shop) — **óptico, -ca** *adj* : optical — ~ *n* : optician
optimismo *nm* : optimism — **optimista** *adj* : optimistic — ~ *nmf* : optimist
optometría *nf* : optometry — **optometrista** *nmf* : optometrist
opuesto *adj* **1** : opposite **2** CONTRADICTORIO : opposed, conflicting
opulencia *nf* : opulence — **opulento, -ta** *adj* : opulent
oración *nf, pl* **-ciones 1** : prayer **2** FRASE : sentence, clause
oráculo *nm* : oracle
orador, -dora *n* : speaker
oral *adj* : oral
orar *vi* : pray
órbita *nf* **1** : orbit (in astronomy) **2** : eye socket — **orbitar** *vi* : orbit
orden *nm, pl* **órdenes 1** : order **2** ~ **del día** : agenda (at a meeting) **3** ~ **público** : law and order — ~ *nf, pl* **órdenes 1** : order (of food) **2** ~ **religiosa** : religious order **3** ~ **de compra** : purchase order
ordenador *nm Spain* : computer
ordenar *vt* **1** : order, command **2** ARREGLAR : put in order **3** : ordain (a priest) — **ordenanza** *nm* : orderly (in the armed forces) — ~ *nf* : ordinance, regulation
ordeñar *vt* : milk
ordinal *adj & nm* : ordinal
ordinario, -ria *adj* **1** : ordinary **2** GROSERO : common, vulgar
orear *vt* : air
orégano *nm* : oregano
oreja *nf* : ear
orfanato *or* **orfelinato** *nm* : orphanage
orfebre *nmf* : goldsmith, silversmith
orgánico, -ca *adj* : organic
organigrama *nm* : flowchart
organismo *nm* **1** : organism **2** ORGANIZACIÓN : agency, organization
organista *nmf* : organist
organizar {21} *vt* : organize — **organizarse** *vr* : get organized — **organización** *nf, pl* **-ciones** : organization — **organizador, -dora** *n* : organizer
órgano *nm* : organ
orgasmo *nm* : orgasm
orgía *nf* : orgy
orgullo *nm* : pride — **orgulloso, -sa** *adj* : proud
orientación *nf, pl* **-ciones 1** : orientation **2** DIRECCIÓN : direction **3** CONSEJO : guidance
oriental *adj* **1** : eastern **2** : oriental — ~ *nmf* : Oriental
orientar *vt* **1** : orient, position **2** GUIAR : guide, direct — **orientarse** *vr* **1** : orient oneself **2** ~ **hacia** : turn towards

oriente *nm* **1** : east, East **2 el Oriente** : the Orient
orificio *nm* : orifice, opening
origen *nm, pl* **orígenes** : origin — **original** *adj & nm* : original — **originalidad** *nf* : originality — **originar** *vt* : give rise to — **originarse** *vr* : originate, arise — **originario, -ria** *adj* **~ de** : native of
orilla *nf* **1** : border, edge **2** : bank (of a river), shore (of the sea)
orinar *vi* : urinate — **orina** *nf* : urine
oriol *nm* : oriole
oriundo, -da *adj* **~ de** : native of
orla *nf* : border
ornamental *adj* : ornamental — **ornamento** *nm* : ornament
ornar *vt* : adorn
ornitología *nf* : ornithology
oro *nm* : gold
orquesta *nf* : orchestra — **orquestar** *vt* : orchestrate
orquídea *nf* : orchid
ortiga *nf* : nettle
ortodoxia *nf* : orthodoxy — **ortodoxo, -xa** *adj* : orthodox
ortografía *nf* : spelling
ortopedia *nf* : orthopedics — **ortopédico, -ca** *adj* : orthopedic
oruga *nf* : caterpillar
orzuelo *nm* : sty (in the eye)
os *pron pl Spain* **1** (*direct or indirect object*) : you, to you **2** (*reflexive*) : yourselves, to yourselves **3** : each other, to each other
osado, -da *adj* : bold, daring — **osadía** *nf* **1** : boldness, daring **2** DESCARO : audacity, nerve
osamenta *nf* : skeleton
osar *vi* : dare
oscilar *vi* **1** : swing, sway **2** FLUCTUAR : fluctuate — **oscilación** *nf, pl* **-ciones 1** : swinging **2** FLUCTUACIÓN : fluctuation
oscuro, -ra *adj* **1** : dark **2** : obscure (of ideas, persons, etc.) **3 a oscuras** : in the dark — **oscurecer** {53} *vt* **1** : darken **2** : confuse, cloud (the mind) **3 al ~** : at nightfall — *v impers* : get dark — **oscurecerse** *vr* : grow dark — **oscuridad** *nf* **1** : darkness **2** : obscurity (of ideas, persons, etc.)
óseo, ósea *adj* : skeletal, bony
oso, osa *n* **1** : bear **2 ~ de peluche** *or* **~ de felpa** : teddy bear
ostensible *adj* : evident, obvious
ostentar *vt* **1** : flaunt, display **2** POSEER : have, hold — **ostentación** *nf, pl* **-ciones** : ostentation — **ostentoso, -sa** *adj* : ostentatious, showy
osteopatía *n* : osteopathy — **osteópata** *nmf* : osteopath
osteoporosis *nf* : osteoporosis
ostra *nf* : oyster
ostracismo *nm* : ostracism
otear *vt* : scan, survey
otoño *nm* : autumn, fall — **otoñal** *adj* : autumn, fall
otorgar {52} *vt* **1** : grant, award **2** : draw up (a legal document)
otro, otra *adj* **1** : another, other **2 otra vez** : again — **~** *pron* **1** : another (one), other (one) **2 los otros, las otras** : the others, the rest
ovación *nf, pl* **-ciones** : ovation
óvalo *nm* : oval — **oval** *or* **ovalado, -da** *adj* : oval
ovario *nm* : ovary
oveja *nf* **1** : sheep, ewe **2 ~ negra** : black sheep
overol *nm Lat* : overalls *pl*
ovillo *nm* **1** : ball (of yarn) **2 hacerse un ~** : curl up (into a ball)
ovni *or* **OVNI** *nm* (*objeto volador no identificado*) : UFO
ovular *vi* : ovulate — **ovulación** *nf, pl* **-ciones** : ovulation
oxidar *vi* : rust — **oxidarse** *vr* : get rusty — **oxidación** *nf, pl* **-ciones** : rusting — **oxidado, -da** *adj* : rusty — **óxido** *nm* : rust
oxígeno *nm* : oxygen
oye → **oír**
oyente *nmf* **1** : listener **2** : auditor (student)
ozono *nm* : ozone

P

p *nf* : p, 17th letter of the Spanish alphabet
pabellón *nm, pl* **-llones 1** : pavilion **2** : block, building (in a hospital complex, etc.) **3** : summerhouse (in a garden, etc.) **4** BANDERA : flag
pabilo *nm* : wick
pacer {48} *v* : graze
paces → **paz**
paciencia *nf* : patience — **paciente** *adj & nmf* : patient
pacificar {72} *vt* : pacify, calm — **paci-**

ficarse *vr* : calm down — **pacífico, -ca** *adj* : peaceful, pacific — **pacifismo** *nm* : pacifism — **pacifista** *adj & nmf* : pacifist
pacotilla *nf* **de ~** : second-rate, trashy
pacto *nm* : pact, agreement — **pactar** *vt* : agree on — *vi* : come to an agreement
padecer {53} *vt* : suffer, endure — *vi* **~ de** : suffer from — **padecimiento** *nm* : suffering
padre *nm* **1** : father **2 ~s** *nmpl* : parents — **~** *adj Lat fam* : great, fantastic — **padrastro** *nm* : stepfather — **padrino** *nm* **1** : godfather **2** : best man (at a wedding)
padrón *nm, pl* **-drones** : register, roll
paella *nf* : paella
paga *nf* : pay, wages *pl* — **pagadero, -ra** *adj* : payable
pagano, -na *adj & n* : pagan, heathen
pagar {52} *vt* : pay, pay for — *vi* : pay — **pagaré** *nm* : IOU
página *nf* : page
pago *nm* : payment
país *nm* **1** : country, nation **2** REGIÓN : region, land — **paisaje** *nm* : scenery, landscape — **paisano, -na** *n* : compatriot
paja *nf* **1** : straw **2** *fam* : nonsense
pájaro *nm* **1** : bird **2 ~ carpintero** : woodpecker — **pajarera** *nf* : aviary
pajita *nf* : (drinking) straw
pala *nf* **1** : shovel, spade **2** : blade (of an oar or a rotor) **3** : paddle, racket (in sports)
palabra *nf* **1** : word **2** HABLA : speech **3 tener la ~** : have the floor — **palabrota** *nf* : swearword
palacio *nm* **1** : palace, mansion **2 ~ de justicia** : courthouse
paladar *nm* : palate — **paladear** *vt* : savor
palanca *nf* **1** : lever, crowbar **2** *fam* : leverage, influence **3 ~ de cambio** *or* **~ de velocidades** : gearshift
palangana *nf* : washbowl
palco *nm* : box (in a theater)
palestino, -na *adj* : Palestinian
paleta *nf* **1** : small shovel, trowel **2** : palette (in art) **3** : paddle (in sports, etc.)
paletilla *nf* : shoulder blade
paliar *vt* : alleviate, ease — **paliativo, -va** *adj* : palliative
pálido, -da *adj* : pale — **palidecer** {53} *vi* : turn pale — **palidez** *nf, pl* **-deces** : paleness, pallor
palillo *nm* **1** : small stick **2** *or* **~ de dientes** : toothpick

paliza *nf* : beating
palma *nf* **1** : palm (of the hand) **2** : palm (tree or leaf) **3 batir ~s** : clap, applaud — **palmada** *nf* **1** : pat, slap **2 ~s** *nfpl* : clapping
palmera *nf* : palm tree
palmo *nm* **1** : span, small amount **2 ~ a ~** : bit by bit
palmotear *vi* : applaud — **palmoteo** *nm* : clapping, applause
palo *nm* **1** : stick **2** MANGO : shaft, handle **3** MÁSTIL : mast **4** POSTE : pole **5** GOLPE : blow **6** : suit (of cards)
paloma *nf* : pigeon, dove — **palomilla** *nf* : moth — **palomitas** *nfpl* : popcorn
palpar *vt* : feel, touch — **palpable** *adj* : palpable
palpitar *vi* : palpitate, throb — **palpitación** *nf, pl* **-ciones** : palpitation
palta *nf Lat* : avocado
paludismo *nm* : malaria
pampa *nf* : pampa
pan *nm* **1** : bread **2** : loaf (of bread, etc.) **3 ~ tostado** : toast
pana *nf* : corduroy
panacea *nf* : panacea
panadería *nf* : bakery, bread shop — **panadero, -ra** *n* : baker
panal *nm* : honeycomb
panameño, -ña *adj* : Panamanian
pancarta *nf* : placard, banner
pancito *nm Lat* : (bread) roll
páncreas *nms & pl* : pancreas
panda *nmf* : panda
pandemonio *nm* : pandemonium
pandero *nm* : tambourine — **pandereta** *nf* : (small) tambourine
pandilla *nf* : gang
panecillo *nm Spain* : (bread) roll
panel *nm* : panel
panfleto *nm* : pamphlet
pánico *nm* : panic
panorama *nm* : panorama — **panorámico, -ca** *adj* : panoramic
panqueque *nm Lat* : pancake
pantaletas *nfpl Lat* : panties
pantalla *nf* **1** : screen **2** : lampshade
pantalón *nm, pl* **-lones 1** *or* **pantalones** *nmpl* : pants *pl,* trousers *pl* **2 pantalones vaqueros** : jeans
pantano *nm* **1** : swamp, marsh **2** EMBALSE : reservoir — **pantanoso, -sa** *adj* : marshy, swampy
pantera *nf* : panther
pantimedias *nfpl Lat* : panty hose
pantomima *nf* : pantomime
pantorrilla *nf* : calf (of the leg)
pantufla *nf* : slipper
panza *nf* : belly, paunch — **panzón, -zona** *adj, mpl* **-zones** : potbellied

pañal *nm* : diaper
paño *nm* **1** : cloth **2** TRAPO : rag, dust cloth **3 ~ de cocina** : dishcloth **4 ~ higiénico** : sanitary napkin **5 ~s menores** : underwear
pañuelo *nm* **1** : handkerchief **2** : scarf, kerchief
papa[1] *nm* : pope
papa[2] *nf Lat* **1** : potato **2 ~s fritas** : potato chips, french fries
papá *nm fam* **1** : dad, pop **2 ~s** *nmpl* : parents, folks
papada *nf* : double chin
papagayo *nm* : parrot
papal *adj* : papal
papalote *nm Lat* : kite
papanatas *nmfs & pl fam* : simpleton
papaya *nf* : papaya
papel *nm* **1** : paper, sheet of paper **2** : role, part (in theater, etc.) **3 ~ de aluminio** : aluminum foil **4 ~ higiénico** *or* **~ de baño** : toilet paper **5 ~ de lija** : sandpaper **6 ~ pintado** : wallpaper — **papeleo** *nm* : paperwork, red tape — **papelera** *nf* : wastebasket — **papelería** *nf* : stationery store — **papeleta** *nf* **1** : ticket, slip **2** : ballot (paper)
paperas *nfpl* : mumps
papilla *nf* **1** : baby food, pap **2 hacer ~** : smash to bits
paquete *nm* **1** : package, parcel **2** : pack (of cigarettes, etc.)
paquistaní *adj* : Pakistani
par *nm* **1** : pair, couple **2** : par (in golf) **3** NOBLE : peer **4 abierto de ~ en ~** : wide open **5 sin ~** : without equal — **~** *adj* : even (in number) — **~** *nf* **1** : par **2 a la ~ que** : at the same time as
para *prep* **1** : for **2** HACIA : towards **3** : (in order) to **4** : around, by (a time) **5 ~ adelante** : forwards **6 ~ atrás** : backwards **7 ~ que** : so (that), in order that
parabienes *nmpl* : congratulations
parábola *nf* : parable
parabrisas *nms & pl* : windshield
paracaídas *nms & pl* : parachute — **paracaidista** *nmf* **1** : parachutist **2** : paratrooper (in the military)
parachoques *nms & pl* : bumper
parada *nf* **1** : stop **2** : (act of) stopping **3** DESFILE : parade — **paradero** *nm* **1** : whereabouts **2** *Lat* : bus stop — **parado, -da** *adj* **1** : idle, stopped **2** *Lat* : standing (up) **3 bien (mal) parado** : in good (bad) shape
paradoja *nf* : paradox
parafernalia *nf* : paraphernalia
parafina *nf* : paraffin
parafrasear *vt* : paraphrase — **paráfrasis** *nfs & pl* : paraphrase
paraguas *nms & pl* : umbrella
paraguayo, -ya *adj* : Paraguayan
paraíso *nm* : paradise
paralelo, -la *adj* : parallel — **paralelo** *nm* : parallel — **paralelismo** *nm* : similarity
parálisis *nfs & pl* : paralysis — **paralítico, -ca** *adj* : paralytic — **paralizar** {21} *vt* : paralyze
parámetro *nm* : parameter
páramo *nm* : barren plateau
parangón *nm, pl* **-gones 1** : comparison **2 sin ~** : matchless
paraninfo *nm* : auditorium, hall
paranoia *nf* : paranoia — **paranoico, -ca** *adj & n* : paranoid
parapeto *nm* : parapet, rampart
parapléjico, -ca *adj & n* : paraplegic
parar *vt* **1** : stop **2** *Lat* : stand, prop — *vi* **1** : stop **2 ir a ~** : end up, wind up — **pararse** *vr* **1** : stop **2** *Lat* : stand up
pararrayos *nms & pl* : lightning rod
parásito, -ta *adj* : parasitic — **parásito** *nm* : parasite
parasol *nm* : parasol
parcela *nf* : parcel, tract (of land) — **parcelar** *vt* : parcel (up)
parche *nm* : patch
parcial *adj* **1** : partial **2 a tiempo ~** : part-time — **parcialidad** *nf* : partiality, bias
parco, -ca *adj* : sparing, frugal
pardo, -da *adj* : brownish grey
parear *vt* : pair (up)
parecer {53} *vi* **1** : seem, look **2** ASEMEJARSE A : look like, seem like **3 me parece que** : I think that, in my opinion **4 ¿qué te parece?** : what do you think? **5 según parece** : apparently — **parecerse** *vr* **~ a** : resemble — **~** *nm* **1** : opinion **2** ASPECTO : appearance **3 al ~** : apparently — **parecido, -da** *adj* **1** : similar **2 bien parecido** : good-looking — **parecido** *nm* : resemblance, similarity
pared *nf* : wall
parejo, -ja *adj* **1** : even, smooth **2** SEMEJANTE : similar — **pareja** *nf* **1** : couple, pair **2** : partner (person)
parentela *nf* : relatives *pl*, kin — **parentesco** *nm* : relationship, kinship
paréntesis *nms & pl* **1** : parenthesis **2** DIGRESIÓN : digression **3 entre ~** : by the way
paria *nmf* : outcast
paridad *nf* : equality
pariente *nmf* : relative, relation

parir *vi* : give birth, have a baby — *vt* : give birth to
parking *nm* : parking lot
parlamentar *vi* : discuss — **parlamentario, -ria** *adj* : parliamentary — **~** *n* : member of parliament — **parlamento** *nm* : parliament
parlanchín, -china *adj, mpl* **-chines** : talkative, chatty — **~** *n* : chatterbox
parlotear *vi fam* : chatter — **parloteo** *nm fam* : chatter
paro *nm* **1** : stoppage, shutdown **2** DESEMPLEO : unemployment **3** *Lat* : strike **4** **~ cardíaco** : cardiac arrest
parodia *nf* : parody — **parodiar** *vt* : parody
párpado *nm* : eyelid — **parpadear** *vi* **1** : blink **2** : flicker (of light), twinkle (of stars) — **parpadeo** *nm* **1** : blink **2** : flicker (of light), twinkling (of stars)
parque *nm* **1** : park **2** **~ de atracciones** : amusement park
parqué *nm* : parquet
parquear *vt Lat* : park
parquedad *nf* : frugality, moderation
parquímetro *nm* : parking meter
parra *nf* : grapevine
párrafo *nm* : paragraph
parranda *nf fam* : party, spree
parrilla *nf* **1** : broiler, grill **2** : grate (of a chimney, etc.) — **parrillada** *nf* : barbecue
párroco *nm* : parish priest — **parroquia** *nf* **1** : parish **2** : parish church — **parroquial** *adj* : parochial — **parroquiano, -na** *nm* **1** : parishioner **2** CLIENTE : customer
parsimonia *nf* **1** : calm **2** FRUGALIDAD : thrift — **parsimonioso, -sa** *adj* **1** : calm, unhurried **2** FRUGAL : thrifty
parte *nf* **1** : part **2** PORCIÓN : share **3** LADO : side **4** : party (in negotiations, etc.) **5** **de ~ de** : on behalf of **6** **¿de ~ de quién?** : who is speaking? **7** **en alguna ~** : somewhere **8** **en todas ~s** : everywhere **9** **tomar ~** : take part — **~** *nm* **1** : report **2** **~ meteorológico** : weather forecast
partero, -ra *n* : midwife
partición *nf, pl* **-ciones** : division, sharing
participar *vi* **1** : participate, take part **2** **~ en** : have a share in — *vt* : notify — **participación** *nf, pl* **-ciones** **1** : participation **2** : share, interest (in a fund, etc.) **3** NOTICIA : notice — **participante** *adj* : participating — **~** *nmf* : participant — **partícipe** *nmf* : participant
participio *nm* : participle
partícula *nf* : particle
particular *adj* **1** : particular **2** PRIVADO : private — **~** *nm* **1** : matter **2** PERSONA : individual — **particularidad** *nf* : peculiarity — **particularizar** {21} *vt* : distinguish, characterize — *vi* : go into details
partir *vt* **1** : split, divide **2** ROMPER : break, crack **3** REPARTIR : share (out) — *vi* **1** : depart **2** **~ de** : start from **3** **a ~ de** : as of, from — **partirse** *vr* **1** : split (open) **2** RAJARSE : crack — **partida** *nf* **1** : departure **2** : entry, item (in a register, etc.) **3** JUEGO : game **4** : group (of persons) **5** **mala ~** : dirty trick **6** **~ de nacimiento** : birth certificate — **partidario, -ria** *n* : follower, supporter — **partido** *nm* **1** : (political) party **2** : game, match (in sports) **3** PARTIDARIOS : following **4** **sacar ~ de** : make the most of
partitura *nf* : (musical) score
parto *nm* **1** : childbirth **2** **estar de ~** : be in labor
parvulario *nm* : nursery school
pasa *nf* **1** : raisin **2** **~ de Corinto** : currant
pasable *adj* : passable
pasada *nf* **1** : pass, wipe, coat (of paint, etc.) **2** **de ~** : in passing **3** **mala ~** : dirty trick — **pasadizo** *nm* : corridor — **pasado, -da** *adj* **1** : past **2** PODRIDO : bad, spoiled **3** ANTICUADO : out-of-date **4** **el año pasado** : last year — **pasado** *nm* : past
pasador *nm* **1** CERROJO : bolt **2** : barrette (for the hair)
pasaje *nm* **1** : passage **2** BILLETE : ticket, fare **3** PASILLO : passageway **4** PASAJEROS : passengers *pl* — **pasajero, -ra** *adj* : passing — **~** *n* : passenger
pasamanos *nms & pl* : handrail, banister
pasaporte *nm* : passport
pasar *vi* **1** : pass, go (by) **2** ENTRAR : come in **3** SUCEDER : happen **4** TERMINARSE : be over, end **5** **~ de** : exceed **6** **¿qué pasa?** : what's the matter? — *vt* **1** : pass **2** : spend (time) **3** CRUZAR : cross **4** TOLERAR : tolerate **5** SUFRIR : go through, suffer **6** : show (a movie, etc.) **7** **pasarlo bien** : have a good time **8** **~ por alto** : overlook, omit — **pasarse** *vr* **1** : pass, go away **2** ESTROPEARSE : spoil, go bad **3** OLVIDARSE : slip one's mind **4** EXCEDERSE : go too far
pasarela *nf* **1** : footbridge **2** : gangway (on a ship)

pasatiempo *nm* : pastime, hobby
Pascua *nf* **1** : Easter (Christian feast) **2** : Passover (Jewish feast) **3** NAVIDAD : Christmas
pase *nm* : pass
pasear *vi* : take a walk, go for a ride — *vt* **1** : take for a walk **2** EXHIBIR : parade, show off — **pasearse** *vr* : go for a walk, go for a ride — **paseo** *nm* **1** : walk, ride **2** *Lat* : outing
pasillo *nm* : passage, corridor
pasión *nf, pl* **-siones** : passion
pasivo, -va *adj* : passive — **pasivo** *nm* : liabilities *pl*
pasmar *vt* : astonish, amaze — **pasmarse** *vr* : be astonished — **pasmado, -da** *adj* : stunned, flabbergasted — **pasmo** *nm* : astonishment — **pasmoso, -sa** *adj* : astonishing
paso[1]**, -sa** *adj* : dried (of fruit)
paso[2] *nm* **1** : step **2** HUELLA : footprint **3** RITMO : pace **4** CRUCE : crossing **5** PASAJE : passage, way through **6** : (mountain) pass **7 de ~** : in passing
pasta *nf* **1** : paste **2** MASA : dough **3** *or* **~s** : pasta **4 ~ de dientes** *or* **~ dentífrica** : toothpaste
pastar *v* : graze
pastel *nm* **1** : cake **2** EMPANADA : pie **3** : pastel (crayon) — **pastelería** *nf* : pastry shop
pasteurizar {21} *vt* : pasteurize
pastilla *nf* **1** : pill, tablet **2** : bar (of chocolate, soap, etc.) **3 ~ para la tos** : lozenge, cough drop
pasto *nm* **1** : pasture **2** *Lat* : grass, lawn — **pastor, -tora** *n* **1** : shepherd **2** : pastor (in religion) — **pastoral** *adj* : pastoral
pata *nf* **1** : paw, leg (of an animal) **2** : foot, leg (of furniture) **3 meter la ~** *fam* : put one's foot in it — **patada** *nf* **1** : kick **2** : stamp (of the foot) — **patalear** *vi* **1** : kick **2** : stamp (one's feet)
patata *nf Spain* : potato
patear *vt* : kick — *vi* **1** : kick **2** : stamp (one's feet)
patentar *vt* : patent — **patente** *adj* : obvious, patent — **~** *nf* : patent
paternal *adj* : fatherly, paternal — **paternidad** *nf* **1** : fatherhood **2** : paternity (in law) — **paterno, -na** *adj* : paternal
patético, -ca *adj* : pathetic, moving
patillas *nfpl* : sideburns
patinar *vi* **1** : skate **2** RESBALAR : slip, slide — **patín** *nm, pl* **-tines** : skate — **patinador, -dora** *n* : skater — **patinaje** *nm* : skating — **patinazo** *nm* **1** : skid **2** *fam* : blunder — **patinete** *nm* : scooter
patio *nm* **1** : courtyard, patio **2** *or* **~ de recreo** : playground
pato, -ta *n* **1** : duck **2 pagar el pato** *fam* : take the blame — **patito, -ta** *n* : duckling
patología *nf* : pathology — **patológico, -ca** *adj* : pathological
patraña *nf* : hoax
patria *nf* : native land
patriarca *nm* : patriarch
patrimonio *nm* **1** : inheritance **2** : (historical or cultural) heritage
patriota *adj* : patriotic — **~** *nmf* : patriot — **patriótico, -ca** *adj* : patriotic — **patriotismo** *nm* : patriotism
patrocinador, -dora *n* : sponsor — **patrocinar** *vt* : sponsor — **patrocinio** *nm* : sponsorship
patrón, -trona *n, mpl* **-trones 1** : patron **2** JEFE : boss **3** : landlord, landlady *f* (of a boarding house, etc.) — **patrón** *nm, pl* **-trones** : pattern (in sewing) — **patronato** *nm* **1** : patronage **2** FUNDACIÓN : foundation, trust
patrulla *nf* **1** : patrol **2** : (police) cruiser — **patrullar** *v* : patrol
paulatino, -na *adj* : gradual
pausa *nf* : pause, break — **pausado, -da** *adj* : slow, deliberate
pauta *nf* : guideline
pavimento *nm* : pavement — **pavimentar** *vt* : pave
pavo, -va *n* **1** : turkey **2 pavo real** : peacock
pavonearse *vr* : strut, swagger
pavor *nm* : dread, terror — **pavoroso, -sa** *adj* : terrifying
payaso, -sa *n* : clown — **payasada** *nf* : antic, buffoonery — **payasear** *vi Lat fam* : clown (around)
paz *nf, pl* **paces 1** : peace **2 dejar en ~** : leave alone **3 hacer las paces** : make up, reconcile
peaje *nm* : toll
peatón *nm, pl* **-tones** : pedestrian
peca *nf* : freckle
pecado *nm* : sin — **pecador, -dora** *adj* : sinful — **~** *n* : sinner — **pecaminoso, -sa** *adj* : sinful — **pecar** {72} *vi* : sin
pecera *nf* : fishbowl, fish tank
pecho *nm* **1** : chest **2** MAMA : breast **3** CORAZÓN : heart, courage **4 dar el ~** : breast-feed **5 tomar a ~** : take to heart — **pechuga** *nf* : breast (of fowl)
pecoso, -sa *adj* : freckled
pectoral *adj* : pectoral
peculiar *adj* **1** : particular **2** RARO : peculiar, odd — **peculiaridad** *nf* : peculiarity

pedagogía *nf* : education, pedagogy — **pedagogo, -ga** *n* : educator, teacher
pedal *nm* : pedal — **pedalear** *vi* : pedal
pedante *adj* : pedantic, pompous
pedazo *nm* **1** : piece, bit **2 hacerse ~s** : fall to pieces
pedernal *nm* : flint
pedestal *nm* : pedestal
pediatra *nmf* : pediatrician
pedigrí *nm* : pedigree
pedir {54} *vt* **1** : ask for, request **2** : order (food, merchandise, etc.) — *vi* **1** : ask **2 ~ prestado** : borrow — **pedido** *nm* **1** : order **2 hacer un ~** : place an order
pedregoso, -sa *adj* : rocky, stony
pedrería *nf* : precious stones *pl*
pegar {52} *vt* **1** : stick, glue, paste **2** : sew on (a button, etc.) **3** JUNTAR : bring together **4** GOLPEAR : hit, strike **5** PROPINAR : deal (a blow, etc.) **6** : transmit (an illness) **7 ~ un grito** : let out a scream — *vi* **1** : adhere, stick **2** GOLPEAR : hit — **pegarse** *vr* **1** : hit oneself, hit each other **2** ADHERIRSE : stick, adhere **3** CONTAGIARSE : be transmitted — **pegadizo, -za** *adj* **1** : catchy **2** CONTAGIOSO : contagious — **pegajoso, -sa** *adj* **1** : sticky **2** *Lat* : catchy — **pegamento** *nm* : glue
peinar *vt* : comb — **peinarse** *vr* : comb one's hair — **peinado** *nm* : hairstyle, hairdo — **peine** *nm* : comb — **peineta** *nf* : ornamental comb
pelado, -da *adj* **1** : shorn, hairless **2** : peeled (of fruit, etc.) **3** *fam* : bare **4** *fam* : broke, penniless
pelaje *nm* : coat (of an animal), fur
pelar *vt* **1** : cut the hair of (a person) **2** MONDAR : peel (fruit) **3** : pluck (a chicken, etc.), skin (an animal) — **pelarse** *vr* **1** : peel **2** *fam* : get a haircut
peldaño *nm* **1** : step (of stairs) **2** : rung (of a ladder)
pelear *vi* **1** : fight **2** DISCUTIR : quarrel — **pelearse** *vr* : have a fight — **pelea** *nf* **1** : fight **2** DISCUSIÓN : quarrel
peletería *nf* : fur shop
peliagudo, -da *adj* : tricky, difficult
pelícano *nm* : pelican
película *nf* : movie, film
peligro *nm* **1** : danger **2** RIESGO : risk — **peligroso, -sa** *adj* : dangerous
pelirrojo, -ja *adj* : red-haired — **~** *n* : redhead
pellejo *nm* : skin, hide
pellizcar {72} *vt* : pinch — **pellizco** *nm* : pinch
pelo *nm* **1** : hair **2** : coat, fur (of an animal) **3** : pile, nap (of fabric) **4 con ~s y señales** : in great detail **5 no tener ~ en la lengua** *fam* : not to mince words **6 tomar el ~ a algn** *fam* : pull someone's leg — **pelón, -lona** *adj fam, mpl* **-lones** : bald
pelota *nf* : ball
pelotón *nm, pl* **-tones** : squad, detachment
peltre *nm* : pewter
peluca *nf* : wig
peluche *nm* **1** : plush **2 oso de ~** : teddy bear
peludo, -da *adj* : hairy, furry
peluquería *nf* : hairdresser's, barber shop — **peluquero, -ra** *n* : barber, hairdresser
pelusa *nf* : fuzz, lint
pelvis *nfs & pl* : pelvis
pena *nf* **1** : penalty **2** TRISTEZA : sorrow **3** DOLOR : suffering, pain **4** *Lat* : embarrassment **5 a duras ~s** : with great difficulty **6 ¡qué ~!** : what a shame! **7 valer la ~** : be worthwhile
penacho *nm* **1** : crest, tuft **2** : plume (ornament)
penal *adj* : penal — **~** *nm* : prison, penitentiary — **penalidad** *nf* **1** : hardship **2** : penalty (in law) — **penalizar** {21} *vt* : penalize
penalty *nm* : penalty (in sports)
penar *vt* : punish — *vi* : suffer
pendenciero, -ra *adj* : quarrelsome
pender *vi* : hang — **pendiente** *adj* **1** : pending **2 estar ~ de** : be watching out for — **~** *nf* : slope — **~** *nm Spain* : earring
pendón *nm, pl* **-dones** : banner
péndulo *nm* : pendulum
pene *nm* : penis
penetrar *vi* **1** : penetrate **2 ~ en** : go into — *vt* **1** : penetrate **2** : pierce (one's heart, etc.) **3** ENTENDER : fathom, grasp — **penetración** *nf, pl* **-ciones 1** : penetration **2** PERSPICACIA : insight — **penetrante** *adj* **1** : penetrating **2** : sharp (of odors, etc.), piercing (of sounds) **3** : deep (of a wound, etc.)
penicilina *nf* : penicillin
península *nf* : peninsula — **peninsular** *adj* : peninsular
penitencia *nf* **1** : penitence **2** CASTIGO : penance — **penitenciaría** *nf* : penitentiary — **penitente** *adj & nmf* : penitent
penoso, -sa *adj* **1** : painful, distressing **2** TRABAJOSO : difficult **3** *Lat* : shy
pensar {55} *vi* **1** : think **2 ~ en** : think about — *vt* **1** : think **2** CONSIDERAR : think about **3 ~ hacer algo** : intend to do sth — **pensador, -dora** *n*

: thinker — **pensamiento** *nm* **1** : thought **2** : pansy (flower) — **pensativo, -va** *adj* : pensive, thoughtful
pensión *nf, pl* **-siones 1** : boarding house **2** : (retirement) pension **3 ~ alimenticia** : alimony — **pensionista** *nmf* **1** : lodger **2** JUBILADO : retiree
pentágono *nm* : pentagon
pentagrama *nm* : staff (in music)
penúltimo, -ma *adj* : next to last, penultimate
penumbra *nf* : half-light
penuria *nf* : dearth, shortage
peña *nf* : rock, crag — **peñasco** *nm* : crag, large rock — **peñón** *nm, pl* **-ñones** : craggy rock
peón *nm, pl* **peones 1** : laborer, peon **2** : pawn (in chess)
peonía *nf* : peony
peor *adv* **1** (*comparative of* **mal**) : worse **2** (*superlative of* **mal**) : worst — **~** *adj* **1** (*comparative of* **malo**) : worse **2** (*superlative of* **malo**) : worst
pepino *nm* : cucumber — **pepinillo** *nm* : pickle, gherkin
pepita *nf* **1** : seed, pip **2** : nugget (of gold, etc.)
pequeño, -ña *adj* : small, little — **pequeñez** *nf, pl* **-ñeces 1** : smallness **2** NIMIEDAD : trifle
pera *nf* : pear — **peral** *nm* : pear tree
percance *nm* : mishap, setback
percatarse *vr* **~ de** : notice
percepción *nf, pl* **-ciones** : perception — **perceptible** *adj* : perceptible
percha *nf* **1** : perch (for birds) **2** : (coat) hanger **3** : coatrack (on a wall)
percibir *vt* **1** : perceive **2** : receive (a salary, etc.)
percusión *nf, pl* **-siones** : percussion
perder {56} *vt* **1** : lose **2** : miss (an opportunity, etc.) **3** DESPERDICIAR : waste (time) — *vi* : lose — **perderse** *vr* **1** : get lost **2** DESAPARECER : disappear **3** DESPERDICIARSE : be wasted — **perdedor, -dora** *n* : loser — **pérdida** *nf* **1** : loss **2** ESCAPE : leak **3 ~ de tiempo** : waste of time — **perdido, -da** *adj* **1** : lost **2 un caso perdido** *fam* : a hopeless case
perdigón *nm, pl* **-gones** : shot, pellet
perdiz *nf, pl* **-dices** : partridge
perdón *nm, pl* **-dones** : forgiveness, pardon — **perdón** *interj* : sorry! — **perdonar** *vt* **1** DISCULPAR : forgive **2** : pardon (in law)
perdurar *vi* : last, endure — **perdurable** *adj* : lasting
perecer {53} *vi* : perish, die — **perecedero, -ra** *adj* : perishable
peregrinación *nf, pl* **-ciones** *or* **peregrinaje** *nm* : pilgrimage — **peregrino, -na** *adj* **1** : migratory **2** RARO : unusual, odd — **~** *n* : pilgrim
perejil *nm* : parsley
perenne *adj & nm* : perennial
pereza *nf* : laziness — **perezoso, -sa** *adj* : lazy
perfección *nf, pl* **-ciones** : perfection — **perfeccionar** *vt* **1** : perfect **2** MEJORAR : improve — **perfeccionista** *nmf* : perfectionist — **perfecto, -ta** *adj* : perfect
perfidia *nf* : treachery — **pérfido, -da** *adj* : treacherous
perfil *nm* **1** : profile **2** CONTORNO : outline **3 ~es** *nmpl* RASGOS : features — **perfilar** *vt* : outline — **perfilarse** *vr* **1** : be outlined **2** CONCRETARSE : take shape
perforar *vt* **1** : perforate **2** : drill, bore (a hole) — **perforación** *nf, pl* **-ciones** : perforation — **perforadora** *nf* : (paper) punch
perfume *nm* : perfume, scent — **perfumar** *vt* : perfume — **perfumarse** *vr* : put perfume on
pergamino *nm* : parchment
pericia *nf* : skill
periferia *nf* : periphery, outskirts (of a city, etc.) — **periférico, -ca** *adj* : peripheral
perilla *nf* **1** : goatee **2** *Lat* : knob **3 venir de ~s** *fam* : come in handy
perímetro *nm* : perimeter
periódico, -ca *adj* : periodic — **periódico** *nm* : newspaper — **periodismo** *nm* : journalism — **periodista** *nmf* : journalist
período *or* **periodo** *nm* : period
periquito *nm* : parakeet
periscopio *nm* : periscope
perito, -ta *adj & n* : expert
perjudicar {72} *vt* : harm, damage — **perjudicial** *adj* : harmful — **perjuicio** *nm* **1** : harm, damage **2 en ~ de** : to the detriment of
perjurar *vi* : perjure oneself — **perjurio** *nm* : perjury
perla *nf* **1** : pearl **2 de ~s** *fam* : great, just fine
permanecer {53} *vi* : remain — **permanencia** *nf* **1** : permanence **2** : stay, staying (in a place) — **permanente** *adj* : permanent — **~** *nf* : permanent (wave)
permeable *adj* : permeable
permitir *vt* **1** : permit, allow **2 ¿me permite?** : may I? — **permitirse** *vr* : allow oneself — **permisible** *adj*

: permissible, allowable — **permisivo, -va** *adj* : permissive — **permiso** *nm* **1** : permission **2** : permit, license (document) **3** : leave (in the military) **4 con ~** : excuse me

permuta *nf* : exchange

pernicioso, -sa *adj* : pernicious, destructive

pero *conj* : but — **~** *nm* **1** : fault **2** REPARO : objection

perorar *vi* : make a speech — **perorata** *nf* : (long-winded) speech

perpendicular *adj & nf* : perpendicular

perpetrar *vt* : perpetrate

perpetuar {3} *vt* : perpetuate — **perpetuo, -tua** *adj* : perpetual

perplejo, -ja *adj* : perplexed — **perplejidad** *nf* : perplexity

perro, -rra *n* **1** : dog, bitch *f* **2 perro caliente** : hot dog — **perrera** *nf* : kennel

perseguir {75} *vt* **1** : pursue, chase **2** ACOSAR : persecute — **persecución** *nf, pl* **-ciones 1** : pursuit, chase **2** ACOSO : persecution

perseverar *vi* : persevere — **perseverancia** *nf* : perseverance

persiana *nf* : (venetian) blind

persistir *vi* : persist — **persistencia** *nf* : persistence — **persistente** *adj* : persistent

persona *nf* : person — **personaje** *nm* **1** : character (in literature, etc.) **2** : important person, celebrity — **personal** *adj* : personal — **~** *nm* : personnel, staff — **personalidad** *nf* : personality — **personificar** {72} *vi* : personify

perspectiva *nf* **1** : perspective **2** VISTA : view **3** POSIBILIDAD : prospect, outlook

perspicacia *nf* : shrewdness, insight — **perspicaz** *adj, pl* **-caces** : shrewd, discerning

persuadir *vt* : persuade — **persuadirse** *vr* : become convinced — **persuasión** *nf, pl* **-siones** : persuasion — **persuasivo, -va** *adj* : persuasive

pertenecer {53} *vi* **~ a** : belong to — **perteneciente** *adj* **~ a** : belonging to — **pertenencia** *nf* **1** : ownership **2 ~s** *nfpl* : belongings

pertinaz *adj, pl* **-naces 1** OBSTINADO : obstinate **2** PERSISTENTE : persistent

pertinente *adj* : pertinent, relevant — **pertinencia** *nf* : relevance

perturbar *vt* : disturb — **perturbación** *nf, pl* **-ciones** : disturbance

peruano, -na *adj* : Peruvian

pervertir {76} *vt* : pervert — **perversión** *nf, pl* **-siones** : perversion — **perverso, -sa** *adj* : perverse — **pervertido, -da** *adj* : perverted, depraved — **~** *n* : pervert

pesa *nf* **1** : weight **2 ~s** : weights (in sports) — **pesadez** *nf, pl* **-deces 1** : heaviness **2** *fam* : tediousness, drag

pesadilla *nf* : nightmare

pesado, -da *adj* **1** : heavy **2** LENTO : sluggish **3** MOLESTO : annoying **4** ABURRIDO : tedious **5** DURO : tough, difficult — **~** *n fam* : bore, pest — **pesadumbre** *nf* : grief, sorrow

pésame *nm* : condolences *pl*

pesar *vt* : weigh — *vi* **1** : weigh, be heavy **2** INFLUIR : carry weight **3 pese a** : despite — **~** *nm* **1** : sorrow, grief **2** REMORDIMIENTO : remorse **3 a ~ de** : in spite of

pescado *nm* : fish — **pesca** *nf* **1** : fishing **2** PECES : fish *pl,* catch **3 ir de ~** : go fishing — **pescadería** *nf* : fish market — **pescador, -dora** *n, mpl* **-dores** : fisherman — **pescar** {72} *vt* **1** : fish for **2** *fam* : catch (a cold, etc.) **3** *fam* : catch hold of, nab — *vi* : fish

pescuezo *nm* : neck (of an animal)

pese a → **pesar**

pesebre *nm* : manger

pesero *nm Lat* : minibus

peseta *nf* : peseta

pesimismo *nm* : pessimism — **pesimista** *adj* : pessimistic — **~** *nmf* : pessimist

pésimo, -ma *adj* : awful

peso *nm* **1** : weight **2** CARGA : burden **3** : peso (currency) **4 ~ pesado** : heavyweight

pesquero, -ra *adj* : fishing

pesquisa *nf* : inquiry

pestaña *nf* : eyelash — **pestañear** *vi* : blink — **pestañeo** *nm* : blink

peste *nm* **1** : plague **2** *fam* : stench, stink **3** *Lat fam* : cold, bug — **pesticida** *nm* : pesticide — **pestilencia** *nf* **1** : stench **2** PLAGA : pestilence

pestillo *nm* : bolt, latch

petaca *nf Lat* : suitcase

pétalo *nm* : petal

petardo *nm* : firecracker

petición *nf, pl* **-ciones** : petition, request

petirrojo *nm* : robin

petrificar {72} *vt* : petrify

petróleo *nm* : oil, petroleum — **petrolero, -ra** *adj* : oil — **petrolero** *nm* : oil tanker

petulante *adj* : insolent, arrogant

peyorativo, -va *adj* : pejorative

pez *nm, pl* **peces 1** : fish **2 ~ de col-**

ores : goldfish **3 ~ espada** : swordfish **4 ~ gordo** *fam* : big shot
pezón *nm, pl* **-zones** : nipple
pezuña *nf* : hoof
piadoso, -sa *adj* **1** : compassionate **2** DEVOTO : pious, devout
piano *nm* : piano — **pianista** *nmf* : pianist, piano player
piar {85} *vi* : chirp, tweet
pibe, -ba *n Lat fam* : kid, child
pica *nf* **1** : pike, lance **2** : spade (in playing cards)
picado, -da *adj* **1** : perforated **2** : minced, chopped (of meat, etc.) **3** : decayed (of teeth) **4** : choppy (of the sea) **5** *fam* : annoyed — **picada** *nf* **1** : bite, sting **2** *Lat* : sharp descent — **picadillo** *nm* : minced meat — **picadura** *nf* **1** : sting, bite **2** : (moth) hole
picante *adj* : hot, spicy
picaporte *nm* **1** : door handle **2** ALDABA : door knocker **3** PESTILLO : latch
picar {72} *vt* **1** : sting, bite **2** : peck at, nibble on (food) **3** PERFORAR : prick, puncture **4** TRITURAR : chop, mince — *vi* **1** : bite, take the bait **2** ESCOCER : sting, itch **3** COMER : nibble **4** : be spicy (of food) — **picarse** *vr* **1** : get a cavity **2** ENFADARSE : take offense
picardía *nf* **1** : craftiness **2** TRAVESURA : prank — **picaresco, -ca** *adj* **1** : picaresque **2** TRAVIESO : roguish — **pícaro, -ra** *adj* **1** : mischievous **2** MALICIOSO : villainous — **~** *n* : rascal, scoundrel
picazón *nf, pl* **-zones** : itch
pichón, -chona *n, mpl* **-chones** : (young) pigeon
picnic *nm, pl* **-nics** : picnic
pico *nm* **1** : beak **2** CIMA : peak **3** PUNTA : (sharp) point **4** : pick, pickax (tool) **5 las siete y ~** : a little after seven — **picotazo** *nm* : peck — **picotear** *vt* : peck — *vi fam* : nibble, pick — **picudo, -da** *adj* : pointy
pie *nm* **1** : foot (in anatomy) **2** : base, bottom, stem **3 al ~ de la letra** : word for word **4 dar ~ a** : give rise to **5 de ~** : standing (up) **6 de ~s a cabeza** : from top to bottom
piedad *nf* **1** : pity, mercy **2** DEVOCIÓN : piety
piedra *nf* **1** : stone **2** : flint (of a lighter) **3** GRANIZO : hailstone **4 ~ angular** : cornerstone **5** → **pómez**
piel *nf* **1** : skin **2** CUERO : leather **3** PELO : fur, pelt
pienso *nm* : feed, fodder
pierna *nf* : leg
pieza *nf* **1** : piece, part **2** *or* **~ de teatro** : play **3** HABITACIÓN : room
pigmento *nm* : pigment — **pigmentación** *nf, pl* **-ciones** : pigmentation
pigmeo, -mea *adj* : pygmy
pijama *nm* : pajamas *pl*
pila *nf* **1** : battery **2** MONTÓN : pile **3** FREGADERO : sink **4** : basin (of a fountain, etc.)
pilar *nm* : pillar
píldora *nf* : pill
pillar *vt* **1** : catch **2** : get (a joke, etc.) — **pillaje** *nm* : pillage — **pillo, -lla** *adj* : crafty — **~** *n* : rascal, scoundrel
piloto *nmf* : pilot — **pilotar** *vt* : pilot
pimienta *nf* : pepper (condiment) — **pimiento** *nm* : pepper (fruit) — **pimentero** *nm* : pepper shaker — **pimentón** *nm, pl* **-tones** **1** : paprika **2** : cayenne pepper
pináculo *nm* : pinnacle
pincel *nm* : paintbrush
pinchar *vt* **1** : pierce, prick **2** : puncture (a tire, etc.) **3** INCITAR : goad — **pinchazo** *nm* **1** : prick **2** : puncture (of a tire, etc.)
pingüino *nm* : penguin
pino *nm* : pine (tree)
pintar *v* : paint — **pintarse** *vr* : put on makeup — **pinta** *nf* **1** : spot **2** : pint (measure) **3** *fam* : appearance — **pintada** *nf* : graffiti — **pinto, -ta** *adj* : speckled, spotted — **pintor, -tora** *n, mpl* **-tores** : painter — **pintoresco, -ca** *adj* : picturesque, quaint — **pintura** *nf* **1** : paint **2** CUADRO : painting
pinza *nf* **1** : clothespin **2** : claw, pincer (of a crab, etc.) **3 ~s** *nfpl* : tweezers
pinzón *nm, pl* **-zones** : finch
piña *nf* **1** : pine cone **2** ANANÁS : pineapple
piñata *nf* : piñata
piñón *nm, pl* **-ñones** : pine nut
pío[1], **pía** *adj* **1** : pious **2** : piebald (of a horse)
pío[2] *nm* : peep, chirp
piojo *nm* : louse
pionero, -ra *n* : pioneer
pipa *nf* **1** : pipe (for smoking) **2** *Spain* : seed, pip
pique *nm* **1** : grudge **2** RIVALIDAD : rivalry **3 irse a ~** : sink, founder
piqueta *nf* : pickax
piquete *nm* : picket (line) — **piquetear** *v* : picket
piragua *nf* : canoe
pirámide *nf* : pyramid
piraña *nf* : piranha
pirata *adj* : bootleg, pirated — **~** *nmf* : pirate — **piratear** *vt* **1** : bootleg, pirate **2** : hack into (a computer)

piropo *nm* : (flirtatious) compliment
pirueta *nf* : pirouette
pirulí *nm* : (cone-shaped) lollipop
pisada *nf* **1** : footstep **2** HUELLA : footprint
pisapapeles *nms & pl* : paperweight
pisar *vt* **1** : step on **2** HUMILLAR : walk all over, abuse — *vi* : step, tread
piscina *nf* **1** : swimming pool **2** : (fish) pond
piso *nm* **1** : floor, story **2** *Lat* : floor (of a room) **3** *Spain* : apartment
pisotear *vt* : trample (on)
pista *nf* **1** : trail, track **2** INDICIO : clue **3** **~ de aterrizaje** : runway, airstrip **4** **~ de baile** : dance floor **5** **~ de hielo** : ice-skating rink
pistacho *nm* : pistachio
pistola *nf* **1** : pistol, gun **2** PULVERIZADOR : spray gun — **pistolera** *nf* : holster — **pistolero** *nm* : gunman
pistón *nm, pl* **-tones** : piston
pito *nm* **1** SILBATO : whistle **2** CLAXON : horn — **pitar** *vi* **1** : blow a whistle **2** : beep, honk (of a horn) — *vt* : whistle at — **pitido** *nm* **1** : whistle, whistling **2** : beep (of a horn) — **pitillo** *nm fam* : cigarette
pitón *nm, pl* **-tones** *nm* : python
pitorro *nm* : spout
pivote *nm* : pivot
piyama *nmf Lat* : pajamas *pl*
pizarra *nf* **1** : slate **2** ENCERADO : blackboard — **pizarrón** *nm, pl* **-rrones** *Lat* : blackboard
pizca *nf* **1** : pinch (of salt) **2** ÁPICE : speck, tiny bit **3** *Lat* : harvest
pizza ['pitsa, 'pisa] *nf* : pizza — **pizzería** *nf* : pizzeria
placa *nf* **1** : sheet, plate **2** INSCRIPCIÓN : plaque **3** : (police) badge
placenta *nf* : placenta
placer {57} *vt* : please — **~** *nm* : pleasure — **placentero, -ra** *adj* : pleasant, agreeable
plácido, -da *adj* : placid, calm
plaga *nf* **1** : plague **2** CALAMIDAD : disaster — **plagar** {52} *vt* : plague, infest
plagiar *vt* : plagiarize — **plagio** *nm* : plagiarism
plan *nm* **1** : plan **2** **en ~ de** : as **3** **no te pongas en ese ~** *fam* : don't be that way
plana *nf* **1** : page **2** **en primera ~** : on the front page
plancha *nf* **1** : iron (for ironing) **2** : grill (for cooking) **3** LÁMINA : sheet, plate — **planchar** *v* : iron — **planchado** *nm* : ironing
planear *vt* : plan — *vi* : glide — **planeador** *nm* : glider
planeta *nm* : planet
planicie *nf* : plain
planificar {72} *vt* : plan — **planificación** *nf, pl* **-ciones** : planning
planilla *nf Lat* : list, roster
plano, -na *adj* : flat — **plano** *nm* **1** : map, plan **2** : plane (surface) **3** NIVEL : level **4** **de ~** : flatly, outright **5** **primer ~** : foreground, close-up (in photography)
planta *nf* **1** : plant **2** PISO : floor, story **3** : sole (of the foot) — **plantación** *nf, pl* **-ciones** **1** : plantation **2** : (action of) planting — **plantar** *vt* **1** : plant **2** *fam* : deal, land — **plantarse** *vr* : stand firm
plantear *vt* **1** : expound, set forth **2** : raise (a question) **3** CAUSAR : create, pose (a problem) — **plantearse** *vr* : think about, consider
plantel *nm* **1** : staff, team **2** *Lat* : educational institution
plantilla *nf* **1** : insole **2** PATRÓN : pattern, template **3** : staff (of a business, etc.)
plasma *nm* : plasma
plástico, -ca *adj* : plastic — **plástico** *nm* : plastic
plata *nf* **1** : silver **2** *Lat fam* : money **3** **~ de ley** : sterling silver
plataforma *nf* **1** : platform **2** **~ petrolífera** : oil rig **3** **~ de lanzamiento** : launching pad
plátano *nm* **1** : banana **2** : plantain
platea *nf* : orchestra, pit (in a theater)
plateado, -da *adj* **1** : silver, silvery (color) **2** : silver-plated
platicar {72} *vi* : talk, chat — **plática** *nf* : chat, conversation
platija *nf* : flatfish, flounder
platillo *nm* **1** : saucer **2** CÍMBALO : cymbal **3** *Lat* : dish, course
platino *nm* : platinum
plato *nm* **1** : plate, dish **2** : course (of a meal) **3** **~ principal** : entrée
platónico, -ca *adj* : platonic
playa *nf* **1** : beach, seashore **2** **~ de estacionamiento** *Lat* : parking lot
plaza *nf* **1** : square, plaza **2** : seat (in transportation) **3** PUESTO : post, position **4** MERCADO : market, marketplace **5** **~ de toros** : bullring
plazo *nm* **1** : period, term **2** PAGO : installment **3** **a largo ~** : long-term
plazoleta *or* **plazuela** *nf* : small square
pleamar *nf* : high tide
plebe *nf* : common people — **plebeyo, -ya** *adj & nm* : plebeian
plegar {49} *vt* : fold, bend — **plegarse** *vr* **1** : give in, yield **2** : jackknife (of a

truck) — **plegable** *or* **plegadizo, -za** *adj* : folding, collapsible
plegaria *nf* : prayer
pleito *nm* **1** : lawsuit **2** *Lat* : dispute, fight
plenilunio *nm* : full moon
pleno, -na *adj* **1** : full, complete **2 en plena forma** : in top form **3 en pleno día** : in broad daylight — **plenitud** *nf* : fullness, abundance
pleuresía *nf* : pleurisy
pliego *nm* : sheet (of paper) — **pliegue** *nm* **1** : crease, fold **2** : pleat (in fabric)
plisar *vt* : pleat
plomería *nf Lat* : plumbing — **plomero, -ra** *n Lat* : plumber
plomo *nm* **1** : lead **2** FUSIBLE : fuse
pluma *nf* **1** : feather **2** : (fountain) pen — **plumaje** *nm* : plumage — **plumero** *nm* : feather duster — **plumilla** *nf* : nib — **plumón** *nm, pl* **-mones** : down
plural *adj & nm* : plural — **pluralidad** *nf* : plurality
pluriempleo *nm* **hacer ~** : have more than one job
plus *nm* : bonus
plusvalía *nf* : appreciation, capital gain
plutocracia *nf* : plutocracy
Plutón *nm* : Pluto
plutonio *nm* : plutonium
pluvial *adj* : rain
poblar {19} *vt* **1** : settle, colonize **2** HABITAR : inhabit — **poblarse** *vr* : become crowded — **población** *nf, pl* **-ciones 1** : city, town, village **2** HABITANTES : population — **poblado, -da** *adj* **1** : populated **2** : thick, bushy (of a beard, eyebrows, etc.) — **poblado** *nm* : village
pobre *adj* **1** : poor **2 ¡~ de mí!** : poor me! — **~** *nmf* **1** : poor person **2 los ~s** : the poor **3 ¡pobre!** : poor thing! — **pobreza** *nf* : poverty
pocilga *nf* : pigsty
poción *nf, pl* **-ciones** *or* **pócima** *nf* : potion
poco, -ca *adj* **1** : little, not much, (a) few **2 pocas veces** : rarely — **~** *pron* **1** : little, few **2 hace poco** : not long ago **3 poco a poco** : bit by bit, gradually **4 por poco** : nearly, just about **5 un poco** : a little, a bit — **poco** *adv* : little, not much
podar *vt* : prune
poder {58} *v aux* **1** : be able to, can **2** (*expressing possibility*) : might, may **3** (*expressing permission*) : can, may **4 ¿cómo puede ser?** : how can it be? **5 ¿puedo pasar?** : may I come in? — *vi* **1** : be possible **2 ~ con** : cope with, manage **3 no puedo más** : I've had enough — **~** *nm* **1** : power **2** POSESIÓN : possession — **poderío** *nm* : power — **poderoso, -sa** *adj* : powerful
podólogo, -ga *n* : chiropodist
podrido, -da *adj* : rotten
poema *nm* : poem — **poesía** *nf* **1** : poetry **2** POEMA : poem — **poeta** *nmf* : poet — **poético, -ca** *adj* : poetic
póker *nm* → **póquer**
polaco, -ca *adj* : Polish
polar *adj* : polar — **polarizar** {21} *vt* : polarize
polea *nf* : pulley
polémica *nf* : controversy — **polémico, -ca** *adj* : controversial — **polemizar** *vt* : argue
polen *nm, pl* **pólenes** : pollen
policía *nf* : police — **~** *nmf* : police officer, policeman *m*, policewoman *f* — **policíaco, -ca** *adj* **1** : police **2 novela policíaca** : detective story
poliéster *nm* : polyester
poligamia *nf* : polygamy — **polígamo, -ma** *n* : polygamist
polígono *nm* : polygon
polilla *nf* : moth
polio *or* **poliomielitis** *nf* : polio, poliomyelitis
politécnico, -ca *adj* : polytechnic
política *nf* **1** : politics **2** POSTURA : policy — **político, -ca** *adj* **1** : political **2 hermano político** : brother-in-law — **~** *n* : politician
póliza *nf or* **~ de seguros** : insurance policy
polizón *nm, pl* **-zones** : stowaway
pollo, -lla *n* **1** : chicken, chick **2** : chicken (for cooking) — **pollera** *nf Lat* : skirt — **pollería** *nf* : poultry shop — **pollito, -ta** *n* : chick
polo *nm* **1** : pole **2** : polo (sport) **3 ~ norte** : North Pole
poltrona *nf* : easy chair
polución *nf, pl* **-ciones** : pollution
polvo *nm* **1** : powder **2** SUCIEDAD : dust **3 ~s** *nmpl* : face powder **4 hacer ~** *fam* : crush, shatter — **polvareda** *nf* : cloud of dust — **polvera** *nf* : compact (for powder) — **pólvora** *nf* : gunpowder — **polvoriento, -ta** *adj* : dusty
pomada *nf* : ointment
pomelo *nm* : grapefruit
pómez *nm or* **piedra ~** *nf* : pumice
pomo *nm* : knob, doorknob
pompa *nf* **1** : (soap) bubble **2** ESPLENDOR : pomp **3 ~s fúnebres** : funeral — **pomposo, -sa** *adj* **1** : pompous **2** ESPLÉNDIDO : splendid
pómulo *nm* : cheekbone

ponchar *vt Lat* : puncture — **ponchadura** *nf Lat* : puncture
ponche *nm* : punch (drink)
poncho *nm* : poncho
ponderar *vt* **1** : consider **2** ALABAR : speak highly of
poner {60} *vt* **1** : put **2** AGREGAR : add **3** CONTRIBUIR : contribute **4** SUPONER : suppose **5** DISPONER : arrange, set out **6** : give (a name), call **7** ENCENDER : turn on **8** ESTABLECER : set up, establish **9** : lay (eggs) — *vi* : lay eggs — **ponerse** *vr* **1** : move (into a position) **2** : put on (clothing, etc.) **3** : set (of the sun) **4** **~ furioso** : become angry
poniente *nm* **1** OCCIDENTE : west **2** : west wind
pontífice *nm* : pontiff
pontón *nm, pl* **-tones** : pontoon
ponzoña *nf* : poison, venom
popa *nf* **1** : stern **2** **a ~** : astern
popelín *nm, pl* **-lines** : poplin
popote *nm Lat* : (drinking) straw
populacho *nm* : rabble, masses *pl*
popular *adj* **1** : popular **2** : colloquial (of language) — **popularidad** *nf* : popularity — **popularizar** {21} *vt* : popularize — **populoso, -sa** *adj* : populous
póquer *nm* : poker (card game)
por *prep* **1** : for **2** (*indicating an approximate time*) : around, during **3** (*indicating an approximate place*) : around, about **4** A TRAVÉS DE : through, along **5** A CAUSA DE : because of **6** (*indicating rate or ratio*) : per **7** *or* **~ medio de** : by means of **8** : times (in mathematics) **9** SEGÚN : as for, according to **10** **estar ~** : be about to **11** **~ ciento** : percent **12** **~ favor** : please **13** **~ lo tanto** : therefore **14** **¿por qué?** : why?
porcelana *nf* : porcelain, china
porcentaje *nm* : percentage
porción *nf, pl* **-ciones** : portion, piece
pordiosero, -ra *n* : beggar
porfiar {85} *vi* : insist — **porfiado, -da** *adj* : obstinate, persistent
pormenor *nm* : detail
pornografía *nf* : pornography — **pornográfico, -ca** *adj* : pornographic
poro *nm* : pore — **poroso, -sa** *adj* : porous
poroto *nm Lat* : bean
porque *conj* **1** : because **2** *or* **por que** : in order that — **porqué** *nm* : reason
porquería *nf* **1** SUCIEDAD : filth **2** : shoddy thing, junk
porra *nf* : nightstick, club — **porrazo** *nm* : blow, whack
portaaviones *nms & pl* : aircraft carrier
portada *nf* **1** : facade **2** : title page (of a book), cover (of a magazine)
portador, -dora *n* : bearer
portaequipajes *nms & pl* : luggage rack
portafolio *or* **portafolios** *nm, pl* **-lios** **1** : portfolio **2** MALETÍN : briefcase
portal *nm* **1** : doorway **2** VESTÍBULO : hall, vestibule
portamonedas *nms & pl* : purse
portar *vt* : carry, bear — **portarse** *vr* : behave
portátil *adj* : portable
portaviones *nm* → **portaaviones**
portavoz *nmf, pl* **-voces** : spokesperson, spokesman *m,* spokeswoman *f*
portazo *nm* **dar un ~** : slam the door
porte *nm* **1** : transport, freight **2** ASPECTO : bearing, appearance **3** **~ pagado** : postage paid
portento *nm* : marvel, wonder — **portentoso, -sa** *adj* : marvelous
porteño, -ña *adj* : of or from Buenos Aires
portería *nf* **1** : superintendent's office **2** : goal, goalposts *pl* (in sports) — **portero, -ra** *n* **1** : goalkeeper, goalie **2** CONSERJE : janitor, superintendent
portezuela *nf* : door (of an automobile)
pórtico *nm* : portico
portilla *nf* : porthole
portugués, -guesa *adj, mpl* **-gueses** : Portuguese — **portugués** *nm* : Portuguese (language)
porvenir *nm* : future
pos: **en ~ de** *adv phr* : in pursuit of
posada *nf* : inn
posaderas *nfpl fam* : backside, bottom
posar *vi* : pose — *vt* : place, lay — **posarse** *vr* : settle, rest
posavasos *nms & pl* : coaster
posdata *nf* : postscript
pose *nf* : pose
poseer {20} *vt* : possess, own — **poseedor, -dora** *n* : possessor, owner — **poseído, -da** *adj* : possessed — **posesión** *nf, pl* **-siones** : possession — **posesionarse** *vr* **~ de** : take possession of, take over — **posesivo, -va** *adj* : possessive
posguerra *nf* : postwar period
posibilidad *nf* : possibility — **posibilitar** *vt* : make possible — **posible** *adj* **1** : possible **2** **de ser ~** : if possible
posición *nf, pl* **-ciones** : position — **posicionar** *vt* : position — **posicionarse** *vr* : take a stand
positivo, -va *adj* : positive
poso *nm* : sediment, (coffee) grounds

posponer {60} *vt* **1** : postpone **2** RELEGAR : put behind, subordinate
postal *adj* : postal — **~** *nf* : postcard
postdata → **posdata**
poste *nm* : post, pole
póster *nm, pl* **-ters** : poster
postergar {52} *vt* **1** : pass over **2** APLAZAR : postpone
posteridad *nf* : posterity — **posterior** *adj* **1** : later, subsequent **2** TRASERO : back, rear — **posteriormente** *adv* : subsequently, later
postigo *nm* **1** : small door **2** CONTRAVENTANA : shutter
postizo, -za *adj* : artificial, false
postrarse *vr* : prostrate oneself — **postrado, -da** *adj* : prostrate
postre *nm* : dessert
postular *vt* **1** : advance, propose **2** *Lat* : nominate — **postulado** *nm* : postulate
póstumo, -ma *adj* : posthumous
postura *nf* : position, stance
potable *adj* : drinkable, potable
potaje *nm* : thick vegetable soup
potasio *nm* : potassium
pote *nm* : jar
potencia *nf* : power — **potencial** *adj & nm* : potential — **potente** *adj* : powerful
potro, -tra *n* : colt *m*, filly *f* — **potro** *nm* : horse (in gymnastics)
pozo *nm* **1** : well **2** : shaft (in a mine)
práctica *nf* **1** : practice **2 en la ~** : in practice — **practicable** *adj* : practicable, feasible — **practicante** *adj* : practicing — **~** *nmf* : practitioner — **practicar** {72} *vt* **1** : practice **2** REALIZAR : perform, carry out — *vi* : practice — **práctico, -ca** *adj* : practical
pradera *nf* : grassland, prairie — **prado** *nm* : meadow
pragmático, -ca *adj* : pragmatic
preámbulo *nm* : preamble
precario, -ria *adj* : precarious
precaución *nf, pl* **-ciones** **1** : precaution **2** PRUDENCIA : caution, care **3 con ~** : cautiously
precaver *vt* : guard against — **precavido, -da** *adj* : prudent, cautious
preceder *v* : precede — **precedencia** *nf* : precedence, priority — **precedente** *adj* : preceding, previous — **~** *nm* : precedent
precepto *nm* : precept
preciado, -da *adj* : prized, valuable — **preciarse** *vr* **~ de** : pride oneself on, boast about
precinto *nm* : seal
precio *nm* : price, cost — **preciosidad** *nf* **1** VALOR : value **2** : beautiful thing — **precioso, -sa** *adj* **1** HERMOSO : beautiful **2** VALIOSO : precious
precipicio *nm* : precipice
precipitar *vt* **1** : hasten, speed up **2** ARROJAR : hurl — **precipitarse** *vr* **1** APRESURARSE : rush **2** : act rashly **3** ARROJARSE : throw oneself — **precipitación** *nf, pl* **-ciones** **1** : precipitation **2** PRISA : haste — **precipitadamente** *adv* : in a rush, hastily — **precipitado, -da** *adj* : hasty
preciso, -sa *adj* **1** : precise **2** NECESARIO : necessary — **precisamente** *adv* : precisely, exactly — **precisar** *vt* **1** : specify, determine **2** NECESITAR : require — **precisión** *nf, pl* **-siones** **1** : precision **2** NECESIDAD : necessity
preconcebido *adj* : preconceived
precoz *adj, pl* **-coces** **1** : early **2** : precocious (of children)
precursor, -sora *n* : forerunner
predecesor, -sora *n* : predecessor
predecir {11} *vt* : foretell, predict
predestinado, -da *adj* : predestined
predeterminar *vt* : predetermine
prédica *nf* : sermon
predicado *nm* : predicate
predicar {72} *v* : preach — **predicador, -dora** *n* : preacher
predicción *nf, pl* **-ciones** **1** : prediction **2** PRONÓSTICO : forecast
predilección *nf, pl* **-ciones** : preference — **predilecto, -ta** *adj* : favorite
predisponer {60} *vt* : predispose — **predisposición** *nf, pl* **-ciones** : predisposition
predominar *vi* : predominate — **predominante** *adj* : predominant, prevailing — **predominio** *nm* : predominance
preeminente *adj* : preeminent
prefabricado, -da *adj* : prefabricated
prefacio *nm* : preface
preferir {76} *vt* : prefer — **preferencia** *nf* **1** : preference **2 de ~** : preferably — **preferente** *adj* : preferential — **preferible** *adj* : preferable — **preferido, -da** *adj* : favorite
prefijo *nm* **1** : prefix **2** *Spain* : area code
pregonar *vt* : proclaim, announce
pregunta *nf* **1** : question **2 hacer ~s** : ask questions — **preguntar** *v* : ask — **preguntarse** *vr* : wonder
prehistórico, -ca *adj* : prehistoric
prejuicio *nm* : prejudice
preliminar *adj & nm* : preliminary
preludio *nm* : prelude
prematrimonial *adj* : premarital

prematuro, -ra *adj* : premature
premeditar *vt* : premeditate — **premeditación** *nf, pl* **-ciones** : premeditation
premenstrual *adj* : premenstrual
premio *nm* **1** : prize **2** RECOMPENSA : reward **3 ~ gordo** : jackpot — **premiado, -da** *adj* : prizewinning — **premiar** *vt* **1** : award a prize to **2** RECOMPENSAR : reward
premisa *nf* : premise
premonición *nf, pl* **-ciones** : premonition
premura *nf* : haste, urgency
prenatal *adj* : prenatal
prenda *nf* **1** : piece of clothing **2** GARANTÍA : pledge **3** : forfeit (in a game) — **prendar** *vt* : captivate — **prendarse** *vr* **~ de** : fall in love with
prender *vt* **1** SUJETAR : pin, fasten **2** APRESAR : capture **3** : light (a match, etc.) **4** *Lat* : turn on (a light, etc.) — *vi* **1** : take root **2** ARDER : catch, burn (of fire) — **prenderse** *vr* : catch fire — **prendedor** *nm Lat* : brooch, pin
prensa *nf* : press — **prensar** *vt* : press
preñado, -da *adj* **1** : pregnant **2 ~ de** : filled with
preocupar *vt* : worry — **preocuparse** *vr* **1** : worry **2 ~ de** : take care of — **preocupación** *nf, pl* **-ciones** : worry
preparar *vt* : prepare — **prepararse** *vr* : get ready — **preparación** *nf, pl* **-ciones** : preparation — **preparado, -da** *adj* : prepared, ready — **preparado** *nm* : preparation — **preparativo, -va** *adj* : preparatory, preliminary — **preparativos** *nmpl* : preparations — **preparatorio, -ria** *adj* : preparatory
preposición *nf, pl* **-ciones** : preposition
prepotente *adj* : arrogant, domineering
prerrogativa *nf* : prerogative
presa *nf* **1** : catch, prey **2** DIQUE : dam **3 hacer ~ en** : seize
presagiar *vt* : presage, forebode — **presagio** *nm* **1** : omen **2** PREMONICIÓN : premonition
presbítero *nm* : presbyter, priest
prescindir *vi* **~ de 1** : do without **2** OMITIR : dispense with
prescribir {33} *vt* : prescribe — **prescripción** *nf, pl* **-ciones** : prescription
presencia *nf* **1** : presence **2** ASPECTO : appearance — **presenciar** *vt* : be present at, witness
presentar *vt* **1** : present **2** OFRECER : offer, give **3** MOSTRAR : show **4** : introduce (persons) — **presentarse** *vr* **1** : show up **2** : arise, come up (of a problem, etc.) **3** : introduce oneself — **presentación** *nf, pl* **-ciones 1** : presentation **2** : introduction (of persons) **3** ASPECTO : appearance — **presentador, -dora** *n* : presenter, host (of a television program, etc.)
presente *adj* **1** : present **2 tener ~** : keep in mind — **~** *nm* **1** : present **2 entre los ~s** : among those present
presentir {76} *vt* : have a presentiment of — **presentimiento** *nm* : premonition
preservar *vt* : preserve, protect — **preservación** *nf, pl* **-ciones** : preservation — **preservativo** *nm* : condom
presidente, -ta *n* **1** : president **2** : chair, chairperson (of a meeting) — **presidencia** *nf* **1** : presidency **2** : chairmanship (of a meeting) — **presidencial** *adj* : presidential
presidio *nm* : prison — **presidiario, -ria** *n* : convict
presidir *vt* **1** : preside over, chair **2** PREDOMINAR : dominate
presión *nf, pl* **-siones 1** : pressure **2 ~ arterial** : blood pressure **3 hacer ~** : press — **presionar** *vt* **1** : press **2** COACCIONAR : put pressure on
preso, -sa *adj* : imprisoned — **~** *n* : prisoner
prestar *vt* **1** : lend, loan **2** : give (aid) **3 ~ atención** : pay attention — **prestado, -da** *adj* **1** : borrowed, on loan **2 pedir ~** : borrow — **prestamista** *nmf* : moneylender — **préstamo** *nm* : loan
prestidigitación *nf, pl* **-ciones** : sleight of hand — **prestidigitador, -dora** *n* : magician
prestigio *nm* : prestige — **prestigioso, -sa** *adj* : prestigious
presto, -ta *adj* : prompt, ready — **presto** *adv* : promptly, right away
presumir *vt* : presume — *vi* : boast, show off — **presumido, -da** *adj* : conceited, vain — **presunción** *nf, pl* **-ciones 1** : presumption **2** VANIDAD : vanity — **presunto, -ta** *adj* : presumed, alleged — **presuntuoso, -sa** *adj* : conceited
presuponer {60} *vt* : presuppose — **presupuesto** *nm* **1** : budget, estimate **2** SUPUESTO : assumption
presuroso, -sa *adj* : hasty, quick
pretender *vt* **1** : try to **2** AFIRMAR : claim **3** CORTEJAR : court, woo **4 ~ que** : expect — **pretencioso, -sa** *adj* : pretentious — **pretendido** *adj* : supposed — **pretendiente** *nmf* **1** : candidate **2** : pretender (to a throne) — **~**

nm : suitor — **pretensión** *nf, pl* **-siones 1** INTENCIÓN : intention, aspiration **2** : claim (to a throne, etc.) **3** **pretensiones** *nfpl* : pretensions
pretérito *nm* : past (in grammar)
pretexto *nm* : pretext, excuse
prevalecer {53} *vi* : prevail — **prevaleciente** *adj* : prevailing, prevalent
prevenir {87} *vt* **1** : prevent **2** AVISAR : warn — **prevenirse** {87} *vr* **~ contra** *or* **~ de** : take precautions against — **prevención** *nf, pl* **-ciones 1** : prevention **2** PRECAUCIÓN : precaution **3** PREJUICIO : prejudice — **prevenido, -da** *adj* **1** : prepared, ready **2** PRECAVIDO : cautious — **preventivo, -va** *adj* : preventive
prever {88} *vt* **1** : foresee **2** PLANEAR : plan
previo, -via *adj* : previous, prior
previsible *adj* : foreseeable — **previsión** *nf, pl* **-siones 1** : foresight **2** PREDICCIÓN : prediction, forecast — **previsor, -sora** *adj* : farsighted, prudent
prieto, -ta *adj* **1** CEÑIDO : tight **2** *Lat fam* : dark-skinned
prima *nf* **1** : bonus **2** : (insurance) premium **3** → **primo**
primario, -ria *adj* **1** : primary **2 escuela primaria** : elementary school
primate *nm* : primate
primavera *nf* **1** : spring (season) **2** : primrose (flower) — **primaveral** *adj* : spring
primero, -ra *adj* (**primer** *before masculine singular nouns*) **1** : first **2** MEJOR : top, leading **3** PRINCIPAL : main, basic **4 de primera** : first-rate — **~** *n* : first (person or thing) — **primero** *adv* **1** : first **2** MÁS BIEN : rather, sooner
primitivo, -va *adj* : primitive
primo, -ma *n* : cousin
primogénito, -ta *adj & n* : firstborn
primor *nm* : beautiful thing
primordial *adj* : basic, fundamental
primoroso, -sa *adj* **1** : exquisite, fine **2** HÁBIL : skillful
princesa *nf* : princess
principado *nm* : principality
principal *adj* : main, principal
príncipe *nm* : prince
principio *nm* **1** : principle **2** COMIENZO : beginning, start **3** ORIGEN : origin **4 al ~** : at first **5 a ~s de** : at the beginning of — **principiante** *nmf* : beginner
pringar {52} *vt* : spatter (with grease) — **pringoso, -sa** *adj* : greasy
prioridad *nf* : priority
prisa *nf* **1** : hurry, rush **2 a ~** *or* **de ~** : quickly **3 a toda ~** : as fast as possible **4 darse ~** : hurry **5 tener ~** : be in a hurry
prisión *nf, pl* **-siones 1** : prison **2** ENCARCELAMIENTO : imprisonment — **prisionero, -ra** *n* : prisoner
prisma *nm* : prism — **prismáticos** *nmpl* : binoculars
privar *vt* **1** : deprive **2** PROHIBIR : forbid **3** *Lat* : knock out — **privarse** *vr* : deprive oneself — **privación** *nf, pl* **-ciones** : deprivation — **privado, -da** *adj* : private — **privativo, -va** *adj* : exclusive
privilegio *nm* : privilege — **privilegiado, -da** *adj* : privileged
pro *prep* : for, in favor of — **~** *nm* **1** : pro, advantage **2 en ~ de** : for, in support of **3 los pros y los contras** : the pros and cons
proa *nf* : bow, prow
probabilidad *nf* : probability — **probable** *adj* : probable, likely — **probablemente** *adv* : probably
probar {19} *vt* **1** : try, test **2** : try on (clothing) **3** DEMOSTRAR : prove **4** DEGUSTAR : taste — *vi* : try — **probarse** *vr* : try on (clothing) — **probeta** *nf* : test tube
problema *nm* : problem — **problemático, -ca** *adj* : problematic
proceder *vi* **1** : proceed, act **2** : be appropriate **3 ~ de** : come from — **procedencia** *nf* : origin — **procedente** *adj* **~ de** : coming from, originating in — **procedimiento** *nm* **1** : procedure, method **2** : proceedings *pl* (in law)
procesar *vt* **1** : prosecute **2** : process (data) — **procesador** *nm* **~ de textos** : word processor — **procesamiento** *nm* : processing — **procesión** *nf, pl* **-siones** : procession — **proceso** *nm* **1** : process **2** : trial, proceedings *pl* (in law)
proclamar *vt* : proclaim — **proclama** *nf* : proclamation — **proclamación** *nf, pl* **-ciones** : proclamation
procrear *vi* : procreate — **procreación** *nf, pl* **-ciones** : procreation
procurar *vt* **1** : try, endeavor **2** CONSEGUIR : obtain, procure — **procurador, -dora** *n* : attorney
prodigar {52} *vt* : lavish — **prodigio** *nm* : wonder, prodigy — **prodigioso, -sa** *adj* : prodigious
pródigo, -ga *adj* : extravagant, prodigal
producir {61} *vt* **1** : produce **2** CAUSAR : cause **3** : yield, bear (interest, fruit, etc.) — **producirse** *vr* : take place —

producción *nf, pl* **-ciones** : production — **productividad** *nf* : productivity — **productivo, -va** *adj* : productive — **producto** *nm* : product — **productor, -tora** *n* : producer
proeza *nf* : exploit
profanar *vt* : profane, desecrate — **profanación** *nf, pl* **-ciones** : desecration — **profano, -na** *adj* : profane
profecía *nf* : prophecy
proferir {76} *vt* **1** : utter **2** : hurl (insults)
profesar *vt* **1** : profess **2** : practice (a profession, etc.) — **profesión** *nf, pl* **-siones** : profession — **profesional** *adj & nmf* : professional — **profesor, -sora** *n* **1** : teacher **2** : professor (at a university, etc.) — **profesorado** *nm* **1** : teaching profession **2** PROFESORES : faculty
profeta *nm* : prophet — **profético, -ca** *adj* : prophetic — **profetista** *nf* : (female) prophet — **profetizar** {21} *vt* : prophesy
prófugo, -ga *adj & n* : fugitive
profundo, -da *adj* **1** HONDO : deep **2** : profound (of thoughts, etc.) — **profundamente** *adv* : deeply, profoundly — **profundidad** *nf* : depth — **profundizar** {21} *vt* : study in depth
profuso, -sa *adj* : profuse — **profusión** *nf, pl* **-siones** : profusion
progenie *nf* : progeny, offspring
programa *nm* **1** : program **2** : curriculum (in education) — **programación** *nf, pl* **-ciones** : programming — **programador, -dora** *n* : programmer — **programar** *vt* **1** : schedule **2** : program (a computer, etc.)
progreso *nm* : progress — **progresar** *vi* : (make) progress — **progresión** *nf, pl* **-ciones** : progression — **progresista** *adj & nmf* : progressive — **progresivo, -va** *adj* : progressive, gradual
prohibir {62} *vt* : prohibit, forbid — **prohibición** *nf, pl* **-ciones** : ban, prohibition — **prohibido, -da** *adj* : forbidden — **prohibitivo, -va** *adj* : prohibitive
prójimo *nm* : neighbor, fellow man
prole *nf* : offspring
proletariado *nm* : proletariat — **proletario, -ria** *adj & n* : proletarian
proliferar *vi* : proliferate — **proliferación** *nf, pl* **-ciones** : proliferation — **prolífico, -ca** *adj* : prolific
prolijo, -ja *adj* : wordy, long-winded
prólogo *nm* : prologue, foreword
prolongar {52} *vt* **1** : prolong **2** ALARGAR : lengthen — **prolongarse** *vr* : last, continue — **prolongación** *nf, pl* **-ciones** : extension
promedio *nm* : average
promesa *nf* : promise — **prometedor, -dora** *adj* : promising, hopeful — **prometer** *vt* : promise — *vi* : show promise — **prometerse** *vr* : get engaged — **prometido, -da** *adj* : engaged — ~ *n* : fiancé *m*, fiancée *f*
prominente *adj* : prominent — **prominencia** *nf* : prominence
promiscuo, -cua *adj* : promiscuous — **promiscuidad** *nf* : promiscuity
promocionar *vt* : promote — **promoción** *nf, pl* **-ciones** : promotion
promontorio *nm* : promontory
promover {47} *vt* **1** : promote **2** CAUSAR : cause — **promotor, -tora** *n* : promoter
promulgar {52} *vt* **1** : proclaim **2** : enact (a law)
pronombre *nm* : pronoun
pronosticar {72} *vt* : predict, forecast — **pronóstico** *nm* **1** : prediction, forecast **2** : (medical) prognosis
pronto, -ta *adj* **1** : quick, prompt **2** PREPARADO : ready — **pronto** *adv* **1** : soon **2** RAPIDAMENTE : quickly, promptly **3 de ~** : suddenly **4 por lo ~** : for the time being **5 tan ~ como** : as soon as
pronunciar *vt* **1** : pronounce **2** : give, deliver (a speech) — **pronunciarse** *vr* **1** : declare oneself **2** SUBLEVARSE : revolt — **pronunciación** *nf, pl* **-ciones** : pronunciation
propagación *nf, pl* **-ciones** : propagation
propaganda *nf* **1** : propaganda **2** PUBLICIDAD : advertising
propagar {52} *vt* : propagate, spread — **propagarse** *vr* : propagate
propano *nm* : propane
propasarse *vr* : go too far
propensión *nf, pl* **-siones** : inclination, propensity — **propenso, -sa** *adj* : prone, inclined
propiamente *adv* : exactly
propicio, -cia *adj* : favorable, propitious
propiedad *nf* **1** : property **2** PERTINENCIA : ownership, possession — **propietario, -ria** *n* : owner, proprietor
propina *nf* : tip
propinar *vt* : give, deal (a blow, etc.)
propio, -pia *adj* **1** : own **2** APROPIADO : proper, appropriate **3** CARACTERÍSTICO : characteristic, typical **4** MISMO : himself, herself, oneself
proponer {60} *vt* **1** : propose **2** : nominate (a person) — **proponerse** *vr* : propose, intend

proporción *nf, pl* **-ciones** : proportion — **proporcionado, -da** *adj* : proportionate — **proporcional** *adj* : proportional — **proporcionar** *vt* **1** : provide **2** AJUSTAR : adapt, proportion

proposición *nf, pl* **-ciones** : proposal, proposition

propósito *nm* **1** : purpose, intention **2 a ~** : incidentally, by the way **3 a ~** : on purpose, intentionally

propuesta *nf* **1** : proposal **2** : offer (of employment, etc.)

propulsar *vt* **1** : propel, drive **2** PROMOVER : promote — **propulsión** *nf, pl* **-siones** : propulsion

prorrogar {52} *vt* **1** : extend **2** APLAZAR : postpone — **prórroga** *nf* **1** : extension, deferment **2** : overtime (in sports)

prorrumpir *vi* : burst forth, break out

prosa *nf* : prose

proscribir {33} *vt* **1** : prohibit, ban **2** DESTERRAR : exile — **proscripción** *nf, pl* **-ciones 1** : ban **2** DESTIERRO : banishment — **proscrito, -ta** *adj* : banned — **~** *n* : exile, outlaw

proseguir {75} *v* : continue — **prosecución** *nf, pl* **-ciones** : continuation

prospección *nf, pl* **-ciones** : prospecting, exploration

prospecto *nm* : prospectus

prosperar *vi* : prosper, thrive — **prosperidad** *nf* : prosperity — **próspero, -ra** *adj* : prosperous, fluorishing

prostituir {41} *vt* : prostitute — **prostitución** *nf, pl* **-ciones** : prostitution — **prostituta** *nf* : prostitute

protagonista *nmf* : protagonist — **protagonizar** *vt* : star in

proteger {15} *vt* : protect — **protegerse** *vr* : protect oneself — **protección** *nf, pl* **-ciones** : protection — **protector, -tora** *adj* : protective — **~** *n* : protector — **protegido, -da** *n* : protégé

proteína *nf* : protein

protestar *v* : protest — **protesta** *nf* : protest — **protestante** *adj & nmf* : Protestant

protocolo *nm* : protocol

prototipo *nm* : prototype

protuberancia *nf* : protuberance — **protuberante** *adj* : protuberant

provecho *nm* **1** : benefit, advantage **2 ¡buen ~!** : enjoy your meal! — **provechoso, -sa** *adj* : profitable, beneficial

proveer {63} *vt* : provide, supply — **proveedor, -dora** *n* : supplier

provenir {87} *vi* **~ de** : come from

proverbio *nm* : proverb — **proverbial** *adj* : proverbial

providencia *nf* **1** : providence **2** PRECAUCIÓN : precaution — **providencial** *adj* : providential

provincia *nf* : province — **provincial** *adj* : provincial — **provinciano, -na** *adj* : provincial, parochial

provisión *nf, pl* **-siones** : provision — **provisional** *adj* : provisional

provocar {72} *vt* **1** : provoke, cause **2** IRRITAR : irritate — **provocación** *nf, pl* **-ciones** : provocation — **provocativo, -va** *adj* : provocative

próximo, -ma *adj* **1** CERCANO : near **2** SIGUIENTE : next — **próximamente** *adv* : shortly, soon — **proximidad** *nf* **1** : proximity **2 ~es** *nfpl* : vicinity

proyectar *vt* **1** : plan **2** LANZAR : throw, hurl **3** : cast (light) **4** : show (a film) — **proyección** *nf, pl* **-ciones** : projection — **proyectil** *nm* : missile — **proyecto** *nm* : plan, project — **proyector** *nm* : projector

prudencia *nf* : prudence, care — **prudente** *adj* : prudent, sensible

prueba *nf* **1** : proof, evidence **2** : test (in education, medicine, etc.) **3** : event (in sports) **4 a ~ de agua** : waterproof

psicoanálisis *nm* : psychoanalysis — **psicoanalista** *nmf* : psychoanalyst — **psicoanalizar** {21} *vt* : psychoanalyze

psicología *nf* : psychology — **psicológico, -ca** *adj* : psychological — **psicólogo, -ga** *n* : psychologist

psicópata *nmf* : psychopath

psicosis *nfs & pl* : psychosis

psicoterapia *nf* : psychotherapy — **psicoterapeuta** *nmf* : psychotherapist

psicótico, -ca *adj & n* : psychotic

psiquiatría *nf* : psychiatry — **psiquiatra** *nmf* : psychiatrist — **psiquiátrico, -ca** *adj* : psychiatric

psíquico, -ca *adj* : psychic

púa *nf* **1** : sharp point **2** : tooth (of a comb) **3** : thorn (of a plant), quill (of a porcupine, etc.) **4** : (guitar) pick

pubertad *nf* : puberty

publicar {72} *vt* **1** : publish **2** DIVULGAR : divulge, disclose — **publicación** *nf, pl* **-ciones** : publication

publicidad *nf* **1** : publicity **2** : advertising (in marketing) — **publicista** *nmf* : publicist — **publicitar** *vt* **1** : publicize **2** : advertise (a product, etc.) — **publicitario, -ria** *adj* : advertising

público, -ca *adj* : public — **público** *nm* **1** : public **2** : audience (of theater, etc.), spectators *pl* (of sports)

puchero *nm* **1** : (cooking) pot **2** GUISADO : stew **3 hacer ~s** : pout

púdico, -ca *adj* : modest

pudiente *adj* : wealthy

pudín *nm, pl* **-dines** : pudding
pudor *nm* : modesty — **pudoroso, -sa** *adj* : modest
pudrir {59} *vt* **1** : rot **2** *fam* : annoy — **pudrirse** *vr* : rot
pueblo *nm* **1** : town, village **2** NACIÓN : people, nation
puente *nm* **1** : bridge **2 hacer ~** : have a long weekend **3 ~ levadizo** : drawbridge
puerco, -ca *n* **1** : pig **2 puerco espín** : porcupine — **~** *adj* : dirty, filthy
pueril *adj* : childish
puerro *nm* : leek
puerta *nf* **1** : door, gate **2 a ~ cerrada** : behind closed doors
puerto *nm* **1** : port **2** : (mountain) pass **3** REFUGIO : haven
puertorriqueño, -ña *adj* : Puerto Rican
pues *conj* **1** : since, because **2** POR LO TANTO : so, therefore **3** (*used interjectionally*) : well, then
puesta *nf* **1 ~ a punto** : tune-up **2 ~ de sol** : sunset **3 ~ en marcha** : starting up — **puesto, -ta** *adj* **1** : put, set **2** VESTIDO : dressed — **puesto** *nm* **1** : place **2** EMPLEO : position, job **3** : stand, stall (in a market) **4 ~ avanzado** : outpost — **~ que** *conj* : since, given that
púgil *nm* : boxer
pugnar *vi* : fight — **pugna** *nf* : fight, battle
pulcro, -cra *adj* : tidy, neat
pulga *nf* **1** : flea **2 tener malas ~s** : have a bad temper
pulgada *nf* : inch — **pulgar** *nm* **1** : thumb **2** : big toe
pulir *vt* **1** : polish **2** REFINAR : touch up, perfect
pulla *nf* : cutting remark, gibe
pulmón *nm, pl* **-mones** : lung — **pulmonar** *adj* : pulmonary — **pulmonía** *nf* : pneumonia
pulpa *nf* : pulp
pulpería *nf Lat* : grocery store
púlpito *nm* : pulpit
pulpo *nm* : octopus
pulsar *vt* **1** : press (a button), strike (a key) **2** : play (music) — **pulsación** *nf, pl* **-ciones 1** : beat, throb **2** : keystroke (on a typewriter, etc.)
pulsera *nf* : bracelet
pulso *nm* **1** : pulse **2** : steadiness (of hand)
pulular *vi* : swarm
pulverizar {21} *vt* **1** : pulverize, crush **2** : spray (a liquid) — **pulverizador** *nm* : atomizer, spray
puma *nf* : puma
punitivo, -va *adj* : punitive
punta *nf* **1** : tip, end **2** : point (of a needle, etc.) **3 ~ del dedo** : fingertip **4 sacar ~ a** : sharpen
puntada *nf* **1** : stitch **2 ~s** *nfpl* : seam
puntal *nm* : prop, support
puntapié *nm* : kick
puntear *vt* : pluck (a guitar)
puntería *nf* : aim, marksmanship
puntiagudo, -da *adj* : sharp, pointed
puntilla *nf* **1** : lace edging **2 de ~s** : on tiptoe
punto *nm* **1** : dot, point **2** : period (in punctuation) **3** ASUNTO : item, question **4** LUGAR : spot, place **5** MOMENTO : moment **6** : point (in a score) **7** PUNTADA : stitch **8 a las dos en ~** : at two o'clock sharp **9 dos ~s** : colon **10 hasta cierto ~** : up to a point **11 ~ de partida** : starting point **12 ~ muerto** : deadlock **13 ~ y coma** : semicolon
puntuación *nf, pl* **-ciones 1** : punctuation **2** : scoring, score (in sports)
puntual *adj* **1** : prompt, punctual **2** EXACTO : accurate, detailed — **puntualidad** *nf* **1** : punctuality **2** EXACTITUD : accuracy
puntuar {3} *vt* : punctuate — *vi* : score (in sports)
punzar {21} *vt* : prick, puncture — **punzada** *nf* **1** PINCHAZO : prick **2** : sharp pain — **punzante** *adj* **1** : sharp **2** MORDAZ : biting, caustic
puñado *nm* **1** : handful **2 a ~s** : by the handful
puñal *nm* : dagger — **puñalada** *nf* : stab
puño *nm* **1** : fist **2** : cuff (of a shirt) **3** : handle, hilt (of a sword, etc.) — **puñetazo** *nm* : punch (with the fist)
pupila *nf* : pupil (of the eye)
pupitre *nm* : desk
puré *nm* **1** : purée **2 ~ de papas** *or* **~ de patatas** *Spain* : mashed potatoes
pureza *nf* : purity
purga *nf* : purge — **purgar** {52} *vt* : purge — **purgatorio** *nm* : purgatory
purificar {72} *vt* : purify — **purificación** *nf, pl* **-ciones** : purification
puritano, -na *adj* : puritanical — **~** *n* : puritan
puro, -ra *adj* **1** : pure **2** SIMPLE : plain, simple **3** *Lat fam* : only, just — **puro** *nm* : cigar
púrpura *nf* : purple — **purpúreo, -rea** *adj* : purple
pus *nm* : pus
pusilánime *adj* : cowardly
puta *nf* : whore
putrefacción *nf, pl* **-ciones** : putrefaction, rot — **pútrido, -da** *adj* : putrid, rotten

Q

q *nf* : q, 18th letter of the Spanish alphabet

que *conj* **1** : that **2** (*in comparisons*) : than **3** (*introducing a reason or cause*) : so that, or else **4 es ~** : the thing is that **5 yo ~ tú** : if I were you — **~** *pron* **1** (*referring to persons*) : who, whom **2** (*referring to things*) : that, which **3 el (la, lo, las, los) ~** : he (she, it, they) who, whoever, the one(s) that

qué *adv* **1** : how, what **2 ¡~ lindo!** : how lovely! — **~** *adj* : what, which — **~** *pron* **1** : what **2 ¿~ crees?** : what do you think?

quebrar {55} *vt* : break — *vi* : go bankrupt — **quebrarse** *vr* : break — **quebrada** *nf* : ravine, gorge — **quebradizo, -za** *adj* : breakable, fragile — **quebrado, -da** *adj* **1** : bankrupt **2** : rough, uneven (of land, etc.) **3** ROTO : broken — **quebrado** *nm* : fraction — **quebradura** *nf* : crack, fissure — **quebrantar** *vt* **1** : break **2** DEBILITAR : weaken — **quebranto** *nm* **1** : harm, damage **2** AFLICCIÓN : grief, pain

queda *nf* → **toque**

quedar *vi* **1** PERMANECER : remain, stay **2** ESTAR : be **3** FALTAR : be left **4** : fit, look (of clothing, etc.) **5 no queda lejos** : it's not far **6 ~ en** : agree to, agree on — **quedarse** *vr* **1** : stay **2 ~ con** : keep

quedo, -da *adj* : quiet, still — **quedo** *adv* : softly, quietly

quehacer *nm* **1** : task **2 ~es** *nmpl* : chores

queja *nf* : complaint — **quejarse** *vr* **1** : complain **2** GEMIR : moan, groan — **quejido** *nm* : moan, whimper — **quejoso, -sa** *adj* : complaining, whining

quemar *vt* **1** : burn **2** MALGASTAR : squander — *vi* : burn — **quemarse** *vr* **1** : burn oneself **2** : burn (up) **3** : get sunburned — **quemado, -da** *adj* **1** : burned **2** AGOTADO : burned-out **3 estar ~** : be fed up — **quemador** *nm* : burner — **quemadura** *nf* : burn — **quemarropa**: **a ~** *adj & adv phr* : point-blank

querella *nf* **1** : dispute, quarrel **2** : charge (in law)

querer {64} *vt* **1** : want **2** AMAR : love **3 ~ decir** : mean **4 ¿quieres pasarme la leche?** : please pass the milk **5 sin ~** : unintentionally — **~** *nm* : love — **querido, -da** *adj* : dear, beloved — **~** *n* **1** : darling **2** AMANTE : lover

queroseno *nm* : kerosene

querubín *nm, pl* **-bines** : cherub

queso *nm* : cheese — **quesadilla** *nf Lat* : quesadilla

quicio *nm* **1 estar fuera de ~** : be beside oneself **2 sacar de ~** : drive crazy

quiebra *nf* **1** : break **2** BANCARROTA : bankruptcy

quien *pron, pl* **quienes 1** (*subject*) : who **2** (*object*) : whom **3** (*indefinite*) : whoever, anyone, some people

quién *pron, pl* **quiénes 1** (*subject*) : who **2** (*object*) : whom **3 ¿de ~ es este lápiz?** : whose pencil is this?

quienquiera *pron, pl* **quienesquiera** : whoever, whomever

quieto, -ta *adj* **1** : calm, quiet **2** INMÓVIL : still — **quietud** *nf* : stillness

quijada *nf* : jaw, jawbone (of an animal)

quilate *nm* : carat, karat

quilla *nf* : keel

quimera *nf* : illusion — **quimérico, -ca** *adj* : fanciful

química *nf* : chemistry — **químico, -ca** *adj* : chemical — **~** *n* : chemist

quince *adj & nm* : fifteen — **quinceañero, -ra** *n* : fifteen-year-old, teenager — **quincena** *nf* : two-week period, fortnight — **quincenal** *adj* : semimonthly, twice a month

quincuagésimo, -ma *adj & n* : fiftieth

quinientos, -tas *adj* : five hundred — **quinientos** *nms & pl* : five hundred

quinina *nf* : quinine

quinqué *nm* : oil lamp

quinta *nf* : country house, villa

quintaesencia *nf* : quintessence

quinteto *nm* : quintet

quinto, -ta *adj & n* : fifth — **quinto** *nm* : fifth

quiosco *nm* : kiosk, newsstand

quiropráctico, -ca *n* : chiropractor

quirúrgico, -ca *adj* : surgical

quisquilloso, -sa *adj* : fastidious, fussy

quiste *nm* : cyst

quitar *vt* **1** : remove, take away **2** : take off (clothes) **3** : get rid of, relieve (pain, etc.) — **quitarse** *vr* **1** : withdraw, leave **2** : take off (one's clothes) **3 ~ de** : give up (a habit) **4 ~ de encima** : get rid of — **quitaesmalte** *nm* : nail-polish remover — **quitamanchas** *nms & pl* : stain remover — **quitanieves** *nm* : snowplow — **quitasol** *nm* : parasol

quizá *or* **quizás** *adv* : maybe, perhaps

R

r *nf* : r, 19th letter of the Spanish alphabet

rábano *nm* **1** : radish **2 ~ picante** : horseradish

rabí *nmf, pl* **-bíes** : rabbi

rabia *nf* **1** : rage, anger **2** : rabies (disease) — **rabiar** *vi* **1** : be furious **2** : be in great pain **3 ~ por** : be dying for — **rabioso, -sa** *adj* **1** : enraged, furious **2** : rabid, having rabies

rabino, -na *n* : rabbi

rabo *nm* **1** : tail **2 el ~ del ojo** : the corner of one's eye

racha *nf* **1** : gust of wind **2** SERIE : series, string — **racheado, -da** *adj* : gusty

racial *adj* : racial

racimo *nm* : bunch, cluster

raciocinio *nm* : reason, reasoning

ración *nf, pl* **-ciones 1** : share, ration **2** : helping (of food)

racional *adj* : rational — **racionalizar** {21} *vt* : rationalize

racionar *vt* : ration — **racionamiento** *nm* : rationing

racismo *nm* : racism — **racista** *adj & nmf* : racist

radar *nm* : radar

radiación *nf, pl* **-ciones** : radiation

radiactivo, -va *adj* : radioactive — **radiactividad** *nf* : radioactivity

radiador *nm* : radiator

radiante *adj* : radiant

radical *adj & nmf* : radical

radicar {72} *vi* **~ en** : lie in, be rooted in

radio *nm* **1** : radius **2** : spoke (of a wheel) **3** : radium (element) — **~** *nmf* : radio

radioactivo, -va *adj* : radioactive — **radioactividad** *nf* : radioactivity

radiodifusión *nf, pl* **-siones** : broadcasting — **radioemisora** *nf* : radio station — **radioescucha** *nmf* : listener — **radiofónico, -ca** *adj* : radio

radiografía *nf* : X ray — **radiografiar** {85} *vt* : x-ray

radiología *nf* : radiology — **radiólogo, -ga** *n* : radiologist

raer {65} *vt* : scrape off

ráfaga *nf* **1** : gust (of wind) **2** : flash (of light)

raído, -da *adj* : worn, shabby

raíz *nf, pl* **raíces 1** : root **2** ORIGEN : origin, source **3 echar raíces** : take root

raja *nf* **1** : crack, slit **2** RODAJA : slice — **rajar** *vt* : crack, split — **rajarse** *vr* **1** : crack, split open **2** *fam* : back out

rajatabla: **a ~** *adv phr* : strictly, to the letter

ralea *nf* : sort, kind

ralentí *nm* : neutral (gear)

rallar *vt* : grate — **rallador** *nm* : grater

rama *nf* : branch — **ramaje** *nm* : branches *pl* — **ramal** *nm* : branch (of a railroad, etc.) — **ramificarse** {72} *vr* : branch (off) — **ramillete** *nm* **1** : bouquet **2** GRUPO : cluster, bunch — **ramo** *nm* **1** : branch **2** RAMILLETE : bouquet

rampa *nf* : ramp, incline

rana *nf* **1** : frog **2 ~ toro** : bullfrog

rancho *nm* : ranch, farm — **ranchero, -ra** *n* : rancher, farmer

rancio, -cia *adj* **1** : rancid **2** : aged (of wine)

rango *nm* **1** : rank **2** : (social) standing

ranúnculo *nm* : buttercup

ranura *nf* : groove, slot

rapar *vt* **1** : shave **2** : crop (hair)

rapaz *adj, pl* **-paces** : rapacious, predatory

rápido, -da *adj* : rapid, quick — **rápidamente** *adv* : rapidly, fast — **rapidez** *nf* : speed — **rápido** *adv* : quickly, fast — **~** *nm* **1** : express train **2 ~s** *nmpl* : rapids

rapiña *nf* **1** : plunder **2 ave de ~** : bird of prey

rapsodia *nf* : rhapsody

raptar *vt* : kidnap — **rapto** *nm* : kidnapping — **raptor, -tora** *n* : kidnapper

raqueta *nf* : racket (in sports)

raro, -ra *adj* **1** : rare **2** EXTRAÑO : odd, strange — **raramente** *adv* : rarely, infrequently — **rareza** *nf* : rarity

ras *nm* **a ~ de** : level with

rascacielos *nms & pl* : skyscraper

rascar {72} *vt* **1** : scratch **2** RASPAR : scrape — **rascarse** *vr* : scratch oneself

rasgar {52} *vt* : rip, tear — **rasgarse** *vr* : rip

rasgo *nm* **1** : stroke (of a pen) **2** CARACTERÍSTICA : trait, characteristic **3 ~s** *nmpl* FACCIONES : features

rasguear *vt* : strum

rasguñar *vt* : scratch — **rasguño** *nm* : scratch

raso, -sa *adj* **1** : level, flat **2** : low (of a flight) **3 soldado raso** : private (in the army) — **raso** *nm* : satin

raspar *vt* **1** : scrape **2** LIMAR : file down, smooth — *vi* : be rough — **raspadura** *nf* **1** : scratch **2 ~s** *nfpl* : scrapings

rastra *nf* **1** : rake **2 a ~s** : unwillingly — **rastrear** *vt* : track, trace — **rastrero, -ra** *adj* **1** : creeping **2** DESPRECIABLE : despicable — **rastrillar** *vt* : rake — **rastrillo** *nm* : rake — **rastro** *nm* **1** : trail, track **2** SEÑAL : sign

rasurar *vt Lat* : shave — **rasurarse** *vr Lat* : shave

rata *nf* : rat

ratear *vt* : steal — **ratero, -ra** *n* : thief

ratificar {72} *vt* : ratify — **ratificación** *nf, pl* **-ciones** : ratification

rato *nm* **1** : while **2 al poco ~** : shortly after **3 pasar el ~** : pass the time

ratón *nm, pl* **-tones** : mouse — **ratonera** *nf* : mousetrap

raudal *nm* **1** : torrent **2 a ~es** : in abundance — **raudo, -da** *adj* : swift

raya *nf* **1** : line **2** LISTA : stripe **3** : part (in the hair) — **rayar** *vt* : scratch — *vi* **1 al ~ el día** : at daybreak **2 ~ en** : border on — **rayarse** *vr* : get scratched

rayo *nm* **1** : ray, beam **2** : bolt of lightning **3 ~s X** : X rays

rayón *nm* : rayon

raza *nf* **1** : (human) race **2** : breed (of animals) **3 de ~** : thoroughbred, pedigreed

razón *nf, pl* **-zones 1** : reason **2 dar ~** : inform **3 en ~ de** : because of **4 tener ~** : be right — **razonable** *adj* : reasonable — **razonamiento** *nm* : reasoning — **razonar** *v* : reason, think

reacción *nf, pl* **-ciones** : reaction — **reaccionar** *vi* : react — **reaccionario, -ria** *adj & n* : reactionary

reacio, -cia *adj* : resistant, stubborn

reactivar *vt* : reactivate, revive

reactor *nm* **1** : jet (airplane) **2 ~ nuclear** : nuclear reactor

reajustar *vt* : readjust — **reajuste** *nm* : readjustment

real *adj* **1** : royal **2** VERDADERO : real, true

realce *nm* **1** : relief **2 dar ~** : highlight

realeza *nf* : royalty

realidad *nf* **1** : reality **2 en ~** : actually, in fact

realismo *nm* : realism — **realista** *adj* : realistic — **~** *nmf* : realist

realizar {21} *vt* **1** : carry out **2** : achieve (a goal) **3** : produce (a film or play) **4** : realize (a profit) — **realizarse** *vr* **1** : fulfill oneself **2** : come true (of a dream, etc.) — **realización** *nf, pl* **-ciones** : execution, realization

realmente *adv* : really, actually

realzar {21} *vt* : highlight, enhance

reanimar *vt* : revive

reanudar *vt* : resume, renew — **reanudarse** *vr* : resume

reaparecer {53} *vi* : reappear — **reaparición** *nf, pl* **-ciones** : reappearance

reavivar *vt* : revive

rebajar *vt* **1** : lower, reduce **2** HUMILLAR : humiliate — **rebajarse** *vr* **1** : humble oneself **2 ~ a** : stoop to — **rebaja** *nf* **1** : reduction **2** DESCUENTO : discount **3 ~s** *nfpl* : sales

rebanada *nf* : slice

rebaño *nm* **1** : herd **2** : flock (of sheep)

rebasar *vt* : surpass, exceed

rebatir *vt* : refute

rebelarse *vr* : rebel — **rebelde** *adj* : rebellious — **~** *nmf* : rebel — **rebeldía** *nf* : rebelliousness — **rebelión** *nf, pl* **-liones** : rebellion

reblandecer *vt* : soften

rebobinar *vt* : rewind

rebosar *vi* **1** : overflow **2 ~ de** : be bursting with — *vt* : overflow with

rebotar *vi* : bounce, rebound — **rebote** *nm* **1** : bounce **2 de ~** : on the rebound

rebozar {21} *vt* : coat in batter

rebuscado, -da *adj* : pretentious

rebuznar *vi* : bray

recabar *vt* **1** : obtain, collect **2 ~ fondos** : raise money

recado *nm* **1** MENSAJE : message **2** *Spain* : errand

recaer {13} *vi* **1** : relapse **2 ~ sobre** : fall on — **recaída** *nf* : relapse

recalcar {72} *vt* : emphasize, stress

recalcitrante *adj* : recalcitrant

recalentar {55} *vt* **1** : overheat **2** : reheat, warm up (food) — **recalentarse** *vr* : overheat

recámara *nf* **1** : chamber (of a firearm) **2** *Lat* : bedroom

recambio *nm* **1** : spare part **2** : refill (for a pen, etc.)

recapitular *vt* : recapitulate, sum up — **recapitulación** *nf, pl* **-ciones** : recapitulation

recargar {52} *vt* **1** : overload **2**

: recharge (a battery), reload (a firearm, etc.) — **recargado, -da** *adj* : overly elaborate — **recargo** *nm* : surcharge

recato *nm* : modesty — **recatado, -da** *adj* : modest, demure

recaudar *vt* : collect — **recaudación** *nf, pl* **-ciones** : collection — **recaudador, -dora** *n* **~ de impuestos** : tax collector

recelar *vt* : distrust, fear — **recelo** *nm* : distrust, suspicion — **receloso, -sa** *adj* : distrustful, suspicious

recepción *nf, pl* **-ciones** : reception — **recepcionista** *nmf* : receptionist

receptáculo *nm* : receptacle

receptivo, -va *adj* : receptive — **receptor, -tora** *n* : recipient — **receptor** *nm* : receiver (of a radio, etc.)

recesión *nf, pl* **-siones** : recession

receso *nm Lat* : recess, adjournment

receta *nf* **1** : recipe **2** : prescription (in medicine)

rechazar {21} *vt* **1** : reject, refuse **2** REPELER : repel **3** : reflect (light) — **rechazo** *nm* : rejection

rechinar *vi* **1** : squeak, creak **2** : grind, gnash (one's teeth)

rechoncho, -cha *adj fam* : chubby

recibir *vt* **1** : receive **2** ACOGER : welcome — *vi* : receive visitors — **recibidor** *nm* : vestibule, entrance hall — **recibimiento** *nm* : reception, welcome — **recibo** *nm* : receipt

reciclar *vt* **1** : recycle **2** : retrain (workers) — **reciclaje** *nm* : recycling

recién *adv* **1** : newly, recently **2 ~ casados** : newlyweds — **reciente** *adj* : recent — **recientemente** *adv* : recently

recinto *nm* **1** : enclosure **2** ÁREA : area, site

recio, -cia *adj* : tough, strong

recipiente *nm* : container, receptacle — **~** *nmf* : recipient

recíproco, -ca *adj* : reciprocal, mutual

recitar *vt* : recite — **recital** *nm* : recital

reclamar *vt* : demand, ask for — *vi* : complain — **reclamación** *nf, pl* **-ciones 1** : claim, demand **2** QUEJA : complaint — **reclamo** *nm* **1** : lure (in hunting) **2** *Lat* : inducement, attraction

reclinar *vt* : rest, lean — **reclinarse** *vr* : recline, lean back

recluir {41} *vt* : confine, lock up — **recluirse** *vr* : shut oneself away — **reclusión** *nf, pl* **-siones** : imprisonment — **recluso, -sa** *n* : prisoner

recluta *nmf* : recruit — **reclutamiento** *nm* : recruitment — **reclutar** *vt* : recruit, enlist

recobrar *vt* : recover, regain — **recobrarse** *vr* **~ de** : recover from

recodo *nm* : bend

recoger {15} *vt* **1** : collect, gather **2** COGER : pick up **3** LIMPIAR, ORDENAR : clean up, tidy (up) — **recogerse** *vr* : retire, withdraw — **recogedor** *nm* : dustpan — **recogido, -da** *adj* : quiet, secluded

recolección *nf, pl* **-ciones 1** : collection **2** COSECHA : harvest

recomendar {55} *vt* : recommend — **recomendación** *nf, pl* **-ciones** : recommendation

recompensar *vt* : reward — **recompensa** *nf* : reward

reconciliar *vt* : reconcile — **reconciliarse** *vr* : be reconciled — **reconciliación** *nf, pl* **-ciones** : reconciliation

recóndito, -ta *adj* : hidden

reconfortar *vt* : comfort

reconocer {18} *vt* **1** : recognize **2** ADMITIR : admit **3** EXAMINAR : examine — **reconocible** *adj* : recognizable — **reconocido, -da** *adj* **1** : recognized, accepted **2** AGRADECIDO : grateful — **reconocimiento** *nm* **1** : recognition **2** AGRADECIMIENTO : gratitude **3** : (medical) examination

reconsiderar *vt* : reconsider

reconstruir {41} *vt* : reconstruct — **reconstrucción** *nf, pl* **-ciones** : reconstruction

recopilar *vt* **1** RECOGER : collect, gather **2** : compile — **recopilación** *nf, pl* **-ciones** : collection, compilation

récord *nm, pl* **-cords** : record

recordar {19} *vt* **1** ACORDARSE DE : remember **2** : remind — *vi* : remember — **recordatorio** *nm* : reminder

recorrer *vt* **1** : travel through **2** : cover (a distance) — **recorrido** *nm* **1** : journey, trip **2** TRAYECTO : route, course

recortar *vt* **1** : reduce **2** CORTAR : cut (out) **3** : trim (hair) — **recortarse** *vr* : stand out — **recorte** *nm* **1** : cut, cutting **2 ~s de periódicos** : newspaper clippings

recostar {19} *vt* : lean, rest — **recostarse** *vr* : lie down

recoveco *nm* **1** : bend **2** RINCÓN : nook, corner

recrear *vt* **1** : recreate **2** ENTRETENER : entertain — **recrearse** *vr* : to enjoy oneself — **recreativo, -va** *adj* : recreational — **recreo** *nm* **1** : recreation, amusement **2** : recess, break (at school)

recriminar *vt* : reproach
recrudecer {53} *vi* : worsen — **recrudecerse** *vr* : intensify, get worse
rectángulo *nm* : rectangle — **rectangular** *adj* : rectangular
rectificar {72} *vt* **1** : rectify, correct **2** AJUSTAR : straighten (out) — **rectitud** *nf* **1** : straightness **2** : (moral) rectitude — **recto, -ta** *adj* **1** : straight **2** ÍNTEGRO : upright, honorable — **recto** *nm* : rectum
rector, -tora *adj* : governing, managing — **~** *n* : rector — **rectoría** *nf* : rectory
recubrir {2} *vt* : cover, coat
recuento *nm* : count, recount
recuerdo *nm* **1** : memory **2** : souvenir, remembrance (of a journey, etc.) **3** **~s** *nmpl* SALUDOS : regards
recuperar *vt* **1** : recover, retrieve **2** **~ el tiempo perdido** : make up for lost time — **recuperarse** *vr* **~ de** : recover from — **recuperación** *nf, pl* **-ciones 1** : recovery **2** **~ de datos** : data retrieval
recurrir *vi* **~ a** : turn to (a person), resort to (force, etc.) — **recurso** *nm* **1** : recourse, resort **2** : appeal (in law) **3** **~s** *nmpl* : resources
red *nf* **1** : net **2** SISTEMA : network, system **3 la Red** : the Internet
redactar *vt* : write (up), draft — **redacción** *nf, pl* **-ciones 1** : writing, drafting **2** : editing (of a newspaper, etc.) — **redactor, -tora** *n* : editor
redada *nf* **1** : (police) raid **2** : catch (in fishing)
redescubrir {2} *vt* : rediscover
redención *nf, pl* **-ciones** : redemption — **redentor, -tora** *adj* : redeeming
redil *nm* : fold, pen
rédito *nm* : interest, yield
redoblar *vt* : redouble
redomado, -da *adj* : out-and-out
redondear *vt* **1** : make round **2** : round off (a number, etc.) — **redonda** *nf* **1** : whole note (in music) **2 a la ~** : in the surrounding area — **redondel** *nm* **1** : ring, circle **2** : bullring — **redondo, -da** *adj* **1** : round **2** PERFECTO : excellent
reducir {61} *vt* : reduce — **reducirse** *vr* **~ a** : come down to, amount to — **reducción** *nf, pl* **-ciones** : reduction — **reducido, -da** *adj* **1** : reduced, limited **2** PEQUEÑO : small
redundante *adj* : redundant — **redundancia** *nf* : reduncancy
reedición *nf, pl* **-ciones** : reprint
reembolsar *vt* : refund, reimburse, repay — **reembolso** *nm* : refund, reimbursement
reemplazar {21} *vt* : replace — **reemplazo** *nm* : replacement
reencarnación *nf, pl* **-ciones** : reincarnation
reencuentro *nm* : reunion
reestructurar *vt* : restructure
refaccionar *vt Lat* : repair, renovate — **refacciones** *nfpl Lat* : repairs, renovations
referir {76} *vt* **1** : tell **2** REMITIR : refer — **referirse** *vr* **~ a** : refer to — **referencia** *nf* **1** : reference **2 hacer ~ a** : refer to — **referéndum** *nm, pl* **-dums** : referendum — **referente** *adj* **~ a** : concerning
refinar *vt* : refine — **refinado, -da** *adj* : refined — **refinamiento** *nm* : refinement — **refinería** *nf* : refinery
reflector *nm* **1** : reflector **2** : spotlight, searchlight, floodlight
reflejar *vt* : reflect — **reflejarse** *vr* : be reflected — **reflejo** *nm* **1** : reflection **2** : (physical) reflex **3** **~s** *nmpl* : highlights (in hair)
reflexionar *vi* : reflect, think — **reflexión** *nf, pl* **-xiones** : reflection, thought — **reflexivo, -va** *adj* **1** : reflective, thoughtful **2** : reflexive (in grammar)
reflujo *nm* : ebb (tide)
reforma *nf* **1** : reform **2** **~s** *nfpl* : renovations — **reformador, -dora** *n* : reformer — **reformar** *vt* **1** : reform **2** : renovate, repair (a house, etc.) — **reformarse** *vr* : mend one's ways — **reformatorio** *nm* : reformatory
reforzar {36} *vt* : reinforce
refrán *nm, pl* **-franes** : proverb, saying
refregar {49} *vt* : scrub
refrenar *vt* **1** : rein in (a horse) **2** CONTENER : restrain — **refrenarse** *vr* : restrain oneself
refrendar *vt* : approve, endorse
refrescar {72} *vt* **1** : refresh, cool **2** : brush up on (knowledge) — *vi* : turn cooler — **refrescante** *adj* : refreshing — **refresco** *nm* : soft drink
refriega *nf* : scuffle, skirmish
refrigerar *vt* **1** : refrigerate **2** CLIMATIZAR : air-condition — **refrigeración** *nf, pl* **-ciones 1** : refrigeration **2** AIRE ACONDICIONADO : air-conditioning — **refrigerador** *nmf Lat* : refrigerator — **refrigerio** *nm* : refreshments *pl*
refrito, -ta *adj* : refried — **refrito** *nm* : rehash
refuerzo *nm* : reinforcement
refugiar *vt* : shelter — **refugiarse** *vr* : take refuge — **refugiado, -da** *n*

: refugee — **refugio** *nm* : refuge, shelter
refulgir {35} *vi* : shine brightly
refunfuñar *vi* : grumble, groan
refutar *vt* : refute
regadera *nf* **1** : watering can **2** *Lat* : shower head, shower
regalar *vt* : give (as a gift) — **regalarse** *vr* **~ con** : treat oneself to
regaliz *nm, pl* **-lices** : licorice
regalo *nm* **1** : gift, present **2** PLACER : pleasure, delight
regañadientes: **a ~** *adv phr* : reluctantly, unwillingly
regañar *vt* : scold — *vi* **1** QUEJARSE : grumble **2** *Spain* : quarrel — **regañon, -ñona** *adj, mpl* **-ñones** *fam* : grumpy, irritable
regar {49} *vt* **1** : irrigate, water **2** ESPARCIR : scatter
regatear *vt* **1** : haggle over **2** ESCATIMAR : skimp on — *vi* : bargain, haggle
regazo *nm* : lap (of a person)
regenerar *vt* : regenerate
regentar *vt* : run, manage
régimen *nm, pl* **regímenes 1** : regime **2** DIETA : diet **3 ~ de vida** : lifestyle
regimiento *nm* : regiment
regio, -gia *adj* : royal, regal
región *nf, pl* **-giones** : region, area — **regional** *adj* : regional
regir {28} *vt* **1** : rule **2** ADMINISTRAR : manage, run **3** DETERMINAR : govern, determine — *vi* : apply, be in force — **regirse** *vr* **~ por** : be guided by
registrar *vt* **1** : register **2** GRABAR : record, tape **3** : search (a house, etc.), frisk (a person) — **registrarse** *vr* **1** : register **2** : be recorded (of temperatures, etc.) — **registrador, -dora** *adj* **caja registradora** : cash register — **~** *n* : registrar — **registro** *nm* **1** : registration **2** : register (book) **3** : registry (office) **4** : range (of a voice, etc.) **5** INSPECCIÓN : search
regla *nf* **1** : rule, regulation **2** : ruler (for measuring) **3** MENSTRUACIÓN : period — **reglamentación** *nf, pl* **-ciones 1** : regulation **2** REGLAS : rules *pl* — **reglamentar** *vt* : regulate — **reglamentario, -ria** *adj* : regulation, official — **reglamento** *nm* : regulations *pl*, rules *pl*
regocijar *vt* : gladden, delight — **regocijarse** *vr* : rejoice — **regocijo** *nm* : delight, rejoicing
regodearse *vr* : be delighted — **regodeo** *nm* : delight
regordete *adj fam* : chubby
regresar *vi* : return, come back, go back — *vt Lat* : give back — **regresión** *nf, pl* **-siones** : regression — **regresivo, -va** *adj* : regressive — **regreso** *nm* **1** : return **2 estar de ~** : be back, be home again
reguero *nm* **1** : irrigation ditch **2** SEÑAL : trail, trace **3 correr como un ~ de pólvora** : spread like wildfire
regular *adj* **1** : regular **2** MEDIANO : medium, average **3 por lo ~** : in general — **~** *vt* : regulate, control — **regulación** *nf, pl* **-ciones** : regulation, control — **regularidad** *nf* : regularity — **regularizar** {21} *vt* : normalize, make regular
rehabilitar *vt* **1** : rehabilitate **2** : reinstate (s.o. in a position) **3** : renovate (a building, etc.) — **rehabilitación** *nf* **1** : rehabilitation **2** : reinstatement (in a position) **3** : renovation (of a building, etc.)
rehacer {40} *vt* **1** : redo **2** REPARAR : repair — **rehacerse** *vr* **1** : recover **2 ~ de** : get over
rehén *nm, pl* **-henes** : hostage
rehuir {41} *vt* : avoid, shun
rehusar {8} *v* : refuse
reimprimir *vt* : reprint — **reimpresión** *nf, pl* **-siones** : reprinting, reprint
reina *nf* : queen — **reinado** *nm* : reign — **reinante** *adj* : reigning — **reinar** *vi* **1** : reign **2** PREVALECER : prevail
reincidir *vi* : backslide, relapse
reino *nm* : kingdom, realm
reintegrar *vt* **1** : reinstate **2** : refund (money), reimburse (expenses, etc.) — **reintegrarse** *vr* **~ a** : return to — **reintegro** *nm* : reimbursement
reír {66} *vi* : laugh — *vt* : laugh at — **reírse** *vr* : laugh
reiterar *vt* : repeat, reiterate
reivindicar {72} *vt* **1** : claim **2** RESTAURAR : restore
reja *nf* : grille, grating — **rejilla** *nf* : grille, grate, screen
rejuvenecer {53} *vt* : rejuvenate — **rejuvenecerse** *vr* : be rejuvenated
relación *nf, pl* **-ciones 1** : relation, connection **2** COMUNICACIÓN : relationship, relations *pl* **3** RELATO : account **4** LISTA : list **5 con ~ a** *or* **en ~ a** : in relation to — **relacionar** *vt* : relate, connect — **relacionarse** *vr* **~ con** : be connected to, interact with
relajar *vt* : relax — **relajarse** *vr* : relax — **relajación** *nf, pl* **-ciones** : relaxation — **relajado, -da** *adj* **1** : relaxed **2** : dissolute, lax (in behavior)
relamerse *vr* : smack one's lips, lick its chops

relámpago *nm* : flash of lightning — **relampaguear** *vi* : flash
relatar *vt* : relate, tell
relativo, -va *adj* **1** : relative **2 en lo relativo a** : with regard to — **relatividad** *nf* : relativity
relato *nm* **1** : account, report **2** CUENTO : story, tale
releer {20} *vt* : reread
relegar {52} *vt* : relegate
relevante *adj* : outstanding, important
relevar *vt* **1** : relieve, take over from **2 ~ de** : exempt from — **relevo** *nm* **1** : relief, replacement **2 carrera de ~s** : relay race
relieve *nm* **1** : relief (in art, etc.) **2** IMPORTANCIA : prominence, importance **3 poner en ~** : emphasize
religión *nf, pl* **-giones** : religion — **religioso, -sa** *adj* : religious — **~** *n* : monk *m*, nun *f*
relinchar *vi* : neigh, whinny — **relincho** *nm* : neigh, whinny
reliquia *nf* **1** : relic **2 ~ de familia** : family heirloom
rellenar *vt* **1** : refill **2** : stuff, fill (in cooking) — **relleno, -na** *adj* : stuffed, filled — **relleno** *nm* : stuffing, filling
reloj *nm* **1** : clock **2** *or* **~ de pulsera** : wristwatch **3 ~ de arena** : hourglass **4 como un ~** : like clockwork
relucir {45} *vi* **1** : glitter, shine **2 sacar a ~** : bring up, mention — **reluciente** *adj* : brilliant, shining
relumbrar *vi* : shine brightly
remachar *vt* **1** : rivet **2** RECALAR : stress, drive home — **remache** *nm* : rivet
remanente *nm* : remainder, surplus
remanso *nm* : pool
remar *vi* : row
rematar *vt* **1** : conclude, finish up **2** MATAR : finish off **3** LIQUIDAR : sell off cheaply **4** *Lat* : auction — *vi* **1** : shoot (in sports) **2** TERMINAR : end — **rematado, -da** *adj* : utter, complete — **remate** *nm* **1** : shot (in sports) **2** FIN : end
remedar *vt* : imitate, mimic
remediar *vt* **1** : remedy, repair **2** : solve (a problem) **3** EVITAR : avoid — **remedio** *nm* **1** : remedy, cure **2** SOLUCIÓN : solution **3 sin ~** : hopeless
rememorar *vi* : recall
remendar {55} *vt* : mend
remesa *nf* **1** : remittance **2** : shipment (of merchandise)
remezón *nm, pl* **-zones** *Lat* : mild earthquake, tremor
remiendo *nm* : mend, patch
remilgado, -da *adj* **1** : prudish **2** AFECTADO : affected — **remilgo** *nm* : primness, affectation
reminiscencia *nf* : reminiscence
remisión *nf, pl* **-siones** : remission
remiso, -sa *adj* **1** : reluctant **2** NEGLIGENTE : remiss
remitir *vt* **1** : send, remit **2 ~ a** : refer to, direct to — *vi* : subside, let up — **remite** *nm* : return address — **remitente** *nmf* : sender (of a letter, etc.)
remo *nm* : paddle, oar
remodelar *vt* **1** : remodel **2** : restructure (an organization)
remojar *vt* : soak, steep — **remojo** *nm* **poner en ~** : soak
remolacha *nf* : beet
remolcar {72} *vt* : tow, tug — **remolcador** *nm* : tugboat
remolino *nm* **1** : whirlwind, whirlpool **2** : crowd (of people) **3** : cowlick (of hair)
remolque *nm* **1** : towing, tow **2** : trailer (vehicle)
remontar *vt* **1** : overcome **2** SUBIR : go up — **remontarse** *vr* **1** : soar **2 ~ a** : date from, go back to
rémora *nf* : hindrance
remorder {47} *vt* : trouble, worry — **remordimiento** *nm* : remorse
remoto, -ta *adj* : remote — **remotamente** *adv* : remotely, slightly
remover {47} *vt* **1** : stir **2** : move around, turn over (earth, embers, etc.) **3** REAVIVIR : bring up again **4** DESPEDIR : fire, dismiss
remunerar *vt* : remunerate
renacer {48} *vi* : be reborn, revive — **renacimiento** *nm* **1** : rebirth, revival **2 el Renacimiento** : the Renaissance
renacuajo *nm* : tadpole, pollywog
rencilla *nf* : quarrel
renco, -ca *adj Lat* : lame
rencor *nm* **1** : rancor, hostility **2 guardar ~** : hold a grudge — **rencoroso, -sa** *adj* : resentful
rendición *nf, pl* **-ciones** : surrender — **rendido, -da** *adj* **1** : submissive **2** AGOTADO : exhausted
rendija *nf* : crack, split
rendir {54} *vt* **1** : render, give **2** PRODUCIR : yield, produce **3** CANSAR : exhaust — *vi* : make progress, go a long way — **rendirse** *vr* : surrender, give up — **rendimiento** *nm* **1** : performance **2** : yield, return (in finance, etc.)
renegar {49} *vt* : deny — *vi* **1** QUEJARSE : grumble **2 ~ de** ABJURAR : renounce, disown — **renegado, -da** *n* : renegade

renglón *nm, pl* **-glones 1** : line (of writing) **2** *Lat* : line (of products)
reno *nm* : reindeer
renombre *nm* : renown — **renombrado, -da** *adj* : famous, renowned
renovar {19} *vt* **1** : renew, restore **2** : renovate (a building, etc.) — **renovación** *nf, pl* **-ciones 1** : renewal **2** : renovation (of a building, etc.)
renquear *vi* : limp, hobble
rentar *vt* **1** : produce, yield **2** *Lat* : rent — **renta** *nf* **1** : income **2** ALQUILER : rent **3 impuesto sobre la ~** : income tax — **rentable** *adj* : profitable
renunciar *vi* **1** : resign **2 ~ a** : renounce, relinquish — **renuncia** *nf* **1** : renunciation **2** DIMISIÓN : resignation
reñir {67} *vi* **~ con** : argue with, fall out with — *vt* **1** : scold **2** DISPUTAR : fight — **reñido, -da** *adj* **1** : hard-fought **2 ~ con** : on bad terms with
reo, rea *n* **1** : accused, defendant **2** CULPABLE : culprit
reojo *nm* **de ~** : out of the corner of one's eye
reorganizar {21} *vt* : reorganize
repantigarse {52} *vr* : sprawl out
reparar *vt* **1** : repair, fix **2** : make amends for (an offense, etc.) — *vi* **1 ~ en** ADVERTIR : take notice of **2 ~ en** CONSIDERAR : consider — **reparación** *nf, pl* **-ciones 1** : reparation, amends **2** ARREGLO : repair — **reparo** *nm* **1** : reservation, objection **2 poner ~s a** : object to
repartir *vt* **1** : allocate **2** DISTRIBUIR : distribute **3** ESPARCIR : spread — **repartición** *nf, pl* **-ciones** : distribution — **repartidor, -dora** *n* : delivery person, distributor — **reparto** *nm* **1** : allocation **2** DISTRIBUCIÓN : delivery **3** : cast (of characters)
repasar *vt* **1** : review, go over **2** ZURCIR : mend — **repaso** *nm* **1** : review **2** : mending (of clothes)
repeler *vt* **1** : repel **2** REPUGNAR : disgust — **repelente** *adj* : repellent, repulsive
repente *nm* **1** : fit, outburst **2 de ~** : suddenly — **repentino, -na** *adj* : sudden
repercutir *vi* **1** : reverberate **2 ~ en** : have repercussions on — **repercusión** *nf, pl* **-siones** : repercussion
repertorio *nm* : repertoire
repetir {54} *vt* **1** : repeat **2** : have a second helping of (food) — **repetirse** *vr* **1** : repeat oneself **2** : recur (of an event, etc.) — **repetición** *nf, pl* **-ciones 1** : repetition **2** : rerun, repeat (of a program, etc.) — **repetido, -da** *adj* **1** : repeated **2 repetidas veces** : repeatedly, time and again — **repetitivo, -va** *adj* : repetitive, repetitious
repicar {72} *vt* : ring — *vi* : ring out, peal — **repique** *nm* : ringing, pealing
repisa *nf* **1** : shelf, ledge **2 ~ de ventana** : windowsill
replegar {49} *vt* : fold — **replegarse** *vr* : retreat, withdraw
repleto, -ta *adj* **1** : replete, full **2 ~ de** : packed with
replicar {72} *vt* : reply, retort — *vi* : answer back — **réplica** *nf* **1** RESPUESTA : reply **2** COPIA : replica, reproduction
repliegue *nm* **1** : fold **2** : (military) withdrawal
repollo *nm* : cabbage
reponer {60} *vt* **1** : replace **2** REPLICAR : reply — **reponerse** *vr* : recover
reportar *vt* **1** : yield, bring **2** *Lat* : report — **reportaje** *nm* : article, (news) report — **reporte** *nm Lat* : report — **reportero, -ra** *n* : reporter
reposar *vi* **1** DESCANSAR : rest **2** : stand, settle (of liquids, dough, etc.) — **reposado, -da** *adj* : calm, relaxed — **reposición** *nf, pl* **-ciones 1** : replacement **2** : rerun, repeat (of a program, etc.) — **reposo** *nm* : rest
repostar *vi* **1** : stock up on **2** : refuel (an airplane, etc.) — *vi* : fill up, refuel
reprender *vt* : reprimand, scold — **reprensible** *adj* : reprehensible
represalia *nf* **1** : reprisal **2 tomar ~s** : retaliate
represar *vt* : dam
representar *vt* **1** : represent **2** : perform (a play, etc.) **3** APARENTAR : look, appear as — **representación** *nf, pl* **-ciones 1** : representation **2** : performance (of a play, etc.) **3 en ~ de** : on behalf of — **representante** *nmf* **1** : representative **2** ACTOR : performer — **representativo, -va** *adj* : representative
represión *nf, pl* **-siones** : repression
reprimenda *nf* : reprimand
reprimir *vt* **1** : repress **2** : suppress (a rebellion, etc.)
reprobar {19} *vt* **1** : reprove, condemn **2** *Lat* : fail (an exam, etc.)
reprochar *vt* : reproach — **reprocharse** *vr* : reproach oneself — **reproche** *nm* : reproach
reproducir {61} *vt* : reproduce — **reproducirse** *vr* **1** : breed, reproduce **2** : recur (of an event, etc.) — **reproducción** *nf, pl* **-ciones** : reproduction — **reproductor, -tora** *adj* : reproductive
reptil *nm* : reptile

república *nf* : republic — **republicano, -na** *adj & n* : republican
repudiar *vt* : repudiate
repuesto *nm* : spare (auto) part
repugnar *vt* : disgust — **repugnancia** *nf* : disgust — **repugnante** *adj* : disgusting
repujar *vt* : emboss
repulsivo, -va *adj* : repulsive
reputar *vt* : consider, deem — **reputación** *nf, pl* **-ciones** : reputation
requerir {76} *vt* **1** : require **2** : summon, send for (a person)
requesón *nm, pl* **-sones** : cottage cheese
réquiem *nm* : requiem
requisito *nm* **1** : requirement **2 ~ previo** : prerequisite
res *nf* **1** : beast, animal **2** *Lat or* **carne de ~** : beef
resabio *nm* **1** VICIO : bad habit, vice **2** DEJO : aftertaste
resaca *nf* **1** : undertow **2 tener ~** : have a hangover
resaltar *vi* **1** : stand out **2 hacer ~** : bring out, highlight — *vt* : emphasize
resarcir {83} *vt* : compensate, repay — **resarcirse** *vr* **~ de** : make up for
resbalar *vi* **1** : slip, slide **2** : skid (of an automobile) — **resbalarse** *vr* : slip, skid — **resbaladizo, -za** *adj* : slippery — **resbalón** *nm, pl* **-lones** : slip — **resbaloso, -sa** *adj Lat* : slippery
rescatar *vt* **1** : rescue, ransom **2** RECUPERAR : recover, get back — **rescate** *nm* **1** : rescue **2** : ransom (money) **3** RECUPERACIÓN : recovery
rescindir *vt* : cancel — **rescisión** *nf, pl* **-siones** : cancellation
rescoldo *nm* : embers *pl*
resecar {72} *vt* : dry (out) — **resecarse** *vr* : dry up — **reseco, -ca** *adj* : dry, dried-up
resentirse {76} *vr* **1** : suffer, be weakened **2** OFENDERSE : be offended **3 ~ de** : feel the effects of — **resentido, -da** *adj* : resentful — **resentimiento** *nm* : resentment
reseñar *vt* **1** : review **2** DESCRIBIR : describe — **reseña** *nf* **1** : review, report **2** DESCRIPCIÓN : description
reservar *vt* **1** : reserve **2** GUARDAR : keep, save — **reservarse** *vr* **1** : save oneself **2** : keep for oneself — **reserva** *nf* **1** : reservation **2** PROVISIÓN : reserve **3 de ~** : spare, in reserve — **reservación** *nf, pl* **-ciones** : reservation — **reservado, -da** *adj* **1** : reserved **2** : confidential (of a document, etc.)
resfriar {85} *vt* : cool — **resfriarse** *vr* **1** : cool off **2** CONSTIPARSE : catch a cold — **resfriado** *nm* CATARRO : cold — **resfrío** *nm Lat* : cold
resguardar *vt* : protect — **resguardarse** *vr* : protect oneself — **resguardo** *nm* **1** : protection **2** RECIBO : receipt
residir *vi* **1** : reside, live **2 ~ en** : lie in — **residencia** *nf* **1** : residence **2** *or* **~ universitaria** : dormitory — **residencial** *adj* : residential — **residente** *adj & nmf* : resident
residuo *nm* **1** : residue **2 ~s** *nmpl* : waste — **residual** *adj* : residual
resignar *vt* : resign — **resignarse** *vr* **~ a** : resign oneself to — **resignación** *nf, pl* **-ciones** : resignation
resina *nf* **1** : resin **2 ~ epoxídica** : epoxy
resistir *vt* **1** AGUANTAR : stand, bear **2** : withstand (temptation, etc.) — *vi* : resist — **resistirse** *vr* **~ a** : be resistant to — **resistencia** *nf* **1** : resistance **2** AGUANTE : endurance, stamina — **resistente** *adj* : resistant, strong, tough
resma *nf* : ream
resollar {19} *vi* : breathe heavily, pant
resolver {89} *vt* **1** : resolve **2** DECIDIR : decide — **resolverse** *vr* : make up one's mind — **resolución** *nf, pl* **-ciones 1** : resolution **2** DECISIÓN : decision **3** FIRMEZA : determination, resolve
resonar {19} *vi* : resound — **resonancia** *nf* **1** : resonance **2** CONSECUENCIAS : impact, repercussions *pl* — **resonante** *adj* : resonant, resounding
resoplar *vi* **1** : puff, pant **2** : snort (with annoyance)
resorte *nm* **1** MUELLE : spring **2 tocar ~s** : pull strings
respaldar *vt* : back, endorse — **respaldarse** *vr* : lean back — **respaldo** *nm* **1** : back (of a chair, etc.) **2** APOYO : support, backing
respectar *vt* : concern, relate to — **respectivo, -va** *adj* : respective — **respecto** *nm* **1 al ~** : in this respect **2 ~ a** : in regard to, concerning
respetar *vt* : respect — **respetable** *adj* : respectable — **respeto** *nm* **1** : respect **2 presentar sus ~s** : pay one's respects — **respetuoso, -sa** *adj* : respectful
respingo *nm* : start, jump
respirar *v* : breathe — **respiración** *nf, pl* **-ciones** : respiration, breathing — **respiratorio, -ria** *adj* : respiratory — **respiro** *nm* **1** : breath **2** DESCANSO : respite, break

resplandecer {53} *vi* : shine — **resplandeciente** *adj* : shining, gleaming — **resplandor** *nm* **1** : brilliance, gleam **2** : flash (of lightning, etc.)
responder *vt* : answer, reply — *vi* **1** : answer **2** REPLICAR : answer back **3** **~ a** : respond to **4** **~ de** : answer for (something)
responsable *adj* : responsible — **responsabilidad** *nf* : responsibility
respuesta *nf* **1** : answer, reply **2** REACCIÓN : response
resquebrajar *vt* : split, crack — **resquebrajarse** *vr* : crack
resquicio *nm* **1** : crack, crevice **2** VESTIGIO : trace, glimmer
resta *nf* : subtraction
restablecer {53} *vt* : reestablish, restore — **restablecerse** *vr* : recover — **restablecimiento** *nm* : restoration, recovery
restallar *vi* : crack, crackle
restar *vt* **1** : deduct, subtract **2** DISMINUIR : minimize — *vi* : be left — **restante** *adj* **1** : remaining **2** **lo ~** : the rest
restauración *nf, pl* **-ciones** : restoration
restaurante *nm* : restaurant
restaurar *vt* : restore
restituir {41} *vt* : return, restore — **restitución** *nf, pl* **-ciones** : restitution
resto *nm* **1** : rest, remainder **2** **~s** *nmpl* : leftovers **3** *or* **~s mortales** : mortal remains
restregar {49} *vt* : rub, scrub — **restregarse** *vr* : rub
restringir {35} *vt* : restrict, limit — **restricción** *nf, pl* **-ciones** : restriction, limitation — **restrictivo, -va** *adj* : restrictive
resucitar *vt* : resuscitate, revive — *vi* : come back to life
resuelto, -ta *adj* : determined, resolved
resuello *nm* : heavy breathing, panting
resultar *vi* **1** : succeed, work out **2** SALIR : turn out (to be) **3** **~ de** : be the result of **4** **~ en** : result in — **resultado** *nm* : result, outcome
resumir *v* : summarize, sum up — **resumen** *nm, pl* **-súmenes** **1** : summary **2** **en ~** : in short
resurgir {35} *vi* : reappear, revive — **resurgimiento** *nm* : resurgence — **resurrección** *nf, pl* **-ciones** : resurrection
retahíla *nf* : string, series
retal *nm* : remnant
retardar *vt* **1** RETRASAR : delay **2** POSPONER : postpone
retazo *nm* **1** : remnant, scrap **2** : fragment (of a text, etc.)
retener {80} *vt* **1** : retain, keep **2** : withhold (funds, etc.) **3** DETENER : detain — **retención** *nf, pl* **-ciones** **1** : retention **2** : deduction, withholding (of funds)
reticente *adj* : reluctant — **reticencia** *nf* : reluctance
retina *nf* : retina
retintín *nm, pl* **-tines** **1** : tinkling, jingle **2** **con ~** : sarcastically
retirar *vt* **1** : remove, take away **2** : withdraw (funds, statements, etc.) — **retirarse** *vr* **1** : retreat, withdraw **2** JUBILARSE : retire — **retirada** *nf* **1** : withdrawal **2** **batirse en ~** : beat a retreat — **retirado, -da** *adj* **1** : remote, secluded **2** JUBILADO : retired — **retiro** *nm* **1** : retreat **2** JUBILACIÓN : retirement **3** *Lat* : withdrawal
reto *nm* : challenge, dare
retocar {72} *vt* : touch up
retoño *nm* : sprout, shoot
retoque *nm* **1** : retouching **2** **el último ~** : the finishing touch
retorcer {14} *vt* **1** : twist, contort **2** : wring out (clothes, etc.) — **retorcerse** *vr* **1** : get twisted up **2** : squirm, writhe (in pain) — **retorcijón** *nm, pl* **-jones** : cramp, spasm — **retorcimiento** *nm* : twisting, wringing out
retórica *nf* : rhetoric — **retórico, -ca** *adj* : rhetorical
retornar *v* : return — **retorno** *nm* : return
retozar {21} *vi* : frolic, romp — **retozón, -zona** *adj* : playful, frisky
retractarse *vr* **1** : withdraw, back down **2** **~ de** : take back, retract
retraer {81} *vt* : retract — **retraerse** *vr* : withdraw — **retraído, -da** *adj* : withdrawn, shy
retrasar *vt* **1** : delay, hold up **2** APLAZAR : postpone **3** : set back (a clock) — **retrasarse** *vr* **1** : be late **2** : fall behind (in work, etc.) — **retrasado, -da** *adj* **1** : retarded **2** : in arrears (of payments) **3** : backward (of a country) **4** : slow (of a clock) — **retraso** *nm* **1** : delay **2** SUBDESARROLLO : backwardness **3** **~ mental** : mental retardation
retratar *vt* **1** : portray **2** FOTOGRAFIAR : photograph **3** DIBUJAR : paint a portrait of — **retrato** *nm* **1** : portrayal **2** DIBUJO : portrait **3** FOTOGRAFÍA : photograph
retrete *nm* : restroom, toilet
retribuir {41} *vt* **1** : pay **2** RECOMPENSAR : reward — **retribución** *nf, pl*

-ciones **1** : payment **2** RECOMPENSA : reward
retroactivo, -va *adj* : retroactive
retroceder *vi* **1** : go back, turn back **2** CEDER : back down — **retroceso** *nm* **1** : backward movement **2** : backing down
retrógrado, -da *adj & nmf* : reactionary
retrospectiva *nf* : hindsight — **retrospectivo, -va** *adj* : retrospective
retrovisor *nm* : rearview mirror
retumbar *vi* : resound, reverberate, rumble
reumatismo *nm* : rheumatism
reunir {68} *vt* **1** : unite, join **2** TENER : have, possess **3** RECOGER : gather, collect — **reunirse** *vr* : meet, gather — **reunión** *nf, pl* **-niones** **1** : meeting **2** : (social) gathering, reunion
revalidar *vt* : confirm, ratify
revancha *nf* **1** : revenge **2** : rematch (in sports)
revelar *vt* **1** : reveal, disclose **2** : develop (film) — **revelación** *nf, pl* **-ciones** : revelation — **revelado** *nm* : developing (of film) — **revelador, -dora** *adj* : revealing
reventar {55} *v* : burst, blow up — **reventarse** *vr* : burst — **reventón** *nm, pl* **-tones** : blowout, flat tire
reverberar *vi* : reverberate — **reverberación** *nf, pl* **-ciones** : reverberation
reverenciar *vt* : revere — **reverencia** *nf* **1** : bow, curtsy **2** VENERACIÓN : reverence — **reverendo, -da** *adj & nmf* : reverend — **reverente** *adj* : reverent
reversa *nf Lat* : reverse (gear)
reverso *nm* **1** : back, reverse **2 el ~ de la medalla** : the complete opposite — **reversible** *adj* : reversible
revertir {76} *vi* **1** : revert **2 ~ en** : result in
revés *nm, pl* **-veses** **1** : back, wrong side **2** CONTRATIEMPO : setback **3** BOFETADA : slap **4** : backhand (in sports) **5 al ~** : the other way around, upside down, inside out
revestir {54} *vt* **1** : coat, cover **2** ASUMIR : take on, assume — **revestimiento** *nm* : covering, coating
revisar *vt* **1** : examine, inspect **2** : check over, overhaul (machinery, etc.) **3** MODIFICAR : revise — **revisión** *nf, pl* **-siones** **1** : revision **2** INSPECCIÓN : inspection, check — **revisor, -sora** *n* : inspector
revistar *vt* : review, inspect (troops, etc.) — **revista** *nf* **1** : magazine, journal **2** : revue (in theater) **3 pasar ~** : review, inspect
revivir *vi* : revive, come alive again — *vt* : relive
revocar {72} *vt* : revoke
revolcar {82} *vt* : knock over, knock down — **revolcarse** *vr* : roll around
revolotear *vi* : flutter, flit — **revoloteo** *nm* : fluttering, flitting
revoltijo *nm* : mess, jumble
revoltoso, -sa *adj* : rebellious
revolución *nf, pl* **-ciones** : revolution — **revolucionar** *vt* : revolutionize — **revolucionario, -ria** *adj & n* : revolutionary
revolver {89} *vt* **1** : mix, stir **2** : upset (one's stomach) **3** DESORGANIZAR : mess up — **revolverse** *vr* **1** : toss and turn **2** VOLVERSE : turn around
revólver *nm* : revolver
revuelo *nm* : commotion
revuelta *nf* : uprising, revolt — **revuelto, -ta** *adj* **1** : choppy, rough **2** DESORDENADO : messed up **3 huevos revueltos** : scrambled eggs
rey *nm* : king
reyerta *nf* : brawl, fight
rezagarse {52} *vr* : fall behind, lag
rezar {21} *vi* **1** : pray **2** DECIR : say — *vt* : say, recite — **rezo** *nm* : prayer
rezongar {52} *vi* : gripe, grumble
rezumar *v* : ooze
ría *nf* : estuary
riachuelo *nm* : brook, stream
riada *nf* : flood
ribera *nf* : bank, shore
ribetear *vt* : border, trim — **ribete** *nm* **1** : border, trim **2** : embellishment
rico, -ca *adj* **1** : rich, wealthy **2** ABUNDANTE : abundant **3** SABROSO : rich, tasty — **~** *n* : rich person
ridiculizar {21} *vt* : ridicule — **ridículo, -la** *adj* : ridiculous — **ridículo** *nm* **1 hacer el ~** : make a fool of oneself **2 poner en ~** : ridicule
riego *nm* : irrigation
riel *nm* : rail
rienda *nf* **1** : rein **2 dar ~ suelta a** : give free rein to
riesgo *nm* : risk
rifa *nf* : raffle — **rifar** *vt* : raffle (off) — **rifarse** *vr fam* : fight over
rifle *nm* : rifle
rígido, -da *adj* **1** : rigid, stiff **2** SEVERO : harsh, strict — **rigidez** *nf, pl* **-deces** **1** : rigidity, stiffness **2** SEVERIDAD : harshness, strictness
rigor *nm* **1** : rigor, harshness **2** EXACTITUD : precision **3 de ~** : essential,

obligatory — **riguroso, -sa** *adj* : rigorous

rima *nf* **1** : rhyme **2** **~s** *nfpl* : verse, poetry — **rimar** *vi* : rhyme

rimbombante *adj* : showy, pompous

rímel *nm* : mascara

rincón *nm, pl* **-cones** : corner, nook

rinoceronte *nm* : rhinoceros

riña *nf* **1** : fight, brawl **2** DISPUTA : dispute, quarrel

riñón *nm, pl* **-ñones** : kidney

río *nm* **1** : river **2** TORRENTE : torrent, stream

riqueza *nf* **1** : wealth **2** ABUNDANCIA : richness **3** **~s naturales** : natural resources

risa *nf* **1** : laughter, laugh **2** **dar ~ a algn** : make s.o. laugh **3** **morirse de la ~** *fam* : die laughing

risco *nm* : crag, cliff

risible *adj* : laughable

ristra *nf* : string, series

risueño, -ña *adj* : cheerful, smiling

ritmo *nm* **1** : rhythm **2** VELOCIDAD : pace, speed — **rítmico, -ca** *adj* : rhythmical

rito *nm* : rite, ritual — **ritual** *adj & nm* : ritual

rival *adj & nmf* : rival — **rivalidad** *nf* : rivalry, competition — **rivalizar** {21} *vi* **~ con** : rival, compete with

rizar {21} *vt* **1** : curl **2** : ripple (a surface) — **rizarse** *vr* : curl — **rizado, -da** *adj* **1** : curly **2** : choppy (of water) — **rizo** *nm* **1** : curl **2** : ripple (in water) **3** : loop (in aviation)

róbalo *nm* : bass (fish)

robar *vt* **1** : steal **2** : burglarize (a house, etc.) **3** SECUESTRAR : kidnap — **robo** *nm* : robbery, theft

roble *nm* : oak

robot *nm, pl* **-bots** : robot — **robótica** *nf* : robotics

robustecer {53} *vt* : make stronger, strengthen — **robusto, -ta** *adj* : robust, sturdy

roca *nf* : rock, boulder

roce *nm* **1** : rubbing, chafing **2** RASGUÑO : graze, scratch **3** **tener un ~ con** : have a brush with

rociar {85} *vt* : spray, sprinkle — **rocío** *nm* : dew

rocoso, -sa *adj* : rocky

rodaja *nf* : slice

rodar {19} *vi* **1** : roll, roll down, roll along **2** GIRAR : turn, go around **3** : travel (of a vehicle) **4** : film (of movies, etc.) — *vt* **1** : film, shoot **2** : break in (a vehicle) — **rodaje** *nm* **1** : filming, shooting **2** : breaking in (of a vehicle)

rodear *vt* **1** : surround, encircle **2** *Lat* : round up (cattle) — **rodearse** *vr* **~ de** : surround oneself with — **rodeo** *nm* **1** : rodeo, roundup **2** DESVÍO : detour **3** **andar con ~s** : beat around the bush

rodilla *nf* : knee

rodillo *nm* **1** : roller **2** : rolling pin (for pastry)

roer {69} *vt* **1** : gnaw **2** ATORMENTAR : eat away at, torment — **roedor** *nm* : rodent

rogar {16} *vt* : beg, request — *vi* : pray

rojo, -ja *adj* **1** : red **2** **ponerse ~** : blush — **rojo** *nm* : red — **rojez** *nf* : redness — **rojizo, -za** *adj* : reddish

rollizo, -za *adj* : plump, chubby

rollo *nm* **1** : roll, coil **2** *fam* : boring speech, lecture

romance *nm* **1** : romance **2** : Romance (language)

romano, -na *adj & n* : Roman

romántico, -ca *adj* : romantic — **romanticismo** *nm* : romanticism

romería *nf* : pilgrimage, procession

romero *nm* : rosemary

romo, -ma *adj* : blunt, dull

rompecabezas *nms & pl* : puzzle

romper {70} *vt* **1** : break **2** RASGAR : rip, tear **3** : break off (relations), break (a contract) — *vi* **1** : break (of the day, waves, etc.) **2** **~ a** : begin to, burst out with **3** **~ con** : break off with — **romperse** *vr* : break

ron *nm* : rum

roncar {72} *vi* : snore — **ronco, -ca** *adj* : hoarse

ronda *nf* **1** : rounds *pl,* patrol **2** : round (of drinks, etc.) — **rondar** *vt* **1** : patrol **2** : hang around (a place) **3** : be approximately (an age, a number, etc.) — *vi* **1** : be on patrol **2** MERODEAR : prowl about

ronquera *nf* : hoarseness

ronquido *nm* : snore

ronronear *vi* : purr — **ronroneo** *nm* : purr, purring

ronzar {21} *vt* : munch, crunch

roña *nf* **1** : mange **2** SUCIEDAD : dirt, filth — **roñoso, -sa** *adj* **1** : mangy **2** SUCIO : dirty **3** *fam* : stingy

ropa *nf* **1** : clothes *pl,* clothing **2** **~ interior** : underwear — **ropaje** *nm* : robes *pl,* regalia — **ropero** *nm* : wardrobe, closet

rosa *nf* : rose (flower) — **~** *adj* : rose-colored — **~** *nm* : rose (color) — **rosado, -da** *adj* **1** : pink **2** **vino rosado** : rosé — **rosado** *nm* : pink (color) — **rosal** *nm* : rosebush

rosario *nm* : rosary
rosbif *nm* : roast beef
rosca *nf* **1** : thread (of a screw) **2** ESPIRAL : ring, coil
roseta *nf* : rosette
rosquilla *nf* : doughnut
rostro *nm* : face
rotación *nf, pl* **-ciones** : rotation — **rotativo, -va** *adj* : rotary, revolving
roto, -ta *adj* : broken, torn
rotonda *nf* : traffic circle, rotary
rótula *nf* : kneecap
rótulo *nm* **1** : heading, title **2** ETIQUETA : label, sign
rotundo, -da *adj* : categorical, absolute
rotura *nf* : break, tear, fracture
rozar {21} *vt* **1** : graze, touch lightly **2** APROXIMARSE DE : touch on, border on — *vi* : scrape, rub — **rozarse** *vr* **1** : rub, chafe **2 ~ con** *fam* : rub elbows with — **rozadura** *nf* : scratch
rubí *nm, pl* **rubíes** : ruby
rubicundo, -da *adj* : ruddy
rubio, -bia *adj & n* : blond
rubor *nm* : flush, blush — **ruborizarse** {21} *vr* : blush
rubrica *nf* **1** : flourish (in writing) **2** TÍTULO : title, heading
rudeza *nf* : roughness, coarseness
rudimentos *nmpl* : rudiments, basics — **rudimentario, -ria** *adj* : rudimentary
rudo, -da *adj* **1** : rough, harsh **2** GROSERO : coarse, unpolished
rueda *nf* **1** : wheel **2** CORRO : circle, ring **3** RODAJA : (round) slice **4 ir sobre ~s** : go smoothly — **ruedo** *nm* : bullring
ruego *nm* : request
rugir {35} *vi* : roar — **rugido** *nm* : roar
rugoso, -sa *adj* **1** : rough **2** ARRUGADO : wrinkled
ruibarbo *nm* : rhubarb
ruido *nm* : noise — **ruidoso, -sa** *adj* : loud, noisy
ruina *nf* **1** : ruin, destruction **2** COLAPSO : collapse **3 ~s** *nfpl* : ruins, remains — **ruinoso, -sa** *adj* : run-down, dilapidated
ruiseñor *nm* : nightingale
ruleta *nf* : roulette
rulo *nm* : curler, roller
rumano, -na *adj* : Romanian, Rumanian
rumba *nf* : rumba
rumbo *nm* **1** : direction, course **2** ESPLENDIDEZ : lavishness **3 con ~ a** : bound for, heading for **4 perder el ~** : go off course
rumiar *vt* : mull over — *vi* : chew the cud — **rumiante** *adj & nm* : ruminant
rumor *nm* **1** : rumor **2** MURMULLO : murmur — **rumorearse** *or* **rumorarse** *vr* : be rumored — **rumoroso, -sa** *adj* : murmuring, babbling
ruptura *nf* **1** : break, rupture **2** : breach (of a contract) **3** : breaking off (of relations)
rural *adj* : rural
ruso, -sa *adj* : Russian — **ruso** *nm* : Russian (language)
rústico, -ca *adj* **1** : rural, rustic **2 en rústica** : in paperback
ruta *nf* : route
rutina *nf* : routine — **rutinario, -ria** *adj* : routine

S

s *nf* : s, 20th letter of the Spanish alphabet
sábado *nm* : Saturday
sábana *nf* : sheet
sabandija *nf* : bug
saber {71} *vt* **1** : know **2** SER CAPAZ DE : know how to, be able to **3** ENTERARSE : learn, find out **4 a ~** : namely — *vi* **1** : taste **2 ~ de** : know about — **~** *nm* : knowledge — **sabelotodo** *nmf fam* : know-it-all — **sabido, -da** *adj* : well-known — **sabiduría** *nf* **1** : wisdom **2** CONOCIMIENTO : learning, knowledge — **sabiendas**: **a ~** *adv phr* : knowingly — **sabio, -bia** *adj* **1** : learned **2** PRUDENTE : wise, sensible
sabor *nm* : flavor, taste — **saborear** *vt* : savor
sabotaje *nm* : sabotage — **saboteador, -dora** *n* : saboteur — **sabotear** *vt* : sabotage
sabroso, -sa *adj* : delicious, tasty
sabueso *nm* **1** : bloodhound **2** *fam* : sleuth
sacacorchos *nms & pl* : corkscrew
sacapuntas *nms & pl* : pencil sharpener
sacar {72} *vt* **1** : take out **2** OBTENER : get, obtain **3** EXTRAER : extract, withdraw **4** : bring out (a book, a product, etc.) **5** : take (photos), make (copies) **6** QUITAR : remove **7 ~ adelante** : bring up (children), carry out (a project,

etc.) **8 ~ la lengua** : stick out one's tongue — *vi* : serve (in sports)
sacarina *nf* : saccharin
sacerdote, -tisa *n* : priest *m,* priestess *f* — **sacerdocio** *nm* : priesthood — **sacerdotal** *adj* : priestly
saciar *vt* : satisfy
saco *nm* **1** : bag, sack **2** : sac (in anatomy) **3** *Lat* : jacket
sacramento *nm* : sacrament — **sacramental** *adj* : sacramental
sacrificar {72} *vt* : sacrifice — **sacrificarse** *vr* : sacrifice oneself — **sacrificio** *nm* : sacrifice
sacrilegio *nm* : sacrilege — **sacrílego, -ga** *adj* : sacrilegious
sacro, -cra *adj* : sacred — **sacrosanto, -ta** *adj* : sacrosanct
sacudir *vt* **1** : shake **2** GOLPEAR : beat **3** CONMOVER : shake up, shock — **sacudirse** *vr* : shake off — **sacudida** *nf* **1** : shaking **2** : jolt (of a train, etc.), tremor (of an earthquake) **3** : (emotional) shock
sádico, -ca *adj* : sadistic — **~** *n* : sadist — **sadismo** *nm* : sadism
saeta *nf* : arrow
safari *nm* : safari
sagaz *adj, pl* **-gaces** : shrewd, sagacious — **sagacidad** *nf* : shrewdness
sagrado, -da *adj* : sacred, holy
sal *nf* : salt
sala *nf* **1** : room, hall **2** : living room (of a house) **3 ~ de espera** : waiting room
salar *vt* : salt — **salado, -da** *adj* **1** : salty **2** GRACIOSO : witty **3 agua salada** : salt water
salario *nm* : salary, wage
salchicha *nf* : sausage — **salchichón** *nf, pl* **-chones** : salami-like cold cut
saldar *vt* **1** : settle, pay off **2** VENDER : sell off — **saldo** *nm* **1** : balance (of an account) **2 ~s** *nmpl* : remainders, sale items
salero *nm* : saltshaker
salir {73} *vi* **1** : go out, come out **2** PARTIR : leave **3** APARECER : appear **4** RESULTAR : turn out **5** : rise (of the sun) **6 ~ adelante** : get by **7 ~ con** : go out with, date **8 ~ de** : come from — **salirse** *vr* **1** : leave **2** ESCAPARSE : leak out, escape **3** SOLTARSE : come off **4 ~ con la suya** : get one's own way — **salida** *nf* **1** : exit **2** : (action of) leaving, departure **3** SOLUCIÓN : way out **4** : leak (of gas, liquid, etc.) **5** OCURRENCIA : witty remark **6 ~ de emergencia** : emergency exit **7 ~ del sol** : sunrise — **saliente** *adj* **1** : departing, outgoing **2** DESTACADO : outstanding
saliva *nf* : saliva
salmo *nm* : psalm
salmón *nm, pl* **-mones** : salmon
salmuera *nf* : brine
salón *nm, pl* **-lones 1** : lounge, sitting room **2 ~ de belleza** : beauty salon **3 ~ de clase** : classroom
salpicar {72} *vt* **1** : splash, spatter **2 ~ de** : pepper with — **salpicadera** *nf Lat* : fender — **salpicadura** *nf* : splash
salsa *nf* **1** : sauce **2** : (meat) gravy **3** : salsa (music)
saltamontes *nms & pl* : grasshopper
saltar *vi* **1** : jump, leap **2** REBOTAR : bounce **3** : come off (of a button, etc.) **4** ROMPERSE : shatter **5** ESTALLAR : explode, blow up — *vt* **1** : jump (over) **2** OMITIR : skip, miss — **saltarse** *vr* **1** : come off **2** OMITIR : skip, miss
saltear *vt* : sauté
saltimbanqui *nmf* : acrobat
salto *nm* **1** : jump, leap **2** : dive (into water) **3 ~ de agua** : waterfall — **saltón, -tona** *adj, mpl* **-tones** : bulging, protruding
salud *nf* **1** : health **2 ¡salud!** : here's to your health! **3 ¡salud!** *Lat* : bless you! (when someone sneezes) — **saludable** *adj* : healthy
saludar *vt* **1** : greet, say hello to **2** : salute (in the military) — **saludo** *nm* **1** : greeting **2** : (military) salute **3 ~s** : best wishes, regards
salva *nf* **~ de aplausos** : round of applause
salvación *nf, pl* **-ciones** : salvation
salvado *nm* : bran
salvador, -dora *n* : savior, rescuer
salvadoreño, -ña *adj* : (El) Salvadoran
salvaguardar *vt* : safeguard
salvaje *adj* **1** : wild **2** PRIMITIVO : savage, primitive — **~** *nmf* : savage
salvar *vt* **1** : save, rescue **2** RECORRER : cover, travel **3** SUPERAR : overcome — **salvarse** *vr* : save oneself — **salvavidas** *nms & pl* **1** : life preserver **2 bote ~** : lifeboat
salvia *nf* : sage (plant)
salvo, -va *adj* : safe — **salvo** *prep* **1** : except (for), save **2 ~ que** : unless
samba *nf* : samba
San → **santo**
sanar *vt* : heal, cure — *vi* : recover — **sanatorio** *nm* **1** : sanatorium **2** HOSPITAL : clinic, hospital
sanción *nf, pl* **-ciones** : sanction — **sancionar** *vt* : sanction
sandalia *nf* : sandal
sándalo *nm* : sandalwood
sandía *nf* : watermelon

sandwich ['sandwitʃ, 'saŋgwitʃ] *nm, pl* **-wiches** [-dwitʃes, -gwi-] : sandwich
saneamiento *nm* : sanitation
sangrar *vt* **1** : bleed **2** : indent (a paragraph) — *vi* : bleed — **sangrante** *adj* : bleeding — **sangre** *nf* **1** : blood **2 a ~ fría** : in cold blood — **sangriento, -ta** *adj* : bloody
sanguijuela *nf* : leech
sanguinario, -ria *adj* : bloodthirsty — **sanguíneo, -nea** *adj* : blood
sano, -na *adj* **1** : healthy **2** : (morally) wholesome **3** ENTERO : intact **4 sano y salvo** : safe and sound — **sanidad** *nf* **1** : health **2** : public health, sanitation — **sanitario, -ria** *adj* : sanitary, health — **sanitario** *nm Lat* : toilet
santiamén *nm* **en un ~** : in no time at all
santo, -ta *adj* **1** : holy **2 Santo, Santa** (**San** *before masculine names except those beginning with D or T*) : Saint — **~** *n* : saint — **santo** *nm* **1** : saint's day **2** *Lat* : birthday — **santidad** *nf* : holiness, sanctity — **santiguarse** {10} *vr* : cross oneself — **santuario** *nm* : sanctuary
saña *nf* **1** : fury **2** BRUTALIDAD : viciousness
sapo *nm* : toad
saque *nm* : serve (in tennis, etc.), throw-in (in soccer)
saquear *vt* : sack, loot — **saqueador, -dora** *n* : looter — **saqueo** *nm* : sacking, looting
sarampión *nm* : measles *pl*
sarape *nm Lat* : serape
sarcasmo *nm* : sarcasm — **sarcástico, -ca** *adj* : sarcastic
sardina *nf* : sardine
sardónico, -ca *adj* : sardonic
sargento *nmf* : sergeant
sarpullido *nm* : rash
sartén *nmf, pl* **-tenes** : frying pan
sastre, -tra *n* : tailor — **sastrería** *nf* **1** : tailoring **2** : tailor's shop
Satanás *nm* : Satan — **satánico, -ca** *adj* : satanic
satélite *nm* : satellite
sátira *nf* : satire — **satírico, -ca** *adj* : satirical
satisfacer {74} *vt* **1** : satisfy **2** CUMPLIR : fulfill, meet **3** PAGAR : pay — **satisfacerse** *vr* **1** : be satisfied **2** VENGARSE : take revenge — **satisfacción** *nf, pl* **-ciones** : satisfaction — **satisfactorio, -ria** *adj* : satisfactory — **satisfecho, -cha** *adj* : satisfied
saturar *vt* : saturate — **saturación** *nf, pl* **-ciones** : saturation
Saturno *nm* : Saturn
sauce *nm* : willow
sauna *nmf* : sauna
savia *nf* : sap
saxofón *nm, pl* **-fones** : saxophone
sazón *nf, pl* **-zones 1** : seasoning **2** MADUREZ : ripeness **3 a la ~** : at that time, then **4 en ~** : ripe, in season — **sazonar** *vt* : season
se *pron* **1** (*reflexive*) : himself, herself, itself, oneself, yourself, yourselves, themselves **2** (*indirect object*) : (to) him, (to) her, (to) you, (to) them **3** : each other, one another **4 ~ dice que** : it is said that **5 ~ habla inglés** : English spoken
sebo *nm* **1** : fat **2** : tallow (for candles, etc.) **3** : suet (for cooking)
secar {72} *v* : dry — **secarse** *vr* : dry (up) — **secador** *nm* : hair dryer — **secadora** *nf* : (clothes) dryer
sección *nf, pl* **-ciones** : section
seco, -ca *adj* **1** : dry **2** : dried (of fruits, etc.) **3** TAJANTE : sharp, brusque **4** *fam* : thin, skinny **5 a secas** : simply, just **6 en seco** : suddenly
secretar *vt* : secrete — **secreción** *nf, pl* **-ciones** : secretion
secretario, -ria *n* : secretary — **secretaría** *nf* : secretariat
secreto, -ta *adj* : secret — **secreto** *nm* **1** : secret **2 en ~** : in confidence
secta *nf* : sect
sector *nm* : sector
secuaz *nmf, pl* **-cuaces** : follower, henchman
secuela *nf* : consequence
secuencia *nf* : sequence
secuestrar *vt* **1** : kidnap **2** : hijack (an airplane, etc.) **3** EMBARGAR : confiscate, seize — **secuestrador, -dora** *n* **1** : kidnapper **2** : hijacker (of an airplane, etc.) — **secuestro** *nm* **1** : kidnapping **2** : hijacking (of an airplane, etc.) **3** : seizure (of goods)
secular *adj* : secular
secundar *vt* : support, second — **secundario, -ria** *adj* : secondary
sed *nf* **1** : thirst **2 tener ~** : be thirsty
seda *nf* : silk
sedal *nm* : fishing line
sedar *vt* : sedate — **sedante** *adj & nm* : sedative
sede *nf* **1** : seat, headquarters **2 Santa Sede** : Holy See
sedentario, -ria *adj* : sedentary
sedición *nf, pl* **-ciones** : sedition — **sedicioso, -sa** *adj* : seditious
sediento, -ta *adj* : thirsty
sedimento *nm* : sediment

sedoso, -sa *adj* : silky, silken
seducir {61} *vt* **1** : seduce **2** ATRAER : captivate, charm — **seducción** *nf, pl* **-ciones** : seduction — **seductor, -tora** *adj* **1** : seductive **2** ENCANTADOR : charming — ~ *n* : seducer
segar {49} *vt* : reap — **segador, -dora** *n* : reaper, harvester
seglar *adj* : lay, secular — ~ *nm* : layperson, layman *m*, laywoman *f*
segmento *nm* : segment
segregar {52} *vt* : segregate — **segregación** *nf, pl* **-ciones** : segregation
seguir {75} *vt* : follow — *vi* : go on, continue — **seguida**: **en** ~ *adv phr* : right away — **seguido** *adv* **1** : straight (ahead) **2** *Lat* : often — **seguido, -da** *adj* **1** : continuous **2** CONSECUTIVO : consecutive — **seguidor, -dora** *n* : follower
según *prep* : according to — ~ *adv* : it depends — ~ *conj* : as, just as
segundo, -da *adj* : second — ~ *n* : second (one) — **segundo** *nm* : second (unit of time)
seguro, -ra *adj* **1** : safe **2** FIRME : secure **3** CIERTO : sure, certain **4** FIABLE : reliable — **seguramente** *adv* : for sure, surely — **seguridad** *nf* **1** : safety **2** GARANTÍA : security **3** CERTEZA : certainty **4** CONFIANZA : confidence — **seguro** *adv* : certainly — ~ *nm* **1** : insurance **2** : safety (device)
seis *adj & nm* : six — **seiscientos, -tas** *adj* : six hundred — **seiscientos** *nms & pl* : six hundred
seísmo *nm* : earthquake
selección *nf, pl* **-ciones** : selection — **seleccionar** *vt* : select, choose — **selectivo, -va** *adj* : selective — **selecto, -ta** *adj* : choice, select
sellar *vt* **1** : seal **2** TIMBRAR : stamp — **sello** *nm* **1** : seal **2** TIMBRE : stamp **3** *or* ~ **distintivo** : hallmark
selva *nf* **1** : jungle **2** BOSQUE : forest
semáforo *nm* : traffic light
semana *nf* : week — **semanal** *adj* : weekly — **semanario** *nm* : weekly
semántica *nf* : semantics — **semántico, -ca** *adj* : semantic
semblante *nm* **1** : countenance, face **2** APARIENCIA : look
sembrar {55} *vt* **1** : sow **2** ~ **de** : strew with
semejar *vi* : resemble — **semejarse** *vr* : look alike — **semejante** *adj* **1** : similar **2** TAL : such — ~ *nm* : fellowman — **semejanza** *nf* : similarity
semen *nm* : semen — **semental** *nm* **1** : stud **2** **caballo** ~ : stallion
semestre *nm* : semester
semiconductor *nm* : semiconductor
semifinal *nf* : semifinal
semilla *nf* : seed — **semillero** *nm* **1** : nursery (for plants) **2** HERVIDERO : hotbed, breeding ground
seminario *nm* **1** : seminary **2** CURSO : seminar, course
sémola *nf* : semolina
senado *nm* : senate — **senador, -dora** *n* : senator
sencillo, -lla *adj* **1** : simple **2** ÚNICO : single — **sencillez** *nf* : simplicity
senda *nf or* **sendero** *nm* : path, way
sendos, -das *adj pl* : each, both
senil *adj* : senile
seno *nm* **1** : breast, bosom **2** : sinus (in anatomy) **3** ~ **materno** : womb
sensación *nf, pl* **-ciones** : feeling, sensation — **sensacional** *adj* : sensational — **sensacionalista** *adj* : sensationalistic, lurid
sensato, -ta *adj* : sensible — **sensatez** *nf* : good sense
sensible *adj* **1** : sensitive **2** APRECIABLE : considerable, significant — **sensibilidad** *nf* : sensitivity — **sensitivo, -va** *or* **sensorial** *adj* : sense, sensory
sensual *adj* : sensual, sensuous — **sensualidad** *nf* : sensuality
sentar {55} *vt* **1** : seat, sit **2** ESTABLECER : establish, set — *vi* **1** : suit **2** ~ **bien a** : agree with (of food or drink) — **sentarse** *vr* : sit (down) — **sentado, -da** *adj* **1** : sitting, seated **2** **dar por sentado** : take for granted
sentencia *nf* **1** FALLO : sentence, judgment **2** MÁXIMA : saying — **sentenciar** *vt* : sentence
sentido, -da *adj* **1** : heartfelt, sincere **2** SENSIBLE : touchy, sensitive — **sentido** *nm* **1** : sense **2** CONOCIMIENTO : consciousness **3** DIRECCIÓN : direction **4** **doble** ~ : double entendre **5** ~ **común** : common sense **6** ~ **del humor** : sense of humor **7** ~ **único** : one-way
sentimiento *nm* **1** : feeling, emotion **2** PESAR : regret — **sentimental** *adj* : sentimental — **sentimentalismo** *nm* : sentimentality
sentir {76} *vt* **1** : feel **2** OÍR : hear **3** LAMENTAR : be sorry for **4** **lo siento** : I'm sorry — *vi* : feel — **sentirse** *vr* : feel
seña *nf* **1** : sign **2** ~**s** *nfpl* DIRECCIÓN : address **3** ~**s particulares** : distinguishing marks
señal *nf* **1** : signal **2** AVISO, INDICIO : sign **3** DEPÓSITO : deposit **4** **dar** ~**es**

de : show signs of **5 en ~ de** : as a token of — **señalado, -da** *adj* : notable — **señalar** *vt* **1** INDICAR : indicate, point out **2** MARCAR : mark **3** FIJAR : fix, set — **señalarse** *vr* : distinguish oneself

señor, -ñora *n* **1** : gentleman *m*, man *m*, lady *f*, woman *f* **2** : Sir *m*, Madam *f* **3** : Mr. *m*, Mrs. *f* **4 señora** : wife *f* **5 el Señor** : the Lord — **señorial** *adj* : stately — **señorita** *nf* **1** : young lady, young woman **2** : Miss

señuelo *nm* **1** : decoy **2** TRAMPA : bait, lure

separar *vt* **1** : separate **2** QUITAR : detach, remove **3** APARTAR : move away **4** DESTITUIR : dismiss — **separarse** *vr* **1** APARTARSE : separate **2** : part company — **separación** *nf, pl* **-ciones** : separation — **separado, -da** *adj* **1** : separate **2** : separated (of persons) **3 por separado** : separately

septentrional *adj* : northern

séptico, -ca *adj* : septic

septiembre *nm* : September

séptimo, -ma *adj* : seventh — **~** *n* : seventh

sepulcro *nm* : tomb, sepulchre — **sepultar** *vt* : bury — **sepultura** *nf* **1** : burial **2** TUMBA : grave

sequedad *nf* : dryness — **sequía** *nf* : drought

séquito *nm* : retinue, entourage

ser {77} *vi* **1** : be **2 a no ~ que** : unless **3 ¿cuánto es?** : how much is it? **4 es más** : what's more **5 ~ de** : belong to **6 ~ de** : come from **7 son las diez** : it's ten o'clock — **~** *nm* **1** ENTE : being **2 ~ humano** : human being

serbio, -bia *adj* : Serb, Serbian

serenar *vt* : calm — **serenarse** *vr* : calm down — **serenata** *nf* : serenade — **serenidad** *nf* : serenity — **sereno, -na** *adj* **1** : serene, calm **2** : fair, clear (of weather) — **sereno** *nm* : night watchman

serie *nf* **1** : series **2 fabricación en ~** : mass production **3 fuera de ~** : extraordinary — **serial** *nm* : serial

serio, -ria *adj* **1** : serious **2** RESPONSABLE : reliable **3 en serio** : seriously — **seriedad** *nf* : seriousness

sermón *nm, pl* **-mones** : sermon — **sermonear** *vt* : lecture, reprimand

serpentear *vi* : twist, wind — **serpiente** *nf* **1** : serpent, snake **2 ~ de cascabel** : rattlesnake

serrado, -da *adj* : serrated

serrano, -na *adj* **1** : mountain **2 jamón serrano** : cured ham

serrar {55} *vt* : saw — **serrín** *nm, pl* **-rrines** : sawdust — **serrucho** *nm* : saw, handsaw

servicio *nm* **1** : service **2 ~s** *nmpl* : restroom — **servicial** *adj* : obliging, helpful — **servidor, -dora** *n* **1** : servant **2 su seguro servidor** : yours truly — **servidumbre** *nf* **1** : servitude **2** CRIADOS : help, servants *pl* — **servil** *adj* : servile

servilleta *nf* : napkin

servir {54} *vt* : serve — *vi* **1** : work, function **2** VALER : be of use — **servirse** *vr* **1** : help oneself **2 sírvase sentarse** : please have a seat

sesenta *adj & nm* : sixty

sesgo *nm* : bias, slant

sesión *nf, pl* **-siones 1** : session **2** : showing (of a film), performance (of a play)

seso *nm* : brain — **sesudo, -da** *adj* **1** : sensible **2** *fam* : brainy

seta *nf* : mushroom

setecientos, -tas *adj* : seven hundred — **setecientos** *nms & pl* : seven hundred

setenta *adj & nm* : seventy

setiembre *nm* → **septiembre**

seto *nm* **1** : fence **2 ~ vivo** : hedge

seudónimo *nm* : pseudonym

severo, -ra *adj* **1** : harsh, severe **2** : strict (of a teacher, etc.) — **severidad** *nf* : severity

sexagésimo, -ma *adj & n* : sixtieth

sexo *nm* : sex — **sexismo** *nm* : sexism — **sexista** *adj & nmf* : sexist

sexteto *nm* : sextet

sexto, -ta *adj & n* : sixth

sexual *adj* : sexual — **sexualidad** *nf* : sexuality

sexy *adj, pl* **sexy** *or* **sexys** : sexy

si *conj* **1** : if **2** (*in indirect questions*) : whether **3 ~ bien** : although **4 ~ no** : otherwise, or else

sí[1] *adv* **1** : yes **2 creo que ~** : I think so **3 porque ~** *fam* : (just) because — **~** *nm* : consent

sí[2] *pron* **1 de por ~** *or* **en ~** : by itself, in itself, per se **2 fuera de ~** : beside oneself **3 para ~ (mismo)** : to himself, to herself, for himself, for herself **4 entre ~** : among themselves

sico- → **psico-**

SIDA *or* **sida** *nm* : AIDS

siderurgia *nf* : iron and steel industry

sidra *nf* : (hard) cider

siega *nf* **1** : harvesting **2** : harvest (time)

siembra *nf* **1** : sowing **2** : sowing season

siempre *adv* **1** : always **2** *Lat* : still **3 para ~** : forever, for good **4 ~ que** : whenever, every time **5 ~ que** *or* **~ y cuando** : provided that
sien *nf* : temple
sierra *nf* **1** : saw **2** CORDILLERA : mountain range **3 la ~** : the mountains *pl*
siervo, -va *n* : slave
siesta *nf* : nap, siesta
siete *adj & nm* : seven
sífilis *nf* : syphilis
sifón *nm, pl* **-fones** : siphon
sigilo *nm* : secrecy
sigla *nf* : acronym, abbreviation
siglo *nm* **1** : century **2 hace ~s** : for ages
significar {72} *vt* **1** : mean, signify **2** EXPRESAR : express — **significación** *nf, pl* **-ciones 1** : significance, importance **2** : meaning (of a word, etc.) — **significado, -da** *adj* : well-known — **significado** *nm* : meaning — **significativo, -va** *adj* : significant
signo *nm* **1** : sign **2 ~ de admiración** : exclamation point **3 ~ de interrogación** : question mark
siguiente *adj* : next, following
sílaba *nf* : syllable
silbar *v* **1** : whistle **2** ABUCHEAR : hiss, boo — **silbato** *nm* : whistle — **silbido** *nm* **1** : whistle, whistling **2** ABUCHEO : hiss, booing
silenciar *vt* : silence — **silenciador** *nm* : muffler — **silencio** *nm* : silence — **silencioso, -sa** *adj* : silent, quiet
silicio *nm* : silicon
silla *nf* **1** : chair **2** *or* **~ de montar** : saddle **3 ~ de ruedas** : wheelchair — **sillón** *nm, pl* **-llones** : armchair, easy chair
silo *nm* : silo
silueta *nf* **1** : silhouette **2** CONTORNO : outline, shape
silvestre *adj* : wild
silvicultura *nf* : forestry
símbolo *nm* : symbol — **simbólico, -ca** *adj* : symbolic — **simbolismo** *nm* : symbolism — **simbolizar** {21} *vt* : symbolize
simetría *nf* : symmetry — **simétrico, -ca** *adj* : symmetrical, symmetric
simiente *nf* : seed
símil *nm* **1** : simile **2** COMPARACIÓN : comparison — **similar** *adj* : similar, alike
simio *nm* : ape
simpatía *nf* **1** : liking, affection **2** AMABILIDAD : friendliness — **simpático, -ca** *adj* **1** : nice, likeable **2** AMABLE : pleasant, kind — **simpatizante** *nmf* : sympathizer — **simpatizar** {21} *vi* **1** : get along, hit it off **2 ~ con** : sympathize with
simple *adj* **1** SENCILLO : simple **2** MERO : pure, sheer **3** TONTO : simpleminded — **~** *n* : fool, simpleton — **simpleza** *nf* **1** : simpleness **2** TONTERÍA : silly thing — **simplicidad** *nf* : simplicity — **simplificar** {72} *vt* : simplify
simposio *or* **simposium** *nm* : symposium
simular *vt* **1** : simulate **2** FINGIR : feign — **simulacro** *nm* : simulation, drill
simultáneo, -nea *adj* : simultaneous
sin *prep* **1** : without **2 ~ que** : without
sinagoga *nf* : synagogue
sincero, -ra *adj* : sincere — **sinceramente** *adv* : sincerely — **sinceridad** *nf* : sincerity
síncopa *nf* : syncopation
sincronizar {21} *vt* : synchronize
sindicato *nm* : (labor) union — **sindical** *adj* : union, labor
síndrome *nm* : syndrome
sinfín *nm* **1** : endless number **2 un ~ de** : no end of
sinfonía *nf* : symphony — **sinfónico, -ca** *adj* : symphonic
singular *adj* **1** : exceptional, outstanding **2** PECULIAR : peculiar **3** : singular (in grammar) — **~** *nm* : singular — **singularizar** {21} *vt* : single out — **singularizarse** *vr* : stand out
siniestro, -tra *adj* **1** : sinister **2** IZQUIERDO : left — **siniestro** *nm* : disaster
sinnúmero *nm* → **sinfín**
sino *conj* **1** : but, rather **2** EXCEPTO : except, save
sinónimo, -ma *adj* : synonymous — **sinónimo** *nm* : synonym
sinopsis *nfs & pl* : synopsis
sinrazón *nf, pl* **-zones** : wrong
síntaxis *nfs & pl* : syntax
síntesis *nfs & pl* : synthesis — **sintético, -ca** *adj* : synthetic — **sintetizar** {21} *vt* **1** : synthesize **2** RESUMIR : summarize
síntoma *nm* : symptom — **sintomático, -ca** *adj* : symptomatic
sintonía *nf* **1** : tuning in (of a radio) **2 en ~ con** : in tune with — **sintonizar** {21} *vt* : tune (in) to
sinuoso, -sa *adj* : winding
sinvergüenza *nmf* : scoundrel
sionismo *nm* : Zionism
siquiera *adv* **1** : at least **2 ni ~** : not even — **~** *conj* : even if
sirena *nf* **1** : mermaid **2** : siren (of an ambulance, etc.)
sirio, -ria *adj* : Syrian

sirviente, -ta *n* : servant, maid *f*
sisear *vi* : hiss — **siseo** *nm* : hiss
sismo *nm* : earthquake — **sísmico, -ca** *adj* : seismic
sistema *nm* **1** : system **2 por ~** : systematically — **sistemático, -ca** *adj* : systematic
sitiar *vt* : besiege
sitio *nm* **1** : place, site **2** ESPACIO : room, space **3** CERCO : siege **4 en cualquier ~** : anywhere
situar {3} *vt* : situate, place — **situarse** *vr* **1** : be located **2** ESTABLECERSE : get oneself established — **situación** *nf, pl* **-ciones** : situation, position — **situado, -da** *adj* : situated, placed
slip *nm* : briefs *pl*, underpants *pl*
smoking *nm* : tuxedo
so *prep* : under
sobaco *nm* : armpit
sobar *vt* **1** : finger, handle **2** : knead (dough) — **sobado, -da** *adj* : worn, shabby
soberanía *nf* : sovereignty — **soberano, -na** *adj & n* : sovereign
soberbia *nf* : pride, arrogance — **soberbio, -bia** *adj* : proud, arrogant
sobornar *vt* : bribe — **soborno** *nm* **1** : bribe **2** : (action of) bribery
sobrar *vi* **1** : be more than enough **2** RESTAR : be left over — **sobra** *nf* **1** : surplus **2 de ~** : to spare **3 ~s** *nfpl* : leftovers — **sobrado, -da** *adj* : more than enough — **sobrante** *adj* : remaining
sobre[1] *nm* : envelope
sobre[2] *prep* **1** : on, on top of **2** POR ENCIMA DE : over, above **3** ACERCA DE : about **4 ~ todo** : especially, above all
sobrecama *nmf Lat* : bedspread
sobrecargar {52} *vt* : overload, overburden
sobrecoger {15} *vt* : startle — **sobrecogerse** *vr* : be startled
sobrecubierta *nf* : dust jacket
sobredosis *nfs & pl* : overdose
sobreentender {56} *vt* : infer, understand — **sobreentenderse** *vr* : be understood
sobreestimar *vt* : overestimate
sobregiro *nm* : overdraft
sobrellevar *vt* : endure, bear
sobremesa *nf* **de ~** : after-dinner
sobrenatural *adj* : supernatural
sobrenombre *nm* : nickname
sobrentender → **sobreentender**
sobrepasar *vt* : exceed
sobreponer {60} *vt* **1** : superimpose **2** ANTEPONER : put before — **sobreponerse** *vr* **~ a** : overcome
sobresalir {73} *vi* **1** : protrude **2** DESTACARSE : stand out — **sobresaliente** *adj* : outstanding
sobresaltar *vt* : startle — **sobresaltarse** *vr* : start, jump up — **sobresalto** *nm* : fright
sobrestimar → **sobreestimar**
sobretodo *nm* : overcoat
sobrevenir {87} *vi* : happen, ensue
sobrevivencia *nf* → **supervivencia**
sobreviviente *adj & nmf* → **superviviente**
sobrevivir *vi* : survive — *vt* : outlive
sobrevolar {19} *vt* : fly over
sobriedad *nf* **1** : sobriety **2** MODERACIÓN : restraint
sobrino, -na *n* : nephew *m*, niece *f*
sobrio, -bria *adj* : sober
socarrón, -rrona *adj, mpl* **-rrones** : sarcastic
socavar *vt* : undermine
sociable *adj* : sociable — **social** *adj* : social — **socialismo** *nm* : socialism — **socialista** *adj & nmf* : socialist — **sociedad** *nf* **1** : society **2** EMPRESA : company **3 ~ anónima** : incorporated company — **socio, -cia** *n* **1** : partner **2** MIEMBRO : member — **sociología** *nf* : sociology — **sociólogo, -ga** *n* : sociologist
socorrer *vt* : help — **socorrista** *nmf* : lifeguard — **socorro** *nm* : help
soda *nf* : soda (water)
sodio *nf* : sodium
sofá *nm* : couch, sofa
sofisticación *nf, pl* **-ciones** : sophistication — **sofisticado, -da** *adj* : sophisticated
sofocar {72} *vt* **1** : suffocate, smother **2** : put out (a fire), stifle (a rebellion, etc.) — **sofocarse** *vr* **1** : suffocate **2** *fam* : get upset — **sofocante** *adj* : suffocating, stifling
sofreír {66} *vt* : sauté
soga *nf* : rope
soja *nf* → **soya**
sojuzgar *vt* : subdue, subjugate
sol *nm* **1** : sun **2 hacer ~** : be sunny
solamente *adv* : only, just
solapa *nf* **1** : lapel (of a jacket) **2** : flap (of an envelope) — **solapado, -da** *adj* : secret, underhanded
solar[1] *adj* : solar, sun
solar[2] *nm* : lot, site
solariego, -ga *adj* : ancestral
solaz *nm, pl* **-laces 1** : solace **2** DESCANSO : relaxation — **solazarse** {21} *vr* : relax
soldado *nm* **1** : soldier **2 ~ raso** : private
soldar {19} *vt* : weld, solder — **solda-**

dor *nm* : soldering iron — **soldador, -dora** *n* : welder
soleado, -da *adj* : sunny
soledad *nf* : loneliness, solitude
solemne *adj* : solemn — **solemnidad** *nf* : solemnity
soler {78} *vi* **1** : be in the habit of **2** **suele llegar tarde** : he usually arrives late
solicitar *vt* **1** : request, solicit **2** : apply for (a job, etc.) — **solicitante** *nmf* : applicant — **solícito, -ta** *adj* : solicitous, obliging — **solicitud** *nf* **1** : concern **2** PETICIÓN : request **3** : application (for a job, etc.)
solidaridad *nf* : solidarity
sólido, -da *adj* **1** : solid **2** : sound (of an argument, etc.) — **sólido** *nm* : solid — **solidez** *nf* : solidity — **solidificar** {72} *vt* : solidify — **solidificarse** *vr* : solidify, harden
soliloquio *nm* : soliloquy
solista *nmf* : soloist
solitario, -ria *adj* **1** : solitary **2** AISLADO : lonely, deserted — **~** *n* : recluse — **solitaria** *nf* : tapeworm — **solitario** *nm* : solitaire
sollozar {21} *vi* : sob — **sollozo** *nm* : sob
solo, -la *adj* **1** : alone **2** AISLADO : lonely **3** **a solas** : alone, by oneself — **solo** *nm* : solo
sólo *adv* : just, only
solomillo *nm* : sirloin
solsticio *nm* : solstice
soltar {19} *vt* **1** : release **2** DEJAR CAER : let go of, drop **3** DESATAR : unfasten, undo — **soltarse** *vr* **1** : break free **2** DESATARSE : come undone
soltero, -ra *adj* : single, unmarried — **~** *n* **1** : bachelor *m*, single woman *f* **2** **apellido de soltera** : maiden name
soltura *nf* **1** : looseness **2** : fluency (in language) **3** AGILIDAD : agility, ease
soluble *adj* : soluble
solución *nf, pl* **-ciones** : solution — **solucionar** *vt* : solve, resolve
solventar *vt* **1** : settle, pay **2** RESOLVER : resolve — **solvente** *adj & nm* : solvent
sombra *nf* **1** : shadow **2** : shade (of a tree, etc.) **3** **~s** *nfpl* : darkness, shadows — **sombreado, -da** *adj* : shady
sombrero *nm* : hat
sombrilla *nf* : parasol, umbrella
sombrío, -bría *adj* : dark, somber, gloomy
somero, -ra *adj* : superficial
someter *vt* **1** : subjugate **2** SUBORDINAR : subordinate **3** : subject (to treatment, etc.) **4** PRESENTAR : submit, present — **someterse** *vr* **1** : submit, yield **2** **~ a** : undergo
somnífero, -ra *adj* : soporific — **somnífero** *nm* : sleeping pill — **somnoliento, -ta** *adj* : drowsy, sleepy
somos → **ser**
son[1] → **ser**
son[2] *nm* **1** : sound **2** **en ~ de** : as, in the manner of
sonajero *nm* : (baby's) rattle
sonámbulo, -la *n* : sleepwalker
sonar {19} *vi* **1** : sound **2** : ring (as a bell) **3** : look or sound familiar **4** **~ a** : sound like — **sonarse** *vr or* **~ las narices** : blow one's nose
sonata *nf* : sonata
sondear *vt* **1** : sound, probe **2** : survey, sound out (opinions, etc.) — **sondeo** *nm* **1** : sounding, probing **2** ENCUESTA : survey, poll
soneto *nm* : sonnet
sónico, -ca *adj* : sonic
sonido *nm* : sound
sonoro, -ra *adj* **1** : resonant, sonorous **2** RUIDOSO : loud
sonreír {66} *vi* : smile — **sonreírse** *vr* : smile — **sonriente** *adj* : smiling — **sonrisa** *nf* : smile
sonrojar *vt* : cause to blush — **sonrojarse** *vr* : blush — **sonrojo** *nm* : blush
sonrosado, -da *adj* : rosy, pink
sonsacar {72} *vt* : wheedle (out)
soñar {19} *v* **1** : dream **2** **~ con** : dream about **3** **~ despierto** : daydream — **soñador, -dora** *adj* : dreamy — **~** *n* : dreamer — **soñoliento, -ta** *adj* : sleepy, drowsy
sopa *nf* : soup
sopesar *vt* : weigh, consider
soplar *vi* : blow — *vt* : blow out, blow off, blow up — **soplete** *nm* : blowtorch — **soplo** *nm* : puff, gust
soplón, -plona *n, pl* **-plones** *fam* : sneak
sopor *nm* : drowsiness — **soporífero, -ra** *adj* : soporific
soportar *vt* **1** SOSTENER : support **2** AGUANTAR : bear — **soporte** *nm* : support
soprano *nmf* : soprano
sor *nf* : Sister (in religion)
sorber *vt* **1** : sip **2** ABSORBER : absorb **3** CHUPAR : suck up — **sorbete** *nm* : sherbet — **sorbo** *nm* **1** : sip, swallow **2** **beber a ~s** : sip
sordera *nf* : deafness
sórdido, -da *adj* : sordid, squalid
sordo, -da *adj* **1** : deaf **2** : muted (of a

sound) — **sordomudo, -da** *n* : deaf-mute

sorna *nf* : sarcasm

sorprender *vt* : surprise — **sorprenderse** *vr* : be surprised — **sorprendente** *adj* : surprising — **sorpresa** *nf* : surprise

sortear *vt* **1** : raffle off, draw lots for **2** ESQUIVAR : dodge — **sorteo** *nm* : drawing, raffle

sortija *nf* **1** : ring **2** : ringlet (of hair)

sortilegio *nm* **1** HECHIZO : spell **2** HECHICERÍA : sorcery

sosegar {49} *vt* : calm, pacify — **sosegarse** *vr* : calm down — **sosegado, -da** *adj* : calm, tranquil — **sosiego** *nm* : calm

soslayo: **de ~** *adv phr* : obliquely, sideways

soso, -sa *adj* **1** : insipid, tasteless **2** ABURRIDO : dull

sospechar *vt* : suspect — **sospecha** *nf* : suspicion — **sospechoso, -sa** *adj* : suspicious — **~** *n* : suspect

sostener {80} *vt* **1** : support **2** SUJETAR : hold **3** MANTENER : sustain, maintain — **sostenerse** *vr* **1** : stand (up) **2** CONTINUAR : remain **3** SUSTENTARSE : support oneself — **sostén** *nm, pl* **-tenes 1** APOYO : support **2** SUSTENTO : sustenance **3** : brassiere, bra — **sostenido, -da** *adj* **1** : sustained **2** : sharp (in music) — **sostenido** *nm* : sharp

sótano *nm* : basement

soterrar {55} *vt* **1** : bury **2** ESCONDER : hide

soto *nm* : grove

soviético, -ca *adj* : Soviet

soy → **ser**

soya *nf* : soy

Sr. *nm* : Mr. — **Sra.** *nf* : Mrs., Ms. — **Srta.** *or* **Srita.** *nf* : Miss, Ms.

su *adj* **1** : his, her, its, their, one's **2** (*formal*) : your

suave *adj* **1** : soft **2** LISO : smooth **3** APACIBLE : gentle, mild — **suavidad** *nf* **1** : softness, smoothness **2** APACIBILIDAD : mildness, gentleness — **suavizar** {21} *vt* : soften, smooth

subalimentado, -da *adj* : undernourished, underfed

subalterno, -na *adj* **1** SUBORDINADO : subordinate **2** SECUNDARIO : secondary — **~** *n* : subordinate

subarrendar {55} *vt* : sublet

subasta *nf* : auction — **subastar** *vt* : auction (off)

subcampeón, -peona *n, mpl* **-peones** : runner-up

subcomité *nm* : subcommittee

subconsciente *adj & nm* : subconscious

subdesarrollado, -da *adj* : underdeveloped

subdirector, -tora *n* : assistant manager

súbdito, -ta *n* : subject

subdividir *vt* : subdivide — **subdivisión** *nf, pl* **-siones** : subdivision

subestimar *vt* : underestimate

subir *vt* **1** : climb, go up **2** LLEVAR : bring up, take up **3** AUMENTAR : raise — *vi* **1** : go up, come up **2 ~ a** : get in (a car), get on (a bus, etc.) — **subirse** *vr* **1** : climb (up) **2 ~ a** : get in (a car), get on (a bus, etc.) **3 ~ a la cabeza** : go to one's head — **subida** *nf* **1** : ascent, climb **2** AUMENTO : rise **3** PENDIENTE : slope — **subido, -da** *adj* **1** : bright, strong **2 ~ de tono** : risqué

súbito, -ta *adj* **1** : sudden **2 de súbito** : all of a sudden, suddenly

subjetivo, -va *adj* : subjective

subjuntivo, -va *adj* : subjunctive — **subjuntivo** *nm* : subjunctive (case)

sublevar *vt* : stir up, incite to rebellion — **sublevarse** *vr* : rebel — **sublevación** *nf, pl* **-ciones** : uprising, rebellion

sublime *adj* : sublime

submarino, -na *adj* : underwater — **submarino** *nm* : submarine — **submarinismo** *nm* : scuba diving

subordinar *vt* : subordinate — **subordinado, -da** *adj & n* : subordinate

subproducto *nm* : by-product

subrayar *vt* **1** : underline **2** ENFATIZAR : emphasize, stress

subrepticio, -cia *adj* : surreptitious

subsanar *vt* **1** : rectify, correct **2** : make up for (a deficiency), overcome (an obstacle)

subscribir → **suscribir**

subsidio *nm* : subsidy, benefit

subsiguiente *adj* : subsequent

subsistir *vi* **1** : live, subsist **2** SOBREVIVIR : survive — **subsistencia** *nf* : subsistence

substancia *nf* → **sustancia**

subterfugio *nm* : subterfuge

subterráneo, -nea *adj* : underground, subterranean — **subterráneo** *nm* : underground passage

subtítulo *nm* : subtitle

suburbio *nm* **1** : suburb **2** : slum (outside a city) — **suburbano, -na** *adj* : suburban

subvencionar *vt* : subsidize — **sub-**

vención *nf, pl* **-ciones** : subsidy, grant
subvertir {76} *vt* : subvert — **subversión** *nf, pl* **-siones** : subversion — **subversivo, -va** *adj & n* : subversive
subyacente *adj* : underlying
subyugar {52} *vt* : subjugate, subdue
succión *nf, pl* **-ciones** : suction — **succionar** *vt* : suck up, draw in
sucedáneo *nm* : substitute
suceder *vi* **1** : happen, occur **2** ~ **a** : follow **3 suceda lo que suceda** : come what may — **sucesión** *nf, pl* **-siones** : succession — **sucesivo, -va** *adj* : successive — **suceso** *nm* **1** : event **2** INCIDENTE : incident — **sucesor, -sora** *n* : successor
suciedad *nf* **1** : dirtiness **2** MUGRE : dirt, filth
sucinto, -ta *adj* : succinct, concise
sucio, -cia *adj* : dirty, filthy
suculento, -ta *adj* : succulent
sucumbir *vi* : succumb
sucursal *nf* : branch (of a business)
sudadera *nf* : sweatshirt — **sudado, -da** *adj* : sweaty
sudafricano, -na *adj* : South African
sudamericano, -na *adj* : South American
sudar *vi* : sweat
sudeste → **sureste**
sudoeste → **suroeste**
sudor *nm* : sweat — **sudoroso, -sa** *adj* : sweaty
sueco, -ca *adj* : Swedish — **sueco** *nm* : Swedish (language)
suegro, -gra *n* **1** : father-in-law *m*, mother-in-law *f* **2 suegros** *nmpl* : in-laws
suela *nf* : sole (of a shoe)
sueldo *nm* : salary, wage
suelo *nm* **1** : ground **2** : floor (in a house) **3** TIERRA : soil, land
suelto, -ta *adj* : loose, free — **suelto** *nm* : loose change
sueño *nm* **1** : dream **2 coger el** ~ : get to sleep **3 tener** ~ : be sleepy
suero *nm* **1** : whey **2** : serum (in medicine)
suerte *nf* **1** : luck, fortune **2** AZAR : chance **3** DESTINO : fate **4** CLASE : sort, kind **5 por** ~ : luckily **6 tener** ~ : be lucky
suéter *nm* : sweater
suficiencia *nf* **1** CAPACIDAD : competence, proficiency **2** PRESUNCIÓN : smugness — **suficiente** *adj* **1** : enough, sufficient **2** PRESUNTUOSO : smug — **suficientemente** *adv* : enough
sufijo *nm* : suffix
sufragio *nm* : suffrage, vote
sufrir *vt* **1** : suffer **2** SOPORTAR : bear, stand — *vi* : suffer — **sufrido, -da** *adj* **1** : long-suffering **2** : sturdy, serviceable (of clothing) — **sufrimiento** *nm* : suffering
sugerir {76} *vt* : suggest — **sugerencia** *nf* : suggestion — **sugestión** *nf, pl* **-tiones** : suggestion — **sugestionable** *adj* : impressionable — **sugestionar** *vt* : influence — **sugestivo, -va** *adj* **1** : suggestive **2** ESTIMULANTE : interesting, stimulating
suicidio *nm* : suicide — **suicida** *adj* : suicidal — ~ *nmf* : suicide (victim) — **suicidarse** *vr* : commit suicide
suite *nf* : suite
suizo, -za *adj* : Swiss
sujetar *vt* **1** : hold (on to) **2** FIJAR : fasten **3** DOMINAR : subdue — **sujetarse** *vr* **1** ~ **a** : hold on to, cling to **2** ~ **a** : abide by — **sujeción** *nf, pl* **-ciones 1** : fastening **2** DOMINACIÓN : subjection — **sujetador** *nm Spain* : brassiere, bra — **sujetapapeles** *nms & pl* : paper clip — **sujeto, -ta** *adj* **1** : fastened **2** ~ **a** : subject to — **sujeto** *nm* **1** : individual **2** : subject (in grammar)
sulfuro *nm* : sulfur — **sulfúrico, -ca** *adj* : sulfuric
sultán *nm, pl* **-tanes** : sultan
suma *nf* **1** : sum, total **2** : addition (in mathematics) **3 en** ~ : in short — **sumamente** *adv* : extremely — **sumar** *vt* **1** : add (up) **2** TOTALIZAR : add up to, total — *vi* : add up — **sumarse** *vr* ~ **a** : join
sumario, -ria *adj* : concise — **sumario** *nm* **1** : summary **2** : indictment (in law)
sumergir {35} *vt* : submerge, plunge — **sumergirse** *vr* : be submerged — **sumergible** *adj* : waterproof (of a watch, etc.)
sumidero *nm* : drain
suministrar *vt* : supply, provide — **suministro** *nm* : supply, provision
sumir *vt* : plunge, immerse — **sumirse** *vr* ~ **en** : sink into
sumisión *nf, pl* **-siones** : submission — **sumiso, -sa** *adj* : submissive
sumo, -ma *adj* **1** : highest, supreme **2 de suma importancia** : of great importance
suntuoso, -sa *adj* : sumptuous, lavish
super *or* **súper** *nm fam* : supermarket
superabundancia *nf* : overabundance
superar *vt* **1** : surpass, outdo **2** VENCER : overcome — **superarse** *vr* : improve oneself

superávit *nm* : surplus
superestructura *nf* : superstructure
superficie *nf* **1** : surface **2** ÁREA : area — **superficial** *adj* : superficial
superfluo, -flua *adj* : superfluous
superintendente *nmf* : supervisor, superintendent
superior *adj* **1** : superior **2** : upper (of a floor, etc.) **3 ~ a** : above, higher than — ~ *nm* : superior — **superioridad** *nf* : superiority
superlativo, -va *adj* : superlative — **superlativo** *nm* : superlative
supermercado *nm* : supermarket
superpoblado, -da *adj* : overpopulated
supersónico, -ca *adj* : supersonic
superstición *nf, pl* **-ciones** : superstition — **supersticioso, -sa** *adj* : superstitious
supervisar *vt* : supervise, oversee — **supervisión** *nf, pl* **-siones** : supervision — **supervisor, -sora** *n* : supervisor
supervivencia *nf* : survival — **superviviente** *adj* : surviving — ~ *nmf* : survivor
suplantar *vt* : supplant, replace
suplemento *nm* : supplement — **suplementario, -ria** *adj* : supplementary
suplente *adj & nmf* : substitute
suplicar {72} *vt* : beg, entreat — **súplica** *nf* : plea, entreaty
suplicio *nm* : ordeal, torture
suplir *vt* **1** : make up for **2** REEMPLAZAR : replace
supo, etc. → **saber**
suponer {60} *vt* **1** : suppose, assume **2** SIGNIFICAR : mean **3** IMPLICAR : involve, entail — **suposición** *nf, pl* **-ciones** : supposition
supositorio *nm* : suppository
supremo, -ma *adj* : supreme — **supremacía** *nf* : supremacy
suprimir *vt* **1** : suppress, eliminate **2** : delete (text) — **supresión** *nf, pl* **-siones 1** : suppression, elimination **2** : deletion (of text)
supuesto, -ta *adj* **1** : supposed, alleged **2 por supuesto** : of course — **supuesto** *nm* : assumption — **supuestamente** *adv* : allegedly
sur *nm* **1** : south, South **2** : south wind **3 del ~** : south, southerly
surafricano, -na → **sudafricano**
suramericano, -na → **sudamericano**
surcar {72} *vt* **1** : plow (earth) **2** : cut through (air, water, etc.) — **surco** *nm* : groove, furrow, rut
sureño, -ña *adj* : southern, Southern — ~ *n* : Southerner
sureste *adj* **1** : southeast, southeastern **2** : southeasterly (of wind, etc.) — ~ *nm* : southeast, Southeast
surf *or* **surfing** *nm* : surfing
surgir {35} *vi* **1** : arise **2** APARECER : appear — **surgimiento** *nm* : rise, emergence
suroeste *adj* **1** : southwest, southwestern **2** : southwesterly (of wind, etc.) — ~ *nm* : southwest, Southwest
surtir *vt* **1** : supply, provide **2 ~ efecto** : have an effect — **surtirse** *vr* **~ de** : stock up on — **surtido, -da** *adj* **1** : assorted, varied **2** : stocked (with merchandise) — **surtido** *nm* : assortment, selection — **surtidor** *nm* : gas pump
susceptible *adj* **1** : susceptible, sensitive **2 ~ de** : capable of — **susceptibilidad** *nf* : sensitivity
suscitar *vt* : provoke, arouse
suscribir {33} *vt* **1** : sign (a formal document) **2** RATIFICAR : endorse — **suscribirse** *vr* **~ a** : subscribe to — **suscripción** *nf, pl* **-ciones** : subscription — **suscriptor, -tora** *n* : subscriber
susodicho, -cha *adj* : aforementioned
suspender *vt* **1** : suspend **2** COLGAR : hang **3** *Spain* : fail (an exam, etc.) — **suspensión** *nf, pl* **-siones** : suspension — **suspenso** *nm* **1** *Spain* : failure (in an exam, etc.) **2** *Lat* : suspense
suspicaz *adj, pl* **-caces** : suspicious
suspirar *vi* : sigh — **suspiro** *nm* : sigh
sustancia *nf* **1** : substance **2 sin ~** : shallow, lacking substance — **sustancial** *adj* : substantial, significant — **sustancioso, -sa** *adj* : substantial, solid
sustantivo *nm* : noun
sustentar *vt* **1** : support **2** ALIMENTAR : sustain, nourish **3** MANTENER : maintain — **sustentarse** *vr* : support oneself — **sustentación** *nf, pl* **-ciones** : support — **sustento** *nm* **1** : means of support, livelihood **2** ALIMENTO : sustenance
sustituir {41} *vt* : replace, substitute — **sustitución** *nf, pl* **-ciones** : replacement, substitution — **sustituto, -ta** *n* : substitute
susto *nm* : fright, scare
sustraer {81} *vt* **1** : remove, take away **2** : subtract (in mathematics) — **sustraerse** *vr* **~ a** : avoid, evade — **sustracción** *nf, pl* **-ciones** : subtraction
susurrar *vi* **1** : whisper **2** : murmur (of water) **3** : rustle (of leaves, etc.) — *vt* : whisper — **susurro** *nm* **1** : whisper **2**

: murmur (of water) **3** : rustle, rustling (of leaves, etc.)
sutil *adj* **1** : delicate, fine **2** : subtle (of fragrances, differences, etc.) — **sutileza** *nf* : subtlety
sutura *nf* : suture
suyo, -ya *adj* **1** : his, her, its, one's, theirs **2** (*formal*) : yours **3 un primo suyo** : a cousin of his/hers — **~** *pron* **1** : his, hers, its (own), one's own, theirs **2** (*formal*) : yours
switch *nm Lat* : switch

T

t *nf* : t, 21st letter of the Spanish alphabet
taba *nf* : anklebone
tabaco *nm* : tobacco — **tabacalero, -ra** *adj* : tobacco
tábano *nm* : horsefly
taberna *nf* : tavern
tabicar {72} *vt* : wall up — **tabique** *nm* : thin wall, partition
tabla *nf* **1** : board, plank **2** LISTA : table, list **3 ~ de planchar** : ironing board **4 ~s** *nfpl* : stage, boards *pl* — **tablado** *nm* **1** : flooring **2** PLATAFORMA : platform **3** : (theater) stage — **tablero** *nm* **1** : bulletin board **2** : board (in games) **3** PIZARRA : blackboard **4 ~ de instrumentos** : dashboard, instrument panel
tableta *nf* **1** : tablet, pill **2** : bar (of chocolate)
tablilla *nf* : slat — **tablón** *nm, pl* **-lones** **1** : plank, beam **2 ~ de anuncios** : bulletin board
tabú *adj* : taboo — **tabú** *nm, pl* **-búes** *or* **-bús** : taboo
tabular *vt* : tabulate
taburete *nm* : stool
tacaño, -na *adj* : stingy, miserly
tacha *nf* **1** : flaw, defect **2 sin ~** : flawless
tachar *vt* **1** : cross out, delete **2 ~ de** : accuse of, label as
tachón *nm, pl* **-chones** : stud, hobnail — **tachuela** *nf* : tack, hobnail
tácito, -ta *adj* : tacit
taciturno, -na *adj* : taciturn
taco *nm* **1** : stopper, plug **2** *Lat* : heel (of a shoe) **3** : cue (in billiards) **4** : taco (in cooking)
tacón *nm, pl* **-cones** **1** : heel (of a shoe) **2 de ~ alto** : high-heeled
táctica *nf* : tactic, tactics *pl* — **táctico, -ca** *adj* : tactical
tacto *nm* **1** : (sense of) touch, feel **2** DELICADEZA : tact
tafetán *nm, pl* **-tanes** : taffeta
tailandés, -desa *adj* : Thai
taimado, -da *adj* : crafty, sly
tajar *vt* : cut, slice — **tajada** *nf* **1** : slice **2 sacar ~** *fam* : get one's share — **tajante** *adj* : categorical — **tajo** *nm* **1** : cut, gash **2** ESCARPA : steep cliff
tal *adv* **1** : so, in such a way **2 con ~ que** : provided that, as long as **3 ¿qué ~?** : how are you?, how's it going? — **~** *adj* **1** : such, such a **2 ~ vez** : maybe, perhaps — **~** *pron* **1** : such a one, such a thing **2 ~ para cual** : two of a kind
taladrar *vt* : drill — **taladro** *nm* : drill
talante *nm* **1** HUMOR : mood **2** VOLUNTAD : willingness
talar *vt* : cut down, fell
talco *nm* : talcum powder
talego *nm* : sack
talento *nm* : talent — **talentoso, -sa** *adj* : talented
talismán *nm, pl* **-manes** : talisman, charm
talla *nf* **1** : sculpture, carving **2** ESTATURA : height **3** : size (in clothing) — **tallar** *vt* **1** : sculpt, carve **2** : measure (someone's height)
tallarín *nf, pl* **-rines** : noodle
talle *nm* **1** : waist, waistline **2** FIGURA : figure **3** : measurements *pl* (of clothing)
taller *nm* **1** : workshop **2** : studio (of an artist)
tallo *nm* : stalk, stem
talón *nm, pl* **-lones** **1** : heel (of the foot) **2** : stub (of a check) — **talonario** *nm* : checkbook
taltuza *nf* : gopher
tamal *nm* : tamale
tamaño, -ña *adj* : such a, such a big — **tamaño** *nm* **1** : size **2 de ~ natural** : life-size
tambalearse *vr* **1** : teeter, wobble **2** : stagger, totter (of persons)
también *adv* : too, as well, also
tambor *nm* : drum — **tamborilear** *vi* : drum
tamiz *nm* : sieve — **tamizar** {21} *vt* : sift
tampoco *adv* : neither, not either
tampón *nm, pl* **-pones** **1** : tampon **2** : ink pad (for stamping)
tan *adv* **1** : so, so very **2 ~ pronto como** : as soon as **3 ~ sólo** : only, merely

tanda *nf* **1** TURNO : turn, shift **2** GRUPO : batch, lot, series
tangente *nf* : tangent
tangible *adj* : tangible
tango *nm* : tango
tanque *nm* : tank
tantear *vt* **1** : feel, grope **2** SOPESAR : size up, weigh — *vi* : feel one's way — **tanteador** *nm* : scoreboard — **tanteo** *nm* **1** : weighing, sizing up **2** PUNTUACIÓN : scoring (in sports)
tanto *adv* **1** : so much **2** (*in expressions of time*) : so long — ~ *nm* **1** : certain amount **2** : goal, point (in sports) **3 un** ~ : somewhat, rather — **tanto, -ta** *adj* **1** : so much, so many **2** (*in comparisons*) : as much, as many **3** *fam* : however many — ~ *pron* **1** : so much, so many **2 entre** ~ : meanwhile **3 por lo** ~ : therefore
tañer {79} *vt* **1** : ring (a bell) **2** : play (a musical instrument)
tapa *nf* **1** : cover, top, lid **2** *Spain* : snack
tapacubos *nms & pl* : hubcap
tapar *vt* **1** : cover, put a lid on **2** OCULTAR : block out **3** ENCUBRIR : cover up — **tapadera** *nf* **1** : cover, lid **2** : front (to hide a deception)
tapete *nm* **1** : small rug, mat **2** : cover (for a table)
tapia *nf* : (adobe) wall, garden wall — **tapiar** *vt* **1** : wall in **2** : block off (a door, etc.)
tapicería *nf* **1** : upholstery **2** TAPIZ : tapestry — **tapicero, -ra** *n* : upholsterer
tapioca *nf* : tapioca
tapiz *nm, pl* **-pices** : tapestry — **tapizar** {21} *vt* : upholster
tapón *nm, pl* **-pones 1** : cork **2** : cap (for a bottle, etc.) **3** : plug, stopper (for a sink)
tapujo *nm* **sin** ~**s** : openly, outright
taquigrafía *nf* : stenography, shorthand — **taquígrafo, -fa** *n* : stenographer
taquilla *nf* **1** : box office **2** RECAUDACIÓN : earnings *pl,* take — **taquillero, -ra** *adj* **un éxito taquillero** : a box-office hit
tarántula *nf* : tarantula
tararear *vt* : hum
tardar *vi* **1** : take a long time, be late **2 a más** ~ : at the latest — *vt* : take (time) — **tardanza** *nf* : lateness, delay — **tarde** *adv* **1** : late **2** ~ **o temprano** : sooner or later — ~ *nf* **1** : afternoon, evening **2 ¡buenas** ~**s!** : good afternoon!, good evening! **3 en la** ~ *or* **por la** ~ : in the afternoon, in the evening — **tardío, -día** *adj* : late, tardy — **tardo, -da** *adj* : slow
tarea *nf* **1** : task, job **2** : homework (in education)
tarifa *nf* **1** : fare, rate **2** LISTA : price list **3** ARANCEL : duty, tariff
tarima *nf* : platform, stage
tarjeta *nf* **1** : card **2** ~ **de crédito** : credit card **3** ~ **postal** : postcard
tarro *nm* : jar, pot
tarta *nf* **1** : cake **2** TORTA : tart
tartamudear *vi* : stammer, stutter — **tartamudeo** *nm* : stutter, stammer
tartán *nm, pl* **-tanes** : tartan, plaid
tártaro *nm* : tartar
tarugo *nm* **1** : block (of wood) **2** *fam* : blockhead, dunce
tasa *nf* **1** : rate **2** IMPUESTO : tax **3** VALORACIÓN : appraisal — **tasación** *nf, pl* **-ciones** : appraisal — **tasar** *vt* **1** : set the price of **2** VALORAR : appraise, value
tasca *nf* : cheap bar, dive
tatuar {3} *vt* : tattoo — **tatuaje** *nm* : tattoo, tattooing
taurino, -na *adj* : bull, bullfighting — **tauromaquia** *nf* : (art of) bullfighting
taxi *nm, pl* **taxis** : taxi, taxicab — **taxista** *nmf* : taxi driver
taza *nf* **1** : cup **2** : (toilet) bowl — **tazón** *nm, pl* **-zones** : bowl
te *pron* **1** (*direct object*) : you **2** (*indirect object*) : for you, to you, from you **3** (*reflexive*) : yourself, for yourself, to yourself, from yourself
té *nm* : tea
teatro *nm* : theater — **teatral** *adj* : theatrical
techo *nm* **1** : roof **2** : ceiling (of a room) **3** LÍMITE : upper limit, ceiling — **techumbre** *nf* : roofing
tecla *nf* : key (of a musical instrument or a machine) — **teclado** *nm* : keyboard — **teclear** *vt* : type in, enter
técnica *nf* **1** : technique, skill **2** TECNOLOGÍA : technology — **técnico, -ca** *adj* : technical — ~ *n* : technician
tecnología *nf* : technology — **tecnológico, -ca** *adj* : technological
tecolote *nm Lat* : owl
tedio *nm* : boredom — **tedioso, -sa** *adj* : tedious, boring
teja *nf* : tile — **tejado** *nm* : roof
tejer *v* **1** : knit, crochet **2** : weave (on a loom)
tejido *nm* **1** : fabric, cloth **2** : tissue (of the body)
tejón *nm, pl* **-jones** : badger
tela *nf* **1** : fabric, material **2** ~ **de araña** : spiderweb — **telar** *nm* : loom — **telaraña** *nf* : spiderweb, cobweb
tele *nf fam* : TV, television

telecomunicación *nf, pl* **-ciones** : telecommunication
teledifusión *nf, pl* **-siones** : television broadcasting
teledirigido, -da *adj* : remote-controlled
telefonear *v* : telephone, call — **telefónico, -ca** *adj* : telephone — **telefonista** *nmf* : telephone operator — **teléfono** *nm* **1** : telephone **2 llamar por ~** : make a phone call
telegrafiar {85} *v* : telegraph — **telegráfico, -ca** *adj* : telegraphic — **telégrafo** *nm* : telegaph
telegrama *nm* : telegram
telenovela *nf* : soap opera
telepatía *nf* : telepathy — **telepático, -ca** *adj* : telepathic
telescopio *nm* : telescope — **telescópico, -ca** *adj* : telescopic
telespectador, -dora *n* : (television) viewer
telesquí *nm, pl* **-squís** : ski lift
televidente *nmf* : (television) viewer
televisión *nf, pl* **-siones** : television, TV — **televisar** *vt* : televise — **televisor** *nm* : television set
telón *nm, pl* **-lones 1** : curtain (in theater) **2 ~ de fondo** : backdrop, background
tema *nm* : theme
temblar {55} *vi* **1** : tremble, shiver **2** : shake (of a building, the ground, etc.) — **temblor** *nm* **1** : shaking, trembling **2** *or* **~ de tierra** : tremor, earthquake — **tembloroso, -sa** *adj* : trembling, shaky
temer *vt* : fear, dread — *vi* : be afraid — **temerario, -ria** *adj* : reckless — **temeridad** *nf* **1** : recklessness **2** : rash act — **temeroso, -sa** *adj* : fearful — **temor** *nm* : fear, dread
temperamento *nm* : temperament — **temperamental** *adj* : temperamental
temperatura *nf* : temperature
tempestad *nf* : storm — **tempestuoso, -sa** *adj* : stormy
templar *vt* **1** : temper (steel) **2** : moderate (temperature) **3** : tune (a musical instrument) — **templarse** *vr* : warm up, cool down — **templado, -da** *adj* **1** : temperate, mild **2** TIBIO : lukewarm **3** VALIENTE : courageous — **templanza** *nf* **1** : moderation **2** : mildness (of weather)
templo *nm* : temple, synagogue
tempo *nm* : tempo
temporada *nf* **1** : season, time **2** PERÍODO : period, spell — **temporal** *adj* **1** : temporal **2** PROVISIONAL : temporary — **~** *nm* : storm — **temporero, -ra** *n* : temporary or seasonal worker
temporizador *nm* : timer
temprano, -na *adj* : early — **temprano** *adv* : early
tenaz *adj, pl* **-naces** : tenacious — **tenaza** *nf or* **tenazas** *nfpl* **1** : pliers **2** : tongs (for the fireplace, etc.) **3** : claw (of a crustacean)
tendedero *nm* : clothesline
tendencia *nf* : tendency, trend
tender {56} *vt* **1** : spread out, stretch out **2** : hang out (clothes) **3** : lay (cables, etc.) **4** : set (a trap) — *vi* **~ a** : have a tendency towards — **tenderse** *vr* : stretch out, lie down
tendero, -ra *n* : shopkeeper
tendido *nm* **1** : laying (of cables, etc.) **2** : seats *pl*, stand (at a bullfight)
tendón *nm, pl* **-dones** : tendon
tenebroso, -sa *adj* **1** : gloomy, dark **2** SINIESTRO : sinister
tenedor, -dora *n* **1** : holder **2 ~ de libros** : bookkeeper — **tenedor** *nm* : table fork — **teneduría** *nf* **~ de libros** : bookkeeping
tener {80} *vt* **1** : have, possess **2** SUJETAR : hold **3** TOMAR : take **4 ~ frío (hambre,** *etc.)* : be cold (hungry, etc.) **5 ~ ... años** : be ... years old **6 ~ por** : think, consider — *v aux* **1 ~ que** : have to, ought to **2 tenía pensado escribirte** : I've been thinking of writing to you — **tenerse** *vr* **1** : stand up **2 ~ por** : consider oneself
tenería *nf* : tannery
tengo → **tener**
tenia *nf* : tapeworm
teniente *nmf* : lieutenant
tenis *nms & pl* **1** : tennis **2 ~** *nmpl* : sneakers — **tenista** *nmf* : tennis player
tenor *nm* **1** : tenor **2** : tone, sense (in style)
tensar *vt* **1** : tense, make taut **2** : draw (a bow) — **tensarse** *vr* : become tense — **tensión** *nf, pl* **-siones 1** : tension **2 ~ arterial** : blood pressure — **tenso, -sa** *adj* : tense
tentación *nf, pl* **-ciones** : temptation
tentáculo *nm* : tentacle
tentar {55} *vt* **1** : feel, touch **2** ATRAER : tempt — **tentador, -dora** *adj* : tempting
tentativa *nf* : attempt
tentempié *nm fam* : snack
tenue *adj* **1** : tenuous **2** : faint, weak (of sounds) **3** : light, fine (of thread, rain, etc.)
teñir {67} *vt* **1** : dye **2 ~ de** : tinge with
teología *nf* : theology — **teólogo, -ga** *n* : theologian

teorema *nm* : theorem
teoría *nf* : theory — **teórico, -ca** *adj* : theoretical
tequila *nm* : tequila
terapia *nf* **1** : therapy **2** ~ **ocupacional** : occupational therapy — **terapeuta** *nmf* : therapist — **terapéutico, -ca** *adj* : therapeutic
tercermundista *adj* : third-world
tercero, -ra *adj* (**tercer** *before masculine singular nouns*) **1** : third **2 el Tercer Mundo** : the Third World — ~ *n* : third (in a series)
terciar *vt* : sling (sth over one's shoulders), tilt (a hat) — *vi* **1** : intervene **2** ~ **en** : take part in
tercio *nm* : third
terciopelo *nm* : velvet
terco, -ca *adj* : obstinate, stubborn
tergiversar *vt* : distort, twist
termal *adj* : thermal, hot — **termas** *nfpl* : hot springs
terminar *vt* : conclude, finish — *vi* **1** : finish **2** ACABARSE : come to an end — **terminarse** *vr* **1** : run out **2** ACABARSE : come to an end — **terminación** *nf, pl* **-ciones** : termination, conclusion — **terminal** *adj* : terminal, final — ~ *nm* (*in some regions f*) : (electric or electronic) terminal — ~ *nf* (*in some regions m*) : terminal, station — **término** *nm* **1** : end **2** PLAZO : period, term **3** ~ **medio** : happy medium **4** ~**s** *nmpl* : terms — **terminología** *nf* : terminology
termita *nf* : termite
termo *nm* : thermos
termómetro *nm* : thermometer
termóstato *nm* : thermostat
ternero, -ra *n* : calf — **ternera** *nf* : veal
ternura *nf* : tenderness
terquedad *nf* : obstinacy, stubbornness
terracota *nf* : terra-cotta
terraplén *nm, pl* **-plenes** : embankment
terráqueo, -quea *adj* : earth, terrestrial
terrateniente *nmf* : landowner
terraza *nf* **1** : terrace **2** BALCÓN : balcony
terremoto *nm* : earthquake
terreno *nm* **1** : terrain **2** SUELO : earth, ground **3** SOLAR : plot, tract of land — **terreno, -na** *adj* : earthly — **terrestre** *adj* : terrestrial
terrible *adj* : terrible
terrier *nmf* : terrier
territorio *nm* : territory — **territorial** *adj* : territorial
terrón *nm, pl* **-rones 1** : clod (of earth) **2** ~ **de azúcar** : lump of sugar
terror *nm* : terror — **terrorífico, -ca** *adj* : terrifying — **terrorismo** *nm* : terrorism — **terrorista** *adj & nmf* : terrorist
terroso, -sa *adj* : earthy
terso, -sa *adj* **1** : smooth **2** : polished, flowing (of a style) — **tersura** *nf* : smoothness
tertulia *nf* : gathering, group
tesis *nfs & pl* : thesis
tesón *nm* : persistence, tenacity
tesoro *nm* **1** : treasure **2** : thesaurus (book) **3 el Tesoro** : the Treasury — **tesorero, -ra** *n* : treasurer
testaferro *nm* : figurehead
testamento *nm* : testament, will — **testamentario, -ria** *n* : executor, executrix *f* — **testar** *vi* : draw up a will
testarudo, -da *adj* : stubborn
testículo *nm* : testicle
testificar {72} *v* : testify — **testigo** *nmf* **1** : witness **2** ~ **ocular** : eyewitness — **testimoniar** *vi* : testify — **testimonio** *nm* : testimony
tétano *or* **tétanos** *nm* : tetanus
tetera *nf* : teapot
tetilla *nf* **1** : teat, nipple (of a man) **2** : nipple (of a baby bottle) — **tetina** *nf* : nipple (of a baby bottle)
tétrico, -ca *adj* : somber, gloomy
textil *adj & nm* : textile
texto *nm* : text — **textual** *adj* **1** : textual **2** EXACTO : literal, exact
textura *nf* : texture
tez *nf, pl* **teces** : complexion
ti *pron* **1** : you **2** ~ **mismo,** ~ **misma** : yourself
tía → **tío**
tianguis *nms & pl Lat* : open-air market
tibio, -bia *adj* : lukewarm
tiburón *nm, pl* **-rones** : shark
tic *nm* : tic
tiempo *nm* **1** : time **2** ÉPOCA : age, period **3** : weather (in meteorology) **4** : halftime (in sports) **5** : tempo (in music) **6** : tense (in grammar)
tienda *nf* **1** : store, shop **2** *or* ~ **de campaña** : tent
tiene → **tener**
tienta *nf* **andar a** ~**s** : feel one's way, grope around
tierno, -na *adj* **1** : tender, fresh, young **2** CARIÑOSO : affectionate
tierra *nf* **1** : land **2** SUELO : ground, earth **3** *or* ~ **natal** : native land **4 la Tierra** : the Earth **5 por** ~ : overland **6** ~ **adentro** : inland
tieso, -sa *adj* **1** : stiff, rigid **2** ERGUIDO : erect **3** ENGREÍDO : haughty
tiesto *nm* : flowerpot
tifoideo, -dea *adj* **fiebre tifoidea** : typhoid fever

tifón *nm, pl* **-fones** : typhoon
tifus *nm* : typhus
tigre, -gresa *n* **1** : tiger, tigress *f* **2** *Lat* : jaguar
tijera *nf or* **tijeras** *nfpl* : scissors — **tijeretada** *nf* : cut, snip
tildar *vt* **~ de** : brand as, call
tilde *nf* **1** : tilde **2** ACENTO : accent mark
tilo *nm* : linden (tree)
timar *vt* : swindle, cheat
timbre *nm* **1** : bell **2** : tone, timbre (of a voice, etc.) **3** SELLO : seal, stamp **4** *Lat* : postage stamp — **timbrar** *vt* : stamp
tímido, -da *adj* : timid, shy — **timidez** *nf* : timidity, shyness
timo *nm fam* : swindle, hoax
timón *nm, pl* **-mones 1** : rudder **2 coger el ~** : take the helm, take charge
tímpano *nm* **1** : eardrum **2 ~s** *nmpl* : timpani, kettledrums
tina *nf* **1** : vat **2** BAÑERA : bathtub
tinieblas *nfpl* **1** : darkness **2 estar en ~ sobre** : be in the dark about
tino *nm* **1** : good judgment, sense **2** TACTO : tact
tinta *nf* **1** : ink **2 saberlo de buena ~** : have it on good authority — **tinte** *nm* **1** : dye, coloring **2** MATIZ : overtone — **tintero** *nm* : inkwell
tintinear *vi* : jingle, tinkle, clink — **tintineo** *nm* : jingle, tinkle, clink
tinto, -ta *adj* **1** : dyed, stained **2** : red (of wine)
tintorería *nf* : dry cleaner (service)
tintura *nf* **1** : dye, tint **2 ~ de yodo** : tincture of iodine
tiña *nf* : ringworm
tío, tía *n* : uncle *m,* aunt *f*
tiovivo *nm* : merry-go-round
típico, -ca *adj* : typical
tiple *nm* : soprano
tipo *nm* **1** : type, kind **2** FIGURA : figure (of a woman), build (of a man) **3** : rate (of interest, etc.) **4** : (printing) type, typeface — **tipo, -pa** *n fam* : guy *m,* gal *f*
tipografía *nf* : typography, printing — **tipográfico, -ca** *adj* : typographical — **tipógrafo, -fa** *n* : printer
tique *or* **tíquet** *nm* : ticket — **tiquete** *nm Lat* : ticket
tira *nf* **1** : strip, strap **2 ~ cómica** : comic strip
tirabuzón *nf, pl* **-zones 1** : corkscrew **2** RIZO : curl, coil
tirada *nf* **1** : throw **2** DISTANCIA : distance **3** IMPRESIÓN : printing, issue — **tirador** *nm* : handle, knob — **tirador, -dora** *n* : marksman *m,* markswoman *f*
tiranía *nf* : tyranny — **tiránico, -ca** *adj* : tyrannical — **tiranizar** {21} *vt* : tyrannize — **tirano, -na** *adj* : tyrannical — **~** *n* : tyrant
tirante *adj* **1** : taut, tight **2** : tense (of a situation, etc.) — **~** *nm* **1** : (shoulder) strap **2 ~s** *nmpl* : suspenders
tirar *vt* **1** : throw **2** DESECHAR : throw away **3** DERRIBAR : knock down **4** DISPARAR : shoot, fire **5** IMPRIMIR : print — *vi* **1** : pull **2** DISPARAR : shoot **3** ATRAER : attract **4** *fam* : get by, manage **5 ~ a** : tend towards — **tirarse** *vr* **1** : throw oneself **2** *fam* : spend (time)
tiritar *vi* : shiver
tiro *nm* **1** : shot, gunshot **2** : shot, kick (in sports) **3** : team (of horses, etc.) **4 a ~** : within range
tiroides *nmf* : thyroid (gland)
tirón *nm, pl* **-rones 1** : pull, yank **2 de un ~** : in one go
tirotear *vt* : shoot at — **tiroteo** *nm* : shooting
tisis *nfs & pl* : tuberculosis
títere *nm* : puppet
titilar *vi* : flicker
titiritero, -ra *n* **1** : puppeteer **2** ACRÓBATA : acrobat
titubear *vi* **1** : hesitate **2** BALBUCEAR : stutter, stammer — **titubeante** *adj* : hesitant, faltering — **titubeo** *nm* : hesitation
titular *vt* : title, call — **titularse** *vr* **1** : be called, be titled **2** LICENCIARSE : receive a degree — **~** *adj* : titular, official — **~** *nm* : headline — **~** *nmf* : holder, incumbent — **título** *nm* **1** : title **2** : degree, qualification (in education)
tiza *nf* : chalk
tiznar *vt* : blacken (with soot, etc.) — **tizne** *nm* : soot
toalla *nf* : towel — **toallero** *nm* : towel rack
tobillo *nm* : ankle
tobogán *nm, pl* **-ganes 1** : toboggan, sled **2** : slide (in a playground, etc.)
tocadiscos *nms & pl* : record player
tocado, -da *adj fam* : touched, not all there — **tocado** *nm* : headgear, headdress
tocador *nm* : dressing table
tocar {72} *vt* **1** : touch, feel **2** MENCIONAR : touch on, refer to **3** : play (a musical instrument) — *vi* **1** : knock, ring **2 ~ en** : touch on, border on
tocayo, -ya *n* : namesake
tocino *nm* **1** : bacon **2** : salt pork (for cooking) — **tocineta** *nf Lat* : bacon
tocólogo, -ga *n* : obstetrician
tocón *nm, pl* **-cones** : stump (of a tree)

todavía *adv* **1** AÚN : still **2** (*in comparisons*) : even **3 ~ no** : not yet
todo, -da *adj* **1** : all **2** CADA, CUALQUIER : every, each **3 a toda velocidad** : at top speed **4 todo el mundo** : everyone, everybody — **~** *pron* **1** : everything, all **2 todos, -das** *pl* : everybody, everyone, all — **todo** *nm* : whole — **todopoderoso, -sa** *adj* : almighty, all-powerful
toga *nf* **1** : toga **2** : gown, robe (of a judge, etc.)
toldo *nm* : awning, canopy
tolerar *vt* : tolerate — **tolerancia** *nf* : tolerance — **tolerante** *adj* : tolerant
toma *nf* **1** : capture **2** DOSIS : dose **3** : take (in film) **4 ~ de corriente** : wall socket, outlet **5 ~ y daca** : give-and-take — **tomar** *vt* **1** : take **2** : have (food or drink) **3** CAPTURAR : capture, seize **4 ~ el sol** : sunbathe **5 ~ tierra** : land — *vi* : drink (alcohol) — **tomarse** *vr* **1** : take (time, etc.) **2** : drink, eat, have (food, drink)
tomate *nm* : tomato
tomillo *nm* : thyme
tomo *nm* : volume
ton *nm* **sin ~ ni son** : without rhyme or reason
tonada *nf* : tune
tonel *nm* : barrel, cask
tonelada *nf* : ton — **tonelaje** *nm* : tonnage
tónica *nf* **1** : tonic (water) **2** TENDENCIA : trend, tone — **tónico, -ca** *adj* : tonic — **tónico** *nm* : tonic (in medicine)
tono *nm* **1** : tone **2** : shade (of colors) **3** : key (in music)
tontería *nf* **1** : silly thing or remark **2** ESTUPIDEZ : foolishness **3 decir ~s** : talk nonsense — **tonto, -ta** *adj* **1** : stupid, silly **2 a tontas y a locas** : haphazardly — **~** *n* : fool, idiot
topacio *nm* : topaz
toparse *vr* **~ con** : run into, come across
tope *nm* **1** : limit, end **2** *or* **~ de puerta** : doorstop 3 *Lat* : bump — **~** *adj* : maximum
tópico, -ca *adj* **1** : topical, external **2** MANIDO : trite — **tópico** *nm* : cliché
topo *nm* : mole (animal)
toque *nm* **1** : (light) touch **2** : ringing, peal (of a bell) **3 ~ de queda** : curfew **4 ~ de diana** : reveille — **toquetear** *vt* : finger, handle
tórax *nms & pl* : thorax
torbellino *nm* : whirlwind
torcer {14} *vt* **1** : twist, bend **2** : turn (a corner) **3** : wring (out) — *vi* : turn — **torcerse** *vr* **1** : twist, sprain **2** FRUSTRARSE : go wrong **3** DESVIARSE : go astray — **torcedura** *nf* **1** : twisting **2** ESGUINCE : sprain — **torcido, -da** *adj* : twisted, crooked
tordo, -da *adj* : dappled — **tordo** *nm* : thrush (bird)
torear *vt* **1** : fight (bulls) **2** ELUDIR : dodge, sidestep — *vi* : fight bulls — **toreo** *nm* : bullfighting — **torero, -ra** *n* : bullfighter
tormenta *nf* : storm — **tormento** *nm* **1** : torture **2** ANGUSTIA : torment, anguish — **tormentoso, -sa** *adj* : stormy
tornado *nm* : tornado
tornar *vt* CONVERTIR : render, turn — *vi* : go back, return — **tornarse** *vr* : become, turn into
torneo *nm* : tournament
tornillo *nm* : screw
torniquete *nm* **1** : turnstile **2** : tourniquet (in medicine)
torno *nm* **1** : winch **2** : (carpenter's) lathe **3 ~ de alfarero** : (potter's) wheel **4 ~ de banco** : vise **5 en ~ a** : around, about
toro *nm* **1** : bull **2 ~s** *nmpl* : bullfight
toronja *nf* : grapefruit
torpe *adj* **1** : clumsy, awkward **2** ESTÚPIDO : stupid, dull
torpedear *vt* : torpedo — **torpedo** *nm* : torpedo
torpeza *nf* **1** : clumsiness, awkwardness **2** ESTUPIDEZ : slowness, stupidity
torre *nf* **1** : tower **2** : turret (on a ship, etc.) **3** : rook, castle (in chess)
torrente *nm* **1** : torrent **2 ~ sanguíneo** : bloodstream — **torrencial** *adj* : torrential
tórrido, -da *adj* : torrid
torsión *nf, pl* **-siones** : twisting
torta *nf* **1** : torte, cake **2** *Lat* : sandwich
tortazo *nm fam* : blow, wallop
tortícolis *nfs & pl* : stiff neck
tortilla *nf* **1** : tortilla **2** *or* **~ de huevo** : omelet
tórtola *nf* : turtledove
tortuga *nf* **1** : turtle, tortoise **2 ~ de agua dulce** : terrapin
tortuoso, -sa *adj* : tortuous, winding
tortura *nf* : torture — **torturar** *vt* : torture
tos *nf* **1** : cough **2 ~ ferina** : whooping cough
tosco, -ca *adj* : rough, coarse
toser *vi* : cough
tosquedad *nf* : coarseness
tostar {19} *vt* **1** : toast **2** BRONCEAR : tan — **tostarse** *vr* : get a tan — **tostada**

nf **1** : piece of toast **2** *Lat* : tostada — **tostador** *nm* : toaster
tostón *nm, pl* **-tones** *Lat* : fried plantain chip
total *adj & nm* : total — **~** *adv* : so, after all — **totalidad** *nf* : whole — **totalitario, -ria** *adj & n* : totalitarian — **totalitarismo** *nm* : totalitarianism — **totalizar** {21} *vt* : total, add up to
tóxico, -ca *adj* : toxic, poisonous — **tóxico** *nm* : poison — **toxicomanía** *nf* : drug addiction — **toxicómano, -na** *n* : drug addict — **toxina** *nf* : toxin
tozudo, -da *adj* : stubborn
traba *nf* : obstacle, hindrance
trabajar *vi* **1** : work **2** : act, perform (in theater, etc.) — *vt* **1** : work (metal) **2** : knead (dough) **3** MEJORAR : work on, work at — **trabajador, -dora** *adj* : hard-working — **~** *n* : worker — **trabajo** *nm* **1** : work **2** EMPLEO : job **3** TAREA : task **4** ESFUERZO : effort **5** **costar ~** : be difficult **6** **~ en equipo** : teamwork **7** **~s** *nmpl* : hardships, difficulties — **trabajoso, -sa** *adj* : hard, laborious
trabalenguas *nms & pl* : tongue twister
trabar *vt* **1** : join, connect **2** OBSTACULIZAR : impede **3** : strike up (a conversation, etc.) **4** : thicken (sauces) — **trabarse** *vr* **1** : jam **2** ENREDARSE : become entangled **3** **se le traba la lengua** : he gets tongue-tied
trabucar {72} *vt* : mix up
tracción *nf* : traction
tractor *nm* : tractor
tradición *nf, pl* **-ciones** : tradition — **tradicional** *adj* : traditional
traducir {61} *vt* : translate — **traducción** *nf, pl* **-ciones** : translation — **traductor, -tora** *n* : translator
traer {81} *vt* **1** : bring **2** CAUSAR : cause, bring about **3** CONTENER : carry, have **4** LLEVAR : wear — **traerse** *vr* **1** : bring along **2** **traérselas** : be difficult
traficar {72} *vi* **~ en** : traffic in — **traficante** *nmf* : dealer, trafficker — **tráfico** *nm* **1** : trade (of merchandise) **2** : traffic (of vehicles)
tragaluz *nf, pl* **-luces** : skylight
tragar {52} *vt* **1** : swallow **2** *fam* : put up with — *vi* : swallow — **tragarse** *vr* **1** : swallow **2** ABSORBER : absorb, swallow up
tragedia *nf* : tragedy — **trágico, -ca** *adj* : tragic
trago *nm* **1** : swallow, swig **2** *fam* : drink, liquor — **tragón, -gona** *adj fam* : greedy — **~** *nmf fam* : glutton
traicionar *vt* : betray — **traición** *nf, pl* **-ciones** **1** : betrayal **2** : treason (in law) — **traidor, -dora** *adj* : traitorous, treacherous — **~** *n* : traitor
trailer *nm* : trailer
traje *nm* **1** : dress, costume **2** : (man's) suit **3** **~ de baño** : bathing suit
trajinar *vi fam* : rush around — **trajín** *nm, pl* **-jines** *fam* : hustle and bustle
trama *nf* **1** : plot **2** : weave, weft (of fabric) — **tramar** *vt* **1** : plot, plan **2** : weave (fabric)
tramitar *vt* : negotiate — **trámite** *nm* : procedure, step
tramo *nm* **1** : stretch, section **2** : flight (of stairs)
trampa *nf* **1** : trap **2** **hacer ~s** : cheat — **trampear** *vt* : cheat
trampilla *nf* : trapdoor
trampolín *nm, pl* **-lines** **1** : diving board **2** : trampoline (in a gymnasium, etc.)
tramposo, -sa *adj* : crooked, cheating — **~** *n* : cheat, swindler
tranca *nf* **1** : cudgel, club **2** : bar (for a door or window)
trance *nm* **1** : critical juncture **2** : (hypnotic) trance **3** **en ~ de** : in the process of
tranquilo, -la *adj* : calm, tranquil — **tranquilidad** *nf* : tranquility, peace — **tranquilizante** *nm* : tranquilizer — **tranquilizar** {21} *vt* : calm, soothe — **tranquilizarse** *vr* : calm down
trans- *see also* **tras-**
transacción *nf, pl* **-ciones** : transaction
transatlántico, -ca *adj* : transatlantic — **transatlántico** *nm* : ocean liner
transbordador *nm* **1** : ferry **2** **~ espacial** : space shuttle — **transbordar** *vt* : transfer — *vi* : change (of trains, etc.) — **transbordo** *nm* **hacer ~** : change (trains, etc.)
transcribir {33} *vt* : transcribe — **transcripción** *nf, pl* **-ciones** : transcription
transcurrir *vi* : elapse, pass — **transcurso** *nm* : course, progression
transeúnte *nmf* : passerby
transferir {76} *vt* : transfer — **transferencia** *nf* : transfer, transference
transformar *vt* **1** : transform, change **2** CONVERTIR : convert — **transformarse** *vr* : be transformed — **transformación** *nf, pl* **-ciones** : transformation — **transformador** *nm* : transformer
transfusión *nf, pl* **-siones** : transfusion
transgredir {1} *vt* : transgress — **transgresión** *nf* : transgression
transición *nf, pl* **-ciones** : transition
transido, -da *adj* : overcome, stricken

transigir {35} *vi* : give in, compromise
transistor *nm* : transistor
transitar *vi* : go, travel — **transitable** *adj* : passable
transitivo, -va *adj* : transitive
tránsito *nm* **1** : transit **2** TRÁFICO : traffic **3 hora de máximo ~** : rush hour — **transitorio, -ria** *adj* : transitory
transmitir *vt* **1** : transmit **2** : broadcast (radio, TV, etc.) **3** CEDER : pass on — **transmisión** *nf, pl* **-siones 1** : broadcast **2** TRANSFERENCIA : transfer **3** : transmission (of an automobile) — **transmisor** *nm* : transmitter
transparentarse *vr* : be transparent — **transparente** *adj* : transparent
transpirar *vi* : perspire, sweat — **transpiración** *nf, pl* **-ciones** : perspiration, sweat
transponer {60} *vt* : transpose, move — **transponerse** *vr* **1** : set (of the sun, etc.) **2** DORMITAR : doze off
transportar *vt* : transport, carry — **transportarse** *vr* : get carried away — **transporte** *nm* : transport, transportation
transversal *adj* **corte ~** : cross section
tranvía *nm* : streetcar, trolley
trapear *vt Lat* : mop
trapecio *nm* : trapeze
trapisonda *nf* : scheme, plot
trapo *nm* **1** : cloth, rag **2 ~s** *nmpl fam* : clothes
tráquea *nf* : trachea, windpipe
traquetear *vi* : rattle around, shake — **traqueteo** *nm* : rattling
tras *prep* **1** DESPUÉS DE : after **2** DÉTRAS DE : behind
tras- *see also* **trans-**
trascender {56} *vi* **1** : leak out, become known **2** EXTENDERSE : spread **3 ~ de** : transcend — **trascendencia** *nf* : importance — **trascendental** *adj* **1** : transcendental **2** IMPORTANTE : important
trasegar *vt* : move around
trasero, -ra *adj* : rear, back — **trasero** *nm* : buttocks *pl*
trasfondo *nm* **1** : background **2** : undercurrent (of suspicion, etc.)
trasladar *vt* **1** : transfer, move **2** POSPONER : postpone — **trasladarse** *vr* : move, relocate — **traslado** *nm* **1** : transfer, move **2** COPIA : copy
traslapar *vt* : overlap — **traslaparse** *vr* : overlap
traslucirse {45} *vr* **1** : be translucent **2** REVELARSE : be revealed — **traslúcido, -da** : translucent
trasnochar *vi* : stay up all night
traspasar *vt* **1** : pierce, go through **2** EXCEDER : go beyond **3** ATRAVESAR : cross, go across **4** : transfer (a business, etc.) — **traspaso** *nm* : transfer, sale
traspié *nm* **1** : stumble, trip **2** ERROR : blunder
trasplantar *vt* : transplant — **trasplante** *nm* : transplant
trasquilar *vt* : shear
traste *nm* **1** : fret (on a guitar, etc.) **2** *Lat* : (kitchen) utensil **3 dar al ~ con** : ruin **4 irse al ~** : fall through
trastos *nmpl fam* : pieces of junk, stuff
trastornar *vt* **1** : disturb, disrupt **2** VOLVER LOCO : drive crazy — **trastornarse** *vr* : go crazy — **trastornado, -da** *adj* : disturbed, deranged — **trastorno** *nm* **1** : disturbance, disruption **2** : (medical or psychological) disorder
trastrocar *vt* : change, switch around
tratable *adj* : friendly, sociable
tratar *vi* **1 ~ con** : deal with **2 ~ de** : try to **3 ~ de** *or* **~ sobre** : be about, concern **4 ~ en** : deal in — *vt* **1** : treat **2** MANEJAR : deal with, handle — **tratarse** *vr* **~ de** : be about, concern — **tratado** *nm* **1** : treatise **2** CONVENIO : treaty — **tratamiento** *nm* : treatment — **trato** *nm* **1** : treatment **2** ACUERDO : deal, agreement **3 ~s** *nmpl* : dealings
trauma *nm* : trauma — **traumático, -ca** *adj* : traumatic
través *nm* **1 a ~ de** : across, through **2 de ~** : sideways
travesaño *nm* : crosspiece
travesía *nf* : voyage, crossing (of the sea)
travesura *nf* **1** : prank **2 ~s** *nfpl* : mischief — **travieso, -sa** *adj* : mischievous, naughty
trayecto *nm* **1** : trajectory, path **2** VIAJE : journey **3** RUTA : route — **trayectoria** *nf* : path, trajectory
traza *nf* **1** : design, plan **2** ASPECTO : appearance — **trazado** *nm* **1** : outline, sketch **2** DISEÑO : plan, layout — **trazar** {21} *vt* **1** : trace, outline **2** : draw up (a plan, etc.) — **trazo** *nm* : stroke, line
trébol *nm* **1** : clover, shamrock **2 ~es** *nmpl* : clubs (in playing cards)
trece *adj & nm* : thirteen — **treceavo, -va** *adj* : thirteenth — **treceavo** *nm* : thirteenth (fraction)
trecho *nm* **1** : stretch, period **2** DISTANCIA : distance **3 de ~ a ~** : at intervals

tregua *nf* **1** : truce **2 sin ~** : without respite
treinta *adj & nm* : thirty — **treintavo, -va** *adj* : thirtieth — **treintavo** *nm* : thirtieth (fraction)
tremendo, -da *adj* : tremendous, enormous
trementina *nf* : turpentine
trémulo, -la *adj* : trembling, flickering
tren *nm* **1** : train **2 ~ de aterrizaje** : landing gear
trenza *nf* : braid, pigtail — **trenzar** {21} *vt* : braid — **trenzarse** *vr Lat* : get involved
trepar *vi* **1** : climb **2** : creep, spread (of a plant) — **treparse** *vr* : climb (up) — **trepador, -dora** *adj* : climbing — **trepadora** *nf* **1** : climbing plant **2** *fam* : social climber
trepidar *vi* : shake, vibrate
tres *adj & nm* : three — **trescientos, -tas** *adj* : three hundred — **trescientos** *nms & pl* : three hundred
treta *nf* : trick
triángulo *nm* : triangle — **triangular** *adj* : triangular
tribu *nf* : tribe — **tribal** *adj* : tribal
tribulación *nf, pl* **-ciones** : tribulation
tribuna *nf* **1** : dais, platform **2** : grandstand, bleachers *pl* (in a stadium)
tribunal *nm* : court, tribunal
tributar *vt* : pay, render — *vi* : pay taxes — **tributo** *nm* **1** : tribute **2** IMPUESTO : tax
triciclo *nm* : tricycle
tricolor *adj* : tricolored
tridimensional *adj* : three-dimensional
trigésimo, -ma *adj & n* : thirtieth
trigo *nm* : wheat
trigonometría *nf* : trigonometry
trillado, -da *adj* : trite
trillar *vt* : thresh — **trilladora** *nf* : threshing machine
trillizo, -za *n* : triplet
trilogía *nf* : trilogy
trimestral *adj* : quarterly
trinar *vi* : warble
trinchar *vt* : carve
trinchera *nf* **1** : trench, ditch **2** IMPERMEABLE : trench coat
trineo *nm* : sled, sleigh
trinidad *nf* : trinity
trino *nm* : trill, warble
trío *nm* : trio
tripa *nf* **1** : gut, intestine **2 ~s** *nfpl fam* : belly, tummy
triple *adj & nm* : triple — **triplicar** {72} *vt* : triple
trípode *nm* : tripod
tripular *vt* : man — **tripulación** *nf, pl* **-ciones** : crew — **tripulante** *nmf* : crew member
tris *nm* **estar en un ~ de** : be within an inch of
triste *adj* **1** : sad **2** SOMBRÍO : dismal, gloomy **3** MISERABLE : sorry, miserable — **tristeza** *nf* : sadness, grief
tritón *nm, pl* **-tones** : newt
triturar *vt* : crush, grind
triunfar *vi* : triumph, win — **triunfal** *adj* : triumphal — **triunfante** *adj* : triumphant — **triunfo** *nm* : triumph, victory
trivial *adj* : trivial
triza *nf* **1** : shred, bit **2 hacer ~s** : smash to pieces
trocar {82} *vt* **1** CONVERTIR : change **2** INTERCAMBIAR : exchange
trocha *nf* : path, trail
trofeo *nm* : trophy
trombón *nm, pl* **-bones 1** : trombone **2** : trombonist (musician)
trombosis *nf* : thrombosis
trompa *nf* **1** : trunk (of an elephant), snout **2** : horn (musical instrument) **3** : tube (in anatomy)
trompeta *nf* : trumpet — **trompetista** *nmf* : trumpet player
trompo *nm* : top (toy)
tronada *nf* : thunderstorm — **tronar** {19} *vi* : thunder, rage — *vt Lat fam* : shoot — *v impers* : thunder
tronchar *vt* **1** : snap **2** TRUNCAR : cut short
tronco *nm* **1** : trunk (of a tree) **2** : torso (of a person) **3 dormir como un ~** : sleep like a log
trono *nm* : throne
tropa *nf* : troops *pl*, soldiers *pl*
tropel *nm* : mob
tropezar {29} *vi* **1** : trip, stumble **2 ~ con** : come up against, run into — **tropezón** *nm, pl* **-zones 1** : stumble **2** EQUIVOCACIÓN : mistake, slip
trópico *nm* : tropic — **tropical** *adj* : tropical
tropiezo *nm* **1** CONTRATIEMPO : snag, setback **2** EQUIVOCACIÓN : mistake, slip
trotar *vi* **1** : trot **2** *fam* : rush about — **trote** *nm* **1** : trot **2** *fam* : rush, bustle **3 al ~** : at a trot, quickly
trozo *nm* : piece, bit, chunk
trucha *nf* : trout
truco *nm* **1** : knack **2** ARDID : trick
trueno *nm* : thunder
trueque *nm* : barter, exchange
trufa *nf* : truffle
truncar {72} *vt* **1** : cut short **2** : thwart, spoil (plans, etc.)

tu *adj* : your
tú *pron* : you
tuba *nf* : tuba
tuberculosis *nf* : tuberculosis
tubo *nm* **1** : tube, pipe **2 ~ de escape** : exhaust pipe (of a vehicle) **3 ~ de desagüe** : drainpipe — **tubería** *nf* : pipes *pl*, tubing
tuerca *nf* : nut (for a screw)
tuerto, -ta *adj* : one-eyed, blind in one eye
tuétano *nm* : marrow
tufo *nm* **1** : vapor **2** *fam* : stench, stink
tugurio *nm* : hovel
tulipán *nm, pl* **-panes** : tulip
tullido, -da *adj* : crippled, paralyzed
tumba *nf* : tomb, grave
tumbar *vt* : knock down, knock over — **tumbarse** *vr* : lie down — **tumbo** *nm* **dar ~s** : jolt, bump around
tumor *nm* : tumor
tumulto *nm* **1** : commotion, tumult **2** MOTÍN : riot — **tumultuoso, -sa** *adj* : tumultuous
tuna *nf* : prickly pear
túnel *nm* : tunnel
túnica *nf* : tunic
tupé *nm* : toupee
tupido, -da *adj* : dense, thick
turba *nf* **1** : peat **2** MUCHEDUMBRE : mob, throng
turbación *nf, pl* **-ciones 1** : disturbance **2** CONFUSIÓN : confusion
turbante *nm* : turban
turbar *vt* **1** : disturb, upset **2** CONFUNDIR : confuse, bewilder
turbina *nf* : turbine
turbio, -bia *adj* **1** : cloudy, murky **2** : blurred (of vision, etc.) — **turbión** *nm, pl* **-biones** : squall
turbulencia *nf* : turbulence — **turbulento, -ta** *adj* : turbulent
turco, -ca *adj* : Turkish — **turco** *nm* : Turkish (language)
turista *nmf* : tourist — **turismo** *nm* : tourism, tourist industry — **turístico, -ca** *adj* : tourist, travel
turnarse *vr* : take turns, alternate — **turno** *nm* **1** : turn **2 ~ de noche** : night shift
turquesa *nf* : turquoise
turrón *nm, pl* **-rrones** : nougat
tutear *vt* : address as *tú*
tutela *nf* **1** : guardianship (in law) **2 bajo la ~ de** : under the protection of
tuteo *nm* : addressing as *tú*
tutor, -tora *n* **1** : guardian **2** : tutor (in education)
tuyo, -ya *adj* : yours, of yours — **~** *pron* **1 el tuyo, la tuya, lo tuyo, los tuyos, las tuyas** : yours **2 los tuyos** : your family, your friends

U

u[1] *nf* : u, 22d letter of the Spanish alphabet
u[2] *conj* (*used before words beginning with o- or ho-*) : or
uapití *nm* : American elk, wapiti
ubicar {72} *vt Lat* **1** COLOCAR : place, position **2** LOCALIZAR : find — **ubicarse** *vr* : be located
ubre *nf* : udder
Ud., Uds. → **usted**
ufanarse *vr* **~ de** : boast about — **ufano, -na** *adj* **1** : proud **2** ENGREÍDO : self-satisfied
ujier *nm* : usher
úlcera *nf* : ulcer
ulterior *adj* : later, subsequent — **ulteriormente** *adv* : subsequently
últimamente *adv* : lately, recently
ultimar *vt* **1** : complete, finish **2** *Lat* : kill — **ultimátum** *nm, pl* **-tums** : ultimatum
último, -ma *adj* **1** : last **2** : latest, most recent (in time) **3** : farthest (in space) **4 por último** : finally
ultrajar *vt* : outrage, insult — **ultraje** *nm* : outrage, insult
ultramar *nm* **de ~** *or* **en ~** : overseas — **ultramarino, -na** *adj* : overseas — **ultramarinos** *nmpl* **tienda de ~** : grocery store
ultranza: **a ~** *adv phr* : to the extreme — **a ~** *adj phr* : out-and-out, complete
ultrasonido *nm* : ultrasound
ultravioleta *adj* : ultraviolet
ulular *vi* **1** : hoot (of an owl) **2** : howl (of a wolf, the wind, etc.) — **ululato** *nm* : hoot (of an owl)
umbilical *adj* : umbilical
umbral *nm* : threshold
un, una *art, mpl* **unos 1** : a, an **2 unos** *or* **unas** *pl* : some, a few **3 unos** *or* **unas** *pl* : about, approximately — **un** *adj* → **uno**

unánime *adj* : unanimous — **unanimidad** *nf* : unanimity
uncir {83} *vt* : yoke
undécimo, -ma *adj & n* : eleventh
ungir {35} *vt* : anoint — **ungüento** *nm* : ointment
único, -ca *adj* **1** : only, sole **2** EXCEPCIONAL : unique — **~** *n* : only one — **únicamente** *adv* : only
unicornio *nm* : unicorn
unidad *nf* **1** : unit **2** ARMONÍA : unity — **unido, -da** *adj* **1** : united **2** : close (of friends, etc.)
unificar {72} *vt* : unify — **unificación** *nf, pl* **-ciones** : unification
uniformar *vt* **1** : standardize **2** : put into uniform — **uniformado, -da** *adj* : uniformed — **uniforme** *adj & nm* : uniform — **uniformidad** *nf* : uniformity
unilateral *adj* : unilateral
unir *vt* **1** : unite, join **2** COMBINAR : combine, mix together — **unirse** *vr* **1** : join together **2 ~ a** : join — **unión** *nf, pl* **uniones 1** : union **2** JUNTURA : joint, coupling
unísono *nm* **al ~** : in unison
unitario, -ria *adj* : unitary
universal *adj* : universal
universidad *nf* : university, college — **universitario, -ria** *adj* : university, college
universo *nm* : universe
uno, una (**un** *before masculine singular nouns*) *adj* : one — **~** *pron* **1** : one **2 unos, unas** *pl* : some **3 uno(s) a otro(s)** : one another, each other **4 uno y otro** : both — **uno** *nm* : one (number)
untar *vt* **1** : smear, grease **2** *fam* : bribe — **untuoso, -sa** *adj* : greasy, sticky
uña *nf* **1** : nail, fingernail **2** : claw (of a cat, etc.), hoof (of a horse, etc.)
uranio *nm* : uranium
Urano *nm* : Uranus
urbano, -na *adj* : urban, city — **urbanidad** *nf* : politeness, courtesy — **urbanización** *nf, pl* **-ciones** : housing development — **urbanizar** *vt* : develop, urbanize — **urbe** *nf* : large city
urdir *vt* **1** : warp **2** PLANEAR : plot — **urdimbre** *nf* : warp (of a fabric)
urgir {35} *v impers* : be urgent, be pressing — **urgencia** *nf* **1** : urgency **2** EMERGENCIA : emergency — **urgente** *adj* : urgent
urinario, -ria *adj* : urinary — **urinario** *nm* : urinal (place)
urna *nf* **1** : urn **2** : ballot box (for voting)
urraca *nf* : magpie
uruguayo, -ya *adj* : Uruguayan
usar *vt* **1** : use **2** LLEVAR : wear — **usarse 1** EMPLEARSE : be used **2** : be worn, be in fashion — **usado, -da** *adj* **1** : used **2** GASTADO : worn, worn-out — **usanza** *nf* : custom, usage — **uso** *nm* **1** : use **2** DESGASTE : wear and tear **3** USANZA : custom, usage
usted *pron* **1** (*used in formal address; often written as* **Ud.** *or* **Vd.**) : you **2 ~es** *pl* (*often written as* **Uds.** *or* **Vds.**) : you (all)
usual *adj* : usual
usuario, -ria *n* : user
usura *nf* : usury — **usurero, -ra** *n* : usurer
usurpar *vt* : usurp
utensilio *nm* : utensil, tool
útero *nm* : uterus, womb
utilizar {21} *vt* : use, utilize — **útil** *adj* : useful — **útiles** *nmpl* : implements, tools — **utilidad** *nf* : utility, usefulness — **utilitario, -ria** *adj* : utilitarian — **utilización** *nf, pl* **-ciones** : utilization, use
uva *nf* : grape

V

v *nf* : v, 23d letter of the Spanish alphabet
va → **ir**
vaca *nf* : cow
vacaciones *nfpl* **1** : vacation **2 estar de ~** : be on vacation **3 irse de ~** : go on vacation
vacante *adj* : vacant — **~** *nf* : vacancy
vaciar {85} *vt* **1** : empty (out) **2** AHUECAR : hollow out **3** : cast, mold (a statue, etc.)
vacilar *vi* **1** : hesitate, waver **2** : flicker (of light) **3** TAMBALEARSE : be unsteady, wobble **4** *fam* : joke, fool around — **vacilación** *nf, pl* **-ciones** : hesitation — **vacilante** *adj* **1** : hesitant **2** OSCILANTE : unsteady
vacío, -cía *adj* : empty — **vacío** *nm* **1** : void **2** : vacuum (in physics) **3** HUECO : space, gap
vacuna *nf* : vaccine — **vacunación** *nf,*

pl **-ciones** : vaccination — **vacunar** *vt* : vaccinate

vacuno, -na *adj* : bovine

vadear *vt* : ford — **vado** *nm* : ford

vagabundear *vi* : wander — **vagabundo, -da** *adj* **1** : vagrant **2** : stray (of a dog, etc.) — ~ *n* : hobo, bum — **vagancia** *nf* **1** : vagrancy **2** PEREZA : laziness, idleness — **vagar** {52} *vi* : roam, wander

vagina *nf* : vagina

vago, -ga *adj* **1** : vague **2** PEREZOSO : lazy, idle — ~ *n* : idler, loafer

vagón *nm, pl* **-gones** : car (of a train)

vahído *nm* : dizzy spell

vaho *nm* **1** : breath **2** VAPOR : vapor, steam

vaina *nf* **1** : sheath, scabbard **2** : pod (in botany) **3** *Lat fam* : bother, pain

vainilla *nf* : vanilla

vaivén *nm, pl* **-venes 1** : swinging, swaying **2** : coming and going (of people, etc.) **3 vaivenes** *nmpl* : ups and downs

vajilla *nf* : dishes *pl*

vale *nm* **1** : voucher **2** PAGARÉ : IOU — **valedero, -ra** *adj* : valid

valentía *nf* : courage, bravery

valer {84} *vt* **1** : be worth **2** COSTAR : cost **3** GANAR : gain, earn **4** EQUIVALER A : be equal to — *vi* **1** : have value, cost **2** SER VÁLIDO : be valid, count **3** SERVIR : be of use **4 hacerse** ~ : assert oneself **5 más vale** : it's better — **valerse** *vr* **1** ~ **de** : take advantage of **2** ~ **solo** *or* ~ **por sí mismo** : look after oneself

valeroso, -sa *adj* : courageous

valga, etc. → **valer**

valía *nf* : worth

validar *vt* : validate — **validez** *nf* : validity — **válido, -da** *adj* : valid

valiente *adj* **1** : brave **2** (*used ironically*) : fine, great

valija *nf* : case, valise

valioso, -sa *adj* : valuable

valla *nf* **1** : fence **2** : hurdle (in sports) — **vallar** *vt* : put a fence around

valle *nm* : valley

valor *nm* **1** : value, worth **2** VALENTÍA : courage, valor **3 objetos de** ~ : valuables **4 sin** ~ : worthless **5** ~**es** *nmpl* : values, principles **6** ~**es** *nmpl* : securities, bonds — **valoración** *nf, pl* **-ciones** : valuation — **valorar** *vt* : evaluate, assess

vals *nm* : waltz

válvula *nf* : valve

vamos → **ir**

vampiro *nm* : vampire

van → **ir**

vanagloriarse *vr* : boast, brag

vándalo *nm* : vandal — **vandalismo** : vandalism

vanguardia *nf* **1** : vanguard **2** : avant-garde (in art, music, etc.) **3 a la** ~ : at/in the forefront

vanidad *nf* : vanity — **vanidoso, -sa** *adj* : vain, conceited

vano, -na *adj* **1** INÚTIL : vain, useless **2** SUPERFICIAL : empty, hollow **3 en vano** : in vain

vapor *nm* **1** : steam, vapor **2 al** ~ : steamed — **vaporizador** *nm* : vaporizer — **vaporizar** {21} *vt* : vaporize

vaquero, -ra *n* : cowboy *m*, cowgirl *f* — **vaqueros** *nmpl* : jeans

vara *nf* **1** : stick, rod **2** : staff (of office)

varado, -da *adj* : stranded

variar {85} *vt* **1** : vary **2** CAMBIAR : change, alter — *vi* : vary, change — **variable** *adj* & *nf* : variable — **variación** *nf, pl* **-ciones** : variation — **variado, -da** *adj* : varied — **variante** *nf* : variant

varicela *nf* : chicken pox

varicoso, -sa *adj* : varicose

variedad *nf* : variety

varilla *nf* : rod, stick

vario, -ria *adj* **1** : varied **2** ~**s** *pl* : several

varita *nf* : wand

variz *nf, pl* **-rices** *or* **várices** : varicose vein

varón *nm, pl* **-rones 1** : man, male **2** NIÑO : boy — **varonil** *adj* : manly

vas → **ir**

vasco, -ca *adj* : Basque — **vasco** *nm* : Basque (language)

vasija *nf* : container, vessel

vaso *nm* **1** : glass **2** : vessel (in anatomy)

vástago *nm* **1** : offspring, descendent **2** BROTE : shoot **3** VARILLA : rod

vasto, -ta *adj* : vast

vaticinar *vt* : prophesy, predict — **vaticinio** *nm* : prophecy

vatio *nm* : watt

vaya, etc. → **ir**

Vd., Vds. → **usted**

ve, etc. → **ir, ver**

vecinal *adj* : local

vecino, -na *n* **1** : neighbor **2** HABITANTE : resident, inhabitant — ~ *adj* : neighboring — **vecindad** *nf* : neighborhood, vicinity — **vecindario** *nm* **1** : neighborhood **2** VECINOS : community, residents *pl*

vedar *vt* : prohibit — **veda** *nf* **1** : prohibition, ban **2** : closed season (for hunt-

ing and fishing) — **vedado** *nm* : preserve (for game, etc.)
vega *nf* : fertile lowland
vegetal *nm* : vegetable, plant — ~ *adj* : vegetable — **vegetación** *nf, pl* **-ciones** : vegetation — **vegetar** *vi* : vegetate — **vegetariano, -na** *adj & n* : vegetarian
vehemente *adj* : vehement
vehículo *nm* : vehicle
veinte *adj & nm* : twenty — **veinteavo, -va** *adj* : twentieth — **veinteavo** *nm* : twentieth — **veintena** *nf* : group of twenty, score
vejar *vt* : mistreat, humiliate — **vejación** *nf, pl* **-ciones** : humiliation
vejez *nf* : old age
vejiga *nf* **1** : bladder **2** AMPOLLA : blister
vela *nf* **1** : candle **2** : sail (of a ship) **3** VIGILIA : vigil **4 pasar la noche en ~** : have a sleepless night
velada *nf* : evening (party)
velar *vt* **1** : hold a wake over **2** CUIDAR : watch over **3** : blur (a photograph) **4** OCULTAR : veil, mask — *vi* **1** : stay awake **2 ~ por** : watch over — **velado, -da** *adj* **1** : veiled, hidden **2** : blurred (of a photograph)
velero *nm* : sailing ship
veleta *nf* : weather vane
vello *nm* **1** : body hair **2** PELUSA : down, fuzz — **vellón** *nm, pl* **-llones** : fleece — **velloso, -sa** *adj* : downy, fluffy — **velludo, -da** *adj* : hairy
velo *nm* : veil
veloz *adj, pl* **-loces** : fast, quick — **velocidad** *nf* **1** : speed, velocity **2** MARCHA : gear (of an automobile) — **velocímetro** *nm* : speedometer
vena *nf* **1** : vein **2** : grain (of wood) **3** DISPOSICIÓN : mood **4 tener ~ de** : have a talent for
venado *nm* **1** : deer **2** : venison (in cooking)
vencer {86} *vt* **1** : beat, defeat **2** SUPERAR : overcome — *vi* **1** : win **2** CADUCAR : expire — **vencerse** *vr* : collapse, give way — **vencedor, -dora** *adj* : winning — ~ *n* : winner — **vencido, -da** *adj* **1** : beaten, defeated **2** CADUCADO : expired **3** : due, payable (in finance) **4 darse por ~** : give up — **vencimiento** *nm* **1** : expiration **2** : maturity (of a loan)
venda *nf* : bandage — **vendaje** *nm* : bandage, dressing — **vendar** *vt* **1** : bandage **2 ~ los ojos** : blindfold
vendaval *nm* : gale
vender *vt* : sell — **venderse** *vr* **1** : be sold **2 se vende** : for sale — **vendedor, -dora** *n* **1** : seller **2** : salesman *m*, saleswoman *f* (in a store)
vendimia *nf* : grape harvest
vendrá, etc. → **venir**
veneno *nm* **1** : poison **2** : venom (of a snake, etc.) — **venenoso, -sa** *adj* : poisonous
venerar *vt* : venerate, revere — **venerable** *adj* : venerable — **veneración** *nf, pl* **-ciones** : veneration, reverence
venéreo, -rea *adj* : venereal
venezolano, -na *adj* : Venezuelan
venga → **venir**
vengar {52} *vt* : avenge — **vengarse** *vr* : get even, take revenge — **venganza** *nf* : vengeance, revenge — **vengativo, -va** *adj* : vindictive, vengeful
venia *nf* **1** : permission **2** : pardon (in law)
venial *adj* : venial, petty
venir {87} *vi* **1** : come **2** LLEGAR : arrive **3** HALLARSE : be, appear **4** QUEDAR : fit **5 que viene** : coming, next **6 ~ a ser** : turn out to be **7 ~ bien** : be suitable — **venirse** *vr* **1** : come **2 ~ abajo** : fall apart, collapse — **venida** *nf* **1** : arrival, coming **2** REGRESO : return — **venidero, -ra** *adj* : coming
venta *nf* **1** : sale, selling **2 en ~** : for sale
ventaja *nf* : advantage — **ventajoso, -sa** *adj* : advantageous
ventana *nf* **1** : window **2 ~ de la nariz** : nostril — **ventanilla** *nf* **1** : window (of a vehicle or airplane) **2** : ticket window, box office (of a theater, etc.)
ventilar *vt* : ventilate, air (out) — **ventilación** *nf, pl* **-ciones** : ventilation — **ventilador** *nm* : fan, ventilator
ventisca *nf* : blizzard — **ventisquero** *nm* : snowdrift
ventoso, -sa *adj* : windy — **ventosidad** *nf* : wind, flatulence
ventrílocuo, -cua *n* : ventriloquist
ventura *nf* **1** : fortune, luck **2** SATISFACCIÓN : happiness **3 a la ~** : at random — **venturoso, -sa** *adj* : fortunate, happy
ver {88} *vt* **1** : see **2** : watch (television, etc.) — *vi* **1** : see **2 a ~** *or* **vamos a ~** : let's see **3 no tener nada que ~ con** : have nothing to do with **4 ya veremos** : we'll see — **verse** *vr* **1** : see oneself **2** HALLARSE : find oneself **3** ENCONTRARSE : see each other, meet
vera *nf* **1** : side, edge **2** : bank (of a river)
veracidad *nf* : truthfulness
verano *nm* : summer — **veraneante** *nmf* : summer vacationer — **veranear**

vi : spend the summer — **veraniego, -ga** *adj* : summer
veras *nfpl* **de ~** : really
veraz *adj, pl* **-races** : truthful
verbal *adj* : verbal
verbena *nf* : festival, fair
verbo *nm* : verb — **verboso, -sa** *adj* : verbose
verdad *nf* **1** : truth **2 de ~** : really, truly **3 ¿verdad?** : right?, isn't that so? — **verdaderamente** *adv* : really, truly — **verdadero, -dera** *adj* : true, real
verde *adj* **1** : green **2** : dirty, risqué (of a joke, etc.) — **~** *nm* : green — **verdor** *nm* : greenness
verdugo *nm* **1** : executioner, hangman **2** : cruel person, tyrant
verdura *nf* : vegetable(s), green(s)
vereda *nf* **1** : path, trail **2** *Lat* : sidewalk
veredicto *nm* : verdict
vergüenza *nf* **1** : shame **2** TIMIDEZ : bashfulness, shyness — **vergonzoso, -sa** *adj* **1** : shameful **2** TÍMIDO : bashful, shy
verídico, -ca *adj* : true, truthful
verificar {72} *vt* **1** : verify, confirm **2** EXAMINAR : test, check out — **verificarse** *vr* **1** : take place **2** : come true (of a prophecy, etc.) — **verificación** *nf, pl* **-ciones** : verification
verja *nf* **1** : (iron) gate **2** : rails *pl* (of a fence) **3** ENREJADO : grating, grille
vermut *nm, pl* **-muts** : vermouth
vernáculo, -la *adj* : vernacular
verosímil *adj* **1** : probable, likely **2** CREÍBLE : credible
verraco *nm* : boar
verruga *nf* : wart
versar *vi* **~ sobre** : deal with, be about — **versado, -da** *adj* **~ en** : versed in
versátil *adj* **1** : versatile **2** VOLUBLE : fickle
versión *nf, pl* **-siones 1** : version **2** TRADUCCIÓN : translation
verso *nm* **1** : poem, verse **2** : line (of poetry)
vértebra *nf* : vertebra
verter {56} *vt* **1** : pour (out) **2** DERRAMAR : spill **3** TIRAR : dump — *vi* : flow — **vertedero** *nm* **1** : dump, landfill **2** DESAGÜE : drain, outlet
vertical *adj & nf* : vertical
vértice *nm* : vertex, apex
vertiente *nf* : slope
vértigo *nm* : vertigo, dizziness — **vertiginoso, -sa** *adj* : dizzy
vesícula *nf* **1** : blister **2 ~ biliar** : gallbladder
vestíbulo *nm* : vestibule, hall, foyer
vestido *nm* **1** : dress **2** ROPA : clothing, clothes *pl*
vestigio *nm* : vestige, trace
vestir {54} *vt* **1** : dress, clothe **2** LLEVAR : wear — *vi* : dress — **vestirse** *vr* : get dressed — **vestimenta** *nf* : clothing — **vestuario** *nm* **1** : wardrobe, clothes *pl* **2** : dressing room (in a theater), locker room (in sports)
veta *nf* **1** : vein, seam **2** : grain (of wood)
vetar *vt* : veto
veteado, -da *adj* : streaked, veined
veterano, -na *adj & n* : veteran
veterinaria *nf* : veterinary medicine — **veterinario, -ria** *adj* : veterinary — **~** *n* : veterinarian
veto *nm* : veto
vetusto, -ta *adj* : ancient
vez *nf, pl* **veces 1** : time **2** TURNO : turn **3 a la ~** : at the same time **4 a veces** : sometimes **5 de una ~** : all at once **6 de una ~ para siempre** : once and for all **7 de ~ en cuando** : from time to time **8 dos veces** : twice **9 en ~ de** : instead of **10 una ~** : once
vía *nf* **1** : way, road, route **2** MEDIO : means **3** : track, line (of a railroad) **4** : (anatomical) tract **5 en ~ de** : in the process of — **~** *prep* : via
viable *adj* : viable, feasible — **viabilidad** *nf* : viability
viaducto *nm* : viaduct
viajar *vi* : travel — **viajante** *nmf* : traveling salesperson — **viaje** *nm* : trip, journey — **viajero, -ra** *adj* : traveling — **~** *n* **1** : traveler **2** PASAJERO : passenger
vial *adj* : road, traffic
víbora *nf* : viper
vibrar *vi* : vibrate — **vibración** *nf, pl* **-ciones** : vibration — **vibrante** *adj* : vibrant
vicario, -ria *n* : vicar
vicepresidente, -ta *n* : vice president
viceversa *adv* : vice versa
vicio *nm* **1** : vice **2** MALA COSTUMBRE : bad habit **3** DEFECTO : defect — **viciado, -da** *adj* **1** : corrupt **2** : stuffy, stale (of air, etc.) — **viciar** *vt* **1** : corrupt **2** ESTROPEAR : spoil, pollute — **vicioso, -sa** *adj* : depraved, corrupt
vicisitud *nf* : vicissitude
víctima *nf* : victim
victoria *nf* : victory — **victorioso, -sa** *adj* : victorious
vid *nf* : vine, grapevine
vida *nf* **1** : life **2** DURACIÓN : lifetime **3 de por ~** : for life **4 estar con ~** : be alive

video *or* **vídeo** *nm* **1** : video **2** : VCR, videocassette recorder
vidrio *nm* : glass — **vidriado** *nm* : glaze — **vidriar** *vt* : glaze — **vidriera** *nf* **1** : stained-glass window **2** : glass door **3** *Lat* : shopwindow — **vidrioso, -sa** *adj* **1** : delicate (of a subject, etc.) **2 ojos vidriosos** : glassy eyes
vieira *nf* : scallop
viejo, -ja *adj* : old — ~ *n* **1** : old man *m*, old woman *f* **2 hacerse** ~ : get old
viene, etc. → **venir**
viento *nm* : wind
vientre *nm* **1** : abdomen, belly **2** MATRIZ : womb **3** INTESTINO : bowels *pl*
viernes *nms & pl* **1** : Friday **2 Viernes Santo** : Good Friday
vietnamita *adj & nm* : Vietnamese
viga *nf* : beam, girder
vigencia *nf* **1** : validity **2 entrar en** ~ : go into effect — **vigente** *adj* : valid, in force
vigésimo, -ma *adj & n* : twentieth
vigía *nmf* : lookout
vigilar *vt* : look after, watch over — *vi* : keep watch — **vigilancia** *nf* **1** : vigilance **2 bajo** ~ : under surveillance — **vigilante** *adj* : vigilant — ~ *nmf* : watchman, guard — **vigilia** *nf* **1** : wakefulness **2** : vigil (in religion)
vigor *nm* **1** : vigor **2 entrar en** ~ : go into effect — **vigorizante** *adj* : invigorating — **vigoroso, -sa** *adj* : vigorous
VIH *nm* : HIV
vil *adj* : vile, despicable — **vileza** *nf* **1** : vileness **2** : despicable act — **vilipendiar** *vt* : revile
villa *nf* **1** : town, village **2** : villa (house)
villancico *nm* : (Christmas) carol
villano, -na *n* : villain
vilo *nm* **en** ~ : suspended, in the air
vinagre *nm* : vinegar — **vinagrera** *nf* : cruet — **vinagreta** *nf* : vinaigrette
vincular *vt* : tie, link — **vínculo** *nm* : link, tie, bond
vindicar *vt* **1** : vindicate **2** VENGAR : avenge
vino[1]**, etc.** → **venir**
vino[2] *nm* : wine
viña *nf or* **viñedo** *nm* : vineyard
vio, etc. → **ver**
viola *nf* : viola
violar *vt* **1** : violate (a law, etc.) **2** : rape (a person) — **violación** *nf, pl* **-ciones 1** : violation, offense **2** : rape (of a person)
violencia *nf* : violence, force — **violentar** *vt* **1** : force **2** : break into (a house, etc.) — **violentarse** *vr* **1** : force oneself **2** AVERGONZARSE : be embarrassed — **violento, -ta** *adj* **1** : violent **2** INCÓMODO : awkward, embarrassing
violeta *adj & nm* : violet (color) — ~ *nf* : violet (flower)
violín *nm, pl* **-lines** : violin — **violinista** *nmf* : violinist — **violoncelista** *or* **violonchelista** *nmf* : cellist — **violoncelo** *or* **violonchelo** *nm* : cello, violoncello
virar *vi* : turn, change direction — **viraje** *nm* **1** : turn, swerve **2** CAMBIO : change
virgen *adj & nmf, pl* **vírgenes** : virgin — **virginal** *adj* : virginal — **virginidad** *nf* : virginity
viril *adj* : virile — **virilidad** *nf* : virility
virtual *adj* : virtual
virtud *nf* **1** : virtue **2 en** ~ **de** : by virtue of — **virtuoso, -sa** *adj* : virtuous — ~ *n* : virtuoso
viruela *nf* **1** : smallpox **2 picado de** ~**s** : pockmarked
virulento, -ta *adj* : virulent
virus *nms & pl* : virus
visa *nf Lat* : visa — **visado** *nm Spain* : visa
vísceras *nfpl* : entrails — **visceral** *adj* : visceral
viscoso, -sa *adj* : viscous — **viscosidad** *nf* : viscosity
visera *nf* : visor
visible *adj* : visible — **visibilidad** *nf* : visibility
visión *nf, pl* **-siones 1** : eyesight **2** APARICIÓN : vision, illusion **3** PUNTO DE VISTA : view, perspective — **visionario, -ria** *adj & n* : visionary
visitar *vt* : visit — **visita** *nf* **1** : visit **2 tener** ~ : have company — **visitante** *adj* : visiting — ~ *nmf* : visitor
vislumbrar *vt* : make out, discern — **vislumbre** *nf* **1** : glimpse, sign **2** RESPLANDOR : glimmer, gleam
viso *nm* **1** : sheen **2 tener** ~**s de** : seem, show signs of
visón *nm, pl* **-sones** : mink
víspera *nf* : eve, day before
vista *nf* **1** : vision, eyesight **2** MIRADA : look, gaze **3** PANORAMA : view, vista **4** : hearing (in court) **5 a primera** ~ *or* **a simple** ~ : at first sight **6 hacer la** ~ **gorda** : turn a blind eye **7 perder de** ~ : lose sight of — **vistazo** *nm* **1** : glance **2 echar un** ~ : have a look
visto, -ta *adj* **1** : clear, obvious **2** COMÚN : commonly seen **3 estar bien** ~ : be approved of **4 estar mal** ~ : be frowned upon **5 nunca** ~ : unheard-

of **6 por lo visto** : apparently **7 visto que** : since, given that — **visto** *nm* **~ bueno** : approval — **~** *pp* → **ver**
vistoso, -sa *adj* : colorful, bright
visual *adj* : visual — **visualizar** {21} *vt* : visualize
vital *adj* : vital — **vitalicio, -cia** *adj* : life, for life — **vitalidad** *nf* : vitality
vitamina *nf* : vitamin
viticultor, -tora *n* : winegrower — **viticultura** *nf* : wine growing
vitorear *vt* : cheer, acclaim
vítreo, -trea *adj* : glassy
vitrina *nf* **1** : showcase, display case **2** *Lat* : shopwindow
vituperar *vt* : censure — **vituperio** *nm* : censure
viudo, -da *n* : widower *m*, widow *f* — **~** *adj* : widowed — **viudez** *nf* : widowerhood, widowhood
viva *nm* **dar ~s** : cheer
vivacidad *nf* : vivacity, liveliness
vivamente *adv* **1** : vividly **2** PROFUNDAMENTE : deeply, acutely
vivaz *adj, pl* **-vaces 1** : lively, vivacious **2** AGUDO : vivid, sharp
víveres *nmpl* : provisions, supplies
vivero *nm* **1** : nursery (for plants) **2** : (fish) hatchery, (oyster) bed
viveza *nf* **1** : liveliness **2** : vividness (of colors, descriptions, etc.) **3** ASTUCIA : sharpness (of mind) — **vívido, -da** *adj* : vivid
vividor, -dora *n* : freeloader
vivienda *nf* **1** : housing **2** MORADA : dwelling
viviente *adj* : living
vivificar {72} *vt* : enliven
vivir *vi* **1** : live, be alive **2 ~ de** : live on — *vt* : experience, live (through) — **~** *nm* **1** : life, lifestyle **2 de mal ~** : disreputable — **vivo, -va** *adj* **1** : alive **2** INTENSO : intense, bright **3** ANIMADO : lively **4** ASTUTO : sharp, quick **5 en vivo** : live
vocablo *nm* : word — **vocabulario** *nm* : vocabulary
vocación *nf, pl* **-ciones** : vocation — **vocacional** *adj* : vocational
vocal *adj* : vocal — **~** *nmf* : member (of a committee, etc.) — **~** *nf* : vowel — **vocalista** *nmf* : singer, vocalist
vocear *v* : shout — **vocerío** *nm* : shouting
vociferar *vi* : shout
vodka *nmf* : vodka
volar {19} *vi* **1** : fly **2** : blow away (of papers, etc.) **3** *fam* : disappear **4 irse volando** : rush off — *vt* : blow up — **volador, -dora** *adj* : flying — **volandas**: **en ~** *adv phr* : in the air — **volante** *adj* : flying — **~** *nm* **1** : steering wheel **2** : shuttlecock (in badminton) **3** : flounce (of fabric) **4** *Lat* : flier, circular
volátil *adj* : volatile
volcán *nm, pl* **-canes** : volcano — **volcánico, -ca** *adj* : volcanic
volcar {82} *vt* **1** : upset, knock over **2** VACIAR : empty out — *vi* : overturn — **volcarse** *vr* **1** : overturn, tip over **2 ~ en** : throw oneself into
voleibol *nm* : volleyball
voltaje *nm* : voltage
voltear *vt* : turn over, turn upside down — **voltearse** *vr Lat* : turn (around) — **voltereta** *nf* : somersault
voltio *nm* : volt
voluble *adj* : fickle
volumen *nm, pl* **-lúmenes** : volume — **voluminoso, -sa** *adj* : voluminous
voluntad *nf* **1** : will **2** DESEO : wish **3** INTENCIÓN : intention **4 a ~** : at will **5 buena ~** : goodwill **6 mala ~** : ill will **7 fuerza de ~** : willpower — **voluntario, -ria** *adj* : voluntary — **~** *n* : volunteer — **voluntarioso, -sa** *adj* **1** : willing **2** TERCO : stubborn, willful
voluptuoso, -sa *adj* : voluptuous
volver {89} *vi* **1** : return, come or go back **2 ~ a** : return to, do again **3 ~ en sí** : come to — *vt* **1** : turn, turn over, turn inside out **2** CONVERTIR EN : turn (into) **3 ~ loco** : drive crazy — **volverse** *vr* **1** : turn (around) **2** HACERSE : become
vomitar *vi* : vomit — *vt* **1** : vomit **2** : spew (out) — **vómito** *nm* **1** : (action of) vomiting **2** : vomit
voraz *adj, pl* **-races** : voracious
vos *pron Lat* : you
vosotros, -tras *pron Spain* : you, yourselves
votar *vi* : vote — *vt* : vote for — **votación** *nf, pl* **-ciones** : vote, voting — **votante** *nmf* : voter — **voto** *nm* **1** : vote **2** : vow (in religion)
voy → **ir**
voz *nf, pl* **voces 1** : voice **2** GRITO : shout, yell **3** VOCABLO : word, term **4** RUMOR : rumor **5 dar voces** : shout **6 en ~ alta** : loudly **7 en ~ baja** : softly
vuelco *nm* : upset, overturning
vuelo *nm* **1** : flight **2** : (action of) flying **3** : flare (of clothing) **4 al ~** : on the wing
vuelta *nf* **1** : turn **2** REVOLUCIÓN : circle, revolution **3** CURVA : bend, curve **4** REGRESO : return **5** : round, lap (in sports)

6 PASEO : walk, drive, ride 7 REVÉS : back, other side 8 *Spain* : change 9 **dar ~s** : spin 10 **estar de ~** : be back — **vuelto** *nm Lat* : change
vuestro, -tra *adj Spain* : your, of yours — ~ *pron Spain* (*with definite article*) : yours
vulgar *adj* 1 : vulgar 2 CORRIENTE : common — **vulgaridad** *nf* 1 : vulgarity 2 BANALIDAD : banality — **vulgo** *nm* **el ~** : the masses, common people
vulnerable *adj* : vulnerable — **vulnerabilidad** *nf* : vulnerability

WXYZ

w *nf* : w, 24th letter of the Spanish alphabet
wáter *nm Spain* : toilet
whisky *nm, pl* **-skys** *or* **-skies** : whiskey
x *nf* : x, 25th letter of the Spanish alphabet
xenofobia *nf* : xenophobia
xilófono *nm* : xylophone
y[1] *nf* : y, 26th letter of the Spanish alphabet
y[2] *conj* : and
ya *adv* 1 : already 2 AHORA : (right) now 3 MÁS TARDE : later, soon 4 **~ no** : no longer 5 **~ que** : now that, since, inasmuch as
yacer {90} *vi* : lie (on or in the ground) — **yacimiento** *nm* : bed, deposit
yanqui *adj & nmf* : Yankee
yate *nm* : yacht
yegua *nf* : mare
yelmo *nm* : helmet
yema *nf* 1 : bud, shoot 2 : yolk (of an egg) 3 *or* **~ del dedo** : fingertip
yerba *nf* 1 *or* **~ mate** : maté 2 → **hierba**
yermo, -ma *adj* : barren, deserted — **yermo** *nm* : wasteland
yerno *nm* : son-in-law
yerro *nm* : blunder, mistake
yerto, -ta *adj* : stiff
yesca *nf* : tinder
yeso *nm* 1 : gypsum 2 : plaster (for art, construction)
yo *pron* 1 (*subject*) : I 2 (*object*) : me 3 **soy ~** : it is I, it's me — ~ *nm* : ego, self
yodo *nm* : iodine
yoga *nm* : yoga
yogurt *or* **yogur** *nm* : yogurt
yuca *nf* : yucca
yugo *nm* : yoke (of oxen)
yugoslavo, -va *adj* : Yugoslavian
yugular *adj* : jugular
yunque *nm* : anvil
yunta *nf* : yoke
yuxtaponer {60} *vt* : juxtapose — **yuxtaposición** *nf, pl* **-ciones** : juxtaposition
z *nf* : z, 27th letter of the Spanish alphabet
zacate *nm Lat* : grass
zafar *vt Lat* : loosen, untie — **zafarse** *vr* 1 : come undone 2 : get free of (an obligation, etc.)
zafio, -fia *adj* : coarse
zafiro *nm* : sapphire
zaga *nf* **a la ~** *or* **en ~** : behind, in the rear
zaguán *nm, pl* **-guanes** : (entrance) hall
zaherir {76} *vt* : hurt (s.o.'s feelings)
zaino, -na *adj* : chestnut (color)
zalamería *nf* : flattery — **zalamero, -ra** *adj* : flattering — ~ *n* : flatterer
zambullirse {38} *vr* : dive, plunge — **zambullida** *nf* : dive, plunge
zanahoria *nf* : carrot
zancada *nf* : stride, step — **zancadilla** *nf* 1 : trip, stumble 2 **hacer una ~ a algn** : trip s.o. up
zancos *nmpl* : stilts
zancudo *nm Lat* : mosquito
zángano, -na *n fam* : lazy person, slacker — **zángano** *nm* : drone (bee)
zanja *nf* : ditch, trench — **zanjar** *vt* : settle, resolve
zapallo *nm Lat* : pumpkin — **zapallito** *nm Lat* : zucchini
zapapico *nm* : pickax
zapato *nm* : shoe — **zapatería** *nf* : shoe store — **zapatero, -ra** *n* : shoemaker, cobbler — **zapatilla** *nf* 1 : slipper 2 : sneaker (for sports, etc.)
zar *nm* : czar
zarandear *vt* 1 : sift 2 SACUDIR : shake
zarcillo *nm* : earring
zarpa *nf* : paw
zarpar *vi* : set sail, raise anchor
zarza *nf* : bramble — **zarzamora** *nf* : blackberry
zigzag *nm, pl* **-zags** *or* **-zagues** : zigzag — **zigzaguear** *vi* : zigzag

zinc *nm* : zinc
zíper *nm Lat* : zipper
zircón *nm, pl* **-cones** : zircon
zócalo *nm* **1** : base (of a column, etc.) **2** : baseboard (of a wall) **3** *Lat* : main square, plaza
zodíaco *nm* : zodiac
zona *nf* : zone, area
zoo *nm* : zoo — **zoología** *nf* : zoology — **zoológico, -ca** *adj* : zoological — **zoológico** *nm* : zoo — **zoólogo, -ga** *n* : zoologist
zopilote *nm Lat* : buzzard
zoquete *nmf fam* : oaf, blockhead
zorrillo *nm Lat* : skunk
zorro, -rra *n* : fox, vixen *f* — **~** *adj* : foxy, sly
zozobra *nf* : anxiety, worry — **zozobrar** *vi* : capsize
zueco *nm* : clog (shoe)
zumbar *vi* : buzz — *vt fam* : hit, beat — **zumbido** *nm* : buzzing
zumo *nf* : juice
zurcir {83} *vt* : darn, mend
zurdo, -da *adj* : left-handed — **~** *n* : left-handed person — **zurda** *nf* : left hand
zutano, -na → **fulano**

English-Spanish Dictionary

A

a[1] [ˈeɪ] *n, pl* **a's** *or* **as** [ˈeɪz] : a *f*, primera letra del alfabeto inglés

a[2] [ə, ˈeɪ] *art* (**an** [ən, ˈæn] *before vowel or silent h*) **1** : un *m*, una *f* **2** PER : por, a la, al

aback [əˈbæk] *adv* **be taken ~** : quedarse desconcertado

abacus [ˈæbəkəs] *n, pl* **abaci** [ˈæbəˌsaɪ, -ˌkiː] *or* **abacuses** : ábaco *m*

abandon [əˈbændən] *vt* **1** DESERT : abandonar **2** GIVE UP : renunciar a — **~** *n* : desenfreno *m* — **abandonment** [əˈbændənmənt] *n* : abandono *m*

abashed [əˈbæʃt] *adj* : avergonzado

abate [əˈbeɪt] *vi* **abated; abating** : amainar, disminuir

abattoir [ˈæbəˌtwɑr] *n* : matadero *m*

abbey [ˈæbi] *n, pl* **-beys** : abadía *f* — **abbot** [ˈæbət] *n* : abad *m*

abbreviate [əˈbriːviˌeɪt] *vt* **-ated; -ating** : abreviar — **abbreviation** [əˌbriːviˈeɪʃən] *n* : abreviatura *f*, abreviación *f*

abdicate [ˈæbdɪˌkeɪt] *v* **-cated; -cating** : abdicar — **abdication** [ˌæbdɪˈkeɪæən] *n* : abdicación *f*

abdomen [ˈæbdəmən, æbˈdoːmən] *n* : abdomen *m*, vientre *m* — **abdominal** [æbˈdɑmənəl] *adj* : abdominal

abduct [æbˈdʌkt] *vt* : secuestrar — **abduction** [æbˈdʌkʃən] *n* : secuestro *m*

aberration [ˌæbəˈreɪʃən] *n* : aberración *f*

abet [əˈbɛt] *vt* **abetted; abetting** *or* **aid and ~** : ser cómplice de

abeyance [əˈbeɪənts] *n* : desuso *m*

abhor [əbˈhɔr, æb-] *vt* **-horred; -horring** : aborrecer

abide [əˈbaɪd] *v* **abode** [əˈboːd] *or* **abided; abiding** *vt* : soportar, tolerar — *vi* **1** DWELL : morar **2 ~ by** : atenerse a

ability [əˈbɪləṭi] *n, pl* **-ties 1** CAPABILITY : aptitud *f*, capacidad *f* **2** SKILL : habilidad *f*

abject [ˈæbˌdʒɛkt, æbˈ-] *adj* : miserable, desdichado

ablaze [əˈbleɪz] *adj* : en llamas

able [ˈeɪbəl] *adj* **abler; ablest 1** CAPABLE : capaz, hábil **2** COMPETENT : competente

abnormal [æbˈnɔrməl] *adj* : anormal — **abnormality** [ˌæbnərˈmæləṭi, -nɔr-] *n, pl* **-ties** : anormalidad *f*

aboard [əˈbord] *adv* : a bordo — **~** *prep* : a bordo de

abode *n* : morada *f*, domicilio *m*

abolish [əˈbɑlɪʃ] *vt* : abolir, suprimir — **abolition** [ˌæbəˈlɪʃən] *n* : abolición *f*

abominable [əˈbɑmənəbəl] *adj* : abominable, aborrecible — **abomination** [əˌbɑməˈneɪʃən] *n* : abominación *f*

aborigine [ˌæbəˈrɪdʒəni] *n* : aborigen *mf*

abort [əˈbɔrt] *vt* : abortar — **abortion** [əˈbɔrʃən] *n* : aborto *m* — **abortive** [əˈbɔrṭɪv] *adj* UNSUCCESSFUL : malogrado

abound [əˈbaʊnd] *vi* **~ in** : abundar en

about [əˈbaʊt] *adv* **1** APPROXIMATELY : aproximadamente, más o menos **2** AROUND : alrededor **3 be ~ to** : estar a punto de **4 be up and ~** : estar levantado — **~** *prep* **1** AROUND : alrededor de **2** CONCERNING : acerca de, sobre

above [əˈbʌv] *adv* : arriba — **~** *prep* **1** : encima de **2 ~ all** : sobre todo — **aboveboard** *adj* : honrado

abrasive [əˈbreɪsɪv] *adj* **1** : abrasivo **2** BRUSQUE : brusco, mordaz

abreast [əˈbrɛst] *adv* **1** : al lado **2 keep ~ of** : mantenerse al corriente de

abridge [əˈbrɪdʒ] *vt* **abridged; abridging** : abreviar

abroad [əˈbrɔd] *adv* **1** : en el extranjero **2** WIDELY : por todas partes **3 go ~** : ir al extranjero

abrupt [əˈbrʌpt] *adj* **1** SUDDEN : repentino **2** BRUSQUE : brusco

abscess [ˈæbˌsɛs] *n* : absceso *m*

absence [ˈæbsənts] *n* **1** : ausencia *f* **2** LACK : falta *f*, carencia *f* — **absent** [ˈæbsənt] *adj* : ausente — **absentee** [ˌæbsənˈtiː] *n* : ausente *mf* — **absent-minded** [ˌæbsəntˈmaɪndəd] *adj* : distraído, despistado

absolute [ˈæbsəˌluːt, ˌæbsəˈluːt] *adj* : absoluto — **absolutely** [ˌæbsəˈluːtli] *adv* : absolutamente

absolve [əbˈzɑlv, æb-, -ˈsɑlv] *vt* **-solved; -solving** : absolver

absorb [əbˈzɔrb, æb-, -ˈsɔrb] *vt* : absorber — **absorbent** [əbˈzɔrbənt, æb-, -ˈsɔr-] *adj* : absorbente — **absorption** [əbˈzɔrpʃən, æb-, -ˈsɔrp-] *n* : absorción *f*

abstain [əbˈsteɪn, æb-] *vi* **~ from** : abstenerse de — **abstinence** [ˈæbstənənts] *n* : abstinencia *f*

abstract [æb'strækt, 'æb,-] *adj* : abstracto — ~ *vt* : extraer — ~ ['æb,strækt] *n* : resumen *m* — **abstraction** [æb'strækʃən] *n* : abstracción *f*
absurd [əb'sərd, -'zərd] *adj* : absurdo — **absurdity** [əb'sərdəṭi, -'zərdəṭi] *n, pl* **-ties** : absurdo *m*
abundant [ə'bʌndənt] *adj* : abundante — **abundance** [ə'bʌndənts] *n* : abundancia *f*
abuse [ə'bju:z] *vt* **abused; abusing 1** MISUSE : abusar de **2** MISTREAT : maltratar **3** REVILE : insultar — ~ [ə'bju:s] *n* **1** : abuso *m* **2** INSULTS : insultos *mpl* — **abusive** [ə'bju:sɪv] *adj* : injurioso
abut [ə'bʌt] *vi* **abutted; abutting ~ on** : colindar con
abyss [ə'bɪs, 'æbɪs] *n* : abismo *m* — **abysmal** [ə'bɪzməl] *adj* : atroz, pésimo
academy [ə'kædəmi] *n, pl* **-mies** : academia *f* — **academic** [,ækə'dɛmɪk] *adj* **1** : académico **2** THEORETICAL : teórico
accelerate [ɪk'sɛlə,reɪt, æk-] *v* **-ated; -ating** : acelerar — **acceleration** [ɪk,sɛlə'reɪʃən, æk-] *n* : aceleración *f*
accent ['æk,sɛnt, æk'sɛnt] *vt* : acentuar — ~ ['æk,sɛnt, sənt] *n* : acento *m* — **accentuate** [ɪk'sɛntʃʊ,eɪt, æk-] *vt* **-ated; -ating** : acentuar, subrayar
accept [ɪk'sɛpt, æk-] *vt* : aceptar — **acceptable** [ɪk'sɛptəbəl, æk-] *adj* : aceptable — **acceptance** [ɪk'sɛptənts, æk-] *n* **1** : aceptación *f* **2** APPROVAL : aprobación *f*
access ['æk,sɛs] *n* : acceso *m* — **accessible** [ɪk'sɛsəbəl, æk-] *adj* : accesible, asequible
accessory *n, pl* **-ries 1** : accesorio *m* **2** ACCOMPLICE : cómplice *mf*
accident ['æksədənt] *n* **1** MISHAP : accidente *m* **2** CHANCE : casualidad *f* — **accidental** [,æksə'dɛntəl] *adj* : accidental — **accidentally** [,æksə'dɛntəli, -'dɛntli] *adv* **1** BY CHANCE : por casualidad **2** UNINTENTIONALLY : sin querer
acclaim [ə'kleɪm] *vt* : aclamar — ~ *n* : aclamación *f*
acclimatize [ə'klaɪmə,taɪz] *vt* **-tized; -tizing** : aclimatar
accommodate [ə'kɑmə,deɪt] *vt* **-dated; -dating 1** ADAPT : acomodar, adaptar **2** SATISFY : complacer, satisfacer **3** HOLD : tener cabida para — **accomodation** [ə,kɑmə'deɪʃən] *n* **1** : adaptación *f* **2 ~s** *npl* LODGING : alojamiento *m*
accompany [ə'kʌmpəni, -'kɑm-] *vt* **-nied; -nying** : acompañar
accomplice [ə'kɑmpləs, -'kʌm-] *n* : cómplice *mf*
accomplish [ə'kɑmplɪʃ, -'kʌm-] *vt* : realizar, llevar a cabo — **accomplishment** [ə'kɑmplɪʃmənt, -'kʌm-] *n* **1** COMPLETION : realización *f* **2** ACHIEVEMENT : logro *m*, éxito *m*
accord *n* **1** AGREEMENT : acuerdo *m* **2 of one's own ~** : voluntariamente — **accordance** [ə'kɔrdənts] *n* **in ~ with** : conforme a, de acuerdo con — **accordingly** [ə'kɔrdɪŋli] *adv* : en consecuencia — **according to** [ə'kɔrdɪŋ] *prep* : según
accordion [ə'kɔrdiən] *n* : acordeón *m*
accost [ə'kɔst] *vt* : abordar
account [ə'kaʊnt] *n* **1** : cuenta *f* **2** REPORT : relato *m*, informe *m* **3** WORTH : importancia *f* **4 on ~ of** : a causa de, debido a **5 on no ~** : de ninguna manera — ~ *vi* **~ for** : dar cuenta de, explicar — **accountable** [ə'kaʊntəbəl] *adj* : responsable — **accountant** [ə'kaʊntənt] *n* : contador *m*, -dora *f Lat;* contable *mf Spain* — **accounting** [ə'kaʊntɪŋ] *n* : contabilidad *f*
accrue [ə'kru:] *vi* **-crued; -cruing** : acumularse
accumulate [ə'kju:mjə,leɪt] *v* **-lated; -lating** *vt* : acumular — *vi* : acumularse — **accumulation** [ə,kju:mjə'leɪʃən] *n* : acumulación *f*
accurate ['ækjərət] *adj* : exacto, preciso — **accuracy** ['ækjərəsi] *n* : exactitud *f*, precisión *f*
accuse [ə'kju:z] *vt* **-cused; -cusing** : acusar — **accusation** [,ækjə'zeɪʃən] *n* : acusación *f*
accustomed [ə'kʌstəmd] *adj* **1** : acostumbrado **2 become ~ to** : acostumbrarse a
ace ['eɪs] *n* : as *m*
ache ['eɪk] *vi* **ached; aching** : doler — ~ *n* : dolor *m*
achieve [ə'tʃi:v] *vt* **achieved; achieving** : lograr, realizar — **achievement** [ə'tʃi:vmənt] *n* : logro *m*, éxito *m*
acid ['æsəd] *adj* : ácido — ~ *n* : ácido *m*
acknowledge [ɪk'nɑlɪdʒ, æk-] *vt* **-edged; -edging 1** ADMIT : admitir **2** RECOGNIZE : reconocer **3 ~ receipt of** : acusar recibo de — **acknowledgment** [ɪk'nɑlɪdʒmənt, æk-] *n* **1** : reconocimiento *m* **2** THANKS : agradecimiento *m* **3 ~ of receipt** : acuse *m* de recibo
acne ['ækni] *n* : acné *m*
acorn ['eɪ,kɔrn, -kərn] *n* : bellota *f*
acoustic [ə'ku:stɪk] *or* **acoustical** [-stɪkəl] *adj* : acústico — **acoustics** [ə'ku:stɪks] *ns & pl* : acústica *f*
acquaint [ə'kweɪnt] *vt* **1 ~ s.o. with**

: poner a algn al corriente de **2 be ~ed with** : conocer a (una persona), saber (un hecho) — **acquaintance** [ə'kweɪntənts] *n* **1** : conocimiento *m* **2** : conocido *m*, -da *f* (persona)
acquire [ə'kwaɪr] *vt* **-quired; -quiring** : adquirir — **acquisition** [ˌækwə'zɪʃən] *n* : adquisición *f*
acquit [ə'kwɪt] *vt* **-quitted; -quitting** : absolver
acre ['eɪkər] *n* : acre *m* — **acreage** ['eɪkərɪdʒ] *n* : superficie *f* en acres
acrid ['ækrəd] *adj* : acre
acrobat ['ækrəˌbæt] *n* : acróbata *mf* — **acrobatic** [ˌækrə'bæt̬ɪk] *adj* : acrobático
acronym ['ækrəˌnɪm] *n* : siglas *fpl*
across [ə'krɔs] *adv* **1** : de un lado a otro **2** CROSSWISE : a través **3 go ~** : atravesar — **~** *prep* **1** : a través de **2 ~ the street** : al otro lado de la calle
acrylic [ə'krɪlɪk] *n* : acrílico *m*
act ['ækt] *vi* **1** : actuar **2** PRETEND : fingir **3** FUNCTION : funcionar **4 ~ as** : servir de — *vt* : interpretar (un papel) — **~** *n* **1** ACTION : acto *m*, acción *f* **2** DECREE : ley *f* **3** : acto *m* (en una obra de teatro), número *m* (en un espectáculo) — **acting** *adj* : interino
action ['ækʃən] *n* **1** : acción *f* **2** LAWSUIT : demanda *f* **3 take ~** : tomar medidas
activate ['æktəˌveɪt] *vt* **-vated; -vating** : activar
active ['æktɪv] *adj* **1** : activo **2** LIVELY : enérgico **3 ~ volcano** : volcán *m* en actividad — **activity** [æk'tɪvət̬i] *n, pl* **-ties** : actividad *f*
actor ['æktər] *n* : actor *m* — **actress** ['æktrəs] *n* : actriz *f*
actual ['æktʃʊəl] *adj* : real, verdadero — **actually** ['æktʃʊəli, -æəli] *adv* : realmente, en realidad
acupuncture ['ækjʊˌpʌŋktʃər] *n* : acupuntura *f*
acute [ə'kju:t] *adj* **acuter; acutest 1** : agudo **2** PERCEPTIVE : perspicaz
ad ['æd] → **advertisement**
adamant ['ædəmənt, -ˌmænt] *adj* : inflexible
adapt [ə'dæpt] *vt* : adaptar — *vi* : adaptarse — **adaptable** [ə'dæptəbəl] *adj* : adaptable — **adaptation** [ˌæˌdæp'teɪʃən, -dəp-] *n* : adaptación *f* — **adapter** [ə'dæptər] *n* : adaptador *m*
add ['æd] *vt* **1** : añadir **2** *or* **~ up** : sumar — *vi* : sumar
addict ['ædɪkt] *n* **1** : adicto *m*, -ta *f* **2** *or* **drug ~** : drogadicto *m*, -ta *f*; toxicómano *m*, -na *f* — **addiction** [ə'dɪkʃən] *n* : dependencia *f*
addition [ə'dɪʃən] *n* **1** : suma *f* (en matemáticas) **2** ADDING : adición *f* **3 in ~** : además — **additional** [ə'dɪʃənəl] *adj* : adicional — **additive** ['ædət̬ɪv] *n* : aditivo *m*
address [ə'drɛs] *vt* **1** : dirigirse a (una persona) **2** : ponerle la dirección a (una carta) **3** : tratar (un asunto) — **~** [ə'drɛs, 'æˌdrɛs] *n* **1** : dirección *f*, domicilio *m* **2** SPEECH : discurso *m*
adept [ə'dɛpt] *adj* : experto, hábil
adequate ['ædɪkwət] *adj* : adecuado, suficiente
adhere [æd'hɪr, əd-] *vi* **-hered; -hering 1** STICK : adherirse **2 ~ to** : observar — **adherence** [æd'hɪrənts, əd-] *n* **1** : adhesión *f* **2** : observancia *f* (de una ley, etc.) — **adhesive** [æd'hi:sɪv, əd-, -zɪv] *adj* : adhesivo — **~** *n* : adhesivo *m*
adjacent [ə'dʒeɪsənt] *adj* : adyacente, contiguo
adjective ['ædʒɪktɪv] *n* : adjetivo *m*
adjoining [ə'dʒɔɪnɪŋ] *adj* : contiguo, vecino
adjourn [ə'dʒərn] *vt* : aplazar, suspender — *vi* : suspenderse
adjust [ə'dʒʌst] *vt* : ajustar, arreglar — *vi* : adaptarse — **adjustable** [ə'dʒʌstəbəl] *adj* : ajustable — **adjustment** [ə'dʒʌstmənt] *n* : ajuste *m* (a una máquina, etc.), adaptación *f* (de una persona)
ad–lib ['æd'lɪb] *v* **-libbed; -libbing** : improvisar
administer [æd'mɪnəstər, əd-] *vt* : administrar — **administration** [ædˌmɪnə'streɪʃən, əd-] *n* : administración *f* — **administrative** [æd'mɪnəˌstreɪt̬ɪv, əd-] *adj* : administrativo — **administrator** [æd'mɪnəˌstreɪt̬ər, əd-] *n* : administrador *m*, -dora *f*
admirable ['ædmərəbəl] *adj* : admirable
admiral ['ædmərəl] *n* : almirante *m*
admire [æd'maɪr] *vt* **-mired; -miring** : admirar — **admiration** [ˌædmə'reɪʃən] *n* : admiración *f* — **admirer** [æd'maɪrər] *n* : admirador *m*, -dora *f*
admit [æd'mɪt, əd-] *vt* **-mitted; -mitting 1** : admitir, dejar entrar **2** ACKNOWLEDGE : reconocer — **admission** [æd'mɪʃən] *n* **1** ADMITTANCE : entrada *f*, admisión *f* **2** ACKNOWLEDGMENT : reconocimiento *m* — **admittance** [æd'mɪtənts, əd-] *n* : admisión *f*, entrada *f*
admonish [æd'mɑnɪʃ, əd-] *vt* : amonestar, reprender
ado [ə'du:] *n* **1** : alboroto *m*, bulla *f* **2 without further ~** : sin más (preámbulos)

adolescent [ˌædəlˈɛsənt] *n* : adolescente *mf* — **adolescence** [ˌædəlˈɛsənts] *n* : adolescencia *f*
adopt [əˈdɑpt] *vt* : adoptar — **adoption** [əˈdɑpʃən] *n* : adopción *f*
adore [əˈdor] *vt* **adored; adoring 1** : adorar **2** LIKE, LOVE : encantarle (algo a uno) — **adorable** [əˈdorəbəl] *adj* : adorable — **adoration** [ˌædəˈreɪæən] *n* : adoración *f*
adorn [əˈdɔrn] *vt* : adornar — **adornment** [əˈdɔrnmənt] *n* : adorno *m*
adrift [əˈdrɪft] *adj & adv* : a la deriva
adroit [əˈdrɔɪt] *adj* : diestro, hábil
adult [əˈdʌlt, ˈæˌdʌlt] *adj* : adulto — ~ *n* : adulto *m*, -ta *f*
adultery [əˈdʌltəri] *n, pl* **-teries** : adulterio *m*
advance [ædˈvænts, əd-] *v* **-vanced; -vancing** *vt* : adelantar — *vi* : avanzar, adelantarse — ~ *n* **1** : avance *m* **2** PROGRESS : adelanto *m* **3 in ~** : por adelantado — **advancement** [ædˈvæntsmənt, əd-] *n* : adelanto *m*, progreso *m*
advantage [ədˈvæntɪdʒ, æd-] *n* **1** : ventaja *f* **2 take ~ of** : aprovecharse de — **advantageous** [ˌædˌvænˈteɪdʒəs, -vən-] *adj* : ventajoso
advent [ˈædˌvɛnt] *n* **1** ARRIVAL : llegada *f* **2 Advent** : Adviento *m*
adventure [ædˈvɛntʃər, əd-] *n* : aventura *f* — **adventurous** [ædˈvɛntʃərəs, əd-] *adj* **1** : intrépido **2** RISKY : arriesgado
adverb [ˈædˌvərb] *n* : adverbio *m*
adversary [ˈædvərˌsɛri] *n, pl* **-saries** : adversario *m*, -ria *f*
adverse [ædˈvərs, ˈæd-,] *adj* : adverso, desfavorable — **adversity** [ædˈvərsət̬i, əd-] *n, pl* **-ties** : adversidad *f*
advertise [ˈædvərˌtaɪz] *v* **-tised; -tising** *vt* : anunciar — *vi* : hacer publicidad — **advertisement** [ˈædvərˌtaɪzmənt] *n* : anuncio *m* — **advertiser** [ˈædvərˌtaɪzər] *n* : anunciante *mf* — **advertising** [ˈædvərˌtaɪzɪŋ] *n* : publicidad *f*
advice [ædˈvaɪs] *n* : consejo *m*
advise [ædˈvaɪz, əd-] *vt* **-vised; -vising 1** COUNSEL : aconsejar, asesorar **2** RECOMMEND : recomendar **3** INFORM : informar — **advisable** [ædˈvaɪzəbəl, əd-] *adj* : aconsejable — **adviser** [ædˈvaɪzər, əd-] *n* : consejero *m*, -ra *f;* asesor *m*, -sora *f* — **advisory** [ædˈvaɪzəri, əd-] *adj* : consultivo
advocate [ˈædvəˌkeɪt] *vt* **-cated; -cating** : recomendar — ~ [ˈædvəkət] *n* : defensor *m*, -sora *f*
aerial [ˈæriəl] *adj* : aéreo — ~ *n* : antena *f*
aerobics [ˌæˈroːbɪks] *ns & pl* : aeróbic *m*
aerodynamic [ˌæroːdaɪˈnæmɪk] *adj* : aerodinámico
aerosol [ˈærəˌsɔl] *n* : aerosol *m*
aesthetic [ɛsˈθɛt̬ɪk] *adj* : estético
afar [əˈfɑr] *adv* : lejos
affable [ˈæfəbəl] *adj* : afable
affair [əˈfær] *n* **1** : asunto *m*, cuestión *f* **2** *or* **love ~** : amorío *m*, aventura *f*
affect [əˈfɛkt, æ-] *vt* **1** : afectar **2** FEIGN : fingir — **affection** [əˈfɛkʃən] *n* : afecto *m*, cariño *m* — **affectionate** [əˈfɛkʃənət] *adj* : afectuoso, cariñoso
affinity [əˈfɪnət̬i] *n, pl* **-ties** : afinidad *f*
affirm [əˈfərm] *vt* : afirmar — **affirmative** [əˈfərmət̬ɪv] *adj* : afirmativo
affix [əˈfɪks] *vt* : fijar, pegar
afflict [əˈflɪkt] *vt* : afligir — **affliction** [əˈflɪkʃən] *n* : aflicción *f*
affluent [ˈæˌfluːənt; æˈfluː-, ə-] *adj* : próspero, adinerado
afford [əˈford] *vt* **1** : tener los recursos para, permitirse (el lujo de) **2** PROVIDE : brindar
affront [əˈfrʌnt] *n* : afrenta *f*
afloat [əˈfloːt] *adv & adj* : a flote
afoot [əˈfʊt] *adj* : en marcha
afraid [əˈfreɪd] *adj* **1 be ~** : tener miedo **2 I'm ~ not** : me temo que no
African [ˈæfrɪkən] *adj* : africano
after [ˈæftər] *adv* **1** AFTERWARD : después **2** BEHIND : detrás, atrás — ~ *conj* : después de (que) — ~ *prep* **1** : después de **2 ~ all** : después de todo **3 it's ten ~ five** : son las cinco y diez
aftereffect [ˈæftərəˌfɛkt] *n* : efecto *m* secundario
aftermath [ˈæftərˌmæθ] *n* : consecuencias *fpl*
afternoon [ˌæftərˈnuːn] *n* : tarde *f*
afterward [ˈæftərwərd] *or* **afterwards** [-wərdz] *adv* : después, más tarde
again [əˈgɛn, -ˈgɪn] *adv* **1** : otra vez, de nuevo **2 ~ and ~** : una y otra vez **3 then ~** : por otra parte
against [əˈgɛntst, -ˈgɪntst] *prep* : contra, en contra de
age [ˈeɪdʒ] *n* **1** : edad *f* **2** ERA : era *f*, época *f* **3 be of ~** : ser mayor de edad **4 for ~s** : hace siglos **5 old ~** : vejez *f* — ~ *vi* **aged; aging** : envejecer — **aged** *adj* **1** [ˈeɪdʒəd, ˈeɪdʒd] OLD : anciano, viejo **2** [ˈeɪdʒd] **children ~ 10 to 17** : niños de 10 a 17 años
agency [ˈeɪdʒəntsi] *n, pl* **-cies** : agencia *f*
agenda [əˈdʒɛndə] *n* : orden *m* del día
agent [ˈeɪdʒənt] *n* : agente *mf*, representante *mf*
aggravate [ˈægrəˌveɪt] *vt* **-vated; -vating**

1 WORSEN : agravar, empeorar 2 ANNOY : irritar
aggregate ['ægrɪgət] *adj* : total, global — ~ *n* : total *m*
aggression [ə'grɛʃən] *n* : agresión *f* — **aggressive** [ə'grɛsɪv] *adj* : agresivo — **aggressor** [ə'grɛsər] *n* : agresor *m*, -sora *f*
aghast [ə'gæst] *adj* : horrorizado
agile ['ædʒəl] *adj* : ágil — **agility** [ə'dʒɪləṭi] *n, pl* **-ties** : agilidad *f*
agitate ['ædʒəˌteɪt] *v* **-tated; -tating** *vt* 1 SHAKE : agitar 2 TROUBLE : inquietar — **agitation** [ˌædʒə'teɪʃən] *n* : agitación *f*, inquietud *f*
agnostic [æg'nɑstɪk] *n* : agnóstico *m*, -ca *f*
ago [ə'go:] *adv* 1 : hace 2 **long** ~ : hace mucho tiempo
agony ['ægəni] *n, pl* **-nies** 1 PAIN : dolor *m* 2 ANGUISH : angustia *f* — **agonize** ['ægəˌnaɪz] *vi* **-nized; -nizing** : atormentarse — **agonizing** ['ægəˌnaɪzɪŋ] *adj* : angustioso
agree [ə'gri:] *v* **agreed; agreeing** *vt* 1 : acordar 2 ~ **that** : estar de acuerdo de que — *vi* 1 : estar de acuerdo 2 CORRESPOND : concordar 3 ~ **to** : acceder a 4 **this climate** ~**s with me** : este clima me sienta bien — **agreeable** [ə'gri:əbəl] *adj* 1 PLEASING : agradable 2 WILLING : dispuesto — **agreement** [ə'gri:mənt] *n* : acuerdo *m*
agriculture ['ægrɪˌkʌltʃər] *n* : agricultura *f* — **agricultural** [ˌægrɪ'kʌltʃərəl] *adj* : agrícola
aground [ə'graʊnd] *adv* **run** ~ : encallar
ahead [ə'hɛd] *adv* 1 IN FRONT : delante, adelante 2 BEFOREHAND : por adelantado 3 LEADING : a la delantera 4 **get** ~ : adelantar — **ahead of** *prep* 1 : delante de, antes de 2 **get** ~ **of** : adelantarse a
aid ['eɪd] *vt* : ayudar — ~ *n* : ayuda *f*, asistencia *f*
AIDS ['eɪdz] *n* : SIDA *m*, sida *m*
ail ['eɪl] *vi* : estar enfermo — **ailment** ['eɪlmənt] *n* : enfermedad *f*
aim ['eɪm] *vt* : apuntar (un arma), dirigir (una observación) — *vi* 1 : apuntar 2 ASPIRE : aspirar — ~ *n* 1 : puntería *f* 2 GOAL : propósito *m*, objetivo *m* — **aimless** ['eɪmləs] *adj* : sin objetivo
air ['ær] *vt or* ~ **out** : airear 2 EXPRESS : expresar 3 BROADCAST : emitir — ~ *n* 1 : aire *m* 2 **be on the** ~ : estar en el aire — **air–conditioning** [ˌærkən'dɪʃənɪŋ] *n* : aire *m* acondicionado — **air conditioned** ['ærkənˌdɪʃənd] *n* : climatizado — **aircraft** ['ærˌkræft] *ns & pl* 1 : avión *m*, aeronave *f* 2 ~ **carrier** : portaaviones *m* — **air force** *n* : fuerza *f* aérea — **airline** ['ærˌlaɪn] *n* : aerolínea *f*, línea *f* aérea — **airliner** ['ærˌlaɪnər] *n* : avión *m* de pasajeros — **airmail** *n* : correo *m* aéreo — **airplane** ['ærˌpleɪn] *n* : avión *m* — **airport** ['ærˌport] *n* : aeropuerto *m* — **airstrip** ['ærˌstrɪp] *n* : pista *f* de aterrizaje — **airtight** ['ær'taɪt] *adj* : hermético — **airy** ['æri] *adj* **airier** [-iər]; **-est** : aireado, bien ventilado
aisle ['aɪl] *n* 1 : pasillo *m* 2 : nave *f* lateral (de una iglesia)
ajar [ə'dʒɑr] *adj* : entreabierto
akin [ə'kɪn] *adj* ~ **to** : semejante a
alarm [ə'lɑrm] *n* 1 : alarma *f* 2 ANXIETY : inquietud *f* — *vt* : alarmar, asustar — **alarm clock** *n* : despertador *m*
alas [ə'læs] *interj* : ¡ay!
album ['ælbəm] *n* : álbum *m*
alcohol ['ælkəˌhɔl] *n* : alcohol *m* — **alcoholic** [ˌælkə'hɔlɪk] *adj* : alcohólico — ~ *n* : alcohólico *m*, -ca *f* — **alcoholism** ['ælkəhɔˌlɪzəm] *n* : alcoholismo *m*
alcove ['ælˌko:v] *n* : nicho *m*, hueco *m*
ale ['eɪl] *n* : cerveza *f*
alert [ə'lərt] *adj* 1 WATCHFUL : alerta, atento 2 LIVELY : vivo — ~ *n* : alerta *f* — ~ *vt* : alertar, poner sobre aviso
alfalfa [æl'fælfə] *n* : alfalfa *f*
alga ['ælgə] *n, pl* **-gae** ['ælˌdʒi:] : alga *f*
algebra ['ældʒəbrə] *n* : álgebra *f*
alias ['eɪliəs] *adv* : alias — ~ *n* : alias *m*
alibi ['æləˌbaɪ] *n* : coartada *f*
alien ['eɪliən] *adj* : extranjero — ~ *n* 1 FOREIGNER : extranjero *m*, -ra *f* 2 EXTRATERRESTRIAL : extraterrestre *mf*
alienate ['eɪliəˌneɪt] *vt* **-ated; -ating** : enajenar — **alienation** [ˌeɪliə'neɪæən] *n* : enajenación *f*
alight [ə'laɪt] *vi* 1 LAND : posarse 2 ~ **from** : apearse de
align [ə'laɪn] *vt* : alinear — **alignment** [ə'laɪnmənt] *n* : alineación *f*
alike [ə'laɪk] *adv* : igual, del mismo modo — ~ *adj* : parecido
alimony ['æləˌmo:ni] *n, pl* **-nies** : pensión *f* alimenticia
alive [ə'laɪv] *adj* 1 LIVING : vivo, viviente 2 LIVELY : animado, activo
all ['ɔl] *adv* 1 COMPLETELY : todo, completamente 2 ~ **the better** : tanto mejor 3 ~ **the more** : aún más, todavía más — ~ *adj* : todo — ~ *pron* 1 : todo, -da 2 ~ **in** ~ : en general 3 **not at** ~ : de ninguna manera —

all–around [ˌɔləˈraʊnd] *adj* VERSATILE : completo
allay [əˈleɪ] *vt* **1** ALLEVIATE : aliviar **2** CALM : aquietar
allege [əˈlɛdʒ] *vt* **-leged; -leging** : alegar — **allegation** [ˌælɪˈgeɪʃən] *n* : alegato *m*, acusación *f* — **alleged** [əˈlɛdʒd, əˈlɛdʒəd] *adj* : presunto — **allegedly** [əˈlɛdʒədli] *adv* : supuestamente
allegiance [əˈli:dʒənts] *n* : lealtad *f*
allegory [ˈæləˌgori] *n, pl* **-ries** : alegoría *f* — **allegorical** [ˌæləˈgɔrɪkəl] *adj* : alegórico
allergy [ˈælərdʒi] *n, pl* **-gies** : alergia *f* — **allergic** [əˈlərdʒɪk] *adj* : alérgico
alleviate [əˈli:viˌeɪt] *vt* **-ated; -ating** : aliviar
alley [ˈæli] *n, pl* **-leys** : callejón *m*
alliance [əˈlaɪənts] *n* : alianza *f*
alligator [ˈæləˌgeɪt̬ər] *n* : caimán *m*
allocate [ˈæləˌkeɪt] *vt* **-cated; -cating** : asignar — **allocation** [ˌæləˈkeɪʃən] *n* : asignación *f*, reparto *m*
allot [əˈlɑt] *vt* **-lotted; -lotting** : asignar — **allotment** [əˈlɑtmənt] *n* : reparto *m*, asignación *f*
allow [əˈlaʊ] *vt* **1** PERMIT : permitir **2** GRANT : dar, conceder **3** ADMIT : admitir **4** CONCEDE : reconocer — *vi* **~ for** : tener en cuenta — **allowance** [əˈlaʊənts] *n* **1** : pensión *f*, subsidio *m* **2 make ~s for** : tener en cuenta, disculpar
alloy [ˈæˌlɔɪ, əˈlɔɪ] *n* : aleación *f*
all right *adv* **1** YES : sí, de acuerdo **2** WELL : bien **3** DEFINITELY : bien, sin duda — **~** *adj* : bien, bueno
allude [əˈlu:d] *vi* **-luded; -luding** : aludir
allure [əˈlʊr] *vt* **-lured; -luring** : atraer — **alluring** [əˈlʊrɪŋ] *adj* : atrayente, seductor
allusion [əˈlu:ʒən] *n* : alusión *f*
ally [əˈlaɪ, ˈæˌlaɪ] *vi* **-lied; -lying ~ oneself with** : aliarse con — **~** [ˈæˌlaɪ, əˈlaɪ] *n* : aliado *m*, **-da** *f*
almanac [ˈɔlməˌnæk, ˈæl-] *n* : almanaque *m*
almighty [ɔlˈmaɪt̬i] *adj* : omnipotente, todopoderoso
almond [ˈɑmənd, ˈɑl-, ˈæ-, ˈæl-] *n* : almendra *f*
almost [ˈɔlˌmo:st, ɔlˈmo:st] *adv* : casi
alms [ˈɑmz, ˈɑlmz, ˈælmz] *ns & pl* : limosna *f*
alone [əˈlo:n] *adv* : sólo, solamente, únicamente — **~** *adj* : solo
along [əˈlɔŋ] *adv* **1** FORWARD : adelante **2 ~ with** : con, junto con **3 all ~** : desde el principio — **~** *prep* : por, a lo largo de — **alongside** [əˌlɔŋˈsaɪd] *adv* : al costado — **~** *or* **~ of** *prep* : al lado de
aloof [əˈlu:f] *adj* : distante, reservado
aloud [əˈlaʊd] *adv* : en voz alta
alphabet [ˈælfəˌbɛt] *n* : alfabeto *m* — **alphabetical** [ˌælfəˈbɛt̬ɪkəl] *or* **alphabetic** [-ˈbɛt̬ɪk] *adj* : alfabético
already [ɔlˈrɛdi] *adv* : ya
also [ˈɔlˌso:] *adv* : también, además
altar [ˈɔltər] *n* : altar *m*
alter [ˈɔltər] *vt* : alterar, modificar — **alteration** [ˌɔltəˈreɪʃən] *n* : alteración *f*, modificación *f*
alternate [ˈɔltərnət] *adj* : alterno — **~** [ˈɔltərˌneɪt] *v* **-nated; -nating** : alternar — **alternating current** *n* : corriente *f* alterna — **alternative** [ɔlˈtərnət̬ɪv] *adj* : alternativo — **~** *n* : alternativa *f*
although [ɔlˈðo:] *conj* : aunque
altitude [ˈæltəˌtu:d, -ˌtju:d] *n* : altitud *f*
altogether [ˌɔltəˈgɛðər] *adv* **1** COMPLETELY : completamente, del todo **2** ON THE WHOLE : en suma, en general
aluminum [əˈlu:mənəm] *n* : aluminio *m*
always [ˈɔlwiz, -ˌweɪz] *adv* **1** : siempre **2** FOREVER : para siempre
am → **be**
amass [əˈmæs] *vt* : amasar, acumular
amateur [ˈæmətʃər, -tər, -ˌtʊr, -ˌtjʊr] *adj* : amateur — **~** *n* : amateur *mf;* aficionado *m*, **-da** *f*
amaze [əˈmeɪz] *vt* **amazed; amazing** : asombrar — **amazement** [əˈmeɪzmənt] *n* : asombro *m* — **amazing** [əˈmeɪzɪŋ] *adj* : asombroso
ambassador [æmˈbæsədər] *n* : embajador *m*, **-dora** *f*
amber [ˈæmbər] *n* : ámbar *m*
ambiguous [æmˈbɪgjʊəs] *adj* : ambiguo — **ambiguity** [ˌæmbəˈgju:ət̬i] *n, pl* **-ties** : ambigüedad *f*
ambition [æmˈbɪʃən] *n* : ambición *f* — **ambitious** [æmˈbɪʃəs] *adj* : ambicioso
ambivalence [æmˈbɪvələnts] *n* : ambivalencia *f* — **ambivalent** [æmˈbɪvələnt] *adj* : ambivalente
amble [ˈæmbəl] *vi or* **~ along** : andar sin prisa
ambulance [ˈæmbjələnts] *n* : ambulancia *f*
ambush [ˈæmˌbʊʃ] *vt* : emboscar — **~** *n* : emboscada *f*
amen [ˈeɪˈmɛn, ˈɑ-] *interj* : amén
amenable [əˈmi:nəbəl, -ˈmɛ-] *adj* **~ to** : receptivo a
amend [əˈmɛnd] *vt* : enmendar — **amendment** [əˈmɛndmənt] *n* : enmienda *f* — **amends** [əˈmɛndz] *ns & pl* **make ~ for** : reparar

amenities [ə'mɛnət̬iz, -'mi:-] *npl* : servicios *mpl*, comodidades *fpl*
American [ə'mɛrɪkən] *adj* : americano
amethyst ['æməθəst] *n* : amatista *f*
amiable ['eɪmi:əbəl] *adj* : amable, agradable
amicable ['æmɪkəbəl] *adj* : amigable, amistoso
amid [ə'mɪd] *or* **amidst** [ə'mɪdst] *prep* : en medio de, entre
amiss [ə'mɪs] *adv* **1** : mal **2 take sth ~** : tomar algo a mal — **~** *adj* **1** WRONG : malo **2 something is ~** : algo anda mal
ammonia [ə'mo:njə] *n* : amoníaco *m*
ammunition [,æmjə'nɪʃən] *n* : municiones *fpl*
amnesia [æm'ni:ʒə] *n* : amnesia *f*
amnesty ['æmnəsti] *n, pl* **-ties** : amnistía *f*
among [ə'mʌŋ] *prep* : entre
amorous ['æmərəs] *adj* : amoroso
amount [ə'maʊnt] *vi* **1 ~ to** : equivaler a **2 ~ to** TOTAL : sumar, ascender a — **~** *n* : cantidad *f*
amphibian [æm'fɪbiən] *n* : anfibio *m* — **amphibious** [æm'fɪbiəs] *adj* : anfibio
amphitheater ['æmfə,θi:ət̬ər] *n* : anfiteatro *m*
ample ['æmpəl] *adj* **-pler**; **-plest 1** SPACIOUS : amplio, extenso **2** ABUNDANT : abundante
amplify ['æmplə,faɪ] *vt* **-fied; -fying** : amplificar — **amplifier** ['æmplə,faɪər] *n* : amplificador *m*
amputate ['æmpjə,teɪt] *vt* **-tated; -tating** : amputar — **amputation** [,æmpjə'teɪʃən] *n* : amputación *f*
amuse [ə'mju:z] *vt* **amused; amusing 1** : hacer reír, divertir **2** ENTERTAIN : entretener — **amusement** [ə'mju:zmənt] *n* : diversión *f* — **amusing** *adj* : divertido
an → **a**²
analogy [ə'nælədʒi] *n, pl* **-gies** : analogía *f* — **analogous** [ə'næləgəs] *adj* : análogo
analysis [ə'næləsəs] *n, pl* **-yses** [-,si:z] : análisis *m* — **analytic** [,ænə'lɪt̬ɪk] *or* **analytical** [-t̬ɪkəl] *adj* : analítico — **analyze** ['ænə,laɪz] *vt* **-lyzed; -lyzing** : analizar
anarchy ['ænərki, -nɑr-] *n* : anarquía *f*
anatomy [ə'næt̬əmi] *n, pl* **-mies** : anatomía *f* — **anatomic** [,ænə'tɑmɪk] *or* **anatomical** [-mɪkəl] *adj* : anatómico
ancestor ['æn,sɛstər] *n* : antepasado *m*, -da *f* — **ancestral** [æn'sɛstrəl] *adj* : ancestral — **ancestry** ['æn,sɛstri] *n* **1** DESCENT : linaje *m*, abolengo *m* **2** ANCESTORS : antepasados *mpl*, -das *fpl*
anchor ['æŋkər] *n* **1** : ancla *f* **2** : presentador *m*, -dora *f* (en televisión) — **~** *vt* **1** : anclar **2** FASTEN : sujetar — *vi* : anclar
anchovy ['æn,tʃo:vi, æn'tʃo:-] *n, pl* **-vies** *or* **-vy** : anchoa *f*
ancient ['eɪntʃənt] *adj* : antiguo, viejo
and ['ænd] *conj* **1** : y (e *before words beginning with i- or hi-*) **2 come ~ see** : ven a ver **3 more ~ more** : cada vez más **4 try ~ finish it soon** : trata de terminarlo pronto
anecdote ['ænɪk,do:t] *n* : anécdota *f*
anemia [ə'ni:miə] *n* : anemia *f* — **anemic** [ə'ni:mɪk] *adj* : anémico
anesthesia [,ænəs'θi:ʒə] *n* : anestesia *f* — **anesthetic** [,ænəs'θɛt̬ɪk] *adj* : anestésico — **~** *n* : anestésico *m*
anew [ə'nu:, -'nju:] *adv* : de nuevo, nuevamente
angel ['eɪndʒəl] *n* : ángel *m* — **angelic** [æn'dʒɛlɪk] *or* **angelical** [-lɪkəl] *adj* : angélico
anger ['æŋgər] *vt* : enojar, enfadar — **~** *n* : ira *f*, enojo *m*, enfado *m*
angle *n* **1** : ángulo *m* **2** POINT OF VIEW : perspectiva *f*, punto *m* de vista — **angler** ['æŋglər] *n* : pescador *m*, -dora *f*
Anglo–Saxon [,æŋglo'sæksən] *adj* : anglosajón
angry ['æŋgri] *adj* **-grier; -est** : enojado, enfadado
anguish ['æŋgwɪʃ] *n* : angustia *f*
angular ['æŋgjələr] *adj* **1** : angular **2 ~ features** : rasgos *mpl* angulosos
animal ['ænəməl] *n* : animal *m*
animate ['ænəmət] *adj* : animado — **~** ['ænə,meɪt] *vt* **-mated; -mating** : animar — **animated** *adj* **1** : animado **2 ~ cartoon** : dibujos *mpl* animados — **animation** [,ænə'meɪʃən] *n* : animación *f*
animosity [,ænə'mɑsət̬i] *n, pl* **-ties** : animosidad *f*
anise ['ænəs] *n* : anís *m*
ankle ['æŋkəl] *n* : tobillo *m*
annals ['ænəlz] *npl* : anales *mpl*
annex [ə'nɛks, 'æ,nɛks] *vt* : anexar — **~** ['æ,nɛks, -nɪks] *n* : anexo *m*
annihilate [ə'naɪə,leɪt] *vt* **-lated; -lating** : aniquilar — **annihilation** [ə,naɪə'leɪʃən] *n* : aniquilación *f*
anniversary [,ænə'vərsəri] *n, pl* **-ries** : aniversario *m*
annotate ['ænə,teɪt] *vt* **-tated; -tating** : anotar — **annotation** [,ænə'teɪʃən] *n* : anotación *f*
announce [ə'naʊnts] *vt* **-nounced;**

-**nouncing** : anunciar — **announcement** [ə'naʊntsmənt] *n* : anuncio *m* — **announcer** [ə'naʊntsər] *n* : locutor *m*, -tora *f*

annoy [ə'nɔɪ] *vt* : fastidiar, molestar — **annoyance** [ə'nɔɪənts] *n* : fastidio *m*, molestia *f* — **annoying** [ə'nɔɪɪŋ] *adj* : molesto, fastidioso

annual ['ænjʊəl] *adj* : anual — ~ *n* : anuario *m*

annuity [ə'nu:əṭi] *n, pl* **-ties** : anualidad *f*

annul [ə'nʌl] *vt* **annulled; annulling** : anular — **annulment** [ə'nʌlmənt] *n* : anulación *f*

anoint [ə'nɔɪnt] *vt* : ungir

anomaly [ə'nɑməli] *n, pl* **-lies** : anomalía *f*

anonymous [ə'nɑnəməs] *adj* : anónimo — **anonymity** [ˌænə'nɪməṭi] *n* : anonimato *m*

another [ə'nʌðər] *adj* **1** : otro **2** **in ~ minute** : en un minuto más — ~ *pron* : otro, otra

answer ['æntsər] *n* **1** REPLY : respuesta *f*, contestación *f* **2** SOLUTION : solución *f* — ~ *vt* **1** : contestar a, responder a **2** **~ the door** : abrir la puerta — *vi* : contestar, responder

ant ['ænt] *n* : hormiga *f*

antagonize [æn'tægəˌnaɪz] *vt* **-nized; -nizing** : provocar la enemistad de — **antagonism** [æn'tægəˌnɪzəm] *n* : antagonismo *m*

antarctic [ænt'ɑrktɪk, -'ɑrṭɪk] *adj* : antártico

antelope ['æntəlˌo:p] *n, pl* **-lope** *or* **-lopes** : antílope *m*

antenna [æn'tɛnə] *n, pl* **-nae** [-ˌni:, -ˌnaɪ] *or* **-nas** : antena *f*

anthem ['ænθəm] *n* : himno *m*

anthology [æn'θɑlədʒi] *n, pl* **-gies** : antología *f*

anthropology [ˌænθrə'pɑlədʒi] *n* : antropología *f*

antibiotic [ˌæntibaɪ'ɑṭɪk, ˌæntaɪ-, -bi-] *adj* : antibiótico — ~ *n* : antibiótico *m*

antibody ['æntiˌbɑdi] *n, pl* **-bodies** : anticuerpo *m*

anticipate [æn'tɪsəˌpeɪt] *vt* **-pated; -pating** **1** FORESEE : anticipar, prever **2** EXPECT : esperar — **anticipation** [ænˌtɪsə'peɪʃən] *n* : anticipación *f*, expectación *f*

antics ['æntɪks] *npl* : payasadas *fpl*

antidote ['æntɪˌdo:t] *n* : antídoto *m*

antifreeze ['æntiˌfri:z] *n* : anticongelante *m*

antipathy [æn'tɪpəθi] *n, pl* **-thies** : antipatía *f*

antiquated ['æntəˌkweɪṭəd] *adj* : anticuado

antique [æn'ti:k] *adj* : antiguo — ~ *n* : antigüedad *f* — **antiquity** [æn'tɪkwəṭi] *n, pl* **-ties** : antigüedad *f*

anti–Semitic [ˌæntisə'mɪṭɪk, ˌæntaɪ-] *adj* : antisemita

antiseptic [ˌæntə'sɛptɪk] *adj* : antiséptico — ~ *n* : antiséptico *m*

antisocial [ˌænti'so:ʃəl, ˌæntaɪ-] *adj* **1** : antisocial **2** UNSOCIABLE : poco sociable

antithesis [æn'tɪθəsɪs] *n, pl* **-eses** [-ˌsi:z] : antítesis *f*

antlers ['æntlərz] *npl* : cornamenta *f*

antonym ['æntəˌnɪm] *n* : antónimo *m*

anus ['eɪnəs] *n* : ano *m*

anvil ['ænvəl, -vɪl] *n* : yunque *m*

anxiety [æŋk'zaɪəṭi] *n, pl* **-eties** **1** APPREHENSION : inquietud *f*, ansiedad *f* **2** EAGERNESS : anhelo *m* — **anxious** ['æŋkʃəs] *adj* **1** WORRIED : inquieto, preocupado **2** EAGER : ansioso — **anxiously** ['æŋkʃəsli] *adv* : con ansiedad

any ['ɛni] *adv* **1** SOMEWHAT : algo, un poco **2** **it's not ~ good** : no sirve para nada **3** **we can't wait ~ longer** : no podemos esperar más — ~ *adj* **1** : alguno **2** (*in negative constructions*) : ningún **3** WHATEVER : cualquier **4** **in ~ case** : en todo caso — ~ *pron* **1** : alguno, -na **2** : ninguno, -na **3** **do you want ~ more rice?** : ¿quieres más arroz?

anybody ['ɛniˌbʌdi, -ˌbɑ-] → **anyone**

anyhow ['ɛniˌhaʊ] *adv* **1** : de todas formas **2** HAPHAZARDLY : de cualquier modo

anymore [ˌɛni'mor] *adv* **not ~** : ya no

anyone ['ɛniˌwʌn] *pron* **1** SOMEONE : alguien **2** WHOEVER : quienquiera **3** **I don't see ~** : no veo a nadie

anyplace ['ɛniˌpleɪs] → **anywhere**

anything ['ɛniˌθɪŋ] *pron* **1** SOMETHING : algo, alguna cosa **2** (*in negative constructions*) : nada **3** WHATEVER : cualquier cosa, lo que sea

anytime ['ɛniˌtaɪm] *adv* : en cualquier momento

anyway ['ɛniˌweɪ] → **anyhow**

anywhere ['ɛniˌhwɛr] *adv* **1** : en cualquier parte, dondequiera **2** (*used in questions*) : en algún sitio **3** **I can't find it ~** : no lo encuentro por ninguna parte

apart [ə'pɑrt] *adv* **1** : aparte **2** **~ from** : excepto, aparte de **3** **fall ~** : deshacerse, hacerse pedazos **4** **live ~** : vivir separados **5** **take ~** : desmontar, desmantelar

apartment [ə'pɑrtmənt] *n* : apartamento *m*
apathy ['æpəθi] *n* : apatía *f* — **apathetic** [ˌæpə'θɛt̬ɪk] *adj* : apático, indiferente
ape *n* : simio *m*
aperture ['æpərtʃər, -ˌtʃʊr] *n* : abertura *f*
apex ['eɪˌpɛks] *n, pl* **apexes** *or* **apices** ['eɪpəˌsiːz, 'æ-] : ápice *m*, cumbre *f*
apiece [ə'piːs] *adv* : cada uno
aplomb [ə'plɑm, -'plʌm] *n* : aplomo *m*
apology [ə'pɑlədʒi] *n, pl* **-gies** : disculpa *f* — **apologetic** [əˌpɑlə'dʒɛt̬ɪk] *adj* : lleno de disculpas — **apologize** [ə'pɑləˌdʒaɪz] *vi* **-gized; -gizing** : disculparse, pedir perdón
apostle [ə'pɑsəl] *n* : apóstol *m*
apostrophe [ə'pɑstrəˌfiː] *n* : apóstrofo *m*
appall [ə'pɔl] *vt* : horrorizar — **appalling** [ə'pɔlɪŋ] *adj* : horroroso
apparatus [ˌæpə'ræt̬əs, -'reɪ-] *n, pl* **-tuses** *or* **-tus** : aparato *m*
apparel [ə'pærəl] *n* : ropa *f*
apparent [ə'pærənt] *adj* **1** OBVIOUS : claro, evidente **2** SEEMING : aparente — **apparently** [ə'pærəntli] *adv* : al parecer, por lo visto
apparition [ˌæpə'rɪʃən] *n* : aparición *f*
appeal [ə'piːl] *vi* **1 ~ for** : solicitar **2 ~ to** : apelar a (la bondad de algn, etc.) **3 ~ to** ATTRACT : atraer a — **~** *n* **1** : apelación *f* (en derecho) **2** REQUEST : llamamiento *m* **3** ATTRACTION : atractivo *m* — **appealing** [ə'piːlɪŋ] *adj* : atractivo
appear [ə'pɪr] *vi* **1** : aparecer **2** : comparecer (ante un tribunal), actuar (en el teatro) **3** SEEM : parecer — **appearance** [ə'pɪrənts] *n* **1** : aparición *f* **2** LOOK : apariencia *f*, aspecto *m*
appease [ə'piːz] *vt* **-peased; -peasing** : apaciguar, aplacar
appendix [ə'pɛndɪks] *n, pl* **-dixes** *or* **-dices** [-dəˌsiːz] : apéndice *m* — **appendicitis** [əˌpɛndə'saɪt̬əs] *n* : apendicitis *f*
appetite ['æpəˌtaɪt] *n* : apetito *m* — **appetizer** ['æpəˌtaɪzər] *n* : aperitivo *m* — **appetizing** ['æpəˌtaɪzɪŋ] *adj* : apetitoso
applaud [ə'plɔd] *v* : aplaudir — **applause** [ə'plɔz] *n* : aplauso *m*
apple ['æpəl] *n* : manzana *f*
appliance [ə'plaɪənts] *n* : aparato *m*
apply [ə'plaɪ] *v* **-plied; -plying** *vt* **1** : aplicar **2 ~ oneself** : aplicarse — *vi* **1** : aplicarse **2 ~ for** : solicitar, pedir — **applicable** ['æplɪkəbəl, ə'plɪkə-] *adj* : aplicable — **applicant** ['æplɪkənt] *n* : solicitante *mf*; candidato *m*, -ta *f* — **application** [ˌæplə'keɪʃən] *n* **1** : aplicación *f* **2** : solicitud *f* (para un empleo, etc.)
appoint [ə'pɔɪnt] *vt* **1** NAME : nombrar **2** FIX, SET : fijar, señalar — **appointment** [ə'pɔɪntmənt] *n* **1** APPOINTING : nombramiento *m* **2** ENGAGEMENT : cita *f*
apportion [ə'porʃən] *vt* : distribuir, repartir
appraise [ə'preɪz] *vt* **-praised; -praising** : evaluar, valorar — **appraisal** [ə'preɪzəl] *n* : evaluación *f*
appreciate [ə'priːʃiˌeɪt, -'prɪ-] *v* **-ated; -ating** *vt* **1** VALUE : apreciar **2** UNDERSTAND : darse cuenta de **3 I ~ your help** : te agradezco tu ayuda — *vi* : aumentar en valor — **appreciation** [əˌpriːʃi'eɪʃən, -ˌprɪ-] *n* **1** GRATITUDE : agradecimiento *m* **2** VALUING : apreciación *f*, valoración *f* — **appreciative** [ə'priːʃət̬ɪv, -'prɪ-; ə'priːʃiˌeɪ-] *adj* **1** : apreciativo **2** GRATEFUL : agradecido
apprehend [ˌæprɪ'hɛnd] *vt* **1** ARREST : aprehender, detener **2** DREAD : temer **3** COMPREHEND : comprender — **apprehension** [ˌæprɪ'hɛntʃən] *n* **1** ARREST : detención *f*, aprehensión *f* **2** ANXIETY : aprensión *f*, temor *m* — **apprehensive** [ˌæprɪ'hɛntsɪv] *adj* : aprensivo, inquieto
apprentice [ə'prɛntɪs] *n* : aprendiz *m*, -diza *f*
approach [ə'proːtʃ] *vt* **1** NEAR : acercarse a **2** : dirigirse a (algn), abordar (un problema, etc.) — *vi* : acercarse — **~** *n* **1** NEARING : acercamiento *m* **2** POSITION : enfoque *m* **3** ACCESS : acceso *m* — **approachable** [ə'proːtʃəbəl] *adj* : accesible, asequible
appropriate [ə'proːpriˌeɪt] *vt* **-ated; -ating** : apropiarse de — **~** [ə'proːpriət] *adj* : apropiado
approve [ə'pruːv] *vt* **-proved; -proving** : aprobar — **approval** [ə'pruːvəl] *n* : aprobación *f*
approximate [ə'prɑksəmət] *adj* : aproximado — **~** [ə'prɑksəˌmeɪt] *vt* **-mated; -mating** : aproximarse a — **approximately** [ə'prɑksəmətli] *adv* : aproximadamente
apricot ['æprəˌkɑt, 'eɪ-] *n* : albaricoque *m*, chabacano *m Lat*
April ['eɪprəl] *n* : abril *m*
apron ['eɪprən] *n* : delantal *m*
apropos [ˌæprə'poː, 'æprəˌpoː] *adv* : a propósito
apt ['æpt] *adj* **1** FITTING : apto, apropiado **2** LIABLE : propenso — **aptitude** ['æptəˌtuːd, -ˌtjuːd] *n* : aptitud *f*

aquarium [əˈkwæriəm] *n, pl* **-iums** *or* **-ia** [-iə] : acuario *m*
aquatic [əˈkwɑt̬ɪk, -ˈkwæ-] *adj* : acuático
aqueduct [ˈækwəˌdʌkt] *n* : acueducto *m*
Arab [ˈærəb] *adj* : árabe — **Arabic** [ˈærəbɪk] *adj* : árabe — ~ *n* : árabe *m* (idioma)
arbitrary [ˈɑrbəˌtrɛri] *adj* : arbitrario
arbitrate [ˈɑrbəˌtreɪt] *v* **-trated; -trating** : arbitrar — **arbitration** [ˌɑrbəˈtreɪʃən] *n* : arbitraje *m*
arc [ˈɑrk] *n* : arco *m*
arcade [ɑrˈkeɪd] *n* **1** : arcada *f* **2 shopping ~** : galería *f* comercial
arch [ˈɑrtʃ] *n* : arco *m* — ~ *vt* : arquear — *vi* : arquearse
archaeology *or* **archeology** [ˌɑrkiˈɑlədʒi] *n* : arqueología *f* — **archaeological** [ˌɑrkiəˈlɑdʒɪkəl] *adj* : arqueológico — **archaeologist** [ˌɑrkiˈɑlədʒɪst] *n* : arqueólogo *m*, -ga *f*
archaic [ɑrˈkeɪɪk] *adj* : arcaico
archbishop [ɑrtæˈbɪʃəp] *n* : arzobispo *m*
archery [ˈɑrtʃəri] *n* : tiro *m* al arco
archipelago [ˌɑrkəˈpɛləˌgoː, ˌɑrtʃə-] *n, pl* **-goes** *or* **-gos** [-goːz] : archipiélago *m*
architecture [ˈɑrkəˌtɛktʃər] *n* : arquitectura *f* — **architect** [ˈɑrkəˌtɛkt] *n* : arquitecto *m*, -ta *f* — **architectural** [ˌɑrkəˈtɛktʃərəl] *adj* : arquitectónico
archives [ˈɑrˌkaɪvz] *npl* : archivo *m*
archway [ˈɑrtʃˌweɪ] *n* : arco *m* (de entrada)
arctic [ˈɑrktɪk, ˈɑrt̬-] *adj* : ártico
ardent [ˈɑrdənt] *adj* : ardiente, fervoroso — **ardor** [ˈɑrdər] *n* : ardor *m*, fervor *m*
arduous [ˈɑrdʒuəs] *adj* : arduo
are → **be**
area [ˈæriə] *n* **1** REGION : área *f*, zona *f* **2** FIELD : campo *m* **3 ~ code** : código *m* de la zona *Lat*, prefijo *m Spain*
arena [əˈriːnə] *n* : arena *f*, ruedo *m*
aren't [ˈɑrnt, ˈɑrənt] (*contraction of* **are not**) → **be**
Argentine [ˈɑrdʒənˌtaɪn, -ˌtiːn] *or* **Argentinean** *or* **Argentinian** [ˌɑrdʒənˈtɪniən] *adj* : argentino
argue [ˈɑrˌgjuː] *v* **-gued; -guing** *vi* **1** QUARREL : discutir **2 ~ against** : argumentar contra — *vt* : argumentar, sostener — **argument** [ˈɑrgjəmənt] *n* **1** QUARREL : disputa *f*, discusión *f* **2** REASONING : argumentos *mpl*
arid [ˈærəd] *adj* : árido — **aridity** [əˈrɪdət̬i, æ-] *n* : aridez *f*
arise [əˈraɪz] *vi* **arose** [əˈroːz]; **arisen** [əˈrɪzən]; **arising 1** : levantarse **2 ~ from** : surgir de
aristocracy [ˌærəˈstɑkrəsi] *n, pl* **-cies** : aristocracia *f* — **aristocrat** [əˈrɪstəˌkræt] *n* : aristócrata *mf* — **aristocratic** [əˌrɪstəˈkræt̬ɪk] *adj* : aristocrático
arithmetic [əˈrɪθməˌtɪk] *n* : aritmética *f*
ark [ˈɑrk] *n* : arca *f*
arm [ˈɑrm] *n* **1** : brazo *m* **2** WEAPON : arma *f* — ~ *vt* : armar — **armament** [ˈɑrməmənt] *n* : armamento *m* — **armchair** [ˈɑrmˌtʃɛr] *n* : sillón *m* — **armed** [ˈɑrmd] *adj* **1 ~ forces** : fuerzas *fpl* armadas **2 ~ robbery** : robo *m* a mano armada
armistice [ˈɑrməstɪs] *n* : armisticio *m*
armor *or Brit* **armour** [ˈɑrmər] *n* : armadura *f* — **armored** *or Brit* **armoured** [ˈɑrmərd] *adj* : blindado, acorazado — **armory** *or Brit* **armoury** [ˈɑrmri, ˈɑrməri] : arsenal *m*
armpit [ˈɑrmˌpɪt] *n* : axila *f*, sobaco *m*
army [ˈɑrmi] *n, pl* **-mies** : ejército *m*
aroma [əˈroːmə] *n* : aroma *m* — **aromatic** [ˌærəˈmæt̬ɪk] *adj* : aromático
around [əˈraʊnd] *adv* **1** : de circunferencia **2** NEARBY : por ahí **3** APPROXIMATELY : más o menos, aproximadamente **4 all ~** : por todos lados, todo alrededor **5 turn ~** : voltearse — ~ *prep* **1** SURROUNDING : alrededor de **2** THROUGHOUT : por **3** NEAR : cerca de **4 ~ the corner** : a la vuelta de la esquina
arouse [əˈraʊz] *vt* **aroused; arousing 1** AWAKE : despertar **2** EXCITE : excitar
arrange [əˈreɪndʒ] *vt* **-ranged; -ranging** : arreglar, poner en orden — **arrangement** [əˈreɪndʒmənt] *n* **1** ORDER : arreglo *m* **2 ~s** *npl* : preparativos *mpl*
array [əˈreɪ] *n* : selección *f*, surtido *m*
arrears [əˈrɪrz] *npl* **1** : atrasos *mpl* **2 be in ~** : estar atrasado en pagos
arrest [əˈrɛst] *vt* : detener — ~ *n* **1** : arresto *m*, detención *f* **2 under ~** : detenido
arrive [əˈraɪv] *vi* **-rived; -riving** : llegar — **arrival** [əˈraɪvəl] *n* : llegada *f*
arrogance [ˈærəgənts] *n* : arrogancia *f* — **arrogant** [ˈærəgənt] *adj* : arrogante
arrow [ˈæro] *n* : flecha *f*
arsenal [ˈɑrsənəl] *n* : arsenal *m*
arsenic [ˈɑrsənɪk] *n* : arsénico *m*
arson [ˈɑrsən] *n* : incendio *m* premeditado
art [ˈɑrt] *n* **1** : arte *m* **2 ~s** *npl* : letras *fpl* (en educación) **3 fine ~s** : bellas artes *fpl*
artefact *Brit* → **artifact**
artery [ˈɑrt̬əri] *n, pl* **-teries** : arteria *f*
artful [ˈɑrtfəl] *adj* : astuto, taimado
arthritis [ɑrˈθraɪt̬əs] *n, pl* **-tides** [ɑrˈθrɪt̬əˌdiːz] : artritis *f* — **arthritic** [ɑrˈθrɪt̬ɪk] *adj* : artrítico

artichoke ['ɑrṭəˌtʃo:k] *n* : alcachofa *f*
article ['ɑrtɪkəl] *n* : artículo *m*
articulate [ɑr'tɪkjəˌleɪt] *vt* **-lated; -lating** : articular — **~** [ɑr'tɪkjələt] *adj* **be ~** : expresarse bien
artifact *or Brit* **artefact** ['ɑrṭəˌfækt] *n* : artefacto *m*
artificial [ˌɑrṭə'fɪʃəl] *adj* : artificial
artillery [ɑr'tɪləri] *n, pl* **-leries** : artillería *f*
artisan ['ɑrṭəzən, -sən] *n* : artesano *m*, -na *f*
artist ['ɑrṭɪst] *n* : artista *mf* — **artistic** [ɑr'tɪstɪk] *adj* : artístico
as ['æz] *adv* **1** : tan, tanto **2 ~ much** : tanto como **3 ~ tall ~** : tan alto como **4 ~ well** : también — **~** *conj* **1** WHILE : mientras **2** (*referring to manner*) : como **3** SINCE : ya que **4** THOUGH : por más que — **~** *prep* **1** : de **2** LIKE : como — **~** *pron* : que
asbestos [æz'bɛstəs, æs-] *n* : asbesto *m*, amianto *m*
ascend [ə'sɛnd] *vi* : ascender, subir — *vt* : subir (a) — **ascent** [ə'sɛnt] *n* : ascensión *f*, subida *f*
ascertain [ˌæsər'teɪn] *vt* : averiguar, determinar
ascribe [ə'skraɪb] *vt* **-cribed; -cribing** : atribuir
as for *prep* : en cuanto a
ash[1] ['æʃ] *n* : ceniza *f*
ash[2] *n* : fresno *m* (árbol)
ashamed [ə'ʃeɪmd] *adj* : avergonzado, apenado *Lat*
ashore [ə'ʃor] *adv* **1** : en tierra **2 go ~** : desembarcar
ashtray ['æʃˌtreɪ] *n* : cenicero *m*
Asian ['eɪʒən, -ʃən] *adj* : asiático
aside [ə'saɪd] *adv* **1** : a un lado **2** APART : aparte **3 set ~** : guardar — **aside from** *prep* **1** BESIDES : además de **2** EXCEPT : aparte de, menos
as if *conj* : como si
ask ['æsk] *vt* **1** : preguntar **2** REQUEST : pedir **3** INVITE : invitar — *vi* : preguntar
askance [ə'skænts] *adv* **look ~** : mirar de soslayo
askew [ə'skju:] *adj* : torcido, ladeado
asleep [ə'sli:p] *adj* **1** : dormido **2 fall ~** : dormirse, quedarse dormido
as of *prep* : desde, a partir de
asparagus [ə'spærəgəs] *n* : espárrago *m*
aspect ['æˌspɛkt] *n* : aspecto *m*
asphalt ['æsˌfɔlt] *n* : asfalto *m*
asphyxiate [æ'sfɪksiˌeɪt] *v* **-ated; -ating** *vt* : asfixiar — **asphyxiation** [æˌsfɪksi'eɪʃən] *n* : asfixia *f*
aspire [ə'spaɪr] *vi* **-pired; -piring** : aspirar — **aspiration** [ˌæspə'reɪʃən] *n* : aspiración *f*
aspirin ['æsprən, 'æspə-] *n, pl* **aspirin** *or* **aspirins** : aspirina *f*
ass ['æs] *n* **1** : asno *m* **2** IDIOT : imbécil *mf*, idiota *mf*
assail [ə'seɪl] *vt* : atacar, asaltar — **assailant** [ə'seɪlənt] *n* : asaltante *mf*, atacante *mf*
assassin [ə'sæsən] *n* : asesino *m*, **-na** *f* — **assassinate** [ə'sæsənˌeɪt] *vt* **-nated; -nating** : asesinar — **assassination** [əˌsæsən'eɪʃən] *n* : asesinato *m*
assault [ə'sɔlt] *n* **1** : ataque *m*, asalto *m* **2** : agresión *f* (contra algn) — **~** *vt* : atacar, asaltar
assemble [ə'sɛmbəl] *v* **-bled; -bling** *vt* **1** GATHER : reunir, juntar **2** CONSTRUCT : montar — *vi* : reunirse — **assembly** [ə'sɛmbli] *n, pl* **-blies 1** MEETING : reunión *f*, asamblea *f* **2** CONSTRUCTING : montaje *m*
assent [ə'sɛnt] *vi* : asentir, consentir — **~** *n* : asentimiento *m*
assert [ə'sərt] *vt* **1** : afirmar **2 ~ oneself** : hacerse valer — **assertion** [ə'sərʃən] *n* : afirmación *f* — **assertive** [ə'sərṭɪv] *adj* : firme, enérgico
assess [ə'sɛs] *vt* : evaluar, valorar — **assessment** [ə'sɛsmənt] *n* : evaluación *f*, valoración *f*
asset ['æˌsɛt] *n* **1** : ventaja *f*, recurso *m* **2 ~s** *npl* : bienes *mpl*, activo *m*
assiduous [ə'sɪdʒuəs] *adj* : asiduo
assign [ə'saɪn] *vt* **1** APPOINT : designar, nombrar **2** ALLOT : asignar — **assignment** [ə'saɪnmənt] *n* **1** TASK : misión *f* **2** HOMEWORK : tarea *f* **3** ASSIGNING : asignación *f*
assimilate [ə'sɪməˌleɪt] *vt* **-lated; -lating** : asimilar
assist [ə'sɪst] *vt* : ayudar — **assistance** [ə'sɪstənts] *n* : ayuda *f* — **assistant** [ə'sɪstənt] *n* : ayudante *mf*
associate [ə'so:ʃiˌeɪt, -si-] *v* **-ated; -ating** *vt* : asociar — *vi* : asociarse — **~** [ə'so:ʃiət, -siət] *n* : asociado *m*, **-da** *f*; socio *m*, -cia *f* — **association** [əˌso:ʃi'eɪʃən, -si-] *n* : asociación *f*
as soon as *conj* : tan pronto como
assorted [ə'sɔrṭəd] *adj* : surtido — **assortment** [ə'sɔrtmənt] *n* : surtido *m*, variedad *f*
assume [ə'su:m] *vt* **-sumed; -suming 1** SUPPOSE : suponer **2** UNDERTAKE : asumir **3** TAKE ON : adquirir, tomar — **assumption** [ə'sʌmpʃən] *n* : suposición *f*
assure [ə'ʃʊr] *vt* **-sured; -suring** : asegurar — **assurance** [ə'ʃʊrənts] *n* **1**

CERTAINTY : certeza *f,* garantía *f* **2** CONFIDENCE : confianza *f,* seguridad *f* (de sí mismo)
asterisk ['æstə,rɪsk] *n* : asterisco *m*
asthma ['æzmə] *n* : asma *m*
as though → **as if**
as to *prep* : sobre, acerca de
astonish [ə'stɑnɪʃ] *vt* : asombrar — **astonishing** [ə'stɑnɪʃɪŋ] *adj* : asombroso — **astonishment** [ə'stɑnɪʃmənt] *n* : asombro *m*
astound [ə'staʊnd] *vt* : asombrar, pasmar — **astounding** [ə'staʊndɪŋ] *adj* : asombroso, pasmoso
astray [ə'streɪ] *adv* **1 go ~** : extraviarse **2 lead ~** : llevar por mal camino
astrology [ə'strɑlədʒi] *n* : astrología *f*
astronaut ['æstrə,nɔt] *n* : astronauta *mf*
astronomy [ə'strɑnəmi] *n, pl* **-mies** : astronomía *f* — **astronomer** [ə'strɑnəmər] *n* : astrónomo *m,* -ma *f* — **astronomical** [,æstrə'nɑmɪkəl] *adj* : astrónómico
astute [ə'stu:t, -'stju:t] *adj* : astuto, sagaz — **astuteness** [ə'stu:tnəs, -'stju:t-] *n* : astucia *f*
as well as *conj* : tanto como — **~** *prep* : además de, aparte de
asylum [ə'saɪləm] *n* **1** : asilo *m* **2 insane ~** : manicomio *m*
at ['æt] *prep* **1** : a **2 ~ home** : en casa **3 ~ night** : en la noche, por la noche **4 ~ two o'clock** : a las dos **5 be angry ~** : estar enojado con **6 laugh ~** : reírse de — **at all** *adv* **not ~** : en absoluto, nada
ate → **eat**
atheist ['eɪθiɪst] *n* : ateo *m,* atea *f* — **atheism** *n* ['eɪθi,ɪzəm] : ateísmo *m*
athlete ['æθ,li:t] *n* : atleta *mf* — **athletic** [æθ'lɛt̬ɪk] *adj* : atlético — **athletics** [æθ'lɛt̬ɪks] *ns & pl* : atletismo *m*
atlas ['ætləs] *n* : atlas *m*
atmosphere ['ætmə,sfɪr] *n* **1** : atmósfera *f* **2** AMBIENCE : ambiente *m* — **atmospheric** [,ætmə'sfɪrɪk, -'sfɛr-] *adj* : atmosférico
atom ['æt̬əm] *n* : átomo *m* — **atomic** [ə'tɑmɪk] *adj* : atómico
atomizer ['æt̬ə,maɪzər] *n* : atomizador *m*
atone [ə'to:n] *vt* **atoned; atoning ~ for** : expiar
atrocity [ə'trɑsət̬i] *n, pl* **-ties** : atrocidad *f* — **atrocious** [ə'tro:ʃəs] *adj* : atroz
atrophy ['ætrəfi] *vi* **-phied; -phying** : atrofiarse
attach [ə'tætʃ] *vt* **1** : sujetar, atar **2** : adjuntar (un documento, etc.) **3 ~ importance to** : atribuir importancia a **4 become ~ed to s.o.** : encariñarse con algn — **attachment** [ə'tætʃmənt] *n* **1** ACCESSORY : accesorio *m* **2** FONDNESS : cariño *m*
attack [ə'tæk] *v* : atacar — **~** *n* : ataque *m* — **attacker** [ə'tækər] *n* : agresor *m,* -sora *f*
attain [ə'teɪn] *vt* : lograr, alcanzar — **attainment** [ə'teɪnmənt] *n* : logro *m*
attempt [ə'tɛmpt] *vt* : intentar — **~** *n* : intento *m*
attend [ə'tɛnd] *vt* : asistir a — vi **1** : asistir **2 ~ to** : ocuparse de — **attendance** [ə'tɛndənts] *n* **1** : asistencia *f* **2** TURNOUT : concurrencia *f* — **attendant** *n* : encargado *m,* -da *f;* asistente *mf*
attention [ə'tɛntʃən] *n* **1** : atención *f* **2 pay ~** : prestar atención, hacer caso — **attentive** [ə'tɛntɪv] *adj* : atento
attest [ə'tɛst] *vt* : atestiguar
attic ['æt̬ɪk] *n* : desván *m*
attire [ə'taɪr] *n* : atavío *m*
attitude ['æt̬ə,tu:d, -,tju:d] *n* **1** : actitud *f* **2** POSTURE : postura *f*
attorney [ə'tərni] *n, pl* **-neys** : abogado *m,* -da *f*
attract [ə'trækt] *vt* : atraer — **attraction** [ə'trækʃən] *n* **1** : atracción *f* **2** APPEAL : atractivo *m* — **attractive** [ə'træktɪv] *adj* : atractivo, atrayente
attribute ['ætrə,bju:t] *n* : atributo *m* — **~** [ə'trɪ,bju:t] *vt* **-tributed; -tributing** : atribuir, imputar
auburn ['ɔbərn] *adj* : castaño rojizo
auction ['ɔkʃən] *n* : subasta *f* — **~** *vt or* **~ off** : subastar
audacious [ɔ'deɪʃəs] *adj* : audaz — **audacity** [ɔ'dæsət̬i] *n, pl* **-ties** : audacia *f,* atrevimiento *m*
audible ['ɔdəbəl] *adj* : audible
audience ['ɔdiənts] *n* **1** INTERVIEW : audiencia *f* **2** PUBLIC : público *m*
audiovisual [,ɔdio'vɪʒʊəl] *adj* : audiovisual
audition [ɔ'dɪʃən] *n* : audición *f*
auditor ['ɔdət̬ər] *n* **1** : auditor *m,* -tora *f* (de finanzas) **2** STUDENT : oyente *mf*
auditorium [,ɔdə'toriəm] *n, pl* **-riums** *or* **-ria** [-riæ] : auditorio *m*
augment [ɔg'mɛnt] *vt* : aumentar
augur ['ɔgər] *vi* **~ well** : ser de buen agüero
August ['ɔgəst] *n* : agosto *m*
aunt ['ænt, 'ant] *n* : tía *f*
aura ['ɔrə] *n* : aura *f*
auspices ['ɔspəsəz, -,si:z] *npl* : auspicios *mpl*
auspicious [ɔ'spɪʃəs] *adj* : propicio, prometedor

austere [ɔ'stɪr] *adj* : austero — **austerity** [ɔ'stɛrəṯi] *n, pl* **-ties** : austeridad *f*
Australian [ɔ'streɪljən] *adj* : australiano
authentic [ə'θɛntɪk, ɔ-] *adj* : auténtico
author ['ɔθər] *n* : autor *m*, -tora *f*
authority [ə'θɔrəṯi, ɔ-] *n, pl* **-ties** : autoridad *f* — **authoritarian** [ɔ,θɔrə'tɛriən, ə-] *adj* : autoritario — **authoritative** [ə'θɔrə,teɪṯɪv, ɔ-] *adj* **1** RELIABLE : autorizado **2** DICTATORIAL : autoritario — **authorization** [,ɔθərə'zeɪʃən] *n* : autorización *f* — **authorize** ['ɔθə,raɪz] *vt* **-rized; -rizing** : autorizar
autobiography [,ɔṯobaɪ'ɑgrəfi] *n, pl* **-phies** : autobiografía *f* — **autobiographical** [,ɔṯo,baɪə'græfɪkəl] *adj* : autobiográfico
autograph ['ɔṯə,græf] *n* : autógrafo *m* — ~ *vt* : autografiar
automatic [,ɔṯə'mæṯɪk] *adj* : automático — **automate** ['ɔṯə,meɪt] *vt* **-mated; -mating** : automatizar — **automation** [,ɔṯə'meɪʃən] *n* : automatización *f*
automobile [,ɔṯəmo'bi:l, -'mo:,bi:l] *n* : automóvil *m*
autonomy [ɔ'tɑnəmi] *n, pl* **-mies** : autonomía *f* — **autonomous** [ɔ'tɑnəməs] *adj* : autónomo
autopsy ['ɔ,tɑpsi, -təp-] *n, pl* **-sies** : autopsia *f*
autumn ['ɔṯəm] *n* : otoño *m*
auxiliary [ɔg'zɪljəri, -'zɪləri] *adj* : auxiliar — ~ *n, pl* **-ries** : auxiliar *mf*
avail [ə'veɪl] *vt* ~ **oneself of** : aprovecharse de — ~ *n* **to no** ~ : en vano — **available** [ə'veɪləbəl] *adj* : disponible — **availability** [ə,veɪlə'bɪləṯi] *n, pl* **-ties** : disponibilidad *f*
avalanche ['ævə,læntʃ] *n* : avalancha *f*
avarice ['ævərəs] *n* : avaricia *f*
avenge [ə'vɛndʒ] *vt* **avenged; avenging** : vengar
avenue ['ævə,nu:, -,nju:] *n* **1** : avenida *f* **2** MEANS : vía *f*
average ['ævrɪdʒ, 'ævə-] *n* : promedio *m* — ~ *adj* **1** MEAN : medio **2** ORDINARY : regular, ordinario — ~ *vt* **-aged; -aging 1** : hacer un promedio de **2** *or* ~ **out** : calcular el promedio de
averse [ə'vərs] *adj* **be** ~ **to** : sentir aversión por — **aversion** [ə'vərʒən] *n* : aversión *f*
avert [ə'vərt] *vt* **1** AVOID : evitar, prevenir **2** ~ **one's eyes** : apartar los ojos
aviation [,eɪvi'eɪʃən] *n* : aviación *f* — **aviator** ['eɪvi,eɪṯər] *n* : aviador *m*, -dora *f*
avid ['ævɪd] *adj* : ávido — **avidly** *adv* : con avidez
avocado [,ævə'kɑdo, ,ɑvə-] *n, pl* **-dos** : aguacate *m*
avoid [ə'vɔɪd] *vt* : evitar — **avoidable** [ə'vɔɪdəbəl] *adj* : evitable
await [ə'weɪt] *vt* : esperar
awake [ə'weɪk] *v* **awoke** [ə'wo:k]; **awoken** [ə'wo:kən] *or* **awaked; awaking** : despertar — ~ *adj* : despierto — **awaken** [ə'weɪkən] *v* → **awake**
award [ə'wɔrd] *vt* **1** : otorgar, conceder (un premio, etc.) **2** : adjudicar (daños y perjuicios) — ~ *n* **1** PRIZE : premio *m* **2** : adjudicación *f*
aware [ə'wær] *adj* **be** ~ **of** : estar consciente de — **awareness** [ə'wærnəs] *n* : conciencia *f*
away [ə'weɪ] *adv* **1** (*referring to distance*) : de aquí, de distancia **2 far** ~ : lejos **3 give** ~ : regalar **4 go** ~ : irse **5 right** ~ : en seguida **6 take** ~ : quitar — ~ *adj* **1** ABSENT : ausente **2** ~ **game** : partido *m* fuera de casa
awe ['ɔ] *n* : temor *m* reverencial — **awesome** ['ɔsəm] *adj* : imponente, formidable
awful ['ɔfəl] *adj* **1** : terrible, espantoso **2 an** ~ **lot** : muchísimo — **awfully** ['ɔfəli] *adv* : terriblemente
awhile [ə'*h*waɪl] *adv* : un rato
awkward ['ɔkwərd] *adj* **1** CLUMSY : torpe **2** EMBARRASSING : embarazoso, delicado **3** DIFFICULT : difícil — **awkwardly** *adv* **1** : con dificultad **2** CLUMSILY : de manera torpe
awning ['ɔnɪŋ] *n* : toldo *m*
awry [ə'raɪ] *adj* **1** ASKEW : torcido **2 go** ~ : salir mal
ax *or* **axe** ['æks] *n* : hacha *f*
axiom ['æksiəm] *n* : axioma *m*
axis ['æksɪs] *n, pl* **axes** [-,si:z] : eje *m*
axle ['æksəl] *n* : eje *m*

B

b ['bi:] *n, pl* **b's** *or* **bs** ['bi:z] : b, segunda letra del alfabeto inglés

babble ['bæbəl] *vi* **-bled; -bling 1** : balbucear **2** MURMUR : murmurar — **~** *n* : balbuceo *m* (de bebé), murmullo *m* (de voces, de un arroyo)

baboon [bæ'bu:n] *n* : babuino *m*

baby ['beɪbi] *n, pl* **-bies** : bebé *m;* niño *m,* **-ña** *f* — **baby** *vt* **-bied; -bying** : mimar, consentir — **babyish** ['beɪbiɪʃ] *adj* : infantil — **baby-sit** ['beɪbi-ˌsɪt] *vi* **-sat** [-ˌsæt]; **-sitting** : cuidar a los niños

bachelor ['bætʃələr] *n* **1** : soltero *m* **2** GRADUATE : licenciado *m,* **-da** *f*

back ['bæk] *n* **1** : espalda *f* **2** REVERSE : reverso *m,* dorso *m,* revés *m* **3** REAR : fondo *m,* parte *f* trasera **4** : defensa *mf* (en deportes) — **~** *adv* **1** : atrás **2** **be ~** : estar de vuelta **3** **go ~** : volver **4** **two years ~** : hace dos años — **~** *adj* **1** REAR : de atrás, trasero **2** OVERDUE : atrasado — **~** *vt* **1** SUPPORT : apoyar **2** *or* **~ up** : darle marcha atrás a (un vehículo) — *vi* **1** **~ down** : volverse atrás **2** **~ up** : retroceder — **backache** ['bækˌeɪk] *n* : dolor *m* de espalda — **backbone** ['bækˌbo:n] *n* : columna *f* vertebral — **backfire** ['bækˌfaɪr] *vi* **-fired; -firing** : petardear — **background** ['bæk-ˌgraʊnd] *n* **1** : fondo *m* (de un cuadro, etc.), antecedentes *mpl* (de una situación) **2** EXPERIENCE : formación *f* — **backhand** ['bækˌhænd] *adv* : de revés, con el revés — **backhanded** ['bækˌhændəd] *adj* : indirecto — **backing** ['bækɪŋ] *n* : apoyo *m,* respaldo *m* — **backlash** ['bækˌlæʃ] *n* : reacción *f* violenta — **backlog** ['bækˌlɔg] *n* : atrasos *mpl* — **backpack** ['bækˌpæk] *n* : mochila *f* — **backstage** [ˌbæk'steɪdʒ, 'bækˌ-] *adv & adj* : entre bastidores — **backtrack** ['bækˌtræk] *vi* : dar marcha atrás — **backup** ['bækˌʌp] *n* **1** SUPPORT : respaldo *m,* apoyo *m* **2** : copia *f* de seguridad (para computadoras) — **backward** ['bækwərd] *or* **backwards** [-wərdz] *adv* **1** : hacia atrás **2** **do it ~** : hacerlo al revés **3** **fall ~** : caer de espaldas **4** **bend over ~s** : hacer todo lo posible — **backward** *adj* **1** : hacia atrás **2** RETARDED : retrasado **3** SHY : tímido **4** UNDERDEVELOPED : atrasado

bacon ['beɪkən] *n* : tocino *m,* tocineta *f Lat,* bacon *m Spain*

bacteria [bæk'tɪriə] : bacterias *fpl*

bad ['bæd] *adj* **worse** ['wərs]; **worst** ['wərst] **1** : malo **2** ROTTEN : podrido **3** SEVERE : grave **4** **from ~ to worse** : de mal en peor **5** **too ~!** : ¡qué lástima! — **~** *adv* → **badly**

badge ['bædʒ] *n* : insignia *f,* chapa *f*

badger ['bædʒər] *n* : tejón *m* — **~** *vt* : acosar

badly ['bædli] *adv* **1** : mal **2** SEVERELY : gravemente **3** **want ~** : desear mucho

baffle ['bæfəl] *vi* **-fled; -fling** : desconcertar

bag ['bæg] *n* **1** : bolsa *f,* saco *m* **2** HANDBAG : bolso *m,* cartera *f Lat* **3** SUITCASE : maleta *f* — **~** *vt* **bagged; bagging** : ensacar, poner en una bolsa

baggage ['bægɪdʒ] *n* : equipaje *m*

baggy ['bægi] *adj* **-gier; -est** : holgado

bail ['beɪl] *n* : fianza *f* — **~** *vt* **1** : achicar (agua de un bote) **2** **~ out** RELEASE : poner en libertad bajo fianza **3** **~ out** EXTRICATE : sacar de apuros

bailiff ['beɪləf] *n* : alguacil *mf*

bait ['beɪt] *vt* **1** : cebar **2** HARASS : acosar — **~** *n* : cebo *m,* carnada *f*

bake ['beɪk] *v* **baked; baking** *vt* : cocer al horno — *vi* : cocerse (al horno) — **baker** ['beɪkər] *n* : panadero *m,* **-ra** *f* — **bakery** ['beɪkəri] *n, pl* **-ries** : panadería *f*

balance ['bælənts] *n* **1** SCALES : balanza *f* **2** COUNTERBALANCE : contrapeso *m* **3** EQUILIBRIUM : equilibrio *m* **4** REMAINDER : resto *m* **5** *or* **bank ~** : saldo *m* — **~** *v* **-anced; -ancing** *vt* **1** : hacer el balance de (una cuenta) **2** EQUALIZE : equilibrar **3** WEIGH : sopesar — *vi* **1** : sostenerse en equilibro **2** : cuadrar (dícese de una cuenta)

balcony ['bælkəni] *n, pl* **-nies 1** : balcón *m* **2** : galería *f* (de un teatro)

bald ['bɔld] *adj* **1** : calvo **2** WORN : pelado **3** **the ~ truth** : la pura verdad

bale *n* : bala *f,* fardo *m*

baleful ['beɪlfəl] *adj* : siniestro

balk ['bɔk] *vi* **~ at** : resistarse a

ball ['bɔl] *n* **1** : pelota *f,* bola *f,* balón *m* **2** DANCE : baile *m* **3** ~ **of string** : ovillo *m* de cuerda
ballad ['bæləd] *n* : balada *f*
ballast *n* : lastre *m*
ball bearing *n* : cojinete *m* de bola
ballerina [ˌbæləˈriːnə] *n* : bailarina *f*
ballet [bæˈleɪ, ˈbæˌleɪ] *n* : ballet *m*
ballistic [bəˈlɪstɪk] *adj* : balístico
balloon *n* : globo *m*
ballot *n* **1** : papeleta *f* (de voto) **2** VOTING : votación *f*
ballpoint pen ['bɔlˌpɔɪnt] *n* : bolígrafo *m*
ballroom ['bɔlˌruːm, -ˌrʊm] *n* : sala *f* de baile
balm ['bɑm, ˈbɑlm] *n* : bálsamo *m* — **balmy** ['bɑmi, ˈbɑl-] *adj* **balmier; -est** : templado, agradable
baloney [bəˈloːni] *n* NONSENSE : tonterías *fpl*
bamboo [bæmˈbuː] *n* : bambú *m*
bamboozle [bæmˈbuːzəl] *vt* **-zled; -zling** : engañar, embaucar
ban ['bæn] *vt* **banned; banning** : prohibir — ~ *n* : prohibición *f*
banal [bəˈnɑl, bəˈnæl, ˈbeɪnəl] *adj* : banal
banana [bəˈnænə] *n* : plátano *m,* banana *f Lat,* banano *m Lat*
band ['bænd] *n* **1** STRIP : banda *f* **2** GROUP : banda *f,* grupo *m,* conjunto *m* — ~ *vi* ~ **together** : unirse, juntarse
bandage ['bændɪdʒ] *n* : vendaje *m,* venda *f* — ~ *vt* **-daged; -daging** : vendar
bandit ['bændət] *n* : bandido *m,* -da *f*
bandy ['bændi] *vt* **-died; -dying** ~ **about** : circular, repetir
bang ['bæŋ] *vt* **1** STRIKE : golpear **2** SLAM : cerrar de un golpe — *vi* **1** SLAM : cerrarse de un golpe **2** ~ **on** : golpear — ~ *n* **1** BLOW : golpe *m* **2** NOISE : estrépito *m* **3** SLAM : portazo *m*
bangle ['bæŋgəl] *n* : brazalete *m,* pulsera *f*
bangs ['bæŋz] *npl* : flequillo *m*
banish ['bænɪʃ] *vt* : desterrar
banister ['bænəstər] *n* : pasamanos *m,* barandal *m*
bank ['bæŋk] *n* **1** : banco *m* **2** : orilla *f,* ribera *f* (de un río) **3** EMBANKMENT : terraplén *m* — ~ *vt* : depositar — *vi* **1** : ladearse (dícese de un avión) **2** : tener una cuenta (en un banco) **3** ~ **on** : contar con — **banker** ['bæŋkər] *n* : banquero *m,* -ra *f* — **banking** ['bæŋkɪŋ] *n* : banca *f*
bankrupt ['bæŋˌkrʌpt] *adj* : en bancarrota, en quiebra — **bankruptcy** ['bæŋˌkrʌptsi] *n, pl* **-cies** : quiebra *f,* bancarrota *f*
banner ['bænər] *n* : bandera *f,* pancarta *f*
banquet ['bæŋkwət] *n* : banquete *m*
banter ['bæntər] *n* : bromas *fpl* — ~ *vi* : hacer bromas
baptize [bæpˈtaɪz, ˈbæpˌtaɪz] *vt* **-tized; -tizing** : bautizar — **baptism** ['bæpˌtɪzəm] *n* : bautismo *m*
bar ['bɑr] *n* **1** : barra *f* **2** BARRIER : barrera *f,* obstáculo *m* **3** COUNTER : mostrador *m,* barra *f* **4** TAVERN : bar *m* **5 behind** ~**s** : entre rejas **6** ~ **of soap** : pastilla *f* de jabón — ~ *vt* **barred; barring 1** OBSTRUCT : obstruir, bloquear **2** EXCLUDE : excluir **3** PROHIBIT : prohibir — ~ *prep* **1** : excepto **2** ~ **none** : sin excepción
barbarian [bɑrˈbæriən] *n* : bárbaro *m,* -ra *f*
barbecue ['bɑrbɪˌkjuː] *vt* **-cued; -cuing** : asar a la parrilla — ~ *n* : barbacoa *f*
barbed wire ['bɑrbdˈwaɪr] *n* : alambre *m* de púas
barber ['bɑrbər] *n* : barbero *m,* -ra *f*
bare ['bær] *adj* **1** : desnudo **2** EMPTY : vacío **3** MINIMUM : mero, esencial — **barefaced** ['bærˌfeɪst] *adj* : descarado — **barefoot** ['bærˌfʊt] *or* **barefooted** [-ˌfʊtəd] *adv & adj* : descalzo — **barely** ['bærli] *adv* : apenas, por poco
bargain ['bɑrgən] *n* **1** AGREEMENT : acuerdo *m* **2** BUY : ganga *f* — ~ *vi* **1** : regatear, negociar **2** ~ **for** : contar con
barge ['bɑrdʒ] *n* : barcaza *f* — ~ *vi* **barged; barging** ~ **in** : entrometerse, interrumpir
baritone ['bærəˌtoːn] *n* : barítono *m*
bark[1] ['bɑrk] *vi* : ladrar — ~ *n* : ladrido *m* (de un perro)
bark[2] *n* : corteza *f* (de un árbol)
barley ['bɑrli] *n* : cebada *f*
barn ['bɑrn] *n* : granero *m* — **barnyard** ['bɑrnˌjɑrd] *n* : corral *m*
barometer [bəˈrɑmətər] *n* : barómetro *m*
baron ['bærən] *n* : barón *m* — **baroness** ['bærənɪs, -nəs, -ˌnɛs] *n* : baronesa *f*
barracks ['bærəks] *ns & pl* : cuartel *m*
barrage [bəˈrɑʒ, -ˈrɑdʒ] *n* **1** : descarga *f* (de artillería) **2** : aluvión *m* (de preguntas, etc.)
barrel ['bærəl] *n* **1** : barril *m,* tonel *m* **2** : cañón *m* (de un arma de fuego)
barren ['bærən] *adj* : estéril
barricade ['bærəˌkeɪd, ˌbærəˈ-] *vt* **-caded; -cading** : cerrar con barricadas — ~ *n* : barricada *f*
barrier ['bæriər] *n* : barrera *f*
barring ['bɑrɪŋ] *prep* : salvo
barrio ['bɑrio, ˈbær-] *n* : barrio *m*

bartender ['bɑr,tɛndər] *n* : camarero *m*, -ra *f*
barter ['bɑrt̬ər] *vt* : cambiar, trocar — ~ *n* : trueque *m*
base ['beɪs] *n, pl* **bases** : base *f* — ~ *vt* **based; basing** : basar, fundamentar — ~ *adj* **baser; basest** : vil
baseball ['beɪs,bɔl] *n* : beisbol *m*, béisbol *m*
basement ['beɪsmənt] *n* : sótano *m*
bash ['bæʃ] *vt* : golpear violentamente — ~ *n* **1** BLOW : golpe *m* **2** PARTY: fiesta *f*
bashful ['bæʃfəl] *adj* : tímido, vergonzoso
basic ['beɪsɪk] *adj* : básico, fundamental — **basically** ['beɪsɪkli] *adv* : fundamentalmente
basil ['beɪzəl, 'bæzəl] *n* : albahaca *f*
basin ['beɪsən] *n* **1** WASHBOWL : palangana *f*, lavabo *m* **2** : cuenca *f* (de un río)
basis ['beɪsəs] *n, pl* **bases** [-,si:z] : base *f*
bask ['bæsk] *vi* ~ **in the sun** : tostarse al sol
basket ['bæskət] *n* : cesta *f*, cesto *m* — **basketball** ['bæskət,bɔl] *n* : baloncesto *m*, basquetbol *m Lat*
bass[1] ['bæs] *n, pl* **bass** *or* **basses** : róbalo *m* (pesca)
bass[2] ['beɪs] *n* : bajo *m* (tono, voz, instrumento)
bassoon [bə'su:n, bæ-] *n* : fagot *m*
bastard ['bæstərd] *n* : bastardo *m*, -da *f*
baste ['beɪst] *vt* **basted; basting 1** STITCH : hilvanar **2** : bañar (carne)
bat[1] ['bæt] *n* : murciélago *m* (animal)
bat[2] *n* : bate *m* — ~ *vt* **batted; batting** : batear
batch ['bætʃ] *n* : hornada *f* (de pasteles, etc.), lote *m* (de mercancías), montón *m* (de trabajo), grupo *m* (de personas)
bath ['bæθ, 'baθ] *n, pl* **baths** ['bæðz, 'bæθs, 'baðz, 'baθs] **1** : baño *m* **2** BATHROOM : baño *m*, cuarto *m* de baño **3 take a** ~ : bañarse — **bathe** ['beɪð] *v* **bathed; bathing** *vt* : bañar, lavar — *vi* : bañarse — **bathrobe** ['bæθ,ro:b] *n* : bata *f* (de baño) — **bathroom** ['bæθ,ru:m, -,rʊm] *n* : baño *m*, cuarto *m* de baño — **bathtub** ['bæθ,tʌb] *n* : bañera *f*, tina *f* (de baño)
baton [bə'tɑn] *n* : batuta *f*
battalion [bə'tæljən] *n* : batallón *m*
batter ['bæt̬ər] *vt* **1** BEAT : golpear **2** MISTREAT : maltratar — ~ *n* **1** : masa *f* para rebozar **2** HITTER : bateador *m*, -dora *f*
battery ['bæt̬əri] *n, pl* **-teries** : batería *f*, pila *f* (de electricidad)
battle ['bæt̬əl] *n* **1** : batalla *f* **2** STRUGGLE : lucha *f* — ~ *vi* **-tled; -tling** : luchar — **battlefield** ['bæt̬əl,fi:ld] *n* : campo *m* de batalla — **battleship** ['bæt̬əl,ʃɪp] *n* : acorazado *m*
bawl ['bɔl] *vi* : llorar a gritos
bay[1] ['beɪ] *n* INLET : bahía *f*
bay[2] *n or* ~ **leaf** : laurel *m*
bay[3] *vi* : aullar — ~ *n* : aullido *m*
bayonet [,beɪə'nɛt, 'beɪə,nɛt] *n* : bayoneta *f*
bay window *n* : ventana *f* en saliente
bazaar [bə'zɑr] *n* **1** : bazar *m* **2** SALE : venta *f* benéfica
be ['bi:] *v* **was** ['wəz, 'wɑz], **were** ['wər]; **been** ['bɪn]; **being; am** ['æm], **is** ['ɪz], **are** ['ɑr] *vi* **1** : ser **2** (*expressing location*) : estar **3** (*expressing existence*) : ser, existir **4** (*expressing a state of being*) : estar, tener — *v impers* **1** (*indicating time*) : ser **2** (*indicating a condition*) : hacer, estar — *v aux* **1** (*expressing occurrence*) : ser **2** (*expressing possibility*) : poderse **3** (*expressing obligation*) : deber **4** (*expressing progression*) : estar
beach ['bi:tʃ] *n* : playa *f*
beacon ['bi:kən] *n* : faro *m*
bead ['bi:d] *n* **1** : cuenta *f* **2** DROP : gota *f* **3** ~**s** *npl* NECKLACE : collar *m*
beak ['bi:k] *n* : pico *m*
beam ['bi:m] *n* **1** : viga *f* (de madera, etc.) **2** RAY : rayo *m* — ~ *vi* SHINE : brillar — *vt* BROADCAST : transmitir, emitir
bean ['bi:n] *n* **1** : habichuela *f*, frijol *m* **2 coffee** ~ : grano *m* **3 string** ~ : judía *f*
bear[1] ['bær] *n, pl* **bears** *or* **bear** : oso *m*, osa *f*
bear[2] *v* **bore** ['bor]; **borne** ['bɔrn]; **bearing** *vt* **1** CARRY : portar **2** ENDURE : soportar — *vi* ~ **right/left** : doble a la derecha/a la izquierda — **bearable** ['bærəbəl] *adj* : soportable
beard ['bɪrd] *n* : barba *f*
bearer ['bærər] *n* : portador *m*, -dora *f*
bearing ['bærɪŋ] *n* **1** MANNER : comportamiento *m* **2** SIGNIFICANCE : relacíon *f*, importancia *f* **3 get one's** ~**s** : orientarse
beast ['bi:st] *n* : bestia *f*
beat ['bi:t] *v* **beat; beaten** ['bi:tən] *or* **beat; beating** *vt* **1** HIT : golpear **2** : batir (huevos, etc.) **3** DEFEAT : derrotar — *vi* : latir (dícese del corazón) — ~ *n* **1** : golpe *m* **2** : latido *m* (del corazón) **3** RHYTHM : ritmo *m*, tiempo *m* — **beating** ['bi:tɪŋ] *n* **1** : paliza *f* **2** DEFEAT : derrota *f*

beauty ['bju:ṭi] *n, pl* **-ties** : belleza *f* — **beautiful** ['bju:ṭɪfəl] *adj* : hermoso, lindo — **beautifully** ['bju:ṭɪfəli] *adv* WONDERFULLY : maravillosamente — **beautify** ['bju:ṭɪˌfaɪ] *vt* **-fied; -fying** : embellecer

beaver ['bi:vər] *n* : castor *m*

because [bɪ'kʌz, -'kɔz] *conj* : porque — **because of** *prep* : por, a causa de, debido a

beckon ['bɛkən] *vt* : llamar, hacer señas a — *vi* : hacer una seña

become [bɪ'kʌm] *v* **-came** [-'keɪm]; **-come; -coming** *vi* : hacerse, ponerse — *vt* SUIT : favorecer — **becoming** [bɪ'kʌmɪŋ] *adj* **1** SUITABLE : apropiado **2** FLATTERING : favorecedor

bed ['bɛd] *n* **1** : cama *f* **2** : cauce *m* (de un río), fondo *m* (del mar) **3** : macizo *m* (de flores) **4 go to ~** : irse a la cama — **bedclothes** ['bɛdˌklo:z, -ˌklo:ðz] *npl* : ropa *f* de cama

bedlam ['bɛdləm] *n* : confusión *f,* caos *m*

bedraggled [bɪ'drægəld] *adj* : desaliñado, sucio

bedridden ['bɛdˌrɪdən] *adj* : postrado en cama

bedroom ['bɛdˌru:m, -ˌrʊm] *n* : dormitorio *m,* recámara *f Lat*

bedspread ['bɛdˌsprɛd] *n* : colcha *f*

bedtime ['bɛdˌtaɪm] *n* : hora *f* de acostarse

bee ['bi:] *n* : abeja *f*

beech ['bi:tʃ] *n, pl* **beeches** *or* **beech** : haya *f*

beef ['bi:f] *n* : carne *f* de vaca, carne *f* de res *Lat* — **beefsteak** ['bi:fˌsteɪk] *n* : bistec *m*

beehive ['bi:ˌhaɪv] *n* : colmena *f*

beeline ['bi:ˌlaɪn] *n* **make a ~ for** : irse derecho a

beep ['bi:p] *n* : pitido *m* — **~** *v* : pitar

beer ['bɪr] *n* : cerveza *f*

beet ['bi:t] *n* : remolacha *f*

beetle ['bi:ṭəl] *n* : escarabajo *m*

before [bɪ'for] *adv* **1** : antes **2 the month ~** : el mes anterior — **~** *prep* **1** (*in space*) : delante de, ante **2** (*in time*) : antes de — **~** *conj* : antes de que — **beforehand** [bɪ'forˌhænd] *adv* : antes

befriend [bɪ'frɛnd] *vt* : hacerse amigo de

beg ['bɛg] *v* **begged; begging** *vt* **1** : pedir, mendigar **2** ENTREAT : suplicar — *vi* : mendigar, pedir limosna — **beggar** ['bɛgər] *n* : mendigo *m,* -ga *f*

begin [bɪ'gɪn] *v* **-gan** [-'gæn]; **-gun** [-'gʌn]; **-ginning** : empezar, comenzar — **beginner** [bɪ'gɪnər] *n* : principiante *mf* — **beginning** [bɪ'gɪnɪŋ] *n* : principio *m,* comienzo *m*

begrudge [bɪ'grʌdʒ] *vt* **-grudged; -grudging 1** : dar de mala gana **2** ENVY : envidiar

behalf [bɪ'hæf, -'haf] *n* **on ~ of** : de parte de, en nombre de

behave [bɪ'heɪv] *vi* **-haved; -having** : comportarse, portarse — **behavior** [bɪ'heɪvjər] *n* : comportamiento *m,* conducta *f*

behind [bɪ'haɪnd] *adv* **1** : detrás **2 fall ~** : atrasarse — **~** *prep* **1** : atrás de, detrás de **2 be ~ schedule** : ir retrasado **3 her friends are ~ her** : tiene el apoyo de sus amigos

behold [bɪ'ho:ld] *vt* **-held; -holding** : contemplar

beige ['beɪʒ] *adj & nm* : beige

being ['bi:ɪŋ] *n* **1** : ser *m* **2 come into ~** : nacer

belated [bɪ'leɪṭəd] *adj* : tardío

belch ['bɛltʃ] *vi* : eructar — **~** *n* : eructo *m*

Belgian ['bɛldʒən] *adj* : belga

belie [bɪ'laɪ] *vt* **-lied; -lying** : contradecir, desmentir

belief [bə'li:f] *n* **1** TRUST : confianza *f* **2** CONVICTION : creencia *f,* convicción *f* **3** FAITH : fe *f* — **believable** [bə'li:vəbəl] *adj* : creíble — **believe** [bə'li:v] *v* **-lieved; -lieving** : creer — **believer** [bə'li:vər] *n* : creyente *mf*

belittle [bɪ'lɪṭəl] *vt* **-littled; -littling** : menospreciar

Belizean [bə'li:ziən] *adj* : beliceño *m,* -ña *f*

bell ['bɛl] *n* **1** : campana *f* **2** : timbre *m* (de teléfono, de la puerta, etc.)

belligerent [bə'lɪdʒərənt] *adj* : beligerante

bellow ['bɛˌlo:] *vi* : bramar, mugir — *vt* *or* **~ out** : gritar

bellows ['bɛˌlo:z] *ns & pl* : fuelle *m*

belly ['bɛli] *n, pl* **-lies** : vientre *m*

belong [bɪ'lɔŋ] *vi* **1 ~ to** : pertenecer a, ser propiedad de **2 ~ to** : ser miembro de (un club, etc.) **3 where does it ~** : ¿dónde va? — **belongings** [bɪ'lɔŋɪŋz] *npl* : pertenencias *fpl,* efectos *mpl* personales

beloved [bɪ'lʌvəd, -'lʌvd] *adj* : querido, amado — **~** *n* : querido *m,* -da *f*

below [bɪ'lo:] *adv* : abajo — **~** *prep* **1** : abajo de, debajo de **2 ~ average** : por debajo del promedio **3 ~ zero** : bajo cero

belt ['bɛlt] *n* **1** : cinturón *m* **2** BAND, STRAP : cinta *f,* correa *f* **3** AREA : frente

m, zona *f* — ~ *vt* **1** : ceñir con un cinturón **2** THRASH : darle una paliza a
bench ['bɛntʃ] *n* **1** : banco *m* **2** WORKBENCH : mesa *f* de trabajo **3** COURT : tribunal *m*
bend ['bɛnd] *v* **bent** ['bɛnt]; **bending** *vt* : doblar, torcer — *vi* **1** : torcerse **2** ~ **over** : inclinarse — ~ *n* : curva *f,* ángulo *m*
beneath [bɪ'ni:θ] *adv* : abajo, debajo — ~ *prep* : bajo, debajo de
benediction [ˌbɛnə'dɪkʃən] *n* : bendición *f*
benefactor ['bɛnəˌfæktər] *n* : benefactor *m,* -tora *f*
benefit ['bɛnəfɪt] *n* **1** ADVANTAGE : ventaja *f,* provecho *m* **2** AID : asistencia *f,* beneficio *m* — ~ *vt* : beneficiar — *vi* : beneficiarse — **beneficial** [ˌbɛnə'fɪʃəl] *adj* : beneficioso — **beneficiary** [ˌbɛnə'fɪʃiˌɛri, -'fɪʃəri] *n, pl* **-ries** : beneficiario *m,* -ria *f*
benevolent [bə'nɛvələnt] *adj* : benévolo
benign [bɪ'naɪn] *adj* **1** KIND : benévolo, amable **2** : benigno (en medicina)
bent ['bɛnt] *adj* **1** : encorvado **2 be** ~ **on** : estar empeñado en — ~ *n* : aptitud *f,* inclinación *f*
bequeath [bɪ'kwi:θ, -'kwi:ð] *vt* : legar — **bequest** [bɪ'kwɛst] *n* : legado *m*
berate [bɪ'reɪt] *vt* **-rated; -rating** : reprender, regañar
bereaved [bɪ'ri:vd] *adj* : desconsolado, a luto
beret [bə'reɪ] *n* : boina *f*
berry ['bɛri] *n, pl* **-ries** : baya *f*
berserk [bər'sərk, -'zərk] *adj* **1** : enloquecido **2 go** ~ : volverse loco
berth ['bərθ] *n* **1** MOORING : atracadero *m* **2** BUNK : litera *f*
beseech [bɪ'si:tʃ] *vt* **-sought** [-'sɔt] *or* **-seeched; -seeching** : suplicar, implorar
beset [bɪ'sɛt] *vt* **-set; -setting 1** HARASS : acosar **2** SURROUND : rodear
beside [bɪ'saɪd] *prep* **1** : al lado de, junto a **2 be** ~ **oneself** : estar fuera de sí — **besides** [bɪ'saɪdz] *adv* : además — ~ *prep* **1** : además de **2** EXCEPT : excepto
besiege [bɪ'si:dʒ] *vt* **-sieged; -sieging** : asediar
best ['bɛst] *adj* (*superlative of* **good**) : mejor — ~ *adv* (*superlative of* **well**) : mejor — ~ *n* **1 at** ~ : a lo más **2 do one's** ~ : hacer todo lo posible **3 the** ~ : lo mejor — **best man** *n* : padrino *m* (de boda)
bestow [bɪ'sto:] *vt* : otorgar, conceder
bet ['bɛt] *n* : apuesta *f* — ~ *v* **bet; betting** *vt* : apostar — *vi* ~ **on sth** : apostarle a algo
betray [bɪ'treɪ] *vt* : traicionar — **betrayal** [bɪ'treɪəl] *n* : traición *f*
better ['bɛt̬ər] *adj* (*comparative of* **good**) **1** : mejor **2 get** ~ : mejorar — ~ *adv* (*comparative of* **well**) **1** : mejor **2 all the** ~ : tanto mejor — ~ *n* **1 the** ~ : el mejor, la mejor **2 get the** ~ **of** : vencer a — ~ *vt* **1** IMPROVE : mejorar **2** SURPASS : superar
between [bɪ'twi:n] *prep* : entre — ~ *adv or* **in** ~ : en medio
beverage ['bɛvrɪdʒ, 'bɛvə-] *n* : bebida *f*
beware [bɪ'wær] *vi* ~ **of** : tener cuidado con
bewilder [bɪ'wɪldər] *vt* : desconcertar — **bewilderment** [bɪ'wɪldərmənt] *n* : desconcierto *m*
bewitch [bɪ'wɪtʃ] *vt* : hechizar, encantar
beyond [bi'jɑnd] *adv* : más allá, más lejos (en el espacio), más adelante (en el tiempo) — ~ *prep* : más allá de
bias ['baɪəs] *n* **1** PREJUDICE : prejuicio *m* **2** TENDENCY : inclinación *f,* tendencia *f* — **biased** ['baɪəst] *adj* : parcial
bib ['bɪb] *n* : babero *m* (para niños)
Bible ['baɪbəl] *n* : Biblia *f* — **biblical** ['bɪblɪkəl] *adj* : bíblico
bibliography [ˌbɪbli'ɑgrəfi] *n, pl* **-phies** : bibliografía *f*
bicarbonate of soda [ˌbaɪ'kɑrbənət, ˌneɪt] *n* : bicarbonato *m* de soda
biceps ['baɪˌsɛps] *ns & pl* : bíceps *m*
bicker ['bɪkər] *vi* : reñir
bicycle ['baɪsɪkəl, -ˌsɪ-] *n* : bicicleta *f* — ~ *vi* **-cled; -cling** : ir en bicicleta
bid ['bɪd] *vt* **bade** ['bæd, 'beɪd] *or* **bid; bidden** ['bɪdən] *or* **bid; bidding 1** OFFER : ofrecer **2** ~ **farewell** : decir adios — ~ *n* **1** OFFER : oferta *f* **2** ATTEMPT : intento *m,* tentativa *f*
bide ['baɪd] *vt* **bode** ['bo:d] *or* **bided; bided; biding** ~ **one's time** : esperar el momento oportuno
bifocals ['baɪˌfo:kəlz] *npl* : anteojos *mpl* bifocales
big ['bɪg] *adj* **bigger; biggest** : grande
bigamy ['bɪgəmi] *n* : bigamía *f*
bigot ['bɪgət] *n* : intolerante *mf* — **bigotry** ['bɪgətri] *n, pl* **-tries** : intolerancia *f,* fanatismo *m*
bike ['baɪk] *n* **1** BICYCLE : bici *f fam* **2** MOTORCYCLE : moto *f*
bikini [bə'ki:ni] *n* : bikini *m*
bile ['baɪl] *n* : bilis *f*
bilingual [baɪ'lɪŋgwəl] *adj* : bilingüe
bill ['bɪl] *n* **1** BEAK : pico *m* **2** INVOICE : cuenta *f,* factura *f* **3** BANKNOTE : billete *m* **4** LAW : proyecto *m* de ley, ley *f*

— ~ *vt* : pasarle la cuenta a — **billboard** ['bɪl,bɔrd] *n* : cartelera *f* — **billfold** ['bɪl,fo:ld] *n* : billetera *f*, cartera *f*

billiards ['bɪljərdz] *n* : billar *m*

billion ['bɪljən] *n, pl* **billions** *or* **billion** : mil millones *mpl*

billow ['bɪlo] *vi* : ondular, hincharse

billy goat ['bɪli,go:t] *n* : macho *m* cabrío

bin ['bɪn] *n* : cubo *m*, cajón *m*

binary ['baɪnəri, -,nɛri] *adj* : binario *m*

bind ['baɪnd] *vt* **bound** ['baʊnd]; **binding 1** TIE : atar **2** OBLIGATE : obligar **3** UNITE : unir **4** BANDAGE : vendar **5** : encuadernar (un libro) — **binder** ['baɪndər] *n* FOLDER : carpeta *f* — **binding** ['baɪndɪŋ] *n* : encuadernación *f* (de libros)

binge ['bɪndʒ] *n* : juerga *f fam*

bingo ['bɪŋ,go:] *n, pl* **-gos** : bingo *m*

binoculars [bə'nɑkjələrz, baɪ-] *npl* : binoculares *mpl*, gemelos *mpl*

biochemistry [,baɪo'kɛmɪstri] *n* : bioquímica *f*

biography [baɪ'ɑgrəfi, bi:-] *n, pl* **-phies** : biografía *f* — **biographer** [baɪ'ɑgrəfər] *n* : biógrafo *m*, **-fa** *f* — **biographical** [,baɪə'græfɪkəl] *adj* : biográfico

biology [baɪ'ɑlədʒi] *n* : biología *f* — **biological** [-dʒɪkəl] *adj* : biológico — **biologist** [baɪ'ɑlədʒɪst] *n* : biólogo *m*, **-ga** *f*

birch ['bərtʃ] *n* : abedul *m*

bird ['bərd] *n* : pájaro *m* (pequeño), ave *f* (grande)

birth ['bərθ] *n* **1** : nacimiento *m*, parto *m* **2 give ~ to** : dar a luz a — **birthday** ['bərθ,deɪ] *n* : cumpleaños *m* — **birthmark** ['bərθ,mɑrk] *n* : mancha *f* de nacimiento — **birthplace** ['bərθ,pleɪs] *n* : lugar *m* de nacimiento — **birthrate** ['bərθ,reɪt] *n* : índice *m* de natalidad

biscuit ['bɪskət] *n* : bizcocho *m*

bisect ['baɪ,sɛkt, ,baɪ'-] *vt* : bisecar

bisexual [,baɪ'sɛkʃəwəl, -'sɛkʃəl] *adj* : bisexual

bishop ['bɪʃəp] *n* : obispo *m*

bison ['baɪzən, -sən] *ns & pl* : bisonte *m*

bit[1] ['bɪt] *n* : bocado *m* (de una brida)

bit[2] **1** : trozo *m*, pedazo *m* **2** : bit *m* (de información) **3 a ~** : un poco

bitch ['bɪtʃ] *n* : perra *f* — ~ *vi* COMPLAIN : quejarse, reclamar

bite ['baɪt] *v* **bit** ['bɪt]; **bitten** ['bɪtən]; **biting** *vt* **1** : morder **2** STING : picar — *vi* : morder — *n* **1** : picadura *f* (de un insecto), mordedura *f* (de un animal) **2** SNACK : bocado *m* — **biting** *adj* **1** PENETRATING : cortante, penetrante **2** CAUSTIC : mordaz

bitter ['bɪt̬ər] *adj* **1** : amargo **2 it's ~ cold** : hace un frío glacial **3 to the ~ end** : hasta el final — **bitterness** ['bɪt̬ərnəs] *n* : amargura *f*

bizarre [bə'zɑr] *adj* : extraño

black ['blæk] *adj* : negro — ~ *n* **1** : negro *m* (color) **2** : negro *m*, **-gra** *f* (persona) — **black-and-blue** [,blækən'blu:] *adj* : amoratado — **blackberry** ['blæk,bɛri] *n, pl* **-ries** : mora *f* — **blackbird** ['blæk,bərd] *n* : mirlo *m* — **blackboard** ['blæk,bɔrd] *n* : pizarra *f*, pizarrón *m Lat* — **blacken** ['blækən] *vt* : ennegrecer — **blackmail** ['blæk,meɪl] *n* : chantaje *m* — ~ *vt* : chantajear — **black market** *n* : mercado *m* negro — **blackout** ['blæk,aʊt] *n* **1** : apagón *m* (de poder eléctrico) **2** FAINT : desmayo *m* — **blacksmith** ['blæk,smɪθ] *n* : herrero *m* — **blacktop** ['blæk,tɑp] *n* : asfalto *m*

bladder ['blædər] *n* : vejiga *f*

blade ['bleɪd] *n* **1** : hoja *f* (de un cuchillo), cuchilla *f* (de un patín) **2** : pala *f* (de un remo, una hélice, etc.) **3 ~ of grass** : brizna *f* (de hierba)

blame ['bleɪm] *vt* **blamed; blaming** : culpar, echar la culpa a — ~ *n* : culpa *f* — **blameless** ['bleɪmləs] *adj* : inocente

bland ['blænd] *adj* : soso, insulso

blank ['blæŋk] *adj* **1** : en blanco (dícese de un papel), liso (dícese de una pared) **2** EMPTY : vacío — ~ *n* : espacio *m* en blanco

blanket ['blæŋkət] *n* **1** : manta *f*, cobija *f Lat* **2 ~ of snow** : manto *m* de nieve — ~ *vt* : cubrir

blare ['blær] *vi* **blared; blaring** : resonar

blasphemy ['blæsfəmi] *n, pl* **-mies** : blasfemia *f*

blast ['blæst] *n* **1** GUST : ráfaga *f* **2** EXPLOSION : explosión *f* **3** : toque *m* (de trompeta, etc.) — ~ *vt* BLOW UP : volar — **blast-off** ['blæst,ɔf] *n* : despegue *m*

blatant ['bleɪtənt] *adj* : descarado

blaze ['bleɪz] *n* **1** FIRE : fuego *m* **2** BRIGHTNESS : resplandor *m*, brillantez *f* **3 ~ of anger** : arranque *m* de cólera — ~ *v* **blazed; blazing** *vi* : arder, brillar — *vt* **~ a trail** : abrir un camino

blazer ['bleɪzər] *n* : chaqueta *f* deportiva

bleach ['bli:tʃ] *vt* : blanquear, decolorar — ~ *n* : lejía *f*, blanqueador *m Lat*

bleachers ['bli:tʃərz] *ns & pl* : gradas *fpl*

bleak ['bli:k] *adj* **1** DESOLATE : desolado **2** GLOOMY : triste, sombrío

bleary-eyed ['blɪri,aɪd] *adj* : con los ojos nublados

bleat ['bli:t] *vi* : balar — ~ *n* : balido *m*

bleed ['bli:d] *v* **bled** ['blɛd]; **bleeding** : sangrar
blemish ['blɛmɪʃ] *vt* : manchar, marcar — ~ *n* : mancha *f*, marca *f*
blend ['blɛnd] *vt* : mezclar, combinar — ~ *n* : mezcla *f*, combinación *f* — **blender** ['blɛndər] *n* : licuadora *f*
bless ['blɛs] *vt* **blessed** ['blɛst]; **blessing** : bendecir — **blessed** ['blɛsəd] *or* **blest** ['blɛst] *adj* : bendito — **blessing** ['blɛsɪŋ] *n* : bendición *f*
blew → **blow**
blind ['blaɪnd] *adj* : ciego — ~ *vt* **1** : cegar, dejar ciego **2** DAZZLE : deslumbrar — ~ *n* **1** : persiana *f* (para una ventana) **2 the** ~ : los ciegos — **blindfold** ['blaɪnd,fo:ld] *vt* : vendar los ojos — ~ *n* : venda *f* (para los ojos) — **blindly** ['blaɪndli] *adv* : ciegamente — **blindness** ['blaɪndnəs] *n* : ceguera *f*
blink ['blɪŋk] *vi* **1** : parpadear **2** FLICKER : brillar intermitentemente — ~ *n* : parpadeo *m* — **blinker** ['blɪŋkər] *n* : intermitente *m*, direccional *f Lat*
bliss ['blɪs] *n* : dicha *f*, felicidad *f* (absoluta) — **blissful** ['blɪsfəl] *adj* : feliz
blister ['blɪstər] *n* : ampolla *f* — ~ *vi* : ampollarse
blitz ['blɪts] *n* : bombardeo *m* aéreo
blizzard ['blɪzərd] *n* : ventisca *f* (de nieve)
bloated ['blo:t̬əd] *adj* : hinchado
blob ['blɑb] *n* **1** DROP : gota *f* **2** SPOT : mancha *f*
block ['blɑk] *n* **1** : bloque *m* **2** OBSTRUCTION : obstrucción *f* **3** : manzana *f*, cuadra *f Lat* (de edificios) **4** *or* **building** ~ : cubo *m* de construcción — ~ *vt* : obstruir, bloquear — **blockade** [blɑ'keɪd] *n* : bloqueo *m* — **blockage** ['blɑkɪdʒ] *n* : obstrucción *f*
blond *or* **blonde** ['blɑnd] *adj* : rubio — ~ *n* : rubio *m*, -bia *f*
blood ['blʌd] *n* : sangre *f* — **bloodhound** ['blʌd,haʊnd] *n* : sabueso *m* — **blood pressure** *n* : tensión *f* (arterial) — **bloodshed** ['blʌd,ʃɛd] *n* : derramamiento *m* de sangre — **bloodshot** ['blʌd,ʃɑt] *adj* : inyectado de sangre — **bloodstained** ['blʌd,steɪnd] *adj* : manchado de sangre — **bloodstream** ['blʌd,stri:m] *n* : sangre *f*, torrente *m* sanguíneo — **bloody** ['blʌdi] *adj* **bloodier; -est** : ensangrentado, sangriento
bloom ['blu:m] *n* **1** : flor *f* **2 in full** ~ : en plena floración — ~ *vi* : florecer
blossom ['blɑsəm] *n* : flor *f* — ~ *vi* : florecer
blot ['blɑt] *n* **1** : borrón *m* (de tinta, etc.) **2** BLEMISH : mancha *f* — ~ *vt* **blotted; blotting 1** : emborronar **2** DRY : secar
blotch ['blɑtʃ] *n* : mancha *f*, borrón *m* — **blotchy** ['blɑtʃi] *adj* **blotchier; -est** : lleno de manchas
blouse ['blaʊs, 'blaʊz] *n* : blusa *f*
blow ['blo:] *v* **blew** ['blu:]; **blown** ['blo:n]; **blowing** *vi* **1** : soplar **2** SOUND : sonar **3** *or* ~ **out** : fundirse (dícese de un fusible eléctrico), reventarse (dícese de una llanta) — *vt* **1** : soplar **2** SOUND : tocar, sonar **3** BUNGLE : echar a perder — ~ *n* : golpe *m* — **blowout** ['blo:,aʊt] *n* : reventón *m* — **blow up** *vi* : estallar, hacer explosión — *vt* **1** EXPLODE : volar **2** INFLATE : inflar
blubber ['blʌbər] *n* : esperma *f* de ballena
bludgeon ['blʌdʒən] *vt* : aporrear
blue ['blu:] *adj* **bluer; bluest 1** : azul **2** MELANCHOLY : triste — ~ *n* : azul *m* — **blueberry** ['blu:,bɛri] *n, pl* **-ries** : arándano *m* — **bluebird** ['blu:,bərd] *n* : azulejo *m* — **blue cheese** *n* : queso *m* azul — **blueprint** ['blu:,prɪnt] *n* PLAN : proyecto *m* — **blues** ['blu:z] *npl* **1** SADNESS : tristeza *f* **2** : blues *m* (en música)
bluff ['blʌf] *vi* : hacer un farol — ~ *n* : farol *m*
blunder ['blʌndər] *vi* : meter la pata *fam* — ~ *n* : metedura *f* de pata *fam*
blunt ['blʌnt] *adj* **1** DULL : desafilado **2** DIRECT : directo, franco
blur ['blər] *n* : imágen *f* borrosa — ~ *vt* **blurred; blurring** : hacer borroso
blurb ['blərb] *n* : nota *f* publicitaria
blurt ['blərt] *vt or* ~ **out** : espetar
blush ['blʌʃ] *n* : rubor *m* — ~ *vi* : ruborizarse
blustery ['blʌstəri] *adj* : borrascoso, tempestuoso
boar ['bor] *n* : cerdo *m* macho
board ['bord] *n* **1** PLANK : tabla *f*, tablón *m* **2** COMMITTEE : junta *f*, consejo *m* **3** : tablero *m* (de juegos) **4 room and** ~ : comida y alojamiento — ~ *vt* **1** : subir a bordo de (una nave, un avión, etc.), subir a (un tren) **2** LODGE : hospedar **3** ~ **up** : cerrar con tablas — **boarder** ['bordər] *n* : huésped *mf*
boast ['bo:st] *n* : jactancia *f* — ~ *vi* : alardear, jactarse — **boastful** ['bo:stfəl] *adj* : jactancioso
boat ['bo:t] *n* : barco *m* (grande), barca *f* (pequeña)
bob ['bɑb] *vi* **bobbed; bobbing** *or* ~ **up and down** : subir y bajar
bobbin ['bɑbən] *n* : bobina *f*, carrete *m*
bobby pin ['bɑbi,pɪn] *n* : horquilla *f*

body ['badi] *n, pl* **bodies 1** : cuerpo *m* **2** CORPSE : cadáver *m* **3** : carrocería (de un automóvil, etc.) **4** COLLECTION : conjunto *m* **5 ~ of water** : masa *f* de agua — **bodily** *adj* : corporal — **bodyguard** ['badi,gard] *n* : guardaespaldas *mf*

bog ['bag, 'bɔg] *n* : ciénaga *f* — **~** *vt* **bogged; bogging** *or* **~ down** : empantanarse

bogus ['bo:gəs] *adj* : falso

boil ['bɔɪl] *v* : hervir — **boiler** ['bɔɪlər] *n* : caldera *f*

bold ['bo:ld] *adj* **1** DARING : audaz **2** IMPUDENT : descarado — **boldness** ['bo:ldnəs] *n* : audacia *f*

Bolivian [bə'lɪviən] *adj* : boliviano *m,* -na *f*

bologna [bə'lo:ni] *n* : salchicha *f* ahumada

bolster ['bo:lstər] *vt* **-stered; -stering** *or* **~ up** : reforzar

bolt ['bo:lt] *n* **1** LOCK : cerrojo *m* **2** SCREW : tornillo *m* **3 ~ of lightning** : relámpago *m,* rayo *m* — **~** *vt* **1** FASTEN : atornillar **2** LOCK : echar el cerrojo a — *vi* FLEE : salir corriendo

bomb ['bam] *n* : bomba *f* — **~** *vt* : bombardear — **bombard** [bam'bard, bəm-] *vt* : bombardear — **bombardment** [bam'bardmənt] *n* : bombardeo *m* — **bomber** ['bamər] *n* : bombardero *m*

bond ['band] *n* **1** TIE : vínculo *m,* lazo *m* **2** SURETY : fianza *f* **3** : bono *m* (en finanzas) — **~** *vi* STICK : adherirse

bondage ['bandɪdʒ] *n* : esclavitud *f*

bone ['bo:n] *n* : hueso *m* — **~** *vt* **boned; boning** : deshuesar

bonfire ['ban,faɪr] *n* : hoguera *f*

bonus ['bo:nəs] *n* **1** PAY : prima *f* **2** BENEFIT : beneficio *m* adicional

bony ['bo:ni] *adj* **bonier; -est 1** : huesudo **2** : lleno de espinas (dícese de pescados)

boo ['bu:] *n, pl* **boos** : abucheo *m* — **~** *vt* : abuchear

book ['bʊk] *n* **1** : libro *m* **2** NOTEBOOK : libreta *f,* cuaderno *m* — **~** *vt* : reservar — **bookcase** ['bʊk,keɪs] *n* : estantería *f* — **bookkeeping** ['bʊk,ki:pɪŋ] *n* : teneduría *f* de libros, contabilidad *f* — **booklet** ['bʊklət] *n* : folleto *m* — **bookmark** ['bʊk,mark] *n* : marcador *m* de libros — **bookseller** ['bʊk,sɛlər] *n* : librero *m,* -ra *f* — **bookshelf** ['bʊk-ʃɛlf] *n, pl* **-shelves** : estante *m* — **bookstore** ['bʊk,stor] *n* : librería *f*

boom ['bu:m] *vi* **1** : tronar, resonar **2** PROSPER : estar en auge, prosperar — **~** *n* **1** : bramido *m,* estruendo *m* **2** : auge *m* (económico)

boon ['bu:n] *n* : ayuda *f,* beneficio *m*

boost ['bu:st] *vt* **1** LIFT : levantar **2** INCREASE : aumentar — **~** *n* **1** INCREASE : aumento *m* **2** ENCOURAGEMENT : estímulo *m*

boot ['bu:t] *n* : bota *f,* botín *m* — **~** *vt* **1** : dar una patada a **2** *or* **~ up** : cargar (un ordenador)

booth ['bu:θ] *n, pl* **booths** ['bu:ðz, 'bu:θs] : cabina *f* (de teléfono, de votar), caseta *f* (de información)

booty ['bu:ṭi] *n, pl* **-ties** : botín *m*

booze ['bu:z] *n* : trago *m,* bebida *f* (alcohólica)

border ['bɔrdər] *n* **1** EDGE : borde *m,* orilla *f* **2** TRIM : ribete *m* **3** FRONTIER : frontera *f*

bore[1] ['bor] *vt* **bored; boring** DRILL : taladrar

bore[2] *vt* TIRE : aburrir — **~** *n* : pesado *m,* -da *fam f* (persona), lata *f fam* (cosa, situación) — **boredom** ['bordəm] *n* : aburrimiento *m* — **boring** ['borɪŋ] *adj* : aburrido, pesado

born ['bɔrn] *adj* **1** : nacido **2 be ~** : nacer

borough ['bəro] *n* : distrito *m* municipal

borrow ['baro] *vt* : pedir prestado, tomar prestado

Bosnian ['bazniən, 'bɔz-] *adj* : bosnio *m,* -nia *f*

bosom ['bʊzəm, 'bu:-] *n* BREAST : pecho *m,* seno *m* — **~** *adj* **~ friend** : amigo *m* intimo

boss ['bɔs] *n* : jefe *m,* -fa *f;* patrón *m,* -trona *f* — **~** *vt* SUPERVISE : dirigir — **bossy** ['bɔsi] *adj* **bossier; -est** : autoritario

botany ['batəni] *n* : botánica *f* — **botanical** [bə'tænɪkəl] *adj* : botánico

botch ['batʃ] *vt* : hacer una chapuza de, estropear

both ['bo:θ] *adj* : ambos, los dos, las dos — **~** *pron* : ambos *m,* -bas *f;* los dos, las dos

bother ['baðər] *vt* **1** TROUBLE : preocupar **2** PESTER : molestar, fastidiar — *vi* **~ to** : molestarse en — **~** *n* : molestia *f*

bottle ['batəl] *n* **1** : botella *f,* frasco *m* **2** *or* **baby ~** : biberón *m* — **~** *vt* **bottled; bottling** : embotellar — **bottleneck** ['batəl,nɛk] *n* : embotellamiento *m*

bottom ['baṭəm] *n* **1** : fondo *m* (de una caja, del mar, etc.), pie *m* (de una escalera, una montaña, etc.), final *m* (de una lista) **2** BUTTOCKS : nalgas *fpl,* trasero *m* — **~** *adj* : más bajo, inferi-

or, de abajo — **bottomless** ['bɑṭəmləs] *adj* : sin fondo
bough ['baʊ] *n* : rama *f*
bought → **buy**
bouillon ['bu:ˌjɑn; 'bʊlˌjɑn, -jən] *n* : caldo *m*
boulder ['bo:ldər] *n* : canto *m* rodado
boulevard ['bʊləˌvɑrd, 'bu:-] *n* : bulevar *m*
bounce ['baʊnʦ] *v* **bounced; bouncing** *vt* : hacer rebotar — *vi* : rebotar — ~ *n* : rebote *m*
bound[1] ['baʊnd] *adj* **be ~ for** : ir rumbo a
bound[2] *adj* **1** OBLIGED : obligado **2** DETERMINED : decidido **3 be ~ to** : tener que
bound[3] *n* **out of ~s** : (en) zona prohibida — **boundary** ['baʊndri, -dəri] *n, pl* **-aries** : límite *m* — **boundless** ['baʊndləs] *adj* : sin límites
bouquet [bo:'keɪ, bu:-] *n* : ramo *m*
bourgeois ['bʊrʒˌwɑ, bʊrʒ'wɑ] *adj* : burgués
bout ['baʊt] *n* **1** : combate *m* (en deportes) **2** : ataque *m* (de una enfermedad) **3** : período *m* (de actividad)
bow[1] ['baʊ] *vi* : inclinarse — *vt* **~ one's head** : inclinar la cabeza — ~ ['baʊ:] *n* : reverencia *f*, inclinación *f*
bow[2] ['bo:] *n* **1** : arco *m* **2 tie a ~** : hacer un lazo
bow[3] ['baʊ] *n* : proa *f* (de un barco)
bowels ['baʊəls] *npl* **1** : intestinos *mpl* **2** DEPTHS : entrañas *fpl*
bowl[1] ['bo:l] *n* : tazón *m*, cuenco *m*
bowl[2] *vi* : jugar a los bolos — **bowling** ['bo:lɪŋ] *n* : bolos *mpl*
box[1] ['bɑks] *vi* FIGHT : boxear — **boxer** ['bɑksər] *n* : boxeador *m*, -dora *f* — **boxing** ['bɑksɪŋ] *n* : boxeo *m*
box[2] *n* **1** : caja *f*, cajón *m* **2** : palco *m* (en el teatro) — ~ *vt* : empaquetar — **box office** *n* : taquilla *f*, boletería *f Lat*
boy ['bɔɪ] *n* : niño *m*, chico *m*
boycott ['bɔɪˌkɑt] *vt* : boicotear — ~ *n* : boicot *m*
boyfriend ['bɔɪˌfrɛnd] *n* : novio *m*
bra ['brɑ] → **brassiere**
brace ['breɪs] *n* **1** SUPPORT : abrazadera *f* **2 ~s** *npl* : aparatos *mpl* (para dientes) — ~ *vi* **~ oneself for** : prepararse para
bracelet ['breɪslət] *n* : brazalete *m*
bracket ['brækət] *n* **1** SUPPORT : soporte *m* **2** : corchete *m* (marca de puntuación) **3** CATEGORY : categoría *f* — ~ *vt* **1** : poner entre corchetes **2** CATEGORIZE : catalogar
brag ['bræg] *vi* **bragged; bragging** : jactarse
braid ['breɪd] *vt* : trenzar — ~ *n* : trenza *f*
braille ['breɪl] *n* : braille *m*
brain ['breɪn] *n* **1** : cerebro *m* **2 ~s** *npl* : inteligencia *f* — **brainstorm** ['breɪnˌstɔrm] *n* : idea *f* genial — **brainwash** ['breɪnˌwɔʃ, -ˌwɑʃ] *vt* : lavar el cerebro — **brainy** ['breɪni] *adj* **brainier; -est** : inteligente, listo
brake ['breɪk] *n* : freno *m* — ~ *v* **braked; braking** : frenar
bramble ['bræmbəl] *n* : zarza *f*
bran ['bræn] *n* : salvado *m*
branch ['bræntʃ] *n* **1** : rama *f* (de una planta) **2** DIVISION : ramal *m* (de un camino, etc.), sucursal *f* (de una empresa), agencia *f* (del gobierno) — ~ *vi or* **~ off** : ramificarse, bifurcarse
brand ['brænd] *n* **1** : marca *f* (de ganado) **2** *or* **~ name** : marca *f* de fábrica — ~ *vt* **1** : marcar (ganado) **2** LABEL : tachar, tildar
brandish ['brændɪʃ] *vt* : blandir
brand–new ['brænd'nu:, -'nju:] *adj* : flamante
brandy ['brændi] *n, pl* **-dies** : brandy *m*, coñac *m*
brass ['bræs] *n* **1** : latón *m* **2** : metales *mpl* (de una orquesta)
brassiere [brə'zɪr, brɑ-] *n* : sostén *m*, brasier *m Lat*
brat ['bræt] *n* : mocoso *m*, -sa *f fam*
bravado [brə'vɑdo] *n, pl* **-does** *or* **-dos** : bravuconadas *fpl*
brave ['breɪv] *adj* **braver; bravest** : valiente, valeroso — ~ *vt* **braved; braving** : afrontar, hacer frente a — ~ *n* : guerrero *m* indio — **bravery** ['breɪvəri] *n* : valor *m*, valentía *f*
brawl ['brɔl] *n* : pelea *f*, reyerta *f*
brawn ['brɔn] *n* : músculos *mpl* — **brawny** ['brɔni] *adj* **brawnier; -est** : musculoso
bray ['breɪ] *vi* : rebuznar
brazen ['breɪzən] *adj* : descarado
Brazilian [brə'zɪljən] *adj* : brasileño *m*, -ña *f*
breach ['bri:tʃ] *n* **1** VIOLATION : infracción *f*, violación *f* **2** GAP : brecha *f*
bread ['brɛd] *n* **1** : pan *m* **2 ~ crumbs** : migajas *fpl*
breadth ['brɛtθ] *n* : anchura *f*
break ['breɪk] *v* **broke** ['bro:k]; **broken** ['bro:kən]; **breaking** *vt* **1** : romper, quebrar **2** VIOLATE : infringir, violar **3** INTERRUPT : interrumpir **4** SURPASS : batir (un récord, etc.) **5 ~ a habit** : quitarse una costumbre **6 ~ the news** : dar la noticia — *vi* **1** : romperse, quebrarse **2 ~ away** : es-

capar **3 ~ down** : estropearse (dícese de una máquina), fallar (dícese de un sistema, etc.) **4 ~ into** : entrar en **5 ~ off** : interrumpirse **6 ~ out of** : escaparse de **7 ~ up** SEPARATE : separarse — **~** *n* **1** : ruptura *f,* fractura *f* **2** GAP : interrupción *f,* claro *m* (entre las nubes) **3 lucky ~** : golpe *m* de suerte **4 take a ~** : tomar(se) un descanso — **breakable** ['breɪkəbəl] *adj* : quebradizo, frágil — **breakdown** ['breɪk,daʊn] *n* **1** : avería *f* (de máquinas), interrupción *f* (de comunicaciones), fracaso *m* (de negociaciones) **2** *or* **nervous ~** : crisis *f* nerviosa

breakfast ['brɛkfəst] *n* : desayuno *m*

breast ['brɛst] *n* **1** : seno *m* (de una mujer) **2** CHEST : pecho *m* — **breast–feed** ['brɛst,fi:d] *vt* **-fed** [-,fɛd]; **-feeding** : amamantar

breath ['brɛθ] *n* : aliento *m,* respiración *f* — **breathe** ['bri:ð] *v* **breathed; breathing** : respirar — **breathless** ['brɛθləs] *adj* : sin aliento, jadeante — **breathtaking** ['brɛθ,teɪkɪŋ] *adj* : impresionante

breed ['bri:d] *v* **bred** ['brɛd]; **breeding** *vt* **1** : criar (animales) **2** ENGENDER : engendrar, producir — *vi* : reproducirse — **~** *n* **1** : raza *f* **2** CLASS : clase *f,* tipo *m*

breeze ['bri:z] *n* : brisa *f* — **breezy** ['bri:zi] *adj* **breezier; -est 1** WINDY : ventoso **2** NONCHALANT : despreocupado

brevity ['brɛvət̬i] *n, pl* **-ties** : brevedad *f*

brew ['bru:] *vt* : hacer (cerveza, etc.), preparar (té) — *vi* **1** : fabricar cerveza **2** : amenazar (dícese de una tormenta) — **brewery** ['bru:əri, 'brʊri] *n, pl* **-eries** : cervecería *f*

bribe ['braɪb] *n* : soborno *m* — **~** *vt* **bribed; bribing** : sobornar — **bribery** ['braɪbəri] *n, pl* **-eries** : soborno *m*

brick ['brɪk] *n* : ladrillo *m* — **bricklayer** ['brɪk,leɪər] *n* : albañil *mf*

bride ['braɪd] *n* : novia *f* — **bridal** ['braɪdəl] *adj* : nupcial, de novia — **bridegroom** ['braɪd,gru:m] *n* : novio *m* — **bridesmaid** ['braɪdz,meɪd] *n* : dama *f* de honor

bridge ['brɪdʒ] *n* **1** : puente *m* **2** : caballete *m* (de la nariz) **3** : bridge *m* (juego de naipes) — **~** *vt* **bridged; bridging 1** : tender un puente sobre **2 ~ the gap** : salvar las diferencias

bridle ['braɪdəl] *n* : brida *f* — **~** *vt* **-dled; -dling** : embridar

brief ['bri:f] *adj* : breve — **~** *n* **1** : resumen *m,* sumario *m* **2 ~s** *npl* UNDERPANTS : calzoncillos *mpl* — **~** *vt* : dar órdenes a, instruir — **briefcase** ['bri:f,keɪs] *n* : portafolio *m,* maletín *m* — **briefly** ['bri:fli] *adv* : brevemente

bright ['braɪt] *adj* **1** : brillante, claro **2** CHEERFUL : alegre, animado **3** INTELLIGENT : listo, inteligente — **brighten** ['braɪtən] *vi* **1** : hacerse más brillante **2** *or* **~ up** : animarse, alegrarse — *vt* **1** ILLUMINATE : iluminar **2** ENLIVEN : alegrar, animar

brilliant ['brɪljənt] *adj* : brillante — **brilliance** ['brɪljənts] *n* **1** BRIGHTNESS : resplandor *m,* brillantez *f* **2** INTELLIGENCE : inteligencia *f*

brim ['brɪm] *n* **1** : borde *m* (de una taza, etc.) **2** : ala *f* (de un sombrero) — **~** *vi* **brimmed; brimming** *or* **~ over** : desbordarse, rebosar

brine ['braɪn] *n* : salmuera *f*

bring ['brɪŋ] *vt* **brought** ['brɔt]; **bringing 1** : traer **2 ~ about** : ocasionar **3 ~ around** PERSUADE : convencer **4 ~ back** : devolver **5 ~ down** : derribar **6 ~ on** CAUSE : provocar **7 ~ out** : sacar **8 ~ to an end** : terminar (con) **9 ~ up** REAR : criar **10 ~ up** MENTION : sacar

brink ['brɪŋk] *n* : borde *m*

brisk ['brɪsk] *adj* **1** FAST : rápido **2** LIVELY : enérgico

bristle ['brɪsəl] *n* : cerda *f* (de un animal), pelo *m* (de una planta) — **~** *vi* **-tled; -tling** : erizarse

British ['brɪt̬ɪʃ] *adj* : británico

brittle ['brɪtəl] *adj* **-tler; -tlest** : frágil, quebradizo

broach ['bro:tʃ] *vt* : abordar

broad ['brɔd] *adj* **1** WIDE : ancho **2** GENERAL : general **3 in ~ daylight** : en pleno día

broadcast ['brɔd,kæst] *vt* **-cast; -casting** : emitir — **~** *n* : emisión *f*

broaden ['brɔdən] *vt* : ampliar, ensanchar — *vi* : ensancharse — **broadly** ['brɔdli] *adv* : en general — **broad–minded** ['brɔd'maɪndəd] *adj* : de miras amplias, tolerante

broccoli ['brɑkəli] *n* : brócoli *m,* brécol *m*

brochure [bro'ʃʊr] *n* : folleto *m*

broil ['brɔɪl] *vt* : asar a la parrilla

broke ['bro:k] → **break** — **~** *adj* : pelado *fam* — **broken** ['bro:kən] *adj* : roto, quebrado — **brokenhearted** [,bro:kən'hɑrt̬əd] *adj* : desconsolado, con el corazón destrozado

broker ['bro:kər] *n* : corredor *m,* **-dora** *f*

bronchitis [brɑn'kaɪt̬əs, brɑŋ-] *n* : bronquitis *f*

bronze ['brɑnz] *n* : bronce *m*
brooch ['bro:tʃ, 'bru:tʃ] *n* : broche *m*
brood ['bru:d] *n* : nidada *f* (de pájaros), camada *f* (de mamíferos) — ~ *vi* **1** INCUBATE : empollar **2** ~ **about** : dar vueltas a, pensar demasiado en
brook ['brʊk] *n* : arroyo *m*
broom ['bru:m, 'brʊm] *n* : escoba *f* — **broomstick** ['bru:m,stɪk, 'brʊm-] *n* : palo *m* de escoba
broth ['brɔθ] *n, pl* **broths** ['brɔθs, 'brɔðz] : caldo *m*
brothel ['brɑθəl, 'brɔ-] *n* : burdel *m*
brother ['brʌðər] *n* : hermano *m* — **brotherhood** ['brʌðər,hʊd] *n* : fraternidad *f* — **brother-in-law** ['brʌðərɪn,lɔ] *n, pl* **brothers-in-law:** cuñado *m* — **brotherly** ['brʌðərli] *adj* : fraternal
brought → **bring**
brow ['braʊ] *n* **1** EYEBROW : ceja *f* **2** FOREHEAD : frente *f* **3** : cima *f* (de una colina)
brown ['braʊn] *adj* : marrón, castaño (dícese del pelo), moreno (dícese de la piel) — ~ *n* : marrón *m* — ~ *vt* : dorar (en cocinar)
browse ['braʊz] *vi* **browsed; browsing** : mirar, echar un vistazo
bruise ['bru:z] *vt* **bruised; bruising 1** : contusionar, magullar (a una persona) **2** : machucar (frutas) — ~ *n* : cardenal *m*, magulladura *f*
brunch ['brʌntʃ] *n* : brunch *m*
brunet *or* **brunette** [bru:'nɛt] *adj* : moreno — ~ *n* : moreno *m*, -na *f*
brunt ['brʌnt] *n* **bear the ~ of** : aguantar el mayor impacto de
brush ['brʌʃ] *n* **1** : cepillo *m*, pincel *m* (de artista), brocha *f* (de pintor) **2** UNDERBRUSH : maleza *f* — ~ *vt* **1** : cepillar **2** GRAZE : rozar **3** ~ **aside** : rechazar **4** ~ **off** DISREGARD : hacer caso omiso de — *vi* ~ **up on** : repasar — **brush-off** ['brʌʃ,ɔf] *n* **give the ~ to** : dar calabazas a
brusque ['brʌsk] *adj* : brusco
brutal ['bru:t̬əl] *adj* : brutal — **brutality** [bru:'tæləṯi] *n, pl* **-ties** : brutalidad *f*
brute ['bru:t] *adj* : bruto — ~ *n* : bestia *f*; bruto *m*, -ta *f*
bubble ['bʌbəl] *n* : burbuja *f* — ~ *vi* **-bled; -bling** : burbujear
buck ['bʌk] *n, pl* **buck** *or* **bucks 1** : animal *m* macho, ciervo *m* (macho) **2** DOLLAR : dólar *m* — ~ *vi* **1** : corcovear (dícese de un caballo) **2** ~ **up** : animarse, levantar el ánimo — *vt* OPPOSE : oponerse a, ir en contra de
bucket ['bʌkət] *n* : cubo *m*
buckle ['bʌkəl] *n* : hebilla *f* — ~ *v* **-led; -ling** *vt* **1** FASTEN : abrochar **2** BEND : combar, torcer — *vi* **1** : combarse, torcerse **2** : doblarse (dícese de las rodillas)
bud ['bʌd] *n* **1** : brote *m* **2** *or* **flower ~** : capullo *m* — ~ *vi* **budded; budding** : brotar, hacer brotes
Buddhism ['bu:,dɪzəm, 'bʊ-] *n* : budismo *m* — **Buddhist** ['bu:dɪst, 'bʊ-] *adj* : budista — ~ *n* : budista *mf*
buddy ['bʌdi] *n, pl* **-dies** : compañero *m*, -ra *f*
budge ['bʌdʒ] *vi* **budged; budging 1** MOVE : moverse **2** YIELD : ceder
budget ['bʌdʒət] *n* : presupuesto *m* — ~ *vi* : presupuestar — **budgetary** ['bʌdʒə,tɛri] *adj* : presupuestario
buff ['bʌf] *n* **1** : beige *m*, color *m* de ante **2** ENTHUSIAST : aficionado *m*, -da *f* — ~ *adj* : beige — ~ *vt* POLISH : pulir
buffalo ['bʌfə,lo:] *n, pl* **-lo** *or* **-loes** : búfalo *m*
buffet [,bʌ'feɪ, ,bu:-] *n* **1** : bufé *m* (comida) **2** SIDEBOARD : aparador *m*
bug ['bʌg] *n* **1** INSECT : bicho *m*, insecto *m* **2** FLAW : defecto *m* **3** GERM : microbio *m* **4** MICROPHONE : micrófono *m* (oculto) — ~ *vt* **bugged; bugging 1** PESTER : fastidiar, molestar **2** : ocultar micrófonos en (una habitación, etc.)
buggy ['bʌgi] *n, pl* **-gies 1** CARRIAGE : calesa *f* **2** *or* **baby ~** : cochecito *m* (para niños)
bugle ['bju:gəl] *n* : clarín *m*, corneta *f*
build ['bɪld] *v* **built** ['bɪlt]; **building** *vt* **1** : construir **2** DEVELOP : desarrollar — *vi* **1** *or* ~ **up** INTENSIFY : aumentar, intensificar **2** *or* ~ **up** ACCUMULATE : acumularse — ~ *n* PHYSIQUE : físico *m*, complexión *f* — **builder** ['bɪldər] *n* : constructor *m*, -tora *f* — **building** ['bɪldɪŋ] *n* **1** STRUCTURE : edificio *m* **2** CONSTRUCTION : construcción *f* — **built-in** ['bɪlt'ɪn] *adj* : empotrado
bulb ['bʌlb] *n* **1** : bulbo *m* (de una planta) **2** LIGHTBULB : bombilla *f*
bulge ['bʌldʒ] *vi* **bulged; bulging** : sobresalir — ~ *n* : bulto *m*, protuberancia *f*
bulk ['bʌlk] *n* **1** VOLUME : volumen *m*, bulto *m* **2 in ~** : en grandes cantidades — **bulky** ['bʌlki] *adj* **bulkier; -est** : voluminoso
bull ['bʊl] *n* **1** : toro *m* **2** MALE : macho *m*
bulldog ['bʊl,dɔg] *n* : buldog *m*
bulldozer ['bʊl,do:zər] *n* : bulldozer *m*
bullet ['bʊlət] *n* : bala *f*
bulletin ['bʊlətən, -lət̬ən] *n* : boletín *m* — **bulletin board** *n* : tablón *m* de anuncios

bulletproof ['bʊlət,pru:f] *adj* : a prueba de balas
bullfight ['bʊl,faɪt] *n* : corrida *f* (de toros) — **bullfighter** ['bʊl,faɪṭər] *n* : torero *m*, -ra *f*; matador *m*
bullion ['bʊljən] *n* : oro *m* en lingotes, plata *f* en lingotes
bull's–eye ['bʊlz,aɪ] *n, pl* **bull's–eyes** : diana *f*
bully ['bʊli] *n, pl* **-lies** : matón *m* — ~ *vt* **-lied; -lying** : intimidar
bum ['bʌm] *n* : vagabundo *m*, -da *f*
bumblebee ['bʌmbəl,bi:] *n* : abejorro *m*
bump ['bʌmp] *n* **1** BULGE : bulto *m*, protuberancia *f* **2** IMPACT : golpe *m* **3** JOLT : sacudida *f* — ~ *vt* : chocar contra — *vi* ~ **into** MEET : encontrarse con — **bumper** ['bʌmpər] *n* : parachoques *mpl* — ~ *adj* : extraordinario, récord — **bumpy** ['bʌmpi] *adj* **bumpier; -est 1** : desigual, lleno de baches (dícese de un camino) **2 a** ~ **flight** : un vuelo agitado
bun ['bʌn] *n* : bollo *m*
bunch ['bʌntʃ] *n* : grupo *m* (de personas), racimo *m* (de frutas, etc.), ramo *m* (de flores), manojo *m* (de llaves) — ~ *vi or* ~ **up** : amontarse, agruparse
bundle ['bʌndəl] *n* **1** : lío *m*, bulto *m*, atado *m*, haz *m* (de palos) **2** PARCEL : paquete *m* **3** ~ **of nerves** : manojo *m* de nervios — ~ *vt* **-dled; -dling** *or* ~ **up** : liar, atar
bungalow ['bʌŋgə,lo:] *n* : casa *f* de un solo piso
bungle ['bʌŋgəl] *vt* **-gled; -gling** : echar a perder
bunion ['bʌnjən] *n* : juanete *m*
bunk ['bʌŋk] *n or* **bunk bed** : litera *f*
bunny ['bʌni] *n, pl* **-nies** : conejo *m*, -ja *f*
buoy ['bu:i, 'bɔɪ] *n* : boya *f* — ~ *vt or* ~ **up** HEARTEN : animar, levantar el ánimo a — **buoyant** ['bɔɪənt, 'bu:jənt] *adj* **1** : boyante, flotante **2** LIGHTHEARTED : alegre, optimista
burden ['bərdən] *n* : carga *f* — ~ *vt* ~ **s.o. with** : cargar a algn con — **burdensome** ['bərdənsəm] *adj* : oneroso
bureau ['bjʊro] *n* **1** : cómoda *f* (mueble) **2** : departamento *m* (del gobierno) **3** AGENCY : agencia *f* — **bureaucracy** [bjʊ'rɑkrəsi] *n, pl* **-cies** : burocracia *f* — **bureaucrat** ['bjʊrə,kræt] *n* : burócrata *mf* — **bureaucratic** [,bjʊrə'kræṭɪk] *adj* : burocrático
burglar ['bərglər] *n* : ladrón *m*, -drona *f* — **burglarize** ['bərglə,raɪz] *vt* **-ized; -izing** : robar — **burglary** ['bərgləri] *n, pl* **-glaries** : robo *m*
burgundy ['bərgəndi] *n, pl* **-dies** : borgoña *m*, vino *m* de Borgoña
burial ['bɛriəl] *n* : entierro *m*
burly ['bərli] *adj* **-lier; -liest** : fornido
burn ['bərn] *v* **burned** ['bərnd, 'bərnt] *or* **burnt** ['bərnt]; **burning** *vt* **1** : quemar **2** *or* ~ **down** : incendiar **3** ~ **up** : consumir — *vi* **1** : arder (dícese de un fuego), quemarse (dícese de la comida, etc.) **2** : estar encendido (dícese de una luz) **3** ~ **out** : apagarse — ~ *n* : quemadura *f* — **burner** ['bərnər] *n* : quemador *m*
burnish ['bərnɪʃ] *vt* : pulir
burp ['bərp] *vi* : eructar — ~ *n* : eructo *m*
burro ['bəro, 'bʊr-] *n, pl* **-os** : burro *m*
burrow ['bəro] *n* : madriguera *f* — ~ *vi* **1** : cavar **2** ~ **into** : hurgar en
bursar ['bərsər] *n* : tesorero *m*, -ra *f*
burst ['bərst] *v* **burst** *or* **bursted; bursting** *vi* : reventarse — *vt* : reventar — ~ *n* **1** EXPLOSION : estallido *m*, explosión *f* **2** OUTBURST : arranque *m*, arrebato *m* **3** ~ **of laughter** : carcajada *f*
bury ['bɛri] *vt* **buried; burying 1** INTER : enterrar **2** HIDE : esconder
bus ['bʌs] *n, pl* **buses** *or* **busses** : autobús *m*, bus *m* — ~ *v* **bused** *or* **bussed** ['bʌst]; **busing** *or* **bussing** ['bʌsɪŋ] *vt* : transportar en autobús — *vi* : viajar en autobús
bush ['bʊʃ] *n* SHRUB : arbusto *m*, mata *f*
bushel ['bʊʃəl] *n* : medida *f* de áridos igual a 35.24 litros
bushy ['bʊʃi] *adj* **bushier; -est** : poblado, espeso
busily ['bɪzəli] *adv* : afanosamente
business ['bɪznəs, -nəz] *n* **1** COMMERCE : negocios *mpl*, comercio *m* **2** COMPANY : empresa *f*, negocio *m* **3 it's none of your** ~ : no es asunto tuyo — **businessman** ['bɪznəs,mæn, -nəz-] *n, pl* **-men** [-mən, -,mɛn] : empresario *m*, hombre *m* de negocios — **businesswoman** ['bɪznəs,wʊmən, -nəz-] *n, pl* **-women** [-,wɪmən] : empresaria *f*, mujer *f* de negocios
bust[1] ['bʌst] *vt* BREAK : romper
bust[2] *n* **1** : busto *m* (en la escultura) **2** BREASTS : pecho *m*, senos *mpl*
bustle ['bʌsəl] *vi* **-tled; -tling** *or* ~ **about** : ir y venir, ajetrearse — ~ *n or* **hustle and** ~ : bullicio *m*, ajetreo *m*
busy ['bɪzi] *adj* **busier; -est 1** : ocupado **2** BUSTLING : concurrido
but ['bʌt] *conj* **1** : pero **2 not one** ~ **two** : no uno sino dos — ~ *prep* : excepto, menos

butcher ['bʊtʃər] *n* : carnicero *m*, -ra *f* — ~ *vt* **1** : matar **2** BOTCH : hacer una carnicería de
butler ['bʌtlər] *n* : mayordomo *m*
butt ['bʌt] *vt* : embestir (con los cuernos), darle un cabezazo a — *vi* ~ **in** : interrumpir — ~ *n* **1** BUTTING : embestida *f* (de cuernos) **2** TARGET : blanco *m* **3** : extremo *m*, culata *f* (de un rifle), colilla *f* (de un cigarillo)
butter ['bʌt̬ər] *n* : mantequilla *f* — ~ *vt* : untar con mantequilla
buttercup ['bʌt̬ər,kʌp] *n* : ranúnculo *m*
butterfly ['bʌt̬ər,flaɪ] *n, pl* **-flies** : mariposa *f*
buttocks ['bʌt̬əks, -,tɑks] *npl* : nalgas *fpl*
button ['bʌtən] *n* : botón *m* — ~ *vt* : abotonar — *vi or* ~ **up** : abotonarse — **buttonhole** ['bʌtən,ho:l] *n* : ojal *m* — ~ *vt* **-holed; -holing** : acorralar
buy ['baɪ] *vt* **bought** ['bɔt]; **buying** : comprar — ~ *n* : compra *f* — **buyer** ['baɪər] *n* : comprador *m*, -dora *f*
buzz ['bʌz] *vi* : zumbar — ~ *n* : zumbido *m*
buzzard ['bʌzərd] *n* : buitre *m*
buzzer ['bʌzər] *n* : timbre *m*
by ['baɪ] *prep* **1** NEAR : cerca de **2** VIA : por **3** PAST : por, por delante de **4** DURING : de, durante **5** (*in expressions of time*) : para **6** (*indicating cause or agent*) : por, de, a — ~ *adv* **1** ~ **and** ~ : poco después **2** ~ **and large** : en general **3 go** ~ : pasar **4 stop** ~ : pasar por casa
bygone ['baɪ,gɔn] *adj* : pasado — ~ *n* **let** ~**s be** ~**s** : lo pasado, pasado está
bypass ['baɪ,pæs] *n* : carretera *f* de circunvalación — ~ *vt* : evitar
by–product ['baɪ,prɑdəkt] *n* : subproducto *m*
bystander ['baɪ,stændər] *n* : espectador *m*, -dora *f*
byte ['baɪt] *n* : byte *m*, octeto *m*
byword ['baɪ,wərd] *n* **be a** ~ **for** : estar sinónimo de

C

c ['si:] *n, pl* **c's** *or* **cs** : c, tercera letra del alfabeto inglés
cab ['kæb] *n* **1** : taxi *m* **2** : cabina *f* (de un camión, etc.)
cabbage ['kæbɪdʒ] *n* : col *f*, repollo *m*
cabin ['kæbən] *n* **1** : cabaña *f* **2** : cabina *f* (de un avión, etc.), camarote *m* (de un barco)
cabinet ['kæbnət] *n* **1** CUPBOARD : armario *m* **2** : gabinete *m* (del gobierno) **3** *or* **medicine** ~ : botiquín *m*
cable ['keɪbəl] *n* : cable *m* — **cable television** *n* : televisión *f* por cable
cackle ['kækəl] *vi* **-led; -ling 1** CLUCK : cacarear **2** LAUGH : reírse a carcajadas
cactus ['kæktəs] *n, pl* **cacti** [-,taɪ] *or* **-tuses** : cactus *m*
cadence ['keɪdənts] *n* : cadencia *f*, ritmo *m*
cadet [kə'dɛt] *n* : cadete *mf*
café [kæ'feɪ, kə-] *n* : café *m*, cafetería *f* — **cafeteria** [,kæfə'tɪriə] *n* : restaurante *m* autoservicio, cantina *f*
caffeine [kæ'fi:n] *n* : cafeína *f*
cage ['keɪdʒ] *n* : jaula *f* — ~ *vt* **caged; caging** : enjaular
cajole [kə'dʒo:l] *vt* **-joled; -joling** : engatusar
cake ['keɪk] *n* **1** : pastel *m*, torta *f* **2** : pastilla *f* (de jabón) **3 take the** ~ : ser el colmo — **caked** ['keɪkt] *adj* ~ **with** : cubierto de
calamity [kə'læmət̬i] *n, pl* **-ties** : calamidad *f*
calcium ['kælsiəm] *n* : calcio *m*
calculate ['kælkjə,leɪt] *v* **-lated; -lating** : calcular — **calculating** ['kælkjə,leɪt̬ɪŋ] *adj* : calculador — **calculation** [,kælkjə'leɪʃən] *n* : cálculo *m* — **calculator** ['kælkjə,leɪt̬ər] *n* : calculadora *f*
calendar ['kæləndər] *n* : calendario *m*
calf[1] ['kæf, 'kaf] *n, pl* **calves** ['kævz, 'kavz] **1** : becerro *m*, -rra *f*; ternero *m*, -ra *f* (de vacunos) **2** : cría *f* (de otros mamíferos)
calf[2] *n, pl* **calves** : pantorrilla *f* (de la pierna)
caliber *or* **calibre** ['kæləbər] *n* : calibre *m*
call ['kɔl] *vi* **1** : llamar **2** VISIT : pasar, hacer (una) visita **3** ~ **for** : requerir — *vt* **1** : llamar **2** ~ **off** : cancelar — ~ *n* **1** : llamada *f* **2** SHOUT : grito *m* **3** VISIT : visita *f* **4** DEMAND : petición *f* — **calling** ['kɔlɪŋ] *n* : vocación *f*
callous ['kæləs] *adj* : insensible, cruel
calm ['kɑm, 'kɑlm] *n* : calma *f*, tranquilidad *f* — ~ *vt* : calmar — *vi or* ~ **down** : calmarse — ~ *adj* : tranquilo, en calma — **calmly** ['kɑmli, 'kɑlm-] *adv* : con calma

calorie [ˈkæləri] *n* : caloría *f*
came → **come**
camel [ˈkæməl] *n* : camello *m*
camera [ˈkæmrə, ˈkæmərə] *n* : cámara *f*
camouflage [ˈkæməˌflɑʒ, -ˌflɑdʒ] *n* : camuflaje *m* — ~ *vt* **-flaged; -flaging** : camuflar
camp [ˈkæmp] *n* **1** : campamento *m* **2** FACTION : bando *m* — ~ *vi* : acampar, ir de camping
campaign [kæmˈpeɪn] *n* : campaña *f* — ~ *vi* : hacer (una) campaña
camping [ˈkæmpɪŋ] *n* : camping *m*
campus [ˈkæmpəs] *n* : ciudad *f* universitaria
can[1] [ˈkæn] *v aux, past* **could** [ˈkʊd]; *present s & pl* **can 1** (*expressing possibility or permission*) : poder **2** (*expressing knowledge or ability*) : saber **3 that cannot be!** : ¡no puede ser!
can[2] [ˈkæn] *n* : lata *f* — ~ *vt* **canned; canning** : enlatar
Canadian [kəˈneɪdiən] *adj* : canadiense
canal [kəˈnæl] *n* : canal *m*
canary [kəˈnɛri] *n, pl* **-naries** : canario *m*
cancel [ˈkæntsəl] *vt* **-celed** *or* **-celled; -celing** *or* **-celling** : cancelar — **cancellation** [ˌkæntsəˈleɪʃən] *n* : cancelación *f*
cancer [ˈkæntsər] *n* : cáncer *m* — **cancerous** [ˈkæntsərəs] *adj* : canceroso
candelabra [ˌkændəˈlɑbrə, -ˈlæ-] *n, pl* **-bra** *or* **-bras** : candelabro *m*
candid [ˈkændɪd] *adj* : franco
candidate [ˈkændəˌdeɪt, -dət] *n* : candidato *m*, -ta *f* — **candidacy** [ˈkændədəsi] *n, pl* **-cies** : candidatura *f*
candle [ˈkændəl] *n* : vela *f* — **candlestick** [ˈkændəlˌstɪk] *n* : candelero *m*
candor *or Brit* **candour** [ˈkændər] *n* : franqueza *f*
candy [ˈkændi] *n, pl* **-dies** : dulce *m*, caramelo *m*
cane [ˈkeɪn] *n* **1** : bastón *m* (para andar), vara *f* (para castigar) **2** REED : caña *f*, mimbre *m* — ~ *vt* **caned; caning 1** : tapizar con mimbre **2** FLOG : azotar
canine [ˈkeɪˌnaɪn] *n or* ~ **tooth** : colmillo *m*, diente *m* canino — ~ *adj* : canino
canister [ˈkænəstər] *n* : lata *f*, bote *m Spain*
cannibal [ˈkænəbəl] *n* : caníbal *mf*
cannon [ˈkænən] *n, pl* **-nons** *or* **-non** : cañón *m*
cannot (can not) [ˈkænˌɑt, kəˈnɑt] → **can**[1]
canny [ˈkæni] *adj* **cannier; -est** : astuto
canoe [kəˈnuː] *n* : canoa *f*, piragua *f* — ~ *vt* **-noed; -noeing** : ir en canoa
canon [ˈkænən] *n* : canon *m* — **canonize** [ˈkænəˌnaɪz] *vt* **-ized; -izing** : canonizar
can opener *n* : abrelatas *m*
canopy [ˈkænəpi] *n, pl* **-pies** : dosel *m*
can't [ˈkænt, ˈkant] (*contraction of* **can not**) → **can**[1]
cantaloupe [ˈkæntəlˌoːp] *n* : melón *m*, cantalupo *m*
cantankerous [kænˈtæŋkərəs] *adj* : irritable, irascible
canteen [kænˈtiːn] *n* **1** FLASK : cantimplora *f* **2** CAFETERIA : cantina *f*
canter [ˈkæntər] *vi* : ir a medio galope — ~ *n* : medio galope *m*
canvas [ˈkænvəs] *n* **1** : lona *f* (tela) **2** : lienzo *m* (de pintar)
canvass [ˈkænvəs] *vt* **1** : solicitar votos de, hacer campaña entre **2** POLL : sondear — ~ *n* **1** : solicitación *f* (de votos) **2** POLL : sondeo *m*
canyon [ˈkænjən] *n* : cañón *m*
cap *n* **1** : gorra *f*, gorro *m* **2** TOP : tapa *f*, tapón *m* (de botellas) **3** LIMIT : tope *m* — ~ [ˈkæp] *vt* **capped; capping 1** COVER : tapar, cubrir **2** OUTDO : superar
capable [ˈkeɪpəbəl] *adj* : capaz, competente — **capability** [ˌkeɪpəˈbɪləṭi] *n, pl* **-ties** : capacidad *f*
capacity [kəˈpæsəṭi] *n, pl* **-ties 1** : capacidad *f* **2** ROLE : calidad *f*
cape[1] [ˈkeɪp] *n* : cabo *m* (en geografía)
cape[2] *n* CLOAK : capa *f*
caper[1] [ˈkeɪpər] *n* : alcaparra *f*
caper[2] *n* PRANK : broma *f*, travesura *f*
capital [ˈkæpəṭəl] *adj* **1** : capital **2** : mayúsculo (dícese de las letras) — ~ *n* **1** *or* ~ **city** : capital *f* **2** WEALTH : capital *m* **3** *or* ~ **letter** : mayúscula *f* — **capitalism** [ˈkæpəṭəlˌɪzəm] *n* : capitalismo *m* — **capitalist** [ˈkæpəṭəlɪst] *or* **capitalistic** [ˌkæpəṭəlˈɪstɪk] *adj* : capitalista — **capitalize** [ˈkæpəṭəlˌaɪz] *vt* **-ized; -izing 1** FINANCE : capitalizar **2** : escribir con mayúscula — *vi* ~ **on** : sacar partido de
capitol [ˈkæpəṭəl] *n* : capitolio *m*
capitulate [kəˈpɪtʃəˌleɪt] *vi* **-lated; -lating** : capitular
capsize [ˈkæpˌsaɪz, kæpˈsaɪz] *v* **-sized; -sizing** *vt* : hacer volcar — *vi* : zozobrar, volcar(se)
capsule [ˈkæpsəl, -ˌsuːl] *n* : cápsula *f*
captain [ˈkæptən] *n* : capitán *m*, -tana *f*
caption [ˈkæpʃən] *n* **1** : leyenda *f* (al pie de una ilustración) **2** SUBTITLE : subtítulo *m*
captivate [ˈkæptəˌveɪt] *vt* **-vated; -vating** : cautivar, encantar

captive ['kæptɪv] *adj* : cautivo — ~ *n* : cautivo *m*, -va *f* — **captivity** [kæp'tɪvət̬i] *n* : cautiverio *m*

capture ['kæpʃər] *n* : captura *f*, apresamiento *m* — ~ *vt* **-tured; -turing 1** SEIZE : capturar, apresar **2 ~ one's interest** : captar el interés de uno

car ['kɑr] *n* **1** : automóvil *m*, coche *m*, carro *m Lat* **2** *or* **railroad ~** : vagón *m*

carafe [kə'ræf, -'rɑf] *n* : garrafa *f*

caramel ['kɑrməl; 'kærəməl, -ˌmɛl] *n* : caramelo *m*, azúcar *f* quemada

carat ['kærət] *n* : quilate *m*

caravan ['kærəˌvæn] *n* : caravana *f*

carbohydrate [ˌkɑrbo'haɪˌdreɪt, -drət] *n* : carbohidrato *m*, hidrato *m* de carbono

carbon ['kɑrbən] *n* : carbono *m* — **carbon copy** *n* : copia *f*, duplicado *m*

carburetor ['kɑrbəˌreɪt̬ər, -bjə-] *n* : carburador *m*

carcass ['kɑrkəs] *n* : cuerpo *m* (de un animal muerto)

card ['kɑrd] *n* **1** : tarjeta *f* **2** *or* **playing ~** : carta *f*, naipe *m* — **cardboard** ['kɑrdˌbord] *n* : cartón *m*

cardiac ['kɑrdiˌæk] *adj* : cardíaco

cardigan ['kɑrdɪgən] *n* : cárdigan *m*

cardinal ['kɑrdənəl] *n* : cardenal *m* — ~ *adj* : cardinal, fundamental

care ['kær] *n* **1** : cuidado *m* **2** WORRY : preocupación **3 take ~ of** : cuidar (de) — ~ *vi* **cared; caring 1** : preocuparse, inquietarse **2 ~ for** TEND : cuidar (de), atender **3 ~ for** LIKE : querer **4 I don't ~** : no me importa

career [kə'rɪr] *n* : carrera *f* — ~ *vi* : ir a toda velocidad

carefree ['kærˌfri:, ˌkær'-] *adj* : despreocupado

careful ['kærfəl] *adj* : cuidadoso — **carefully** ['kærfəli] *adv* : con cuidado, cuidadosamente — **careless** ['kærləs] *adj* : descuidado — **carelessness** ['kærləsnəs] *n* : descuido *m*

caress [kə'rɛs] *n* : caricia *f* — ~ *vt* : acariciar

cargo ['kɑrˌgo:] *n, pl* **-goes** *or* **-gos** : cargamento *m*, carga *f*

caricature ['kærɪkəˌtʃʊr] *n* : caricatura *f* — ~ *vt* **-tured; -turing** : caricaturizar

caring ['kærɪŋ] *adj* : solícito, afectuoso

carnage ['kɑrnɪdʒ] *n* : matanza *f*, carnicería *f*

carnal ['kɑrnəl] *adj* : carnal

carnation [kɑr'neɪʃən] *n* : clavel *m*

carnival ['kɑrnəvəl] *n* : carnaval *m*

carol ['kærəl] *n* : villancico *m*

carp ['kɑrp] *vi* **~ at** : quejarse de

carpenter ['kɑrpəntər] *n* : carpintero *m*, -ra *f* — **carpentry** ['kɑrpəntri] *n* : carpintería *f*

carpet ['kɑrpət] *n* : alfombra *f*

carriage ['kærɪdʒ] *n* **1** : transporte *m* (de mercancías) **2** BEARING : porte *m* **3** *or* **baby ~** : cochecito *m* **4** *or* **horse-drawn ~** : carruaje *m*, coche *m*

carrier ['kæriər] *n* **1** : transportista *mf*, empresa *f* de transportes **2** : portador *m*, -dora *f* (de una enfermedad)

carrot ['kærət] *n* : zanahoria *f*

carry ['kæri] *v* **-ried; -rying** *vt* **1** : llevar **2** TRANSPORT : transportar **3** STOCK : vender **4** ENTAIL : acarrear, implicar **5 ~ oneself** : portarse — *vi* : oírse (dícese de sonidos) — **carry away** *vt* **get carried away** : exaltarse, entusiasmarse — **carry on** *vt* CONDUCT : realizar — *vi* **1** : portarse inapropiadamente **2** CONTINUE : seguir, continuar — **carry out** *vt* **1** PERFORM : llevar a cabo, realizar **2** FULFILL : cumplir

cart ['kɑrt] *n* : carreta *f*, carro *m* — ~ *vt* *or* **~ around** : acarrear

cartilage ['kɑrt̬əlɪdʒ] *n* : cartílago *m*

carton ['kɑrtən] *n* : caja *f* (de cartón)

cartoon [kɑr'tu:n] *n* **1** : caricatura *f* **2** COMIC STRIP : historieta *f* **3** *or* **animated ~** : dibujos *mpl* animados

cartridge ['kɑrtrɪdʒ] *n* : cartucho *m*

carve ['kɑrv] *vt* **carved; carving 1** : tallar, esculpir **2** : trinchar (carne)

case *n* **1** : caso *m* **2** BOX : caja *f* **3 in any ~** : en todo caso **4 in ~ of** : en caso de **5 just in ~** : por si acaso

cash ['kæʃ] *n* : efectivo *m*, dinero *m* en efectivo — ~ *vt* : convertir en efectivo, cobrar

cashew ['kæˌʃu:, kə'ʃu:] *n* : anacardo *m*

cashier [kæ'ʃɪr] *n* : cajero *m*, -ra *f*

cashmere ['kæʒˌmɪr, 'kæʃ-] *n* : cachemira *f*

cash register *n* : caja *f* registradora

casino [kə'si:ˌno:] *n, pl* **-nos** : casino *m*

cask ['kæsk] *n* : barril *m*

casket ['kæskət] *n* : ataúd *m*

casserole ['kæsəˌro:l] *n* **1** *or* **~ dish** : cazuela *f* **2** : guiso *m* (comida)

cassette [kə'sɛt, kæ-] *n* : cassette *mf*

cast ['kæst] *vt* **cast; casting 1** THROW : arrojar, lanzar **2** : depositar (un voto) **3** : repartir (papeles dramáticos) **4** MOLD : fundir — ~ *n* **1** : elenco *m*, reparto *m* (de actores) **2** *or* **plaster ~** : molde *m* de yeso, escayola *f*

castanets [ˌkæstə'nɛts] *npl* : castañuelas *fpl*

castaway ['kæstəˌweɪ] *n* : náufrago *m*, -ga *f*

cast iron *n* : hierro *m* fundido

castle ['kæsəl] *n* **1** : castillo *m* **2** : torre *f* (en ajedrez)
castrate ['kæs,treɪt] *vt* **-trated; -trating** : castrar
casual ['kæʒuəl] *adj* **1** CHANCE : casual, fortuito **2** INDIFFERENT : despreocupado **3** INFORMAL : informal — **casually** ['kæʒuəli, 'kæʒəli] *adv* **1** : de manera despreocupada **2** INFORMALLY : informalmente
casualty ['kæʒuəlti, 'kæʒəl-] *n, pl* **-ties 1** : accidente *m* **2** VICTIM : víctima *f;* herido *m,* -da *f* **3 casualties** *npl* : bajas *fpl* (militares)
cat ['kæt] *n* : gato *m,* -ta *f*
catalog *or* **catalogue** ['kæṭə,lɔg] *n* : catálogo *m* — ~ *vt* **-loged** *or* **-logued; -loging** *or* **-loguing** : catalogar
catapult ['kæṭə,pʌlt, -,pʊlt] *n* : catapulta *f*
cataract ['kæṭə,rækt] *n* : catarata *f*
catastrophe [kə'tæstrə,fi:] *n* : catástrofe *f* — **catastrophic** [,kæṭə'strɑfɪk] *adj* : catastrófico
catch ['kætʃ, 'kɛtʃ] *v* **caught** ['kɔt]; **catching** *vt* **1** CAPTURE, TRAP : capturar, atrapar **2** SURPRISE : sorprender **3** GRASP : agarrar, captar **4** SNAG : enganchar **5** : tomar (un tren, etc.) **6** ~ **a cold** : resfriarse — *vi* **1** SNAG : engancharse **2** ~ **fire** : prender fuego — **catching** ['kætʃɪŋ, 'kɛ-] *adj* : contagioso — **catchy** ['kætʃi, 'kɛ-] *adj* **catchier; -est** : pegadizo, pegajoso *Lat*
category ['kæṭə,gori] *n, pl* **-ries** : categoría *f* — **categorical** [,kæṭə'gɔrɪkəl] *adj* : categórico
cater ['keɪṭər] *vi* **1** : proveer comida **2** ~ **to** : atender a — **caterer** ['keɪṭərər] *n* : proveedor *m,* -dora *f* de comida
caterpillar ['kæṭər,pɪlər] *n* : oruga *f*
catfish ['kæt,fɪʃ] *n* : bagre *m*
cathedral [kə'θi:drəl] *n* : catedral *f*
catholic ['kæθəlɪk] *adj* **1** : universal **2 Catholic** : católico — **catholicism** [kə'θɑlə,sɪzəm] *n* : catolicismo *m*
cattle ['kæṭəl] *npl* : ganado *m* (vacuno)
caught → **catch**
cauldron ['kɔldrən] *n* : caldera *f*
cauliflower ['kɑlɪ,flauər, 'kɔ-] *n* : coliflor *f*
cause ['kɔz] *n* **1** : causa *f* **2** REASON : motivo *m* — ~ *vt* **caused; causing** : causar
caustic ['kɔstɪk] *adj* : cáustico
caution ['kɔʃən] *n* **1** WARNING : advertencia *f* **2** CARE : precaución *f,* cautela *f* — ~ *vt* : advertir — **cautious** ['kɔʃəs] *adj* : cauteloso, precavido — **cautiously** ['kɔʃəsli] *adv* : con precaución
cavalier [,kævə'lɪr] *adj* : arrogante, desdeñoso
cavalry ['kævəlri] *n, pl* **-ries** : caballería *f*
cave ['keɪv] *n* : cueva *f* — ~ *vi* **caved; caving** *or* ~ **in** : hundirse
cavern ['kævərn] *n* : caverna *f*
cavity ['kævəṭi] *n, pl* **-ties 1** : cavidad *f* **2** : caries *f* (dental)
cavort [kə'vɔrt] *vi* : brincar
CD [,si:'di:] *n* : CD *m,* disco *m* compacto
cease ['si:s] *v* **ceased; ceasing** *vt* : dejar de — *vi* : cesar — **cease-fire** ['si:s'faɪr] *n* : alto *m* el fuego — **ceaseless** ['si:sləs] *adj* : incesante
cedar ['si:dər] *n* : cedro *m*
ceiling ['si:lɪŋ] *n* : techo *m*
celebrate ['sɛlə,breɪt] *v* **-brated; -brating** *vt* : celebrar — *vi* : divertirse — **celebrated** ['sɛlə,breɪṭəd] *adj* : célebre — **celebration** [,sɛlə'breɪʃən] *n* **1** : celebración *f* **2** FESTIVITY : fiesta *f* — **celebrity** [sə'lɛbrəṭi] *n, pl* **-ties** : celebridad *f*
celery ['sɛləri] *n, pl* **-eries** : apio *m*
cell ['sɛl] *n* **1** : célula *f* **2** : celda *f* (en una cárcel, etc.)
cellar ['sɛlər] *n* **1** BASEMENT : sótano *m* **2** : bodega *f* (de vinos)
cello ['tʃɛ,lo:] *n, pl* **-los** : violoncelo *m*
cellular ['sɛljələr] *adj* : celular
cement [sɪ'mɛnt] *n* : cemento *m* — ~ *vt* : cementar
cemetery ['sɛmə,tɛri] *n, pl* **-teries** : cementerio *m*
censor ['sɛntsər] *vt* : censurar — **censorship** ['sɛntsər,ʃɪp] *n* : censura *f* — **censure** ['sɛntʃər] *n* : censura *f* — ~ *vt* **-sured; -suring** : censurar, criticar
census ['sɛntsəs] *n* : censo *m*
cent ['sɛnt] *n* : centavo *m*
centennial [sɛn'tɛniəl] *n* : centenario *m*
center *or Brit* **centre** ['sɛntər] *n* : centro *m* — ~ *v* **centered** *or Brit* **centred; centering** *or Brit* **centring** *vt* : centrar — *vi* ~ **on** : centrarse en
centigrade ['sɛntə,greɪd, 'sɑn-] *adj* : centígrado
centimeter ['sɛntə,mi:ṭər, 'sɑn-] *n* : centímetro *m*
centipede ['sɛntə,pi:d] *n* : ciempiés *m*
central ['sɛntrəl] *adj* **1** : central **2 a** ~ **location** : un lugar céntrico — **centralize** ['sɛntrə,laɪz] *vt* **-ized; -izing** : centralizar
centre ['sɛntər] → **center**
century ['sɛntʃəri] *n, pl* **-ries** : siglo *m*
ceramics [sə'ræmɪks] *npl* : cerámica *f*

cereal ['sɪriəl] *n* : cereal *m*
ceremony ['sɛrə,mo:ni] *n, pl* **-nies** : ceremonia *f* — **ceremonial** [,sɛrə'mo:niəl] *adj* : ceremonial
certain ['sərtən] *adj* **1** : cierto **2 be ~ of** : estar seguro de **3 for ~** : seguro, con toda seguridad **4 make ~ of** : asegurarse de — **certainly** ['sərtənli] *adv* : desde luego, por supuesto — **certainty** ['sərtənti] *n, pl* **-ties** : certeza *f*, seguridad *f*
certify ['sərt̬ə,faɪ] *vt* **-fied; -fying** : certificar — **certificate** [sər'tɪfɪkət] *n* : certificado *m*, partida *f*, acta *f*
chafe ['tʃeɪf] *v* **chafed; chafing** *vi* : rozarse — *vt* : rozar
chain ['tʃeɪn] *n* **1** : cadena *f* **2 ~ of events** : serie *f* de acontecimientos — **~** *vt* : encadenar
chair ['tʃɛr] *n* **1** : silla *f* **2** : cátedra *f* (en una universidad) — **~** *vt* : presidir — **chairman** ['tʃɛrmən] *n, pl* **-men** [-mən, -,mɛn] : presidente *m* — **chairperson** ['tʃɛr,pərsən] *n* : presidente *m*, -ta *f*
chalk ['tʃɔk] *n* : tiza *f*, gis *m Lat*
challenge ['tʃælɪndʒ] *vt* **-lenged; -lenging 1** DISPUTE : disputar, poner en duda **2** DARE : desafiar — **~** *n* : reto *m*, desafío *m* — **challenging** ['tʃælɪndʒɪŋ] *adj* : estimulante
chamber ['tʃeɪmbər] *n* : cámara *f* — **chambermaid** ['tʃeɪmbər,meɪd] *n* : camarera *f*
champagne [ʃæm'peɪn] *n* : champaña *m*, champán *m*
champion ['tʃæmpiən] *n* : campeón *m*, -peona *f* — **~** *vt* : defender — **championship** ['tʃæmpiən,ʃɪp] *n* : campeonato *m*
chance ['tʃænts] *n* **1** LUCK : azar *m*, suerte *f* **2** OPPORTUNITY : oportunidad *f* **3** LIKELIHOOD : probabilidad *f* **4 by ~** : por casualidad **5 take a ~** : arriesgarse — **~** *vt* **chanced; chancing** RISK : arriesgar — **~** *adj* : fortuito
chandelier [,ʃændə'lɪr] *n* : araña *f* (de luces)
change ['tʃeɪndʒ] *v* **changed; changing** *vt* **1** : cambiar **2** SWITCH : cambiar de — *vi* **1** : cambiar **2** *or* **~ clothes** : cambiarse (de ropa) — **~** *n* : cambio *m* — **changeable** ['tʃeɪndʒəbəl] *adj* : cambiable
channel ['tʃænəl] *n* **1** : canal *m* **2** : cauce *m* (de un río) **3** MEANS : vía *f*, medio *m*
chant ['tʃænt] *v* : cantar — **~** *n* : canto *m*
chaos ['keɪ,ɑs] *n* : caos *m* — **chaotic** [keɪ'ɑt̬ɪk] *adj* : caótico
chap[1] ['tʃæp] *vi* **chapped; chapping** : agrietarse
chap[2] *n* : tipo *m fam*
chapel ['tʃæpəl] *n* : capilla *f*
chaperon *or* **chaperone** ['ʃæpə,ro:n] *n* : acompañante *mf*
chaplain ['tʃæplɪn] *n* : capellán *m*
chapter ['tʃæptər] *n* : capítulo *m*
char ['tʃɑr] *vt* **charred; charring** : carbonizar
character ['kærɪktər] *n* **1** : carácter *m* **2** : personaje *m* (en una novela, etc.) — **characteristic** [,kærɪktə'rɪstɪk] *adj* : característico — **~** *n* : característica *f* — **characterize** ['kærɪktə,raɪz] *vt* **-ized; -izing** : caracterizar
charcoal ['tʃɑr,ko:l] *n* : carbón *m*
charge ['tʃɑrdʒ] *n* **1** : carga *f* (eléctrica) **2** COST : precio *m* **3** BURDEN : carga *f*, peso *m* **4** ACCUSATION : cargo *m*, acusación *f* **5 in ~ of** : encargado de **6 take ~ of** : hacerse cargo de — **~** *v* **charged; charging** *vt* **1** : cargar **2** ENTRUST : encargar **3** COMMAND : ordenar, mandar **4** ACCUSE : acusar — *vi* **1** : cargar **2 ~ too much** : cobrar demasiado
charisma [kə'rɪzmə] *n* : carisma *m* — **charismatic** [,kærəz'mætɪk] *adj* : carismático
charity ['tʃærət̬i] *n, pl* **-ties 1** : organización *f* benéfica **2** GOODWILL : caridad *f*
charlatan ['ʃɑrlətən] *n* : charlatán *m*, -tana *f*
charm ['tʃɑrm] *n* **1** : encanto *m* **2** SPELL : hechizo *m* — **~** *vt* : encantar, cautivar — **charming** ['tʃɑrmɪŋ] *adj* : encantador
chart ['tʃɑrt] *n* **1** MAP : carta *f* **2** DIAGRAM : gráfico *m*, tabla *f* — **~** *vt* : trazar un mapa de
charter ['tʃɑrt̬ər] *n* : carta *f* — **~** *vt* : alquilar, fletar
chase ['tʃeɪs] *n* : persecución *f* — **~** *vt* **chased; chasing 1** PURSUE : perseguir **2** *or* **~ away** : ahuyentar
chasm ['kæzəm] *n* : abismo *m*
chaste ['tʃeɪst] *adj* **chaster; -est** : casto — **chastity** ['tʃæstət̬i] *n* : castidad *f*
chat ['tʃæt] *vi* **chatted; chatting** : charlar — **~** *n* : charla *f* — **chatter** ['tʃæt̬ər] *vi* **1** : parlotear *fam* **2** : castañetear (dícese de los dientes) — **~** *n* : parloteo *m*, cháchara *f* — **chatterbox** ['tʃæt̬ər,bɑks] *n* : parlanchín *m*, -china *f* — **chatty** ['tʃæt̬i] *adj* **chattier; chattiest 1** : parlanchín **2** INFORMAL : familiar
chauffeur ['ʃo:fər, ʃo'fər] *n* : chofer *mf*
chauvinist ['ʃo:vənɪst] *or* **chauvinistic**

[ˌʃoːvəˈnɪstɪk] *adj* : chauvinista, patriotero

cheap [ˈtʃiːp] *adj* **1** INEXPENSIVE : barato **2** SHODDY : de baja calidad — ~ *adv* : barato — **cheapen** [ˈtʃiːpən] *vt* : rebajar — **cheaply** [ˈtʃiːpli] *adv* : barato, a precio bajo

cheat [ˈtʃiːt] *vt* : defraudar, estafar — *vi* **1** : hacer trampa(s) **2** ~ **on s.o.** : engañar a algn — ~ *or* **cheater** [ˈtʃiːt̬ər] *n* : tramposo *m*, -sa *f*

check [ˈtʃɛk] *n* **1** RESTRAINT : freno *m* **2** INSPECTION : inspección *f*, comprobación *f* **3** DRAFT : cheque *m* **4** BILL : cuenta *f* **5** : jaque *m* (en ajedrez) **6** : tela *f* a cuadros — ~ *vt* **1** RESTRAIN : frenar, contener **2** INSPECT : revisar **3** VERIFY : comprobar **4** : dar jaque (en ajedrez) **5** ~ **in** : enregistrarse (en un hotel) **6** ~ **out** : irse (de un hotel) **7** ~ **out** VERIFY : verificar, comprobar

checkers [ˈtʃɛkərz] *n* : damas *fpl*

checkmate [ˈtʃɛkˌmeɪt] *n* : jaque *m* mate

checkpoint [ˈtʃɛkˌpɔɪnt] *n* : puesto *m* de control

checkup [ˈtʃɛkˌʌp] *n* : chequeo *m*, examen *m* médico

cheek [ˈtʃiːk] *n* : mejilla *f*

cheer [ˈtʃɪr] *n* **1** CHEERFULNESS : alegría *f* **2** APPLAUSE : aclamación *f* **3** ~**s!** : ¡salud! — ~ *vt* **1** GLADDEN : alegrar **2** APPLAUD, SHOUT : aclamar, aplaudir — **cheerful** [ˈtʃɪrfəl] *adj* : alegre

cheese [ˈtʃiːz] *n* : queso *m*

cheetah [ˈtʃiːt̬ə] *n* : guepardo *m*

chef [ˈʃɛf] *n* : chef *m*

chemical [ˈkɛmɪkəl] *adj* : químico — ~ *n* : sustancia *f* química — **chemist** [ˈkɛmɪst] *n* : químico *m*, -ca *f* — **chemistry** [ˈkɛmɪstri] *n*, *pl* **-tries** : química *f*

cheque [ˈtʃɛk] *Brit* → **check**

cherish [ˈtʃɛrɪʃ] *vt* **1** : querer, apreciar **2** HARBOR : abrigar (un recuerdo, una esperanza, etc.)

cherry [ˈtʃɛri] *n*, *pl* **-ries** : cereza *f*

chess [ˈtʃɛs] *n* : ajedrez *m*

chest [ˈtʃɛst] *n* **1** BOX : cofre *m* **2** : pecho *m* (del cuerpo) **3** *or* ~ **of drawers** : cómoda *f*

chestnut [ˈtʃɛstˌnʌt] *n* : castaña *f*

chew [ˈtʃuː] *vt* : masticar, mascar — **chewing gum** *n* : chicle *m*

chic [ˈʃiːk] *adj* : elegante

chick [ˈtʃɪk] *n* : polluelo *m*, -la *f* — **chicken** [ˈtʃɪkən] *n* : pollo *m* — **chicken pox** *n* : varicela *f*

chicory [ˈtʃɪkəri] *n*, *pl* **-ries 1** : endivia *f* (para ensaladas) **2** : achicoria *f* (aditivo de café)

chief [ˈtʃiːf] *adj* : principal — ~ *n* : jefe *m*, -fa *f* — **chiefly** [ˈtʃiːfli] *adv* : principalmente

child [ˈtʃaɪld] *n*, *pl* **children** [ˈtʃɪldrən] **1** : niño *m*, -ña *f* **2** OFFSPRING : hijo *m*, -ja *f* — **childbirth** [ˈtʃaɪldˌbərθ] *n* : parto *m* — **childhood** [ˈtʃaɪldˌhʊd] *n* : infancia *f*, niñez *f* — **childish** [ˈtʃaɪldɪʃ] *adj* : infantil — **childlike** [ˈtʃaɪldˌlaɪk] *adj* : infantil, inocente — **childproof** [ˈtʃaɪldˌpruːf] *adj* : a prueba de niños

Chilean [ˈtʃɪliən, tʃɪˈleɪən] *adj* : chileno

chili *or* **chile** *or* **chilli** [ˈtʃɪli] *n*, *pl* **chilies** *or* **chiles** *or* **chillies 1** *or* ~ **pepper** : chile *m* **2** : chile *m* con carne

chill [ˈtʃɪl] *n* **1** CHILLINESS : frío *m* **2** **catch a** ~ : resfriarse **3** **there's a** ~ **in the air** : hace fresco — ~ *adj* : frío — ~ *v* : enfriar — **chilly** [ˈtʃɪli] *adj* **chillier; -est** : fresco, frío

chime [ˈtʃaɪm] *vi* **chimed; chiming** : repicar, sonar — ~ *n* : carillón *m*

chimney [ˈtʃɪmni] *n*, *pl* **-neys** : chimenea *f*

chimpanzee [ˌtʃɪmˌpænˈziː, ˌʃɪm-; tʃɪmˈpænzi, ʃɪm-] *n* : chimpancé *m*

chin [ˈtʃɪn] *n* : barbilla *f*

china [ˈtʃaɪnə] *n* : porcelana *f*, loza *f*

Chinese [ˈtʃaɪˈniːz, -ˈniːs] *adj* : chino — ~ *n* : chino *m* (idioma)

chink [ˈtʃɪŋk] *n* : grieta *f*

chip [ˈtʃɪp] *n* **1** : astilla *f* (de madera o vidrio), lasca *f* (de piedra) **2** : ficha *f* (de póker, etc.) **3** NICK : desportilladura *f* **4** *or* **computer** ~ : chip *m* **5** → **potato chips** — ~ *v* **chipped; chipping** *vt* : desportillar — *vi* **1** : desportillarse **2** ~ **in** : contribuir

chipmunk [ˈtʃɪpˌmʌŋk] *n* : ardilla *f* listada

chiropodist [kəˈrɑpədɪst, ʃə-] *n* : podólogo *m*, -ga *f*

chiropractor [ˈkaɪrəˌpræktər] *n* : quiropráctico *m*, -ca *f*

chirp [ˈtʃərp] *vi* : piar, gorjear

chisel [ˈtʃɪzəl] *n* : cincel *m* (para piedras, etc.), formón *m*, escoplo *m* (para madera) — ~ *vt* **-eled** *or* **-elled; -eling** *or* **-elling** : cincelar, tallar

chit [ˈtʃɪt] *n* : nota *f*

chitchat [ˈtʃɪtˌtʃæt] *n* : cháchara *f fam*

chivalrous [ˈʃɪvəlrəs] *adj* : caballeroso — **chivalry** [ˈʃɪvəlri] *n*, *pl* **-ries** : caballerosidad *f*

chive [ˈtʃaɪv] *n* : cebollino *m*

chlorine [ˈklorˌiːn] *n* : cloro *m*

chock–full [ˈtʃɑkˈfʊl, ˈtʃʌk-] *adj* : repleto, atestado

chocolate [ˈtʃɑkələt, ˈtʃɔk-] *n* : chocolate *m*

choice [ˈtʃɔɪs] *n* **1** : elección *f*, selección

f **2** PREFERENCE : preferencia *f* — **~** *adj* **choicer; -est** : selecto
choir ['kwaɪr] *n* : coro *m*
choke ['tʃo:k] *v* **choked; choking** *vt* **1** : asfixiar, estrangular **2** BLOCK : atascar — *vi* : asfixiarse, atragantarse (con comida) — **~** *n* : estárter *m* (de un motor)
choose ['tʃu:z] *v* **chose** ['tʃo:z]; **chosen** ['tʃo:zən]; **choosing** *vt* **1** SELECT : escoger, elegir **2** DECIDE : decidir — *vi* : escoger — **choosy** *or* **choosey** ['tʃu:zi] *adj* **choosier; -est** : exigente
chop ['tʃɑp] *vt* **chopped; chopping 1** : cortar, picar (carne, etc.) **2 ~ down** : talar — **~** *n* : chuleta *f* (de cerdo, etc.) — **choppy** ['tʃɑpi] *adj* **-pier; -est** : picado, agitado
chopsticks ['tʃɑp,stɪks] *npl* : palillos *mpl*
chord ['kɔrd] *n* : acorde *m* (en música)
chore ['tʃor] *n* **1** : tarea *f* **2 household ~s** : faenas *fpl* domésticas
choreography [,kori'ɑgrəfi] *n, pl* **-phies** : coreografía *f*
chortle ['tʃɔrṭəl] *vi* **-tled; -tling** : reírse (con satisfacción o júbilo)
chorus ['korəs] **1** : coro *m* (grupo de personas) **2** REFRAIN : estribillo *m*
chose, chosen → **choose**
christen ['krɪsən] *vt* : bautizar — **christening** ['krɪsənɪŋ] *n* : bautizo *m*
Christian ['krɪstʃən] *n* : cristiano *m*, -na *f* — **~** *adj* : cristiano — **Christianity** [,krɪstʃi'ænəṭi, ,krɪs'tʃæ-] *n* : cristianismo *m*
Christmas ['krɪsməs] *n* : Navidad *f*
chrome ['kro:m] *n* : cromo *m*
chronic ['krɑnɪk] *adj* : crónico
chronicle ['krɑnɪkəl] *n* : crónica *f*
chronology [krə'nɑləʤi] *n, pl* **-gies** : cronología *f* — **chronological** [,krɑnəl'ɑʤɪkəl] *adj* : cronológico
chrysanthemum [krɪ'sæntθəməm] *n* : crisantemo *m*
chubby ['tʃʌbi] *adj* **-bier; -est** : regordete *fam*, rechoncho *fam*
chuck ['tʃʌk] *vt* : tirar, arrojar
chuckle ['tʃʌkəl] *vi* **-led; -ling** : reírse (entre dientes) — **~** *n* : risa *f* ahogada
chum ['tʃʌm] *n* : amigo *m*, -ga *f*; compinche *mf fam* — **chummy** ['tʃʌmi] *adj* **-mier; -est** : muy amigable
chunk ['tʃʌnk] *n* : trozo *m*, pedazo *m*
church ['tʃərtʃ] *n* : iglesia *f*
churn ['tʃərn] *n* : mantequera *f* — **~** *vt* **1** : agitar **2 ~ out** : producir en grandes cantidades
chute ['ʃu:t] *n* **1** : vertedor *m* **2** SLIDE : tobogán *m*
cider ['saɪdər] *n* : sidra *f*
cigar [sɪ'gɑr] *n* : puro *m* — **cigarette** [,sɪgə'rɛt, 'sɪgə,rɛt] *n* : cigarrillo *m*, cigarro *m*
cinch ['sɪntʃ] *n* **it's a ~** : es pan comido
cinema ['sɪnəmə] *n* : cine *m*
cinnamon ['sɪnəmən] *n* : canela *f*
cipher ['saɪfər] *n* **1** ZERO : cero *m* **2** CODE : cifra *f*
circa ['sərkə] *prep* : hacia
circle ['sərkəl] *n* : círculo *m* — **~** *v* **-cled; -cling** *vt* **1** : dar vueltas alrededor de **2** : trazar un círculo alrededor de (un número, etc.) — *vi* : dar vueltas
circuit ['sərkət] *n* : circuito *m* — **circuitous** [,sər'kju:əṭəs] *adj* : tortuoso
circular ['sərkjələr] *adj* : circular — **~** *n* LEAFLET : circular *f*
circulate ['sərkjə,leɪt] *v* **-lated; -lating** *vt* : hacer circular — *vi* : circular — **circulation** [,sərkjə'leɪʃən] *n* **1** : circulación *f* **2** : tirada *f* (de una publicación)
circumcise ['sərkəm,saɪz] *vt* **-cised; -cising** : circuncidar — **circumcision** [,sərkəm'sɪʒən, 'sərkəm,-] *n* : circuncisión *f*
circumference [sər'kʌmpfrənts] *n* : circunferencia *f*
circumspect ['sərkəm,spekt] *adj* : circunspecto, prudente
circumstance ['sərkəm,stænts] *n* **1** : circunstancia *f* **2 under no ~s** : bajo ningún concepto
circus ['sərkəs] *n* : circo *m*
cistern ['sɪstərn] *n* : cisterna *f*
cite ['saɪt] *vt* **cited; citing** : citar — **citation** [saɪ'teɪʃən] *n* : citación *f*
citizen ['sɪṭəzən] *n* : ciudadano *m*, -na *f* — **citizenship** ['sɪṭəzən,ʃɪp] *n* : ciudadanía *f*
citrus ['sɪtrəs] *n, pl* **-rus** *or* **-ruses** *or* **~ fruit** : cítrico *m*
city ['sɪṭi] *n, pl* **cities** : ciudad *f*
civic ['sɪvɪk] *adj* : cívico — **civics** ['sɪvɪks] *ns & pl* : civismo *m*
civil ['sɪvəl] *adj* : civil — **civilian** [sə'vɪljən] *n* : civil *mf* — **civility** [sə'vɪləṭi] *n, pl* **-ties** : cortesía *f* — **civilization** [,sɪvələ'zeɪʃən] *n* : civilización *f* — **civilize** ['sɪvə,laɪz] *vt* **-lized; -lizing** : civilizar
clad ['klæd] *adj* **~ in** : vestido de
claim ['kleɪm] *vt* **1** DEMAND : reclamar **2** MAINTAIN : afirmar, sostener **3 ~ responsibility** : atribuirse la responsabilidad — **~** *n* **1** DEMAND : demanda *f*, reclamación *f* **2** ASSERTION : afirmación *f*
clam ['klæm] *n* : almeja *f*

clamber ['klæmbər] *vi* : trepar (con torpeza)
clammy ['klæmi] *adj* **-mier; -est** : húmedo y algo frío
clamor ['klæmər] *n* : clamor *m* — **~** *vi* : clamar
clamp ['klæmp] *n* : abrazadera *f* — **~** *vt* : sujetar con abrazaderas — *vi* **~ down on** : reprimir
clan ['klæn] *n* : clan *m*
clandestine [klæn'destɪn] *adj* : clandestino
clang ['klæŋ] *n* : ruido *m* metálico
clap ['klæp] *v* **clapped; clapping** *vt* **1** : aplaudir **2 ~ one's hands** : dar palmadas — *vi* : aplaudir — **~** *n* : palmada *f*
clarify ['klærə,faɪ] *vt* **-fied; -fying** : aclarar — **clarification** [,klærəfə'keɪʃən] *n* : clarificación *f*
clarinet [,klærə'nɛt] *n* : clarinete *m*
clarity ['klærət̬i] *n* : claridad *f*
clash ['klæʃ] *vi* **1** : chocar, enfrentarse **2** CONFLICT : estar en conflicto — **~** *n* **1** CRASH : choque *m* **2** CONFLICT : conflicto *m*
clasp ['klæsp] *n* : broche *m*, cierre *m* — **~** *vt* **1** : abrazar (a una persona), agarrar (una cosa) **2** FASTEN : abrochar
class ['klæs] *n* : clase *f*
classic ['klæsɪk] *or* **classical** ['klæsɪkəl] *adj* : clásico — **classic** *n* : clásico *m*
classify ['klæsə,faɪ] *vt* **-fied; -fying** : clasificar — **classification** [,klæsəfə'keɪʃən] *n* : clasificación *f* — **classified** ['klæsə,faɪd] *adj* RESTRICTED : secreto
classmate ['klæs,meɪt] *n* : compañero *m*, **-ra** *f* de clase
classroom ['klæs,ru:m] *n* : aula *f*, salón *m* de clase
clatter ['klæt̬ər] *vi* : hacer ruido — **~** *n* : estrépito *m*
clause ['klɔz] *n* : cláusula *f*
claustrophobia [,klɔstrə'fo:biə] *n* : claustrofobia *f*
claw ['klɔ] *n* : garra *f*, uña *f* (de un gato), pinza *f* (de un crustáceo) — **~** *v* : arañar
clay ['kleɪ] *n* : arcilla *f*
clean ['kli:n] *adj* **1** : limpio **2** UNADULTERATED : puro **3** SPOTLESS : impecable — **~** *vt* : limpiar — **~** *adv* : limpio — **cleaner** ['kli:nər] *n* **1** : limpiador *m*, **-dora** *f* **2** DRY CLEANER : tintorería *f* — **cleanliness** ['klɛnlinəs] *n* : limpieza *f* — **cleanse** ['klɛnz] *vt* **cleansed; cleansing** : limpiar, purificar
clear ['klɪr] *adj* **1** : claro **2** TRANSPARENT : transparente **3** UNOBSTRUCTED : despejado, libre — **~** *vt* **1** : despejar (una superficie), desatascar (un tubo, etc.) **2** EXONERATE : absolver **3** : saltar por encima de (un obstáculo) **4 ~ the table** : levantar la mesa **5 ~ up** RESOLVE : aclarar, resolver — *vi* **1 ~ up** BRIGHTEN : despejarse (dícese del tiempo, etc.) **2 ~ up** VANISH : desaparecer (dícese de una infección, etc.) — **~** *adv* **1 make oneself ~** : explicarse **2 stand ~ !** : ¡aléjate! — **clearance** ['klɪrənts] *n* **1** SPACE : espacio *m* (libre) **2** AUTHORIZATION : autorización *f* **3 ~ sale** : liquidación *f* — **clearing** ['klɪrɪŋ] *n* : claro *m* — **clearly** ['klɪrli] *adv* **1** DISTINCTLY : claramente **2** OBVIOUSLY : obviamente
cleaver ['kli:vər] *n* : cuchillo *m* de carnicero
clef ['klɛf] *n* : clave *f*
cleft ['klɛft] *n* : hendidura *f*, grieta *f*
clement ['klɛmənt] *adj* : clemente — **clemency** ['klɛməntsi] *n* : clemencia *f*
clench ['klɛntʃ] *vt* : apretar
clergy ['klərdʒi] *n*, *pl* **-gies** : clero *m* — **clergyman** ['klərdʒimən] *n*, *pl* **-men** [-mən, -,mɛn] : clérigo *m* — **clerical** ['klɛrɪkəl] *adj* **1** : clerical **2 ~ work** : trabajo *m* de oficina
clerk ['klərk, *Brit* 'klɑrk] *n* **1** : oficinista *mf;* empleado *m*, **-da** *f* de oficina **2** SALESPERSON : dependiente *m*, **-ta** *f*
clever ['klɛvər] *adj* **1** SKILLFUL : ingenioso, hábil **2** SMART : listo, inteligente — **cleverly** ['klɛvərli] *adv* : ingeniosamente — **cleverness** ['klɛvərnəs] *n* **1** SKILL : ingenio *m* **2** INTELLIGENCE : inteligencia *f*
cliché [kli'ʃeɪ] *n* : cliché *m*
click ['klɪk] *vt* : chasquear — *vi* **1** : chasquear **2** GET ALONG : llevarse bien — **~** *n* : chasquido *m*
client ['klaɪənt] *n* : cliente *m*, **-ta** *f* — **clientele** [,klaɪən'tɛl, ,kli:-] *n* : clientela *f*
cliff ['klɪf] *n* : acantilado *m*
climate ['klaɪmət] *n* : clima *m*
climax ['klaɪ,mæks] *n* : clímax *m*, punto *m* culminante
climb ['klaɪm] *vt* : escalar, subir a, trepar a — *vi* **1** RISE : subir **2** *or* **~ up** : subirse, treparse — **~** *n* : subida *f*
clinch ['klɪntʃ] *vt* : cerrar (un acuerdo, etc.)
cling ['klɪŋ] *vi* **clung** ['klʌŋ]; **clinging** : adherirse, pegarse
clinic ['klɪnɪk] *n* : clínica *f* — **clinical** ['klɪnɪkəl] *adj* : clínico
clink ['klɪŋk] *vi* : tintinear
clip ['klɪp] *vt* **clipped; clipping 1** CUT

: cortar, recortar **2** FASTEN : sujetar (con un clip) — **~** *n* **1** FASTENER : clip *m* **2 at a good ~** : a buen trote **3** → **paper clip** — **clippers** ['klɪpərz] *npl* **1** : maquinilla *f* para cortar el pelo **2** *or* **nail ~** : cortauñas *m*

cloak ['klo:k] *n* : capa *f*

clock ['klɑk] **1** : reloj *m* (de pared) **2 around the ~** : las veinticuatro horas — **clockwise** ['klɑk,waɪz] *adv & adj* : en el sentido de las agujas del reloj — **clockwork** ['klɑk,wərk] *n* **1** : mecanismo *m* de relojería **2 like ~** : con precisión

clog ['klɑg] *n* : zueco *m* — **~** *v* **clogged; clogging** *vt* : atascar, obstruir — *vi or* **~ up** : atascarse

cloister ['klɔɪstər] *n* : claustro *m*

close[1] ['klo:z] *v* **closed; closing** *vt* : cerrar — *vi* **1** : cerrarse **2** TERMINATE : terminar **3 ~ in** : acercarse — **~** *n* : final *m*

close[2] ['klo:s] *adj* **closer; closest 1** NEAR : cercano, próximo **2** INTIMATE : íntimo **3** STRICT : estricto **4** STUFFY : sofocante **5 a ~ game** : un juego reñido — **~** *adv* : cerca, de cerca — **closely** ['klo:sli] *adv* : cerca, de cerca — **closeness** ['klo:snəs] *n* **1** NEARNESS : cercanía *f* **2** INTIMACY : intimidad *f*

closet ['klɑzət] *n* : armario *m*, clóset *m Lat*

closure ['klo:ʒər] *n* : cierre *m*

clot ['klɑt] *n* : coágulo *m* — **~** *v* **clotted; clotting** *vt* : coagular, cuajar — *vi* : coagularse

cloth ['klɔθ] *n, pl* **cloths** ['klɔðz, 'klɔθs] **1** FABRIC : tela *f* **2** RAG : trapo *m*

clothe ['klo:ð] *vt* **clothed** *or* **clad** ['klæd]; **clothing** : vestir — **clothes** ['klo:z, 'klo:ðz] *npl* **1** : ropa *f* **2 put on one's ~** : vestirse — **clothespin** ['klo:z,pɪn] *n* : pinza *f* (para la ropa) — **clothing** ['klo:ðɪŋ] *n* : ropa *f*

cloud ['klaʊd] *n* : nube *f* — **~** *vt* : nublar — *vi or* **~ over** : nublarse — **cloudy** ['klaʊdi] *adj* **cloudier; -est** : nublado

clout ['klaʊt] *n* **1** BLOW : golpe *m*, tortazo *m fam* **2** INFLUENCE : influencia *f*

clove ['klo:v] *n* **1** : clavo *m* **2** : diente *m* (de ajo)

clover ['klo:vər] *n* : trébol *m*

clown ['klaʊn] *n* : payaso *m*, -sa *f* — **~** *or* **~ around** *vi* : payasear

cloying ['klɔɪɪŋ] *adj* : empalagoso

club ['klʌb] *n* **1** : garrote *m*, porra *f* **2** ASSOCIATION : club *m* **3 ~s** *mpl* : tréboles *mpl* (en los naipes) — **~** *vt* **clubbed; clubbing** : aporrear

cluck ['klʌk] *vi* : cloquear

clue ['klu:] *n* **1** : pista *f*, indicio *m* **2 I haven't got a ~** : no tengo la menor idea

clump ['klʌmp] *n* : grupo *m* (de arbustos)

clumsy ['klʌmzi] *adj* **-sier; -est** : torpe — **clumsiness** ['klʌmzinəs] *n* : torpeza *f*

cluster ['klʌstər] *n* : grupo *m*, racimo *m* (de uvas, etc.) — **~** *vi* : agruparse

clutch ['klʌtʃ] *vt* : agarrar, asir — *vi* **~ at** : tratar de agarrarse de — **~** *n* : embrague *m*, clutch *m Lat* (de un automóvil)

clutter ['klʌţər] *vt* : llenar desordenadamente — **~** *n* : desorden *m*, revoltijo *m*

coach ['ko:tʃ] *n* **1** CARRIAGE : carruaje *m*, carroza *f* **2** : vagón *m* de pasajeros (de un tren) **3** BUS : autobús *m* **4** : pasaje *m* aéreo de segunda clase **5** TRAINER : entrenador *m*, -dora *f* — *vt* : entrenar (un atleta), dar clases particulares a (un alumno)

coagulate [ko'ægjə,leɪt] *v* **-lated; -lating** *vt* : coagular — *vi* : coagularse

coal ['ko:l] *n* : carbón *m*

coalition [,ko:ə'lɪʃən] *n* : coalición *f*

coarse ['kors] *adj* **coarser; -est 1** : tosco, basto **2** CRUDE, VULGAR : grosero, ordinario — **coarseness** ['korsnəs] *n* : aspereza *f*, tosquedad *f*

coast ['ko:st] *n* : costa *f* — **~** *vi* : ir en punto muerto (dícese de un automóvil), deslizarse (dícese de una bicicleta) — **coastal** ['ko:stəl] *adj* : costero

coaster ['ko:stər] *n* : posavasos *m*

coast guard *n* : guardacostas *mpl*

coastline ['ko:st,laɪn] *n* : litoral *m*

coat ['ko:t] *n* **1** : abrigo *m* **2** : pelaje *m* (de un animal) **3** : mano *f* (de pintura) — **~** *vt* : cubrir, revestir — **coating** ['ko:ţɪŋ] *n* : capa *f* — **coat of arms** *n* : escudo *m* de armas

coax ['ko:ks] *vt* : engatusar

cob ['kɑb] → **corncob**

cobblestone ['kɑbəl,sto:n] *n* : adoquín *m*

cobweb ['kɑb,wɛb] *n* : telaraña *f*

cocaine [ko:'keɪn, 'ko:,keɪn] *n* : cocaína *f*

cock ['kɑk] *n* **1** ROOSTER : gallo *m* **2** FAUCET : grifo *m* **3** : martillo *m* (de un arma de fuego) — **~** *vt* **1** : amartillar (un arma de fuego) **2 ~ one's head** : ladear la cabeza — **cockeyed** ['kɑk,aɪd] *adj* **1** ASKEW : ladeado **2** ABSURD : absurdo

cockpit ['kɑk,pɪt] *n* : cabina *f*

cockroach ['kɑk,ro:tʃ] *n* : cucaracha *f*

cocktail ['kɑk,teɪl] *n* : coctel *m*, cóctel *m*
cocky ['kɑki] *adj* **cockier; -est** : engreído, arrogante
cocoa ['ko:,ko:] *n* **1** : cacao *m* **2** : chocolate *m* (bebida)
coconut ['ko:kə,nʌt] *n* : coco *m*
cocoon [kə'ku:n] *n* : capullo *m*
cod ['kɑd] *ns & pl* : bacalao *m*
coddle ['kɑdəl] *vt* **-dled; -dling** : mimar
code ['ko:d] *n* : código *m*
coeducational [,ko:,ɛdʒə'keɪʃənəl] *adj* : mixto
coerce [ko'ərs] *vt* **-erced; -ercing** : coaccionar, forzar — **coercion** [ko-'ərʒən, -ʃən] *n* : coacción *f*
coffee ['kɔfi] *n* : café *m* — **coffeepot** ['kɔfi,pɑt] *n* : cafetera *f*
coffer ['kɔfər] *n* : cofre *m*
coffin ['kɔfən] *n* : ataúd *m*, féretro *m*
cog ['kɑg] *n* : diente *m* (de una rueda)
cogent ['ko:dʒənt] *adj* : convincente, persuasivo
cognac ['ko:n,jæk] *n* : coñac *m*
cogwheel ['kɑg,hwi:l] *n* : rueda *f* dentada
coherent [ko'hɪrənt] *adj* : coherente
coil ['kɔɪl] *vt* : enrollar — *vi* : enrollarse — ~ *n* **1** ROLL : rollo *m* **2** : tirabuzón *m* (de pelo), espiral *f* (de humo)
coin ['kɔɪn] *n* : moneda *f* — ~ *vt* : acuñar
coincide [,ko:ɪn'saɪd, 'ko:ɪn,saɪd] *vi* **-cided; -ciding** : coincidir — **coincidence** [ko'ɪntsədənts] *n* : coincidencia *f*, casualidad *f* — **coincidental** [ko-,ɪntsə'dentəl] *adj* : casual, fortuito
coke ['ko:k] *n* : coque *m* (combustible)
colander ['kɑləndər, 'kʌ-] *n* : colador *m*
cold ['ko:ld] *adj* **1** : frío **2 be ~** : tener frío **3 it's ~ today** : hace frío hoy — ~ *n* **1** : frío *m* **2** : resfriado *m* (en medicina) **3 catch a ~** : resfriarse
coleslaw ['ko:l,slɔ] *n* : ensalada *f* de col
colic ['kɑlɪk] *n* : cólico *m*
collaborate [kə'læbə,reɪt] *vi* **-rated; -rating** : colaborar — **collaboration** [kə,læbə'reɪʃən] *n* : colaboración *f* — **collaborator** [kə'læbə,reɪʈər] *n* : colaborador *m*, -dora *f*
collapse [kə'læps] *vi* **-lapsed; -lapsing** **1** : derrumbarse, hundirse **2** : sufrir un colapso (físico o mental) — ~ *n* **1** FALL : derrumbamiento *m* **2** BREAKDOWN : colapso *m* — **collapsible** [kə-'læpsəbəl] *adj* : plegable
collar ['kɑlər] *n* : cuello *m* (de camisa, etc.), collar *m* (para animales) — **collarbone** ['kɑlər,bo:n] *n* : clavícula *f*
colleague ['kɑ,li:g] *n* : colega *mf*
collect [kə'lekt] *vt* **1** GATHER : reunir **2** : coleccionar, juntar (timbres, etc.) **3** : recaudar (fondos, etc.) — *vi* **1** ACCUMULATE : acumularse, juntarse **2** CONGREGATE : congregarse, reunirse — ~ *adv* **call ~** : llamar a cobro revertido, llamar por cobrar *Lat* — **collection** [kə'lɛkʃən] *n* **1** : colección *f* **2** : colecta *f* (de contribuciones) — **collective** [kə'lɛktɪv] *adj* : colectivo — **collector** [kə'lɛktər] *n* **1** : coleccionista *mf* **2** : cobrador *m*, -dora *f* (de deudas)
college ['kɑlɪdʒ] *n* **1** : instituto *m* (a nivel universitario) **2** : colegio *m* (electoral, etc.)
collide [kə'laɪd] *vi* **-lided; -liding** : chocar, colisionar — **collision** [kə-'lɪʒən] *n* : choque *m*, colisión *f*
colloquial [kə'lo:kwiəl] *adj* : coloquial, familiar
cologne [kə'lo:n] *n* : colonia *f*
Colombian [kə'lʌmbiən] *adj* : colombiano
colon[1] ['ko:lən] *n, pl* **colons** *or* **cola** [-lə] : colon *m* (en anatomía)
colon[2] *n, pl* **colons** : dos puntos *mpl* (signo de puntuación)
colonel ['kərnəl] *n* : coronel *m*
colony ['kɑləni] *n, pl* **-nies** : colonia *f* — **colonial** [kə'lo:niəl] *adj* : colonial — **colonize** ['kɑlə,naɪz] *vt* **-nized; -nizing** : colonizar
color *or Brit* **colour** ['kʌlər] *n* : color *m* — ~ *vt* : colorear, pintar — *vi* BLUSH : sonrojarse — **color-blind** *or Brit* **colour-blind** ['kʌlər,blaɪnd] *adj* : daltónico — **colored** *or Brit* **coloured** ['kʌlərd] *adj* : de color — **colorful** *or Brit* **colourful** ['kʌlərfəl] *adj* **1** : de vivos colores **2** PICTURESQUE : pintoresco — **colorless** *or Brit* **colourless** ['kʌlərləs] *adj* : incoloro
colossal [kə'lɑsəl] *adj* : colosal
colt ['ko:lt] *n* : potro *m*
column ['kɑləm] *n* : columna *f* — **columnist** ['kɑləmnɪst, -ləmɪst] *n* : columnista *mf*
coma ['ko:mə] *n* : coma *m*
comb ['ko:m] *n* **1** : peine *m* **2** : cresta *f* (de un gallo) — ~ *vt* : peinar
combat ['kɑm,bæt] *n* : combate *m* — ~ [kəm'bæt, 'kɑm,bæt] *vt* **-bated** *or* **-batted; -bating** *or* **-batting** : combatir — **combatant** [kəm'bætənt] *n* : combatiente *mf*
combine [kəm'baɪn] *v* **-bined; -bining** *vt* : combinar — *vi* : combinarse — ~ ['kɑm,baɪn] *n* HARVESTER : cosechadora *f* — **combination** [,kɑmbə'neɪʃən] *n* : combinación *f*
combustion [kəm'bʌstʃən] *n* : combustión *f*

come [ˈkʌm] *vi* **came** [ˈkeɪm]; **come; coming 1** : venir **2** ARRIVE : llegar **3 ~ about** : suceder **4 ~ back** : regresar, volver **5 ~ from** : venir de, provenir de **6 ~ in** : entrar **7 ~ out** : salir **8 ~ to** REVIVE : volver en sí **9 ~ on!** : ¡ándale! **10 ~ up** OCCUR : surgir **11 how ~?** : ¿por qué? — **comeback** [ˈkʌmˌbæk] *n* **1** RETURN : retorno *m* **2** RETORT : réplica *f*

comedy [ˈkɑmədi] *n, pl* **-dies** : comedia *f* — **comedian** [kəˈmiːdiən] *n* : cómico *m,* **-ca** *f*

comet [ˈkɑmət] *n* : cometa *m*

comfort [ˈkʌmpfərt] *vt* : consolar — **~** *n* **1** : comodidad *f* **2** SOLACE : consuelo *m* — **comfortable** [ˈkʌmpfərt̬əbəl, ˈkʌmpftə-] *adj* : cómodo

comic [ˈkɑmɪk] *or* **comical** [ˈkɑmɪkəl] *adj* : cómico — **~** *n* **1** COMEDIAN : cómico *m,* **-ca** *f* **2** *or* **~ book** : revista *f* de historietas, cómic *m* — **comic strip** *n* : tira *f* cómica, historieta *f*

coming [ˈkʌmɪŋ] *adj* : próximo, que viene

comma [ˈkɑmə] *n* : coma *f*

command [kəˈmænd] *vt* **1** ORDER : ordenar, mandar **2** : estar al mando de (un barco, etc.) **3 ~ respect** : inspirar (el) respeto — *vi* : dar órdenes — **~** *n* **1** ORDER : orden *f* **2** LEADERSHIP : mando *m* **3** MASTERY : maestría *f,* dominio *m* — **commander** [kəˈmændər] *n* : comandante *mf* — **commandment** [kəˈmændmənt] *n* : mandamiento *m*

commemorate [kəˈmɛməˌreɪt] *vt* **-rated; -rating** : conmemorar — **commemoration** [kəˌmɛməˈreɪʃən] *n* : conmemoración *f*

commence [kəˈmɛnts] *v* **-menced; -mencing** : comenzar, empezar — **commencement** [kəˈmɛntsmənt] *n* **1** BEGINNING : comienzo *m* **2** GRADUATION : ceremonia *f* de graduación

commend [kəˈmɛnd] *vt* **1** ENTRUST : encomendar **2** PRAISE : alabar — **commendable** [kəˈmɛndəbəl] *adj* : loable

comment [ˈkɑˌmɛnt] *n* : comentario *m,* observación *f* — **~** *vi* : hacer comentarios — **commentary** [ˈkɑmənˌtɛri] *n, pl* **-taries** : comentario *m* — **commentator** [ˈkɑmənˌteɪt̬ər] *n* : comentarista *mf*

commerce [ˈkɑmərs] *n* : comercio *m* — **commercial** [kəˈmərʃəl] *adj* : comercial — **~** *n* : anuncio *m,* aviso *m Lat* — **commercialize** [kəˈmərʃəˌlaɪz] *vt* **-ized; -izing** : comercializar

commiserate [kəˈmɪzəˌreɪt] *vi* **-ated; -ating** : compadecerse

commission [kəˈmɪʃən] *n* : comisión *f* — **~** *vt* : encargar (una obra de arte) — **commissioner** [kəˈmɪʃənər] *n* : comisario *m,* **-ria** *f*

commit [kəˈmɪt] *vt* **-mitted; -mitting 1** ENTRUST : confiar **2** : cometer (un crimen) **3** : internar (a algn en un hospital) **4 ~ oneself** : comprometerse **5 ~ to memory** : aprender de memoria — **commitment** [kəˈmɪtmənt] *n* : compromiso *m*

committee [kəˈmɪt̬i] *n* : comité *m,* comisión *f*

commodity [kəˈmɑdət̬i] *n, pl* **-ties** : artículo *m* de comercio, producto *m*

common [ˈkɑmən] *adj* **1** : común **2** ORDINARY : ordinario, común y corriente — **~** *n* **in ~** : en común — **commonly** [ˈkɑmənli] *adv* : comúnmente — **commonplace** [ˈkɑmənˌpleɪs] *adj* : común, banal — **common sense** *n* : sentido *m* común

commotion [kəˈmoːʃən] *n* : alboroto *m,* jaleo *m*

commune¹ [ˈkɑˌmjuːn, kəˈmjuːn] *n* : comuna *f* — **communal** [kəˈmjuːnəl] *adj* : comunal

commune² [kəˈmjuːn] *vi* **-muned; -muning ~ with** : comunicarse con

communicate [kəˈmjuːnəˌkeɪt] *v* **-cated; -cating** *vt* : comunicar — *vi* : comunicarse — **communicable** [kəˈmjuːnɪkəbəl] *adj* : transmisible — **communication** [kəˌmjuːnəˈkeɪʃən] *n* : comunicación *f* — **communicative** [kəˈmjuːnɪˌkeɪt̬ɪv, -kət̬ɪv] *adj* : comunicativo

communion [kəˈmjuːnjən] *n* : comunión *f*

Communism [ˈkɑmjəˌnɪzəm] *n* : comunismo *m* — **Communist** [ˈkɑmjəˌnɪst] *adj* : comunista — **~** *n* : comunista *mf*

community [kəˈmjuːnət̬i] *n, pl* **-ties** : comunidad *f*

commute [kəˈmjuːt] *v* **-muted; -muting** *vt* : conmutar, reducir (una sentencia) — *vi* : viajar de la residencia al trabajo

compact [kəmˈpækt, ˈkɑmˌpækt] *adj* : compacto — **~** [ˈkɑmˌpækt] *n* **1** *or* **~ car** : auto *m* compacto **2** *or* **powder ~** : polvera *f* — **compact disc** [ˈkɑmˌpæktˈdɪsk] *n* : disco *m* compacto

companion [kəmˈpænjən] *n* : compañero *m,* **-ra** *f* — **companionship** [kəmˈpænjənˌʃɪp] *n* : compañerismo *m*

company [ˈkʌmpəni] *n, pl* **-nies 1** : compañía *f* **2** GUESTS : visita *f*

compare [kəmˈpær] *v* **-pared; -paring**

vt : comparar — *vi* ~ **with** : poderse comparar con — **comparable** ['kɑmpərəbəl] *adj* : comparable — **comparative** [kəm'pærəṭiv] *adj* : comparativo, relativo — **comparison** [kəm'pærəsən] *n* : comparación *f*
compartment [kəm'pɑrtmənt] *n* : compartimento *m*
compass ['kʌmpəs, 'kɑm-] *n* **1** : compás *m* **2 points of the ~** : puntos *mpl* cardinales
compassion [kəm'pæʃən] *n* : compasión *f* — **compassionate** [kəm'pæʃənət] *adj* : compasivo
compatible [kəm'pæṭəbəl] *adj* : compatible, afín — **compatibility** [kəm,pæṭə'bɪləṭi] *n* : compatibilidad *f*
compel [kəm'pɛl] *vt* **-pelled; -pelling** : obligar — **compelling** [kəm'pɛlɪŋ] *adj* : convincente
compensate ['kɑmpən,seɪt] *v* **-sated; -sating** *vi* ~ **for** : compensar — *vt* : indemnizar, compensar — **compensation** [,kɑmpən'seɪʃən] *n* : compensación *f*, indemnización *f*
compete [kəm'pi:t] *vi* **-peted; -peting** : competir — **competent** ['kɑmpəṭənt] *adj* : competente — **competition** [,kɑmpə'tɪʃən] *n* **1** : competencia *f* **2** CONTEST : concurso *m* — **competitor** [kəm'pɛṭəṭər] *n* : competidor *m*, -dora *f*
compile [kəm'paɪl] *vt* **-piled; -piling** : compilar, recopilar
complacency [kəm'pleɪsəntsi] *n* : satisfacción *f* consigo mismo — **complacent** [kəm'pleɪsənt] *adj* : satisfecho de sí mismo
complain [kəm'pleɪn] *vi* : quejarse — **complaint** [kəm'pleɪnt] *n* **1** : queja *f* **2** AILMENT : enfermedad *f*
complement ['kɑmpləmənt] *n* : complemento *m* — ~ ['kɑmplə,mɛnt] *vt* : complementar — **complementary** [,kɑmplə'mɛntəri] *adj* : complementario
complete [kəm'pli:t] *adj* **-pleter; -est 1** WHOLE : completo, entero **2** FINISHED : terminado **3** TOTAL : total — ~ *vt* **-pleted; -pleting** : completar — **completion** [kəm'pli:ʃən] *n* : conclusión *f*
complex [kɑm'plɛks, kəm-; 'kɑm,plɛks] *adj* : complejo — ~ ['kɑm,plɛks] *n* : complejo *m*
complexion [kəm'plɛkʃən] *n* : cutis *m*, tez *f*
complexity [kəm'plɛksəṭi, kɑm-] *n, pl* **-ties** : complejidad *f*
compliance [kəm'plaɪənts] *n* **1** : acatamiento *m* **2 in ~ with** : conforme a — **compliant** [kəm'plaɪənt] *adj* : sumiso
complicate ['kɑmplə,keɪt] *vt* **-cated; -cating** : complicar — **complicated** ['kɑmplə,keɪṭəd] *adj* : complicado — **complication** [,kɑmplə'keɪʃən] *n* : complicación *f*
compliment ['kɑmpləmənt] *n* **1** : cumplido *m* **2 ~s** *npl* : saludos *mpl* — ~ ['kɑmplə,mɛnt] *vt* : felicitar — **complimentary** [,kɑmplə'mɛntəri] *adj* **1** FLATTERING : halagador, halagueño **2** FREE : de cortesía, gratis
comply [kəm'plaɪ] *vi* **-plied; -plying ~ with** : cumplir, obedecer
component [kəm'po:nənt, 'kɑm,po:-] *n* : componente *m*
compose [kəm'po:z] *vt* **-posed; -posing 1** : componer **2 ~ oneself** : serenarse — **composer** [kəm'po:zər] *n* : compositor *m*, -tora *f* — **composition** [,kɑmpə'zɪʃən] *n* **1** : composición *f* **2** ESSAY : ensayo *m* — **composure** [kəm'po:ʒər] *n* : calma *f*
compound[1] [kɑm'paʊnd, kəm-; 'kɑm,paʊnd] *vt* **1** COMPOSE : componer **2** : agravar (un problema, etc.) — ~ ['kɑm,paʊnd; kɑm'paʊnd, kəm-] *adj* : compuesto — ~ ['kɑm,paʊnd] *n* : compuesto *m*
compound[2] ['kɑm,paʊnd] *n* ENCLOSURE : recinto *m*
comprehend [,kɑmprɪ'hɛnd] *vt* : comprender — **comprehension** [,kɑmprɪ'hɛntʃən] *n* : comprensión *f* — **comprehensive** [,kɑmprɪ'hɛntsɪv] *adj* **1** INCLUSIVE : inclusivo **2** BROAD : amplio
compress [kəm'prɛs] *vt* : comprimir — **compression** [kəm'prɛʃən] *n* : compresión *f*
comprise [kəm'praɪz] *vt* **-prised; -prising** : comprender
compromise ['kɑmprə,maɪz] *n* : acuerdo *m*, arreglo *m* — ~ *v* **-mised; -mising** *vi* : llegar a un acuerdo — *vt* : comprometer
compulsion [kəm'pʌlʃən] *n* **1** COERCION : coacción *f* **2** URGE : impulso *m* — **compulsive** [kəm'pʌlsɪv] *adj* : compulsivo — **compulsory** [kəm'pʌlsəri] *adj* : obligatorio
compute [kəm'pju:t] *vt* **-puted; -puting** : computar — **computer** [kəm'pju:ṭər] *n* : computadora *f*, computador *m*, ordenador *m Spain* — **computerize** [kəm'pju:ṭə,raɪz] *vt* **-ized; -izing** : informatizar
comrade ['kɑm,ræd] *n* : camarada *mf*
con ['kɑn] *vt* **conned; conning** : estafar — ~ *n* **1** SWINDLE : estafa *f* **2 the pros and ~s** : los pros y los contras
concave [kɑn'keɪv, 'kɑn,keɪv] *adj* : cóncavo

conceal [kən'si:l] *vt* : ocultar
concede [kən'si:d] *vt* **-ceded; -ceding** : conceder, admitir
conceit [kən'si:t] *n* : vanidad *f* — **conceited** [kən'si:t̬əd] *adj* : engreído
conceive [kən'si:v] *v* **-ceived; -ceiving** *vt* : concebir — *vi* ~ **of** : concebir — **conceivable** [kən'si:vəbəl] *adj* : concebible
concentrate ['kɑntsənˌtreɪt] *v* **-trated; -trating** *vt* : concentrar — *vi* : concentrarse — **concentration** [ˌkɑntsən'treɪʃən] *n* : concentración *f*
concept ['kɑnˌsɛpt] *n* : concepto *m* — **conception** [kən'sɛpʃən] *n* : concepción *f*
concern [kən'sərn] *vt* **1** : concernir **2** ~ **oneself about** : preocuparse por — ~ *n* **1** AFFAIR : asunto *m* **2** WORRY : preocupación *f* **3** BUSINESS : negocio *m* — **concerned** [kən'sərnd] *adj* **1** ANXIOUS : ansioso **2 as far as I'm** ~ : en cuanto a mí — **concerning** [kən'sərnɪŋ] *prep* : con respecto a
concert ['kɑnˌsərt] *n* : concierto *m* — **concerted** [kən'sərt̬əd] *adj* : concertado
concession [kən'sɛʃən] *n* : concesión *f*
concise [kən'saɪs] *adj* : conciso
conclude [kən'klu:d] *v* **-cluded; -cluding** : concluir — **conclusion** [kən'klu:ʒən] *n* : conclusión *f* — **conclusive** [kən'klu:sɪv] *adj* : concluyente
concoct [kən'kɑkt, kɑn-] *vt* **1** PREPARE : confeccionar **2** DEVISE : inventarse, tramar — **concoction** [kən'kɑkʃən] *n* : mezcla *f*, brebaje *m*
concourse ['kɑnˌkors] *n* : vestíbulo *m*, salón *m*
concrete [kɑn'kri:t, 'kɑnˌkri:t] *adj* : concreto — ~ ['kɑnˌkri:t, kɑn'kri:t] *n* : hormigón *m*, concreto *m Lat*
concur [kən'kər] *vi* **concurred; concurring** AGREE : estar de acuerdo
concussion [kən'kʌʃən] *n* : conmoción *f* cerebral
condemn [kən'dɛm] *vt* : condenar — **condemnation** [ˌkɑnˌdɛm'neɪʃən] *n* : condenación *f*
condense [kən'dɛnts] *v* **-densed; -densing** *vt* : condensar — *vi* : condensarse — **condensation** [ˌkɑnˌdɛn'seɪʃən, -dən-] *n* : condensación *f*
condescending [ˌkɑndɪ'sɛndɪŋ] *adj* : condescendiente
condiment ['kɑndəmənt] *n* : condimento *m*
condition [kən'dɪʃən] *n* **1** : condición *f* **2 in good** ~ : en buen estado — **conditional** [kən'dɪʃənəl] *adj* : condicional
condolences [kən'do:ləntsəz] *npl* : pésame *m*
condom ['kɑndəm] *n* : condón *m*
condominium [ˌkɑndə'mɪniəm] *n, pl* **-ums** : condominio *m Lat*
condone [kən'do:n] *vt* **-doned; -doning** : aprobar
conducive [kən'du:sɪv, -'dju:-] *adj* : propicio, favorable
conduct ['kɑnˌdʌkt] *n* : conducta *f* — ~ [kən'dʌkt] *vt* **1** DIRECT, GUIDE : conducir, dirigir **2** CARRY OUT : llevar a cabo **3** ~ **oneself** : conducirse, comportarse — **conductor** [kən'dʌktər] *n* : revisor *m*, -sora *f* (en un tren); cobrador *m*, -dora *f* (en un autobús); director *m*, -tora *f* (de una orquesta)
cone ['ko:n] *n* **1** : cono *m* **2** *or* **ice-cream** ~ : cucurucho *m*, barquillo *m Lat*
confection [kən'fɛkʃən] *n* : dulce *m*
confederation [kənˌfɛdə'reɪʃən] *n* : confederación *f*
confer [kən'fər] *v* **-ferred; -ferring** *vt* : conferir, otorgar — *vi* ~ **with** : consultar — **conference** ['kɑnfrənts, -fərənts] *n* : conferencia *f*
confess [kən'fɛs] *vt* : confesar — *vi* **1** : confesarse **2** ~ **to** : confesar, admitir — **confession** [kən'fɛʃən] *n* : confesión *f*
confetti [kən'fɛt̬i] *n* : confeti *m*
confide [kən'faɪd] *v* **-fided; -fiding** : confiar — **confidence** ['kɑnfədənts] *n* **1** TRUST : confianza *f* **2** SELF-ASSURANCE : confianza *f* en sí mismo **3** SECRET : confidencia *f* — **confident** ['kɑnfədənt] *adj* **1** SURE : seguro **2** SELF-ASSURED : confiado, seguro de sí mismo — **confidential** [ˌkɑnfə'dɛntʃəl] *adj* : confidencial
confine [kən'faɪn] *vt* **-fined; -fining 1** LIMIT : confinar, limitar **2** IMPRISON : encerrar — **confines** ['kɑnˌfaɪnz] *npl* : confines *mpl*
confirm [kən'fərm] *vt* : confirmar — **confirmation** [ˌkɑnfər'meɪʃən] *n* : confirmación *f* — **confirmed** *adj* : inveterado
confiscate ['kɑnfəˌskeɪt] *vt* **-cated; -cating** : confiscar
conflict ['kɑnˌflɪkt] *n* : conflicto *m* — ~ [kən'flɪkt] *vi* : estar en conflicto, oponerse
conform [kən'fɔrm] *vi* **1** COMPLY : ajustarse **2** ~ **with** : corresponder a — **conformity** [kən'fɔrmət̬i] *n, pl* **-ties** : conformidad *f*
confound [kən'faʊnd, kɑn-] *vt* : confundir, desconcertar

confront [kən'frʌnt] *vt* : afrontar, encarar — **confrontation** [ˌkɑnfrən'teɪʃən] *n* : confrontación *f*
confuse [kən'fju:z] *vt* **-fused; -fusing** : confundir — **confusing** [kən'fju:zɪŋ] *adj* : confuso, desconcertante — **confusion** [kən'fju:ʒən] *n* : confusión *f*, desconcierto *m*
congeal [kən'dʒi:l] *vi* : coagularse
congenial [kən'dʒi:niəl] *adj* : agradable
congested [kən'dʒɛstəd] *adj* : congestionado — **congestion** [kən'dʒɛstʃən] *n* : congestión *f*
congratulate [kən'grædʒəˌleɪt, -'grætʃə-] *vt* **-lated; -lating** : felicitar — **congratulations** [kənˌgrædʒə'leɪʃən, -ˌgrætʃə-] *npl* : felicitaciones *fpl*
congregate ['kɑŋgrɪˌgeɪt] *vi* **-gated; -gating** : congregarse — **congregation** [ˌkɑŋgrɪ'geɪʃən] *n* : feligreses *mpl* (en religión)
congress ['kɑŋgrəs] *n* : congreso *m* — **congressional** [kən'grɛʃənəl, kɑn-] *adj* : del congreso — **congressman** ['kɑŋgrəsmən] *n, pl* **-men** [-mən, -ˌmɛn] : congresista *mf*
conjecture [kən'dʒɛktʃər] *n* : conjetura *f*, presunción *f* — ~ *v* **-tured; -turing** *vt* : conjeturar — *vi* : hacer conjeturas
conjugal ['kɑndʒɪgəl, kən'dʒu:-] *adj* : conyugal
conjugate ['kɑndʒəˌgeɪt] *vt* **-gated; -gating** : conjugar — **conjugation** [ˌkɑndʒə'geɪʃən] *n* : conjugación *f*
conjunction [kən'dʒʌŋkʃən] *n* **1** : conjunción *f* **2 in ~ with** : en combinación con
conjure ['kɑndʒər, 'kʌn-] *v* **-jured; -juring** *vi* : hacer juegos de manos — ~ *vt or* ~ **up** : evocar
connect [kə'nɛkt] *vi* : conectarse — *vt* **1** JOIN : conectar, juntar **2** ASSOCIATE : asociar — **connection** [kə'nɛkʃən] *n* **1** : conexión *f* **2** : enlace *m* (con un tren, etc.) **3 ~s** *npl* : relaciones *fpl* (personas)
connoisseur [ˌkɑnə'sər, -'sʊr] *n* : conocedor *m*, -dora *f*
connote [kə'no:t] *vt* **-noted; -noting** : connotar, implicar
conquer ['kɑŋkər] *vt* : conquistar — **conqueror** ['kɑŋkərər] *n* : conquistador *m*, -dora *f* — **conquest** ['kɑnˌkwɛst, 'kɑŋ-] *n* : conquista *f*
conscience ['kɑntʃənts] *n* : conciencia *f* — **conscientious** [ˌkɑntʃi'ɛntʃəs] *adj* : concienzudo
conscious ['kɑntʃəs] *adj* **1** AWARE : consciente **2** INTENTIONAL : intencional — **consciously** *adv* : deliberadamente — **consciousness** ['kɑntʃəsnəs] *n* **1** AWARENESS : consciencia *f* **2 lose ~** : perder el conocimiento
consecrate ['kɑntsəˌkreɪt] *vt* **-crated; -crating** : consagrar — **consecration** [ˌkɑntsə'kreɪʃən] *n* : consagración *f*
consecutive [kən'sɛkjət̬ɪv] *adj* : consecutivo, sucesivo
consensus [kən'sɛntsəs] *n* : consenso *m*
consent [kən'sɛnt] *vi* : consentir — ~ *n* : consentimiento *m*
consequence ['kɑntsəˌkwɛnts, -kwənts] *n* **1** : consecuencia *f* **2 of no ~** : sin importancia — **consequent** ['kɑntsəkwənt, -ˌkwɛnt] *adj* : consiguiente — **consequently** ['kɑntsəkwəntli, -ˌkwɛnt-] *adv* : por consiguiente
conserve [kən'sərv] *vt* **-served; -serving** : conservar, preservar — **conservation** [ˌkɑntsər'veɪʃən] *n* : conservación *f* — **conservative** [kən'sərvət̬ɪv] *adj* **1** : conservador **2** CAUTIOUS : moderado, prudente — ~ *n* : conservador *m*, -dora *f* — **conservatory** [kən'sərvəˌtori] *n, pl* **-ries** : conservatorio *m*
consider [kən'sɪdər] *vt* **1** : considerar **2 all things considered** : teniéndolo todo en cuenta — **considerable** [kən'sɪdərəbəl] *adj* : considerable — **considerate** [kən'sɪdərət] *adj* : considerado — **consideration** [kənˌsɪdə'reɪʃən] *n* **1** : consideración *f* **2 take into ~** : tener en cuenta — **considering** [kən'sɪdərɪŋ] *prep* : teniendo en cuenta
consign [kən'saɪn] *vt* **1** : relegar **2** SEND : enviar — **consignment** [kən'saɪnmənt] *n* : envío *m*
consist [kən'sɪst] *vi* **1 ~ in** : consistir en **2 ~ of** : constar de, componerse de — **consistency** [kən'sɪstəntsi] *n, pl* **-cies 1** TEXTURE : consistencia *f* **2** COHERENCE : coherencia *f* **3** UNIFORMITY : regularidad *f* — **consistent** [kən'sɪstənt] *adj* **1** UNCHANGING : constante, regular **2 ~ with** : consecuente con
console [kən'so:l] *vt* **-soled; -soling** : consolar — **consolation** [ˌkɑntsə'leɪʃən] *n* **1** : consuelo *m* **2 ~ prize** : premio *m* de consolación
consolidate [kən'sɑləˌdeɪt] *vt* **-dated; -dating** : consolidar — **consolidation** [kənˌsɑlə'deɪʃən] *n* : consolidación *f*
consonant ['kɑntsənənt] *n* : consonante *f*
conspicuous [kən'spɪkjʊəs] *adj* **1** OBVIOUS : visible, evidente **2** STRIKING : llamativo — **conspicuously** [kən'spɪkjʊəsli] *adv* : de manera llamativa

conspire [kən'spaɪr] *vi* **-spired; -spiring** : conspirar — **conspiracy** [kən'spɪrəsi] *n, pl* **-cies** : conspiración *f*
constant ['kɑntstənt] *adj* : constante — **constantly** ['kɑntstəntli] *adv* : constantemente
constellation [ˌkɑntstə'leɪʃən] *n* : constelación *f*
constipated ['kɑntstəˌpeɪtəd] *adj* : estreñido — **constipation** [ˌkɑntstə'peɪʃən] *n* : estreñimiento *m*
constituent [kən'stɪtʃʊənt] *n* **1** COMPONENT : componente *m* **2** VOTER : elector *m*, -tora *f*; votante *mf*
constitute ['kɑntstəˌtuːt, -ˌtjuːt] *vt* **-tuted; -tuting** : constituir — **constitution** [ˌkɑntstə'tuːʃən, -'tjuː-] *n* : constitución *f* — **constitutional** [ˌkɑntstə'tuːʃənəl, -'tjuː-] *adj* : constitucional
constraint [kən'streɪnt] *n* : restricción *f*, limitación *f*
construct [kən'strʌkt] *vt* : construir — **construction** [kən'strʌkʃən] *n* : construcción *f* — **constructive** [kən'strʌktɪv] *adj* : constructivo
construe [kən'struː] *vt* **-strued; -struing** : interpretar
consul ['kɑntsəl] *n* : cónsul *mf* — **consulate** ['kɑntsələt] *n* : consulado *m*
consult [kən'sʌlt] *v* : consultar — **consultant** [kən'sʌltənt] *n* : asesor *m*, -sora *f*; consultor *m*, -tora *f* — **consultation** [ˌkɑntsəl'teɪʃən] *n* : consulta *f*
consume [kən'suːm] *vt* **-sumed; -suming** : consumir — **consumer** [kən'suːmər] *n* : consumidor *m*, -dora *f* — **consumption** [kən'sʌmpʃən] *n* : consumo *m*
contact ['kɑnˌtækt] *n* : contacto *m* — **~** ['kɑnˌtækt, kən'-] *vt* : ponerse en contacto con — **contact lens** ['kɑnˌtækt'lɛnz] *n* : lente *mf* (de contacto)
contagious [kən'teɪdʒəs] *adj* : contagioso
contain [kən'teɪn] *vt* **1** : contener **2 ~ oneself** : contenerse — **container** [kən'teɪnər] *n* : recipiente *m*, envase *m*
contaminate [kən'tæməˌneɪt] *vt* **-nated; -nating** : contaminar — **contamination** [kənˌtæmə'neɪʃən] *n* : contaminación *f*
contemplate ['kɑntəmˌpleɪt] *v* **-plated; -plating** *vt* **1** : contemplar **2** CONSIDER : considerar, pensar en — *vi* : reflexionar — **contemplation** [ˌkɑntəm'pleɪʃən] *n* : contemplación *f*
contemporary [kən'tɛmpəˌrɛri] *adj* : contemporáneo — **~** *n, pl* **-raries** : contemporáneo *m*, -nea *f*
contempt [kən'tɛmpt] *n* : desprecio *m* — **contemptible** [kən'tɛmptəbəl] *adj* : despreciable — **contemptuous** [kən'tɛmptʃʊəs] *adj* : desdeñoso
contend [kən'tɛnd] *vi* **1** COMPETE : contender, competir **2 ~ with** : enfrentarse a — *vt* : sostener, afirmar — **contender** [kən'tɛndər] *n* : contendiente *mf*
content[1] ['kɑnˌtɛnt] *n* **1** : contenido *m* **2 table of ~s** : índice *m* de materias
content[2] [kən'tɛnt] *adj* : contento — **~** *vt* **~ oneself with** : contentarse con — **contented** [kən'tɛntəd] *adj* : satisfecho, contento
contention [kən'tɛntʃən] *n* **1** DISPUTE : disputa *f* **2** OPINION : argumento *m*, opinión *f*
contentment [kən'tɛntmənt] *n* : satisfacción *f*
contest [kən'tɛst] *vt* : disputar — **~** ['kɑnˌtɛst] *n* **1** STRUGGLE : contienda *f* **2** COMPETITION : concurso *m*, competencia *f* — **contestant** [kən'tɛstənt] *n* : concursante *mf*, contendiente *mf*
context ['kɑnˌtɛkst] *n* : contexto *m*
continent ['kɑntənənt] *n* : continente *m* — **continental** [ˌkɑntən'ɛntəl] *adj* : continental
contingency [kən'tɪndʒəntsi] *n, pl* **-cies** : contingencia *f*
continue [kən'tɪnjuː] *v* **-tinued; -tinuing** : continuar — **continual** [kən'tɪnjʊəl] *adj* : continuo, constante — **continuation** [kənˌtɪnjʊ'eɪʃən] *n* : continuación *f* — **continuity** [ˌkɑntən'uːəṭi, -'juː-] *n, pl* **-ties** : continuidad *f* — **continuous** [kən'tɪnjʊəs] *adj* : continuo
contort [kən'tɔrt] *vt* : retorcer — **contortion** [kən'tɔrʃən] *n* : contorsión *f*
contour ['kɑnˌtʊr] *n* **1** : contorno *m* **2** *or* **~ line** : curva *f* de nivel
contraband ['kɑntrəˌbænd] *n* : contrabando *m*
contraception [ˌkɑntrə'sɛpʃən] *n* : anticoncepción *f* — **contraceptive** [ˌkɑntrə'sɛptɪv] *adj* : anticonceptivo — **~** *n* : anticonceptivo *m*
contract ['kɑnˌtrækt] *n* : contrato *m* — **~** [kən'trækt] *vt* : contraer — *vi* : contraerse — **contraction** [kən'trækʃən] *n* : contracción *f* — **contractor** ['kɑnˌtræktər, kən'træk-] *n* : contratista *mf*
contradiction [ˌkɑntrə'dɪkʃən] *n* : contradicción *f* — **contradict** [ˌkɑntrə'dɪkt] *vt* : contradecir — **contradictory** [ˌkɑntrə'dɪktəri] *adj* : contradictorio
contraption [kən'træpʃən] *n* : artilugio *m*, artefacto *m*
contrary ['kɑnˌtrɛri] *n, pl* **-traries 1** : contrario **2 on the ~** : al contrario

— ~ ['kɑnˌtrɛri] *adj* **1** : contrario, opuesto **2** **~ to** : en contra de
contrast [kən'træst] *v* : contrastar — **~** ['kɑnˌtræst] *n* : contraste *m*
contribute [kən'trɪbjət] *v* **-uted; -uting** : contribuir — **contribution** [ˌkɑntrə'bjuːʃən] *n* : contribución *f* — **contributor** [kən'trɪbjət̬ər] *n* **1** : contribuyente *mf* **2** : colaborador *m*, -dora *f* (en periodismo)
contrite ['kɑnˌtraɪt, kən'traɪt] *adj* : arrepentido
contrive [kən'traɪv] *vt* **-trived; -triving** **1** DEVISE : idear **2** **~ to do sth** : lograr hacer algo
control [kən'troːl] *vt* **-trolled; -trolling** : controlar — **~** *n* **1** : control *m* **2** **~s** *npl* : mandos *mpl*
controversy ['kɑntrəˌvərsi] *n, pl* **-sies** : controversia *f* — **controversial** [ˌkɑntrə'vərʃəl, -siəl] *adj* : polémico
convalescence [ˌkɑnvə'lɛsənts] *n* : convalecencia *f* — **convalescent** [ˌkɑnvə'lɛsənt] *adj* : convaleciente — **~** *n* : convaleciente *mf*
convene [kən'viːn] *v* **-vened; -vening** *vt* : convocar — *vi* : reunirse
convenience [kən'viːnjənts] *n* : conveniencia *f*, comodidad *f* — **convenient** [kən'viːnjənt] *adj* : conveniente
convent ['kɑnvənt, -ˌvɛnt] *n* : convento *m*
convention [kən'vɛntʃən] *n* : convención *f* — **conventional** [kən'vɛntʃənəl] *adj* : convencional
converge [kən'vərdʒ] *vi* **-verged; -verging** : converger, convergir
converse[1] [kən'vərs] *vi* **-versed; -versing** : conversar — **conversation** [ˌkɑnvər'seɪʃən] *n* : conversación *f* — **conversational** [ˌkɑnvər'seɪʃənəl] *adj* : familiar
converse[2] [kən'vərs, 'kɑnˌvərs] *adj* : contrario, opuesto — **conversely** [kən'vərsli, 'kɑnˌvərs-] *adv* : a la inversa
conversion [kən'vərʒən] *n* : conversión *f* — **convert** [kən'vərt] *vt* : convertir — *vi* : convertirse — **convertible** [kən'vərt̬əbəl] *adj* : convertible — **~** *n* : descapotable *m*, convertible *m Lat*
convex [kɑn'vɛks, 'kɑn-, kən'-] *adj* : convexo
convey [kən'veɪ] *vt* **1** TRANSPORT : llevar, transportar **2** TRANSMIT : comunicar
convict [kən'vɪkt] *vt* : declarar culpable a — **~** ['kɑnˌvɪkt] *n* : presidiario *m*, -ria *f* — **conviction** [kən'vɪkʃən] *n* **1** : condena *f* (de un acusado) **2** BELIEF : convicción *f*
convince [kən'vɪnts] *vt* **-vinced; -vincing** : convencer — **convincing** [kən'vɪntsɪŋ] *adj* : convincente
convoke [kən'voːk] *vt* **-voked; -voking** : convocar
convoluted ['kɑnvəˌluːt̬əd] *adj* : complicado
convulsion [kən'vʌlʃən] *n* : convulsión *f* — **convulsive** [kən'vʌlsɪv] *adj* : convulsivo
cook ['kʊk] *n* : cocinero *m*, -ra *f* — **~** *vi* : cocinar, guisar — *vt* : preparar (comida) — **cookbook** ['kʊkˌbʊk] *n* : libro *m* de cocina
cookie *or* **cooky** ['kʊki] *n, pl* **-ies** : galleta *f* (dulce)
cooking *n* : cocina *f*
cool ['kuːl] *adj* **1** : fresco **2** CALM : tranquilo **3** UNFRIENDLY : frío — **~** *vt* : enfriar — *vi* : enfriarse — **~** *n* **1** : fresco *m* **2** COMPOSURE : calma *f* — **cooler** ['kuːlər] *n* : nevera *f* portátil — **coolness** ['kuːlnəs] *n* : frescura *f*
coop ['kuːp, 'kʊp] *n* : gallinero *m* — **~** *vt or* **~ up** : encerrar
cooperate [ko'ɑpəˌreɪt] *vi* **-ated; -ating** : cooperar — **cooperation** [koˌɑpə'reɪʃən] *n* : cooperación *f* — **cooperative** [ko'ɑpərət̬ɪv, -'ɑpəˌreɪt̬ɪv] *adj* : cooperativo
coordinate [ko'ɔrdənˌeɪt] *v* **-nated; -nating** *vt* : coordinar — **coordination** [koˌɔrdən'eɪʃən] *n* : coordinación *f*
cop ['kɑp] *n* **1** : poli *mf fam* **2** **the ~s** : la poli *fam*
cope ['koːp] *vi* **coped; coping** **1** : arreglárselas **2** **~ with** : hacer frente a, poder con
copier ['kɑpiər] *n* : fotocopiadora *f*
copious ['koːpiəs] *adj* : copioso
copper ['kɑpər] *n* : cobre *m*
copy ['kɑpi] *n, pl* **copies** **1** : copia *f* **2** : ejemplar *m* (de un libro), número *m* (de una revista) — **~** *vt* **copied; copying** **1** DUPLICATE : hacer una copia de **2** IMITATE : copiar — **copyright** ['kɑpiˌraɪt] *n* : derechos *mpl* de autor
coral ['kɔrəl] *n* : coral *m*
cord ['kɔrd] *n* **1** : cuerda *f* **2** *or* **electric ~** : cable *m* (eléctrico)
cordial ['kɔrdʒəl] *adj* : cordial
corduroy ['kɔrdəˌrɔɪ] *n* : pana *f*
core ['kor] *n* **1** : corazón *m* (de una fruta) **2** CENTER : núcleo *m*, centro *m*
cork ['kɔrk] *n* : corcho *m* — **corkscrew** ['kɔrkˌskruː] *n* : sacacorchos *m*
corn ['kɔrn] *n* **1** : grano *m* **2** *or* **Indian ~** : maíz *m* **3** : callo *m* (del pie) — **corncob** ['kɔrnˌkɑb] *n* : mazorca *f*

corner ['kɔrnər] *n* **:** ángulo *m*, rincón *m* (en una habitación), esquina *f* (de una intersección) — **~** *vt* **1** TRAP **:** acorralar **2** MONOPOLIZE **:** acaparar (un mercado) — **cornerstone** ['kɔrnərˌsto:n] *n* **:** piedra *f* angular

cornmeal ['kɔrnˌmi:l] *n* **:** harina *f* de maíz — **cornstarch** ['kɔrnˌstɑrtʃ] *n* **:** maicena *f*

corny ['kɔrni] *adj* **:** cursi, sentimental

coronary ['kɔrəˌnɛri] *n, pl* **-naries** **:** trombosis *f* coronaria

coronation [ˌkɔrə'neɪʃən] *n* **:** coronación *f*

corporal ['kɔrpərəl] *n* **:** cabo *m*

corporation [ˌkɔrpə'reɪʃən] *n* **:** sociedad *f* anónima, compañía *f* — **corporate** ['kɔrpərət] *adj* **:** corporativo

corps ['kor] *n, pl* **corps** ['korz] **:** cuerpo *m*

corpse ['kɔrps] *n* **:** cadáver *m*

corpulent ['kɔrpjələnt] *adj* **:** obeso, gordo

corpuscle ['kɔrˌpʌsəl] *n* **:** glóbulo *m*

corral [kə'ræl] *n* **:** corral *m* — **~** *vt* **-ralled; -ralling** **:** acorralar

correct [kə'rɛkt] *vt* **:** corregir — **~** *adj* **:** correcto — **correction** [kə'rɛkʃən] *n* **:** corrección *f*

correlation [ˌkɔrə'leɪʃən] *n* **:** correlación *f*

correspond [ˌkɔrə'spɑnd] *vi* **1** WRITE **:** corresponderse **2 ~ to** **:** corresponder a — **correspondence** [ˌkɔrə'spɑndənts] *n* **:** correspondencia *f*

corridor ['kɔrədər, -ˌdɔr] *n* **:** pasillo *m*

corroborate [kə'rɑbəˌreɪt] *vt* **-rated; -rating** **:** corroborar

corrode [kə'ro:d] *v* **-roded; -roding** *vt* **:** corroer — *vi* **:** corroerse — **corrosion** [kə'ro:ʒən] *n* **:** corrosión *f* — **corrosive** [kə'ro:sɪv] *adj* **:** corrosivo

corrugated ['kɔrəˌgeɪt̬əd] *adj* **:** ondulado

corrupt [kə'rʌpt] *vt* **:** corromper — **~** *adj* **:** corrupto, corrompido — **corruption** [kə'rʌpʃən] *n* **:** corrupción *f*

corset ['kɔrsət] *n* **:** corsé *m*

cosmetic [kɑz'mɛt̬ɪk] *n* **:** cosmético *m* — **~** *adj* **:** cosmético

cosmic ['kɑzmɪk] *adj* **:** cósmico

cosmopolitan [ˌkɑzmə'pɑlətən] *adj* **:** cosmopolita

cosmos ['kɑzməs, -ˌmo:s, -ˌmɑs] *n* **:** cosmos *m*

cost ['kɔst] *n* **:** costo *m*, coste *m* — **~** *vi* **cost; costing 1** **:** costar **2 how much does it ~?** **:** ¿cuánto cuesta?, ¿cuánto vale?

Costa Rican [ˌkɔstə'ri:kən] *adj* **:** costarricense

costly ['kɔstli] *adj* **:** costoso

costume ['kɑsˌtu:m, -ˌtju:m] *n* **1** OUTFIT **:** traje *m* **2** DISGUISE **:** disfraz *m*

cot ['kɑt] *n* **:** catre *m*

cottage ['kɑt̬ɪdʒ] *n* **:** casita *f* (de campo) — **cottage cheese** *n* **:** requesón *m*

cotton ['kɑtən] *n* **:** algodón *m*

couch ['kaʊtʃ] *n* **:** sofá *m*

cough ['kɔf] *vi* **:** toser — **~** *n* **:** tos *f*

could ['kʊd] → **can**[1]

council ['kaʊntsəl] *n* **1** **:** concejo *m* **2** *or* **city ~** **:** ayuntamiento *m* — **councillor** *or* **councilor** ['kaʊntsələr] *n* **:** concejal *m*, **-jala** *f*

counsel *n* **1** ADVICE **:** consejo *m* **2** LAWYER **:** abogado *m*, **-da** *f* — **~** ['kaʊntsəl] *vt* **-seled** *or* **-selled; -seling** *or* **-selling** **:** aconsejar — **counselor** *or* **counsellor** ['kaʊntsələr] *n* **:** consejero *m*, **-ra** *f*

count[1] ['kaʊnt] *vt* **:** contar — *vi* **1** **:** contar **2 ~ on** **:** contar con **3 that doesn't ~** **:** eso no vale — **~** *n* **1** **:** recuento *m* **2 keep ~ of** **:** llevar la cuenta de

count[2] *n* **:** conde *m* (noble)

counter[1] ['kaʊntər] *n* **1** **:** mostrador *m* (de un negocio) **2** TOKEN **:** ficha *f* (de un juego)

counter[2] *vt* **:** oponerse a — *vi* **:** contraatacar — **~** *adv* **~ to** **:** contrario a — **counteract** [ˌkaʊntər'ækt] *vt* **:** contrarrestar — **counterattack** ['kaʊntərəˌtæk] *n* **:** contraataque *m* — **counterbalance** [ˌkaʊntər'bæləntsl] *n* **:** contrapeso *m* — **counterclockwise** [ˌkaʊntər'klɑkˌwaɪz] *adv & adj* **:** en sentido opuesto a las agujas del reloj — **counterfeit** ['kaʊntərˌfɪt] *vt* **:** falsificar — **~** *adj* **:** falsificado — **~** *n* **:** falsificación *f* — **counterpart** ['kaʊntərˌpɑrt] *n* **:** homólogo *m* (de una persona), equivalente *m* (de una cosa) — **counterproductive** [ˌkaʊntərprə'dʌktɪv] *adj* **:** contraproducente

countess ['kaʊntɪs] *n* **:** condesa *f*

countless ['kaʊntləs] *adj* **:** incontable, innumerable

country ['kʌntri] *n, pl* **-tries 1** NATION **:** país *m* **2** COUNTRYSIDE **:** campo *m* — **~** *adj* **:** campestre, rural — **countryman** ['kʌntrimən] *n, pl* **-men** [-mən, -ˌmɛn] *or* **fellow ~** **:** compatriota *mf* — **countryside** ['kʌntriˌsaɪd] *n* **:** campo *m*, campiña *f*

county ['kaʊnti] *n, pl* **-ties** **:** condado *m*

coup ['ku:] *n, pl* **coups** ['ku:z] *or* **~ d'etat** **:** golpe *m* (de estado)

couple ['kʌpəl] *n* **1** **:** pareja *f* (de per-

sonas) **2 a ~ of** : un par de — **~** *vt* **-pled; -pling** : acoplar, unir
coupon [ˈkuːˌpɑn, ˈkjuː-] *n* : cupón *m*
courage [ˈkərɪdʒ] *n* : valor *m* — **courageous** [kəˈreɪdʒəs] *adj* : valiente
courier [ˈkʊriər, ˈkəriər] *n* : mensajero *m*, -ra *f*
course [ˈkors] *n* **1** : curso *m* **2** : plato *m* (de una cena) **3** *or* **golf ~** : campo *m* de golf **4 in the ~ of** : en el transcurso de **5 of ~** : desde luego, por supuesto
court [ˈkort] *n* **1** : corte *f* (de un rey, etc.) **2** : cancha *f*, pista *f* (en deportes) **3** TRIBUNAL : corte *f*, tribunal *m* — **~** *vt* : cortejar
courteous [ˈkərt̬iəs] *adj* : cortés — **courtesy** [ˈkərt̬əsi] *n, pl* **-sies** : cortesía *f*
courthouse [ˈkortˌhaʊs] *n* : palacio *m* de justicia, juzgado *m* — **courtroom** [ˈkortˌruːm] *n* : sala *f* (de un tribunal)
courtship [ˈkortˌʃɪp] *n* : cortejo *m*, noviazgo *m*
courtyard [ˈkortˌjɑrd] *n* : patio *m*
cousin [ˈkʌzən] *n* : primo *m*, -ma *f*
cove [ˈkoːv] *n* : ensenada *f*, cala *f*
covenant [ˈkʌvənənt] *n* : pacto *m*, convenio *m*
cover [ˈkʌvər] *vt* **1** : cubrir **2** *or* **~ up** : encubrir, ocultar **3** TREAT : tratar — **~** *n* **1** : cubierta *f* **2** SHELTER : abrigo *m*, refugio *m* **3** LID : tapa *f* **4** : cubierta *f* (de un libro), portada *f* (de una revista) **5 ~s** *npl* BEDCLOTHES : mantas *fpl*, cobijas *fpl Lat* **6 take ~** : ponerse a cubierto **7 under ~ of** : al amparo de — **coverage** [ˈkʌvərɪdʒ] *n* : cobertura *f* — **covert** [ˈkoːˌvərt, ˈkʌvərt] *adj* : encubierto — **cover-up** [ˈkʌvərˌʌp] *n* : encubrimiento *m*
covet [ˈkʌvət] *vt* : codiciar — **covetous** [ˈkʌvət̬əs] *adj* : codicioso
cow [ˈkaʊ] *n* : vaca *f* — **~** *vt* : intimidar, acobardar
coward [ˈkaʊərd] *n* : cobarde *mf* — **cowardice** [ˈkaʊərdɪs] *n* : cobardía *f* — **cowardly** [ˈkaʊərdli] *adj* : cobarde
cowboy [ˈkaʊˌbɔɪ] *n* : vaquero *m*
cower [ˈkaʊər] *vi* : encogerse (de miedo)
coy [ˈkɔɪ] *adj* : tímido y coqueto
coyote [kaɪˈoːt̬i, ˈkaɪˌoːt] *n, pl* **coyotes** *or* **coyote** : coyote *m*
cozy [ˈkoːzi] *adj* **-zier; -est** : acogedor
crab [ˈkræb] *n* : cangrejo *m*, jaiba *f Lat*
crack [ˈkræk] *vt* **1** SPLIT : rajar, partir **2** : cascar (nueces, huevos) **3** : chasquear (un látigo, etc.) **4 ~ down on** : tomar medidas enérgicas contra — *vi* **1** SPLIT : rajarse, agrietarse **2** : chasquear (dícese de un látigo) **3 ~ up** : sufrir una crisis nerviosa — **~** *n* **1** CRACKING : chasquido *m*, crujido *m* **2** CREVICE : raja *f*, grieta *f* **3 have a ~ at** : intentar
cracker [ˈkrækər] *n* : galleta *f* (de soda, etc.)
crackle [ˈkrækəl] *vi* **-led; -ling** : crepitar, chisporrotear — **~** *n* : crujido *m*, chisporroteo *m*
cradle [ˈkreɪdəl] *n* : cuna *f* — **~** *vt* **-dled; -dling** : acunar
craft [ˈkræft] *n* **1** TRADE : oficio *m* **2** CUNNING : astucia *f* **3** → **craftsmanship 4** *pl usually* **craft** BOAT : embarcación *f* — **craftsman** [ˈkræftsmən] *n, pl* **-men** [-mən, -ˌmɛn] : artesano *m*, -na *f* — **craftsmanship** [ˈkræftsmənˌʃɪp] *n* : artesanía *f*, destreza *f* — **crafty** [ˈkræfti] *adj* **craftier; -est** : astuto, taimado
crag [ˈkræg] *n* : peñasco *m*
cram [ˈkræm] *v* **crammed; cramming** *vt* **1** STUFF : embutir **2 ~ with** : atiborrar de — *vi* : estudiar a última hora
cramp [ˈkræmp] *n* **1** : calambre *m*, espasmo *m* (de los músculos) **2 ~s** *npl* : retorcijones *mpl*
cranberry [ˈkrænˌbɛri] *n, pl* **-berries** : arándano *m* (rojo y agrio)
crane [ˈkreɪn] *n* **1** : grulla *f* (ave) **2** : grúa *f* (máquina) — **~** *vt* **craned; craning** : estirar (el cuello)
crank [ˈkræŋk] *n* **1** : manivela *f* **2** ECCENTRIC : excéntrico *m*, -ca *f* — **cranky** [ˈkræŋki] *adj* **crankier; -est** : malhumorado
crash [ˈkræʃ] *vi* **1** : caerse con estrépito **2** COLLIDE : estrellarse, chocar — *vt* : estrellar — **~** *n* **1** DIN : estrépito *m* **2** COLLISION : choque *m*
crass [ˈkræs] *adj* : burdo, grosero
crate [ˈkreɪt] *n* : cajón *m* (de madera)
crater [ˈkreɪt̬ər] *n* : cráter *m*
crave [ˈkreɪv] *vt* **craved; craving** : ansiar — **craving** [ˈkreɪvɪŋ] *n* : ansia *f*
crawl [ˈkrɔl] *vi* : arrastrarse, gatear (dícese de un bebé) — **~** *n* **at a ~** : a paso lento
crayon [ˈkreɪˌɑn, -ən] *n* : lápiz *m* de cera
craze [ˈkreɪz] *n* : moda *f* pasajera, manía *f*
crazy [ˈkreɪzi] *adj* **-zier; -est 1** : loco **2 go ~** : volverse loco — **craziness** [ˈkreɪzinəs] *n* : locura *f*
creak [ˈkriːk] *vi* : chirriar, crujir — **~** *n* : chirrido *m*, crujido *m*
cream [ˈkriːm] *n* : crema *f*, nata *f Spain* — **cream cheese** *n* : queso *m* crema

— **creamy** ['kri:mi] *adj* **creamier; -est** : cremoso

crease ['kri:s] *n* : pliegue *m*, raya *f* (del pantalón) — ~ *vt* **creased; creasing** : plegar, poner una raya en (el pantalón)

create [kri'eɪt] *vt* **-ated; -ating** : crear — **creation** [kri'eɪʃən] *n* : creación *f* — **creative** [kri'eɪṭɪv] *adj* : creativo — **creator** [kri'eɪṭər] *n* : creador *m*, -dora *f*

creature ['kri:tʃər] *n* : criatura *f*, animal *m*

credence ['kri:dənts] *n* **lend ~ to** : dar crédito a

credentials [krɪ'dɛntʃəlz] *npl* : credenciales *fpl*

credible ['krɛdəbəl] *adj* : creíble — **credibility** [ˌkrɛdə 'bɪləṭi] *n* : credibilidad *f*

credit ['krɛdɪt] *n* **1** : crédito *m* **2** RECOGNITION : reconocimiento *m* **3 be a ~ to** : ser el orgullo de — ~ *vt* **1** BELIEVE : creer **2** : abonar (en una cuenta) **3 ~ s.o. with sth** : atribuir algo a algn — **credit card** *n* : tarjeta *f* de crédito

credulous ['krɛdʒələs] *adj* : crédulo

creed ['kri:d] *n* : credo *m*

creek ['kri:k, 'krɪk] *n* : arroyo *m*, riachuelo *m*

creep ['kri:p] *vi* **crept** ['krɛpt]; **creeping 1** CRAWL : arrastrarse **2** SLINK : ir a hurtadillas — ~ *n* **1** CRAWL : paso *m* lento **2 the ~s** : escalofríos *mpl* — **creeping** *adj* **~ plant** : planta *f* trepadora

cremate ['kri:ˌmeɪt] *vt* **-mated; -mating** : incinerar

crescent ['krɛsənt] *n* : media luna *f*

cress ['krɛs] *n* : berro *m*

crest ['krɛst] *n* : cresta *f* — **crestfallen** ['krɛstˌfɔlən] *adj* : alicaído

crevice ['krɛvɪs] *n* : grieta *f*

crew ['kru:] *n* **1** : tripulación *f* (de una nave) **2** TEAM : equipo *m*

crib ['krɪb] *n* : cuna *f* (de un bebé)

cricket ['krɪkət] *n* **1** : grillo *m* (insecto) **2** : críquet *m* (juego)

crime ['kraɪm] *n* : crimen *m* — **criminal** ['krɪmənəl] *adj* : criminal — ~ *n* : criminal *mf*

crimp ['krɪmp] *vt* : rizar

crimson ['krɪmzən] *n* : carmesí *m*

cringe ['krɪndʒ] *vi* **cringed; cringing** : encogerse

crinkle ['krɪŋkəl] *vt* **-kled; -kling** : arrugar

cripple ['krɪpəl] *vt* **-pled; -pling 1** DISABLE : lisiar, dejar inválido **2** INCAPACITATE : inutilizar, paralizar

crisis ['kraɪsɪs] *n, pl* **crises** [-ˌsi:z] : crisis *f*

crisp ['krɪsp] *adj* **1** CRUNCHY : crujiente **2** : frío y vigorizante (dícese del aire) — **crispy** ['krɪspi] *adj* **crispier; -est** : crujiente

crisscross ['krɪsˌkrɔs] *vt* : entrecruzar

criterion [kraɪ'tɪriən] *n, pl* **-ria** [-iə] : criterio *m*

critic ['krɪṭɪk] *n* : crítico *m*, **-ca** *f* — **critical** ['krɪṭɪkəl] *adj* : crítico — **criticism** ['krɪṭəˌsɪzəm] *n* : crítica *f* — **criticize** ['krɪṭəˌsaɪz] *vt* **-cized; -cizing** : criticar

croak ['kro:k] *vi* : croar

crock ['krɑk] *n* : vasija *f* de barro — **crockery** ['krɑkəri] *n* : vajilla *f*, loza *f*

crocodile ['krɑkəˌdaɪl] *n* : cocodrilo *m*

crony ['kro:ni] *n, pl* **-nies** : amigote *m fam*

crook ['krʊk] *n* **1** STAFF : cayado *m* **2** THIEF : ratero *m*, -ra *f*; ladrón *m*, -drona *f* **3** BEND : pliegue *m* — **crooked** ['krʊkəd] *adj* **1** BENT : torcido, chueco *Lat* **2** DISHONEST : deshonesto

crop ['krɑp] *n* **1** WHIP : fusta *f* **2** HARVEST : cosecha *f* **3** : cultivo *m* (de maíz, tabaco, etc.) — ~ *v* **cropped; cropping** *vt* TRIM : recortar, cortar — *vi* **~ up** : surgir

cross ['krɔs] *n* **1** : cruz *f* **2** HYBRID : cruce *m* — ~ *vt* **1** : cruzar, atravesar **2** CROSSBREED : cruzar **3** *or* **~ out** : tachar — ~ *adj* **1** : que atraviesa **2** ANGRY : enojado — **crossbreed** ['krɔsˌbri:d] *vt* **-bred** [-bred]; **-breeding** : cruzar — **cross–examine** *vt* : interrogar — **cross–eyed** ['krɔsˌaɪd] *adj* : bizco — **cross fire** *n* : fuego *m* cruzado — **crossing** ['krɔsɪŋ] *n* **1** INTERSECTION : cruce *m*, paso *m* **2** VOYAGE : travesía *f* (del mar) — **cross–reference** [ˌkrɔs'rɛfrənts, -'rɛfərənts] *n* : referencia *f* — **crossroads** ['krɔsˌro:dz] *n* : cruce *m* — **cross section** *n* **1** : corte *m* transversal **2** SAMPLE : muestra *f* representativa — **crosswalk** ['krɔsˌwɔk] *n* : cruce *m* peatonal, paso *m* de peatones — **crossword puzzle** ['krɔsˌwərd] *n* : crucigrama *m*

crotch ['krɑtʃ] *n* : entrepierna *f*

crouch ['kraʊtʃ] *vi* : agacharse

crouton ['kru:ˌtɑn] *n* : crutón *m*

crow ['kro:] *n* : cuervo *m* — ~ *vi* **crowed** *or Brit* **crew; crowing** : cacarear

crowbar ['kro:ˌbɑr] *n* : palanca *f*

crowd ['kraʊd] *vi* : amontonarse — *vt* : atestar, llenar — ~ *n* : multitud *f*, muchedumbre *f*

crown ['kraʊn] *n* **1** : corona *f* **2** : cima *f* (de una colina) — ~ *vt* : coronar
crucial ['kru:ʃəl] *adj* : crucial
crucify ['kru:sə,faɪ] *vt* **-fied; -fying** : crucificar — **crucifix** ['kru:sə,fɪks] *n* : crucifijo *m* — **crucifixion** [,kru:sə'fɪkʃən] *n* : crucifixión *f*
crude ['kru:d] *adj* **cruder; -est 1** RAW : crudo **2** VULGAR : grosero **3** ROUGH : tosco, rudo
cruel ['kru:əl] *adj* **-eler** *or* **-eller; -elest** *or* **-ellest** : cruel — **cruelty** ['kru:əlti] *n, pl* **-ties** : crueldad *f*
cruet ['kru:ɪt] *n* : vinagrera *f*
cruise ['kru:z] *vi* **cruised; cruising 1** : hacer un crucero **2** : ir a velocidad de crucero — ~ *n* : crucero *m* — **cruiser** ['kru:zər] *n* **1** WARSHIP : crucero *m* **2** : patrulla *f* (de policía)
crumb ['krʌm] *n* : miga *f*, migaja *f*
crumble ['krʌmbəl] *v* **-bled; -bling** *vt* : desmenuzar — *vi* : desmenuzarse, desmoronarse
crumple ['krʌmpəl] *vt* **-pled; -pling** : arrugar
crunch ['krʌntʃ] *vt* : ronzar (con los dientes), hacer crujir (con los pies, etc.) — **crunchy** ['krʌntʃi] *adj* **crunchier; -est** : crujiente
crusade [kru:'seɪd] *n* : cruzada *f*
crush ['krʌʃ] *vt* : aplastar, apachurrar *Lat* — ~ *n* **have a ~ on** : estar chiflado por
crust ['krʌst] *n* : corteza *f*
crutch ['krʌtʃ] *n* : muleta *f*
crux ['krʌks, 'krʊks] *n* : quid *m*
cry ['kraɪ] *vi* **cried; crying 1** SHOUT : gritar **2** WEEP : llorar — ~ *n, pl* **cries** : grito *m*
crypt ['krɪpt] *n* : cripta *f*
crystal ['krɪstəl] *n* : cristal *m*
cub ['kʌb] *n* : cachorro *m*, -rra *f*
Cuban ['kju:bən] *adj* : cubano
cube ['kju:b] *n* : cubo *m* — **cubic** ['kju:bɪk] *adj* : cúbico
cubicle ['kju:bɪkəl] *n* : cubículo *m*
cuckoo ['ku:,ku:, 'kʊ-] *n* : cuco *m*, cuclillo *m*
cucumber ['kju:,kʌmbər] *n* : pepino *m*
cuddle ['kʌdəl] *v* **-dled; -dling** *vi* : acurrucarse, abrazarse — *vt* : abrazar
cudgel ['kʌdʒəl] *n* : porra *f* — ~ *vt* **-geled** *or* **-gelled; -geling** *or* **-gelling** : aporrear
cue[1] ['kju:] *n* SIGNAL : señal *f*
cue[2] *n* : taco *m* (de billar)
cuff[1] ['kʌf] **1** : puño *m* (de una camisa) **2** **~s** *npl* → **handcuffs**
cuff[2] *vt* : bofetear — ~ *n* SLAP : bofetada *f*
cuisine [kwɪ'zi:n] *n* : cocina *f*
culinary ['kʌlə,nɛri, 'kju:lə-] *adj* : culinario
cull ['kʌl] *vt* : seleccionar, entresacar
culminate ['kʌlmə,neɪt] *vi* **-nated; -nating** : culminar — **culmination** [,kʌlmə'neɪʃən] *n* : culminación *f*
culprit ['kʌlprɪt] *n* : culpable *mf*
cult ['kʌlt] *n* : culto *m*
cultivate ['kʌltə,veɪt] *vt* **-vated; -vating** : cultivar — **cultivation** [,kʌltə'veɪʃən] *n* : cultivo *m*
culture ['kʌltʃər] *n* **1** : cultura *f* **2** : cultivo *m* (en biología) — **cultural** ['kʌltʃərəl] *adj* : cultural — **cultured** ['kʌltʃərd] *adj* : culto
cumbersome ['kʌmbərsəm] *adj* : torpe (y pesado), difícil de manejar
cumulative ['kju:mjələṭiv, -,leɪṭɪv] *adj* : acumulativo
cunning ['kʌnɪŋ] *adj* : astuto, taimado — ~ *n* : astucia *f*
cup ['kʌp] *n* **1** : taza *f* **2** TROPHY : copa *f*
cupboard ['kʌbərd] *n* : alacena *f*, armario *m*
curator ['kjʊr,eɪṭər, kjʊ'reɪṭər] *n* : conservador *m*, -dora *f*; director *m*, -tora *f*
curb ['kərb] *n* **1** RESTRAINT : freno *m* **2** : borde *m* de la acera — ~ *vt* : refrenar
curdle ['kərdəl] *v* **-dled; -dling** *vi* : cuajarse — *vt* : cuajar
cure ['kjʊr] *n* : cura *f*, remedio *m* — ~ *vt* **cured; curing** : curar
curfew ['kər,fju:] *n* : toque *m* de queda
curious ['kjʊriəs] *adj* : curioso — **curio** ['kjʊri,o:] *n, pl* **-rios** : curiosidad *f* — **curiosity** [,kjʊri'ɑsəṭi] *n, pl* **-ties** : curiosidad *f*
curl ['kərl] *vt* **1** : rizar **2** COIL : enrollar, enroscar — *vi* **1** : rizarse **2 ~ up** : acurrucarse — ~ *n* : rizo *m* — **curler** ['kərlər] *n* : rulo *m* — **curly** ['kərli] *adj* **curlier; -est** : rizado
currant ['kərənt] *n* **1** : grosella *f* (fruta) **2** RAISIN : pasa *f* de Corinto
currency ['kərəntsi] *n, pl* **-cies 1** MONEY : moneda *f* **2 gain ~** : ganar aceptación
current ['kərənt] *adj* **1** PRESENT : actual **2** PREVALENT : corriente — ~ *n* : corriente *f*
curriculum [kə'rɪkjələm] *n, pl* **-la** [-lə] : plan *m* de estudios
curry ['kəri] *n, pl* **-ries** : curry *m*
curse ['kərs] *n* : maldición *f* — ~ *v* **cursed; cursing** : maldecir
cursor ['kərsər] *n* : cursor *m*
cursory ['kərsəri] *adj* : superficial
curt ['kərt] *adj* : corto, seco

curtail [kər'teɪl] *vt* : acortar
curtain ['kərtən] *n* : cortina *f* (de una ventana), telón *m* (en un teatro)
curtsy ['kərtsi] *vi* **-sied** *or* **-seyed; -sying** *or* **-seying** : hacer una reverencia — ~ *n* : reverencia *f*
curve ['kərv] *v* **curved; curving** *vi* : hacer una curva — *vt* : encorvar — ~ *n* : curva *f*
cushion ['kuʃən] *n* : cojín *m* — ~ *vt* : amortiguar
custard ['kʌstərd] *n* : natillas *fpl*
custody ['kʌstədi] *n, pl* **-dies 1** : custodia *f* **2 be in ~** : estar detenido — **custodian** [ˌkʌ'sto:diən] *n* : custodio *m*, -dia *f*; guardián, -diana *f*
custom ['kʌstəm] *n* : costumbre *f* — **customary** ['kʌstəˌmɛri] *adj* : habitual, acostumbrado — **customer** ['kʌstəmər] *n* : cliente *m*, -ta *f* — **customs** ['kʌstəmz] *npl* : aduana *f*
cut ['kʌt] *v* **cut; cutting** *vt* **1** : cortar **2** REDUCE : reducir, rebajar **3 ~ oneself** : cortarse **4 ~ up** : cortar en pedazos — *vi* **1** : cortar **2 ~ in** : interrumpir — ~ *n* **1** : corte *m* **2** REDUCTION : rebaja *f*, reducción *f*
cute ['kju:t] *adj* **cuter; -est** : mono *fam*, lindo
cutlery ['kʌtləri] *n* : cubiertos *mpl*
cutlet ['kʌtlət] *n* : chuleta *f*
cutting ['kʌṭɪŋ] *adj* : cortante, mordaz
cyanide ['saɪəˌnaɪd, -nɪd] *n* : cianuro *m*
cycle ['saɪkəl] *n* **1** : ciclo *m* **2** BICYCLE : bicicleta *f* — ~ *vi* **-cled; -cling** : ir en bicicleta — **cyclic** ['saɪklɪk, 'sɪ-] *or* **cyclical** [-klɪkəl] *adj* : cíclico — **cyclist** ['saɪklɪst] *n* : ciclista *mf*
cyclone ['saɪˌklo:n] *n* : ciclón *m*
cylinder ['sɪləndər] *n* : cilindro *m* — **cylindrical** [sə'lɪndrɪkəl] *adj* : cilíndrico
cymbal ['sɪmbəl] *n* : platillo *m*, címbalo *m*
cynic ['sɪnɪk] *n* : cínico *m*, -ca *f* — **cynical** ['sɪnɪkəl] *adj* : cínico — **cynicism** ['sɪnəˌsɪzəm] *n* : cinismo *m*
cypress ['saɪprəs] *n* : ciprés *m*
cyst ['sɪst] *n* : quiste *m*
czar ['zɑr, 'sɑr] *n* : zar *m*
Czech ['tʃɛk] *adj* : checo — ~ *n* : checo *m* (idioma)

D

d ['di:] *n, pl* **d's** *or* **ds** ['di:z] : d *f*, cuarta letra del alfabeto inglés
dab ['dæb] *n* : toque *m* — ~ *vt* **dabbed; dabbing** : dar toques ligeros a, aplicar suavemente
dabble ['dæbəl] *vi* **-bled; -bling ~ in** : interesarse superficialmente en — **dabbler** *n* : aficionado *m*, -da *f*
dad ['dæd] *n* : papá *m fam* — **daddy** ['dædi] *n, pl* **-dies** : papá *m fam*
daffodil ['dæfəˌdɪl] *n* : narciso *m*
dagger ['dægər] *n* : daga *f*, puñal *m*
daily ['deɪli] *adj* : diario — ~ *adv* : diariamente
dainty ['deɪnti] *adj* **-tier; -est** : delicado
dairy ['dæri] *n, pl* **-ies 1** : lechería *f* (tienda) **2** *or* **~ farm** : granja *f* lechera
daisy ['deɪzi] *n, pl* **-sies** : margarita *f*
dam ['dæm] *n* : presa *f* — ~ *vt* **dammed; damming** : represar
damage ['dæmɪdʒ] *n* **1** : daño *m*, perjuicio *m* **2 ~s** *npl* : daños y perjuicios *mpl* — ~ *vt* **-aged; -aging** : dañar
damn ['dæm] *vt* **1** CONDEMN : condenar **2** CURSE : maldecir — ~ *n* **not give a ~** : no importarse un comino *fam* — ~ *or* **damned** ['dæmd] *adj* : maldito *fam*
damp ['dæmp] *adj* : húmedo — **dampen** ['dæmpən] *vt* **1** MOISTEN : humedecer **2** DISCOURAGE : desalentar, desanimar — **dampness** ['dæmpnəs] *n* : humedad *f*
dance ['dænts] *v* **danced; dancing** : bailar — ~ *n* : baile *m* — **dancer** ['dæntsər] *n* : bailarín *m*, -rina *f*
dandelion ['dændəlˌaɪən] *n* : diente *m* de león
dandruff ['dændrəf] *n* : caspa *f*
dandy ['dændi] *adj* **-dier; -est** : de primera, excelente
danger ['deɪndʒər] *n* : peligro *m* — **dangerous** ['deɪndʒərəs] *adj* : peligroso
dangle ['dæŋgəl] *v* **-gled; -gling** *vi* HANG : colgar, pender — *vt* : hacer oscilar
Danish ['deɪnɪʃ] *adj* : danés — ~ *n* : danés *m* (idioma)
dank ['dæŋk] *adj* : frío y húmedo
dare ['dær] *v* **dared; daring** *vt* : desafiar — *vi* : osar — ~ *n* : desafío *m* — **daredevil** ['dærˌdɛvəl] *n* : persona *f* temeraria — **daring** ['dærɪŋ] *adj* : atrevido, audaz — ~ *n* : audacia *f*
dark ['dɑrk] *adj* **1** : oscuro **2** : moreno (dícese del pelo o de la piel) **3** GLOOMY : sombrío **4 get ~** : hacerse de noche — **darken** ['dɑrkən] *vt* : oscurecer — *vi* : oscurecerse — **darkness** ['dɑrknəs] *n* : oscuridad *f*

darling ['dɑrlɪŋ] *n* BELOVED : querido *m*, -da *f* — ~ *adj* : querido
darn ['dɑrn] *vt* : zurcir — ~ *adj* : maldito *fam*
dart ['dɑrt] *n* **1** : dardo *m* **2** ~**s** *npl* : juego *m* de dardos — ~ *vi* : precipitarse
dash ['dæʃ] *vt* **1** SMASH : romper **2** HURL : lanzar **3** ~ **off** : hacer (algo) rápidamente — *vi* : lanzarse, irse corriendo — ~ *n* **1** : guión *m* largo (signo de puntuación) **2** PINCH : poquito *m*, pizca *f* **3** RACE : carrera *f* — **dashboard** ['dæʃˌbord] *n* : tablero *m* de instrumentos — **dashing** ['dæʃɪŋ] *adj* : gallardo, apuesto
data ['deɪṭə, 'dæ-, 'dɑ-] *ns & pl* : datos *mpl* — **database** ['deɪṭəˌbeɪs, 'dæ-, 'dɑ-] *n* : base *f* de datos
date[1] ['deɪt] *n* : dátil *m* (fruta)
date[2] *n* **1** : fecha *f* **2** APPOINTMENT : cita *f* — ~ *v* **dated; dating** *vt* **1** : fechar (una carta, etc.) **2** : salir con (algn) — *vi* ~ **from** : datar de — **dated** ['deɪṭəd] *adj* : pasado de moda
daub ['dɔb] *vt* : embadurnar
daughter ['dɔṭər] *n* : hija *f* — **daughter–in–law** ['dɔṭərɪnˌlɔ] *n, pl* **daughters–in–law** : nuera *f*
daunt ['dɔnt] *vt* : intimidar
dawdle ['dɔdəl] *vi* **-dled; -dling** : entretenerse, perder tiempo
dawn ['dɔn] *vi* **1** : amanecer **2 it** ~**ed on him that** : cayó en la cuenta de que — ~ *n* : amanecer *m*
day ['deɪ] *n* **1** : día *m* **2** *or* **working** ~ : jornada *f* **3 the** ~ **before** : el día anterior **4 the** ~ **before yesterday** : anteayer **5 the** ~ **after** : el día siguiente **6 the** ~ **after tomorrow** : pasada mañana — **daybreak** ['deɪˌbreɪk] *n* : amanecer *m* — **daydream** ['deɪˌdri:m] *n* : ensueño *m* — ~ *vi* : soñar despierto — **daylight** ['deɪˌlaɪt] *n* : luz *f* del día — **daytime** ['deɪˌtaɪm] *n* : día *m*
daze ['deɪz] *vt* **dazed; dazing** : aturdir — ~ *n* **in a** ~ : aturdido
dazzle ['dæzəl] *vt* **-zled; -zling** : deslumbrar
dead ['dɛd] *adj* **1** LIFELESS : muerto **2** NUMB : entumecido — ~ *n* **1 in the** ~ **of night** : en plena noche **2 the** ~ : los muertos — ~ *adv* ABSOLUTELY : absolutamente — **deaden** ['dɛdən] *vt* **1** : atenuar (dolores) **2** MUFFLE : amortiguar — **dead end** ['dɛd'ɛnd] *n* : callejón *m* sin salida — **deadline** ['dɛdˌlaɪn] *n* : fecha *f* límite — **deadlock** ['dɛdˌlɑk] *n* : punto *m* muerto — **deadly** ['dɛdli] *adj* **-lier; -est 1** : mortal, letal **2** ACCURATE : certero, preciso
deaf ['dɛf] *adj* : sordo — **deafen** ['dɛfən] *vt* : ensordecer — **deafness** ['dɛfnəs] *n* : sordera *f*
deal ['di:l] *n* **1** TRANSACTION : trato *m*, transacción *f* **2** : reparto *m* (de naipes) **3 a good** ~ : mucho — ~ *v* **dealt; dealing** *vt* **1** : dar **2** : repartir, dar (naipes) **3** ~ **a blow** : asestar un golpe — *vi* **1** : dar, repartir (en juegos de naipes) **2** ~ **in** : comerciar en **3** ~ **with** CONCERN : tratar de **4** ~ **with s.o.** : tratar con algn — **dealer** ['di:lər] *n* : comerciante *mf* — **dealings** *npl* : trato *m*, relaciones *fpl*
dean ['di:n] *n* : decano *m*, -na *f*
dear ['dɪr] *adj* : querido — ~ *n* : querido *m*, -da *f* — **dearly** ['dɪrli] *adv* **1** : mucho **2 pay** ~ : pagar caro
death ['dɛθ] *n* : muerte *f*
debar [di'bɑr] *vt* : excluir
debate [di'beɪt] *n* : debate *m*, discusión *f* — ~ *vt* **-bated; -bating** : debatir, discutir
debit ['dɛbɪt] *vt* : adeudar, cargar — ~ *n* : débito *m*, debe *m*
debris [də'bri:, deɪ-; 'deɪˌbri:] *n, pl* **-bris** [-'bri:z, -ˌbri:z] : escombros *mpl*
debt ['dɛt] *n* : deuda *f* — **debtor** ['dɛṭər] *n* : deudor *m*, -dora *f*
debunk [di'bʌŋk] *vt* : desmentir
debut [deɪ'bju:, 'deɪˌbju:] *n* : debut *m* — ~ *vi* : debutar
decade ['dɛˌkeɪd, dɛ'keɪd] *n* : década *f*
decadence ['dɛkədənts] *n* : decadencia *f* — **decadent** ['dɛkədənt] *adj* : decadente
decal ['di:ˌkæl, di'kæl] *n* : calcomanía *f*
decanter [di'kæntər] *n* : licorera *f*
decapitate [di'kæpəˌteɪt] *vt* **-tated; -tating** : decapitar
decay [di'keɪ] *vi* **1** DECOMPOSE : descomponerse **2** DETERIORATE : deteriorarse **3** : cariarse (dícese de los dientes) — ~ *n* **1** : descomposición *f* **2** : deterioro *m* (de un edificio, etc.) **3** : caries *f* (de los dientes)
deceased [di'si:st] *adj* : difunto — ~ *n* **the** ~ : el difunto, la difunta
deceive [di'si:v] *vt* **-ceived; -ceiving** : engañar — **deceit** [di'si:t] *n* : engaño *m* — **deceitful** [di'si:tfəl] *adj* : engañoso
December [di'sɛmbər] *n* : diciembre *m*
decent ['di:sənt] *adj* **1** : decente **2** KIND : bueno, amable — **decency** ['disəntsi] *n, pl* **-cies** : decencia *f*
deception [di'sɛpʃən] *n* : engaño *m* — **deceptive** [di'sɛptɪv] *adj* : engañoso

decide [dɪ'saɪd] *v* **-cided; -ciding** *vt* : decidir — *vi* : decidirse — **decided** [dɪ'saɪdəd] *adj* **1** UNQUESTIONABLE : indudable **2** RESOLUTE : decidido — **decidedly** [dɪ'saɪdədli] *adv* **1** DEFINITELY : decididamente **2** RESOLUTELY : con decisión

decimal ['dɛsəməl] *adj* : decimal — ~ *n* : número *m* decimal — **decimal point** *n* : coma *f* decimal

decipher [dɪ'saɪfər] *vt* : descifrar

decision [dɪ'sɪʒən] *n* : decisión *f* — **decisive** [dɪ'saɪsɪv] *adj* **1** RESOLUTE : decidido **2** CONCLUSIVE : decisivo

deck ['dɛk] *n* **1** : cubierta *f* (de un barco) **2** *or* ~ **of cards** : baraja *f* (de naipes) **3** TERRACE : entarimado *m*

declare [dɪ'klær] *vt* **-clared; -claring** : declarar — **declaration** [ˌdɛklə'reɪʃən] *n* : declaración *f*

decline [dɪ'klaɪn] *v* **-clined; -clining** *vt* REFUSE : declinar, rehusar — *vi* DECREASE : disminuir — ~ *n* **1** DETERIORATION : decadencia *f*, deterioro *m* **2** DECREASE : disminución *f*

decode [dɪ'koːd] *vt* **-coded; -coding** : descodificar

decompose [ˌdiːkəm'poːz] *vt* **-posed; -posing** : descomponer — *vi* : descomponerse

decongestant [ˌdiːkən'dʒɛstənt] *n* : descongestionante *m*

decorate ['dɛkəˌreɪt] *vt* **-rated; -rating** : decorar — **decor** *or* **décor** [deɪ'kɔr, 'deɪˌkɔr] *n* : decoración *f* — **decoration** [ˌdɛkə'reɪʃən] *n* : decoración *f* — **decorator** ['dɛkəˌreɪt̬ər] *n* : decorador *m*, -dora *f*

decoy ['diːˌkɔɪ, dɪ'-] *n* : señuelo *m*

decrease [dɪ'kriːs] *v* **-creased; -creasing** : disminuir — ~ ['diːˌkriːs] *n* : disminución *f*

decree [dɪ'kriː] *n* : decreto *m* — ~ *vt* **-creed; -creeing** : decretar

decrepit [dɪ'krɛpɪt] *adj* **1** FEEBLE : decrépito **2** DILAPIDATED : ruinoso

dedicate ['dɛdɪˌkeɪt] *vt* **-cated; -cating 1** : dedicar **2** ~ **oneself to** : consagrarse a — **dedication** [ˌdɛdɪ'keɪʃən] *n* **1** DEVOTION : dedicación *f* **2** INSCRIPTION : dedicatoria *f*

deduce [dɪ'duːs, -'djuːs] *vt* **-duced; -ducing** : deducir — **deduct** [dɪ'dʌkt] *vt* : deducir — **deduction** [dɪ'dʌkʃən] *n* : deducción *f*

deed ['diːd] *n* : acción *f*, hecho *m*

deem ['diːm] *vt* : considerar, juzgar

deep ['diːp] *adj* : hondo, profundo — ~ *adv* **1** DEEPLY : profundamente **2** ~ **down** : en el fondo **3 dig** ~ : cavar hondo — **deepen** ['diːpən] *vt* : ahondar — *vi* : hacerse más profundo — **deeply** ['diːpli] *adv* : hondo, profundamente

deer ['dɪr] *ns & pl* : ciervo *m*

deface [dɪ'feɪs] *vt* **-faced; -facing** : desfigurar

default [dɪ'fɔlt, 'diːˌfɔlt] *n* **by** ~ : en rebeldía — ~ *vi* **1** ~ **on** : no pagar (una deuda) **2** : no presentarse (en deportes)

defeat [dɪ'fiːt] *vt* **1** BEAT : vencer, derrotar **2** FRUSTRATE : frustrar — ~ *n* : derrota *f*

defect ['diːˌfɛkt, dɪ'fɛkt] *n* : defecto *m* — ~ [dɪ'fɛkt] *vi* : desertar — **defective** [dɪ'fɛktɪv] *adj* : defectuoso

defend [dɪ'fɛnd] *vt* : defender — **defendant** [dɪ'fɛndənt] *n* : acusado *m*, -da *f* — **defense** *or Brit* **defence** [dɪ'fɛnts, 'diːˌfɛnts] *n* : defensa *f* — **defenseless** *or Brit* **defenceless** *adj* : indefenso — **defensive** [dɪ'fɛntsɪv] *adj* : defensivo — ~ *n* **on the** ~ : a la defensiva

defer [dɪ'fər] *v* **-ferred; -ferring** *vt* : diferir, aplazar — *vi* ~ **to** : deferir a — **deference** ['dɛfərənts] *n* : deferencia *f* — **deferential** [ˌdɛfə'rɛntʃəl] *adj* : deferente

defiance [dɪ'faɪənts] *n* **1** : desafío *m* **2 in** ~ **of** : a despecho de — **defiant** [dɪ'faɪənt] *adj* : desafiante

deficiency [dɪ'fɪʃəntsi] *n, pl* **-cies** : deficiencia *f* — **deficient** [dɪ'fɪʃənt] *adj* : deficiente

deficit ['dɛfəsɪt] *n* : déficit *m*

defile [dɪ'faɪl] *vt* **-filed; -filing 1** DIRTY : ensuciar **2** DESECRATE : profanar

define [dɪ'faɪn] *vt* **-fined; -fining** : definir — **definite** ['dɛfənɪt] *adj* **1** : definido **2** CERTAIN : seguro, incuestionable — **definition** [ˌdɛfə'nɪʃən] *n* : definición *f* — **definitive** [dɪ'fɪnət̬ɪv] *adj* : definitivo

deflate [dɪ'fleɪt] *v* **-flated; -flating** *vt* : desinflar (una llanta, etc.) — *vi* : desinflarse

deflect [dɪ'flɛkt] *vt* : desviar — *vi* : desviarse

deform [dɪ'fɔrm] *vt* : deformar — **deformity** [dɪ'fɔrmət̬i] *n, pl* **-ties** : deformidad *f*

defraud [dɪ'frɔd] *vt* : defraudar

defrost [dɪ'frɔst] *vt* : descongelar — *vi* : descongelarse

deft ['dɛft] *adj* : hábil, diestro

defy [dɪ'faɪ] *vt* **-fied; -fying 1** CHALLENGE : desafiar **2** RESIST : resistir

degenerate [dɪ'dʒɛnəˌreɪt] *vi* : degenerar — ~ [dɪ'dʒɛnərət] *adj* : degenerado

degrade [di'greɪd] *vt* **-graded; -grading** : degradar — **degrading** *adj* : degradante
degree [di'gri:] *n* **1** : grado *m* **2** *or* **academic ~** : título *m*
dehydrate [di'haɪˌdreɪt] *vt* **-drated; -drating** : deshidratar
deign ['deɪn] *vi* **~ to** : dignarse (a)
deity ['di:əţi, 'deɪ-] *n, pl* **-ties** : deidad *f*
dejected [di'dʒɛktəd] *adj* : abatido — **dejection** [di'dʒɛkʃən] *n* : abatimiento *m*
delay [di'leɪ] *n* : retraso *m* — **~** *vt* **1** POSTPONE : aplazar **2** HOLD UP : retrasar — *vi* : demorar
delectable [di'lɛktəbəl] *adj* : delicioso
delegate ['dɛlɪgət, -ˌgeɪt] *n* : delegado *m*, -da *f* — **~** ['dɛlɪˌgeɪt] *v* **-gated; -gating** : delegar — **delegation** [ˌdɛlɪ'geɪʃən] *n* : delegación *f*
delete [di'li:t] *vt* **-leted; -leting** : borrar
deliberate [dɪ'lɪbəˌreɪt] *v* **-ated; -ating** *vt* : deliberar sobre — *vi* : deliberar — **~** [dɪ'lɪbərət] *adj* : deliberado — **deliberately** [dɪ'lɪbərətli] *adv* INTENTIONALLY : a propósito — **deliberation** [dɪˌlɪbə'reɪʃən] *n* : deliberación *f*
delicacy ['dɛlɪkəsi] *n, pl* **-cies 1** : delicadeza *f* **2** FOOD : manjar *m*, exquisitez *f* — **delicate** ['dɛlɪkət] *adj* : delicado
delicatessen [ˌdɛlɪkə'tɛsən] *n* : charcutería *f*
delicious [di'lɪʃəs] *adj* : delicioso
delight [dɪ'laɪt] *n* : placer *m*, deleite *m* — **~** *vt* : deleitar, encantar — *vi* **~ in** : deleitarse con — **delightful** [dɪ'laɪtfəl] *adj* : delicioso, encantador
delinquent [di'lɪŋkwənt] *adj* : delincuente — **~** *n* : delincuente *mf*
delirious [di'lɪriəs] *adj* : delirante — **delirium** [di'lɪriəm] *n* : delirio *m*
deliver [di'lɪvər] *vt* **1** DISTRIBUTE : entregar, repartir **2** FREE : liberar **3** : asistir en el parto de (un niño) **4** : pronunciar (un discurso, etc.) **5** DEAL : asestar (un golpe, etc.) — **delivery** [di'lɪvəri] *n, pl* **-eries 1** DISTRIBUTION : entrega *f*, reparto *m* **2** LIBERATION : liberación *f* **3** CHILDBIRTH : parto *m*, alumbramiento *m*
delude [di'lu:d] *vt* **-luded; -luding 1** : engañar **2 ~ oneself** : engañarse
deluge ['dɛlˌju:dʒ, -ju:ʒ] *n* : diluvio *m*
delusion [di'lu:ʒən] *n* : ilusión *f*
deluxe [di'lʌks, -'lʊks] *adj* : de lujo
delve ['dɛlv] *vi* **delved; delving 1** : escarbar **2 ~ into** PROBE : investigar
demand [di'mænd] *n* **1** REQUEST : petición *f* **2** CLAIM : reclamación *f*, exigencia *f* **3** → **supply** — **~** *vt* : exigir — **demanding** *adj* : exigente
demean [di'mi:n] *vt* **~ oneself** : rebajarse
demeanor [di'mi:nər] *n* : comportamiento *m*
demented [di'mɛntəd] *adj* : demente, loco
demise [dɪ'maɪz] *n* : fallecimiento *m*
democracy [di'mɑkrəsi] *n, pl* **-cies** : democracia *f* — **democrat** ['dɛməˌkræt] *n* : demócrata *mf* — **democratic** [ˌdɛmə'kræţɪk] *adj* : democrático
demolish [di'mɑlɪʃ] *vt* : demoler — **demolition** [ˌdɛmə'lɪʃən, ˌdi:-] *n* : demolición *f*
demon ['di:mən] *n* : demonio *m*
demonstrate ['dɛmənˌstreɪt] *v* **-strated; -strating** *vt* : demostrar — *vi* RALLY : manifestarse — **demonstration** [ˌdɛmən'streɪʃən] *n* **1** : demostración *f* **2** RALLY : manifestación *f*
demoralize [di'mɔrəˌlaɪz] *vt* **-ized; -izing** : desmoralizar
demote [di'mo:t] *vt* **-moted; -moting** : bajar de categoría
demure [di'mjʊr] *adj* : recatado
den ['dɛn] *n* LAIR : guarida *f*
denial [di'naɪəl] *n* **1** : negación *f*, rechazo *m* **2** REFUSAL : denegación *f*
denim ['dɛnəm] *n* : tela *f* vaquera, mezclilla *f Lat*
denomination [dɪˌnɑmə'neɪʃən] *n* **1** : confesión *f* (religiosa) **2** : valor *m* (de una moneda)
denounce [di'naʊnts] *vt* **-nounced; -nouncing** : denunciar
dense ['dɛnts] *adj* **denser; -est 1** THICK : denso **2** STUPID : estúpido — **density** ['dɛntsəţi] *n, pl* **-ties** : densidad *f*
dent ['dɛnt] *vt* : abollar — **~** *n* : abolladura *f*
dental ['dɛntəl] *adj* : dental — **dental floss** *n* : hilo *m* dental — **dentist** ['dɛntɪst] *n* : dentista *mf* — **dentures** ['dɛntʃərz] *npl* : dentadura *f* postiza
deny [di'naɪ] *vt* **-nied; -nying 1** : negar **2** REFUSE : denegar
deodorant [di'o:dərənt] *n* : desodorante *m*
depart [di'pɑrt] *vi* **1** : salir **2 ~ from** : apartarse de (la verdad, etc.)
department [di'pɑrtmənt] *n* : sección *f* (de una tienda, etc.), departamento *m* (de una empresa, etc.), ministerio *m* (del gobierno) — **department store** *n* : grandes almacenes *mpl*
departure [di'pɑrtʃər] *n* **1** : salida *f* **2** DEVIATION : desviación *f*
depend [di'pɛnd] *vi* **1 ~ on** : depender

de **2 ~ on s.o.** : contar con algn **3 that ~s** : eso depende — **dependable** [di'pɛndəbəl] *adj* : digno de confianza — **dependence** [di'pɛndənts] *n* : dependencia *f* — **dependent** [di'pɛndənt] *adj* : dependiente
depict [di'pɪkt] *vt* **1** PORTRAY : representar **2** DESCRIBE : describir
deplete [di'pli:t] *vt* **-pleted; -pleting** : agotar, reducir
deplore [di'plor] *vt* **-plored; -ploring** : deplorar, lamentar — **deplorable** [di'plorəbəl] *adj* : lamentable
deploy [di'plɔɪ] *vt* : desplegar
deport [di'port] *vt* : deportar, expulsar (de un país) — **deportation** [ˌdiˌpor'teɪʃən] *n* : deportación *f*
depose [di'po:z] *vt* **-posed; -posing** : deponer
deposit [di'pɑzət] *vt* **-ited; -iting** : depositar — **~** *n* **1** : depósito *m* **2** DOWN PAYMENT : entrega *f* inicial
depot [*in sense 1 usu* 'dɛˌpo:, *2 usu* 'di:-] *n* **1** WAREHOUSE : almacén *m*, depósito *m* **2** STATION : terminal *mf*
depreciate [di'pri:ʃiˌeɪt] *vi* **-ated; -ating** : depreciarse — **depreciation** [diˌpri:ʃi'eɪʃən] *n* : depreciación *f*
depress [di'prɛs] *vt* **1** : deprimir **2** PRESS : apretar — **depressed** [di'prɛst] *adj* : abatido, deprimido — **depressing** [di'prɛsɪŋ] *adj* : deprimente — **depression** [di'prɛʃən] *n* : depresión *f*
deprive [di'praɪv] *vt* **-prived; -priving** : privar
depth ['dɛpθ] *n, pl* **depths** ['dɛpθs, 'dɛps] **1** : profundidad *f* **2 in the ~s of night** : en lo más profundo de la noche
deputy ['dɛpjuṭi] *n, pl* **-ties** : suplente *mf;* sustituto *m*, -ta *f*
derail [di'reɪl] *vt* : hacer descarrilar
deranged [di'reɪndʒd] *adj* : trastornado
derelict ['dɛrəˌlɪkt] *adj* : abandonado
deride [di'raɪd] *vt* **-rided; -riding** : burlarse de — **derision** [di'rɪʒən] *n* : mofa *f*
derive [di'raɪv] *vi* **-rived; -riving** : derivar — **derivation** [ˌdɛrə'veɪʃən] *n* : derivación *f*
derogatory [di'rɑgəˌtori] *adj* : despectivo
descend [di'sɛnd] *v* : descender, bajar — **descendant** [di'sɛndənt] *n* : descendiente *mf* —**descent** [di'sɛnt] *n* **1** : descenso *m* **2** LINEAGE : descendencia *f*
describe [di'skraɪb] *vt* **-scribed; -scribing** : describir — **description** [di'skrɪpʃən] *n* : descripción *f* — **descriptive** [di'skrɪptɪv] *adj* : descriptivo
desecrate ['dɛsɪˌkreɪt] *vt* **-crated; -crating** : profanar
desert ['dɛzərt] *n* : desierto *m* — **~** *adj* **~ island** : isla *f* desierta — **~** [di'zərt] *vt* : abandonar — *vi* : desertar — **deserter** [di'zərṭər] *n* : desertor *m*, -tora *f*
deserve [di'zərv] *vt* **-served; -serving** : merecer
design [di'zaɪn] *vt* **1** DEVISE : diseñar **2** PLAN : proyectar — **~** *n* **1** : diseño *m* **2** PLAN : plan *m*, proyecto *m*
designate ['dɛzɪgˌneɪt] *vt* **-nated; -nating** : nombrar, designar
designer [di'zaɪnər] *n* : diseñador *m*, -dora *f*
desire [di'zaɪr] *vt* **-sired; -siring** : desear — **~** *n* : deseo *m* — **desirable** [di'zaɪrəbəl] *adj* : deseable
desk ['dɛsk] *n* : escritorio *m*, pupitre *m* (en la escuela)
desolate ['dɛsələt, -zə-] *adj* : desolado
despair [di'spær] *vi* : desesperar — **~** *n* : desesperación *f*
desperate ['dɛspərət] *adj* : desesperado — **desperation** [ˌdɛspə'reɪʃən] *n* : desesperación *f*
despise [di'spaɪz] *vt* **-spised; -spising** : despreciar — **despicable** [di'spɪkəbəl, 'dɛspɪ-] *adj* : despreciable
despite [də'spaɪt] *prep* : a pesar de
despondent [di'spɑndənt] *adj* : desanimado
dessert [di'zərt] *n* : postre *m*
destination [ˌdɛstə'neɪʃən] *n* : destino *m* — **destined** ['dɛstənd] *adj* **1** : destinado **2 ~ for** : con destino a — **destiny** ['dɛstəni] *n, pl* **-nies** : destino *m*
destitute ['dɛstəˌtu:t, -ˌtju:t] *adj* : indigente
destroy [di'strɔɪ] *vt* : destruir — **destruction** [di'strʌkʃən] *n* : destrucción *f* — **destructive** [di'strʌktɪv] *adj* : destructivo
detach [di'tætʃ] *vt* : separar — **detached** [di'tætʃt] *adj* **1** : separado **2** IMPARTIAL : objetivo
detail [di'teɪl, 'di:ˌteɪl] *n* **1** : detalle *m* **2 go into ~** : entrar en detalles — **~** *vt* : detallar — **detailed** *adj* : detallado
detain [di'teɪn] *vt* **1** : detener (un prisionero) **2** DELAY : entretener
detect [di'tɛkt] *vt* : detectar — **detection** [di'tɛkʃən] *n* : detección *f*, descubrimiento *m* — **detective** [di'tɛktɪv] *n* : detective *mf*
detention [di'tɛntʃən] *n* : detención *m*
deter [di'tər] *vt* **-terred; -terring** : disuadir
detergent [di'tərdʒənt] *n* : detergente *m*

deteriorate [di'tɪriə,reɪt] *vi* **-rated; -rating** : deteriorarse — **deterioration** [di,tɪriə'reɪʃən] *n* : deterioro *m*
determine [di'tərmən] *vt* **-mined; -mining** : determinar — **determined** [di'tərmənd] *adj* RESOLUTE : decidido — **determination** [dɪ,tərmə'neɪʃən] *n* : determinación *f*
deterrent [di'tərənt] *n* : medida *f* disuasiva
detest [di'tɛst] *vt* : detestar — **detestable** [di'tɛstəbəl] *adj* : odioso
detonate ['dɛtən,eɪt] *v* **-nated; -nating** *vt* : hacer detonar — *vi* EXPLODE : detonar, estallar — **detonation** [,dɛtə'neɪʃən, 'dɛtə,-] *n* : detonación *f*
detour ['di:,tʊr, di'tʊr] *n* **1** : desviación *f* **2 make a ~** : dar un rodeo — **~** *vi* : desviarse
detract [di'trækt] *vi* **~ from** : aminorar, restar importancia a
detrimental [,dɛtrə'mɛntəl] *adj* : perjudicial
devalue [di'væl,ju:] *vt* **-ued; -uing** : devaluar
devastate ['dɛvə,steɪt] *vt* **-tated; -tating** : devastar — **devastating** *adj* : devastador — **devastation** [,dɛvə'steɪʃən] *n* : devastación *f*
develop [di'vɛləp] *vt* **1** : desarrollar **2 ~ an illness** : contraer una enfermedad — *vi* **1** GROW : desarrollarse **2** HAPPEN : aparecer — **development** [di'vɛləpmənt] *n* : desarrollo *m*
deviate ['di:vi,eɪt] *v* **-ated; -ating** *vi* : desviarse — **deviation** [,di:vi'eɪʃən] *n* : desviación *f*
device [di'vaɪs] *n* : dispositivo *m*, mecanismo *m*
devil ['dɛvəl] *n* : diablo *m*, demonio *m* — **devilish** ['dɛvəlɪʃ] *adj* : diabólico
devious ['di:viəs] *adj* **1** CRAFTY : taimado **2** WINDING : tortuoso
devise [di'vaɪz] *vt* **-vised; -vising** : idear, concebir
devoid [di'vɔɪd] *adj* **~ of** : desprovisto de
devote [di'vo:t] *vt* **-voted; -voting** : consagrar, dedicar — **devoted** [di'vo:t̬əd] *adj* : leal — **devotee** [,dɛvə'ti:, -'teɪ] *n* : devoto *m*, -ta *f* — **devotion** [di'vo:ʃən] *n* **1** : devoción *f*, dedicación *f* **2** : oración *f* (en religión)
devour [di'vaʊər] *vt* : devorar
devout [di'vaʊt] *adj* : devoto
dew ['du:, 'dju:] *n* : rocío *m*
dexterity [dɛk'stɛrət̬i] *n, pl* **-ties** : destreza *f*
diabetes [,daɪə'bi:t̬iz] *n* : diabetes *f* — **diabetic** [,daɪə'bɛt̬ɪk] *adj* : diabético — **~** *n* : diabético *m*, -ca *f*
diabolic [,daɪə'bɑlɪk] *or* **diabolical** [-lɪkəl] *adj* : diabólico
diagnosis [,daɪɪg'no:sɪs] *n, pl* **-noses** [-'no:,si:z] : diagnóstico *m* — **diagnose** ['daɪɪg,no:s, ,daɪɪg'no:s] *vt* **-nosed; -nosing** : diagnosticar — **diagnostic** [,daɪɪg'nɑstɪk] *adj* : diagnóstico
diagonal [daɪ'ægənəl] *adj* : diagonal, en diagonal — **~** *n* : diagonal *f*
diagram ['daɪə,græm] *n* : diagrama *m*
dial ['daɪl] *n* : esfera *f* (de un reloj), dial *m* (de un radio, etc.) — **~** *v* **dialed** *or* **dialled; dialing** *or* **dialling** : marcar
dialect ['daɪə,lɛkt] *n* : dialecto *m*
dialogue ['daɪə ,lɔg] *n* : diálogo *m*
diameter [daɪ'æmət̬ər] *n* : diámetro *m*
diamond ['daɪmənd, 'daɪə-] *n* **1** : diamante *m* **2** : rombo *m* (forma) **3** *or* **baseball ~** : cuadro *m*, diamante *m*
diaper ['daɪpər, 'daɪə-] *n* : pañal *m*
diaphragm ['daɪə,fræm] *n* : diafragma *m*
diarrhea [,daɪə'ri:ə] *n* : diarrea *f*
diary ['daɪəri] *n, pl* **-ries**: diario *m*
dice ['daɪs] *ns & pl* : dados *mpl* (juego)
dictate ['dɪk,teɪt, dɪk'teɪt] *vt* **-tated; -tating** : dictar — **dictation** [dɪk'teɪʃən] *n* : dictado *m* — **dictator** ['dɪk,teɪt̬ər] *n* : dictador *m*, -dora *f* — **dictatorship** [dɪk'teɪt̬ər,ʃɪp, 'dɪk,-] *n* : dictadura *f*
dictionary ['dɪkʃə,nɛri] *n, pl* **-naries** : diccionario *m*
did → **do**
die[1] ['daɪ] *vi* **died** ['daɪd]; **dying** ['daɪɪŋ] **1** : morir **2 ~ down** : amainar, disminuir **3 ~ out** : extinguirse **4 be dying for** : morirse por
die[2] ['daɪ] *n* **1** *pl* **dice** ['daɪs] : dado *m* (para jugar) **2** *pl* **dies** ['daɪz] MOLD : molde *m*
diesel ['di:zəl, -səl] *n* : diesel *m*
diet ['daɪət] *n* **1** FOOD : alimentación *f* **2 go on a ~** : ponerse a régimen — **~** *vi* : estar a régimen
differ ['dɪfər] *vi* **-ferred; -ferring 1** : diferir, ser distinto **2** DISAGREE : no estar de acuerdo — **difference** ['dɪfrənts, 'dɪfərənts] *n* : diferencia *f* — **different** ['dɪfrənt, 'dɪfərənt] *adj* : distinto, diferente — **differentiate** [,dɪfə'rɛntʃi,eɪt] *v* **-ated; -ating** *vt* : diferenciar — *vi* : distinguir — **differently** ['dɪfrəntli, 'dɪfərənt-] *adv* : de otra manera
difficult ['dɪfɪ,kʌlt] *adj* : difícil — **difficulty** ['dɪfɪ,kʌlti] *n, pl* **-ties** : dificultad *f*
diffident ['dɪfədənt] *adj* : tímido, que falta confianza

dig ['dɪg] *v* **dug** ['dʌg]; **digging** *vt* **1** : cavar **2** ~ **up** : desenterrar — *vi* : cavar — ~ *n* **1** GIBE : pulla *f* **2** EXCAVATION : excavación *f*

digest ['daɪ,dʒɛst] *n* : resumen *m* — ~ [daɪ'dʒɛst] *vt* **1** : digerir **2** SUMMARIZE : resumir — **digestible** [daɪ'dʒɛstəbəl, dɪ-] *adj* : digerible — **digestion** [daɪ'dʒɛstʃən, dɪ-] *n* : digestión *f* — **digestive** [daɪ'dʒɛstɪv, dɪ-] *adj* : digestivo

digit ['dɪdʒət] *n* **1** NUMERAL : dígito *m*, número *m* **2** FINGER, TOE : dedo *m* — **digital** ['dɪdʒət̬əl] *adj* : digital

dignity ['dɪgnət̬i] *n, pl* **-ties** : dignidad *f* — **dignified** ['dɪgnə,faɪd] *adj* : digno, decoroso

digress [daɪ'grɛs, də-] *vi* : desviarse del tema, divagar — **digression** [daɪ'grɛʃən, də-] *n* : digresión *f*

dike ['daɪk] *n* : dique *m*

dilapidated [də'læpə,deɪt̬əd] *adj* : ruinoso

dilate [daɪ'leɪt, 'daɪ,leɪt] *v* **-lated; -lating** *vt* : dilatar — *vi* : dilatarse

dilemma [dɪ'lɛmə] *n* : dilema *m*

diligence ['dɪlədʒənts] *n* : diligencia *f* — **diligent** ['dɪlədʒənt] *adj* : diligente

dilute [daɪ'lu:t, də-] *vt* **-luted; -luting** : diluir

dim ['dɪm] *v* **dimmed; dimming** *vt* : atenuar — *vi* : irse atenuando — ~ *adj* **dimmer; dimmest 1** DARK : oscuro **2** FAINT : débil, tenue

dime ['daɪm] *n* : moneda *f* de diez centavos

dimension [də'mɛntʃən, daɪ-] *n* : dimensión *f*

diminish [də'mɪnɪʃ] *v* : disminuir

diminutive [də'mɪnjut̬ɪv] *adj* : diminuto

dimple ['dɪmpəl] *n* : hoyuelo *m*

din ['dɪn] *n* : estrépito *m*

dine ['daɪn] *vi* **dined; dining** : cenar — **diner** ['daɪnər] *n* **1** : comensal *mf* (persona) **2** : cafetería *f* (restaurante)

dingy ['dɪndʒi] *adj* **-gier; -est** : sucio, deslucido

dinner ['dɪnər] *n* : cena *f*, comida *f*

dinosaur ['daɪnə,sɔr] *n* : dinosaurio *m*

dint ['dɪnt] *n* **by** ~ **of** : a fuerza de

dip ['dɪp] *v* **dipped; dipping** *vt* : mojar — *vi* : bajar, descender — ~ *n* **1** DROP : descenso *m*, caída *f* **2** SWIM : chapuzón *m* **3** SAUCE : salsa *f*

diploma [də'plo:mə] *n, pl* **-mas** : diploma *m*

diplomacy [də'plo:məsi] *n* : diplomacia *f* — **diplomat** ['dɪplə,mæt] *n* : diplomático *m*, -ca *f* — **diplomatic** [,dɪplə'mæt̬ɪk] *adj* : diplomático

dire ['daɪr] *adj* **direr; direst 1** : grave, terrible **2** EXTREME : extremo

direct [də'rɛkt, daɪ-] *vt* **1** : dirigir **2** ORDER : mandar — ~ *adj* **1** STRAIGHT : directo **2** FRANK : franco — ~ *adv* : directamente — **direct current** *n* : corriente *f* continua — **direction** [də'rɛkʃən, daɪ-] *n* **1** : dirección *f* **2 ask ~s** : pedir indicaciones — **directly** [də'rɛktli, daɪ-] *adv* **1** STRAIGHT : directamente **2** IMMEDIATELY : en seguida — **director** [də'rɛktər, daɪ-] *n* **1** : director *m*, -tora *f* **2 board of ~s** : directorio *m* — **directory** [də'rɛktəri, daɪ-] *n, pl* **-ries** : guía *f* (telefónica)

dirt ['dərt] *n* **1** : suciedad *f* **2** SOIL : tierra *f* — **dirty** ['dərt̬i] *adj* **dirtier; -est 1** : sucio **2** INDECENT : obsceno, cochino *fam*

disability [,dɪsə'bɪlət̬i] *n, pl* **-ties** : minusvalía *f*, invalidez *f* — **disable** [dɪs'eɪbəl] *vt* **-abled; -abling** : incapacitar — **disabled** [dɪs'eɪbəld] *adj* : minusválido

disadvantage [,dɪsəd'væntɪdʒ] *n* : desventaja *f*

disagree [,dɪsə'gri:] *vi* **1** : no estar de acuerdo (con algn) **2** CONFLICT : no coincidir — **disagreeable** [,dɪsə'gri:əbəl] *adj* : desagradable — **disagreement** [,dɪsə'gri:mənt] *n* **1** : desacuerdo *m* **2** ARGUMENT : discusión *f*

disappear [,dɪsə'pɪr] *vi* : desaparecer — **disappearance** [,dɪsə'pɪrənts] *n* : desaparición *f*

disappoint [,dɪsə'pɔɪnt] *vt* : decepcionar, desilusionar — **disappointment** [,dɪsə'pɔɪntmənt] *n* : decepción *f*, desilusión *f*

disapprove [,dɪsə'pru:v] *vi* **-proved; -proving** ~ **of** : desaprobar — **disapproval** [,dɪsə'pru:vəl] *n* : desaprobación *f*

disarm [dɪs'ɑrm] *vt* : desarmar — **disarmament** [dɪs'ɑrməmənt] *n* : desarme *m*

disarray [,dɪsə'reɪ] *n* : desorden *m*

disaster [dɪ'zæstər] *n* : desastre *m* — **disastrous** [dɪ'zæstrəs] *adj* : desastroso

disbelief [,dɪsbɪ'li:f] *n* : incredulidad *f*

disc → **disk**

discard [dɪs'kɑrd, 'dɪs,kɑrd] *vt* : desechar, deshacerse de

discern [dɪ'sərn, -'zərn] *vt* : percibir, discernir — **discernible** [dɪ'sərnəbəl, -'zər-] *adj* : perceptible

discharge [dɪs'tʃɑrdʒ, 'dɪs,-] *vt* **-charged; -charging 1** UNLOAD : descargar **2** RELEASE : liberar, poner en libertad **3** DISMISS : despedir **4**

CARRY OUT : cumplir con (una obligación) — ~ ['dɪs,tʃɑrdʒ, dɪs'-] *n* **1** : descarga *f* (de electricidad), emisión *f* (de humo, etc.) **2** DISMISSAL : despido *m* **3** RELEASE : alta *f* (de un paciente), puesta *f* en libertad (de un preso) **4** : supuración *f* (en medicina)
disciple [dɪ'saɪpəl] *n* : discípulo *m*, -la *f*
discipline ['dɪsəplən] *n* **1** : disciplina *f* **2** PUNISHMENT : castigo *m* — ~ *vt* **-plined; -plining 1** CONTROL : disciplinar **2** PUNISH : castigar
disclaim [dɪs'kleɪm] *vt* : negar
disclose [dɪs'klo:z] *vt* **-closed; -closing** : revelar — **disclosure** [dɪs'klo:ʒər] *n* : revelación *f*
discomfort [dɪs'kʌmfərt] *n* **1** : incomodidad *f* **2** PAIN : malestar *m* **3** UNEASINESS : inquietud *f*
disconcert [,dɪskən'sərt] *vt* : desconcertar
disconnect [,dɪskə'nɛkt] *vt* : desconectar
disconsolate [dɪs'kɑntsələt] *adj* : desconsolado
discontented [,dɪskən'tɛntəd] *adj* : descontento
discontinue [,dɪskən'tɪn,ju:] *vt* **-ued; -uing** : suspender, descontinuar
discount ['dɪs,kaʊnt, dɪs'-] *n* : descuento *m*, rebaja *f* — ~ *vt* **1** : descontar (precios) **2** DISREGARD : descartar
discourage [dɪs'kərɪdʒ] *vt* **-aged; -aging** : desalentar, desanimar — **discouragement** [dɪs'kərɪdʒmənt] *n* : desánimo *m*, desaliento *m*
discover [dɪs'kʌvər] *vt* : descubrir — **discovery** [dɪs'kʌvəri] *n, pl* **-ries** : descubrimiento *m*
discredit [dɪs'krɛdət] *vt* : desacreditar — ~ *n* : descrédito *m*
discreet [dɪs'kri:t] *adj* : discreto
discrepancy [dɪs'krɛpəntsi] *n, pl* **-cies** : discrepancia *f*
discretion [dɪs'krɛʃən] *n* : discreción *f*
discriminate [dɪs'krɪmə,neɪt] *vi* **-nated; -nating 1 ~ against** : discriminar **2 ~ between** : distinguir entre — **discrimination** [dɪs,krɪmə'neɪʃən] *n* **1** PREJUDICE : discriminación *f* **2** DISCERNMENT : discernimiento *m*
discuss [dɪs'kʌs] *vt* : hablar de, discutir — **discussion** [dɪs'kʌʃən] *n* : discusión *f*
disdain [dɪs'deɪn] *n* : desdén *m* — ~ *vt* : desdeñar
disease [dɪ'zi:z] *n* : enfermedad *f* — **diseased** [dɪ'zi:zd] *adj* : enfermo
disembark [,dɪsɪm'bɑrk] *vi* : desembarcar
disengage [,dɪsɪn'geɪdʒ] *vt* **-gaged; -gaging 1** RELEASE : soltar **2 ~ the clutch** : desembragar
disentangle [,dɪsɪn'tæŋgəl] *vt* **-gled; -gling** : desenredar
disfavor [dɪs'feɪvər] *n* : desaprobación *f*
disfigure [dɪs'fɪgjər] *vt* **-ured; -uring** : desfigurar
disgrace [dɪ'skreɪs] *vt* **-graced; -gracing** : deshonrar — ~ *n* **1** DISHONOR : deshonra *f* **2** SHAME : vergüenza *f* — **disgraceful** [dɪ'skreɪsfəl] *adj* : vergonzoso, deshonroso
disgruntled [dɪs'grʌntəld] *adj* : descontento
disguise [dɪ'skaɪz] *vt* **-guised; -guising** : disfrazar — ~ *n* : disfraz *m*
disgust [dɪ'skʌst] *n* : asco *m*, repugnancia *f* — ~ *vt* : asquear — **disgusting** [dɪ'skʌstɪŋ] *adj* : asqueroso
dish ['dɪʃ] *n* **1** : plato *m* **2** *or* **serving ~** : fuente *f* **3 wash the ~es** : lavar los platos — ~ *vt or* **~ up** : servir — **dishcloth** ['dɪʃ,klɔth] *n* : paño *m* de cocina (para secar), trapo *m* de fregar (para lavar)
dishearten [dɪs'hɑrtən] *vt* : desanimar
disheveled *or* **dishevelled** [dɪ'ʃɛvəld] *adj* : desaliñado, despeinado (dícese del pelo)
dishonest [dɪ'sɑnəst] *adj* : deshonesto — **dishonesty** [dɪ'sɑnəsti] *n, pl* **-ties** : falta *f* de honradez
dishonor [dɪ'sɑnər] *n* : deshonra *f* — ~ *vt* : deshonrar — **dishonorable** [dɪ'sɑnərəbəl] *adj* : deshonroso
dishwasher ['dɪʃ,wɔʃər] *n* : lavaplatos *m*, lavavajillas *m*
disillusion [,dɪsə'lu:ʒən] *vt* : desilusionar — **disillusionment** [,dɪsə'lu:ʒənmənt] *n* : desilusión *f*
disinfect [,dɪsɪn'fɛkt] *vt* : desinfectar — **disinfectant** [,dɪsɪn'fɛktənt] *n* : desinfectante *m*
disintegrate [dɪs'ɪntə,greɪt] *vi* **-grated; -grating** : desintegrarse
disinterested [dɪs'ɪntərəstəd, -,rɛs-] *adj* : desinteresado
disk *or* **disc** ['dɪsk] *n* : disco *m*
dislike [dɪs'laɪk] *n* : aversión *f*, antipatía *f* — ~ *vt* **-liked; -liking 1** : tener aversión a **2 I ~ dancing** : no me gusta bailar
dislocate ['dɪslo,keɪt, dɪs'lo:-] *vt* **-cated; -cating** : dislocar
dislodge [dɪs'lɑdʒ] *vt* **-lodged; -lodging** : sacar, desalojar
disloyal [dɪs'lɔɪəl] *adj* : desleal — **disloyalty** [dɪs'lɔɪəlti] *n, pl* **-ties** : deslealtad *f*

dismal ['dɪzməl] *adj* : sombrío, deprimente
dismantle [dɪs'mæntəl] *vt* **-tled; -tling** : desmontar, desarmar
dismay [dɪs'meɪ] *vt* : consternar — ~ *n* : consternación *f*
dismiss [dɪs'mɪs] *vt* **1** DISCHARGE : despedir, destituir **2** REJECT : descartar, rechazar — **dismissal** [dɪs'mɪsəl] *n* **1** : despido *m* (de un empleado), destitución *f* (de un funcionario) **2** REJECTION : rechazo *m*
dismount [dɪs'maʊnt] *vi* : desmontar
disobey [ˌdɪsə'beɪ] *v* : desobedecer — **disobedience** [ˌdɪsə'biːdiənts] *n* : desobediencia *f* — **disobedient** [-ənt] *adj* : desobediente
disorder [dɪs'ɔrdər] *n* **1** : desorden *m* **2** AILMENT : afección *f*, problema *m* — **disorderly** [dɪs'ɔrdərli] *adj* : desordenado
disorganize [dɪs'ɔrgəˌnaɪz] *vt* **-nized; -nizing** : desorganizar
disown [dɪs'oːn] *vt* : renegar de
dispassionate [dɪs'pæʃənət] *adj* : desapasionado
dispatch [dɪs'pætʃ] *vt* : despachar, enviar
dispel [dɪs'pɛl] *vt* **-pelled; -pelling** : disipar
dispensation [ˌdɪspen'seɪʃən] *n* EXEMPTION : exención *m*, dispensa *f*
dispense [dɪs'pɛnts] *v* **-pensed; -pensing** *vt* : repartir, distribuir — *vi* ~ **with** : prescindir de
disperse [dɪs'pərs] *v* **-persed; -persing** *vt* : dispersar — *vi* : dispersarse
displace [dɪs'pleɪs] *vt* **-placed; -placing** **1** : desplazar **2** REPLACE : reemplazar
display [dɪs'pleɪ] *vt* **1** EXHIBIT : exponer, exhibir **2** ~ **anger** : manifestar la ira — ~ *n* : muestra *f*, exposición *f*
displease [dɪs'pliːz] *vt* **-pleased; -pleasing** : desagradar — **displeasure** [dɪs'plɛʒər] *n* : desagrado *m*
dispose [dɪs'poːz] *v* **-posed; -posing** *vt* : disponer — *vi* ~ **of** : deshacerse de — **disposable** [dɪs'poːzəbəl] *adj* : desechable — **disposal** [dɪs'poːzəl] *n* **1** REMOVAL : eliminación *f* **2 have at one's** ~ : tener a su disposición — **disposition** [ˌdɪspə'zɪʃən] *n* **1** ARRANGEMENT : disposición *f* **2** TEMPERAMENT : temperamento *m*, carácter *m*
disprove [dɪs'pruːv] *vt* **-proved; -proving** : refutar
dispute [dɪs'pjuːt] *v* **-puted; -putting** *vt* QUESTION : cuestionar — *vi* ARGUE : discutir — ~ *n* : disputa *f*, conflicto *m*
disqualification [dɪsˌkwɑləfə'keɪʃən] *n* : descalificación *f* — **disqualify** [dɪs'kwɑləˌfaɪ] *vt* **-fied; -fying** : descalificar
disregard [ˌdɪsrɪ'gɑrd] *vt* : ignorar, hacer caso omiso de — ~ *n* : indiferencia *f*
disrepair [ˌdɪsrɪ'pær] *n* : mal estado *m*
disreputable [dɪs'rɛpjʊt̬əbəl] *adj* : de mala fama
disrespect [ˌdɪsrɪ'spɛkt] *n* : falta *f* de respeto — **disrespectful** [ˌdɪsrɪ'spɛktfəl] *adj* : irrespetuoso
disrupt [dɪs'rʌpt] *vt* : trastornar, perturbar — **disruption** [dɪs'rʌpʃən] *n* : trastorno *m*
dissatisfaction [dɪsˌsæt̬əs'fækʃən] *n* : descontento *m* — **dissatisfied** [dɪs'sæt̬əsˌfaɪd] *adj* : descontento
dissect [dɪ'sɛkt] *vt* : disecar
disseminate [dɪ'sɛməˌneɪt] *vt* **-nated; -nating** : diseminar, difundir
dissent [dɪ'sɛnt] *vi* : disentir — ~ *n* : disentimiento *m*
dissertation [ˌdɪsər'teɪʃən] THESIS : tesis *f*
disservice [dɪs'sərvɪs] *n* **do a** ~ **to** : no hacer justicia a
dissident ['dɪsədənt] *n* : disidente *mf*
dissimilar [dɪ'sɪmələr] *adj* : distinto
dissipate ['dɪsəˌpeɪt] *vt* **-pated; -pating** **1** DISPEL : disipar **2** SQUANDER : desperdiciar
dissolve [dɪ'zɑlv] *v* **-solved; -solving** *vt* : disolver — *vi* : disolverse
dissuade [dɪ'sweɪd] *vt* **-suaded; -suading** : disuadir
distance ['dɪstənts] *n* **1** : distancia *f* **2 in the** ~ : a lo lejos — **distant** ['dɪstənt] *adj* : distante
distaste [dɪs'teɪst] *n* : desagrado *m* — **distasteful** [dɪs'teɪstfəl] *adj* : desagradable
distend [dɪs'tɛnd] *vt* : dilatar — *vi* : dilatarse
distill [dɪ'stɪl] *or Brit* **distil** *vt* **-tilled; -tilling** : destilar
distinct [dɪ'stɪŋkt] *adj* **1** DIFFERENT : distinto **2** CLEAR : claro — **distinction** [dɪ'stɪŋkʃən] *n* : distinción *f* — **distinctive** [dɪ'stɪŋktɪv] *adj* : distintivo
distinguish [dɪs'tɪŋgwɪʃ] *vt* : distinguir — **distinguished** [dɪs'tɪŋgwɪʃt] *adj* : distinguido
distort [dɪ'stɔrt] *vt* : deformar, distorsionar — **distortion** [dɪ'stɔrʃən] *n* : deformación *f*
distract [dɪ'strækt] *vt* : distraer — **distraction** [dɪ'strækʃən] *n* : distracción *f*
distraught [dɪ'strɔt] *adj* : muy afligido
distress [dɪ'strɛs] *n* **1** : angustia *f*, aflicción *f* **2 in** ~ : en peligro — ~ *vt*

: afligir — **distressing** [dɪ'strɛsɪŋ] *adj* : penoso
distribute [dɪ'strɪ,bju:t, -bjʊt] *vt* **-uted; -uting** : distribuir, repartir — **distribution** [,dɪstrə'bju:ʃən] *n* : distribución *f* — **distributor** [dɪ'strɪbjʊt̬ər] *n* : distribuidor *m*, -dora *f*
district ['dɪs,trɪkt] *n* **1** REGION : región *f*, zona *f*, barrio *m* (de una ciudad) **2** : distrito *m* (zona política)
distrust [dɪs'trʌst] *n* : desconfianza *f* — **~** *vt* : desconfiar de
disturb [dɪ'stərb] *vt* **1** BOTHER : molestar, perturbar **2** WORRY : inquietar — **disturbance** [dɪ'stərbənts] *n* **1** COMMOTION : alboroto *m*, disturbio *m* **2** INTERRUPTION : interrupción *f*
disuse [dɪs'ju:s] *n* **fall into ~** : caer en desuso
ditch ['dɪtʃ] *n* : zanja *f*, cuneta *f* — **~** *vt* DISCARD : deshacerse de, botar
ditto ['dɪt̬o:] *n, pl* **-tos 1** : ídem *m* **2 ~ marks** : comillas *fpl*
dive ['daɪv] *vi* **dived** *or* **dove** ['do:v]; **dived; diving 1** : zambullirse, tirarse al agua **2** DESCEND : bajar en picada (dícese de un avión, etc.) — **~** *n* **1** : zambullida *f*, clavado *m Lat* **2** DESCENT : descenso *m* en picada — **diver** ['daɪvər] *n* : saltador *m*, -dora *f*
diverge [də'vərdʒ, daɪ-] *vi* **-verged; -verging** : divergir
diverse [daɪ'vərs, də-, 'daɪ,vərs] *adj* : diverso — **diversify** [daɪ'vərsə,faɪ, də-] *v* **-fied; -fying** *vt* : diversificar — *vi* : diversificarse
diversion [daɪ'vərʒən, də-] *n* **1** : desviación *f* **2** AMUSEMENT : diversión *f*, distracción *f*
diversity [daɪ'vərsət̬i, də-] *n, pl* **-ties** : diversidad *f*
divert [də'vərt, daɪ-] *vt* **1** : desviar **2** DISTRACT : distraer **3** AMUSE : divertir
divide [də'vaɪd] *v* **-vided; -viding** *vt* : dividir — *vi* : dividirse
dividend ['dɪvə,dɛnd, -dənd] *n* : dividendo *m*
divine [də'vaɪn] *adj* **-viner; -est** : divino — **divinity** [də'vɪnət̬i] *n, pl* **-ties** : divinidad *f*
division [dɪ'vɪʒən] *n* : división *f*
divorce [də'vors] *n* : divorcio *m* — **~** *v* **-vorced; -vorcing** *vt* : divorciar — *vi* : divorciarse — **divorcée** [dɪ,vor'seɪ, -'si:; -'vor,-] *n* : divorciada *f*
divulge [də'vʌldʒ, daɪ-] *vt* **-vulged; -vulging** : revelar, divulgar
dizzy ['dɪzi] *adj* **dizzier; -est 1** : mareado **2 a ~ speed** : una velocidad vertiginosa — **dizziness** ['dɪzinəs] *n* : mareo *m*, vértigo *m*
DNA [,di:,ɛn'eɪ] *n* : AND *m*
do ['du:] *v* **did** ['dɪd]; **done** ['dʌn]; **doing; does** ['dʌz] *vt* **1** : hacer **2** PREPARE : preparar — *vi* **1** BEHAVE : hacer **2** FARE : estar, ir, andar **3** SUFFICE : ser suficiente **4 ~ away with** : abolir, eliminar **5 how are you doing?** : ¿cómo estás? — *v aux* **1** (*used in interrogative sentences*) **do you know her?** : ¿la conoces? **2** (*used in negative statements*) **I don't know** : yo no se **3** (*used as a substitute verb to avoid repetition*) **do you speak English? yes, I do** : ¿habla inglés? sí
dock ['dɑk] *n* : muelle *m* — **~** *vt* : descontar dinero de (un sueldo) — *vi* ANCHOR : fondear, atracar
doctor ['dɑktər] *n* **1** : doctor *m*, -tora *f* (en derecho, etc.) **2** PHYSICIAN : médico *m*, -ca; doctor *m*, -tora *f* — **~** *vt* ALTER : alterar, falsificar
doctrine ['dɑktrɪn] *n* : doctrina *f*
document ['dɑkjʊmənt] *n* : documento *m* — **~** ['dɑkjʊ,mɛnt] *vt* : documentar — **documentary** [,dɑkjʊ'mɛntəri] *n, pl* **-ries** : documental *m*
dodge ['dɑdʒ] *n* : artimaña *f*, truco *m* — **~** *v* **dodged; dodging** *vt* : esquivar, eludir — *vi* : echarse a un lado
doe ['do:] *n, pl* **does** *or* **doe** : gama *f*, cierva *f*
does → **do**
dog ['dɔg, 'dɑg] *n* : perro *m*, -rra *f* — **~** *vt* **dogged; dogging** : perseguir — **dogged** ['dɔgəd] *adj* : tenaz
dogma ['dɔgmə] *n* : dogma *m* — **dogmatic** [dɔg'mæt̬ɪk] *adj* : dogmático
doily ['dɔɪli] *n, pl* **-lies** : tapete *m*
doings ['du:ɪŋz] *npl* : actividades *fpl*
doldrums ['do:ldrəmz, 'dɑl-] *npl* **be in the ~** : estar abatido
dole ['do:l] *n* : subsidio *m* de desempleo — **~** *vt* **doled; doling** *or* **~ out** : repartir
doleful ['do:lfəl] *adj* : triste, lúgubre
doll ['dɑl, 'dɔl] *n* : muñeco *m*, -ca *f*
dollar ['dɑlər] *n* : dólar *m*
dolphin ['dɑlfən, 'dɔl-] *n* : delfín *m*
domain [do'meɪn, də-] *n* **1** TERRITORY : dominio *m* **2** FIELD : campo *m*, esfera *f*
dome ['do:m] *n* : cúpula *f*
domestic [də'mɛstɪk] *adj* **1** : doméstico **2** INTERNAL : nacional — **~** *n* SERVANT : empleado *m* doméstico, empleada *f* doméstica — **domesticate** [də'mɛstɪ,keɪt] *vt* **-cated; -cating** : domesticar
domination [,dɑmə'neɪʃən] *n* : domi-

nación *f* — **dominant** ['dɑmənənt] *adj* : dominante — **dominate** ['dɑmə,neɪt] *v* **-nated; -nating** : dominar — **domineer** [,dɑmə'nɪr] *vi* : dominar, tiranizar

dominos ['dɑmə,no:z] *n* : dominó *m* (juego)

donate ['do:,neɪt, do:'-] *vt* **-nated; -nating** : donar, hacer un donativo de — **donation** [do:'neɪʃən] *n* : donativo *m*

done ['dʌn] → **do** — ~ *adj* **1** FINISHED : terminado, hecho **2** COOKED : cocido

donkey ['dɑŋki, 'dʌŋ-] *n, pl* **-keys** : burro *m*

donor ['do:nər] *n* : donante *mf*

don't ['do:nt] (*contraction of* **do not**) → **do**

doodle ['du:dəl] *v* **-dled; -dling** : garabatear — ~ *n* : garabato *m*

doom ['du:m] *n* : perdición *f*, fatalidad *f* — ~ *vt* : condenar

door ['dor] *n* **1** : puerta *f* **2** ENTRANCE : entrada *f* — **doorbell** ['dor,bɛl] *n* : timbre *m* — **doorknob** ['dor,nɑb] *n* : pomo *m* — **doorman** ['dormən] *n, pl* **-men** [-mən, -,mɛn] : portero *m* — **doormat** ['dor,mæt] *n* : felpudo *m* — **doorstep** ['dor,stɛp] *n* : umbral *m* — **doorway** ['dor,weɪ] *n* : entrada *f*, portal *m*

dope ['do:p] *n* **1** DRUG : droga *f* **2** IDIOT : idiota *mf* — ~ *vt* **doped; doping** : drogar

dormant ['dɔrmənt] *adj* : inactivo, latente

dormitory ['dɔrmə,tori] *n, pl* **-ries** : dormitorio *m*

dose ['do:s] *n* : dosis *f* — **dosage** ['do:sɪdʒ] *n* : dosis *f*

dot ['dɑt] *n* **1** : punto *m* **2 on the** ~ : en punto

dote ['do:t] *vi* **doted; doting** ~ **on** : adorar

double ['dʌbəl] *adj* : doble — ~ *v* **-bled; -bling** *vt* : doblar — *vi* : doblarse — ~ *adv* : (el) doble — ~ *n* : doble *mf* — **double bass** *n* : contrabajo *m* — **double–cross** [,dʌbəl-'krɔs] *vt* : traicionar — **doubly** ['dʌbli] *adv* : doblemente

doubt ['daʊt] *vt* **1** : dudar **2** DISTRUST : desconfiar de, dudar de — ~ *n* : duda *f* — **doubtful** ['daʊtfəl] *adj* : dudoso — **doubtless** ['daʊtləs] *adv* : sin duda

dough ['do:] *n* : masa *f* — **doughnut** ['do:,nʌt] *n* : rosquilla *f*, dona *f Lat*

douse ['daʊs, 'daʊz] *vt* **doused; dousing 1** DRENCH : empapar, mojar **2** EXTINGUISH : apagar

dove[1] ['do:v] → **dive**

dove[2] ['dʌv] *n* : paloma *f*

dowdy ['daʊdi] *adj* **dowdier; -est** : poco elegante

down ['daʊn] *adv* **1** DOWNWARD : hacia abajo **2 come/go** ~ : bajar **3** ~ **here** : aquí abajo **4 fall** ~ : caer **5 lie** ~ : acostarse **6 sit** ~ : sentarse — ~ *prep* **1** ALONG : a lo largo de **2** THROUGH : a través de **3** ~ **the hill** : cuesta abajo — ~ *adj* **1** DESCENDING : de bajada **2** DOWNCAST : abatido — ~ *n* : plumón *m* — **downcast** ['daʊn,kæst] *adj* : triste, abatido — **downfall** ['daʊn,fɔl] *n* : ruina *f* — **downhearted** ['daʊn,hɑrṭəd] *adj* : desanimado — **downhill** ['daʊn'hɪl] *adv & adj* : cuesta abajo — **down payment** *n* : entrega *f* inicial — **downpour** ['daʊn,por] *n* : chaparrón *m* — **downright** ['daʊn,raɪt] *adv* : absolutamente — ~ *adj* : absoluto, categórico — **downstairs** ['daʊn'stærz] *adv* : abajo — ~ ['daʊn,stærz] *adj* : de abajo — **downstream** ['daʊn'stri:m] *adv* : río abajo — **down–to–earth** [,daʊntu'ərθ] *adj* : realista — **downtown** [,daʊn'taʊn, 'daʊn,taʊn] *n* : centro *m* (de la ciudad) — ~ [,daʊn'taʊn] *adv* : al centro, en el centro — ~ *adj* : del centro — **downward** ['daʊnwərd] *or* **downwards** [-wərdz] *adv & adj* : hacia abajo

dowry ['daʊri] *n, pl* **-ries** : dote *f*

doze ['do:z] *vi* **dozed; dozing** : dormitar

dozen ['dʌzən] *n, pl* **dozens** *or* **dozen** : docena *f*

drab ['dræb] *adj* **drabber; drabbest** : monótono, apagado

draft ['dræft, 'draft] *n* **1** : corriente *f* de aire **2** *or* **rough** ~ : borrador *m* **3** : conscripción *f* (militar) **4** *or* ~ **beer** : cerveza *f* de barril — ~ *vt* **1** SKETCH : hacer el borrador de **2** CONSCRIPT : reclutar — **drafty** ['dræfti] *adj* **draftier; -est** : con corrientes de aire

drag ['dræg] *v* **dragged; dragging** *vt* **1** : arrastrar **2** DREDGE : dragar — *vi* : arrastrar(se) — ~ *n* **1** RESISTANCE : resistencia *f* (aerodinámica) **2** BORE : pesadez *f*, plomo *m fam*

dragon ['drægən] *n* : dragón *m* — **dragonfly** ['drægən,flaɪ] *n, pl* **-flies** : libélula *f*

drain ['dreɪn] *vt* **1** EMPTY : vaciar, drenar **2** EXHAUST : agotar — *vi* **1** : escurrir(se) (se dice de los platos) **2** *or* ~ **away** : desaparecer poco a poco — ~ *n* **1** : desagüe *m* **2** SEWER : alcantarilla *f* **3** DEPLETION : agotamiento *m* — **drainage** ['dreɪnɪdʒ] *n* : drenaje *m* — **drainpipe** ['dreɪn,paɪp] *n* : tubo *m* de desagüe

drama ['drɑmə, 'dræ-] *n* : drama *m* —

dramatic [drəˈmæt̬ɪk] *adj* : dramático — **dramatist** [ˈdræmət̬ɪst, ˈdrɑ-] *n* : dramaturgo *m*, -ga *f* — **dramatize** [ˈdræmə͵taɪz, ˈdrɑ-] *vt* **-tized; -tizing** : dramatizar

drank → **drink**

drape [ˈdreɪp] *vt* **draped; draping 1** COVER : cubrir (con tela) **2** HANG : drapear —**drapes** *npl* CURTAINS : cortinas *fpl*

drastic [ˈdræstɪk] *adj* : drástico

draught [ˈdræft, ˈdraft] → **draft**

draw [ˈdrɔ] *v* **drew** [ˈdruː]; **drawn** [ˈdrɔn]; **drawing** *vt* **1** PULL : tirar de **2** ATTRACT : atraer **3** SKETCH : dibujar, trazar **4** : sacar (una espada, etc.) **5 ~ a conclusion** : llegar a una conclusión **6 ~ up** DRAFT : redactar — *vi* **1** SKETCH : dibujar **2 ~ near** : acercarse — **~** *n* **1** DRAWING : sorteo *m* **2** TIE : empate *m* **3** ATTRACTION : atracción *f* — **drawback** [ˈdrɔ͵bæk] *n* : desventaja *f* — **drawer** [ˈdrɔr, ˈdrɔər] *n* : gaveta *f*, cajón *m* (en un mueble) — **drawing** [ˈdrɔɪŋ] *n* **1** LOTTERY : sorteo *m* **2** SKETCH : dibujo *m*

drawl [ˈdrɔl] *n* : habla *f* lenta y con vocales prolongadas

dread [ˈdrɛd] *vt* : temer — **~** *n* : pavor *m*, temor *m* — **dreadful** [ˈdrɛdfəl] *adj* : espantoso, terrible

dream [ˈdriːm] *n* : sueño *m* — **~** *v* **dreamed** [ˈdrɛmpt, ˈdriːmd] *or* **dreamt** [ˈdrɛmpt]; **dreaming** *vi* : soñar — *vt* **1** : soñar **2 ~ up** : idear — **dreamer** [ˈdriːmər] *n* : soñador *m*, -dora *f* — **dreamy** [ˈdriːmi] *adj* **dreamier; -est** : soñador

dreary [ˈdrɪri] *adj* **-rier; -est** : sombrío, deprimente

dredge [ˈdrɛdʒ] *vt* **dredged; dredging** : dragar — **~** *n* : draga *f*

dregs [ˈdrɛgz] *npl* : heces *fpl*

drench [ˈdrɛntʃ] *vt* : empapar

dress [ˈdrɛs] *vt* **1** : vestir **2** : preparar (pollo o pescado), aliñar (ensalada) — *vi* **1** : vestirse **2 ~ up** : ponerse elegante — **~** *n* **1** CLOTHING : ropa *f* **2** : vestido *m* (de mujer) — **dresser** [ˈdrɛsər] *n* : cómoda *f* con espejo — **dressing** [ˈdrɛsɪŋ] *n* **1** : aliño *m* (de ensalada), relleno *m* (de pollo) **2** BANDAGE : vendaje *m* — **dressmaker** [ˈdrɛs͵meɪkər] *n* : modista *mf* — **dressy** [ˈdrɛsi] *adj* **dressier; -est** : elegante

drew → **draw**

dribble [ˈdrɪbəl] *vi* **-bled; -bling 1** DRIP : gotear **2** DROOL : babear **3** : driblar (en basquetbol) — **~** *n* **1** TRICKLE : goteo *m*, hilo *m* **2** DROOL : baba *f*

drier, driest → **dry**

drift [ˈdrɪft] *n* **1** MOVEMENT : movimiento *m* **2** HEAP : montón *m* (de arena, etc.), ventisquero *m* (de nieve) **3** MEANING : sentido *m* — **~** *vi* **1** : ir a la deriva **2** ACCUMULATE : amontonarse

drill [ˈdrɪl] *n* **1** : taladro *m* **2** : ejercicio *m* (en educación), simulacro *m* (de incendio, etc.) — **~** *vt* **1** : perforar, taladrar **2** TRAIN : instruir por repetición — *vi* **~ for** : perforar en busca de

drink [ˈdrɪŋk] *v* **drank** [ˈdræŋk]; **drunk** [ˈdrʌŋk] *or* **drank; drinking** : beber — **~** *n* : bebida *f*

drip [ˈdrɪp] *vi* **dripped; dripping** : gotear — **~** *n* **1** DROP : gota *f* **2** DRIPPING : goteo *m*

drive [ˈdraɪv] *v* **drove** [ˈdroːv]; **driven** [ˈdrɪvən]; **driving** *vt* **1** : manejar **2** IMPEL : impulsar **3 ~ crazy** : volver loco **4 ~ s.o. to (do sth)** : llevar a algn a (hacer algo) — *vi* : manejar, conducir — **~** *n* **1** : paseo *m* (en coche) **2** CAMPAIGN : campaña *f* **3** VIGOR : energía *f* **4** NEED : instinto *m*

drivel [ˈdrɪvəl] *n* : tonterías *fpl*

driver [ˈdraɪvər] *n* : conductor *m*, -tora *f*; chofer *m*

driveway [ˈdraɪv͵weɪ] *n* : camino *m* de entrada

drizzle [ˈdrɪzəl] *n* : llovizna *f* — **~** *vi* **-zled; -zling** : lloviznar

drone [ˈdroːn] *n* **1** BEE : zángano *m* **2** HUM : zumbido *m* — **~** *vi* **droned; droning 1** BUZZ : zumbar **2** *or* **~ on** : hablar con monotonía

drool [ˈdruːl] *vi* : babear — **~** *n* : baba *f*

droop [ˈdruːp] *vi* : inclinarse (dícese de la cabeza), encorvarse (dícese de los escombros), marchitarse (dícese de las flores)

drop [ˈdrɑp] *n* **1** : gota *f* (de líquido) **2** DECLINE, FALL : caída *f* — **~** *v* **dropped; dropping** *vt* **1** : dejar caer **2** LOWER : bajar **3** ABANDON : abandonar, dejar **4 ~ off** LEAVE : dejar — *vi* **1** FALL : caer(se) **2** DECREASE : bajar, descender **3 ~ by** *or* **~ in** : pasar

drought [ˈdraʊt] *n* : sequía *f*

drove → **drive**

droves [ˈdroːvz] *n* **in ~** : en manada

drown [ˈdraʊn] *vt* : ahogar — *vi* : ahogarse

drowsy [ˈdraʊzi] *adj* **drowsier; -est** : somnoliento

drudgery [ˈdrʌdʒəri] *n, pl* **-eries** : trabajo *m* pesado

drug [ˈdrʌg] *n* **1** MEDICATION : medicamento *m* **2** NARCOTIC : droga *f*, estupefaciente *m* — **~** *vt* **drugged; drugging** : drogar — **drugstore** [ˈdrʌg͵stor] *n* : farmacia *f*

drum ['drʌm] *n* **1** : tambor *m* **2** *or* **oil ~** : bidón *m* (de petróleo) — **~** *v* **drummed; drumming** *vi* : tocar el tambor — *vt* : tamborilear con (los dedos, etc.) — **drumstick** ['drʌm,stɪk] *n* **1** : palillo *m* (de tambor) **2** : muslo *m* (de pollo)

drunk ['drʌŋk] → **drink** — **~** *adj* : borracho — **~** *or* **drunkard** ['drʌŋkərd] *n* : borracho *m*, -cha *f* — **drunken** ['drʌŋkən] *adj* : borracho, ebrio

dry ['draɪ] *adj* **drier; driest** : seco — **~** *v* **dried; drying** *vt* : secar — *vi* : secarse — **dry–clean** ['draɪ,kli:n] *vt* : limpiar en seco — **dry cleaner** *n* : tintorería *f* (servicio) — **dry cleaning** *n* : limpieza *f* en seco — **dryer** ['draɪər] *n* : secadora *f* — **dryness** ['draɪnəs] *n* : sequedad *f*, aridez *f*

dual ['du:əl, 'dju:-] *adj* : doble

dub ['dʌb] *vt* **dubbed; dubbing 1** CALL : apodar **2** : doblar (una película)

dubious ['du:biəs, 'dju:-] *adj* **1** UNCERTAIN : dudoso **2** QUESTIONABLE : sospechoso

duchess ['dʌtʃəs] *n* : duquesa *f*

duck ['dʌk] *n, pl* **duck** *or* **ducks** : pato *m*, -ta *f* — **~** *vt* **1** LOWER : agachar, bajar **2** EVADE : eludir, esquivar — *vi* : agacharse — **duckling** ['dʌklɪŋ] *n* : patito *m*, -ta *f*

duct ['dʌkt] *n* : conducto *m*

due ['du:, 'dju:] *adj* **1** PAYABLE : pagadero **2** APPROPRIATE : debido, apropiado **3** EXPECTED : esperado **4 ~ to** : debido a — **~** *n* **1 give s.o. their ~** : hacer justicia a algn **2 ~s** *npl* : cuota *f* — **~** *adv* **~ east** : justo al este

duel ['du:əl, 'dju:-] *n* : duelo *m*

duet [du'ɛt, dju-] *n* : dúo *m*

dug → **dig**

duke ['du:k, 'dju:k] *n* : duque *m*

dull ['dʌl] *adj* **1** STUPID : torpe **2** BLUNT : desafilado **3** BORING : aburrido **4** LACKLUSTER : apagado — **~** *vt* : entorpecer (los sentidos), aliviar (el dolor)

dumb ['dʌm] *adj* **1** MUTE : mudo **2** STUPID : estúpido

dumbfound *or* **dumfound** [,dʌm'faʊnd] *vt* : dejar sin habla

dummy ['dʌmi] *n, pl* **-mies 1** SHAM : imitación *f* **2** MANNEQUIN : maniquí *m* **3** IDIOT : tonto *m*, -ta *f*

dump ['dʌmp] *vt* : descargar, verter — **~** *n* **1** : vertedero *m*, tiradero *m Lat* **2 down in the ~s** : triste, deprimido

dumpling ['dʌmplɪŋ] *n* : bola *f* de masa hervida

dumpy ['dʌmpi] *adj* **dumpier; -est** : regordete

dunce ['dʌnts] *n* : burro *m*, -rra *f fam*

dune ['du:n, 'dju:n] *n* : duna *f*

dung ['dʌŋ] *n* **1** : excrementos *mpl* **2** MANURE : estiércol *m*

dungarees [,dʌŋgə'ri:] *npl* JEANS : vaqueros *mpl*, jeans *mpl*

dungeon ['dʌndʒən] *n* : calabozo *m*

dunk ['dʌŋk] *vt* : mojar

duo ['du:o:, 'dju:-] *n, pl* **duos** : dúo *m*

dupe ['du:p, dju:p] *vt* **duped; duping** : engañar — **~** *n* : inocentón *m*, -tona *f*

duplex ['du:,plɛks, 'dju:-] *n* : casa *f* de dos viviendas, dúplex *m*

duplicate ['du:plɪkət, 'dju:-] *adj* : duplicado — **~** ['du:plɪ,keɪt, 'dju:-] *vt* **-cated; -cating** : duplicar, hacer copias de — **~** ['du:plɪkət, 'dju:-] *n* : duplicado *m*, copia *f*

durable ['dʊrəbəl, 'djʊr-] *adj* : duradero

duration [dʊ'reɪʃən, djʊ-] *n* : duración *f*

duress [dʊ'rɛs, djʊ-] *n* : coacción *f*

during ['dʊrɪŋ, 'djʊr-] *prep* : durante

dusk ['dʌsk] *n* : anochecer *m*, crepúsculo *m*

dust ['dʌst] *n* : polvo *m* — **~** *vt* **1** : quitar el polvo a **2** SPRINKLE : espolvorear — **dustpan** ['dʌst,pæn] *n* : recogedor *m* — **dusty** ['dʌsti] *adj* **dustier; -est** : polvoriento

Dutch ['dʌtʃ] *adj* : holandés — **~** *n* **1** : holandés *m* (idioma) **2 the ~** : los holandeses

duty ['du:ṭi, 'dju:-] *n, pl* **-ties 1** OBLIGATION : deber *m* **2** TAX : impuesto *m* **3 on ~** : de servicio — **dutiful** ['du:ṭɪfəl, 'dju:-] *adj* : obediente

dwarf ['dwɔrf] *n, pl* **dwarfs** ['dwɔrfs] *or* **dwarves** ['dwɔrvz] : enano *m*, -na *f* — **~** *vt* : hacer parecer pequeño

dwell ['dwɛl] *vi* **dwelled** *or* **dwelt** ['dwɛlt]; **dwelling 1** RESIDE : morar, vivir **2 ~ on** : pensar demasiado en — **dweller** ['dwɛlər] *n* : habitante *mf* — **dwelling** ['dwɛlɪŋ] *n* : morada *f*, vivienda *f*

dwindle ['dwɪndəl] *vi* **-dled; -dling** : disminuir

dye ['daɪ] *n* : tinte *m* — **~** *vt* **dyed; dyeing** : teñir

dying → **die**[1]

dynamic [daɪ'næmɪk] *adj* : dinámico

dynamite ['daɪnə,maɪt] *n* : dinamita *f*

dynamo ['daɪnə,mo:] *n, pl* **-mos** : dínamo *m*

dynasty ['daɪnəsti, -,næs-] *n, pl* **-ties** : dinastía *f*

dysentery ['dɪsən,tɛri] *n, pl* **-teries** : disentería *f*

E

e ['iː] *n, pl* **e's** *or* **es** ['iːz] : e *f*, quinta letra del alfabeto inglés
each ['iːtʃ] *adj* : cada — **~** *pron* **1** : cada uno *m*, cada una *f* **2** **~ other** : el uno al otro **3 they hate ~ other** : se odian — **~** *adv* : cada uno, por persona
eager ['iːgər] *adj* **1** ENTHUSIASTIC : entusiasta **2** IMPATIENT : impaciente — **eagerness** ['iːgərnəs] *n* : entusiasmo *m*, impaciencia *f*
eagle ['iːgəl] *n* : águila *f*
ear ['ɪr] *n* **1** : oreja *f* **2 ~ of corn** : mazorca *f*, choclo *m Lat* — **eardrum** ['ɪrˌdrʌm] *n* : tímpano *m*
earl ['ərl] *n* : conde *m*
earlobe ['ɪrˌloːb] *n* : lóbulo *m* de la oreja
early ['ərli] *adv* **earlier; -est 1** : temprano **2 as ~ as possible** : lo más pronto posible **3 ten minutes ~** : diez minutos de adelanto — **~** *adj* **earlier; -est 1** FIRST : primero **2** ANCIENT : primitivo, antiguo **3 an ~ death** : una muerte prematura **4 be ~** : llegar temprano **5 in the ~ spring** : a principios de la primavera
earmark ['ɪrˌmɑrk] *vt* : destinar
earn ['ərn] *vt* **1** : ganar **2** DESERVE : merecer
earnest ['ərnəst] *adj* : serio — **~** *n* **in ~** : en serio
earnings ['ərnɪŋz] *npl* **1** WAGES : ingresos *mpl* **2** PROFITS : ganancias *fpl*
earphone ['ɪrˌfoːn] *n* : audífono *m*
earring ['ɪrˌrɪŋ] *n* : pendiente *m*, arete *m Lat*
earshot ['ɪrˌʃɑt] *n* **within ~** : al alcance del oído
earth ['ərθ] *n* : tierra *f* — **earthenware** ['ərθən ˌwær, -ðən-] *n* : loza *f* — **earthly** ['ərθli] *adj* : terrenal — **earthquake** ['ərθˌkweɪk] *n* : terremoto *m* — **earthworm** ['ərθˌwərm] *n* : lombriz *f* (de tierra) — **earthy** ['ərθi] *adj* **earthier; -est 1** : terroso **2** COARSE, CRUDE : grosero
ease ['iːz] *n* **1** FACILITY : facilidad *f* **2** COMFORT : comodidad *f* **3 feel at ~** : sentir cómodo — **~** *v* **eased; easing** *vt* **1** ALLEVIATE : aliviar, calmar **2** FACILITATE : facilitar — *vi* **1** : calmarse **2 ~ up** : disminuir
easel ['iːzəl] *n* : caballete *m*
easily ['iːzəli] *adv* **1** : fácilmente, con facilidad **2** UNQUESTIONABLY : con mucho, de lejos *Lat*
east ['iːst] *adv* : al este — **~** *adj* : este, del este — **~** *n* **1** : este *m* **2 the East** : el Oriente
Easter ['iːstər] *n* : Pascua *f*
easterly ['iːstərli] *adv & adj* : del este
eastern ['iːstərn] *adj* **1** : del este **2 Eastern** : oriental, del este
easy ['iːzi] *adj* **easier; -est 1** : fácil **2** RELAXED : relajado — **easygoing** [ˌiːzi'goːɪŋ] *adj* : tolerante, relajado
eat ['iːt] *v* **ate** ['eɪt]; **eaten** ['iːtən]; **eating** *vt* : comer — *vi* **1** : comer **2 ~ into** CORRODE : corroer **3 ~ into** DEPLETE : comerse — **eatable** ['iːt̬əbəl] *adj* : comestible
eaves ['iːvz] *npl* : alero *m* — **eavesdrop** ['iːvzˌdrɑp] *vi* **-dropped; -dropping** : escuchar a escondidas
ebb ['ɛb] *n* : reflujo *m* — **~** *vi* **1** : bajar (dícese de la marea) **2** DECLINE : decaer
ebony ['ɛbəni] *n, pl* **-nies** : ébano *m*
eccentric [ɪk'sentrɪk] *adj* : excéntrico — **~** *n* : ecéntrico *m*, **-ca** *f* — **eccentricity** [ˌɛkˌsen'trɪsət̬i] *n, pl* **-ties** : excentricidad *f*
echo ['ɛˌkoː] *n, pl* **echoes** : eco *m* — **~** *v* **echoed; echoing** *vt* : repetir — *vi* : hacer eco, resonar
eclipse [ɪ'klɪps] *n* : eclipse *m* — **~** *vt* **eclipsed; eclipsing** : eclipsar
ecology [i'kɑlədʒi, ɛ-] *n, pl* **-gies** : ecología *f* — **ecological** *adj* [ˌiːkə'lɑdʒɪkəl, ˌɛkə-] : ecológico
economy [i'kɑnəmi] *n, pl* **-mies** : economía *f* — **economic** [ˌiːkə'nɑmɪk, ˌɛkə-] *or* **economical** [ˌiːkə'nɑmɪkəl, ˌɛkə-] *adj* : económico — **economics** [ˌiːkə'nɑmɪks, ˌɛkə-] *n* : economía *f* — **economist** [i'kɑnəmɪst] *n* : economista *mf* — **economize** [i'kɑnəˌmaɪz] *v* **-mized; -mizing** : economizar
ecstasy ['ɛkstəsi] *n, pl* **-sies** : éxtasis *m* — **ecstatic** [ɛk'stæt̬ɪk, ɪk-] *adj* : extático
Ecuadoran [ˌɛkwə'dorən] *or* **Ecuadorean** *or* **Ecuadorian** [ˌɛkwə'doriən] *adj* : ecuatoriano
edge ['ɛdʒ] *n* **1** BORDER : borde *m* **2** : filo *m* (de un cuchillo) **3** ADVANTAGE : ventaja *f* — **~** *v* **edged; edging** *vt* : bor-

dear, ribetear — *vi* : avanzar poco a poco — **edgewise** ['ɛdʒˌwaɪz] *adv* : de lado — **edgy** ['ɛdʒi] *adj* **edgier; -est** : nervioso

edible ['ɛdəbəl] *adj* : comestible

edit ['ɛdɪt] *vt* **1** : editar, redactar, corregir **2 ~ out** : suprimir, cortar — **edition** [ɪ'dɪʃən] *n* : edición *f* — **editor** ['ɛdɪṭər] *n* : director *m*, -tora *f* (de un periódico); redactor *m*, -tora *f* (de un libro) — **editorial** [ˌɛdɪ'toriəl] *n* : editorial *m*

educate ['ɛdʒəˌkeɪt] *vt* **-cated; -cating 1** TEACH : educar, instruir **2** INFORM : informar — **education** [ˌɛdʒə'keɪʃən] *n* : educación *f* — **educational** [ˌɛdʒə'keɪʃənəl] *adj* **1** : educativo, instructivo **2** TEACHING : docente — **educator** ['ɛdʒəˌkeɪṭər] *n* : educador *m*, -dora *f*

eel ['i:l] *n* : anguila *f*

eerie ['ɪri] *adj* **-rier; -est** : extraño e inquietante, misterioso

effect [ɪ'fɛkt] *n* **1** : efecto *m* **2 go into ~** : entrar en vigor — **~** *vt* : efectuar, llevar a cabo — **effective** [ɪ'fɛktɪv] *adj* **1** : eficaz **2** ACTUAL : efectivo, vigente — **effectiveness** [ɪ'fɛktɪvnəs] *n* : eficacia *f*

effeminate [ə'fɛmənət] *adj* : afeminado

effervescent [ˌɛfər'vɛsənt] *adj* : efervescente

efficient [ɪ'fɪʃənt] *adj* : eficiente — **efficiency** [ɪ'fɪʃəntsi] *n, pl* **-cies** : eficiencia *f*

effort ['ɛfərt] *n* **1** : esfuerzo *m* **2 it's not worth the ~** : no vale la pena — **effortless** ['ɛfərtləs] *adj* : fácil, sin esfuerzo

egg ['ɛg] *n* : huevo *m* — **~** *vt* **~ on** : incitar — **eggplant** ['ɛgˌplænt] *n* : berenjena *f* — **eggshell** ['ɛgˌʃɛl] *n* : cascarón *m*

ego ['i:ˌgo:] *n, pl* **egos 1** SELF : ego *m*, yo *m* **2** SELF-ESTEEM : amor *m* propio — **egotism** ['i:gəˌtɪzəm] *n* : egotismo *m* — **egotist** ['i:gətɪst] *n* : egotista *mf* — **egotistic** [ˌi:gə'tɪstɪk] *or* **egotistical** [-'tɪstɪkəl] *adj* : egotista

eiderdown ['aɪdərˌdaʊn] *n* **1** DOWN : plumón *m* **2** COMFORTER : edredón *m*

eight ['eɪt] *n* : ocho *m* — **~** *adj* : ocho — **eight hundred** *n* : ochocientos *m*

eighteen [eɪt'ti:n] *n* : dieciocho *m* — **~** *adj* : dieciocho — **eighteenth** [eɪt'ti:nθ] *adj* : decimoctavo — **~** *n* **1** : decimoctavo *m*, -va *f* (en una serie) **2** : dieciochoavo *m*, dieciochoava parte *f*

eighth ['eɪtθ] *n* **1** : octavo *m*, -va *f* (en una serie) **2** : octavo *m*, octava parte *f* — **~** *adj* : octavo

eighty ['eɪṭi] *n, pl* **eighties** : ochenta *m* — **~** *adj* : ochenta

either ['i:ðər, 'aɪ-] *adj* **1** : cualquiera (de los dos) **2** (*in negative constructions*) : ninguno (de los dos) **3** EACH : cada — **~** *pron* **1** : cualquiera *mf* (de los dos) **2** (*in negative constructions*) : ninguno *m*, -na *f* (de los dos) **3** *or* **~ one** : algún *m*, alguna *f* — **~** *conj* **1** : o **2** (*in negative constructions*) : ni

eject [i'dʒɛkt] *vt* : expulsar, expeler

eke ['i:k] *vt* **eked; eking** *or* **~ out** : ganar a duras penas

elaborate [i'læbərət] *adj* **1** DETAILED : detallado **2** COMPLEX : complicado — **~** [i'læbəˌreɪt] *v* **-rated; -rating** *vt* : elaborar — *vi* : entrar en detalles

elapse [i'læps] *vi* **elapsed; elapsing** : transcurrir

elastic [i'læstɪk] *adj* : elástico — **~** *n* **1** : elástico *m* **2** RUBBER BAND : goma *f* (elástica) — **elasticity** [iˌlæs'tɪsəṭi, ˌi:ˌlæs-] *n, pl* **-ties** : elasticidad *f*

elated [i'leɪṭəd] *adj* : regocijado

elbow ['ɛlˌbo:] *n* : codo *m*

elder ['ɛldər] *adj* : mayor — **~** *n* **1** : mayor *mf* **2** : anciano *m*, -na *f* (de un tribu, etc.) — **elderly** ['ɛldərli] *adj* : mayor, anciano

elect [i'lɛkt] *vt* : elegir — **~** *adj* : electo — **election** [i'lɛkʃən] *n* : elección *f* — **electoral** [i'lɛktərəl] *adj* : electoral — **electorate** [i'lɛktərət] *n* : electorado *m*

electricity [iˌlɛk'trɪsəṭi] *n, pl* **-ties** : electricidad *f* — **electric** [i'lɛktrɪk] *or* **electrical** [-trɪkəl] *adj* : eléctrico — **electrician** [iˌlɛk'trɪʃən] *n* : electricista *mf* — **electrify** [i'lɛktrəˌfaɪ] *vt* **-fied; -fying** : electrificar — **electrocute** [i'lɛktrəˌkju:t] *vt* **-cuted; -cuting** : electrocutar

electron [i'lɛkˌtrɑn] *n* : electrón *m* — **electronic** [iˌlɛk'trɑnɪk] *adj* : electrónico — **electronic mail** *n* : correo *m* electrónico — **electronics** [iˌlɛk'trɑnɪks] *n* : electrónica *f*

elegant ['ɛlɪgənt] *adj* : elegante — **elegance** ['ɛlɪgənts] *n* : elegancia *f*

element ['ɛləmənt] *n* **1** : elemento *m* **2 ~s** *npl* BASICS : elementos *mpl*, rudimentos *mpl* — **elementary** [ˌɛlə'mɛntri] *adj* : elemental — **elementary school** *n* : escuela *f* primaria

elephant ['ɛləfənt] *n* : elefante *m*, -ta *f*

elevate ['ɛləˌveɪt] *vt* **-vated; -vating** : elevar — **elevator** ['ɛləˌveɪṭər] *n* : ascensor *m*

eleven [ɪ'lɛvən] *n* : once *m* — **~** *adj* : once — **eleventh** [ɪ'lɛvəntθ] *adj* : undécimo — **~** *n* **1** : undécimo *m*, -ma *f*

(en una serie) **2** : onceavo *m*, onceava parte *f*
elf ['ɛlf] *n, pl* **elves** ['ɛlvz] : duende *m*
elicit [ɪ'lɪsət] *vt* : provocar
eligible ['ɛlədʒəbəl] *adj* : elegible
eliminate [ɪ'lɪmə,neɪt] *vt* **-nated; -nating** : eliminar — **elimination** [ɪ,lɪmə'neɪʃən] *n* : eliminación *f*
elite [eɪ'li:t, i-] *n* : elite *f*
elk ['ɛlk] *n* : alce *m* (de Europa), uapití *m* (de América)
elliptical [ɪ'lɪptɪkəl, ɛ-] *or* **elliptic** [-tɪk] *adj* : elíptico
elm ['ɛlm] *n* : olmo *m*
elongate [i'lɔŋ,geɪt] *vt* **-gated; -gating** : alargar
elope [i'lo:p] *vi* **eloped; eloping** : fugarse — **elopement** [i'lo:pmənt] *n* : fuga *f*
eloquence ['ɛləkwənts] *n* : elocuencia *f* — **eloquent** ['ɛləkwənt] *adj* : elocuente
else ['ɛls] *adv* **1 how ~ ?** : ¿de qué otro modo? **2 where ~ ?** : ¿en qué otro sitio? **3 or ~** : si no, de lo contrario — **~** *adj* **1 everyone ~** : todos los demás **2 nobody ~** : ningún otro, nadie más **3 nothing ~** : nada más **4 what ~ ?** : ¿qué más? — **elsewhere** ['ɛls,hwɛr] *adv* : en otra parte
elude [i'lu:d] *vt* **eluded; eluding** : eludir, esquivar — **elusive** [i'lu:sɪv] *adj* : esquivo
elves → **elf**
emaciated [i'meɪʃi,eɪt̬əd] *adj* : esquálido, demacrado
E-mail ['i:,meɪl] → **electronic mail**
emanate ['ɛmə,neɪt] *vi* **-nated; -nating** : emanar
emancipate [i'mæntsə,peɪt] *vt* **-pated; -pating** : emancipar — **emancipation** [i,mæntsə'peɪʃən] *n* : emancipación *f*
embalm [ɪm'bɑm, ɛm-, -'bɑlm] *vt* : embalsamar
embankment [ɪm'bæŋkmənt, ɛm-] *n* : terraplén *m*, dique *m* (de un río)
embargo [ɪm'bɑrgo, ɛm-] *n, pl* **-goes** : embargo *m*
embark [ɪm'bɑrk, ɛm-] *vt* : embarcar — *vi* **1** : embarcarse **2 ~ upon** : emprender — **embarkation** [,ɛm,bɑr'keɪʃən] *n* : embarque *m*, embarco *m*
embarrass [ɪm'bærəs, ɛm-] *vt* : avergonzar — **embarrassing** [ɪm'bærəsɪŋ, ɛm-] *adj* : embarazoso — **embarrassment** [ɪm'bærəsmənt, ɛm-] *n* : vergüenza *f*
embassy ['ɛmbəsi] *n, pl* **-sies** : embajada *f*
embed [ɪm'bed, ɛm-] *vt* **-bedded; -bedding** : incrustar, enterrar
embellish [ɪm'bɛlɪʃ, ɛm-] *vt* : adornar, embellecer — **embellishment** [ɪm'bɛlɪʃmənt, ɛm-] *n* : adorno *m*
embers ['ɛmbərz] *npl* : ascuas *fpl*
embezzle [ɪm'bɛzəl, ɛm-] *vt* **-zled; -zling** : desfalcar, malversar — **embezzlement** [ɪm'bɛzəlmənt, ɛm-] *n* : desfalco *m*, malversación *f*
emblem ['ɛmbləm] *n* : emblema *m*
embody [ɪm'bɑdi, ɛm-] *vt* **-bodied; -bodying** : encarnar, personificar
emboss [ɪm'bɑs, ɛm-, -'bɔs] *vt* : repujar, grabar en relieve
embrace [ɪm'breɪs, ɛm-] *v* **-braced; -bracing** *vt* : abrazar — *vi* : abrazarse — **~** *n* : abrazo *m*
embroider [ɪm'brɔɪdər, ɛm-] *vt* : bordar — **embroidery** [ɪm'brɔɪdəri, ɛm-] *n, pl* **-deries** : bordado *m*
embryo ['ɛmbri,o:] *n, pl* **embryos** : embrión *m*
emerald ['ɛmrəld, 'ɛmə-] *n* : esmeralda *f*
emerge [i'mərdʒ] *vi* **emerged; emerging** : salir, aparecer — **emergence** [i'mərdʒənts] *n* : aparición *f*
emergency [i'mərdʒəntsi] *n, pl* **-cies 1** : emergencia *f* **2 ~ exit** : salida *f* de emergencia **3 ~ room** : sala *f* de urgencias, sala *f* de guardia
emery ['ɛməri] *n, pl* **-eries 1** : esmeril *m* **2 ~ board** : lima *f* de uñas
emigrant ['ɛmɪgrənt] *n* : emigrante *mf* — **emigrate** ['ɛmə,greɪt] *vi* **-grated; -grating** : emigrar — **emigration** [,ɛmə'greɪʃən] *n* : emigración *f*
eminence ['ɛmənənts] *n* : eminencia *f* — **eminent** ['ɛmənənt] *adj* : eminente
emission [i'mɪʃən] *n* : emisión *f* — **emit** [i'mɪt] *vt* **emitted; emitting** : emitir
emotion [i'mo:ʃən] *n* : emoción *f* — **emotional** [i'mo:ʃənəl] *adj* **1** : emocional **2** MOVING : emotivo
emperor ['ɛmpərər] *n* : emperador *m*
emphasis ['ɛmfəsɪs] *n, pl* **-phases** [-,si:z] : énfasis *m* — **emphasize** ['ɛmfə,saɪz] *vt* **-sized; -sizing** : subrayar, hacer hincapié en — **emphatic** [ɪm'fætɪk, ɛm-] *adj* : enérgico, categórico
empire ['ɛm,paɪr] *n* : imperio *m*
employ [ɪm'plɔɪ, ɛm-] *vt* : emplear — **employee** [ɪm,plɔɪ'i:, ɛm-, -'plɔɪ,i:] *n* : empleado *m*, -da *f* — **employer** [ɪm'plɔɪər, ɛm-] *n* : patrón *m*, -trona *f*; empleador *m*, -dora *f* — **employment** [ɪm'plɔɪmənt, ɛm-] *n* : trabajo *m*, empleo *m*
empower [ɪm'paʊər, ɛm-] *vt* : autorizar
empress ['ɛmprəs] *n* : emperatriz *f*
empty ['ɛmpti] *adj* **emptier; -est 1** : vacío **2** MEANINGLESS : vano — **~** *v*

-tied; -tying *vt* : vaciar — *vi* : vaciarse — **emptiness** ['ɛmptinəs] *n* : vacío *m*
emulate ['ɛmjəˌleɪt] *vt* **-lated; -lating** : emular
enable [ɪ'neɪbəl, ɛ-] *vt* **-abled; -abling** : hacer posible, permitar
enact [ɪ'nækt, ɛ-] *vt* **1** : promulgar (un ley o un decreto) **2** PERFORM : representar
enamel [ɪ'næməl] *n* : esmalte *m*
encampment [ɪn'kæmpmənt, ɛn-] *n* : campamento *m*
encase [ɪn'keɪs, ɛn-] *vt* **-cased; -casing** : encerrar, revestir
enchant [ɪn'tʃænt, ɛn-] *vt* : encantar — **enchanting** [ɪn'tʃæntɪŋ, ɛn-] *adj* : encantador — **enchantment** [ɪn'tʃæntmənt, ɛn-] *n* : encanto *m*
encircle [ɪn'sərkəl, ɛn-] *vt* **-cled; -cling** : rodear
enclose [ɪn'klo:z, ɛn-] *vt* **-closed; -closing 1** SURROUND : encerrar, cercar **2** INCLUDE : adjuntar (a una carta) — **enclosure** [ɪn'klo:ʒər, ɛn-] *n* **1** AREA : recinto *m* **2** : anexo *m* (con una carta)
encompass [ɪn'kʌmpəs, ɛn-, -'kɑm-] *vt* **1** ENCIRCLE : cercar **2** INCLUDE : abarcar
encore ['ɑnˌkor] *n* : bis *m*
encounter [ɪn'kaʊntər, ɛn-] *vt* : encontrar — **~** *n* : encuentro *m*
encourage [ɪn'kərɪdʒ, ɛn-] *vt* **-aged; -aging 1** : animar, alentar **2** FOSTER : promover, fomentar — **encouragement** [ɪn'kərɪdʒmənt, ɛn-] *n* **1** : aliento *m* **2** PROMOTION : fomento *m*
encroach [ɪn'kro:tʃ, ɛn-] *vi* **~ on** : invadir, usurpar, quitar (el tiempo)
encyclopedia [ɪnˌsaɪklə'pi:diə, ɛn-] *n* : enciclopedia *f*
end ['ɛnd] *n* **1** : fin **2** EXTREMITY : extremo *m*, punta *f* **3 come to an ~** : llegar a su fin **4 in the ~** : por fin — **~** *vt* : terminar, poner fin a — *vi* : terminar(se)
endanger [ɪn'deɪndʒər, ɛn-] *vt* : poner en peligro
endearing [ɪn'dɪrɪŋ, ɛn-] *adj* : simpático
endeavor *or Brit* **endeavour** [ɪn'dɛvər, ɛn-] *vt* **~ to** : esforzarse por — **~** *n* : esfuerzo *m*
ending ['ɛndɪŋ] *n* : final *m*, desenlace *m*
endive ['ɛnˌdaɪv, ˌɑn'di:v] *n* : endibia *f*, endivia *f*
endless ['ɛndləs] *adj* **1** INTERMINABLE : interminable **2** INNUMERABLE : innumerable **3 ~ possibilities** : posibilidades *fpl* infinitas
endorse [ɪn'dɔrs, ɛn-] *vt* **-dorsed; -dorsing 1** SIGN : endosar **2** APPROVE : aprobar — **endorsement** [ɪn'dɔrsmənt, ɛn-] *n* APPROVAL : aprobación *f*
endow [ɪn'daʊ, ɛn-] *vt* : dotar
endure [ɪn'dʊr, ɛn-, -'djʊr] *v* **-dured; -during** *vt* : soportar, aguantar — *vi* LAST : durar — **endurance** [ɪn'dʊrənts, ɛn-, -'djʊr-] *n* : resistencia *f*
enemy ['ɛnəmi] *n, pl* **-mies** : enemigo *m*, -ga *f*
energy ['ɛnərdʒi] *n, pl* **-gies** : energía *f* — **energetic** [ˌɛnər'dʒɛt̬ɪk] *adj* : enérgico
enforce [ɪn'fors, ɛn-] *vt* **-forced; -forcing 1** : hacer cumplir (un ley, etc.) **2** IMPOSE : imponer — **enforced** *adj* : forzoso — **enforcement** [ɪn'forsmənt, ɛn-] *n* : imposición *f* del cumplimiento
engage [ɪn'geɪdʒ, ɛn-] *v* **-gaged; -gaging** *vt* **1** : captar, atraer (la atención, etc.) **2 ~ the clutch** : embragar — *vi* **~ in** : dedicarse a, entrar en — **engagement** [ɪn'geɪdʒmənt, ɛn-] *n* **1** APPOINTMENT : cita *f*, hora *f* **2** BETROTHAL : compromiso *m* — **engaging** [ɪn'geɪdʒɪŋ, ɛn-] *adj* : atractivo
engine ['ɛndʒən] *n* **1** : motor *m* **2** LOCOMOTIVE : locomotora *f* — **engineer** [ˌɛndʒə'nɪr] *n* **1** : ingeniero *m*, -ra *f* **2** : maquinista *mf* (de locomotoras) — **~** *vt* **1** CONSTRUCT : construir **2** CONTRIVE : tramar — **engineering** [ˌɛndʒə'nɪrɪŋ] *n* : ingeniería *f*
English ['ɪŋglɪʃ, 'ɪŋlɪʃ] *adj* : inglés — **~** *n* : inglés *m* (idioma) — **Englishman** ['ɪŋglɪʃmən, 'ɪŋlɪʃ-] *n* : inglés *m* — **Englishwoman** ['ɪŋglɪʃˌwʊmən, 'ɪŋlɪʃ-] *n* : inglesa *f*
engrave [ɪn'greɪv, ɛn-] *vt* **-graved; -graving** : grabar — **engraving** [ɪn'greɪvɪŋ, ɛn-] *n* : grabado *m*
engross [ɪn'gro:s, ɛn-] *vt* : absorber
engulf [ɪn'gʌlf, ɛn-] *vt* : envolver
enhance [ɪn'hænts, ɛn-] *vt* **-hanced; -hancing** : aumentar, mejorar
enjoy [ɪn'dʒɔɪ, ɛn-] *vt* **1** : disfrutar, gozar de **2 ~ oneself** : divertirse — **enjoyable** [ɪn'dʒɔɪəbəl, ɛn-] *adj* : agradable — **enjoyment** [ɪn'dʒɔɪmənt, ɛn-] *n* : placer *m*
enlarge [ɪn'lɑrdʒ, ɛn-] *v* **-larged; -larging** *vt* : agrandar, ampliar — *vi* **1** : agrandarse **2 ~ upon** : extenderse sobre — **enlargement** [ɪn'lɑrdʒmənt, ɛn-] *n* : ampliación *f*
enlighten [ɪn'laɪtən, ɛn-] *vt* : aclarar, iluminar
enlist [ɪn'lɪst, ɛn-] *vt* **1** ENROLL : alistar **2** OBTAIN : conseguir — *vi* : alistarse
enliven [ɪn'laɪvən, ɛn-] *vt* : animar

enmity ['ɛnməṯi] *n, pl* **-ties** : enemistad *f*
enormous [ɪ'nɔrməs] *adj* : enorme
enough [ɪ'nʌf] *adj* : bastante, suficiente — ~ *adv* : bastante — ~ *pron* **1** : (lo) suficiente, (lo) bastante **2 it's not ~** : no basta **3 I've had ~ !** : ¡estoy harto!
enquire [ɪn'kwaɪr, ɛn-], **enquiry** ['ɪn,kwaɪri, 'ɛn-, -kwəri; ɪn'kwaɪri, ɛn'-] → **inquire, inquiry**
enrage [ɪn'reɪdʒ, ɛn-] *vt* **-raged; -raging** : enfurecer
enrich [ɪn'rɪtʃ, ɛn-] *vt* : enriquecer
enroll *or* **enrol** [ɪn'ro:l, ɛn-] *v* **-rolled; -rolling** *vt* : matricular, inscribir — *vi* : matricularse, inscribirse
ensemble [ɑn'sɑmbəl] *n* : conjunto *m*
ensign ['ɛntsən, 'ɛn,saɪn] *n* **1** FLAG : enseña *f* **2** : alférez *mf* (de fragata)
enslave [ɪn'sleɪv, ɛn-] *vt* **-slaved; -slaving** : esclavizar
ensue [ɪn'su:, ɛn-] *vi* **-sued; -suing** : seguir, resultar
ensure [ɪn'ʃʊr, ɛn-] *vt* **-sured; -suring** : asegurar
entail [ɪn'teɪl, ɛn-] *vt* : suponer, conllevar
entangle [ɪn'tæŋgəl, ɛn-] *vt* **-gled; -gling** : enredar — **entanglement** [ɪn'tæŋgəlmənt, ɛn-] *n* : enredo *m*
enter ['ɛntər] *vt* **1** : entrar en **2** RECORD : inscribir — *vi* **1** : entrar **2 ~ into** : firmar (un acuerdo), entablar (negociaciones, etc.)
enterprise ['ɛntər,praɪz] *n* **1** : empresa *f* **2** INITIATIVE : iniciativa *f* — **enterprising** ['ɛntər,praɪzɪŋ] *adj* : emprendedor
entertain [,ɛntər'teɪn] *vt* **1** AMUSE : entretener, divertir **2** CONSIDER : considerar **3 ~ guests** : recibir invitados — **entertainment** [,ɛntər'teɪnmənt] *n* : entretenimiento *m*, diversión *f*
enthrall *or* **enthral** [ɪn'θrɔl, ɛn-] *vt* **-thralled; -thralling** : cautivar, embelesar
enthusiasm [ɪn'θu:zi,æzəm, ɛn-, -'θju:-] *n* : entusiasmo *m* — **enthusiast** [ɪn'θu:zi,æst, ɛn-, -'θju:-, -əst] *n* : entusiasta *mf* — **enthusiastic** [ɪn,θu:zi'æstɪk, ɛn-, -,θju:-] *adj* : entusiasta
entice [ɪn'taɪs, ɛn-] *vt* **-ticed; -ticing** : atraer, tentar
entire [ɪn'taɪr, ɛn-] *adj* : entero, completo — **entirely** [ɪn'taɪrli, ɛn-] *adv* : completamente — **entirety** [ɪn'taɪrṯi, ɛn-, -'taɪrəṯi] *n, pl* **-ties** : totalidad *f*
entitle [ɪn'taɪṯəl, ɛn-] *vt* **-tled; -tling 1** NAME : titular **2** AUTHORIZE : dar derecho a — **entitlement** [ɪn'taɪṯəlmənt, ɛn-] *n* : derecho *m*
entity ['ɛntəṯi] *n, pl* **-ties** : entidad *f*
entrails ['ɛn,treɪlz, -trəlz] *npl* : entrañas *fpl*, vísceras *fpl*
entrance[1] [ɪn'træns, ɛn-] *vt* **-tranced; -trancing** : encantar, fascinar
entrance[2] ['ɛntrənts] *n* : entrada *f* — **entrant** ['ɛntrənt] *n* : participante *mf*
entreat [ɪn'tri:t, ɛn-] *vt* : suplicar
entrée *or* **entree** ['ɑn,treɪ, ,ɑn'-] *n* : plato *m* principal
entrepreneur [,ɑntrəprə'nər, -'njʊr] *n* : empresario *m*, -ria *f*
entrust [ɪn'trʌst, ɛn-] *vt* : confiar
entry ['ɛntri] *n, pl* **-tries 1** ENTRANCE : entrada *f* **2** NOTATION : entrada *f*, anotación *f*
enumerate [ɪ'nu:mə,reɪt, ɛ-, -'nju:-] *vt* **-ated; -ating** : enumerar
enunciate [i'nʌntsi,eɪt, ɛ-] *vt* **-ated; -ating 1** STATE : enunciar **2** PRONOUNCE : articular
envelop [ɪn'vɛləp, ɛn-] *vt* : envolver — **envelope** ['ɛnvə,lo:p, 'ɑn-] *n* : sobre *m*
envious ['ɛnviəs] *adj* : envidioso — **enviously** *adv* : con envidia
environment [ɪn'vaɪrənmənt, ɛn-, -'vaɪərn-] *n* : medio *m* ambiente — **environmental** [ɪn,vaɪrən'mɛntəl, ɛn-, -,vaɪərn-] *adj* : ambiental — **environmentalist** [ɪn,vaɪrən'mɛntəlɪst, ɛn-, -,vaɪərn-] *n* : ecologista *mf*
envision [ɪn'vɪʒən, ɛn-] *vt* : prever, imaginar
envoy ['ɛn,vɔɪ, 'ɑn-] *n* : enviado *m*, -da *f*
envy ['ɛnvi] *n, pl* **envies** : envidia *f* — ~ *vt* **-vied; -vying** : envidiar
enzyme ['ɛn,zaɪm] *n* : enzima *f*
epic ['ɛpɪk] *adj* : épico — ~ *n* : epopeya *f*
epidemic [,ɛpə'dɛmɪk] *n* : epidemia *f* — ~ *adj* : epidémico
epilepsy ['ɛpə,lɛpsi] *n, pl* **-sies** : epilepsia *f* — **epileptic** [,ɛpə'lɛptɪk] *adj* : epiléptico — ~ *n* : epiléptico *m*, -ca *f*
episode ['ɛpə,so:d] *n* : episodio *m*
epitaph ['ɛpə,tæf] *n* : epitafio *m*
epitome [ɪ'pɪṯəmi] *n* : personificación *f* — **epitomize** [ɪ'pɪṯə,maɪz] *vt* **-mized; -mizing** : ser la personificación de, personificar
epoch ['ɛpək, 'ɛ,pɑk, 'i:,pɑk] *n* : época *f*
equal ['i:kwəl] *adj* **1** SAME : igual **2 be ~ to** : estar a la altura de (una tarea, etc.) — ~ *n* : igual *mf* — ~ *vt* **equaled** *or* **equalled; equaling** *or* **equalling 1** : igualar **2** : ser igual a (en matématicas) — **equality** [ɪ'kwɑləṯi] *n, pl* **-ties** : igualdad *f* — **equalize** ['i:kwə,laɪz] *vt* **-ized; -izing** : igualar — **equally** ['i:kwəli] *adv* **1** : igual-

mente **2 ~ important** : igual de importante
equate [ɪ'kweɪt] *vt* **equated; equating ~ with** : equiparar con — **equation** [ɪ'kweɪʒən] *n* : ecuación *f*
equator [ɪ'kweɪt̬ər] *n* : ecuador *m*
equilibrium [ˌiːkwə'lɪbriəm, ˌɛ-] *n, pl* **-riums** *or* **-ria** [-briə] : equilibrio *m*
equinox ['iːkwəˌnɑks, 'ɛ-] *n* : equinoccio *m*
equip [ɪ'kwɪp] *vt* **equipped; equipping** : equipar — **equipment** [ɪ'kwɪpmənt] *n* : equipo *m*
equity ['ɛkwət̬i] *n, pl* **-ties 1** FAIRNESS : equidad *f* **2 equities** *npl* STOCKS : acciones *fpl* ordinarias
equivalent [ɪ'kwɪvələnt] *adj* : equivalente — **~** *n* : equivalente *m*
era ['ɪrə, 'ɛrə, 'iːrə] *n* : era *f*, época *f*
eradicate [ɪ'rædəˌkeɪt] *vt* **-cated; -cating** : erradicar
erase [ɪ'reɪs] *vt* **erased; erasing** : borrar — **eraser** [ɪ'reɪsər] *n* : goma *f* de borrar, borrador *m*
erect [ɪ'rɛkt] *adj* : erguido — **~** *vt* : erigir, levantar — **erection** [ɪ'rɛkʃən] *n* **1** BUILDING : construcción *f* **2** : erección *f* (en fisiología)
erode [ɪ'roːd] *vt* **eroded; eroding** : erosionar (el suelo), corroer (metales) — **erosion** [ɪ'roːʒən] *n* : erosión *f*, corrosión *f*
erotic [ɪ'rɑt̬ɪk] *adj* : erótico
err ['ɛr, 'ər] *vi* : equivocarse, errar
errand ['ɛrənd] *n* : mandado *m*, recado *m Spain*
erratic [ɪ'ræt̬ɪk] *adj* : errático, irregular
error ['ɛrər] *n* : error *m* — **erroneous** [ɪ'roːniəs, ɛ-] *adj* : erróneo
erupt [ɪ'rʌpt] *vi* **1** : hacer erupción (dícese de un volcán) **2** : estallar (dícese de la cólera, la violencia, etc.) — **eruption** [ɪ'rʌpʃən] *n* : erupción *f*
escalate ['ɛskəˌleɪt] *vi* **-lated; -lating** : intensificarse
escalator ['ɛskəˌleɪt̬ər] *n* : escalera *f* mecánica
escapade ['ɛskəˌpeɪd] *n* : aventura *f*
escape [ɪ'skeɪp, ɛ-] *v* **-caped; -caping** *vt* : escapar a, evitar — *vi* : escaparse, fugarse — **~** *n* **1** : fuga *f* **2 ~ from reality** : evasión *f* de la realidad — **escapee** [ɪˌskeɪ'piː, ˌɛ-] *n* : fugitivo *m*, -va *f*
escort ['ɛsˌkɔrt] *n* **1** GUARD : escolta *f* **2** COMPANION : acompañante *mf* — **~** [ɪ'skɔrt, ɛ-] *vt* **1** : escoltar **2** ACCOMPANY : acompañar
Eskimo ['ɛskəˌmoː] *adj* : esquimal
especially [ɪ'spɛʃəli] *adv* : especialmente
espionage ['ɛspiəˌnɑʒ, -ˌnɑdʒ] *n* : espionaje *m*
espresso [ɛ'sprɛˌsoː] *n, pl* **-sos** : café *m* exprés
essay ['ɛˌseɪ] *n* : ensayo *m* (literario), composición *f* (académica)
essence ['ɛsənts] *n* : esencia *f* — **essential** [ɪ'sɛntʃəl] *adj* : esencial — **~** *n* **1** : elemento *m* esencial **2 the ~s** : lo indispensable
establish [ɪ'stæblɪʃ, ɛ-] *vt* : establecer — **establishment** [ɪ'stæblɪʃmənt, ɛ-] *n* : establecimiento *m*
estate [ɪ'steɪt, ɛ-] *n* **1** POSSESSIONS : bienes *mpl* **2** LAND, PROPERTY : finca *f*
esteem [ɪ'stiːm, ɛ-] *n* : estima *f* — **~** *vt* : estimar
esthetic [ɛs'θɛt̬ɪk] → **aesthetic**
estimate ['ɛstəˌmeɪt] *vt* **-mated; -mating** : calcular, estimar — **~** ['ɛstəmət] *n* **1** : cálculo *m* (aproximado) **2** *or* **~ of costs** : presupuesto *m* — **estimation** [ˌɛstə'meɪʃən] *n* **1** JUDGMENT : juicio *m* **2** ESTEEM : estima *f*
estuary ['ɛstʃʊˌwɛri] *n, pl* **-aries** : estuario *m*, ría *f*
eternal [ɪ'tərnəl, iː-] *adj* : eterno — **eternity** [ɪ'tərnət̬i, iː-] *n, pl* **-ties** : eternidad *f*
ether ['iːθər] *n* : éter *m*
ethical ['ɛθɪkəl] *adj* : ético — **ethics** ['ɛθɪks] *ns & pl* : ética *f*, moralidad *f*
ethnic ['ɛθnɪk] *adj* : étnico
etiquette ['ɛt̬ɪkət, -ˌkɛt] *n* : etiqueta *f*
Eucharist ['juːkərɪst] *n* : Eucaristía *f*
eulogy ['juːlədʒi] *n, pl* **-gies** : elogio *m*, panegírico *m*
euphemism ['juːfəˌmɪzəm] *n* : eufemismo *m*
euphoria [jʊ'foriə] *n* : euforia *f*
European [ˌjʊrə'piːən, -piːn] *adj* : europeo
evacuate [ɪ'vækjʊˌeɪt] *vt* **-ated; -ating** : evacuar — **evacuation** [ɪˌvækjʊ'eɪʃən] *n* : evacuación *f*
evade [ɪ'veɪd] *vt* **evaded; evading** : evadir, eludir
evaluate [ɪ'væljʊˌeɪt] *vt* **-ated; -ating** : evaluar
evaporate [ɪ'væpəˌreɪt] *vi* **-rated; -rating** : evaporarse
evasion [ɪ'veɪʒən] *n* : evasión *f* — **evasive** [ɪ'veɪsɪv] *adj* : evasivo
eve ['iːv] *n* : víspera *f*
even ['iːvən] *adj* **1** REGULAR, STEADY : regular, constante **2** LEVEL : plano, llano **3** SMOOTH : liso **4** EQUAL : igual **5 ~ number** : número *m* par **6 get ~ with** : desquitarse con — **~** *adv* **1** : hasta, incluso **2 ~ better** : aún

mejor, todavía mejor **3 ~ if** : aunque **4 ~ so** : aun así — **~** *vt* : igualar — *vi or* **~ out** : nivelarse
evening ['i:vnɪŋ] *n* : tarde *f*, noche *f*
event [ɪ'vɛnt] *n* **1** : acontecimiento *m*, suceso *m* **2** : prueba *f* (en deportes) **3 in the ~ of** : en caso de — **eventful** [ɪ'vɛntfəl] *adj* : lleno de incidentes
eventual [ɪ'vɛntʃuəl] *adj* : final — **eventuality** [ɪ,vɛntʃu'æləṭi] *n, pl* **-ties** : eventualidad *f* — **eventually** [ɪ-'vɛntʃuəli] *adv* : al fin, finalmente
ever ['ɛvər] *adv* **1** ALWAYS : siempre **2 ~ since** : desde entonces **3 hardly ~** : casi nunca **4 have you ~ done it?** : ¿lo has hecho alguna vez?
evergreen ['ɛvər,gri:n] *n* : planta *f* de hoja perenne
everlasting [,ɛvər'læstɪŋ] *adj* : eterno
every ['ɛvri] *adj* **1** EACH : cada **2 ~ month** : todos los meses **3 ~ other day** : cada dos días — **everybody** ['ɛvri,bʌdi, -,bɑ-] *pron* : todos *mpl*, -das *fpl;* todo el mundo — **everyday** [,ɛvri-'deɪ, 'ɛvri,-] *adj* : cotidiano, de todos los días — **everyone** ['ɛvri,wʌn] → **everybody** — **everything** ['ɛvri ,θɪŋ] *pron* : todo — **everywhere** ['ɛvri ,hwɛr] *adv* : en todas partes, por todas partes
evict [ɪ'vɪkt] *vt* : desahuciar, desalojar — **eviction** [ɪ'vɪkʃən] *n* : desahucio *m*
evidence ['ɛvədənts] *n* **1** PROOF : pruebas *fpl* **2** TESTIMONY : testimonio *m*, declaración *f* — **evident** ['ɛvidənt] *adj* : evidente — **evidently** ['ɛvidəntli, ,ɛvi-'dɛntli] *adv* **1** OBVIOUSLY : obviamente **2** APPARENTLY : evidentemente, al parecer
evil ['i:vəl, -vɪl] *adj* **eviler** *or* **eviller; evilest** *or* **evillest** : malvado, malo — **~** *n* : mal *m*, maldad *f*
evoke [i'vo:k] *vt* **evoked; evoking** : evocar
evolution [,ɛvə'lu:ʃən, ,i:-] *n* : evolución *f*, desarrollo *m* — **evolve** [i'vɑlv] *vi* **evolved; evolving** : evolucionar, desarrollarse
exact [ɪg'zækt, ɛg-] *adj* : exacto, preciso — **~** *vt* : exigir — **exacting** [ɪg-'zæktɪŋ, ɛg-] *adj* : exigente — **exactly** [ɪg'zæktli, ɛg-] *adv* : exactamente
exaggerate [ɪg'zædʒə,reɪt, ɛg-] *v* **-ated; -ating** : exagerar — **exaggeration** [ɪg-,zædʒə'reɪʃən, ɛg-] *n* : exageración *f*
examine [ɪg'zæmən, ɛg-] *vt* **-ined; -ining 1** : examinar **2** INSPECT : revisar **3** QUESTION : interrogar — **exam** [ɪg-'zæm, ɛg-] *n* : examen *m* — **examination** [ɪg,zæmə'neɪʃən, ɛg-] *n* : examen *m*
example [ɪg'zæmpəl, ɛg-] *n* : ejemplo *m*
exasperate [ɪg'zæspə,reɪt, ɛg-] *vt* **-ated; -ating** : exasperar — **exasperation** [ɪg,zæspə'reɪʃən, ɛg-] *n* : exasperación *f*
excavate ['ɛkskə,veɪt] *vt* **-vated; -vating** : excavar — **excavation** [,ɛkskə'veɪʃən] *n* : excavación *f*
exceed [ɪk'si:d, ɛk-] *vt* : exceder, sobrepasar — **exceedingly** [ɪk'si:dɪŋli, ɛk-] *adv* : extremadamente
excel [ɪk'sɛl, ɛk-] *v* **-celled; -celling** *vi* : sobresalir — *vt* SURPASS : superar — **excellence** ['ɛksələnts] *n* : excelencia *f* — **excellent** ['ɛksələnt] *adj* : excelente
except [ɪk'sɛpt] *prep or* **~ for** : excepto, menos, salvo — **~** *vt* : exceptuar — **exception** [ɪk'sɛpʃən] *n* : excepción *f* — **exceptional** [ɪk'sɛpʃənəl] *adj* : excepcional
excerpt ['ɛk,sərpt, 'ɛg,zərpt] *n* : extracto *m*
excess [ɪk'sɛs, 'ɛk,sɛs] *n* : exceso *m* — **~** ['ɛk,sɛs, ɪk'sɛs] *adj* : excesivo, de sobra — **excessive** [ɪk'sɛsɪv, ɛk-] *adj* : excesivo
exchange [ɪks'tʃeɪndʒ, ɛks-; 'ɛks,tʃeɪndʒ] *n* **1** : intercambio *m* **2** : cambio *m* (en finanzas) — **~** *vt* **-changed; -changing** : cambiar, intercambiar
excise [ɪk'saɪz, ɛk-] *n* **~ tax** : impuesto *m* interno, impuesto *m* sobre el consumo
excite [ɪk'saɪt, ɛk-] *vt* **-cited; -citing** : excitar, emocionar — **excited** [ɪk-'saɪṭəd, ɛk-] *adj* : excitado, entusiasmado — **excitement** [ɪk'saɪtmənt, ɛk-] *n* : entusiasmo *m*, emoción *f*
exclaim [ɪks'kleɪm, ɛk-] *v* : exclamar — **exclamation** [,ɛksklə'meɪʃən] *n* : exclamación *f* — **exclamation point** *n* : signo *m* de admiración
exclude [ɪks'klu:d, ɛks-] *vt* **-cluded; -cluding** : excluir — **excluding** [ɪks-'klu:dɪŋ, ɛks-] *prep* : excepto, con excepción de — **exclusion** [ɪks'klu:ʒən, ɛks-] *n* : exclusión *f* — **exclusive** [ɪks-'klu:sɪv, ɛks-] *adj* : exclusivo
excrement ['ɛkskrəmənt] *n* : excremento *m*
excruciating [ɪk'skru:ʃi,eɪṭɪŋ, ɛk-] *adj* : insoportable, atroz
excursion [ɪk'skərʒən, ɛk-] *n* : excursión *f*
excuse [ɪk'skju:z, ɛk-] *vt* **-cused; -cusing 1** : perdonar **2 ~ me** : perdóne, perdón — **~** [ɪk'skju:s, ɛk-] *n* : excusa *f*
execute ['ɛksɪ,kju:t] *vt* **-cuted; -cuting** : ejecutar — **execution** [,ɛksɪ'kju:ʃən] *n* : ejecución *f* — **executioner** [,ɛksɪ-'kju:ʃənər] *n* : verdugo *m*

executive [ɪg'zɛkjət̬ɪv, ɛg-] *adj* : ejecutivo — ~ *n* **1** MANAGER : ejecutivo *m*, -va *f* **2** *or* ~ **branch** : poder *m* ejecutivo

exemplify [ɪg'zɛmplə,faɪ, ɛg-] *vt* **-fied; -fying** : ejemplificar — **exemplary** [ɪg'zɛmpləri, ɛg-] *adj* : ejemplar

exempt [ɪg'zɛmpt, ɛg-] *adj* : exento — ~ *vt* : dispensar — **exemption** [ɪg'zɛmpʃən, ɛg-] *n* : exención *f*

exercise ['ɛksər,saɪz] *n* : ejercicio *m* — ~ *v* **-cised; -cising** *vt* USE : ejercer, hacer uso de — *vi* : hacer ejercicio

exert [ɪg'zərt, ɛg-] *vt* **1** : ejercer **2** ~ **oneself** : esforzarse — **exertion** [ɪg'zərʃən, ɛg-] *n* : esfuerzo *m*

exhale [ɛks'heɪl] *v* **-haled; -haling** : exhalar

exhaust [ɪg'zɔst, ɛg-] *vt* : agotar — ~ *n* **1** *or* ~ **fumes** : gases *mpl* de escape **2** *or* ~ **pipe** : tubo *m* de escape — **exhaustion** [ɪg'zɔstʃən, ɛg-] *n* : agotamiento *m* — **exhaustive** [ɪg'zɔstɪv, ɛg-] *adj* : exhaustivo

exhibit [ɪg'zɪbət, ɛg-] *vt* **1** DISPLAY : exponer **2** SHOW : mostrar — ~ *n* **1** : objeto *m* expuesto **2** EXHIBITION : exposición *f* — **exhibition** [,ɛksə'bɪʃən] *n* : exposición *f*

exhilarate [ɪg'zɪlə,reɪt, ɛg-] *vt* **-rated; -rating** : alegrar — **exhilaration** [ɪg,zɪlə'reɪʃən, ɛg-] *n* : regocijo *m*

exile ['ɛg,zaɪl, 'ɛk,saɪl] *n* **1** : exilio *m* **2** OUTCAST : exiliado *m*, -da *f* — ~ *vt* **exiled; exiling** : exiliar

exist [ɪg'zɪst, ɛg-] *vi* : existir — **existence** [ɪg'zɪstənts, ɛg-] *n* : existencia *f* — **existing** *adj* : existente

exit ['ɛgzət, 'ɛksət] *n* : salida *f* — ~ *vi* : salir

exodus ['ɛksədəs] *n* : éxodo *m*

exonerate [ɪg'zɑnə,reɪt, ɛg-] *vt* **-ated; -ating** : exonerar, disculpar

exorbitant [ɪg'zɔrbətənt, ɛg-] *adj* : exorbitante, excesivo

exotic [ɪg'zɑtɪk, ɛg-] *adj* : exótico

expand [ɪk'spænd, ɛk-] *vt* **1** : ampliar, extender **2** : dilatar (metales, etc.) — *vi* **1** : ampliarse, extenderse **2** : dilatarse (dícese de metales, etc.) — **expanse** [ɪk'spænts, ɛk-] *n* : extensión *f* — **expansion** [ɪk'spæntʃən, ɛk-] *n* : expansión *f*

expatriate [ɛks'peɪtriət, -,eɪt] *n* : expatriado *m*, -da *f* — ~ *adj* : expatriado

expect [ɪk'spɛkt, ɛk-] *vt* **1** : esperar **2** REQUIRE : contar con — *vi* **be expecting** : estar embarazada — **expectancy** [ɪk'spɛktəntsi, ɛk-] *n, pl* **-cies** : esperanza *f* — **expectant** [ɪk'spɛktənt, ɛk-] *adj* **1** : expectante **2** ~ **mother** : futura madre *f* — **expectation** [,ɛk,spɛk'teɪʃən] *n* : esperanza *f*

expedient [ɪk'spi:diənt, ɛk-] *adj* : conveniente — ~ *n* : expediente *m*, recurso *m*

expedition [,ɛkspə'dɪʃən] *n* : expedición *f*

expel [ɪk'spɛl, ɛk-] *vt* **-pelled; -pelling** : expulsar (a una persona), expeler (humo, etc.)

expend [ɪk'spɛnd, ɛk-] *vt* : gastar — **expendable** [ɪk'spɛndəbəl, ɛk-] *adj* : prescindible — **expenditure** [ɪk'spɛndɪtʃər, ɛk-, -,tʃʊr] *n* : gasto *m* — **expense** [ɪk'spɛnts, ɛk-] *n* **1** : gasto *m* **2** ~**s** *npl* : gastos *mpl*, expensas *fpl* **3 at the** ~ **of** : a expensas de — **expensive** [ɪk'spɛntsɪv, ɛk-] *adj* : caro

experience [ɪk'spɪriənts, ɛk-] *n* : experiencia *f* — ~ *vt* **-enced; -encing** : experimentar — **experienced** [ɪk'spɪriəntst, ɛk-] *adj* : experimentado — **experiment** [ɪk'spɛrəmənt, ɛk-, -'spɪr-] *n* : experimento *m* — ~ *vi* : experimentar — **experimental** [ɪk,spɛrə'mɛntəl, ɛk-, -,spɪr-] *adj* : experimental

expert ['ɛk,spərt, ɪk'spərt] *adj* : experto — ~ ['ɛk,spərt] *n* : experto *m*, -ta *f* — **expertise** [,ɛkspər'ti:z] *n* : pericia *f*, competencia *f*

expire [ɪk'spaɪr, ɛk-] *vi* **-pired; -piring 1** : caducar, vencer **2** DIE : expirar, morir — **expiration** [,ɛkspə'reɪʃən] *n* : vencimiento *m*, caducidad *f*

explain [ɪk'spleɪn, ɛk-] *vt* : explicar — **explanation** [,ɛksplə'neɪʃən] *n* : explicación *f* — **explanatory** [ɪk'splænə,tori, ɛk-] *adj* : explicativo

explicit [ɪk'splɪsət, ɛk-] *adj* : explícito

explode [ɪk'splo:d, ɛk-] *v* **-ploded; -ploding** *vt* : hacer explotar — *vi* : explotar, estallar

exploit ['ɛk,splɔɪt] *n* : hazaña *f*, proeza *f* — ~ [ɪk'splɔɪt, ɛk-] *vt* : explotar — **exploitation** [,ɛk,splɔɪ'teɪʃən] *n* : explotación *f*

exploration [,ɛksplə'reɪʃən] *n* : exploración *f* — **explore** [ɪk'splor, ɛk-] *vt* **-plored; -ploring** : explorar — **explorer** [ɪk'splorər, ɛk-] *n* : explorador *m*, -dora *f*

explosion [ɪk'splo:ʒən, ɛk-] *n* : explosión *f* — **explosive** [ɪk'splo:sɪv, ɛk-] *adj* : explosivo — ~ *n* : explosivo *m*

export [ɛk'sport, 'ɛk,sport] *vt* : exportar — ~ ['ɛk,sport] *n* : exportación *f*

expose [ɪk'spo:z, ɛk-] *vt* **-posed; -posing 1** : exponer **2** REVEAL : descubrir, revelar — **exposed** [ɪk'spo:zd, ɛk-] *adj*

: expuesto, al descubierto — **exposure** [ɪk'spo:ʒər, ɛk-] *n* : exposición *f*

express [ɪk'sprɛs, ɛk-] *adj* **1** SPECIFIC : expreso, específico **2** FAST : expreso, rápido — ~ *adv* : por correo urgente — ~ *n or* ~ **train** : expreso *m* — ~ *vt* : expresar — **expression** [ɪk'sprɛʃən, ɛk-] *n* : expresión *f* — **expressive** [ɪk'sprɛsɪv, ɛk-] *adj* : expresivo — **expressly** [ɪk'sprɛsli, ɛk-] *adv* : expresamente — **expressway** [ɪk'sprɛs,weɪ, ɛk-] *n* : autopista *f*

expulsion [ɪk'spʌlʃən, ɛk-] *n* : expulsión *f*

exquisite [ɛk'skwɪzət, 'ɛk,skwɪ-] *adj* : exquisito

extend [ɪk'stɛnd, ɛk-] *vt* **1** STRETCH : extender **2** LENGTHEN : prolongar **3** ENLARGE : ampliar **4** ~ **one's hand** : tender la mano — *vi* : extenderse — **extension** [ɪk'stɛntʃən, ɛk-] *n* **1** : extensión *f* **2** LENGTHENING : prolongación *f* **3** ANNEX : ampliación *f*, anexo *m* **4** ~ **cord** : alargador *m* — **extensive** [ɪk'stɛntsɪv, ɛk-] *adj* : extenso — **extent** [ɪk'stɛnt, ɛk-] *n* **1** SIZE : extensión *f* **2** DEGREE : alcance *m*, grado *m* **3** **to a certain** ~ : hasta cierto punto

extenuating [ɪk'stɛnjə,weɪṭɪŋ, ɛk-] *adj* ~ **circumstances** : circunstancias *fpl* atenuantes

exterior [ɛk'stɪriər] *adj* : exterior — ~ *n* : exterior *m*

exterminate [ɪk'stərmə,neɪt, ɛk-] *vt* **-nated; -nating** : exterminar — **extermination** [ɪk,stərmə'neɪʃən, ɛk-] *n* : exterminación *f*

external [ɪk'stərnəl, ɛk-] *adj* : externo — **externally** [ɪk'stərnəli, ɛk-] *adv* : exteriormente

extinct [ɪk'stɪŋkt, ɛk-] *adj* : extinto — **extinction** [ɪk'stɪŋkʃən, ɛk-] *n* : extinción *f*

extinguish [ɪk'stɪŋgwɪʃ, ɛk-] *vt* : extinguir, apagar — **extinguisher** [ɪk'stɪŋgwɪʃər, ɛk-] *n* : extintor *m*

extol [ɪk'sto:l, ɛk-] *vt* **-tolled; -tolling** : ensalzar, alabar

extort [ɪk'stɔrt, ɛk-] *vt* : arrancar (algo a algn) por la fuerza — **extortion** [ɪk'stɔrʃən, ɛk-] *n* : extorsión *f*

extra ['ɛkstrə] *adj* : suplementario, de más — ~ *n* : extra *m* — ~ *adv* **1** : extra, más **2** ~ **special** : super especial

extract [ɪk'strækt, ɛk-] *vt* : extraer, sacar — ~ ['ɛk,strækt] *n* : extracto *m* — **extraction** [ɪk'strækʃən, ɛk-] *n* : extracción *f*

extracurricular [,ɛkstrəkə'rɪkjələr] *adj* : extracurricular

extradite ['ɛkstrə,daɪt] *vt* **-dited; -diting** : extraditar

extraordinary [ɪk'strɔrdən,ɛri, ,ɛkstrə'ɔrd-] *adj* : extraordinario

extraterrestrial [,ɛkstrətə'rɛstriəl] *adj* : extraterrestre — ~ *n* : extraterrestre *mf*

extravagant [ɪk'strævɪgənt, ɛk-] *adj* **1** WASTEFUL : despilfarrador, derrochador **2** EXAGGERATED : extravagante, exagerado — **extravagance** [ɪk'strævɪgənts, ɛk-] *n* **1** WASTEFULNESS : derroche *m*, despilfarro *m* **2** LUXURY : lujo *m* **3** EXAGGERATION : extravagancia *f*

extreme [ɪk'stri:m, ɛk-] *adj* : extremo — ~ *n* : extremo *m* — **extremely** [ɪk'stri:mli, ɛk-] *adv* : extremadamente — **extremity** [ɪk'strɛməṭi, ɛk-] *n, pl* **-ties** : extremidad *f*

extricate ['ɛkstrə,keɪt] *vt* **-cated; -cating** : librar, (lograr) sacar

extrovert ['ɛkstrə,vərt] *n* : extrovertido *m*, -da *f* — **extroverted** ['ɛkstrə,vərṭəd] *adj* : extrovertido

exuberant [ɪg'zu:bərənt, ɛg-] *adj* **1** JOYOUS : eufórico **2** LUSH : exuberante — **exuberance** [ɪg'zu:bərənts, ɛg-] *n* **1** JOYOUSNESS : euforia *f* **2** VIGOR : exuberancia *f*

exult [ɪg'zʌlt, ɛg-] *vi* : exultar

eye ['aɪ] *n* **1** : ojo *m* **2** VISION : visión *f*, vista *f* **3** GLANCE : mirada *f* — ~ *vt* **eyed; eyeing** *or* **eying** : mirar — **eyeball** ['aɪ,bɔl] *n* : globo *m* ocular — **eyebrow** ['aɪ,braʊ] *n* : ceja *f* — **eyeglasses** ['aɪ,glæsəz] *npl* : anteojos *mpl*, lentes *mpl* — **eyelash** ['aɪ,læʃ] *n* : pestaña *f* — **eyelid** ['aɪ,lɪd] *n* : párpado *m* — **eyesight** ['aɪ,saɪt] *n* : vista *f*, visión *f* — **eyesore** ['aɪ,sor] *n* : monstruosidad *f* — **eyewitness** ['aɪ'wɪtnəs] *n* : testigo *mf* ocular

F

f ['ɛf] *n, pl* **f's** *or* **fs** ['ɛfs] : f, sexta letra del alfabeto inglés
fable ['feɪbəl] *n* : fábula *f*
fabric ['fæbrɪk] *n* : tela *f*, tejido *m*
fabulous ['fæbjələs] *adj* : fabuloso
facade [fə'sɑd] *n* : fachada *f*
face ['feɪs] *n* **1** : cara *f*, rostro *m* (de una persona) **2** APPEARANCE : fisonomía *f*, aspecto *m* **3** : cara *f* (de una moneda), fachada *f* (de un edificio) **4** **~ value** : valor *m* nominal **5** **in the ~ of** : en medio de, ante **6** **lose ~** : desprestigiarse **7** **make ~s** : hacer muecas — **~ faced; facing** *vt* **1** : estar frente a **2** CONFRONT : enfrentarse a **3** OVERLOOK : dar a — *vi* **~ to the north** : mirar hacia el norte — **facedown** ['feɪs,daʊn] *adv* : boca abajo — **faceless** ['feɪsləs] *adj* : anónimo — **face–lift** ['feɪs,lɪft] *n* : estiramiento *m* facial
facet ['fæsət] *n* : faceta *f*
face–to–face *adv & adj* : cara a cara
facial ['feɪʃəl] *adj* : de la cara, facial — **~** *n* : limpieza *f* de cutis
facetious [fə'siːʃəs] *adj* : gracioso, burlón
facility [fə'sɪləṭi] *n, pl* **-ties** **1** EASE : facilidad *f* **2** CENTER : centro *m* **3** **facilities** *npl* : comodidades *fpl*, servicios *mpl*
facsimile [fæk'sɪməli] *n* : facsímile *m*, facsímil *m*
fact ['fækt] *n* **1** : hecho *m* **2** **in ~** : en realidad, de hecho
faction ['fækʃən] *n* : facción *m*, bando *m*
factor ['fæktər] *n* : factor *m*
factory ['fæktəri] *n, pl* **-ries** : fábrica *f*
factual ['fæktʃʊəl] *adj* : basado en hechos
faculty ['fækəlti] *n, pl* **-ties** : facultad *f*
fad ['fæd] *n* : moda *f* pasajera, manía *f*
fade ['feɪd] *v* **faded; fading** *vi* **1** WITHER : marchitarse **2** DISCOLOR : desteñirse, decolorarse **3** DIM : apagarse **4** VANISH : desvanecerse — *vt* : desteñir
fail ['feɪl] *vi* **1** : fracasar (dícese de una empresa, un matrimonio, etc.) **2** BREAK DOWN : fallar **3** **~ in** : faltar a, no cumplir con **4** FLUNK : suspender *Spain*, ser reprobado *Lat* **5** **~ to do sth** : no hacer algo — *vt* **1** DISAPPOINT : fallar **2** FLUNK : suspender *Spain*, reprobar *Lat* — **~** *n* **without ~** : sin falta — **failing** ['feɪlɪŋ] *n* : defecto *m* — **failure** ['feɪljər] *n* **1** : fracaso *m* **2** BREAKDOWN : falla *f*
faint ['feɪnt] *adj* **1** WEAK : débil **2** INDISTINCT : tenue, indistinto **3** **feel ~** : estar mareado — **~** *vi* : desmayarse — **~** *n* : desmayo *m* — **fainthearted** ['feɪnt'hɑrṭəd] *adj* : cobarde, pusilánime — **faintly** ['feɪntli] *adv* **1** WEAKLY : débilmente **2** SLIGHTLY : ligeramente, levemente
fair[1] ['fær] *n* : feria *f*
fair[2] *adj* **1** BEAUTIFUL : bello, hermoso **2** : bueno (dícese del tiempo) **3** JUST : justo **4** : rubio (dícese del pelo), blanco (dícese de la tez) **5** ADEQUATE : adecuado — **~** *adv* **play ~** : jugar limpio — **fairly** ['færli] *adv* **1** JUSTLY : justamente **2** QUITE : bastante — **fairness** ['færnəs] *n* : justicia *f*
fairy ['færi] *n, pl* **fairies** **1** : hada *f* **2** **~ tale** : cuento *m* de hadas
faith ['feɪθ] *n, pl* **faiths** ['feɪθs, 'feɪðz] : fe *f* — **faithful** ['feɪθfəl] *adj* : fiel — **faithfully** *adv* : fielmente — **faithfulness** ['feɪθfəlnəs] *n* : fidelidad *f*
fake ['feɪk] *v* **faked; faking** *vt* **1** FALSIFY : falsificar, falsear **2** FEIGN : fingir — *vi* PRETEND : fingir — **~** *adj* : falso — **~** *n* **1** IMITATION : falsificación *f* **2** IMPOSTOR : impostor *m*, **-tora** *f*
falcon ['fælkən, 'fɔl-] *n* : halcón *m*
fall ['fɔl] *vi* **fell** ['fel]; **fallen** [fɔlən]; **falling** **1** : caer, bajar (dícese de los precios), descender (dícese de la temperatura) **2** **~ asleep** : dormirse **3** **~ back** : retirarse **4** **~ back on** : recurrir a **5** **~ down** : caerse **6** **~ in love** : enamorarse **7** **~ out** QUARREL : pelearse **8** **~ through** : fracasar — **~** *n* **1** : caída *f*, bajada *f* (de precios), descenso *m* (de temperatura) **2** AUTUMN : otoño *m* **3** **~s** *npl* WATERFALL : cascada *f*, catarata *f*
fallacy ['fæləsi] *n, pl* **-cies** : concepto *m* erróneo
fallible ['fæləbəl] *adj* : falible
fallow ['fælo] *adj* **lie ~** : estar en barbecho
false ['fɔls] *adj* **falser; falsest** **1** : falso **2** **~ alarm** : falsa alarma *f* **3** **~ teeth** : dentadura *f* postiza — **falsehood** ['fɔls,hʊd] *n* : mentira — **falseness**

['fɔlsnəs] *n* : falsedad *f* — **falsify** ['fɔlsə,faɪ] *vt* **-fied; fying** : falsificar, falsear

falter ['fɔltər] *vi* **-tered; -tering 1** STUMBLE : tambalearse **2** WAVER : vacilar

fame ['feɪm] *n* : fama *f*

familiar [fə'mɪljər] *adj* **1** : familiar **2 be ~ with** : estar familiarizado con — **familiarity** [fə,mɪli'ærət̬i, -,mɪl'jær-] *n, pl* **-ties** : familiaridad *f* — **familiarize** [fə'mɪljə,raɪz] *vt* **-ized; -izing ~ oneself** : familiarizarse

family ['fæmli, 'fæmə-] *n, pl* **-lies** : familia *f*

famine ['fæmən] *n* : hambre *f,* hambruna *f*

famished ['fæmɪʃt] *adj* : famélico

famous ['feɪməs] *adj* : famoso

fan ['fæn] *n* **1** : ventilador *m,* abanico *m* **2** : aficionado *m,* **-da** *f* (a un pasatiempo); admirador *m,* **-dora** *f* (de una persona) — **~** *vt* **fanned; fanning** : abanicar (a una persona), avivar (un fuego)

fanatic [fə'næt̬ɪk] *or* **fanatical** [-t̬ɪkəl] *adj* : fanático — **~** *n* : fanático *m,* -ca *f* — **fanaticism** [fə'næt̬ə,sɪzəm] *n* : fanatismo *m*

fancy ['fæntsi] *vt* **-cied; -cying 1** IMAGINE : imaginarse **2** DESIRE : apetecerle (algo a uno) — **~** *adj* **-cier; -est 1** ELABORATE : elaborado **2** LUXURIOUS : lujoso, elegante — **~** *n, pl* **-cies 1** WHIM : capricho *m* **2** IMAGINATION : imaginación *f* **3 take a ~ to** : aficionarse a (una cosa), tomar cariño a (una persona) — **fanciful** ['fæntsɪfəl] *adj* **1** CAPRICIOUS : caprichoso **2** IMAGINATIVE : imaginativo

fanfare ['fæn,fær] *n* : fanfarria *f*

fang ['fæŋ] *n* : colmillo *m* (de un animal), diente *m* (de una serpiente)

fantasy ['fæntəsi] *n, pl* **-sies** : fantasía *f* — **fantasize** ['fæntə,saɪz] *vi* **-sized; -sizing** : fantasear — **fantastic** [fæn'tæstɪk] *adj* : fantástico

far ['fɑr] *adv* **farther** ['fɑrðər] *or* **further** ['fər-]; **farthest** *or* **furthest** [-ðəst] **1** : lejos **2** MUCH : muy, mucho **3 as ~ as** : hasta (un lugar), con respecto a (un tema) **4 by ~** : con mucho **5 ~ and wide** : por todas partes **6 ~ away** : a lo lejos **7 ~ from it!** : ¡todo lo contrario! **8 so ~** : hasta ahora, todavía — **~** *adj* **farther** *or* **further; farthest** *or* **furthest 1** REMOTE : lejano **2** EXTREME : extremo — **faraway** ['fɑrə,weɪ] *adj* : remoto, lejano

farce ['fɑrs] *n* : farsa *f*

fare ['fær] *vi* **fared; faring** : irle a uno — **~** *n* **1** : precio *m* del pasaje **2** FOOD : comida *f*

farewell [fær'wɛl] *n* : despedida *f* — **~** *adj* : de despedida

far–fetched ['fɑr'fɛtʃt] *adj* : improbable, exagerado

farm ['fɑrm] *n* : granja *f,* hacienda *f* — **~** *vt* : cultivar (la tierra), criar (animales) — *vi* : ser agricultor — **farmer** ['fɑrmər] *n* : agricultor *m,* **-tora** *f;* granjero *m,* **-jera** *f* — **farmhand** ['fɑrm,hænd] *n* : peón *m* — **farmhouse** ['fɑrm,haʊs] *n* : granja *f,* casa *f* de hacienda — **farming** ['fɑrmɪŋ] *n* : agricultura *f,* cultivo *m* (de plantas), crianza *f* (de animales) — **farmyard** ['fɑrm,jɑrd] *n* : corral *m*

far–off ['fɑr,ɔf, -'ɔf] *adj* : lejano

far–reaching ['fɑr'riːtʃɪŋ] *adj* : de gran alcance

farsighted ['fɑr,saɪt̬əd] *adj* **1** : hipermétrope **2** PRUDENT : previsor

farther ['fɑrðər] *adv* **1** : más lejos **2** MORE : más — *adj* : más lejano — **farthest** *adv* **1** : lo más lejos **2** MOST : más — *adj* : más lejano

fascinate ['fæsən,eɪt] *vt* **-nated; -nating** : fascinar — **fascination** [,fæsən'eɪʃən] *n* : fascinación *f*

fascism ['fæʃ,ɪzəm] *n* : fascismo *m* — **fascist** ['fæʃɪst] *adj* : fascista — **~** *n* : fascista *mf*

fashion ['fæʃən] *n* **1** MANNER : manera *f* **2** STYLE : moda *f* **3 out of ~** : pasada de moda — **fashionable** ['fæʃənəbəl] *adj* : de moda

fast[1] ['fæst] *vi* : ayunar — **~** *n* : ayuno *m*

fast[2] *adj* **1** SWIFT : rápido **2** SECURE : firme, seguro **3** : adelantado (dícese de un reloj) **4 ~ friends** : amigos *mpl* leales — **~** *adv* **1** SECURELY : firmemente **2** SWIFTLY : rápidamente **3 ~ asleep** : profundamente dormido

fasten ['fæsən] *vt* : sujetar (papeles, etc.), abrochar (una blusa, etc.), cerrar (una maleta, etc.) — *vi* : abrocharse, cerrar — **fastener** ['fæsənər] *n* : cierre *m*

fat ['fæt] *adj* **fatter; fattest 1** : gordo **2** THICK : grueso — **~** *n* : grasa *f*

fatal ['feɪt̬əl] *adj* **1** : mortal **2** FATEFUL : fatal, fatídico — **fatality** [feɪ'tæləti, fə-] *n, pl* **-ties** : víctima *f* mortal

fate ['feɪt] *n* **1** : destino *m* **2** LOT : suerte *f* — **fateful** ['feɪtfəl] *adj* : fatídico

father ['fɑðər] *n* : padre *m* — **~** *vt* : engendrar — **fatherhood** ['fɑðər,hʊd] *n* : paternidad *f* — **father–in–law** ['fɑðərɪn,lɔ] *n, pl* **fathers–in–law** : sue-

gro *m* — **fatherly** ['fɑðərli] *adj* : paternal
fathom ['fæðəm] *vt* : comprender
fatigue [fə'ti:g] *n* : fatiga *f* — ~ *vt* **-tigued; -tiguing** : fatigar
fatten ['fætən] *vt* : engordar — **fattening** *adj* : que engorda
fatty ['fæṭi] *adj* **fattier; -est** : graso
faucet ['fɔsət] *n* : llave *f Lat,* grifo *m Spain*
fault ['fɔlt] *n* **1** FLAW : defecto *m* **2** RESPONSIBILITY : culpa *f* **3** : falla *f* (geológica) — *vt* : encontrar defectos a — **faultless** ['fɔltləs] *adj* : impecable — **faulty** ['fɔlti] *adj* **faultier; -est** : defectuoso
fauna ['fɔnə] *n* : fauna *f*
favor *or Brit* **favour** ['feɪvər] *n* **1** : favor *m* **2 in ~ of** : a favor de — ~ *vt* **1** : favorecer **2** SUPPORT : estar a favor de **3** PREFER : preferir — **favorable** *or Brit* **favourable** ['feɪvərəbəl] *adj* : favorable — **favorite** *or Brit* **favourite** ['feɪvərət] *n* : favorito *m,* -ta *f* — ~ *adj* : favorito — **favoritism** *or Brit* **favouritism** ['feɪvərə,tɪzəm] *n* : favoritismo *m*
fawn[1] ['fɔn] *vi* ~ **over** : adular
fawn[2] *n* : cervato *m*
fax ['fæks] *n* : fax *m* — ~ *vt* : faxear, enviar por fax
fear ['fɪr] *v* : temer — ~ *n* **1** : miedo *m,* temor *m* **2 for ~ of** : por temor a — **fearful** ['fɪrfəl] *adj* **1** FRIGHTENING : espantoso **2** AFRAID : temeroso
feasible ['fi:zəbəl] *adj* : viable, factible
feast ['fi:st] *n* **1** BANQUET : banquete *m,* festín *m* **2** FESTIVAL : fiesta *f* — ~ *vi* **1** : banquetear **2 ~ upon** : darse un festín de
feat ['fi:t] *n* : hazaña *f*
feather ['feðər] *n* : pluma *f*
feature ['fi:tʃər] *n* **1** : rasgo *m* (de la cara) **2** CHARACTERISTIC : característica *f* **3** : artículo *m* (en un periódico) **4 ~ film** : largometraje *m* — *v* **-tured; -turing** *vt* **1** PRESENT : presentar **2** EMPHASIZE : destacar — *vi* : figurar
February ['fɛbju,ɛri, 'fɛbu-, 'fɛbru-] *n* : febrero *m*
feces ['fi:,si:z] *npl* : excremento *mpl*
federal ['fɛdrəl, -dərəl] *adj* : federal — **federation** [,fɛdə'reɪʃən] *n* : federación *f*
fed up *adj* : harto
fee ['fi:] *n* **1** : honorarios *mpl* **2 entrance ~** : entrada *f*
feeble ['fi:bəl] *adj* **-bler; -blest 1** : débil **2 a ~ excuse** : una pobre excusa
feed ['fi:d] *v* **fed** ['fɛd]; **feeding** *vt* **1** : dar de comer a, alimentar **2** SUPPLY : alimentar — *vi* : comer, alimentarse — ~ *n* : pienso *m*
feel ['fi:l] *v* **felt** ['fɛlt]; **feeling** *vt* **1** : sentir (una sensación, etc.) **2** TOUCH : tocar, palpar **3** BELIEVE : creer — *vi* **1** : sentirse (bien, cansado, etc.) **2** SEEM : parecer **3 ~ hot/thirsty** : tener calor/sed **4 ~ like doing** : tener ganas de hacer — ~ *n* : tacto *m,* sensación *f* — **feeling** ['fi:lɪŋ] *n* **1** SENSATION : sensación *f* **2** EMOTION : sentimiento *m* **3** OPINION : opinión *f* **4 hurt s.o.'s ~s** : herir los sentimientos de algn
feet → **foot**
feign ['feɪn] *vt* : fingir
feline ['fi:,laɪn] *adj* : felino — ~ *n* : felino *m,* -na *f*
fell[1] → **fall**
fell[2] ['fɛl] *vt* : talar (un árbol)
fellow ['fɛ,lo:] *n* **1** COMPANION : compañero *m,* -ra *f* **2** MEMBER : socio *m,* -cia *f* **3** MAN : tipo *m* — **fellowship** ['fɛlo,ʃɪp] *n* **1** : compañerismo *m* **2** ASSOCIATION : fraternidad *f* **3** GRANT : beca *f*
felon ['fɛlən] *n* : criminal *mf* — **felony** ['fɛləni] *n, pl* **-nies** : delito *m* grave
felt[1] → **feel**
felt[2] ['fɛlt] *n* : fieltro *m*
female ['fi:,meɪl] *adj* : femenino — ~ *n* **1** : hembra *f* (animal) **2** WOMAN : mujer *f*
feminine ['fɛmənən] *adj* : femenino — **femininity** [,fɛm'nɪnəṭi] *n* : femineidad *f* — **feminism** ['fɛmə,nɪzəm] *n* : feminismo *m* — **feminist** ['fɛmənɪst] *adj* : feminista — ~ *n* : feminista *mf*
fence ['fɛnts] *n* : cerca *f,* valla *f,* cerco *m Lat* — ~ *v* **fenced; fencing** *vt or* **~ in** : vallar, cercar — *vi* : hacer esgrima — **fencing** ['fɛntsɪŋ] *n* : esgrima *m* (deporte)
fend ['fɛnd] *vt* **~ off** : rechazar (un enemigo), eludir (una pregunta) — *vi* **~ for oneself** : valerse por sí mismo
fender ['fɛndər] *n* : guardabarros *mpl*
fennel ['fɛnəl] *n* : hinojo *m*
ferment [fər'mɛnt] *v* : fermentar — **fermentation** [,fərmən'teɪʃən, -,mɛn-] *n* : fermentación *f*
fern ['fərn] *n* : helecho *m*
ferocious [fə'ro:ʃəs] *adj* : feroz — **ferocity** [fə'rɑsəṭi] *n* : ferocidad *f*
ferret ['fɛrət] *n* : hurón *m* — ~ *vt* **~ out** : descubrir
Ferris wheel ['fɛrɪs] *n* : noria *f*
ferry ['fɛri] *vt* **-ried; -rying** : transportar — ~ *n, pl* **-ries** : ferry *m*

fertile ['fərt̬əl] *adj* : fértil — **fertility** [fər'tɪləṭi] *n* : fertilidad *f* — **fertilize** ['fərt̬əl,aɪz] *vt* **-ized; -izing** : fecundar (un huevo), abonar (el suelo) — **fertilizer** ['fərt̬əl,aɪzər] *n* : fertilizante *m*, abono *m*

fervent ['fərvənt] *adj* : ferviente — **fervor** *or Brit* **fervour** ['fərvər] *n* : fervor *m*

fester ['fɛstər] *vi* : enconarse

festival ['fɛstəvəl] *n* **1** : fiesta *f* **2 film ~** : festival *m* de cine — **festive** ['fɛstɪv] *adj* : festivo — **festivity** [fɛs'tɪvəṭi] *n, pl* **-ties** : festividad *f*

fetch ['fɛtʃ] *vt* **1** : ir a buscar **2** : venderse por (un precio)

fête ['feɪt, 'fɛt] *n* : fiesta *f*

fetid ['fɛṭəd] *adj* : fétido

fetish ['fɛṭɪʃ] *n* : fetiche *m*

fetters ['fɛṭərz] *npl* : grillos *mpl* — **fetter** ['fɛṭər] *vt* : encadenar

fetus ['fi:ṭəs] *n* : feto *m*

feud ['fju:d] *n* : enemistad *f* (entre familiares) — **~** *vi* : pelear

feudal ['fju:dəl] *adj* : feudal — **feudalism** ['fju:dəl,ɪzəm] *n* : feudalismo *m*

fever ['fi:vər] *n* : fiebre *f* — **feverish** ['fi:vərɪʃ] *adj* : febril

few ['fju:] *adj* **1** : pocos **2 a ~ times** : varias veces — **~** *pron* **1** : pocos **2 a ~** : algunos, unos cuantos **3 quite a ~** : muchos — **fewer** ['fju:ər] *adj & pron* : menos

fiancé, fiancée [,fi:ɑn'seɪ, ,fi:'ɑn,seɪ] *n* : prometido *m*, -da *f*; novio *m*, -via *f*

fiasco [fi'æs,ko:] *n, pl* **-coes** : fiasco *m*

fib ['fɪb] *n* : mentirilla *f* — **~** *vi* **fibbed; fibbing** : decir mentirillas

fiber *or* **fibre** ['faɪbər] *n* : fibra *f* — **fiberglass** ['faɪbər,glæs] *n* : fibra *f* de vidrio — **fibrous** ['faɪbrəs] *adj* : fibroso

fickle ['fɪkəl] *adj* : inconstante

fiction ['fɪkʃən] *n* : ficción *f* — **fictional** ['fɪkʃənəl] *or* **fictitious** [fɪk'tɪʃəs] *adj* : ficticio

fiddle ['fɪdəl] *n* : violín *m* — **~** *vi* **-dled; -dling 1** : tocar el violín **2 ~ with** : juguetear con

fidelity [fə'dɛləṭi, faɪ-] *n, pl* **-ties** : fidelidad *f*

fidget ['fɪdʒət] *vi* **1** : estarse inquieto, moverse **2 ~ with** : juguetear con — **fidgety** ['fɪdʒəṭi] *adj* : inquieto, nervioso

field ['fi:ld] *n* : campo *m* — **~** *vt* : interceptar (una pelota), sortear (una pregunta) — **field glasses** *n* : binoculares *mpl*, gemelos *mpl* — **field trip** *n* : viaje *m* de estudio

fiend ['fi:nd] *n* **1** : demonio *m* **2** FANATIC : fanático *m*, -ca *f* — **fiendish** ['fi:ndɪʃ] *adj* : diabólico

fierce ['fɪrs] *adj* **fiercer; -est 1** : feroz **2** INTENSE : fuerte (dícese del viento), acalorado (dícese de un debate) — **fierceness** ['fɪrsnəs] *n* : ferocidad *f*

fiery ['faɪəri] *adj* **fierier; -est 1** BURNING : llameante **2** SPIRITED : ardiente, fogoso — **fieriness** ['faɪərinəs] *n* : pasión *f*, ardor *m*

fifteen [fɪf'ti:n] *n* : quince *m* — **~** *adj* : quince — **fifteenth** [fɪf'ti:nθ] *adj* : decimoquinto — **~** *n* **1** : decimoquinto *m*, -ta *f* (en una serie) **2** : quinceavo *m* (en matemáticas)

fifth ['fɪfθ] *n* **1** : quinto *m*, -ta *f* (en una serie) **2** : quinto *m* (en matemáticas) — **~** *adj* : quinto

fiftieth ['fɪftiəθ] *adj* : quincuagésimo — **~** *n* **1** : quincuagésimo *m*, -ma *f* (en una serie) **2** : cincuentavo *m* (en matemáticas)

fifty ['fɪfti] *n, pl* **-ties** : cincuenta *m* — **~** *adj* : cincuenta — **fifty–fifty** [,fɪfti'fɪfti] *adv* : a medias, mitad y mitad — **~** *adj* **a ~ chance** : un cincuenta por ciento de posibilidades

fig ['fɪg] *n* : higo *m*

fight ['faɪt] *v* **fought** ['fɔt]; **fighting** *vi* **1** BATTLE : luchar **2** QUARREL : pelear **3 ~ back** : defenderse — *vt* : luchar contra — **~** *n* **1** STRUGGLE : lucha *f* **2** QUARREL : pelea *f* — **fighter** ['faɪṭər] *n* **1** : luchador *m*, -dora *f* **2** *or* **~ plane** : avión *m* de caza

figment ['fɪgmənt] *n* **~ of the imagination** : producto *m* de la imaginación

figurative ['fɪgjərəṭɪv, -gə-] *adj* : figurado

figure ['fɪgjər, -gər] *n* **1** NUMBER : número *m*, cifra *f* **2** PERSON, SHAPE : figura *f* **3 ~ of speech** : figura *f* retórica **4 watch one's ~** : cuidar la línea — **~** *v* **-ured; -uring** *vt* : calcular — *vi* **1** : figurar **2 that ~s!** : ¡no me extraña! — **figurehead** ['fɪgjər,hɛd, -gər] *n* : testaferro *m* — **figure out** *vt* **1** UNDERSTAND : entender **2** RESOLVE : resolver

file[1] ['faɪl] *n* : lima *f* (instrumento) — **~** *vt* **filed; filing** : limar

file[2] *vt* **filed; filing 1** : archivar (documentos) **2 ~ charges** : presentar cargos — **~** *n* : archivo *m*

file[3] *n* LINE : fila *f* — **~** *vi* **~ in/out** : entrar/salir en fila

fill ['fɪl] *vt* **1** : llenar, rellenar **2** : cumplir con (un requisito) **3** : tapar (un agujero), empastar (un diente) — *vi* **1 ~ in for** : reemplazar **2** *or* **~ up**

: llenarse — ~ *n* **1 eat one's ~** : comer lo suficiente **2 have one's ~ of** : estar harto de
fillet ['fɪlət, fɪ'leɪ, 'fɪˌleɪ] *n* : filete *m*
filling ['fɪlɪŋ] *n* **1** : relleno *m* **2** : empaste *m* (de dientes) **3 ~ station** → **service station**
filly ['fɪli] *n, pl* **-lies** : potra *f*
film ['fɪlm] *n* : película *f* — ~ *vt* : filmar
filter ['fɪltər] *n* : filtro *m* — ~ *vt* : filtrar
filth ['fɪlθ] *n* : mugre *f* — **filthy** ['fɪlθi] *adj* **filthier; -est 1** : mugriento **2** OBSCENE : obsceno
fin ['fɪn] *n* : aleta *f*
final ['faɪnəl] *adj* **1** LAST : último **2** DEFINITIVE : definitivo **3** ULTIMATE : final — ~ *n* **1** : final *f* (en deportes) **2 ~s** *npl* : exámenes *mpl* finales — **finalist** ['faɪnəlɪst] *n* : finalista *mf* — **finalize** ['faɪnəlˌaɪz] *vt* **-ized; -izing** : finalizar — **finally** ['faɪnəli] *adv* : finalmente
finance [fə'nænts, 'faɪˌnænts] *n* **1** : finanzas *fpl* **2 ~s** *npl* : recursos *mpl* financieros — ~ *vt* **-nanced; -nancing** : financiar — **financial** [fə'næntʃəl, faɪ-] *adj* : financiero — **financially** [fə'næntʃəli, faɪ-] *adv* : económicamente
find ['faɪnd] *vt* **found** ['faʊnd]; **finding 1** LOCATE : encontrar **2** REALIZE : darse cuenta de **3 ~ guilty** : declarar culpable **4** *or* **~ out** : descubrir — *vi* **~ out** : enterarse — ~ *n* : hallazgo *m* — **finding** ['faɪndɪŋ] *n* **1** FIND : hallazgo *m* **2 ~s** *npl* : conclusiones *fpl*
fine[1] ['faɪn] *n* : multa *f* — ~ *vt* **fined; fining** : multar
fine[2] *adj* **finer; -est 1** DELICATE : fino **2** EXCELLENT : excelente **3** SUBTLE : sutil **4** : bueno (dícese del tiempo) **5 ~ print** : letra *f* menuda **6 it's ~ with me** : me parece bien — ~ *adv* OK : bien — **fine arts** *npl* : bellas artes *fpl* — **finely** ['faɪnli] *adv* **1** EXCELLENTLY : excelentemente **2** PRECISELY : con precisión **3** MINUTELY : fino, menudo
finger ['fɪŋgər] *n* : dedo *m* — ~ *vt* : tocar, toquetear — **fingernail** ['fɪŋgərˌneɪl] *n* : uña *f* — **fingerprint** ['fɪŋgərˌprɪnt] *n* : huella *f* digital — **fingertip** ['fɪŋgərˌtɪp] *n* : punta *f* del dedo
finicky ['fɪnɪki] *adj* : maniático, mañoso *Lat*
finish ['fɪnɪʃ] *v* : acabar, terminar — ~ *n* **1** END : fin *m*, final *m* **2** *or* **~ line** : meta *f* **3** SURFACE : acabado *m*
finite ['faɪˌnaɪt] *adj* : finito
fir ['fər] *n* : abeto *m*
fire ['faɪr] *n* **1** : fuego *m* **2** CONFLAGRATION : incendio *m* **3 catch ~** : incendiarse (dícese de bosques, etc.), prenderse (dícese de fósforos, etc.) **4 on ~** : en llamas **5 open ~ on** : abrir fuego sobre — ~ *vt* **fired; firing 1** DISMISS : despedir **2** SHOOT : disparar — *vi* : disparar — **fire alarm** *n* : alarma *f* contra incendios — **firearm** ['faɪrˌɑrm] *n* : arma *f* de fuego — **firecracker** ['faɪrˌkrækər] *n* : petardo *m* — **fire engine** *n* : carro *m* de bomberos *Lat*, coche *m* de bomberos *Spain* — **fire escape** *n* : escalera *f* de incendios — **fire extinguisher** *n* : extintor *m* (de incendios) — **firefighter** ['faɪrˌfaɪt̬ər] *n* : bombero *m*, -ra *f* — **firefly** ['faɪrˌflaɪ] *n, pl* **-flies** : luciérnaga *f* — **firehouse** → **fire station** — **fireman** ['faɪrmən] *n, pl* **-men** [-mən, -ˌmɛn] → **firefighter** — **fireplace** ['faɪrˌpleɪs] *n* : hogar *m*, chimenea *f* — **fireproof** ['faɪrˌpru:f] *adj* : ignífugo — **fireside** ['faɪrˌsaɪd] *n* : hogar *m* — **fire station** *n* : estación *f* de bomberos *Lat*, parque *m* de bomberos *Spain* — **firewood** ['faɪrˌwʊd] *n* : leña *f* — **fireworks** ['faɪrˌwərk] *npl* : fuegos *mpl* artificiales
firm[1] ['fərm] *n* : empresa *f*
firm[2] *adj* : firme — **firmly** ['fərmli] *adv* : firmemente — **firmness** ['fərmnəs] *n* : firmeza *f*
first ['fərst] *adj* **1** : primero **2 at ~ sight** : a primera vista **3 for the ~ time** : por primera vez — ~ *adv* **1** : primero **2 ~ and foremost** : ante todo **3 ~ of all** : en primer lugar — ~ *n* **1** : primero *m*, -ra *f* **2 at ~** : al principio — **first aid** *n* : primeros auxilios *mpl* — **first-class** ['fərst'klæs] *adv* : en primera — ~ *adj* : de primera *f* — **firsthand** ['fərst'hænd] *adv* : directamente — ~ *adj* : de primera mano — **firstly** ['fərstli] *adv* : en primer lugar — **first name** *n* : nombre *m* de pila — **first-rate** ['fərst'reɪt] *adj* → **first-class**
fiscal ['fɪskəl] *adj* : fiscal
fish ['fɪʃ] *n, pl* **fish** *or* **fishes** : pez *m* (vivo), pescado *m* (para comer) — ~ *vi* **1** : pescar **2 ~ for** SEEK : buscar **3 go ~ing** : ir de pesca — **fisherman** ['fɪʃərmən] *n, pl* **-men** [-mən, -ˌmɛn] : pescador *m*, -dora *f* — **fishhook** ['fɪʃˌhʊk] *n* : anzuelo *m* — **fishing** ['fɪʃɪŋ] *n* : pesca *f* — **fishing pole** *n* : caña *f* de pescar — **fish market** *n* : pescadería *f* — **fishy** ['fɪʃi] *adj* **fishier; -est 1** : a pescado (dícese de sabores, etc.) **2** SUSPICIOUS : sospechoso
fist ['fɪst] *n* : puño *m*
fit[1] ['fɪt] *n* **1** : ataque *m* **2 he had a ~** : le dio un ataque

fit[2] *adj* **fitter; fittest 1** SUITABLE : apropiado **2** HEALTHY : en forma **3 be ~ for** : ser apto para — **~** *v* **fitted; fitting** *vt* **1** : encajar en (un hueco, etc.) **2** *(relating to clothing)* : quedar bien a **3** SUIT : ser apropiado para **4** MATCH : coincidir con **5** *or* **~ out** : equipar — *vi* **1** : caber (en una caja, etc.), encajar (en un hueco, etc.) **2** *or* **~ in** BELONG : encajar **3 this dress doesn't ~** : este vestido no me queda bien — **~** *n* **it's a good fit** : me queda bien — **fitful** [ˈfɪtfəl] *adj* : irregular — **fitness** [ˈfɪtnəs] *n* **1** HEALTH : salud *f* **2** SUITABILITY : idoneidad *f* — **fitting** [ˈfɪtɪŋ] *adj* : apropiado

five [ˈfaɪv] *n* : cinco *m* — **~** *adj* : cinco — **five hundred** *n* : quinientos *m* — **~** *adj* : quinientos

fix [ˈfɪks] *vt* **1** ATTACH : fijar, sujetar **2** REPAIR : arreglar **3** PREPARE : preparar — **~** *n* PREDICAMENT : aprieto *m,* apuro *m* — **fixed** [ˈfɪkst] *adj* : fijo — **fixture** [ˈfɪkstʃər] *n* : instalación *f*

fizz [ˈfɪz] *vi* : burbujear — **~** *n* : efervescencia *f*

fizzle [ˈfɪzəl] *vi* **-zled; -zling** *or* **~ out** : quedar en nada

flabbergasted [ˈflæbərˌgæstəd] *adj* : estupefacto, pasmado

flabby [ˈflæbi] *adj* **-bier; -est** : fofo

flaccid [ˈflæksəd, ˈflæsəd] *adj* : fláccido

flag[1] [ˈflæg] *vi* WEAKEN : flaquear

flag[2] *n* : bandera *f* — **~** *vt* **flagged; flagging** *or* **~ down** : hacer señales de parada a — **flagpole** [ˈflægˌpoːl] *n* : asta *f*

flagrant [ˈfleɪgrənt] *adj* : flagrante

flair [ˈflær] *n* : don *m,* facilidad *f*

flake [ˈfleɪk] *n* : copo *m* (de nieve), escama *f* (de pintura, de la piel) — **~** *vi* **flaked; flaking** : pelarse

flamboyant [flæmˈbɔɪənt] *adj* : extravagante

flame [ˈfleɪm] *n* **1** : llama *f* **2 burst into ~s** : estallar en llamas **3 go up in ~s** : incendiarse

flamingo [fləˈmɪŋgo] *n, pl* **-gos** : flamenco *m*

flammable [ˈflæməbəl] *adj* : inflamable

flank [ˈflæŋk] *n* : ijado *m* (de un animal), flanco *m* (militar) — **~** *vt* : flanquear

flannel [ˈflænəl] *n* : franela *f*

flap [ˈflæp] *n* : solapa *f* (de un sobre, un libro, etc.), tapa *f* (de un recipiente) — **~** *v* **flapped; flapping** *vi* : agitarse — *vt* : batir, agitar

flapjack [ˈflæpˌdʒæk] → **pancake**

flare [ˈflær] *vi* **flared; flaring 1 ~ up** BLAZE : llamear **2 ~ up** EXPLODE, ERUPT : estallar, explotar — **~** *n* **1** BLAZE : llamarada *f* **2** SIGNAL : (luz *f* de) bengala *f*

flash [ˈflæʃ] *vi* **1** : brillar, destellar **2 ~ past** : pasar como un rayo — *vt* **1** : dirigir (una luz) **2** SHOW : mostrar **3 ~ a smile** : sonreír — **~** *n* **1** : destello *m* **2 ~ of lightning** : relámpago *m* **3 in a ~** : de repente — **flashlight** [ˈflæʃˌlaɪt] *n* : linterna *f* — **flashy** [ˈflæʃi] *adj* **flashier; -est** : ostentoso

flask [ˈflæsk] *n* : frasco *m*

flat [ˈflæt] *adj* **flatter; flattest 1** LEVEL : plano, llano **2** DOWNRIGHT : categórico **3** FIXED : fijo **4** MONOTONOUS : monótono **5** : bemol (en la música) **6 ~ tire** : neumático *m* desinflado — **~** *n* **1** : bemol *m* (en la música) **2** *Brit* APARTMENT : apartamento *m,* departamento *m Lat* **3** PUNCTURE : pinchazo *m* — **~** *adv* **1 ~ broke** : pelado **2 in one hour ~** : en una hora justa — **flatly** [ˈflætli] *adv* : categóricamente — **flat–out** [ˈflætˈaʊt] *adj* **1** : frenético **2** DOWNRIGHT : categórico — **flatten** [ˈflætən] *vt* **1** LEVEL : aplanar, allanar **2** KNOCK DOWN : arrasar

flatter [ˈflæţər] *vt* **1** : halagar **2** BECOME : favorecer — **flatterer** [ˈflæţərər] *n* : adulador *m,* -dora *f* — **flattering** [ˈflæţərɪŋ] *adj* **1** : halagador **2** BECOMING : favorecedor — **flattery** [ˈflæţəri] *n, pl* **-ries** : halagos *mpl*

flaunt [ˈflɔnt] *vt* : hacer alarde de

flavor *or Brit* **flavour** [ˈfleɪvər] *n* : gusto *m,* sabor *m* — **~** *vt* : sazonar — **flavorful** *or Brit* **flavourful** [ˈfleɪvərfəl] *adj* : sabroso — **flavoring** *or Brit* **flavouring** [ˈfleɪvərɪŋ] *n* : condimento *m,* sazón *f*

flaw [ˈflɔ] *n* : defecto *m* — **flawless** [ˈflɔləs] *adj* : perfecto

flax [ˈflæks] *n* : lino *m*

flea [ˈfliː] *n* : pulga *f*

fleck [ˈflɛk] *n* **1** PARTICLE : mota *f* **2** SPOT : pinta *f*

flee [ˈfliː] *v* **fled** [ˈflɛd]; **fleeing** *vi* : huir — *vt* : huir de

fleece [ˈfliːs] *n* : vellón *m* — **~** *vt* **fleeced; fleecing 1** SHEAR : esquilar **2** DEFRAUD : desplumar

fleet [ˈfliːt] *n* : flota *f*

fleeting [ˈfliːţɪŋ] *adj* : fugaz

Flemish [ˈflɛmɪʃ] *adj* : flamenco

flesh [ˈflɛʃ] *n* **1** : carne *f* **2** PULP : pulpa *f* **3 in the ~** : en persona — **fleshy** [ˈflɛʃi] *adj* **fleshier; -est 1** : gordo **2** PULPY : carnoso

flew → **fly**

flex [ˈflɛks] *vt* : flexionar — **flexibility**

[ˌflɛksəˈbɪləṭi] *n, pl* **-ties** : flexibilidad *f* — **flexible** [ˈflɛksəbəl] *adj* : flexible
flick [ˈflɪk] *n* : golpecito *m* — ~ *vt* : dar un golpecito a — *vi* ~ **through** : hojear
flicker [ˈflɪkər] *vi* : parpadear — ~ *n* **1** : parpadeo *m* **2 a ~ of hope** : un rayo de esperanza
flier [ˈflaɪər] *n* **1** AVIATOR : aviador *m*, -dora *f* **2** *or* **flyer** LEAFLET : folleto *m*, volante *m Lat*
flight[1] [ˈflaɪt] *n* **1** : vuelo *m* **2** TRAJECTORY : trayectoria *f* **3 ~ of stairs** : tramo *m*
flight[2] *n* ESCAPE : huida *f*
flimsy [flɪmzi] *adj* **flimsier; -est 1** LIGHT : ligero **2** SHAKY : poco sólido **3 a ~ excuse** : una excusa floja
flinch [ˈflɪntʃ] *vi* ~ **from** : encogerse ante
fling [ˈflɪŋ] *vt* **flung** [ˈflʌŋ]; **flinging 1** : arrojar **2 ~ open** : abrir de un golpe — ~ *n* **1** AFFAIR : aventura *f* **2 have a ~ at** : intentar
flint [ˈflɪnt] *n* : pedernal *m*
flip [ˈflɪp] *v* **flipped; flipping** *vt* **1** *or* **~ over** : dar la vuelta a **2 ~ a coin** : echarlo a cara o cruz — *vi* **1** *or* **~ over** : volcarse **2 ~ through** : hojear — ~ *n* SOMERSAULT : voltereta *f*
flippant [ˈflɪpənt] *adj* : ligero, frívolo
flipper [ˈflɪpər] *n* : aleta *f*
flirt [ˈflərt] *vi* : coquetear — ~ *n* : coqueto *m*, -ta *f* — **flirtatious** [ˌflərˈteɪʃəs] *adj* : coqueto
flit [ˈflɪt] *vi* **flitted; flitting** : revolotear
float [ˈfloːt] *n* **1** : flotador *m* **2** : carroza *f* (en un desfile) — ~ *vi* : flotar — *vt* : hacer flotar
flock [ˈflɑk] *n* : rebaño *m* (de ovejas), bandada *f* (de pájaros) — ~ *vi* : congregarse
flog [ˈflɑg] *vt* **flogged; flogging** : azotar
flood [ˈflʌd] *n* **1** : inundación *f* **2** : torrente *m* (de palabras, de lágrimas, etc.) — ~ *vt* : inundar — **floodlight** [ˈflʌdˌlaɪt] *n* : foco *m*
floor [ˈflor] *n* **1** : suelo *m*, piso *m Lat* **2** STORY : piso *m* **3 dance ~** : pista *f* de baile **4 ground ~** : planta *f* baja — ~ *vt* **1** KNOCK DOWN : derribar **2** NONPLUS : desconcertar — **floorboard** [ˈflorˌbord] *n* : tabla *f* del suelo
flop [ˈflɑp] *vi* **flopped; flopping 1** FLAP : agitarse **2** COLLAPSE : dejarse caer **3** FAIL : fracasar — ~ *n* FAILURE : fracaso *m* — **floppy** [ˈflɑpi] *adj* **-pier; -est** : flojo, flexible — **floppy disk** *n* : diskette *m*, disquete *m*
flora [ˈflorə] *n* : flora *f* — **floral** [ˈflorəl] *adj* : floral — **florid** [ˈflorɪd] *adj* **1** FLOWERY : florido **2** RUDDY : rojizo — **florist** [ˈflorɪst] *n* : florista *mf*
floss [ˈflɔs] *n* → **dental floss**
flounder[1] [ˈflaʊndər] *n, pl* **flounder** *or* **flounders** : platija *f*
flounder[2] *vi* **1** *or* **~ about** : resbalarse, revolcarse **2** : titubear (en un discurso)
flour [ˈflaʊər] *n* : harina *f*
flourish [ˈflərɪʃ] *vi* : florecer — *vt* BRANDISH : blandir — ~ *n* : floritura *f* — **flourishing** [ˈflərɪʃɪŋ] *adj* : floreciente
flout [ˈflaʊt] *vt* : desacatar, burlarse de
flow [ˈfloː] *vi* : fluir, correr — ~ *n* **1** : flujo *m*, circulación *f* **2** : corriente *f* (de información, etc.)
flower [ˈflaʊər] *n* : flor *f* — ~ *vi* : florecer — **flowered** [ˈflaʊərd] *adj* : floreado — **flowerpot** [ˈflaʊərˌpɑt] *n* : maceta *f* — **flowery** [ˈflaʊəri] *adj* : florido
flown → **fly**
flu [ˈfluː] *n* : gripe *f*
fluctuate [ˈflʌktʃʊˌeɪt] *vi* **-ated; -ating** : fluctuar — **fluctuation** [ˌflʌktʃʊˈeɪʃən] *n* : fluctuación *f*
fluency [ˈfluːən*t*si] *n* : fluidez *f* — **fluent** [ˈfluːənt] *adj* **1** : fluido **2 be ~ in** : hablar con fluidez — **fluently** [ˈfluːəntli] *adv* : con fluidez
fluff [ˈflʌf] *n* : pelusa *f* — **fluffy** [ˈflʌfi] *adj* **fluffier; -est** : de pelusa, velloso
fluid [ˈfluːɪd] *adj* : fluido — ~ *n* : fluido *m*
flung → **fling**
flunk [ˈflʌŋk] *vt* : reprobar *Lat*, suspender *Spain* — *vi* : ser reprobado *Lat*, suspender *Spain*
fluorescence [ˌflʊrˈɛsən*t*s, ˌflɔr-] *n* : fluorescencia *f* — **fluorescent** [ˌflʊrˈɛsənt, ˌflɔr-] *adj* : fluorescente
flurry [ˈfləri] *n, pl* **-ries 1** GUST : ráfaga *f* **2** *or* **snow ~** : nevisca *f* **3 ~ of questions** : aluvión *m* de preguntas
flush [ˈflʌʃ] *vi* BLUSH : ruborizarse, sonrojarse — *vt* **~ the toilet** : tirar de la cadena, jalarle a la cadena *Lat* — ~ *n* BLUSH : rubor *m*, sonrojo *m* — ~ *adj* **~ with** : a nivel con, a ras de — ~ *adv* : al mismo nivel, a ras
fluster [ˈflʌstər] *vt* : poner nervioso
flute [ˈfluːt] *n* : flauta *f*
flutter [ˈflʌṭər] *vi* **1** FLIT : revolotear **2** WAVE : ondear **3** *or* **~ about** : ir y venir — ~ *n* **1** : revoloteo *m* (de alas) **2** STIR : revuelo *m*
flux [ˈflʌks] *n* **be in a state of ~** : cambiar continuamente
fly[1] [ˈflaɪ] *v* **flew** [ˈfluː]; **flown** [ˈfloːn]; **flying** *vi* **1** : volar **2** TRAVEL : ir en avión **3** WAVE : ondear **4** RUSH : correr **5 ~**

by : pasar volando — *vt* **1** PILOT : pilotar **2** : hacer volar (una cometa), enarbolar (una bandera) — **~** *n, pl* **flies** : bragueta *f* (de un pantalón)
fly[2] *n, pl* **flies** : mosca *f* (insecto)
flyer → **flier**
flying saucer *n* : platillo *m* volador *Lat,* platillo *m* volante *Spain*
flyswatter ['flaɪˌswɑṭər] *n* : matamoscas *m*
foal ['fo:l] *n* : potro *m,* -tra *f*
foam ['fo:m] *n* : espuma *f* — **~** *vi* : hacer espuma — **foamy** ['fo:mi] *adj* **foamier; -est** : espumoso
focus ['fo:kəs] *n, pl* **-ci** ['fo:ˌsaɪ, -ˌkaɪ] **1** : foco *m* **2 be in ~** : estar enfocado **3 ~ of attention** : centro *m* de atención — **~** *v* **-cused** *or* **-cussed; -cusing** *or* **-cussing** *vt* **1** : enfocar **2** : centrar (la atención, etc.) — *vi* **~ on** : enfocar (con los ojos), concentrarse en (con la mente)
fodder ['fɑdər] *n* : forraje *m*
foe ['fo:] *n* : enemigo *m,* -ga *f*
fog ['fɔg, 'fɑg] *n* : niebla *f* — **~** *v* **fogged; fogging** *vt* : empañar — *vi or* **~ up** : empañarse — **foggy** ['fɔgi, 'fɑ-] *adj* **foggier; -est** : nebuloso — **foghorn** ['fɔgˌhɔrn, 'fɑg-] *n* : sirena *f* de niebla
foil[1] ['fɔɪl] *vt* : frustrar
foil[2] *n or* **aluminum ~** : papel *m* de aluminio
fold[1] ['fo:ld] *n* **1** : redil *m* (para ovejas) **2 return to the ~** : volver al redil
fold[2] *vt* **1** : doblar, plegar **2 ~ one's arms** : cruzar los brazos — *vi* **1** *or* **~ up** : doblarse, plegarse **2** FAIL : fracasar — **~** *n* : pliegue *m* — **folder** ['fo:ldər] *n* : carpeta *f*
foliage ['fo:liɪdʒ, -lɪdʒ] *n* : follaje *m*
folk ['fo:k] *n, pl* **folk** *or* **folks 1** : gente *f* **2 ~s** *npl* PARENTS : padres *mpl* — **~** *adj* **1** : popular **2 ~ dance** : danza *f* folklórica — **folklore** ['fo:kˌlor] *n* : folklore *m*
follow ['fɑlo] *vt* **1** : seguir **2** UNDERSTAND : entender **3 ~ up** : seguir — *vi* **1** : seguir **2** UNDERSTAND : entender **3 ~ up on** : seguir con — **follower** ['fɑloər] *n* : seguidor *m,* -dora *f* — **following** ['fɑloɪŋ] *adj* : siguiente — **~** *n* : seguidores *mpl* — **~** *prep* : después de
folly ['fɑli] *n, pl* **-lies** : locura *f*
fond ['fɑnd] *adj* **1** : cariñoso **2 be ~ of sth** : ser aficionado a algo **3 be ~ of s.o.** : tener cariño a algn
fondle ['fɑndəl] *vt* **-dled; -dling** : acariciar
fondness ['fɑndnəs] *n* **1** LOVE : cariño *m* **2** LIKING : afición *f*
food ['fu:d] *n* : comida *f,* alimento *m* — **foodstuffs** ['fu:dˌstʌfs] *npl* : comestibles *mpl*
fool ['fu:l] *n* **1** : idiota *mf* **2** JESTER : bufón *m,* -fona *f* — **~** *vi* **1** JOKE : bromear **2 ~ around** : perder el tiempo — *vt* TRICK : engañar — **foolhardy** ['fu:lˌhɑrdi] *adj* : temerario — **foolish** ['fu:lɪʃ] *adj* : tonto — **foolishness** ['fu:lɪʃnəs] *n* : tontería *f* — **foolproof** ['fu:lˌpru:f] *adj* : infalible
foot ['fʊt] *n, pl* **feet** ['fi:t] : pie *m* — **footage** ['fʊṭɪdʒ] *n* : secuencias *fpl* (cinemáticas) — **football** ['fʊtˌbɔl] *n* : fútbol *m* americano — **footbridge** ['fʊtˌbrɪdʒ] *n* : pasarela *f,* puente *m* peatonal — **foothills** ['fʊtˌhɪlz] *npl* : estribaciones *fpl* — **foothold** ['fʊtˌho:ld] *n* : punto *m* de apoyo — **footing** ['fʊṭɪŋ] *n* **1** BALANCE : equilibrio *m* **2 on equal ~** : en igualdad — **footlights** ['fʊtˌlaɪts] *npl* : candilejas *fpl* — **footnote** ['fʊtˌno:t] *n* : nota *f* al pie de la página — **footpath** ['fʊtˌpæθ] *n* : sendero *m* — **footprint** ['fʊtˌprɪnt] *n* : huella *f* — **footstep** ['fʊtˌstɛp] *n* : paso *m* — **footstool** ['fʊtˌstu:l] *n* : escabel *m* — **footwear** ['fʊtˌwær] *n* : calzado *m*
for ['fɔr] *prep* **1** (*indicating purpose, etc.*) : para **2** (*indicating motivation, etc.*) : por **3** (*indicating duration*) : durante **4 we walked ~ 3 miles** : andamos 3 millas **5** AS FOR : con respecto a — **~** *conj* : puesto que, porque
forage ['fɔrɪdʒ] *n* : forraje *m* — **~** *vi* **-aged; -aging 1** : forrajear **2 ~ for** : buscar
foray ['fɔrˌeɪ] *n* : incursión *f*
forbid [fər'bɪd] *vt* **-bade** [-'bæd, -'beɪd] *or* **-bad** [-'bæd]; **-bidden** [-'bɪdən]; **-bidding** : prohibir — **forbidding** [fər'bɪdɪŋ] *adj* : intimidante, severo
force ['fors] *n* **1** : fuerza *f* **2 by ~** : por la fuerza **3 in ~** : en vigor, en vigencia **4 armed ~s** : fuerzas *fpl* armadas — **~** *vt* **forced; forcing 1** : forzar **2** OBLIGATE : obligar — **forced** ['forst] *adj* : forzado, forzoso — **forceful** ['forsfəl] *adj* : fuerte, energético
forceps ['fɔrsəps, -ˌsɛps] *ns & pl* : fórceps *m*
forcibly [-bli] *adv* : por la fuerza
ford ['ford] *n* : vado *m* — **~** *vt* : vadear
fore ['for] *n* **come to the ~** : empezar a destacarse
forearm ['forˌɑrm] *n* : antebrazo *m*
foreboding [for'bo:dɪŋ] *n* : premonición *f,* presentimiento *m*

forecast ['for,kæst] *vt* **-cast; -casting** : predecir, pronosticar — **~** *n* : predicción *f*, pronóstico *m*
forefathers ['for,fɑðərz] *n* : antepasados *mpl*
forefinger ['for,fɪŋgər] *n* : índice *m*, dedo *m* índice
forefront ['for,frʌnt] *n* **at/in the ~** : a la vanguardia
forego [for'go:] → **forgo**
foregone [for'gɔn] *adj* **~ conclusion** : resultado *m* inevitable
foreground ['for,graʊnd] *n* : primer plano *m*
forehead ['fɔrəd, 'for,hɛd] *n* : frente *f*
foreign ['fɔrən] *adj* **1** : extranjero **2 ~ trade** : comercio *m* exterior — **foreigner** ['fɔrənər] *n* : extranjero *m*, -ra *f*
foreman ['formən] *n, pl* **-men** [-mən, -,mɛn] : capataz *mf*
foremost ['for,mo:st] *adj* : principal — **~** *adv* **first and ~** : ante todo
forensic [fə'rɛntsɪk] *adj* : forense
forerunner ['for,rʌnər] *n* : precursor *m*, -sora *f*
foresee [for'si:] *vt* **-saw; -seen; -seeing** : prever — **foreseeable** [for'si:əbəl] *adj* : previsible
foreshadow [for'ʃædo:] *vt* : presagiar
foresight ['for,saɪt] *n* : previsión *f*
forest ['fɔrəst] *n* : bosque *m* — **forestry** ['fɔrəstri] *n* : silvicultura *f*
foretaste ['for,teɪst] *n* : anticipo *m*
foretell [for'tɛl] *vt* **-told; -telling** : predecir
forethought ['for,θɔt] *n* : reflexión *f* previa
forever [fɔr'ɛvər] *adv* **1** ETERNALLY : para siempre **2** CONTINUALLY : siempre, constantemente
forewarn [for'wɔrn] *vt* : advertir, prevenir
foreword ['forwərd] *n* : prólogo *m*
forfeit ['fɔrfət] *n* **1** PENALTY : pena *f* **2** : prenda *f* (en un juego) — **~** *vt* : perder
forge ['fordʒ] *n* : forja *f* — **~** *v* **forged; forging** *vt* **1** : forjar (metal, etc.) **2** COUNTERFEIT : falsificar — *vi* **~ ahead** : avanzar, seguir adelante — **forger** ['fordʒər] *n* : falsificador *m*, -dora *f* — **forgery** ['fordʒəri] *n, pl* **-eries** : falsificación *f*
forget [fər'gɛt] *v* **-got** [-'gɑt]; **-gotten** [-'gɑtən] *or* **-got; -getting** *vt* : olvidar, olvidarse de — *vi* **1** : olvidarse **2 I forgot** : se me olvidó — **forgetful** [fər'gɛtfəl] *adj* : olvidadizo
forgive [fər'gɪv] *vt* **-gave** [-'geɪv]; **-given** [-'gɪvən]; **-giving** : perdonar — **forgiveness** [fər'gɪvnəs] *n* : perdón *m*
forgo *or* **forego** [for'go:] *vt* **-went; -gone; -going** : privarse de, renunciar a
fork ['fɔrk] *n* **1** : tenedor *m* **2** PITCHFORK : horca *f* **3** : bifurcación *f* (de un camino, etc.) — *vi* : ramificarse, bifurcarse — *vt* **~ over** : desembolsar
forlorn [fɔr'lɔrn] *adj* : triste
form ['fɔrm] *n* **1** : forma *f* **2** DOCUMENT : formulario *m* **3** KIND : tipo *m* — **~** *vt* **1** : formar **2 ~ a habit** : adquirir un hábito — *vi* : formarse
formal ['fɔrməl] *adj* : formal — **~** *n* **1** BALL : baile *m* (formal) **2** *or* **~ dress** : traje *m* de etiqueta — **formality** [fɔr'mæləṭi] *n, pl* **-ties** : formalidad *f*
format ['fɔr,mæt] *n* : formato *m* — **~** *vt* **-matted; -matting** : formatear
formation [fɔr'meɪʃən] *n* **1** : formación *f* **2** SHAPE : forma *f*
former ['fɔrmər] *adj* **1** PREVIOUS : antiguo, anterior **2** : primero (de dos) — **formerly** ['fɔrmərli] *adv* : anteriormente, antes
formidable ['fɔrmədəbəl, fɔr'mɪdə-] *adj* : formidable
formula ['fɔrmjələ] *n, pl* **-las** *or* **-lae** [-,li:, -,laɪ] **1** : fórmula *f* **2** *or* **baby ~** : preparado *m* para biberón
forsake [fər'seɪk] *vt* **-sook** [-'sʊk]; **-saken** [-'seɪkən]; **-saking** : abandonar
fort ['fort] *n* : fuerte *m*
forth ['forθ] *adv* **1 and so ~** : etcétera **2 back and ~** → **back 3 from this day ~** : de hoy en adelante — **forthcoming** [forθ'kʌmɪŋ, 'forθ,-] *adj* **1** COMING : próximo **2** OPEN : comunicativo — **forthright** ['forθ,raɪt] *adj* : directo, franco
fortieth ['fɔrṭiəθ] *adj* : cuadragésimo — **~** *n* **1** : cuadragésimo *m*, -ma *f* (en una serie) **2** : cuarentavo *m*, cuarentava parte *f*
fortify ['fɔrṭə,faɪ] *vt* **-fied; -fying** : fortificar — **fortification** [,fɔrṭəfə'keɪʃən] *n* : fortificación *f*
fortitude ['fɔrṭə,tu:d, -,tju:d] *n* : fortaleza *f*
fortnight ['fort,naɪt] *n* : quince días *mpl*, quincena *f*
fortress ['fɔrtrəs] *n* : fortaleza *f*
fortunate ['fɔrtʃənət] *adj* : afortunado — **fortunately** ['fɔrtʃənətli] *adv* : afortunadamente — **fortune** ['fɔrtʃən] *n* : fortuna *f* — **fortune–teller** ['fɔrtʃən,tɛlər] *n* : adivino *m*, -na *f*
forty ['fɔrṭi] *n, pl* **forties** : cuarenta *m* — **~** *adj* : cuarenta

forum ['forəm] *n, pl* **-rums** : foro *m*
forward ['fɔrwərd] *adj* **1** : hacia adelante (en dirección), delantero (en posición) **2** BRASH : descarado — **~** *adv* **1** : (hacia) adelante **2 from this day ~** : de aquí en adelante — **~** *vt* : remitir, enviar — **~** *n* : delantero *m*, -ra *f* (en deportes) — **forwards** ['fɔrwərdz] *adv* → **forward**
fossil ['fɑsəl] *n* : fósil *m*
foster ['fɔstər] *adj* : adoptivo — **~** *vt* : promover, fomentar
fought → **fight**
foul ['faʊl] *adj* **1** REPULSIVE : asqueroso **2 ~ language** : palabrotas *fpl* **3 ~ play** : actos *mpl* criminales **4 ~ weather** : mal tiempo *m* — **~** *n* : falta *f* (en deportes) — **~** *vi* : cometer faltas (en deportes) — *vt* : ensuciar
found[1] ['faʊnd] → **find**
found[2] *vt* : fundar, establecer — **foundation** [faʊn'deɪʃən] *n* **1** : fundación *f* **2** BASIS : fundamento *m* **3** : cimientos *mpl* (de un edificio)
founder[1] ['faʊndər] *n* : fundador *m*, -dora *f*
founder[2] *vi* SINK : hundirse
fountain ['faʊntən] *n* : fuente *f*
four ['for] *n* : cuatro *m* — **~** *adj* : cuatro — **fourfold** ['for,fo:ld, -'fo:ld] *adj* : cuadruple — **four hundred** *adj* : cuatrocientos — **~** *n* : cuatrocientos *m*
fourteen [for'ti:n] *n* : catorce *m* — **~** *adj* : catorce — **fourteenth** [for'ti:nθ] *adj* : decimocuarto — **~** *n* **1** : decimocuarto *m*, **-ta** *f* (en una serie) **2** : catorceavo *m*, catorceava parte *f*
fourth ['forθ] *n* **1** : cuarto *m*, -ta *f* (en una serie) **2** : cuarto *m*, cuarta parte *f* — **~** *adj* : cuarto
fowl ['faʊl] *n, pl* **fowl** *or* **fowls** : ave *f*
fox ['fɑks] *n, pl* **foxes** : zorro *m*, -ra *f* — **~** *vt* TRICK : engañar — **foxy** ['fɑksi] *adj* **foxier; -est** SHREWD : astuto
foyer ['fɔɪər, 'fɔɪ,jeɪ] *n* : vestíbulo *m*
fraction ['frækʃən] *n* : fracción *f*
fracture ['fræktʃər] *n* : fractura *f* — **~** *vt* **-tured; -turing** : fracturar
fragile ['frædʒəl, -,dʒaɪl] *adj* : frágil
fragment ['frægmənt] *n* : fragmento *m*
fragrant ['freɪgrənt] *adj* : fragante — **fragrance** ['freɪgrənts] *n* : fragancia *f*, aroma *m*
frail ['freɪl] *adj* : débil, delicado
frame ['freɪm] *vt* **framed; framing 1** ENCLOSE : enmarcar **2** COMPOSE, DRAFT : formular **3** INCRIMINATE : incriminar — **~** *n* **1** : armazón *mf* (de un edificio, etc.) **2** : marco *m* (de un cuadro, una puerta, etc.) **3** *or* **~s** *npl* : montura *f* (para anteojos) **4 ~ of mind** : estado *m* de ánimo — **framework** ['freɪm,wərk] *n* : armazón *f*
franc ['fræŋk] *n* : franco *m*
frank ['fræŋk] *adj* : franco — **frankly** *adv* : francamente — **frankness** ['fræŋknəs] *n* : franqueza *f*
frantic ['fræntɪk] *adj* : frenético
fraternal [frə'tərnəl] *adj* : fraterno, fraternal — **fraternity** [frə'tərnəṭi] *n, pl* **-ties** : fraternidad *f* — **fraternize** ['fræṭər,naɪz] *vi* **-nized; -nizing** : confraternizar
fraud ['frɔd] *n* **1** DECEIT : fraude *m* **2** IMPOSTOR : impostor *m*, -tora *f* — **fraudulent** ['frɔdʒələnt] *adj* : fraudulento
fraught ['frɔt] *adj* **~ with** : lleno de, cargado de
fray[1] ['freɪ] *n* **1 join the ~** : salir a la palestra **2 return to the ~** : volver a la carga
fray[2] *vt* : crispar (los nervios) — *vi* : deshilacharse
freak ['fri:k] *n* **1** ODDITY : fenómeno *m* **2** ENTHUSIAST : entusiasta *mf* — **freakish** ['fri:kɪʃ] *adj* : anormal
freckle ['frɛkəl] *n* : peca *f*
free ['fri:] *adj* **freer; freest 1** : libre **2** *or* **~ of charge** : gratuito, gratis **3** LOOSE : suelto — **~** *vt* **freed; freeing 1** : liberar, poner en libertad **2** RELEASE, UNFASTEN : soltar, desatar — **~** *adv or* **for ~** : gratis — **freedom** ['fri:dəm] *n* : libertad *f* — **freelance** ['fri:,lænts] *adj* : por cuenta propia — **freely** ['fri:li] *adv* **1** : libremente **2** LAVISHLY : con generosidad — **freeway** ['fri:,weɪ] *n* : autopista *f* — **free will** *n* **1** : libre albedrío *m* **2 of one's own ~** : por su propia voluntad
freeze ['fri:z] *v* **froze** ['fro:z]; **frozen** ['fro:zən]; **freezing** *vi* **1** : congelarse, helarse **2** STOP : quedarse inmóvil — *vt* : helar (agua, etc.), congelar (alimentos, precios, etc.) — **freeze-dry** ['fri:z'draɪ] *vt* **-dried; -drying** : liofilizar — **freezer** ['fri:zər] *n* : congelador *m* — **freezing** ['fri:zɪŋ] *adj* **1** CHILLY : helado **2 it's freezing!** : ¡hace un frío espantoso!
freight ['freɪt] *n* **1** SHIPPING : porte *m*, flete *m Lat* **2** CARGO : carga *f*
French ['frɛntʃ] *adj* : francés — **~** *n* **1** : francés *m* (idioma) **2 the ~** *npl* : los franceses — **Frenchman** ['frɛntʃmən] *n* : francés *m* — **Frenchwoman** ['frɛntʃ,wʊmən] *n* : francesa *f* — **french fries** ['frɛntʃ,fraɪz] *npl* : papas *fpl* fritas
frenetic [frɪ'nɛṭɪk] *adj* : frenético

frenzy ['frɛnzi] *n, pl* **-zies** : frenesí *m* — **frenzied** ['frɛnzid] *adj* : frenético

frequent [fri'kwɛnt, 'fri:kwənt] *vt* : frecuentar — ~ ['fri:kwənt] *adj* : frecuente — **frequency** ['fri:kwəntsi] *n, pl* **-cies** : frecuencia *f* — **frequently** *adv* : a menudo, frecuentemente

fresco ['frɛs,ko:] *n, pl* **-coes** : fresco *m*

fresh ['frɛʃ] *adj* **1** : fresco **2** IMPUDENT : descarado **3** CLEAN : limpio **4** NEW : nuevo **5** ~ **water** : agua *m* dulce — **freshen** ['frɛʃən] *vt* : refrescar — *vi* ~ **up** : arreglarse — **freshly** ['frɛʃli] *adv* : recién — **freshman** ['frɛʃmən] *n, pl* **-men** [-mən, -,mɛn] : estudiante *mf* de primer año — **freshness** ['frɛʃnəs] *n* : frescura *f*

fret ['frɛt] *vi* **fretted; fretting** : preocuparse — **fretful** ['frɛtfəl] *adj* : nervioso, irritable

friar ['fraɪər] *n* : fraile *m*

friction ['frɪkʃən] *n* : fricción *f*

Friday ['fraɪ,deɪ, -di] *n* : viernes *m*

friend ['frɛnd] *n* : amigo *m*, -ga *f* — **friendliness** ['frɛndlinəs] *n* : simpatía *f* — **friendly** ['frɛndli] *adj* **-lier; -est** : simpático, amable — **friendship** [frɛnd,ʃɪp] *n* : amistad *f*

frigate ['frɪgət] *n* : fragata *f*

fright ['fraɪt] *n* : miedo *m*, susto *m* — **frighten** ['fraitən] *vt* : asustar, espantar — **frightened** ['fraitənd] *adj* **1** : asustado, temeroso **2 be** ~ **of** : tener miedo de — **frightening** ['fraitənɪŋ] *adj* : espantoso — **frightful** ['fraɪtfəl] *adj* : espantoso, terrible

frigid ['frɪdʒɪd] *adj* : frío, glacial

frill ['frɪl] *n* **1** RUFFLE : volante *m* **2** LUXURY : lujo *m*

fringe ['frɪndʒ] *n* **1** : fleco *m* **2** EDGE : periferia *f*, margen *m* **3** ~ **benefits** : incentivos *mpl*, extras *mpl*

frisk ['frɪsk] *vt* SEARCH : cachear, registrar — **frisky** ['frɪski] *adj* **friskier; -est** : retozón, juguetón

fritter ['frɪţər] *n* : buñuelo *m* — ~ *vt or* ~ **away** : malgastar (dinero), desperdiciar (tiempo)

frivolous ['frɪvələs] *adj* : frívolo — **frivolity** [frɪ'vɑləţi] *n, pl* **-ties** : frivolidad *f*

frizzy ['frɪzi] *adj* **frizzier; -est** : rizado, crespo

fro ['fro:] *adv* **to and** ~ → **to**

frock ['frɑk] *n* : vestido *m*

frog ['frɔg, 'frɑg] *n* **1** : rana *f* **2 have a** ~ **in one's throat** : tener carraspera

frolic ['frɑlɪk] *vi* **-icked; -icking** : retozar

from ['frʌm, 'frɑm] *prep* **1** : de **2** (*indicating a starting point*) : desde **3** (*indicating a cause*) : de, por **4** ~ **now on** : a partir de ahora

front ['frʌnt] *n* **1** : parte *f* delantera **2** : delantera *f* (de un vestido, etc.), fachada *f* (de un edificio), frente *m* (militar) **3 cold** ~ : frente *m* frío **4 in** ~ **of** : delante de, adelante de *Lat* — ~ *vi or* ~ **on** : dar a, estar orientado a — ~ *adj* **1** : delantero, de adelante **2 the** ~ **row** : la primera fila

frontier [,frʌn'tɪr] *n* : frontera *f*

frost ['frɔst] *n* **1** : helada *f* **2** : escarcha *f* (en una superficie) — ~ *vt* ICE : bañar (pasteles) — **frostbite** ['frɔst,baɪt] *n* : congelación *f* — **frosting** ['frɔstɪŋ] *n* ICING : baño *m* — **frosty** ['frɔsti] *adj* **frostier; -est 1** : cubierto de escarcha **2** CHILLY : helado, frío

froth ['frɔθ] *n, pl* **froths** ['frɔθs, 'frɔðz] : espuma *f* — **frothy** ['frɔθi] *adj* **frothier; -est** : espumoso

frown ['fraʊn] *vi* **1** : fruncir el ceño, fruncir el entrecejo **2** ~ **at** : mirar con ceño **3** ~ **upon** : desaprobar — ~ *n* : ceño *m* (fruncido)

froze, frozen → **freeze**

frugal ['fru:gəl] *adj* : frugal

fruit ['fru:t] *n* **1** : fruta *f* **2** PRODUCT, RESULT : fruto *m* — **fruitcake** ['fru:t,keɪk] *n* : pastel *m* de frutas — **fruitful** ['fru:tfəl] *adj* : fructífero — **fruition** [fru'ɪʃən] *n* **come to** ~ : realizarse — **fruitless** ['fru:tləs] *adj* : infructuoso — **fruity** ['fru:ţi] *adj* **fruitier; -est** : (con sabor) a fruta

frustrate ['frʌs,treɪt] *vt* **-trated; -trating** : frustrar — **frustrating** ['frʌs,treɪţɪŋ] *adj* : frustrante — **frustration** [,frʌs'treɪʃən] *n* : frustración *f*

fry ['fraɪ] *vt* **fried; frying** : freír — ~ *n, pl* **fries 1 small** ~ : gente *f* de poca monta **2 fries** *npl* → **french fries** — **frying pan** *n* : sartén *mf*

fudge ['fʌdʒ] *n* : dulce *m* blando de chocolate y leche

fuel ['fju:əl] *n* : combustible *m* — ~ *vt* **-eled** *or* **-elled; -eling** *or* **-elling 1** : alimentar (un horno), abastecer de combustible (un avión) **2** STIMULATE : estimular

fugitive ['fju:dʒəţɪv] *n* : fugitivo *m*, -va *f*

fulfill *or* **fulfil** [fʊl'fɪl] *vt* **-filled; -filling 1** : cumplir con (una obligación), desarrollar (potencial) **2** FILL, MEET : cumplir — **fulfillment** [fʊl'fɪlmənt] *n* **1** ACCOMPLISHMENT : cumplimiento *m* **2** SATISFACTION : satisfacción *f*

full ['fʊl, 'fʌl] *adj* **1** FILLED : lleno **2** COMPLETE : complete, detallado **3** : redondo (dícese de la cara), amplio (dícese de ropa) **4 at ~ speed** : a toda velocidad **5 in ~ bloom** : en plena flor — **~** *adv* **1** DIRECTLY : de lleno **2 know ~ well** : saber muy bien — **~** *n* **1 pay in ~** : pagar en su totalidad **2 to the ~** : al máximo — **full–fledged** ['fʊl'flɛdʒd] *adj* : hecho y derecho — **fully** ['fʊli] *adv* **1** COMPLETELY : completamente **2** AT LEAST : al menos, por lo menos

fumble ['fʌmbəl] *vi* **-bled; -bling 1** RUMMAGE : hurgar **2 ~ with** : manejar con torpeza

fume ['fju:m] *vi* **fumed; fuming 1** SMOKE : echar humo, humear **2** RAGE : estar furioso — **fumes** *npl* : gases *mpl*

fumigate ['fju:məˌgeɪt] *vt* **-gated; -gating** : fumigar

fun ['fʌn] *n* **1** AMUSEMENT : diversión *f* **2 have ~** : divertirse **3 make ~ of** : reírse de, burlarse de — **~** *adj* : divertido

function ['fʌŋkʃən] *n* **1** : función *f* **2** GATHERING : recepción *f*, reunión *f* social — **~** *vi* : funcionar — **functional** ['fʌŋkʃənəl] *adj* : funcional

fund ['fʌnd] *n* **1** : fondo *m* **2 ~s** *npl* RESOURCES : fondos *mpl* — **~** *vt* : financiar

fundamental [ˌfʌndə'mɛntəl] *adj* : fundamental — **fundamentals** *npl* : fundamentos *mpl*

funeral ['fju:nərəl] *adj* : funeral, fúnebre — **~** *n* : funeral *m*, funerales *mpl* — **funeral home** *or* **funeral parlor** *n* : funeraria *f*

fungus ['fʌŋgəs] *n, pl* **fungi** ['fʌnˌdʒaɪ, 'fʌŋˌgaɪ] : hongo *m*

funnel ['fʌnəl] *n* **1** : embudo *m* **2** SMOKESTACK : chimenea *f*

funny ['fʌni] *adj* **funnier; -est 1** : divertido, gracioso **2** STRANGE : extraño, raro — **funnies** ['fʌniz] *npl* : tiras *fpl* cómicas

fur ['fər] *n* **1** : pelaje *m*, pelo *m* (de un animal) **2** *or* **~ coat** : (prenda *f* de) piel *f* — **~** *adj* : de piel

furious ['fjʊriəs] *adj* : furioso

furnace ['fərnəs] *n* : horno *m*

furnish ['fərnɪʃ] *vt* **1** SUPPLY : proveer **2** : amueblar (una casa, etc.) — **furnishings** ['fərnɪʃɪŋz] *npl* : muebles *mpl*, mobiliario *m* — **furniture** ['fərnɪtʃər] *n* : muebles *mpl*, mobiliario *m*

furrow ['fəro:] *n* : surco *m*

furry ['fəri] *adj* **furrier; -est** : peludo (dícese de un animal), de peluche (dícese de un juguete, etc.)

further ['fərðər] *adv* **1** FARTHER : más lejos **2** MOREOVER : además **3** MORE : más — **~** *vt* : promover, fomentar — **~** *adj* **1** FARTHER : más lejano **2** ADDITIONAL : adicional, más **3 until ~ notice** : hasta nuevo aviso — **furthermore** ['fərðərˌmor] *adv* : además — **furthest** ['fərðəst] → **farthest**

furtive ['fərṭɪv] *adj* : furtivo

fury ['fjʊri] *n, pl* **-ries** : furia *f*

fuse[1] *or* **fuze** ['fju:z] *n* : mecha *f* (de una bomba, etc.)

fuse[2] *v* **fused; fusing** *vt* **1** MELT : fundir **2** UNITE : fusionar — *vi* : fundirse, fusionarse — **~** *n* **1** : fusible *m* **2 blow a ~** : fundir un fusible — **fusion** ['fju:ʒən] *n* : fusión *f*

fuss ['fʌs] *n* **1** : jaleo *m*, alboroto *m* **2 make a ~** : armar un escándalo — **~** *vi* **1** WORRY : preocuparse **2** COMPLAIN : quejarse — **fussy** ['fʌsi] *adj* **fussier; -est 1** IRRITABLE : irritable **2** ELABORATE : recargado **3** FINICKY : quisquilloso

futile ['fju:ṭəl, 'fju:ˌtaɪl] *adj* : inútil, vano — **futility** [fju'tɪləṭi] *n, pl* **-ties** : inutilidad *f*

future ['fju:tʃər] *adj* : futuro — **~** *n* : futuro *m*

fuze → **fuse**[1]

fuzz ['fʌz] *n* : pelusa *f* — **fuzzy** ['fʌzi] *adj* **fuzzier; -est 1** FURRY : con pelusa, peludo **2** BLURRY : borroso **3** VAGUE : confuso

G

g ['dʒi:] *n, pl* **g's** *or* **gs** ['dʒi:z] : g *f*, séptima letra del alfabeto inglés

gab ['gæb] *vi* **gabbed; gabbing** : charlar, cotorrear *fam* — **~** *n* CHATTER : charla *f*

gable ['geɪbəl] *n* : aguilón *m*

gadget ['gædʒət] *n* : artilugio *m*

gag ['gæg] *v* **gagged; gagging** *vt* : amordazar — *vi* CHOKE : atragantarse — **~** *n* **1** : mordaza *f* **2** JOKE : chiste *m*

gage → **gauge**

gaiety ['geɪəṭi] *n, pl* **-eties** : alegría *f* — **gaily** ['geɪli] *adv* : alegremente

gain ['geɪn] *n* **1** PROFIT : ganancia *f* **2** INCREASE : aumento *m* — **~** *vt* **1** OBTAIN : ganar, adquirir **2 ~ weight** : aumen-

tar de peso — *vi* 1 PROFIT : beneficiarse 2 : adelantar(se) (dícese de un reloj) — **gainful** ['geɪnfəl] *adj* : lucrativo
gait ['geɪt] *n* : modo *m* de andar
gala ['geɪlə, 'gæ-, 'gɑ-] *n* : fiesta *f*
galaxy ['gæləksi] *n, pl* **-axies** : galaxia *f*
gale ['geɪl] *n* 1 : vendaval *f* 2 **~s of laughter** : carcajadas *fpl*
gall ['gɔl] *n* **have the ~ to** : tener el descaro de
gallant ['gælənt] *adj* 1 BRAVE : valiente 2 CHIVALROUS : galante
gallbladder ['gɔl,blædər] *n* : vesícula *f* biliar
gallery ['gæləri] *n, pl* **-leries** : galería *f*
gallon ['gælən] *n* : galón *m*
gallop ['gæləp] *vi* : galopar — **~** *n* : galope *m*
gallows ['gæ,lo:z] *n, pl* **-lows** *or* **-lowses** [-,lo:zəz] : horca *f*
gallstone ['gɔl,sto:n] *n* : cálculo *m* biliar
galore [gə'lor] *adj* : en abundancia
galoshes [gə'lɑʃ] *n* : galochas *fpl*, chanclos *mpl*
galvanize ['gælvən,aɪz] *vt* **-nized; -nizing** : galvanizar
gamble ['gæmbəl] *v* **-bled; -bling** *vi* : jugar — *vt* : jugarse — **~** *n* 1 BET : apuesta *f* 2 RISK : riesga *f* — **gambler** ['gæmbələr] *n* : jugador *m*, -dora *f*
game ['geɪm] *n* 1 : juego *m* 2 MATCH : partido *m* 3 *or* **~ animals** : caza *f* — **~** *adj* READY : listo, dispuesto
gamut ['gæmət] *n* : gama *f*
gang ['gæŋ] *n* : banda *f*, pandilla *f* — **~** *vi* **~ up on** : unirse contra
gangplank ['gæŋ,plæŋk] *n* : pasarela *f*
gangrene ['gæŋ,gri:n, 'gæn-; gæŋ'-, gæn'-] *n* : gangrena *f*
gangster ['gæŋstər] *n* : gángster *mf*
gangway ['gæŋ,weɪ] *n* → **gangplank**
gap ['gæp] *n* 1 OPENING : espacio *m* 2 INTERVAL : intervalo *m* 3 DISPARITY : brecha *f*, distancia *f* 4 DEFICIENCY : laguna *f*
gape ['geɪp] *vi* **gaped; gaping** 1 OPEN : estar abierto 2 STARE : mirar boquiabierto
garage [gə'rɑʒ, -'rɑdʒ] *n* : garaje *m* — **~** *vt* **-raged; -raging** : dejar en un garaje
garb ['gɑrb] *n* : vestido *m*
garbage ['gɑrbɪdʒ] *n* : basura *f* — **garbage can** *n* : cubo *m* de la basura
garble ['gɑrbəl] *vt* **-bled; -bling** : tergiversar — **garbled** ['gɑrbəld] *adj* : confuso, incomprensible
garden ['gɑrdən] *n* : jardín *m* — **~** *vi* : trabajar en el jardín — **gardener** ['gɑrdənər] *n* : jardinero *m*, -ra *f* — **gardening** ['gɑrdənɪŋ] *n* : jardinería *f*
gargle ['gɑrgəl] *vi* **-gled; -gling** : hacer gárgaras
garish ['gærɪʃ] *adj* : chillón
garland ['gɑrlənd] *n* : guirnalda *f*
garlic ['gɑrlɪk] *n* : ajo *m*
garment ['gɑrmənt] *n* : prenda *f*
garnish ['gɑrnɪʃ] *vt* : guarnecer — **~** *n* : adorno *m*, guarnición *f*
garret ['gærət] *n* : buhardilla *f*
garrison ['gærəsən] *n* : guarnición *f*
garrulous ['gærələs] *adj* : charlatán, parlanchín
garter ['gɑrtər] *n* : liga *f*
gas ['gæs] *n, pl* **gases** ['gæsəz] 1 : gas *m* 2 GASOLINE : gasolina *f* — **~** *v* **gassed; gassing** *vt* : asfixiar con gas — *vi* **~ up** : llenar el tanque con gasolina
gash ['gæʃ] *n* : tajo *m* — **~** *vt* : hacer un tajo en, cortar
gasket ['gæskət] *n* : junta *f*
gasoline ['gæsə,li:n, ,gæsə'-] *n* : gasolina *f*
gasp ['gæsp] *vi* 1 : dar un grito ahogado 2 PANT : jadear — **~** *n* : grito *m* ahogado
gas station *n* : gasolinera *f*
gastric ['gæstrɪk] *adj* : gástrico
gastronomy [gæs'trɑnəmi] *n* : gastronomía *f*
gate ['geɪt] *n* 1 DOOR : puerta *f* 2 BARRIER : barrera *f* — **gateway** ['geɪt,weɪ] *n* : puerta *f*
gather ['gæðər] *vt* 1 ASSEMBLE : reunir 2 COLLECT : recoger 3 CONCLUDE : deducir 4 : fruncir (una tela) 5 **~ speed** : acelerar — *vi* : reunirse (dícese de personas), acumularse (dícese de cosas) — **gathering** ['gæðərɪŋ] *n* : reunión *f*
gaudy ['gɔdi] *adj* **gaudier; -est** : chillón, llamativo
gauge ['geɪdʒ] *n* 1 INDICATOR : indicador *m* 2 CALIBER : calibre *m* — **~** *vt* **gauged; gauging** 1 MEASURE : medir 2 ESTIMATE : calcular, evaluar
gaunt ['gɔnt] *adj* : demacrado, descarnado
gauze ['gɔz] *n* : gasa *f*
gave → **give**
gawky ['gɔki] *adj* **gawkier; -est** : desgarbado
gay ['geɪ] *adj* 1 : alegre 2 HOMOSEXUAL : gay, homosexual
gaze ['geɪz] *vi* **gazed; gazing** : mirar (fijamente) — **~** *n* : mirada *f*
gazelle [gə'zel] *n* : gacela *f*
gazette [gə'zɛt] *n* : gaceta *f*
gear ['gɪr] *n* 1 EQUIPMENT : equipo *m* 2 POSSESSIONS : efectos *mpl* personales

3 : marcha *f* (de un vehículo) **4** *or* ~ **wheel** : rueda *f* dentada — ~ *vt* : orientar, adaptar — *vi* ~ **up** : prepararse — **gearshift** ['gɪr,ʃɪft] *n* : palanca *f* de cambio, palanca *f* de velocidades *Lat*

geese → **goose**

gelatin ['dʒɛlətən] *n* : gelatina *f*

gem ['dʒɛm] *n* : gema *f*, piedra *f* preciosa — **gemstone** ['dʒɛm,sto:n] *n* : piedra *f* preciosa

gender ['dʒɛndər] *n* **1** SEX : sexo *m* **2** : género *m* (en la gramática)

gene ['dʒi:n] *n* : gen *m*, gene *m*

genealogy [,dʒi:ni'ɑlədʒi, ,dʒɛ-, -'æ-] *n, pl* **-gies** : genealogía *f*

general ['dʒɛnrəl, 'dʒɛnə-] *adj* : general — ~ *n* **1** : general *mf* (militar) **2 in** ~ : en general, por lo general — **generalize** ['dʒɛnrə,laɪz, 'dʒɛnərə-] *v* **-ized; -izing** : generalizar — **generally** ['dʒɛnrəli, 'dʒɛnərə-] *adv* : generalmente, en general — **general practitioner** *n* : médico *m*, -ca *f* de cabecera

generate ['dʒɛnə,reɪt] *vt* **-ated; -ating** : generar — **generation** [,dʒɛnə'reɪʃən] *n* : generación *f* — **generator** ['dʒɛnə,reɪt̬ər] *n* : generador *m*

generous ['dʒɛnərəs] *adj* **1** : generoso **2** AMPLE : abundante — **generosity** [,dʒɛnə'rɑsət̬i] *n, pl* **-ties** : generosidad *f*

genetic [dʒə'nɛt̬ɪk] *adj* : genético — **genetics** [dʒə'nɛt̬ɪks] *n* : genética *f*

genial ['dʒi:niəl] *adj* : afable, simpático

genital ['dʒɛnət̬əl] *adj* : genital — **genitals** ['dʒɛnət̬əlz] *npl* : genitales *mpl*

genius ['dʒi:njəs] *n* : genio *m*

genocide ['dʒɛnə,saɪd] *n* : genocidio *m*

genteel [dʒɛn'ti:l] *adj* : refinado

gentle ['dʒɛntəl] *adj* **-tler; -tlest 1** MILD : suave, dulce **2** LIGHT : ligero **3 a** ~ **hint** : una indirecta discreta — **gentleman** ['dʒɛntəlmən] *n, pl* **-men** [-mən, -,mɛn] **1** MAN : caballero *m*, señor *m* **2 a perfect** ~ : un perfecto caballero — **gentleness** ['dʒɛntəlnəs] *n* : delicadeza *f*, ternura *f*

genuine ['dʒɛnjʊwən] *adj* **1** AUTHENTIC : verdadero, auténtico **2** SINCERE : sincero

geography [dʒi'ɑgrəfi] *n, pl* **-phies** : geografía *f* — **geographic** [,dʒi:ə'græfɪk] *or* **geographical** [-fɪkəl] *adj* : geográfico

geology [dʒi'ɑlədʒi] *n* : geología *f* — **geologic** [,dʒi:ə'lɑdʒɪk] *or* **geological** [-dʒɪkəl] *adj* : geológico

geometry [dʒi'ɑmətri] *n, pl* **-tries** : geometría *f* — **geometric** [,dʒi:ə'mɛtrɪk] *or* **geometrical** [-trɪkəl] *adj* : geométrico

geranium [dʒə'reɪniəm] *n* : geranio *m*

geriatric [,dʒɛri'ætrɪk] *adj* : geriátrico — **geriatrics** [,dʒɛri'ætrɪks] *n* : geriatría *f*

germ ['dʒərm] *n* **1** : germen *m* **2** MICROBE : microbio *m*

German ['dʒərmən] *adj* : alemán — ~ *n* : alemán *m* (idioma)

germinate ['dʒərmə,neɪt] *v* **-nated; -nating** *vi* : germinar — *vt* : hacer germinar

gestation [dʒɛ'steɪʃən] *n* : gestación *f*

gesture ['dʒɛstʃər] *n* : gesto *m* — ~ *vi* **-tured; -turing 1** : hacer gestos **2** ~ **to** : hacer señas a

get ['gɛt] *v* **got** ['gɑt]; **got** *or* **gotten** ['gɑtən]; **getting** *vt* **1** OBTAIN : conseguir, obtener **2** RECEIVE : recibir **3** EARN : ganar **4** FETCH : traer **5** CATCH : coger, agarrar *Lat* **6** UNDERSTAND : entender **7** PREPARE : preparar **8** ~ **one's hair cut** : cortarse el pelo **9** ~ **s.o. to do sth** : lograr que uno haga algo **10 have got** : tener **11 have got to** : tener que — *vi* **1** BECOME : ponerse, hacerse **2** GO, MOVE : ir **3** PROGRESS : avanzar **4** ~ **ahead** : progresar **5** ~ **at** MEAN : querer decir **6** ~ **away** : escaparse **7** ~ **away with** : salir impune de **8** ~ **back at** : desquitarse con **9** ~ **by** : arreglárselas **10** ~ **home** : llegar a casa **11** ~ **out** : salir **12** ~ **over** : reponerse de, consolarse de **13** ~ **together** : reunirse **14** ~ **up** : levantarse — **getaway** ['gɛt̬ə,weɪ] *n* : fuga *f*, huida *f* — **get-together** *n* : reunión *f*

geyser ['gaɪzər] *n* : géiser *m*

ghastly ['gæstli] *adj* **-lier; -est** : horrible, espantoso

ghetto ['gɛt̬o:] *n, pl* **-tos** *or* **-toes** : gueto *m*

ghost ['go:st] *n* : fantasma *f*, espectro *m* — **ghostly** ['go:stli] *adv* : fantasmal

giant ['dʒaɪənt] *n* : gigante *m*, -ta *f* — ~ *adj* : gigantesco

gibberish ['dʒɪbərɪʃ] *n* : galimatías *m*, jerigonza *f*

gibe ['dʒaɪb] *vi* **gibed; gibing** ~ **at** : mofarse de — ~ *n* : pulla *f*, mofa *f*

giblets ['dʒɪbləts] *npl* : menudillos *mpl*

giddy ['gɪdi] *adj* **-dier; -est** : mareado, vertiginoso — **giddiness** ['gɪdinəs] *n* : vértigo *m*

gift ['gɪft] *n* **1** PRESENT : regalo *m* **2** TALENT : don *m* — **gifted** ['gɪftəd] *adj* : talentoso, de talento

gigantic [dʒaɪ'gæntɪk] *adj* : gigantesco

giggle ['gɪgəl] *vi* **-gled; -gling** : reírse tontamente — ~ *n* : risa *f* tonta

gild ['gɪld] *vt* **gilded** ['gɪldəd] *or* **gilt** ['gɪlt]; **gilding** : dorar
gill ['gɪl] *n* : agalla *f*, branquia *f*
gilt ['gɪlt] *adj* : dorado
gimmick ['gɪmɪk] *n* : truco *m*, ardid *m*
gin ['dʒɪn] *n* : ginebra *f*
ginger ['dʒɪndʒər] *n* : jengibre *m* — **ginger ale** *n* : refresco *m* de jengibre — **gingerbread** ['dʒɪndʒərˌbrɛd] *n* : pan *m* de jengibre — **gingerly** ['dʒɪndʒərli] *adv* : con cuidado, cautelosamente
giraffe [dʒə'ræf] *n* : jirafa *f*
girder ['gərdər] *n* : viga *f*
girdle ['gərdəl] *n* CORSET : faja *f*
girl ['gərl] *n* **1** : niña *f*, muchacha *f*, chica *f* — **girlfriend** ['gərlˌfrɛnd] *n* : novia *f*, amiga *f*
girth ['gərθ] *n* : circunferencia *f*
gist ['dʒɪst] *n* **get the ~ of** : comprender lo esencial de
give ['gɪv] *v* **gave** ['geɪv]; **given** ['gɪvən]; **giving** *vt* **1** : dar **2** INDICATE : señalar **3** PRESENT : presentar **4 ~ away** : regalar **5 ~ back** : devolver **6 ~ out** : repartir **7 ~ up smoking** : dejar de fumar — *vi* **1** YIELD : ceder **2** COLLAPSE : romperse **3 ~ out** : agotarse **4 ~ up** : rendirse — **~** *n* : elasticidad *f* — **given** ['gɪvən] *adj* **1** SPECIFIED : determinado **2** INCLINED : dado, inclinado — **given name** *n* : nombre *m* de pila
glacier ['gleɪʃər] *n* : glaciar *m*
glad ['glæd] *adj* **gladder; gladdest 1** : alegre, contento **2 be ~** : alegrarse **3 ~ to meet you!** : ¡mucho gusto! — **gladden** ['glædən] *vt* : alegrar — **gladly** ['glædli] *adv* : con mucho gusto — **gladness** ['glædnəs] *n* : alegría *f*, gozo *m*
glade ['gleɪd] *n* : claro *m*
glamor *or* **glamour** ['glæmər] *n* : atractivo *m*, encanto *m* — **glamorous** ['glæmərəs] *adj* : atractivo
glance ['glænts] *vi* **glanced; glancing 1 ~ at** : mirar, dar un vistazo a **2 ~ off** : rebotar en — **~** *n* : mirada *f*, vistazo *m*
gland ['glænd] *n* : glándula *f*
glare ['glær] *vi* **glared; glaring 1** : brillar, relumbrar **2 ~ at** : lanzar una mirada feroz a — **~** *n* **1** : luz *f* deslumbrante **2** STARE : mirada *f* feroz — **glaring** ['glærɪŋ] *adj* **1** BRIGHT : deslumbrante **2** FLAGRANT : flagrante
glass ['glæs] *n* **1** : vidrio *m*, cristal *m* **2 a ~ of milk** : un vaso de leche **3 ~es** *npl* SPECTACLES : anteojos *mpl*, lentes *fpl* — **~** *adj* : de vidrio — **glassware** ['glæsˌwær] *n* : cristalería *f* — **glassy** ['glæsi] *adj* **glassier; -est 1** : vítreo **2 ~ eyes** : ojos *mpl* vidriosos
glaze ['gleɪz] *vt* **glazed; glazing 1** : poner vidrios a (una ventana, etc.) **2** : vidriar (cerámica) **3** ICE : glasear — **~** *n* **1** : vidriado *m*, barniz *m* (de cerámica) **2** ICING : glaseado *m*
gleam ['gli:m] *n* **1** : destello *m* **2 a ~ of hope** : un rayo de esperanza — **~** *vi* : destellar, relucir
glee ['gli:] *n* : alegría *f* — **gleeful** ['gli:fəl] *adj* : lleno de alegría
glib ['glɪb] *adj* **glibber; glibbest 1** : de mucha labia **2 a ~ reply** : una respuesta simplista — **glibly** ['glɪbli] *adv* : con mucha labia
glide ['glaɪd] *vi* **glided; gliding** : deslizarse (en una superficie), planear (en el aire) — **glider** ['glaɪdər] *n* : planeador *m*
glimmer ['glɪmər] *vi* : brillar con luz trémula — **~** *n* : luz *f* trémula, luz *f* tenue
glimpse ['glɪmps] *vt* **glimpsed; glimpsing** : vislumbrar — **~** *n* : vislumbre
glint ['glɪnt] *vi* : destellar — **~** *n* : destello *m*
glisten ['glɪsən] *vi* : brillar
glitter ['glɪt̬ər] *vi* : relucir, brillar
gloat ['glo:t] *vi* **~ over** : regodearse con
globe ['glo:b] *n* : globo *m* — **global** ['glo:bəl] *adj* : global, mundial
gloom ['glu:m] *n* **1** DARKNESS : oscuridad *f* **2** SADNESS : tristeza *f* — **gloomy** ['glu:mi] *adj* **gloomier; -est 1** DARK : sombrío, tenebroso **2** DISMAL : deprimente, lúgubre **3** PESSIMISTIC : pesimista
glory ['glori] *n, pl* **-ries** : gloria *f* — **glorify** ['gloraˌfaɪ] *vt* **-fied; -fying** : glorificar — **glorious** ['gloriəs] *adj* : glorioso, espléndido
gloss ['glɔs, 'glɑs] *n* : lustre *m*, brillo *m* — **~** *vt* **~ over** : minimizar (la importancia de algo)
glossary ['glɔsəri, 'glɑ-] *n, pl* **-ries** : glosario *m*
glossy ['glɔsi, 'glɑ-] *adj* **glossier; -est** : lustroso, brillante
glove ['glʌv] *n* : guante *m*
glow ['glo:] *vi* **1** : brillar, resplandecer **2 ~ with health** : rebosar de salud — **~** *n* : resplandor *m*, brillo *m*
glue ['glu:] *n* : pegamento *m*, cola *f* — **~** *vt* **glued; gluing** *or* **glueing** : pegar
glum ['glʌm] *adj* **glummer; glummest** : sombrío, triste
glut ['glʌt] *n* : superabundancia *f*, exceso *m*

glutton ['glʌtən] *n* : glotón *m*, -tona *f* — **gluttonous** ['glʌtənəs] *adj* : glotón — **gluttony** ['glʌtəni] *n, pl* **-tonies** : glotonería *f*

gnarled ['nɑrld] *adj* : nudoso

gnash ['næʃ] *vt* **~ one's teeth** : hacer rechinar los dientes

gnat ['næt] *n* : jején *m*

gnaw ['nɔ] *vt* : roer

go ['go:] *v* **went** ['wɛnt]; **gone** ['gɔn, 'gɑn]; **going; goes** ['go:z] *vi* **1** : ir **2** LEAVE : irse, salir **3** EXTEND : ir, extenderse **4** SELL : venderse **5** FUNCTION : funcionar, marchar **6** DISAPPEAR : desaparecer **7 ~ back on one's word** : faltar a su palabra **8 ~ crazy** : volverse loco **9 ~ for** LIKE : gustar **10 ~ off** EXPLODE : estallar **11 ~ with** MATCH : armonizar con **12 ~ without** : pasar sin — *v aux* **be going to** : ir a — **~** *n, pl* **goes 1 be on the ~** : no parar **2 have a ~ at** : intentar

goad ['go:d] *vt* : aguijonear (un animal), incitar (a una persona)

goal ['go:l] *n* **1** AIM : meta *m*, objetivo *m* **2** : gol *m* (en deportes) — **goalkeeper** ['go:l,ki:pər] *or* **goalie** ['go:li] *n* : portero *m*, -ra *f;* arquero *m*, -ra *f*

goat ['go:t] *n* : cabra *f*

goatee [go:'ti:] *n* : barbita *f* de chivo

gobble ['gɑbəl] *vt* **-bled; -bling** *or* **~ up** : engullir

goblet ['gɑblət] *n* : copa *f*

goblin ['gɑblən] *n* : duende *m*

god ['gɑd, 'gɔd] *n* **1** : dios *m* **2 God** : Dios *m* — **goddess** ['gɑdəs, 'gɔ-] *n* : diosa *f* — **godchild** ['gɑd,tʃaɪld, 'gɔd-] *n, pl* **-children** : ahijado *m*, -da *f* — **godfather** ['gɑd,fɑðər, 'gɔd-] *n* : padrino *m* — **godmother** ['gɑd,mʌðər, 'gɔd-] *n* : madrina *f* — **godparents** ['gɑd,pærənt, 'gɔd-] *npl* : padrinos *mpl* — **godsend** ['gɑd,sɛnd, 'gɔd-] *n* : bendición *f* (del cielo)

goes → **go**

goggles ['gɑgəlz] *npl* : gafas *fpl* (protectoras), anteojos *mpl*

goings-on [,go:ɪŋz'ɑn, -'ɔn] *npl* : sucesos *mpl*

gold ['go:ld] *n* : oro *m* — **golden** ['go:ldən] *adj* **1** : (hecho) de oro **2** : dorado, de color oro — **goldfish** ['go:ld,fɪʃ] *n* : pez *m* de colores — **goldsmith** ['go:ld,smɪθ] *n* : orfebre *mf*

golf ['gɑlf, 'gɔlf] *n* : golf *m* — **~** *vi* : jugar (al) golf — **golf ball** *n* : pelota *f* de golf — **golf course** *n* : campo *m* de golf — **golfer** ['gɑlfər, 'gɔl-] *n* : golfista *mf*

gone ['gɔn] *adj* **1** : ido, pasado **2** DEAD : muerto **3** LOST : desaparecido

good ['gʊd] *adj* **better** ['bɛt̬ər]; **best** ['bɛst] **1** : bueno **2** KIND : amable **3 ~ afternoon (evening)** : buenas tardes **4 be ~ at** : tener facilidad para **5 feel ~** : sentirse bien **6 ~ for a cold** : beneficioso para los resfriados **7 have a ~ time** : divertirse **8 ~ morning** : buenos días **9 ~ night** : buenas noches — **~** *n* **1** : bien *m* **2** GOODNESS : bondad *f* **3 ~s** *npl* PROPERTY : bienes *mpl* **4 ~s** *npl* WARES : mercancías *fpl*, mercaderías *fpl* **5 for ~** : para siempre — **~** *adv* : bien — **good-bye** *or* **good-by** [gʊd'baɪ] *n* : adiós *m* — **Good Friday** *n* : Viernes *m* Santo — **good-looking** ['gʊd'lʊkɪŋ] *adj* : bello, guapo — **goodness** ['gʊdnəs] *n* **1** : bondad *f* **2 thank ~!** : ¡gracias a Dios!, ¡menos mal! — **goodwill** [,gʊd'wɪl] *n* : buena voluntad *f* — **goody** ['gʊdi] *n, pl* **goodies** : golosina *f*

gooey ['gu:i] *adj* **gooier; gooiest** : pegajoso

goof *n* ['gu:f] : pifia *f fam* — **~** *vi* **1** *or* **~ up** : cometer un error **2 ~ around** : hacer tonterías

goose ['gu:s] *n, pl* **geese** ['gi:s] : ganso *m*, -sa *f;* oca *f* — **goose bumps** *or* **goose pimples** *npl* : carne *f* de gallina

gopher ['go:fər] *n* : taltuza *f*

gore[1] ['gor] *n* BLOOD : sangre *f*

gore[2] *vt* **gored; goring** : cornear

gorge ['gɔrdʒ] *n* RAVINE : cañon *m* — **~** *vt* **gorged; gorging ~ oneself** : hartarse

gorgeous ['gɔrdʒəs] *adj* : magnífico, espléndido

gorilla [gə'rɪlə] *n* : gorila *m*

gory ['gori] *adj* **gorier; -est** : sangriento

gospel ['gɑspəl] *n* **1** : evangelio *m* **2 the Gospel** : el Evangelio

gossip ['gɑsɪp] *n* **1** : chismoso *m*, -sa *f* (persona) **2** RUMOR : chisme *m* — **~** *vi* : chismear, contar chismes — **gossipy** ['gɑsɪpi] *adj* : chismoso

got → **get**

Gothic ['gɑθɪk] *adj* : gótico

gotten → **get**

gourmet ['gʊr,meɪ, gʊr'meɪ] *n* : gastrónomo *m*, -ma *f*

gout ['gaʊt] *n* : gota *f*

govern ['gʌvərn] *v* : gobernar — **governess** ['gʌvərnəs] *n* : institutriz *f* — **government** ['gʌvərmənt] *n* : gobierno *m* — **governor** ['gʌvənər, 'gʌvərnər] *n* : gobernador *m*, -dora *f*

gown ['gaʊn] *n* **1** : vestido *m* **2** : toga *f* (de magistrados, etc.)

grab ['græb] *v* **grabbed; grabbing** *vt* : agarrar, arrebatar

grace ['greɪs] *n* **1** : gracia *f* **2 say ~** : bendecir la mesa — **~** *vt* **graced; gracing 1** HONOR : honrar **2** ADORN : adornar — **graceful** ['greɪsfəl] *adj* : lleno de gracia, grácil — **gracious** ['greɪʃəs] *adj* : cortés, gentil

grade ['greɪd] *n* **1** QUALITY : calidad *f* **2** RANK : grado *m,* rango *m* (militar) **3** YEAR : grado *m,* año *m* (a la escuela) **4** MARK : nota *f* **5** SLOPE : cuesta *f* — **~** *vt* **graded; grading 1** CLASSIFY : clasificar **2** MARK : calificar (exámenes, etc.) — **grade school** → **elementary school**

gradual ['grædʒʊəl] *adj* : gradual — **gradually** ['grædʒʊəli, 'grædʒəli] *adv* : gradualmente, poco a poco

graduate ['grædʒʊət] *n* : licenciado *m,* -da *f* (de la universidad), bachiller *mf* (de la escuela secondaria) — **~** ['grædʒʊˌeɪt] *v* **-ated; -ating** *vi* : graduarse, licenciarse — *vt* CALIBRATE : graduar — **graduation** [ˌgrædʒʊ'eɪʃən] *n* : graduación *f*

graffiti [grə'fi:ţi, græ-] *npl* : graffiti *mpl*

graft ['græft] *n* : injerto *m* — **~** *vt* : injertar

grain ['greɪn] *n* **1** : grano *m* **2** CEREALS : cereales *mpl* **3** : veta *f,* vena *f* (de madera)

gram ['græm] *n* : gramo *m*

grammar ['græmər] *n* : gramática *f* — **grammar school** → **elementary school**

grand ['grænd] *adj* **1** : magnífico, espléndido **2** FABULOUS, GREAT : fabuloso, estupendo — **grandchild** ['grændˌtʃaɪld] *n, pl* **-children** : nieto *m,* -ta *f* — **granddaughter** ['grændˌdɔţər] *n* : nieta *f* — **grandeur** ['grændʒər] *n* : grandiosidad *f* — **grandfather** ['grændˌfɑðər] *n* : abuelo *m* — **grandiose** ['grændiˌo:s, ˌgrændi'-] *adj* : grandioso — **grandmother** ['grændˌmʌðər] *n* : abuela *f* — **grandparents** ['grændˌpærənt] *npl* : abuelos *mpl* — **grandson** ['grændˌsʌn] *n* : nieto *m* — **grandstand** ['grændˌstænd] *n* : tribuna *f*

granite ['grænɪt] *n* : granito *m*

grant ['grænt] *vt* **1** : conceder **2** ADMIT : reconocer, admitir **3 take for granted** : dar (algo) por sentado — **~** *n* **1** SUBSIDY : subvención *f* **2** SCHOLARSHIP : beca *f*

grape ['greɪp] *n* : uva *f*

grapefruit ['greɪpˌfru:t] *n* : toronja *f,* pomelo *m*

grapevine ['greɪpˌvaɪn] *n* **1** : vid *f,* parra *f* **2 I heard it through the ~** : me lo dijo un pajarito *fam*

graph ['græf] *n* : gráfica *f,* gráfico *m* — **graphic** ['græfɪk] *adj* : gráfico

grapple ['græpəl] *vi* **-pled; -pling ~ with** : forcejear con (una persona), luchar con (un problema)

grasp ['græsp] *vt* **1** : agarrar **2** UNDERSTAND : comprender, captar — **~** *n* **1** : agarre *m* **2** UNDERSTANDING : comprensión *f* **3** REACH : alcance *m*

grass ['græs] *n* **1** : hierba *f* (planta) **2** LAWN : césped *m,* pasto *m Lat* — **grasshopper** ['græsˌhɑpər] *n* : saltamontes *m* — **grassy** ['græsi] *adj* **grassier; -est** : cubierto de hierba

grate[1] ['greɪt] *v* **grated; -ing** *vt* **1** : rallar (en cocina) **2 ~ one's teeth** : hacer rechinar los dientes — *vi* RASP : chirriar

grate[2] *n* GRATING : reja *f,* rejilla *f*

grateful ['greɪtfəl] *adj* : agradecido — **gratefully** ['greɪtfəli] *adv* : con agradecimiento — **gratefulness** ['greɪtfəlnəs] *n* : gratitud *f,* agradecimiento *m*

grater ['greɪţər] *n* : rallador *m*

gratify ['græţəˌfaɪ] *vt* **-fied; -fying 1** PLEASE : complacer **2** SATISFY : satisfacer

grating ['greɪţɪŋ] *n* : reja *f,* rejilla *f*

gratitude ['græţəˌtu:d, -ˌtju:d] *n* : gratitud *f*

gratuitous [grə'tu:əţəs] *adj* : gratuito

grave[1] ['greɪv] *n* : tumba *f,* sepultura *f*

grave[2] *adj* **graver; -est** : grave

gravel ['grævəl] *n* : grava *f,* gravilla *f*

gravestone ['greɪvˌsto:n] *n* : lápida *f* — **graveyard** ['greɪvˌjɑrd] *n* : cementerio *m*

gravity ['grævəţi] *n, pl* **-ties** : gravedad *f*

gravy ['greɪvi] *n, pl* **-vies** : salsa *f* (preparada con jugo de carne)

gray ['greɪ] *adj* **1** : gris **2 ~ hair** : pelo *m* canoso — **~** *n* : gris *m* — **~** *vi or* **turn ~** : encanecer, ponerse gris

graze[1] ['greɪz] *vi* **grazed; grazing** : pastar, pacer

graze[2] *vt* **1** TOUCH : rozar **2** SCRATCH : rasguñarse

grease ['gri:s] *n* : grasa *f* — **~** ['gri:s, 'gri:z] *vt* **greased; greasing** : engrasar — **greasy** ['gri:si, -zi] *adj* **greasier; -est 1** : grasiento **2** OILY : graso, grasoso

great ['greɪt] *adj* **1** : grande **2** FANTASTIC : estupendo, fabuloso — **great-grandchild** [ˌgreɪt'grændˌtʃaɪld] *n, pl*

-children [-ˌtʃɪldrən] : bisnieto *m*, -ta *f* — **great–grandfather** [ˌgreɪt'grændˌfɑðər] *n* : bisabuelo *m* — **great-grandmother** [ˌgreɪt'grændˌmʌðər] *n* : bisabuela *f* — **greatly** ['greɪtli] *adv* **1** MUCH : mucho **2** VERY : muy — **greatness** ['greɪtnəs] *n* : grandeza *f*

greed ['gri:d] *n* **1** : codicia *f*, avaricia *f* **2** GLUTTONY : glotonería *f* — **greedily** ['gri:dəli] *adv* : con avaricia — **greedy** ['gri:di] *adj* **greedier; -est 1** : codicioso, avaro **2** GLUTTONOUS : glotón

Greek ['gri:k] *adj* : griego — ~ *n* : griego *m* (idioma)

green ['gri:n] *adj* **1** : verde **2** INEXPERIENCED : novato — ~ *n* **1** : verde *m* (color) **2 ~s** *npl* : verduras *fpl* — **greenery** ['gri:nəri] *n, pl* **-eries** : vegetación *f* — **greenhouse** ['gri:nˌhaʊs] *n* : invernadero *m*

greet ['gri:t] *vt* **1** : saludar **2** WELCOME : recibir — **greeting** ['gri:t̬ɪŋ] *n* **1** : saludo *m* **2 ~s** *npl* REGARDS : saludos *mpl*, recuerdos *mpl*

gregarious [grɪ'gæriəs] *adj* : sociable

grenade [grə'neɪd] *n* : granada *f*

grew → **grow**

grey → **gray**

greyhound ['greɪˌhaʊnd] *n* : galgo *m*

grid ['grɪd] *n* **1** GRATING : rejilla *f* **2** NETWORK : red *f* **3** : cuadriculado *m* (de un mapa)

griddle ['grɪdəl] *n* : plancha *f*

grief ['gri:f] *n* : dolor *m*, pesar *m* — **grievance** ['gri:vənts] *n* : queja *f* — **grieve** ['gri:v] *v* **grieved; grieving** *vt* : entristecer — *vi* ~ **for** : llorar (a), lamentar — **grievous** ['gri:vəs] *adj* : grave, doloroso

grill ['grɪl] *vt* **1** : asar a la parrilla **2** INTERROGATE : interrogar — ~ *n* : parrilla *f* (para cocinar) — **grille** *or* **grill** ['grɪl] GRATING *n* : reja *f*, rejilla *f*

grim ['grɪm] *adj* **grimmer; grimmest 1** STERN : severo **2** GLOOMY : sombrío

grimace ['grɪməs, grɪ'meɪs] *n* : mueca *f* — ~ *vi* **-maced; -macing** : hacer muecas

grime ['graɪm] *n* : mugre *f*, suciedad *f* — **grimy** ['graɪmi] *adj* **grimier; -est** : mugriento, sucio

grin ['grɪn] *vi* **grinned; grinning** : sonreír (abiertamente) — ~ *n* : sonrisa *f* (abierta)

grind ['graɪnd] *v* **ground** ['graʊnd]; **grinding** *vt* **1** : moler (el café, etc.) **2** SHARPEN : afilar **3 ~ one's teeth** : rechinar los dientes — *vi* : rechinar — ~ *n* **the daily ~** : la rutina diaria — **grinder** ['graɪndər] *n* : molinillo *m*

grip ['grɪp] *vt* **gripped; gripping 1** : agarrar, asir **2** INTEREST : captar el interés de — ~ *n* **1** GRASP : agarre *m* **2** CONTROL : control *m*, dominio *m* **3** HANDLE : empuñadura *f* **4 come to ~s with** : llegar a entender de

gripe ['graɪp] *vi* **griped; griping** : quejarse — ~ *n* : queja *f*

grisly ['grɪzli] *adj* **-lier; -est** : espeluznante, horrible

gristle ['grɪsəl] *n* : cartílago *m*

grit ['grɪt] *n* **1** : arena *f*, grava *f* **2** GUTS : agallas *fpl fam* **3 ~s** *npl* : sémola *f* de maíz — ~ *vt* **gritted; gritting ~ one's teeth** : acorazarse

groan ['gro:n] *vi* : gemir — ~ *n* : gemido *m*

grocery ['gro:səri, -ʃəri] *n, pl* **-ceries 1** *or* ~ **store** : tienda *f* de comestibles, tienda *f* de abarrotes *Lat* **2 groceries** *npl* : comestibles *mpl*, abarrotes *mpl Lat* — **grocer** ['gro:sər] *n* : tendero *m*, -ra *f*

groggy ['grɑgi] *adj* **-gier; -est** : atontado, grogui *fam*

groin ['grɔɪn] *n* : ingle *f*

groom ['gru:m, 'grʊm] *n* BRIDEGROOM : novio *m* — ~ *vt* **1** : almohazar (un animal) **2** PREPARE : preparar

groove ['gru:v] *n* : ranura *f*, surco *m*

grope ['gro:p] *vi* **groped; groping 1** : andar a tientas **2 ~ for:** buscar a tientas

gross ['gro:s] *adj* **1** SERIOUS : grave **2** OBESE : obeso **3** TOTAL : bruto **4** VULGAR : grosero, basto — ~ *n* **1** *or* ~ **income** : ingresos *mpl* brutos **2** *pl* ~ : gruesa *f* (12 docenas) — **grossly** ['gro:sli] *adv* **1** EXTREMELY : enormemente **2** CRUDELY : groseramente

grotesque [gro:'tɛsk] *adj* : grotesco

grouch ['graʊtʃ] *n* : gruñón *m*, -ñona *f fam* — **grouchy** ['graʊtʃi] *adj* **grouchier; -est** : gruñon *fam*

ground[1] ['graʊnd] → **grind**

ground[2] *n* **1** : suelo *m*, tierra *f* **2** *or* **~s** LAND : terreno *m* **3 ~s** REASON : razón *f*, motivos *mpl* **4 ~s** DREGS : pozo *m* (de café) — ~ *vt* **1** BASE : fundar, basar **2** : conectar a tierra (un aparato eléctrico) **3** : restringir (un avión o un piloto) a la tierra — **groundhog** ['graʊndˌhɔg] *n* : marmota *f* (de América) — **groundless** ['graʊndləs] *adj* : infundado — **groundwork** ['graʊndˌwərk] *n* : trabajo *m* preparatorio

group ['gru:p] *n* : grupo *m* — ~ *vt* : agrupar — *vi or* ~ **together** : agruparse

grove ['gro:v] *n* : arboleda *f*

grovel ['grɑvəl, 'grʌ-] *vi* **-eled** *or* **-elled; -eling** *or* **-elling** : arrastrarse, humillarse
grow ['gro:] *v* **grew** ['gru:]; **grown** ['gro:n]; **growing** *vi* **1** : crecer **2** INCREASE : aumentar **3** BECOME : volverse, ponerse **4** ~ **dark** : oscurecerse **5** ~ **up** : hacerse mayor — *vt* **1** CULTIVATE : cultivar **2** : dejarse crecer (el pelo, etc.) — **grower** ['gro:ər] *n* : cultivador *m*, **-dora** *f*
growl ['graʊl] *vi* : gruñir — ~ *n* : gruñido *m*
grown–up ['gro:n,əp] *adj* : mayor — ~ *n* : persona *f* mayor
growth ['gro:θ] *n* **1** : crecimiento *m* **2** INCREASE : aumento *m* **3** DEVELOPMENT : desarrollo *m* **4** TUMOR : tumor *m*
grub ['grʌb] *n* **1** LARVA : larva *f* **2** FOOD : comida *f*
grubby ['grʌbi] *adj* **grubbier; -est** : mugriento, sucio
grudge ['grʌdʒ] *vt* **grudged; grudging** : dar de mala gana — ~ *n* **hold a** ~ : guardar rencor
grueling *or* **gruelling** ['gru:lɪŋ, 'gru:ə-] *adj* : extenuante, agotador
gruesome ['gru:səm] *adj* : horripilante
gruff ['grʌf] *adj* **1** BRUSQUE : brusco **2** HOARSE : bronco
grumble ['grʌmbəl] *vi* **-bled; -bling** : refunfuñar, rezongar
grumpy ['grʌmpi] *adj* **grumpier; -est** : malhumorado, gruñón *fam*
grunt ['grʌnt] *vi* : gruñir — ~ *n* : gruñido *m*
guarantee [,gærən'ti:] *n* : garantía *f* — ~ *vt* **-teed; -teeing** : garantizar
guard ['gɑrd] *n* **1** : guardia *f* **2** PRECAUTION : protección *f* — ~ *vt* : proteger, vigilar — *vi* ~ **against** : protegerse contra — **guardian** ['gɑrdiən] *n* **1** : tutor *m*, **-tora** *f* (de niños) **2** PROTECTOR : guardián *m*, **-diana** *f*
guava ['gwɑvə] *n* : guayaba *f*
guerrilla *or* **guerilla** [gə'rɪlə] *n* **1** : guerrillero *m*, **-ra** *f* **2** ~ **warfare** : guerra *f* de guerrillas
guess ['gɛs] *vt* **1** : adivinar **2** SUPPOSE : suponer, creer — *vi* ~ **at** : adivinar — ~ *n* : conjetura *f*, suposición *f*
guest ['gɛst] *n* **1** : invitado *m*, **-da** *f* **2** : huésped *mf* (a un hotel)
guide ['gaɪd] *n* : guía *mf* (persona), guía *f* (libro, etc.) — ~ *vt* **guided; guiding** : guiar — **guidance** ['gaɪdənts] *n* : orientación *f* — **guidebook** ['gaɪd,bʊk] *n* : guía *f* — **guideline** ['gaɪd,laɪn] *n* : pauta *f*, directriz *f*
guild ['gɪld] *n* : gremio *m*
guile ['gaɪl] *n* : astucia *f*
guilt ['gɪlt] *n* : culpa *f*, culpabilidad *f* — **guilty** ['gɪlti] *adj* **guiltier; -est** : culpable
guinea pig ['gɪni-] *n* : conejillo *m* de Indias, cobaya *f*
guise ['gaɪz] *n* : apariencia *f*
guitar [gə'tɑr, gɪ-] *n* : guitarra *f*
gulf ['gʌlf] *n* **1** : golfo *m* **2** ABYSS : abismo *m*
gull ['gʌl] *n* : gaviota *f*
gullet ['gʌlət] *n* **1** THROAT : garganta *f* **2** ESOPHAGUS : esófago *m*
gullible ['gʌlɪbəl] *adj* : crédulo
gully ['gʌli] *n, pl* **-lies** : barranco *m*
gulp ['gʌlp] *vt or* ~ **down** : tragarse, engullir — *vi* : tragar saliva — ~ *n* : trago *m*
gum[1] ['gʌm] *n* : encía *f* (de la boca)
gum[2] *n* **1** : resina *f* (de plantas) **2** CHEWING GUM : goma *f* de mascar, chicle *m*
gumption ['gʌmpʃən] *n* : iniciativa *f*, agallas *fpl fam*
gun ['gʌn] *n* **1** FIREARM : arma *f* de fuego **2** *or* **spray** ~ : pistola *f* **3** → **cannon, pistol, revolver, rifle** — ~ *vt* **gunned; gunning 1** *or* ~ **down** : matar a tiros, asesinar **2** ~ **the engine** : acelerar (el motor) — **gunboat** ['gʌn,bo:t] *n* : cañonero *m* — **gunfire** ['gʌn,faɪr] *n* : disparos *mpl* — **gunman** ['gʌnmən] *n, pl* **-men** [-mən, -,mɛn] : pistolero *m*, gatillero *m Lat* — **gunpowder** ['gʌn,paʊdər] *n* : pólvora *f* — **gunshot** ['gʌn,ʃɑt] *n* : disparo *m*, tiro *m*
gurgle ['gərgəl] *vi* **-gled; -gling 1** : borbotar, gorgotear **2** : gorjear (dícese de un niño)
gush ['gʌʃ] *vi* **1** SPOUT : salir a chorros **2** ~ **with praise** : deshacerse en elogios
gust ['gʌst] *n* : ráfaga *f*
gusto ['gʌs,to:] *n, pl* **gustoes** : entusiasmo *m*
gusty ['gʌsti] *adj* **gustier; -est** : racheado, ventoso
gut ['gʌt] *n* **1** : intestino *m* **2** ~**s** *npl* INNARDS : tripas *fpl* **3** ~**s** *npl* COURAGE : agallas *fpl fam* — ~ *vt* **gutted; gutting 1** EVISCERATE : destripar (un pollo, etc.), limpiar (un pescado) **2** : destruir el interior de (un edificio)
gutter ['gʌt̬ər] *n* : canaleta *f* (de un techo), cuneta *f* (de una calle)
guy ['gaɪ] *n* : tipo *m fam*
guzzle ['gʌzəl] *vt* **-zled; -zling** : chupar *fam*, tragar
gym ['dʒɪm] *or* **gymnasium** [dʒɪm'neɪziəm, -ʒəm] *n, pl* **-siums** *or* **-sia** [-ziːə, -ʒə] : gimnasio *m* — **gymnast**

H

h ['eɪtʃ] *n, pl* **h's** *or* **hs** ['eɪtʃəz] : h *f*, octava letra del alfabeto inglés

habit ['hæbɪt] *n* **1** CUSTOM : hábito *m*, costumbre *f* **2** : hábito *m* (religioso)

habitat ['hæbɪ,tæt] *n* : hábitat *m*

habitual [hə'bɪtʃʊəl] *adj* **1** CUSTOMARY : habitual **2** INVETERATE : empedernido

hack[1] ['hæk] *n* **1** : caballo *m* de alquiler **2** *or* **~ writer** : escritorzuelo *m*, -la *f*

hack[2] *vt* : cortar — *vi or* **~ into** : piratear (un sistema informático)

hackneyed ['hæknid] *adj* : manido, trillado

hacksaw ['hæk,sɔ] *n* : sierra *f* para metales

had → **have**

haddock ['hædək] *ns & pl* : eglefino *m*

hadn't ['hædənt] (*contraction of* **had not**) → **have**

hag ['hæg] *n* : bruja *f*

haggard ['hægərd] *adj* : demacrado

haggle ['hægəl] *vi* **-gled; -gling** : regatear

hail[1] ['heɪl] *vt* **1** GREET : saludar **2** : llamar (un taxi)

hail[2] *n* : granizo *m* (en meteorología) — **~** *vi* : granizar — **hailstone** ['heɪl,sto:n] *n* : piedra *f* de granizo

hair ['hær] *n* **1** : pelo *m*, cabello *m* **2** : vello *m* (en las piernas, etc.) — **hairbrush** ['hær,brʌʃ] *n* : cepillo *m* (para el pelo) — **haircut** ['hær,kʌt] *n* **1** : corte *m* de pelo **2 get a ~** : cortarse el pelo — **hairdo** ['hær,du:] *n, pl* **-dos** : peinado *m* — **hairdresser** ['hær,drɛsər] *n* : peluquero *m*, -ra *f* — **hairless** ['hærləs] *adj* : sin pelo, calvo — **hairpin** ['hær,pɪn] *n* : horquilla *f* — **hair–raising** ['hær,reɪzɪŋ] *adj* : espeluznante — **hairstyle** ['hær,staɪl] → **hairdo** — **hair spray** *n* : laca *f* (para el pelo) — **hairy** ['hæri] *adj* **hairier; -est** : peludo, velludo

hale ['heɪl] *adj* : saludable, robusto

half ['hæf, 'haf] *n, pl* **halves** ['hævz, 'havz] **1** : mitad *f* **2** *or* **halftime** : tiempo *m* (en deportes) **3 in ~** : por la mitad — **~** *adj* **1** : medio **2 ~ an hour** : una media hora — **~** *adv* : medio — **half brother** *n* : medio hermano *m*, hermanastro *m* — **halfhearted** ['hæf'hɑrtəd] *adj* : sin ánimo, poco entusiasta — **half sister** *n* : media hermana *f*, hermanastra *f* — **halfway** ['hæf'weɪ] *adv* : a medio camino — **~** *adj* : medio

halibut ['hælɪbət] *ns & pl* : halibut *m*

hall ['hɔl] *n* **1** HALLWAY : corredor *m*, pasillo *m* **2** AUDITORIUM : sala *f* **3** LOBBY : vestíbulo *m* **4** DORMITORY : residencia *f* universitaria

hallmark ['hɔl,mɑrk] *n* : sello *m* (distintivo)

Halloween [,hælə'wi:n, ,hɑ-] *n* : víspera *f* de Todos los Santos

hallucination [hə,lu:sən'eɪʃən] *n* : alucinación *f*

hallway ['hɔl,weɪ] *n* **1** ENTRANCE : entrada *f* **2** CORRIDOR : corredor *m*, pasillo *m*

halo ['heɪ,lo:] *n, pl* **-los** *or* **-loes** : aureola *f*, halo *m*

halt ['hɔlt] *n* **1 call a ~ to** : poner fin a **2 come to a ~** : pararse — **~** *vi* : pararse — *vt* : parar

halve ['hæv, 'hav] *vt* **halved; halving 1** DIVIDE : partir por la mitad **2** REDUCE : reducir a la mitad — **halves** → **half**

ham ['hæm] *n* : jamón *m*

hamburger ['hæm,bərgər] *or* **hamburg** [-,bərg] *n* **1** : carne *f* molida **2** *or* **~ patty** : hamburguesa *f*

hammer ['hæmər] *n* : martillo *m* — **~** *v* : martillar, martillear

hammock ['hæmək] *n* : hamaca *f*

hamper[1] ['hæmpər] *vt* : obstaculizar, dificultar

hamper[2] *n* : cesto *m*, canasta *f* (para ropa sucia)

hamster ['hæmpstər] *n* : hámster *m*

hand ['hænd] *n* **1** : mano *f* **2** : manecilla *f*, aguja *f* (de un reloj, etc.) **3** HANDWRITING : letra *f*, escritura *f* **4** WORKER : obrero *m*, -ra *f* **5 by ~** : a mano **6 lend a ~** : echar una mano **7 on ~** : a mano, disponible **8 on the other ~** : por otro lado — **~** *vt* **1** : pasar, dar **2 ~ out** : distribuir **3 ~ over** : entregar — **handbag** ['hænd,bæg] *n* : cartera *f Lat*, bolso *m Spain* — **handbook** ['hænd,bʊk] *n* : manual *m* — **handcuffs** ['hænd,kʌfs] *npl* : esposas *fpl* — **handful** ['hænd,fʊl] *n* : puñado *m* — **handgun** ['hænd,gʌn] *n* : pistola *f*, revólver *m*

handicap ['hændi,kæp] *n* **1** : minusvalía *f*

(física) **2** : hándicap *m* (en deportes) — ~ *vt* **-capped; -capping 1** : asignar un handicap a (en deportes) **2** HAMPER : obstaculizar — **handicapped** [ˈhændiˌkæpt] *adj* : minusválido

handicrafts [ˈhændiˌkræfts] *npl* : artesanía(s) *f(pl)*

handiwork [ˈhændiˌwərk] *n* : trabajo *m* (manual)

handkerchief [ˈhæŋkərtʃəf, -ˌtʃiːf] *n, pl* **-chiefs** : pañuelo *m*

handle [ˈhændəl] *n* : asa *m* (de una taza, etc.), mango *m* (de un utensilio), pomo *m* (de una puerta), tirador *m* (de un cajón) — ~ *vt* **-dled; -dling 1** TOUCH : tocar **2** MANAGE : tratar, manejar — **handlebars** [ˈhændəlˌbɑrz] *npl* : manillar *m*, manubrio *m Lat*

handmade [ˈhændˌmeɪd] *adj* : hecho a mano

handout [ˈhændˌaʊt] *n* **1** ALMS : dádiva *f*, limosna *f* **2** LEAFLET : folleto *m*

handrail [ˈhændˌreɪl] *n* : pasamanos *m*

handshake [ˈhændˌʃeɪk] *n* : apretón *m* de manos

handsome [ˈhæntsəm] *adj* **-somer; -est 1** ATTRACTIVE : apuesto, guapo **2** GENEROUS : generoso **3** SIZABLE : considerable

handwriting [ˈhændˌraɪţɪŋ] *n* : letra *f*, escritura *f* — **handwritten** [ˈhændˌrɪtən] *adj* : escrito a mano

handy [ˈhændi] *adj* **handier; -est 1** NEARBY : a mano **2** USEFUL : práctico, útil **3** DEFT : habilidoso — **handyman** [ˈhændimən] *n, pl* **-men** [-mən, -ˌmɛn] : hombre *m* habilidoso

hang [ˈhæŋ] *v* **hung** [ˈhʌŋ]; **hanging** *vt* **1** : colgar **2** (*past tense often* **hanged**) EXECUTE : ahorcar **3** ~ **one's head** : bajar la cabeza — *vi* **1** : colgar, pender **2** : caer (dícese de la ropa, etc.) **3** ~ **up on s.o.** : colgar a algn — ~ *n* **1** DRAPE : caída *f* **2 get the** ~ **of** : agarrar la onda de

hangar [ˈhæŋər, ˈhæŋgər] *n* : hangar *m*

hanger [ˈhæŋər] *n* : percha *f*, gancho *m* (para ropa) *Lat*

hangover [ˈhæŋˌoːvər] *n* : resaca *f*

hanker [ˈhæŋkər] *vi* ~ **for** : tener ansias de — **hankering** [ˈhæŋkərɪŋ] *n* : ansia *f*, anhelo *m*

haphazard [hæpˈhæzərd] *adj* : casual, fortuito

happen [ˈhæpən] *vi* **1** : pasar, suceder, ocurrir **2** ~ **to do sth** : hacer algo por casualidad **3 it so happens that...** : da la casualidad de que... — **happening** [ˈhæpənɪŋ] *n* : suceso *m*, acontecimiento *m*

happy [ˈhæpi] *adj* **-pier; -est 1** : feliz **2 be** ~ : alegrarse **3 be** ~ **with** : estar contento con **4 be** ~ **to do sth** : hacer algo con mucho gusto — **happily** [ˈhæpəli] *adv* : alegremente — **happiness** [ˈhæpinəs] *n* : felicidad *f* — **happy–go–lucky** [ˈhæpigoːˈlʌki] *adj* : despreocupado

harass [həˈræs, ˈhærəs] *vt* : acosar — **harassment** [həˈræsmənt, ˈhærəsmənt] *n* : acoso *m*

harbor *or Brit* **harbour** [ˈhɑrbər] *n* : puerto *m* — *vt* **1** SHELTER : albergar **2** ~ **a grudge against** : guardar rencor a

hard [ˈhɑrd] *adj* **1** : duro **2** DIFFICULT : difícil **3 be a** ~ **worker** : ser muy trabajador **4** ~ **liquor** : bebidas *fpl* fuertes **5** ~ **water** : agua *f* dura — ~ *adv* **1** FORCEFULLY : fuerte **2 work** ~ : trabajar duro **3 take sth** ~ : tomarse algo muy mal — **harden** [ˈhɑrdən] *vt* : endurecer — **hardheaded** [ˌhɑrdˈhɛdəd] *adj* : testarudo, terco — **hard–hearted** [ˌhɑrdˈhɑrţəd] *adj* : duro de corazón — **hardly** [ˈhɑrdli] *adv* **1** : apenas **2** ~ **ever** : casi nunca — **hardness** [ˈhɑrdnəs] *n* **1** : dureza *f* **2** DIFFICULTY : dificultad *f* — **hardship** [ˈhɑrdˌʃɪp] *n* : dificultad *f* — **hardware** [ˈhɑrdˌwær] *n* **1** : ferretería *f* **2** : hardware *m* (en informática) — **hardworking** [ˈhɑrdˈwərkɪŋ] *adj* : trabajador

hardy [ˈhɑrdi] *adj* **-dier; -est** : fuerte (dícese de personas), resistente (dícese de las plantas)

hare [ˈhær] *n, pl* **hare** *or* **hares** : liebre *f*

harm [ˈhɑrm] *n* : daño *m* — ~ *vt* : hacer daño a (una persona), dañar (una cosa), perjudicar (la reputación de algn, etc.) — **harmful** [ˈhɑrmfəl] *adj* : perjudicial — **harmless** [ˈhɑrmləs] *adj* : inofensivo

harmonica [hɑrˈmɑnɪkə] *n* : armónica *f*

harmony [ˈhɑrməni] *n, pl* **-nies** : armonía *f* — **harmonious** [hɑrˈmoːniəs] *adj* : armonioso — **harmonize** [ˈhɑrməˌnaɪz] *v* **-nized; -nizing** : armonizar

harness [ˈhɑrnəs] *n* : arnés *m* — ~ *vt* **1** : enjaezar **2** UTILIZE : utilizar

harp [ˈhɑrp] *n* : arpa *m* — ~ *vi* ~ **on** : insistir sobre

harpoon [hɑrˈpuːn] *n* : arpón *m*

harpsichord [ˈhɑrpsɪˌkɔrd] *n* : clavicémbalo *m*

harsh [ˈhɑrʃ] *adj* **1** ROUGH : áspero **2** SEVERE : duro, severo **3** : fuerte (dícese de una luz), discordante (dícese de sonidos) — **harshness** [ˈhɑrʃnəs] *n* : severidad *f*

harvest ['hɑrvəst] *n* : cosecha *f* — **~** *v* : cosechar
has → **have**
hash ['hæʃ] *vt* **1** CHOP : picar **2 ~ over** DISCUSS : discutir — **~** *n* : picadillo *m* (comida)
hasn't ['hæzənt] (*contraction of* **has not**) → **has**
hassle ['hæsəl] *n* : problemas *mpl,* lío *m* — **~** *vt* **-sled; -sling** : fastidiar
haste ['heɪst] *n* **1** : prisa *f,* apuro *m Lat* **2 make ~** : darse prisa, apurarse *Lat* — **hasten** ['heɪsən] *vt* : acelerar — *vi* : apresurarse, apurarse *Lat* — **hasty** ['heɪsti] *adj* **hastier; -est** : precipitado
hat ['hæt] *n* : sombrero *m*
hatch ['hætʃ] *n* : escotilla *f* — **~** *vt* **1** : empollar (huevos) **2** CONCOCT : tramar — *vi* : salir del cascarón
hatchet ['hætʃət] *n* : hacha *f*
hate ['heɪt] *n* : odio *m* — **~** *vt* **hated; hating** : odiar, aborrecer — **hateful** ['heɪtfəl] *adj* : odioso, aborrecible — **hatred** ['heɪtrəd] *n* : odio *m*
haughty ['hɔt̬i] *adj* **-tier; -est** : altanero, altivo
haul ['hɔl] *vt* : arrastrar, jalar *Lat* — **~** *n* **1** CATCH : redada *f* (de peces) **2** LOOT : botín *m* **3 a long ~** : un trayecto largo
haunch ['hɔntʃ] *n* : cadera *f* (de una persona), anca *f* (de un animal)
haunt ['hɔnt] *vt* **1** : frecuentar, rondar **2** TROUBLE : inquietar — **~** *n* : sitio *m* predilecto — **haunted** ['hɔntəd] *adj* : embrujado
have ['hæv, *in sense 3 as an auxiliary verb usu* 'hæf] *v* **had** ['hæd]; **having; has** ['hæz, *in sense 3 as an auxiliary verb usu* 'hæs] *vt* **1** : tener **2** CONSUME : comer, tomar **3** ALLOW : permitir **4** : dar (una fiesta, etc.), convocar (una reunión) **5 ~ one's hair cut** : cortarse el pelo **6 ~ sth done** : mandar hacer algo — *v aux* **1** : haber **2 ~ just done sth** : acabar de hacer algo **4 you've finished, haven't you?** : has terminado, ¿no?
haven ['heɪvən] *n* : refugio *m*
havoc ['hævək] *n* : estragos *mpl*
hawk[1] ['hɔk] *n* : halcón *m*
hawk[2] *vt* : pregonar (mercancías)
hay ['heɪ] *n* : heno *m* — **hay fever** *n* : fiebre *f* del heno — **haystack** ['heɪˌstæk] *n* : almiar *m* — **haywire** ['heɪˌwaɪr] *adj* **go ~** : estropearse
hazard ['hæzərd] *n* : peligro *m,* riesgo *m* — **~** *vt* : arriesgar, aventurar — **hazardous** ['hæzərdəs] *adj* : arriesgado, peligroso
haze ['heɪz] *n* : bruma *f,* neblina *f*
hazel ['heɪzəl] *n* : color *m* avellana — **hazelnut** ['heɪzəlˌnʌt] *n* : avellana *f*
hazy ['heɪzi] *adj* **hazier; -est** : nebuloso
he ['hi:] *pron* : él
head ['hɛd] *n* **1** : cabeza *f* **2** END, TOP : cabeza *f* (de un clavo, etc.), cabecera *f* (de una mesa) **3** LEADER : jefe *m,* -fa *f* **4 be out of one's ~** : estar loco **5 come to a ~** : llegar a un punto crítico **6 ~s or tails** : cara o cruz **7 per ~** : por cabeza — **~** *adj* MAIN : principal — **~** *vt* : encabezar — *vi* : dirigirse — **headache** ['hɛdˌeɪk] *n* : dolor *m* de cabeza — **headband** ['hɛdˌbænd] *n* : cinta *f* del pelo — **headdress** ['hɛdˌdrɛs] *n* : tocado *m* — **headfirst** ['hɛd'fərst] *adv* : de cabeza — **heading** ['hɛdɪŋ] *n* : encabezamiento *m,* título *m* — **headland** ['hɛdlənd, -ˌlænd] *n* : cabo *m* — **headlight** ['hɛdˌlaɪt] *n* : faro *m* — **headline** ['hɛdˌlaɪn] *n* : titular *m* — **headlong** ['hɛd'lɔŋ] *adv* **1** HEADFIRST : de cabeza **2** HASTILY : precipitadamente — **headmaster** ['hɛdˌmæstər] *n* : director *m* — **headmistress** ['hɛdˌmɪstrəs, -'mɪs-] *n* : directora *f* — **head-on** ['hɛd'ɑn, -'ɔn] *adv & adj* : de frente — **headphones** ['hɛdˌfo:nz] *npl* : auriculares *mpl,* audífonos *mpl Lat* — **headquarters** ['hɛdˌkwɔrt̬ərz] *ns & pl* : oficina *f* central (de una compañía), cuartel *m* general (de los militares) — **head start** *n* : ventaja *f* — **headstrong** ['hɛd'strɔŋ] *adj* : testarudo, obstinado — **headwaiter** ['hɛd'weɪt̬ər] *n* : jefe *m,* -fa *f* de comedor — **headway** ['hɛdˌweɪ] *n* **1** : progreso *m* **2 make ~** : avanzar — **heady** ['hɛdi] *adj* **headier; -est** : embriagador
heal ['hi:l] *vt* : curar — *vi* : cicatrizar
health ['hɛlθ] *n* : salud *f* — **healthy** ['hɛlθi] *adj* **healthier; -est** : sano, saludable
heap ['hi:p] *n* : montón *m* — **~** *vt* : amontonar
hear ['hɪr] *v* **heard** ['hərd]; **hearing** *vt* : oír — *vi* **1** : oír **2 ~ about** : enterarse de **3 ~ from** : tener noticias de — **hearing** ['hɪrɪŋ] *n* **1** : oído *m* **2** : vista *f* (en un tribunal) — **hearing aid** *n* : audífono *m* — **hearsay** ['hɪrˌseɪ] *n* : rumores *mpl*
hearse ['hərs] *n* : coche *m* fúnebre
heart ['hɑrt] *n* **1** : corazón *m* **2 at ~** : en el fondo **3 by ~** : de memoria **4 lose ~** : descorazonarse **5 take ~** : animarse — **heartache** ['hɑrt̬ˌeɪk] *n* : pena *f,* dolor *m* — **heart attack** *n* : infarto *m,* ataque *m* al corazón — **heartbeat**

['hɑrt,bi:t] *n* : latido *m* (del corazón) — **heartbreak** ['hɑrt,breɪk] *n* : congoja *f*, angustia *f* — **heartbroken** ['hɑrt,bro:kən] *adj* : desconsolado — **heartburn** ['hɑrt,bərn] *n* : acidez *f* estomacal

hearth ['hɑrθ] *n* : hogar *m*

heartily ['hɑrṭəli] *adv* : de buena gana

heartless ['hɑrtləs] *adj* : de mal corazón, cruel

hearty ['hɑrṭi] *adj* **heartier; -est 1** : cordial, caluroso **2** : abundante (dícese de una comida)

heat ['hi:t] *vt* : calentar — *vi* or **~ up** : calentarse — **~** *n* **1** : calor *m* **2** HEATING : calefacción *f* — **heated** ['hi:ṭəd] *adj* : acalorado — **heater** ['hi:ṭər] *n* : calentador *m*

heath ['hi:θ] *n* : brezal *m*

heathen ['hi:ðən] *adj* : pagano — **~** *n*, *pl* **-thens** *or* **-then** : pagano *m*, -na *f*

heather ['hɛðər] *n* : brezo *m*

heave ['hi:v] *v* **heaved** *or* **hove** ['ho:v]; **heaving** *vt* **1** LIFT : levantar (con esfuerzo) **2** HURL : lanzar, tirar **3 ~ a sigh** : suspirar — **~** *vi or* **~ up** : levantarse

heaven ['hɛvən] *n* : cielo *m* — **heavenly** ['hɛvənli] *adj* **1** : celestial **2 ~ body** : cuerpo *m* celeste

heavy ['hɛvi] *adj* **heavier; -est 1** : pesado **2** INTENSE : fuerte **3 ~ sigh** : suspiro *m* profundo **4 ~ traffic** : tráfico *m* denso — **heavily** ['hɛvəli] *adv* **1** : pesadamente **2** EXCESSIVELY : mucho — **heaviness** ['hɛvinəs] *n* : peso *m*, pesadez *f* — **heavyweight** ['hɛvi,weɪt] *n* : peso *m* pesado

Hebrew ['hi:,bru:] *adj* : hebreo — **~** *n* : hebreo *m* (idioma)

heckle ['hɛkəl] *vt* **-led; -ling** : interrumpir (a un orador) con preguntas molestas

hectic ['hɛktɪk] *adj* : agitado, ajetreado

he'd ['hi:d] (*contraction of* **he had** *or* **he would**) → **have, would**

hedge ['hɛdʒ] *n* : seto *m* vivo — **~** *v* **hedged; hedging** *vt* **~ one's bets** : cubrirse — *vi* : contestar con evasivas — **hedgehog** ['hɛdʒ,hɔg, -hɑg] *n* : erizo *m*

heed ['hi:d] *vt* : prestar atención a, hacer caso de — **~** *n* **take ~** : tener cuidado — **heedless** ['hi:dləs] *adj* **be ~ of** : hacer caso omiso **de**

heel ['hi:l] *n* : talón *m* (del pie), tacón *m* (de un zapato)

hefty ['hɛfti] *adj* **heftier; -est** : robusto y pesado

heifer ['hɛfər] *n* : novilla *f*

height ['haɪt] *n* **1** : estatura *f* (de una persona), altura *f* (de un objeto) **2** PEAK : cumbre *f* **3 the ~ of folly** : el colmo de la locura **4 what is your ~ ?** : ¿cuánto mides? — **heighten** ['haɪtən] *vt* : aumentar, intensificar

heir ['ær] *n* : heredero *m*, -ra *f* — **heiress** ['ærəs] *n* : heredera *f* — **heirloom** ['ær,lu:m] *n* : reliquia *f* de familia

held → **hold**

helicopter ['hɛlə,kɑptər] *n* : helicóptero *m*

hell ['hɛl] *n* : infierno *m* — **hellish** ['hɛlɪʃ] *adj* : infernal

he'll ['hi:l, 'hɪl] (*contraction of* **he shall** *or* **he will**) → **shall, will**

hello [hə'lo:, hɛ-] *interj* : ¡hola!

helm ['hɛlm] *n* : timón *m*

helmet ['hɛlmət] *n* : casco *m*

help ['hɛlp] *vt* **1** : ayudar **2 ~ oneself** : servirse **3 I can't ~ it** : no lo puedo remediar — **~** *n* **1** : ayuda *f* **2** STAFF : personal *m* **3 help!** : ¡socorro!, ¡auxilio! — **helper** ['hɛlpər] *n* : ayudante *mf* — **helpful** ['hɛlpfəl] *adj* **1** OBLIGING : servicial, amable **2** USEFUL : útil — **helping** ['hɛlpɪŋ] *n* : porción *f* — **helpless** ['hɛlpləs] *adj* **1** POWERLESS : incapaz **2** DEFENSELESS : indefenso

hem ['hɛm] *n* : dobladillo *m* — **~** *vt* **hemmed; hemming ~ in** : encerrar

hemisphere ['hɛmə,sfɪr] *n* : hemisferio *m*

hemorrhage ['hɛmərɪdʒ] *n* : hemorragia *f*

hemorrhoids ['hɛmə,rɔɪdz, 'hɛm,rɔɪdz] *npl* : hemorroides *fpl*, almorranas *fpl*

hemp ['hɛmp] *n* : cáñamo *m*

hen ['hɛn] *n* : gallina *f*

hence ['hɛnts] *adv* **1** : de aquí, de ahí **2** THEREFORE : por lo tanto **3 ten years ~** : de aquí a 10 años — **henceforth** ['hɛnts,forθ, ,hɛnts'-] *adv* : de ahora en adelante

henpeck ['hɛn,pɛk] *vt* : dominar (al marido)

hepatitis [,hɛpə'taɪṭəs] *n*, *pl* **-titides** [-'tɪṭə,di:z] : hepatitis *f*

her ['hər] *adj* : su, sus — **~** ['hər, ər] *pron* **1** (*used as direct object*) : la **2** (*used as indirect object*) : le, se **3** (*used as object of a preposition*) : ella

herald ['hɛrəld] *vt* : anunciar

herb ['ərb, 'hərb] *n* : hierba *f*

herd ['hərd] *n* : manada *f* — **~** *vt* : conducir (en manada) — *vi or* **~ together** : reunir

here ['hɪr] *adv* **1** : aquí, acá **2 ~ you are!** : ¡toma! — **hereabouts** ['hɪrə,baʊts] *or* **hereabout** [-,baʊt] *adv* : por aquí (cerca) — **hereafter** [hɪr'æftər]

adv : en el futuro — **hereby** [hɪr'baɪ] *adv* : por este medio
hereditary [hə'rɛdə,tɛri] *adj* : hereditario — **heredity** [hə'rɛdəṯi] *n* : herencia *f*
heresy ['hɛrəsi] *n, pl* **-sies** : herejía *f*
herewith [hɪr'wɪθ] *adv* : adjunto
heritage ['hɛrəṯɪdʒ] *n* **1** : herencia *f* **2** : patrimonio *m* (nacional)
hermit ['hərmət] *n* : ermitaño *m*, -ña *f*
hernia ['hərniə] *n, pl* **-nias** *or* **-niae** [-ni,iː, -ni,aɪ] : hernia *f*
hero ['hiː,roː, 'hɪr,oː] *n, pl* **-roes** : héroe *m* — **heroic** [hɪ'roːɪk] *adj* : heroico — **heroine** ['hɛroən] *n* : heroína *f* — **heroism** ['hɛro,ɪzəm] *n* : heroísmo *m*
heron ['hɛrən] *n* : garza *f*
herring ['hɛrɪŋ] *n, pl* **-ring** *or* **-rings** : arenque *m*
hers ['hərz] *pron* **1** : (el) suyo, (la) suya, (los) suyos, (las) suyas **2 some friends of ~** : unos amigos suyos, unos amigos de ella — **herself** [hər-'sɛlf] *pron* **1** (*used reflexively*) : se **2** (*used emphatically*) : ella misma
he's ['hiːz] (*contraction of* **he is** *or* **he has**) → **be, have**
hesitant ['hɛzəṯənt] *adj* : titubeante, vacilante — **hesitate** ['hɛzə,teɪt] *vi* **-tated; -tating** : vacilar, titubear — **hesitation** [,hɛzə'teɪʃən] *n* : vacilación *f*, titubeo *m*
heterosexual [,hɛṯəro'sɛkʃuəl] *adj* : heterosexual — **~** *n* : heterosexual *mf*
hexagon ['hɛksə,gɑn] *n* : hexágono *m*
hey ['heɪ] *interj* : ¡eh!, ¡oye!
heyday ['heɪ,deɪ] *n* : auge *m*, apogeo *m*
hi ['haɪ] *interj* : ¡hola!
hibernate ['haɪbər,neɪt] *vi* **-nated; -nating** : hibernar
hiccup ['hɪkəp] *n* **have the ~s** : tener hipo — **~** *vi* **-cuped; -cuping** : tener hipo
hide[1] ['haɪd] *n* : piel *f*, cuero *m*
hide[2] *v* **hid** ['hɪd]; **hidden** ['hɪdən] *or* **hid; hiding** *vt* **1** : esconder **2** : ocultar (motivos, etc.) — *vi* : esconderse — **hide-and-seek** ['haɪdənd̮siːk] *n* : escondite *m*, escondidas *fpl Lat*
hideous ['hɪdiəs] *adj* : horrible, espantoso
hideout ['haɪd,aut] *n* : escondite *m*, guarida *f*
hierarchy ['haɪə,rɑrki] *n, pl* **-chies** : jerarquía *f* — **hierarchical** [,haɪə'rɑrkɪkəl] *adj* : jerárquico
high ['haɪ] *adj* **1** : alto **2** INTOXICATED : borracho, drogado **3 a ~ voice** : una voz aguda **4 it's two feet ~** : tiene dos pies de alto **5 ~ winds** : fuertes vientos *mpl* — **~** *adv* : alto — **~** *n* : récord *m*, máximo *m* — **higher** ['haɪər] *adj* **1** : superior **2 ~ education** : enseñanza *f* superior — **highlight** ['haɪ,laɪt] *n* : punto *m* culminante — **highly** ['haɪli] *adv* **1** VERY : muy, sumamente **2 think ~ of** : tener en mucho a — **Highness** ['haɪnəs] *n* **His/Her ~** : Su Alteza *f* — **high school** *n* : escuela *f* superior, escuela *f* secundaria — **high-strung** [,haɪ'strʌŋ] *adj* : nervioso, excitable — **highway** ['haɪ,weɪ] *n* : carretera *f*
hijack ['haɪ,dʒæk] *vt* : secuestrar — **hijacker** ['haɪ,dʒækər] *n* : secuestrador *m*, -dora *f* — **hijacking** *n* : secuestro *m*
hike ['haɪk] *v* **hiked; hiking** *vi* : ir de caminata — *vt or* **~ up** RAISE : subir — **~** *n* : caminata *f*, excursión *f* — **hiker** ['haɪkər] *n* : excursionista *mf*
hilarious [hɪ'lærɪəs, haɪ'-] *adj* : muy divertido — **hilarity** [hɪ'lærəṯi, haɪ-] *n* : hilaridad *f*
hill ['hɪl] *n* **1** : colina *f*, cerro *m* **2** SLOPE : cuesta *f* — **hillside** ['hɪl,saɪd] *n* : ladera *f*, cuesta *f* — **hilly** ['hɪli] *adj* **hillier; -est** : accidentado
hilt ['hɪlt] *n* : puño *m*
him ['hɪm, əm] *pron* **1** (*used as direct object*) : lo **2** (*used as indirect object*) : le, se **3** (*used as object of a preposition*) : él — **himself** [hɪm'sɛlf] *pron* **1** (*used reflexively*) : se **2** (*used emphatically*) : él mismo
hind ['haɪnd] *adj* : trasero, posterior
hinder ['hɪndər] *vt* : dificultar, estorbar — **hindrance** ['hɪndrənts] *n* : obstáculo *m*
hindsight ['haɪnd,saɪt] *n* **in ~** : en retrospectiva
Hindu ['hɪn,duː] *adj* : hindú
hinge ['hɪndʒ] *n* : bisagra *f*, gozne *m* — **~** *vi* **hinged; hinging ~ on** : depender de
hint ['hɪnt] *n* **1** : indirecta *f* **2** TIP : consejo *m* **3** TRACE : asomo *m*, toque *m* — **~** *vt* : dar a entender — *vi* **~ at** : insinuar
hip ['hɪp] *n* : cadera *f*
hippopotamus [,hɪpə'pɑṯəməs] *n, pl* **-muses** *or* **-mi** [-,maɪ] : hipopótamo *m*
hire ['haɪr] *n* **1** : alquiler *m* **2 for ~** : se alquila — **~** *vt* **hired; hiring 1** EMPLOY : contratar, emplear **2** RENT : alquilar
his ['hɪz, ɪz] *adj* : su, sus, de él — **~** *pron* **1** : (el) suyo, (la) suya, (los) suyos, (las) suyas **2 some friends of ~** : unos amigos suyos, unos amigos de él

Hispanic [hɪ'spænɪk] *adj* : hispano, hispánico

hiss ['hɪs] *vi* : silbar — *n* : silbido *m*

history ['hɪstəri] *n, pl* **-ries 1** : historia *f* **2** BACKGROUND : historial *m* — **historian** [hɪ'stɔriən] *n* : historiador *m*, -dora *f* — **historic** [hɪ'stɔrɪk] *or* **historical** [-ɪkəl] *adj* : histórico

hit ['hɪt] *v* **hit; hitting** *vt* **1** : golpear, pegar **2** : dar (con un proyectil) **3** AFFECT : afectar **4** REACH : alcanzar **5 the car ~ a tree** : el coche chocó contra un árbol — *vi* : pegar — **~** *n* **1** : golpe *m* **2** SUCCESS : éxito *m*

hitch ['hɪtʃ] *vt* **1** ATTACH : enganchar **2** *or* **~ up** RAISE : subirse **3 ~ a ride** : hacer autostop — **~** *n* PROBLEM : problema *m* — **hitchhike** ['hɪtʃ,haɪk] *vi* **-hiked; -hiking** : hacer autostop — **hitchhiker** ['hɪtʃ,haɪkər] *n* : autostopista *mf*

hitherto ['hɪðər,tu:, ,hɪðər'-] *adv* : hasta ahora

HIV [,eɪtʃ,aɪ'vi:] *n* : VIH *m*, virus *m* del sida

hive ['haɪv] *n* : colmena *f*

hives ['haɪvz] *ns & pl* : urticaria *f*

hoard ['hord] *n* : tesoro *m* (de dinero), reserva *f* (de provisiones) — **~** *vt* : acumular

hoarse ['hors] *adj* **hoarser; -est** : ronco

hoax ['ho:ks] *n* : engaño *m*

hobble ['hɑbəl] *vi* **-bled; -bling** : cojear

hobby ['hɑbi] *n, pl* **-bies** : pasatiempo *m*

hobo ['ho:,bo:] *n, pl* **-boes** : vagabundo *m*, -da *f*

hockey ['hɑki] *n* : hockey *m*

hoe ['ho:] *n* : azada *f* — **~** *vt* **hoed; hoeing** : azadonar

hog ['hɔg, 'hɑg] *n* : cerdo *m* — **~** *vt* **hogged; hogging** MONOPOLIZE : acaparar

hoist ['hɔɪst] *vt* **1** : izar (una vela, etc.) **2** LIFT : levantar — **~** *n* : grúa *f*

hold[1] ['ho:ld] *n* : bodega *f* (en un barco o un avión)

hold[2] *v* **held** ['hɛld]; **holding** *vt* **1** GRIP : agarrar **2** POSSESS : tener **3** SUPPORT : sostener **4** : celebrar (una reunión, etc.), mantener (una conversación) **5** CONTAIN : contener **6** CONSIDER : considerar **7** *or* **~ back** : detener **8 ~ hands** : agarrarse de la mano **9 ~ up** ROB : atracar **10 ~ up** DELAY : retrasar — *vi* **1** LAST : durar, continuar **2** APPLY : ser válido — **~** *n* **1** GRIP : agarre *m* **2 get ~ of** : conseguir **3 get ~ of oneself** : controlarse — **holder** ['ho:ldər] *n* : tenedor *m*, -dora *f* — **holdup** ['ho:ld,ʌp] *n* **1** ROBBERY : atraco *m* **2** DELAY : retraso *m*, demora *f*

hole ['ho:l] *n* : agujero *m*, hoyo *m*

holiday ['hɑlə,deɪ] *n* **1** : día *m* feriado, fiesta *f* **2** *Brit* VACATION : vacaciones *fpl*

holiness ['ho:linəs] *n* : santidad *f*

holler ['hɑlər] *vi* : gritar — **~** *n* : grito *m*

hollow ['hɑ,lo:] *n* **1** : hueco *m* **2** VALLEY : hondonada *f* — **~** *adj* **-lower; -est 1** : hueco **2** FALSE : vacío, falso — **~** *vt* *or* **~ out** : ahuecar

holly ['hɑli] *n, pl* **-lies** : acebo *m*

holocaust ['hɑlə,kɔst, 'ho:-, 'hɔ-] *n* : holocausto *m*

holster ['ho:lstər] *n* : pistolera *f*

holy ['ho:li] *adj* **-lier; -est** : santo, sagrado

homage ['ɑmɪdʒ, 'hɑ-] *n* : homenaje *m*

home ['ho:m] *n* **1** : casa *f* **2** FAMILY : hogar *m* **3** INSTITUTION : residencia *f*, asilo *m* **4 at ~ and abroad** : dentro y fuera del país — **~** *adv* **go ~** : ir a casa — **homeland** ['ho:m,lænd] *n* : patria *f* — **homeless** ['ho:mləs] *adj* : sin hogar — **homely** ['ho:mli] *adj* **-lier; -est 1** DOMESTIC : casero **2** UGLY : feo — **homemade** ['ho:m'meɪd] *adj* : casero, hecho en casa — **homemaker** ['ho:m,meɪkər] *n* : ama *f* de casa — **home run** *n* : jonrón *m* — **homesick** ['ho:m,sɪk] *adj* **be ~** : echar de menos a la familia — **homeward** ['ho:mwərd] *adj* : de vuelta, de regreso — **homework** ['ho:m,wərk] *n* : tarea *f*, deberes *mpl* — **homey** ['ho:mi] *adj* **homier; -est** : hogareño, acogedor

homicide ['hɑmə,saɪd, 'ho:-] *n* : homicidio *m*

homogeneous [,ho:mə'dʒi:niəs, **-njəs**] *adj* : homogéneo

homosexual [,ho:mə'sɛkʃuəl] *adj* : homosexual — **~** *n* : homosexual *mf* — **homosexuality** [,ho:mə,sɛkʃʊ'æləṭi] *n* : homosexualidad *f*

honest ['ɑnəst] *adj* **1** : honrado **2** FRANK : sincero — **honestly** *adv* : sinceramente — **honesty** ['ɑnəsti] *n, pl* **-ties** : honradez *f*

honey ['hʌni] *n, pl* **-eys** : miel *f* — **honeycomb** ['hʌni,ko:m] *n* : panal *m* — **honeymoon** ['hʌni,mu:n] *n* : luna *f* de miel

honk ['hɑŋk, 'hɔŋk] *vi* : tocar la bocina — **~** *n* : bocinazo *m*

honor *or Brit* **honour** ['ɑnər] *n* : honor *m* — **~** *vt* **1** : honrar **2** : aceptar (un cheque, etc.), cumplir con (una promesa) — **honorable** *or Brit* **honourable** ['ɑnərəbəl] *adj* : honorable, honroso — **honorary** ['ɑnə,rɛri] *adj* : honorario

hood ['hʊd] *n* **1 :** capucha *f* (de un abrigo, etc.) **2 :** capó *m* (de un automóvil)
hoodlum ['hʊdləm, 'hu:d-] *n* **:** matón *m*
hoodwink ['hʊd,wɪŋk] *vt* **:** engañar
hoof ['hʊf, 'hu:f] *n, pl* **hooves** ['hʊvz, 'hu:vz] *or* **hoofs :** pezuña *f* (de una vaca, etc.), casco *m* (de un caballo)
hook ['hʊk] *n* **1 :** gancho *m* **2** *or* **~ and eye :** corchete *m* **3** → **fishhook 4 off the ~ :** descolgado — **~** *vt* **:** enganchar — *vi* **:** engancharse
hoop ['hu:p] *n* **:** aro *m*
hooray [hʊ'reɪ] → **hurrah**
hoot ['hu:t] *vi* **1 :** ulular (dícese de un búho) **2 ~ with laughter :** reírse a carcajadas — **~** *n* **1 :** ululato *m* (de un búho) **2 I don't give a ~ :** me importa un comino
hop[1] ['hɑp] *vi* **hopped; hopping :** saltar a la pata coja — **~** *n* **:** salto *m* a la pata coja
hop[2] *n* **~s :** lúpulo *m* (planta)
hope ['ho:p] *v* **hoped; hoping** *vi* **:** esperar — *vt* **:** esperar que — **~** *n* **:** esperanza *f* — **hopeful** ['ho:pfəl] *adj* **:** esperanzado — **hopefully** *adv* **1 :** con esperanza **2 ~ it will help :** se espera que ayude — **hopeless** ['ho:pləs] *adj* **:** desesperado — **hopelessly** ['ho:pləsli] *adv* **:** desesperadamente
horde ['hord] *n* **:** horda *f*
horizon [hə'raɪzən] *n* **:** horizonte *m* — **horizontal** [,hɔrə'zɑntəl] *adj* **:** horizontal
hormone ['hɔr,mo:n] *n* **:** hormona *f*
horn ['hɔrn] *n* **1 :** cuerno *m* (de un animal) **2 :** trompa *f* (instrumento musical) **3 :** bocina *f*, claxon *m* (de un vehículo)
hornet ['hɔrnət] *n* **:** avispón *m*
horoscope ['hɔrə,sko:p] *n* **:** horóscopo *m*
horror ['hɔrər] *n* **:** horror *m* — **horrendous** [hɔ'rendəs] *adj* **:** horrendo — **horrible** ['hɔrəbəl] *adj* **:** horrible — **horrid** ['hɔrɪd] *adj* **:** horroroso, horrible — **horrify** ['hɔrə,faɪ] *vt* **-fied; -fying :** horrorizar
hors d'oeuvre [ɔr'dərv] *n, pl* **hors d'oeuvres** [-'dərvz] **:** entremés *m*
horse ['hɔrs] *n* **:** caballo *m* — **horseback** ['hɔrs,bæk] *n* **on ~ :** a caballo — **horsefly** ['hɔrs,flaɪ] *n, pl* **-flies :** tábano *m* — **horseman** ['hɔrsmən] *n, pl* **-men** [-mən, -,men] **:** jinete *m* — **horseplay** ['hɔrs,pleɪ] *n* **:** payasadas *fpl* — **horsepower** ['hɔrs,paʊər] *n* **:** caballo *m* de fuerza — **horseradish** ['hɔrs,rædɪʃ] *n* **:** rábano *m* picante — **horseshoe** ['hɔrs,ʃu:] *n* **:** herradura *f* — **horsewoman** ['hɔrs,wʊmən] *n, pl* **-women** [-,wɪmən] **:** jinete *f*
horticulture ['hɔrṭə,kʌltʃər] *n* **:** horticultura *f*
hose ['ho:z] *n* **1** *pl* **hoses :** manguera *f*, manga *f* **2 hose** *pl* STOCKINGS **:** medias *fpl* — **~** *vt* **hosed; hosing :** regar (con manguera) — **hosiery** ['ho:ʒəri, 'ho:zə-] *n* **:** calcetería *f*
hospice ['hɑspəs] *n* **:** hospicio *m*
hospital ['hɑs,pɪṭəl] *n* **:** hospital *m* — **hospitable** [hɑ'spɪṭəbəl, 'hɑs,pɪ-] *adj* **:** hospitalario — **hospitality** [,hɑspə'tæləṭi] *n, pl* **-ties :** hospitalidad *f* — **hospitalize** ['hɑs,pɪṭəl,aɪz] *vt* **-ized; -izing :** hospitalizar
host[1] ['ho:st] *n* **a ~ of :** toda una serie de
host[2] *n* **1 :** anfitrión *m*, -triona *f* **2 :** presentador *m*, -dora *f* (de televisión, etc.) — **~** *vt* **:** presentar (un programa de televisión, etc.)
host[3] *n* EUCHARIST **:** hostia *f*, Eucaristía *f*
hostage ['hɑstɪdʒ] *n* **:** rehén *m*
hostel ['hɑstəl] *n* *or* **youth ~ :** albergue *m* juvenil
hostess ['ho:stɪs] *n* **:** anfitriona *f*
hostile ['hɑstəl, -,taɪl] *adj* **:** hostil — **hostility** [hɑs'tɪləṭi] *n, pl* **-ties :** hostilidad *f*
hot ['hɑt] *adj* **hotter; hottest 1 :** caliente, caluroso (dícese del tiempo), cálido (dícese del clima) **2** SPICY **:** picante **3 feel ~ :** tener calor **4 have a ~ temper :** tener mal genio **5 ~ news :** noticias *fpl* de última hora **6 it's ~ today :** hace calor
hot dog *n* **:** perro *m* caliente
hotel [ho:'tɛl] *n* **:** hotel *m*
hotheaded ['hɑt'hɛdəd] *adj* **:** exaltado
hound ['haʊnd] *n* **:** perro *m* (de caza) — **~** *vt* **:** acosar, perseguir
hour ['aʊər] *n* **:** hora *f* — **hourglass** ['aʊər,glæs] *n* **:** reloj *m* de arena — **hourly** ['aʊərli] *adv & adj* **:** cada hora, por hora
house ['haʊs] *n, pl* **houses** ['haʊzəz, -səz] **1 :** casa *f* **2 :** cámara *f* (del gobierno) **3 publishing ~ :** editorial *f* — **~** ['haʊz] *vt* **housed; housing :** albergar — **houseboat** ['haʊs,bo:t] *n* **:** casa *f* flotante — **housefly** ['haʊs,flaɪ] *n, pl* **-flies :** mosca *f* común — **household** ['haʊs,ho:ld] *adj* **1 :** doméstico **2 ~ name :** nombre *m* muy conocido — **~** *n* **:** casa *f* — **housekeeper** ['haʊs,ki:pər] *n* **:** ama *f* de llaves — **housekeeping** ['haʊs,ki:pɪŋ] *n* **:** gobierno *m* de la casa — **housewarming** ['haʊs,wɔrmɪŋ] *n* **:** fiesta *f* de estreno de

una casa — **housewife** ['haʊs,waɪf] *n, pl* **-wives** : ama *f* de casa — **housework** ['haʊs,wərk] *n* : faenas *fpl* domésticas — **housing** ['haʊzɪŋ] *n* **1** : viviendas *fpl* **2** CASE : caja *f* protectora

hove → **heave**

hovel ['hʌvəl, 'hɑ-] *n* : casucha *f,* tugurio *m*

hover ['hʌvər, 'hɑ-] *vi* **1** : cernerse **2** ~ **about** : rondar

how ['haʊ] *adv* **1** : cómo **2** (*used in exclamations*) : qué **3** ~ **are you?** : ¿cómo está Ud.? **4** ~ **come** : por qué **5** ~ **much** : cuánto **6** ~ **do you do?** : mucho gusto **7** ~ **old are you?** : ¿cuántos años tienes? — ~ *conj* : como

however [haʊ'ɛvər] *conj* **1** : de cualquier manera que **2** ~ **you like** : como quieras — ~ *adv* **1** NEVERTHELESS : sin embargo, no obstante **2** ~ **difficult it is** : por díficil que sea **3** ~ **hard I try** : por más que me esfuerce

howl ['haʊl] *vi* : aullar — ~ *n* : aullido *m*

hub ['hʌb] *n* **1** CENTER : centro *m* **2** : cubo *m* (de una rueda)

hubbub ['hʌ,bʌb] *n* : alboroto *m,* jaleo *m*

hubcap ['hʌb,kæp] *n* : tapacubos *m*

huddle ['hʌdəl] *vi* **-dled; -dling** *or* ~ **together** : apiñarse

hue ['hju:] *n* : color *m,* tono *m*

huff ['hʌf] *n* **be in a** ~ : estar enojado

hug ['hʌg] *vt* **hugged; hugging** : abrazar — ~ *n* : abrazo *m*

huge ['hju:dʒ] *adj* **huger; hugest** : inmenso, enorme

hull ['hʌl] *n* : casco *m* (de un barco, etc.)

hum ['hʌm] *v* **hummed; humming** *vi* **1** : tararear **2** BUZZ : zumbar — *vt* : tararear (una melodía) — ~ *n* : zumbido *m*

human ['hju:mən, 'ju:-] *adj* : humano — ~ *n* : (ser *m*) humano *m* — **humane** [hju:'meɪn, ju:-] *adj* : humano, humanitario — **humanitarian** [hju:,mænə'tɛriən, ju:-] *adj* : humanitario — **humanity** [hju:'mænəṭi, ju:-] *n, pl* **-ties** : humanidad *f*

humble ['hʌmbəl] *vt* **-bled; -bling 1** : humillar **2** ~ **oneself** : humillarse — ~ *adj* **-bler; -blest** : humilde

humdrum ['hʌm,drʌm] *adj* : monótono, rutinario

humid ['hju:məd, 'ju:-] *adj* : húmedo — **humidity** [hju:'mɪdəṭi, ju:-] *n, pl* **-ties** : humedad *f*

humiliate [hju:'mɪli,eɪt, ju:-] *vt* **-ated; -ating** : humillar — **humiliating** [hju:'mɪli,eɪṭɪŋ, ju:-] *adj* : humillante — **humiliation** [hju:,mɪli'eɪʃən, ju:-] *n* : humillación *f* — **humility** [hju:'mɪləṭi, ju:-] *n* : humildad *f*

humor *or Brit* **humour** ['hju:mər, 'ju:-] *n* : humor *m* — ~ *vt* : seguir la corriente a, complacer — **humorous** ['hju:mərəs, 'ju:-] *adj* : humorístico, cómico

hump ['hʌmp] *n* : joroba *f*

hunch ['hʌntʃ] *vi or* ~ **over** : encorvarse — ~ *n* : presentimiento *m*

hundred ['hʌndrəd] *adj* : cien, ciento — ~ *n, pl* **-dreds** *or* **-dred** : ciento *m* — **hundredth** ['hʌndrədθ] *adj* : centésimo — ~ *n* **1** : centésimo *m,* -ma *f* (en una serie) **2** : centésimo *m* (en matemáticas)

hung → **hang**

Hungarian [hʌŋ'gæriən] *adj* : húngaro — ~ *n* : húngaro *m* (idioma)

hunger ['hʌŋgər] *n* : hambre *m* — ~ *vi* **1** : tener hambre **2** ~ **for** : ansiar, anhelar — **hungry** ['hʌŋgri] *adj* **-grier; -est 1** : hambriento **2 be** ~ : tener hambre

hunk ['hʌŋk] *n* : pedazo *m* (grande)

hunt ['hʌnt] *vt* **1** : cazar **2** ~ **for** : buscar — ~ *n* **1** : caza *f,* cacería *f* **2** SEARCH : búsqueda *f,* busca *f* — **hunter** ['hʌntər] *n* : cazador *m,* -dora *f* — **hunting** ['hʌntɪŋ] *n* **1** : caza *f* **2 go** ~ : ir de caza

hurdle ['hərdəl] *n* **1** : valla *f* (en deportes) **2** OBSTACLE : obstáculo *m*

hurl ['hərl] *vt* : lanzar, arrojar

hurrah [hʊ'rɑ, -'rɔ] *interj* : ¡hurra!

hurricane ['hərə,keɪn] *n* : huracán *m*

hurry ['həri] *n* : prisa *f,* apuro *f Lat* — *v* **-ried; -rying** *vi* : darse prisa, apurarse *Lat* — *vt* : apurar, dar prisa a — **hurried** ['hərid] *adj* : apresurado — **hurriedly** ['hərədli] *adv* : apresuradamente, de prisa

hurt ['hərt] *v* **hurt; hurting** *vt* **1** INJURE : hacer daño a, lastimar **2** OFFEND : ofender, herir — *vi* **1** : doler **2 my foot** ~**s** : me duele el pie — ~ *n* **1** INJURY : herida *f* **2** DISTRESS : dolor *m,* pena *f* — **hurtful** ['hərtfəl] *adj* : hiriente, doloroso

hurtle ['hərṭəl] *vi* **-tled; -tling** : lanzarse, precipitarse

husband ['hʌzbənd] *n* : esposo *m,* marido *m*

hush ['hʌʃ] *vt* : hacer callar, acallar — ~ *n* : silencio *m*

husk ['hʌsk] *n* : cáscara *f*

husky[1] ['hʌski] *adj* **-kier; -est** HOARSE : ronco

husky[2] *n, pl* **-kies** : perro *m,* -rra *f* esquimal

husky[3] *adj* BURLY : fornido
hustle ['həsəl] *v* **-tled; -tling** *vt* : dar prisa a, apurar *Lat* — *vi* : darse prisa, apurarse *Lat* — ~ *n* ~ **and bustle** : ajetreo *m,* bullicio *m*
hut ['hʌt] *n* : cabaña *f*
hutch ['hʌtʃ] *n or* **rabbit** ~ : conejera *f*
hyacinth ['haɪə,sɪnθ] *n* : jacinto *m*
hybrid ['haɪbrɪd] *n* : híbrido *m* — ~ *adj* : híbrido
hydrant ['haɪdrənt] *n or* **fire** ~ : boca *f* de incendios
hydraulic [haɪ'drɔlɪk] *adj* : hidráulico
hydroelectric [,haɪdroɪ'lɛktrɪk] *adj* : hidroeléctrico
hydrogen ['haɪdrədʒən] *n* : hidrógeno *m*
hyena [haɪ'i:nə] *n* : hiena *f*
hygiene ['haɪ,dʒi:n] *n* : higiene *f* — **hygienic** [haɪ'dʒɛnɪk, -'dʒi:-; ,haɪdʒi'ɛnɪk] *adj* : higiénico
hymn ['hɪm] *n* : himno *m*
hyperactive [,haɪpər'æktɪv] *adj* : hiperactivo
hyphen ['haɪfən] *n* : guión *m*
hypnosis [hɪp'no:sɪs] *n, pl* **-noses** [-,si:z] : hipnosis *f* — **hypnotic** [hɪp'nɑtɪk] *adj* : hipnótico — **hypnotism** ['hɪpnə,tɪzəm] *n* : hipnotismo *m* — **hypnotize** ['hɪpnə,taɪz] *vt* **-tized; -tizing** : hipnotizar
hypochondriac [,haɪpə'kɑndri,æk] *n* : hipocondríaco *m,* -ca *f*
hypocrisy [hɪp'ɑkrəsi] *n, pl* **-sies** : hipocresía *f* — **hypocrite** ['hɪpə,krɪt] *n* : hipócrita *mf* — **hypocritical** [,hɪpə'krɪtɪkəl] *adj* : hipócrita
hypothesis [haɪ'pɑθəsɪs] *n, pl* **-eses** [-,si:z] : hipótesis *f* — **hypothetical** [,haɪpə'θɛtɪkəl] *adj* : hipotético
hysteria [hɪs'tɛriə, -tɪr-] *n* : histeria *f,* histerismo *m* — **hysterical** [hɪs'tɛrɪkəl] *adj* : histérico

I

i ['aɪ] *n, pl* **i's** *or* **is** ['aɪz] : i *f,* novena letra del alfabeto inglés
I ['aɪ] *pron* : yo
ice ['aɪs] *n* : hielo *m* — ~ *v* **iced; icing** *vt* **1** FREEZE : congelar **2** CHILL : enfriar **3** : bañar (pasteles, etc.) — ~ *vi or* ~ **up** : helarse, congelarse — **iceberg** ['aɪs,bərg] *n* : iceberg *m* — **icebox** ['aɪs,bɑks] → **refrigerator** — **ice–cold** ['aɪs'ko:ld] *adj* : helado — **ice cream** *n* : helado *m* — **ice cube** *n* : cubito *m* de hielo — **ice–skate** ['aɪs,skeɪt] *vi* **-skated; -skating** : patinar — **ice skate** *n* : patín *m* de cuchilla — **icicle** ['aɪ,sɪkəl] *n* : carámbano *m* — **icing** ['aɪsɪŋ] *n* : baño *m*
icon ['aɪ,kɑn, -kən] *n* : icono *m*
icy ['aɪsi] *adj* **icier; -est 1** : cubierto de hielo (dícese de pavimento, etc.) **2** FREEZING : helado
I'd ['aɪd] (*contraction of* **I should** *or* **I would**) → **should, would**
idea [aɪ'di:ə] *n* : idea *f*
ideal [aɪ'di:əl] *adj* : ideal — ~ *n* : ideal *m* — **idealist** [aɪ'di:əlɪst] *n* : idealista *mf* — **idealistic** [aɪ,di:ə'lɪstɪk] *adj* : idealista — **idealize** [aɪ'di:ə,laɪz] *vt* **-ized; -izing** : idealizar
identity [aɪ'dɛntəṭi] *n, pl* **-ties** : identidad *f* — **identical** [aɪ'dɛntɪkəl] *adj* : idéntico — **identify** [aɪ'dɛntə,faɪ] *v* **-fied; -fying** *vt* : identificar — *vi* ~ **with** : identificarse con — **identification** [aɪ,dɛntəfə'keɪʃən] *n* **1** : identificación *f* **2** ~ **card** : carnet *m,* carné *m*
ideology [,aɪdi'ɑlədʒi, ,ɪ-] *n, pl* **-gies** : ideología *f* — **ideological** [,aɪdiə'lɑdʒɪkəl, ,ɪ-] *adj* : ideológico
idiocy ['ɪdiəsi] *n, pl* **-cies** : idiotez *f*
idiom ['ɪdiəm] *n* EXPRESSION : modismo *m* — **idiomatic** [,ɪdiə'mæṭɪk] *adj* : idiomático
idiosyncrasy [,ɪdio'sɪŋkrəsi] *n, pl* **-sies** : idiosincrasia *f*
idiot ['ɪdiət] *n* : idiota *mf* — **idiotic** [,ɪdi'ɑṭɪk] *adj* : idiota
idle ['aɪdəl] *adj* **idler; idlest 1** LAZY : haragán, holgazán **2** INACTIVE : parado (dícese de una máquina) **3** UNEMPLOYED : desocupado **4** VAIN : frívolo, vano **5 out of** ~ **curiosity** : por pura curiosidad — ~ *v* **idled; idling** *vi* : andar al ralentí (dícese de un motor) — *vt* ~ **away the hours** : pasar el rato — **idleness** ['aɪdəlnəs] *n* : ociosidad *f*
idol ['aɪdəl] *n* : ídolo *m* — **idolize** ['aɪdəlaɪz] *vt* **-ized; -izing** : idolatrar
idyllic [aɪ'dɪlɪk] *adj* : idílico
if ['ɪf] *conj* **1** : si **2** THOUGH : aunque, si bien **3** ~ **so** : si es así
igloo ['ɪ,glu:] *n, pl* **-loos** : iglú *m*
ignite [ɪg'naɪt] *v* **-nited; -niting** *vt* : encender — *vi* : encenderse — **ignition** [ɪg'nɪʃən] *n* **1** : ignición *f* **2** *or* ~ **switch** : encendido *m*

ignore [ɪg'nor] *vt* **-nored; -noring** : ignorar, no hacer caso de — **ignorance** [ˌɪgnərənts] *n* : ignorancia *f* — **ignorant** ['ɪgnərənt] *adj* **1** : ignorante **2 be ~ of** : desconocer, ignorar

ilk ['ɪlk] *n* : tipo *m*, clase *f*

ill ['ɪl] *adj* **worse** ['wərs]; **worst** ['wərst] **1** SICK : enfermo **2** BAD : malo — *adv* **worse; worst** : mal — **ill–advised** [ˌɪlæd'vaɪzd, -əd-] *adj* : imprudente — **ill at ease** *adj* : incómodo

I'll ['aɪl] (*contraction of* **I shall** *or* **I will**) → **shall, will**

illegal [ɪl'li:gəl] *adj* : ilegal

illegible [ɪl'lɛdʒəbəl] *adj* : ilegible

illegitimate [ˌɪlɪ'dʒɪṭəmət] *adj* : ilegítimo — **illegitimacy** [ˌɪlɪ'dʒɪṭəməsi] *n* : ilegitimidad *f*

illicit [ɪl'lɪsət] *adj* : ilícito

illiterate [ɪl'lɪṭərət] *adj* : analfabeto — **illiteracy** [ɪl'lɪṭərəsi] *n, pl* **-cies** : analfabetismo *m*

ill–mannered [ˌɪl'mænərd] *adj* : descortés, maleducado

ill–natured [ˌɪl'neɪtʃərd] *adj* : de mal genio

illness ['ɪlnəs] *n* : enfermedad *f*

illogical [ɪl'lɑdʒɪkəl] *adj* : ilógico

ill–treat [ˌɪl'tri:t] *vt* : maltratar

illuminate [ɪ'lu:məˌneɪt] *vt* **-nated; -nating** : iluminar — **illumination** [ɪˌlu:mə'neɪʃən] *n* : iluminación *f*

illusion [ɪ'lu:ʒən] *n* : ilusión *f* — **illusory** [ɪ'lu:səri, -zəri] *adj* : ilusorio

illustrate ['ɪləsˌtreɪt] *v* **-trated; -trating** : ilustrar — **illustration** [ˌɪlə'streɪʃən] *n* **1** : ilustración *f* **2** EXAMPLE : ejemplo *m* — **illustrative** [ɪ'lʌstrəṭɪv, 'ɪləˌstreɪṭɪv] *adj* : ilustrativo

illustrious [ɪ'lʌstriəs] *adj* : ilustre, glorioso

ill will *n* : animadversión *f*, mala voluntad *f*

I'm ['aɪm] (*contraction of* **I am**) → **be**

image ['ɪmɪdʒ] *n* : imagen *f* — **imaginary** [ɪ'mædʒəˌnɛri] *adj* : imaginario — **imagination** [ɪˌmædʒə'neɪʃən] *n* : imaginación *f* — **imaginative** [ɪ'mædʒənəṭɪv, -əˌneɪṭɪv] *adj* : imaginativo — **imagine** [ɪ'mædʒən] *vt* **-ined; -ining** : imaginar(se)

imbalance [ɪm'bæləntsl] *n* : desequilibrio *m*

imbecile ['ɪmbəsəl, -ˌsɪl] *n* : imbécil *mf*

imbue [ɪm'bju:] *vt* **-bued; -buing** : imbuir

imitation [ˌɪmə'teɪʃən] *n* : imitación *f* — **~** *adj* : de imitación, artificial — **imitate** ['ɪməˌteɪt] *vt* **-tated; -tating** : imitar, remedar — **imitator** ['ɪməˌteɪṭər] *n* : imitador *m*, -dora *f*

immaculate [ɪ'mækjələt] *adj* : inmaculado

immaterial [ˌɪmə'tɪriəl] *adj* : irrelevante, sin importancia

immature [ˌɪmə'tʃʊr, -'tjʊr, -'tʊr] *adj* : inmaduro — **immaturity** [ˌɪmə'tʃʊrəṭi, -'tjʊr-, -'tʊr-] *n, pl* **-ties** : inmadurez *f*

immediate [ɪ'mi:diət] *adj* : inmediato — **immediately** [ɪ'mi:diətli] *adv* : inmediatamente

immense [ɪ'mɛnts] *adj* : inmenso — **immensity** [ɪ'mɛntsəṭi] *n, pl* **-ties** : inmensidad *f*

immerse [ɪ'mərs] *vt* **-mersed; -mersing** : sumergir — **immersion** [ɪ'mərʒən] *n* : inmersión *f*

immigrate ['ɪməˌgreɪt] *vi* **-grated; -grating** : inmigrar — **immigrant** ['ɪmɪgrənt] *n* : inmigrante *mf* — **immigration** [ˌɪmə'greɪʃən] *n* : inmigración *f*

imminent ['ɪmənənt] *adj* : inminente — **imminence** ['ɪmənənts] *n* : inminencia *f*

immobile [ɪm'o:bəl] *adj* : inmóvil — **immobilize** [ɪ'mo:bəˌlaɪz] *vt* **-lized; -lizing** : inmovilizar

immoral [ɪ'mɔrəl] *adj* : inmoral — **immorality** [ˌɪmɔ'ræləṭi, ˌɪmə-] *n, pl* **-ties** : inmoralidad *f*

immortal [ɪ'mɔrtəl] *adj* : inmortal — **~** *n* : inmortal *mf* — **immortality** [ˌɪˌmɔr'tæləṭi] *n* : inmortalidad *f*

immune [ɪ'mju:n] *adj* : inmune — **immunity** [ɪ'mju:nəṭi] *n, pl* **-ties** : inmunidad *f* — **immunization** [ˌɪmjʊnə'zeɪʃən] *n* : inmunización *f* — **immunize** ['ɪmjʊˌnaɪz] *vt* **-nized; -nizing** : inmunizar

imp ['ɪmp] *n* RASCAL : diablillo *m*

impact ['ɪmˌpækt] *n* : impacto *m*

impair [ɪm'pær] *vt* : dañar, perjudicar

impart [ɪm'pɑrt] *vt* : impartir (información), conferir (una calidad, etc.)

impartial [ɪm'pɑrʃəl] *adj* : imparcial — **impartiality** [ɪmˌpɑrʃi'æləṭi] *n, pl* **-ties** : imparcialidad *f*

impassable [ɪm'pæsəbəl] *adj* : intransitable

impasse ['ɪmˌpæs] *n* : impasse *m*

impassioned [ɪm'pæʃənd] *adj* : apasionado

impassive [ɪm'pæsɪv] *adj* : impasible

impatience [ɪm'peɪʃənts] *n* : impaciencia *f* — **impatient** [ɪm'peɪʃənt] *adj* : impaciente — **impatiently** [ɪm'peɪʃəntli] *adv* : con impaciencia

impeccable [ɪm'pɛkəbəl] *adj* : impecable

impede [ɪmˈpiːd] *vt* **-peded; -peding** : dificultar — **impediment** [ɪmˈpɛdəmənt] *n* : impedimento *m,* obstáculo *m*
impel [ɪmˈpɛl] *vt* **-pelled; -pelling** : impeler
impending [ɪmˈpɛndɪŋ] *adj* : inminente
impenetrable [ɪmˈpɛnətrəbəl] *adj* : impenetrable
imperative [ɪmˈpɛrət̬ɪv] *adj* **1** COMMANDING : imperativo **2** NECESSARY : imprescindible — **~** *n* : imperativo *m*
imperceptible [ˌɪmpərˈsɛptəbəl] *adj* : imperceptible
imperfection [ɪmˌpərˈfɛkʃən] *n* : imperfección *f* — **imperfect** [ɪmˈpərfɪkt] *adj* : imperfecto — **~** *n or* **~ tense** : imperfecto *m*
imperial [ɪmˈpɪriəl] *adj* : imperial — **imperialism** [ɪmˈpɪriəˌlɪzəm] *n* : imperialismo *m* — **imperious** [ɪmˈpɪriəs] *adj* : imperioso
impersonal [ɪmˈpərsənəl] *adj* : impersonal
impersonate [ɪmˈpərsənˌeɪt] *vt* **-ated; -ating** : hacerse pasar por, imitar — **impersonation** [ɪmˌpərsənˈeɪʃən] *n* : imitación *f* — **impersonator** [ɪmˈpərsənˌeɪt̬ər] *n* : imitador *m,* -dora *f*
impertinent [ɪmˈpərtənənt] *adj* : impertinente — **impertinence** [ɪmˈpərtənənts] *n* : impertinencia *f*
impervious [ɪmˈpərviəs] *adj* **~ to** : impermeable a
impetuous [ɪmˈpɛtʃʊəs] *adj* : impetuoso, impulsivo
impetus [ˈɪmpət̬əs] *n* : ímpetu *m,* impulso *m*
impinge [ɪmˈpɪndʒ] *vi* **-pinged; -pinging ~ on** : afectara, incidir en
impish [ˈɪmpɪʃ] *adj* : pícaro, travieso
implant [ɪmˈplænt] *vt* : implantar
implausible [ɪmˈplɔzəbəl] *adj* : inverosímil
implement [ˈɪmpləmənt] *n* : instrumento *m,* implemento *m Lat* — **~** [ˈɪmpləˌmɛnt] *vt* : poner en práctica
implicate [ˈɪmpləˌkeɪt] *vt* **-cated; -cating** : implicar — **implication** [ˌɪmpləˈkeɪʃən] *n* **1** INVOLVEMENT : implicación *f* **2** CONSEQUENCE : consecuencia *f* **3 by ~** : de forma indirecta
implicit [ɪmˈplɪsət] *adj* **1** : implícito **2** UNQUESTIONING : absoluto, incondicional
implore [ɪmˈplor] *vt* **-plored; -ploring** : implorar, suplicar
imply [ɪmˈplaɪ] *vt* **-plied; -plying 1** HINT : insinuar **2** ENTAIL : implicar
impolite [ˌɪmpəˈlaɪt] *adj* : descortés, maleducado
import [ɪmˈport] *vt* : importar (mercancías) — **important** [ɪmˈpɔrtənt] *adj* : importante — **importance** [ɪmˈportənts] *n* : importancia *f* — **importation** [ˌɪmˌpɔrˈteɪʃən] *n* : importación *f* — **importer** [ɪmˈport̬ər] *n* : importador *m,* -dora *f*
impose [ɪmˈpoːz] *v* **-posed; -posing** *vt* : imponer — *vi* **~ on** : importunar, molestar — **imposing** [ɪmˈpoːzɪŋ] *adj* : imponente — **imposition** [ˌɪmpəˈzɪʃən] *n* **1** ENFORCEMENT : imposición *f* **2 be an ~ on** : molestar
impossible [ɪmˈpɑsəbəl] *adj* : imposible — **impossibility** [ɪmˌpɑsəˈbɪlət̬i] *n, pl* **-ties** : imposibilidad *f*
impostor *or* **imposter** [ɪmˈpɑstər] *n* : impostor *m,* -tora *f*
impotent [ˈɪmpətənt] *adj* : impotente — **impotence** [ˈɪmpətənts] *n* : impotencia *f*
impound [ɪmˈpaʊnd] *vt* : incautar, embargar
impoverished [ɪmˈpɑvərɪʃt] *adj* : empobrecido
impracticable [ɪmˈpræktɪkəbəl] *adj* : impracticable
impractical [ɪmˈpræktɪkəl] *adj* : poco práctico
imprecise [ˌɪmprɪˈsaɪs] *adj* : impreciso — **imprecision** [ˌɪmprɪˈsɪʒən] *n* : imprecisión *f*
impregnable [ɪmˈprɛgnəbəl] *adj* : impenetrable
impregnate [ɪmˈprɛgˌneɪt] *vt* **-nated; -nating 1** : impregnar **2** FERTILIZE : fecundar
impress [ɪmˈprɛs] *vt* **1** : causar una buena impresión a **2** AFFECT : impresionar **3 ~ sth on s.o.** : recalcar algo a algn — *vi* : impresionar — **impression** [ɪmˈprɛʃən] *n* : impresión *f* — **impressionable** [ɪmˈprɛʃənəbəl] *adj* : impresionable — **impressive** [ɪmˈprɛsɪv] *adj* : impresionante
imprint [ɪmˈprɪnt, ˈɪm,-] *vt* : imprimir — **~** [ˈɪmˌprɪnt] *n* MARK : impresión *f,* huella *f*
imprison [ɪmˈprɪzən] *vt* : encarcelar — **imprisonment** [ɪmˈprɪzənmənt] *n* : encarcelamiento *m*
improbable [ɪmˈprɑbəbəl] *adj* : improbable — **improbability** [ɪmˌprɑbəˈbɪlət̬i] *n, pl* **-ties** : improbabilidad *f*
impromptu [ɪmˈprɑmpˌtuː, -ˌtjuː] *adj* : improvisado
improper [ɪmˈprɑpər] *adj* **1** UNSEEMLY : indecoroso **2** INCORRECT : impropio

— **impropriety** [ˌɪmprəˈpraɪət̬i] *n, pl* **-eties** : inconveniencia *f*
improve [ɪmˈpruːv] *v* **-proved; -proving** : mejorar — **improvement** [ɪmˈpruːvmənt] *n* : mejora *f*
improvise [ˈɪmprəˌvaɪz] *v* **-vised; -vising** : improvisar — **improvisation** [ɪmˌprɑvəˈzeɪʃən, ˌɪmprəvə-] *n* : improvisación *f*
impudent [ˈɪmpjədənt] *adj* : insolente — **impudence** [ˈɪmpjədənts] *n* : insolencia *f*
impulse [ˈɪmˌpʌls] *n* **1** : impulso *m* **2 on ~** : sin reflexionar — **impulsive** [ɪmˈpʌlsɪv] *adj* : impulsivo — **impulsiveness** [ɪmˈpʌlsɪvnəs] *n* : impulsividad *f*
impunity [ɪmˈpjuːnət̬i] *n* **1** : impunidad *f* **2 with ~** : impunemente
impure [ɪmˈpjʊr] *adj* : impuro — **impurity** [ɪmˈpjʊrət̬i] *n, pl* **-ties** : impureza *f*
in [ˈɪn] *prep* **1** : en **2** DURING : por, en *Lat* **3** WITHIN : dentro de **4 dressed ~ red** : vestido de rojo **5 ~ the rain** : bajo la lluvia **6 ~ the sun** : al sol **7 ~ this way** : de esta manera **8 the best ~ the world** : el mejor del mundo **9 written ~ ink/French** : escrito con tinta/en francés — *adv* **1** INSIDE : dentro, adentro **2 be ~** : estar (en casa) **3 be ~ on** : participar en **4 come in!** : ¡entre!, ¡pase! **5 he's ~ for a shock** : se va a llevar un shock — **~** *adj* : de moda
inability [ˌɪnəˈbɪlət̬i] *n, pl* **-ties** : incapacidad *f*
inaccessible [ˌɪnɪkˈsɛsəbəl] *adj* : inaccesible
inaccurate [ɪnˈækjərət] *n* : inexacto
inactive [ɪnˈæktɪv] *n* : inactivo — **inactivity** [ˌɪnˌækˈtɪvət̬i] *n, pl* **-ties** : inactividad *f*
inadequate [ɪnˈædɪkwət] *adj* : insuficiente
inadvertently [ˌɪnədˈvərtəntli] *adv* : sin querer
inadvisable [ˌɪnædˈvaɪzəbəl] *adj* : desaconsejable
inane [ɪˈneɪn] *adj* **inaner; -est** : estúpido, tonto
inanimate [ɪnˈænəmət] *adj* : inanimado
inapplicable [ɪnˈæplɪkəbəl, ˌɪnəˈplɪkəbəl] *adj* : inaplicable
inappropriate [ˌɪnəˈproːpriət] *adj* : impropio, inoportuno
inarticulate [ˌɪnɑrˈtɪkjələt] *adj* : incapaz de expresarse
inasmuch as [ˌɪnæzˈmʌtʃæz] *conj* : ya que, puesto que
inattentive [ˌɪnəˈtentɪv] *adj* : poco atento
inaudible [ɪnˈodəbəl] *adj* : inaudible
inaugural [ɪˈnɔgjərəl, -gərəl] *adj* **1** : inaugural **2 ~ address** : discurso *m* de investidura — **inaugurate** [ɪˈnɔgjəˌreɪt, -gə-] *vt* **-rated; -rating 1** : investir (a un presidente, etc.) **2** BEGIN : inaugurar — **inauguration** [ɪˌnɔgjəˈreɪʃən, -gə-] *n* : investidura *f* (de una persona), inauguración *f* (de un edificio, etc.)
inborn [ˈɪnˌbɔrn] *adj* : innato
inbred [ˈɪnˌbrɛd] *adj* INNATE : innato
incalculable [ɪnˈkælkjələbəl] *adj* : incalculable
incapable [ɪnˈkeɪpəbəl] *adj* : incapaz — **incapacitate** [ˌɪnkəˈpæsəˌteɪt] *vt* **-tated; -tating** : incapacitar — **incapacity** [ˌɪnkəˈpæsət̬i] *n, pl* **-ties** : incapacidad *f*
incarcerate [ɪnˈkɑrsəˌreɪt] *vt* **-ated; -ating** : encarcelar
incarnate [ɪnˈkɑrnət, -ˌneɪt] *adj* : encarnado — **incarnation** [ˌɪnˌkɑrˈneɪʃən] *n* : encarnación *f*
incendiary [ɪnˈsɛndiˌeri] *adj* : incendiario
incense[1] [ˈɪnˌsɛnts] *n* : incienso *m*
incense[2] [ɪnˈsɛnts] *vt* **-censed; -censing** : indignar, enfurecer
incentive [ɪnˈsentɪv] *n* : incentivo *m*
inception [ɪnˈsɛpʃən] *n* : comienzo *m*, principio *m*
incessant [ɪnˈsɛsənt] *adj* : incesante
incest [ˈɪnˌsɛst] *n* : incesto *m* — **incestuous** [ɪnˈsɛstʃʊəs] *adj* : incestuoso
inch [ˈɪntʃ] *n* : pulgada *f* — **~** *v* : avanzar poco a poco
incident [ˈɪntsədənt] *n* : incidente *m* — **incidence** [ˈɪntsədənts] *n* : índice *m* (de crímenes, etc.) — **incidental** [ˌɪntsəˈdentəl] *adj* **1** MINOR : incidental **2** CHANCE : casual — **incidentally** [ˌɪntsəˈdentəli, -ˈdentli] *adv* : a propósito
incinerate [ɪnˈsɪnəˌreɪt] *vt* **-ated; -ating** : incinerar — **incinerator** [ɪnˈsɪnəˌreɪt̬ər] *n* : incinerador *m*
incision [ɪnˈsɪʒən] *n* : incisión *f*
incite [ɪnˈsaɪt] *vt* **-cited; -citing** : incitar, instigar
incline [ɪnˈklaɪn] *v* **-clined; -clining** *vt* **1** BEND : inclinar **2 be ~ed to** : inclinarse a, tender a — **~** *vi* : inclinarse — **~** [ˈɪnˌklaɪn] *n* : pendiente *f* — **inclination** [ˌɪnkləˈneɪʃən] *n* **1** : inclinación *f* **2** DESIRE : deseo *m*, ganas *fpl*
include [ɪnˈkluːd] *vt* **-cluded; -cluding** : incluir — **inclusion** [ɪnˈkluːʒən] *n* : inclusión *f* — **inclusive** [ɪnˈkluːsɪv] *adj* : inclusivo
incognito [ˌɪnˌkɑgˈniːt̬o, ɪnˈkɑgnəˌtoː] *adv & adj* : de incógnito
incoherent [ˌɪnkoˈhɪrənt, -ˈhɛr-] *adj* : in-

coherente — **incoherence** [ˌɪnko-ˈhɪrənts, -ˈhɛr-] *n* : incoherencia *f*
income [ˈɪnˌkʌm] *n* : ingresos *mpl* — **income tax** *n* : impuesto *m* sobre la renta
incomparable [ɪnˈkɑmpərəbəl] *adj* : incomparable
incompatible [ˌɪnkəmˈpæt̬əbəl] *adj* : incompatible
incompetent [ɪnˈkɑmpət̬ənt] *adj* : incompetente — **incompetence** [ɪn-ˈkɑmpət̬ənts] *n* : incompetencia *f*
incomplete [ˌɪnkəmˈpliːt] *adj* : incompleto
incomprehensible [ˌɪnˌkɑmpriˈhɛntsəbəl] *adj* : incomprensible
inconceivable [ˌɪnkənˈsiːvəbəl] *adj* : inconcebible
inconclusive [ˌɪnkənˈkluːsɪv] *adj* : no concluyente
incongruous [ɪnˈkɑŋgruəs] *adj* : incongruente
inconsiderate [ˌɪnkənˈsɪdərət] *adj* : desconsiderado
inconsistent [ˌɪnkənˈsɪstənt] *adj* **1** : inconsecuente **2 be ~ with** : no concordar con — **inconsistency** [ˌɪnkən-ˈsɪstəntsi] *n, pl* **-cies** : inconsecuencia *f*
inconspicuous [ˌɪnkənˈspɪkjuəs] *adj* : que no llama la atención
inconvenient [ˌɪnkənˈviːnjənt] *adj* : incómodo, inconveniente — **inconvenience** [ˌɪnkənˈviːnjənts] *n* **1** BOTHER : incomodidad *f,* molestia *f* **2** DRAWBACK : inconveniente *m* — **~** *vt* **-nienced; -niencing** *vt* : importunar, molestar
incorporate [ɪnˈkɔrpəˌreɪt] *vt* **-rated; -rating** : incorporar
incorrect [ˌɪnkəˈrɛkt] *adj* : incorrecto
increase [ˈɪnˌkriːs, ɪnˈkriːs] *n* : aumento *m* — **~** [ɪnˈkriːs, ˈɪnˌkriːs] *v* **-creased; -creasing** : aumentar — **increasingly** [ɪnˈkriːsɪŋli] *adv* : cada vez más
incredible [ɪnˈkrɛdəbəl] *adj* : increíble
incredulous [ɪnˈkrɛdʒələs] *adj* : incrédulo
incriminate [ɪnˈkrɪməˌneɪt] *vt* **-nated; -nating** : incriminar
incubator [ˈɪŋkjʊˌbeɪt̬ər, ˈɪn-] *n* : incubadora *f*
incumbent [ɪnˈkʌmbənt] *n* : titular *mf*
incur [ɪnˈkər] *vt* **incurred; incurring** : provocar (al enojo, etc.), incurrir en (gastos)
incurable [ɪnˈkjʊrəbəl] *adj* : incurable
indebted [ɪnˈdɛt̬əd] *adj* **1** : endeudado **2 be ~ to s.o.** : estar en deuda con algn
indecent [ɪnˈdiːsənt] *adj* : indecente — **indecency** [ɪnˈdiːsəntsi] *n, pl* **-cies** : indecencia *f*
indecisive [ˌɪndɪˈsaɪsɪv] *adj* : indeciso
indeed [ɪnˈdiːd] *adv* **1** TRULY : verdaderamente, sin duda **2** IN FACT : en efecto **3 ~?** : ¿de veras?
indefinite [ɪnˈdɛfənət] *adj* **1** : indefinido **2** VAGUE : impreciso — **indefinitely** [ɪnˈdɛfənətli] *adv* : indefinidamente
indelible [ɪnˈdɛləbəl] *adj* : indeleble
indent [ɪnˈdɛnt] *vt* : sangrar (un párrafo) — **indentation** [ˌɪnˌdɛnˈteɪʃən] *n* DENT, NOTCH : mella *f*
independent [ˌɪndəˈpɛndənt] *adj* : independiente — **independence** [ˌɪndə-ˈpɛndənts] *n* : independencia *f*
indescribable [ˌɪndɪˈskraɪbəbəl] *adj* : indescriptible
indestructible [ˌɪndɪˈstrʌktəbəl] *adj* : indestructible
index [ˈɪnˌdɛks] *n, pl* **-dexes** *or* **-dices** [ˈɪndəˌsiːz] : índice *m* — **~** *vt* : incluir en un índice — **index finger** *n* : dedo *m* índice
Indian [ˈɪndiən] *adj* : indio *m,* -dia *f*
indication [ˌɪndəˈkeɪʃən] *n* : indicio *m,* señal *f* — **indicate** [ˈɪndəˌkeɪt] *vt* **-cated; -cating** : indicar — **indicative** [ɪnˈdɪkət̬ɪv] *adj* : indicativo — **indicator** [ˈɪndəˌkeɪt̬ər] *n* : indicador *m*
indict [ɪnˈdaɪt] *vt* : acusar (de un crimen) — **indictment** [ɪnˈdaɪtmənt] *n* : acusación *f*
indifferent [ɪnˈdɪfrənt, -ˈdɪfə-] *adj* **1** : indiferente **2** MEDIOCRE : mediocre — **indifference** [ɪnˈdɪfrənts, -ˈdɪfə-] *n* : indiferencia *f*
indigenous [ɪnˈdɪdʒənəs] *adj* : indígena
indigestion [ˌɪndaɪˈdʒɛstʃən, -dɪ-] *n* : indigestión *f* — **indigestible** [ˌɪndaɪ-ˈdʒɛstəbəl, -dɪ-] *adj* : indigesto
indignation [ˌɪndɪgˈneɪʃən] *n* : indignación *f* — **indignant** [ɪnˈdɪgnənt] *adj* : indignado — **indignity** [ɪnˈdɪgnət̬i] *n, pl* **-ties** : indignidad *f*
indigo [ˈɪndɪˌgoː] *n, pl* **-gos** *or* **-goes** : añil *m*
indirect [ˌɪndəˈrɛkt, -daɪ-] *adj* : indirecto
indiscreet [ˌɪndɪˈskriːt] *adj* : indiscreto — **indiscretion** [ˌɪndɪˈskrɛʃən] *n* : indiscreción *f*
indiscriminate [ˌɪndɪˈskrɪmənət] *adj* : indiscriminado
indispensable [ˌɪndɪˈspɛntsəbəl] *adj* : indispensable, imprescindible
indisputable [ˌɪndɪˈspjuːt̬əbəl, ɪnˈdɪspjʊt̬ə-] *adj* : indiscutible
indistinct [ˌɪndɪˈstɪŋkt] *adj* : indistinto
individual [ˌɪndəˈvɪdʒuəl] *adj* **1** : individual **2** PARTICULAR : particular — **~** *n* : individuo *m* — **individuality** [ˌɪndəˌvɪdʒʊˈælət̬i] *n, pl* **-ties** : individualidad

f — **individually** [ˌɪndəˈvɪdʒuəli, -dʒəli] *adv* : individualmente

indoctrinate [ɪnˈdɑktrəˌneɪt] *vt* **-nated; -nating** : adoctrinar — **indoctrination** [ɪnˌdɑktrəˈneɪʃən] *n* : adoctrinamiento *m*

indoor [ˈɪnˈdor] *adj* **1** : (de) interior **2 ~ plant** : planta *f* de interior **3 ~ pool** : piscina *f* cubierta **4 ~ sports** : deportes *mpl* bajo techo — **indoors** [ˈɪnˈdorz] *adv* : adentro, dentro

induce [ɪnˈduːs, -ˈdjuːs] *vt* **-duced; -ducing 1** : inducir **2** CAUSE : provocar — **inducement** [ɪnˈduːsmənt, -ˈdjuːs-] *n* : incentivo *m*

indulge [ɪnˈdʌldʒ] *v* **-dulged; -dulging** *vt* **1** GRATIFY : satisfacer **2** PAMPER : consentir — *vi* **~ in** : permitirse — **indulgence** [ɪnˈdʌldʒənts] *n* **1** : indulgencia *f* **2** SATISFYING : satisfacción *f* — **indulgent** [ɪnˈdʌldʒənt] *adj* : indulgente

industry [ˈɪndəstri] *n, pl* **-tries 1** : industria *f* **2** DILIGENCE : diligencia *f* — **industrial** [ɪnˈdʌstriəl] *adj* : industrial — **industrialize** [ɪnˈdʌstriəˌlaɪz] *vt* **-ized; -izing** : industrializar — **industrious** [ɪnˈdʌstriəs] *adj* : diligente, trabajador

inebriated [ɪˈniːbriˌeɪt̬əd] *adj* : ebrio, embriagado

inedible [ɪˈnɛdəbəl] *adj* : no comestible

ineffective [ˌɪnɪˈfɛktɪv] *adj* **1** : ineficaz **2** INCOMPETENT : incompetente — **ineffectual** [ˌɪnɪˈfɛktʃuəl] *adj* : inútil, ineficaz

inefficient [ˌɪnɪˈfɪʃənt] *adj* **1** : ineficiente **2** INCOMPETENT : incompetente — **inefficiency** [ˌɪnɪˈfɪʃəntsi] *n, pl* **-cies** : ineficiencia *f*

ineligible [ɪˈnɛlədʒəbəl] *adj* : ineligible

inept [ɪˈnɛpt] *adj* **1** : inepto **2 ~ at** : incapaz para

inequality [ˌɪnɪˈkwɑlət̬i] *n, pl* **-ties** : desigualdad *f*

inert [ɪˈnərt] *adj* : inerte — **inertia** [ɪˈnərʃə] *n* : inercia *f*

inescapable [ˌɪnɪˈskeɪpəbəl] *adj* : ineludible

inevitable [ɪˈnɛvət̬əbəl] *adj* : inevitable — **inevitably** [-bli] *adv* : inevitablemente

inexcusable [ˌɪnɪkˈskjuːzəbəl] *adj* : inexcusable

inexpensive [ˌɪnɪkˈspɛntsɪv] *adj* : barato, económico

inexperienced [ˌɪnɪkˈspɪriəntst] *adj* : inexperto

inexplicable [ˌɪnɪkˈsplɪkəbəl] *adj* : inexplicable

infallible [ɪnˈfæləbəl] *adj* : infalible

infamous [ˈɪnfəməs] *adj* : infame

infancy [ˈɪnfəntsi] *n, pl* **-cies** : infancia *f* — **infant** [ˈɪnfənt] *n* : bebé *m;* niño *m,* -ña *f* — **infantile** [ˈɪnfənˌtaɪl, -təl, -ˌtiːl] *adj* : infantil

infantry [ˈɪnfəntri] *n, pl* **-tries** : infantería *f*

infatuated [ɪnˈfætʃuˌeɪt̬əd] *adj* **be ~ with** : estar encaprichado con — **infatuation** [ɪnˌfætʃuˈeɪʃən] *n* : encaprichamiento *m*

infect [ɪnˈfɛkt] *vt* : infectar — **infection** [ɪnˈfɛkʃən] *n* : infección *f* — **infectious** [ɪnˈfɛkʃəs] *adj* : contagioso

infer [ɪnˈfər] *vt* **inferred; inferring** : deducir, inferir — **inference** [ˈɪnfərənts] *n* : deducción *f*

inferior [ɪnˈfɪriər] *adj* : inferior — **~** *n* : inferior *mf* — **inferiority** [ɪnˌfɪriˈɔrət̬i] *n, pl* **-ties** : inferioridad *f*

infernal [ɪnˈfərnəl] *adj* : infernal — **inferno** [ɪnˈfərˌnoː] *n, pl* **-nos** : infierno *m*

infertile [ɪnˈfərt̬əl, -ˌtaɪl] *adj* : estéril — **infertility** [ˌɪnfərˈtɪlət̬i] *n* : esterilidad *f*

infest [ɪnˈfɛst] *vt* : infestar

infidelity [ˌɪnfəˈdɛlət̬i, -faɪ-] *n, pl* **-ties** : infidelidad *f*

infiltrate [ɪnˈfɪlˌtreɪt, ˈɪnfɪl-] *v* **-trated; -trating** *vt* : infiltrar — *vi* : infiltrarse

infinite [ˈɪnfənət] *adj* : infinito

infinitive [ɪnˈfɪnət̬ɪv] *n* : infinitivo *m*

infinity [ɪnˈfɪnət̬i] *n, pl* **-ties 1** : infinito *m* **2 an ~ of** : una infinidad de

infirm [ɪnˈfərm] *adj* : enfermizo, endeble — **infirmary** [ɪnˈfərməri] *n, pl* **-ries** : enfermería *f* — **infirmity** [ɪnˈfərmət̬i] *n, pl* **-ties 1** FRAILTY : endeblez *f* **2** AILMENT : enfermedad *f*

inflame [ɪnˈfleɪm] *vt* **-flamed; -flaming** : inflamar — **inflammable** [ɪnˈflæməbəl] *adj* : inflamable — **inflammation** [ˌɪnfləˈmeɪʃən] *n* : inflamación *f* — **inflammatory** [ɪnˈflæməˌtori] *adj* : inflamatorio

inflate [ɪnˈfleɪt] *vt* **-flated; -flating** : inflar — **inflation** [ɪnˈfleɪʃən] *n* : inflación *f* — **inflationary** [ɪnˈfleɪʃəˌnɛri] *adj* : inflacionario, inflacionista

inflexible [ɪnˈflɛksɪbəl] *adj* : inflexible

inflict [ɪnˈflɪkt] *vt* : infligir

influence [ˈɪnˌfluːənts, ɪnˈfluːənts] *n* **1** : influencia *f* **2 under the ~** : embriagado — **~** *vt* **-enced; -encing** : influir en, influenciar — **influential** [ˌɪnfluˈɛntʃəl] *adj* : influyente

influenza [ˌɪnfluˈɛnzə] *n* : gripe *f,* influenza *f*

influx [ˈɪnˌflʌks] *n* : afluencia *f*

inform [ɪnˈfɔrm] *vt* **1** : informar **2 keep me ~ed** : manténme al corriente — *vi* **~ on** : delatar, denunciar

informal [ɪn'fɔrməl] *adj* **1** : informal **2** : familiar (dícese del lenguaje) — **informality** [,ɪnfɔr'mæləṭi, -fər-] *n, pl* **-ties** : falta *f* de ceremonia — **informally** [ɪn'fɔrməli] *adv* : de manera informal
information [,ɪnfər'meɪʃən] *n* : información *f* — **informative** [ɪn'fɔrməṭɪv] *adj* : informativo — **informer** [ɪn'fɔrmər] *n* : informante *mf*
infrared [,ɪnfrə'rɛd] *adj* : infrarrojo
infrastructure ['ɪnfrə,strʌktʃər] *n* : infraestructura *f*
infrequent [ɪn'fri:kwənt] *adj* : infrequente — **infrequently** [ɪn'fri:kwəntli] *adv* : raramente
infringe [ɪn'frɪndʒ] *v* **-fringed; -fringing** *vt* : infringir — *vi* ~ **on** : violar — **infringement** [ɪn'frɪndʒmənt] *n* : violación *f*
infuriate [ɪn'fjʊri,eɪt] *vt* **-ated; -ating** : enfurecer, poner furioso — **infuriating** [ɪn'fjʊri,eɪṭɪŋ] *adj* : exasperante
infuse [ɪn'fju:z] *vt* **-fused; -fusing** : infundir — **infusion** [ɪn'fju:ʒən] *n* : infusión *f*
ingenious [ɪn'dʒi:njəs] *adj* : ingenioso — **ingenuity** [,ɪndʒə'nu:əṭi, -'nju:-] *n, pl* **-ities** : ingenio
ingenuous [ɪn'dʒenjʊəs] *adj* : ingenuo
ingest [ɪn'dʒɛst] *vt* : ingerir
ingot ['ɪŋgət] *n* : lingote *m*
ingrained [ɪn'greɪnd] *adj* : arraigado
ingratiate [ɪn'greɪʃi,eɪt] *vt* **-ated; -ating** ~ **oneself with** : congraciarse con
ingratitude [ɪn'græṭə,tu:d, -,tju:d] *n* : ingratitud *f*
ingredient [ɪn'gri:diənt] *n* : ingrediente *m*
ingrown ['ɪn,gro:n] *adj* ~ **nail** : uña *f* encarnada
inhabit [ɪn'hæbət] *vt* : habitar — **inhabitant** [ɪn'hæbəṭənt] *n* : habitante *mf*
inhale [ɪn'heɪl] *v* **-haled; -haling** *vt* : inhalar, aspirar — *vi* : inspirar
inherent [ɪn'hɪrənt, -'hɛr-] *adj* : inherente — **inherently** [ɪn'hɪrəntli, -'hɛr-] *adv* : intrínsecamente
inherit [ɪn'hɛrət] *vt* : heredar — **inheritance** [ɪn'hɛrəṭənts] *n* : herencia *f*
inhibit [ɪn'hɪbət] *vt* IMPEDE : inhibir — **inhibition** [,ɪnhə'bɪʃən, ,ɪnə-] *n* : inhibición *f*
inhuman [ɪn'hju:mən, -'ju:-] *adj* : inhumano — **inhumane** [,ɪnhju'meɪn, -ju-] *adj* : inhumano — **inhumanity** [,ɪnhju'mænəṭi, -ju-] *n, pl* **-ties** : inhumanidad *f*
initial [ɪ'nɪʃəl] *adj* : inicial — *n* : inicial *f* — *vt* **-tialed** *or* **-tialled; -tialing** *or* **-tialling** : poner las iniciales a
initiate [ɪ'nɪʃi,eɪt] *vt* **-ated; -ating 1** BEGIN : iniciar **2** ~ **s.o. into sth** : iniciar a algn en algo — **initiation** [ɪ,nɪʃi'eɪʃən] *n* : iniciación *f* — **initiative** [ɪ'nɪʃəṭɪv] *n* : iniciativa *f*
inject [ɪn'dʒɛkt] *vt* : inyectar — **injection** [ɪn'dʒɛkʃən] *n* : inyección *f*
injure ['ɪndʒər] *vt* **-jured; -juring 1** : herir **2** ~ **oneself** : hacerse daño — **injurious** [ɪn'dʒʊriəs] *adj* : perjudicial — **injury** ['ɪndʒəri] *n, pl* **-ries 1** : herida *f* **2** HARM : perjuicio *m*
injustice [ɪn'dʒʌstəs] *n* : injusticia *f*
ink ['ɪŋk] *n* : tinta *f* — **inkwell** ['ɪŋk,wɛl] *n* : tintero *m*
inland ['ɪn,lænd, -lənd] *adj* : interior — ~ *adv* : hacia el interior, tierra adentro
in–laws ['ɪn,lɔz] *npl* : suegros *mpl*
inlet ['ɪn,lɛt, -lət] *n* : ensenada *f*, cala *f*
inmate ['ɪn,meɪt] *n* **1** PATIENT : paciente *mf* **2** PRISONER : preso *m*, -sa *f*
inn ['ɪn] *n* : posada *f*, hostería *f*
innards ['ɪnərdz] *npl* : entrañas *fpl*, tripas *fpl fam*
innate [ɪ'neɪt] *adj* : innato
inner ['ɪnər] *adj* : interior, interno — **innermost** ['ɪnər,mo:st] *adj* : más íntimo, más profundo
inning ['ɪnɪŋ] *n* : entrada *f*
innocent ['ɪnəsənt] *adj* : inocente — ~ *n* : inocente *mf* — **innocence** ['ɪnəsənts] *n* : inocencia *f*
innocuous [ɪ'nɑkjəwəs] *adj* : inocuo
innovate ['ɪnə,veɪt] *vi* **-vated; -vating** : innovar — **innovation** [,ɪnə'veɪʃən] *n* : innovación *f* — **innovative** ['ɪnə,veɪṭɪv] *adj* : innovador — **innovator** ['ɪnə,veɪṭər] *n* : innovador *m*, -dora *f*
innuendo [,ɪnjʊ'endo] *n, pl* **-dos** *or* **-does** : insinuación *f*, indirecta *f*
innumerable [ɪ'nu:mərəbəl, -'nju:-] *adj* : innumerable
inoculate [ɪ'nɑkjə,leɪt] *vt* **-lated; -lating** : inocular — **inoculation** [ɪ,nɑkjə'leɪʃən] *n* : inoculación *f*
inoffensive [,ɪnə'fɛntsɪv] *adj* : inofensivo
inpatient ['ɪn,peɪʃənt] *n* : paciente *mf* hospitalizado
input ['ɪn,pʊt] *n* **1** : contribución *f* **2** : entrada *f* (de datos) — ~ *vt* **-putted** *or* **-put; -putting** : entrar (datos, etc.)
inquire [ɪn'kwaɪr] *v* **-quired; -quiring** *vt* : preguntar — *vi* **1** ~ **about** : informarse sobre **2** ~ **into** : investigar — **inquiry** ['ɪn,kwaɪri, ɪn'kwaɪri; 'ɪnkwəri, 'ɪŋ-] *n, pl* **-ries 1** QUESTION : pregunta *f* **2** INVESTIGATION : investigación *f* — **inquisition** [,ɪnkwə'zɪʃən, ,ɪŋ-] *n* : in-

quisición *f* — **inquisitive** [ɪnˈkwɪzət̬ɪv] *adj* : curioso
insane [ɪnˈseɪn] *adj* : loco — **insanity** [ɪnˈsænət̬i] *n, pl* **-ties** : locura *f*
insatiable [ɪnˈseɪʃəbəl] *adj* : insaciable
inscribe [ɪnˈskraɪb] *vt* **-scribed; -scribing** : inscribir — **inscription** [ɪnˈskrɪpʃən] *n* : inscripción *f*
inscrutable [ɪnˈskruːt̬əbəl] *adj* : inescrutable
insect [ˈɪn,sɛkt] *n* : insecto *m* — **insecticide** [ɪnˈsɛktə,saɪd] *n* : insecticida *m*
insecure [,ɪnsɪˈkjʊr] *adj* : inseguro, poco seguro — **insecurity** [,ɪnsɪˈkjʊrət̬i] *n, pl* **-ties** : inseguridad *f*
insensitive [ɪnˈsɛntsət̬ɪv] *adj* : insensible — **insensitivity** [ɪn,sɛntsəˈtɪvət̬i] *n, pl* **-ties** : insensibilidad *f*
inseparable [ɪnˈsɛpərəbəl] *adj* : inseparable
insert [ɪnˈsərt] *vt* : insertar (texto), introducir (una moneda, etc.)
inside [ɪnˈsaɪd, ˈɪn,saɪd] *n* **1** : interior *m* **2** ~ **out** : al revés — *adv* : dentro, adentro — ~ *adj* : interior — ~ *prep* **1** *or* ~ **of** : dentro de **2** ~ **an hour** : en menos de una hora
insidious [ɪnˈsɪdiəs] *adj* : insidioso
insight [ˈɪn,saɪt] *n* : perspicacia *f*
insignia [ɪnˈsɪgniə] *or* **insigne** [-,niː] *n, pl* **-nia** *or* **-nias** : insignia *f*, enseña *f*
insignificant [,ɪnsɪgˈnɪfɪkənt] *adj* : insignificante
insincere [,ɪnsɪnˈsɪr] *adj* : insincero
insinuate [ɪnˈsɪnjʊ,eɪt] *vt* **-ated; -ating** : insinuar — **insinuation** [ɪn,sɪnjʊˈeɪʃən] *n* : insinuación *f*
insipid [ɪnˈsɪpəd] *adj* : insípido
insist [ɪnˈsɪst] *v* : insistir — **insistent** [ɪnˈsɪstənt] *adj* : insistente
insofar as [,ɪnsoˈfɑræz] *conj* : en la medida en que
insole [ˈɪn,soːl] *n* : plantilla *f*
insolent [ˈɪntsələnt] *adj* : insolente — **insolence** [ˈɪntsələnts] *n* : insolencia *f*
insolvent [ɪnˈsɑlvənt] *adj* : insolvente
insomnia [ɪnˈsɑmniə] *n* : insomnio *m*
inspect [ɪnˈspɛkt] *vt* : inspeccionar, revisar — **inspection** [ɪnˈspɛkʃən] *n* : inspección *f* — **inspector** [ɪnˈspɛktər] *n* : inspector *m*, **-tora** *f*
inspire [ɪnˈspaɪr] *vt* **-spired; -spiring** : inspirar — **inspiration** [,ɪntspəˈreɪʃən] *n* : inspiración *f* — **inspirational** [,ɪntspəˈreɪʃənəl] *adj* : inspirador
instability [,ɪntstəˈbɪlət̬i] *n, pl* **-ties** : inestabilidad *f*
install [ɪnˈstɔl] *vt* **-stalled; -stalling** : instalar — **installation** [,ɪntstəˈleɪʃən] *n* : instalación *f* — **installment** [ɪnˈstɔlmənt] *n* **1** PAYMENT : plazo *m*, cuota *f* **2** : entrega *f* (de una publicación o telenovela)
instance [ˈɪntstənts] *n* **1** : ejemplo *m* **2 for** ~ : por ejemplo **3 in this** ~ : en este caso
instant [ˈɪntstənt] *n* : instante *m* — ~ *adj* **1** IMMEDIATE : inmediato **2** ~ **coffee** : café *m* instantáneo — **instantaneous** [,ɪntstənˈteɪniəs] *adj* : instantáneo — **instantly** [ˈɪntstəntli] *adv* : al instante, instantáneamente
instead [ɪnˈstɛd] *adv* **1** : en cambio **2 I went** ~ : fui en su lugar — **instead of** *prep* : en vez de, en lugar de
instep [ˈɪn,stɛp] *n* : empeine *m*
instigate [ˈɪntstə,geɪt] *vt* **-gated; -gating** : instigar a — **instigation** [,ɪntstəˈgeɪʃən] *n* : instigación *f* — **instigator** [ˈɪntstə,geɪt̬ər] *n* : instigador *m*, **-dora** *f*
instill [ɪnˈstɪl] *or Brit* **instil** *vt* **-stilled; -stilling** : inculcar, infundir
instinct [ˈɪn,stɪŋkt] *n* : instinto *m* — **instinctive** [ɪnˈstɪŋktɪv] *or* **instinctual** [ɪnˈstɪŋktʃʊəl] *adj* : instintivo
institute [ˈɪntstə,tuːt, -,tjuːt] *vt* **-tuted; -tuting 1** : instituir **2** INITIATE : iniciar — ~ *n* : instituto *m* — **institution** [,ɪntstəˈtuːʃən, -ˈtjuː-] *n* : institución *f*
instruct [ɪnˈstrʌkt] *vt* **1** : instruir **2** COMMAND : mandar — **instruction** [ɪnˈstrʌkʃən] *n* : instrucción *f* — **instructor** [ɪnˈstrʌktər] *n* : instructor *m*, **-tora** *f*
instrument [ˈɪntstrəmənt] *n* : instrumento *m* — **instrumental** [,ɪntstrəˈmɛntəl] *adj* **1** : instrumental **2 be** ~ **in** : jugar un papel fundamental en
insubordinate [,ɪnsəˈbɔrdənət] *adj* : insubordinado — **insubordination** [,ɪnsə,bɔrdənˈeɪʃən] *n* : insubordinación *f*
insufferable [ɪnˈsʌfərəbəl] *adj* : insoportable
insufficient [,ɪnsəˈfɪʃənt] *adj* : insuficiente
insular [ˈɪntsʊlər, -sjʊ-] *adj* **1** : insular **2** NARROW-MINDED : estrecho de miras
insulate [ˈɪntsə,leɪt] *vt* **-lated; -lating** : aislar — **insulation** [,ɪntsəˈleɪʃən] *n* : aislamiento *m*
insulin [ˈɪntsələn] *n* : insulina *f*
insult [ɪnˈsʌlt] *vt* : insultar — ~ [ˈɪn,sʌlt] *n* : insulto *m* — **insulting** [ɪnˈsʌltɪŋ] *adj* : insultante, ofensivo
insure [ɪnˈʃʊr] *vt* **-sured; -suring** : asegurar — **insurance** [ɪnˈʃʊrənts, ˈɪn,ʃʊr-] *n* : seguro *m*
insurmountable [,ɪnsərˈmaʊntəbəl] *adj* : insuperable
intact [ɪnˈtækt] *adj* : intacto

intake ['ɪn,teɪk] *n* : consumo *m* (de alimentos), entrada *f* (de aire, etc.)
intangible [ɪn'tændʒəbəl] *adj* : intangible
integral ['ɪntɪgrəl] *adj* : integral
integrate ['ɪntə,greɪt] *v* **-grated; -grating** *vt* : integrar — *vi* : integrarse
integrity [ɪn'tɛgrəṭi] *n* : integridad *f*
intellect ['ɪntəl,ɛkt] *n* : intelecto *m* — **intellectual** [,ɪntə'lɛktʃuəl] *adj* : intelectual — ~ *n* : intelectual *mf* — **intelligence** [ɪn'tɛlədʒənts] *n* : inteligencia *f* — **intelligent** [ɪn'tɛlədʒənt] *adj* : inteligente — **intelligible** [ɪn'tɛlədʒəbəl] *adj* : inteligible
intend [ɪn'tɛnd] *vt* **1 be ~ed for** : ser para **2 ~ to do** : pensar hacer, tener la intención de hacer — **intended** [ɪn'tɛndəd] *adj* : intencionado, deliberado
intense [ɪn'tɛnts] *adj* : intenso — **intensely** [ɪn'tɛntsli] *adv* : sumamente, profundamente — **intensify** [ɪn'tɛntsə,faɪ] *v* **-fied; -fying** *vt* : intensificar — *vi* : intensificarse — **intensity** [ɪn'tɛntsəṭi] *n, pl* **-ties** : intensidad *f* — **intensive** [ɪn'tɛntsɪv] *adj* : intensivo
intent [ɪn'tɛnt] *n* : intención *f* — ~ *adj* **1** : atento, concentrado **2 ~ on doing** : resuelto a hacer — **intention** [ɪn'tɛntʃən] *n* : intención *f* — **intentional** [ɪn'tɛntʃənəl] *adj* : intencional, deliberado — **intently** [ɪn'tɛntli] *adv* : atentamente, fijamente
interact [,ɪntər'ækt] *vi* **1** : interactuar **2 ~ with** : relacionarse con — **interaction** [,ɪntər'ækʃən] *n* : interacción *f* — **interactive** [,ɪntər'æktɪv] *adj* : interactivo
intercede [,ɪntər'si:d] *vi* **-ceded; -ceding** : interceder
intercept [,ɪntər'sɛpt] *vt* : interceptar
interchange [,ɪntər'tʃeɪndʒ] *vt* **-changed; -changing** : intercambiar — ~ ['ɪntər,tʃeɪndʒ] *n* **1** : intercambio *m* **2** JUNCTION : enlace *m* — **interchangeable** [,ɪntər'tʃeɪndʒəbəl] *adj* : intercambiable
intercourse ['ɪntər,kors] *n* : relaciones *fpl* (sexuales)
interest ['ɪntrəst, -tə,rɛst] *n* : interés *m* — ~ *vt* : interesar — **interested** [-əd] *adj* : interesado — **interesting** ['ɪntrəstɪŋ, -tə,rɛstɪŋ] *adj* : interesante
interface ['ɪntər,feɪs] *n* : interfaz *mf* (de una computadora)
interfere [,ɪntər'fɪr] *vi* **-fered; -fering 1 ~ in** : entrometerse en, interferir en **2 ~ with** DISRUPT : afectar (una actividad, etc.) — **interference** [,ɪntər'fɪrənts] *n* **1** : interferencia *f* **2** : intromisión *f* (en el radio, etc.)
interim ['ɪntərəm] *n* **1** : interín *m* **2 in the ~** : mientras tanto — ~ *adj* : interino, provisional
interior [ɪn'tɪriər] *adj* : interior — ~ *n* : interior *m*
interjection [,ɪntər'dʒɛkʃən] *n* : interjección *f*
interlock [,ɪntər'lɑk] *vt* : engranar
interloper [,ɪntər'lo:pər] *n* : intruso *m*, -sa *f*
interlude ['ɪntər,lu:d] *n* **1** : intervalo *m* **2** : interludio *m* (en música, etc.)
intermediate [,ɪntər'mi:diət] *adj* : intermedio — **intermediary** [,ɪntər'mi:di,ɛri] *n, pl* **-aries** : intermediario *m*, -ria *f*
interminable [ɪn'tərmənəbəl] *adj* : interminable
intermission [,ɪntər'mɪʃən] *n* : intervalo *m*, intermedio *m*
intermittent [,ɪntər'mɪtənt] *adj* : intermitente
intern[1] ['ɪn,tərn, ɪn'tərn] *vt* : confinar
intern[2] ['ɪn,tərn] *vi* : hacer las prácticas — ~ *n* : interno *m*, -na *f*
internal [ɪn'tərnəl] *adj* : interno
international [,ɪntər'næʃənəl] *adj* : internacional
interpret [ɪn'tərprət] *vt* : interpretar — **interpretation** [ɪn,tərprə'teɪʃən] *n* : interpretación *f* — **interpreter** [ɪn'tərprəṭər] *n* : intérprete *mf*
interrogate [ɪn'tɛrə,geɪt] *vt* **-gated; -gating** : interrogar — **interrogation** [ɪn,tɛrə'geɪʃən] *n* QUESTIONING : interrogatorio *m* — **interrogative** [,ɪntə'rɑgəṭɪv] *adj* : interrogativo
interrupt [,ɪntə'rʌpt] *v* : interrumpir — **interruption** [,ɪntə'rʌpʃən] *n* : interrupción *f*
intersect [,ɪntər'sɛkt] *vt* : cruzar (dícese de calles), cortar (dícese de líneas) — *vi* : cruzarse, cortarse — **intersection** [,ɪntər'sɛkʃən] *n* : cruce *m*, intersección *f*
intersperse [,ɪntər'spərs] *vt* **-spersed; -spersing** : intercalar
interstate [,ɪntər'steɪt] *n or* **~ highway** : carretera *f* interestatal
intertwine [,ɪntər'twaɪn] *vi* **-twined; -twining** : entrelazarse
interval ['ɪntərvəl] *n* : intervalo *m*
intervene [,ɪntər'vi:n] *vi* **-vened; -vening 1** : intervenir **2** ELAPSE : transcurrir, pasar — **intervention** [,ɪntər'vɛntʃən] *n* : intervención *f*
interview ['ɪntər,vju:] *n* : entrevista *f* — ~ *vt* : entrevistar — **interviewer** ['ɪntər,vju:ər] *n* : entrevistador *m*, -dora *f*

intestine [ɪn'tɛstən] *n* : intestino *m* — **intestinal** [ɪn'tɛstənəl] *adj* : intestinal
intimate[1] ['ɪntə,meɪt] *vt* **-mated; -mating** : insinuar, dar a entender
intimate[2] ['ɪntəmət] *adj* : íntimo — **intimacy** ['ɪntəməsi] *n, pl* **-cies** : intimidad *f*
intimidate [ɪn'tɪmə,deɪt] *vt* **-dated; -dating** : intimidar — **intimidation** [ɪn,tɪmə'deɪʃən] *n* : intimidación *f*
into ['ɪn,tu:] *prep* **1** : en, a **2 bump ~** : darse contra **3** (*used in mathematics*) **3 ~ 12** : 12 dividido por 3
intolerable [ɪn'tɑlərəbəl] *adj* : intolerable — **intolerance** [ɪn'tɑlərənts] *n* : intolerancia *f* — **intolerant** [ɪn'tɑlərənt] *adj* : intolerante
intoxicate [ɪn'tɑksə,keɪt] *vt* **-cated; -cating** : embriagar — **intoxicated** [ɪn'tɑksə,keɪt̬əd] *adj* **1** : embriagado **2 ~ with** : ebrio de
intransitive [ɪn'træntsət̬ɪv, -'trænzə-] *adj* : intransitivo
intravenous [,ɪntrə'vi:nəs] *adj* : intravenoso
intrepid [ɪn'trɛpəd] *adj* : intrépido
intricate ['ɪntrɪkət] *adj* : complicado, intrincado — **intricacy** ['ɪntrɪkəsi] *n, pl* **-cies** : complejidad *f*
intrigue ['ɪn,tri:g, ɪn'tri:g] *n* : intriga *f* — **~** [ɪn'tri:g] *v* **-trigued; -triguing** : intrigar — **intriguing** [ɪn'tri:gɪŋli] *adj* : intrigante
intrinsic [ɪn'trɪnzɪk, -'trɪntsɪk] *adj* : intrínseco
introduce [,ɪntrə'du:s, -'dju:s] *vt* **-duced; -ducing 1** : introducir **2** : presentar (a una persona) — **introduction** [,ɪntrə'dʌkʃən] *n* **1** : introducción *f* **2** : presentación *f* (de una persona) — **introductory** [,ɪntrə'dʌktəri] *adj* : introductorio
introvert ['ɪntrə,vərt] *n* : introvertido *m*, -da *f* — **introverted** ['ɪntrə,vərt̬əd] *adj* : introvertido
intrude [ɪn'tru:d] *vi* **-truded; -truding 1** : entrometerse **2 ~ on s.o.** : molestar a algn — **intruder** [ɪn'tru:dər] *n* : intruso *m*, -sa *f* — **intrusion** [ɪn'tru:ʒən] *n* : intrusión *f* — **intrusive** [ɪn'tru:sɪv] *adj* : intruso
intuition [,ɪntʊ'ɪʃən, -tjʊ-] *n* : intuición *f* — **intuitive** [ɪn'tu:ət̬ɪv, -'tju:-] *adj* : intuitivo
inundate ['ɪnən,deɪt] *vt* **-dated; -dating** : inundar
invade [ɪn'veɪd] *vt* **-vaded; -vading** : invadir
invalid[1] [ɪn'væləd] *adj* : inválido
invalid[2] ['ɪnvələd] *n* : inválido *m*, -da *f*
invaluable [ɪn'væljəbəl, -'væljʊə-] *adj* : inestimable, invalorable *Lat*
invariable [ɪn'væriəbəl] *adj* : invariable
invasion [ɪn'veɪʒən] *n* : invasión *f*
invent [ɪn'vɛnt] *vt* : inventar — **invention** [ɪn'vɛntʃən] *n* : invención *f* — **inventive** [ɪn'vɛntɪv] *adj* : inventivo — **inventor** [ɪn'vɛntər] *n* : inventor *m*, -tora *f*
inventory ['ɪnvən,tɔri] *n, pl* **-ries** : inventario *m*
invert [ɪn'vərt] *vt* : invertir
invertebrate [ɪn'vərt̬əbrət, -,breɪt] *adj* : invertebrado — **~** *n* : invertebrado *m*
invest [ɪn'vɛst] *vt* : invertir
investigate [ɪn'vɛstə,geɪt] *v* **-gated; -gating** : investigar — **investigation** [ɪn,vɛstə'geɪʃən] *n* : investigación *f* — **investigator** [ɪn'vɛstə,geɪt̬ər] *n* : investigador *m*, -dora *f*
investment [ɪn'vɛstmənt] *n* : inversión *f* — **investor** [ɪn'vɛstər] *n* : inversor *m*, -sora *f*
inveterate [ɪn'vɛt̬ərət] *adj* : inveterado
invigorating [ɪn'vɪgə,reɪt̬ɪŋ] *adj* : vigorizante
invincible [ɪn'vɪntsəbəl] *adj* : invencible
invisible [ɪn'vɪzəbəl] *adj* : invisible
invitation [,ɪnvə'teɪʃən] *n* : invitación *f* — **invite** [ɪn'vaɪt] *vt* **-vited; -viting 1** : invitar **2** SEEK : buscar (problemas, etc.) — **inviting** [ɪn'vaɪt̬ɪŋ] *adj* : atrayente
invoice ['ɪn,vɔɪs] *n* : factura *f*
invoke [ɪn'vo:k] *vt* **-voked; -voking** : invocar
involuntary [ɪn'vɑlən,tɛri] *adj* : involuntario
involve [ɪn'vɑlv] *vt* **-volved; -volving 1** CONCERN : concernir, afectar **2** ENTAIL : suponer — **involved** [ɪn'vɑlvd] *adj* **1** COMPLEX : complicado **2** CONCERNED : afectado — **involvement** [ɪn'vɑlvmənt] *n* : participación *f*
invulnerable [ɪn'vʌlnərəbəl] *adj* : invulnerable
inward ['ɪnwərd] *adj* INNER : interior, interno — **~** *or* **inwards** [-wərdz] *adv* : hacia adentro, hacia el interior
iodine ['aɪə,daɪn, -dən] *n* : yodo *m*, tintura *f* de yodo
ion ['aɪən, 'aɪ,ɑn] *n* : ion *m*
iota [aɪ'o:t̬ə] *n* : pizca *f*, ápice *m*
IOU [,aɪ,o'ju:] *n* : pagaré *m*, vale *m*
Iranian [ɪ'reɪniən, -'ræ-, -'rɑ-; aɪ'-] *adj* : iraní
Iraqi [ɪ'rɑki, -'ræk-] *adj* : iraquí
ire ['aɪr] *n* : ira *f* — **irate** [aɪ'reɪt] *adj* : furioso
iris ['aɪrəs] *n, pl* **irises** *or* **irides** ['aɪrə-

ˌdiːz, ˈɪr-] **1 :** iris *m* (del ojo) **2 :** lirio *m* (planta)
Irish [ˈaɪrɪʃ] *adj* **:** irlandés
irksome [ˈərksəm] *adj* **:** irritante, fastidioso
iron [ˈaɪərn] *n* **1 :** hierro *m,* fierro *m Lat* (metal) **2 :** plancha *f* (para la ropa) — **~** *v* **:** planchar
ironic [aɪˈrɑnɪk] *or* **ironical** [-nɪkəl] *adj* **:** irónico
ironing board *n* **:** tabla *f* (de planchar)
irony [ˈaɪrəni] *n, pl* **-nies :** ironía *f*
irrational [ɪˈræʃənəl] *adj* **:** irracional
irreconcilable [ɪˌrɛkənˈsaɪləbəl] *adj* **:** irreconciliable
irrefutable [ˌɪrɪˈfjuːţəbəl, ɪrˈrɛfjə-] *adj* **:** irrefutable
irregular [ɪˈrɛgjələr] *adj* **:** irregular — **irregularity** [ɪˌrɛgjəˈlærəţi] *n, pl* **-ties :** irregularidad *f*
irrelevant [ɪˈrɛləvənt] *adj* **:** irrelevante
irreparable [ɪˈrɛpərəbəl] *adj* **:** irreparable
irreplaceable [ˌɪrɪˈpleɪsəbəl] *adj* **:** irreemplazable
irresistible [ˌɪrɪˈzɪsţəbəl] *adj* **:** irresistible
irresolute [ɪˈrɛzəˌluːt] *adj* **:** irresoluto
irrespective of [ˌɪrɪˈspɛktɪvəv] *prep* **:** sin tener en cuenta
irresponsible [ˌɪrɪˈspɑntsəbəl] *adj* **:** irresponsable — **irresponsibility** [ˌɪrɪˌspɑntsəˈbɪləţi] *n, pl* **-ties :** irresponsabilidad *f*
irreverent [ɪˈrɛvərənt] *adj* **:** irreverente
irreversible [ˌɪrɪˈvərsəbəl] *adj* **:** irreversible, irrevocable
irrigate [ˈɪrəˌgeɪt] *vt* **-gated; -gating :** irrigar, regar — **irrigation** [ˌɪrəˈgeɪʃən] *n* **:** irrigación *f,* riego *m*
irritate [ˈɪrəˌteɪt] *vt* **-tated; -tating :** irritar — **irritable** [ˈɪrəţəbəl] *adj* **:** irritable — **irritably** [ˈɪrəţəbli] *adv* **:** con irritación — **irritating** [ˈɪrəˌteɪţɪŋ] *adj* **:** irritante — **irritation** [ˌɪrəˈteɪʃən] *n* **:** irritación *f*
is → **be**
Islam [ɪsˈlɑm, ɪz-, -ˈlæm; ˈɪsˌlɑm, ˈɪz-, -ˌlæm] *n* **:** el Islam — **Islamic** [ɪsˈlɑmɪk, ɪz-, -ˈlæ-] *adj* **:** islámico
island [ˈaɪlənd] *n* **:** isla *f* — **isle** [ˈaɪl] *n* **:** isla *f*
isolate [ˈaɪsəˌleɪt] *vt* **-lated; -lating :** aislar — **isolation** [ˌaɪsəˈleɪʃən] *n* **:** aislamiento *m*
Israeli [ɪzˈreɪli] *adj* **:** israelí
issue [ˈɪˌʃuː] *n* **1** MATTER **:** asunto *m,* cuestión *f* **2 :** número *m* (de una revista, etc.) **3 make an ~ of :** insistir demasiado sobre **4 take ~ with :** disentir de — **~** *v* **-sued; -suing** *vi* **~ from :** surgir de — *vt* **1 :** emitir (sellos, etc.), distribuir (provisiones, etc.) **2** PUBLISH **:** publicar
isthmus [ˈɪsməs] *n* **:** istmo *m*
it [ˈɪt] *pron* **1** (*as subject*) **:** él, ella **2** (*as indirect object*) **:** le, se **3** (*as direct object*) **:** lo, la **4** (*as object of a preposition*) **:** él, ella **5 it's raining :** está lloviendo **6 it's 8 o'clock :** son las ocho **7 it's hot out :** hace calor **8 ~ is necessary :** es necesario **9 who is ~? :** ¿quién es? **10 it's me :** soy yo
Italian [ɪˈtæliən, aɪ-] *adj* **:** italiano — **~** *n* **:** italiano *m* (idioma)
italics [ɪˈtælɪks, aɪ-] *n* **:** cursiva *f*
itch [ˈɪtʃ] *vi* **1 :** picar **2 be ~ing to :** morirse por — **~** *n* **:** picazón *f* — **itchy** [ˈɪtʃi] *adj* **itchier; -est :** que pica
it'd [ˈɪţəd] (*contraction of* **it had** *or* **it would**) → **have, would**
item [ˈaɪţəm] *n* **1 :** artículo *m* **2 :** punto *m* (en una agenda) **3 ~ of clothing :** prenda *f* de vestir **4 news ~ :** noticia *f* — **itemize** [ˈaɪţəˌmaɪz] *vt* **-ized; -izing :** detallar, enumerar
itinerant [aɪˈtɪnərənt] *adj* **:** ambulante
itinerary [aɪˈtɪnəˌrɛri] *n, pl* **-aries :** itinerario *m*
it'll [ˈɪţəl] (*contraction of* **it shall** *or* **it will**) → **shall, will**
its [ˈɪts] *adj* **:** su, sus
it's [ˈɪts] (*contraction of* **it is** *or* **it has**) → **be, have**
itself [ɪtˈsɛlf] *pron* **1** (*used reflexively*) **:** se **2** (*used for emphasis*) **:** (él) mismo, (ella) misma, sí (mismo) **3 by ~ :** solo
I've [ˈaɪv] (*contraction of* **I have**) → **have**
ivory [ˈaɪvəri] *n, pl* **-ries :** marfil *m*
ivy [ˈaɪvi] *n, pl* **ivies :** hiedra *f*

J

j ['dʒeɪ] *n, pl* **j's** *or* **js** ['dʒeɪz] : j *f*, décima letra del alfabeto inglés

jab ['dʒæb] *vt* **jabbed; jabbing 1** PIERCE : pinchar **2** POKE : golpear (con la punta de algo) — **~** *n* **1** PRICK : pinchazo *m* **2** POKE : golpe *m* abrupto

jabber ['dʒæbər] *vi* : farfullar

jack ['dʒæk] *n* **1** : gato *m* (mecanismo) **2** : sota *f* (de naipes) — **~** *vt or* **~ up 1** : levantar (con un gato) **2** INCREASE : subir

jackal ['dʒækəl] *n* : chacal *m*

jackass ['dʒæk,æs] *n* : asno *m*, burro *m*

jacket ['dʒækət] *n* **1** : chaqueta *f* **2** : sobrecubierta *f* (de un libro), carátula *f* (de un disco)

jackhammer ['dʒæk,hæmər] *n* : martillo *m* neumático

jackknife ['dʒæk,naɪf] *n* : navaja *f* — **~** *vi* **-knifed; -knifing** : plegarse (dícese de un camión)

jack–o'–lantern ['dʒækə,læntərn] *n* : linterna *f* hecha de una calabaza

jackpot ['dʒæk,pɑt] *n* : premio *m* gordo

jaded ['dʒeɪdəd] *adj* **1** TIRED : agotado **2** BORED : hastiado

jagged ['dʒægəd] *adj* : dentado

jail ['dʒeɪl] *n* : cárcel *f* — **~** *vt* : encarcelar — **jailer** *or* **jailor** ['dʒeɪlər] *n* : carcelero *m*, -ra *f*

jalapeño [,hɑlə'peɪnjo, ,hæ-, -'pi:no] *n* : jalapeño *m Lat*

jam[1] ['dʒæm] *v* **jammed; jamming** *vt* **1** CRAM : apiñar, embutir **2** BLOCK : atascar, atorar — *vi* : atascarse, atrancarse — **~** *n* **1** *or* **traffic ~** : embotellamiento *m* (de tráfico) **2** FIX : lío *m*, aprieto *m*

jam[2] *n* PRESERVES : mermelada *f*

jangle ['dʒæŋgəl] *v* **-gled; -gling** *vi* : hacer un ruido metálico — *vt* : hacer sonar — **~** *n* : ruido *m* metálico

janitor ['dʒænəṯər] *n* : portero *m*, -ra *f*; conserje *mf*

January ['dʒænjʊ,ɛri] *n* : enero *m*

Japanese [,dʒæpə'ni:z, -'ni:s] *adj* : japonés — **~** *n* : japonés *m* (idioma)

jar[1] ['dʒɑr] *v* **jarred; jarring** *vi* **1** GRATE : chirriar **2** CLASH : desentonar **3 ~ on** IRRITATE : crispar, enervar (a algn) — *vt* JOLT : sacudir — **~** *n* : sacudida *f*

jar[2] *n* : tarro *m*

jargon ['dʒɑrgən] *n* : jerga *f*

jaundice ['dʒɔndɪs] *n* : ictericia *f*

jaunt ['dʒɔnt] *n* : excursión *f*

jaunty ['dʒɔnti] *adj* **-tier; -est** : garboso, desenvuelto

jaw ['dʒɔ] *n* : mandíbula *f* (de una persona), quijada *f* (de un animal) — **jawbone** ['dʒɔ,bo:n] *n* : mandíbula *f*, quijada *f*

jay ['dʒeɪ] *n* : arrendajo *m*

jazz ['dʒæz] *n* : jazz *m* — **~** *vt or* **~ up** : animar, alegrar — **jazzy** ['dʒæzi] *adj* **jazzier; -est** FLASHY : llamativo

jealous ['dʒɛləs] *adj* : celoso — **jealousy** ['dʒɛləsi] *n* : celos *mpl*, envidia *f*

jeans ['dʒi:nz] *npl* : jeans *mpl*, vaqueros *mpl*

jeer ['dʒɪr] *vt* **1** BOO : abuchear **2** MOCK : mofarse de — *vi* **~ at** : mofarse de — **~** *n* : mofa *f*

jell ['dʒɛl] *vi* : cuajar

jelly ['dʒɛli] *n, pl* **-lies** : jalea *f* — **jellyfish** ['dʒɛli,fɪʃ] *n* : medusa *f*

jeopardy ['dʒɛpərdi] *n* : peligro *m*, riesgo *m* — **jeopardize** ['dʒɛpər,daɪz] *vt* **-dized; -dizing** : arriesgar, poner en peligro

jerk ['dʒərk] *n* **1** JOLT : sacudida *f* brusca **2** FOOL : idiota *mf* — **~** *vt* : sacudir — *vi* JOLT : dar sacudidas

jersey ['dʒərzi] *n, pl* **-seys** : jersey *m*

jest ['dʒɛst] *n* : broma *f* — **~** *vi* : bromear — **jester** ['dʒɛstər] *n* : bufón *m*

Jesus ['dʒi:zəs, -zəz] *n* : Jesús *m*

jet ['dʒɛt] *n* **1** STREAM : chorro *m* **2** *or* **~ airplane** : avión *m* a reacción, reactor *m* — **jet–propelled** *adj* : a reacción

jettison ['dʒɛṯəsən] *vt* **1** : echar al mar **2** DISCARD : deshacerse de

jetty ['dʒɛṯi] *n, pl* **-ties** : desembarcadero *m*, muelle *m*

jewel ['dʒu:əl] *n* **1** : joya *f* **2** GEM : piedra *f* preciosa — **jeweler** *or* **jeweller** ['dʒu:ələr] *n* : joyero *m*, -ra *f* — **jewelry** ['dʒu:əlri] *n* : joyas *fpl*, alhajas *fpl*

Jewish ['dʒu:ɪʃ] *adj* : judío

jibe ['dʒaɪb] *vi* **jibed; jibing** AGREE : concordar

jiffy ['dʒɪfi] *n, pl* **-fies** : santiamén *m*, segundo *m*

jig ['dʒɪg] *n* : giga *f*

jiggle ['dʒɪgəl] *vt* **-gled; -gling** : sacudir, zarandear — **~** *n* : sacudida *f*

jigsaw ['dʒɪg,sɔ] *n* **1** : sierra *f* de vaivén **2** *or* ~ **puzzle** : rompecabezas *m*
jilt ['dʒɪlt] *vt* : dejar plantado
jingle ['dʒɪŋgəl] *v* **-gled; -gling** *vi* : tintinear — *vt* : hacer sonar — ~ *n* TINKLE : tintineo *m*
jinx ['dʒɪŋks] *n* CURSE : maldición *f*
jitters ['dʒɪt̬ərz] *npl* **have the** ~ : estar nervioso — **jittery** ['dʒɪt̬əri] *adj* : nervioso
job ['dʒɑb] *n* **1** EMPLOYMENT : empleo *m*, trabajo *m* **2** TASK : trabajo *m*
jockey ['dʒɑki] *n, pl* **-eys** : jockey *mf*
jog ['dʒɑg] *v* **jogged; jogging** *vt* ~ **s.o.'s memory** : refrescar la memoria a algn — *vi* : hacer footing — **jogging** *n* : footing *m*
join ['dʒɔɪn] *vt* **1** UNITE : unir, juntar **2** MEET : reunirse con **3** : hacerse socio de (una organización, etc.) — *vi* **1** *or* ~ **together** : unirse **2** : hacerse socio (de una organización, etc.)
joint ['dʒɔɪnt] *n* **1** : articulación *f* (en anatomía) **2** JUNCTURE : juntura *f*, unión *f* — ~ *adj* : conjunto — **jointly** ['dʒɔɪntli] *adv* : conjuntamente
joke ['dʒo:k] *n* : chiste *m*, broma *f* — ~ *vi* **joked; joking** : bromear — **joker** ['dʒo:kər] *n* **1** : bromista *mf* **2** : comodín *m* (en los naipes)
jolly ['dʒɑli] *adj* **-lier; -est** : alegre, jovial
jolt ['dʒo:lt] *vt* : sacudir — ~ *n* **1** : sacudida *f* brusca **2** SHOCK : golpe *m* (emocional)
jostle ['dʒɑsəl] *v* **-tled; -tling** *vt* : empujar, dar empujones — *vi* : empujarse
jot ['dʒɑt] *vt* **jotted; jotting** *or* ~ **down** : anotar, apuntar
journal ['dʒərnəl] *n* **1** DIARY : diario *m* **2** PERIODICAL : revista *f* — **journalism** ['dʒərnəl,ɪzəm] *n* : periodismo *m* — **journalist** ['dʒərnəlɪst] *n* : periodista *mf*
journey ['dʒərni] *n, pl* **-neys** : viaje *m* — ~ *vi* **-neyed; -neying** : viajar
jovial ['dʒo:viəl] *adj* : jovial
joy ['dʒɔɪ] *n* : alegría *f* — **joyful** ['dʒɔɪfəl] *adj* : alegre, feliz — **joyous** ['dʒɔɪəs] *adj* : jubiloso, alegre
jubilant ['dʒu:bələnt] *adj* : jubiloso — **jubilee** ['dʒu:bə,li:] *n* : aniversario *m* especial
Judaism ['dʒu:də,ɪzəm, 'dʒu:di-, 'dʒu:,deɪ-] *n* : judaísmo *m*
judge ['dʒʌdʒ] *vt* **judged; judging** : juzgar — ~ *n* : juez *mf* — **judgment** *or* **judgement** ['dʒʌdʒmənt] *n* **1** RULING : fallo *m*, sentencia *f* **2** VIEW : juicio *m*
judicial [dʒʊ'dɪʃəl] *adj* : judicial — **judicious** [dʒʊ'dɪʃəs] *adj* : juicioso
jug ['dʒʌg] *n* : jarra *f*
juggle ['dʒʌgəl] *vi* **-gled; -gling** : hacer juegos malabares — **juggler** ['dʒʌgələr] *n* : malabarista *mf*
jugular vein ['dʒʌgjʊlər-] *n* : vena *f* yugular
juice ['dʒu:s] *n* : jugo *m* — **juicy** ['dʒu:si] *adj* **juicier; -est** : jugoso
jukebox ['dʒu:k,bɑks] *n* : máquina *f* de discos
July [dʒʊ'laɪ] *n* : julio *m*
jumble ['dʒʌmbəl] *vt* **-bled; -bling** : mezclar — ~ *n* : revoltijo *m*
jumbo ['dʒʌm,bo:] *adj* : gigante
jump ['dʒʌmp] *vi* **1** LEAP : saltar **2** START : sobresaltarse **3** RISE : subir de un golpe **4** ~ **at** : no dejar escapar (una oportunidad, etc.) — *vt* : saltar — ~ *n* **1** LEAP : salto *m* **2** INCREASE : aumento *m* — **jumper** ['dʒʌmpər] *n* **1** : saltador *m*, **-dora** *f* (en deportes) **2** : jumper *m* (vestido) — **jumpy** ['dʒʌmpi] *adj* **jumpier; -est** : nervioso
junction ['dʒʌŋkʃən] *n* **1** JOINING : unión *f* **2** : cruce *m* (de calles), empalme *m* (de un ferrocarril) — **juncture** ['dʒʌŋktʃər] *n* : coyuntura *f*
June ['dʒu:n] *n* : junio *m*
jungle ['dʒʌŋgəl] *n* : selva *f*
junior ['dʒu:njər] *adj* **1** YOUNGER : más joven **2** SUBORDINATE : subalterno — ~ *n* **1** : persona *f* de menor edad **2** SUBORDINATE : subalterno *m*, **-na** *f* **3** : estudiante *mf* de penúltimo año
junk ['dʒʌŋk] *n* : trastos *mpl* (viejos) — ~ *vt* : echar a la basura
junta ['hʊntə, 'dʒʌn-, 'hʌn-] *n* : junta *f* (militar)
jurisdiction [,dʒʊrəs'dɪkʃən] *n* : jurisdicción *f*
jury ['dʒʊri] *n, pl* **-ries** : jurado *m* — **juror** ['dʒʊrər] *n* : jurado *mf*
just ['dʒʌst] *adj* : justo — ~ *adv* **1** BARELY : apenas **2** EXACTLY : exactamente **3** ONLY : sólo, solamente **4** ~ **now** : ahora mismo **5** **she has** ~ **left** : acaba de salir **6** **we were** ~ **leaving** : justo íbamos a salir
justice ['dʒʌstɪs] *n* **1** : justicia *f* **2** JUDGE : juez *mf*
justify ['dʒʌstə,faɪ] *vt* **-fied; -fying** : justificar — **justification** [,dʒʌstəfə'keɪʃən] *n* : justificación *f*
jut ['dʒʌt] *vi* **jutted; jutting** *or* ~ **out** : sobresalir
juvenile ['dʒu:və,naɪl, -vənəl] *adj* **1** YOUNG : juvenil **2** CHILDISH : infantil — ~ *n* : menor *mf*
juxtapose ['dʒʌkstə,po:z] *vt* **-posed; -posing** : yuxtaponer

K

k ['keɪ] *n, pl* **k's** *or* **ks** ['keɪz] : k *f*, undécima letra del alfabeto inglés
kaleidoscope [kə'laɪdə,sko:p] *n* : calidoscopio *m*
kangaroo [,kæŋgə'ru:] *n, pl* **-roos** : canguro *m*
karat ['kærət] *n* : quilate *m*
karate [kə'rɑṭi] *n* : karate *m*
keel ['ki:l] *n* : quilla *f* — ~ *vi or* ~ **over** : volcarse (dícese de un barco), desplomarse (dícese de una persona)
keen ['ki:n] *adj* **1** SHARP : afilado **2** PENETRATING : cortante, penetrante **3** ENTHUSIASTIC : entusiasta **4** ~ **eyesight** : visión *f* aguda
keep ['ki:p] *v* **kept** ['kɛpt]; **keeping** *vt* **1** : guardar **2** : cumplir (una promesa), acudir a (una cita) **3** DETAIN : hacer quedar, detener **4** PREVENT : impedir **5** ~ **up** : mantener — *vi* **1** REMAIN : mantenerse **2** LAST : conservarse **3** *or* ~ **on** CONTINUE : no dejar — ~ *n* **1** **earn one's** ~ : ganarse el pan **2** **for** ~**s** : para siempre — **keeper** ['ki:pər] *n* : guarda *mf* — **keeping** ['ki:pɪŋ] *n* **1** CARE : cuidado *m* **2** **in** ~ **with** : de acuerdo con — **keepsake** ['ki:p,seɪk] *n* : recuerdo *m*
keg ['kɛg] *n* : barril *m*
kennel ['kenəl] *n* : caseta *f* para perros, perrera *f*
kept → **keep**
kerchief ['kərtʃəf, -,tʃi:f] *n* : pañuelo *m*
kernel ['kərnəl] *n* **1** : almendra *f* **2** CORE : meollo *m*
kerosene *or* **kerosine** ['kɛrə,si:n, ,kɛrə'-] *n* : queroseno *m*
ketchup ['kɛtʃəp, 'kæ-] *n* : salsa *f* de tomate
kettle ['kɛṭəl] *n* : hervidor *m*, tetera *f* (para hervir)
key ['ki:] *n* **1** : llave *f* **2** : tecla *f* (de un piano o una máquina) — ~ *vt* **be keyed up** : estar nervioso — ~ *adj* : clave — **keyboard** ['ki:,bord] *n* : teclado *m* — **keyhole** ['ki:,ho:l] *n* : ojo *m* (de la cerradura) — **keynote** ['ki:-,no:t] *n* : tónica *f* — **key ring** *n* : llavero *m*
khaki ['kæki, 'kɑ-] *adj* : caqui
kick ['kɪk] *vt* **1** : dar una patada a **2** ~ **out** : echar a patadas — *vi* **1** : dar patadas (dícese de una persona), cocear (dícese de un animal) **2** RECOIL : dar un culatazo — ~ *n* **1** : patada *f*, coz *f* (de un animal) **2** RECOIL : culatazo *m* **3** PLEASURE, THRILL : placer *m*
kid ['kɪd] *n* **1** GOAT : chivo *m*, -va *f*; cabrito *m* **2** CHILD : niño *m*, -ña *f* — ~ *v* **kidded; kidding** *vi or* ~ **around** : bromear — *vt* TEASE : tomar el pelo a — **kidnap** ['kɪd,næp] *vt* **-napped** *or* **-naped** [-,næpt]; **-napping** *or* **-naping** [-,næpɪŋ] : secuestrar, raptar
kidney ['kɪdni] *n, pl* **-neys** : riñón *m*
kidney bean *n* : frijol *m*
kill ['kɪl] *vt* **1** : matar **2** DESTROY : acabar con **3** ~ **time** : matar el tiempo — ~ *n* **1** KILLING : matanza *f* **2** PREY : presa *f* — **killer** ['kɪlər] *n* : asesino *m*, -na *f* — **killing** ['kɪlɪŋ] *n* **1** : matanza *f* **2** MURDER : asesinato *m*
kiln ['kɪl, 'kɪln] *n* : horno *m*
kilo ['ki:,lo:] *n, pl* **-los** : kilo *m* — **kilogram** ['kɪlə,græm, 'ki:-] *n* : kilogramo *m* — **kilometer** [kɪ'lɑməṭər, 'kɪlə,mi:-] *n* : kilómetro *m* — **kilowatt** ['kɪlə,wɑt] *n* : kilovatio *m*
kin ['kɪn] *n* : parientes *mpl*
kind ['kaɪnd] *n* : tipo *m*, clase *f* — ~ *adj* : amable
kindergarten ['kɪndər,gɑrtən, -dən] *n* : jardín *m* infantil, jardín *m* de niños *Lat*
kindhearted [,kaɪnd'hɑrṭəd] *adj* : de buen corazón
kindle ['kɪndəl] *vt* **-dled; -dling** **1** : encender (un fuego) **2** AROUSE : despertar
kindly ['kaɪndli] *adj* **-lier; -est** : bondadoso, amable — ~ *adv* **1** : amablemente **2** **take** ~ **to** : aceptar de buena gana **3** **we** ~ **ask you not smoke** : les rogamos que no fumen — **kindness** ['kaɪndnəs] *n* : bondad *f* — **kind of** *adv* SOMEWHAT : un tanto, algo
kindred ['kɪndrəd] *adj* **1** : emparentado **2** ~ **spirit** : alma *f* gemela
king ['kɪŋ] *n* : rey *m* — **kingdom** ['kɪŋdəm] *n* : reino *m*
kink ['kɪŋk] *n* **1** TWIST : vuelta *f*, curva *f* **2** FLAW : problema *m*
kinship ['kɪn,ʃɪp] *n* : parentesco *m*
kiss ['kɪs] *vt* : besar — *vi* : besarse — ~ *n* : beso *m*
kit ['kɪt] *n* **1** : juego *m*, kit *m* **2** **first–aid**

~ : botiquín *m* **3 tool ~** : caja *f* de herramientas
kitchen ['kɪtʃən] *n* : cocina *f*
kite ['kaɪt] *n* : cometa *f,* papalote *m Lat*
kitten ['kɪtən] *n* : gatito *m,* **-ta** *f* — **kitty** ['kɪt̬i] *n, pl* **-ties** FUND : fondo *m* común
knack ['næk] *n* : maña *f,* facilidad *f*
knapsack ['næp,sæk] *n* : mochila *f*
knead ['ni:d] *vt* **1** : amasar, sobar **2** MASSAGE : masajear
knee ['ni:] *n* : rodilla *f* — **kneecap** ['ni:,kæp] *n* : rótula *f*
kneel ['ni:l] *vi* **knelt** ['nɛlt] *or* **kneeled** ['ni:ld]; **kneeling** : arrodillarse
knew → **know**
knickknack ['nɪk,næk] *n* : chuchería *f*
knife ['naɪf] *n, pl* **knives** ['naɪvz] : cuchillo *m* — **~** *vt* **knifed** ['naɪft]; **knifing** : acuchillar
knight ['naɪt] *n* **1** : caballero *m* **2** : caballo *m* (en ajedrez) — **knighthood** ['naɪt,hʊd] *n* : título *m* de Sir
knit ['nɪt] *v* **knit** *or* **knitted** ['nɪt̬əd]; **knitting** *v* : tejer — **~** *n* : prenda *f* tejida
knob ['nɑb] *n* : tirador *m,* botón *m,* perilla *f Lat*
knock ['nɑk] *vt* **1** : golpear **2** CRITICIZE : criticar **3 ~ down** : derribar, echar al suelo — *vi* **1** : dar un golpe, llamar (a la puerta) **2** COLLIDE : darse, chocar — **~** *n* : golpe *m,* llamada *f* (a la puerta)
knot ['nɑt] *n* : nudo *m* — **~** *vt* **knotted; knotting** : anudar — **knotty** ['nɑt̬i] *adj* **-tier; -est 1** : nudoso **2** : enredado (dícese de un problema)
know ['no:] *v* **knew** ['nu:, 'nju:]; **known** ['no:n]; **knowing** *vt* **1** : saber **2** : conocer (a una persona, un lugar) **3 ~ how to** : saber — *vi* : saber — **knowing** ['no:ɪŋ] *adj* : cómplice — **knowingly** ['no:ɪŋli] *adv* **1** : de manera cómplice **2** DELIBERATELY : a sabiendas — **know–it–all** ['no:ɪt̬,ɔl] *n* : sabelotodo *mf fam* — **knowledge** ['nɑlɪdʒ] *n* **1** : conocimiento *m* **2** LEARNING : conocimientos *mpl,* saber *m* — **knowledgeable** ['nɑlɪdʒəbəl] *adj* : informado, entendido
knuckle ['nʌkəl] *n* : nudillo *m*
Koran [kə'rɑn, -'ræn] *n* **the Koran** : el Corán *m*
Korean [kə'ri:ən] *adj* : coreano *m,* **-na** *f* — **~** *n* : coreano *m* (idioma)
kosher ['ko:ʃər] *adj* : aprobado por la ley judía

L

l ['ɛl] *n, pl* **l's** *or* **ls** ['ɛlz] : l *f,* duodécima letra del alfabeto inglés
lab ['læb] → **laboratory**
label ['leɪbəl] *n* **1** TAG : etiqueta *f* **2** BRAND : marca *f* — **~** *vt* **-beled** *or* **-belled; -beling** *or* **-belling** : etiquetar
labor ['leɪbər] *n* **1** : trabajo *m* **2** WORKERS : mano *f* de obra **3 in ~** : de parto — **~** *vi* **1** : trabajar **2** STRUGGLE : avanzar penosamente — *vt* BELABOR : insistir en (un punto)
laboratory ['læbrə,tori, lə'bɔrə-] *n, pl* **-ries** : laboratorio *m*
laborer ['leɪbərər] *n* : trabajador *m,* **-dora** *f*
laborious [lə'boriəs] *adj* : laborioso
lace ['leɪs] *n* **1** : encaje *m* **2** SHOELACE : cordón *m* (de zapatos), agujeta *f Lat* — **~** *vt* **laced; lacing 1** TIE : atar **2 be laced with** : echar licor a (una bebida, etc.)
lacerate ['læsə,reɪt] *vt* **-ated; -ating** : lacerar
lack ['læk] *vt* : carecer de, no tener — *vi* **be lacking** : faltar — **~** *n* : falta *f,* carencia *f*
lackadaisical [,lækə'deɪzɪkəl] *adj* : apático, indolente
lackluster ['læk,lʌstər] *adj* : sin brillo, apagado
laconic [lə'kɑnɪk] *adj* : lacónico
lacquer ['lækər] *n* : laca *f*
lacrosse [lə'krɔs] *n* : lacrosse *f*
lacy ['leɪsi] *adj* **lacier; -est** : como de encaje
lad ['læd] *n* : muchacho *m,* niño *m*
ladder ['lædər] *n* : escalera *f*
laden ['leɪdən] *adj* : cargado
ladle ['leɪdəl] *n* : cucharón *m* — **~** *vt* **-dled; -dling** : servir con cucharón
lady ['leɪdi] *n, pl* **-dies** : señora *f,* dama *f* — **ladybug** ['leɪdi,bʌg] *n* : mariquita *f* — **ladylike** ['leɪdi,laɪk] *adj* : elegante, como señora
lag ['læg] *n* **1** DELAY : retraso *m* **2** INTERVAL : intervalo *m* — **~** *vi* **lagged; lagging** : quedarse atrás, rezagarse
lager ['lɑgər] *n* : cerveza *f* rubia
lagoon [lə'gu:n] *n* : laguna *f*
laid *pp* → **lay**[1]
lain *pp* → **lie**[1]
lair ['lær] *n* : guarida *f*

lake ['leɪk] *n* : lago *m*
lamb ['læm] *n* : cordero *m*
lame ['leɪm] *adj* **lamer; lamest 1** : cojo, renco **2 a ~ excuse** : una excusa poco convincente
lament [lə'mɛnt] *vt* **1** MOURN : llorar **2** DEPLORE : lamentar — **~** *n* : lamento *m* — **lamentable** ['læməntəbəl, lə-'mɛntə-] *adj* : lamentable
laminate ['læmə,neɪt] *vt* **-nated; -nating** : laminar
lamp ['læmp] *n* : lámpara *f* — **lamppost** ['læmp,po:st] *n* : farol *m* — **lampshade** ['læmp,ʃeɪd] *n* : pantalla *f*
lance ['lænts] *n* : lanza *f* — **~** *vt* **lanced; lancing** : abrir con lanceta (en medecina)
land ['lænd] *n* **1** : tierra *f* **2** COUNTRY : país *m* **3** *or* **plot of ~** : terreno *m* — **~** *vt* **1** : desembarcar (pasajeros de un barco), hacer aterrizar (un avión) **2** CATCH : sacar (un pez) del agua **3** SECURE : conseguir (empleo, etc.) — *vi* **1** : aterrizar (dícese de un avión) **2** FALL : caer — **landing** ['lændɪŋ] *n* **1** : aterrizaje *m* (de aviones) **2** : desembarco *m* (de barcos) **3** : descanso *m* (de una escalera) — **landlady** ['lænd,leɪdi] *n, pl* **-dies** : casera *f* — **landlord** ['lænd,lɔrd] *n* : casero *m* — **landmark** ['lænd,mɑrk] *n* **1** : punto *m* de referencia **2** MONUMENT : monumento *m* histórico — **landowner** ['lænd,o:nər] *n* : hacendado *m*, -da *f*; terrateniente *mf* — **landscape** ['lænd,skeɪp] *n* : paisaje *m* — **~** *vt* **-scaped; -scaping** : ajardinar — **landslide** ['lænd,slaɪd] *n* **1** : desprendimiento *m* de tierras **2** *or* **~ victory** : victoria *f* arrolladora
lane ['leɪn] *n* **1** : carril *m* (de una carretera) **2** PATH, ROAD : camino *m*
language ['læŋgwɪdʒ] *n* **1** : idioma *m*, lengua *f* **2** SPEECH : lenguaje *m*
languid ['læŋgwɪd] *adj* : lánguido — **languish** ['læŋgwɪʃ] *vi* : languidecer
lanky ['læŋki] *adj* **lankier; -est** : delgado, larguirucho *fam*
lantern ['læntərn] *n* : linterna *f*
lap ['læp] *n* **1** : regazo *m* (de una persona) **2** : vuelta *f* (en deportes) — **~** *v* **lapped; lapping** *vt* *or* **~ up** : beber a lengüetadas — *vi* **~ against** : lamer
lapel [lə'pɛl] *n* : solapa *f*
lapse ['læps] *n* **1** : lapsus *m*, falla *f* (de memoria, etc.) **2** INTERVAL : lapso *m*, intervalo *m* — **~** *vi* **lapsed; lapsing 1** EXPIRE : caducar **2** ELAPSE : transcurrir, pasar **3 ~ into** : caer en
laptop ['læp,tɑp] *adj* : portátil
larceny ['lɑrsəni] *n, pl* **-nies** : robo *m*
lard ['lɑrd] *n* : manteca *f* de cerdo
large ['lɑrdʒ] *adj* **larger; largest 1** : grande **2 at ~** : en libertad **3 by and ~** : por lo general — **largely** ['lɑrdʒli] *adv* : en gran parte
lark ['lɑrk] *n* **1** : alondra *f* (pájaro) **2 for a ~** : por divertirse
larva ['lɑrvə] *n, pl* **-vae** [-,vi:, -,vaɪ] : larva *f*
larynx ['lærɪŋks] *n, pl* **-rynges** [lə'rɪn-,dʒi:z] *or* **-ynxes** ['lærɪŋksəz] : laringe *f* — **laryngitis** [,lærən'dʒaɪṭəs] *n* : laringitis *f*
lasagna [lə'zɑnjə] *n* : lasaña *f*
laser ['leɪzər] *n* : láser *m*
lash ['læʃ] *vt* **1** WHIP : azotar **2** BIND : amarrar — *vi* **~ out at** : arremeter contra — **~** *n* **1** BLOW : latigazo *m* (con un látigo) **2** EYELASH : pestaña *f*
lass ['læs] *or* **lassie** ['læsi] *n* : muchacha *f*, chica *f*
lasso ['læ,so:, læ'su:] *n, pl* **-sos** *or* **-soes** : lazo *m*
last ['læst] *vi* : durar — **~** *n* **1** : último *m*, -ma *f* **2 at ~** : por fin, finalmente — **~** *adv* **1** : por última vez, en último lugar **2 arrive ~** : llegar el último — **~** *adj* **1** : último **2 ~ year** : el año pasado — **lastly** ['læstli] *adv* : por último, finalmente
latch ['lætʃ] *n* : picaporte *m*, pestillo *m*
late ['leɪt] *adj* **later; latest 1** : tarde **2** : avanzado (dícese de la hora) **3** DECEASED : difunto **4** RECENT : reciente — **~** *adv* **later; latest** : tarde — **lately** ['leɪtli] *adv* : recientemente, últimamente — **lateness** ['leɪtnəs] *n* **1** : retraso *m* **2** : lo avanzado (de la hora)
latent ['leɪtənt] *adj* : latente
lateral ['læṭərəl] *adj* : lateral
latest ['leɪtəst] *n* **at the ~** : a más tardar
lathe ['leɪð] *n* : torno *m*
lather ['læðər] *n* : espuma *f* — **~** *vt* : enjabonar — *vi* : hacer espuma
Latin–American ['lætənə'mɛrikən] *adj* : latinoamericano
latitude ['læṭə,tu:d, -,tju:d] *n* : latitud *f*
latter ['læṭər] *adj* **1** : último **2** SECOND : segundo — **~** *pron* **the ~** : éste, ésta, éstos *pl*, éstas *pl*
lattice ['læṭəs] *n* : enrejado *m*
laugh ['læf] *vi* : reír(se) — **~** *n* : risa *f* — **laughable** ['læfəbəl] *adj* : risible, ridículo — **laughter** ['læftər] *n* : risa *f*, risas *fpl*
launch ['lɔntʃ] *vt* : lanzar — **~** *n* : lanzamiento *m*
launder ['lɔndər] *vt* **1** : lavar y planchar (ropa) **2** : blanquear, lavar (dinero) — **laundry** ['lɔndri] *n, pl* **-dries 1** : ropa *f*

sucia **2** : lavandería *f* (servicio) **3 do the ~** : lavar la ropa
lava ['lɑvə, 'læ-] *n* : lava *f*
lavatory ['lævə,tori] *n, pl* **-ries** BATHROOM : baño *m*, cuarto *m* de baño
lavender ['lævəndər] *n* : lavanda *f*
lavish ['lævɪʃ] *adj* **1** EXTRAVAGANT : pródigo **2** ABUNDANT : abundante **3** LUXURIOUS : lujoso — **~** *vt* : prodigar
law ['lɔ] *n* **1** : ley *f* **2** : derecho *m* (profesión, etc.) **3 practice ~** : ejercer la abogacía — **lawful** ['lɔfəl] *adj* : legal, legítimo
lawn ['lɔn] *n* : césped *m* — **lawn mower** *n* : cortadora *f* de césped
lawsuit ['lɔ,su:t] *n* : pleito *m*
lawyer ['lɔɪər, 'lɔjər] *n* : abogado *m*, -da *f*
lax ['læks] *adj* : poco estricto, relajado
laxative ['læksət̬ɪv] *n* : laxante *m*
lay[1] ['leɪ] *vt* **laid** ['leɪd]; **laying 1** PLACE, PUT : poner, colocar **2 ~ eggs** : poner huevos **3 ~ off** : dispedir (un empleado) **4 ~ out** PRESENT : presentar, exponer **5 ~ out** DESIGN : diseñar (el trazado de)
lay[2] *pp* → **lie**[1]
lay[3] *adj* **1** SECULAR : laico **2** NONPROFESSIONAL : lego, profano
layer ['leɪər] *n* : capa *f*
layman ['leɪmən] *n, pl* **-men** : lego *m*, laico *m* (en religión)
layout ['leɪ,aʊt] *n* ARRANGEMENT : disposición *f*
lazy ['leɪzi] *adj* **-zier; -est** : perezoso — **laziness** ['leɪzinəs] *n* : pereza *f*
lead[1] ['li:d] *vt* **led** ['lɛd]; **leading 1** GUIDE : conducir **2** DIRECT : dirigir **3** HEAD : encabezar, ir al frente de — *vi* : llevar, conducir (a algo) — **~** *n* **1** : delantera *f* **2 follow s.o.'s ~** : seguir el ejemplo de algn
lead[2] ['lɛd] *n* **1** : plomo *m* (metal) **2** GRAPHITE : mina *f* — **leaden** ['lɛdən] *adj* **1** : de plomo **2** HEAVY : pesado
leader ['li:dər] *n* : jefe *m*, -fa *f* — **leadership** ['li:dər,ʃɪp] *n* : mando *m*, dirección *f*
leaf ['li:f] *n, pl* **leaves** ['li:vz] **1** : hoja *f* **2 turn over a new ~** : hacer borrón y cuenta nueva — **~** *vi* **~ through** : hojear (un libro, etc.) — **leaflet** ['li:flət] *n* : folleto *m*
league ['li:g] *n* **1** : liga *f* **2 be in ~ with** : estar confabulado con
leak ['li:k] *vt* **1** : dejar escapar (un líquido o un gas) **2** : filtrar (información) — *vi* **1** : gotear, escaparse (dícese de un líquido o un gas) **2** : filtrarse (dícese de información) — **~** *n* **1** : agujero *m* (de un cubo, etc.), gotera *f* (de un techo) **2** : fuga *f*, escape *m* (de un líquido o un gas) **3** : filtración *f* (de información) — **leaky** ['li:ki] *adj* **leakier; -est** : que hace agua
lean[1] ['li:n] *v* **leaned** *or Brit* **leant** ['lɛnt]; **leaning** *vi* **1** BEND : inclinarse **2 ~ against** : apoyarse contra — *vt* : apoyar
lean[2] *adj* **1** THIN : delgado **2** : sin grasa (dícese de la carne)
leaning ['li:nɪŋ] *n* : inclinación *f*
leanness ['li:nnəs] *n* : delgadez *f* (de una persona), lo magro (de la carne)
leap ['li:p] *vi* **leapt** *or* **leaped** ['li:pt, 'lɛpt]; **leaping** : saltar, brincar — **~** *n* : salto *m*, brinco *m* — **leap year** *n* : año *m* bisiesto
learn ['lərn] *v* **learned** ['lərnd, 'lərnt]; **learning** : aprender — **learned** ['lərnəd] *adj* : sabio, erudito — **learner** ['lərnər] *n* : principiante *mf*, estudiante *mf* — **learning** ['lərnɪŋ] *n* : erudición *f*, saber *m*
lease ['li:s] *n* : contrato *m* de arrendamiento — **~** *vt* **leased; leasing** : arrendar
leash ['li:ʃ] *n* : correa *f*
least ['li:st] *adj* **1** : menor **2** SLIGHTEST : más minimo — **~** *n* **1 at ~** : por lo menos **2 the ~** : lo menos **3 to say the ~** : por no decir más — **~** *adv* : menos
leather ['lɛðər] *n* : cuero *m*
leave ['li:v] *v* **left** ['lɛft]; **leaving** *vt* **1** : dejar **2** : salir(se) de (un lugar) **3 ~ out** : omitir — *vi* DEPART : irse — **~** *n* **1** *or* **~ of absence** : permiso *m*, licencia *f* **2 take one's ~** : despedirse
leaves → **leaf**
lecture ['lɛktʃər] *n* **1** TALK : conferencia *f* **2** REPRIMAND : sermón *m*, reprimenda *f* — **~** *v* **-tured; -turing** *vt* : sermonear — *vi* : dar clase, dar una conferencia
led *pp* → **lead**[1]
ledge ['lɛdʒ] *n* : antepecho *m* (de una ventana), saliente *m* (de una montaña)
leech ['li:tʃ] *n* : sanguijuela *f*
leek ['li:k] *n* : puerro *m*
leer ['lɪr] *vi* : lanzar una mirada lascivia — **~** *n* : mirada *f* lasciva
leery ['lɪri] *adj* : receloso
leeway ['li:,weɪ] *n* : libertad *f* de acción, margen *m*
left[1] → **leave**
left[2] ['lɛft] *adj* : izquierdo — **~** *adv* : a la izquierda — **~** *n* : izquierda *f* — **left–handed** ['lɛft'handəd] *adj* : zurdo
leftovers ['lɛft,o:vərz] *npl* : restos *mpl*, sobras *fpl*

leg ['lɛg] *n* **1** : pierna *f* (de una persona, de ropa), pata *f* (de un animal, de muebles) **2** : etapa *f* (de un viaje)
legacy ['lɛgəsi] *n, pl* **-cies** : legado *m*
legal ['li:gəl] *adj* **1** LAWFUL : legítimo, legal **2** JUDICIAL : legal, jurídico — **legality** [li'gæləṭi] *n, pl* **-ties** : legalidad *f* — **legalize** ['li:gə,laɪz] *vt* **-ized; -izing** : legalizar
legend ['lɛdʒənd] *n* : leyenda *f* — **legendary** ['lɛdʒən,dɛri] *adj* : lengendario
legible ['lɛdʒəbəl] *adj* : legible
legion ['li:dʒən] *n* : legión *f*
legislate ['lɛdʒəs,leɪt] *vi* **-lated; -lating** : legislar — **legislation** [,lɛdʒəs'leɪʃən] *n* : legislación *f* — **legislative** ['lɛdʒəs,leɪṭɪv] *adj* : legislativo, legislador — **legislature** ['lɛdʒəs,leɪtʃər] *n* : asamblea *f* legislativa
legitimate [lɪ'dʒɪṭəmət] *adj* : legítimo — **legitimacy** [lɪ'dʒɪṭəməsi] *n* : legitimidad *f*
leisure ['li:ʒər, 'lɛ-] *n* **1** : ocio *m*, tiempo *m* libre **2 at your ~** : cuando te venga bien — **leisurely** ['li:ʒərli, 'lɛ-] *adj & adv* : lento, sin prisas
lemon ['lɛmən] *n* : limón *m* — **lemonade** [,lɛmə'neɪd] *n* : limonada *f*
lend ['lɛnd] *vt* **lent** ['lɛnt]; **lending** : prestar
length ['lɛŋ*k*θ] *n* **1** : largo *m* **2** DURATION : duración *f* **3 at ~** FINALLY : por fin **4 at ~** : EXTENSIVELY : extensamente **5 go to any ~s** : hacer todo lo posible — **lengthen** ['lɛŋ*k*θən] *vt* **1** : alargar **2** PROLONG : prolongar — *vi* : alargarse — **lengthways** ['lɛŋ*k*θ,weɪz] *or* **lengthwise** ['lɛŋ*k*θ,waɪz] *adv* : a lo largo — **lengthy** ['lɛŋ*k*θi] *adj* **lengthier; -est** : largo
lenient ['li:niənt] *adj* : indulgente — **leniency** ['li:niəntsi] *n, pl* **-cies** : indulgencia *f*
lens ['lɛnz] *n* **1** : cristalino *m* (del ojo) **2** : lente *mf* (de un instrumento) **3** → **contact lens**
Lent ['lɛnt] *n* : Cuaresma *f*
lentil ['lɛntəl] *n* : lenteja *f*
leopard ['lɛpərd] *n* : leopardo *m*
leotard ['li:ə,tɑrd] *n* : leotardo *m*, malla *f*
lesbian ['lɛzbiən] *n* : lesbiana *f*
less ['lɛs] *adv* (*comparative of* **little**) : menos — **~** *adj* (*comparative of* **little**) : menos — **~** *pron* : menos — **~** *prep* MINUS : menos — **lessen** ['lɛsən] *v* : disminuir — **lesser** ['lɛsər] *adj* : menor
lesson ['lɛsən] *n* **1** CLASS : clase *f*, curso *m* **2 learn one's ~** : aprender la lección
lest ['lɛst] *conj* **~ we forget** : para que no olvidemos
let ['lɛt] *vt* **let; letting 1** ALLOW : dejar, permitir **2** RENT : alquilar **3 ~'s go!** : ¡vamos!, ¡vámonos! **4 ~ down** DISAPPOINT : fallar **5 ~ in** : dejar entrar **6 ~ off** FORGIVE : perdonar **7 ~ up** ABATE : amainar, disminuir
letdown ['lɛt,daʊn] *n* : chasco *m*, decepción *f*
lethal ['li:θəl] *adj* : letal
lethargic [lɪ'θɑrdʒɪk] *adj* : letárgico
let's ['lɛts] (*contraction of* **let us**) → **let**
letter ['lɛṭər] *n* **1** : carta *f* **2** : letra *f* (del alfabeto)
lettuce ['lɛṭəs] *n* : lechuga *f*
letup ['lɛt,əp] *n* : pausa *f*, descanso *m*
leukemia [lu:'ki:miə] *n* : leucemia *f*
level ['lɛvəl] *n* **1** : nivel *m* **2 be on the ~** : ser honrado — **~** *vt* **-eled** *or* **-elled; -eling** *or* **-elling 1** : nivelar **2** AIM : apuntar **3** RAZE : arrasar — **~** *adj* **1** FLAT : llano, plano **2** : nivel (de altura) — **levelheaded** ['lɛvəl'hɛdəd] *adj* : sensato, equilibrado
lever ['lɛvər, 'li:-] *n* : palanca *f* — **leverage** ['lɛvərɪdʒ, 'li:-] *n* **1** : apalancamiento *m* (en física) **2** INFLUENCE : influencia *f*
levity ['lɛvəṭi] *n* : ligereza *f*
levy ['lɛvi] *n, pl* **levies** : impuesto *m* — **~** *vt* **levied; levying** : imponer, exigir (un impuesto)
lewd ['lu:d] *adj* : lascivo
lexicon ['lɛksɪ,kɑn] *n, pl* **-ica** [-kə] *or* **-icons** : léxico *m*, lexicón *m*
liable ['laɪəbəl] *adj* **1** : responsable **2** LIKELY : probable **3** SUSCEPTIBLE : propenso — **liability** [,laɪə'bɪləṭi] *n, pl* **-ties 1** RESPONSIBILITY : responsabilidad *f* **2** DRAWBACK : desventaja *f* **3 liabilities** *npl* DEBTS : deudas *fpl*, pasivo *m*
liaison ['li:ə,zɑn, li'eɪ-] *n* **1** : enlace *m* **2** AFFAIR : amorío *m*
liar ['laɪər] *n* : mentiroso *m*, **-sa** *f*
libel ['laɪbəl] *n* : libelo *m*, difamación *f* — **~** *vt* **-beled** *or* **-belled; -beling** *or* **-belling** : difamar
liberal ['lɪbrəl, 'lɪbərəl] *adj* : liberal — **~** *n* : liberal *mf*
liberate ['lɪbə,reɪt] *vt* **-ated; -ating** : liberar — **liberation** [,lɪbə'reɪʃən] *n* : liberación *f*
liberty ['lɪbərṭi] *n, pl* **-ties** : libertad *f*
library ['laɪ,brɛri] *n, pl* **-braries** : biblioteca *f* — **librarian** [laɪ'brɛriən] *n* : bibliotecario *m*, **-ria** *f*
lice → **louse**
license *or* **licence** ['laɪsənts] *n* **1** PERMIT

: licencia *f* **2** FREEDOM : libertad *f* **3** AUTHORIZATION : permiso *m* — ~ *vt* **licensed; licensing** : autorizar

lick ['lɪk] *vt* **1** : lamer **2** DEFEAT : dar una paliza a *fam* — ~ *n* : lamida *f*

licorice ['lɪkərɪʃ, -rəs] *n* : regaliz *m*

lid ['lɪd] *n* **1** : tapa *f* **2** EYELID : párpado *m*

lie¹ ['laɪ] *vi* **lay** ['leɪ]; **lain** ['leɪn]; **lying** ['laɪɪŋ] **1** *or* ~ **down** : acostarse, echarse **2** BE : estar, encontrarse

lie² *vi* **lied; lying** ['laɪɪŋ] : mentir — ~ *n* : mentira *f*

lieutenant [luːˈtɛnənt] *n* : teniente *mf*

life ['laɪf] *n, pl* **lives** ['laɪvz] : vida *f* — **lifeboat** ['laɪfˌboːt] *n* : bote *m* salvavidas — **lifeguard** ['laɪfˌgɑrd] *n* : socorrista *mf* — **lifeless** ['laɪfləs] *adj* : sin vida — **lifelike** ['laɪfˌlaɪk] *adj* : natural, realista — **lifelong** ['laɪflɔŋ] *adj* : de toda la vida — **life preserver** *n* : salvavidas *m* — **lifestyle** ['laɪfˌstaɪl] *n* : estilo *m* de vida — **lifetime** ['laɪfˌtaɪm] *n* : vida *f*

lift ['lɪft] *vt* **1** RAISE : levantar **2** STEAL : robar — *vi* **1** CLEAR UP : despejarse **2** *or* ~ **off** : despegar (dícese de un avión, etc.) — ~ *n* **1** LIFTING : levantamiento *m* **2 give s.o. a** ~ : llevar en coche a algn — **liftoff** ['lɪftˌɔf] *n* : despegue *m*

light¹ ['laɪt] *n* **1** : luz *f* **2** LAMP : lámpara *f* **3** HEADLIGHT : faro *m* **4 do you have a** ~**?** : ¿tienes fuego? — ~ *adj* **1** BRIGHT : bien iluminado **2** : claro (dícese de los colores), rubio (dícese del pelo) — ~ *v* **lit** ['lɪt] *or* **lighted; lighting** *vt* **1** : encender (un fuego) **2** ILLUMINATE : iluminar — *vi or* ~ **up** : iluminarse — **lightbulb** ['laɪtˌbʌlb] *n* : bombilla *f,* bombillo *m Lat* — **lighten** ['laɪtən] *vt* BRIGHTEN : iluminar — **lighter** ['laɪt̬ər] *n* : encendedor *m* — **lighthouse** ['laɪtˌhaʊs] *n* : faro *m* — **lighting** ['laɪt̬ɪŋ] *n* : alumbrado *m* — **lightning** ['laɪtnɪŋ] *n* : relámpago *m,* rayo *m* — **light–year** ['laɪtˌjɪr] *n* : año *m* luz

light² *adj* : ligero — **lighten** ['laɪtən] *vt* : aligerar — **lightly** ['laɪtli] *adv* **1** : suavemente **2 let off** ~ : tratar con indulgencia — **lightness** ['laɪtnəs] *n* : ligereza *f* — **lightweight** ['laɪtˈweɪt] *adj* : ligero

like¹ ['laɪk] *v* **liked; liking** *vt* **1** : gustarle (a uno) **2** WANT : querer — *vi* **if you** ~ : si quieres — **likes** *npl* : preferencias *fpl,* gustos *mpl* — **likable** *or* **likeable** ['laɪkəbəl] *adj* : simpático

like² *adj* SIMILAR : parecido — ~ *prep* : como — ~ *conj* **1** AS : como **2** AS IF : como si — **likelihood** ['laɪkliˌhʊd] *n* : probabilidad *f* — **likely** ['laɪkli] *adj* **-lier; -est** : probable — **liken** ['laɪkən] *vt* : comparar — **likeness** ['laɪknəs] *n* : semejanza *f,* parecido *m* — **likewise** ['laɪkˌwaɪz] *adv* **1** : lo mismo **2** ALSO : también

liking ['laɪkɪŋ] *n* : afición *f* (por una cosa), simpatía *f* (por una persona)

lilac ['laɪlək, -ˌlæk, -ˌlɑk] *n* : lila *f*

lily ['lɪli] *n, pl* **lilies** : lirio *m,* azucena *f* — **lily of the valley** *n* : lirio *m* de los valles

lima bean ['laɪmə] *n* : frijol *m* de media luna

limb ['lɪm] *n* **1** : miembro *m* (en anatomía) **2** : rama *f* (de un arból)

limber ['lɪmbər] *vi or* ~ **up** : calentarse, hacer ejercicios preliminares — ~ *adj* : ágil

limbo ['lɪmˌboː] *n, pl* **-bos** : limbo *m*

lime ['laɪm] *n* : lima *f,* limón *m* verde *Lat*

limelight ['laɪmˌlaɪt] *n* **be in the** ~ : estar en el candelero

limerick ['lɪmərɪk] *n* : poema *m* jocoso de cinco versos

limestone ['laɪmˌstoːn] *n* : (piedra *f*) caliza *f*

limit ['lɪmət] *n* : límite *m* — ~ *vt* : limitar, restringir — **limitation** [ˌlɪməˈteɪʃən] *n* : limitación *f,* restricción *f* — **limited** ['lɪmət̬əd] *adj* : limitado

limousine ['lɪməˌziːn, ˌlɪməˈ-] *n* : limusina *f*

limp¹ ['lɪmp] *vi* : cojear — ~ *n* : cojera *f*

limp² *adj* : flojo, fláccido

line ['laɪn] *n* **1** : línea *f* **2** ROPE : cuerda *f* **3** ROW : fila *f* **4** QUEUE : cola *f* **5** WRINKLE : arruga *f* **6 drop a** ~ : mándar unas líneas — ~ *v* **lined; lining** *vt* **1** : forrar (un vestido, etc.), cubrir (las paredes, etc.) **2** MARK : rayar, trazar líneas en **3** BORDER : bordear — *vi* ~ **up** : ponerse in fila, hacer cola

lineage ['lɪniɪdʒ] *n* : linaje *m*

linear ['lɪniər] *adj* : lineal

linen ['lɪnən] *n* : lino *m*

liner ['laɪnər] *n* **1** LINING : forro *m* **2** SHIP : buque *m,* transatlántico *m*

lineup ['laɪnˌəp] *n* **1** *or* **police** ~ : fila *f* de sospechosos **2** : alineación *f* (en deportes)

linger ['lɪŋgər] *vi* **1** : quedarse, entretenerse **2** PERSIST : persistir

lingerie [ˌlɑndʒəˈreɪ, ˌlænʒəˈriː] *n* : ropa *f* íntima femenina, lencería *f*

lingo ['lɪŋgo] *n, pl* **-goes** JARGON : jerga *f*

linguistics [lɪŋˈgwɪstɪks] *n* : lingüística *f* — **linguist** ['lɪŋgwɪst] *n* : lingüista *mf*

— **linguistic** [lɪŋ'gwɪstɪk] *adj* : lingüístico
lining ['laɪnɪŋ] *n* : forro *m*
link ['lɪŋk] *n* **1** : eslabón *m* (de una cadena) **2** BOND : lazo *m* **3** CONNECTION : conexión *f* — ~ *vt* : enlazar, conectar — *vi* ~ **up** : unirse, conectar
linoleum [lə'no:liəm] *n* : linóleo *m*
lint ['lɪnt] *n* : pelusa *f*
lion ['laɪən] *n* : león *m* — **lioness** ['laɪənɪs] *n* : leona *f*
lip ['lɪp] *n* **1** : labio *m* **2** EDGE : borde *m* — **lipstick** ['lɪp,stɪk] *n* : lápiz *m* de labios
liqueur [lɪ'kʊr, -'kər, -'kjʊr] *n* : licor *m*
liquid ['lɪkwəd] *adj* : líquido — ~ *n* : líquido *m* — **liquidate** ['lɪkwə,deɪt] *vt* **-dated; -dating** : liquidar — **liquidation** [,lɪkwə'deɪʃən] *n* : liquidación *f*
liquor ['lɪkər] *n* : bebidas *fpl* alcohólicas
lisp ['lɪsp] *vi* : cecear — ~ *n* : ceceo *m*
list[1] ['lɪst] *n* : lista *f* — ~ *vt* **1** ENUMERATE : hacer una lista de, enumerar **2** INCLUDE : incluir (en una lista)
list[2] *vi* : escorar (dícese de un barco)
listen ['lɪsən] *vi* **1** : escuchar **2** ~ **to** HEED : hacer caso de **3** ~ **to reason** : atender a razones — **listener** ['lɪsənər] *n* : oyente *mf*
listless ['lɪstləs] *adj* : apático
lit ['lɪt] *pp* → **light**
litany ['lɪtəni] *n, pl* **-nies** : letanía *f*
liter ['li:t̬ər] *n* : litro *m*
literacy ['lɪt̬ərəsi] *n* : alfabetismo *m*
literal ['lɪt̬ərəl] *adj* : literal — **literally** *adv* : literalmente, al pie de la letra
literate ['lɪt̬ərət] *adj* : alfabetizado
literature ['lɪt̬ərə,tʃʊr, -tʃər] *n* : literatura *f* — **literary** ['lɪt̬ə,rɛri] *adj* : literario
lithe ['laɪð, 'laɪθ] *adj* : ágil y grácil
litigation [,lɪt̬ə'geɪʃən] *n* : litigio *m*
litre → **liter**
litter ['lɪt̬ər] *n* **1** RUBBISH : basura *f* **2** : camada *f* (de animales) **3** *or* **kitty** ~ : arena *f* higiénica — ~ *vt* : tirar basura en, ensuciar — *vi* : tirar basura
little ['lɪtəl] *adj* **littler** *or* **less** ['lɛs] *or* **lesser** ['lɛsər]; **littlest** *or* **least** ['li:st] **1** SMALL : pequeño **2 a** ~ SOME : un poco de **3 he speaks** ~ **English** : habla poco inglés — ~ *adv* **less** ['lɛs]; **least** ['li:st] : poco — ~ *pron* **1** : poco *m*, -ca *f* **2** ~ **by** ~ : poco a poco
liturgy ['lɪt̬ərdʒi] *n, pl* **-gies** : liturgia *f* — **liturgical** [lə'tərdʒɪkəl] *adj* : litúrgico
live ['lɪv] *vi* **lived; living 1** : vivir **2** RESIDE : residir **3** ~ **on** : vivir de — *vt* : vivir, llevar (una vida) — ~ ['laɪv] *adj* **1** : vivo **2** : con corriente (dícese de cables eléctricos) **3** : en vivo, en directo (dícese de programas de televisión, etc.) — **livelihood** ['laɪvli,hʊd] *n* : sustento *m*, medio *m* de vida — **lively** ['laɪvli] *adj* **-lier; -est** : animado, alegre — **liven** ['laɪvən] *vt or* ~ **up** : animar — *vi* : animarse
liver ['lɪvər] *n* : hígado *m*
livestock ['laɪv,stɑk] *n* : ganado *m*
livid ['lɪvəd] *adj* **1** : lívido **2** ENRAGED : furioso
living ['lɪvɪŋ] *adj* : vivo — ~ *n* **make a** ~ : ganarse la vida — **living room** *n* : living *m*, sala *f* (de estar)
lizard ['lɪzərd] *n* : lagarto *m*
llama ['lɑmə, 'jɑ-] *n* : llama *f*
load ['lo:d] *n* **1** CARGO : carga *f* **2** BURDEN : carga *f*, peso *m* **3** ~**s of** : un montón de — ~ *vt* : cargar
loaf[1] ['lo:f] *n, pl* **loaves** ['lo:vz] : pan *m*, barra *f* (de pan)
loaf[2] *vi* : holgazanear — **loafer** ['lo:fər] *n* **1** : holgazán *m*, -zana *f* **2** : mocasín *m* (zapato)
loan ['lo:n] *n* : préstamo *m* — ~ *vt* : prestar
loathe ['lo:ð] *vt* **loathed; loathing** : odiar — **loathsome** ['lo:θsəm, 'lo:ð-] *adj* : odioso
lobby ['lɑbi] *n, pl* **-bies 1** : vestíbulo *m* **2** *or* **political** ~ : grupo *m* de presión, lobby *m* — ~ *v* **-bied; -bying** *vt* : ejercer presión sobre
lobe ['lo:b] *n* : lóbulo *m*
lobster ['lɑbstər] *n* : langosta *f*
local ['lo:kəl] *adj* : local — ~ *n* **the** ~**s** : los vecinos del lugar — **locale** [lo-'kæl] *n* : escenario *m* — **locality** [lo-'kæləţi] *n, pl* **-ties** : localidad *f*
locate ['lo:,keɪt, lo'keɪt] *vt* **-cated; -cating 1** SITUATE : situar, ubicar **2** FIND : localizar — **location** [lo'keɪʃən] *n* : situación *f*, lugar *m*
lock[1] ['lɑk] *n* : mechón *m* (de pelo)
lock[2] *n* **1** : cerradura *f* (de una puerta, etc.) **2** : esclusa *f* (de un canal) — ~ *vt* **1** : cerrar (con llave) **2** *or* ~ **up** CONFINE : encerrar — *vi* **1** : cerrarse con llave **2** : bloquearse (dícese de una rueda, etc.) — **locker** ['lɑkər] *n* : armario *m* — **locket** ['lɑkət] *n* : medallón *m* — **locksmith** ['lɑk,smɪθ] *n* : cerrajero *m*, -ra *f*
locomotive [,lo:kə'mo:t̬ɪv] *n* : locomotora *f*
locust ['lo:kəst] *n* : langosta *f*, chapulín *m Lat*
lodge ['lɑdʒ] *v* **lodged; lodging** *vt* **1** HOUSE : hospedar, alojar **2** FILE : presentar — *vi* : hospedarse, alojarse — ~ *n* : pabellón *m* — **lodger** ['lɑdʒər] *n*

: huésped *m,* -peda *f* — **lodging** ['lɑdʒɪŋ] *n* **1** : alojamiento *m* **2 ~s** *npl* : habitaciones *fpl*

loft ['lɔft] *n* **1** : desván *m* (en una casa) **2** HAYLOFT : pajar *m* — **lofty** ['lɔfti] *adj* **loftier; -est 1** : noble, elevado **2** HAUGHTY : altanero

log ['lɔg, 'lɑg] *n* **1** : tronco *m,* leño *m* **2** RECORD : diario *m* — **~** *vi* **logged; logging 1** : talar (árboles) **2** RECORD : registrar, anotar **3 ~ on** : entrar (en el sistema) **4 ~ off** : salir (del sistema) — **logger** ['lɔgər, 'lɑ-] *n* : leñador *m,* -dora *f*

logic ['lɑdʒɪk] *n* : lógica *f* — **logical** ['lɑdʒɪkəl] *adj* : lógico — **logistics** [lə-'dʒɪstɪks, lo-] *ns & pl* : logística *f*

logo ['lo:,go:] *n, pl* **logos** [-,go:z] : logotipo *m*

loin ['lɔɪn] *n* : lomo *m*

loiter ['lɔɪt̬ər] *vi* : vagar, holgazanear

lollipop *or* **lollypop** ['lɑli,pɑp] *n* : pirulí *m,* chupete *m Lat*

lone ['lo:n] *adj* : solitario — **loneliness** ['lo:nlinəs] *n* : soledad *f* — **lonely** ['lo:nli] *adj* **-lier; -est** : solitario, solo — **loner** ['lo:nər] *n* : solitario *m,* -ria *f* — **lonesome** ['lo:nsəm] *adj* : solo, solitario

long[1] ['lɔŋ] *adj* **longer** ['lɔngər]; **longest** ['lɔŋgəst] : largo — **~** *adv* **1** : mucho tiempo **2 all day ~** : todo el día **3 as ~ as** : mientras **4 no ~er** : ya no **5 so ~!** : ¡hasta luego!, ¡adiós! — **~** *n* **1 before ~** : dentro de poco **2 the ~ and the short** : lo esencial

long[2] *vi* **~ for** : anhelar, desear

longevity [lɑn'dʒɛvət̬i] *n* : longevidad *f*

longing [lɔŋɪŋ] *n* : ansia *f,* anhelo *m*

longitude ['lɑndʒə,tu:d, -,tju:d] *n* : longitud *f*

look ['lʊk] *vi* **1** : mirar **2** SEEM : parecer **3 ~ after** : cuidar (de) **4 ~ for** EXPECT : esperar **5 ~ for** SEEK : buscar **6 ~ into** : investigar **7 ~ out** : tener cuidado **8 ~ over** EXAMINE : revisar **9 ~ up to** : respetar — *vt* : mirar — **~** *n* **1** : mirada *f* **2** APPEARANCE : aspecto *m,* aire *m* — **lookout** ['lʊk,aʊt] *n* **1** : puesto *m* de observación **2** WATCHMAN : vigía *mf* **3 be on the ~ for** : estar al acecho de

loom[1] ['lu:m] *n* : telar *m*

loom[2] *vi* **1** APPEAR : aparecer, surgir **2** APPROACH : ser inminente

loop ['lu:p] *n* : lazada *f,* lazo *m* — **~** *vt* : hacer lazadas con — **loophole** ['lu:p-,ho:l] *n* : escapatoria *f*

loose ['lu:s] *adj* **looser; -est 1** MOVABLE : flojo, suelto **2** SLACK : flojo **3** ROOMY : holgado **4** APPROXIMATE : libre, aproximado **5** FREE : suelto **6** IMMORAL : relajado — **loosely** ['lu:sli] *adv* **1** : sin apretar **2** ROUGHLY : aproximadamente — **loosen** ['lu:sən] *vt* : aflojar

loot ['lu:t] *n* : botín *m* — **~** *vt* : saquear, robar — **looter** ['lu:t̬ər] *n* : saqueador *m,* -dora *f* — **looting** ['lu:t̬ɪŋ] *n* : saqueo *m*

lop ['lɑp] *vt* **lopped; lopping** : cortar, podar

lopsided ['lɑp,saɪdəd] *adj* : torcido, chueco *Lat*

lord ['lɔrd] *n* **1** : señor *m,* noble *m* **2 the Lord** : el Señor

lore ['lor] *n* : saber *m* popular, tradición *f*

lose ['lu:z] *v* **lost** ['lɔst]; **losing** ['lu:zɪŋ] *vt* **1** : perder **2 ~ one's way** : perderse **3 ~ time** : atrasarse (dícese de un reloj) — *vi* : perder — **loser** ['lu:zər] *n* : perdedor *m,* -dora *f* — **loss** ['lɔs] *n* **1** : pérdida *f* **2** DEFEAT : derrota *f* **3 be at a ~ for words** : no encontrar palabras — **lost** ['lɔst] *adj* **1** : perdido **2 get ~** : perderse

lot ['lɑt] *n* **1** FATE : suerte *f* **2** PLOT : solar *m* **3 a ~ of** *or* **~s of** : mucho, un montón de

lotion ['lo:ʃən] *n* : loción *f*

lottery ['lɑt̬əri] *n, pl* **-teries** : lotería *f*

loud ['laʊd] *adj* **1** : alto, fuerte **2** NOISY : ruidoso **3** FLASHY : llamativo — **~** *adv* **1** : fuerte **2 out ~** : en voz alta — **loudly** ['laʊdli] *adv* : en voz alta — **loudspeaker** ['laʊd,spi:kər] *n* : altavoz *m*

lounge ['laʊndʒ] *vi* **lounged; lounging 1** : repantigarse **2** *or* **~ about** : holgazanear — **~** *n* : salón *m*

louse ['laʊs] *n, pl* **lice** ['laɪs] : piojo *m* — **lousy** ['laʊzi] *adj* **lousier; -est 1** : piojoso **2** BAD : pésimo, muy malo

love ['lʌv] *n* **1** : amor *m* **2 fall in ~** : enamorarse — **~** *v* **loved; loving** : querer, amar — **lovable** ['lʌvəbəl] *adj* : adorable, amoroso *Lat* — **lovely** ['lʌvli] *adj* **-lier; -est** : lindo, precioso — **lover** ['lʌvər] *n* : amante *mf* — **loving** ['lʌvɪŋ] *adj* : cariñoso

low ['lo:] *adj* **lower** ['lo:ər]; **-est 1** : bajo **2** SCARCE : escaso **3** DEPRESSED : deprimido — **~** *adv* **1** : bajo **2 turn the lights down ~** : bajar las luces — **~** *n* **1** : punto *m* bajo **2** *or* **~ gear** : primera velocidad *f* — **lower** ['lo:ər] *adj* : inferior, más bajo — **~** *vt* : bajar — **lowly** ['lo:li] *adj* **-lier; -est** : humilde

loyal ['lɔɪəl] *adj* : leal, fiel — **loyalty** ['lɔɪəlti] *n, pl* **-ties** : lealtad *f*

lozenge [ˈlɑzəndʒ] *n* : pastilla *f*
lubricate [ˈluːbrɪˌkeɪt] *vt* **-cated; -cating** : lubricar — **lubricant** [ˈluːbrɪkənt] *n* : lubricante *m* — **lubrication** [ˌluːbrɪˈkeɪʃən] *n* : lubricación *f*
lucid [ˈluːsəd] *adj* : lúcido — **lucidity** [luːˈsɪdət̬i] *n* : lucidez *f*
luck [ˈlʌk] *n* **1** : suerte *f* **2 good ~!**: ¡buena suerte! — **luckily** [ˈlʌkəli] *adv* : afortunadamente — **lucky** [ˈlʌki] *adj* **luckier; -est 1** : afortunado **2 ~ charm** : amuleto *m* (de la suerte)
lucrative [ˈluːkrət̬ɪv] *adj* : lucrativo
ludicrous [ˈluːdəkrəs] *adj* : ridículo, absurdo
lug [ˈlʌg] *vt* **lugged; lugging** : arrastrar
luggage [ˈlʌgɪdʒ] *n* : equipaje *m*
lukewarm [ˈluːkˈwɔrm] *adj* : tibio
lull [ˈlʌl] *vt* **1** CALM : calmar **2 ~ to sleep** : adormecer — **~** *n* : período *m* de calma, pausa *f*
lullaby [ˈlʌləˌbaɪ] *n, pl* **-bies** : canción *f* de cuna, nana *f*
lumber [ˈlʌmbər] *n* : madera *f* — **lumberjack** [ˈlʌmbərˌdʒæk] *n* : leñador *m*, -dora *f*
luminous [ˈluːmənəs] *adj* : luminoso
lump [ˈlʌmp] *n* **1** CHUNK, PIECE : pedazo *m*, trozo *m* **2** SWELLING : bulto *m* **3** : grumo *m* (en un líquido) — **~** *vt or* **~ together** : juntar, agrupar — **lumpy** [ˈlʌmpi] *adj* **lumpier; -est** : grumoso (dícese de una salsa), lleno de bultos (dícese de un colchón)
lunacy [ˈluːnəsi] *n, pl* **-cies** : locura *f*
lunar [ˈluːnər] *adj* : lunar
lunatic [ˈluːnəˌtɪk] *n* : loco *m*, -ca *f*
lunch [ˈlʌntʃ] *n* : almuerzo *m*, comida *f* — **~** *vi* : almorzar, comer — **luncheon** [ˈlʌntʃən] *n* : comida *f*, almuerzo *m*
lung [ˈlʌŋ] *n* : pulmón *m*
lunge [ˈlʌndʒ] *vi* **lunged; lunging 1** : lanzarse **2 ~ at** : arremeter contre
lurch[1] [ˈlərtʃ] *vi* **1** STAGGER : tambalearse **2** : dar bandazos (dícese de un vehículo)
lurch[2] *n* **leave in a ~** : dejar en la estacada
lure [ˈlʊr] *n* **1** BAIT : señuelo *m* **2** ATTRACTION : atractivo *m* — **~** *vt* **lured; luring** : atraer
lurid [ˈlʊrəd] *adj* **1** GRUESOME : espeluznante **2** SENSATIONAL : sensacionalista **3** GAUDY : chillón
lurk [ˈlərk] *vi* : estar al acecho
luscious [ˈlʌʃəs] *adj* : delicioso, exquisito
lush [ˈlʌʃ] *adj* : exuberante, suntuoso
lust [ˈlʌst] *n* **1** : lujuria *f* **2** CRAVING : ansia *f*, anhelo *m* — **~** *vi* **~ after** : desear (a una persona), codiciar (riquezas, etc.)
luster *or* **lustre** [ˈlʌstər] *n* : lustre *m*
lusty [ˈlʌsti] *adj* **lustier; -est** : fuerte, vigoroso
luxurious [ˌlʌgˈʒʊriəs, ˌlʌkˈʃʊr-] *adj* : lujoso — **luxury** [ˈlʌkʃəri, ˈlʌgʒə-] *n, pl* **-ries** : lujo *m*
lye [ˈlaɪ] *n* : lejía *f*
lying → **lie**
lynch [ˈlɪntʃ] *vt* : linchar
lynx [ˈlɪŋks] *n* : lince *m*
lyric [ˈlɪrɪk] *or* **lyrical** [ˈlɪrɪkəl] *adj* : lírico — **lyrics** *npl* : letra *f* (de una canción)

M

m [ˈɛm] *n, pl* **m's** *or* **ms** [ˈɛmz] : m *f*, decimotercera letra del alfabeto inglés
ma'am [ˈmæm] → **madam**
macabre [məˈkɑb, -ˈkɑbər, -ˈkɑbrə] *adj* : macabro
macaroni [ˌmækəˈroːni] *n* : macarrones *mpl*
mace [ˈmeɪs] *n* **1** : maza *f* (arma o símbolo) **2** : macis *f* (especia)
machete [məˈʃɛt̬i] *n* : machete *m*
machine [məˈʃiːn] *n* : máquina *f* — **machinery** [məˈʃiːnəri] *n, pl* **-eries 1** : maquinaria *f* **2** WORKS : mecanismo *m* — **machine gun** *n* : ametralladora *f*
mad [ˈmæd] *adj* **madder; maddest 1** INSANE : loco **2** FOOLISH : insensato **3** ANGRY : furioso
madam [ˈmædəm] *n, pl* **mesdames** [meɪˈdɑm] : señora *f*
madden [ˈmædən] *vt* : enfurecer
made → **make**
madly [ˈmædli] *adv* : como un loco, locamente — **madman** [ˈmædˌmæn, -mən] *n, pl* **-men** [-mən, -ˌmɛn] : loco *m* — **madness** [ˈmædnəs] *n* : locura *f*
Mafia [ˈmɑfiə] *n* : Mafia *f*
magazine [ˈmægəˌziːn] *n* **1** PERIODICAL : revista *f* **2** : recámara *f* (de un arma de fuego)
maggot [ˈmægət] *n* : gusano *m*
magic [ˈmædʒɪk] *n* : magia *f* — **~** *or* **magical** [ˈmædʒɪkəl] *adj* : mágico — **magician** [məˈdʒɪʃən] *n* : mago *m*, -ga *f*

magistrate ['mædʒəˌstreɪt] *n* : magistrado *m*, -da *f*
magnanimous [mæg'nænəməs] *adj* : magnánimo
magnate ['mægˌneɪt, -nət] *n* : magnate *mf*
magnet ['mægnət] *n* : imán *m* — **magnetic** [mæg'nɛt̬ɪk] *adj* : magnético — **magnetism** ['mægnəˌtɪzəm] *n* : magnetismo *m* — **magnetize** ['mægnəˌtaɪz] *vt* **-tized; -tizing** : magnetizar
magnificent [mæg'nɪfəsənt] *adj* : magnífico — **magnificence** [mæg'nɪfəsənts] *n* : magnificencia *f*
magnify ['mægnəˌfaɪ] *vt* **-fied; -fying 1** ENLARGE : ampliar **2** EXAGGERATE : exagerar — **magnifying glass** *n* : lupa *f*
magnitude ['mægnəˌtuːd, -ˌtjuːd] *n* : magnitud *f*
magnolia [mæg'noːljə] *n* : magnolia *f*
mahogany [mə'hɑgəni] *n, pl* **-nies** : caoba *f*
maid ['meɪd] *n* : sirvienta *f*, criada *f*, muchacha *f* — **maiden** ['meɪdən] *adj* FIRST : inaugural — **maiden name** *n* : nombre *m* de soltera
mail ['meɪl] *n* **1** : correo *m* **2** LETTERS : correspondencia *f* — **~** *vt* : enviar por correo — **mailbox** ['meɪlˌbɑks] *n* : buzón *m* — **mailman** ['meɪlˌmæn, -mən] *n, pl* **-men** [-mən, -ˌmɛn] : cartero *m*
maim ['meɪm] *vt* : mutilar
main ['meɪn] *n* : tubería *f* principal (de agua o gas), cable *m* principal (de un circuito) — **~** *adj* : principal — **mainframe** ['meɪnˌfreɪm] *n* : computadora *f* central — **mainland** ['meɪnˌlænd, -lənd] *n* : continente *m* — **mainly** ['meɪnli] *adv* : principalmente — **mainstay** ['meɪnˌsteɪ] *n* : sostén *m* (principal) — **mainstream** ['meɪnˌstriːm] *n* : corriente *f* principal — **~** *adj* : dominante, convencional
maintain [meɪn'teɪn] *vt* : mantener — **maintenance** ['meɪntənənts] *n* : mantenimiento *m*
maize ['meɪz] *n* : maíz *m*
majestic [mə'dʒɛstɪk] *adj* : majestuoso — **majesty** ['mædʒəsti] *n, pl* **-ties** : majestad *f*
major ['meɪdʒər] *adj* **1** : muy importante, principal **2** : mayor (en música) — **~** *n* **1** : mayor *mf*, comandante *mf* (en las fuerzas armadas) **2** : especialidad *f* (universitaria) — **~** *vi* **-jored; -joring** : especializarse — **majority** [mə'dʒɔrət̬i] *n, pl* **-ties** : mayoría *f*
make ['meɪk] *v* **made** ['meɪd]; **making** *vt* **1** : hacer **2** MANUFACTURE : fabricar **3** CONSTITUTE : constituir **4** PREPARE : preparar **5** RENDER : poner **6** COMPEL : obligar **7 ~ a decision** : tomar una decisión **8 ~ a living** : ganar la vida — *vi* **1 ~ do** : arreglárselas **2 ~ for** : dirigirse a **3 ~ good** SUCCEED : tener éxito — **~** *n* BRAND : marca *f* — **make–believe** [ˌmeɪkbə'liːv] *n* : fantasía *f* — **~** *adj* : imaginario — **make out** *vt* **1** : hacer (un cheque, etc.) **2** DISCERN : distinguir **3** UNDERSTAND : comprender — *vi* **how did you ~?** : ¿qué tal te fue? — **maker** ['meɪkər] *n* MANUFACTURER : fabricante *mf* — **makeshift** ['meɪkˌʃɪft] *adj* : improvisado — **makeup** ['meɪkˌʌp] *n* **1** COMPOSITION : composición *f* **2** COSMETICS : maquillaje *m* — **make up** *vt* **1** PREPARE : preparar **2** INVENT : inventar **3** CONSTITUTE : formar — *vi* RECONCILE : hacer las paces
maladjusted [ˌmælə'dʒʌstəd] *adj* : inadaptado
malaria [mə'lɛriə] *n* : malaria *f*, paludismo *m*
male ['meɪl] *n* : macho *m* (de animales o plantas), varón *m* (de personas) — **~** *adj* **1** : macho **2** MASCULINE : masculino
malevolent [mə'lɛvələnt] *adj* : malévolo
malfunction [mæl'fʌŋkʃən] *vi* : funcionar mal — **~** *n* : mal funcionamiento *m*
malice ['mælɪs] *n* : mala intención *f*, rencor *m* — **malicious** [mə'lɪʃəs] *adj* : malicioso
malign [mə'laɪn] *adj* : maligno — **~** *vt* : calumniar
malignant [mə'lɪgnənt] *adj* : maligno
mall ['mɔl] *n or* **shopping ~** : centro *m* comercial
malleable ['mæliəbəl] *adj* : maleable
mallet ['mælət] *n* : mazo *m*
malnutrition [ˌmælnʊ'trɪʃən, -njʊ-] *n* : desnutrición *f*
malpractice [ˌmæl'præktəs] *n* : mala práctica *f*, negligencia *f*
malt ['mɔlt] *n* : malta *f*
mama *or* **mamma** ['mɑmə] *n* : mamá *f*
mammal ['mæməl] *n* : mamífero *m*
mammogram ['mæməˌgræm] *n* : mamografía *f*
mammoth ['mæməθ] *adj* : gigantesco
man ['mæn] *n, pl* **men** ['mɛn] : hombre *m* — **~** *vt* **manned; manning** : tripular (un barco o avión), encargarse de (un servicio)
manage ['mænɪdʒ] *v* **-aged; -aging** *vt* **1** HANDLE : manejar **2** DIRECT : administrar, dirigir — *vi* COPE : arreglárselas

— **manageable** ['mænɪdʒəbəl] *adj* : manejable — **management** ['mænɪdʒmənt] *n* : dirección *f* — **manager** ['mænɪdʒər] *n* : director *m*, -tora *f*; gerente *mf* — **managerial** [ˌmænə'dʒɪriəl] *adj* : directivo
mandarin ['mændərən] *n or* ~ **orange** : mandarina *f*
mandate ['mænˌdeɪt] *n* : mandato *m* — **mandatory** ['mændəˌtori] *adj* : obligatorio
mane ['meɪn] *n* : crin *f* (de un caballo), melena *f* (de un león)
maneuver [mə'nuːvər, -'njuː-] *n* : maniobra *f* — ~ *v* **-vered; -vering** : maniobrar
mangle ['mæŋgəl] *vt* **-gled; -gling** : destrozar
mango ['mæŋˌgoː] *n, pl* **-goes** : mango *m*
mangy ['meɪndʒi] *adj* **mangier; -est** : sarnoso
manhandle ['mænˌhændəl] *vi* **-dled; -dling** : maltratar
manhole ['mænˌhoːl] *n* : boca *f* de alcantarilla
manhood ['mænˌhʊd] *n* **1** : madurez *f* (de un hombre) **2** VIRILITY : virilidad *f*
mania ['meɪniə, -njə] *n* : manía *f* — **maniac** ['meɪniˌæk] *n* : maníaco *m*, -ca *f*
manicure ['mænəˌkjʊr] *n* : manicura *f* — ~ *vt* **-cured; -curing** : hacer la manicura a
manifest ['mænəˌfɛst] *adj* : manifiesto, patente — ~ *vt* : manifestar — **manifesto** [ˌmænə'fɛsˌtoː] *n, pl* **-tos** *or* **-toes** : manifiesto *m*
manipulate [mə'nɪpjəˌleɪt] *vt* **-lated; -lating** : manipular — **manipulation** [məˌnɪpjə'leɪʃən] *n* : manipulación *f*
mankind ['mæn'kaɪnd, ˌkaɪnd] *n* : género *m* humano, humanidad *f*
manly ['mænli] *adj* **-lier; -est** : viril — **manliness** ['mænlinəs] *n* : virilidad *f*
man–made ['mæn'meɪd] *adj* : artificial
mannequin ['mænɪkən] *n* : maniquí *m*
manner ['mænər] *n* **1** : manera *f* **2** KIND : clase *f* **3** ~**s** *npl* ETIQUETTE : modales *mpl*, educación *f* — **mannerism** ['mænəˌrɪzəm] *n* : peculiaridad *f* (de una persona)
manoeuvre *Brit* → **maneuver**
manor ['mænər] *n* : casa *f* solariega
manpower ['mænˌpaʊər] *n* : mano *f* de obra
mansion ['mæntʃən] *n* : mansión *f*
manslaughter ['mænˌslɔt̬ər] *n* : homicidio *m* sin premeditación
mentel ['mæntəl] *or* **mantelpiece** ['mæntəlˌpiːs] *n* : repisa *f* de la chimenea
manual ['mænjʊəl] *adj* : manual — ~ *n* : manual *m*
manufacture [ˌmænjə'fæktʃər] *n* : fabricación *f* — ~ *vt* **-tured; -turing** : fabricar — **manufacturer** [ˌmænjə'fæktʃərər] *n* : fabricante *mf*
manure [mə'nʊr, -'njʊr] *n* : estiércol *m*
manuscript ['mænjəˌskrɪpt] *n* : manuscrito *m*
many ['mɛni] *adj* **more** ['mor]; **most** ['moːst] **1** : muchos **2 as** ~ : tantos **3 how** ~ : cuántos **4 too** ~ : demasiados — ~ *pron* : muchos *pl*, -chas *pl*
map ['mæp] *n* : mapa *m* — ~ *vt* **mapped; mapping 1** : trazar el mapa de **2** *or* ~ **out** : planear, proyectar
maple ['meɪpəl] *n* : arce *m*
mar ['mɑr] *vt* **marred; marring** : estropear
marathon ['mærəˌθɑn] *n* : maratón *m*
marble ['mɑrbəl] *n* **1** : mármol *m* **2** ~**s** *npl* : canicas *fpl* (para jugar)
march ['mɑrtʃ] *n* : marcha *f* — ~ *vi* : marchar, desfilar
March ['mɑrtʃ] *n* : marzo *m*
mare ['mær] *n* : yegua *f*
margarine ['mɑrdʒərən] *n* : margarina *f*
margin ['mɑrdʒən] *n* : margen *m* — **marginal** ['mɑrdʒənəl] *adj* : marginal
marigold ['mærəˌgoːld] *n* : caléndula *f*
marijuana [ˌmærə'hwɑnə] *n* : marihuana *f*
marinate ['mærəˌneɪt] *vt* **-nated; -nating** : marinar
marine [mə'riːn] *adj* : marino — ~ *n* : soldado *m* de marina
marionette [ˌmæriə'nɛt] *n* : marioneta *f*
marital ['mærət̬əl] *adj* **1** : matrimonial **2** ~ **status** : estado *m* civil
maritime ['mærəˌtaɪm] *adj* : marítimo
mark ['mɑrk] *n* **1** : marca *f* **2** STAIN : mancha *f* **3** IMPRINT : huella *f* **4** TARGET : blanco *m* **5** GRADE : nota *f* — ~ *vt* **1** : marcar **2** STAIN : manchar **3** POINT OUT : señalar **4** : calificar (un examen, etc.) **5** COMMEMORATE : conmemorar **6** CHARACTERIZE : caracterizar **7** ~ **off** : delimitar — **marked** ['mɑrkt] *adj* : marcado, notable — **markedly** ['mɑrkədli] *adv* : notablemente — **marker** ['mɑrkər] *n* : marcador *m*
market ['mɑrkət] *n* : mercado *m* — ~ *vt* : vender, comercializar — **marketable** ['mɑrkət̬əbəl] *adj* : vendible — **marketplace** ['mɑrkətˌpleɪs] *n* : mercado *m*
marksman ['mɑrksmən] *n, pl* **-men** [-mən, -ˌmɛn] : tirador *m* — **marksmanship** ['mɑrksmənʃɪp] *n* : puntería *f*
marmalade ['mɑrməˌleɪd] *n* : mermelada *f*

maroon[1] [mə'ru:n] *vt* : abandonar, aislar
maroon[2] *n* : rojo *m* oscuro
marquee [mɑr'ki:] *n* CANOPY : marquesina *f*
marriage ['mærɪdʒ] *n* **1** : matrimonio *m* **2** WEDDING : casamiento *m*, boda *f* — **married** ['mærid] *adj* **1** : casado **2 get ~** : casarse
marrow ['mæro:] *n* : médula *f*, tuétano *m*
marry ['mæri] *v* **-ried; -rying** *vt* **1** : casar **2** WED : casarse con — *vi* : casarse
Mars ['mɑrz] *n* : Marte *m*
marsh ['mɑrʃ] *n* **1** : pantano *m* **2** *or* **salt ~** : marisma *f*
marshal ['mɑrʃəl] *n* : mariscal *m* (en el ejército); jefe *m*, -fa *f* (de policía, de bomberos, etc.) — **~** *vt* **-shaled** *or* **-shalled; -shaling** *or* **-shalling** : poner en orden (los pensamientos, etc.), reunir (las tropas)
marshmallow ['mɑrʃ,mɛlo:, -,mælo:] *n* : malvavisco *m*
marshy ['mɑrʃi] *adj* **marshier; -est** : pantanoso
mart ['mɑrt] *n* : mercado *m*
martial ['mɑrʃəl] *adj* : marcial
martyr ['mɑrt̬ər] *n* : mártir *mf* — **~** *vt* : martirizar
marvel ['mɑrvəl] *n* : maravilla *f* — **~** *vi* **-veled** *or* **-velled; -veling** *or* **-velling** : maravillarse — **marvelous** ['mɑrvələs] *or* **marvellous** *adj* : maravilloso
mascara [mæs'kærə] *n* : rímel *m*
mascot ['mæs,kɑt, -kət] *n* : mascota *f*
masculine ['mæskjələn] *adj* : masculino — **masculinity** [,mæskjə'lɪnət̬i] *n* : masculinidad *f*
mash ['mæʃ] *vt* **1** CRUSH : aplastar, majar **2** PUREE : hacer puré de — **mashed potatoes** *npl* : puré *m* de patatas, puré *m* de papas *Lat*
mask ['mæsk] *n* : máscara *f* — **~** *vt* : enmascarar
masochism ['mæsə,kɪzəm, 'mæzə-] *n* : masoquismo *m* — **masochist** ['mæsə,kɪst, 'mæzə-] *n* : masoquista *mf* — **masochistic** [,mæsə'kɪstɪk, ,mæzə-] *adj* : masoquista
mason ['meɪsən] *n* : albañil *mf* — **masonry** ['meɪsənri] *n, pl* **-ries** : albañilería *f*
masquerade [,mæskə'reɪd] *n* : mascarada *f* — **~** *vi* **-aded; -ading ~ as** : disfrazarse de, hacerse pasar por
mass ['mæs] *n* **1** : masa *f* **2** MULTITUDE : cantidad *f* **3 the ~es** : las masas
Mass ['mæs] *n* : misa *f*
massacre ['mæsɪkər] *n* : masacre *f* — **~** *vt* **-cred; -cring** : masacrar
massage [mə'sɑʒ, -'sɑdʒ] *n* : masaje *m* — **~** *vt* **-saged; -saging** : dar masaje a, masajear — **masseur** [mæ'sər] *n* : masajista *m* — **masseuse** [mæ'səz, -'sərz, -'su:z] *n* : masajista *f*
massive ['mæsɪv] *adj* **1** BULKY, SOLID : macizo **2** HUGE : enorme, masivo
mast ['mæst] *n* : mástil *m*
master ['mæstər] *n* **1** : amo *m*, señor *m* (de la casa) **2** EXPERT : maestro *m*, -tra *f* **3 ~'s degree** : maestría *f* — **~** *vt* : dominar — **masterful** ['mæstərfəl] *adj* : magistral — **masterpiece** ['mæstər,pi:s] *n* : obra *f* maestra — **mastery** ['mæstəri] *n* : maestría *f*
masturbate ['mæstər,beɪt] *v* **-bated; -bating** *vi* : masturbarse — **masturbation** [,mæstər'beɪʃən] *n* : masturbación *f*
mat ['mæt] *n* **1** DOORMAT : felpudo *m* **2** RUG : estera *f*
matador ['mæt̬ə,dɔr] *n* : matador *m*
match ['mætʃ] *n* **1** EQUAL : igual *mf* **2** : fósforo *m*, cerilla *f* (para encender) **3** GAME : partido *m*, combate *m* (en boxeo) **4 be a good ~** : hacer buena pareja — **~** *vt* **1** *or* **~ up** : emparejar **2** EQUAL : igualar **3** : combinar con, hacer juego con (ropa, colores, etc.) — *vi* : concordar, coincidir
mate ['meɪt] *n* **1** COMPANION : compañero *m*, -ra *f*; amigo *m*, -ga *f* **2** : macho *m*, hembra *f* (de animales) — **~** *vi* **mated; mating** : aparearse
material [mə'tɪriəl] *adj* **1** : material **2** IMPORTANT : importante — **~** *n* **1** : material *m* **2** CLOTH : tela *f*, tejido *m* — **materialistic** [mə,tɪriə'lɪstɪk] *adj* : materialista — **materialize** [mə'tɪriə,laɪz] *vi* **-ized; -izing** : aparecer
maternal [mə'tərnəl] *adj* : maternal — **maternity** [mə'tərnət̬i] *n, pl* **-ties** : maternidad *f* — **~** *adj* **1** : de maternidad **2 ~ clothes** : ropa *f* de futura mamá
math ['mæθ] → **mathematics**
mathematics [,mæθə'mæt̬ɪks] *ns & pl* : matemáticas *fpl* — **mathematical** [,mæθə'mæt̬ɪkəl] *adj* : matemático — **mathematician** [,mæθəmə'tɪʃən] *n* : matemático *m*, -ca *f*
matinee *or* **matinée** [,mætən'eɪ] *n* : matiné(e) *f*, fonción *f* de tarde
matrimony ['mætrə,mo:ni] *n* : matrimonio *m* — **matrimonial** [,mætrə'mo:niəl] *adj* : matrimonial
matrix ['meɪtrɪks] *n, pl* **-trices** ['meɪtrə,si:z, 'mæ-] *or* **-trixes** ['meɪtrɪksəz] : matriz *f*
matte ['mæt] *adj* : mate
matter ['mæt̬ər] *n* **1** SUBSTANCE : materia

f 2 QUESTION : asunto *m,* cuestión *f* 3 **as a ~ of fact** : en efecto, en realidad 4 **for that ~** : de hecho 5 **to make ~s worse** : para colmo de males 6 **what's the ~?** : ¿qué pasa? — ~ *vi* : importar

mattress ['mætrəs] *n* : colchón *m*

mature [mə'tʊr, -'tjʊr, -'tʃʊr] *adj* **-turer; -est** : maduro — ~ *vi* **-tured; -turing** : madurar — **maturity** [mə'tʊrət̬i, -'tjʊr-, -'tʃʊr-] *n* : madurez *f*

maul ['mɔl] *vt* : maltratar, aporrear

mauve ['mo:v, 'mɔv] *n* : malva *m*

maxim ['mæksəm] *n* : máxima *f*

maximum ['mæksəməm] *n, pl* **-ma** ['mæksəmə] *or* **-mums** : máximo *m* — ~ *adj* : máximo — **maximize** ['mæksə,maɪz] *vt* **-mized; -mizing** : llevar al máximo

may ['meɪ] *v aux, past* **might** ['maɪt]; *present s & pl* **may** 1 : poder 2 **come what ~** : pase lo que pase 3 **it ~ happen** : puede pasar 4 **~ the best man win** : que gane el mejor

May ['meɪ] *n* : mayo *m*

maybe ['meɪbi] *adv* : quizás, tal vez

mayhem ['meɪ,hɛm, 'meɪəm] *n* : alboroto *m*

mayonnaise ['meɪə,neɪz] *n* : mayonesa *f*

mayor ['meɪər, 'mɛr] *n* : alcalde *m,* -desa *f*

maze ['meɪz] *n* : laberinto *m*

me ['mi:] *pron* 1 : me 2 **for ~** : para mí 3 **give it to ~!** : ¡dámelo! 4 **it's ~** : soy yo 5 **with ~** : conmigo

meadow ['mɛdo:] *n* : prado *m,* pradera *f*

meager ['mi:gər] *or* **meagre** *adj* : escaso

meal ['mi:l] *n* 1 : comida *f* 2 : harina *f* (de maíz, etc.) — **mealtime** ['mi:l,taɪm] *n* : hora *f* de comer

mean[1] ['mi:n] *vt* **meant** ['mɛnt]; **meaning** 1 SIGNIFY : querer decir 2 INTEND : querer, tener la intención de 3 **be meant for** : estar destinado a 4 **he didn't ~ it** : no lo dijo en serio

mean[2] *adj* 1 UNKIND : malo 2 STINGY : mezquino, tacaño 3 HUMBLE : humilde

mean[3] *adj* AVERAGE : medio — ~ *n* : promedio *m*

meander [mi'ændər] *vi* **-dered; -dering** 1 WIND : serpentear 2 WANDER : vagar

meaning ['mi:nɪŋ] *n* : significado *m,* sentido *m* — **meaningful** ['mi:nɪŋfəl] *adj* : significativo — **meaningless** ['mi:nɪŋləs] *adj* : sin sentido

meanness ['mi:nnəs] *n* 1 UNKINDNESS : maldad *f* 2 STINGINESS : mezquinidad *f*

means ['mi:nz] *n* 1 : medio *m* 2 **by all ~** : por supuesto 3 **by ~ of** : por medio de 4 **by no ~** : de ninguna manera

meantime ['mi:n,taɪm] *n* 1 : interín *m* 2 **in the ~** : mientras tanto — ~ *adv* → **meanwhile**

meanwhile ['mi:n,*h*waɪl] *adv* : mientras tanto — ~ *n* → **meantime**

measles ['mi:zəlz] *npl* : sarampión *m*

measly ['mi:zli] *adj* **-slier; -est** : miserable, mísero

measure ['mɛʒər, 'meɪ-] *n* : medida *f* — ~ *v* **-sured; -suring** : medir — **measurable** ['mɛʒərəbəl, 'meɪ-] *adj* : mensurable — **measurement** ['mɛʒərmənt, 'meɪ-] *n* : medida *f* — **measure up** *vi* **~ to** : estar a la altura de

meat ['mi:t] *n* : carne *f* — **meatball** ['mi:t,bɔl] *n* : albóndiga *f* — **meaty** ['mi:t̬i] *adj* **meatier; -est** 1 : carnoso 2 SUBSTANTIAL : sustancioso

mechanic [mɪ'kænɪk] *n* : mecánico *m,* -ca *f* — **mechanical** [mɪ'kænɪkəl] *adj* : mecánico — **mechanics** [mɪ'kænɪks] *ns & pl* 1 : mecánica *f* 2 WORKINGS : mecanismo *m* — **mechanism** ['mɛkə,nɪzəm] *n* : mecanismo *m* — **mechanize** ['mɛkə,naɪz] *vt* **-nized; -nizing** : mecanizar

medal ['mɛdəl] *n* : medalla *f* — **medallion** [mə'dæljən] *n* : medallón *m*

meddle ['mɛdəl] *vi* **-dled; -dling** : entrometerse

media ['mi:diə] *or* **mass ~** *npl* : medios *mpl* de comunicación

median ['mi:diən] *adj* : medio

mediate ['mi:di,eɪt] *vi* **-ated; -ating** : mediar — **mediation** [,mi:di'eɪʃən] *n* : mediación *f* — **mediator** ['mi:di,eɪt̬ər] *n* : mediador *m,* -dora *f*

medical ['mɛdɪkəl] *adj* : médico — **medicated** ['mɛdə,keɪt̬əd] *adj* : medicinal — **medication** [,mɛdə'keɪʃən] *n* : medicamento *m* — **medicinal** [mə'dɪsənəl] *adj* : medicinal — **medicine** ['mɛdəsən] *n* 1 : medicina *f* 2 MEDICATION : medicina *f,* medicamento *m*

medieval *or* **mediaeval** [mɪ'di:vəl, ,mi:-, ,mɛ-, -di'i:vəl] *adj* : medieval

mediocre [,mi:di'o:kər] *adj* : mediocre — **mediocrity** [,mi:di'ɑkrət̬i] *n, pl* **-ties** : mediocridad *f*

meditate ['mɛdə,teɪt] *vi* **-tated; -tating** : meditar — **meditation** [,mɛdə'teɪʃən] *n* : meditación *f*

medium ['mi:diəm] *n, pl* **-diums** *or* **-dia** ['mi:diə] 1 MEANS : medio *m* 2 MEAN : punto *m* medio, término *m* medio 3 → **media** — ~ *adj* : mediano

medley ['mɛdli] *n, pl* **-leys 1 :** mezcla *f* **2 :** popurrí *m* (de canciones)
meek ['mi:k] *adj* **:** dócil
meet ['mi:t] *v* **met** ['mɛt]; **meeting** *vt* **1** ENCOUNTER **:** encontrarse con **2** SATISFY **:** satisfacer **3 pleased to ~ you :** encantado de conocerlo — *vi* **1 :** encontrarse **2** ASSEMBLE **:** reunirse **3** BE INTRODUCED **:** conocerse — **~** *n* **:** encuentro *m* — **meeting** ['mi:ṯɪŋ] *n* **:** reunión *f*
megabyte ['mɛgə,baɪt] *n* **:** megabyte *m*
megaphone ['mɛgə,fo:n] *n* **:** megáfono *m*
melancholy ['mɛlən,kɑli] *n, pl* **-cholies :** melancolía *f* — **~** *adj* **:** melancólico, triste
mellow ['mɛlo:] *adj* **1 :** suave, dulce **2** CALM **:** apacible **3 :** maduro (dícese de frutas), añejo (dícese de vinos) — **~** *vt* **:** suavizar, endulzar — *vi* **:** suavizarse
melody ['mɛlədi] *n, pl* **-dies :** melodía *f*
melon ['mɛlən] *n* **:** melón *m*
melt ['mɛlt] *vi* **:** derretirse, fundirse — *vt* **:** derretir
member ['mɛmbər] *n* **:** miembro *m* — **membership** ['mɛmbər,ʃɪp] *n* **1 :** calidad *f* de miembro **2** MEMBERS **:** miembros *mpl*
membrane ['mɛm,breɪn] *n* **:** membrana *f*
memory ['mɛmri, 'mɛmə-] *n, pl* **-ries 1 :** memoria *f* **2** RECOLLECTION **:** recuerdo *m* — **memento** [mɪ'mɛn,to:] *n, pl* **-tos** *or* **-toes :** recuerdo *m* — **memo** ['mɛmo:] *n, pl* **memos** *or* **memorandum** [,mɛmə'rændəm] *n, pl* **-dums** *or* **-da** [-də] **:** memorándum *m* — **memoirs** ['mɛm,wɑrz] *npl* **:** memorias *fpl* — **memorable** ['mɛmərəbəl] *adj* **:** memorable — **memorial** [mə'moriəl] *adj* **:** conmemorativo — **~** *n* **:** monumento *m* (conmemorativo) — **memorize** ['mɛmə,raɪz] *vt* **-rized; -rizing :** aprender de memoria
men → **man**
menace ['mɛnəs] *n* **:** amenaza *f* — **~** *vt* **-aced; -acing :** amenazar — **menacing** ['mɛnəsɪŋ] *adj* **:** amenazador
mend ['mɛnd] *vt* **1 :** reparar, arreglar **2** DARN **:** zurcir — *vi* HEAL **:** curarse
menial ['mi:niəl] *adj* **:** servil, bajo
meningitis [,mɛnən'dʒaɪṯəs] *n, pl* **-gitides** [-'dʒɪṯə,di:z] **:** meningitis *f*
menopause ['mɛnə,pɔz] *n* **:** menopausia *f*
menstruate ['mɛntstrʊ,eɪt] *vi* **-ated; -ating :** menstruar — **menstruation** [,mɛntstrʊ'eɪʃən] *n* **:** menstruación *f*
mental ['mɛntəl] *adj* **:** mental — **mentality** [mɛn'tæləṯi] *n, pl* **-ties :** mentalidad *f*
mention ['mɛntʃən] *n* **:** mención *f* — **mention** *vt* **1 :** mencionar **2 don't ~ it! :** ¡de nada!, ¡no hay de qué!
menu ['mɛn,ju:] *n* **:** menú *m*
meow [mi:'aʊ] *n* **:** maullido *m,* miau *m* — **~** *vi* **:** maullar
mercenary ['mərsən,ɛri] *n, pl* **-naries :** mercenario *m,* **-ria** *f* — **~** *adj* **:** mercenario
merchant ['mərtʃənt] *n* **:** comerciante *mf* — **merchandise** ['mərtʃən,daɪz, -,daɪs] *n* **:** mercancía *f,* mercadería *f*
merciful ['mərsɪfəl] *adj* **:** misericordioso, compasivo — **merciless** ['mərsɪləs] *adj* **:** despiadado
mercury ['mərkjəri] *n, pl* **-ries :** mercurio *m*
Mercury *n* **:** Mercurio *m*
mercy ['mərsi] *n, pl* **-cies 1 :** misericordia *f,* compasión *f* **2 at the ~ of :** a merced de
mere ['mɪr] *adj, superlative* **merest :** mero, simple — **merely** ['mɪrli] *adv* **:** simplemente
merge ['mərdʒ] *v* **merged; merging** *vi* **:** unirse, fusionarse (dícese de las compañías), confluir (dícese de los ríos, las calles, etc.) — *vt* **:** unir, fusionar, combinar — **merger** ['mərdʒər] *n* **:** unión *f,* fusión *f*
merit ['mɛrət] *n* **:** mérito *m* — **~** *vt* **:** merecer
mermaid ['mər,meɪd] *n* **:** sirena *f*
merry ['mɛri] *adj* **-rier; -est :** alegre — **merry-go-round** ['mɛrigo,raʊnd] *n* **:** tiovivo *m*
mesa ['meɪsə] *n* **:** mesa *f*
mesh ['mɛʃ] *n* **:** malla *f*
mesmerize ['mɛzmə,raɪz] *vt* **-ized; -izing :** hipnotizar
mess ['mɛs] *n* **1 :** desorden *m* **2** MUDDLE **:** lío *m* **3 :** rancho *m* (militar) — **~** *vt* **1** *or* **~ up** SOIL **:** ensuciar **2 ~ up** DISARRANGE **:** desordenar **3 ~ up** BUNGLE **:** echar a perder — *vi* **1 ~ around** PUTTER **:** entretenerse **2 ~ with** PROVOKE **:** meterse con
message ['mɛsɪdʒ] *n* **:** mensaje *m* — **messenger** ['mɛsəndʒər] *n* **:** mensajero *m,* **-ra** *f*
messy ['mɛsi] *adj* **messier; -est :** desordenado, sucio
met → **meet**
metabolism [mə'tæbə,lɪzəm] *n* **:** metabolismo *m*
metal ['mɛṯəl] *n* **:** metal *m* — **metallic** [mə'tælɪk] *adj* **:** metálico

metamorphosis [ˌmɛt̬əˈmɔrfəsɪs] *n, pl* **-phoses** [-ˌsi:z] : metamorfosis *f*
metaphor [ˈmɛt̬əˌfɔr, -fər] *n* : metáfora *f*
meteor [ˈmi:t̬iər, -t̬i:ˌɔr] *n* : meteoro *m* — **meteorological** [ˌmi:t̬iˌɔrəˈlɑdʒɪkəl] *adj* : meteorológico — **meteorologist** [ˌmi:t̬iəˈrɑlədʒɪst] *n* : meteorólogo *m*, -ga *f* — **meteorology** [ˌmi:t̬iəˈrɑlədʒi] *n* : meteorología *f*
meter *or Brit* **metre** [ˈmi:t̬ər] *n* **1** : metro *m* **2** : contador *m* (de electricidad, etc.)
method [ˈmɛθəd] *n* : método *m* — **methodical** [məˈθɑdɪkəl] *adj* : metódico
meticulous [məˈtɪkjələs] *adj* : meticuloso
metric [ˈmɛtrɪk] *or* **metrical** [-trɪkəl] *adj* : métrico
metropolis [məˈtrɑpələs] *n* : metrópoli *f* — **metropolitan** [ˌmɛtrəˈpɑlətən] *adj* : metropolitano
Mexican [ˈmɛksɪkən] *adj* : mexicano
mice → **mouse**
microbe [ˈmaɪˌkro:b] *n* : microbio *m*
microfilm [ˈmaɪkroˌfɪlm] *n* : microfilm *m*
microphone [ˈmaɪkrəˌfo:n] *n* : micrófono *m*
microscope [ˈmaɪkrəˌsko:p] *n* : microscopio *m* — **microscopic** [ˌmaɪkrəˈskɑpɪk] *adj* : microscópico
microwave [ˈmaɪkrəˌweɪv] *n or* **~ oven** : microondas *m*
mid [ˈmɪd] *adj* **1 ~ morning** : a media mañana **2 in ~-August** : a mediados de agosto **3 she is in her mid thirties** : tiene alrededor de 35 años — **midair** [ˈmɪdˈær] *n* **in ~** : en el aire — **midday** [ˈmɪdˈdeɪ] *n* : mediodía *m*
middle [ˈmɪdəl] *adj* : de en medio, del medio — **~** *n* **1** : medio *m*, centro *m* **2 in the ~ of** : en medio de (un espacio), a mitad de (una actividad) **3 in the ~ of the month** : a mediados del mes — **middle–aged** [ˌmɪdəlˈeɪdʒd] *adj* : de mediana edad — **Middle Ages** *npl* : Edad *f* Media — **middle class** *n* : clase *f* media — **middleman** [ˈmɪdəlˌmæn] *n, pl* **-men** [-mən, -ˌmɛn] : intermediario *m*, -ria *f*
midget [ˈmɪdʒət] *n* : enano *m*, -na *f*
midnight [ˈmɪdˌnaɪt] *n* : medianoche *f*
midriff [ˈmɪdˌrɪf] *n* : diafragma *m*
midst [ˈmɪdst] *n* **1 in the ~ of** : en medio de **2 in our ~** : entre nosotros
midsummer [ˈmɪdˈsʌmər, -ˌsʌ-] *n* : pleno verano *m*
midway [ˈmɪdˌweɪ] *adv* : a mitad de camino, a medio camino
midwife [ˈmɪdˌwaɪf] *n, pl* **-wives** [-ˌwaɪvz] : comadrona *f*
midwinter [ˈmɪdˈwɪntər, -ˌwɪn-] *n* : pleno invierno *m*
miff [ˈmɪf] *vt* : ofender
might[1] [ˈmaɪt] (*used to express permission or possibility or as a polite alternative to* **may**) → **may**
might[2] *n* : fuerza *f*, poder *m* — **mighty** [ˈmaɪt̬i] *adj* **mightier; -est 1** : fuerte, poderoso **2** GREAT : enorme — **~** *adv* : muy
migraine [ˈmaɪˌgreɪn] *n* : jaqueca *f*, migraña *f*
migrate [ˈmaɪˌgreɪt] *vi* **-grated; -grating** : emigrar — **migrant** [ˈmaɪgrənt] *n* : trabajador *m*, -dora *f* ambulante
mild [ˈmaɪld] *adj* **1** GENTLE : suave **2** LIGHT : leve **3 a ~ climate** : una clima templada
mildew [ˈmɪlˌdu:, -ˌdju:] *n* : moho *m*
mildly [ˈmaɪldli] *adv* : ligeramente, suavemente — **mildness** [ˈmaɪldnəs] *n* : apacibilidad *f* (de personas), suavedad *f* (de sabores, etc.)
mile [ˈmaɪl] *n* : milla *f* — **mileage** [ˈmaɪlɪdʒ] *n* : distancia *f* recorrida (en millas), kilometraje *m* — **milestone** [ˈmaɪlˌsto:n] *n* : hito *m*
military [ˈmɪləˌtɛri] *adj* : militar — **~** *n* **the ~** : las fuerzas armadas — **militant** [ˈmɪlətənt] *adj* : militante — **~** *n* : militante *mf* — **militia** [məˈlɪʃə] *n* : milicia *f*
milk [ˈmɪlk] *n* : leche *f* — **~** *vt* **1** : ordeñar (una vaca, etc.) **2** EXPLOIT : explotar — **milky** [ˈmɪlki] *adj* **milkier; -est** : lechoso — **Milky Way** *n* **the ~** : la Vía Láctea
mill [ˈmɪl] *n* **1** : molino *m* **2** FACTORY : fábrica *f* **3** GRINDER : molinillo *m* — **~** *vt* : moler — *vi or* **~ about** : arremolinarse
millennium [məˈlɛniəm] *n, pl* **-nia** [-niə] *or* **-niums** : milenio *m*
miller [ˈmɪlər] *n* : molinero *m*, -ra *f*
milligram [ˈmɪləˌgræm] *n* : miligramo *m* — **millimeter** *or Brit* **millimetre** [ˈmɪləˌmi:t̬ər] *n* : milímetro *m*
million [ˈmɪljən] *n, pl* **millions** *or* **million 1** : millón *m* **2 a ~ people** : un millón de personas — **~** *adj* **a ~** : un millón de — **millionaire** [ˌmɪljəˈnær, ˈmɪljəˌnær] *n* : millonario *m*, -ria *f* — **millionth** [ˈmɪljənθ] *adj* : millonésimo
mime [ˈmaɪm] *n* **1** : mimo *mf* **2** PANTOMIME : pantomima *f* — **~** *v* **mimed; miming** *vt* : imitar — *vi* : hacer la mímica — **mimic** [ˈmɪmɪk] *vt* **-icked; -icking** : imitar, remedar — **~** *n* : imitador *m*, -dora *f* — **mimicry** [ˈmɪmɪkri] *n, pl* **-ries** : imitación *f*

mince ['mɪnts] *v* **minced; mincing** *vt* **1** : picar, moler **2 not to ~ one's words** : no tener pelos en la lengua
mind ['maɪnd] *n* **1** : mente *f* **2** INTELLECT : capacidad *f* intelectual **3** OPINION : opinión *f* **4** REASON : razón *f* **5 have a ~ to** : tener intención de — **~** *vt* **1** TEND : cuidar **2** OBEY : obedecer **3** WATCH : tener cuidado con **4 I don't ~ the heat** : no me molesta el calor — *vi* **1** OBEY : obedecer **2 I don't ~** : no me importa, me es igual — **mindful** ['maɪndfəl] *adj* : atento — **mindless** ['maɪndləs] *adj* **1** SENSELESS : estúpido, sin sentido **2** DULL : aburrido
mine[1] ['maɪn] *pron* **1** : (el) mío, (la) mía, (los) míos, (las) mías **2 a friend of ~** : un amigo mío
mine[2] *n* : mina *f* — **~** *vt* **mined; mining 1** : extraer (oro, etc.) **2** : minar (con artefactos explosivos) — **minefield** ['maɪn.fi:ld] *n* : campo *m* de minas — **miner** ['maɪnər] *n* : minero *m*, -ra *f*
mineral ['mɪnərəl] *n* : mineral *m*
mingle ['mɪŋgəl] *v* **-gled; -gling** *vt* : mezclar — *vi* **1** : mezclarse **2** : circular (a una fiesta, etc.)
miniature ['mɪniə,tʃʊr, 'mɪnɪ,tʃʊr, -tʃər] *n* : miniatura *f* — **~** *adj* : en miniatura
minimal ['mɪnəməl] *adj* : mínimo — **minimize** ['mɪnə,maɪz] *vt* **-mized; -mizing** : minimizar — **minimum** ['mɪnəməm] *adj* : mínimo — **~** *n, pl* **-ma** ['mɪnəmə] *or* **-mums** : mínimo *m*
mining ['maɪnɪŋ] *n* : minería *f*
minister ['mɪnəstər] *n* **1** : pastor *m*, -tora *f* (de una iglesia) **2** : ministro *m*, -tra *f* (en política) — **~** *vi* **~ to** : cuidar (de), atender a — **ministerial** [,mɪnə'stɪriəl] *adj* : ministerial — **ministry** ['mɪnəstri] *n, pl* **-tries** : ministerio *m*
mink ['mɪŋk] *n, pl* **mink** *or* **minks** : visón *m*
minnow ['mɪno:] *n, pl* **-nows** : pececillo *m* de agua dulce
minor ['maɪnər] *adj* **1** : menor **2** INSIGNIFICANT : sin importancia — **~** *n* **1** : menor *mf* (de edad) **2** : asignatura *f* secundaria (de estudios) — **minority** [mə'nɔrəṭi, maɪ-] *n, pl* **-ties** : minoría *f*
mint[1] ['mɪnt] *n* **1** : menta *f* (planta) **2** : pastilla *f* de menta (dulce)
mint[2] *n* **1 the U.S. Mint** : la casa de la moneda de los EE.UU. **2 be worth a ~** : valer un dineral — **~** *vt* : acuñar — **~** *adj* **in ~ condition** : como nuevo
minus ['maɪnəs] *prep* **1** : menos **2** WITHOUT : sin — **~** *n or* **~ sign** : signo *m* de menos
minuscule ['mɪnəs,kju:l, mɪ'nʌs-] *adj* : minúsculo
minute[1] [maɪ'nu:t, mɪ-, -'nju:t] *n* **1** : minuto *m* **2** MOMENT : momento *m* **3 ~s** *npl* : actas *fpl* (de una reunión)
minute[2] ['mɪnət] *adj* **-nuter; -est 1** TINY : diminuto, minúsculo **2** DETAILED : minucioso
miracle ['mɪrɪkəl] *n* : milagro *m* — **miraculous** [mə'rækjələs] *adj* : milagroso
mirage [mɪ'rɑʒ, 'mɪr,ɑʒ] *n* : espejismo *m*
mire ['maɪr] *n* : lodo *m*, fango *m*
mirror ['mɪrər] *n* : espejo *m* — **~** *vt* : reflejar
mirth ['mərθ] *n* : alegría *f*, risas *fpl*
misapprehension [,mɪs,æprə'hɛntʃən] *n* : malentendido *m*
misbehave [,mɪsbi'heɪv] *vi* **-haved; -having** : portarse mal — **misbehavior** [,mɪsbi'heɪvjər] *n* : mala conducta *f*
miscalculate [mɪs'kælkjə,leɪt] *v* **-lated; -lating** : calcular mal
miscarriage [,mɪs'kærɪdʒ, 'mɪs,kærɪdʒ] *n* **1** : aborto *m* **2 ~ of justice** : error *m* judicial
miscellaneous [,mɪsə'leɪniəs] *adj* : diverso, vario
mischief ['mɪstʃəf] *n* : travesuras *fpl* — **mischievous** ['mɪstʃəvəs] *adj* : travieso
misconception [,mɪskən'sɛpʃən] *n* : concepto *m* erróneo
misconduct [mɪs'kɑndəkt] *n* : mala conducta *f*
misdeed [mɪs'di:d] *n* : fechoría *f*
misdemeanor [,mɪsdɪ'mi:nər] *n* : delito *m* menor
miser ['maɪzər] *n* : avaro *m*, -ra *f*; tacaño *m*, -ña *f*
miserable ['mɪzərəbəl] *adj* **1** UNHAPPY : triste **2** WRETCHED : miserable **3 ~ weather** : tiempo *m* malo
miserly ['maɪzərli] *adj* : mezquino
misery ['mɪzəri] *n, pl* **-eries 1** : sufrimiento *m* **2** WRETCHEDNESS : miseria *f*
misfire [mɪs'faɪr] *vi* **-fired; -firing** : fallar
misfit ['mɪs,fɪt, mɪs'fɪt] *n* : inadaptado *m*, -da *f*
misfortune [mɪs'fɔrtʃən] *n* : desgracia *f*
misgiving [mɪs'gɪvɪŋ] *n* : duda *f*
misguided [mɪs'gaɪdəd] *adj* : descaminado, equivocado
mishap ['mɪs,hæp] *n* : contratiempo *m*
misinform [,mɪsɪn'fɔrm] *vt* : informar mal
misinterpret [,mɪsɪn'tərprət] *vt* : interpretar mal
misjudge [mɪs'dʒʌdʒ] *vt* **-judged; -judging** : juzgar mal

mislay [mɪsˈleɪ] *vt* **-laid** [-leɪd]; **-laying** : extraviar, perder
mislead [mɪsˈliːd] *vt* **-led** [-ˈlɛd]; **-leading** : engañar — **misleading** [mɪsˈliːdɪŋ] *adj* : engañoso
misnomer [mɪsˈnoːmər] *n* : nombre *m* inapropiado
misplace [mɪsˈpleɪs] *vt* **-placed; -placing** : extraviar, perder
misprint [ˈmɪsˌprɪnt, mɪsˈ-] *n* : errata *f*, error *m* de imprenta
miss [ˈmɪs] *vt* **1** : errar, faltar **2** OVERLOOK : pasar por alto **3** : perder (una oportunidad, un vuelo, etc.) **4** AVOID : evitar **5** OMIT : saltarse **6 I ~ you** : te echo de menos — **~** *n* **1** : fallo *m* (de un tiro, etc.) **2** FAILURE : fracaso *m*
Miss [ˈmɪs] *n* : señorita *f*
missile [ˈmɪsəl] *n* **1** : misil *m* **2** PROJECTILE : proyectil *m*
missing [ˈmɪsɪŋ] *adj* : perdido, desaparecido
mission [ˈmɪʃən] *n* : misión *f* — **missionary** [ˈmɪʃəˌnɛri] *n, pl* **-aries** : misionero *m*, -ra *f*
misspell [mɪsˈspɛl] *vt* : escribir mal
mist [ˈmɪst] *n* : neblina *f*, bruma *f*
mistake [mɪˈsteɪk] *vt* **mistook** [-ˈstʊk]; **mistaken** [-ˈsteɪkən]; **-taking 1** MISINTERPRET : entender mal **2** CONFUSE : confundir — **~** *n* **1** : error *m* **2 make a ~** : equivocarse — **mistaken** [mɪˈsteɪkən] *adj* : equivocado
mister [ˈmɪstər] *n* : señor *m*
mistletoe [ˈmɪsəlˌtoː] *n* : muérdago *m*
mistreat [mɪsˈtriːt] *vt* : maltratar
mistress [ˈmɪstrəs] *n* **1** : dueña *f*, señora *f* (de una casa) **2** LOVER : amante *f*
mistrust [mɪsˈtrʌst] *n* : desconfianza *f* — **~** *vt* : desconfiar de
misty [ˈmɪsti] *adj* **mistier; -est** : neblinoso, nebuloso
misunderstand [ˌmɪsˌʌndərˈstænd] *vt* **-stood; -standing** : entender mal — **misunderstanding** [ˌmɪsˌʌndərˈstændɪŋ] *n* : malentendido *m*
misuse [mɪsˈjuːz] *vt* **-used; -using 1** : emplear mal **2** MISTREAT : maltratar — **~** [mɪsˈjuːs] *n* : mal empleo *m*, abuso *m*
mitigate [ˈmɪt̬əˌgeɪt] *vt* **-gated; -gating** : mitigar
mitt [ˈmɪt] *n* : manopla *f*, guante *m* (de béisbol) — **mitten** [ˈmɪtən] *n* : manopla *f*, mitón *m*
mix [ˈmɪks] *vt* **1** : mezclar **2 ~ up** : confundir — *vi* : mezclarse — **~** *n* : mezcla *f* — **mixture** [ˈmɪkstʃər] *n* : mezcla *f* — **mix–up** [ˈmɪksˌʌp] *n* : confusión *f*, lío *m fam*
moan [ˈmoːn] *n* : gemido *m* — **~** *vi* : gemir
mob [ˈmɑb] *n* : muchedumbre *f* — **~** *vt* **mobbed; mobbing** : acosar
mobile [ˈmoːbəl, -ˌbiːl, -ˌbaɪl] *adj* : móvil — **~** [ˈmoˌbiːl] *n* : móvil *m* — **mobile home** *n* : caravana *f* — **mobility** [moˈbɪlət̬i] *n* : movilidad *f* — **mobilize** [ˈmoːbəˌlaɪz] *vt* **-lized; -lizing** : movilizar
moccasin [ˈmɑkəsən] *n* : mocasín *m*
mock [ˈmɑk, ˈmɔk] *vt* : burlarse de, mofarse de — **~** *adj* : falso — **mockery** [ˈmɑkəri, ˈmɔ-] *n, pl* **-eries** : burla *f* — **mock–up** [ˈmɑkˌʌp] *n* : maqueta *f*
mode [ˈmoːd] *n* **1** : modo *m* **2** FASHION : moda *f*
model [ˈmɑdəl] *n* **1** : modelo *m* **2** MOCK-UP : maqueta *f* **3** : modelo *mf* (persona) — **~** *v* **-eled** *or* **-elled; -eling** *or* **-elling** *vt* **1** SHAPE : modelar **2** WEAR : lucir — *vi* : trabajar de modelo — **~** *adj* : modelo
modem [ˈmoːdəm, -ˌdɛm] *n* : módem *m*
moderate [ˈmɑdərət] *adj* : moderado — **~** *n* : moderado *m*, -da *f* — **~** [ˈmɑdəˌreɪt] *v* **-ated; -ating** *vt* : moderar — *vi* : moderarse — **moderation** [ˌmɑdəˈreɪʃən] *n* : moderación *f* — **moderator** [ˈmɑdəˌreɪt̬ər] *n* : moderador *m*, -dora *f*
modern [ˈmɑdərn] *adj* : moderno — **modernize** [ˈmɑdərˌnaɪz] *vt* **-ized; -izing** : modernizar
modest [ˈmɑdəst] *adj* : modesto — **modesty** [ˈmɑdəsti] *n* : modestia *f*
modify [ˈmɑdəˌfaɪ] *vt* **-fied; -fying** : modificar
moist [ˈmɔɪst] *adj* : húmedo — **moisten** [ˈmɔɪsən] *vt* : humedecer — **moisture** [ˈmɔɪstʃər] *n* : humedad *f* — **moisturizer** [ˈmɔɪtʃəˌraɪzər] *n* : crema *f* hidratante
molar [ˈmoːlər] *n* : muela *f*
molasses [məˈlæsəz] *n* : melaza *f*
mold[1] [ˈmoːld] *n* FORM : molde *m* — **~** *vt* : moldear, formar
mold[2] *n* FUNGUS : moho *m* — **moldy** [ˈmoːldi] *adj* **moldier; -est** : mohoso
mole[1] [ˈmoːl] *n* : lunar *m* (en la piel)
mole[2] *n* : topo *m* (animal)
molecule [ˈmɑlɪˌkjuːl] *n* : molécula *f*
molest [məˈlɛst] *vt* **1** HARASS : importunar **2** : abusar (sexualmente)
molten [ˈmoːltən] *adj* : fundido
mom [ˈmɑm, ˈmʌm] *n* : mamá *f*
moment [ˈmoːmənt] *n* : momento *m* — **momentarily** [ˌmoːmənˈtɛrəli] *adv* **1** : momentáneamente **2** SOON : dentro de poco, pronto — **momentary** [ˈmoːmənˌtɛri] *adj* : momentáneo

momentous [mo'mɛntəs] *adj* : muy importante
momentum [mo'mɛntəm] *n, pl* **-ta** [-tə] *or* **-tums 1** : momento *m* (en física) **2** IMPETUS : ímpetu *m*
monarch ['mɑ,nɑrk, -nərk] *n* : monarca *mf* — **monarchy** ['mɑ,nɑrki, -nər-] *n, pl* **-chies** : monarquía *f*
monastery ['mɑnə,stɛri] *n, pl* **-teries** : monasterio *m*
Monday ['mʌn,deɪ, -di] *n* : lunes *m*
money ['mʌni] *n, pl* **-eys** *or* **-ies** ['mʌniz] : dinero *m* — **monetary** ['mɑnə,tɛri, 'mʌnə-] *adj* : monetario — **money order** *n* : giro *m* postal
mongrel ['mɑŋgrəl, 'mʌŋ-] *n* : perro *m* mestizo
monitor ['mɑnət̬ər] *n* : monitor *m* (de una computadora, etc.) — ~ *vt* : controlar
monk ['mʌŋk] *n* : monje *m*
monkey ['mʌŋki] *n, pl* **-keys** : mono *m*, -na *f* — **monkey wrench** *n* : llave *f* inglesa
monogram ['mɑnə,græm] *n* : monograma *m*
monologue ['mɑnə,lɔg] *n* : monólogo *m*
monopoly [mə'nɑpəli] *n, pl* **-lies** : monopolio *m* — **monopolize** [mə'nɑpə,laɪz] *vt* **-lized; -lizing** : monopolizar
monotonous [mə'nɑtənəs] *adj* : monótono — **monotony** [mə'nɑtəni] *n* : monotonía *f*
monster ['mɑntstər] *n* : monstruo *m* — **monstrosity** [mɑn'strɑsət̬i] *n, pl* **-ties** : monstruosidad *f* — **monstrous** ['mɑntstrəs] *adj* **1** : monstruoso **2** HUGE : gigantesco
month ['mʌnθ] *n* : mes *m* — **monthly** ['mʌnθli] *adv* : mensualmente — ~ *adj* : mensual
monument ['mɑnjəmənt] *n* : monumento *m* — **monumental** [,mɑnjə'mɛntəl] *adj* : monumental
moo ['mu:] *vi* : mugir — ~ *n* : mugido *m*
mood ['mu:d] *n* : humor *m* — **moody** ['mu:di] *adj* **moodier; -est 1** GLOOMY : melancólico, deprimido **2** IRRITABLE : malhumorado **3** TEMPERAMENTAL : de humor variable
moon ['mu:n] *n* : luna *f* — **moonlight** ['mu:n,laɪt] *n* : luz *f* de la luna
moor[1] ['mʊr, 'mɔr] *n* : brezal *m*, páramo *m*
moor[2] *vt* : amarrar — **mooring** ['mʊrɪŋ, 'mɔr-] *n* DOCK : atracadero *m*
moose ['mu:s] *ns & pl* : alce *m*
moot ['mu:t] *adj* : discutible
mop ['mɑp] *n* **1** : trapeador *m Lat*, fregona *f Spain* **2** *or* ~ **of hair** : pelambrera *f* — ~ *vt* **mopped; mopping** : trapear *Lat*, pasar la fregona a *Spain*
mope ['mo:p] *vi* **moped; moping** : andar deprimido
moped ['mo:,pɛd] *n* : ciclomotor *m*
moral ['mɔrəl] *adj* : moral — ~ *n* **1** : moraleja *f* (de un cuento, etc.) **2** ~**s** *npl* : moral *f*, moralidad *f* — **morale** [mə'ræl] *n* : moral *f* — **morality** [mə'ræləṭi] *n, pl* **-ties** : moralidad *f*
morbid ['mɔrbɪd] *adj* : morboso
more ['mor] *adj* : más — ~ *adv* **1** : más **2** ~ **and** ~ : cada vez más **3** ~ **or less** : más o menos **4 once** ~ : una vez más — ~ *n* : más *m* — ~ *pron* : más — **moreover** [mor'o:vər] *adv* : además
morgue ['mɔrg] *n* : depósito *m* de cadáveres
morning ['mɔrnɪŋ] *n* **1** : mañana *f* **2** **good** ~! : ¡buenos días! **3 in the** ~ : por la mañana
moron ['mor,ɑn] *n* : estúpido *m*, -da *f*; imbécil *mf*
morose [mə'ro:s] *adj* : malhumorado
morphine ['mɔr,fi:n] *n* : morfina *f*
morsel ['mɔrsəl] *n* **1** BITE : bocado *m* **2** FRAGMENT : pedazo *m*
mortal ['mɔrt̬əl] *adj* : mortal — ~ *n* : mortal *mf* — **mortality** [mɔr'tæləṭi] *n* : mortalidad *f*
mortar ['mɔrt̬ər] *n* : mortero *m*
mortgage ['mɔrgɪdʒ] *n* : hipoteca *f* — ~ *vt* **-gaged; -gaging** : hipotecar
mortify ['mɔrt̬ə,faɪ] *vt* **-fied; -fying 1** : mortificar **2** HUMILIATE : avergonzar
mosaic [mo'zeɪɪk] *n* : mosaico *m*
Moslem ['mɑzləm] → **Muslim**
mosque ['mɑsk] *n* : mezquita *f*
mosquito [mə'ski:t̬o] *n, pl* **-toes** : mosquito *m*, zancudo *m Lat*
moss ['mɔs] *n* : musgo *m*
most ['mo:st] *adj* **1** : la mayoría de, la mayor parte de **2 (the)** ~ : más — ~ *adv* : más — ~ *n* : más *m*, máximo *m* — ~ *pron* : la mayoría, la mayor parte — **mostly** ['mo:stli] *adv* **1** MAINLY : en su mayor parte, principalmente **2** USUALLY : normalmente
motel [mo'tɛl] *n* : motel *m*
moth ['mɔθ] *n* : palomilla *f*, polilla *f*
mother ['mʌðər] *n* : madre *f* — ~ *vt* **1** : cuidar de **2** SPOIL : mimar — **motherhood** ['mʌðər,hʊd] *n* : maternidad *f* — **mother-in-law** ['mʌðərɪn,lɔ] *n, pl* **mothers-in-law** : suegra *f* — **motherly** ['mʌðərli] *adj* : maternal — **mother-of-pearl** [,mʌðərəv'pərl] *n* : nácar *m*
motif [mo'ti:f] *n* : motivo *m*

motion ['mo:ʃən] *n* **1** : movimiento *m* **2** PROPOSAL : moción *f* **3 set in ~** : poner en marcha — **~** *vi* **~ to s.o.** : hacer una señal a algn — **motionless** ['mo:ʃənləs] *adj* : inmóvil — **motion picture** *n* : película *f*

motive ['mo:t̬ɪv] *n* : motivo *m* — **motivate** ['mo:t̬əˌveɪt] *vt* **-vated; -vating** : motivar — **motivation** [ˌmo:t̬ə'veɪʃən] *n* : motivación *f*

motor ['mo:t̬ər] *n* : motor *m* — **motorbike** ['mo:t̬ərˌbaɪk] *n* : motocicleta *f* (pequeña), moto *f* — **motorboat** ['mo:t̬ərˌbo:t] *n* : lancha *f* motora — **motorcycle** ['mo:t̬ərˌsaɪkəl] *n* : motocicleta *f* — **motorcyclist** ['mo:t̬ərˌsaɪkəlɪst] *n* : motociclista *mf* — **motorist** ['mo:t̬ərɪst] *n* : automovilista *mf*, motorista *mf Lat*

motto ['mɑt̬o:] *n, pl* **-toes** : lema *m*

mould ['mo:ld] → **mold**

mound ['maʊnd] *n* **1** PILE : montón *m* **2** HILL : montículo *m*

mount[1] ['maʊnt] *n* **1** HORSE : montura *f* **2** SUPPORT : soporte *m* — **~** *vt* : montar (un caballo, etc.), subir (una escalera) — *vi* INCREASE : aumentar

mount[2] *n* HILL : monte *m* — **mountain** ['maʊntən] *n* : montaña *f* — **mountainous** ['maʊntənəs] *adj* : montañoso

mourn ['morn] *vt* : llorar (por) — *vi* : lamentarse — **mourner** ['mornər] *n* : doliente *mf* — **mournful** ['mornfəl] *adj* : triste — **mourning** ['mornɪŋ] *n* : luto *m*

mouse ['maʊs] *n, pl* **mice** ['maɪs] : ratón *m* — **mousetrap** ['maʊsˌtræp] *n* : ratonera *f*

moustache ['mʌˌstæʃ, mə'stæʃ] → **mustache**

mouth ['maʊθ] *n* : boca *f* (de una persona o un animal), desembocadura *f* (de un río) — **mouthful** ['maʊθˌfʊl] *n* : bocado *m* — **mouthpiece** ['maʊθˌpi:s] *n* : boquilla *f* (de un instrumento musical)

move ['mu:v] *v* **moved; moving** *vi* **1** GO : ir **2** RELOCATE : mudarse **3** STIR : moverse **4** ACT : tomar medidas — *vt* **1** : mover **2** AFFECT : conmover **3** TRANSPORT : transportar, trasladar **4** PROPOSE : proponer — **~** *n* **1** MOVEMENT : movimiento *m* **2** RELOCATION : mudanza *f* **3** STEP : medida *f* — **movable** ['mu:vəbəl] *or* **moveable** *adj* : movible, móvil — **movement** ['mu:vmənt] *n* : movimiento *m*

movie ['mu:vi] *n* **1** : película *f* **2 ~s** *npl* : cine *m*

mow ['mo:] *vt* **mowed; mowed** *or* **mown** ['mo:n]; **mowing** : cortar (la hierba) — **mower** ['mo:ər] → **lawn mower**

Mr. ['mɪstər] *n, pl* **Messrs.** ['mɛsərz] : señor *m*

Mrs. ['mɪsəz, -səs, *esp South* 'mɪzəz, -zəs] *n, pl* **Mesdames** [meɪ'deɪm, -'dæm] : señora *f*

Ms. ['mɪz] *n* : señora *f*, señorita *f*

much ['mʌtʃ] *adj* **more; most** : mucho — **~** *adv* **more** ['mor]; **most** ['mo:st] **1** : mucho **2 as ~ as** : tanto como **3 how ~?** : ¿cuánto? **4 too ~** : demasiado — **~** *pron* : mucho, -cha

muck ['mʌk] *n* **1** DIRT : mugre *f*, suciedad *f* **2** MANURE : estiércol *m*

mucus ['mju:kəs] *n* : mucosidad *f*

mud ['mʌd] *n* : barro *m*, lodo *m*

muddle ['mʌdəl] *v* **-dled; -dling** *vt* **1** CONFUSE : confundir **2** JUMBLE : desordenar — *vi* **~ through** : arreglárselas — **~** *n* : confusión *f*, lío *m fam*

muddy ['mʌdi] *adj* **-dier; -est** : fangoso, lleno de barro

muffin ['mʌfən] *n* : mollete *m*

muffle ['mʌfəl] *vt* **-fled; -fling** : amortiguar (un sonido) — **muffler** ['mʌflər] *n* **1** SCARF : bufanda *f* **2** : silenciador *m*, mofle *m Lat* (de un automóvil)

mug ['mʌg] *n* CUP : tazón *m* — **~** *vt* : asaltar, atracar — **mugger** ['mʌgər] *n* : atracador *m*, -dora *f*

muggy ['mʌgi] *adj* **-gier; -est** : bochornoso

mule ['mju:l] *n* : mula *f*

mull ['mʌl] *vt or* **~ over** : reflexionar sobre

multicolored [ˌmʌlti'kʌlərd, ˌmʌltaɪ-] *adj* : multicolor

multimedia [ˌmʌlti'mi:diə, ˌmʌltaɪ-] *adj* : multimedia

multinational [ˌmʌlti'næʃənəl, ˌmʌltaɪ-] *adj* : multinacional

multiple ['mʌltəpəl] *adj* : múltiple — **~** *n* : múltiplo *m* — **multiplication** [ˌmʌltəplə'keɪʃən] *n* : multiplicación *f* — **multiply** ['mʌltəˌplaɪ] *v* **-plied; -plying** *vt* : multiplicar — *vi* : multiplicarse

multitude ['mʌltəˌtu:d, -ˌtju:d] *n* : multitud *f*

mum ['mʌm] *adj* **keep ~** : guardar silencio

mumble ['mʌmbəl] *v* **-bled; -bling** *vt* : mascullar — *vi* : hablar entre dientes

mummy ['mʌmi] *n, pl* **-mies** : momia *f*

mumps ['mʌmps] *ns & pl* : paperas *fpl*

munch ['mʌntʃ] *v* : mascar, masticar

mundane [ˌmʌn'deɪn, 'mʌnˌ-] *adj* : rutinario, ordinario

municipal [mjʊˈnɪsəpəl] *adj* : municipal — **municipality** [mjʊˌnɪsəˈpæləṭi] *n, pl* **-ties** : municipio *m*
munitions [mjʊˈnɪʃənz] *npl* : municiónes *fpl*
mural [ˈmjʊrəl] *n* : mural *m*
murder [ˈmərdər] *n* : asesinato *m*, homicidio *m* — **~** *vt* : asesinar, matar — *vi* : matar — **murderer** [ˈmərdərər] *n* : asesino *m*, -na *f;* homicida *mf* — **murderous** [ˈmərdərəs] *adj* : asesino, homicida
murky [ˈmərki] *adj* **-kier; -est** : turbio, oscuro
murmur [ˈmərmər] *n* : murmullo *m* — **murmur** *v* : mumurar
muscle [ˈmʌsəl] *n* : músculo *m* — **~** *vi* **-cled; -cling** *or* **~ in** : meterse por la fuerza en — **muscular** [ˈmʌskjələr] *adj* **1** : muscular **2** STRONG : musculoso
muse[1] [ˈmju:z] *n* : musa *f*
muse[2] *vi* **mused; musing** : meditar
museum [mjʊˈzi:əm] *n* : museo *m*
mushroom [ˈmʌʃˌru:m, -ˌrʊm] *n* **1** : hongo *m*, seta *f* **2** : champiñón *m* (en la cocina) — **~** *vi* GROW : crecer rápidamente, multiplicarse
mushy [ˈmʌʃi] *adj* **mushier; -est 1** SOFT : blando **2** MAWKISH : sensiblero
music [ˈmju:zɪk] *n* : música *f* — **musical** [ˈmju:zɪkəl] *adj* : musical — **~** *n* : comedia *f* musical — **musician** [mjʊˈzɪʃən] *n* : músico *m*, -ca *f*
Muslim [ˈmʌzləm, ˈmʊs-, ˈmʊz-] *adj* : musulmán — **~** *n* : musulmán *m*, -mana *f*
muslin [ˈmʌzlən] *n* : muselina *f*
mussel [ˈmʌsəl] *n* : mejillón *m*
must [ˈmʌst] *v aux* **1** : deber, tener que **2 you ~ come** : tienes que venir **3 you ~ be tired** : debes (de) estar cansado — **~** *n* : necesidad *f*
mustache [ˈmʌˌstæʃ, mʌˈstæʃ] *n* : bigote *m*, bigotes *mpl*
mustang [ˈmʌˌstæŋ] *n* : mustang *m*
mustard [ˈmʌstərd] *n* : mostaza *f*
muster [ˈmʌstər] *vt* **1** : reunir **2** *or* **~ up** : armarse de, cobrar (valor, fuerzas, etc.)
musty [ˈmʌsti] *adj* **mustier; -est** : que huele a cerrado
mute [ˈmju:t] *adj* **muter; mutest** : mudo — **~** *n* : mudo *m*, -da *f*
mutilate [ˈmju:ṭəˌleɪt] *vt* **-lated; -lating** : mutilar
mutiny [ˈmju:təni] *n, pl* **-nies** : motín *m* — **~** *vi* **-nied; -nying** : amotinarse
mutter [ˈmʌṭər] *vi* : murmurar
mutton [ˈmʌtən] *n* : carne *f* de carnero
mutual [ˈmju:tʃʊəl] *adj* **1** : mutuo **2** COMMON : común — **mutually** [ˈmju:tʃʊəli, -tʃəli] *adv* : mutuamente
muzzle [ˈmʌzəl] *n* **1** SNOUT : hocico *m* **2** : bozal *m* (para un perro, etc.) **3** : boca *f* (de un arma de fuego) — **~** *vt* **-zled; -zling** : poner un bozal a (un animal)
my [ˈmaɪ] *adj* : mi
myopia [maɪˈo:piə] *n* : miopía *f* — **myopic** [maɪˈo:pɪk, -ˈɑ-] *adj* : miope
myself [maɪˈsɛlf] *pron* **1** (*reflexive*) : me **2** (*emphatic*) : yo mismo **3 by ~** : solo
mystery [ˈmɪstəri] *n, pl* **-teries** : misterio *m* — **mysterious** [mɪˈstɪriəs] *adj* : misterioso
mystic [ˈmɪstɪk] *adj or* **mystical** [ˈmɪstɪkəl] : místico
mystify [ˈmɪstəˌfaɪ] *vt* **-fied; -fying** : dejar perplejo, confundir
mystique [mɪˈsti:k] *n* : aura *f* de misterio
myth [ˈmɪθ] *n* : mito *m* — **mythical** [ˈmɪθɪkəl] *adj* : mítico

N

n [ˈɛn] *n, pl* **n's** *or* **ns** [ˈɛnz] : n *f*, decimocuarta letra del alfabeto inglés
nab [ˈnæb] *vt* **nabbed; nabbing 1** ARREST : pescar *fam* **2** GRAB : agarrar
nag [ˈnæg] *v* **nagged; nagging** *vi* COMPLAIN : quejarse — *vt* **1** ANNOY : fastidiar, dar la lata a **2** SCOLD : regañar — **nagging** *adj* : persistente
nail [ˈneɪl] *n* **1** : clavo *m* **2** : uña *f* (de un dedo) — **~** *vt or* **~ down** : clavar — **nail file** *n* : lima *f* de uñas
naive *or* **naïve** [nɑˈi:v] *adj* **-iver; -est** : ingenuo — **naïveté** [ˌnɑi:vəˈteɪ, nɑˈi:vəˌ-] *n* : ingenuidad *f*
naked [ˈneɪkəd] *adj* **1** : desnudo **2 the ~ truth** : la pura verdad **3 to the ~ eye** : a simple vista
name [ˈneɪm] *n* **1** : nombre *m* **2** REPUTATION : fama *f* **3 what is your ~?** : ¿cómo se llama? **4** → **first name, surname** — **~** *vt* **named; naming 1** : poner nombre a **2** APPOINT : nombrar **3 ~ a price** : fijar un precio — **nameless** [ˈneɪmləs] *adj* : anónimo — **namely** [ˈneɪmli] *adv* : a saber — **namesake** [ˈneɪmˌseɪk] *n* : tocayo *m*, -ya *f*
nap[1] [ˈnæp] *vi* **napped; napping** : echarse una siesta — **~** *n* : siesta *f*

nap² *n* : pelo *m* (de una tela)
nape ['neɪp, 'næp] *n or* ~ **of the neck** : nuca *f*
napkin ['næpkən] *n* **1** : servilleta *f* **2** → **sanitary napkin**
narcotic [nɑr'kɑţɪk] *n* : narcótico *m,* estupefaciente *m*
narrate ['nær,eɪt] *vt* **-rated; -rating** : narrar — **narration** [næ'reɪʃən] *n* : narración *f* — **narrative** ['nærəţɪv] *n* : narración *f* — **narrator** ['nær,eɪţər] *n* : narrador *m,* **-dora** *f*
narrow ['nær,o:] *adj* **1** : estrecho, angosto **2** RESTRICTED : limitado — ~ *vi* : estrecharse — *vt* **1** : estrechar **2** *or* ~ **down** : limitar — **narrowly** ['næroli] *adv* : por poco — **narrow–minded** [,næro'maɪndəd] *adj* : de miras estrechas
nasal ['neɪzəl] *adj* : nasal
nasty ['næsti] *adj* **-tier; -est 1** MEAN : malo, cruel **2** UNPLEASANT : desagradable **3** REPUGNANT : asqueroso — **nastiness** ['næstinəs] *n* : maldad *f*
nation ['neɪʃən] *n* : nación *f* — **national** ['næʃənəl] *adj* : nacional — **nationalism** ['næʃənə,lɪzəm] *n* : nacionalismo *m* — **nationality** [,næʃə'næləţi] *n, pl* **-ties** : nacionalidad *f* — **nationalize** ['næʃənə,laɪz] *vt* **-ized; -izing** : nacionalizar — **nationwide** ['neɪʃən-'waɪd] *adj* : por todo el país
native ['neɪţɪv] *adj* **1** : natal (dícese de un país, etc.) **2** INNATE : innato **3** ~ **language** : lengua *f* materna — ~ *n* **1** : nativo *m,* **-va** *f* **2 be a** ~ **of** : ser natural de — **Native American** : indio *m* americano, india *f* americana — **nativity** [nə'tɪvəţi, neɪ-] *n, pl* **-ties the Nativity** : la Navidad
nature ['neɪtʃər] *n* **1** : naturaleza *f* **2** KIND : índole *f,* clase *f* **3** DISPOSITION : carácter *m,* natural *m* — **natural** ['nætʃərəl] *adj* : natural — **naturalize** ['nætʃərə,laɪz] *vt* **-ized; -izing** : naturalizar — **naturally** ['nætʃərəli] *adv* : naturalmente
naught ['nɔt] *n* **1** NOTHING : nada *f* **2** ZERO : cero *m*
naughty ['nɔţi] *adj* **-tier; -est 1** : travieso, pícaro **2** RISQUÉ : picante
nausea ['nɔziə, 'nɔʃə] *n* : náuseas *fpl* — **nauseating** *adj* : nauseabundo — **nauseous** ['nɔʃəs, -ziəs] *adj* **1 feel** ~ : sentir náuseas **2** SICKENING : nauseabundo
nautical ['nɔţɪkəl] *adj* : náutico
naval ['neɪvəl] *adj* : naval
nave ['neɪv] *n* : nave *f* (de una iglesia)
navel ['neɪvəl] *n* : ombligo *m*
navigate ['nævə,geɪt] *v* **-gated; -gating** *vi* : navegar — *vt* **1** : gobernar (un barco), pilotar (un avión) **2** : navegar por (un río, etc.) — **navigable** ['nævɪgəbəl] *adj* : navegable — **navigation** [,nævə-'geɪʃən] *n* : navegación *f* — **navigator** ['nævə,geɪţər] *n* : navegante *mf*
navy ['neɪvi] *n, pl* **-vies 1** : marina *f* de guerra **2** *or* ~ **blue** : azul *m* marino
near ['nɪr] *adv* : cerca — ~ *prep* : cerca de — ~ *adj* : cercano, próximo — ~ *vt* : acercarse a — **nearby** [nɪr'baɪ, 'nɪr-,baɪ] *adv* : cerca — ~ *adj* : cercano — **nearly** ['nɪrli] *adv* : casi — **nearsighted** ['nɪr,saɪţəd] *adj* : miope, corto de vista
neat ['ni:t] *adj* **1** TIDY : muy arreglado **2** CLEVER : hábil, ingenioso — **neatly** ['ni:tli] *adv* **1** : ordenadamente **2** CLEVERLY : hábilmente — **neatness** ['ni:tnəs] *n* : pulcritud *f,* orden *m*
nebulous ['nɛbjʊləs] *adj* : nebuloso
necessary ['nɛsə,sɛri] *adj* : necesario — **necessarily** [,nɛsə'sɛrəli] *adv* : necesariamente — **necessitate** [nɪ'sɛsə-,teɪt] *vt* **-tated; -tating** : exigir, requerir — **necessity** [nɪ'sɛsəţi] *n, pl* **-ties 1** : necesidad *f* **2 necessities** *npl* : cosas *fpl* indispensables
neck ['nɛk] *n* **1** : cuello *m* (de una persona o una botella), pescuezo *m* (de un animal) **2** COLLAR : cuello *m* — **necklace** ['nɛkləs] *n* : collar *m* — **necktie** ['nɛk,taɪ] *n* : corbata *f*
nectar ['nɛktər] *n* : néctar *m*
nectarine [,nɛktə'ri:n] *n* : nectarina *f*
need ['ni:d] *n* **1** : necesidad *f* **2 if** ~ **be** : si hace falta — ~ *vt* **1** : necesitar, exigir **2** ~ **to** : tener que — *v aux* : tener que
needle ['ni:dəl] *n* : aguja *f* — ~ *vt* **-dled; -dling** : pinchar
needless ['ni:dləs] *adj* **1** : innecesario **2** ~ **to say** : de más está decir
needlework ['ni:dəl,wərk] *n* : bordado *m*
needn't ['ni:dənt] (*contraction of* **need not**) → **need**
needy ['ni:di] **needier; -est** *adj* : necesitado
negative ['nɛgəţɪv] *adj* : negativo — ~ *n* **1** : negación *f* (en gramática) **2** : negativo *m* (en fotografía)
neglect [nɪ'glɛkt] *vt* : descuidar — ~ *n* : descuido *m,* abandono *m*
negligee [,nɛglə'ʒeɪ] *n* : negligé *m*
negligence ['nɛglɪdʒənts] *n* : negligencia *f,* descuido *m* — **negligent** ['nɛglɪdʒənt] *adj* : negligente, descuidado
negligible ['nɛglɪdʒəbəl] *adj* : insignificante

negotiate [nɪˈgoːʃiˌeɪt] *v* **-ated; -ating** : negociar — **negotiable** [nɪˈgoːʃəbəl, -ʃiə-] *adj* : negociable — **negotiation** [nɪˌgoːʃiˈeɪʃən, -siˈeɪ-] *n* : negociación *f* — **negotiator** [nɪˈgoːʃiˌeɪt̬ər, -siˌeɪ-] *n* : negociador *m*, -dora *f*

Negro [ˈniːˌgroː] *n, pl* **-groes** *sometimes considered offensive* : negro *m*, -gra *f*

neigh [ˈneɪ] *vi* : relinchar — ~ *n* : relincho *m*

neighbor *or Brit* **neighbour** [ˈneɪbər] *n* : vecino *m*, -na *f* — **neighborhood** *or Brit* **neighbourhood** [ˈneɪbərˌhʊd] *n* **1** : barrio *m*, vecindario *m* **2 in the ~ of** : alrededor de — **neighborly** *or Brit* **neighbourly** [ˈneɪbərli] *adv* : amable

neither [ˈniːðər, ˈnaɪ-] *conj* **1 ~...nor** : ni...ni **2 ~ am/do I** : yo tampoco — ~ *pron* : ninguno, -na — ~ *adj* : ninguno (de los dos)

neon [ˈniːˌɑn] *n* : neón *m*

nephew [ˈnɛˌfjuː, *chiefly British* ˈnɛˌvjuː] *n* : sobrino *m*

Neptune [ˈnɛpˌtuːn, -ˌtjuːn] *n* : Neptuno *m*

nerve [ˈnərv] *n* **1** : nervio *m* **2** COURAGE : coraje *m* **3** GALL : descaro *m* **4 ~s** *npl* JITTERS : nervios *mpl* — **nervous** [ˈnərvəs] *adj* : nervioso — **nervousness** [ˈnərvəsnəs] *n* : nerviosismo *m* — **nervy** [ˈnərvi] *adj* **nervier; -est** : descarado

nest [ˈnɛst] *n* : nido *m* — ~ *vi* : anidar

nestle [ˈnɛsəl] *vi* **-tled; -tling** : acurrucarse

net¹ [ˈnɛt] *n* : red *f* — ~ *vt* **netted; netting** : pescar, atrapar (con una red)

net² *adj* : neto — ~ *vt* **netted; netting** YIELD : producir neto

nettle [ˈnɛt̬əl] *n* : ortiga *f*

network [ˈnɛtˌwərk] *n* : red *f*

neurology [nʊˈrɑlədʒi, njʊ-] *n* : neurología *f*

neurosis [nʊˈroːsɪs, njʊ-] *n, pl* **-roses** [-ˌsiːz] : neurosis *f* — **neurotic** [nʊˈrɑt̬ɪk, njʊ-] *adj* : neurótico

neuter [ˈnuːt̬ər, ˈnjuː-] *adj* : neutro — ~ *vt* : castrar

neutral [ˈnuːtrəl, ˈnjuː-] *n* : punto *m* muerto (de un automóvil) — ~ *adj* **1** : neutral **2** : neutro (en electrotecnia o química) — **neutrality** [nuːˈtræləṭiː, njuː-] *n* : neutralidad *f* — **neutralize** [ˈnuːtrəˌlaɪz, ˈnjuː-] *vt* **-ized; -izing** : neutralizar

neutron [ˈnuːˌtrɑn, ˈnjuː-] *n* : neutrón *m*

never [ˈnɛvər] *adv* **1** : nunca, jamás **2** NOT : no **3 ~ again** : nunca más **4 ~ mind** : no importa — **nevermore** [ˌnɛvərˈmor] *adv* : nunca jamás — **nevertheless** [ˌnɛvərðəˈlɛs] *adv* : sin embargo, no obstante

new [ˈnuː, ˈnjuː] *adj* : nuevo — **newborn** [ˈnuːˌbɔrn, ˈnjuː-] *adj* : recién nacido — **newcomer** [ˈnuːˌkʌmər, ˈnjuː-] *n* : recién llegado *m*, -da *f* — **newly** [ˈnuːli, ˈnjuː-] *adv* : recién, recientemente — **newlywed** [ˈnuːliˌwɛd, ˈnjuː-] *n* : recién casado *m*, -da *f* — **news** [ˈnuːz, ˈnjuːz] *n* : noticias *fpl* — **newscast** [ˈnuːzˌkæst, ˈnjuːz-] *n* : noticiario *m*, noticiero *m Lat* — **newscaster** [ˈnuːzˌkæstər, ˈnjuːz-] *n* : presentador *m*, -dora *f* (de un noticiario) — **newsletter** [ˈnuːzˌlɛt̬ər, ˈnjuːz-] *n* : boletín *m* informativo — **newspaper** [ˈnuːzˌpeɪpər, ˈnjuːz-] *n* : periódico *m*, diario *m* — **newsstand** [ˈnuːzˌstænd, ˈnjuːz-] *n* : puesto *m* de periódicos

newt [ˈnuːt, ˈnjuːt] *n* : tritón *m*

New Year's Day *n* : día *m* del Año Nuevo

next [ˈnɛkst] *adj* **1** : próximo **2** FOLLOWING : siguiente — ~ *adv* **1** : la próxima vez **2** AFTERWARD : después, luego **3** NOW : ahora — **next–door** [ˈnɛkstˈdor] *adj* : de al lado — **next to** *adv* ALMOST : casi — ~ *prep* BESIDE : al lado de

nib [ˈnɪb] *n* : plumilla *f*

nibble [ˈnɪbəl] *vt* **-bled; -bling** : mordisquear

Nicaraguan [ˌnɪkəˈrɑgwən] *adj* : nicaragüense

nice [ˈnaɪs] *adj* **nicer; nicest 1** PLEASANT : agradable, bueno **2** KIND : amable — **nicely** [ˈnaɪsli] *adv* **1** WELL : bien **2** KINDLY : amablemente — **niceness** [ˈnaɪsnəs] *n* : amabilidad *f* — **niceties** [ˈnaɪsət̬iz] *npl* : detalles *mpl*, sutilezas *fpl*

niche [ˈnɪtʃ] *n* **1** : nicho *m* **2 find one's ~** : hacerse su hueco

nick [ˈnɪk] *n* **1** : corte *m* pequeño, muesca *f* **2 in the ~ of time** : justo a tiempo — ~ *vt* : hacer una muesca en

nickel [ˈnɪkəl] *n* **1** : níquel *m* (metal) **2** : moneda *f* de cinco centavos

nickname [ˈnɪkˌneɪm] *n* : apodo *m*, sobrenombre *m* — ~ *vt* **-named; -naming** : apodar

nicotine [ˈnɪkəˌtiːn] *n* : nicotina *f*

niece [ˈniːs] *n* : sobrina *f*

niggling [ˈnɪgəlɪŋ] *adj* **1** PETTY : insignificante **2** PERSISTENT : constante

night [ˈnaɪt] *n* **1** : noche *f* **2 at ~** : de noche **3 last ~** : anoche **4 tomorrow ~** : mañana por la noche — **nightclub** [ˈnaɪtˌklʌb] *n* : club *m* nocturno — **nightfall** [ˈnaɪtˌfɔl] *n* : anochecer *m* — **nightgown** [ˈnaɪtˌgaʊn] *n* : camisón *m* (de noche) — **nightly** ['naɪt] *adj* : de todas las noches — ~ *adv* : cada noche — **nightmare** ['naɪt,mær] *n* : pesadilla *f* — **nighttime** ['naɪt,taɪm] *n* : noche *f*

nil ['nɪl] *n* NOTHING : nada *f*

nimble ['nɪmbəl] *adj* **-bler; -blest** : ágil

nine ['naɪn] *adj* : nueve — ~ *n* : nueve *m* — **nine hundred** *adj* : novecientos — ~ *n* : novecientos *m* — **nineteen** [naɪn'ti:n] *adj* : diecinueve — ~ *n* : diecinueve *m* — **nineteenth** [naɪn'ti:nθ] *adj* : decimonoveno, decimonono — ~ *n* **1** : decimonoveno *m,* -na *f;* decimonono *m,* -na *f* (en una serie) **2** : diecinueveavo *m* (en matemáticas) — **ninetieth** ['naɪnt̬iəθ] *adj* : nonagésimo — ~ *n* **1** : nonagésimo *m,* -ma *f* (en una serie) **2** : noventavo *m* (en matemáticas) — **ninety** ['naɪnt̬i] *adj* : noventa — ~ *n, pl* **-ties** : noventa *m* — **ninth** ['naɪnθ] *adj* : noveno — ~ *n* **1** : noveno *m,* -na *f* (en una serie) **2** : noveno *m* (en matemáticas)

nip ['nɪp] *vt* **nipped; nipping 1** PINCH : pellizcar **2** BITE : mordisquear **3** ~ **in the bud** : cortar de raíz — ~ *n* **1** PINCH : pellizco *m* **2** NIBBLE : mordisco *m*

nipple ['nɪpəl] *n* **1** : pezón *m* (de una mujer) **2** : tetilla *f* (de un hombre o un biberón)

nitrogen ['naɪtrədʒən] *n* : nitrógen *m*

nitwit ['nɪt,wɪt] *n* : idiota *mf*

no ['no:] *adv* : no — ~ *adj* **1** : ninguno **2 I have ~ money** : no tengo dinero **3 it's ~ trouble** : no es ningún problema **4 ~ smoking** : prohibido fumar — ~ *n, pl* **noes** *or* **nos** ['no:z] : no *m*

noble ['no:bəl] *adj* **-bler; -blest** : noble — ~ *n* : noble *mf* — **nobility** [no'bɪlət̬i] *n* : nobleza *f*

nobody ['no:bədi, -,badi] *pron* : nadie

nocturnal [nɑk'tərnəl] *adj* : nocturno

nod ['nɑd] *v* **nodded; nodding** *vi* **1** *or* **~ yes** : asentir con la cabeza **2 ~ off** : dormirse — *vt* **~ one's head** : asentir con la cabeza — ~ *n* : señal *m* con la cabeza

noes → **no**

noise ['nɔɪz] *n* : ruido *m* — **noisily** ['nɔɪzəli] *adv* : ruidosamente — **noisy** ['nɔɪzi] *adj* **noisier; -est** : ruidoso

nomad ['no:,mæd] *n* : nómada *mf* — **nomadic** [no'mædɪk] *adj* : nómada

nominal ['nɑmənəl] *adj* : nominal

nominate ['nɑmə,neɪt] *vt* **-nated; -nating 1** : proponer, postular *Lat* **2** APPOINT : nombrar — **nomination** [,nɑmə'neɪʃən] *n* **1** : propuesta *f,* postulación *f Lat* **2** APPOINTMENT : nombramiento *m*

nonalcoholic [,nɑn,ælkə'hɔlɪk] *adj* : no alcohólico

nonchalant [,nɑnʃə'lɑnt] *adj* : despreocupado

noncommissioned officer [,nɑnkə'mɪʃənd] *n* : suboficial *mf*

noncommittal [,nɑnkə'mɪt̬əl] *adj* : evasivo

nondescript [,nɑndɪ'skrɪpt] *adj* : anodino, soso

none ['nʌn] *pron* **1** : ninguno, ninguna **2 there are ~ left** : no hay más — ~ *adv* **1 be ~ the worse** : no sufrir daño alguno **2 ~ too happy** : nada contento **3 ~ too soon** : a buena hora

nonentity [,nɑn'ɛntət̬i] *n, pl* **-ties** : persona *f* insignificante

nonetheless [,nʌnðə'lɛs] *adv* : sin embargo, no obstante

nonexistent [,nɑnɪg'zɪstənt] *adj* : inexistente

nonfat [,nɑn'fæt] *adj* : sin grasa

nonfiction [,nɑn'fɪkʃən] *n* : no ficción *f*

nonprofit [,nɑn'prɑfət] *adj* : sin fines lucrativos

nonsense ['nɑn,sɛnts, 'nɑntsənts] *n* : tonterías *fpl,* disparates *mpl* — **nonsensical** [nɑn'sɛntsɪkəl] *adj* : absurdo

nonsmoker [,nɑn'smo:kər] *n* : no fumador *m,* -dora *f*

nonstop [,nɑn'stɑp] *adj* : directo — ~ *adv* : sin parar

noodle ['nu:dəl] *n* : fideo *m*

nook ['nʊk] *n* : rincón *m*

noon ['nu:n] *n* : mediodía *m*

no one *pron* : nadie

noose ['nu:s] *n* **1** : dogal *m,* soga *f* **2** LASSO : lazo *m*

nor ['nɔr] *conj* **1 neither...~** : ni...ni **2 ~ I** : yo tampoco

norm ['nɔrm] *n* **1** : norma *f* **2 the ~** : lo normal — **normal** ['nɔrməl] *adj* : normal — **normality** [nɔr'mælət̬i] *n* : normalidad *f* — **normally** *adv* : normalmente

north ['nɔrθ] *adv* : al norte — ~ *adj* : norte, del norte — ~ *n* **1** : norte *m* **2 the North** : el Norte — **North American** *adj* : norteamericano — **northeast** [nɔrθ'i:st] *adv* : hacia el nordeste — ~ *adj* : nordeste, del nordeste — ~ *n* : nordeste *m,* noreste *m* — **northeastern** [nɔrθ'i:stərn] *adj* : nordeste, del nordeste — **northerly** ['nɔrðərli] *adj* : del norte — **northern** ['nɔrðərn] *adj* : del norte, norteño — **northwest** [,nɔrθ'wɛst] *adv* : hacia el noroeste —

~ *adj* : noroeste, del noroeste — ~ *n* : noroeste *m* — **northwestern** [ˌnɔrθ-ˈwɛstərn] *adj* : noroeste, del noroeste
Norwegian [nɔrˈwiːdʒən] *adj* : noruego
nose [ˈnoːz] *n* **1** : nariz *f* (de una persona), hocico *m* (de un animal) **2 blow one's ~** : sonarse las narices — ~ *vi* **nosed; nosing** *or* **~ around** : meter las narices — **nosebleed** [ˈnoːzˌbliːd] *n* : hemorragia *f* nasal — **nosedive** [ˈnoːzˌdaɪv] *n* : descenso *m* en picada
nostalgia [nɑˈstældʒə, nə-] *n* : nostalgia *f* — **nostalgic** [nɑˈstældʒɪk, nə-] *adj* : nostálgico
nostril [ˈnɑstrəl] *n* : ventana *f* de la nariz
nosy *or* **nosey** [ˈnoːzi] *adj* **nosier; -est** : entrometido
not [ˈnɑt] *adv* **1** : no **2 he's ~ tired** : no esta cansado **3 I hope ~** : espero que no **4 ~ ... anything** : no...nada
notable [ˈnoːt̬əbəl] *adj* : notable — ~ *n* : personaje *m* — **notably** [ˈnoːt̬əbli] *adv* : notablemente
notary public [ˈnoːt̬əri-] *n, pl* **notaries public** *or* **notary publics** : notario *m*, -ria *f*
notation [noˈteɪʃən] *n* : anotación *f*
notch [ˈnɑtʃ] *n* : muesca *f*, corte *m* — ~ *vt* : hacer un corte en
note [ˈnoːt] *vt* **noted; noting 1** NOTICE : observar, notar **2** RECORD : anotar — ~ *n* **1** : nota *f* **2 of ~** : destacado **3 take ~ of** : prestar atención a **4 take ~s** : apuntar — **notebook** [ˈnoːtˌbʊk] *n* : libreta *f*, cuaderno *m* — **noted** [ˈnoːt̬əd] *adj* : renombrado, célebre — **noteworthy** [ˈnoːtˌwərði] *adj* : notable
nothing [ˈnʌθɪŋ] *pron* **1** : nada **2 be ~ but** : no ser más que **3 for ~** FREE : gratis — ~ *n* **1** ZERO : zero *m* **2** TRIFLE : nimiedad *f*
notice [ˈnoːt̬ɪs] *n* **1** SIGN : letrero *m*, aviso *m* **2 at a moment's ~** : sin previo aviso **3 be given one's ~** : ser despedido **4 take ~ of** : prestar atención a — ~ *vt* **-ticed; -ticing** : notar — **noticeable** [ˈnoːt̬ɪsəbəl] *adj* : perceptible, evidente
notify [ˈnoːt̬əˌfaɪ] *vt* **-fied; -fying** : notificar, avisar — **notification** [ˌnoːt̬əfəˈkeɪʃən] *n* : notificación *f*, aviso *m*
notion [ˈnoːʃən] *n* **1** : noción *f*, idea *f* **2 ~s** *npl* : artículos *mpl* de mercería
notorious [noˈtoːriəs] *adj* : de mala fama — **notoriety** [ˌnoːt̬əˈraɪət̬i] *n* : mala fama *f*, notoriedad *f*
notwithstanding [ˌnɑtwɪθˈstændɪŋ, -wɪð-] *prep* : a pesar de, no obstante — ~ *adv* : sin embargo — ~ *conj* : a pesar de que
nougat [ˈnuːgət] *n* : turrón *m*
nought [ˈnɔt, ˈnɑt] → **naught**
noun [ˈnaʊn] *n* : nombre *m*, sustantivo *m*
nourish [ˈnərɪʃ] *vt* : nutrir — **nourishing** [ˈnərɪʃɪŋ] *adj* : nutritivo — **nourishment** [ˈnərɪʃmənt] *n* : alimento *m*
novel [ˈnɑvəl] *adj* : original, novedoso — ~ *n* : novela *f* — **novelist** [ˈnɑvəlɪst] *n* : novelista *mf* — **novelty** [ˈnɑvəlt̬i] *n, pl* **-ties** : novedad *f*
November [noˈvɛmbər] *n* : noviembre *m*
novice [ˈnɑvɪs] *n* : novato *m*, -ta *f*; principiante *mf*
now [ˈnaʊ] *adv* **1** : ahora **2** THEN : entonces **3 from ~ on** : de ahora en adelante **4 ~ and then** : de vez en cuando **5 right ~** : ahora mismo — ~ *conj or* **~ that** : ahora que, ya que — ~ *n* **1 a year from ~** : dentro de un año **2 by ~** : ya **3 until ~** : hasta ahora — **nowadays** [ˈnaʊəˌdeɪz] *adv* : hoy en día
nowhere [ˈnoːˌhwɛr] *adv* **1** (*indicating location*) : por ninguna parte, por ningún lado **2** (*indicating motion*) : a ninguna parte, a ningún lado **3 I'm ~ near finished** : aún me falta mucho para terminar **4 it's ~ near here** : queda bastante lejos de aquí — ~ *n* : ninguna parte *f*
nozzle [ˈnɑzəl] *n* : boca *f* (de una manguera, etc.)
nuance [ˈnuːˌɑnts, ˈnjuː-] *n* : matiz *m*
nucleus [ˈnuːkliəs, ˈnjuː-] *n, pl* **-clei** [-kliˌaɪ] : núcleo *m* — **nuclear** [ˈnuːkliər, ˈnjuː-] *adj* : nuclear
nude [ˈnuːd, ˈnjuːd] *adj* **nuder; nudest** : desnudo — ~ *n* : desnudo *m*
nudge [ˈnʌdʒ] *vt* **nudged; nudging** : dar un codazo a — ~ *n* : toque *m* (con el codo)
nudity [ˈnuːdət̬i, ˈnjuː-] *n* : desnudez *f*
nugget [ˈnʌgət] *n* : pepita *f* (de oro, etc.)
nuisance [ˈnuːsənts, ˈnjuː-] *n* **1** ANNOYANCE : fastidio *m*, molestia *f* **2** PEST : pesado *m*, -da *f fam*
null [ˈnʌl] *adj* **~ and void** : nulo y sin efecto
numb [ˈnʌm] *adj* **1** : entumecido, dormido **2 ~ with fear** : paralizado de miedo — ~ *vt* : entumecer, adormecer
number [ˈnʌmbər] *n* **1** : número *m* **2 a ~ of** : varios — ~ *vt* **1** : numerar **2** INCLUDE : contar, incluir **3** TOTAL : ascender a
numeral [ˈnuːmərəl, ˈnjuː-] *n* : número *m* — **numeric** [nʊˈmɛrɪk, njʊ-] *or* **numerical** [nʊˈmɛrɪkəl, njʊ-] *adj* : numérico — **numerous** [ˈnuːmərəs, ˈnjuː-] *adj* : numeroso

nun ['nʌn] *n* : monja *f*
nuptial ['nʌpʃəl] *adj* : nupcial
nurse ['nərs] *n* **1** : enfermero *m*, -ra *f* **2** → **nursemaid** — ~ *vt* **nursed; nursing 1** : cuidar (de), atender **2** SUCKLE : amamantar — **nursemaid** ['nərs-ˌmeɪd] *n* : niñera *f* — **nursery** ['nərsəri] *n, pl* **-eries 1** : cuarto *m* de los niños **2** *or* **day** ~ : guardería *f* **3** : vivero *m* (de plantas) — **nursing home** *n* : asilo *m* de ancianos
nurture ['nərtʃər] *vt* **-tured; -turing 1** NOURISH : nutrir **2** EDUCATE : criar, educar **3** FOSTER : alimentar
nut ['nʌt] *n* **1** : nuez *f* **2** LUNATIC : loco *m*, -ca *f* **3** ENTHUSIAST : fanático *m*, -ca *f* **4** ~**s and bolts** : tuercas y tornillos — **nutcracker** ['nʌtˌkrækər] *n* : cascanueces *m*
nutmeg ['nʌtˌmɛg] *n* : nuez *f* moscada
nutrient ['nu:triənt, 'nju:-] *n* : nutriente *m*
nutrition [nʊ'trɪʃən, njʊ-] *n* : nutrición *f* — **nutritional** [nʊ'trɪʃənəl, njʊ-] *adj* : nutritivo — **nutritious** [nʊ'trɪʃəs, njʊ-] *adj* : nutritivo
nuts ['nʌts] *adj* : loco
nutshell ['nʌtˌʃɛl] *n* **1** : cáscara *f* de nuez **2 in a** ~ : en pocas palabras
nutty ['nʌṭi] *adj* **-tier; -tiest** : loco
nuzzle ['nʌzəl] *v* **-zled; -zling** *vi* : acurrucarse — *vt* : acariciar con el hocico
nylon ['naɪˌlɑn] *n* **1** : nilón *m* **2** ~**s** *npl* : medias *fpl* de nilón
nymph ['nɪmpf] *n* : ninfa *f*

O

o ['o:] *n, pl* **o's** *or* **os** ['o:z] **1** : o *f*, decimoquinta letra del alfabeto inglés **2** ZERO : cero *m*
O ['o:] → **oh**
oaf ['o:f] *n* : zoquete *m*
oak ['o:k] *n, pl* **oaks** *or* **oak** : roble *m*
oar ['or] *n* : remo *m*
oasis [o'eɪsɪs] *n, pl* **oases** [-ˌsi:z] : oasis *m*
oath ['o:θ] *n, pl* **oaths** ['o:ðz, 'o:θs] **1** : juramento *m* **2** SWEARWORD : palabrota *f*
oats ['o:ts] *npl* : avena *f* — **oatmeal** ['o:t-ˌmi:l] *n* : harina *f* de avena
obedient [o'bi:diənt] *adj* : obediente — **obedience** [o'bi:diənts] *n* : obediencia *f*
obese [o'bi:s] *adj* : obeso — **obesity** [o'bi:səṭi] *n* : obesidad *f*
obey [o'beɪ] *v* **obeyed; obeying** : obedecer
obituary [ə'bɪtʃʊˌɛri] *n, pl* **-aries** : obituario *m*
object ['ɑbdʒɪkt] *n* **1** : objeto *m* **2** AIM : objetivo *m* **3** : complemento *m* (en gramática) — ~ [əb'dʒɛkt] *vt* : objetar — *vi* ~ **to** : oponerse a — **objection** [əb'dʒɛkʃən] *n* : objeción *f* — **objectionable** [əb'dʒɛkʃənəbəl] *adj* : desagradable — **objective** [əb'dʒɛktɪv] *adj* : objetivo — ~ *n* : objetivo *m*
oblige [ə'blaɪdʒ] *vt* **obliged; obliging 1** : obligar **2 be much** ~**d** : estar muy agradecido **3** ~ **s.o.** : hacer un favor a algn — **obligation** [ˌɑblə'geɪʃən] *n* : obligación *f* — **obligatory** [ə'blɪgə-ˌtori] *adj* : obligatorio — **obliging** [ə'blaɪdʒɪŋ] *adj* : atento, servicial
oblique [o'bli:k] *adj* **1** SLANTING : oblicuo **2** INDIRECT : indirecto
obliterate [ə'blɪṭəˌreɪt] *vt* **-ated; -ating 1** ERASE : borrar **2** DESTROY : arrasar
oblivion [ə'blɪviən] *n* : olvido *m* — **oblivious** [ə'blɪviəs] *adj* : inconsciente
oblong ['ɑˌblɔŋ] *adj* : oblongo — ~ *n* : rectángulo *m*
obnoxious [ɑb'nɑkʃəs, əb-] *adj* : odioso
oboe ['o:ˌbo:] *n* : oboe *m*
obscene [ɑb'si:n, əb-] *adj* : obsceno — **obscenity** [ɑb'sɛnəṭi, əb-] *n, pl* **-ties** : obscenidad *f*
obscurity [ɑb'skjʊrəṭi, əb-] *n, pl* **-ties** : oscuridad *f* — **obscure** [ɑb'skjʊr, əb-] *adj* : oscuro — ~ *vt* **-scured; -scuring 1** DARKEN : oscurecer **2** HIDE : ocultar
observe [əb'zərv] *v* **-served; -serving** *vt* : observar — *vi* WATCH : mirar — **observance** [əb'zərvənts] *n* **1** : observancia *f* **2 religious** ~**s** : prácticas *fpl* religiosas — **observant** [əb'zərvənt] *adj* : observador — **observation** [ˌɑbsər'veɪʃən, -zər-] *n* : observación *f* — **observatory** [əb'zərvəˌtori] *n, pl* **-ries** : observatorio *m*
obsess [əb'sɛs] *vt* : obsesionar — **obsession** [ɑb'sɛʃən, əb-] *n* : obsesión *f* — **obsessive** [ɑb'sɛsɪv, əb-] *adj* : obsesivo
obsolete [ˌɑbsə'li:t, 'ɑbsəˌ-] *adj* : obsoleto, desusado
obstacle ['ɑbstɪkəl] *n* : obstáculo *m*
obstetrics [əb'stɛtrɪks] *n* : obstetricia *f*
obstinate ['ɑbstənət] *adj* : obstinado
obstruct [əb'strʌkt] *vt* **1** BLOCK : obstru-

ir **2** HINDER : obstaculizar — **obstruction** [əb'strʌkʃən] *n* : obstrucción *f*
obtain [əb'teɪn] *vt* : obtener, conseguir — **obtainable** [əb'teɪnəbəl] *adj* : asequible
obtrusive [əb'tru:sɪv] *adj* : entrometido (dícese de las personas), demasiado prominente (dícese de las cosas)
obtuse [ɑb'tu:s, əb-, -'tju:s] *adj* : obtuso
obvious ['ɑbviəs] *adj* : obvio, evidente — **obviously** ['ɑbviəsli] *adv* **1** CLEARLY : obviamente **2** OF COURSE : claro, por supuesto
occasion [ə'keɪʒən] *n* **1** : ocasión *f* **2 on ~** : de vez en cuando — **~** *vt* : ocasionar — **occasional** [ə'keɪʒənəl] *adj* : poco frecuente, ocasional — **occasionally** [ə'keɪʒənəli] *adv* : de vez en cuando
occult [ə'kʌlt, 'ɑ,kʌlt] *adj* : oculto
occupy ['ɑkjə,paɪ] *vt* **-pied; -pying 1** : ocupar **2 ~ oneself** : entretenerse — **occupancy** ['ɑkjəpəntsi] *n, pl* **-cies** : ocupación *f* — **occupant** ['ɑkjəpənt] *n* : ocupante *mf* — **occupation** [,ɑkjə'peɪʃən] *n* : ocupación *f* — **occupational** [,ɑkjə'peɪʃənəl] *adj* : profesional
occur [ə'kər] *vi* **occurred; occurring 1** : ocurrir **2** APPEAR : encontrarse **3 ~ to s.o.** : occurirse a algn — **occurrence** [ə'kərənts] *n* **1** EVENT : acontecimiento *m*, suceso *m* **2** INCIDENCE : incidencia *f*
ocean ['o:ʃən] *n* : océano *m*
ocher *or* **ochre** ['o:kər] *n* : ocre *m*
o'clock [ə'klɑk] *adv* **1 at 6 ~** : a las seis **2 it's one ~** : es la una **3 it's ten ~** : son las diez
octagon ['ɑktə,gɑn] *n* : octágono *m* — **octagonal** [ɑk'tægənəl] *adj* : octagonal
octave ['ɑktɪv] *n* : octava *f*
October [ɑk'to:bər] *n* : octubre *m*
octopus ['ɑktə,pus, -pəs] *n, pl* **-puses** *or* **-pi** [-,paɪ] : pulpo *m*
oculist ['ɑkjəlɪst] *n* : oculista *mf*
odd ['ɑd] *adj* **1** STRANGE : extraño, raro **2** : sin pareja (dícese de un calcetín, etc.) **3 forty ~ years** : cuarenta y tantos años **4 ~ jobs** : algunos trabajos *mpl* **5 ~ number** : número *m* impar — **oddity** ['ɑdəṭi] *n, pl* **-ties** : rareza *f* — **oddly** ['ɑdli] *adv* : de manera extraña — **odds** ['ɑdz] *npl* **1** CHANCES : probabilidades *fpl* **2 at ~** : en desacuerdo **3 five to one ~** : cinco contra uno (en apuestas) — **odds and ends** *npl* : cosas *fpl* sueltas
ode ['o:d] *n* : oda *f*
odious ['o:diəs] *adj* : odioso
odor *or Brit* **odour** ['o:dər] *n* : olor *m* — **odorless** *or Brit* **odourless** ['o:dərləs] *adj* : inodoro
of ['ʌv, 'ɑv] *prep* **1** : de **2 five minutes ~ ten** : las diez menos cinco **3 the eighth ~ April** : el ocho de abril
off ['ɔf] *adv* **1 be ~** LEAVE : irse **2 cut ~** : cortar **3 day ~** : día *m* de descanso **4 fall ~** : caerse **5 doze ~** : dormirse **6 far ~** : lejos **7 ~ and on** : de vez en cuando **8 shut ~** : apagar **9 ten miles ~** : a diez millas de aquí — **~** *prep* **1** : de **2 be ~ duty** : estar libre **3 ~ center** : descentrado — **~** *adj* **1** CANCELED : cancelado **2** OUT : apagado **3 an ~ chance** : una posibilidad remota
offend [ə'fɛnd] *vt* : ofender — **offender** [ə'fɛndər] *n* : delincuente *mf* — **offense** *or* **offence** [ə'fɛnts, 'ɔ,fɛnts] *n* **1** AFFRONT : afrenta *f* **2** ASSAULT : ataque *m* **3** : ofensiva *f* (en deportes) **4** CRIME : delito *m* **5 take ~** : ofenderse — **offensive** [ə'fɛntsɪv,'ɔ,fɛnt-] *adj* : ofensivo — **~** *n* : ofensiva *f*
offer ['ɔfər] *vt* : ofrecer — **~** *n* : oferta *f* — **offering** ['ɔfərɪŋ] *n* : ofrenda *f*
offhand ['ɔf'hænd] *adv* : de improviso, en este momento — **~** *adj* : improvisado
office ['ɔfəs] *n* **1** : oficina *f* **2** POSITION : cargo *m* **3 run for ~** : presentarse como candidato — **officer** ['ɔfəsər] *n* **1** : oficial *mf* **2** *or* **police ~** : agente *mf* (de policía) — **official** [ə'fɪʃəl] *n* : funcionario *m*, -ria *f* — **~** *adj* : oficial
offing ['ɔfɪŋ] *n* **in the ~** : en perspectiva
offset ['ɔf,sɛt] *vt* **-set; -setting** : compensar
offshore ['ɔf'ʃor] *adv* : a una distancia de la costa
offspring ['ɔf,sprɪŋ] *ns & pl* : prole *f*, progenie *f*
often ['ɔfən, 'ɔftən] *adv* **1** : muchas veces, a menudo, con frecuencia **2 every so ~** : de vez en cuando
ogle ['o:gəl] *vt* **ogled; ogling** : comerse con los ojos
ogre ['o:gər] *n* : ogro *m*
oh ['o:] *interj* **1** : ¡oh!, ¡ah! **2 ~ no!** : ¡ay no! **3 ~ really?** : ¿de veras?
oil ['ɔɪl] *n* **1** : aceite *m* **2** PETROLEUM : petróleo *m* **3** *or* **~ painting** : óleo *m* — **~** *vt* : lubricar — **oilskin** ['ɔɪl,skɪn] *n* : hule *m* — **oily** ['ɔɪli] *adj* **oilier; -est** : aceitoso, grasiento
ointment ['ɔɪntmənt] *n* : ungüento *m*, pomada *f*
OK *or* **okay** [,o:'keɪ] *adv* **1** : muy bien **2 ~!** : ¡de acuerdo!, ¡bueno! — **~** *adj* **1**

ALL RIGHT : bien **2 it's ~ with me** : por mí no hay problema — ~ *n* : visto *m* bueno — ~ [ˌoːˈkeɪ] *vt* **OK'd** *or* **okayed** [ˌoːˈkeɪd]; **OK'ing** *or* **okaying** : dar el visto bueno a

okra [ˈoːkrə, *South also* -kri] *n* : quingombó *m*

old [ˈoːld] *adj* **1** : viejo **2** FORMER : antiguo **3 any ~** : cualquier **4 be ten years ~** : tener diez años (de edad) **5 ~ age** : vejez *f* **6 ~ man** : anciano *m* **7 ~ woman** : anciana *f* — ~ *n* **the ~** : los viejos, los ancianos — **old–fashioned** [ˈoːldˈfæʃənd] *adj* : anticuado

olive [ˈɑlɪv, -ləv] *n* **1** : aceituna *f* (fruta) **2** *or* **~ green** : verde *m* oliva

Olympic [oˈlɪmpɪk] *adj* : olímpico — **Olympics** [oˈlɪmpɪks] *npl* **the ~** : las Olimpiadas, las Olimpíadas

omelet *or* **omelette** [ˈɑmlət, ˈɑmə-] *n* : omelette *mf Lat,* tortilla *f* francesa *Spain*

omen [ˈoːmən] *n* : agüero *m* — **ominous** [ˈɑmənəs] *adj* : ominoso, de mal agüero

omit [oˈmɪt] *vt* **omitted; omitting** : omitir — **omission** [oˈmɪʃən] *n* : omisión *f*

omnipotent [ɑmˈnɪpəṭənt] *adj* : omnipotente

on [ˈɑn, ˈɔn] *prep* **1** : en **2** ABOUT : sobre **3 ~ foot** : a pie **4 ~ Monday** : el lunes **5 ~ the right** : a la derecha **6 ~ vacation** : de vacaciones **7 talk ~ the phone** : hablar por teléfono — ~ *adv* **1 and so ~** : etcétera **2 from that moment ~** : a partir de ese momento **3 keep ~** : seguir **4 later ~** : más tarde **5 ~ and ~** : sin parar **6 put ~** : ponerse (ropa), poner (música, etc.) **7 turn ~** : encender (una luz, etc.), abrir (una llave) — ~ *adj* **1** : encendido (dícese de luces, etc.), abierto (dícese de llaves) **2 be ~ to** : estar enterado de

once [ˈwʌnts] *adv* **1** : una vez **2** FORMERLY : antes — ~ *n* **1 at ~** TOGETHER : al mismo tiempo **2 at ~** IMMEDIATELY : inmediatamente — ~ *conj* : una vez que

oncoming [ˈɑnˌkʌmɪŋ, ˈɔn-] *adj* : que viene

one [ˈwʌn] *adj* **1** : un, uno **2** ONLY : único **3** *or* **~ and the same** : el mismo — ~ *n* **1** : uno *m* (número) **2 ~ by ~** : uno a uno — ~ *pron* **1** : uno, una **2 ~ another** : el uno al otro **3 ~ never knows** : nunca se sabe **4 that ~** : aquél, aquella **5 which ~?** : ¿cuál? — **oneself** [ˌwʌnˈsɛlf] *pron* **1** (*used reflexively*) : se **2** (*used after prepositions*) : sí mismo, sí misma **3** (*used emphatically*) : uno mismo, una misma **4 by ~** : solo — **one–sided** [ˈwʌnˈsaɪdəd] *adj* **1** UNEQUAL : desigual **2** BIASED : parcial — **one–way** [ˈwʌnˈweɪ] *adj* **1** : de sentido único (dícese de una calle) **2 ~ ticket** : boleto *m* de ida

ongoing [ˈɑnˌgoːɪŋ] *adj* : en curso, corrinte

onion [ˈʌnjən] *n* : cebolla *f*

only [ˈoːnli] *adj* : único — ~ *adv* **1** : sólo, solamente **2 if ~** : ojalá, por lo menos — ~ *conj* BUT : pero

onset [ˈɑnˌsɛt] *n* : comienzo *m,* llegada *f*

onslaught [ˈɑnˌslɔt, ˈɔn-] *n* : ataque *m,* arremetida *f*

onto [ˈɑnˌtuː, ˈɔn-] *prep* : sobre

onus [ˈoːnəs] *n* : responsabilidad *f*

onward [ˈɑnwərd, ˈɔn-] *adv & adj* : hacia adelante

onyx [ˈɑnɪks] *n* : ónix *m*

ooze [ˈuːz] *v* **oozed; oozing** : rezumar

opal [ˈoːpəl] *n* : ópalo *m*

opaque [oˈpeɪk] *adj* : opaco

open [ˈoːpən] *adj* **1** : abierto **2** AVAILABLE : vacante, libre **3 an ~ question** : una cuestión pendiente — ~ *vt* : abrir — *vi* **1** : abrirse **2** BEGIN : comenzar — ~ *n* **in the ~ 1** OUTDOORS : al aire libre **2** KNOWN : sacado a la luz — **open–air** [ˈoːpənˈær] *adj* : al aire libre — **opener** [ˈoːpənər] *n* **1** : abridor *m* **2** *or* **bottle ~** : abrebotellas *m* **3** *or* **can ~** : abrelatas *m* — **opening** [ˈoːpənɪŋ] *n* **1** : abertura *f* **2** BEGINNING : comienzo *m,* apertura *f* **3** OPPORTUNITY : opportunidad *f* — **openly** [ˈoːpənli] *adv* : abiertamente

opera [ˈɑprə, ˈɑpərə] *n* : ópera *f*

operate [ˈɑpəˌreɪt] *v* **-ated; -ating** *vi* **1** FUNCTION : funcionar **2 ~ on s.o.** : operar a algn — *vt* **1** : hacer funcionar (una máquina) **2** MANAGE : dirigir, manejar — **operation** [ˌɑpəˈreɪʃən] *n* **1** : operación *f* **2** FUNCTIONING : funcionamiento *m* — **operational** [ˌɑpəˈreɪʃənəl] *adj* : operacional — **operative** [ˈɑpərəṭɪv, -ˌreɪ-] *adj* : en vigor — **operator** [ˈɑpəˌreɪṭər] *n* **1** : operador *m,* -dora *f* **2** *or* **machine ~** : operario *m,* -ria *f*

opinion [əˈpɪnjən] *n* : opinión *f* — **opinionated** [əˈpɪnjəˌneɪṭəd] *adj* : dogmático

opium [ˈoːpiəm] *n* : opio *m*

opossum [əˈpɑsəm] *n* : zarigüeya *f,* opossum *m*

opponent [əˈpoːnənt] *n* : adversario *m,* -ria *f;* contrincante *mf* (en deportes)

opportunity [ˌɑpərˈtuːnət̬i, -ˈtjuː-] *n, pl* **-ties** : oportunidad *f* — **opportune** [ˌɑpərˈtuːn, -ˈtjuːn] *adj* : oportuno — **opportunist** [ˌɑpərˈtuːnɪst, -ˈtjuː-] *n* : oportunista *mf*

oppose [əˈpoːz] *vt* **-posed; -posing** : oponerse a — **opposed** *adj* **~ to** : en contra de

opposite [ˈɑpəzət] *adj* **1** FACING : de enfrente **2** CONTRARY : opuesto — **~** *n* **the ~** : lo contrario, lo opuesto — **~** *adv* : enfrente — **~** *prep* : enfrente de, frente a — **opposition** [ˌɑpəˈzɪʃən] *n* **1** : oposición *f* **2 in ~ to** : en contra de

oppress [əˈprɛs] *vt* : oprimir — **oppression** [əˈprɛʃən] *n* : opresión *f* — **oppressive** [əˈprɛsɪv] *adj* **1** : opresivo **2** STIFLING : agobiante — **oppressor** [əˈprɛsər] *n* : opresor *m*, -sora *f*

opt [ˈɑpt] *vi* **~ for** : optar por

optic [ˈɑptɪk] *or* **optical** [-tɪkəl] *adj* : óptico — **optician** [ɑpˈtɪʃən] *n* : óptico *m*, -ca *f*

optimism [ˈɑptəˌmɪzəm] *n* : optimismo *m* — **optimist** [ˈɑptəmɪst] *n* : optimista *mf* — **optimistic** [ˌɑptəˈmɪstɪk] *adj* : optimista

optimum [ˈɑptəməm] *n, pl* **-ma** [-ˈmə] : lo óptimo, lo ideal

option [ˈɑpʃən] *n* **1** : opción *f* **2 have no ~** : no tener más remedio — **optional** [ˈɑpʃənəl] *adj* : facultativo, opcional

opulence [ˈɑpjələnts] *n* : opulencia *f* — **opulent** [ˈɑpjələnt] *adj* : opulento

or [ˈɔr] *conj* **1** (*indicating an alternative*) : o (u *before* o- *or* ho-) **2** (*following a negative*) : ni **3 ~ else** : si no

oracle [ˈɔrəkəl] *n* : oráculo *m*

oral [ˈorəl] *adj* : oral

orange [ˈɔrɪndʒ] *n* **1** : naranja *f* (fruta) **2** : naranja *m* (color)

orator [ˈɔrət̬ər] *n* : orador *m*, -dora *f*

orbit [ˈɔrbət] *n* : órbita *f* — **~** *vt* : girar alrededor de — *vi* : orbitar

orchard [ˈɔrtʃərd] *n* : huerto *m*

orchestra [ˈɔrkəstrə] *n* : orquesta *f*

orchid [ˈɔrkɪd] *n* : orquídea *f*

ordain [ɔrˈdeɪn] *vt* **1** : ordenar (un sacerdote, etc.) **2** DECREE : decretar

ordeal [ɔrˈdiːl, ˈɔrˌdiːl] *n* : prueba *f* dura

order [ˈɔrdər] *vt* **1** : ordenar **2** : pedir (mercancías, etc.) — *vi* : hacer un pedido — **~** *n* **1** ARRANGEMENT : orden *m* **2** COMMAND : orden *f* **3** REQUEST : pedido *m* **4** : orden *f* (religiosa) **5 in ~ that** : para que **6 in ~ to** : para **7 out of ~** : averiado, descompuesto *Lat* — **orderly** [ˈɔrdərli] *adj* : ordenado — **~** *n, pl* **-lies 1** : ordenanza *m* (en el ejército) **2** : camillero *m* (en un hospital)

ordinary [ˈɔrdənˌɛri] *adj* **1** : normal, corriente **2** MEDIOCRE : ordinario — **ordinarily** [ˌɔrdənˈɛrəli] *adv* : generalmente

ore [ˈor] *n* : mena *f*

oregano [əˈrɛgəˌnoː] *n* : orégano *m*

organ [ˈɔrgən] *n* : órgano *m* — **organic** [ɔrˈgænɪk] *adj* : orgánico — **organism** [ˈɔrgəˌnɪzəm] *n* : organismo *m* — **organist** [ˈɔrgənɪst] *n* : organista *mf* — **organize** [ˈɔrgəˌnaɪz] *vt* **-nized; -nizing** : organizar — **organization** [ˌɔrgənəˈzeɪʃən] *n* : organización *f* — **organizer** [ˈɔrgəˌnaɪzər] *n* : organizador *m*, -dora *f*

orgasm [ˈɔrˌgæzəm] *n* : orgasmo *m*

orgy [ˈɔrdʒi] *n, pl* **-gies** : orgía *f*

Orient [ˈoriˌɛnt] *n* **the ~** : el Oriente — **orient** *vt* : orientar — **oriental** [ˌoriˈɛntəl] *adj* : del Oriente, oriental — **orientation** [ˌoriənˈteɪʃən] *n* : orientación *f*

orifice [ˈɔrəfəs] *n* : orificio *m*

origin [ˈɔrədʒən] *n* : origen *m* — **original** [əˈrɪdʒənəl] *n* : original *m* — **~** *adj* : original — **originality** [əˌrɪdʒəˈnælət̬i] *n* : originalidad *f* — **originally** [əˈrɪdʒənəli] *adv* : originariamente — **originate** [əˈrɪdʒəˌneɪt] *v* **-nated; -nating** *vt* : originar — *vi* **1** : originarse **2 ~ from** : provenir de — **originator** [əˈrɪdʒəˌneɪt̬ər] *n* : creador *m*, -dora *f*

ornament [ˈɔrnəmənt] *n* : adorno *m* — **~** *vt* : adornar — **ornamental** [ˌɔrnəˈmɛntəl] *adj* : ornamental, de adorno — **ornate** [ɔrˈneɪt] *adj* : elaborado, adornado

ornithology [ˌɔrnəˈθɑlədʒi] *n, pl* **-gies** : ornitología *f*

orphan [ˈɔrfən] *n* : huérfano *m*, -na *f* — **~** *vt* : dejar huérfano — **orphanage** [ˈɔrfənɪdʒ] *n* : orfelinato *m*, orfanato *m*

orthodox [ˈɔrθəˌdɑks] *adj* : ortodoxo — **orthodoxy** [ˈɔrθəˌdɑksi] *n, pl* **-doxies** : ortodoxia *f*

orthopedic [ˌɔrθəˈpiːdɪk] *adj* : ortopédico

oscillation [ˌɑsəˈleɪʃən] *n* : oscilación *f* — **oscillate** [ˈɑsəˌleɪt] *vi* **-lated; -lating** : oscilar

ostensible [ɑˈstɛntsəbəl] *adj* : aparente, ostensible

ostentation [ˌɑstənˈteɪʃən] *n* : ostentación *f* — **ostentatious** [ˌɑstənˈteɪʃəs] *adj* : ostentoso

osteopath [ˈɑstiəˌpæθ] *n* : osteópata *f*

ostracism [ˈɑstrəˌsɪzəm] *n* : ostracismo *m* — **ostracize** [ˈɑstrəˌsaɪz] *vt* **-cized; -cizing** : aislar

ostrich [ˈɑstrɪtʃ, ˈɔs-] *n* : avestruz *m*

other ['ʌðər] *adj* **1** : otro **2 every ~ day** : cada dos días **3 on the ~ hand** : por otra parte, por otro lado — **~** *pron* **1** : otro, otra **2 the ~s** : los otros, las otras, los demás, las demás — **other than** *prep* : aparte de, fuera de — **otherwise** ['ʌðər,waɪz] *adv* **1** : eso aparte, por lo demás **2** DIFFERENTLY : de otro modo **3** OR ELSE : si no

otter ['ɑṭər] *n* : nutria *f*

ought ['ɔt] *v aux* **1** : deber **2 you ~ to have done it** : deberías haberlo hecho

ounce ['aʊnts] *n* : onza *f*

our ['ɑr, 'aʊr] *adj* : nuestro — **ours** ['aʊrz, 'ɑrz] *pron* **1** : (el) nuestro, (la) nuestra, (los) nuestros, (las) nuestras **2 a friend of ~** : un amigo nuestro — **ourselves** [ɑr'sɛlvz, aʊr-] *pron* **1** (*used reflexively*) : nos **2** (*used after prepositions*) : nosotros, nosotras **3** (*used for emphasis*) : nosotros mismos, nosotras mismas

oust ['aʊst] *vt* : desbancar

out ['aʊt] *adv* **1** OUTSIDE : fuera, afuera **2 cry ~** : gritar **3 eat ~** : comer afuera **4 go ~** : salir **5 look ~** : mirar para afuera **6 run ~ of** : agotar **7 turn ~** : apagar (una luz) **8 take ~** REMOVE : sacar — **~** *prep* → **out of** — **~** *adj* **1** ABSENT : ausente **2** UNFASHIONABLE : fuera de moda **3** EXTINGUISHED : apagado **4 the sun is ~** : hace sol

outboard motor ['aʊt,bord] *n* : motor *m* fuera de borde

outbreak ['aʊt,breɪk] *n* : brote *m* (de una enfermedad), comienzo *m* (de guerra)

outburst ['aʊt,bərst] *n* : arranque *m*, arrebato *m*

outcast ['aʊt,kæst] *n* : paria *mf*

outcome ['aʊt,kʌm] *n* : resultado *m*

outcry ['aʊt,kraɪ] *n, pl* **-cries** : protesta *f*

outdated [,aʊt'deɪṭəd] *adj* : anticuado

outdo [,aʊt'du:] *vt* **-did** [-'dɪd]; **-done** [-'dʌn]; **-doing**; **-does** [-'dʌz] : superar

outdoor ['aʊt'dor] *adj* : al aire libre — **outdoors** ['aʊt'dorz] *adv* : al aire libre

outer ['aʊṭər] *adj* : exterior — **outer space** *n* : espacio *m* exterior

outfit ['aʊt,fɪt] *n* **1** EQUIPMENT : equipo *m* **2** CLOTHES : conjunto *m* — **~** *vt* **-fitted; -fitting** EQUIP : equipar

outgoing ['aʊt,go:ɪŋ] *adj* **1** SOCIABLE : extrovertido **2 ~ mail** : correo *m* (para enviar) **3 ~ president** : presidente *m*, -ta *f* saliente

outgrow [,aʊt'gro:] *vt* **-grew** [-'gru:]; **-grown** [-'gro:n]; **-growing** : crecer más que

outing ['aʊṭɪŋ] *n* : excursión *f*

outlandish [aʊt'lændɪʃ] *adj* : estrafalario

outlast [,aʊt'læst] *vt* : durar más que

outlaw ['aʊt,lɔ] *n* : forajido *m*, -da *f* — **~** *vt* : declarar ilegal

outlay ['aʊt,leɪ] *n* : desembolso *m*

outlet ['aʊt,lɛt, -lət] *n* **1** EXIT : salida *f* **2** RELEASE : desahogo *m* **3** *or* **electrical ~** : toma *f* de corriente **4** *or* **retail ~** : tienda *f* al por menor

outline ['aʊt,laɪn] *n* **1** CONTOUR : contorno *m* **2** SKETCH : bosquejo *m*, boceto *m* **3** SUMMARY : esquema *m* — **~** *vt* **-lined; -lining 1** SKETCH : bosquejar **2** EXPLAIN : delinear, esbozar

outlive [,aʊt'lɪv] *vt* **-lived; -living** : sobrevivir a

outlook ['aʊt,lʊk] *n* **1** PROSPECTS : perspectivas *fpl* **2** VIEWPOINT : punto *m* de vista

outlying ['aʊt,laɪɪŋ] *adj* : alejado, distante

outmoded [,aʊt'mo:dəd] *adj* : pasado de moda, anticuado

outnumber [,aʊt'nʌmbər] *vt* : superar en número a

out of *prep* **1** FROM : de **2** THROUGH : por **3** WITHOUT : sin **4 ~ curiosity** : por curiosidad **5 ~ control** : fuera de control **6 one ~ four** : uno de cada cuatro — **out–of–date** [,aʊṭəv'deɪt] *adj* : anticuado — **out–of–door** [,aʊṭəv'dor] *or* **out–of–doors** [-'dorz] *adj* → **outdoor**

outpatient ['aʊt,peɪʃənt] *n* : paciente *m* externo

outpost ['aʊt,po:st] *n* : puesto *m* avanzado

output ['aʊt,pʊt] *n* **1** : producción *f*, rendimiento *m* **2** : salida *f* (informática) — **~** *vt* **-putted** *or* **-put; -putting** : producir

outrage ['aʊt,reɪdʒ] *n* **1** : atrocidad *f*, escándalo *m* **2** ANGER : ira *f*, indignación *f* — **~** *vt* **-raged; -raging** : ultrajar — **outrageous** [,aʊt'reɪdʒəs] *adj* : escandaloso

outright [,aʊt'raɪt] *adv* **1** COMPLETELY : por completo **2** INSTANTLY : en el acto — **~** ['aʊt,raɪt] *adj* : completo, absoluto

outset ['aʊt,sɛt] *n* : comienzo *m*, principio *m*

outside [,aʊt'saɪd, 'aʊt,-] *n* **1** : exterior *m* **2 from the ~** : desde fuera, desde afuera — **~** *adj* **1** : exterior, externo **2 an ~ chance** : una posibilidad remota — **~** *adv* : fuera, afuera — **~** *prep* *or* **~ of** : fuera de — **outsider** [,aʊt'saɪdər] *n* : forastero *m*, -ra *f*

outskirts ['aut,skərts] *npl* : afueras *fpl*, alrededores *mpl*
outspoken [,aut'spo:kən] *adj* : franco, directo
outstanding [,aut'stændɪŋ] *adj* **1** UNPAID : pendiente **2** EXCELLENT : excepcional
outstretched [,aut'strɛtʃt] *adj* : extendido
outstrip [,aut'strɪp] *vt* **-stripped** *or* **-stript** [-'strɪpt]; **-stripping** : aventajar
outward ['autwərd] *adj* **1** : hacia afuera **2** EXTERNAL : externo, external — ~ *or* **outwards** [-wərdz] *adv* : hacia afuera — **outwardly** ['autwərdli] *adv* APPARENTLY : aparentemente
outweigh [,aut'weɪ] *vt* : pesar más que
outwit [,aut'wɪt] *vt* **-witted; -witting** : ser más listo que
oval ['o:vəl] *n* : óvalo *m* — ~ *adj* : ovalado
ovary ['o:vəri] *n, pl* **-ries** : ovario *m*
ovation [o'veɪʃən] *n* : ovación *f*
oven ['ʌvən] *n* : horno *m*
over ['o:vər] *adv* **1** ABOVE : por encima **2** AGAIN : otra vez, de nuevo **3** MORE : más **4 all** ~ : por todas partes **5 ask** ~ : invitar **6 cross** ~ : cruzar **7 fall** ~ : caerse **8** ~ **and** ~ : una y otra vez **9** ~ **here** : aquí **10** ~ **there** : allí — ~ *prep* **1** ABOVE, UPON : encima de, sobre **2** ACROSS : por encima de, sobre **3** DURING : en, durante **4 fight** ~ : pelearse por **5** ~ **$5** : más de $5 **6** ~ **the phone** : por teléfono — ~ *adj* : terminado, acabado
overall [,o:vər'ɔl] *adv* GENERALLY : en general — *adj* : total, en conjunto — **overalls** ['o:vər,ɔlz] *npl* : overol *m Lat*
overbearing [,o:vər'bærɪŋ] *adj* : dominante, imperioso
overboard ['o:vər,bord] *adv* **fall** ~ : caer al agua
overburden [,o:vər'bərdən] *vt* : sobrecargar
overcast [,o:vər,kæst] *adj* : nublado
overcharge [,o:vər'tʃɑrdʒ] *vt* **-charged; -charging** : cobrar demasiado
overcoat ['o:vər,ko:t] *n* : abrigo *m*
overcome [,o:vər'kʌm] *v* **-came** [-'keɪm]; **-come; -coming** *vt* **1** CONQUER : vencer **2** OVERWHELM : agobiar — *vi* : vencer
overcook [,o:vər'kuk] *vt* : cocer demasiado
overcrowded [,o:vər'kraudəd] *adj* : abarrotado de gente
overdo [,o:vər'du:] *vt* **-did** [-'dɪd]; **-done** [-'dʌn]; **-doing; -does** [-'dʌz] **1** : hacer demasiado **2** EXAGGERATE : exagerar **3** → **overcook**
overdose ['o:vər,do:s] *n* : sobredosis *f*
overdraw [,o:vər'drɔ] *vt* **-drew** [-'dru:]; **-drawn** [-'drɔn]; **-drawing** : girar en descubierto — **overdraft** ['o:vər,dræft] *n* : sobregiro *m*, descubierto *m*
overdue [,o:vər'du:] *adj* : fuera de plazo (dícese de pagos, libros, etc.)
overeat [,o:vər'i:t] *vi* **-ate** [-'eɪt]; **-eaten** [-'eɪtən]; **-eating** : comer demasiado
overestimate [,o:vər'ɛstə,meɪt] *vt* **-mated; -mating** : sobreestimar
overflow [,o:vər'flo:] *vt* : desbordar — *vi* : desbordarse — ~ ['o:vər,flo:] *n* : desbordamiento *m* (de un río)
overgrown [,o:vər'gro:n] *adj* : cubierto (de malas hierbas, etc.)
overhand ['o:vər,hænd] *adv* : por encima de la cabeza
overhang [,o:vər'hæŋ] *v* **-hung** [-'hʌŋ]; **-hanging** : sobresalir
overhaul [,o:vər'hɔl] *vt* : revisar (un motor, etc.)
overhead [,o:vər'hɛd] *adv* : por encima — ~ ['o:vər,hɛd] *adj* : de arriba — ~ ['o:vər,hɛd] *n* : gastos *mpl* generales
overhear [,o:vər'hɪr] *vt* **-heard; -hearing** : oír por casualidad
overheat [,o:vər'hi:t] *vt* : calentar demasiado — *vi* : recalentarse
overjoyed [,o:vər'dʒɔɪd] *adj* : encantado
overland ['o:vər,lænd, -lənd] *adv & adj* : por tierra
overlap [,o:vər'læp] *v* **-lapped; -lapping** *vt* : traslapar — *vi* : traslaparse
overload [,o:vər'lo:d] *vt* : sobrecargar
overlook [,o:vər'luk] *vt* **1** : dar a (un jardín, el mar, etc.) **2** MISS : pasar por alto
overly ['o:vərli] *adv* : demasiado
overnight [,o:vər'naɪt] *adv* **1** : por la noche **2** SUDDENLY : de la noche a la mañana — ~ ['o:vər'naɪt] *adj* **1** : de noche **2** SUDDEN : repentino
overpass ['o:vər,pæs] *n* : paso *m* elevado
overpopulated [,o:vər'pɑpjə,leɪţəd] *adj* : superpoblado
overpower [,o:vər'pauər] *vt* **1** SUBDUE : dominar **2** OVERWHELM : agobiar, abrumar
overrated [,o:vər'reɪţəd] *adj* : sobreestimado
override [,o:vər'raɪd] *vt* **-rode** [-'ro:d]; **-ridden** [-'rɪdən]; **-riding 1** : predominar sobre **2** : anular (una decisión, etc.)
overrule [,o:vər'ru:l] *vt* **-ruled; -ruling** : anular (una decisión), rechazar (una protesta)
overrun [,o:vər'rʌn] *vt* **-ran** [-'ræn]; **-running 1** INVADE : invadir **2** EXCEED : exceder

overseas [ˌo:vərˈsi:z] *adv* : en el extranjero — ~ [ˈo:vərˌsi:z] *adj* : extranjero, exterior
oversee [ˌo:vərˈsi:] *vt* **-saw** [-ˈsɔ]; **-seen** [-ˈsi:n]; **-seeing** : supervisar
overshadow [ˌo:vərˈʃæˌdo:] *vt* : eclipsar
oversight [ˈo:vərˌsaɪt] *n* : descuido *m*
oversleep [ˌo:vərˈsli:p] *vi* **-slept** [-ˈslɛpt]; **-sleeping** : quedarse dormido
overstep [ˌo:vərˈstɛp] *vt* **-stepped**; **-stepping** : sobrepasar
overt [oˈvərt, ˈo:ˌvərt] *adj* : manifiesto
overtake [ˌo:vərˈteɪk] *vt* **-took** [-ˈtʊk]; **-taken** [-ˈteɪkən]; **-taking 1** PASS : adelantar **2** SURPASS : superar
overthrow [ˌo:vərˈθro:] *vt* **-threw** [-ˈθru:]; **-thrown** [-ˈθro:n]; **-throwing** : derrocar
overtime [ˈo:vərˌtaɪm] *n* **1** : horas *fpl* extras (de trabajo) **2** : prórroga *f* (en deportes)
overtone [ˈo:vərˌto:n] *n* SUGGESTION : tinte *m*, insinuación *f*
overture [ˈo:vərˌtʃʊr, -tʃər] *n* : obertura *f* (en música)
overturn [ˌo:vərˈtərn] *vt* **1** : dar la vuelta a **2** NULLIFY : anular — *vi* : volcar
overweight [ˌo:vərˈweɪt] *adj* : demasiado gordo
overwhelm [ˌo:vərˈhwɛlm] *vt* **1** : abrumar, agobiar **2** : aplastar (a un enemigo) — **overwhelming** [ˌo:vərˈhwɛlmɪŋ] *adj* : abrumador, apabullante
overwork [ˌo:vərˈwərk] *vt* : hacer trabajar demasiado — *vi* : trabajar demasiado
overwrought [ˌo:vərˈrɔt] *adj* : alterado, sobreexitado
owe [ˈo:] *vt* **owed; owing** : deber — **owing to** *prep* : debido a
owl [ˈaʊl] *n* : búho *m*
own [ˈo:n] *adj* : propio — ~ *vt* : poseer, tener — *vi* ~ **up** : confesar — ~ *pron* **1 my (your, his/her/their, our)** ~ : el mío, la mía; el tuyo, la tuya; el suyo, la suya; el nuestro, la nuestra **2 be on one's** ~ : estar solo **3 to each his** ~ : cada uno a lo suyo — **owner** [ˈo:nər] *n* : propietario *m*, -ria *f* — **ownership** [ˈo:nərˌʃɪp] *n* : propiedad *f*
ox [ˈɑks] *n, pl* **oxen** [ˈɑksən] : buey *m*
oxygen [ˈɑksɪdʒən] *n* : oxígeno *m*
oyster [ˈɔɪstər] *n* : ostra *f*
ozone [ˈo:ˌzo:n] *n* : ozono *m*

P

p [ˈpi:] *n, pl* **p's** *or* **ps** [ˈpi:z] : p *f*, decimosexta letra del alfabeto inglés
pace [ˈpeɪs] *n* **1** STEP : paso *m* **2** RATE : ritmo *m* **3 keep** ~ **with** : andar al mismo paso que — ~ *vi* **paced; pacing** *or* ~ **up and down** : caminar de arriba para abajo
pacify [ˈpæsəˌfaɪ] *vt* **-fied; -fying** : apaciguar — **pacifier** [ˈpæsəˌfaɪər] *n* : chupete *m* — **pacifist** [ˈpæsəfɪst] *n* : pacifista *mf*
pack [ˈpæk] *n* **1** BUNDLE : fardo *m* **2** BACKPACK : mochila *f* **3** PACKAGE : paquete *m* **4** : baraja *f* (de naipes) **5** : manada *f* (de lobos, etc.), jauría *f* (de perros) — ~ *vt* **1** PACKAGE : empaquetar **2** FILL : llenar **3** : hacer (una maleta) — *vi* : hacer las maletas — **package** [ˈpækɪdʒ] *vt* **-aged; -aging** : empaquetar — ~ *n* : paquete *m* — **packet** [ˈpækət] *n* : paquete *m*
pact [ˈpækt] *n* : pacto *m*, acuerdo *m*
pad [ˈpæd] *n* **1** CUSHION : almohadilla *f* **2** TABLET : bloc *m* (de papel) **3** *or* **ink** ~ : tampón *m* **4 launching** ~ : plataforma *f* (de lanzamiento) — ~ *vt* **padded; padding** : rellenar — **padding** [ˈpædɪŋ] *n* **1** : relleno *m* **2** : paja *f* (en un discurso, etc.)
paddle [ˈpædəl] *n* **1** : canalete *m* (de una canoa) **2** : pala *f*, paleta *f* (en deportes) — ~ *vt* **-dled; -dling** : hacer avanzar (una canoa) con canalete
padlock [ˈpædˌlɑk] *n* : candado *m* — ~ *vt* : cerrar con candado
pagan [ˈpeɪgən] *n* : pagano *m*, -na *f* — ~ *adj* : pagano
page[1] [ˈpeɪdʒ] *vt* **paged; paging** : llamar por altavoz
page[2] *n* : página *f* (de un libro, etc.)
pageant [ˈpædʒənt] *n* : espectáculo *m* — **pageantry** [ˈpædʒəntri] *n* : pompa *f*, boato *m*
paid → **pay**
pail [ˈpeɪl] *n* : cubo *m Spain*, cubeta *f Lat*
pain [ˈpeɪn] *n* **1** : dolor *m* **2** : pena *f* (mental) **3** ~**s** *npl* EFFORT : esfuerzos *mpl* — ~ *vt* : doler — **painful** [ˈpeɪnfəl] *adj* : doloroso — **painkiller** [ˈpeɪnˌkɪlər] *n* : analgésico *m* — **painless** [ˈpeɪnləs] *adj* : indoloro, sin dolor — **painstaking** [ˈpeɪnˌsteɪkɪŋ] *adj* : meticuloso, esmerado
paint [ˈpeɪnt] *v* : pintar — ~ *n* : pintura

f — **paintbrush** ['peɪnt,brʌʃ] *n* : pincel *m* (de un artista), brocha *f* (para pintar casas, etc.) — **painter** ['peɪntər] *n* : pintor *m*, -tora *f* — **painting** ['peɪntɪŋ] *n* : pintura *f*
pair ['pær] *n* **1** : par *m* **2** COUPLE : pareja *f* — ~ *vt* : emparejar
pajamas [pə'dʒɑməz, -'dʒæ-] *npl* : pijama *m*, piyama *mf Lat*
Pakistani [,pækɪ'stæni, ,pɑkɪ'stɑni] *adj* : paquistaní
pal ['pæl] *n* : amigo *m*, -ga *f*
palace ['pæləs] *n* : palacio *m*
palate ['pælət] *n* : paladar *m* — **palatable** ['pælət̬əbəl] *adj* : sabroso
pale ['peɪl] *adj* **paler; palest 1** PALLID : pálido **2** : claro (dícese de los colores, etc.) — ~ *vi* **paled; paling** : palidecer — **paleness** ['peɪlnəs] *n* : palidez *f*
Palestinian [,pælə'stɪniən] *adj* : palestino
palette ['pælət] *n* : paleta *f*
pallbearer ['pɔl,bɛrər] *n* : portador *m*, -dora *f* del féretro
pallid ['pæləd] *adj* : pálido — **pallor** ['pælər] *n* : palidez *f*
palm[1] ['pɑm, 'pɑlm] *n* : palma *f* (de la mano)
palm[2] *or* ~ **tree** : palmera *f* — **Palm Sunday** *n* : Domingo *m* de Ramos
palpitate ['pælpə,teɪt] *vi* **-tated; -tating** : palpitar — **palpitation** [,pælpə'teɪʃən] *n* : palpitación *f*
paltry ['pɔltri] *adj* **-trier; -est** : mísero, mezquino
pamper ['pæmpər] *vt* : mimar
pamphlet ['pæmpflət] *n* : panfleto *m*, folleto *m*
pan ['pæn] *n* **1** SAUCEPAN : cacerola *f* **2** FRYING PAN : sartén *mf* — ~ *vt* **panned; panning** CRITICIZE : poner por los suelos
pancake ['pæn,keɪk] *n* : crepe *mf*, panqueque *m Lat*
panda ['pændə] *n* : panda *mf*
pandemonium [,pændə'mo:niəm] *n* : pandemonio *m*
pander ['pændər] *vi* ~ **to** : complacer a
pane ['peɪn] *n* : cristal *m*, vidrio *m*
panel ['pænəl] *n* **1** : panel *m* **2** GROUP : jurado *m* **3** *or* **instrument** ~ : tablero *m* (de instrumentos) — ~ *vt* **-eled** *or* **-elled; -eling** *or* **-elling** : adornar con paneles — **paneling** ['pænəlɪŋ] *n* : paneles *mpl*
pang ['pæŋ] *n* : punzada *f*
panic ['pænɪk] *n* : pánico *m* — ~ *v* **-icked; -icking** *vt* : llenar del pánico — *vi* : ser presa del pánico — **panicky** ['pænɪki] *adj* : presa de pánico
panorama [,pænə'ræmə, -'rɑ-] *n* : panorama *m* — **panoramic** [,pænə'ræmɪk, -'rɑ-] *adj* : panorámico
pansy ['pænzi] *n, pl* **-sies** : pensamiento *m*
pant ['pænt] *vi* : jadear, resoplar
panther ['pænθər] *n* : pantera *f*
panties ['pæntiz] *npl* : bragas *fpl Spain*, calzones *mpl Lat*
pantomime ['pæntə,maɪm] *n* : pantomima *f*
pantry ['pæntri] *n, pl* **-tries** : despensa *f*
pants ['pænts] *npl* TROUSERS : pantalón *m*, pantalones *mpl*
papa ['pɑpə] *n* : papá *m fam*
papal ['peɪpəl] *adj* : papal
papaya [pə'paɪə] *n* : papaya *f*
paper ['peɪpər] *n* **1** : papel *m* **2** DOCUMENT : documento *m* **3** NEWSPAPER : periódico *m* — ~ *vt* WALLPAPER : empapelar — ~ *adj* : de papel — **paperback** ['peɪpər,bæk] *n* : libro *m* en rústica — **paper clip** *n* : clip *m*, sujetapapeles *m* — **paperweight** ['peɪpər,weɪt] *n* : pisapapeles *m* — **paperwork** ['peɪpər,wərk] *n* : papeleo *m*
paprika [pə'pri:kə, pæ-] *n* : pimentón *m*
par ['pɑr] *n* **1** : par *m* (en golf) **2 below** ~ : debajo de la par **3 on a** ~ **with** : al nivel de
parable ['pærəbəl] *n* : parábola *f*
parachute ['pærə,ʃu:t] *n* : paracaídas *m* — ~ *vi* **-chuted; -chuting** : lanzarse en paracaídas
parade [pə'reɪd] *n* **1** : desfile *m* **2** DISPLAY : alarde *m* — ~ *v* **-raded; -rading** *vi* MARCH : desfilar — *vt* DISPLAY : hacer alarde de
paradise ['pærə,daɪs, -,daɪz] *n* : paraíso *m*
paradox ['pærə,dɑks] *n* : paradoja *f* — **paradoxical** [,pærə'dɑksɪkəl] *adj* : paradójico
paraffin ['pærəfən] *n* : parafina *f*
paragraph ['pærə,græf] *n* : párrafo *m*
Paraguayan [,pærə'gwaɪən, -'gweɪ-] *adj* : paraguayo
parakeet ['pærə,ki:t] *n* : periquito *m*
parallel ['pærə,lɛl, -ləl] *adj* : paralelo — ~ *n* **1** : paralelo *m* (en geografía) **2** SIMILARITY : paralelismo *m*, semejanza *f* — ~ *vt* : ser paralelo a
paralysis [pə'ræləsɪs] *n, pl* **-yses** [-,si:z] : parálisis *f* — **paralyze** *or Brit* **paralise** ['pærə,laɪz] *vt* **-lyzed** *or Brit* **-lised; -lyzing** *or Brit* **-lising** : paralizar
parameter [pə'ræmət̬ər] *n* : parámetro *m*
paramount ['pærə,maʊnt] *adj* **of** ~ **importance** : de suma importancia

paranoia [ˌpærəˈnɔɪə] *n* : paranoia *f* — **paranoid** [ˈpærəˌnɔɪd] *adj* : paranoico

paraphernalia [ˌpærəfəˈneɪljə, -fər-] *ns & pl* : parafernalia *f*

paraphrase [ˈpærəˌfreɪz] *n* : paráfrasis *f* — ~ *vt* **-phrased; -phrasing** : parafrasear

paraplegic [ˌpærəˈpli:dʒɪk] *n* : parapléjico *m*, -ca *f*

parasite [ˈpærəˌsaɪt] *n* : parásito *m*

paratrooper [ˈpærəˌtru:pər] *n* : paracaidista *mf* (militar)

parcel [ˈpɑrsəl] *n* : paquete *m*

parch [ˈpɑrtʃ] *vt* : resecar

parchment [ˈpɑrtʃmənt] *n* : pergamino *m*

pardon [ˈpɑrdən] *n* **1** : perdón *m* **2** REPRIEVE : indulto *m* **3 I beg your** ~ : perdone Ud., disculpe Ud. *Lat* — ~ *vt* **1** : perdonar **2** REPRIEVE : indultar (a un delincuente)

parent [ˈpærənt] *n* **1** : madre *f*, padre *m* **2** ~**s** *npl* : padres *mpl* — **parental** [pəˈrentəl] *adj* : de los padres

parenthesis [pəˈrenθəsɪs] *n, pl* **-theses** [-ˌsi:z] : paréntesis *m*

parish [ˈpærɪʃ] *n* : parroquia *f* — **parishioner** [pəˈrɪʃənər] *n* : feligrés *m*, -gresa *f*

parity [ˈpærəţi] *n, pl* **-ties** : igualidad *f*

park [ˈpɑrk] *n* : parque *m* — ~ *v* : estacionar, parquear *Lat*

parka [ˈpɑrkə] *n* : parka *f*

parking [ˈpɑrkɪŋ] *n* : estacionamiento *m*

parliament [ˈpɑrləmənt, ˈpɑrljə-] *n* : parlamento *m* — **parliamentary** [ˌpɑrləˈmentəri, ˌpɑrljə-] *adj* : parlamentario

parlor *or Brit* **parlour** [ˈpɑrlər] *n* : salón *m*

parochial [pəˈro:kiəl] *adj* **1** : parroquial **2** PROVINCIAL : de miras estrechas

parody [ˈpærədi] *n, pl* **-dies** : parodia *f* — ~ *vt* **-died; -dying** : parodiar

parole [pəˈro:l] *n* : libertad *f* condicional

parrot [ˈpærət] *n* : loro *m*, papagayo *m*

parry [ˈpæri] *vt* **-ried; -rying 1** : parar (un golpe) **2** EVADE : eludir (una pregunta, etc.)

parsley [ˈpɑrsli] *n* : perejil *m*

parsnip [ˈpɑrsnɪp] *n* : chirivía *f*

parson [ˈpɑrsən] *n* : clérigo *m*

part [ˈpɑrt] *n* **1** : parte *f* **2** PIECE : pieza *f* **3** ROLE : papel *m* **4** : raya *f* (del pelo) — ~ *vi* **1** *or* ~ **company** : separarse **2** ~ **with** : dehacerse de — *vt* SEPARATE : separar

partake [pɑrˈteɪk, pər-] *vi* **-took; -taken; -taking** ~ **in** : participar en

partial [ˈpɑrʃəl] *adj* **1** : parcial **2 be** ~ **to** : ser aficionado a

participate [pərˈtɪsəˌpeɪt, pɑr-] *vi* **-pated; -pating** : participar — **participant** [pərˈtɪsəpənt, pɑr-] *n* : participante *mf*

participle [ˈpɑrţəˌsɪpəl] *n* : participio *m*

particle [ˈpɑrţɪkəl] *n* : partícula *f*

particular [pɑrˈtɪkjələr] *adj* **1** : particular **2** FUSSY : exigente — ~ *n* **1 in** ~ : en particular, en especial **2** ~**s** *npl* DETAILS : detalles *mpl* — **particularly** [pɑrˈtɪkjələrli] *adv* : especialmente

partisan [ˈpɑrţəzən, -sən] *n* : partidario *m*, -ria *f*

partition [pərˈtɪʃən, pɑr-] *n* **1** DISTRIBUTION : partición *f* **2** DIVIDER : tabique *m* — ~ *vt* : dividir

partly [ˈpɑrtli] *adv* : en parte

partner [ˈpɑrtnər] *n* **1** : pareja *f* (en un juego, etc.) **2** *or* **business** ~ : socio *m*, -cia *f* — **partnership** [ˈpɑrtnərˌʃɪp] *n* : asociación *f*

party [ˈpɑrţi] *n, pl* **-ties 1** : partido *m* (político) **2** GATHERING : fiesta *f* **3** GROUP : grupo *m*

pass [ˈpæs] *vi* **1** : pasar **2** CEASE : pasarse **3** : aprobar (en un examen) **4** *or* ~ **away** DIE : morir **5** ~ **for** : pasar por **6** ~ **out** FAINT : desmayarse — *vt* **1** : pasar **2** *or* ~ **in front of** : pasar por **3** OVERTAKE : adelantar **4** : aprobar (un examen, una ley, etc.) **5** ~ **down** : transmitir — ~ *n* **1** PERMIT : pase *m*, permiso *m* **2** : pase *m* (en deportes) **3** *or* **mountain** ~ : paso *m* de montaña — **passable** [ˈpæsəbəl] *adj* **1** ADEQUATE : adecuado **2** : transitable (dícese de un camino, etc.) — **passage** [ˈpæsɪdʒ] *n* **1** : paso *m* **2** CORRIDOR : pasillo *m* (dentro de un edificio), pasaje *m* (entre edificios) **3** VOYAGE : travesía *f* (por el mar) — **passageway** [ˈpæsɪdʒˌweɪ] *n* : pasillo *m*, corredor *m*

passenger [ˈpæsəndʒər] *n* : pasajero *m*, -ra *f*

passerby [ˌpæsərˈbaɪ, ˈpæsərˌ-] *n, pl* **passersby** : transeúnte *mf*

passion [ˈpæʃən] *n* : pasión *f* — **passionate** [ˈpæʃənət] *adj* : apasionado

passive [ˈpæsɪv] *adj* : pasivo

Passover [ˈpæsˌo:vər] *n* : Pascua *f* (en el judaísmo)

passport [ˈpæsˌport] *n* : pasaporte *m*

password [ˈpæsˌwərd] *n* : contraseña *f*

past [ˈpæst] *adj* **1** : pasado **2** FORMER : anterior **3 the** ~ **few months** : los últimos meses — ~ *prep* **1** IN FRONT OF : por delante de **2** BEYOND : más allá de **3 half** ~ **two** : las dos y media — ~ *n* : pasado *m* — ~ *adv* : por delante

pasta ['pɑstə, 'pæs-] *n* : pasta *f*
paste ['peɪst] *n* **1** : pasta *f* **2** GLUE : engrudo *m* — ~ *vt* **pasted; pasting** : pegar
pastel [pæ'stɛl] *n* : pastel *m* — ~ *adj* : pastel
pasteurize ['pæstʃə,raɪz, 'pæstjə-] *vt* **-ized; -izing** : pasteurizar
pastime ['pæs,taɪm] *n* : pasatiempo *m*
pastor ['pæstər] *n* : pastor *m*, -tora *f*
pastry ['peɪstri] *n, pl* **-ries** : pasteles *mpl*
pasture ['pæstʃər] *n* : pasto *m*
pasty ['peɪsti] *adj* **pastier; -est** **1** DOUGHY : pastoso **2** PALLID : pálido
pat ['pæt] *n* **1** : palmadita *f* **2 a ~ of butter** : una porción de mantequilla — ~ *vt* **patted; patting** : dar palmaditas a — ~ *adv* **have down ~** : saberse de memoria — ~ *adj* GLIB : fácil
patch ['pætʃ] *n* **1** : parche *m*, remiendo *m* (para la ropa) **2** SPOT : mancha *f*, trozo *m* **3** PLOT : parcela *f* (de tierra) — ~ *vt* **1** MEND : remender **2 ~ up** : arreglar — **patchy** ['pætʃi] *adj* **patchier; -est** **1** : desigual **2** INCOMPLETE : parcial, incompleto
patent *adj* ['pætənt] **1** *or* **patented** ['pætəntəd] : patentado **2** ['pætənt, 'peɪt-] OBVIOUS : patente, evidente — ~ ['pætənt] *n* : patente *f* — ~ ['pætənt] *vt* : patentar
paternal [pə'tərnəl] *adj* **1** FATHERLY : paternal **2 ~ grandmother** : abuela *f* paterna — **paternity** [pə'tərnəṭi] *n* : paternidad *f*
path ['pæθ, 'paθ] *n* **1** TRACK, TRAIL : camino *m*, sendero *m* **2** COURSE : trayectoria *f*
pathetic [pə'θɛṭɪk] *adj* : patético
pathology [pə'θɑlədʒi] *n, pl* **-gies** : patología *f*
pathway ['pæθ,weɪ] *n* : camino *m*, sendero *m*
patience ['peɪʃənts] *n* : paciencia *f* — **patient** ['peɪʃənt] *adj* : paciente — ~ *n* : paciente *mf* — **patiently** *adv* : con paciencia
patio ['pæṭi,o:] *n, pl* **-tios** : patio *m*
patriot ['peɪtriət] *n* : patriota *mf* — **patriotic** [,peɪtri'ɑṭɪk] *adj* : patriótico
patrol [pə'tro:l] *n* : patrulla *f* — ~ *v* **-trolled; -trolling** : patrullar
patron ['peɪtrən] *n* **1** SPONSOR : patrocinador *m*, -dora *f* **2** CUSTOMER : cliente *m*, -ta *f* — **patronage** ['peɪtrənɪdʒ, 'pæ-] *n* **1** SPONSORSHIP : patrocinio *m* **2** CLIENTELE : clientela *f* — **patronize** ['peɪtrə,naɪz, 'pæ-] *vt* **-ized; -izing** **1** : ser cliente de (una tienda, etc.) **2** : tratar (a algn) con condescencia
patter ['pæṭər] *n* : tamborileo *m* (de la lluvia), correteo *m* (de los pies)
pattern ['pæṭərn] *n* **1** MODEL : modelo *m* **2** DESIGN : diseño *m* **3** STANDARD : pauta *f*, modo *m* **4** : patrón *m* (en costura) — ~ *vt* : basar (en un modelo)
paunch ['pɔntʃ] *n* : panza *f*
pause ['pɔz] *n* : pausa *f* — ~ *vi* **paused; pausing** : hacer una pausa
pave ['peɪv] *vt* **paved; paving** : pavimentar — **pavement** ['peɪvmənt] *n* : pavimento *m*
pavilion [pə'vɪljən] *n* : pabellón *m*
paw ['pɔ] *n* **1** : pata *f* **2** : garra *f* (de un gato) — ~ *vt* : tocar con la pata
pawn[1] ['pɔn] *n* : peón *m* (en ajedrez)
pawn[2] *vt* : empeñar — **pawnbroker** ['pɔn,bro:kər] *n* : prestamista *mf* — **pawnshop** ['pɔn,ʃɑp] *n* : casa *f* de empeños
pay ['peɪ] *v* **paid** ['peɪd]; **paying** *vt* **1** : pagar **2 ~ attention** : prestar atención **3 ~ back** : devolver **4 ~ one's respects** : presentar uno sus respetos **5 ~ a visit** : hacer una visita — *vi* **1** : pagar **2 crime doesn't ~** : no hay crimen sin castigo — ~ *n* : paga *f* — **payable** ['peɪəbəl] *adj* : pagadero — **paycheck** ['peɪ,tʃɛk] *n* : cheque *m* del sueldo — **payment** ['peɪmənt] *n* **1** : pago *m* **2** INSTALLMENT : plazo *m*, cuota *f Lat* — **payroll** *n* : nómina *f*
PC [,pi:'si:] *n, pl* **PCs** *or* **PC's** : PC *mf*, computadora *f* personal
pea ['pi:] *n* : guisante *m*, arveja *f Lat*
peace ['pi:s] *n* : paz *f* — **peaceful** ['pi:sfəl] *adj* **1** : pacífico **2** CALM : tranquilo
peach ['pi:tʃ] *n* : melocotón *m*, durazno *m Lat*
peacock ['pi:,kɑk] *n* : pavo *m* real
peak ['pi:k] *n* **1** SUMMIT : cumbre *f*, cima *f*, pico *m* (de una montaña) **2** APEX : nivel *m* máximo — ~ *adj* : máximo — ~ *vi* : alcanzar su nivel máximo
peal ['pi:l] *n* **1** : repique *m* **2 ~s of laughter** : carcajadas *fpl*
peanut ['pi:,nʌt] *n* : cacajuete *m*, maní *m Lat*
pear ['pær] *n* : pera *f*
pearl ['pərl] *n* : perla *f*
peasant ['pɛzənt] *n* : campesino *m*, -na *f*
peat ['pi:t] *n* : turba *f*
pebble ['pɛbəl] *n* : guijarro *m*
pecan [pɪ'kɑn, -'kæn, 'pi:,kæn] *n* : pacana *f*, nuez *f Lat*
peck ['pɛk] *vt* : picar, picotear — ~ *n* **1** : picotazo *m* (de un pájaro) **2** KISS : besito
peculiar [pɪ'kju:ljər] *adj* **1** DISTINCTIVE

: peculiar, característico **2** STRANGE : extraño, raro — **peculiarity** [pɪ,kju:l'jærət̬i, -,kju:li'ær-] *n, pl* **-ties 1** : peculiaridad *f* **2** ODDITY : rareza *f*

pedal ['pɛdəl] *n* : pedal *m* — ~ *vi* **-aled** *or* **-alled; -aling** *or* **-alling** : pedalear

pedantic [pɪ'dæntɪk] *adj* : pedante

peddle ['pɛdəl] *vt* **-dled; -dling** : vender en las calles — **peddler** ['pɛdlər] *n* : vendedor *m,* -dora *f* ambulante

pedestal ['pɛdəstəl] *n* : pedestal *m*

pedestrian [pə'dɛstriən] *n* : peatón *m,* -tona *f* — ~ *adj* ~ **crossing** : paso *m* de peatones

pediatrics [,pi:di'ætrɪks] *ns & pl* : pediatría *f* — **pediatrician** [,pi:diə'trɪʃən] *n* : pediatra *mf*

pedigree ['pɛdə,gri:] *n* : pedigrí *m* (de un animal), linaje *m* (de una persona)

peek ['pi:k] *vi* : mirar a hurtadillas — ~ *n* : miradita *f* (furtiva)

peel ['pi:l] *vt* : pelar (fruta, etc.) — *vi* : pelarse (dícese de la piel), desconcharse (dícese de la pintura) — ~ *n* : piel *f,* cáscara *f*

peep[1] ['pi:p] *vi* CHEEP : piar — ~ *n* : pío *m* (de un pajarito)

peep[2] *vi* **1** PEEK : mirar a hurtadillas **2** *or* ~ **out** : asomar — ~ *n* GLANCE : mirada *f* (furtiva)

peer[1] ['pɪr] *n* : par *mf*

peer[2] *vi* : mirar (con atención)

peeve ['pi:v] *vt* : irritar — **peevish** ['pi:vɪʃ] *adj* : malhumorado

peg ['pɛg] *n* **1** : clavija *f* **2** HOOK : gancho *m*

pelican ['pɛlɪkən] *n* : pelícano *m*

pellet ['pɛlət] *n* **1** : bolita *f* **2** SHOT : perdigón *m*

pelt[1] ['pɛlt] *n* : piel *f* (de un animal)

pelt[2] *vt* : lanzar (algo a algn)

pelvis ['pɛlvɪs] *n, pl* **-vises** *or* **-ves** ['pɛl,vi:z] : pelvis *f* — **pelvic** ['pɛlvɪk] *adj* : pélvico

pen[1] ['pɛn] *vt* **penned; penning** ENCLOSE : encerrar — ~ *n* : corral *m,* redil *m*

pen[2] *n* **1** *or* **ballpoint** ~ : bolígrafo *m* **2** *or* **fountain** ~ : pluma *f*

penal ['pi:nəl] *adj* : penal — **penalize** ['pi:nəl,aɪz, 'pɛn-] *vt* **-ized; -izing** : penalizar — **penalty** ['pɛnəlti] *n, pl* **-ties 1** : pena *f,* castigo *m* **2** : penalty *m* (en deportes)

penance ['pɛnənts] *n* : penitencia *f*

pencil ['pɛntsəl] *n* : lápiz *m* — **pencil sharpener** *n* : sacapuntas *m*

pendant ['pɛndənt] *n* : colgante *m*

pending ['pɛndɪŋ] *adj* : pendiente — ~ *prep* : en espera de

penetrate ['pɛnə,treɪt] *v* **-trated; -trating** : penetrar — **penetrating** ['pɛnə,treɪt̬ɪŋ] *adj* : penetrante — **penetration** [,pɛnə'treɪʃən] *n* : penetración *f*

penguin ['pɛŋgwɪn, 'pɛn-] *n* : pingüino *m*

penicillin [,pɛnə'sɪlən] *n* : penicilina *f*

peninsula [pə'nɪntsələ, -'nɪntʃʊlə] *n* : península *f*

penis ['pi:nəs] *n, pl* **-nes** [-,ni:z] *or* **-nises** : pene *m*

penitentiary [,pɛnə'tɛntʃəri] *n, pl* **-ries** : penitenciaría *f*

pen name *n* : seudónimo *m*

pennant ['pɛnənt] *n* : banderín *m*

penny ['pɛni] *n, pl* **-nies** *or* **pence** ['pɛnts] : centavo *m* (de los Estados Unidos), penique *m* (del Reino Unido) — **penniless** ['pɛniləs] *adj* : sin un centavo

pension ['pɛntʃən] *n* : pensión *m,* jubilación *f*

pensive ['pɛntsɪv] *adj* : pensativo

pentagon ['pɛntə,gɑn] *n* : pentágono *m*

penthouse ['pɛnt,haʊs] *n* : ático *m*

pent-up ['pɛnt,ʌp] *adj* : reprimado

people ['pi:pəl] *ns & pl* **1 people** *npl* : gente *f,* personas *fpl* **2** *pl* ~**s** : pueblo *m*

pep ['pɛp] *n* : energía *f,* vigor *m* — ~ *vt* *or* ~ **up** : animar

pepper ['pɛpər] *n* **1** : pimienta *f* (condimento) **2** : pimiento *m* (fruta) — **peppermint** ['pɛpər,mɪnt] *n* : menta *f*

per ['pər] *prep* **1** : por **2** ACCORDING TO : según **3** ~ **day** : al día **4 miles** ~ **hour** : millas *fpl* por hora

perceive [pər'si:v] *vt* **-ceived; -ceiving** : percibir

percent [pər'sɛnt] *adv* : por ciento — **percentage** [pər'sɛntɪdʒ] *n* : porcentaje *m*

perception [pər'sɛpʃən] *n* : percepción *f* — **perceptive** [pər'sɛptɪv] *adj* : perspicaz

perch[1] ['pərtʃ] *n* : percha *f* (para los pájaros) — ~ *vi* : posarse

perch[2] *n* : perca *f* (pez)

percolate ['pərkə,leɪt] *vi* **-lated; -lating** : filtrarse — **percolator** ['pərkə,leɪt̬ər] *n* : cafetera *f* de filtro

percussion [pər'kʌʃən] *n* : percusión *f*

perennial [pə'rɛniəl] *adj* : perenne — ~ *n* : planta *f* perenne

perfect ['pərfɪkt] *adj* : perfecto — ~ [pər'fɛkt] *vt* : perfeccionar — **perfection** [pər'fɛkʃən] *n* : perfección *f* — **perfectionist** [pər'fɛkʃənɪst] *n* : perfeccionista *mf*

perforate ['pərfə,reɪt] *vt* **-rated; -rating** : perforar
perform [pər'fɔrm] *vt* **1** CARRY OUT : realizar, hacer **2** : representar (una obra teatral), interpretar (una obra musical) — *vi* **1** FUNCTION : funcionar **2** ACT : actuar — **performance** [pər'fɔrmənts] *n* **1** : realización *f* **2** INTERPRETATION : interpretación *f* **3** PRESENTATION : representación *f* — **performer** [pər'fɔrmər] *n* : actor *m*, -triz *f*; intérprete *mf* (de música)
perfume ['pər,fju:m, pər'-] *n* : perfume *m*
perhaps [pər'hæps] *adv* : tal vez, quizá, quizás
peril ['pɛrəl] *n* : peligro *m* — **perilous** ['pɛrələs] *adj* : peligroso
perimeter [pə'rɪmət̬ər] *n* : perímetro *m*
period ['pɪriəd] *n* **1** : período *m* (de tiempo) **2** : punto *m* (en puntuación) **3** ERA : época *f* — **periodic** [,pɪri'ɑdɪk] *adj* : periódico — **periodical** [,pɪri'ɑdɪkəl] *n* : revista *f*
peripheral [pə'rɪfərəl] *adj* : periférico
perish ['pɛrɪʃ] *vi* : perecer — **perishable** ['pɛrɪʃəbəl] *adj* : perecedero — **perishables** ['pɛrɪʃəbəlz] *npl* : productos *mpl* perecederos
perjury ['pərdʒəri] *n* : perjurio *m*
perk ['pərk] *vi* ~ **up** : animarse, reanimarse — ~ *n* : extra *m* — **perky** ['pərki] *adj* **perkier; -est** : alegre
permanence ['pərmənənts] *n* : permanencia *f* — **permanent** ['pərmənənt] *adj* : permanente — ~ *n* : permanente *f*
permeate ['pərmi,eɪt] *v* **-ated; -ating** : penetrar
permission [pər'mɪʃən] *n* : permiso *m* — **permissible** [pər'mɪsəbəl] *adj* : permisible — **permissive** [pər'mɪsɪv] *adj* : permisivo — **permit** [pər'mɪt] *vt* **-mitted; -mitting** : permitir — ~ ['pər,mɪt, pər'-] *n* : permiso *m*
peroxide [pə'rɑk,saɪd] *n* : peróxido *m*
perpendicular [,pərpən'dɪkjələr] *adj* : perpendicular
perpetrate ['pərpə,treɪt] *vt* **-trated; -trating** : cometer — **perpetrator** ['pərpə,treɪt̬ər] *n* : autor *m*, -tora *f* (de un delito)
perpetual [pər'pɛtʃuəl] *adj* : perpetuo
perplex [pər'plɛks] *vt* : dejar perplejo — **perplexing** [pər'plɛksɪŋ] *adj* : desconcertante — **perplexity** [pər'plɛksət̬i] *n*, *pl* **-ties** : perplejidad *f*
persecute ['pərsɪ,kju:t] *vt* **-cuted; -cuting** : perseguir — **persecution** [,pərsɪ'kju:ʃən] *n* : persecución *f*
persevere [,pərsə'vɪr] *vi* **-vered; -vering** : perseverar — **perseverance** [,pərsə'vɪrənts] *n* : perseverancia *f*
persist [pər'sɪst] *vi* : persistir — **persistence** [pər'sɪstənts] *n* : persistencia *f* — **persistent** [pər'sɪstənt] *adj* : persistente
person ['pərsən] *n* : persona *f* — **personal** ['pərsənəl] *adj* : personal — **personality** [,pərsən'æləţi] *n*, *pl* **-ties** : personalidad *f* — **personally** ['pərsənəli] *adv* : personalmente, en persona — **personnel** [,pərsən'ɛl] *n* : personal *m*
perspective [pər'spɛktɪv] *n* : perspectiva *f*
perspiration [,pərspə'reɪʃən] *n* : transpiración *f* — **perspire** [pər'spaɪr] *vi* **-spired; -spiring** : transpirar
persuade [pər'sweɪd] *vt* **-suaded; -suading** : persuadir — **persuasion** [pər'sweɪʒən] *n* : persuasión *f*
pertain [pər'teɪn] *vi* ~ **to** : estar relacionado con — **pertinent** ['pərtənənt] *adj* : pertinente
perturb [pər'tərb] *vt* : perturbar
Peruvian [pə'ru:viən] *adj* : peruano
pervade [pər'veɪd] *vt* **-vaded; -vading** : penetrar — **pervasive** [pər'veɪsɪv, -zɪv] *adj* : penetrante
perverse [pər'vərs] *adj* **1** CORRUPT : perverso **2** STUBBORN : obstinado — **pervert** ['pər,vərt] *n* : pervertido *m*, -da *f*
peso ['peɪ,so:] *n*, *pl* **-sos** : peso *m*
pessimism ['pɛsə,mɪzəm] *n* : pesimismo *m* — **pessimist** ['pɛsəmɪst] *n* : pesimista *mf* — **pessimistic** [,pɛsə'mɪstɪk] *adj* : pesimista
pest ['pɛst] *n* **1** : insecto *m* nocivo, animal *m* nocivo **2** : peste *f fam* (persona)
pester ['pɛstər] *vt* **-tered; -tering** : molestar
pesticide ['pɛstə,saɪd] *n* : pesticida *m*
pet ['pɛt] *n* **1** : animal *m* doméstico **2** FAVORITE : favorito *m*, -ta *f* — ~ *vt* **petted; petting** : acariciar
petal ['pɛţəl] *n* : pétalo *m*
petite [pə'ti:t] *adj* : chiquita
petition [pə'tɪʃən] *n* : petición *f* — ~ *vt* : dirigir una petición a
petrify ['pɛtrə,faɪ] *vt* **-fied; -fying** : petrificar
petroleum [pə'tro:liəm] *n* : petróleo *m*
petticoat ['pɛţi,ko:t] *n* : enagua *f*, fondo *m Lat*
petty ['pɛţi] *adj* **-tier; -est** **1** UNIMPORTANT : insignificante, nimio **2** MEAN : mezquino — **pettiness** ['pɛţinəs] *n* : mezquindad *f*
petulant ['pɛtʃələnt] *adj* : irritable, de mal genio
pew ['pju:] *n* : banco *m* (de iglesia)

pewter ['pju:t̬ər] *n* : peltre *m*
phallic ['fælɪk] *adj* : fálico
phantom ['fæntəm] *n* : fantasma *m*
pharmacy ['fɑrməsi] *n, pl* **-cies** : farmacia *f* — **pharmacist** ['fɑrməsɪst] *n* : farmacéutico *m,* -ca *f*
phase ['feɪz] *n* : fase *f* — ~ *vt* **phased; phasing 1** ~ **in** : introducir progresivamente **2** ~ **out** : retirar progresivamente
phenomenon [fɪ'nɑməˌnɑn, -nən] *n, pl* **-na** [-nə] *or* **-nons** : fenómeno *m* — **phenomenal** [fɪ'nɑmənəl] *adj* : fenomenal
philanthropy [fə'lænᵗθrəpi] *n, pl* **-pies** : filantropía *f* — **philanthropist** [fə'lænᵗθrəpɪst] *n* : filántropo *m,* -pa *f*
philosophy [fə'lɑsəfi] *n, pl* **-phies** : filosofía *f* — **philosopher** [fə'lɑsəfər] *n* : filósofo *m,* -fa *f*
phlegm ['flɛm] *n* : flema *f*
phobia ['fo:biə] *n* : fobia *f*
phone ['fo:n] → **telephone**
phonetic [fə'nɛt̬ɪk] *adj* : fonético
phony *or* **phoney** ['fo:ni] *adj* **-nier; -est** : falso — ~ *n, pl* **-nies** : farsante *mf*
phosphorus ['fɑsfərəs] *n* : fósforo *m*
photo ['fo:t̬o:] *n, pl* **-tos** : foto *f* — **photocopier** ['fo:t̬oˌkɑpiər] *n* : fotocopiadora *f* — **photocopy** ['fo:t̬oˌkɑpi] *n, pl* **-copies** : fotocopia *f* — ~ *vt* **-copied; -copying** : fotocopiar — **photograph** ['fo:t̬əˌgræf] *n* : fotografía *f,* foto *f* — ~ *vt* : fotografiar — **photographer** [fə'tɑgrəfər] *n* : fotógrafo *m,* -fa *f* — **photographic** [ˌfo:t̬ə'græfɪk] *adj* : fotográfico — **photography** [fə'tɑgrəfi] *n* : fotografía *f*
phrase ['freɪz] *n* : frase *f* — ~ *vt* **phrased; phrasing** : expresar
physical ['fɪzɪkəl] *adj* : físico — ~ *n* : reconocimiento *m* médico
physician [fə'zɪʃən] *n* : médico *m,* -ca *f*
physics ['fɪzɪks] *ns & pl* : física *f* — **physicist** ['fɪzəsɪst] *n* : físico *m,* -ca *f*
physiology [ˌfɪzi'ɑlədʒi] *n* : fisiología *f*
physique [fə'zi:k] *n* : físico *m*
piano [pi'æno:] *n, pl* **-anos** : piano *m* — **pianist** [pi'ænɪst, 'pi:ənɪst] *n* : pianista *mf*
pick ['pɪk] *vt* **1** CHOOSE : escoger **2** GATHER : recoger **3** REMOVE : quitar (poco a poco) **4** ~ **a fight** : buscar camorra — *vi* **1** ~ **and choose** : ser exigente **2** ~ **on** : meterse con — ~ *n* **1** CHOICE : selección *f* **2** *or* **pickax** ['pɪkˌæks] : pico *m* **3 the** ~ **of** : lo mejor de
picket ['pɪkət] *n* **1** STAKE : estaca *f* **2** *or* ~ **line** : piquete *m* — ~ *v* : piquetear
pickle ['pɪkəl] *n* **1** : pepinillo *m* (encurtido) **2** JAM : lío *m fam,* apuro *m* — ~ *vt* **-led; -ling** : encurtir
pickpocket ['pɪkˌpɑkət] *n* : carterista *mf*
pickup ['pɪkˌəp] *n* **1** IMPROVEMENT : mejora *f* **2** *or* ~ **truck** : camioneta *f* — **pick up** *vt* **1** LIFT : levantar **2** TIDY : arreglar, ordenar — *vi* IMPROVE : mejorar
picnic ['pɪkˌnɪk] *n* : picnic *m* — ~ *vi* **-nicked; -nicking** : ir de picnic
picture ['pɪktʃər] *n* **1** PAINTING : cuadro *m* **2** DRAWING : dibujo *m* **3** PHOTO : fotografía *f* **4** IMAGE : imagen *f* **5** MOVIE : película *f* — ~ *vt* **-tured; -turing 1** DEPICT : representar **2** IMAGINE : imaginarse — **picturesque** [ˌpɪktʃə'rɛsk] *adj* : pintoresco
pie ['paɪ] *n* : pastel *m* (con fruta o carne), empanada *f* (con carne)
piece ['pi:s] *n* **1** : pieza *f* **2** FRAGMENT : trozo *m,* pedazo *m* **3 a** ~ **of advice** : un consejo — ~ *vt* **pieced; piecing** *or* ~ **together** : juntar, componer — **piecemeal** ['pi:sˌmi:l] *adv* : poco a poco — ~ *adj* : poco sistemático
pier ['pɪr] *n* : muelle *m*
pierce ['pɪrs] *vt* **pierced; piercing** : perforar — **piercing** *adj* : penetrante
piety ['paɪət̬i] *n, pl* **-eties** : piedad *f*
pig ['pɪg] *n* : cerdo *m,* -da *f;* puerco *m,* -ca *f*
pigeon ['pɪdʒən] *n* : paloma *f* — **pigeonhole** ['pɪdʒənˌho:l] *n* : casilla *f*
piggyback ['pɪgiˌbæk] *adv & adj* : a cuestas
pigment ['pɪgmənt] *n* : pigmento *m*
pigpen ['pɪgˌpɛn] *n* : pocilga *f*
pigtail ['pɪgˌteɪl] *n* : coleta *f,* trenza *f*
pile[1] ['paɪl] *n* HEAP : montón *m,* pila *f* — ~ *v* **piled; piling** *vt* : amontonar, apilar — *vi* ~ **up** : amontonarse, acumularse
pile[2] *n* NAP : pelo *m* (de telas)
pilfer ['pɪlfər] *vt* : robar, hurtar
pilgrim ['pɪlgrəm] *n* : peregrino *m,* -na *f* — **pilgrimage** ['pɪlgrəmɪdʒ] *n* : peregrinación *f*
pill ['pɪl] *n* : pastilla *f,* píldora *f*
pillage ['pɪlɪdʒ] *n* : saqueo *m* — ~ *vt* **-laged; -laging** : saquear
pillar ['pɪlər] *n* : pilar *m,* columna *f*
pillow ['pɪˌlo:] *n* : almohada *f* — **pillowcase** ['pɪˌlo:ˌkeɪs] *n* : funda *f* (de almohada)
pilot ['paɪlət] *n* : piloto *mf* — ~ *vt* : pilotar, pilotear — **pilot light** *n* : piloto *m*
pimp ['pɪmp] *n* : proxeneta *m*
pimple ['pɪmpəl] *n* : grano *m*
pin ['pɪn] *n* **1** : alfiler *m* **2** BROOCH

: broche *m* 3 *or* **bowling ~** : bolo *m* — ~ *vt* **pinned; pinning 1** FASTEN : prender, sujetar (con alfileres) **2** *or* **~ down** : inmovilizar

pincers [ˈpɪntsərz] *npl* : tenazas *fpl*

pinch [ˈpɪntʃ] *vt* **1** : pellizcar **2** STEAL : robar — *vi* : apretar — ~ *n* **1** : pellizco *m* **2** BIT : pizca *f* **3 in a ~** : en caso necesario

pine[1] [ˈpaɪn] *n* : pino *m* (árbol)

pine[2] *vi* **pined; pining 1** LANGUISH : languidecer **2 ~ for** : suspirar por

pineapple [ˈpaɪnˌæpəl] *n* : piña *f*, ananás *m*

pink [ˈpɪŋk] *n* : rosa *m*, rosado *m* — ~ *adj* : rosa, rosado

pinnacle [ˈpɪnɪkəl] *n* : pináculo *m*

pinpoint [ˈpɪnˌpɔɪnt] *vt* : localizar, precisar

pint [ˈpaɪnt] *n* : pinta *f*

pioneer [ˌpaɪəˈnɪr] *n* : pionero *m*, -ra *f*

pious [ˈpaɪəs] *adj* : piadoso

pipe [ˈpaɪp] *n* **1** : tubo *m*, caño *m* **2** : pipa *f* (para fumar) — **pipeline** [ˈpaɪpˌlaɪn] *n* **1** : conducto *m*, oleoducto *m* (para petróleo)

piquant [ˈpiːkənt, ˈpɪkwənt] *adj* : picante

pique [ˈpiːk] *n* : resentimiento *m*

pirate [ˈpaɪrət] *n* : pirata *mf*

pistachio [pəˈstæʃiˌoː, -ˈstɑ-] *n, pl* **-chios** : pistacho *m*

pistol [ˈpɪstəl] *n* : pistola *f*

piston [ˈpɪstən] *n* : pistón *m*

pit [ˈpɪt] *n* **1** HOLE : hoyo *m*, fosa *f* **2** MINE : mina *f* **3** : hueso *m* (de una fruta) **4 ~ of the stomach** : boca *f* del estómago — ~ *vt* **pitted; pitting 1** : marcar de hoyos **2** : deshuesar (una fruta) **3 ~ against** : enfrentar a

pitch [ˈpɪtʃ] *vt* **1** : armar (una tienda) **2** THROW : lanzar — *vi* **1** *or* **~ forward** : caerse **2** LURCH : cabecear (dícese de un barco o un avión) — ~ *n* **1** DEGREE, LEVEL : grado *m*, punto *m* **2** TONE : tono *m* **3** THROW : lanzamiento *m* **4** *or* **sales ~** : presentación *f* (de un vendedor)

pitcher [ˈpɪtʃər] *n* **1** JUG : jarro *m* **2** : lanzador *m*, -dora *f* (en béisbol, etc.)

pitchfork [ˈpɪtʃˌfɔrk] *n* : horquilla *f*, horca *f*

pitfall [ˈpɪtˌfɔl] *n* : riesgo *m*, dificultad *f*

pith [ˈpɪθ] *n* **1** : médula *f* (de un hueso, etc.) **2** CORE : meollo *m* — **pithy** [ˈpɪθi] *adj* **pithier; -est** : conciso y sustancioso

pity [ˈpɪti] *n, pl* **pities 1** COMPASSION : compasión *f* **2 what a ~!** : ¡qué lástima! — ~ *vt* **pitied; pitying** : compadecerse de — **pitiful** [ˈpɪtɪfəl] *adj* : lastimoso — **pitiless** [ˈpɪtɪləs] *adj* : despiadado

pivot [ˈpɪvət] *n* : pivote *m* — ~ *vi* **1** : girar sobre un eje **2 ~ on** : depender de

pizza [ˈpiːtsə] *n* : pizza *f*

placard [ˈplækərd, -ˌkɑrd] *n* POSTER : cartel *m*, póster *m*

placate [ˈpleɪˌkeɪt, ˈplæ-] *vt* **-cated; -cating** : apaciguar

place [ˈpleɪs] *n* **1** : sitio *m*, lugar *m* **2** SEAT : asiento *m* **3** POSITION : puesto *m* **4** ROLE : papel *m* **5 take ~** : tener lugar **6 take the ~ of** : sustituir a — ~ *vt* **placed; placing 1** PUT, SET : poner, colocar **2** IDENTIFY : identificar, recordar **3 ~ an order** : hacer un pedido — **placement** [ˈpleɪsmənt] *n* : colocación *f*

placid [ˈplæsəd] *adj* : plácido, tranquilo

plagiarism [ˈpleɪdʒəˌrɪzəm] *n* : plagio *m* — **plagiarize** [ˈpleɪdʒəˌraɪz] *vt* **-rized; -rizing** : plagiar

plague [ˈpleɪg] *n* **1** : plaga *f* (de insectos, etc.) **2** : peste *f* (en medicina)

plaid [ˈplæd] *n* : tela *f* escocesa — ~ *adj* : escocés

plain [ˈpleɪn] *adj* **1** SIMPLE : sencillo **2** CLEAR : claro, evidente **3** CANDID : franco **4** HOMELY : poco atractivo **5 in ~ sight** : a la vista (de todos) — ~ *n* : llanura *f*, planicie *f* — **plainly** [ˈpleɪnli] *adv* **1** CLEARLY : claramente **2** FRANKLY : francamente **3** SIMPLY : sencillamente

plaintiff [ˈpleɪntɪf] *n* : demandante *mf*

plan [ˈplæn] *n* **1** : plan *m*, proyecto *m* **2** DIAGRAM : plano *m* — ~ *v* **planned; planning** *vt* **1** : planear, proyectar **2** INTEND : tener planeado — *vi* : hacer planes

plane[1] [ˈpleɪn] *n* **1** LEVEL : plano *m*, nivel *m* **2** AIRPLANE : avión *m*

plane[2] *n or* **carpenter's ~** : cepillo *m*

planet [ˈplænət] *n* : planeta *f*

plank [ˈplæŋk] *n* : tabla *f*

planning [ˈplænɪŋ] *n* : planificación *f*

plant [ˈplænt] *vt* : plantar (flores, árboles), sembrar (semillas) — ~ *n* **1** : planta *f* **2** FACTORY : fábrica *f*

plantain [ˈplæntən] *n* : plátano *m* (grande)

plantation [plænˈteɪʃən] *n* : plantación *f*

plaque [ˈplæk] *n* : placa *f*

plaster [ˈplæstər] *n* : yeso *m* — ~ *vt* **1** : enyesar **2** COVER : cubrir — **plaster cast** *n* : escayola *f*

plastic [ˈplæstɪk] *adj* **1** : de plástico **2** FLEXIBLE : plástico, flexible **3 ~ surgery** : cirugía *f* plástica — ~ *n* : plástico *m*

plate ['pleɪt] *n* **1** SHEET : placa *f* **2** DISH : plato *m* **3** ILLUSTRATION : lámina *f* — ~ *vt* **plated; plating** : chapar (en metal)
plateau [plæ'to:] *n, pl* **-teaus** *or* **-teaux** [-'to:z] : meseta *f*
platform ['plæt,fɔrm] *n* **1** : plataforma *f* **2** : andén *m* (de una estación de ferrocarril) **3** *or* **political** ~ : programa *m* electoral
platinum ['plætənəm] *n* : platino *m*
platitude ['plæṭə,tu:d, -,tju:d] *n* : lugar *m* común
platoon [plə'tu:n] *n* : sección *f* (en el ejército)
platter ['plæṭər] *n* : fuente *f*
plausible ['plɔzəbəl] *adj* : creíble, verosímil
play ['pleɪ] *n* **1** : juego *m* **2** DRAMA : obra *f* de teatro — ~ *vi* **1** : jugar **2** ~ **in a band** : tocar en un grupo — *vt* **1** : jugar (deportes, etc.), jugar a (juegos) **2** : tocar (música o un instrumento) **3** ~ **the role of** : representar el papel de — **player** ['pleɪər] *n* **1** : jugador *m*, -dora *f* **2** ACTOR : actor *m*, actriz *f* **3** MUSICIAN : músico *m*, -ca *f* — **playful** ['pleɪfəl] *adj* : juguetón — **playground** ['pleɪ,graʊnd] *n* : patio *m* de recreo — **playing card** *n* : naipe *m*, carta *f* — **playmate** ['pleɪ,meɪt] *n* : compañero *m*, -ra *f* de juego — **play–off** ['pleɪ,ɔf] *n* : desempate *m* — **playpen** ['pleɪ,pɛn] *n* : corral *m* (para niños) — **plaything** ['pleɪ,θɪŋ] *n* : juguete *m* — **playwright** ['pleɪ,raɪt] *n* : dramaturgo *m*, -ga *f*
plea ['pli:] *n* **1** : acto *m* de declararse (en derecho) **2** APPEAL : ruego *m*, súplica *f* — **plead** ['pli:d] *v* **pleaded** *or* **pled** ['plɛd]; **pleading** *vi* **1** ~ **for** : suplicar **2** ~ **guilty** : declararse culpable **3** ~ **not guilty** : negar la acusación — *vt* **1** : alegar, pretextar **2** ~ **a case** : defender un caso
pleasant ['plɛzənt] *adj* : agradable, grato — **please** ['pli:z] *v* **pleased; pleasing** *vt* **1** GRATIFY : complacer **2** SATISFY : satisfacer — *vi* **1** : agradar **2** **do as you** ~ : haz lo que quieras — ~ *adv* : por favor — **pleased** ['pli:zd] *adj* : contento — **pleasing** ['pli:zɪŋ] *adj* : agradable — **pleasure** ['plɛʒər] *n* : placer *m*, gusto *m*
pleat ['pli:t] *vt* : plisar — ~ *n* : pliegue *m*
pledge ['plɛdʒ] *n* **1** SECURITY : prenda *f* **2** PROMISE : promesa *f* — ~ *vt* **pledged; pledging** **1** PAWN : empeñar **2** PROMISE : prometer
plenty ['plɛnti] *n* **1** : abundancia *f* **2** ~ **of time** : tiempo *m* de sobra — **plentiful** ['plɛntɪfəl] *adj* : abundante
pliable ['plaɪəbəl] *adj* : flexible
pliers ['plaɪərz] *npl* : alicates *mpl*
plight ['plaɪt] *n* : situación *f* difícil
plod ['plɑd] *vi* **plodded; plodding** **1** : caminar con paso pesado **2** DRUDGE : trabajar laboriosamente
plot ['plɑt] *n* **1** LOT : parcela *f* **2** : argumento *m* (de una novela, etc.) **3** CONSPIRACY : complot *m*, intriga *f* — ~ *v* **plotted; plotting** *vt* : tramar (un plan), trazar (una gráfica, etc.) — *vi* CONSPIRE : conspirar
plow *or* **plough** ['plaʊ] *n* **1** : arado *m* **2** → **snowplow** — ~ *v* : arar
ploy ['plɔɪ] *n* : estratagema *f*
pluck ['plʌk] *vt* **1** : arrancar **2** : desplumar (un pollo, etc.) **3** : recoger (flores) **4** ~ **one's eyebrows** : depilarse las cejas
plug ['plʌg] *n* **1** STOPPER : tapón *m* **2** : enchufe *m* (eléctrico) — ~ *vt* **plugged; plugging** **1** BLOCK : tapar **2** ADVERTISE : dar publicidad a **3** ~ **in** : enchufar
plum ['plʌm] *n* : ciruela *f*
plumb ['plʌm] *adj* : a plomo, vertical — **plumber** ['plʌmər] *n* : fontanero *m*, -ra *f*; plomero *m*, -ra *f Lat* — **plumbing** ['plʌmɪŋ] *n* **1** : fontanería *f*, plomería *f Lat* **2** PIPES : cañerías *fpl*
plume ['plu:m] *n* : pluma *f*
plummet ['plʌmət] *vi* : caer en picado
plump ['plʌmp] *adj* : rechoncho *fam*
plunder ['plʌndər] *vi* : saquear, robar — ~ *n* : botín *m*
plunge ['plʌndʒ] *v* **plunged; plunging** *vt* **1** IMMERSE : sumergir **2** THRUST : hundir — *vi* **1** : zambullirse (en el agua) **2** DESCEND : descender en picada — ~ *n* **1** DIVE : zambullida *f* **2** DROP : descenso *m* abrupto
plural ['plʊrəl] *adj* : plural — ~ *n* : plural *m*
plus ['plʌs] *adj* : positivo — ~ *n* **1** *or* ~ **sign** : signo *m* (de) más **2** ADVANTAGE : ventaja *f* — ~ *prep* : más — ~ *conj* : y, además
plush ['plʌʃ] *n* : felpa *f* — ~ *adj* **1** : de felpa **2** LUXURIOUS : lujoso
plutonium [plu:'to:niəm] *n* : plutonio *m*
ply ['plaɪ] *vt* **plied; plying** **1** : ejercer (un oficio) **2** ~ **with questions** : acosar con preguntas
plywood ['plaɪ,wʊd] *n* : contrachapado *m*
pneumatic [nʊ'mæṭɪk, njʊ-] *adj* : neumático

pneumonia [nʊˈmoːnjə, njʊ-] *n* : pulmonía *f*
poach[1] [ˈpoːtʃ] *vt* : cocer a fuego lento
poach[2] *vt or* ~ **game** : cazar ilegalmente — **poacher** [ˈpoːtʃər] *n* : cazador *m* furtivo, cazadora *f* furtiva
pocket [ˈpɑkət] *n* : bolsillo *m* — ~ *vt* : meterse en el bolsillo — **pocketbook** [ˈpɑkətˌbʊk] *n* : cartera *f*, bolsa *f Lat* — **pocketknife** [ˈpɑkətˌnaɪf] *n, pl* **-knives** : navaja *f*
pod [ˈpɑd] *n* : vaina *f*
poem [ˈpoːəm] *n* : poema *m* — **poet** [ˈpoːət] *n* : poeta *mf* — **poetic** [poˈɛt̬ɪk] *or* **poetical** [-t̬ɪkəl] *adj* : poético — **poetry** [ˈpoːətri] *n* : poesía *f*
poignant [ˈpɔɪnjənt] *adj* : conmovedor
point [ˈpɔɪnt] *n* **1** : punto *m* **2** PURPOSE : sentido *m* **3** TIP : punta *f* **4** FEATURE : cualidad *f* **5 be beside the** ~ : no venir al caso **6 there's no** ~ ... : no sirve de nada...— ~ *vt* **1** AIM : apuntar **2** *or* ~ **out** : señalar, indicar — *vi* ~ **at** : señalar (con el dedo) — **point–blank** [ˈpɔɪntˈblæŋk] *adv* : a quemarropa — **pointer** [ˈpɔɪntər] *n* **1** NEEDLE : aguja *f* **2** : perro *m* de muestra **3** TIP : consejo *m* — **pointless** [ˈpɔɪntləs] *adj* : inútil — **point of view** *n* : perspectiva *f*, punto *m* de vista
poise [ˈpɔɪz] *n* **1** : elegancia *f* **2** COMPOSURE : aplomo *m*
poison [ˈpɔɪzən] *n* : veneno *m* — ~ *vt* : envenenar — **poisonous** [ˈpɔɪzənəs] *adj* : venenoso (dícese de una culebra, etc.), tóxico (dícese de una sustancia)
poke [ˈpoːk] *vt* **poked; poking 1** JAB : golpear (con la punta de algo), dar **2** THRUST : introducir, asomar — ~ *n* : golpe *m* abrupto (con la punta de algo)
poker[1] [ˈpoːkər] *n* : atizador *m* (para el fuego)
poker[2] *n* : póquer *m* (juego de naipes)
polar [ˈpoːlər] *adj* : polar — **polar bear** *n* : oso *m* blanco — **polarize** [ˈpoːləˌraɪz] *vt* **-ized; -izing** : polarizar
pole[1] [ˈpoːl] *n* : palo *m*, poste *m*
pole[2] *n* : polo *m* (en geografía)
police [pəˈliːs] *vt* **-liced; -licing** : mantener el orden en — ~ *ns & pl* **the** ~ : la policía — **policeman** [pəˈliːsmən] *n, pl* **-men** [-mən, -ˌmɛn] : policía *m* — **police officer** *n* : policía *mf*, agente *mf* de policía — **policewoman** [pəˈliːsˌwʊmən] *n, pl* **-women** [-ˌwɪmən] : (mujer *f*) policía *f*
policy [ˈpɑləsi] *n, pl* **-cies 1** : política *f* **2** *or* **insurance** ~ : póliza *f* de seguros
polio [ˈpoːliˌoː] *or* **poliomyelitis** [ˌpoːliˌoːˌmaɪəˈlaɪt̬əs] *n* : polio *f*, poliomielitis *f*
polish [ˈpɑlɪʃ] *vt* **1** : pulir **2** : limpiar (zapatos), encerar (un suelo) — ~ *n* **1** LUSTER : brillo *m*, lustre *m* **2** : betún *m* (para zapatos), cera *f* (para suelos y muebles), esmalte *m* (para las uñas)
Polish [ˈpoːlɪʃ] *adj* : polaco — ~ *n* : polaco *m* (idioma)
polite [pəˈlaɪt] *adj* **-liter; -est** : cortés — **politeness** [pəˈlaɪtnəs] *n* : cortesía *f*
political [pəˈlɪt̬ɪkəl] *adj* : político — **politician** [ˌpɑləˈtɪʃən] *n* : político *m*, -ca *f* — **politics** [ˈpɑləˌtɪks] *ns & pl* : política *f*
polka [ˈpoːlkə, ˈpoːkə] *n* : polka *f* — **polka dot** [ˈpoːkəˌdɑt] *n* : lunar *m*
poll [ˈpoːl] *n* **1** : encuesta *f*, sondeo *m* **2 the** ~**s** : las urnas — ~ *vt* **1** : obtener (votos) **2** CANVASS : encuestar, sondear
pollen [ˈpɑlən] *n* : polen *m*
pollute [pəˈluːt] *vt* **-luted; -luting** : contaminar — **pollution** [pəˈluːʃən] *n* : contaminación *f*
polyester [ˈpɑliˌɛstər, ˌpɑliˈ-] *n* : poliéster *m*
polygon [ˈpɑliˌgɑn] *n* : polígono *m*
pomegranate [ˈpɑməˌgrænət, ˈpɑmˌgrænət] *n* : granada *f*
pomp [ˈpɑmp] *n* : pompa *f* — **pompous** [ˈpɑmpəs] *adj* : pomposo
pond [ˈpɑnd] *n* : charca *f* (natural), estanque *m* (artificial)
ponder [ˈpɑndər] *vt* : considerar — *vi* ~ **over** : reflexionar sobre
pony [ˈpoːni] *n, pl* **-nies** : poni *m* — **ponytail** [ˈpoːniˌteɪl] *n* : cola *f* de caballo
poodle [ˈpuːdəl] *n* : caniche *m*
pool [ˈpuːl] *n* **1** PUDDLE : charco *m* **2** : fondo *m* común (de recursos) **3** BILLIARDS : billar *m* **4** *or* **swimming** ~ : piscina *f* — ~ *vt* : hacer un fondo común de
poor [ˈpʊr, ˈpor] *adj* **1** : pobre **2** INFERIOR : malo **3 the** ~ : los pobres — **poorly** [ˈpʊrli, ˈpor-] *adv* : mal
pop[1] [ˈpɑp] *v* **popped; popping** *vt* **1** : hacer reventar **2** ~ **sth into** : meter algo en — *vi* **1** BURST : reventarse, estallar **2** ~ **in** : entrar (un momento) **3** ~ **out** : saltar (dícese de los ojos) **4** ~ **up** APPEAR : aparecer — ~ *n* **1** : ruido *m* seco **2** → **soda pop**
pop[2] *n or* ~ **music** : música *f* popular
popcorn [ˈpɑpˌkɔrn] *n* : palomitas *fpl*
pope [ˈpoːp] *n* : papa *m*
poplar [ˈpɑplər] *n* : álamo *m*
poppy [ˈpɑpi] *n, pl* **-pies** : amapola *f*
popular [ˈpɑpjələr] *adj* : popular — **pop-**

ularity [ˌpɑpjəˈlærət̬i] *n* : popularidad *f* — **popularize** [ˈpɑpjələˌraɪz] *vt* **-ized; -izing** : popularizar
populate [ˈpɑpjəˌleɪt] *vt* **-lated; -lating** : poblar — **population** [ˌpɑpjəˈleɪʃən] *n* : población *f*
porcelain [ˈporsələn] *n* : porcelana *f*
porch [ˈportʃ] *n* : porche *m*
porcupine [ˈpɔrkjəˌpaɪn] *n* : puerco *m* espín
pore[1] [ˈpor] *vi* **pored; poring ~ over** : estudiar esmeradamente
pore[2] *n* : poro *m*
pork [ˈpork] *n* : carne *f* de cerdo
pornography [pɔrˈnɑgrəfi] *n* : pornografía *f* — **pornographic** [ˌpɔrnəˈgræfɪk] *adj* : pornográfico
porous [ˈporəs] *adj* : poroso
porpoise [ˈpɔrpəs] *n* : marsopa *f*
porridge [ˈpɔrɪdʒ] *n* : avena *f* (cocida), gachas *fpl* (de avena)
port[1] [ˈport] *n* HARBOR : puerto *m*
port[2] *n or* **~ side** : babor *m*
port[3] *n* : oporto *m* (vino)
portable [ˈport̬əbəl] *adj* : portátil
portent [ˈpɔrˌtɛnt] *n* : presagio *m*
porter [ˈport̬ər] *n* : maletero *m*, mozo *m* (de estación)
portfolio [portˈfoːliˌo] *n, pl* **-lios** : cartera *f*
porthole [ˈportˌhoːl] *n* : portilla *f*
portion [ˈporʃən] *n* : porción *f*
portrait [ˈportrət, -ˌtreɪt] *n* : retrato *m*
portray [porˈtreɪ] *vt* **1** : representar, retratar **2** : interpretar (un personaje)
Portuguese [ˌportʃəˈgiːz, -ˈgiːs] *adj* : portugués — **~** *n* : portugués *m* (idioma)
pose [ˈpoːz] *v* **posed; posing** *vt* : plantear (una pregunta, etc.), representar (una amenaza) — *vi* **1** : posar **2 ~ as** : hacerse pasar por — **~** *n* : pose *f*
posh [ˈpɑʃ] *adj* : elegante, de lujo
position [pəˈzɪʃən] *n* **1** : posición *f* **2** JOB : puesto *m* — **~** *vt* : colocar, situar
positive [ˈpɑzət̬ɪv] *adj* **1** : positivo **2** CERTAIN : seguro
possess [pəˈzɛs] *vt* : poseer — **possession** [pəˈzɛʃən] *n* **1** : posesión *f* **2 ~s** *npl* BELONGINGS : bienes *mpl* — **possessive** [pəˈzɛsɪv] *adj* : posesivo
possible [ˈpɑsəbəl] *adj* : posible — **possibility** [ˌpɑsəˈbɪlət̬i] *n, pl* **-ties** : posibilidad *f* — **possibly** [ˈpɑsəbli] *adv* : posiblemente
post[1] [ˈpoːst] *n* POLE : poste *m*, palo *m*
post[2] *n* POSITION : puesto *m*
post[3] *n* MAIL : cartas *fpl* — **~** *vt* **1** : echar al correo **2 keep ~ed** : tener al corriente — **postage** [ˈpoːstɪdʒ] *n* : franqueo *m* — **postal** [ˈpoːstəl] *adj* : postal — **postcard** [ˈpoːstˌkɑrd] *n* : tarjeta *f* postal
poster [ˈpoːstər] *n* : cartel *m*
posterity [pɑˈstɛrət̬i] *n* : posteridad *f*
posthumous [ˈpɑstʃəməs] *adj* : póstumo
postman [ˈpoːstmən, -ˌmæn] → **mailman** — **post office** *n* : oficina *f* de correos
postpone [ˌpoːstˈpoːn] *vt* **-poned; -poning** : aplazar — **postponement** [ˌpoːstˈpoːnmənt] *n* : aplazamiento *m*
postscript [ˈpoːstˌskrɪpt] *n* : posdata *f*
posture [ˈpɑstʃər] *n* : postura *f*
postwar [ˌpoːstˈwɔr] *adj* : de (la) posguerra
pot [ˈpɑt] *n* **1** : olla *f* (de cocina) **2** FLOWERPOT : maceta *f* **3 ~s and pans** : cacharros *mpl*
potassium [pəˈtæsiəm] *n* : potasio *m*
potato [pəˈteɪt̬o] *n, pl* **-toes** : patata *f*, papa *f Lat*
potent [ˈpoːtənt] *adj* **1** POWERFUL : poderoso **2** EFFECTIVE : eficaz
potential [pəˈtɛntʃəl] *adj* : potencial — **~** *n* : potencial *m*
pothole [ˈpɑtˌhoːl] *n* : bache *m*
potion [ˈpoːʃən] *n* : poción *f*
pottery [ˈpɑt̬əri] *n, pl* **-teries** : cerámica *f*
pouch [ˈpaʊtʃ] *n* **1** BAG : bolsa *f* pequeña **2** : bolsa *f* (de un animal)
poultry [ˈpoːltri] *n* : aves *fpl* de corral
pounce [ˈpaʊnts] *vi* **pounced; pouncing** : abalanzarse
pound[1] [ˈpaʊnd] *n* : libra *f* (unidad de dinero o de peso)
pound[2] *n or* **dog ~** : perrera *f*
pound[3] *vt* **1** CRUSH : machacar **2** HIT : golpear — *vi* : palpitar (dícese del corazón)
pour [ˈpor] *vt* : verter — *vi* **1** FLOW : fluir, salir **2 it's ~ing** : está lloviendo a cántaros
pout [ˈpaʊt] *vi* : hacer pucheros — **~** *n* : puchero *m*
poverty [ˈpɑvərt̬i] *n* : pobreza *f*
powder [ˈpaʊdər] *vt* **1** : empolvar **2** CRUSH : pulverizar — **~** *n* **1** : polvo *m* **2** *or* **face ~** : polvos *mpl* — **powdery** [ˈpaʊdəri] *adj* : polvoriento
power [ˈpaʊər] *n* **1** CONTROL : poder *m* **2** ABILITY : capacidad *f* **3** STRENGTH : fuerza *f* **4** : potencia *f* (política) **5** ENERGY : energía *f* **6** ELECTRICITY : electricidad *f* — **~** *vt* : impulsar — **powerful** [ˈpaʊərfəl] *adj* : poderoso — **powerless** [ˈpaʊərləs] *adj* : impotente
practical [ˈpræktɪkəl] *adj* : práctico — **practically** [ˈpræktɪkli] *adv* : casi, prácticamente
practice *or* **practise** [ˈpræktəs] *v* **-ticed**

or **-tised; -ticing** *or* **-tising** *vt* **1** : practicar **2** : ejercer (una profesión) — *vi* : practicar — **practice** *n* **1** : práctica *f* **2** CUSTOM : costumbre *f* **3** : ejercicio *m* (de una profesión) **4 be out of ~** : no estar en forma — **practitioner** [præk'tɪʃənər] *n* **1** : profesional *mf* **2 general ~** : médico *m*, -ca *f* de medicina general

pragmatic [præg'mæṭɪk] *adj* : pragmático

prairie ['prɛri] *n* : pradera *f*

praise ['preɪz] *vt* **praised; praising** : elogiar, alabar — **~** *n* : elogio *m*, alabanza *f* — **praiseworthy** ['preɪz,wərði] *adj* : loable

prance ['prænts] *vi* **pranced; prancing** : hacer cabriolas

prank ['præŋk] *n* : travesura *f*

prawn ['prɔn] *n* : gamba *f*

pray ['preɪ] *vi* **1** : rezar **2 ~ for** : rogar — **prayer** ['prɛr] *n* : oración *f*

preach ['pri:tʃ] *v* : predicar — **preacher** ['pri:tʃər] *n* MINISTER : pastor *m*, -tora *f*

precarious [pri'kæriəs] *adj* : precario

precaution [pri'kɔʃən] *n* : precaución *f*

precede [pri'si:d] *vt* **-ceded; -ceding** : preceder a — **precedence** ['prɛsədənts, prɪ'si:dənts] *n* : precedencia *f* — **precedent** ['prɛsədənt] *n* : precedente *m*

precinct ['pri:,sɪŋkt] *n* **1** DISTRICT : distrito *m* **2 ~s** *npl* : recinto *m*

precious ['prɛʃəs] *adj* : precioso

precipice ['prɛsəpəs] *n* : precipicio *m*

precipitate [pri'sɪpə,teɪt] *vt* **-tated; -tating** : precipitar — **precipitation** [pri,sɪpə'teɪʃən] *n* **1** HASTE : precipitación *f* **2** : precipitaciones *fpl* (en meteorología)

precise [pri'saɪs] *adj* : preciso — **precisely** *adv* : precisamente — **precision** [pri'sɪʒən] *n* : precisión *f*

preclude [pri'klu:d] *vt* **-cluded; -cluding** **1** PREVENT : impedir **2** EXCLUDE : excluir

precocious [pri'ko:ʃəs] *adj* : precoz

preconceived [,pri:kən'si:v] *adj* : preconcebido

predator ['prɛdəṭər] *n* : depredador *m*

predecessor ['prɛdə,sɛsər, 'pri:-] *n* : antecesor *m*, -sora *f*; predecesor *m*, -sora *f*

predicament [pri'dɪkəmənt] *n* : apuro *m*

predict [pri'dɪkt] *vt* : pronosticar, predecir — **predictable** [pri'dɪktəbəl] *adj* : previsible — **prediction** [pri'dɪkʃən] *n* : pronóstico *m*, predicción *f*

predispose [,pri:dɪ'spo:z] *vt* **-posed; -posing** : predisponer

predominant [pri'dɑmənənt] *adj* : predominante

preeminent [pri'ɛmənənt] *adj* : preeminente

preempt [pri'ɛmpt] *vt* : adelantarse a (un ataque, etc.)

preen ['pri:n] *vt* **1** : arreglarse (las plumas) **2 ~ oneself** : acicalarse

prefabricated [,pri:'fæbrə,keɪṭəd] *adj* : prefabricado

preface ['prɛfəs] *n* : prefacio *m*, prólogo *m*

prefer [pri'fər] *vt* **-ferred; -ferring** : preferir — **preferable** ['prɛfərəbəl] *adj* : preferible — **preference** ['prɛfrənts, 'prɛfər-] *n* : preferencia *f* — **preferential** [,prɛfə'rɛntʃəl] *adj* : preferente

prefix ['pri:,fɪks] *n* : prefijo *m*

pregnancy ['prɛgnəntsi] *n, pl* **-cies** : embarazo *m* — **pregnant** ['prɛgnənt] *adj* : embarazada

prehistoric [,pri:hɪs'tɔrɪk] *or* **prehistorical** [-ɪkəl] *adj* : prehistórico

prejudice ['prɛdʒədəs] *n* **1** BIAS : prejuicio *m* **2** HARM : perjuicio *m* — **~** *vt* **-diced; -dicing** **1** BIAS : predisponer **2** HARM : perjudicar — **prejudiced** ['prɛdʒədəst] *adj* : parcial

preliminary [pri'lɪmə,nɛri] *adj* : preliminar

prelude ['prɛ,lu:d, 'prɛl,ju:d; 'preɪ,lu:d, 'pri:-] *n* : preludio *m*

premarital [,pri:'mærəṭəl] *adj* : prematrimonial

premature [,pri:mə'tʊr, -'tjʊr, -'tʃʊr] *adj* : prematuro

premeditated [pri'mɛdə,teɪṭəd] *adj* : premeditado

premier [pri'mɪr, -'mjɪr; 'pri:miər] *adj* : principal — **~** *n* PRIME MINISTER : primer ministro *m*, primera ministra *f*

premiere [prɪ'mjɛr, -'mɪr] *n* : estreno *m*

premise ['prɛmɪs] *n* **1** : premisa *f* (de un argumento) **2 ~s** *npl* : recinto *m*, local *m*

premium ['pri:miəm] *n* **1** : premio *m* **2** *or* **insurance ~** : prima *f* (de seguro)

preoccupied [pri'ɑkjə,paɪd] *adj* : preocupado

prepare [pri'pær] *v* **-pared; -paring** *vt* : preparar — *vi* : prepararse — **preparation** [,prɛpə'reɪʃən] *n* **1** : preparación *f* **2 ~s** *npl* ARRANGEMENTS : preparativos *mpl* — **preparatory** [pri'pærə,tori] *adj* : preparatorio

prepay [,pri:'peɪ] *vt* **-paid; -paying** : pagar por adelantado

preposition [,prɛpə'zɪʃən] *n* : preposición *f*

preposterous [pri'pastərəs] *adj* : absurdo, ridículo
prerequisite [pri'rɛkwəzət] *n* : requisito *m* previo
prerogative [pri'ragəṭɪv] *n* : prerrogativa *f*
prescribe [pri'skraɪb] *vt* **-scribed; -scribing 1** : prescribir **2** : recetar (en medicina) — **prescription** [pri'skrɪpʃən] *n* : receta *f*
presence ['prɛzənts] *n* : presencia *f*
present[1] ['prɛzənt] *adj* **1** CURRENT : actual **2 be ~ at** : estar presente en — **~** *n* **1** : presente *m* **2 at ~** : actualmente
present[2] ['prɛzənt] *n* GIFT : regalo *m* — **~** [pri'zɛnt] *vt* **1** INTRODUCE : presentar **2** GIVE : entregar — **presentation** [ˌpri:ˌzɛn'teɪʃən, ˌprɛzən-] *n* **1** : presentación *f* **2** *or* **~ ceremony** : ceremonia *f* de entrega
presently ['prɛzəntli] *adv* **1** SOON : dentro de poco **2** NOW : actualmente
preserve [pri'zərv] *vt* **-served; -serving 1** : conservar **2** MAINTAIN : mantener — **~** *n* **1** JAM : confitura *f* **2** *or* **game ~** : coto *m* de caza — **preservation** [ˌprɛzər'veɪʃən] *n* : preservación *f*, conservación *f* — **preservative** [pri'zərvəṭɪv] *n* : conservante *m*
president ['prɛzədənt] *n* : presidente *m*, -ta *f* — **presidency** ['prɛzədəntsi] *n, pl* **-cies** : presidencia *f* — **presidential** [ˌprɛzə'dɛntʃəl] *adj* : presidencial
press ['prɛs] *n* : prensa *f* — **~** *vt* **1** : apretar **2** IRON : planchar — *vi* **1** : apretar **2** URGE : presionar — **pressing** ['prɛsɪŋ] *adj* : urgente — **pressure** ['prɛʃər] *n* : presión *f* — **~** *vt* **-sured; -suring** : presionar, apremiar
prestige [prɛ'sti:ʒ, -'sti:dʒ] *n* : prestigio *m* — **prestigious** [prɛ'stɪdʒəs] *adj* : prestigioso
presume [pri'zu:m] *vt* **-sumed; -suming** : presumir — **presumably** [pri'zu:məbli] *adv* : es de suponer, supuestamente — **presumption** [pri'zʌmpʃən] *n* : presunción *f* — **presumptuous** [pri'zʌmptʃʊəs] *adj* : presuntuoso
pretend [pri'tɛnd] *vt* **1** CLAIM : pretender **2** FEIGN : fingir — *vi* : fingir — **pretense** *or* **pretence** ['pri:ˌtɛnts, pri'tɛnts] *n* **1** CLAIM : pretensión *f* **2 under false ~s** : con pretextos falsos — **pretentious** [pri'tɛntʃəs] *adj* : pretencioso
pretext ['pri:ˌtɛkst] *n* : pretexto *m*
pretty ['prɪṭi] *adj* **-tier; -est** : lindo, bonito — **~** *adv* FAIRLY : bastante
pretzel ['prɛtsəl] *n* : galleta *f* salada
prevail [pri'veɪl] *vi* **1** TRIUMPH : prevalecer **2** PREDOMINATE : predominar **3 ~ upon** : persuadir — **prevalent** ['prɛvələnt] *adj* : extendido
prevent [pri'vɛnt] *vt* : impedir — **prevention** [pri'vɛntʃən] *n* : prevención *f* — **preventive** [pri'vɛntɪv] *adj* : preventivo
preview ['pri:ˌvju] *n* : preestreno *m*
previous ['pri:viəs] *adj* : previo, anterior — **previously** ['pri:viəsli] *adv* : anteriormente
prey ['preɪ] *n, pl* **preys** : presa *f* — **prey on** *vt* **1** : alimentarse de **2 ~ on one's mind** : atormentar a algn
price ['praɪs] *n* : precio *m* — **~** *vt* **priced; pricing** : poner un precio a — **priceless** ['praɪsləs] *adj* : inestimable
prick ['prɪk] *n* : pinchazo *m* — **~** *vt* **1** : pinchar **2 ~ up one's ears** : levantar las orejas — **prickly** ['prɪkəli] *adj* : espinoso
pride ['praɪd] *n* : orgullo *m* — **~** *vt* **prided; priding ~ oneself on** : enorgullecerse de
priest ['pri:st] *n* : sacerdote *m* — **priesthood** ['pri:stˌhʊd] *n* : sacerdocio *m*
prim ['prɪm] *adj* **primmer; primmest** : remilgado
primary ['praɪˌmɛri, 'praɪməri] *adj* **1** FIRST : primario **2** PRINCIPAL : principal — **primarily** [praɪ'mɛrəli] *adv* : principalmente
prime[1] ['praɪm] *vt* **primed; priming 1** : cebar (un arma de fuego, etc.) **2** PREPARE : preparar
prime[2] *n* **the ~ of one's life** : la flor de la vida — **~** *adj* **1** MAIN : principal, primero **2** EXCELLENT : excelente — **prime minister** *n* : primero ministro *m*, primera ministra *f*
primer[1] ['praɪmər] *n* : base *f* (de pintura)
primer[2] ['prɪmər] *n* READER : cartilla *f*
primitive ['prɪməṭɪv] *adj* : primitivo
primrose ['prɪmˌro:z] *n* : primavera *f*
prince ['prɪnts] *n* : príncipe *m* — **princess** ['prɪntsəs, 'prɪnˌsɛs] *n* : princesa *f*
principal ['prɪntsəpəl] *adj* : principal — **~** *n* : director *m*, -tora *f* (de un colegio)
principle ['prɪntsəpəl] *n* : principio *m*
print ['prɪnt] *n* **1** MARK : huella *f* **2** LETTERING : letra *f* **3** ENGRAVING : grabado *m* **4** : estampado *m* (de tela) **5** : copia *f* (en fotografía) **6 out of ~** : agotado — **~** *vt* : imprimir (libros, etc.) — *vi* : escribir con letra de molde — **printer** ['prɪntər] *n* **1** : impresor *m*, -sora *f* (persona) **2** : impresora *f* (máquina) — **printing** ['prɪntɪŋ] *n* **1** : impresión *f* **2**

: imprenta *f* (profesión) **3** LETTERING : letras *fpl* de molde
prior ['praɪər] *adj* **1** : previo **2** ~ **to** : antes de — **priority** [praɪ'ɔrəṭi] *n, pl* **-ties** : prioridad *f*
prison ['prɪzən] *n* : prisión *f,* cárcel *f* — **prisoner** ['prɪzənər] *n* **1** : preso *m,* -sa *f* **2** ~ **of war** : prisionero *m,* -ra *f* de guerra
privacy ['praɪvəsi] *n, pl* **-cies** : intimidad *f* — **private** ['praɪvət] *adj* **1** : privado **2** SECRET : secreto — ~ *n* : soldado *m* raso — **privately** ['praɪvətli] *adv* : en privado
privilege ['prɪvlɪdʒ, 'prɪvə-] *n* : privilegio *m* — **privileged** ['prɪvlɪdʒd, 'prɪvə-] *adj* : privilegiado
prize ['praɪz] *n* : premio *m* — ~ *adj* : premiado — ~ *vt* **prized; prizing** : valorar, apreciar — **prizefighter** ['praɪz,faɪṭər] *n* : boxeador *m,* -dora *f* profesional — **prizewinning** ['praɪz-,wɪnɪŋ] *adj* : premiado
pro ['pro:] *n* **1** → **professional 2 the** ~**s and cons** : los pros y los contras
probability [,prɑbə'bɪləṭi] *n, pl* **-ties** : probabilidad *f* — **probable** ['prɑbəbəl] *adj* : probable — **probably** [-bli] *adv* : probablemente
probation [pro'beɪʃən] *n* **1** : período *m* de prueba (de un empleado, etc.) **2** : libertad *f* condicional (de un preso)
probe ['pro:b] *n* **1** : sonda *f* (en medicina, etc.) **2** INVESTIGATION : investigación *f* — ~ *vt* **probed; probing 1** : sondar **2** INVESTIGATE : investigar
problem ['prɑbləm] *n* : problema *m*
procedure [prə'si:dʒər] *n* : procedimiento *m*
proceed [pro'si:d] *vi* **1** ACT : proceder **2** CONTINUE : continuar **3** ADVANCE : avanzar — **proceedings** [pro'si:dɪŋz] *npl* **1** EVENTS : actos *mpl* **2** : proceso *m* (en derecho) — **proceeds** ['pro:,si:dz] *npl* : ganancias *fpl*
process ['prɑ,sɛs, 'pro:-] *n, pl* **-cesses** ['prɑ,sɛsəz, 'pro:-, -səsəz, -sə,si:z] **1** : proceso *m* **2** **in the** ~ **of** : en vías de — ~ *vt* : procesar — **procession** [prə-'sɛʃən] *n* : desfile *m*
proclaim [pro'kleɪm] *vt* : proclamar — **proclamation** [,prɑklə'meɪʃən] *n* : proclamación *f*
procrastinate [prə'kræstə,neɪt] *vi* **-nated; -nating** : demorar, aplazar
procure [prə'kjʊr] *vt* **-cured; -curing** : obtener
prod ['prɑd] *vt* **prodded; prodding** : pinchar, aguijonear
prodigal ['prɑdɪgəl] *adj* : pródigo
prodigy ['prɑdədʒi] *n, pl* **-gies** : prodigio *m*
produce [prə'du:s, -'dju:s] *vt* **-duced; -ducing 1** : producir **2** CAUSE : causar **3** SHOW : presentar, mostrar **4** : poner en escena (una obra de teatro) — ~ ['prɑ,du:s, 'pro:-, -,dju:s] *n* : productos *mpl* agrícolas — **producer** [prə'du:sər, -'dju:-] *n* : productor *m,* -tora *f* — **product** ['prɑ,dʌkt] *n* : producto *m* — **productive** [prə'dʌktɪv] *adj* : productivo
profane [pro'feɪn] *adj* **1** : profano **2** IRREVERENT : blasfemo — **profanity** [pro'fænəṭi] *n, pl* **-ties** : blasfemia *f*
profess [prə'fɛs] *vt* : profesar — **profession** [prə'fɛʃən] *n* : profesión *f* — **professional** [prə'fɛʃənəl] *adj* : profesional — ~ *n* : profesional *mf* — **professor** [prə'fɛsər] *n* : profesor *m,* -sora *f*
proficiency [prə'fɪʃəntsi] *n* : competencia *f* — **proficient** [prə'fɪʃənt] *adj* : competente
profile ['pro:,faɪl] *n* **1** : perfil *m* **2 keep a low** ~ : no llamar la atención
profit ['prɑfət] *n* : beneficio *m,* ganancia *f* — ~ *vi* : sacar provecho (de), beneficiarse (de) — **profitable** ['prɑfəṭəbəl] *adj* : provechoso
profound [prə'faʊnd] *adj* : profundo
profuse [prə'fju:s] *adj* : profuso — **profusion** [prə'fju:ʒən] *n* : profusión *f*
prognosis [prɑg'no:sɪs] *n, pl* **-noses** [-,si:z] : pronóstico *m*
program ['pro:,græm, -grəm] *n* : programa *m* — ~ *vt* **-grammed** *or* **-gramed; -gramming** *or* **-graming** : programar
progress ['prɑgrəs, -,grɛs] *n* **1** : progreso *m* **2** ADVANCE : avance *m* — ~ [prə-'grɛs] *vi* : progresar, avanzar — **progressive** [prə'grɛsɪv] *adj* **1** : progresista (dícese de la política, etc.) **2** INCREASING : progresiva
prohibit [pro'hɪbət] *vt* : prohibir — **prohibition** [,pro:ə'bɪʃən, ,pro:hə-] *n* : prohibición *f*
project ['prɑ,dʒɛkt, -dʒɪkt] *n* : proyecto *m* — ~ [prə'dʒɛkt] *vt* : proyectar — *vi* PROTRUDE : sobresalir — **projectile** [prə'dʒɛktəl, -,taɪl] *n* : proyectil *m* — **projection** [prə'dʒɛkʃən] *n* **1** : proyección *f* **2** PROTRUSION : saliente *m* — **projector** [prə'dʒɛktər] *n* : proyector *m*
proliferate [prə'lɪfə,reɪt] *vi* **-ated; -ating** : proliferar — **proliferation** [prə,lɪfə-'reɪʃən] *n* : proliferación *f* — **prolific** [prə'lɪfɪk] *adj* : prolífico
prologue ['pro:,lɔg] *n* : prólogo *m*
prolong [prə'lɔŋ] *vt* : prolongar

prom ['prɑm] *n* : baile *m* formal (en un colegio)

prominent ['prɑmənənt] *adj* : prominente — **prominence** ['prɑmənənts] *n* **1** : prominencia *f* **2** IMPORTANCE : eminencia *f*

promiscuous [prə'mɪskjʊəs] *adj* : promiscuo

promise ['prɑməs] *n* : promesa *f* — ~ *v* **-ised; -ising** : prometer — **promising** ['prɑməsɪŋ] *adj* : prometedor

promote [prə'mo:t] *vt* **-moted; -moting** **1** : ascender (a un alumno o un empleado) **2** FURTHER : promover, fomentar **3** ADVERTISE : promocionar — **promoter** [prə'mo:t̬ər] *n* : promotor *m*, -tora *f*; empresario *m*, -ria *f* (en deportes) — **promotion** [prə'mo:ʃən] *n* **1** : ascenso *m* (de un alumno o un empleado) **2** ADVERTISING : publicidad *f*, propaganda *f*

prompt ['prɑmpt] *vt* **1** INCITE : provocar (una cosa), inducir (a una persona) **2** : apuntar (a un actor, etc.) — ~ *adj* **1** : rápido **2** PUNCTUAL : puntual

prone ['pro:n] *adj* **1** : boca abajo, decúbito prono **2 be ~ to** : ser propenso a

prong ['prɔŋ] *n* : punta *f*, diente *m*

pronoun ['pro:ˌnaʊn] *n* : pronombre *m*

pronounce [prə'naʊnts] *vt* **-nounced; -nouncing** : pronunciar — **pronouncement** [prə'naʊntsmənt] *n* : declaración *f* — **pronunciation** [prəˌnʌntsi'eɪʃən] *n* : pronunciación *f*

proof ['pru:f] *n* : prueba *f* — ~ *adj* ~ **against** : a prueba de — **proofread** ['pru:fˌri:d] *vt* **-read; -reading** : corregir

prop ['prɑp] *n* **1** SUPPORT : puntal *m*, apoyo *m* **2** : accesorio *m* (en teatro) — ~ *vt* **propped; propping** **1** ~ **against** : apoyar contra **2** ~ **up** SUPPORT : apoyar

propaganda [ˌprɑpə'gændə, ˌpro:-] *n* : propaganda *f*

propagate ['prɑpəˌgeɪt] *v* **-gated; -gating** *vt* : propagar — *vi* : propagarse

propel [prə'pɛl] *vt* **-pelled; -pelling** : propulsar — **propeller** [prə'pɛlər] *n* : hélice *f*

propensity [prə'pɛntsət̬i] *n, pl* **-ties** : propensión *f*

proper ['prɑpər] *adj* **1** SUITABLE : apropiado **2** REAL : verdadero **3** CORRECT : correcto **4** GENTEEL : cortés **5** ~ **name** : nombre *m* propio — **properly** ['prɑpərli] *adv* : correctamente

property ['prɑpərt̬i] *n, pl* **-ties** **1** : propiedad *f* **2** BUILDING : inmueble *m* **3** LAND, LOT : parcela *f*

prophet ['prɑfət] *n* : profeta *m*, profetisa *f* — **prophecy** ['prɑfəsi] *n, pl* **-cies** : profecía *f* — **prophesy** ['prɑfəˌsaɪ] *v* **-sied; -sying** *vt* : profetizar — *vi* : hacer profecías — **prophetic** [prə'fɛt̬ɪk] *adj* : profético

proportion [prə'porʃən] *n* **1** : proporción *f* **2** SHARE : parte *f* — **proportional** [prə'porʃənəl] *adj* : proporcional — **proportionate** [prə'porʃənət] *adj* : proporcional

proposal [prə'po:zəl] *n* : propuesta *f*

propose [prə'po:z] *v* **-posed; -posing** *vt* **1** SUGGEST : proponer **2** ~ **to do sth** : pensar hacer algo — *vi* : proponer matrimonio — **proposition** [ˌprɑpə'zɪʃən] *n* : proposición *f*

proprietor [prə'praɪət̬ər] *n* : propietario *m*, -ria *f*

propriety [prə'praɪət̬i] *n, pl* **-eties** : decencia *f*, decoro *m*

propulsion [prə'pʌlʃən] *n* : propulsión *f*

prose ['pro:z] *n* : prosa *f*

prosecute ['prɑsɪˌkju:t] *vt* **-cuted; -cuting** : procesar — **prosecution** [ˌprɑsɪ'kju:ʃən] *n* **1** : procesamiento *m* **2 the ~** : la acusación — **prosecutor** ['prɑsɪˌkju:t̬ər] *n* : acusador *m*, -dora *f*

prospect ['prɑˌspɛkt] *n* **1** : perspectiva *f* **2** POSSIBILITY : posibilidad *f* — **prospective** [prə'spɛktɪv, 'prɑˌspɛk-] *adj* : futuro, posible

prosper ['prɑspər] *vi* : prosperar — **prosperity** [prɑ'spɛrət̬i] *n* : prosperidad *f* — **prosperous** ['prɑspərəs] *adj* : próspero

prostitute ['prɑstəˌtu:t, -ˌtju:t] *n* : prostituta *f* — **prostitution** [ˌprɑstə'tu:ʃən, -'tju:-] *n* : prostitución *f*

prostrate ['prɑˌstreɪt] *adj* : postrado

protagonist [pro'tægənɪst] *n* : protagonista *mf*

protect [prə'tɛkt] *vt* : proteger — **protection** [prə'tɛkʃən] *n* : protección *f* — **protective** [prə'tɛktɪv] *adj* : protector — **protector** [prə'tɛktər] *n* : protector *m*, -tora *f*

protégé ['pro:t̬əˌʒeɪ] *n* : protegido *m*, -da *f*

protein ['pro:ˌti:n] *n* : proteína *f*

protest ['pro:ˌtɛst] *n* : protesta *f* — ~ [pro'tɛst] *vt* : protestar — *vi* ~ **against** : protestar contra — **Protestant** ['prɑt̬əstənt] *n* : protestante *mf* — **protester** *or* **protestor** ['pro:ˌtɛstər, prə'-] *n* : manifestante *mf*

protocol ['pro:t̬əˌkɔl] *n* : protocolo *m*

prototype ['pro:t̬əˌtaɪp] *n* : prototipo *m*

protract [pro'trækt] *vt* : prolongar

protrude [pro'tru:d] *vi* **-truded; -truding** : sobresalir

proud ['praud] *adj* : orgulloso

prove ['pru:v] *v* **proved; proved** *or* **proven** ['pru:vən]; **proving** *vt* : probar — *vi* : resultar

proverb ['prɑ,vərb] *n* : proverbio *m*, refrán *m* — **proverbial** [prə'vərbiəl] *adj* : proverbial

provide [prə'vaɪd] *v* **-vided; -viding** *vt* : proveer — *vi* ~ **for** SUPPORT : mantener — **provided** [prə'vaɪdəd] *or* ~ **that** *conj* : con tal (de) que, siempre que — **providence** ['prɑvədənts] *n* : providencia *f*

province ['prɑvɪnts] *n* **1** : provincia *f* **2** SPHERE : campo *m*, competencia *f* — **provincial** [prə'vɪntʃəl] *adj* : provinciano

provision [prə'vɪʒən] *n* **1** : provisión *f*, suministro *m* **2** STIPULATION : condición *f* **3** ~**s** *npl* : víveres *mpl* — **provisional** [prə'vɪʒənəl] *adj* : provisional — **proviso** [prə'vaɪ,zo:] *n, pl* **-sos** *or* **-soes** : condición *f*

provoke [prə'vo:k] *vt* **-voked; -voking** : provocar — **provocation** [,prɑvə'keɪʃən] *n* : provocación *f* — **provocative** [prə'vɑkət̬ɪv] *adj* : provocador, provocativo

prow ['prau] *n* : proa *f*

prowess ['prauəs] *n* **1** BRAVERY : valor *m* **2** SKILL : habilidad *f*

prowl ['praul] *vi* : merodear, rondar — *vt* : merodear por — **prowler** ['praulər] *n* : merodeador *m*, -dora *f*

proximity [prɑk'sɪmət̬i] *n* : proximidad *f* — **proxy** ['prɑksi] *n, pl* **proxies by** ~ : por poder

prude ['pru:d] *n* : mojigato *m*, -ta *f*

prudence ['pru:dənts] *n* : prudencia *f* — **prudent** ['pru:dənt] *adj* : prudente

prune[1] ['pru:n] *n* : ciruela *f* pasa

prune[2] *vt* **pruned; pruning** : podar (arbustos, etc.)

pry ['praɪ] *v* **pried; prying** *vi* ~ **into** : entrometerse en — *vt or* ~ **open** : abrir (a la fuerza)

psalm ['sɑm, 'sɑlm] *n* : salmo *m*

pseudonym ['su:də,nɪm] *n* : seudónimo *m*

psychiatry [sə'kaɪətri, saɪ-] *n* : psiquiatría *f* — **psychiatric** [,saɪki'ætrɪk] *adj* : psiquiátrico — **psychiatrist** [sə'kaɪətrɪst, saɪ-] *n* : psiquiatra *mf*

psychic ['saɪkɪk] *adj* : psíquico

psychoanalysis [,saɪkoə'næləsɪs] *n, pl* **-yses** : psicoanálisis *m* — **psychoanalyst** [,saɪko'ænəlɪst] *n* : psicoanalista *mf* — **psychoanalyze** [,saɪko'ænəl,aɪz] *vt* **-lyzed; -lyzing** : psicoanalizar

psychology [saɪ'kɑlədʒi] *n, pl* **-gies** : psicología *f* — **psychological** [,saɪkə'lɑdʒɪkəl] *adj* : psicológico — **psychologist** [saɪ'kɑlədʒɪst] *n* : psicólogo *m*, -ga *f*

psychopath ['saɪkə,pæθ] *n* : psicópata *mf*

psychotherapy [,saɪko'θɛrəpi] *n, pl* **-pies** : psicoterapia *f*

psychotic [saɪ'kɑt̬ɪk] *adj* : psicótico

puberty ['pju:bərt̬i] *n* : pubertad *f*

pubic ['pju:bɪk] *adj* : púbico

public ['pʌblɪk] *adj* : público — ~ *n* : público *m* — **publication** [,pʌblə'keɪʃən] *n* : publicación *f* — **publicity** [pə'blɪsət̬i] *n* : publicidad *f* — **publicize** ['pʌblə,saɪz] *vt* **-cized; -cizing** : publicitar, divulgar

publish ['pʌblɪʃ] *vt* : publicar — **publisher** ['pʌblɪʃər] *n* **1** : editor *m*, -tora *f* (persona) **2** : casa *f* editorial (negocio)

pucker ['pʌkər] *vt* : fruncir, arrugar — *vi* : arrugarse

pudding ['pudɪŋ] *n* : budín *m*, pudín *m*

puddle ['pʌdəl] *n* : charco *m*

pudgy ['pʌdʒi] *adj* **pudgier; -est** : rechoncho *fam*

Puerto Rican [,pwɛrt̬ə'ri:kən, ,port̬ə-] *adj* : puertorriqueño

puff ['pʌf] *vi* **1** BLOW : soplar **2** PANT : resoplar **3** ~ **up** SWELL : hincharse — *vt* ~ **out** : hinchar — ~ *n* **1** : bocanada *f* (de humo) **2** : chupada *f* (a un cigarrillo) **3** *or* **cream** ~ : pastelito *m* de crema **4** *or* **powder** ~ : borla *f* — **puffy** ['pʌfi] *adj* **puffier; -est** : hinchado

pull ['pul, 'pʌl] *vt* **1** : tirar de **2** EXTRACT : sacar **3** TEAR : desgarrarse (un músculo, etc.) **4** ~ **off** REMOVE : quitar **5** ~ **oneself together** : calmarse **6** ~ **up** : levantar, subir — *vi* **1** : tirar **2** ~ **through** RECOVER : reponerse **3** ~ **together** COOPERATE : reunir **4** ~ **up** STOP : parar — ~ *n* **1** : tirón *m* **2** INFLUENCE : influencia *f* — **pulley** ['puli] *n, pl* **-leys** : polea *f* — **pullover** ['pul,o:vər] *n* : suéter *m*

pulp ['pʌlp] *n* **1** : pulpa *f* (de frutas, etc.) **2** *or* **wood** ~ : pasta *f* de papel

pulpit ['pul,pɪt] *n* : púlpito *m*

pulsate ['pʌl,seɪt] *vi* **-sated; -sating** : palpitar — **pulse** ['pʌls] *n* : pulso *m*

pulverize ['pʌlvə,raɪz] *vt* **-ized; -izing** : pulverizar

pummel ['pʌməl] *vt* **-meled; -meling** : aporrear

pump[1] ['pʌmp] *n* : bomba *f* — ~ *vt* **1** : bombear **2** ~ **up** : inflar

pump[2] *n* SHOE : zapato *m* de tacón

pumpernickel ['pʌmpər,nɪkəl] *n* : pan *m* negro de centeno

pumpkin ['pʌmpkɪn, 'pʌŋkən] *n* : calabaza *f*, zapallo *m Lat*

pun ['pʌn] *n* : juego *m* de palabras — ~ *vi* **punned; punning** : hacer juegos de palabras

punch[1] ['pʌntʃ] *vt* **1** : dar un puñetazo a **2** PERFORATE : perforar (papeles, etc.), picar (un boleto) — ~ *n* **1** : golpe *m*, puñetazo *m* **2** *or* **paper ~** : perforadora *f*

punch[2] *n* : ponche *m* (bebida)

punctual ['pʌŋktʃʊəl] *adj* : puntual — **punctuality** [ˌpʌŋktʃʊ'æləṭi] *n* : puntualidad *f*

punctuate ['pʌŋktʃʊˌeɪt] *vt* **-ated; -ating** : puntuar — **punctuation** [ˌpʌŋktʃʊ'eɪʃən] *n* : puntuación *f*

puncture ['pʌŋktʃər] *n* : pinchazo *m*, ponchadura *f Lat* — ~ *vt* **-tured; -turing** : pinchar, ponchar *Lat*

pungent ['pʌndʒənt] *adj* : acre

punish ['pʌnɪʃ] *vt* : castigar — **punishment** ['pʌnɪʃmənt] *n* : castigo *m* — **punitive** ['pju:nəṭɪv] *adj* : punitivo

puny ['pju:ni] *adj* **-nier; -est** : enclenque

pup ['pʌp] *n* : cachorro *m*, -rra *f* (de un perro); cría *f* (de otros animales)

pupil[1] ['pju:pəl] *n* : alumno *m*, -na *f* (de colegio)

pupil[2] *n* : pupila *f* (del ojo)

puppet ['pʌpət] *n* : títere *m*

puppy ['pʌpi] *n, pl* **-pies** : cachorro *m*, -rra *f*

purchase ['pərtʃəs] *vt* **-chased; -chasing** : comprar — ~ *n* : compra *f*

pure ['pjʊr] *adj* **purer; purest** : puro

puree [pjʊ'reɪ, -'ri:] *n* : puré *m*

purely ['pjʊrli] *adv* : puramente

purgatory ['pərgəˌtori] *n, pl* **-ries** : purgatorio *m* — **purge** ['pərdʒ] *vt* **purged; purging** : purgar — ~ *n* : purga *f*

purify ['pjʊrəˌfaɪ] *vt* **-fied; -fying** : purificar — **purification** [ˌpjʊrəfə'keɪʃən] *n* : purificación *f*

puritanical [ˌpju:rə'tænɪkəl] *adj* : puritano

purity ['pjʊrəṭi] *n* : pureza *f*

purple ['pərpəl] *n* : morado *m*

purport [pər'port] *vt* ~ **to be** : pretender ser

purpose ['pərpəs] *n* **1** : propósito *m* **2** RESOLUTION : determinación *f* **3 on ~** : a propósito — **purposeful** ['pərpəsfəl] *adj* : resuelto — **purposely** ['pərpəsli] *adv* : a propósito

purr ['pər] *n* : ronroneo *m* — ~ *vi* : ronronear

purse ['pərs] *n* **1** *or* **change ~** : monedero *m* **2** HANDBAG : cartera *f*, bolso *m Spain*, bolsa *f Lat* — ~ *vt* **pursed; pursing** : fruncir

pursue [pər'su:] *vt* **-sued; -suing 1** CHASE : perseguir **2** SEEK : buscar — **pursuer** [pər'su:ər] *n* : perseguidor *m*, -dora *f* — **pursuit** [pər'su:t] *n* **1** CHASE : persecución *f* **2** SEARCH : búsqueda *f* **3** OCCUPATION : actividad *f*

pus ['pʌs] *n* : pus *m*

push ['pʊʃ] *vt* **1** SHOVE : empujar **2** PRESS : apretar **3** URGE : presionar **4 ~ around** BULLY : mangonear — *vi* **1** : empujar **2 ~ for** : presionar para — ~ *n* **1** SHOVE : empujón *m* **2** DRIVE : dinamismo *m* **3** EFFORT : esfuerzo *m* — **pushy** ['pʊʃi] *adj* **pushier; -est** : mandón, prepotente

pussy ['pʊsi] *n, pl* **pussies** : gatito *m*, -ta *f*; minino *m*, -na *f*

put ['pʊt] *v* **put; putting** *vt* **1** : poner **2** INSERT : meter **3** EXPRESS : decir **4 ~ one's mind to sth** : proponerse hacer algo — *vi* **~ up with** : aguantar — **put away** *vt* **1** STORE : guardar **2** *or* **~ aside** : dejar a un lado — **put down** *vt* **1** SUPPRESS : aplastar, sofocar **2** ATTRIBUTE : atribuir — **put off** *vt* DEFER : aplazar, posponer — **put on** *vt* **1** ASSUME : adoptar **2** PRESENT : presentar (una obra de teatro, etc.) **3** WEAR : ponerse — **put out** *vt* INCONVENIENCE : incomodar — **put up** *vt* **1** BUILD : construir **2** LODGE : alojar **3** PROVIDE : poner (dinero)

putrefy ['pju:trəˌfaɪ] *vi* **-fied; -fying** : pudrirse

putty ['pʌṭi] *n, pl* **-ties** : masilla *f*

puzzle ['pʌzəl] *v* **-zled; -zling** *vt* : confundir, dejar perplejo — *vi* **~ over** : tratar de descifrar — ~ *n* **1** : rompecabezas *m* **2** MYSTERY : enigma *m*

pylon ['paɪˌlɑn, -lən] *n* : pilón *m*

pyramid ['pɪrəˌmɪd] *n* : pirámide *f*

python ['paɪˌθɑn, -θən] *n* : pitón *f*

Q

q ['kju:] *n, pl* **q's** *or* **qs** ['kju:z] : q *f*, decimoséptima letra del alfabeto inglés
quack¹ ['kwæk] *vi* : graznar (dícese del pato) — **~** *n* : graznido *m*
quack² *n* CHARLATAN : charlatán *m*, -tana *f*
quadruple [kwɑ'dru:pəl, -'drʌ-; 'kwɑdrə-] *v* **-pled; -pling** *vt* : cuadruplicar — *vi* : cuadruplicarse
quagmire ['kwæg,maɪr, 'kwɑg-] *n* : atolladero *m*
quail ['kweɪl] *n, pl* **quail** *or* **quails** : codorniz *f*
quaint ['kweɪnt] *adj* **1** ODD : curioso **2** PICTURESQUE : pintoresco
quake ['kweɪk] *vi* **quaked; quaking** : temblar — **~** *n* → **earthquake**
qualify ['kwɑlə,faɪ] *v* **-fied; -fying** *vt* **1** LIMIT : matizar **2** : calificar (en gramática) **3** EQUIP : habilitar — *vi* **1** : titularse (de abogado, etc.) **2** : clasificarse (en deportes) — **qualification** [,kwɑləfə'keɪʃən] *n* **1** REQUIREMENT : requisito *m* **2** **~s** *npl* ABILITY : capacidad *f* **3** **without ~** : sin reservas — **qualified** ['kwɑlə,faɪd] *adj* : capacitado
quality ['kwɑləṭi] *n, pl* **-ties** **1** : calidad *f* **2** PROPERTY : cualidad *f*
qualm ['kwɑm, 'kwɑlm, 'kwɔm] *n* **1** DOUBT : duda *f* **2** **have no ~s about** : no tener ningún escrúpulo en
quandary ['kwɑndri] *n, pl* **-ries** : dilema *m*
quantity ['kwɑntəṭi] *n, pl* **-ties** : cantidad *f*
quarantine ['kwɔrən,ti:n] *n* : cuarentena *f* — **~** *vt* **-tined; -tining** : poner en cuarentena
quarrel ['kwɔrəl] *n* : pelea *f*, riña *f* — **~** *vi* **-reled** *or* **-relled; -reling** *or* **-relling** : pelearse, reñir — **quarrelsome** ['kwɔrəlsəm] *adj* : pendenciero
quarry¹ ['kwɔri] *n, pl* **quarries** PREY : presa *f*
quarry² *n, pl* **quarries** EXCAVATION : cantera *f*
quart ['kwɔrt] *n* : cuarto *m* de galón
quarter ['kwɔrṭər] *n* **1** : cuarto *m* (en matemáticas) **2** : moneda *f* de 25 centavos **3** DISTRICT : barrio *m* **4** **~ after three** : las tres y cuarto **5** **~s** *npl* LODGING : alojamiento *m* — **~** *vt* **1** : dividir en cuatro partes **2** : acuartelar (tropas) — **quarterly** ['kwɔrṭərli] *adv* : cada tres meses — **~** *adj* : trimestral — **~** *n, pl* **-lies** : publicación *f* trimestral
quartet [kwɔr'tɛt] *n* : cuarteto *m*
quartz ['kwɔrts] *n* : cuarzo *m*
quash ['kwɑʃ, 'kwɔʃ] *vt* **1** ANNUL : anular **2** SUPPRESS : aplastar, sofocar
quaver ['kweɪvər] *vi* : temblar
quay ['ki:, 'keɪ, 'kweɪ] *n* : muelle *m*
queasy ['kwi:zi] *adj* **-sier; -est** : mareado
queen ['kwi:n] *n* : reina *f*
queer ['kwɪr] *adj* ODD : extraño
quell ['kwɛl] *vt* SUPPRESS : sofocar, aplastar
quench ['kwɛntʃ] *vt* **1** EXTINGUISH : apagar **2** **~ one's thirst** : quitar la sed
query ['kwɪri, 'kwɛr-] *n, pl* **-ries** : pregunta *f* — **~** *vt* **-ried; -rying** **1** ASK : preguntar **2** QUESTION : cuestionar
quest ['kwɛst] *n* : búsqueda *f*
question ['kwɛstʃən] *n* **1** QUERY : pregunta *f* **2** ISSUE : cuestión *f* **3** **be out of the ~** : ser indiscutible **4** **call into ~** : poner en duda **5** **without ~** : sin duda — **~** *vt* **1** ASK : preguntar **2** DOUBT : cuestionar **3** INTERROGATE : interrogar — *vi* : preguntar — **questionable** ['kwɛstʃənəbəl] *adj* : discutible — **question mark** *n* : signo *m* de interrogación — **questionnaire** [,kwɛstʃə'nær] *n* : cuestionario *m*
queue ['kju:] *n* : cola *f* — **~** *vi* **queued; queuing** *or* **queueing** : hacer cola
quibble ['kwɪbəl] *vi* **-bled; -bling** : discutir, quejarse por nimiedades
quick ['kwɪk] *adj* **1** : rápido **2** CLEVER : agudo — **~** *n* **to the ~** : en lo vivo — **~** *adv* : rápidamente — **quicken** ['kwɪkən] *vt* : acelerar — **quickly** ['kwɪkli] *adv* : rápidamente — **quicksand** ['kwɪk,sænd] *n* : arena *f* movediza — **quick–tempered** ['kwɪk'tɛmpərd] *adj* : irascible — **quick–witted** ['kwɪk'wɪṭəd] *adj* : agudo
quiet ['kwaɪət] *n* **1** : silencio *m* **2** CALM : tranquilidad *f* — **~** *adj* **1** : silencioso **2** CALM : tranquilo **3** RESERVED : callado **4** : discreto (dícese de colores, etc.) — **~** *vt* **1** SILENCE : hacer callar **2** CALM : calmar — *vi or* **~ down** : cal-

marse — **quietly** *adv* **1** : silenciosamente **2** CALMLY : tranquilamente
quilt ['kwɪlt] *n* : edredón *m*
quintet [kwɪn'tɛt] *n* : quinteto *m*
quip ['kwɪp] *n* : ocurrencia *f*, salida *f* — ~ *vt* **quipped; quipping** : decir bromeando
quirk ['kwərk] *n* : peculiaridad *f*
quit ['kwɪt] *v* **quit; quitting** *vt* **1** LEAVE : dejar, abandonar **2** ~ **doing** : dejar de hacer — *vi* **1** STOP : parar **2** RESIGN : dimitir, renunciar
quite ['kwaɪt] *adv* **1** COMPLETELY : completamente **2** RATHER : bastante
quits ['kwɪts] *adj* **call it** ~ : quedar en paz
quiver ['kwɪvər] *vi* : temblar
quiz ['kwɪz] *n, pl* **quizzes** TEST : prueba *f* — ~ *vt* **quizzed; quizzing** : interrogar
quota ['kwo:ţə] *n* : cuota *f*, cupo *m*
quotation [kwo'teɪʃən] *n* **1** : cita *f* **2** ESTIMATE : presupuesto *m* — **quotation marks** *npl* : comillas *fpl* — **quote** ['kwo:t] *vt* **quoted; quoting 1** CITE : citar **2** : cotizar (en finanzas) — ~ *n* **1** → **quotation 2** ~**s** *npl* → **quotation marks**
quotient ['kwo:ʃənt] *n* : cociente *m*

R

r ['ɑr] *n, pl* **r's** *or* **rs** ['ɑrz] : r *f*, decimoctava letra del alfabeto inglés
rabbi ['ræ,baɪ] *n* : rabino *m*, -na *f*
rabbit ['ræbət] *n, pl* **-bit** *or* **-bits** : conejo *m*, -ja *f*
rabble ['ræbəl] *n* : chusma *f*, populacho *m*
rabies ['reɪbi:z] *ns & pl* : rabia *f* — **rabid** ['ræbɪd] *adj* **1** : rabioso **2** FANATIC : fanático
raccoon [ræ'ku:n] *n, pl* **-coon** *or* **-coons** : mapache *m*
race[1] ['reɪs] *n* **1** : raza *f* **2 human** ~ : género *m* humano
race[2] *n* : carrera *f* (competitiva) — ~ *vi* **raced; racing 1** : correr (en una carrera) **2** RUSH : ir corriendo — **racehorse** ['reɪs,hors] *n* : caballo *m* de carreras — **racetrack** ['reɪs,træk] *n* : pista *f* (de carreras)
racial ['reɪʃəl] *adj* : racial — **racism** ['reɪ,sɪzəm] *n* : racismo *m* — **racist** ['reɪsɪst] *n* : racista *mf*
rack ['ræk] *n* **1** SHELF : estante *m* **2 luggage** ~ : portaequipajes *m* — ~ *vt* **1** ~**ed with** : atormentado por **2** ~ **one's brains** : devanarse los sesos
racket[1] ['rækət] *n* : raqueta *f* (en deportes)
racket[2] *n* **1** DIN : alboroto *m*, bulla *f* **2** SWINDLE : estafa *f*
racy ['reɪsi] *adj* **racier; -est** : subido de tono, picante
radar ['reɪ,dɑr] *n* : radar *m*
radiant ['reɪdiənt] *adj* : radiante — **radiance** ['reɪdiənts] *n* : resplandor *m* — **radiate** ['reɪdi,eɪt] *v* **-ated; -ating** *vt* : irradiar — *vi* **1** : irradiar **2** *or* ~ **out** : extenderse (desde un centro) — **radiation** [,reɪdi'eɪʃən] *n* : radiación *f* — **radiator** ['reɪdi,eɪţər] *n* : radiador *m*
radical ['rædɪkəl] *adj* : radical — ~ *n* : radical *mf*
radii → **radius**
radio ['reɪdi,o:] *n, pl* **-dios** : radio *mf* (aparato), radio *f* (medio) — ~ *vt* : transmitir por radio — **radioactive** ['reɪdio'æktɪv] *adj* : radioactivo, radiactivo
radish ['rædɪʃ] *n* : rábano *m*
radius ['reɪdiəs] *n, pl* **radii** [-di,aɪ] : radio *m*
raffle ['ræfəl] *vt* **-fled; -fling** : rifar — ~ *n* : rifa *f*
raft ['ræft] *n* : balsa *f*
rafter ['ræftər] *n* : cabrio *m*
rag ['ræg] *n* **1** : trapo *m* **2** ~**s** *npl* TATTERS : harapos *mpl*, andrajos *mpl*
rage ['reɪdʒ] *n* **1** : cólera *f*, rabia *f* **2 be all the** ~ : hacer furor — ~ *vi* **raged; raging 1** : estar furioso **2** : bramar (dícese del viento, etc.)
ragged ['rægəd] *adj* **1** UNEVEN : irregular **2** TATTERED : andrajoso, harapiento
raid ['reɪd] *n* **1** : invasión *f* (militar) **2** : asalto *m* (por delincuentes), redada *f* (por la policía) — ~ *vt* **1** INVADE : invadir **2** ROB : asaltar **3** : hacer una redada en (dícese de la policía) — **raider** ['reɪdər] *n* ATTACKER : asaltante *mf*
rail[1] ['reɪl] *vi* ~ **at s.o.** : recriminar a algn
rail[2] *n* **1** BAR : barra *f* **2** HANDRAIL : pasamanos *m* **3** TRACK : riel *m* **4 by** ~ : por ferrocarril — **railing** ['reɪlɪŋ] *n* **1** : baranda *f* (de un balcón), pasamanos *m* (de una escalera) **2**

RAILS : reja *f* — **railroad** ['reɪl,ro:d] *n* : ferrocarril *m* — **railway** ['reɪl,weɪ] → **railroad**
rain ['reɪn] *n* : lluvia *f* — ~ *vi* : llover — **rainbow** ['reɪn,bo:] *n* : arco *m* iris — **raincoat** ['reɪn,ko:t] *n* : impermeable *m* — **rainfall** ['reɪn,fɔl] *n* : precipitación *f* — **rainy** ['reɪni] *adj* **rainier; -est** : lluvioso
raise ['reɪz] *vt* **raised; raising 1** : levantar **2** COLLECT : recaudar **3** REAR : criar **4** GROW : cultivar **5** INCREASE : aumentar **6** : sacar (objeciones, etc.) — ~ *n* : aumento *m*
raisin ['reɪzən] *n* : pasa *f*
rake ['reɪk] *n* : rastrillo *m* — ~ *vt* **raked; raking** : rastrillar
rally ['ræli] *v* **-lied; -lying** *vi* **1** : unirse, reunirse **2** RECOVER : recuperarse — *vt* : conseguir (apoyo), unir a (la gente) — ~ *n, pl* **-lies** : reunión *f,* mitin *m*
ram *n* ['ræm] : carnero *m* (animal) — ~ *vt* **rammed; ramming 1** CRAM : meter con fuerza **2** *or* ~ **into** : chocar contra
RAM ['ræm] *n* : RAM *f*
ramble ['ræmbəl] *vi* **-bled; -bling 1** WANDER : pasear **2** *or* ~ **on** : divagar — ~ *n* : paseo *m,* excursión *f*
ramp ['ræmp] *n* : rampa *f*
rampage ['ræm,peɪdʒ, ræm'peɪdʒ] *vi* **-paged; -paging** : andar arrasando todo — ~ ['ræm,peɪdʒ] *n* : frenesí *m* (de violencia)
rampant ['ræmpənt] *adj* : desenfrenado
rampart ['ræm,pɑrt] *n* : muralla *f*
ramshackle ['ræm,ʃækəl] *adj* : destartalado
ran → **run**
ranch ['ræntʃ] *n* : hacienda *f* — **rancher** ['ræntʃər] *n* : hacendado *m,* -da *f*
rancid ['ræntsɪd] *adj* : rancio
rancor ['ræŋkər] *n* : rencor *m*
random ['rændəm] *adj* **1** : aleatorio **2 at** ~ : al azar
rang → **ring**
range ['reɪndʒ] *n* **1** GRASSLAND : pradera *f* **2** STOVE : cocina *f* **3** VARIETY : gama *f* **4** SCOPE : amplitud *f* **5** *or* **mountain** ~ : cordillera *f* — ~ *vi* **ranged; ranging 1** EXTEND : extenderse **2** ~ **from...to...** : variar entre...y... — **ranger** ['reɪndʒər] *n or* **forest** ~ : guardabosque *mf*
rank[1] ['ræŋk] *adj* **1** SMELLY : fétido **2** OUTRIGHT : completo
rank[2] *n* **1** ROW : fila *f* **2** : rango *m* (militar) **3** ~**s** *npl* : soldados *mpl* rasos **4 the** ~ **and file** : las bases — ~ *vt* RATE : clasificar — *vi* : clasificarse
rankle ['ræŋkəl] *vi* **-kled; -kling** : causar rencor, doler
ransack ['ræn,sæk] *vt* **1** SEARCH : registrar **2** LOOT : saquear
ransom ['ræntsəm] *n* : rescate *m* — ~ *vt* : rescatar
rant ['rænt] *vi or* ~ **and rave** : despotricar
rap[1] ['ræp] *n* KNOCK : golpecito *m* — ~ *v* **rapped; rapping** : golpear
rap[2] *n or* ~ **music** : rap *m*
rapacious [rə'peɪʃəs] *adj* : rapaz
rape ['reɪp] *vt* **raped; raping** : violar — ~ *n* : violación *f*
rapid ['ræpɪd] *adj* : rápido — **rapids** ['ræpɪdz] *npl* : rápidos *mpl*
rapist ['reɪpɪst] *n* : violador *m,* -dora *f*
rapport [ræ'pɔr] *n* **have a good** ~ : entenderse bien
rapt ['ræpt] *adj* : absorto, embelesado
rapture ['ræptʃər] *n* : éxtasis *m*
rare ['rær] *adj* **rarer; rarest 1** FINE : excepcional **2** UNCOMMON : raro **3** : poco cocido (dícese de la carne) — **rarely** ['rærli] *adv* : raramente — **rarity** ['rærəṭi] *n, pl* **-ties** : rareza *f*
rascal ['ræskəl] *n* : pillo *m,* -lla *f;* pícaro *m,* -ra *f*
rash[1] ['ræʃ] *adj* : imprudente, precipitado
rash[2] *n* : sarpullido *m,* erupción *f*
rasp ['ræsp] *vt* SCRAPE : raspar — ~ *n* : escofina *f*
raspberry ['ræz,bɛri] *n, pl* **-ries** : frambuesa *f*
rat ['ræt] *n* : rata *f*
rate ['reɪt] *n* **1** PACE : velocidad *f,* ritmo *m* **2** : tipo *m,* tasa *m* (de interés, etc.) **3** PRICE : tarifa *f* **4 at any** ~ : de todos modos **5 birth** ~ : índice *m* de natalidad — ~ *vt* **rated; rating 1** REGARD : considerar **2** DESERVE : merecer
rather ['ræðər, 'rʌ-, 'rɑ-] *adv* **1** FAIRLY : bastante **2 I'd** ~... : prefiero... **3 or** ~ : o mejor dicho
ratify ['ræṭə,faɪ] *vt* **-fied; -fying** : ratificar — **ratification** [,ræṭəfə'keɪʃən] *n* : ratificación *f*
rating ['reɪṭɪŋ] *n* **1** : clasificación *f* **2** ~**s** *npl* : índice *m* de audiencia
ratio ['reɪʃio] *n, pl* **-tios** : proporción *f*
ration ['ræʃən, 'reɪʃən] *n* **1** : ración *f* **2** ~**s** *npl* PROVISIONS : víveres *mpl* — ~ *vt* **rationed; rationing** : racionar
rational ['ræʃənəl] *adj* : racional — **rationale** [,ræʃə'næl] *n* : lógica *f,* razones *fpl* — **rationalize** ['ræʃənə,laɪz] *vt* **-ized; -izing** : racionalizar
rattle ['ræṭəl] *v* **-tled; -tling** *vi* : traquetear — *vt* **1** SHAKE : agitar **2** UPSET : de-

sconcertar **3 ~ off** : decir de corrido — ~ *n* **1** : traqueteo *m* **2** *or* **baby's ~** : sonajero *m* — **rattlesnake** ['ræṭəl-ˌsneɪk] *n* : serpiente *f* de cascabel

raucous ['rɔkəs] *adj* **1** HOARSE : ronco **2** BOISTEROUS : bullicioso

ravage ['rævɪdʒ] *vt* **-aged; -aging** : estragar, asolar — **ravages** ['rævɪdʒəz] *npl* : estragos *mpl*

rave ['reɪv] *vi* **raved; raving 1** : delirar **2 ~ about** : hablar con entusiasmo sobre

raven ['reɪvən] *n* : cuervo *m*

ravenous ['rævənəs] *adj* **1** HUNGRY : hambriento **2** VORACIOUS : voraz

ravine [rə'vi:n] *n* : barranco *m*

ravishing ['rævɪʃɪŋ] *adj* : encantador

raw ['rɔ] *adj* **rawer; rawest 1** UNCOOKED : crudo **2** INEXPERIENCED : inexperto **3** CHAFED : en carne viva **4** : frío y húmedo (dícese del tiempo) **5 ~ deal** : trato *m* injusto **6 ~ materials** : materias *fpl* primas

ray ['reɪ] *n* : rayo *m*

rayon ['reɪˌɑn] *n* : rayón *m*

raze ['reɪz] *vt* **razed; razing** : arrasar

razor ['reɪzər] *n* : maquinilla *f* de afeitar — **razor blade** *n* : hoja *f* de afeitar

reach ['ri:tʃ] *vt* **1** : alcanzar **2** *or* **~ out** : extender **3** : llegar a (un acuerdo, un límite, etc.) **4** CONTACT : contactar — *vi* **1** : extenderse **2 ~ for** : tratar de agarrar — ~ *n* **1** : alcance *m* **2 within ~** : al alcance

react [ri'ækt] *vi* : reaccionar — **reaction** [ri'ækʃən] *n* : reacción *f* — **reactionary** [ri'ækʃəˌneri] *adj* : reaccionario — ~ *n, pl* **-ries** : reaccionario *m*, -ria *f* — **reactor** [ri'æktər] *n* : reactor *m*

read ['ri:d] *v* **read** ['rɛd]; **reading** *vt* **1** : leer **2** INTERPRET : interpretar **3** SAY : decir **4** INDICATE : marcar — *vi* **1** : leer **2 it ~s as follows** : dice lo siguiente — **readable** ['ri:dəbəl] *adj* : legible — **reader** ['ri:dər] *n* : lector *m*, -tora *f*

readily ['rɛdəli] *adv* **1** WILLINGLY : de buena gana **2** EASILY : fácilmente

reading ['ri:dɪŋ] *n* : lectura *f*

readjust [ˌri:ə'dʒʌst] *vt* : reajustar — *vi* : volverse a adaptar

ready ['rɛdi] *adj* **readier; -est 1** : listo, preparado **2** WILLING : dispuesto **3** AVAILABLE : disponible **4 get ~** : prepararse — ~ *vt* **readied; readying** : preparar

real ['ri:l] *adj* **1** : verdadero, real **2** GENUINE : auténtico — ~ *adv* VERY : muy — **real estate** *n* : propiedad *f* inmobiliaria, bienes *mpl* raíces — **realism** ['ri:əˌlɪzəm] *n* : realismo *m* — **realist** ['ri:əlɪst] *n* : realista *mf* — **realistic** [ˌri:ə'lɪstɪk] *adj* : realista — **reality** [ri-'æləṭi] *n, pl* **-ties** : realidad *f*

realize ['ri:əˌlaɪz] *vt* **-ized; -izing 1** : darse cuenta de **2** ACHIEVE : realizar — **realization** [ˌri:ələ'zeɪʃən] *n* **1** : comprensión *f* **2** FULFILLMENT : realización *f*

really ['rɪli, 'ri:-] *adv* : verdaderamente

realm ['rɛlm] *n* **1** KINGDOM : reino *m* **2** SPHERE : esfera *f*

ream ['ri:m] *n* : resma *f* (de papel)

reap ['ri:p] *v* : cosechar

reappear [ˌri:ə'pɪr] *vi* : reaparecer

rear[1] ['rɪr] *vt* **1** RAISE : levantar **2** : criar (niños, etc.) — *vi or* **~ up** : encabritarse

rear[2] *n* **1** BACK : parte *f* de atrás **2** BUTTOCKS : trasero *m fam* — ~ *adj* : trasero, posterior

rearrange [ˌri:ə'reɪndʒ] *vt* **-ranged; -ranging** : reorganizar, cambiar

reason ['ri:zən] *n* : razón *f* — ~ *vt* THINK : pensar — *vi* : razonar — **reasonable** ['ri:zənəbəl] *adj* : razonable — **reasoning** ['ri:zənɪŋ] *n* : razonamiento *m*

reassure [ˌri:ə'ʃʊr] *vt* **-sured; -suring** : tranquilizar — **reassurance** [ˌri:ə-'ʃʊrənts] *n* : (palabras *fpl* de) consuelo *m*

rebate ['ri:ˌbeɪt] *n* : reembolso *m*

rebel ['rɛbəl] *n* : rebelde *mf* — ~ [rɪ'bɛl] *vi* **-belled; -belling** : rebelarse — **rebellion** [rɪ'bɛljən] *n* : rebelión *f* — **rebellious** [rɪ'bɛljəs] *adj* : rebelde

rebirth [ˌri:'bərθ] *n* : renacimiento *m*

rebound ['ri:ˌbaʊnd, ˌri:'baʊnd] *vi* : rebotar — ~ ['ri:ˌbaʊnd] *n* : rebote *m*

rebuff [ri'bʌf] *vt* : rechazar — ~ *n* : desaire *m*

rebuild [ˌri:'bɪld] *vt* **-built; -building** : reconstruir

rebuke [ri'bju:k] *vt* **-buked; -buking** : reprender — ~ *n* : reprimenda *f*

rebut [ri'bʌt] *vt* **-butted; -butting** : rebatir — **rebuttal** [ri'bʌṭəl] *n* : refutación *f*

recall [ri'kɔl] *vt* **1** : llamar (al servicio, etc.) **2** REMEMBER : recordar **3** REVOKE : revocar — ~ [ri'kɔl, 'ri:ˌkɔl] *n* **1** : retirada *f* **2** MEMORY : memoria *f*

recant [ri'kænt] *vi* : retractarse

recapitulate [ˌri:kə'pɪtʃəˌleɪt] *v* **-lated; -lating** : recapitular

recapture [ˌri:'kæptʃər] *vt* **-tured; -turing 1** : recobrar **2** RELIVE : revivir

recede [ri'si:d] *vi* **-ceded; -ceding** : retirarse

receipt [ri'si:t] *n* **1** : recibo *m* **2 ~s** *npl* : ingresos *mpl*
receive [ri'si:v] *vt* **-ceived; -ceiving** : recibir — **receiver** [ri'si:vər] *n* **1** : receptor *m* (de radio, etc.) **2** *or* **telephone ~** : auricular *m*
recent ['ri:sənt] *adj* : reciente — **recently** [-li] *adv* : recientemente
receptacle [ri'sɛptɪkəl] *n* : receptáculo *m*, recipiente *m*
reception [ri'sɛpʃən] *n* : recepción *f* — **receptionist** [ri'sɛpʃənɪst] *n* : recepcionista *mf* — **receptive** [ri'sɛptɪv] *adj* : receptivo
recess ['ri:ˌsɛs, rɪ'sɛs] *n* **1** ALCOVE : hueco *m* **2** : recreo *m* (escolar) **3** ADJOURNMENT : suspensión *f* de actividades *Spain*, receso *m Lat* — **recession** [ri'sɛʃən] *n* : recesión *f*
recharge [ˌri:'tʃɑrdʒ] *vt* **-charged; -charging** : recargar — **rechargeable** [ˌri:'tʃɑrdʒəbəl] *adj* : recargable
recipe ['rɛsəˌpi:] *n* : receta *f*
recipient [ri'sɪpiənt] *n* : recipiente *mf*
reciprocal [ri'sɪprəkəl] *adj* : recíproco
recite [ri'saɪt] *vt* **-cited; -citing 1** : recitar (un poema, etc.) **2** LIST : enumerar — **recital** [ri'saɪṭəl] *n* : recital *m*
reckless ['rɛkləs] *adj* : imprudente — **recklessness** ['rɛkləsnəs] *n* : imprudencia *f*
reckon ['rɛkən] *vt* **1** COMPUTE : calcular **2** CONSIDER : considerar — **reckoning** ['rɛkənɪŋ] *n* : cálculos *mpl*
reclaim [ri'kleɪm] *vt* **1** : reclamar **2** RECOVER : recuperar
recline [ri'klaɪn] *vi* **-clined; -clining** : reclinarse — **reclining** *adj* : reclinable (dícese de un asiento, etc.)
recluse ['rɛˌklu:s, ri'klu:s] *n* : solitario *m*, -ria *f*
recognition [ˌrɛkɪg'nɪʃən] *n* : reconocimiento *m* — **recognizable** ['rɛkɪgˌnaɪzəbəl] *adj* : reconocible — **recognize** ['rɛkɪgˌnaɪz] *vt* **-nized; -nizing** : reconocer
recoil [ri'kɔɪl] *vi* : retroceder — **~** ['ri:ˌkɔɪl, ri'-] *n* : culatazo *m* (de un arma de fuego)
recollect [ˌrɛkə'lɛkt] *v* : recordar — **recollection** [ˌrɛkə'lɛkʃən] *n* : recuerdo *m*
recommend [ˌrɛkə'mɛnd] *vt* : recomendar — **recommendation** [ˌrɛkəmən'deɪʃən] *n* : recomendación *f*
reconcile ['rɛkənˌsaɪl] *v* **-ciled; -ciling** *vt* **1** : reconciliar (personas), conciliar (datos, etc.) **2 ~ oneself to** : resignarse a — *vi* MAKE UP : reconciliarse — **reconciliation** [ˌrɛkənˌsɪli'eɪʃən] *n* : reconciliación *f*
reconnaissance [ri'kɑnəzənts, -sənts] *n* : reconocimiento *m* (militar)
reconsider [ˌri:kən'sɪdər] *vt* : reconsiderar
reconstruct [ˌri:kən'strʌkt] *vt* : reconstruir
record [ri'kɔrd] *vt* **1** WRITE DOWN : anotar, apuntar **2** REGISTER : registrar **3** : grabar (música, etc.) — **~** ['rɛkərd] *n* **1** DOCUMENT : documento *m* **2** REGISTER : registro *m* **3** HISTORY : historial *m* **4** : disco *m* (de música, etc.) **5 criminal ~** : antecedentes *mpl* penales **6 world ~** : récord *m* mundial — **recorder** [ri'kɔrdər] *n* **1** : flauta *f* dulce **2** *or* **tape ~** : grabadora *f* — **recording** [-ɪŋ] *n* : disco *m* — **record player** *n* : tocadiscos *m*
recount[1] [ri'kaʊnt] *vt* NARRATE : narrar, relatar
recount[2] ['ri:ˌkaʊnt, ˌri'-] *vt* : volver a contar (votos, etc.) **~** — *n* : recuento *m*
recourse ['ri:ˌkors, ri'-] *n* **1** : recurso *m* **2 have ~ to** : recurrir a
recover [ri'kʌvər] *vt* : recobrar — *vi* RECUPERATE : recuperarse — **recovery** [ri'kʌvəri] *n, pl* **-eries** : recuperación *f*
recreation [ˌrɛkri'eɪʃən] *n* : recreo *m* — **recreational** [ˌrɛkri'eɪʃənəl] *adj* : de recreo
recruit [ri'kru:t] *vt* : reclutar — **~** *n* : recluta *mf* — **recruitment** [ri'kru:tmənt] *n* : reclutamiento *m*
rectangle ['rɛkˌtæŋgəl] *n* : rectángulo *m* — **rectangular** [rɛk'tæŋgjələr] *adj* : rectangular
rectify ['rɛktəˌfaɪ] *vt* **-fied; -fying** : rectificar
rector ['rɛktər] *n* **1** : parroco *m* (clérigo) **2** : rector *m*, -tora *f* (de una universidad) — **rectory** ['rɛktəri] *n, pl* **-ries** : rectoría *f*
rectum ['rɛktəm] *n, pl* **-tums** *or* **-ta** [-tə] : recto *m*
recuperate [ri'ku:pəˌreɪt, -'kju:-] *v* **-ated; -ating** *vt* : recuperar — *vi* : recuperarse — **recuperation** [riˌku:pə'reɪʃən, -ˌkju:-] *n* : recuperación *f*
recur [ri'kər] *vi* **-curred; -curring** : repetirse — **recurrence** [ri'kərənts] *n* : repetición *f* — **recurrent** [ri'kərənt] *adj* : que se repite
recycle [ri'saɪkəl] *vt* **-cled; -cling** : reciclar
red ['rɛd] *adj* : rojo — **~** *n* : rojo *m* — **redden** ['rɛdən] *vt* : enrojecer — *vi* : enrojecerse — **reddish** ['rɛdɪʃ] *adj* : rojizo
redecorate [ˌri:'dɛkəˌreɪt] *vt* **-rated; -rating** : pintar de nuevo
redeem [ri'di:m] *vt* **1** SAVE : salvar,

rescatar **2** : desempeñar (de un monte de piedad) **3** : canjear (cupones, etc.) — **redemption** [ri'dɛmpʃən] *n* : redención *f*

red–handed ['rɛd'hændəd] *adv or adj* : con las manos en la masa

redhead ['rɛd,hɛd] *n* : pelirrojo *m*, -ja *f*

red–hot ['rɛd'hɑt] *adj* : al rojo vivo

redness ['rɛdnəs] *n* : rojez *f*

redo [,ri:'du:] *vt* **-did** [-dɪd]; **-done** [-'dʌn]; **-doing** : hacer de nuevo

redouble [ri'dʌbəl] *vt* **-bled; -bling** : redoblar

red tape *n* : papeleo *m*

reduce [ri'du:s, -'dju:s] *v* **-duced; -ducing** *vt* : reducir — *vi* SLIM : adelgazar — **reduction** [ri'dʌkʃən] *n* : reducción *f*

redundant [ri'dʌndənt] *adj* : redundante

reed ['ri:d] *n* **1** : caña *f* **2** : lengüeta *f* (de un instrumento)

reef ['ri:f] *n* : arrecife *m*

reek ['ri:k] *vi* : apestar

reel ['ri:l] *n* : carrete *m* (de hilo, etc.) — **~** *vt* **1** **~ in** : enrollar (un sedal), sacar (un pez) del agua **2** **~ off** : enumerar — *vi* **1** SPIN : dar vueltas **2** STAGGER : tambalearse

reestablish [,ri:ɪ'stæblɪʃ] *vt* : restablecer

refer [ri'fər] *v* **-ferred; -ferring** *vt* **1** DIRECT : enviar, mandar **2** SUBMIT : remitir — *vi* **~ to** **1** MENTION : referirse a **2** CONSULT : consultar

referee [,rɛfə'ri:] *n* : árbitro *m*, -tra *f* — **~** *v* **-eed; -eeing** : arbitrar

reference ['rɛfrənts, 'rɛfə-] *n* **1** : referencia *f* **2** CONSULTATION : consulta *f* **3** *or* **~ book** : libro *m* de consulta **4** **in ~ to** : con referencia a

refill [,ri:'fɪl] *vt* : rellenar — **~** ['ri:,fɪl] *n* : recambio *m*

refine [ri'faɪn] *vt* **-fined; -fining** : refinar — **refined** [ri'faɪnd] *adj* : refinado — **refinement** [ri'faɪnmənt] *n* : refinamiento *m* — **refinery** [ri'faɪnəri] *n, pl* **-eries** : refinería *f*

reflect [ri'flɛkt] *vt* : reflejar — *vi* **1** : reflejarse **2** **~ badly on** : desacreditar **3** **~ upon** : reflexionar sobre — **reflection** [ri'flɛkʃən] *n* **1** : reflexión *f* **2** IMAGE : reflejo *m* — **reflector** [ri'flɛktər] *n* : reflector *m*

reflex ['ri:,flɛks] *n* : reflejo *m*

reflexive [ri'flɛksɪv] *adj* : reflexivo

reform [ri'fɔrm] *vt* : reformar — *vi* : reformarse — **~** *n* : reforma *f* — **reformer** [ri'fɔrmər] *n* : reformador *m*, -dora *f*

refrain[1] [ri'freɪn] *vi* **~ from** : abstenerse de

refrain[2] *n* : estribillo *m* (en música)

refresh [ri'frɛʃ] *vt* : refrescar — **refreshments** [ri'frɛʃmənts] *npl* : refrigerio *m*

refrigerate [ri'frɪdʒə,reɪt] *vt* **-ated; -ating** : refrigerar — **refrigeration** [ri,frɪdʒə'reɪʃən] *n* : refrigeración *f* — **refrigerator** [ri'frɪdʒə,reɪt̬ər] *n* : nevera *f*, refrigerador *m Lat*, frigorífico *m Spain*

refuel [ri:'fju:əl] *v* **-eled** *or* **-elled; -eling** *or* **-elling** *vt* : llenar de carburante — *vi* : repostar

refuge ['rɛ,fju:dʒ] *n* : refugio *m* — **refugee** [,rɛfjʊ'dʒi:] *n* : refugiado *m*, -da *f*

refund [ri'fʌnd, 'ri:,fʌnd] *vt* : reembolsar — **~** ['ri:,fʌnd] *n* : reembolso *m*

refurbish [ri'fərbɪʃ] *vt* : renovar, restaurar

refuse[1] [ri'fju:z] *v* **-fused; -fusing** *vt* **1** : rehusar, rechazar **2** **~ to do sth** : negarse a hacer algo — *vi* : negarse — **refusal** [ri'fju:zəl] *n* : negativa *f*

refuse[2] ['rɛ,fju:s, -,fju:z] *n* : residuos *mpl*, desperdicios *mpl*

refute [ri'fju:t] *vt* **-futed; -futing** : refutar

regain [ri:'geɪn] *vt* : recuperar, recobrar

regal ['ri:gəl] *adj* : regio, majestuoso — **regalia** [ri'geɪljə] *n* : ropaje *m*, insignias *fpl*

regard [ri'gɑrd] *n* **1** : consideración *f* **2** ESTEEM : estima *f* **3** **in this ~** : en este sentido **4** **~s** *npl* : saludos *mpl* **5** **with ~ to** : respecto a — **~** *vt* **1** : mirar (con recelo, etc.) **2** HEED : tener en cuenta **3** ESTEEM : estimar **4** **as ~s** : en lo que se refiere a **5** **~ as** : considerar — **regarding** [ri'gɑrdɪŋ] *prep* : respecto a — **regardless** [ri'gɑrdləs] *adv* : a pesar de todo — **regardless of** *prep* **1** : sin tener en cuenta **2** IN SPITE OF : a pesar de

regent ['ri:dʒənt] *n* : regente *mf*

regime [reɪ'ʒi:m, rɪ-] *n* : régimen *m* — **regimen** ['rɛdʒəmən] *n* : régimen *m*

regiment ['rɛdʒəmənt] *n* : regimiento *m*

region ['ri:dʒən] *n* : región *f* — **regional** ['ri:dʒənəl] *adj* : regional

register ['rɛdʒəstər] *n* : registro *m* — **~** *vt* **1** : registrar (a personas), matricular (vehículos) **2** SHOW : marcar, manifestar **3** : certificar (correo) — *vi* ENROLL : inscribirse, matricularse — **registrar** ['rɛdʒə,strɑr] *n* : registrador *m*, -dora *f* oficial — **registration** [,rɛdʒə'streɪʃən] *n* **1** : inscripción *f*, matriculación *f* **2** *or* **~ number** : número *m* de matrícula — **registry** ['rɛdʒəstri] *n, pl* **-tries** : registro *m*

regret [ri'grɛt] *vt* **-gretted; -gretting** : lamentar — **~** *n* **1** REMORSE : arrepentimiento *m* **2** SORROW : pesar *m*

— **regrettable** [ri'grɛt̬əbəl] *adj* : lamentable
regular ['rɛgjələr] *adj* **1** : regular **2** CUSTOMARY : habitual — ~ *n* : cliente *mf* habitual — **regularity** [ˌrɛgjə'lærət̬i] *n, pl* **-ties** : regularidad *f* — **regularly** ['rɛgjələrli] *adv* : regularmente — **regulate** ['rɛgjəˌleɪt] *vt* **-lated; -lating** : regular — **regulation** [ˌrɛgjə'leɪʃən] *n* **1** CONTROL : regulación *f* **2** RULE : regla *f*
rehabilitate [ˌri:hə'bɪləˌteɪt, ˌri:ə-] *vt* **-tated; -tating** : rehabilitar — **rehabilitation** [ˌri:həˌbɪlə'teɪʃən, ˌri:ə-] *n* : rehabilitación *f*
rehearse [ri'hərs] *v* **-hearsed; -hearsing** : ensayar — **rehearsal** [ri'hərsəl] *n* : ensayo *m*
reign ['reɪn] *n* : reinado *m* — ~ *vi* : reinar
reimburse [ˌri:əm'bərs] *vt* **-bursed; -bursing** : reembolsar — **reimbursement** [ˌri:əm'bərsmənt] *n* : reembolso *m*
rein ['reɪn] *n* : rienda *f*
reincarnation [ˌri:ɪnˌkɑr'neɪʃən] *n* : reencarnación *f*
reindeer ['reɪnˌdɪr] *n* : reno *m*
reinforce [ˌri:ən'fors] *vt* **-forced; -forcing** : reforzar — **reinforcement** [ˌri:ən'forsmənt] *n* : refuerzo *m*
reinstate [ˌri:ən'steɪt] *vt* **-stated; -stating** **1** : restablecer **2** : restituir (a algn en su cargo)
reiterate [ri'ɪt̬əˌreɪt] *vt* **-ated; -ating** : reiterar
reject [ri'dʒɛkt] *vt* : rechazar — **rejection** [ri'dʒɛkʃən] *n* : rechazo *m*
rejoice [ri'dʒɔɪs] *vi* **-joiced; -joicing** : regocijarse
rejuvenate [ri'dʒu:vəˌneɪt] *vt* **-nated; -nating** : rejuvenecer
rekindle [ˌri:'kɪndəl] *vt* **-dled; -dling** : reavivar
relapse ['ri:ˌlæps, ri'læps] *n* : recaída *f* — ~ [ri'læps] *vi* **-lapsed; -lapsing** : recaer
relate [ri'leɪt] *v* **-lated; -lating** *vt* **1** TELL : relatar **2** ASSOCIATE : relacionar — *vi* ~ **to** **1** CONCERN : estar relacionado con **2** UNDERSTAND : identificarse con **3** : relacionarse con (socialmente) — **related** [ri'leɪt̬əd] *adj* ~ **to** : emparentado con — **relation** [ri'leɪʃən] *n* **1** CONNECTION : relación *f* **2** RELATIVE : pariente *mf* **3** **in** ~ **to** : en relación con **4** ~**s** *npl* : relaciones *fpl* — **relationship** [ri'leɪʃənˌʃɪp] *n* **1** : relación *f* **2** KINSHIP : parentesco *m* — **relative** ['rɛlət̬ɪv] *n* : pariente *mf* — ~ *adj* : relativo — **relatively** *adv* : relativamente
relax [ri'læks] *vt* : relajar — *vi* : relajarse — **relaxation** [ˌri:ˌlæk'seɪʃən] *n* **1** : relajación *f* **2** RECREATION : esparcimiento *m*
relay ['ri:ˌleɪ] *n* **1** : relevo *m* **2** *or* ~ **race** : carrera *f* de relevos — ~ ['ri:ˌleɪ, ri'leɪ] *vt* **-layed; -laying** : transmitir
release [ri'li:s] *vt* **-leased; -leasing** **1** FREE : liberar, poner en libertad **2** : soltar (un freno, etc.) **3** EMIT : despedir **4** : sacar (un libro, etc.), estrenar (una película) — ~ *n* **1** : liberación *f* **2** : estreno *m* (de una película), publicación *f* (de un libro) **3** : fuga *f* (de gases)
relegate ['rɛləˌgeɪt] *vt* **-gated; -gating** : relegar
relent [ri'lɛnt] *vi* : ceder — **relentless** [ri'lɛntləs] *adj* : implacable
relevant ['rɛləvənt] *adj* : pertinente — **relevance** ['rɛləvənts] *n* : pertinencia *f*
reliable [ri'laɪəbəl] *adj* : fiable (dícese de personas), fidedigno (dícese de información, etc.) — **reliability** [riˌlaɪə'bɪlət̬i] *n, pl* **-ties** : fiabilidad *f* (de una cosa), responsabilidad *f* (de una persona) — **reliance** [ri'laɪənts] *n* **1** : dependencia *f* **2** TRUST : confianza *f* — **reliant** [ri'laɪənt] *adj* : dependente
relic ['rɛlɪk] *n* : reliquia *f*
relief [ri'li:f] *n* **1** : alivio *m* **2** AID : ayuda *f* **3** : relieve *m* (en la escultura) **4** REPLACEMENT : relevo *m* — **relieve** [ri'li:v] *vt* **-lieved; -lieving** **1** : aliviar **2** REPLACE : relevar (a algn) **3** ~ **s.o. of** : liberar a algn de
religion [ri'lɪdʒən] *n* : religión *f* — **religious** [ri'lɪdʒəs] *adj* : religioso
relinquish [ri'lɪŋkwɪʃ, -'lɪn-] *vt* : renunciar a, abandonar
relish ['rɛlɪʃ] *n* **1** : salsa *f* (condimento) **2** **with** ~ : con gusto — ~ *vt* : saborear
relocate [ˌri:'lo:ˌkeɪt, ˌri:lo'keɪt] *vt* **-cated; -cating** : trasladar — *vi* : trasladarse — **relocation** [ˌri:lo'keɪʃən] *n* : traslado *m*
reluctance [ri'lʌktənts] *n* : reticencia *f*, desgana *f* — **reluctant** [ri'lʌktənt] *adj* : reacio, reticente — **reluctantly** [ri'lʌktəntli] *adv* : a regañadientes
rely [ri'laɪ] *vi* **-lied; -lying** ~ **on** **1** DEPEND ON : depender de **2** TRUST : confiar (en)
remain [ri'meɪn] *vi* **1** : quedar **2** STAY : quedarse **3** CONTINUE : seguir, continuar — **remainder** [ri'meɪndər] *n* : resto *m* — **remains** [ri'meɪnz] *npl* : restos *mpl*
remark [ri'mɑrk] *n* : comentario *m*, observación *f* — ~ *vt* : observar — *vi* ~

on : observar — **remarkable** [ri'mɑrkəbəl] *adj* : extraordinario, notable
remedy ['rɛmədi] *n, pl* **-dies** : remedio *m* — ~ *vt* **-died; -dying** : remediar — **remedial** [ri'mi:diəl] *adj* : correctivo
remember [ri'mɛmbər] *vt* **1** : acordarse de, recordar **2** ~ **to** : acordarse de — *vi* : acordarse, recordar — **remembrance** [ri'mɛmbrənts] *n* : recuerdo *m*
remind [ri'maɪnd] *vt* : recordar — **reminder** [ri'maɪndər] *n* : recordatorio *m*
reminiscence [ˌrɛmə'nɪsənts] *n* : recuerdo *m*, reminiscencia *f* — **reminisce** [ˌrɛmə'nɪs] *vi* **-nisced; -niscing** : rememorar los viejos tiempos — **reminiscent** [ˌrɛmə'nɪsənt] *adj* **be ~ of** : recordar
remiss [ri'mɪs] *adj* : negligente, remiso
remit [ri'mɪt] *vt* **-mitted; -mitting 1** PARDON : perdonar **2** : enviar (dinero) — **remission** [ri'mɪʃən] *n* : remisión *f*
remnant ['rɛmnənt] *n* **1** : resto *m* **2** TRACE : vestigio *m*
remorse [ri'mɔrs] *n* : remordimiento *m* — **remorseful** [ri'mɔrsfəl] *adj* : arrepentido
remote [ri'mo:t] *adj* **-moter; -est 1** : remoto **2** ALOOF : distante **3 ~ from** : apartado de, alejado de — **remote control** *n* : control *m* remoto — **remotely** [ri'mo:tli] *adv* SLIGHTLY : remotamente
remove [ri'mu:v] *vt* **-moved; -moving 1** : quitar (una tapa, etc.), quitarse (ropa) **2** EXTRACT : sacar **3** DISMISS : destituir **4** ELIMINATE : eliminar — **removable** [ri'mu:vəbəl] *adj* : separable, de quita y pon — **removal** [ri'mu:vəl] *n* **1** : eliminación *f* **2** EXTRACTION : extracción *f*
remunerate [ri'mju:nəˌreɪt] *vt* **-ated; -ating** : remunerar
render ['rɛndər] *vt* **1** : rendir (homenaje), prestar (ayuda) **2** MAKE : hacer **3** TRANSLATE : traducir
rendezvous ['rɑndɪˌvu:, -deɪ-] *ns & pl* : cita *f*
rendition [rɛn'dɪʃən] *n* : interpretación *f*
renegade ['rɛnɪˌgeɪd] *n* : renegado *m*, -da *f*
renew [ri'nu:, -'nju:] *vt* **1** : renovar **2** RESUME : reanudar — **renewal** [ri'nu:əl, -'nju:-] *n* : renovación *f*
renounce [ri'naʊnts] *vt* **-nounced; -nouncing** : renunciar a
renovate ['rɛnəˌveɪt] *vt* **-vated; -vating** : renovar — **renovation** [ˌrɛnə'veɪʃən] *n* : renovación *f*
renown [ri'naʊn] *n* : renombre *m* — **renowned** [ri'naʊnd] *adj* : célebre, renombrado
rent ['rɛnt] *n* **1** : alquiler *m*, arrendamiento *m*, renta *f* **2 for ~** : se alquila — ~ *vt* : alquilar — **rental** ['rɛntəl] *n* : alquiler *m* — ~ *adj* : de alquiler — **renter** ['rɛntər] *n* : arrendatario *m*, -ria *f*
renunciation [riˌnʌntsi'eɪʃən] *n* : renuncia *f*
reopen [ˌri:'o:pən] *vt* : volver a abrir
reorganize [ˌri:'ɔrgənˌaɪz] *vt* **-nized; -nizing** : reorganizar — **reorganization** [ˌri:ˌɔrgənə'zeɪʃən] *n* : reorganización *f*
repair [ri'pær] *vt* : reparar, arreglar — ~ *n* **1** : reparación *f*, arreglo *m* **2 in bad ~** : en mal estado
repay [ri'peɪ] *vt* **-paid; -paying 1** : devolver (dinero), pagar (una deuda) **2** : corresponder a (un favor, etc.)
repeal [ri'pi:l] *vt* : abrogar, revocar — ~ *n* : abrogación *f*, revocación *f*
repeat [ri'pi:t] *vt* : repetir — ~ *n* : repetición *f* — **repeatedly** [ri'pi:ţədli] *adv* : repetidas veces
repel [ri'pɛl] *vt* **-pelled; -pelling** : repeler — **repellent** [ri'pɛlənt] *n* : repelente *m*
repent [ri'pɛnt] *vi* : arrepentirse — **repentance** [ri'pɛntənts] *n* : arrepentimiento *m*
repercussion [ˌri:pər'kʌʃən, ˌrɛpər-] *n* : repercusión *f*
repertoire ['rɛpərˌtwɑr] *n* : repertorio *m*
repetition [ˌrɛpə'tɪʃən] *n* : repetición *f* — **repetitious** [ˌrɛpə'tɪʃəs] *adj* : repetitivo — **repetitive** [ri'pɛţəţɪv] *adj* : repetitivo
replace [ri'pleɪs] *vt* **-placed; -placing 1** : reponer **2** SUBSTITUTE : reemplazar, sustituir **3** EXCHANGE : cambiar — **replacement** [ri'pleɪsmənt] *n* **1** : sustitución *f* **2** : sustituto *m*, -ta *f* (persona) **3** *or* **~ part** : repuesto *m*
replenish [ri'plɛnɪʃ] *vt* **1** : reponer **2** REFILL : rellenar
replete [ri'pli:t] *adj* **~ with** : repleto de
replica ['rɛplɪkə] *n* : réplica *f*
reply [ri'plaɪ] *vi* **-plied; -plying** : contestar, responder — ~ *n, pl* **-plies** : respuesta *f*
report [ri'port] *n* **1** : informe *m* **2** RUMOR : rumor *m* **3** *or* **news ~** : reportaje *m* **4 weather ~** : boletín *m* meteorológico — ~ *vt* **1** RELATE : anunciar **2 ~ a crime** : denunciar un delito **3** *or* **~ on** : informar sobre — *vi* **1** : informar **2 ~ for duty** : presentarse — **report card** *n* : boletín *m* de calificaciones — **reportedly** [ri'porţədli] *adv*

: según se dice — **reporter** [ri'port̬ər] *n* : periodista *mf;* reportero *m,* -ra *f*
repose [ri'po:z] *vi* **-posed; -posing** : reposar — ~ *n* : reposo *m*
reprehensible [ˌrɛpri'hɛntsəbəl] *adj* : reprensible
represent [ˌrɛprɪ'zɛnt] *vt* **1** : representar **2** PORTRAY : presentar — **representation** [ˌrɛprɪˌzɛn'teɪʃən, -zən-] *n* : representación *f* — **representative** [ˌrɛprɪ'zɛntət̬ɪv] *adj* : representativo — ~ *n* : representante *mf*
repress [ri'prɛs] *vt* : reprimir — **repression** [ri'prɛʃən] *n* : represión *f*
reprieve [ri'pri:v] *n* : indulto *m*
reprimand ['rɛprəˌmænd] *n* : reprimenda *f* — ~ *vt* : reprender
reprint [ri'prɪnt] *vt* : reimprimir — ~ ['ri:ˌprɪnt, ri'prɪnt] *n* : reedición *f*
reprisal [ri'praɪzəl] *n* : represalia *f*
reproach [ri'pro:tʃ] *n* **1** : reproche *m* **2 beyond** ~ : irreprochable — ~ *vt* : reprochar — **reproachful** [ri'pro:tʃfəl] *adj* : de reproche
reproduce [ˌri:prə'du:s, -'dju:s] *v* **-duced; -ducing** *vt* : reproducir — *vi* : reproducirse — **reproduction** [ˌri:prə'dʌkʃən] *n* : reproducción *f* — **reproductive** [ˌri:prə'dʌktɪv] *adj* : reproductor
reproof [ri'pru:f] *n* : reprobación *f*
reptile ['rɛpˌtaɪl] *n* : reptil *m*
republic [ri'pʌblɪk] *n* : república *f* — **republican** [ri'pʌblɪkən] *n* : republicano *m,* -na *f* — ~ *adj* : republicano
repudiate [ri'pju:diˌeɪt] *vt* **-ated; -ating** : repudiar
repugnant [ri'pʌgnənt] *adj* : repugnante, asqueroso — **repugnance** [ri'pʌgnənts] *n* : repugnancia *f*
repulse [ri'pʌls] *vt* **-pulsed; -pulsing** : repeler, rechazar — **repulsive** [ri'pʌlsɪv] *adj* : repulsivo
reputation [ˌrɛpjə'teɪʃən] *n* : reputación *f* — **reputable** ['rɛpjət̬əbəl] *adj* : de confianza, acreditado — **reputed** [ri'pju:t̬əd] *adj* : supuesto
request [ri'kwɛst] *n* : petición *f* — ~ *vt* : pedir
requiem ['rɛkwiəm, 'reɪ-] *n* : réquiem *m*
require [ri'kwaɪr] *vt* **-quired; -quiring 1** CALL FOR : requerir **2** NEED : necesitar — **requirement** [ri'kwaɪrmənt] *n* **1** NEED : necesidad *f* **2** DEMAND : requisito *m* — **requisite** ['rɛkwəzɪt] *adj* : necesario
resale ['ri:ˌseɪl, ˌri:'seɪl] *n* : reventa *f*
rescind [ri'sɪnd] *vt* : rescindir (un contrato), revocar (una ley, etc.)
rescue ['rɛsˌkju:] *vt* **-cued; -cuing** : rescatar, salvar — ~ *n* : rescate *m* — **rescuer** ['rɛskjuər] *n* : salvador *m,* -dora *f*
research [ri'sərtʃ, 'ri:ˌsərtʃ] *n* : investigación *f* — ~ *vt* : investigar — **researcher** [ri'sərtʃər, 'ri:ˌ-] *n* : investigador *m,* -dora *f*
resemble [ri'zɛmbəl] *vt* **-sembled; -sembling** : parecerse a — **resemblance** [ri'zɛmbləns] *n* : parecido *m*
resent [ri'zɛnt] *vt* : resentirse de, ofenderse por — **resentful** [ri'zɛntfəl] *adj* : resentido — **resentment** [ri'zɛntmənt] *n* : resentimiento *m*
reserve [ri'zərv] *vt* **-served; -serving** : reservar — ~ *n* **1** : reserva *f* **2** ~**s** *npl* : reservas *fpl* (militares) — **reservation** [ˌrɛzər'veɪʃən] *n* : reserva *f* — **reserved** [ri'zərvd] *adj* : reservado — **reservoir** ['rɛzərˌvwɑr, -ˌvwɔr, -ˌvɔr] *n* : embalse *m*
reset [ˌri:'sɛt] *vt* **-set; -setting** : volver a poner (un reloj, etc.)
residence ['rɛzədənts] *n* : residencia *f* — **reside** [ri'zaɪd] *vi* **-sided; -siding** : residir — **resident** ['rɛzədənt] *adj* : residente — ~ *n* : residente *mf* — **residential** [ˌrɛzə'dɛntʃəl] *adj* : residencial
residue ['rɛzəˌdu:, -ˌdju:] *n* : residuo *m*
resign [ri'zaɪn] *vt* **1** QUIT : dimitir **2** ~ **oneself to** : resignarse a — **resignation** [ˌrɛzɪg'neɪʃən] *n* **1** : dimisión *f* **2** ACCEPTANCE : resignación *f*
resilient [ri'zɪljənt] *adj* **1** : resistente (dícese de personas) **2** ELASTIC : elástico — **resilience** [ri'zɪljənts] *n* **1** : resistencia *f* **2** ELASTICITY : elasticidad *f*
resin ['rɛzən] *n* : resina *f*
resist [ri'zɪst] *vt* : resistir — *vi* : resistirse — **resistance** [ri'zɪstənts] *n* : resistencia *f* — **resistant** [ri'zɪstənt] *adj* : resistente
resolve [ri'zɑlv] *vt* **-solved; -solving** : resolver — ~ *n* : resolución *f* — **resolution** [ˌrɛzə'lu:ʃən] *n* **1** : resolución *f* **2** DECISION, INTENTION : propósito *m* — **resolute** ['rɛzəˌlu:t] *adj* : resuelto
resonance ['rɛzənənts] *n* : resonancia *f* — **resonant** ['rɛzənənt] *adj* : resonante
resort [ri'zɔrt] *n* **1** RECOURSE : recurso *m* **2** *or* **tourist** ~ : centro *m* turístico — ~ *vi* ~ **to** : recurrir a
resounding [ri'zaʊndɪŋ] *adj* **1** RESONANT : resonante **2** ABSOLUTE : rotundo
resource ['ri:ˌsors, ri'sors] *n* : recurso *m* — **resourceful** [ri'sorsfəl, -'zors-] *adj* : ingenioso
respect [ri'spɛkt] *n* **1** ESTEEM : respeto *m* **2 in some** ~**s** : en algún sentido **3 pay one's** ~**s** : presentar uno sus re-

spetos **4 with ~ to** : (con) respecto a — ~ *vt* : respetar — **respectable** [ri'spɛktəbəl] *adj* : respetable — **respectful** [ri'spɛktfəl] *adj* : respetuoso — **respective** [ri'spɛktɪv] *adj* : respectivo — **respectively** *adv* : respectivamente

respiration [ˌrɛspə'reɪʃən] *n* : respiración *f* — **respiratory** ['rɛspərəˌtori, rɪ'spaɪrə-] *adj* : respiratorio

respite ['rɛspɪt, rɪ'spaɪt] *n* : respiro *m*

response [ri'spɑnts] *n* : respuesta *f* — **respond** [ri'spɑnd] *vi* : responder — **responsibility** [riˌspɑntsə'bɪləṭi] *n, pl* **-ties** : responsabilidad *f* — **responsible** [ri'spɑntsəbəl] *adj* : responsable — **responsive** [ri'spɑntsɪv] *adj* : sensible, receptivo

rest[1] ['rɛst] *n* **1** : descanso *m* **2** SUPPORT : apoyo *m* **3** : silencio *m* (en música) — ~ *vi* **1** : descansar **2** LEAN : apoyarse **3 ~ on** DEPEND ON : depender de — *vt* **1** RELAX : descansar **2** LEAN : apoyar

rest[2] *n* REMAINDER : resto *m*

restaurant ['rɛstəˌrɑnt, -rənt] *n* : restaurante *m*

restful ['rɛstfəl] *adj* : tranquilo, apacible

restitution [ˌrɛstə'tu:ʃən, -'tju:-] *n* : restitución *f*

restless ['rɛstləs] *adj* : inquieto, agitado

restore [ri'stor] *vt* **-stored; -storing 1** RETURN : devolver **2** REESTABLISH : restablecer **3** REPAIR : restaurar — **restoration** [ˌrɛstə'reɪʃən] *n* **1** : restablecimiento *m* **2** REPAIR : restauración *f*

restrain [ri'streɪn] *vt* **1** : contener **2 ~ oneself** : contenerse — **restrained** [ri'streɪnd] *adj* : comedido, moderado — **restraint** [ri'streɪnt] *n* **1** : restricción *f* **2** SELF-CONTROL : moderación *f*, control *m* de sí mismo

restriction [ri'strɪkʃən] *n* : restricción *f* — **restrict** [ri'strɪkt] *vt* : restringir — **restricted** [ri'strɪktəd] *adj* : restringido — **restrictive** [ri'strɪktɪv] *adj* : restrictivo

result [ri'zʌlt] *vi* : resultar — ~ *n* **1** : resultado *m* **2 as a ~ of** : como consecuencia de

resume [ri'zu:m] *v* **-sumed; -suming** *vt* : reanudar — *vi* : reanudarse

résumé *or* **resume** *or* **resumé** ['rɛzəˌmeɪ, ˌrɛzə'-] *n* : currículum *m* (vitae)

resumption [ri'zʌmpʃən] *n* : reanudación *f*

resurgence [ri'sərdʒənts] *n* : resurgimiento *m*

resurrection [ˌrɛzə'rɛkʃən] *n* : resurrección *f* — **resurrect** [ˌrɛzə'rɛkt] *vt* : resucitar

resuscitate [ri'sʌsəˌteɪt] *vt* **-tated; -tating** : resucitar

retail ['ri:ˌteɪl] *vt* : vender al por menor — ~ *n* : venta *f* al por menor — ~ *adj* : detallista, minorista — ~ *adv* : al detalle, al por menor — **retailer** ['ri:ˌteɪlər] *n* : detallista *mf*, minorista *mf*

retain [ri'teɪn] *vt* : retener

retaliate [ri'tæliˌeɪt] *vi* **-ated; -ating** : tomar represalias — **retaliation** [riˌtæli'eɪʃən] *n* : represalias *fpl*

retard [ri'tɑrd] *vt* : retardar, retrasar — **retarded** [ri'tɑrdəd] *adj* : retrasado

retention [ri'tɛntʃən] *n* : retención *f*

reticence ['rɛṭəsənts] *n* : reticencia *f* — **reticent** ['rɛṭəsənt] *adj* : reticente

retina ['rɛtənə] *n, pl* **-nas** *or* **-nae** [-əni, -əˌnaɪ] : retina *f*

retinue ['rɛtənˌu:, -ju:] *n* : séquito *m*

retire [ri'taɪr] *vi* **-tired; -tiring 1** WITHDRAW : retirarse **2** : jubilarse, retirarse (de un trabajo) **3** : acostarse (en la cama) — **retirement** [ri'taɪrmənt] *n* : jubilación *f* — **retiring** [ri'taɪrɪŋ] *adj* SHY : retraído

retort [ri'tɔrt] *vt* : replicar — ~ *n* : réplica *f*

retrace [ˌri:'treɪs] *vt* **-traced; -tracing ~ one's steps** : volver sobre sus pasos

retract [ri'trækt] *vt* **1** WITHDRAW : retirar **2** : retraer (garras, etc.) — *vi* : retractarse

retrain [ˌri:'treɪn] *vt* : reciclar

retreat [ri'tri:t] *n* **1** : retirada *f* **2** REFUGE : refugio *m* — ~ *vi* : retirarse

retribution [ˌrɛtrə'bju:ʃən] *n* : castigo *m*

retrieve [ri'tri:v] *vt* **-trieved; -trieving 1** : cobrar, recuperar **2** RESCUE : salvar — **retrieval** [ri'tri:vəl] *n* : recuperación *f* — **retriever** [ri'tri:vər] *n* : perro *m* cobrador

retroactive [ˌrɛtro'æktɪv] *adj* : retroactivo

retrospect ['rɛtrəˌspɛkt] *n* **in ~** : mirando hacia atrás — **retrospective** [ˌrɛtrə'spɛktɪv] *adj* : retrospectivo

return [ri'tərn] *vi* **1** : volver, regresar **2** REAPPEAR : reaparecer — *vt* **1** : devolver **2** YIELD : producir — ~ *n* **1** : regreso *m*, vuelta *f* **2** : devolución *f* (de algo prestado) **3** YIELD : rendimiento *m* **4 in ~ for** : a cambio de **5** *or* **tax ~** : declaración *f* de impuestos — ~ *adj* : de vuelta

reunite [ˌri:jʊ'naɪt] *vt* **-nited; -niting** : reunir — **reunion** [ri'ju:njən] *n* : reunión *f*

revamp [ˌri'væmp] *vt* : renovar

reveal [ri'vi:l] *vt* **1** : revelar **2** SHOW : dejar ver

revel ['rɛvəl] *vi* **-eled** *or* **-elled; -eling** *or* **-elling ~ in** : deleitarse en
revelation [ˌrɛvə'leɪʃən] *n* : revelación *f*
revelry ['rɛvəlri] *n, pl* **-ries** : jolgorio *m,* regocijos *mpl*
revenge [ri'vɛndʒ] *vt* **-venged; -venging** : vengar — **~** *n* **1** : venganza *f* **2 take ~ on** : vengarse de
revenue ['rɛvəˌnu:, -ˌnju:] *n* : ingresos *mpl*
reverberate [ri'vərbəˌreɪt] *vi* **-ated; -ating** : retumbar, resonar
reverence ['rɛvərənts] *n* : reverencia *f,* veneración *f* — **revere** [ri'vɪr] *vt* **-vered; -vering** : venerar — **reverend** ['rɛvərənd] *adj* : reverendo — **reverent** ['rɛvərənt] *adj* : reverente
reverie ['rɛvəri] *n, pl* **-eries** : ensueño *m*
reverse [ri'vərs] *adj* : inverso, contrario — **~** *v* **-versed; -versing** *vt* **1** : invertir **2** : cambiar (una política), revocar (una decisión) **3** : dar marcha atrás a (un automóvil) — *vi* : invertirse — **~** *n* **1** BACK : dorso *m,* revés *m* **2** *or* **~ gear** : marcha *f* atrás **3 the ~** : lo contrario — **reversible** [ri'vərsəbəl] *adj* : reversible — **reversal** ['rɛvərsəl] *n* **1** : inversión *f* **2** CHANGE : cambio *m* total **3** SETBACK : revés *m* — **revert** [ri'vərt] *vi* : revertir
review [ri'vju:] *n* **1** : revisión *f* **2** OVERVIEW : resumen *m* **3** CRITIQUE : reseña *f,* crítica *f* **4** : repaso *m* (para un examen) — **~** *vt* **1** EXAMINE : examinar **2** : repasar (una lección) **3** CRITIQUE : reseñar — **reviewer** [ri'vju:ər] *n* : crítico *m,* -ca *f*
revile [ri'vaɪl] *vt* **-viled; -viling** : injuriar
revise [ri'vaɪz] *vt* **-vised; -vising 1** : modificar (una política, etc.) **2** : revisar, corregir (una publicación) — **revision** [ri'vɪʒən] *n* : corrección *f,* modificación *f*
revive [ri'vaɪv] *v* **-vived; -viving** *vt* **1** : reanimar, reactivar **2** : resucitar (a una persona) **3** RESTORE : restablecer — *vi* **1** : reanimarse, reactivarse **2** COME TO : volver en sí — **revival** [ri'vaɪvəl] *n* : reanimación *f,* reactivación *f*
revoke [ri'vo:k] *vt* **-voked; -voking** : revocar
revolt [ri'vo:lt] *vi* : rebelarse, sublevarse — *vt* : dar asco a — **~** *n* : revuelta *f,* sublevación *f* — **revolting** [ri'vo:ltɪŋ] *adj* : asqueroso
revolution [ˌrɛvə'lu:ʃən] *n* : revolución *f* — **revolutionary** [ˌrɛvə'lu:ʃəˌnɛri] *adj* : revolucionario — **~** *n, pl* **-aries** : revolucionario *m,* -ria *f* — **revolutionize** [ˌrɛvə'lu:ʃəˌnaɪz] *vt* **-ized; -izing** : revolucionar
revolve [ri'vɑlv] *v* **-volved; -volving** *vt* : hacer girar — *vi* : girar
revolver [ri'vɑlvər] *n* : revólver *m*
revue [ri'vju:] *n* : revista *f* (teatral)
revulsion [ri'vʌlʃən] *n* : repugnancia *f*
reward [ri'wɔrd] *vt* : recompensar — **~** *n* : recompensa *f*
rewrite [ˌri:'raɪt] *vt* **-wrote; -written; -writing** : volver a escribir
rhetoric ['rɛt̬ərɪk] *n* : retórica *f* — **rhetorical** [rɪ'tɔrɪkəl] *adj* : retórico
rheumatism ['ru:məˌtɪzəm, 'rʊ-] *n* : reumatismo *m* — **rheumatic** [rʊ'mæt̬ɪk] *adj* : reumático
rhino ['raɪˌno:] *n, pl* **-no** *or* **-nos** → **rhinoceros** — **rhinoceros** [raɪ'nɑsərəs] *n, pl* **-noceroses** *or* **-noceros** *or* **-noceri** [-ˌraɪ] : rinoceronte *m*
rhubarb ['ru:ˌbɑrb] *n* : ruibarbo *m*
rhyme ['raɪm] *n* **1** : rima *f* **2** VERSE : verso *m* (en rima) — **~** *vi* **rhymed; rhyming** : rimar
rhythm ['rɪðəm] *n* : ritmo *m* — **rhythmic** ['rɪðmɪk] *or* **rhythmical** [-mɪkəl] *adj* : rítmico
rib ['rɪb] *n* : costilla *f* — **~** *vt* TEASE : tomar el pelo a
ribbon ['rɪbən] *n* : cinta *f*
rice ['raɪs] *n* : arroz *m*
rich ['rɪtʃ] *adj* **1** : rico **2 ~ foods** : comidas *fpl* pesadas — **riches** ['rɪtʃəz] *npl* : riquezas *fpl* — **richness** ['rɪtʃnəs] *n* : riqueza *f*
rickety ['rɪkət̬i] *adj* : desvencijado, destartalado
ricochet ['rɪkəˌʃeɪ, -ʃɛt] *n* : rebote *m* — **~** *vi* **-cheted** [-ʃeɪd] *or* **-chetted** [-ʃɛt̬əd]; **-cheting** [-ʃeɪɪŋ] *or* **-chetting** [-ʃɛt̬ɪŋ] : rebotar
rid ['rɪd] *vt* **rid; ridding 1** : librar **2 get ~ of** : deshacerse de — **riddance** ['rɪdənts] *n* **good ~!** : ¡adiós y buen viaje!
riddle[1] ['rɪdəl] *n* : acertijo *m,* adivinanza *f*
riddle[2] *vt* **-dled; -dling 1** : acribillar **2 riddled with** : lleno de
ride ['raɪd] *v* **rode** ['ro:d]; **ridden** ['rɪdən]; **riding** *vt* **1** : montar (a caballo, en bicicleta), ir (en autobús, etc.) **2** TRAVERSE : recorrer — *vi* **1** *or* **~ horseback** : montar a caballo **2** : ir (en auto, etc.) — **~** *n* **1** : paseo *m,* vuelta *f* **2** : aparato *m* (en un parque de diversiones) — **rider** ['raɪdər] *n* **1** : jinete *mf* (a caballo) **2** CYCLIST : ciclista *mf,* motociclista *mf*
ridge ['rɪdʒ] *n* : cadena *f* (de montañas)
ridiculous [rə'dɪkjələs] *adj* : ridículo — **ridicule** ['rɪdəˌkju:l] *n* : burlas *fpl* — **~** *vt* **-culed; -culing** : ridiculizar

rife ['raɪf] *adj* **1** : extendido **2 be ~ with** : estar plagado de
rifle[1] ['raɪfəl] *vi* **-fled; -fling ~ through** : revolver
rifle[2] *n* : rifle *m,* fusil *m*
rift ['rɪft] *n* **1** : grieta *f* **2** : ruptura *f* (entre personas)
rig[1] ['rɪg] *vt* : amañar (una elección)
rig[2] *vt* **rigged; rigging 1** : aparejar (un barco) **2** EQUIP : equipar **3** *or* **~ out** DRESS : vestir **4** *or* **~ up** CONSTRUCT : construir — **~** *n* **1** : aparejo *m* (de un barco) **2** *or* **oil ~** : plataforma *f* petrolífera — **rigging** ['rɪgɪŋ, -gən] *n* : aparejo *m*
right ['raɪt] *adj* **1** JUST : bueno, justo **2** CORRECT : correcto **3** APPROPRIATE : apropiado, adecuado **4** STRAIGHT : recto **5 be ~** : tener razón **6** → **right–hand** — **~** *n* **1** GOOD : bien *m* **2** ENTITLEMENT : derecho *m* **3 on the ~** : a la derecha **4** *or* **~ side** : derecha *f* — **~** *adv* **1** WELL : bien **2** PRECISELY : justo **3** DIRECTLY : derecho **4** IMMEDIATELY : inmediatamente **5** COMPLETELY : completamente **6** *or* **to the ~** : a la derecha — **~** *vt* **1** STRAIGHTEN : enderezar **2 ~ a wrong** : reparar un daño — **right angle** *n* : ángulo *m* recto — **righteous** ['raɪtʃəs] *adj* : recto, honrado — **rightful** ['raɪt̬fəl] *adj* : legítimo — **right–hand** ['raɪt'hænd] *adj* : derecho — **right–handed** ['raɪt'hændəd] *adj* : diestro — **rightly** ['raɪtli] *adv* **1** : justamente **2** CORRECTLY : correctamente — **right–wing** ['raɪt'wɪŋ] *adj* : derechista
rigid ['rɪdʒɪd] *adj* : rígido
rigor *or Brit* **rigour** ['rɪgər] *n* : rigor *m* — **rigorous** ['rɪgərəs] *adj* : riguroso
rim ['rɪm] *n* **1** EDGE : borde *m* **2** : llanta *f* (de una rueda) **3** : montura *f* (de anteojos)
rind ['raɪnd] *n* : corteza *f*
ring[1] ['rɪŋ] *v* **rang** ['ræŋ]; **rung** ['rʌŋ]; **ringing** *vi* **1** : sonar (dícese de un timbre, etc.) **2** RESOUND : resonar — *vt* : tocar (un timbre, etc.) — **~** *n* **1** : toque *m* (de un timbre, etc.) **2** CALL : llamada *f* (por teléfono)
ring[2] *n* **1** : anillo *m,* sortija *f* **2** BAND, HOOP : aro *m* **3** CIRCLE : círculo *m* **4** *or* **boxing ~** : cuadrilátero *m* **5** NETWORK : red *f* — **~** *vt* : cercar, rodear — **ringleader** ['rɪŋˌli:dər] *n* : cabecilla *mf*
ringlet ['rɪŋlət] *n* : rizo *m,* bucle *m*
rink ['rɪŋk] *n* : pista *f* (de patinaje)
rinse ['rɪnts] *vt* **rinsed; rinsing** : enjuagar — **~** *n* : enjuague *m*
riot ['raɪət] *n* : disturbio *m* — **~** *vi* : causar disturbios — **rioter** ['raɪət̬ər] *n* : alborotador *m,* -dora *f*
rip ['rɪp] *v* **ripped; ripping** *vt* **1** : rasgar, desgarrar **2 ~ off** : arrancar — *vi* : rasgarse — **~** *n* : rasgón *m,* desgarrón *m*
ripe ['raɪp] *adj* **riper; ripest 1** : maduro **2 ~ for** : listo por — **ripen** ['raɪpən] *v* : madurar — **ripeness** ['raɪpnəs] *n* : madurez *f*
rip–off ['rɪpˌɔf] *n* : timo *m fam*
ripple ['rɪpəl] *v* **-pled; -pling** *vi* : rizarse (dícese de agua) — *vt* : rizar — **~** *n* : onda *f,* rizo *m*
rise ['raɪz] *vi* **rose** ['ro:z]; **risen** ['rɪzən]; **rising 1** GET UP : levantarse **2** : salir (dícese del sol, etc.) **3** ASCEND : subir **4** INCREASE : aumentar **5 ~ up** REBEL : sublevarse — **~** *n* **1** ASCENT : subida *f* **2** INCREASE : aumento *m* **3** SLOPE : cuesta *f* — **riser** ['raɪzər] *n* **1 early ~** : madrugador *m,* -dora *f* **2 late ~** : dormilón *m,* -lona *f*
risk ['rɪsk] *n* : riesgo *m* — **~** *vt* : arriesgar — **risky** ['rɪski] *adj* **riskier; -est** : arriesgado, riesgoso *Lat*
rite ['raɪt] *n* : rito *m* — **ritual** ['rɪtʃʊəl] *adj* : ritual — **~** *n* : ritual *m*
rival ['raɪvəl] *n* : rival *mf* — **~** *adj* : rival — **~** *vt* **-valed** *or* **-valled; -valing** *or* **-valling** : rivalizar con — **rivalry** ['raɪvəlri] *n, pl* **-ries** : rivalidad *f*
river ['rɪvər] *n* : río *m*
rivet ['rɪvət] *n* : remache *m* — **~** *vt* **1** : remachar **2** FIX : fijar (los ojos, etc.) **3 be ~ed by** : estar fascinado con
roach ['ro:tʃ] → **cockroach**
road ['ro:d] *n* **1** : carretera *f* **2** STREET : calle *f* **3** PATH : camino *m* — **roadblock** ['ro:dˌblɑk] *n* : control *m* — **roadside** ['ro:dˌsaɪd] *n* : borde *m* de la carretera — **roadway** ['ro:dˌweɪ] *n* : carretera *f*
roam ['ro:m] *vi* : vagar — *vt* : vagar por
roar ['ror] *vi* **1** : rugir **2 ~ with laughter** : reírse a carcajadas — *vt* : decir a gritos — **~** *n* : rugido *m* (de un animal), estruendo *m* (de un avión, etc.)
roast ['ro:st] *vt* : asar (carne, etc.), tostar (café, etc.) — *vi* : asarse — **~** *n* : asado *m* — **~** *adj* : asado — **roast beef** *n* : rosbif *m*
rob ['rɑb] *v* **robbed; robbing** *vt* **1** : robar **2 ~ of** : privar de — *vi* : robar — **robber** ['rɑbər] *n* : ladrón *m,* -drona *f* — **robbery** ['rɑbəri] *n, pl* **-beries** : robo *m*
robe ['ro:b] *n* **1** : toga *f* (de un magistrado, etc.) **2** → **bathrobe**
robin ['rɑbən] *n* : petirrojo *m*

robot ['ro:ˌbɑt, -bət] *n* : robot *m*
robust [ro'bʌst, 'ro:ˌbʌst] *adj* : robusto
rock[1] ['rɑk] *vt* **1** : acunar (a un niño), mecer (una cuna) **2** SHAKE : sacudir — *vi* : mecerse — **~** *n or* **~ music** : música *f* rock
rock[2] *n* **1** : roca *f* (sustancia) **2** BOULDER : peña *f*, peñasco *m* **3** STONE : piedra *f*
rocket ['rɑkət] *n* : cohete *m*
rocking chair *n* : mecedora *f*
rocky ['rɑki] *adj* **rockier; -est 1** : rocoso **2** SHAKY : tambaleante
rod ['rɑd] *n* **1** : varilla *f* **2** *or* **fishing ~** : caña *f* de pescar
rode → **ride**
rodent ['ro:dənt] *n* : roedor *m*
rodeo ['ro:diˌo:, ro'deɪˌo:] *n, pl* **-deos** : rodeo *m*
roe ['ro:] *n* : hueva *f*
rogue ['ro:g] *n* : pícaro *m*, -ra *f*
role ['ro:l] *n* : papel *m*
roll ['ro:l] *n* **1** : rollo *m* (de película, etc.) **2** LIST : lista *f* **3** : redoble *m* (de un tambor) **4** SWAYING : balanceo *m* **5** BUN : pancito *m Lat*, panecillo *m Spain* — **~** *vt* **1** : hacer rodar **2** *or* **~ out** : estirar (masa) **3 ~ up** : enrollar (papel, etc.), arremangar (una manga) — *vi* **1** : rodar **2** SWAY : balancearse **3 ~ around** : revolcarse **4 ~ over** : darse la vuelta — **roller** ['ro:lər] *n* **1** : rodillo *m* **2** CURLER : rulo *m* — **roller coaster** ['ro:lərˌko:stər] *n* : montaña *f* rusa — **roller–skate** ['ro:lərˌskeɪt] *vi* **-skated; -skating** : patinar (sobre ruedas) — **roller skate** *n* : patín *m* (de ruedas)
Roman ['ro:mən] *adj* : romano — **Roman Catholic** *adj* : católico
romance [ro'mænts, 'ro:ˌmænts] *n* **1** : novela *f* romántica **2** AFFAIR : romance *m*
Romanian [rʊ'meɪniən, ro-] *adj* : rumano — **~** *n* : rumano *m* (idioma)
romantic [ro'mæntɪk] *adj* : romántico
romp ['rɑmp] *n* : retozo *m* — **~** *vi* : retozar
roof ['ru:f, 'rʊf] *n, pl* **roofs** ['ru:fs, 'rʊfs; 'ru:vz, 'rʊvz] **1** : tejado *m*, techo *m* **2 ~ of the mouth** : paladar *m* — **roofing** ['ru:fɪŋ, 'rʊfɪŋ] *n* : techumbre *f* — **rooftop** ['ru:fˌtɑp, 'rʊf-] *n* : tejado *m*, techo *m*
rook[1] ['rʊk] *n* : grajo *m* (ave)
rook[2] *n* : torre *f* (en ajedrez)
rookie ['rʊki] *n* : novato *m*, -ta *f*
room ['ru:m, 'rʊm] *n* **1** : cuarto *m*, habitación *f* **2** BEDROOM : dormitorio *m* **3** SPACE : espacio *m* **4** OPPORTUNITY : posibilidad *f* — **roommate** ['ru:mˌmeɪt, 'rʊm-] *n* : compañero *m*, -ra *f* de cuarto — **roomy** ['ru:mi, 'rʊmi] *adj* **roomier; -est** : espacioso
roost ['ru:st] *n* : percha *f* — **~** *vi* : posarse — **rooster** ['ru:stər, 'rʊs-] *n* : gallo *m*
root[1] ['ru:t, 'rʊt] *n* : raíz *f* — **~** *vt* **~ out** : extirpar
root[2] *vi* **~ around in** : hurgar en
root[3] *vi* **~ for** SUPPORT : alentar
rope ['ro:p] *n* : cuerda *f* — **~** *vt* **roped; roping 1** : atar (con cuerda) **2 ~ off** : acordonar
rosary ['ro:zəri] *n, pl* **-ries** : rosario *m*
rose[1] → **rise**
rose[2] ['ro:z] *n* : rosa *f* (flor), rosa *m* (color) — **~** *adj* : rosa — **rosebush** ['ro:zˌbʊʃ] *n* : rosal *m*
rosemary ['ro:zˌmɛri] *n, pl* **-maries** : romero *m*
Rosh Hashanah [ˌrɑʃhɑ'ʃɑnə, ˌro:ʃ-] *n* : el Año Nuevo judío
roster ['rɑstər] *n* : lista *f*
rostrum ['rɑstrəm] *n, pl* **-tra** *or* **-trums** [-trə] : tribuna *f*
rosy ['ro:zi] *adj* **rosier; -est 1** : sonrosado **2** PROMISING : halagüeno
rot ['rɑt] *v* **rotted; rotting** *vi* : pudrirse — *vt* : pudrir — **~** *n* : putrefacción *f*
rotary ['ro:t̬əri] *adj* : rotativo — **~** *n* : rotonda *f*, glorieta *f Spain*
rotate ['ro:ˌteɪt] *v* **-tated; -tating** *vi* : girar — *vt* **1** : girar **2** ALTERNATE : alternar — **rotation** [ro'teɪʃən] *n* : rotación *f*
rote ['ro:t] *n* **by ~** : de memoria
rotor ['ro:t̬ər] *n* : rotor *m*
rotten ['rɑtən] *adj* **1** : podrido **2** BAD : malo
rouge ['ru:ʒ, 'ru:dʒ] *n* : colorete *m*
rough ['rʌf] *adj* **1** COARSE : áspero **2** RUGGED : accidentado **3** CHOPPY : agitado **4** DIFFICULT : duro **5** FORCEFUL : brusco **6** APPROXIMATE : aproximado **7** UNREFINED : tosco **8 ~ draft** : borrador *m* — **~** *vt* **1** → **roughen 2 ~ up** BEAT : dar una paliza a — **roughage** ['rʌfɪdʒ] *n* : fibra *f* — **roughen** ['rʌfən] *vt* : poner áspero — *vi* : ponerse áspero — **roughly** ['rʌfli] *adv* **1** : bruscamente **2** ABOUT : aproximadamente — **roughness** ['rʌfnəs] *n* COARSENESS : aspereza *f*
roulette [ru:'lɛt] *n* : ruleta *f*
round ['raʊnd] *adj* : redondo — **~** *adv* → **around** — **~** *n* **1** : círculo *m* **2** : ronda *f* (de bebidas, negociaciones, etc.) **3** : asalto *m* (en boxeo), vuelta *f* (en juegos) **4 ~ of applause** : aplauso *m* **5 ~s** *npl* : visitas *fpl* (de un médico), rondas *fpl* (de un policía, etc.) — **~** *vt* **1** TURN : doblar **2 ~ off**

: redondear **3 ~ off** *or* **~ out** COMPLETE : rematar **4 ~ up** GATHER : reunir (personas), rodear (ganado) — **~** *prep* → **around** — **roundabout** ['raʊndə,baʊt] *adj* : indirecto — **round–trip** ['raʊnd,trɪp] *n* : viaje *m* de ida y vuelta — **roundup** ['raʊnd,ʌp] *n* : rodeo *m* (de animales), redada *f* (de delincuentes, etc.)

rouse ['raʊz] *vt* **roused; rousing 1** AWAKEN : despertar **2** EXCITE : excitar

rout ['raʊt] *n* : derrota *f* aplastante — **~** *vt* : derrotar

route ['ru:t, 'raʊt] *n* **1** : ruta *f* **2** *or* **delivery ~** : recorrido *m*

routine [ru:'ti:n] *n* : rutina *f* — **~** *adj* : rutinario

rove ['ro:v] *v* **roved; roving** *vi* : errar, vagar — *vt* : errar por

row[1] ['ro:] *vt* **1** : llevar a remo **2 ~ a boat** : remar — *vi* : remar

row[2] *n* **1** : fila *f* (de gente o asientos), hilera *f* (de casas, etc.) **2 in a ~** SUCCESSIVELY : seguido

row[3] ['raʊ] *n* **1** RACKET : bulla *f* **2** QUARREL : pelea *f*

rowboat ['ro:,bo:t] *n* : bote *m* de remos

rowdy ['raʊdi] *adj* **-dier; -est** : escandaloso, alborotador — **~** *n, pl* **-dies** : alborotador *m*, -dora *f*

royal ['rɔɪəl] *adj* : real — **royalty** ['rɔɪəlti] *n, pl* **-ties 1** : realeza *f* **2 royalties** *npl* : derechos *mpl* de autor

rub ['rʌb] *v* **rubbed; rubbing** *vt* **1** : frotar **2** CHAFE : rozar **3 ~ in** : aplicar frotando — *vi* **1 ~ against** : rozar **2 ~ off** : salir (al frotar) — **~** *n* : frotamiento *m*

rubber ['rʌbər] *n* **1** : goma *f*, caucho *m* **2 ~s** *npl* : chanclos *mpl* — **rubber band** *n* : goma *f* (elástica) — **rubber stamp** *n* : sello *m* (de goma) — **rubbery** ['rʌbəri] *adj* : gomoso

rubbish ['rʌbɪʃ] *n* **1** : basura *f* **2** NONSENSE : tonterías *fpl*

rubble ['rʌbəl] *n* : escombros *mpl*

ruby ['ru:bi] *n, pl* **-bies** : rubí *m*

rudder ['rʌdər] *n* : timón *m*

ruddy ['rʌdi] *adj* **-dier; -est** : rubicundo

rude ['ru:d] *adj* **ruder; rudest 1** IMPOLITE : grosero, mal educado **2** ABRUPT : brusco — **rudely** ['ru:dli] *adv* : groseramente — **rudeness** ['ru:dnəs] *n* : mala educación *f*

rudiment ['ru:dəmənt] *n* : rudimento *m* — **rudimentary** [,ru:də'mɛntəri] *adj* : rudimentario

rue ['ru:] *vt* **rued; ruing** : lamentar — **rueful** ['ru:fəl] *adj* : triste, arrepentido

ruffle ['rʌfəl] *vt* **-fled; -fling 1** : despeinar (pelo), erizar (plumas) **2** VEX : alterar, contrariar — **~** *n* : volante *m* (de un vestido, etc.)

rug ['rʌg] *n* : alfombra *f*, tapete *m*

rugged ['rʌgəd] *adj* **1** : escabroso (dícese del terreno), escarpado (dícese de montañas) **2** HARSH : duro **3** STURDY : fuerte

ruin ['ru:ən] *n* : ruina *f* — **~** *vt* : arruinar

rule ['ru:l] *n* **1** : regla *f* **2** CONTROL : dominio *m* **3 as a ~** : por lo general — **~** *v* **ruled; ruling** *vt* **1** GOVERN : gobernar **2** : fallar (dícese de un juez) **3 ~ out** : descartar — *vi* : gobernar, reinar — **ruler** ['ru:lər] *n* **1** : gobernante *mf;* soberano *m*, -na *f* **2** : regla *f* (para medir) — **ruling** ['ru:lɪŋ] *n* VERDICT : fallo *m*

rum ['rʌm] *n* : ron *m*

Rumanian [rʊ'meɪniən] → **Romanian**

rumble ['rʌmbəl] *vi* **-bled; -bling 1** : retumbar **2** : hacer ruidos (dícese del estómago) — **~** *n* : retumbo *m*, estruendo *m*

rummage ['rʌmɪdʒ] *vi* **-maged; -maging** : hurgar

rumor ['ru:mər] *n* : rumor *m* — **~** *vt* **be ~ed** : rumorearse

rump ['rʌmp] *n* **1** : grupa *f* (de un animal) **2 ~ steak** : filete *m* de cadera

rumpus ['rʌmpəs] *n* : lío *m*, jaleo *m fam*

run ['rʌn] *v* **ran** ['ræn]; **run; running** *vi* **1** : correr **2** FUNCTION : funcionar **3** LAST : durar **4** : desteñir (dícese de colores) **5** EXTEND : correr, extenderse **6** : presentarse (como candidato) **7 ~ away** : huir **8 ~ into** ENCOUNTER : tropezar con **9 ~ into** HIT : chocar contra **10 ~ late** : ir retrasado **11 ~ out of** : quedarse sin **12 ~ over** : atropellar — *vt* **1** : correr **2** OPERATE : hacer funcionar **3** : hacer correr (agua) **4** MANAGE : dirigir **5 ~ a fever** : tener fiebre — **~** *n* **1** : carrera *f* **2** TRIP : viaje *m*, paseo *m* (en coche) **3** SERIES : serie *f* **4 in the long ~** : a la larga **5 in the short ~** : a corto plazo — **runaway** ['rʌnə,weɪ] *n* : fugitivo *m*, -va *f* — **~** *adj* : fugitivo — **rundown** ['rʌn,daʊn] *n* : resumen *m* — **run–down** ['rʌn'daʊn] *adj* **1** : destartalado **2** EXHAUSTED : agotado

rung[1] → **ring**[1]

rung[2] ['rʌŋ] *n* : peldaño *m* (de una escalera, etc.)

runner ['rʌnər] *n* **1** : corredor *m*, -dora *f* **2** : patín *m* (de un trineo), riel *m* (de un cajón, etc.) — **runner–up** [,rʌnər'ʌp] *n, pl* **runners–up** : subcampeón *m*, -peona *f* — **running** ['rʌnɪŋ] *adj* **1**

FLOWING : corriente **2** CONTINUOUS : continuo **3** CONSECUTIVE : seguido
runt ['rʌnt] *n* : animal *m* más pequeño (de una camada)
runway ['rʌn,weɪ] *n* : pista *f* de aterrizaje
rupture ['rʌptʃər] *n* : ruptura *f* — ~ *v* **-tured; -turing** *vt* : romper — *vi* : reventar
rural ['rʊrəl] *adj* : rural
ruse ['ru:s, 'ru:z] *n* : ardid *m*
rush[1] ['rʌʃ] *n* : junco *m* (planta)
rush[2] *vi* : ir de prisa — *vt* **1** : apresurar, apurar **2** ATTACK : asaltar **3** : llevar rápidamente (al hospital, etc.) — ~ *n* **1** : prisa *f,* apuro *m* **2** : ráfaga *f* (de aire), torrente *m* (de agua) — ~ *adj* : urgente — **rush hour** *n* : hora *f* punta
russet ['rʌsət] *n* : color *m* rojizo
Russian ['rʌʃən] *adj* : ruso — ~ *n* : ruso *m* (idioma)
rust ['rʌst] *n* : herrumbre *f,* óxido *m* — ~ *vi* : oxidarse — *vt* : oxidar
rustic ['rʌstɪk] *adj* : rústico
rustle ['rʌsəl] *v* **-tled; -tling** *vt* **1** : hacer susurrar **2** : robar (ganado) — *vi* : susurrar — ~ *n* : susurro *m*
rusty ['rʌsti] *adj* **rustier; -est** : oxidado
rut ['rʌt] *n* **1** : surco *m* **2 be in a ~** : ser esclavo de la rutina
ruthless ['ru:θləs] *adj* : despiadado, cruel
rye ['raɪ] *n* : centeno *m*

S

s ['ɛs] *n, pl* **s's** *or* **ss** ['ɛsəz] : s *f,* decimonovena letra del alfabeto inglés
Sabbath ['sæbəθ] *n* **1** : sábado *m* (día santo judío) **2** : domingo *m* (día santo cristiano)
sabotage ['sæbə,tɑʒ] *n* : sabotaje *m* — ~ *vt* **-taged; -taging** : sabotear
saccharin ['sækərən] *n* : sacarina *f*
sack ['sæk] *n* : saco *m* — ~ *vt* **1** FIRE : despedir **2** PLUNDER : saquear
sacrament ['sækrəmənt] *n* : sacramento *m*
sacred ['seɪkrəd] *adj* : sagrado
sacrifice ['sækrə,faɪs] *n* : sacrificio *m* — ~ *vt* **-ficed; -ficing** : sacrificar
sacrilege ['sækrəlɪdʒ] *n* : sacrilegio *m* — **sacrilegious** [,sækrə'lɪdʒəs, -'li:-] *adj* : sacrílego
sad ['sæd] *adj* **sadder; saddest** : triste — **sadden** ['sædən] *vt* : entristecer
saddle ['sædəl] *n* : silla *f* (de montar) — ~ *vt* **-dled; -dling 1** : ensillar (un caballo, etc.) **2 ~ s.o. with sth** : cargar a algn con algo
sadistic [sə'dɪstɪk] *adj* : sádico
sadness ['sædnəs] *n* : tristeza *f*
safari [sə'fɑri, -'fær-] *n* : safari *m*
safe ['seɪf] *adj* **safer; safest 1** : seguro **2** UNHARMED : ileso **3** CAREFUL : prudente **4 ~ and sound** : sano y salvo — ~ *n* : caja *f* fuerte — **safeguard** ['seɪf,gɑrd] *n* : salvaguarda *f* — ~ *vt* : salvaguardar — **safely** ['seɪfli] *adv* **1** : sin peligro **2 arrive ~** : llegar sin novedad — **safety** ['seɪfti] *n, pl* **-ties** : seguridad *f* — **safety belt** *n* : cinturón *m* de seguridad — **safety pin** *n* : imperdible *m*
saffron ['sæfrən] *n* : azafrán *m*
sag ['sæg] *vi* **sagged; sagging 1** : combarse **2** GIVE : aflojarse **3** FLAG : flaquear
saga ['sɑgə, 'sæ-] *n* : saga *f*
sage[1] ['seɪdʒ] *n* : salvia *f* (planta)
sage[2] *adj* **sager; -est** : sabio — ~ *n* : sabio *m,* **-bia** *f*
said → **say**
sail ['seɪl] *n* **1** : vela *f* (de un barco) **2 go for a ~** : salir a navegar **3 set ~** : zarpar — ~ *vi* : navegar — *vt* : gobernar (un barco), navegar (el mar) — **sailboat** ['seɪl,bo:t] *n* : velero *m* — **sailor** ['seɪlər] *n* : marinero *m*
saint ['seɪnt, *before a name* ,seɪnt *or* sənt] *n* : santo *m,* **-ta** *f* — **saintly** ['seɪntli] *adj* **saintlier; -est** : santo
sake ['seɪk] *n* **1 for goodness' ~!** : ¡por Dios! **2 for the ~ of** : por (el bien de)
salad ['sæləd] *n* : ensalada *f*
salamander ['sælə,mændər] *n* : salamandra *f*
salami [sə'lɑmi] *n* : salami *m*
salary ['sæləri] *n, pl* **-ries** : sueldo *m*
sale ['seɪl] *n* **1** : venta *f* **2 for ~** : se vende **3 on ~** : de rebaja — **salesman** ['seɪlzmən] *n, pl* **-men** [-mən, -,mɛn] : vendedor *m,* dependiente *m* — **saleswoman** ['seɪlz,wʊmən] *n, pl* **-women** [-,wɪmən] : vendedora *f,* dependienta *f*
salient ['seɪljənt] *adj* : saliente
saliva [sə'laɪvə] *n* : saliva *f*
sallow ['sælo:] *adj* : amarillento, cetrino
salmon ['sæmən] *ns & pl* : salmón *m*
salon [sə'lɑn, 'sæ,lɑn] *n* → **beauty salon**

saloon [sə'lu:n] *n* : bar *m*
salsa ['sɔlsə, 'sɑl-] *n* : salsa *f* mexicana, salsa *f* picante
salt ['sɔlt] *n* : sal *f* — ~ *vt* : salar — **saltwater** ['sɔlt,wɔt̬ər, -,wɑ-] *adj* : de agua salada — **salty** ['sɔlti] *adj* **saltier; -est** : salado
salute [sə'lu:t] *v* **-luted; -luting** *vt* : saludar — *vi* : hacer un saludo — ~ *n* : saludo *m*
salvage ['sælvɪdʒ] *n* : salvamento *m* — ~ *vt* **-vaged; -vaging** : salvar
salvation [sæl'veɪʃən] *n* : salvación *f*
salve ['sæv, 'sav] *n* : ungüento *m*
same ['seɪm] *adj* **1** : mismo **2 be the ~ (as)** : ser igual (que) **3 the ~ thing (as)** : la misma cosa (que) — ~ *pron* **1 all the ~** : igual **2 the ~** : lo mismo — ~ *adv* **the ~** : igual
sample ['sæmpəl] *n* : muestra *f* — ~ *vt* **-pled; -pling** : probar
sanatorium [,sænə'toriəm] *n, pl* **-riums** *or* **-ria** [-iə] : sanatorio *m*
sanctify ['sæŋktə,faɪ] *vt* **-fied; -fying** : santificar
sanction *n* ['sæŋkʃən] : sanción *f* — ~ *vt* : sancionar
sanctity ['sæŋktət̬i] *n, pl* **-ties** : santidad *f*
sanctuary ['sæŋktʃu,eri] *n, pl* **-aries** : santuario *m*
sand ['sænd] *n* : arena *f* — ~ *vt* : lijar (madera)
sandal ['sændəl] *n* : sandalia *f*
sandpaper ['sænd,peɪpər] *n* : papel *m* de lija — ~ *vt* : lijar
sandwich ['sænd,wɪtʃ] *n* : sandwich *m*, bocadillo *m Spain* — ~ *vt* ~ **between** : meter entre
sandy ['sændi] *adj* **sandier; -est** : arenoso
sane ['seɪn] *adj* **saner; sanest 1** : cuerdo **2** SENSIBLE : sensato
sang → **sing**
sanitarium [,sænə'tɛriəm] *n, pl* **-iums** *or* **-ia** [-iə] → **sanatorium**
sanitary ['sænətɛri] *adj* **1** : sanitario **2** HYGIENIC : higiénico — **sanitary napkin** *n* : compresa *f* (higiénica) — **sanitation** [,sænə'teɪʃən] *n* : sanidad *f*
sanity ['sænət̬i] *n* : cordura *f*
sank → **sink**
Santa Claus ['sæntə,klɔz] *n* : Papá *m* Noel
sap[1] ['sæp] *n* **1** : savia *f* (de una planta) **2** SUCKER : inocentón *m*, -tona *f*
sap[2] *vt* **sapped; sapping** : minar (la fuerza, etc.)
sapphire ['sæ,faɪr] *n* : zafiro *m*
sarcasm ['sɑr,kæzəm] *n* : sarcasmo *m* — **sarcastic** [sɑr'kæstɪk] *adj* : sarcástico
sardine [sɑr'di:n] *n* : sardina *f*
sash ['sæʃ] *n* : faja *f* (de un vestido), fajín *m* (de un uniforme)
sat → **sit**
satanic [sə'tænɪk, seɪ-] *adj* : satánico
satchel ['sætʃəl] *n* : cartera *f*
satellite ['sæt̬ə,laɪt] *n* : satélite *m*
satin ['sætən] *n* : raso *m*
satire ['sæ,taɪr] *n* : sátira *f* — **satiric** [sə'tɪrɪk] *or* **satirical** [-ɪkəl] *adj* : satírico
satisfaction [,sæt̬əs'fækʃən] *n* : satisfacción *f* — **satisfactory** [,sæt̬əs'fæktəri] *adj* : satisfactorio — **satisfy** ['sæt̬əs,faɪ] *v* **-fied; -fying** *vt* **1** : satisfacer **2** CONVINCE : convencer — **satisfying** *adj* : satisfactorio
saturate ['sætʃə,reɪt] *vt* **-rated; -rating 1** : saturar **2** DRENCH : empapar — **saturation** [,sætʃə'reɪʃən] *n* : saturación *f*
Saturday ['sæt̬ər,deɪ, -di] *n* : sábado *m*
Saturn ['sæt̬ərn] *n* : Saturno *m*
sauce ['sɔs] *n* : salsa *f* — **saucepan** ['sɔs,pæn] *n* : cacerola *f* — **saucer** ['sɔsər] *n* : platillo *m* — **saucy** ['sɔsi] *adj* **saucier; -est** IMPUDENT : descarado
sauna ['sɔnə, 'saʊnə] *n* : sauna *mf*
saunter ['sɔntər, 'sɑn-] *vi* : pasear
sausage ['sɔsɪdʒ] *n* : salchicha *f*
sauté [sɔ'teɪ, so:-] *vt* **-téed** *or* **-téd; -téing** : saltear, sofreír
savage ['sævɪdʒ] *adj* : salvaje, feroz — ~ *n* : salvaje *mf* — **savagery** ['sævɪdʒri, -dʒəri] *n, pl* **-ries** : ferocidad *f*
save ['seɪv] *vt* **saved; saving 1** RESCUE : salvar **2** RESERVE : guardar **3** : ahorrar (dinero, tiempo, etc.) — ~ *prep* EXCEPT : salvo
savior ['seɪvjər] *n* : salvador *m*, -dora *f*
savor ['seɪvər] *vt* : saborear — **savory** ['seɪvəri] *adj* : sabroso
saw[1] → **see**
saw[2] ['sɔ] *n* : sierra *f* — ~ *vt* **sawed; sawed** *or* **sawn; sawing** : serrar — **sawdust** ['sɔ,dʌst] *n* : serrín *m*, aserrín *m*
saxophone ['sæksə,fo:n] *n* : saxofón *m*
say ['seɪ] *v* **said** ['sɛd]; **saying; says** ['sɛz] *vt* **1** : decir **2** INDICATE : marcar (dícese de relojes, etc.) — *vi* **1** : decir **2 that is to ~** : es decir — ~ *n, pl* **says** ['seɪz] **1 have no ~** : no tener ni voz ni voto **2 have one's ~** : dar su opinión — **saying** ['seɪɪŋ] *n* : refrán *m*
scab ['skæb] *n* **1** : costra *f* (en una herida) **2** STRIKEBREAKER : esquirol *mf*
scaffold ['skæfəld, -,fo:ld] *n* : andamio *m* (en construcción)
scald ['skɔld] *vt* : escaldar

scale[1] ['skeɪl] *n* : balanza *f* (para pesar)
scale[2] *n* : escama *f* (de un pez, etc.) — ~ *vt* **scaled; scaling** : escamar
scale[3] *vt* **scaled; scaling 1** CLIMB : escalar **2** ~ **down** : reducir — ~ *n* : escala *f* (musical, salarial, etc.)
scallion ['skæljən] *n* : cebolleta *f*
scallop ['skɑləp, 'skæ-] *n* : vieira *f*
scalp ['skælp] *n* : cuero *m* cabelludo
scam ['skæm] *n* : estafa *f*, timo *m fam*
scamper ['skæmpər] *vi* ~ **away** : irse corriendo
scan ['skæn] *vt* **scanned; scanning 1** : escandir (versos) **2** EXAMINE : escudriñar **3** SKIM : echar un vistazo a **4** : escanear (en informática)
scandal ['skændəl] *n* **1** : escándalo *m* **2** GOSSIP : habladurías *fpl* — **scandalous** ['skændələs] *adj* : escandaloso
Scandinavian [ˌskændə'neɪviən] *adj* : escandinavo
scant ['skænt] *adj* : escaso
scapegoat ['skeɪpˌgoːt] *n* : chivo *m* expiatorio
scar ['skɑr] *n* : cicatriz *f* — ~ *v* **scarred; scarring** *vt* : dejar una cicatriz en — *vi* : cicatrizar
scarce ['skɛrs] *adj* **scarcer; -est** : escaso — **scarcely** ['skɛrsli] *adv* : apenas — **scarcity** ['skɛrsət̬i] *n, pl* **-ties** : escasez *f*
scare ['skɛr] *vt* **scared; scaring 1** : asustar **2 be ~d of** : tener miedo a — ~ *n* **1** FRIGHT : susto *m* **2** ALARM : pánico *m* — **scarecrow** ['skɛrˌkroː] *n* : espantapájaros *m*, espantajo *m*
scarf ['skɑrf] *n, pl* **scarves** ['skɑrvz] *or* **scarfs 1** : bufanda *f* **2** KERCHIEF : pañuelo *m*
scarlet ['skɑrlət] *adj* : escarlata — **scarlet fever** *n* : escarlatina *f*
scary ['skɛri] *adj* **scarier; -est** : que da miedo
scathing ['skeɪðɪŋ] *adj* : mordaz
scatter ['skæt̬ər] *vt* **1** STREW : esparcir **2** DISPERSE : dispersar — *vi* : dispersarse
scavenger ['skævəndʒər] *n* : carroñero *m*, -ra *f* (animal)
scenario [sə'næriˌoː, -'nɑr-] *n, pl* **-ios 1** : guión *m* (cinemático) **2 the worst-case** ~ : el peor de los casos
scene ['siːn] *n* **1** : escena *f* **2 behind the ~s** : entre bastidores **3 make a** ~ : armar un escándalo — **scenery** ['siːnəri] *n, pl* **-eries 1** : decorado *m* **2** LANDSCAPE : paisaje *m* — **scenic** ['siːnɪk] *adj* : pintoresco
scent ['sɛnt] *n* **1** : aroma *m* **2** PERFUME : perfume *m* **3** TRAIL : rastro *m* — **scented** ['sɛntəd] *adj* : perfumado
sceptic ['skɛptɪk] → **skeptic**
schedule ['skɛˌdʒuːl, -dʒəl, *esp Brit* 'ʃɛdjuːl] *n* **1** : programa *m* **2** TIMETABLE : horario *m* **3 behind** ~ : atrasado, con retraso **4 on** ~ : según lo previsto — ~ *vt* **-uled; -uling** : planear, programar
scheme ['skiːm] *n* **1** PLAN : plan *m* **2** PLOT : intriga *f* **3** DESIGN : esquema *f* — ~ *vi* **schemed; scheming** : intrigar
schism ['sɪzəm, 'skɪ-] *n* : cisma *m*
schizophrenia [ˌskɪtsə'friːniə, ˌskɪzə-, -'frɛ-] *n* : esquizofrenia *f* — **schizophrenic** [ˌskɪtsə'frɛnɪk, ˌskɪzə-] *adj* : esquizofrénico
scholar ['skɑlər] *n* : erudito *m*, -ta *f* — **scholarly** ['skɑlərli] *adj* : erudito — **scholarship** ['skɑlərˌʃɪp] *n* **1** : erudición *f* **2** GRANT : beca *f*
school[1] ['skuːl] *n* : banco *m* (de peces)
school[2] *n* **1** : escuela *f* **2** COLLEGE : universidad *f* **3** DEPARTMENT : facultad *f* — ~ *vt* : instruir — **schoolboy** ['skuːlˌbɔɪ] *n* : colegial *m* — **schoolgirl** ['skuːlˌgərl] *n* : colegiala *f* — **schoolteacher** ['skuːlˌtiːtʃər] *n* → **teacher**
science ['saɪənts] *n* : ciencia *f* — **scientific** [ˌsaɪən'tɪfɪk] *adj* : científico — **scientist** ['saɪəntɪst] *n* : científico *m*, -ca *f*
scissors ['sɪzərz] *npl* : tijeras *fpl*
scoff ['skɑf] *vi* ~ **at** : burlarse de, mofarse de
scold ['skoːld] *vt* : regañar
scoop ['skuːp] *n* **1** : pala *f* **2** : noticia *f* exclusiva (en periodismo) — ~ *vt* **1** : sacar (con pala) **2** ~ **out** : ahuecar **3** ~ **up** : recoger
scoot ['skuːt] *vi* : ir rápidamente — **scooter** ['skuːt̬ər] *n* **1** : patinete *m* **2** *or* **motor** ~ : escúter *m*
scope ['skoːp] *n* **1** RANGE : alcance *m* **2** OPPORTUNITY : posibilidades *fpl*
scorch ['skɔrtʃ] *vt* : chamuscar
score ['skor] *n, pl* **scores 1** : tanteo *m* (en deportes) **2** RATING : puntuación *f* **3** : partitura *f* (musical) **4** *or pl* **score** TWENTY : veintena *f* **5 keep** ~ : llevar la cuenta **6 on that** ~ : en ese sentido — ~ *v* **scored; scoring** *vt* **1** : marcar, anotarse *Lat* (un tanto) **2** : sacar (una nota) — *vi* : marcar (en deportes)
scorn ['skɔrn] *n* : desdén *m* — ~ *vt* : desdeñar — **scornful** ['skɔrnfəl] *adj* : desdeñoso
scorpion ['skɔrpiən] *n* : alacrán *m*, escorpión *m*
Scot ['skɑt] *n* : escocés *m*, -cesa *f* — **Scotch** ['skɑtʃ] *adj* → **Scottish** — ~ *n or* ~ **whiskey** : whisky *m* escocés — **Scottish** ['skɑt̬ɪʃ] *adj* : escocés

scoundrel ['skaʊndrəl] *n* : sinvergüenza *mf*
scour ['skaʊər] *vt* **1** SCRUB : fregar **2** SEARCH : registrar
scourge ['skərdʒ] *n* : azote *m*
scout ['skaʊt] *n* : explorador *m*, -dora *f*
scowl ['skaʊl] *vi* : fruncir el ceño — **~** *n* : ceño *m* fruncido
scram ['skræm] *vi* **scrammed; scramming** : largarse
scramble ['skræmbəl] *v* **-bled; -bling** *vi* **1** CLAMBER : trepar **2 ~ for** : pelearse por — *vt* : mezclar — **~** *n* : rebatiña *f*, pelea *f* — **scrambled eggs** *npl* : huevos *mpl* revueltos
scrap[1] ['skræp] *n* **1** PIECE : pedazo *m* **2** *or* **~ metal** : chatarra *f* **3 ~s** *npl* : sobras — **~** *vt* **scrapped; scrapping** : desechar
scrap[2] *n* FIGHT : pelea *f*
scrapbook ['skræp,bʊk] *n* : álbum *m* de recortes
scrape ['skreɪp] *v* **scraped; scraping** *vt* **1** : rascar **2** : rasparse (la rodilla, etc.) **3** *or* **~ off** : raspar **4 ~ together** : reunir — *vi* **1** RUB : rozar **2 ~ by** : arreglárselas — **~** *n* **1** : rasguño *m* **2** PREDICAMENT : apuro *m*
scratch ['skrætʃ] *vt* **1** CLAW : arañar **2** MARK : rayar **3** : rascarse (la cabeza, etc.) **4 ~ out** : tachar — **~** *n* **1** : arañazo *m* **2** MARK : rayón *m* **3 start from ~** : empezar desde cero
scrawl ['skrɔl] *v* : garabatear — **~** *n* : garabato *m*
scrawny ['skrɔni] *adj* **scrawnier; -est** : escuálido
scream ['skri:m] *vi* : gritar, chillar — **~** *n* : grito *m*, chillido *m*
screech ['skri:tʃ] *n* **1** : chillido *m* (de personas) **2** : chirrido *m* (de frenos, etc.) — **~** *vi* **1** : chillar **2** : chirriar (dícese de los frenos, etc.)
screen ['skri:n] *n* **1** : pantalla *f* **2** PARTITION : mampara *f* **3** *or* **window ~** : mosquitero *m* — **~** *vt* **1** SHIELD : proteger **2** HIDE : ocultar **3** : seleccionar (candidatos, etc.)
screw ['skru:] *n* : tornillo *m* — **~** *vt* **1** : atornillar **2 ~ up** RUIN : fastidiar — **screwdriver** ['skru:,draɪvər] *n* : destornillador *m*
scribble ['skrɪbəl] *v* **-bled; -bling** : garabatear — **~** *n* : garabato *m*
script ['skrɪpt] *n* **1** HANDWRITING : escritura *f* **2** : guión *m* (de cine, etc.) — **scripture** ['skrɪptʃər] *n* **1** : escritos *mpl* sagrados **2 the Scriptures** *npl* : las Escrituras *fpl*
scroll ['skro:l] *n* : rollo *m* (de pergamino, etc.)
scrounge ['skraʊndʒ] *v* **scrounged; scrounging** *vt* : gorrear *fam* — *vi* **~ around for sth** : andar buscando algo
scrub[1] ['skrʌb] *n* UNDERBRUSH : maleza *f*
scrub[2] *vt* **scrubbed; scrubbing** SCOUR : fregar — **~** *n* : fregado *m*
scruff ['skrʌf] *n* **by the ~ of the neck** : por el pescuezo
scruple ['skru:pəl] *n* : escrúpulo *m* — **scrupulous** ['skru:pjələs] *adj* : escrupuloso
scrutiny ['skru:təni] *n, pl* **-nies** : análisis *m* cuidadoso — **scrutinize** ['skru:tən,aɪz] *vt* **-nized; -nizing** : escudriñar
scuff ['skʌf] *vt* : raspar, rayar
scuffle ['skʌfəl] *n* : refriega *f*
sculpture ['skʌlptʃər] *n* : escultura *f* — **sculpt** ['skʌlpt] *v* : esculpir — **sculptor** ['skʌlptər] *n* : escultor *m*, -tora *f*
scum ['skʌm] *n* **1** FROTH : espuma *f* **2** : escoria *f* (dícese de personas)
scurry ['skəri] *vi* **-ried; -rying** : corretear
scuttle[1] ['skʌt̬əl] *n* : cubo *m* (para carbón)
scuttle[2] *vt* **-tled; -tling** : hundir (un barco)
scuttle[3] *vi* SCAMPER : corretear
sea ['si:] *n* **1** : mar *mf* **2 at ~** : en el mar — **~** *adj* : del mar — **seafarer** ['si:,færər] *n* : marinero *m* — **seafood** ['si:,fu:d] *n* : mariscos *mpl* — **seagull** ['si:,gʌl] *n* : gaviota *f*
seal[1] ['si:l] *n* : foca *f* (animal)
seal[2] *n* **1** STAMP : sello *m* **2** CLOSURE : cierre *m* (hermético) — **~** *vt* : sellar
seam ['si:m] *n* **1** : costura *f* **2** VEIN : veta *f*
seaman ['si:mən] *n, pl* **-men** [-mən, -,mɛn] : marinero *m*
seamy ['si:mi] *adj* **seamier; -est** : sórdido
seaplane ['si:,pleɪn] *n* : hidroavión *m*
seaport ['si:,port] *n* : puerto *m* marítimo
search ['sərtʃ] *vt* : registrar — *vi* **~ for** : buscar — **~** *n* **1** : registro *m* **2** HUNT : búsqueda *f* — **searchlight** ['sərtʃ,laɪt] *n* : reflector *m*
seashell ['si:,ʃɛl] *n* : concha *f* (marina) — **seashore** ['si:,ʃor] *n* : orilla *f* del mar — **seasick** ['si:,sɪk] *adj* **1** : mareado **2 be ~** : marearse — **seasickness** ['si:,sɪknəs] *n* : mareo *m*
season ['si:zən] *n* **1** : estación *f* (del año) **2** : temporada *f* (en deportes, etc.) — **~** *vt* **1** FLAVOR : sazonar **2** : secar (madera) — **seasonal** ['si:zənəl] *adj*

: estacional — **seasoned** *adj* EXPERIENCED : veterano — **seasoning** ['si:zənɪŋ] *n* : condimento *m*

seat ['si:t] *n* **1** : asiento *m* **2** : fondillos *mpl* (de un pantalón) **3** BUTTOCKS : trasero *m* **4** CENTER : sede *f* — **~** *vt* **1 be ~ed** : sentarse **2 the bus ~s 30** : el autobús tiene cabida para 30 — **seat belt** *n* : cinturón *m* de seguridad

seaweed ['si:ˌwi:d] *n* : alga *f* marina

secede [sɪ'si:d] *vi* **-ceded; -ceding** : separarse (de una nación, etc.)

secluded [sɪ'klu:dəd] *adj* : aislado — **seclusion** [sɪ'klu:ʒən] *n* : aislamiento *m*

second ['sɛkənd] *adj* : segundo — **~** *or* **secondly** ['sɛkəndli] *adv* : en segundo lugar — **~** *n* **1** : segundo *m*, **-da** *f* **2** MOMENT : segundo *m* **3 have ~s** : repetir (en una comida) — **~** *vt* : secundar — **secondary** ['sɛkənˌdɛri] *adj* : secundario — **secondhand** ['sɛkənd'hænd] *adj* : de segunda mano — **second–rate** ['sɛkənd'reɪt] *adj* : mediocre

secret ['si:krət] *adj* : secreto — **~** *n* : secreto *m* — **secrecy** ['si:krəsi] *n, pl* **-cies** : secreto *m*

secretary ['sɛkrəˌtɛri] *n, pl* **-taries 1** : secretario *m*, -ria *f* **2** : ministro *m*, -tra *f* (del gobierno)

secretion [sɪ'kri:ʃən] *n* : secreción *f* — **secrete** [sɪ'kri:t] *vt* **-creted; -creting** : secretar

secretive ['si:krəţɪv, sɪ'kri:ţɪv] *adj* : reservado — **secretly** ['si:krətli] *adv* : en secreto

sect ['sɛkt] *n* : secta *f*

section ['sɛkʃən] *n* : sección *f*, parte *f*

sector ['sɛktər] *n* : sector *m*

secular ['sɛkjələr] *adj* : secular

security [sɪ'kjʊrəţi] *n, pl* **-ties 1** : seguridad *f* **2** GUARANTEE : garantía *f* **3 securities** *npl* : valores *mpl* — **secure** [sɪ'kjʊr] *adj* **-curer; -est** : seguro — **~** *vt* **-cured; -curing 1** FASTEN : asegurar **2** GET : conseguir

sedan [sɪ'dæn] *n* : sedán *m*

sedate [sɪ'deɪt] *adj* : sosegado

sedative ['sɛdəţɪv] *adj* : sedante — **~** *n* : sedante *m*

sedentary ['sɛdənˌtɛri] *adj* : sedentario

sediment ['sɛdəmənt] *n* : sedimento *m*

seduce [sɪ'du:s, -'dju:s] *vt* **-duced; -ducing** : seducir — **seduction** [sɪ'dʌkʃən] *n* : seducción *f* — **seductive** [sɪ'dʌktɪv] *adj* : seductor

see ['si:] *v* **saw** ['sɔ]; **seen** ['si:n]; **seeing** *vt* **1** : ver **2** UNDERSTAND : entender **3** ESCORT : acompañar **4 ~ s.o. off** : despedirse de algn **5 ~ sth through** : llevar algo a cabo **6 ~ you later!** : ¡hasta luego! — *vi* **1** : ver **2** UNDERSTAND : entender **3 let's ~** : vamos a ver **4 ~ to** : ocuparse de

seed ['si:d] *n, pl* **seed** *or* **seeds 1** : semilla *f* **2** SOURCE : germen *m* — **seedy** ['si:di] *adj* **seedier; -est** SQUALID : sórdido

seek ['si:k] *v* **sought** ['sɔt]; **seeking** *vt* **1** *or* **~ out** : buscar **2** REQUEST : pedir **3 ~ to** : tratar de — *vi* SEARCH : buscar

seem ['si:m] *vi* : parecer

seep ['si:p] *vi* : filtrarse

seesaw ['si:ˌsɔ] *n* : balancín *m*

seethe ['si:ð] *vi* **seethed; seething** : rabiar, estar furioso

segment ['sɛgmənt] *n* : segmento *m*

segregate ['sɛgrɪˌgeɪt] *vt* **-gated; -gating** : segregar — **segregation** [ˌsɛgrɪ'geɪʃən] *n* : segregación *f*

seize ['si:z] *v* **seized; seizing** *vt* **1** GRASP : agarrar **2** CAPTURE : tomar **3** : aprovechar (una oportunidad) — *vi* *or* **~ up** : agarrotarse — **seizure** ['si:ʒər] *n* **1** CAPTURE : toma *f* **2** : ataque *m* (en medicina)

seldom ['sɛldəm] *adv* : pocas veces, raramente

select [sə'lɛkt] *adj* : selecto — **~** *vt* : seleccionar — **selection** [sə'lɛkʃən] *n* : selección *f* — **selective** [sə'lɛktɪv] *adj* : selectivo

self ['sɛlf] *n, pl* **selves** ['sɛlvz] **1** : ser *m* **2 her better ~** : su lado bueno — **self–addressed** [ˌsɛlfə'drɛst] *adj* : con la dirección del remitente — **self–assured** [ˌsɛlfə'ʃʊrd] *adj* : seguro de sí mismo — **self–centered** [ˌsɛlf'sɛntərd] *adj* : egocéntrico — **self–confidence** [ˌsɛlf'kɑnfədənts] *n* : confianza *f* en sí mismo — **self–confident** [ˌsɛlf'kɑnfədənt] *adj* : seguro de sí mismo — **self–conscious** [ˌsɛlf'kɑntʃəs] *adj* : cohibido — **self–control** [ˌsɛlfkən'tro:l] *n* : dominio *m* de sí mismo — **self–defense** [ˌsɛlfdɪ'fɛnts] *n* : defensa *f* propia — **self–employed** [ˌsɛlfɪm'plɔɪd] *adj* : que trabaja por cuenta propia — **self–esteem** [ˌsɛlfɪ'sti:m] *n* : amor *m* propio — **self–evident** [ˌsɛlf'ɛvədənt] *adj* : evidente — **self–help** [ˌsɛlf'hɛlp] *n* : autoayuda *f* — **self–important** [ˌsɛlfɪm'pɔrtənt] *adj* : presumido — **self–interest** [ˌsɛlf'ɪntrəst, -təˌrɛst] *n* : interés *m* personal — **selfish** ['sɛlfɪʃ] *adj* : egoísta — **selfishness** ['sɛlfɪʃnəs] *n* : egoísmo *m* — **selfless** ['sɛlfləs] *adj* : desinteresado — **self–pity** [ˌsɛlf'pɪţi] *n, pl* **-ties** : autocompasión *f* — **self–portrait** [ˌsɛlf-

'pɔrtrət] *n* : autorretrato *m* — **self–respect** [ˌsɛlfri'spɛkt] *n* : amor *m* propio — **self–righteous** [ˌsɛlfraɪtʃəs] *adj* : santurrón — **self–service** [ˌsɛlf'sərvɪs] *adj* : de autoservicio — **self–sufficient** [ˌsɛlfsə'fɪʃənt] *adj* : autosuficiente — **self–taught** [ˌsɛlftɔt] *adj* : autodidacta

sell ['sɛl] *v* **sold** ['so:ld]; **selling** *vt* : vender — *vi* : venderse — **seller** ['sɛlər] *n* : vendedor *m*, -dora *f*

selves → **self**

semantics [sɪ'mæntɪks] *ns & pl* : semántica *f*

semblance ['sɛmbləntś] *n* : apariencia *f*

semester [sə'mɛstər] *n* : semestre *m*

semicolon ['sɛmiˌko:lən, 'sɛˌmaɪ-] *n* : punto y coma *m*

semifinal ['sɛmiˌfaɪnəl, 'sɛˌmaɪ-] *n* : semifinal *f*

seminary ['sɛməˌnɛri] *n, pl* **-naries** : seminario *m* — **seminar** ['sɛməˌnɑr] *n* : seminario *m*

senate ['sɛnət] *n* : senado *m* — **senator** ['sɛnət̬ər] *n* : senador *m*, -dora *f*

send ['sɛnd] *vt* **sent** ['sɛnt]; **sending** **1** : mandar, enviar **2 ~ away for** : pedir **3 ~ back** : devolver (mercancías, etc.) **4 ~ for** : mandar a buscar — **sender** ['sɛndər] *n* : remitente *mf*

senile ['si:ˌnaɪl] *adj* : senil — **senility** [sɪ'nɪlət̬i] *n* : senilidad *f*

senior ['si:njər] *n* **1** SUPERIOR : superior *m* **2** : estudiante *mf* de último año (en educación) **3** *or* **~ citizen** : persona *f* mayor **4 be s.o.'s ~** : ser mayor que algn — **~** *adj* **1** : superior (en rango) **2** ELDER : mayor — **seniority** [ˌsi:'njɔrət̬i] *n* : antigüedad *f*

sensation [sɛn'seɪʃən] *n* : sensación *f* — **sensational** [sɛn'seɪʃənəl] *adj* : sensacional

sense ['sɛnts] *n* **1** : sentido *m* **2** FEELING : sensación *f* **3** COMMON SENSE : sentido *m* común **4 make ~** : tener sentido — **~** *vt* **sensed; sensing** : sentir — **senseless** ['sɛntsləs] *adj* **1** : sin sentido **2** UNCONSCIOUS : inconsciente — **sensible** ['sɛntsəbəl] *adj* : sensato, práctico — **sensibility** [ˌsɛntsə'bɪlət̬i] *n, pl* **-ties** : sensibilidad *f* — **sensitive** ['sɛntsət̬ɪv] *adj* **1** : sensible **2** TOUCHY : susceptible — **sensitivity** [ˌsɛntsə'tɪvət̬i] *n, pl* **-ties** : sensibilidad *f* — **sensual** ['sɛntʃuəl] *adj* : sensual — **sensuous** ['sɛntʃuəs] *adj* : sensual

sent → **send**

sentence ['sɛntənts, -ənz] *n* **1** : frase *f* **2** JUDGMENT : sentencia *f* — **~** *vt* **-tenced; -tencing** : sentenciar

sentiment ['sɛntəmənt] *n* **1** : sentimiento *m* **2** BELIEF : opinión *f* — **sentimental** [ˌsɛntə'mɛntəl] *adj* : sentimental — **sentimentality** [ˌsɛntəˌmɛn'tælət̬i] *n, pl* **-ties** : sentimentalismo *m*

sentry ['sɛntri] *n, pl* **-tries** : centinela *m*

separation [ˌsɛpə'reɪʃən] *n* : separación *f* — **separate** ['sɛpəˌreɪt] *v* **-rated; -rating** *vt* **1** : separar **2** DISTINGUISH : distinguir — *vi* : separarse — **~** ['sɛprət, 'sɛpə-] *adj* **1** : separado **2** DETACHED : aparte **3** DISTINCT : distinto — **separately** ['sɛprətli, 'sɛpə-] *adv* : por separado

September [sɛp'tɛmbər] *n* : septiembre *m*, setiembre *m*

sequel ['si:kwəl] *n* **1** : continuación *f* **2** CONSEQUENCE : secuela *f*

sequence ['si:kwənts] *n* **1** ORDER : orden *m* **2** : secuencia *f* (de números o escenas)

Serb ['sərb] *or* **Serbian** ['sərbiən] *adj* : serbio

serene [sə'ri:n] *adj* : sereno — **serenity** [sə'rɛnət̬i] *n* : serenidad *f*

sergeant ['sɑrdʒənt] *n* : sargento *mf*

serial ['sɪriəl] *adj* : seriado — **~** *n* : serial *m* — **series** ['sɪrˌi:z] *n, pl* **series** : serie *f*

serious ['sɪriəs] *adj* : serio — **seriously** ['sɪriəsli] *adv* **1** : seriamente **2** GRAVELY : gravemente **3 take ~** : tomar en serio

sermon ['sərmən] *n* : sermón *m*

serpent ['sərpənt] *n* : serpiente *f*

servant ['sərvənt] *n* : criado *m*, -da *f*

serve ['sərv] *v* **served; serving** *vi* **1** : servir **2** : sacar (en deportes) **3 ~ as** : servir de — *vt* **1** : servir **2 ~ time** : cumplir una condena — **server** ['sərvər] *n* **1** WAITER : camarero *m*, -ra *f* **2** : servidor *m* (en informática)

service ['sərvəs] *n* **1** : servicio *m* **2** CEREMONY : oficio *m* **3** MAINTENANCE : revisión *f* **4 armed ~s** : fuerzas *fpl* armadas — **~** *vt* **-viced; -vicing** : revisar (un vehículo, etc.) — **serviceman** ['sərvəsˌmæn, -mən] *n, pl* **-men** [-mən, -ˌmɛn] : militar *m* — **service station** *n* : estación *f* de servicio — **serving** ['sərvɪŋ] *n* : porción *f*, ración *f*

session ['sɛʃən] *n* : sesión *f*

set ['sɛt] *n* **1** : juego *m* (de platos, etc.) **2** : set *m* (en tenis, etc.) **3** *or* **stage ~** : decorado *m* **4 television ~** : aparato *m* de televisión — **~** *v* **set; setting** *vt* **1** *or* **~ down** : poner **2** : poner en hora (un reloj) **3** FIX : fijar (una fecha, etc.) **4 ~ fire to** : prender fuego a **5 ~ free** : poner en libertad **6 ~ off**

: hacer sonar (una alarma), hacer estallar (una bomba) 7 ~ **out to (do sth)** : proponerse (hacer algo) 8 ~ **up** ASSEMBLE : montar, armar 9 ~ **up** ESTABLISH : establecer — *vi* 1 : cuajarse (dícese de la gelatina, etc.), fraguar (dícese del cemento) 2 : ponerse (dícese del sol, etc.) 3 ~ **in** BEGIN : empezar 4 ~ **off** *or* ~ **out** : salir (de viaje) — ~ *adj* 1 FIXED : fijo 2 READY : listo, preparado — **setback** ['sɛt,bæk] *n* : revés *m* — **setting** ['sɛt̬ɪŋ] *n* 1 : posición *f* (de un control) 2 MOUNTING : engaste *m* (de joyas) 3 SCENE : escenario *m*

settle ['sɛt̬əl] *v* **settled; settling** *vi* 1 : asentarse (dícese de polvo, colonos, etc.) 2 ~ **down** RELAX : calmarse 3 ~ **for** : conformarse con 4 ~ **in** : instalarse — *vt* 1 DECIDE : fijar, decidir 2 RESOLVE : resolver 3 PAY : pagar 4 CALM : calmar 5 COLONIZE : colonizar — **settlement** ['sɛt̬əlmənt] *n* 1 PAYMENT : pago *m* 2 COLONY : colonia *f*, poblado *m* 3 AGREEMENT : acuerdo *m* — **settler** ['sɛt̬ələr] *n* : colono *m*, -na *f*

seven ['sɛvən] *adj* : siete — ~ *n* : siete *m* — **seven hundred** *adj* : setecientos — ~ *n* : setecientos *m* — **seventeen** [,sɛvən'ti:n] *adj* : diecisiete — ~ *n* : diecisiete *m* — **seventeenth** [,sɛvən'ti:nθ] *adj* : decimoséptimo — ~ *n* 1 : decimoséptimo *m*, -ma *f* (en una serie) 2 : diecisieteavo *m* (en matemáticas) — **seventh** ['sɛvənθ] *adj* : séptimo — ~ *n* 1 : séptimo *m*, -ma *f* (en una serie) 2 : séptimo *m* (en matemáticas) — **seventieth** ['sɛvəntiəθ] *adj* : septuagésimo — ~ *n* 1 : septuagésimo *m*, -ma *f* (en una serie) 2 : setentavo *m* (en matemáticas) — **seventy** ['sɛvənt̬i] *adj* : setenta — ~ *n*, *pl* **-ties** : setenta *m*

sever ['sɛvər] *vt* **-ered; -ering** : cortar, romper

several ['sɛvrəl, 'sɛvə-] *adj* : varios — ~ *pron* : varios, varias

severance ['sɛvrənts, sɛvə-] *n* : ruptura *f*

severe [sə'vɪr] *adj* **severer; -est** 1 : severo 2 SERIOUS : grave — **severely** *adv* 1 : severamente 2 SERIOUSLY : gravemente — **severity** [sə'vɛrət̬i] *n* 1 : severidad *f* 2 SERIOUSNESS : gravedad *f*

sew ['so:] *v* **sewed; sewn** ['so:n] *or* **sewed; sewing** : coser

sewer ['su:ər] *n* : cloaca *f* — **sewage** ['su:ɪdʒ] *n* : aguas *fpl* negras

sewing ['so:ɪŋ] *n* : costura *f*

sex ['sɛks] *n* 1 : sexo *m* 2 INTERCOURSE : relaciones *fpl* sexuales — **sexism** ['sɛk,sɪzəm] *n* : sexismo *m* — **sexist** ['sɛksɪst] *adj* : sexista — **sexual** ['sɛkʃuəl] *adj* : sexual — **sexuality** [,sɛkʃu'ælət̬i] *n* : sexualidad *f* — **sexy** ['sɛksi] *adj* **sexier; -est** : sexy

shabby ['ʃæbi] *adj* **shabbier; -est** 1 WORN : gastado 2 UNFAIR : malo, injusto

shack ['ʃæk] *n* : choza *f*

shackle ['ʃækəl] *n* : grillete *m*

shade ['ʃeɪd] *n* 1 : sombra *f* 2 : tono *m* (de un color) 3 NUANCE : matiz *m* 4 *or* **lampshade** : pantalla *f* 5 *or* **window** ~ : persiana *f* — ~ *vt* **shaded; shading** : proteger de la luz — **shadow** ['ʃædo:] *n* : sombra *f* — **shadowy** ['ʃædowi] *adj* INDISTINCT : vago — **shady** ['ʃeɪdi] *adj* **shadier; -est** 1 : sombreado 2 DISREPUTABLE : sospechoso

shaft ['ʃæft] *n* 1 : asta *f* (de una flecha, etc.) 2 HANDLE : mango *m* 3 AXLE : eje *m* 4 : rayo *m* (de luz) 5 *or* **mine** ~ : pozo *m*

shaggy ['ʃægi] *adj* **shaggier; -est** : peludo

shake ['ʃeɪk] *v* **shook** ['ʃuk]; **shaken** ['ʃeɪkən]; **shaking** *vt* 1 : sacudir 2 MIX : agitar 3 ~ **hands with s.o.** : dar la mano a algn 4 ~ **one's head** : negar con la cabeza 5 ~ **up** UPSET : afectar — *vi* : temblar — ~ *n* 1 : sacudida *f* 2 → **handshake** — **shaker** ['ʃeɪkər] *n* 1 **salt** ~ : salero *m* 2 **pepper** ~ : pimentero *m* — **shaky** ['ʃeɪki] *adj* **shakier; -est** 1 : tembloroso 2 UNSTABLE : poco firme

shall ['ʃæl] *v aux*, *past* **should** ['ʃud]; *pres sing & pl* **shall** 1 (*expressing volition or futurity*) → **will** 2 (*expressing possibility or obligation*) → **should** 3 ~ **we go?** : ¿nos vamos?

shallow ['ʃælo:] *adj* 1 : poco profundo 2 SUPERFICIAL : superficial

sham ['ʃæm] *n* : farsa *f* — ~ *v* **shammed; shamming** : fingir

shambles ['ʃæmbəlz] *ns & pl* : caos *m*, desorden *m*

shame ['ʃeɪm] *n* 1 : vergüenza *f* 2 **what a ~!** : ¡qué lástima! — ~ *vt* **shamed; shaming** : avergonzar — **shameful** ['ʃeɪmfəl] *adj* : vergonzoso — **shameless** ['ʃeɪmləs] *adj* : desvergonzado

shampoo [ʃæm'pu:] *vt* : lavar (el pelo) — ~ *n*, *pl* **-poos** : champú *m*

shamrock ['ʃæm,rɑk] *n* : trébol

shan't ['ʃænt] (*contraction of* **shall not**) → **shall**

shape [ˈʃeɪp] *v* **shaped; shaping** *vt* **1** : formar **2** DETERMINE : determinar **3** **be ~d like** : tener forma de — *vi or* **~ up** : tomar forma — **~** *n* **1** : forma *f* **2** **get in ~** : ponerse en forma — **shapeless** [ˈʃeɪpləs] *adj* : informe

share [ˈʃɛr] *n* **1** : porción *f* **2** : acción *f* (en una compañía) — **~** *v* **shared; sharing** *vt* **1** : compartir **2** DIVIDE : dividir — *vi* : compartir — **shareholder** [ˈʃɛrˌhoːldər] *n* : accionista *mf*

shark [ˈʃɑrk] *n* : tiburón *m*

sharp [ˈʃɑrp] *adj* **1** : afilado **2** POINTY : puntiagudo **3** ACUTE : agudo **4** HARSH : duro, severo **5** CLEAR : nítido **6** : sostenido (en música) **7** **a ~ curve** : una curva cerrada — **~** *adv* **at two o'clock ~** : a las dos en punto — **~** *n* : sostenido (en música) — **sharpen** [ˈʃɑrpən] *vt* : afilar (un cuchillo, etc.), sacar punta a (un lápiz) — **sharpener** [ˈʃɑrpənər] *n* **1** *or* **knife ~** : afilador *m* **2** *or* **pencil ~** : sacapuntas *m* — **sharply** [ˈʃɑrpli] *adv* : bruscamente

shatter [ˈʃæt̬ər] *vt* **1** : hacer añicos **2** DEVASTATE : destrozar — *vi* : hacerse añicos

shave [ˈʃeɪv] *v* **shaved; shaved** *or* **shaven** [ˈʃeɪvən]; **shaving** *vt* **1** : afeitar **2** SLICE : cortar — *vi* : afeitarse — **~** *n* : afeitada *f* — **shaver** [ˈʃeɪvər] *n* : máquina *f* de afeitar

shawl [ˈʃɔl] *n* : chal *m*

she [ˈʃiː] *pron* : ella

sheaf [ˈʃiːf] *n, pl* **sheaves** [ˈʃiːvz] **1** : gavilla *f* **2** : fajo *m* (de papeles)

shear [ˈʃɪr] *vt* **sheared; sheared** *or* **shorn** [ˈʃorn]; **shearing** : esquilar — **shears** [ˈʃɪrz] *npl* : tijeras *fpl* (grandes)

sheath [ˈʃiːθ] *n, pl* **sheaths** [ˈʃiːðz, ˈʃiːθs] : funda *f*, vaina *f*

shed[1] [ˈʃɛd] *v* **shed; shedding** *vt* **1** : derramar (lágrimas, etc.) **2** : mudar (de piel, etc.), quitarse (ropa) **3** **~ light on** : aclarar

shed[2] *n* : cobertizo *m*

she'd [ˈʃiːd] (*contraction of* **she had** *or* **she would**) → **have, would**

sheen [ˈʃiːn] *n* : brillo *m*, lustre *m*

sheep [ˈʃiːp] *n, pl* **sheep** : oveja *f* — **sheepish** [ˈʃiːpɪʃ] *adj* : avergonzado

sheer [ˈʃɪr] *adj* **1** THIN : transparente **2** PURE : puro **3** STEEP : escarpado

sheet [ˈʃiːt] *n* **1** : sábana *f* (de la cama) **2** : hoja *f* (de papel) **3** : capa *f* (de hielo, etc.) **4** PLATE : placa *f*, lámina *f*

shelf [ˈʃɛlf] *n, pl* **shelves** [ˈʃɛlvz] : estante *m*

shell [ˈʃɛl] *n* **1** : concha *f* **2** : caparazón *m* (de un crustáceo, etc.) **3** : cáscara *f* (de un huevo, etc.) **4** : armazón *mf* (de un edificio, etc.) **5** POD : vaína *f* **6** MISSILE : proyectil *m* — **~** *vt* **1** : pelar (nueces, etc.) **2** BOMBARD : bombardear

she'll [ˈʃiːl, ˈʃɪl] (*contraction of* **she shall** *or* **she will**) → **shall, will**

shellfish [ˈʃɛlˌfɪʃ] *n* : marisco *m*

shelter [ˈʃɛltər] *n* **1** : refugio *m* **2** **take ~** : refugiarse — **~** *vt* **1** PROTECT : proteger **2** HARBOR : albergar

shelve [ˈʃɛlv] *vt* **shelved; shelving** DEFER : dar carpetazo a

shepherd [ˈʃɛpərd] *n* : pastor *m* — **~** *vt* GUIDE : conducir, guiar

sherbet [ˈʃərbət] *n* : sorbete *m*

sheriff [ˈʃɛrɪf] *n* : sheriff *mf*

sherry [ˈʃɛri] *n, pl* **-ries** : jerez *m*

she's [ˈʃiːz] (*contraction of* **she is** *or* **she has**) → **be, have**

shield [ˈʃiːld] *n* : escudo *m* — **~** *vt* : proteger

shier, shiest → **shy**

shift [ˈʃɪft] *vt* **1** MOVE : mover **2** SWITCH : transferir — *vi* **1** CHANGE : cambiar **2** MOVE : moverse **3** *or* **~ gears** : cambiar de velocidad — **~** *n* **1** CHANGE : cambio *m* **2** : turno *m* (de trabajo) — **shiftless** [ˈʃɪftləs] *adj* : holgazán — **shifty** [ˈʃɪfti] *adj* **shiftier; -est** : sospechoso

shimmer [ˈʃɪmər] *vi* : brillar, relucir

shin [ˈʃɪn] *n* : espinilla *f*

shine [ˈʃaɪn] *v* **shone** [ˈʃoːn] *or* **shined; shining** *vi* : brillar — *vt* **1** : alumbrar (una luz) **2** POLISH : sacar brillo a — **~** *n* : brillo *m*

shingle [ˈʃɪŋgəl] *n* : teja *f* plana y delgada (en construcción) — **~** *vt* **-gled; -gling** : techar — **shingles** [ˈʃɪŋgəlz] *npl* : herpes *m*

shiny [ˈʃaɪni] *adj* **shinier; -est** : brillante

ship [ˈʃɪp] *n* **1** : barco *m*, buque *m* **2** → **spaceship** — **~** *vt* **shipped; shipping** : transportar, enviar (por barco) — **shipbuilding** [ˈʃɪpˌbɪldɪŋ] *n* : construcción *f* naval — **shipment** [ˈʃɪpmənt] *n* : envío *m* — **shipping** [ˈʃɪpɪŋ] *n* **1** : transporte *m* **2** SHIPS : barcos *mpl* — **shipshape** [ˈʃɪpˈʃeɪp] *adj* : ordenado — **shipwreck** [ˈʃɪpˌrɛk] *n* : naufragio *m* — **~** *vt* **be ~ed** : naufragar — **shipyard** [ˈʃɪpˌjɑrd] *n* : astillero *m*

shirk [ˈʃərk] *vt* : esquivar

shirt [ˈʃərt] *n* : camisa *f*

shiver [ˈʃɪvər] *vi* : temblar (del frío, etc.) — **~** *n* : escalofrío *m*

shoal [ˈʃoːl] *n* : banco *m*

shock [ˈʃɑk] *n* **1** IMPACT : choque *m* **2** SURPRISE, UPSET : golpe *m* emocional **3** : shock *m* (en medicina) **4** *or* **electric ~** : descarga *f* (eléctrica) — **~** *vt* : escandalizar — **shock absorber** *n* : amortiguador *m* — **shocking** [ˈʃɑkɪŋ] *adj* : escandaloso

shoddy [ˈʃɑdi] *adj* **shoddier; -est** : de mala calidad

shoe [ˈʃuː] *n* : zapato *m* — **~** *vt* **shod** [ˈʃɑd]; **shoeing** : herrar (un caballo) — **shoelace** [ˈʃuːˌleɪs] *n* : cordón *m* (de zapato) — **shoemaker** [ˈʃuːˌmeɪkər] *n* : zapatero *m*, -ra *f*

shone → **shine**

shook → **shake**

shoot [ˈʃuːt] *v* **shot** [ˈʃɑt]; **shooting** *vt* **1** : disparar **2** : echar (una mirada) **3** PHOTOGRAPH : fotografiar **4** FILM : rodar — *vi* **1** : disparar **2 ~ by** : pasar como una bala — **~** *n* : brote *m*, retoño *m* (de una planta) — **shooting star** *n* : estrella *f* fugaz

shop [ˈʃɑp] *n* **1** : tienda *f* **2** WORKSHOP : taller *m* — **~** *vi* **shopped; shopping 1** : hacer compras **2 go shopping** : ir de compras — **shopkeeper** [ˈʃɑpˌkiːpər] *n* : tendero *m*, -ra *f* — **shoplift** [ˈʃɑpˌlɪft] *vi* : hurtar mercancía (en tiendas) — **shoplifter** [ˈʃɑpˌlɪftər] *n* : ladrón *m*, -drona *f* (que roba en tiendas) — **shopper** [ˈʃɑpər] *n* : comprador *m*, -dora *f*

shore [ˈʃor] *n* : orilla *f*

shorn → **shear**

short [ˈʃɔrt] *adj* **1** : corto **2** : bajo (de estatura) **3** CURT : brusco **4 a ~ time ago** : hace poco **5 be ~ of** : estar corto de — **~** *adv* **1 stop ~** : parar en seco **2 fall ~** : quedarse corto — **shortage** [ˈʃɔrtɪdʒ] *n* : escasez *f*, carencia *f* — **shortcake** [ˈʃɔrtˌkeɪk] *n* : tarta *f* de fruta — **shortcoming** [ˈʃɔrtˌkʌmɪŋ] *n* : defecto *m* — **shortcut** [ˈʃɔrtˌkʌt] *n* : atajo *m* — **shorten** [ˈʃɔrtən] *vt* : acortar — **shorthand** [ˈʃɔrtˌhænd] *n* : taquigrafía *f* — **short-lived** [ˈʃɔrtˈlɪvd, -ˈlaɪvd] *adj* : efímero — **shortly** [ˈʃɔrtli] *adv* : dentro de poco — **shortness** [ˈʃɔrtnəs] *n* **1** : lo corto (de una cosa), baja estatura *f* (de una persona) **2 ~ of breath** : falta *f* de aliento — **shorts** *npl* : shorts *mpl*, pantalones *mpl* cortos — **shortsighted** [ˈʃɔrtˌsaɪtəd] → **nearsighted**

shot [ˈʃɑt] *n* **1** : disparo *m*, tiro *m* **2** : tiro *m* (en deportes) **3** ATTEMPT : intento *m* **4** PHOTOGRAPH : foto *f* **5** INJECTION : inyección *f* **6** : trago *m* (de licor) — **shotgun** [ˈʃɑtˌgʌn] *n* : escopeta *f*

should [ˈʃʊd] *past of* **shall 1 if she ~ call** : si llama **2 I ~ have gone** : debería haber ido **3 they ~ arrive soon** : deben llegar pronto **4 what ~ we do?** : ¿qué hacemos?

shoulder [ˈʃoːldər] *n* **1** : hombro *m* **2** : arcén *m* (de una carretera) — **~** *vt* : cargar con (la responsabilidad, etc.) — **shoulder blade** *n* : omóplato *m*

shouldn't [ˈʃʊdənt] (*contraction of* **should not**) → **should**

shout [ˈʃaʊt] *v* : gritar — **~** *n* : grito *m*

shove [ˈʃʌv] *v* **shoved; shoving** : empujar — **~** *n* : empujón *m*

shovel [ˈʃʌvəl] *n* : pala *f* — **~** *vt* **-veled** *or* **-velled; -veling** *or* **-velling 1** : mover (tierra, etc.) con una pala **2** DIG : cavar (con una pala)

show [ˈʃoː] *v* **showed; shown** [ˈʃoːn] *or* **showed; showing** *vt* **1** : mostrar **2** TEACH : enseñar **3** PROVE : demostrar **4** ESCORT : acompañar **5** : proyectar (una película), dar (un programa de televisión) **6 ~ off** : hacer alarde de — *vi* **1** : notarse, verse **2 ~ off** : lucirse **3 ~ up** ARRIVE : aparecer — **~** *n* **1** : demostración *f* **2** EXHIBITION : exposición *f* **3** : espectáculo *m* (teatral), programa *m* (de televisión, etc.) — **showdown** [ˈʃoːˌdaʊn] *n* : confrontación *f*

shower [ˈʃaʊər] *n* **1** : ducha *f* **2** : chaparrón *m* (en meteorología) **3** PARTY : fiesta *f* — **~** *vt* **1** SPRAY : regar **2 ~ s.o. with** : colmar a algn de — *vi* **1** : ducharse **2** RAIN : llover

showy [ˈʃoːi] *adj* **showier; -est** : llamativo, ostentoso

shrank → **shrink**

shrapnel [ˈʃræpnəl] *ns & pl* : metralla *f*

shred [ˈʃrɛd] *n* **1** : tira *f* (de tela, etc.) **2** IOTA : pizca *f* — **~** *vt* **shredded; shredding 1** : hacer tiras **2** GRATE : rallar

shrewd [ˈʃruːd] *adj* : astuto

shriek [ˈʃriːk] *vi* : chillar — **~** *n* : chillido *m*, alarido *m*

shrill [ˈʃrɪl] *adj* : agudo, estridente

shrimp [ˈʃrɪmp] *n* : camarón *m*

shrine [ˈʃraɪn] *n* **1** TOMB : sepulcro *m* **2** SANCTUARY : santuario *m*

shrink [ˈʃrɪŋk] *v* **shrank** [ˈʃræŋk]; **shrunk** [ˈʃrʌŋk] *or* **shrunken** [ˈʃrʌŋkən]; **shrinking** *vt* : encoger — *vi* **1** : encogerse (dícese de ropa), reducirse (dícese de números, etc.) **2** *or* **~ back** : retroceder

shrivel [ˈʃrɪvəl] *vi* **-veled** *or* **-velled; -veling** *or* **-velling** *or* **~ up** : arrugarse, marchitarse

shroud ['ʃraʊd] *n* **1** : sudario *m,* mortaja *f* **2** VEIL : velo *m* — **~** *vt* : envolver
shrub ['ʃrʌb] *n* : arbusto *m,* mata *f*
shrug ['ʃrʌg] *vi* **shrugged; shrugging** : encogerse de hombros
shrunk → **shrink**
shudder ['ʃʌdər] *vi* : estremecerse — **~** *n* : estremecimiento *m*
shuffle ['ʃʌfəl] *v* **-fled; -fling** *vt* : barajar (naipes), revolver (papeles, etc.) — *vi* : caminar arrastrando los pies
shun ['ʃʌn] *vi* **shunned; shunning** : evitar, esquivar
shut ['ʃʌt] *v* **shut; shutting** *vt* **1** CLOSE : cerrar **2 ~ off** → **turn off 3 ~ up** CONFINE : encerrar — *vi* **1** *or* **~ down** : cerrarse **2 ~ up!** : ¡cállate! — **shutter** ['ʃʌṭər] *n* **1** *or* **window ~** : contraventana *f* **2** : obturador *m* (de una cámara)
shuttle ['ʃʌṭəl] *n* **1** : lanzadera *f* (para tejer) **2** *or* **~ bus** : autobús *m* (de corto recorrido) **3** → **space shuttle** — **~** *v* **-tled; -tling** *vt* : transportar — *vi* : ir y venir
shy ['ʃaɪ] *adj* **shier** *or* **shyer** ['ʃaɪər]; **shiest** *or* **shyest** ['ʃaɪəst] : tímido — **~** *vi* **shied; shying** *or* **~ away** : retroceder — **shyness** ['ʃaɪnəs] *n* : timidez *f*
sibling ['sɪblɪŋ] *n* : hermano *m,* hermana *f*
sick ['sɪk] *adj* **1** : enfermo **2 be ~** VOMIT : vomitar **3 be ~ of** : estar harto de **4 feel ~** : tener náuseas — **sicken** ['sɪkən] *vt* DISGUST : dar asco a — **sickening** ['sɪkənɪŋ] *adj* : nauseabundo
sickle ['sɪkəl] *n* : hoz *f*
sickly ['sɪkli] *adj* **sicklier; -est 1** UNHEALTHY : enfermizo **2** → **sickening** — **sickness** ['sɪknəs] *n* : enfermedad *f*
side ['saɪd] *n* **1** : lado *m* **2** : costado *m* (de una persona), ijada *f* (de un animal) **3** : parte *f* (en una disputa, etc.) **4 ~ by ~** : uno al lado de otro **5 take ~s** : tomar partido — **~** *vi* **~ with** : ponerse de parte de — **sideboard** ['saɪd,bord] *n* : aparador *m* — **sideburns** ['saɪd,bərnz] *npl* : patillas *fpl* — **side effect** *n* : efecto *m* secundario — **sideline** ['saɪd,laɪn] *n* : línea *f* de banda (en deportes) — **sidestep** ['saɪd,stɛp] *vt* **-stepped; -stepping** : eludir, esquivar — **sidetrack** ['saɪd,træk] *vt* **get ~ed** : distraerse — **sidewalk** ['saɪd,wɔk] *n* : acera *f* — **sideways** ['saɪd,weɪz] *adj & adv* : de lado — **siding** ['saɪdɪŋ] *n* : revestimiento *m* exterior
siege ['si:dʒ, 'si:ʒ] *n* : sitio *m*
sieve ['sɪv] *n* : tamiz *m,* cedazo *m*
sift ['sɪft] *vt* **1** : cerner, tamizar **2** *or* **~ through** : pasar por el tamiz
sigh ['saɪ] *vi* : suspirar — **~** *n* : suspiro *m*
sight ['saɪt] *n* **1** : vista *f* **2** SPECTACLE : espectáculo *m* **3** : lugar *m* de interés (turístico) **4 catch ~ of** : avistar — **~** *vt* : avistar — **sightseer** ['saɪt,si:ər] *n* : turista *mf*
sign ['saɪn] *n* **1** : signo *m* **2** NOTICE : letrero *m* **3** GESTURE : seña *f,* señal *f* — **~** *vt* : firmar (un cheque, etc.) — *vi* **1** : firmar **2 ~ up** ENROLL : inscribirse
signal ['sɪgnəl] *n* : señal *f* — **~** *v* **-naled** *or* **-nalled; -naling** *or* **-nalling** *vt* **1** : hacer señas a **2** INDICATE : señalar — *vi* **1** : hacer señas **2** : señalizar (en un vehículo)
signature ['sɪgnə,tʃʊr] *n* : firma *f*
significance [sɪg'nɪfɪkənts] *n* **1** : significado *m* **2** IMPORTANCE : importancia *f* — **significant** [sɪg'nɪfɪkənt] *adj* : importante — **signify** ['sɪgnə,faɪ] *vt* **-fied; -fying** : significar
sign language *n* : lenguaje *m* gestual — **signpost** ['saɪn,po:st] *n* : poste *m* indicador
silence ['saɪlənts] *n* : silencio *m* — **~** *vt* **-lenced; -lencing** : silenciar — **silent** ['saɪlənt] *adj* **1** : silencioso **2** MUM : callado **3** : mudo (dícese de películas y letras)
silhouette [,sɪlə'wɛt] *n* : silueta *f* — **~** *vt* **-etted; -etting be ~d against** : perfilarse contra
silicon ['sɪlɪkən, -,kɑn] *n* : silicio *m*
silk ['sɪlk] *n* : seda *f* — **silky** ['sɪlki] *adj* **silkier; -est** : sedoso
sill ['sɪl] *n* : alféizar *m* (de una ventana), umbral *m* (de una puerta)
silly ['sɪli] *adj* **sillier; -est** : tonto, estúpido
silt ['sɪlt] *n* : cieno *m*
silver ['sɪlvər] *n* **1** : plata *f* **2** → **silverware** — **~** *adj* : de plata — **silverware** ['sɪlvər,wær] *n* : plata *f* — **silvery** ['sɪlvəri] *adj* : plateado
similar ['sɪmələr] *adj* : similar, parecido — **similarity** [,sɪmə'lærəṭi] *n, pl* **-ties** : semejanza *f,* parecido *m*
simmer ['sɪmər] *v* : hervir a fuego lento
simple ['sɪmpəl] *adj* **simpler; -plest 1** : simple **2** EASY : sencillo — **simplicity** [sɪm'plɪsəṭi] *n* : simplicidad *f,* sencillez *f* — **simplify** ['sɪmplə,faɪ] *vt* **-fied; -fying** : simplificar — **simply** ['sɪmpli] *adv* **1** : sencillamente **2** ABSOLUTELY : realmente

simulate ['sɪmjəˌleɪt] *vt* **-lated; -lating** : simular
simultaneous [ˌsaɪməl'teɪniəs] *adj* : simultáneo
sin ['sɪn] *n* : pecado *m* — ~ *vi* **sinned; sinning** : pecar
since ['sɪnts] *adv* **1** *or* ~ **then** : desde entonces **2 long** ~ : hace mucho — ~ *conj* **1** : desde que **2** BECAUSE : ya que, como **3 it's been years** ~... : hace años que... — ~ *prep* : desde
sincere [sɪn'sɪr] *adj* **-cerer; -est** : sincero — **sincerely** *adv* : sinceramente — **sincerity** [sɪn'serəṭi] *n* : sinceridad *f*
sinful ['sɪnfəl] *adj* : pecador (dícese de las personas), pecaminoso (dícese de las acciones)
sing ['sɪŋ] *v* **sang** ['sæŋ] *or* **sung** ['sʌŋ]; **sung; singing** : cantar
singe ['sɪndʒ] *vt* **singed; singeing** : chamuscar
singer ['sɪŋər] *n* : cantante *mf*
single ['sɪŋgəl] *adj* **1** : solo, único **2** UNMARRIED : soltero **3 every** ~ **day** : cada día, todos los días — ~ *n* **1** : soltero *m*, **-ra** *f* **2** *or* ~ **room** : habitación *f* individual — ~ *vt* **-gled; -gling** ~ **out 1** SELECT : escoger **2** DISTINGUISH : señalar — **single-handed** ['sɪŋgəl'hændəd] *adj* : sin ayuda, solo
singular ['sɪŋgjələr] *adj* : singular — ~ *n* : singular *m*
sinister ['sɪnəstər] *adj* : siniestro
sink ['sɪŋk] *v* **sank** ['sæŋk] *or* **sunk** ['sʌŋk]; **sunk; sinking** *vi* **1** : hundirse (en un líquido) **2** DROP : bajar, caer — *vt* **1** : hundir **2** ~ **sth into** : clavar algo en — ~ *n* **1** *or* **kitchen** ~ : fregadero *m* **2** *or* **bathroom** ~ : lavabo *m*, lavamanos *m*
sinner ['sɪnər] *n* : pecador *m*, **-dora** *f*
sip ['sɪp] *v* **sipped; sipping** *vt* : sorber — *vi* : beber a sorbos — ~ *n* : sorbo *m*
siphon ['saɪfən] *n* : sifón *m* — ~ *vt* : sacar con sifón
sir ['sər] *n* **1** (*in titles*) : sir *m* **2** (*as a form of address*) : señor *m* **3 Dear Sir** : Estimado señor
siren ['saɪrən] *n* : sirena *f*
sirloin ['sərˌlɔɪn] *n* : solomillo *m*
sissy ['sɪsi] *n, pl* **-sies** : mariquita *mf fam*
sister ['sɪstər] *n* : hermana *f* — **sister-in-law** ['sɪstərɪnˌlɔ] *n, pl* **sisters-in-law** : cuñada *f*
sit ['sɪt] *v* **sat** ['sæt]; **sitting** *vi* **1** *or* ~ **down** : sentarse **2** LIE : estar (ubicado) **3** MEET : estar en sesión **4** *or* ~ **up** : incorporarse — *vt* : sentar
site ['saɪt] *n* **1** : sitio *m*, lugar *m* **2** LOT : solar *m*
sitting room → **living room**
sitter ['sɪṭər] → **baby-sitter**
situated ['sɪtʃuˌeɪṭəd] *adj* : ubicado, situado — **situation** [ˌsɪtʃu'eɪʃən] *n* : situación *f*
six ['sɪks] *adj* : seis — ~ *n* : seis *m* — **six hundred** *adj* : seiscientos — ~ *n* : seiscientos *m* — **sixteen** [sɪks'tiːn] *adj* : dieciséis — ~ *n* : dieciséis *m* — **sixteenth** [sɪks'tiːnθ] *adj* : decimosexto — ~ *n* **1** : decimosexto *m*, **-ta** *f* (en una serie) **2** : dieciseisavo *m*, dieciseisava parte *f* — **sixth** ['sɪksθ, 'sɪkst] *adj* : sexto — ~ *n* **1** : sexto *m*, **-ta** *f* (en una serie) **2** : sexto *m* (en matemáticas) — **sixtieth** ['sɪksṭiəθ] *adj* : sexagésimo — ~ *n* **1** : sexagésimo *m*, **-ma** *f* (en una serie) **2** : sesentavo *m* (en matemáticas) — **sixty** ['sɪksṭi] *adj* : sesenta — ~ *n, pl* **-ties** : sesenta *m*
size ['saɪz] *n* **1** : tamaño *m*, talla *f* (de ropa), número *m* (de zapatos) **2** EXTENT : magnitud *f* — ~ *vt* **sized; sizing** ~ **up** : evaluar — **sizable** *or* **sizeable** ['saɪzəbəl] *adj* : considerable
sizzle ['sɪzəl] *vi* **-zled; -zling** : chisporrotear
skate[1] ['skeɪt] *n* : raya *f* (pez)
skate[2] *n* : patín *m* — ~ *vi* **skated; skating** : patinar — **skateboard** ['skeɪtˌbord] *n* : monopatín *m* — **skater** ['skeɪṭər] *n* : patinador *m*, **-dora** *f*
skeleton ['skɛlətən] *n* : esqueleto *m*
skeptic ['skɛptɪk] *n* : escéptico *m*, **-ca** *f* — **skeptical** ['skɛptɪkəl] *adj* : escéptico — **skepticism** ['skɛptəˌsɪzəm] *n* : escepticismo *m*
sketch ['skɛtʃ] *n* **1** : esbozo *m*, bosquejo *m* **2** SKIT : sketch *m* — ~ *vt* : bosquejar — *vi* : hacer bosquejos — **sketchy** ['skɛtʃi] *adj* **sketchier; -est** : incompleto
skewer ['skjuːər] *n* : brocheta *f*, broqueta *f*
ski ['skiː] *n, pl* **skis** : esquí *m* — ~ *vi* **skied; skiing** : esquiar
skid ['skɪd] *n* : derrape *m*, patinazo *m* — ~ *vi* **skidded; skidding** : derrapar, patinar
skier ['skiːər] *n* : esquiador *m*, **-dora** *f*
skill ['skɪl] *n* **1** : habilidad *f*, destreza *f* **2** TECHNIQUE : técnica *f* — **skilled** ['skɪld] *adj* : hábil
skillet ['skɪlət] *n* : sartén *mf*
skillful ['skɪlfəl] *adj* : hábil, diestro
skim ['skɪm] *vt* **skimmed; skimming 1** : espumar (sopa, etc.), descremar (leche) **2** : pasar rozando (una superfi-

cie) **3** *or* **~ through** : echar un vistazo a — **~** *adj* : descremado

skimp ['skɪmp] *vi* **~ on** : escatimar — **skimpy** ['skɪmpi] *adj* **skimpier; -est 1** : exiguo, escaso **2** : brevísimo (dícese de ropa)

skin ['skɪn] *n* : piel *f* — **~** *vt* **skinned; skinning** : despellejar — **skin diving** *n* : buceo *m*, submarinismo *m* — **skinny** ['skɪni] *adj* **skinnier; -est** : flaco

skip ['skɪp] *v* **skipped; skipping** *vi* : ir brincando — *vt* OMIT : saltarse — **~** *n* : brinco *m*, salto *m*

skipper ['skɪpər] *n* : capitán *m*, -tana *f*

skirmish ['skərmɪʃ] *n* : escaramuza *f*

skirt ['skərt] *n* : falda *f* — **~** *vt* **1** BORDER : bordear **2** EVADE : eludir

skull ['skʌl] *n* : cráneo *m* (de una persona viva), calavera *f* (de un esqueleto)

skunk ['skʌŋk] *n* : mofeta *f*, zorrillo *m* *Lat*

sky ['skaɪ] *n*, *pl* **skies** : cielo *m* — **skylight** ['skaɪˌlaɪt] *n* : claraboya *f*, tragaluz *m* — **skyline** ['skaɪˌlaɪn] *n* : horizonte *m* — **skyscraper** ['skaɪˌskreɪpər] *n* : rascacielos *m*

slab ['slæb] *n* : bloque *m* (de piedra, etc.)

slack ['slæk] *adj* **1** LOOSE : flojo **2** CARELESS : descuidado — **~** *n* **1 take up the ~** : tensar (una cuerda, etc.) **2 ~s** *npl* : pantalones *mpl* — **slacken** ['slækən] *vt* : aflojar — *vi* : aflojarse

slain → **slay**

slam ['slæm] *n* : golpe *m*, portazo *m* (de una puerta) — **~** *v* **slammed; slamming** *vt* **1** *or* **~ down** : tirar, plantar **2** *or* **~ shut** : cerrar de golpe **3 ~ the door** : dar un portazo — *vi* **1** : cerrarse de golpe **2 ~ into** : chocar contra

slander ['slændər] *vt* : calumniar, difamar — **~** *n* : calumnia *f*, difamación *f*

slang ['slæŋ] *n* : argot *m*

slant ['slænt] *n* : inclinación *f* — **~** *vi* : inclinarse

slap ['slæp] *vt* **slapped; slapping 1** : dar una bofetada a **2 ~ s.o. on the back** : dar una palmada en la espalda a algn — **~** *n* : bofetada *f*, cachetada *f* *Lat*

slash ['slæʃ] *vt* **1** : hacer un tajo en **2** : rebajar (precios) drásticamente — **~** *n* : tajo *m*

slat ['slæt] *n* : tablilla *f*

slate ['sleɪt] *n* : pizarra *f*

slaughter ['slɔt̬ər] *n* : matanza *f* — **~** *vt* **1** : matar (animales) **2** MASSACRE : masacrar — **slaughterhouse** ['slɔt̬ərˌhaʊs] *n* : matadero *m*

slave ['sleɪv] *n* : esclavo *m*, -va *f* — **~** *vi* **slaved; slaving** : trabajar como un burro — **slavery** ['sleɪvəri] *n* : esclavitud *f*

Slavic ['slɑvɪk, 'slæ-] *adj* : eslavo

slay ['sleɪ] *vt* **slew** ['slu:]; **slain** ['sleɪn]; **slaying** : asesinar

sleazy ['sli:zi] *adj* **sleazier; -est** : sórdido

sled ['slɛd] *n* : trineo *m*

sledgehammer ['slɛdʒˌhæmər] *n* : almádena *f*

sleek ['sli:k] *adj* : liso y brillante

sleep ['sli:p] *n* **1** : sueño *m* **2 go to ~** : dormirse — **~** *vi* **slept** ['slɛpt]; **sleeping** : dormir — **sleeper** ['sli:pər] *n* **be a light ~** : tener el sueño ligero — **sleepless** ['sli:pləs] *adj* **have a ~ night** : pasar la noche en blanco — **sleepwalker** ['sli:pˌwɔkər] *n* : sonámbulo *m*, -la *f* — **sleepy** ['sli:pi] *adj* **sleepier; -est 1** : somnoliento, soñoliento **2 be ~** : tener sueño

sleet ['sli:t] *n* : aguanieve *f* — **~** *vi* : caer aguanieve

sleeve ['sli:v] *n* : manga *f* — **sleeveless** ['sli:vləs] *adj* : sin mangas

sleigh ['sleɪ] *n* : trineo *m*

slender ['slɛndər] *adj* : delgado

slew ['slu:] → **slay**

slice ['slaɪs] *vt* **sliced; slicing** : cortar — **~** *n* : trozo *m*, rebanada *f* (de pan, etc.), tajada *f* (de carne)

slick ['slɪk] *adj* SLIPPERY : resbaladizo, resbaloso *Lat*

slide ['slaɪd] *v* **slid** ['slɪd]; **sliding** ['slaɪdɪŋ] *vi* : deslizarse — *vt* : deslizar — **~** *n* **1** : deslizamiento *m* **2** : tobogán *m* (para niños) **3** : diapositiva *f* (fotográfica) **4** DECLINE : descenso *m*

slier, sliest → **sly**

slight ['slaɪt] *adj* **1** : ligero, leve **2** SLENDER : delgado — **~** *vt* : desairar — **slightly** ['slaɪtli] *adv* : ligeramente, un poco

slim ['slɪm] *adj* **slimmer; slimmest 1** : delgado **2 a ~ chance** : escasas posibilidades *fpl* — **~** *v* **slimmed; slimming** : adelgazar

slime ['slaɪm] *n* **1** : baba *f* (de un caracol, etc.) **2** MUD : limo *m* — **slimy** ['slaɪmi] *adj* **slimier; -est** : viscoso

sling ['slɪŋ] *vt* **slung** ['slʌŋ]; **slinging 1** THROW : lanzar **2** HANG : colgar — **~** *n* **1** : honda *f* **2** : cabestrillo *m* (en medicina) — **slingshot** ['slɪŋˌʃɑt] *n* : tirachinas *m*

slink ['slɪŋk] *vi* **slunk** ['slʌŋk]; **slinking** : andar furtivamente

slip[1] ['slɪp] *v* **slipped; slipping** *vi* **1** SLIDE : resbalarse **2 let sth ~** : dejar

escapar algo **3 ~ away** : escabullirse **4 ~ up** : equivocarse — *vt* **1** : deslizar **2 ~ into** : ponerse (una prenda) **3 it slipped my mind** : se me olvidó — **~** *n* **1** MISTAKE : error *m,* desliz *m* **2 ~ of the tongue** : lapsus *m* **3** PETTICOAT : enagua *f*
slip[2] *n* **~ of paper** : papelito *m*
slipper ['slɪpər] *n* : zapatilla *f,* pantufla *f*
slippery ['slɪpəri] *adj* **slipperier; -est** : resbaladizo, resbaloso *Lat*
slit ['slɪt] *n* **1** OPENING : rendija *f* **2** CUT : corte *m,* raja *f* — **~** *vt* **slit; slitting** : cortar
slither ['slɪðər] *vi* : deslizarse
sliver ['slɪvər] *n* : astilla *f*
slogan ['slo:gən] *n* : eslogan *m*
slop ['slɑp] *v* **slopped; slopping** *vt* : derramar — *vi* : derramarse
slope ['slo:p] *vi* **sloped; sloping** : inclinarse — **~** *n* : pendiente *f,* declive *m*
sloppy ['slɑpi] *adj* **sloppier; -est 1** CARELESS : descuidado **2** UNKEMPT : desaliñado
slot ['slɑt] *n* : ranura *f*
sloth ['slɔθ, 'slo:θ] *n* : pereza *f*
slouch ['slaʊtʃ] *vi* : andar con los hombros caídos (en una silla)
slovenly ['slɑvənli, 'slʌv-] *adj* : desaliñado
slow ['slo:] *adj* **1** : lento **2 be ~** : estar atrasado (dícese de un reloj) — **~** *adv* → **slowly** — **~** *vt* : retrasar, retardar — *vi or* **~ down** : ir más despacio — **slowly** ['slo:li] *adv* : lentamente, despacio — **slowness** ['slo:nəs] *n* : lentitud *f*
sludge ['slʌdʒ] *n* SEWAGE : aguas *fpl* negras
slug[1] ['slʌg] *n* **1** : babosa *f* (molusco) **2** BULLET : bala *f* **3** TOKEN : ficha *f*
slug[2] *vt* **slugged; slugging** : pegar un porrazo a
sluggish ['slʌgɪʃ] *adj* : lento
slum ['slʌm] *n* : barrio *m* bajo
slumber ['slʌmbər] *vi* : dormir — **~** *n* : sueño *m*
slump ['slʌmp] *vi* **1** DROP : bajar **2** COLLAPSE : dejarse caer **3** → **slouch** — **~** *n* : bajón *m*
slung → **sling**
slunk → **slink**
slur[1] ['slər] *n* ASPERSION : calumnia *f,* difamación *f*
slur[2] *vt* **slurred; slurring** : arrastrar (las palabras)
slurp ['slərp] *v* : beber haciendo ruido — **~** *n* : sorbo *m* (ruidoso)
slush ['slʌʃ] *n* : nieve *f* medio derretida
sly ['slaɪ] *adj* **slier** ['slaɪər]; **sliest** ['slaɪəst] **1** : astuto, taimado **2 on the ~** : a escondidas
smack[1] ['smæk] *vi* **~ of** : oler a
smack[2] *vt* **1** : pegar una bofetada a **2** KISS : besar **3 ~ one's lips** : relamerse — **~** *n* : **1** SLAP : bofetada *f* **2** KISS : beso *m* — **~** *adv* : justo, exactamente
small ['smɔl] *adj* : pequeño, chico — **smallpox** ['smɔl,pɑks] *n* : viruela *f*
smart ['smɑrt] *adj* **1** : listo, inteligente **2** STYLISH : elegante — **~** *vi* STING : escocer — **smartly** ['smɑrtli] *adv* : elegantemente
smash ['smæʃ] *n* **1** BLOW : golpe *m* **2** COLLISION : choque *m* **3** BANG, CRASH : estrépito *m* — **~** *vt* **1** BREAK : romper **2** DESTROY : aplastar — *vi* **1** SHATTER : hacerse pedazos **2 ~ into** : estrellarse contra
smattering ['smæt̬ərɪŋ] *n* : nociones *fpl*
smear ['smɪr] *n* : mancha *f* — **~** *vt* **1** : embadurnar (de pinta, etc.), untar (de aceite, etc.) **2** SMUDGE : manchar
smell ['smɛl] *v* **smelled** *or* **smelt** ['smɛlt]; **smelling** : oler — **~** *n* **1** : (sentido *m* del) olfato *m* **2** ODOR : olor *m* — **smelly** ['smɛli] *adj* **smellier; -est** : maloliente
smelt ['smɛlt] *vt* : fundir
smile ['smaɪl] *vi* **smiled; smiling** : sonreír — **~** *n* : sonrisa *f*
smirk ['smərk] *vi* : sonreír con suficiencia — **~** *n* : sonrisa *f* satisfecha
smitten ['smɪtən] *adj* **be ~ with** : estar enamorado de
smith ['smɪθ] → **blacksmith**
smock ['smɑk] *n* : blusón *m,* bata *f*
smog ['smɑg, 'smɔg] *n* : smog *m*
smoke ['smo:k] *n* : humo *m* — **~** *v* **smoked; smoking** *vi* **1** : humear (dícese de fuegos, etc.) **2** : fumar (dícese de personas) — *vt* **1** : ahumar (carne, etc.) **2** : fumar (cigarillos) — **smoker** ['smo:kər] *n* : fumador *m,* -dora *f* — **smokestack** ['smo:k,stæk] *n* : chimenea *f* — **smoky** ['smo:ki] *adj* **smokier; -est 1** : lleno de humo **2** : a humo (dícese de sabores, etc.)
smolder ['smo:ldər] *vi* : arder (sin llama)
smooth ['smu:ð] *adj* **1** : liso (dícese de superficies), suave (dícese de movimientos), tranquilo (dícese del mar) **2** : sin grumos (dícese de salsas, etc.) — **~** *vt* : alisar — **smoothly** ['smu:ðli] *adv* : suavemente — **smoothness** ['smu:ðnəs] *n* : suavidad *f*
smother ['smʌðər] *vt* : asfixiar (a algn), sofocar (llamas, etc.)
smudge ['smʌdʒ] *v* **smudged; smudg-**

ing *vt* : emborronar — *vi* : correrse — ~ *n* : mancha *f*, borrón *m*
smug ['smʌg] *adj* **smugger; smuggest** : suficiente
smuggle ['smʌgəl] *vt* **-gled; -gling** : pasar de contrabando — **smuggler** ['smʌgələr] *n* : contrabandista *mf*
snack ['snæk] *n* : refrigerio *m*, tentempié *m fam*
snag ['snæg] *n* : problema *m* — ~ *v* **snagged; snagging** *vt* : enganchar — *vi* : engancharse
snail ['sneɪl] *n* : caracol *m*
snake ['sneɪk] *n* : culebra *f*, serpiente *f*
snap ['snæp] *v* **snapped; snapping** *vi* **1** BREAK : romperse **2** : intentar morder (dícese de un perro, etc.) **3** ~ **at** : contestar bruscamente a — *vt* **1** BREAK : romper **2** ~ **one's fingers** : chasquear los dedos **3** ~ **open/shut** : abrir/cerrar de golpe — ~ *n* **1** : chasquido *m* **2** FASTENER : broche *m* (de presión) **3 be a** ~ : ser facilísimo — **snappy** ['snæpi] *adj* **snappier; -est 1** FAST : rápido **2** STYLISH : elegante — **snapshot** ['snæp,ʃɑt] *n* : instantánea *f*
snare ['snær] *n* : trampa *f* — ~ *vt* **snared; snaring** : atrapar
snarl[1] ['snɑrl] *vi* TANGLE : enmarañar, enredar — ~ *n* : enredo *m*, maraña *f*
snarl[2] *vi* GROWL : gruñir — *n* : gruñido *m*
snatch ['snætʃ] *vt* : arrebatar
sneak ['sni:k] *vi* : ir a hurtadillas — *vt* : hacer furtivamente — ~ *n* : soplón *m*, -plona *f fam* — **sneakers** ['sni:kərz] *npl* : tenis *mpl*, zapatillas *fpl* — **sneaky** ['sni:ki] *adj* **sneakier; -est** : solapado
sneer ['snɪr] *vi* : sonreír con desprecio — ~ *n* : sonrisa *f* de desprecio
sneeze ['sni:z] *vi* **sneezed; sneezing** : estornudar — ~ *n* : estornudo *m*
snide ['snaɪd] *adj* : sarcástico
sniff ['snɪf] *vi* : oler — *vt* **1** : oler **2** → **sniffle** — ~ *n* : aspiración *f* por la nariz — **sniffle** ['snɪfəl] *vi* **-fled; -fling** : sorberse la nariz — **sniffles** ['snɪfəlz] *npl* **have the** ~ : estar resfriado
snip ['snɪp] *n* : tijeretada *f* — ~ *vt* **snipped; snipping** : cortar (con tijeras)
snivel ['snɪvəl] *vi* **-veled** *or* **-velled; -veling** *or* **-velling** : lloriquear
snob ['snɑb] *n* : esnob *mf* — **snobbish** ['snɑbɪʃ] *adj* : esnob
snoop ['snu:p] *vi* : husmear — ~ *n* : fisgón *m*, -gona *f*
snooze ['snu:z] *vi* **snoozed; snoozing** : dormitar — ~ *n* : siestecita *f*, siestita *f*
snore ['snor] *vi* **snored; snoring** : roncar — ~ *n* : ronquido *m*
snort ['snɔrt] *vi* : bufar — ~ *n* : bufido *m*
snout ['snaʊt] *n* : hocico *m*, morro *m*
snow ['sno:] *n* : nieve *f* — ~ *vi* : nevar — **snowfall** ['sno:,fɔl] *n* : nevada *f* — **snowflake** ['sno:,fleɪk] *n* : copo *m* de nieve — **snowman** ['sno:,mæn] *n* : muñeco *m* de nieve — **snowplow** ['sno:,plaʊ] *n* : quitanieves *m* — **snowshoe** ['sno:,ʃu:] *n* : raqueta *f* (para nieve) — **snowstorm** ['sno:,stɔrm] *n* : tormenta *f* de nieve — **snowy** ['sno:i] *adj* **snowier; -est 1 a** ~ **day** : un día nevoso **2** ~ **mountains** : montañas *fpl* nevadas
snub ['snʌb] *vt* **snubbed; snubbing** : desairar — ~ *n* : desaire *m*
snuff ['snʌf] *vt or* ~ **out** : apagar
snug ['snʌg] *adj* **snugger; snuggest 1** : cómodo **2** TIGHT : ajustado — **snuggle** ['snʌgəl] *vi* **-gled; -gling** : acurrucarse
so ['so:] *adv* **1** LIKEWISE : también **2** THUS : así **3** THEREFORE : por lo tanto **4** *or* ~ **much** : tanto **5** *or* ~ **very** : tan **6 and** ~ **on** : etcétera **7 I think** ~ : creo que sí **8 I told you** ~ : te lo dije — ~ *conj* **1** THEREFORE : así que **2** *or* ~ **that** : para que **3** ~ **what?** : ¿y qué? — ~ *adj* TRUE : cierto — ~ *pron* **or** ~ : más o menos
soak ['so:k] *vi* : estar en remojo — *vt* **1** : poner en remojo **2** ~ **up** : absorber — ~ *n* : remojo *m*
soap ['so:p] *n* : jabón *m* — ~ *vt or* ~ **up** : enjabonar — **soapy** ['so:pi] **soapier; -est** *adj* : jabonoso
soar ['sor] *vi* **1** : planear **2** SKYROCKET : dispararse
sob ['sɑb] *vi* **sobbed; sobbing** : sollozar — ~ *n* : sollozo *m*
sober ['so:bər] *adj* **1** : sobrio **2** SERIOUS : serio — **sobriety** [sə'braɪəṭi, so-] *n* **1** : sobriedad *f* **2** SERIOUSNESS : seriedad *f*
so–called ['so:'kɔld] *adj* : supuesto, presunto
soccer ['sɑkər] *n* : futbol *m*, fútbol *m*
social ['so:ʃəl] *adj* : social — ~ *n* : reunión *f* social — **sociable** ['so:ʃəbəl] *adj* : sociable — **socialism** ['so:ʃə,lɪzəm] *n* : socialismo *m* — **socialist** ['so:ʃəlɪst] *n* : socialista *mf* — ~ *adj* : socialista — **socialize** ['so:ʃə,laɪz] *v* **-ized; -izing** *vt* : socializar — *vi* ~ **with** : alternar con — **society** [sə'saɪəṭi] *n*, *pl* **-eties** : sociedad *f* — **sociology** [,so:si'ɑlədʒi] *n* : sociología *f*

sock[1] ['sɑk] *n, pl* **socks** *or* **sox** ['sɑks] : calcetín *m*
sock[2] *vt* : pegar, golpear — ~ *n* PUNCH : puñetazo *m*
socket ['sɑkət] *n* **1** *or* **electric** ~ : enchufe *m*, toma *f* de corriente **2** *or* **eye** ~ : órbita *f*, cuenca *f* **3** : glena *f* (de una articulación)
soda ['so:də] *n* **1** *or* ~ **pop** : refresco *m*, gaseosa *f* **2** *or* ~ **water** : soda *f*
sodium ['so:diəm] *n* : sodio *m*
sofa ['so:fə] *n* : sofá *m*
soft ['sɔft] *adj* **1** : blando **2** SMOOTH : suave — **softball** ['sɔft,bɔl] *n* : softbol *m* — **soft drink** *n* : refresco *m* — **soften** ['sɔfən] *vt* **1** : ablandar **2** EASE, SMOOTH : suavizar — *vi* **1** : ablandarse **2** EASE : suavizarse — **softly** ['sɔftli] *adv* : suavemente — **software** ['sɔft,wær] *n* : software *m*
soggy ['sɑgi] *adj* **soggier; -est** : empapado
soil ['sɔɪl] *vt* : ensuciar — ~ *n* DIRT : tierra *f*
solace ['sɑləs] *n* : consuelo *m*
solar ['so:lər] *adj* : solar
sold → **sell**
solder ['sɑdər, 'sɔ-] *n* : soldadura *f* — ~ *vt* : soldar
soldier ['so:ldʒər] *n* : soldado *mf*
sole[1] ['so:l] *n* : lenguado *m* (pez)
sole[2] *n* : planta *f* (del pie), suela *f* (de un zapato)
sole[3] *adj* : único — **solely** ['so:li] *adv* : únicamente, sólo
solemn ['sɑləm] *adj* : solemne — **solemnity** [sə'lɛmnət̬i] *n, pl* **-ties** : solemnidad *f*
solicit [sə'lɪsət] *vt* : solicitar
solid ['sɑləd] *adj* **1** : sólido **2** UNBROKEN : continuo **3** ~ **gold** : oro *m* macizo **4** **two** ~ **hours** : dos horas seguidas — ~ *n* : sólido *m* — **solidarity** [,sɑlə'dærət̬i] *n* : solidaridad *f* — **solidify** [sə'lɪdə,faɪ] *v* **-fied; -fying** *vt* : solidificar — *vi* : solidificarse — **solidity** [sə'lɪdət̬i] *n, pl* **-ties** : solidez *f*
solitary ['sɑlə,tɛri] *adj* : solitario — **solitude** ['sɑlə,tu:d, -,tju:d] *n* : soledad *f*
solo ['so:,lo:] *n, pl* **solos** : solo *m* — **soloist** ['so:loɪst] *n* : solista *mf*
solution [sə'lu:ʃən] *n* : solución *f* — **soluble** ['sɑljəbəl] *adj* : soluble — **solve** ['sɑlv] *vt* **solved; solving** : resolver — **solvent** ['sɑlvənt] *n* : solvente *m*
somber ['sɑmbər] *adj* : sombrío
some ['sʌm] *adj* **1** (*of unspecified identity*) : un **2** (*of an unspecified amount*) : algo de, un poco de **3** (*of an unspecified number*) : unos **4** CERTAIN : algunos **5** **that was** ~ **game!** : ¡fue un partidazo! — ~ *pron* **1** SEVERAL : algunos, unos **2** PART : un poco, algo — ~ *adv* ~ **twenty people** : unas veinte personas — **somebody** ['sʌmbədi, -,bɑdi] *pron* : alguien — **someday** ['sʌm,deɪ] *adv* : algún día — **somehow** ['sʌm,haʊ] *adv* **1** : de algún modo **2** ~ **or other** : de alguna manera u otra — **someone** ['sʌm,wʌn] *pron* : alguien
somersault ['sʌmər,sɔlt] *n* : voltereta *f*, salto *m* mortal
something ['sʌmθɪŋ] *pron* **1** : algo **2** ~ **else** : otra cosa — **sometime** ['sʌm,taɪm] *adv* **1** : algún día, en algún momento **2** ~ **next month** : (durante) el mes que viene — **sometimes** ['sʌm,taɪmz] *adv* : a veces — **somewhat** ['sʌm,hwʌt, -,hwɑt] *adv* : algo — **somewhere** ['sʌm,hwɛr] *adv* **1** : en alguna parte, en algún lado **2** ~ **around** : alrededor de **3** ~ **else** → **elsewhere**
son ['sʌn] *n* : hijo *m*
song ['sɔŋ] *n* : canción *f*
son–in–law ['sʌnɪn,lɔ] *n, pl* **sons–in–law** : yerno *m*
sonnet ['sɑnət] *n* : soneto *m*
soon ['su:n] *adv* **1** : pronto **2** SHORTLY : dentro de poco **3** **as** ~ **as** : en cuanto **4** **as** ~ **as possible** : lo más pronto posible **5** ~ **after** : poco después **6** ~**er or later** : tarde o temprano **7** **the** ~**er the better** : cuanto antes mejor
soot ['sʊt, 'su:t, 'sʌt] *n* : hollín *m*
soothe ['su:ð] *vt* **soothed; soothing** **1** CALM : calmar **2** RELIEVE : aliviar
sop ['sɑp] *vt* **sopped; sopping** ~ **up** : absorber
sophistication [sə,fɪstə'keɪʃən] *n* : sofisticación *f* — **sophisticated** [sə'fɪstə,keɪt̬əd] *adj* : sofisticado
sophomore ['sɑf,mor, 'sɑfə,mor] *n* : estudiante *mf* de segundo año
soprano [sə'præ,no:] *n, pl* **-nos** : soprano *mf*
sorcerer ['sɔrsərər] *n* : hechicero *m*, brujo *m* — **sorcery** ['sɔrsəri] *n* : hechicería *f*, brujería *f*
sordid ['sɔrdɪd] *adj* : sórdido
sore ['sor] *adj* **sorer; sorest** **1** : dolorido **2** ANGRY : enfadado **3** ~ **throat** : dolor *m* de garganta **4** **I have a** ~ **throat** : me duele la garganta — ~ *n* : llaga *f* — **sorely** ['sorli] *adv* : muchísimo — **soreness** ['sornəs] *n* : dolor *m*
sorrow ['sɑr,o:] *n* : pesar *m*, pena *f* — **sorry** ['sɑri] *adj* **sorrier; -est** **1** PITIFUL : lamentable **2** **feel** ~ **for** : compadecer **3** **I'm** ~ : lo siento

sort ['sɔrt] *n* **1** : tipo *m*, clase *f* **2 a ~ of** : una especie de — **~** *vt* : clasificar — **sort of** *adv* **1** SOMEWHAT : algo **2** MORE OR LESS : más o menos
SOS [ˌɛsˌoːˈɛs] *n* : SOS *m*
so–so [ˈsoːˈsoː] *adj & adv* : así así *fam*
soufflé [suːˈfleɪ] *n* : suflé *m*
sought → **seek**
soul [ˈsoːl] *n* : alma *f*
sound[1] [ˈsaʊnd] *adj* **1** HEALTHY : sano **2** FIRM : sólido **3** SENSIBLE : lógico **4 a ~ sleep** : un sueño profundo **5 safe and ~** : sano y salvo
sound[2] *n* : sonido *m* — *vt* : hacer sonar, tocar (una trompeta, etc.) — *vi* **1** : sonar **2** SEEM : parecer
sound[3] *n* CHANNEL : brazo *m* de mar — **~** *vt* **1** : sondar (en navegación) **2** *or* **~ out** : sondear
soundly [ˈsaʊndli] *adv* **1** SOLIDLY : sólidamente **2** DEEPLY : profundamente
soundproof [ˈsaʊndˌpruːf] *adj* : insonorizado
soup [ˈsuːp] *n* : sopa *f*
sour [ˈsaʊər] *adj* **1** : agrio **2 ~ milk** : leche *f* cortada — **~** *vt* : agriar
source [ˈsors] *n* : fuente *f*, origen *m*
south [ˈsaʊθ] *adv* : al sur — **~** *adj* : (del) sur — **~** *n* : sur *m* — **South African** *adj* : sudafricano — **South American** *adj* : sudamericano — **southeast** [saʊˈθiːst] *adv* : hacia el sureste — **~** *adj* : (del) sureste — **~** *n* : sureste *m*, sudeste *m* — **southeastern** [saʊˈθiːstərn] *adj* → **southeast** — **southerly** [ˈsʌðərli] *adv & adj* : del sur — **southern** [ˈsʌðərn] *adj* : del sur, meridional — **southwest** [saʊθˈwɛst] *adv* : hacia el suroeste — **~** *adj* : (del) suroeste — **~** *n* : suroeste *m*, sudoeste *m* — **southwestern** [saʊθˈwɛstərn] *adj* → **southwest**
souvenir [ˌsuːvəˈnɪr, ˈsuːvəˌ-] *n* : recuerdo *m*
sovereign [ˈsɑvərən] *n* : soberano *m*, -na *f* — **~** *adj* : soberano — **sovereignty** [ˈsɑvərənti] *n, pl* **-ties** : soberanía *f*
Soviet [ˈsoːviˌɛt, ˈsɑ-, -viət] *adj* : soviético
sow[1] [ˈsaʊ] *n* : cerda *f*
sow[2] [ˈsoː] *vt* **sowed; sown** [ˈsoːn] *or* **sowed; sowing** : sembrar
sox → **sock**
soybean [ˈsɔɪˌbiːn] *n* : soya *f*, soja *f*
spa [ˈspɑ] *n* : balneario *m*
space [ˈspeɪs] *n* **1** : espacio *m* **2** ROOM, SPOT : sitio *m*, lugar *m* — **~** *vt* **spaced; spacing** : espaciar — **spaceship** [ˈspeɪsˌʃɪp] *n* : nave *f* espacial — **space shuttle** *n* : transbordador *m* espacial — **spacious** [ˈspeɪʃəs] *adj* : espacioso, amplio
spade[1] [ˈspeɪd] *n* SHOVEL : pala *f*
spade[2] *n* : pica *f* (naipe)
spaghetti [spəˈgɛţi] *n* : espaguetis *mpl*
span [ˈspæn] *n* **1** PERIOD : espacio *m* **2** : luz *f* (entre dos soportes) — **~** *vt* **spanned; spanning 1** : abarcar (un período) **2** CROSS : extenderse sobre
Spaniard [ˈspænjərd] *n* : español *m*, -ñola *f*
spaniel [ˈspænjəl] *n* : spaniel *m*
Spanish [ˈspænɪʃ] *adj* : español — **~** *n* : español *m* (idioma)
spank [ˈspæŋk] *vt* : dar palmadas a (en las nalgas)
spar [ˈspɑr] *vi* **sparred; sparring** : entrenarse (en boxeo)
spare [ˈspær] *vt* **spared; sparing 1** PARDON : perdonar **2** SAVE : ahorrar **3 can you ~ a dollar?** : ¿me das un dólar? **4 I can't ~ the time** : no tengo tiempo **5 ~ no expense** : no reparar en gastos **6 to ~** : de sobra — **~** *adj* **1** : de repuesto **2** EXCESS : de más **3** LEAN : delgado — **~** *n or* **~ part** : repuesto *m* — **spare time** *n* : tiempo *m* libre — **sparing** [ˈspærɪŋ] *adj* : parco, económico
spark [ˈspɑrk] *n* : chispa *f* — **~** *vi* : chispear, echar chispas — *vt* : despertar (interés), provocar (crítica) — **sparkle** [ˈspɑrkəl] *vi* **-kled; -kling** : destellar, centellear — **~** *n* : destello *m*, centelleo *m* — **spark plug** *n* : bujía *f*
sparrow [ˈspæroː] *n* : gorrión *m*
sparse [ˈspɑrs] *adj* **sparser; -est** : escaso
spasm [ˈspæzəm] *n* : espasmo *m*
spat[1] → **spit**
spat[2] *n* QUARREL : disputa *f*, pelea *f*
spatter [ˈspæţər] *vt* : salpicar
spawn [ˈspɔn] *vi* : desovar — *vt* : engendrar, producir — **~** *n* : hueva *f*
speak [ˈspiːk] *v* **spoke** [ˈspoːk]; **spoken** [ˈspoːkən]; **speaking** *vi* **1** : hablar **2 ~ out against** : denunciar **3 ~ up** : hablar más alto **4 ~ up for** : defender — *vt* **1** : decir **2** : hablar (un idioma) — **speaker** [ˈspiːkər] *n* **1** ORATOR : orador *m*, -dora *f* **2** : hablante *mf* (de un idioma) **3** LOUDSPEAKER : altavoz *m*
spear [ˈspɪr] *n* : lanza *f* — **spearhead** [ˈspɪrˌhɛd] *n* : punta *f* de lanza — **~** *vt* : encabezar — **spearmint** [ˈspɪrmɪnt] *n* : menta *f* verde
special [ˈspɛʃəl] *adj* : especial — **specialist** [ˈspɛʃəlɪst] *n* : especialista *mf* — **specialization** [ˌspɛʃələˈzeɪʃən] *n* : especialización *f* — **specialize** [ˈspɛʃə-

ˌlaɪz] *vi* **-ized; -izing** : especializarse — **specially** *adv* : especialmente — **specialty** ['spɛʃəlṯi] *n, pl* **-ties** : especialidad *f*
species ['spiːˌʃiːz, -ˌsiːz] *ns & pl* : especie *f*
specify ['spɛsəˌfaɪ] *vt* **-fied; -fying** : especificar — **specific** [spɪ'sɪfɪk] *adj* : específico — **specifically** [spɪ'sɪfɪkli] *adv* **1** : específicamente **2** EXPLICITLY : expresamente — **specification** [ˌspɛsəfə'keɪʃən] *n* : especificación *f*
specimen ['spɛsəmən] *n* : espécimen *m*
speck ['spɛk] *n* **1** SPOT : mancha *f* **2** BIT : mota *f* — **speckled** ['spɛkəld] *adj* : moteado
spectacle ['spɛktɪkəl] *n* **1** : espectáculo *m* **2 ~s** *npl* GLASSES : gafas *fpl,* lentes *fpl,* anteojos *mpl* — **spectacular** [spɛk'tækjələr] *adj* : espectacular — **spectator** ['spɛkˌteɪṯər] *n* : espectador *m,* -dora *f*
specter *or* **spectre** ['spɛktər] *n* : espectro *m*
spectrum ['spɛktrəm] *n, pl* **-tra** [-trə] *or* **-trums 1** : espectro *m* **2** RANGE : gama *f*
speculation [ˌspɛkjə'leɪʃən] *n* : especulación *f*
speech ['spiːtʃ] *n* **1** : habla *f* **2** ADDRESS : discurso *m* — **speechless** ['spiːtʃləs] *adj* : mudo
speed ['spiːd] *n* **1** : rapidez *f* **2** VELOCITY : velocidad *f* — **~** *v* **sped** ['spɛd] *or* **speeded; speeding** *vi* **1** : conducir a exceso de velocidad **2 ~ off** : irse a toda velocidad **3 ~ up** : acelerarse — *vt or* **~ up** : acelerar — **speed limit** *n* : velocidad *f* máxima — **speedometer** [spɪ'dɑməṯər] *n* : velocímetro *m* — **speedy** ['spiːdi] *adj* **speedier, -est** : rápido
spell[1] ['spɛl] *vt* **1** : escribir (las letras de) **2** *or* **~ out** : deletrear **3** MEAN : significar
spell[2] *n* ENCHANTMENT : hechizo *m*
spell[3] *n* : período *m* (de tiempo)
spellbound ['spɛlˌbaʊnd] *adj* : embelesado
spelling ['spɛlɪŋ] *n* : ortografía *f*
spend ['spɛnd] *vt* **spent** ['spɛnt]; **spending 1** : gastar (dinero) **2** : pasar (las vacaciones, etc.) **3 ~ time on** : dedicar tiempo a
sperm ['spərm] *n, pl* **sperm** *or* **sperms** : esperma *mf*
spew ['spjuː] *vt* : vomitar, arrojar (lava, etc.)
sphere ['sfɪr] *n* : esfera *f* — **spherical** ['sfɪrɪkəl, 'sfɛr-] *adj* : esférico
spice ['spaɪs] *n* : especia *f* — **~** *vt* **spiced; spicing** : condimentar, sazonar — **spicy** ['spaɪsi] *adj* **spicier; -est** : picante
spider ['spaɪdər] *n* : araña *f*
spigot ['spɪgət, -kət] *n* : grifo *m Spain,* llave *f Lat*
spike ['spaɪk] *n* **1** : clavo *m* (grande) **2** POINT : punta *f* — **spiky** ['spaɪki] *adj* : puntiagudo
spill ['spɪl] *vt* : derramar — *vi* : derramarse
spin ['spɪn] *v* **spun** ['spʌn]; **spinning** *vi* : girar — *vt* **1** : hilar (lana, etc.) **2** TWIRL : hacer girar — **~** *n* **1** : vuelta *f,* giro *m* **2 go for a ~** : dar una vuelta (en auto)
spinach ['spɪnɪtʃ] *n* : espinacas *fpl*
spinal cord ['spaɪnəl] *n* : médula *f* espinal
spindle ['spɪndəl] *n* : huso *m* (para hilar) — **spindly** ['spɪndli] *adj* : larguirucho *fam*
spine ['spaɪn] *n* **1** : columna *f* vertebral **2** QUILL : púa *f* **3** THORN : espina *f* **4** : lomo *m* (de un libro)
spinster ['spɪntstər] *n* : soltera *f*
spiral ['spaɪrəl] *adj* : de espiral, en espiral — **~** *n* : espiral *f* — **~** *vi* **-raled** *or* **-ralled; -raling** *or* **-ralling** : ir en espiral
spire ['spaɪr] *n* : aguja *f*
spirit ['spɪrət] *n* **1** : espíritu *m* **2 in good ~s** : animado **3 ~s** *npl* : licores *mpl* — **spirited** ['spɪrəṯəd] *adj* : animado — **spiritual** ['spɪrɪtʃʊəl, -tʃəl] *adj* : espiritual — **spirituality** [ˌspɪrɪtʃʊ'æləṯi] *n, pl* **-ties** : espiritualidad *f*
spit[1] ['spɪt] *n* ROTISSERIE : asador *m*
spit[2] *v* **spit** *or* **spat** ['spæt]; **spitting** : escupir — *n* SALIVA : saliva *f*
spite ['spaɪt] *n* **1** : rencor *m* **2 in ~ of** : a pesar de — **~** *vt* **spited; spiting** : fastidiar — **spiteful** ['spaɪtfəl] *adj* : rencoroso
spittle ['spɪṯəl] *n* : saliva *f*
splash ['splæʃ] *vt* : salpicar — *vi* **1** : salpicar **2** *or* **~ about** : chapotear — **~** *n* **1** : salpicadura *f* **2** : mancha *f* (de color, etc.)
splatter ['splæṯər] → **spatter**
spleen ['spliːn] *n* : bazo *m* (órgano)
splendor ['splɛndər] *n* : esplendor *m* — **splendid** ['splɛndəd] *adj* : espléndido
splint ['splɪnt] *n* : tablilla *f*
splinter ['splɪntər] *n* : astilla *f* — *vi* : astillarse
split ['splɪt] *v* **split; splitting** *vt* **1** : partir **2** BURST : reventar **3** *or* **~ up** : dividir — *vi* **1** : partirse, rajarse **2** *or* **~ up**

: dividirse — ~ *n* **1** CRACK : rajadura *f* **2** *or* ~ **seam** : descosido *m* **3** DIVISION : división *f*

splurge ['splərdʒ] *vi* **splurged; splurging** : derrochar dinero

spoil ['spɔɪl] *vt* **spoiled** *or* **spoilt** ['spɔɪlt]; **spoiling 1** RUIN : estropear **2** PAMPER : consentir, mimar — **spoils** *npl* : botín *m*

spoke[1] ['spo:k] → **speak**

spoke[2] *n* : rayo *m* (de una rueda)

spoken → **speak**

spokesman ['spo:ksmən] *n, pl* **-men** [-mən, -ˌmen] : portavoz *mf* — **spokeswoman** ['spo:ksˌwʊmən] *n, pl* **-women** [-ˌwɪmən] : portavoz *f*

sponge ['spʌndʒ] *n* : esponja *f* — ~ *vt* **sponged; sponging** : limpiar con una esponja — **spongy** ['spʌndʒi] *adj* **spongier; -est** : esponjoso

sponsor ['spɑntsər] *n* : patrocinador *m*, -dora *f* — ~ *vt* : patrocinar — **sponsorship** ['spɑntsərˌʃɪp] *n* : patrocinio *m*

spontaneity [ˌspɑntə'ni:əṭi, -'neɪ-] *n* : espontaneidad *f* — **spontaneous** [spɑn'teɪniəs] *adj* : espontáneo

spooky ['spu:ki] *adj* **spookier; -est** : espeluzante

spool ['spu:l] *n* : carrete *m*

spoon ['spu:n] *n* : cuchara *f* — **spoonful** ['spu:nˌfʊl] *n* : cucharada *f*

sporadic [spə'rædɪk] *adj* : esporádico

spore ['spor] *n* : espora *f*

sport ['sport] *n* **1** : deporte *m* **2 be a good** ~ : tener espíritu deportivo — **sportsman** ['sportsmən] *n, pl* **-men** [-mən, -ˌmen] : deportista *m* — **sportswoman** ['sportsˌwʊmən] *n, pl* **-women** [-ˌwɪmən] : deportista *f* — **sporty** ['sporṭi] *adj* **sportier; -est** : deportivo

spot ['spɑt] *n* **1** : mancha *f* **2** DOT : punto *m* **3** PLACE : lugar *m*, sitio *m* **4 in a tight** ~ : en apuros **5 on the** ~ INSTANTLY : en ese mismo momento — ~ *vt* **spotted; spotting 1** STAIN : manchar **2** DETECT, NOTICE : ver, descubrir — **spotless** ['spɑtləs] *adj* : impecable — **spotlight** ['spɑtˌlaɪt] *n* **1** : foco *m*, reflector *m* **2 be in the** ~ : ser el centro de atención — **spotty** ['spɑṭi] *adj* **spottier; -est** : irregular

spouse ['spaʊs] *n* : cónyuge *mf*

spout ['spaʊt] *vi* : salir a chorros — ~ *n* **1** : pico *m* (de una jarra, etc.) **2** STREAM : chorro *m*

sprain ['spreɪn] *n* : esguince *m* — ~ *vt* : sufrir un esguince en

sprawl ['sprɔl] *vi* **1** : repantigarse (en un sillón, etc.) **2** EXTEND : extenderse — ~ *n* : extensión *f*

spray[1] ['spreɪ] *n* BOUQUET : ramillete *m*

spray[2] *n* **1** MIST : rocío *m* **2** *or* **aerosol** ~ : spray *m* **3** *or* ~ **bottle** : atomizador *m* — ~ *vt* : rociar (una superficie), pulverizar (un líquido)

spread ['sprɛd] *v* **spread; spreading** *vt* **1** : propagar (enfermedades), difundir (noticias, etc.) **2** *or* ~ **out** : extender **3** : untar (con mantequilla, etc.) — *vi* **1** : propagarse, difundirse **2** *or* ~ **out** : extenderse — ~ *n* **1** : propagación *f*, difusión *f* **2** PASTE : pasta *f* (para untar) — **spreadsheet** ['sprɛdˌʃi:t] *n* : hoja *f* de cálculo

spree ['spri] *n* **go on a** ~ : ir de juerga *fam*

sprig ['sprɪg] *n* : ramito *m*

sprightly ['spraɪtli] *adj* **sprightlier; -est** : vivo

spring ['sprɪŋ] *v* **sprang** ['spræŋ] *or* **sprung** ['sprʌŋ]; **sprung; springing** *vi* **1** : saltar **2** ~ **from** : surgir de **3** ~ **up** : surgir — *vt* **1** ACTIVATE : accionar **2** ~ **a leak** : hacer agua **3** ~ **sth on s.o.** : sorprender a algn con algo — ~ *n* **1** : manantial *m* (de aguas) **2** : primavera *f* (estación) **3** LEAP : salto *m* **4** RESILIENCE : elasticidad *f* **5** : resorte *m* (mecanismo) **6** *or* **bedspring** : muelle *m* — **springboard** ['sprɪŋˌbord] *n* : trampolín *m* — **springtime** ['sprɪŋˌtaɪm] *n* : primavera *f* — **springy** ['sprɪŋi] *adj* **springier; -est** : mullido

sprinkle ['sprɪŋkəl] *vt* **-kled; -kling 1** : salpicar, rociar **2** DUST : espolvorear — ~ *n* : llovizna *f* — **sprinkler** ['sprɪŋkələr] *n* : aspersor *m*

sprint ['sprɪnt] *vi* **1** : correr **2** : esprintar (en deportes) — ~ *n* : esprint *m* (en deportes)

sprout ['spraʊt] *vi* : brotar — ~ *n* : brote *m*

spruce[1] ['spru:s] *vt* **spruced; sprucing** ~ **up** : arreglar

spruce[2] *n* : picea *f* (árbol)

spry ['spraɪ] *adj* **sprier** *or* **spryer** ['spraɪər]; **spriest** *or* **spryest** ['spraɪəst] : ágil, activo

spun → **spin**

spur ['spər] *n* **1** : espuela *f* **2** STIMULUS : acicate *m* **3 on the** ~ **of the moment** : sin pensarlo — ~ *vt* **spurred; spurring** *or* ~ **on 1** : espolear (un caballo) **2** MOTIVATE : motivar

spurn ['spərn] *vt* : desdeñar, rechazar

spurt[1] ['spərt] *vi* : salir a chorros — ~ *n* : chorro *m*

spurt[2] *n* **1** : arranque *m* (de energía, etc.) **2 work in** ~**s** : trabajar por rachas

spy ['spaɪ] *v* **spied; spying** *vt* : ver, divisar — *vi* ~ **on s.o.** : espiar a algn — ~ *n* : espía *mf*
squabble ['skwɑbəl] *n* : riña *f*, pelea *f* — ~ *vi* **-bled; -bling** : reñir, pelearse
squad ['skwɑd] *n* : pelotón *m* (militar), brigada *f* (de policías)
squadron ['skwɑdrən] *n* : escuadrón *m* (de soldados), escuadra *f* (de aviones o naves)
squalid ['skwɑlɪd] *adj* : miserable
squall ['skwɔl] *n* : turbión *m*
squalor ['skwɑlər] *n* : miseria *f*
squander ['skwɑndər] *vt* : derrochar (dinero, etc.), desperdiciar (oportunidades, etc.)
square ['skwær] *n* **1** : cuadrado *m* **2** : plaza *f* (de una ciudad) — ~ *adj* **squarer; -est 1** : cuadrado **2** HONEST : justo **3** EVEN : en paz **4 a ~ meal** : una comida decente — ~ *vt* **squared; squaring 1** : elevar al cuadrado (un número) **2** : saldar (una cuenta) — **square root** *n* : raíz *f* cuadrada
squash[1] ['skwɑʃ, 'skwɔʃ] *vt* **1** : aplastar **2** : acallar (protestas, etc.) — ~ *n* : squash *m* (deporte)
squash[2] *n, pl* **squashes** *or* **squash** : calabaza *f* (vegetal)
squat ['skwɑt] *vi* **squatted; squatting 1** *or* ~ **down** : ponerse en cuclillas **2** : ocupar un lugar sin derecho — ~ *adj* **squatter; squattest** : achaparrado
squawk ['skwɔk] *n* : graznido *m* — ~ *vi* : graznar
squeak ['skwi:k] *vi* **1** : chillar **2** CREAK : chirriar — ~ *n* **1** : chillido *m* **2** CREAK : chirrido *m* — **squeaky** ['skwi:ki] *adj* **squeakier; -est** : chirriante
squeal ['skwi:l] *vi* **1** : chillar (dícese de personas, etc.), chirriar (dícese de frenos, etc.) **2** PROTEST : quejarse — ~ *n* : chillido *m* (de una persona), chirrido *m* (de frenos, etc.)
squeamish ['skwi:mɪʃ] *adj* : impresionable, delicado
squeeze ['skwi:z] *vt* **squeezed; squeezing 1** : apretar **2** : exprimir (frutas, etc.) **3** : extraer (jugo, etc.) — ~ *n* : apretón *m*
squid ['skwɪd] *n, pl* **squid** *or* **squids** : calamar *m*
squint ['skwɪnt] *vi* : entrecerrar los ojos — ~ *n* : estrabismo *m*
squirm ['skwərm] *vi* : retorcerse
squirrel ['skwərəl] *n* : ardilla *f*
squirt ['skwərt] *vt* : lanzar un chorro de — *vi* : salir a chorros — ~ *n* : chorrito *m*
stab ['stæb] *n* **1** : puñalada *f* **2 ~ of pain** : pinchazo *m* **3 take a ~ at** : intentar — ~ *vt* **stabbed; stabbing 1** KNIFE : apuñalar **2** STICK : clavar
stable ['steɪbəl] *n* **1** : establo *m* (para ganado) **2** *or* **horse ~** : caballeriza *f* — ~ *adj* **-bler; -blest** : estable — **stability** [stə'bɪləṭi] *n, pl* **-ties** : estabilidad *f* — **stabilize** ['steɪbə,laɪz] *vt* **-lized; -lizing** : estabilizar
stack ['stæk] *n* : montón *m*, pila *f* — ~ *vt* : amontonar, apilar
stadium ['steɪdiəm] *n, pl* **-dia** *or* **-diums** : estadio *m*
staff ['stæfs, stævz] *n, pl* **staffs** *or* **staves** ['stævz, 'steɪvz] **1** : bastón *m* **2** *pl* **staffs** PERSONNEL : personal *m* **3** *pl* **staffs** : pentagrama *m* (en música) — ~ ['stæf] *vt* : proveer de personal
stag ['stæg] *n, pl* **stags** *or* **stag** : ciervo *m*, venado *m* — ~ *adj* : sólo para hombres — ~ *adv* **go ~** : ir solo
stage ['steɪdʒ] *n* **1** : escenario *m* (de un teatro) **2** PHASE : etapa *f* **3 the ~** : el teatro — ~ *vt* **staged; staging 1** : poner en escena **2** ARRANGE : montar — **stagecoach** ['steɪdʒ,ko:tʃ] *n* : diligencia *f*
stagger ['stægər] *vi* : tambalearse — *vt* **1** : escalonar (turnos, etc.) **2 be ~ed by** : quedarse estupefacto por — ~ *n* : tambaleo *m* — **staggering** ['stægərɪŋ] *adj* : asombroso
stagnant ['stægnənt] *adj* : estancado — **stagnate** ['stæg,neɪt] *vi* **-nated; -nating** : estancarse
stain ['steɪn] *vt* **1** : manchar **2** : teñir (madera) — ~ *n* **1** : mancha *f* **2** DYE : tinte *m*, tintura *f* — **stainless steel** ['steɪnləs-] *n* : acero *m* inoxidable
stair ['stær] *n* **1** STEP : escalón *m*, peldaño *m* **2 ~s** *npl* : escalera(s) *f(pl)* — **staircase** ['stær,keɪs] *n* : escalera(s) *f(pl)* — **stairway** ['stær,weɪ] *n* : escalera(s) *f(pl)*
stake ['steɪk] *n* **1** POST : estaca *f* **2** BET : apuesta *f* **3** INTEREST : intereses *mpl* **4 be at ~** : estar en juego — ~ *vt* **staked; staking 1** : estacar **2** BET : jugarse **3 ~ a claim to** : reclamar
stale ['steɪl] *adj* **staler; stalest 1** : duro (dícese del pan) **2** OLD : viejo **3** STUFFY : viciado
stalk[1] ['stɔk] *n* : tallo *m* (de una planta)
stalk[2] *vt* : acechar — *vi or* ~ **off** : irse con altivez
stall[1] ['stɔl] *n* **1** : compartimiento *m* (de un establo) **2** STAND : puesto *m* — ~ *vt* : parar (un motor) — *vi* : pararse

stall[2] *vt* DELAY : entretener — *vi* : andar con rodeos
stallion ['stæljən] *n* : caballo *m* semental
stalwart ['stɔlwərt] *adj* **1** STRONG : fornido **2** ~ **supporter** : partidario *m* leal
stamina ['stæmənə] *n* : resistencia *f*
stammer ['stæmər] *vi* : tartamudear — ~ *n* : tartamudeo *m*
stamp ['stæmp] *n* **1** SEAL : sello *m* **2** DIE : cuño *m* **3** *or* **postage** ~ : sello *m*, estampilla *f Lat*, timbre *m Lat* — ~ *vt* **1** : franquear (una carta) **2** IMPRINT : sellar **3** MINT : acuñar **4** ~ **one's foot** : dar una patada (en el suelo)
stampede [stæm'pi:d] *n* : estampida *f* — ~ *vi* **-peded; -peding** : salir en estampida
stance ['stænts] *n* : postura *f*
stand ['stænd] *v* **stood** ['stʊd]; **standing** *vi* **1** : estar de pie, estar parado *Lat* **2** BE : estar **3** CONTINUE : seguir vigente **4** LIE, REST : reposar **5** ~ **aside** *or* ~ **back** : apartarse **6** ~ **out** : sobresalir **7** *or* ~ **up** : ponerse de pie, pararse *Lat* — *vt* **1** PLACE : poner, colocar **2** ENDURE : soportar **3** ~ **a chance** : tener una posibilidad — **stand by** *vt* **1** : mantener (una promesa, etc.) **2** SUPPORT : apoyar — **stand for** *vt* **1** MEAN : significar **2** PERMIT : permitir — **stand up** *vi* **1** ~ **for** : defender **2** ~ **up to** : resistir a — ~ *n* **1** RESISTANCE : resistencia *f* **2** STALL : puesto *m* **3** BASE : base *f* **4** POSITION : posición *f* **5** ~**s** *npl* : tribuna *f*
standard ['stændərd] *n* **1** : norma *f* **2** BANNER : estandarte *m* **3** CRITERION : criterio *m* **4** ~ **of living** : nivel *m* de vida — ~ *adj* : estándar — **standardize** ['stændər,daɪz] *vt* **-ized; -izing** : estandarizar
standing ['stændɪŋ] *n* **1** RANK : posición *f* **2** DURATION : duración *f*
standpoint ['stænd,pɔint] *n* : punto *m* de vista
standstill ['stænd,stɪl] *n* **1 be at a** ~ : estar paralizado **2 come to a** ~ : pararse
stank → **stink**
stanza ['stænzə] *n* : estrofa *f*
staple[1] ['steɪpəl] *n* : producto *m* principal — ~ *adj* : principal, básico
staple[2] *n* : grapa *f* (para papeles) — ~ *vt* **-pled; -pling** : grapar, engrapar *Lat* — **stapler** ['steɪplər] *n* : grapadora *f*, engrapadora *f Lat*
star ['stɑr] *n* : estrella *f* — ~ *v* **starred; starring** *vt* FEATURE : estar protagonizado por — *vi* ~ **in** : protagonizar
starboard ['stɑrbərd] *n* : estribor *m*
starch ['stɑrtʃ] *vt* : almidonar — ~ *n* **1** : almidón *m* **2** : fécula *f* (comida)
stardom ['stɑrdəm] *n* : estrellato *m*
stare ['stær] *vi* **stared; staring** : mirar fijamente — ~ *n* : mirada *f* fija
starfish ['stɑr,fɪʃ] *n* : estrella *f* de mar
stark ['stɑrk] *adj* **1** PLAIN : austero **2** HARSH : severo, duro **3** SHARP : marcado — ~ *adv* **1** : completamente **2** ~ **naked** : en cueros (vivos)
starlight ['stɑr,laɪt] *n* : luz *f* de las estrellas
starling ['stɑrlɪŋ] *n* : estornino *m*
starry ['stɑri] *adj* **starrier; -est** : estrellado
start ['stɑrt] *vi* **1** : empezar, comenzar **2** SET OUT : salir **3** JUMP : sobresaltarse **4** *or* ~ **up** : arrancar — *vt* **1** : empezar, comenzar **2** CAUSE : provocar **3** *or* ~ **up** ESTABLISH : montar **4** *or* ~ **up** : arrancar (un motor, etc.) — ~ *n* **1** : principio *m* **2 get an early** ~ : salir temprano **3 give s.o. a** ~ : asustar a algn — **starter** ['stɑrt̬ər] *n* : motor *m* de arranque (de un vehículo)
startle ['stɑrt̬əl] *vt* **-tled; -tling** : asustar
starve ['stɑrv] *v* **starved; starving** *vi* : morirse de hambre — *vt* : privar de comida — **starvation** [stɑr'veɪʃən] *n* : inanición *f*, hambre *f*
stash ['stæʃ] *vt* : esconder
state ['steɪt] *n* **1** : estado *m* **2 the States** : los Estados Unidos — ~ *vt* **stated; stating 1** SAY : decir **2** REPORT : exponer — **stately** ['steɪtli] *adj* **statelier; -est** : majestuoso — **statement** ['steɪtmənt] *n* **1** : declaración *f* **2** *or* **bank** ~ : estado *m* de cuenta — **statesman** ['steɪtsmən] *n, pl* **-men** [-mən, -,mɛn] : estadista *mf*
static ['stæt̬ɪk] *adj* : estático — ~ *n* : estática *f*
station ['steɪʃən] *n* **1** : estación *f* (de trenes, etc.) **2** RANK : condición *f* (social) **3** : canal *m* (de televisión), emisora *f* (de radio) **4** → **fire station, police station** — *vt* : apostar, estacionar — **stationary** ['steɪʃə,nɛri] *adj* : estacionario
stationery ['steɪʃə,nɛri] *n* : papel *m* y sobres *mpl* (para cartas)
station wagon *n* : camioneta *f* (familiar)
statistic [stə'tɪstɪk] *n* : estadística *f* — **statistical** [stə'tɪstɪkəl] *adj* : estadístico
statue ['stæ,tʃu:] *n* : estatua *f*
stature ['stætʃər] *n* : estatura *f*, talla *f*
status ['steɪt̬əs, 'stæ-] *n* **1** : situación *f* **2** *or* **social** ~ : estatus *m* **3 marital** ~ : estado *m* civil

statute ['stæ,tʃu:t] *n* : estatuto *m*
staunch ['stɔntʃ] *adj* : leal
stave ['steɪv] *vt* **staved** *or* **stove** ['sto:v]; **staving 1 ~ in** : romper **2 ~ off** : evitar
staves → **staff**
stay[1] ['steɪ] *vi* **1** REMAIN : quedarse, permanecer **2** LODGE : alojarse **3 ~ awake** : mantenerse despierto **4 ~ in** : quedarse en casa — *vt* : suspender (una ejecución, etc.) — **~** *n* **1** : estancia *f*, estadía *f Lat* **2** SUSPENSION : suspensión *f*
stay[2] *n* SUPPORT : soporte *m*
stead ['stɛd] *n* **1 in s.o.'s ~** : en lugar de algn **2 stand s.o. in good ~** : ser muy útil a algn — **steadfast** ['stɛd,fæst] *adj* **1** FIRM : firme **2** LOYAL : leal, fiel — **steadily** ['stɛdəli] *adv* **1** : progresivamente **2** INCESSANTLY : sin parar **3** FIXEDLY : fijamente — **steady** ['stɛdi] *adj* **steadier; -est 1** FIRM, SURE : firme, seguro **2** FIXED : fijo **3** DEPENDABLE : responsable **4** CONSTANT : constante — **~** *vt* **steadied; steadying 1** : mantener firme **2** : calmar (los nervios)
steak ['steɪk] *n* : bistec *m*, filete *m*
steal ['sti:l] *v* **stole** ['sto:l]; **stolen** ['sto:lən]; **stealing** *vt* : robar — *vi* **1** : robar **2 ~ away** : escabullirse
stealth ['stɛlθ] *n* : sigilo *m* — **stealthy** ['stɛlθi] *adj* **stealthier; -est** : furtivo, sigiloso
steam ['sti:m] *n* **1** : vapor *m* **2 let off ~** : desahogarse — **~** *vi* : echar vapor — *vt* **1** : cocer al vapor **2 ~ up** : empañar — **steam engine** *n* : motor *m* de vapor — **steamship** ['sti:m,ʃɪp] *n* : (barco *m* de) vapor *m* — **steamy** ['sti:mi] *adj* **steamier; -est 1** : lleno de vapor **2** PASSIONATE : tórrido
steel ['sti:l] *n* : acero *m* — **~** *vt* **~ oneself** : armarse de valor — **~** *adj* : de acero
steep[1] ['sti:p] *adj* **1** : empinado **2** CONSIDERABLE : considerable **3** : muy alto (dícese de precios)
steep[2] *vt* : dejar (té, etc.) en infusión
steeple ['sti:pəl] *n* : aguja *f*, campanario *m*
steer[1] ['stɪr] *n* : buey *m*
steer[2] *vt* : dirigir (un auto, etc.), pilotear (un barco) — **steering wheel** *n* : volante
stem[1] ['stɛm] *n* : tallo *m* (de una planta), pie *m* (de una copa) — **~** *vi* **~ from** : provenir de
stem[2] *vt* **stemmed; stemming** : contener, detener
stench ['stɛntʃ] *n* : hedor *m*, mal olor *m*
stencil ['stɛntsəl] *n* : plantilla *f* (para marcar)
step ['stɛp] *n* **1** : paso *m* **2** RUNG, STAIR : escalón *m* **3 ~ by ~** : paso por paso **4 take ~s** : tomar medidas **5 watch your ~** : mira por dónde caminas — **~** *vi* **stepped; stepping 1** : dar un paso **2 ~ back** : retoceder **3 ~ down** RESIGN : retirarse **4 ~ in** : intervenir **5 ~ out** : salir (por un momento) **6 ~ this way** : pase por aquí — **step up** *vt* INCREASE : aumentar
stepbrother ['stɛp,brʌðər] *n* : hermanastro *m* — **stepdaughter** ['stɛp,dɔṭər] *n* : hijastra *f* — **stepfather** ['stɛp,fɑðər, -,fa-] *n* : padrastro *m*
stepladder ['stɛp,lædər] *n* : escalera *f* de tijera
stepmother ['stɛp,mʌðər] *n* : madrastra *f* — **stepsister** ['stɛp,sɪstər] *n* : hermanastra *f* — **stepson** ['stɛp,sʌn] *n* : hijastro *m*
stereo ['stɛri,o:, 'stɪr-] *n, pl* **stereos** : estéreo *m* — **~** *adj* : estéreo
stereotype ['stɛrio,taɪp, 'stɪr-] *vt* **-typed; -typing** : estereotipar — **~** *n* : estereotipo *m*
sterile ['stɛrəl] *adj* : estéril — **sterility** [stə'rɪləṭi] *n* : esterilidad *f* — **sterilization** [,stɛrələ'zeɪʃən] *n* : esterilización *f* — **sterilize** ['stɛrə,laɪz] *vt* **-ized; -izing** : esterilizar
sterling ['stərlɪŋ] *adj* : excelente — **sterling silver** *n* : plata *f* de ley
stern[1] ['stərn] *adj* : severo, adusto
stern[2] *n* : popa *f*
stethoscope ['stɛθə,sko:p] *n* : estetoscopio *m*
stew ['stu:, 'stju:] *n* : estofado *m*, guiso *m* — **~** *vt* : estofar, guisar — *vi* **1** : cocer **2** FRET : preocuparse
steward ['stu:ərd, 'stju:-] *n* **1** : administrador *m*, -dora *f* **2** : auxiliar *m* de vuelo (en un avión) **3** : camarero *m* (en un barco) — **stewardess** ['stu:ərdəs, 'stju:-] *n* **1** : auxiliar *f* de vuelo, azafata *f* (en un avión) **2** : camarera *f* (en un barco)
stick[1] ['stɪk] *n* **1** : palo *m* **2** TWIG : ramita *f* (suelta) **3** WALKING STICK : bastón *m*
stick[2] *v* **stuck** ['stʌk]; **sticking** *vt* **1** : pegar **2** STAB : clavar **3** PUT : poner **4 ~ out** : sacar (la lengua, etc.) — *vi* **1** : pegarse **2** JAM : atascarse **3 ~ around** : quedarse **4 ~ out** PROTRUDE : sobresalir **5 ~ out** SHOW : asomar **6 ~ up** : sobresalir **7 ~ up for** : defender — **sticker** ['stɪkər] *n* : etiqueta *f*

adhesiva — **stickler** ['stɪklər] *n* **be a ~ for** : insistir mucho en — **sticky** ['stɪki] *adj* **stickier; -est** : pegajoso

stiff ['stɪf] *adj* **1** RIGID : rígido, tieso **2** STILTED : forzado **3** STRONG : fuerte **4** DIFFICULT : difícil **5** : entumecido (dícese de músculos) — **stiffen** ['stɪfən] *vt* : fortalecer, hacer más duro — *vi* **1** HARDEN : endurecerse **2** : entumecerse (dícese de músculos) — **stiffness** ['stɪfnəs] *n* : rigidez *f*

stifle ['staɪfəl] *vt* **-fled; -fling** : sofocar

stigmatize ['stɪgməˌtaɪz] *vt* **-tized; -tizing** : estigmatizar

still ['stɪl] *adj* **1** : inmóvil **2** SILENT : callado — **~** *adv* **1** : todavía, aún **2** NEVERTHELESS : de todos modos, aún así **3 sit ~!** : ¡quédate quieto! — **~** *n* : quietud *f*, calma *f* — **stillborn** ['stɪlˌbɔrn] *adj* : nacido muerto — **stillness** ['stɪlnəs] *n* : calma *f*, silencio *m*

stilt ['stɪlt] *n* : zanco *m* — **stilted** ['stɪltəd] *adj* : forzado

stimulate ['stɪmjəˌleɪt] *vt* **-lated; -lating** : estimular — **stimulant** ['stɪmjələnt] *n* : estimulante *m* — **stimulation** [ˌstɪmjə'leɪʃən] *n* : estimulación *f* — **stimulus** ['stɪmjələs] *n, pl* **-li** [-ˌlaɪ] : estímulo *m*

sting ['stɪŋ] *v* **stung** ['stʌŋ]; **stinging** : picar — **~** *n* : picadura *f* — **stinger** ['stɪŋər] *n* : aguijón *m*

stingy ['stɪndʒi] *adj* **stingier; -est** : tacaño — **stinginess** ['stɪndʒinəs] *n* : tacañería *f*

stink ['stɪŋk] *vi* **stank** ['stæŋk] *or* **stunk** ['stʌŋk]; **stunk; stinking** : apestar, oler mal — **~** *n* : hedor *m*, peste *f fam*

stint ['stɪnt] *vi* **~ on** : escatimar — **~** *n* : período *m*

stipulate ['stɪpjəˌleɪt] *vt* **-lated; -lating** : estipular

stir ['stər] *v* **stirred; stirring** *vt* **1** : remover, revolver **2** MOVE : mover **3** INCITE : incitar **4** *or* **~ up** : despertar (memorias, etc.), provocar (ira, etc.) — *vi* : moverse, agitarse — **~** *n* COMMOTION : revuelo *m*

stirrup ['stərəp, 'stɪr-] *n* : estribo *m*

stitch ['stɪtʃ] *n* **1** : puntada *f* **2** PAIN : punzada *f* (en el costado) — **~** *v* : coser

stock ['stɑk] *n* **1** INVENTORY : existencias *fpl* **2** SECURITIES : acciones *fpl* **3** ANCESTRY : linaje *m*, estirpe *f* **4** BROTH : caldo *m* **5 out of ~** : agotado **6 take ~ of** : evaluar — **~** *vt* : surtir, abastecer — *vi* **~ up on** : abastecerse de — **stockbroker** ['stɑkˌbroːkər] *n* : corredor *m*, -dora *f* de bolsa

stocking ['stɑkɪŋ] *n* : media *f*

stock market *n* : bolsa *f* — **stockpile** ['stɑkˌpaɪl] *n* : reservas *fpl* — **~** *vt* **-piled; -piling** : almacenar — **stocky** ['stɑki] *adj* **stockier; -est** : robusto, fornido

stodgy ['stɑdʒi] *adj* **stodgier; -est 1** DULL : pesado **2** OLD-FASHIONED : anticuado

stoic ['stoːɪk] *n* : estoico *m*, -ca *f* — **~** *or* **stoical** [-ɪkəl] *adj* : estoico — **stoicism** ['stoːəˌsɪzəm] *n* : estoicismo *m*

stoke ['stoːk] *vt* **stoked; stoking** : echar carbón o leña a

stole[1] ['stoːl] → **steal**

stole[2] *n* : estola *f*

stolen → **steal**

stomach ['stʌmɪk] *n* : estómago *m* — **~** *vt* : aguantar, soportar — **stomachache** ['stʌmɪkˌeɪk] *n* : dolor *m* de estómago

stone ['stoːn] *n* **1** : piedra *f* **2** : hueso *m* (de una fruta) — **~** *vt* **stoned; stoning** : apedrear — **stony** ['stoːni] *adj* **stonier; -est 1** : pedregoso **2 a ~ silence** : un silencio sepulcral

stood → **stand**

stool ['stuːl] *n* : taburete *m*

stoop ['stuːp] *vi* **1** : agacharse **2 ~ to** : rebajarse a — **~** *n* **have a ~** : ser encorvado

stop ['stɑp] *v* **stopped; stopping** *vt* **1** PLUG : tapar **2** PREVENT : impedir **3** HALT : parar, detener **4** CEASE : dejar de — *vi* **1** : detenerse, parar **2** CEASE : cesar, dejar **3 ~ by** : visitar — **~** *n* **1** : parada *f*, alto *m* **2 come to a ~** : pararse, detenerse **3 put a ~ to** : poner fin a — **stopgap** ['stɑpˌgæp] *n* : arreglo *m* provisorio — **stoplight** ['stɑpˌlaɪt] *n* : semáforo *m* — **stoppage** ['stɑpɪdʒ] *n* *or* **work ~** : paro *m* — **stopper** ['stɑpər] *n* : tapón *m*

store ['stor] *vt* **stored; storing** : guardar (comida, etc.), almacenar (datos, mercancías, etc.) — **~** *n* **1** SUPPLY : reserva *f* **2** SHOP : tienda *f* — **storage** ['storɪdʒ] *n* : almacenamiento *m* — **storehouse** ['storˌhaus] *n* : almacén *m* — **storekeeper** ['storˌkiːpər] *n* : tendero *m*, -ra *f* — **storeroom** ['storˌruːm, -ˌrum] *n* : almacén *m*

stork ['stɔrk] *n* : cigüeña *f*

storm ['stɔrm] *n* : tormenta *f*, tempestad *f* — **~** *vi* **1** RAGE : ponerse furioso **2 ~ in/out** : entrar/salir furioso — *vt* ATTACK : asaltar — **stormy** ['stɔrmi] *adj* **stormier; -est** : tormentoso

story[1] ['stori] *n, pl* **stories 1** TALE : cuento *m* **2** ACCOUNT : historia *f* **3** RUMOR : rumor *m*

story[2] *n* FLOOR : piso *m*, planta *f*
stout ['staut] *adj* **1** BRAVE : valiente **2** RESOLUTE : tenaz **3** STURDY : fuerte **4** FAT : corpulento
stove[1] ['sto:v] *n* **1** : estufa *f* (para calentar) **2** RANGE : cocina *f*
stove[2] → **stave**
stow ['sto:] *vt* **1** : guardar **2** LOAD : cargar — *vi* **~ away** : viajar de polizón — **stowaway** ['sto:əˌweɪ] *n* : polizón *m*
straddle ['strædəl] *vt* **-dled; -dling** : sentarse a horcajadas sobre
straggle ['strægəl] *vi* **-gled; -gling** : rezagarse, quedarse atrás — **straggler** ['strægələr] *n* : rezagado *m*, -da *f*
straight ['streɪt] *adj* **1** : recto, derecho **2** : lacio (dícese del pelo) **3** HONEST : franco **4** TIDY : arreglado — **~** *adv* **1** DIRECTLY : derecho **2** EXACTLY : justo **3** CLEARLY : con claridad **4** FRANKLY : con franqueza — **straightaway** ['streɪt'weɪ, -ˌweɪ] *adv* : inmediatamente — **straighten** ['streɪtən] *vt* **1** : enderezar **2 ~ up** : arreglar — **straightforward** [streɪt'fɔrwərd] *adj* **1** FRANK : franco **2** CLEAR : claro, sencillo
strain[1] ['streɪn] *n* **1** LINEAGE : linaje *m* **2** STREAK : veta *f* **3** VARIETY : variedad *f* **4 ~s** *npl* : acordes *mpl* (de música)
strain[2] *vt* **1** : forzar (la vista o la voz) **2** FILTER : colar **3** : tensar (relaciones, etc.) **4 ~ a muscle** : sufrir un esguince **5 ~ oneself** : hacerse daño — *vi* : esforzarse (por) — **~** *n* **1** STRESS : tensión *f* **2** SPRAIN : esguince *m* — **strainer** ['streɪnər] *n* : colador *m*
strait ['streɪt] *n* **1** : estrecho *m* **2 in dire ~s** : en grandes apuros
strand[1] ['strænd] *vt* **be ~ed** : quedar(se) varado
strand[2] *n* **1** : hebra *f* **2 a ~ of hair** : un pelo
strange ['streɪndʒ] *adj* **stranger; -est 1** : extraño, raro **2** UNFAMILIAR : desconocido — **strangely** ['streɪndʒli] *adv* : de manera extraña — **strangeness** ['streɪndʒnəs] *n* **1** : rareza *f* **2** UNFAMILIARITY : lo desconocido — **stranger** ['streɪndʒər] *n* : desconocido *m*, -da *f*
strangle ['stræŋgəl] *vt* **-gled; -gling** : estrangular
strap ['stræp] *n* **1** : correa *f* **2** *or* **shoulder ~** : tirante *m* — **~** *vt* **strapped; strapping** : sujetar con una correa — **strapless** ['stræpləs] *n* : sin tirantes — **strapping** ['stræpɪŋ] *adj* : robusto, fornido
strategy ['stræṭədʒi] *n, pl* **-gies** : estrategia *f* — **strategic** [strə'ti:dʒɪk] *adj* : estratégico
straw ['strɔ] *n* **1** : paja *f* **2** *or* **drinking ~** : pajita *f* **3 the last ~** : el colmo
strawberry ['strɔˌberi] *n, pl* **-ries** : fresa *f*
stray ['streɪ] *n* : animal *m* perdido — **~** *vi* **1** : perderse, extraviarse **2** : apartarse (de un grupo, etc.) **3** DEVIATE : desviarse — **~** *adj* : perdido
streak ['stri:k] *n* **1** : raya *f* **2** VEIN : veta *f* **3 ~ of luck** : racha *f* de suerte — *vi* **~ by** : pasar como una flecha
stream ['stri:m] *n* **1** : arroyo *m*, riachuelo *m* **2** FLOW : chorro *m*, corriente *f* — **~** *vi* : correr — **streamer** ['stri:mər] *n* **1** PENNANT : banderín *m* **2** : serpentina *f* (de papel) — **streamlined** ['stri:mˌlaɪnd] *adj* **1** : aerodinámico **2** EFFICIENT : eficiente
street ['stri:t] *n* : calle *f* — **streetcar** ['stri:tˌkɑr] *n* : tranvía *m* — **streetlight** ['stri:tˌlaɪt] *n* : farol *m*
strength ['streŋkθ] *n* **1** : fuerza *f* **2** FORTITUDE : fortaleza *f* **3** TOUGHNESS : resistencia *f*, solidez *f* **4** INTENSITY : intensidad *f* **5 ~s and weaknesses** : virtudes y defectos — **strengthen** ['streŋkθən] *vt* **1** : fortalecer **2** REINFORCE : reforzar **3** INTENSIFY : intensificar
strenuous ['strenjuəs] *adj* **1** : enérgico **2** ARDUOUS : duro, riguroso
stress ['strɛs] *n* **1** : tensión *f* **2** EMPHASIS : énfasis *m* **3** : acento *m* (en lingüística) — **~** *vt* **1** EMPHASIZE : enfatizar **2** *or* **~ out** : estresar — **stressful** ['stresfəl] *adj* : estresante
stretch ['stretʃ] *vt* **1** : estirar (músculos, elástico, etc.) **2** EXTEND : extender **3 ~ the truth** : forzar la verdad — *vi* **1** : estirarse **2** EXTEND : extenderse — **~** *n* **1** : extensión *f* **2** ELASTICITY : elasticidad *f* **3** EXPANSE : tramo *m* **4** : período *m* (de tiempo) — **stretcher** ['stretʃər] *n* : camilla *f*
strew ['stru:] *vt* **strewed; strewed** *or* **strewn** ['stru:n]; **strewing** : esparcir (semillas, etc.), desparramar (papeles, etc.)
stricken ['strɪkən] *adj* **~ with** : aquejado de (una enfermedad), afligido por (tristeza, etc.)
strict ['strɪkt] *adj* : estricto — **strictly** *adv* **~ speaking** : en rigor
stride ['straɪd] *vi* **strode** ['stro:d]; **stridden** ['strɪdən]; **striding** : ir dando zancadas — **~** *n* **1** : zancada *f* **2 make great ~s** : hacer grandes progresos
strident ['straɪdənt] *adj* : estridente
strife ['straɪf] *n* : conflictos *mpl*

strike ['straɪk] *v* **struck** ['strʌk]; **struck; striking** *vt* **1** HIT : golpear **2** *or* **~ against** : chocar contra **3** *or* **~ out** DELETE : tachar **4** : dar (la hora) **5** IMPRESS : impresionar **6** : descubrir (oro o petróleo) **7 it ~s me as...** : me parece... **8 ~ up** START : entablar — *vi* **1** : golpear **2** ATTACK : atacar **3** : declararse en huelga **4** : sobrevenir (dícese de una enfermedad, etc.) — **~** *n* **1** BLOW : golpe *m* **2** : huelga *f*, paro *m Lat* (de trabajadores) **3** ATTACK : ataque *m* — **strikebreaker** ['straɪk-ˌbreɪkər] *n* : esquirol *mf* — **striker** ['straɪkər] *n* : huelgista *mf* — **striking** ['straɪkɪŋ] *adj* : notable, llamativo

string ['strɪŋ] *n* **1** : cordel *m* **2** : sarta *f* (de perlas, insultos, etc.), serie *f* (de eventos, etc.) **3 ~s** *npl* : cuerdas *fpl* (en música) — **~** *vt* **strung** ['strʌŋ]; **stringing 1** : ensartar **2** *or* **~ up** : colgar — **string bean** *n* : habichuela *f* verde

stringent ['strɪndʒənt] *adj* : estricto, severo

strip[1] ['strɪp] *v* **stripped; stripping** *vt* **1** REMOVE : quitar **2** UNDRESS : desnudar **3 ~ s.o. of sth** : despojar a algn de algo — *vi* UNDRESS : desnudarse

strip[2] *n* : tira *f*

stripe ['straɪp] *n* : raya *f*, lista *f* — **striped** ['straɪpt, 'straɪpəd] *adj* : a rayas, rayado

strive ['straɪv] *vi* **strove** ['stro:v]; **striven** ['strɪvən] *or* **strived; striving 1 ~ for** : luchar por **2 ~ to** : esforzarse por

strode → **stride**

stroke ['stro:k] *vt* **stroked; stroking** : acariciar — **~** *n* **1** : golpe *m* **2** : derrame *m* cerebral (en medicina)

stroll ['stro:l] *vi* : pasearse — **~** *n* : paseo *m* — **stroller** ['stro:lər] *n* : cochecito *m* (para niños)

strong ['strɔŋ] *adj* : fuerte — **stronghold** ['strɔŋˌho:ld] *n* : bastión *m* — **strongly** ['strɔŋli] *adv* **1** DEEPLY : profundamente **2** WHOLEHEARTEDLY : totalmente **3** VIGOROUSLY : enérgicamente

strove → **strive**

struck → **strike**

structure ['strʌktʃər] *n* : estructura *f* — **structural** ['strʌktʃərəl] *adj* : estructural

struggle ['strʌgəl] *vi* **-gled; -gling 1** : forcejear **2** STRIVE : luchar — **~** *n* : lucha *f*

strum ['strʌm] *vt* **strummed; strumming** : rasguear

strung → **string**

strut ['strʌt] *vi* **strutted; strutting** : pavonearse — **~** *n* : puntal *m* (en construcción)

stub ['stʌb] *n* : colilla *f* (de un cigarillo), cabo *m* (de un lápiz, etc.), talón *m* (de un cheque) — **~** *vt* **stubbed; stubbing ~ one's toe** : darse en el dedo

stubble ['stʌbəl] *n* : barba *f* de varios días

stubborn ['stʌbərn] *adj* **1** : terco, obstinado **2** PERSISTENT : tenaz

stucco ['stʌko:] *n, pl* **stuccos** *or* **stuccoes** : estuco *m*

stuck → **stick** — **stuck-up** ['stʌk'ʌp] *adj* : engreído, creído *fam*

stud[1] ['stʌd] *n* : semental *m* (animal)

stud[2] *n* **1** NAIL, TACK : tachuela *f*, tachón *m* **2** *or* **~ earring** : arete *m Lat*, pendiente *m Spain* **3** : montante *m* (en construcción)

student ['stu:dənt, 'stju:-] *n* : estudiante *mf*; alumno *m*, **-na** *f* (de un colegio) — **studio** ['stu:diˌo:, 'stju:-] *n, pl* **studios** : estudio *m* — **study** ['stʌdi] *n, pl* **studies** : estudio *m* — **~** *v* **studied; studying** : estudiar — **studious** ['stu:diəs, 'stju:-] *adj* : estudioso

stuff ['stʌf] *n* **1** : cosas *fpl* **2** MATTER, SUBSTANCE : cosa *f* **3 know one's ~** : ser experto — **~** *vt* **1** FILL : rellenar **2** CRAM : meter — **stuffing** ['stʌfɪŋ] *n* : relleno *m* — **stuffy** ['stʌfi] *adj* **stuffier; -est 1** STODGY : pesado, aburrido **2** : tapado (dícese de la nariz) **3 ~ rooms** : salas *fpl* mal ventiladas

stumble ['stʌmbəl] *vi* **-bled; -bling 1** : tropezar **2 ~ across** *or* **upon** : tropezar con

stump ['stʌmp] *n* **1** : muñón *m* (de una pierna, etc.) **2** *or* **tree ~** : tocón *m* — **~** *vt* : dejar perplejo

stun ['stʌn] *vt* **stunned; stunning 1** : aturdir (con un golpe) **2** ASTONISH : dejar atónito

stung → **sting**

stunk → **stink**

stunning ['stʌnɪŋ] *adj* **1** : increíble, sensacional **2** STRIKING : imponente

stunt[1] ['stʌnt] *vt* : atrofiar

stunt[2] *n* : proeza *f* (acrobática)

stupendous [stʊ'pendəs, stjʊ-] *adj* : estupendo

stupid ['stu:pəd, 'stju:-] *adj* **1** : estúpido **2** SILLY : tonto, bobo — **stupidity** [stʊ'pɪdəṭi, stjʊ-] *n* : tontería *f*, estupidez *f*

sturdy ['stərdi] *adj* **sturdier; -est 1** : fuerte, resistente **2** ROBUST : robusto

stutter ['stʌṭər] *vi* : tartamudear — **~** *n* : tartamudeo *m*

sty ['staɪ] *n* **1** *pl* **sties** PIGPEN : pocilga *f*

2 *pl* **sties** *or* **styes :** orzuelo *m* (en el ojo)
style ['staɪl] *n* **1 :** estilo *m* **2** FASHION **:** moda *f* **3 be in ~ :** estar de moda — **~** *vt* **styled; styling :** peinar (pelo), diseñar (vestidos, etc.) — **stylish** ['staɪlɪʃ] *adj* **:** elegante, chic — **stylist** ['staɪlɪst] *n* **:** estilista *mf*
suave ['swɑv] *adj* **:** refinado y afable
sub[1] ['sʌb] *vi* **subbed; subbing → substitute** — **~** *n* **→ substitute**
sub[2] *n* **→ submarine**
subconscious [səb'kɑntʃəs] *adj* **:** subconsciente — **~** *n* **:** subconsciente *m*
subdivide [ˌsʌbdə'vaɪd, 'sʌbdəˌvaɪd] *vt* **-vided; -viding :** subdividir — **subdivision** ['sʌbdəˌvɪʒən] *n* **:** subdivisión *f*
subdue [səb'du:, -'dju:] *vt* **-dued; -duing 1** CONQUER **:** sojuzgar **2** CONTROL **:** dominar **3** SOFTEN **:** atenuar — **subdued** *adj* **:** apagado
subject ['sʌbdʒɪkt] *n* **1 :** sujeto *m* **2 :** súbdito *m*, -ta *f* (de un gobierno) **3** TOPIC **:** tema *m* — **~** *adj* **1 :** sometido **2 ~ to :** sujeto a — **~** [səb'dʒɛkt] *vt* **~ to :** someter a — **subjective** [səb'dʒɛktɪv] *adj* **:** subjetivo
subjunctive [səb'dʒʌŋktɪv] *n* **:** subjuntivo *m* — **subjunctive** *adj* **:** subjuntivo
sublime [sə'blaɪm] *adj* **:** sublime
submarine ['sʌbməˌri:n, ˌsʌbmə'-] *adj* **:** submarino — **~** *n* **:** submarino *m*
submerge [səb'mərdʒ] *v* **-merged; -merging** *vt* **:** sumergir — *vi* **:** sumergirse
submit [səb'mɪt] *v* **-mitted; -mitting** *vi* **1** YIELD **:** rendirse **2 ~ to :** someterse a — *vt* **:** presentar — **submission** [səb'mɪʃən] *n* **1 :** sumisión *f* **2** PRESENTATION **:** presentación *f* — **submissive** [səb'mɪsɪv] *adj* **:** sumiso
subordinate [sə'bɔrdənət] *adj* **:** subordinado — **~** *n* **:** subordinado *m*, -da *f* — **~** [sə'bɔrdənˌeɪt] *vt* **-nated; -nating :** subordinar
subpoena [sə'pi:nə] *n* **:** citación *f*
subscribe [səb'skraɪb] *vi* **-scribed; -scribing ~ to :** suscribirse a (una revista, etc.), suscribir (una opinión, etc.) — **subscriber** [səb'skraɪbər] *n* **:** suscriptor *m*, -tora *f* (de una revista, etc.); abonado *m*, -da *f* (de un servicio) — **subscription** [səb'skrɪpʃən] *n* **:** suscripción *f*
subsequent ['sʌbsɪkwənt, -səˌkwent] *adj* **1 :** subsiguiente **2 ~ to :** posterior a — **subsequently** ['sʌbˌkwentli, -kwənt-] *adv* **:** posteriormente
subservient [səb'sərviənt] *adj* **:** servil
subside [səb'saɪd] *vi* **-sided; -siding 1** SINK **:** hundirse **2 :** amainar (dícese de tormentas, pasiones, etc.), remitir (dícese de fiebres, etc.)
subsidiary [səb'sɪdiˌɛri] *adj* **:** secundario — **~** *n, pl* **-ries :** filial *f*
subsidy ['sʌbsədi] *n, pl* **-dies :** subvención *f* — **subsidize** ['sʌbsəˌdaɪz] *vt* **-dized; -dizing :** subvencionar
subsistence [səb'sɪstənts] *n* **:** subsistencia *f* — **subsist** [səb'sɪst] *vi* **:** subsistir
substance ['sʌbstənts] *n* **:** sustancia *f*
substandard [ˌsʌb'stændərd] *adj* **:** inferior
substantial [səb'stæntʃəl] *adj* **1** CONSIDERABLE **:** considerable **2** STURDY **:** sólido **3 :** sustancioso (dícese de una comida, etc.) — **substantially** [səb'stæntʃəli] *adv* **:** considerablemente
substitute ['sʌbstəˌtu:t, -ˌtju:t] *n* **:** sustituto *m*, -ta *f* (de una persona); sucedáneo *m* (de una cosa) — **~** *vt* **-tuted; -tuting :** sustituir — **substitution** [ˌsʌbstə'tu:ʃən, -'tju:-] *n* **:** sustitución *f*
subterranean [ˌsʌbtə'reɪniən] *adj* **:** subterráneo
subtitle ['sʌbˌtaɪt̬əl] *n* **:** subtítulo *m*
subtle ['sʌt̬əl] *adj* **-tler; -tlest :** sutil — **subtlety** ['sʌt̬əlti] *n, pl* **-ties :** sutileza *f*
subtraction [səb'trækʃən] *n* **:** resta *f* — **subtract** [səb'trækt] *vt* **:** restar
suburb ['sʌˌbərb] *n* **1 :** barrio *m* residencial, suburbio *m* **2 the ~s :** las afueras — **suburban** [sə'bərbən] *adj* **:** de las afueras (de una ciudad)
subversion [səb'vərʒən] *n* **:** subversión *f* — **subversive** [səb'vərsɪv] *adj* **:** subversivo
subway ['sʌbˌweɪ] *n* **:** metro *m*
succeed [sək'si:d] *vt* **:** suceder a — *vi* **:** tener éxito (dícese de personas), dar resultado (dícese de planes, etc.) — **success** [sək'sɛs] *n* **:** éxito *m* — **successful** [sək'sɛsfəl] *adj* **:** de éxito, exitoso *Lat* — **successfully** *adv* **:** con éxito
succession [sək'sɛʃən] *n* **1 :** sucesión *f* **2 in ~ :** sucesivamente, seguidos — **successive** [sək'sɛsɪv] *adj* **:** sucesivo — **successor** [sək'sɛsər] *n* **:** sucesor *m*, -sora *f*
succinct [sək'sɪŋkt, sə'sɪŋkt] *adj* **:** sucinto
succulent ['sʌkjələnt] *adj* **:** suculento
succumb [sə'kʌm] *vi* **:** sucumbir
such ['sʌtʃ] *adj* **1 :** tal **2 ~ as :** como **3 ~ a pity! :** ¡qué lástima! — **~** *pron* **1 :** tal **2 and ~ :** y cosas por el estilo **3 as ~ :** como tal — **~** *adv* **1** VERY **:** muy **2 ~ a nice man! :** ¡qué hombre tan simpático! **3 ~ that :** de tal manera que

suck ['sʌk] *vt* **1** *or* **~ on** : chupar **2** *or* **~ up** : sorber (bebidas), aspirar (con una máquina) — **sucker** ['sʌkər] *n* **1** SHOOT : chupón *m* **2** FOOL : imbécil *mf* — **suckle** ['sʌkəl] *vt* **-led; -ling** : amamantar — **suction** ['sʌkʃən] *n* : succión *f*
sudden ['sʌdən] *adj* **1** : repentino **2 all of a ~** : de repente — **suddenly** ['sʌdənli] *adv* : de repente
suds ['sʌdz] *npl* : espuma *f* (de jabón)
sue ['su:] *vt* **sued; suing** : demandar (por)
suede ['sweɪd] *n* : ante *m,* gamuza *f*
suet ['su:ət] *n* : sebo *m*
suffer ['sʌfər] *vi* : sufrir — *vt* **1** : sufrir **2** BEAR : tolerar — **suffering** ['sʌfərɪŋ] *n* : sufrimiento *m*
suffice [sə'faɪs] *vi* **-ficed; -ficing** : bastar — **sufficient** [sə'fɪʃənt] *adj* : suficiente — **sufficiently** [sə'fɪʃəntli] *adv* : (lo) suficientemente
suffix ['sʌˌfɪks] *n* : sufijo *m*
suffocate ['sʌfəˌkeɪt] *v* **-cated; -cating** *vt* : asfixiar — *vi* : asfixiarse — **suffocation** [ˌsʌfə'keɪʃən] *n* : asfixia *f*
suffrage ['sʌfrɪdʒ] *n* : sufragio *m*
sugar ['ʃʊgər] *n* : azúcar *mf* — **sugarcane** ['ʃʊgərˌkeɪn] *n* : caña *f* de azúcar — **sugary** ['ʃʊgəri] *adj* : azucarado
suggestion [səg'dʒɛstʃən, sə-] *n* **1** : sugerencia *f* **2** TRACE : indicio *m* — **suggest** [səg'dʒɛst, sə-] *vt* **1** : sugerir **2** INDICATE : indicar
suicide ['su:əˌsaɪd] *n* **1** : suicidio *m* (acto) **2** : suicida *mf* (persona) — **suicidal** [ˌsu:ə'saɪdəl] *adj* : suicida
suit ['su:t] *n* **1** LAWSUIT : pleito *m* **2** : traje *m* (ropa) **3** : palo *m* (de naipes) — **~** *vt* **1** ADAPT : adaptar **2** BEFIT : ser apropiado para **3 ~ s.o.** : convenir a algn (dícese de fechas, etc.), quedar bien a algn (dícese de ropa) — **suitable** ['su:ţəbəl] *adj* : apropiado — **suitcase** ['su:tˌkeɪs] *n* : maleta *f,* valija *f Lat*
suite ['swi:t, *for* 2 *also* 'su:t] *n* **1** : suite *f* (de habitaciones) **2** : juego *m* (de muebles)
suitor ['su:ţər] *n* : pretendiente *m*
sulfur ['sʌlfər] *n* : azufre *m*
sulk ['sʌlk] *vi* : enfurruñarse *fam* — **sulky** ['sʌlki] *adj* **sulkier; -est** : malhumorado
sullen ['sʌlən] *adj* : hosco
sultry ['sʌltri] *adj* **sultrier; -est 1** : bochornoso **2** SENSUAL : sensual
sum ['sʌm] *n* : suma *f* — **~** *vt* **summed; summing ~ up** : resumir — **summarize** ['sʌməˌraɪz] *v* **-rized; -rizing** : resumir — **summary** ['sʌməri] *n, pl* **-ries** : resumen *m*
summer ['sʌmər] *n* : verano *m*
summit ['sʌmət] *n* : cumbre *f*
summon ['sʌmən] *vt* **1** : llamar (a algn), convocar (una reunión) **2** : citar (en derecho) — **summons** ['sʌmənz] *n, pl* **summonses** SUBPOENA : citación *f*
sumptuous ['sʌmptʃʊəs] *adj* : suntuoso
sun ['sʌn] *n* : sol *m* — **sunbathe** ['sʌnˌbeɪð] *vi* **-bathed; -bathing** : tomar el sol — **sunbeam** ['sʌnˌbi:m] *n* : rayo *m* de sol — **sunburn** ['sʌnˌbərn] *n* : quemadura *f* de sol
Sunday ['sʌnˌdeɪ, -di] *n* : domingo *m*
sundry ['sʌndri] *adj* : varios, diversos
sunflower ['sʌnˌflaʊər] *n* : girasol *m*
sung → **sing**
sunglasses ['sʌnˌglæsəz] *npl* : gafas *fpl* de sol, lentes *mpl* de sol
sunk → **sink** — **sunken** ['sʌŋkən] *adj* : hundido
sunlight ['sʌnˌlaɪt] *n* : (luz *f* del) sol *m* — **sunny** ['sʌni] *adj* **-nier; -est** : soleado — **sunrise** ['sʌnˌraɪz] *n* : salida *f* del sol — **sunset** ['sʌnˌsɛt] *n* : puesta *f* del sol — **sunshine** ['sʌnˌʃaɪn] *n* : sol *m,* luz *f* del sol — **suntan** ['sʌnˌtæn] *n* : bronceado *m*
super ['su:pər] *adj* : súper *fam*
superb [sʊ'pərb] *adj* : magnífico, espléndido
superficial [ˌsu:pər'fɪʃəl] *adj* : superficial
superfluous [sʊ'pərfluəs] *adj* : superfluo
superimpose [ˌsu:pərɪm'po:z] *vt* **-posed; -posing** : sobreponer
superintendent [ˌsu:pərɪn'tɛndənt] *n* **1** : superintendente *mf* (de policía) **2** *or* **building ~** : portero *m,* -ra *f* **3** *or* **school ~** : director *m,* -tora *f* (de un colegio)
superior [sʊ'pɪriər] *adj* : superior — **~** *n* : superior *m* — **superiority** [sʊˌpɪri'ɔrəţi] *n, pl* **-ties** : superioridad *f*
superlative [sʊ'pərləţɪv] *adj* **1** : superlativo (en gramática) **2** EXCELLENT : excepcional — **~** *n* : superlativo *m*
supermarket ['su:pərˌmɑrkət] *n* : supermercado *m*
supernatural [ˌsu:pər'nætʃərəl] *adj* : sobrenatural
superpower ['su:pərˌpaʊər] *n* : superpotencia *f*
supersede [ˌsu:pər'si:d] *vt* **-seded; -seding** : reemplazar, suplantar
supersonic [ˌsu:pər'sɑnɪk] *adj* : supersónico
superstition [ˌsu:pər'stɪʃən] *n* : superstición *f* — **superstitious** [ˌsu:pər'stɪʃəs] *adj* : supersticioso
supervisor ['su:pərˌvaɪzər] *n* : supervisor

m, -sora *f* — **supervise** ['su:pər,vaɪz] *vt* **-vised; -vising** : supervisar — **supervision** [,su:pər'vɪʒən] *n* : supervisión *f* — **supervisory** [,su:pər'vaɪzəri] *adj* : de supervisor

supper ['sʌpər] *n* : cena *f,* comida *f*

supplant [sə'plænt] *vt* : suplantar

supple ['sʌpəl] *adj* **-pler; -plest** : flexible

supplement ['sʌpləmənt] *n* : suplemento *m* — ~ ['sʌplə,mɛnt] *vt* : complementar — **supplementary** [,sʌplə'mɛntəri] *adj* : suplementario

supply [sə'plaɪ] *vt* **-plied; -plying 1** : suministrar **2** ~ **with** : proveer de — ~ *n, pl* **-plies 1** : suministro *m,* provisión *f* **2** ~ **and demand** : oferta y demanda **3 supplies** *npl* PROVISIONS : provisiones *fpl,* víveres *mpl* — **supplier** [sə'plaɪər] *n* : proveedor *m,* -dora *f*

support [sə'port] *vt* **1** BACK : apoyar **2** : mantener (una familia, etc.) **3** PROP UP : sostener — ~ *n* **1** : apoyo *m* (moral), ayuda *f* (económica) **2** PROP : soporte *m* — **supporter** [sə'porṭər] *n* : partidario *m,* -ria *f*

suppose [sə'po:z] *vt* **-posed; -posing 1** : suponer **2 be ~d to (do sth)** : tener que (hacer algo) — **supposedly** *adv* : supuestamente

suppress [sə'prɛs] *vt* **1** : reprimir **2** : suprimir (noticias, etc.) — **suppression** [sə'prɛʃən] *n* **1** : represión *f* **2** : supresión *f* (de información)

supreme [su'pri:m] *adj* : supremo — **supremacy** [su'prɛməsi] *n, pl* **-cies** : supremacía *f*

sure ['ʃur] *adj* **surer; -est 1** : seguro **2 make ~ that** : asegurarse de que — ~ *adv* **1** OF COURSE : por supuesto, claro **2 it ~ is hot!** : ¡qué calor! — **surely** ['ʃurli] *adv* : seguramente

surfing ['sərfɪŋ] *n* : surf *m,* surfing *m*

surface ['sərfəs] *n* : superficie *f* — ~ *v* **-faced; -facing** *vi* : salir a la superficie — *vt* : revestir

surfeit ['sərfət] *n* : exceso *m*

surfing ['sərfɪŋ] *n* : surf *m,* surfing *m*

surge ['sərdʒ] *vi* **surged; surging 1** SWELL : hincharse (dícese del mar) **2** SWARM : moverse en tropel — ~ *n* **1** : oleaje *m* (del mar), oleada *f* (de gente) **2** INCREASE : aumento *m* (súbito)

surgeon ['sərdʒən] *n* : cirujano *m,* -na *f* — **surgery** ['sərdʒəri] *n, pl* **-geries** : cirugía *f* — **surgical** ['sərdʒɪkəl] *adj* : quirúrgico

surly ['sərli] *adj* **surlier; -est** : hosco, arisco

surmount [sər'maʊnt] *vt* : superar

surname ['sər,neɪm] *n* : apellido *m*

surpass [sər'pæs] *vt* : superar

surplus ['sər,plʌs] *n* : excedente *m*

surprise [sə'praɪz, sər-] *n* **1** : sorpresa *f* **2 take by ~** : sorprender — ~ *vt* **-prised; -prising** : sorprender — **surprising** [sə'praɪzɪŋ, sər-] *adj* : sorprendente

surrender [sə'rɛndər] *vt* : entregar, rendir — *vi* : rendirse — ~ *n* : rendición *m* (de una ciudad, etc.), entrega *f* (de posesiones)

surrogate ['sərəgət, -,geɪt] *n* : sustituto *m*

surround [sə'raʊnd] *vt* : rodear — **surroundings** [sə'raʊndɪŋz] *npl* : ambiente *m*

surveillance [sər'veɪlənts, -'veɪljənts, -'veɪənts] *n* : vigilancia *f*

survey [sər'veɪ] *vt* **-veyed; -veying 1** : medir (un solar) **2** INSPECT : inspeccionar **3** POLL : sondear — ~ ['sər,veɪ] *n, pl* **-veys 1** INSPECTION : inspección *f* **2** : medición *f* (de un solar) **3** POLL : encuesta *f,* sondeo *m* — **surveyor** [sər'veɪər] *n* : agrimensor *m,* -sora *f*

survive [sər'vaɪv] *v* **-vived; -viving** *vi* : sobrevivir — *vt* : sobrevivir a — **survival** [sər'vaɪvəl] *n* : supervivencia *f* — **survivor** [sər'vaɪvər] *n* : superviviente *mf*

susceptible [sə'sɛptəbəl] *adj* ~ **to** : propenso a — **susceptibility** [sə,sɛptə'bɪləṭi] *n, pl* **-ties** : propensión *f* (a enfermedades, etc.)

suspect ['sʌs,pɛkt, sə'spɛkt] *adj* : sospechoso — ~ ['sʌs,pɛkt] *n* : sospechoso *m,* -sa *f* — ~ [sə'spɛkt] *vt* : sospechar (algo), sospechar de (algn)

suspend [sə'spɛnd] *vt* : suspender — **suspense** [sə'spɛnts] *n* **1** : incertidumbre *m* **2** : suspenso *m Lat,* suspense *m Spain* (en el cine, etc.) — **suspension** [sə'spɛntʃən] *n* : suspensión *f*

suspicion [sə'spɪʃən] *n* : sospecha *f* — **suspicious** [sə'spɪʃəs] *adj* **1** QUESTIONABLE : sospechoso **2** DISTRUSTFUL : suspicaz

sustain [sə'steɪn] *vt* **1** : sostener **2** SUFFER : sufrir

swagger ['swægər] *vi* : pavonearse

swallow[1] ['swɑlo:] *v* : tragar — ~ *n* : trago *m*

swallow[2] *n* : golondrina *f* (pájaro)

swam → **swim**

swamp ['swɑmp] *n* : pantano *m,* ciénaga *f* — ~ *vt* : inundar — **swampy** ['swɑmpi] *adj* **swampier; -est** : pantanoso, cenagoso

swan ['swɑn] *n* : cisne *f*

swap ['swɑp] *vt* **swapped; swapping 1**

: intercambiar **2 ~ sth for sth** : cambiar algo por algo **3 ~ sth with s.o.** : cambiar algo a algn — **~** *n* : cambio *m*

swarm ['swɔrm] *n* : enjambre *m* — **~** *vi* : enjambrar

swat ['swɑt] *vt* **swatted; swatting** : aplastar (un insecto)

sway ['sweɪ] *n* **1** : balanceo *m* **2** INFLUENCE : influjo *m* — **~** *vi* : balancearse — *vt* : influir en

swear ['swær] *v* **swore** ['swor]; **sworn** ['sworn]; **swearing** *vi* **1** : jurar **2** CURSE : decir palabrotas — *vt* : jurar — **swearword** ['swær,wərd] *n* : palabrota *f*

sweat ['swɛt] *vi* **sweat** *or* **sweated; sweating** : sudar — **~** *n* : sudor *m* — **sweater** ['swɛṭər] *n* : suéter *m* — **sweatshirt** ['swɛt,ʃərt] *n* : sudadera *f* — **sweaty** ['swɛṭi] *adj* **sweatier; -est** : sudado

Swedish ['swi:dɪʃ] *adj* : sueco — **~** *n* : sueco *m* (idioma)

sweep ['swi:p] *v* **swept** ['swɛpt]; **sweeping** *vt* **1** : barrer **2 ~ aside** : apartar **3 ~ through** : extenderse por — *vi* : barrer — **~** *n* **1** : barrido *m* **2** : movimiento *m* circular (de la mano, etc.) **3** SCOPE : alcance *m* — **sweeping** ['swi:pɪŋ] *adj* **1** WIDE : amplio **2** EXTENSIVE : extenso — **sweepstakes** ['swi:p,steɪks] *ns & pl* : lotería *f*

sweet ['swi:t] *adj* **1** : dulce **2** PLEASANT : agradable — **~** *n* : dulce *m* — **sweeten** ['swi:tən] *vt* : endulzar — **sweetener** ['swi:tənər] *n* : endulzante *m* — **sweetheart** ['swi:t,hɑrt] *n* **1** : novio *m*, -via *f* **2** (*used as a form of address*) : cariño *m* — **sweetness** ['swi:tnəs] *n* : dulzura *f* — **sweet potato** *n* : batata *f*, boniato *m*

swell ['swɛl] *vi* **swelled; swelled** *or* **swollen** ['swo:lən, 'swʌl-]; **swelling 1** *or* **~ up** : hincharse **2** INCREASE : aumentar, crecer — **~** *n* : oleaje *m* (del mar) — **swelling** ['swɛlɪŋ] *n* : hinchazón *f*

sweltering ['swɛltərɪŋ] *adj* : sofocante

swept → **sweep**

swerve ['swərv] *vi* **swerved; swerving** : virar bruscamente

swift ['swɪft] *adj* : rápido — **swiftly** *adv* : rápidamente

swig ['swɪg] *n* : trago *m* — **~** *vi* **swigged; swigging** : beber a tragos

swim ['swɪm] *vi* **swam** ['swæm]; **swum** ['swʌm]; **swimming 1** : nadar **2** REEL : dar vueltas — **~** *n* **1** : baño *m* **2 go for a ~** : ir a nadar — **swimmer** ['swɪmər] *n* : nadador *m*, -dora *f*

swindle ['swɪndəl] *vt* **-dled; -dling** : estafar, timar — **~** *n* : estafa *f*, timo *m fam*

swine ['swaɪn] *ns & pl* : cerdo *m*, -da *f*

swing ['swɪŋ] *v* **swung** ['swʌŋ]; **swinging** *vt* **1** : balancear, hacer oscilar **2** MANAGE : arreglar — *vi* **1** : balancearse, oscilar **2** SWIVEL : girar — **~** *n* **1** : vaivén *m*, balanceo *m* **2** SHIFT : cambio *m* **3** : columpio *m* (para niños) **4 in full ~** : en pleno proceso

swipe ['swaɪp] *v* **swiped; swiping** *vt* STEAL : birlar *fam*, robar — *vi* **~ at** : intentar pegar

swirl ['swərl] *vi* : arremolinarse — **~** *n* **1** EDDY : remolino *m* **2** SPIRAL : espiral *f*

swish ['swɪʃ] *vt* : agitar (haciendo un sonido) — *vi* **1** RUSTLE : hacer frufrú **2 ~ by** : pasar silbando

Swiss ['swɪs] *adj* : suizo

switch ['swɪtʃ] *n* **1** WHIP : vara *f* **2** CHANGE : cambio *m* **3** : interruptor *m*, llave *f* (de la luz, etc.) — **~** *vt* **1** CHANGE : cambiar de **2** EXCHANGE : intercambiar **3 ~ on** : encender, prender *Lat* **4 ~ off** : apagar — *vi* **1** : sacudir (la cola, etc.) **2** CHANGE : cambiar **3** SWAP : intercambiarse — **switchboard** ['swɪtʃ,bord] *n* : centralita *f*, conmutador *m Lat*

swivel ['swɪvəl] *vi* **-veled** *or* **-velled; -veling** *or* **-velling** : girar (sobre un pivote)

swollen → **swell**

swoon ['swu:n] *vi* : desvanecerse

swoop ['swu:p] *vi* **~ down on** : abatirse sobre — **~** *n* : descenso *m* en picada

sword ['sɔrd] *n* : espada *f*

swordfish ['sɔrd,fɪʃ] *n* : pez *m* espada

swore, sworn → **swear**

swum → **swim**

swung → **swing**

syllable ['sɪləbəl] *n* : sílaba *f*

syllabus ['sɪləbəs] *n, pl* **-bi** [-,baɪ] *or* **-buses** : programa *m* (de estudios)

symbol ['sɪmbəl] *n* : símbolo *m* — **symbolic** [sɪm'bɑlɪk] *adj* : simbólico — **symbolism** ['sɪmbə,lɪzəm] *n* : simbolismo *m* — **symbolize** ['sɪmbə,laɪz] *vt* **-ized; -izing** : simbolizar

symmetry ['sɪmətri] *n, pl* **-tries** : simetría *f* — **symmetrical** [sə'mɛtrɪkəl] *adj* : simétrico

sympathy ['sɪmpəθi] *n, pl* **-thies 1** COMPASSION : compasión *f* **2** UNDERSTANDING : comprensión *f* **3** CONDOLENCES : pésame *m* **4 sympathies** *npl* LOYALTY : simpatías *fpl* — **sympathize** ['sɪmpə,θaɪz] *vi* **-thized; -thizing 1 ~ with** PITY : compadecerse de **2 ~**

with UNDERSTAND : comprender — **sympathetic** [ˌsɪmpəˈθeṭɪk] *adj* **1** COMPASSIONATE : compasivo **2** UNDERSTANDING : comprensivo
symphony [ˈsɪmpfəni] *n, pl* **-nies** : sinfonía *f*
symposium [sɪmˈpoːziəm] *n, pl* **-sia** [-ziə] *or* **-siums** : simposio *m*
symptom [ˈsɪmptəm] *n* : síntoma *m* — **symptomatic** [ˌsɪmptəˈmæṭɪk] *adj* : sintomático
synagogue [ˈsɪnəˌgɑg, -ˌgɔg] *n* : sinagoga *f*
synchronize [ˈsɪŋkrəˌnaɪz, ˈsɪn-] *vt* **-nized; -nizing** : sincronizar
syndrome [ˈsɪnˌdroːm] *n* : síndrome *m*
synonym [ˈsɪnəˌnɪm] *n* : sinónimo *m* — **synonymous** [səˈnɑnəməs] *adj* : sinónimo
synopsis [səˈnɑpsɪs] *n, pl* **-opses** [-ˌsiːz] : sinopsis *f*
syntax [ˈsɪnˌtæks] *n* : sintaxis *f*
synthesis [ˈsɪnθəsɪs] *n, pl* **-theses** [-ˌsiːz] : síntesis *f* — **synthesize** [ˈsɪnθəˌsaɪz] *vt* **-sized; -sizing** : sintetizar — **synthetic** [sɪnˈθɛṭɪk] *adj* : sintético
syphilis [ˈsɪfələs] *n* : sífilis *f*
Syrian [ˈsɪriən] *adj* : sirio
syringe [səˈrɪndʒ, ˈsɪrɪndʒ] *n* : jeringa *f*, jeringuilla *f*
syrup [ˈsərəp, ˈsɪrəp] *n* : jarabe *m*
system [ˈsɪstəm] *n* **1** : sistema *m* **2** BODY : organismo *m* **3 digestive ~** : aparato *m* digestivo — **systematic** [ˌsɪstəˈmæṭɪk] *adj* : sistemático

T

t [ˈtiː] *n, pl* **t's** *or* **ts** [ˈtiːz] : t *f*, vigésima letra del alfabeto inglés
tab [ˈtæb] *n* **1** TAG : etiqueta *f* **2** FLAP : lengüeta *f* **3** ACCOUNT : cuenta *f* **4 keep ~s on** : vigilar
table [ˈteɪbəl] *n* **1** : mesa *f* **2** LIST : tabla *f* **3 ~ of contents** : índice *m* de materias — **tablecloth** [ˈteɪbəlˌklɔθ] *n* : mantel *m* — **tablespoon** [ˈteɪbəlˌspuːn] *n* **1** : cuchara *f* grande **2** : cucharada *f* (cantidad)
tablet [ˈtæblət] *n* **1** PAD : bloc *m* **2** PILL : pastilla *f* **3** *or* **stone ~** : lápida *f*
tabloid [ˈtæˌblɔɪd] *n* : tabloide *m*
taboo [təˈbuː, tæ-] *adj* : tabú — **~** *n* : tabú *m*
tacit [ˈtæsɪt] *adj* : tácito
taciturn [ˈtæsɪˌtərn] *adj* : taciturno
tack [ˈtæk] *vt* **1** : fijar con tachuelas **2 ~ on** ADD : añadir — **~** *n* **1** : tachuela *f* **2 change ~** : cambiar de rumbo
tackle [ˈtækəl] *n* **1** GEAR : aparejo *m* **2** : placaje *m*, tacle *m Lat* (acción) — **~** *vt* **-led; -ling 1** : placar, taclear *Lat* **2** CONFRONT : abordar
tacky [ˈtæki] *adj* **tackier; -est 1** : pegajoso **2** GAUDY : de mal gusto
tact [ˈtækt] *n* : tacto *m* — **tactful** [ˈtæktfəl] *adj* : diplomático, discreto
tactical [ˈtæktɪkəl] *adj* : táctico — **tactic** [ˈtæktɪk] *n* : táctica *f* — **tactics** [ˈtæktɪks] *ns & pl* : táctica *f*
tactless [ˈtæktləs] *adj* : indiscreto
tadpole [ˈtædˌpoːl] *n* : renacuajo *m*
tag[1] [ˈtæg] *n* LABEL : etiqueta *f* — **~** *v* **tagged; tagging** *vt* : etiquetar — *vi* **~ along with s.o.** : acompañar a algn
tag[2] *vt* : tocar (en varios juegos)
tail [ˈteɪl] *n* **1** : cola *f* **2 ~s** *npl* : cruz *f* (de una moneda) — **~** *vt* FOLLOW : seguir
tailor [ˈteɪlər] *n* : sastre *m*, **-tra** *f* — **~** *vt* **1** : confeccionar (ropa) **2** ADAPT : adaptar
taint [ˈteɪnt] *vt* : contaminar
take [ˈteɪk] *v* **took** [ˈtʊk]; **taken** [ˈteɪkən]; **taking** *vt* **1** : tomar **2** BRING : llevar **3** REMOVE : sacar **4** BEAR : soportar, aguantar **5** ACCEPT : aceptar **6 I ~ it that...** : supongo que... **7 ~ a bath** : bañarse **8 ~ a walk** : dar un paseo **9 ~ back** : retirar (palabras, etc.) **10 ~ in** ALTER : achicar **11 ~ in** GRASP : entender **12 ~ in** TRICK : engañar **13 ~ off** REMOVE : quitar, quitarse (ropa) **14 ~ on** : asumir (una responsabilidad, etc.) **15 ~ out** : sacar **16 ~ over** : tomar el poder de **17 ~ place** : tener lugar **18 ~ up** SHORTEN : acortar **19 ~ up** OCCUPY : ocupar — *vi* **1** : prender (dícese de una vacuna, etc.) **2 ~ off** : despegar (dícese de aviones, etc.) **3 ~ over** : asumir el mando — **~** *n* **1** PROCEEDS : ingresos *mpl* **2** : toma *f* (en el cine) — **takeoff** [ˈteɪkˌɔf] *n* : despegue *m* (de un avión, etc.) — **takeover** [ˈteɪkˌoːvər] *n* : toma *f* (de poder, etc.), adquisición *f* (de una empresa)
talcum powder [ˈtælkəm] *n* : polvos *mpl* de talco
tale [ˈteɪl] *n* : cuento *m*

talent ['tælənt] *n* : talento *m* — **talented** ['tæləntəd] *adj* : talentoso

talk ['tɔk] *vi* **1** : hablar **2** ~ **about** : hablar de **3** ~ **to/with** : hablar con — *vt* **1** SPEAK : hablar **2** ~ **over** : hablar de, discutir — ~ *n* **1** CHAT : conversación *f* **2** SPEECH : charla *f* — **talkative** ['tɔkəṭɪv] *adj* : hablador

tall ['tɔl] *adj* **1** : alto **2 how** ~ **are you?** : ¿cuánto mides?

tally ['tæli] *n, pl* **-lies** : cuenta *f* — ~ *v* **-lied; -lying** *vt* RECKON : calcular — *vi* MATCH : concordar, cuadrar

talon ['tælən] *n* : garra *f*

tambourine [ˌtæmbə'ri:n] *n* : pandereta *f*

tame ['teɪm] *adj* **tamer; -est 1** : domesticado **2** DOCILE : manso **3** DULL : insípido, soso — ~ *vt* **tamed; taming** : domar

tamper ['tæmpər] *vi* ~ **with** : forzar (una cerradura), amañar (documentos, etc.)

tampon ['tæmˌpɑn] *n* : tampón *m*

tan ['tæn] *v* **tanned; tanning** *vt* : curtir (cuero) — *vi* : broncearse — ~ *n* **1** SUNTAN : bronceado *m* **2** : (color *m*) café *m* con leche

tang ['tæŋ] *n* : sabor *m* fuerte

tangent ['tændʒənt] *n* : tangente *f*

tangerine ['tændʒəˌri:n, ˌtændʒə'-] *n* : mandarina *f*

tangible ['tændʒəbəl] *adj* : tangible

tangle ['tæŋgəl] *v* **-gled; -gling** *vt* : enredar — *vi* : enredarse — ~ *n* : enredo *m*

tango ['tæŋˌgo:] *n, pl* **-gos** : tango *m*

tank ['tæŋk] *n* **1** : tanque *m*, depósito *m* **2** : tanque *m* (militar) — **tanker** ['tæŋkər] *n* **1** : buque *m* tanque **2** *or* ~ **truck** : camión *m* cisterna

tantalizing ['tæntəˌlaɪzɪŋ] *adj* : tentador

tantrum ['tæntrəm] *n* **throw a** ~ : hacer un berrinche

tap[1] ['tæp] *n* FAUCET : llave *f*, grifo *m Spain* — ~ *vt* **tapped; tapping 1** : sacar (un líquido, etc.), sangrar (un árbol) **2** : intervenir (un teléfono)

tap[2] *vt* **tapped; tapping** STRIKE : tocar, dar un golpecito en — ~ *n* : golpecito *m*, toque *m*

tape ['teɪp] *n* : cinta *f* — ~ *vt* **taped; taping 1** : pegar con cinta **2** RECORD : grabar — **tape measure** *n* : cinta *f* métrica

taper ['teɪpər] *n* : vela *f* (larga) — ~ *vi* **1** NARROW : estrecharse **2** *or* ~ **off** : disminuir

tapestry ['tæpəstri] *n, pl* **-tries** : tapiz *m*

tar ['tɑr] *n* : alquitrán *m* — ~ *vt* **tarred; tarring** : alquitranar

tarantula [tə'ræntʃələ, -'ræntələ] *n* : tarántula *f*

target ['tɑrgət] *n* **1** : blanco *m* **2** GOAL : objetivo *m*

tariff ['tærɪf] *n* : tarifa *f*, arancel *m*

tarnish ['tɑrnɪʃ] *vt* **1** : deslustrar **2** : empañar (una reputación, etc.) — *vi* : deslustrarse

tart[1] ['tɑrt] *adj* SOUR : ácido, agrio

tart[2] *n* : pastel *m*

tartan ['tɑrtən] *n* : tartán *m*

task ['tæsk] *n* : tarea *f*

tassel ['tæsəl] *n* : borla *f*

taste ['teɪst] *v* **tasted; tasting** *vt* TRY : probar — *vi* **1** : saber **2** ~ **like** : saber a — ~ *n* **1** FLAVOR : gusto *m*, sabor *m* **2 have a** ~ **of** : probar **3 in good/bad** ~ : de buen/mal gusto — **tasteful** ['teɪstfəl] *adj* : de buen gusto — **tasteless** ['teɪstləs] *adj* **1** : sin sabor **2** COARSE : de mal gusto — **tasty** ['teɪsti] *adj* **tastier; -est** : sabroso

tatters ['tæṭər] *npl* : harapos *mpl* — **tattered** ['tæṭərd] *adj* : harapiento

tattle ['tæṭəl] *vi* **-tled; -tling** ~ **on s.o.** : acusar a algn

tattoo [tæ'tu:] *vt* : tatuar — ~ *n* : tatuaje *m*

taught → **teach**

taunt ['tɔnt] *n* : pulla *f*, burla *f* — ~ *vt* : mofarse de, burlarse de

taut ['tɔt] *adj* : tirante, tenso

tavern ['tævərn] *n* : taberna *f*

tax ['tæks] *vt* **1** : gravar **2** STRAIN : poner a prueba — ~ *n* **1** : impuesto *m* **2** BURDEN : carga *f* — **taxable** ['tæksəbəl] *adj* : imponible — **taxation** [tæk'seɪʃən] *n* : impuestos *mpl* — **tax-exempt** ['tæksɪg'zɛmpt, -ɛg-] *adj* : libre de impuestos

taxi ['tæksi] *n, pl* **taxis** : taxi *m* — ~ *vi* **taxied; taxiing** *or* **taxying; taxis** *or* **taxies** : rodar por la pista (dícese de un avión)

taxpayer ['tæksˌpeɪər] *n* : contribuyente *mf*

tea ['ti:] *n* : té *m*

teach ['ti:tʃ] *v* **taught** ['tɔt]; **teaching** *vt* : enseñar, dar clases de (una asignatura) — *vi* : dar clases — **teacher** ['ti:tʃər] *n* : profesor *m*, **-sora** *f*; maestro *m*, **-tra** *f* (de niños pequeños) — **teaching** ['ti:tʃɪŋ] *n* : enseñanza *f*

teacup ['ti:ˌkʌp] *n* : taza *f* de té

team ['ti:m] *n* : equipo *m* — ~ *vi or* ~ **up** : asociarse — **teammate** ['ti:mˌmeɪt] *n* : compañero *m*, **-ra** *f* de equipo — **teamwork** ['ti:mˌwərk] *n* : trabajo *m* de equipo

teapot ['ti:ˌpɑt] *n* : tetera *f*

tear[1] ['tær] *v* **tore** ['tor]; **torn** ['torn]; **tearing** *vt* **1** : romper, rasgar **2** ~ **apart** : destrozar **3** ~ **down** : derribar **4** ~ **off** *or* ~ **out** : arrancar **5** ~ **up** : romper (papel, etc.) — *vi* **1** : romperse, rasgarse **2** RUSH : ir a toda velocidad — ~ *n* : desgarro *m,* rasgón *m*
tear[2] ['tɪr] *n* : lágrima *f* — **tearful** ['tɪrfəl] *adj* : lloroso
tease ['ti:z] *vt* **teased; teasing 1** : tomar el pelo a, burlarse de **2** ANNOY : fastidiar
teaspoon ['ti:ˌspu:n] *n* **1** : cucharita *f* **2** : cucharadita *f* (cantidad)
technical ['tɛknɪkəl] *adj* : técnico — **technicality** [ˌtɛknə'kæləţi] *n, pl* **-ties** : detalle *m* técnico — **technically** [-kli] *adv* : técnicamente — **technician** [tɛk'nɪʃən] *n* : técnico *m,* -ca *f*
technique [tɛk'ni:k] *n* : técnica *f*
technological [ˌtɛknə'lɑdʒɪkəl] *adj* : tecnológico — **technology** [tɛk'nɑlədʒi] *n, pl* **-gies** : tecnología *f*
teddy bear ['tɛdi] *n* : oso *m* de peluche
tedious ['ti:diəs] *adj* : tedioso, aburrido — **tedium** ['ti:diəm] *n* : tedio *m*
tee ['ti:] *n* : tee *m* (en deportes)
teem ['ti:m] *vi* **1** POUR : llover a cántaros **2 be ~ing with** : estar repleto de
teenage ['ti:nˌeɪdʒ] *or* **teenaged** [-ˌeɪdʒd] *adj* : adolescente — **teenager** ['ti:nˌeɪdʒər] *n* : adolescente *mf* — **teens** ['ti:nz] *npl* : adolescencia *f*
teepee → **tepee**
teeter ['ti:ţər] *vi* : tambalearse
teeth → **tooth** — **teethe** ['ti:ð] *vi* **teethed; teething** : echar los dientes
telecommunication ['tɛləkəˌmju:nə'keɪʃən] *n* : telecomunicación *f*
telegram ['tɛləˌgræm] *n* : telegrama *m*
telegraph ['tɛləˌgræf] *n* : telégrafo *m* — ~ *v* : telegrafiar
telephone ['tɛləˌfo:n] *n* : teléfono *m* — ~ *v* **-phoned; -phoning** : llamar por teléfono
telescope ['tɛləˌsko:p] *n* : telescopio *m*
televise ['tɛləˌvaɪz] *vt* **-vised; -vising** : televisar — **television** ['tɛləˌvɪʒən] *n* : televisión *f*
tell ['tɛl] *v* **told** ['to:ld]; **telling** *vt* **1** : decir **2** RELATE : contar **3** DISTINGUISH : distinguir **4 ~ s.o. off** : regañar a algn — *vi* **1** : decir **2** KNOW : saber **3** SHOW : tener efecto **4 ~ on s.o.** : acusar a algn — **teller** ['tɛlər] *n or* **bank ~** : cajero *m,* -ra *f*
temp ['tɛmp] *n* : empleado *m,* -da *f* temporal
temper ['tɛmpər] *vt* MODERATE : temperar — ~ *n* **1** MOOD : humor *m* **2 have a bad ~** : tener mal genio **3 lose one's ~** : perder los estribos — **temperament** ['tɛmpərmənt, -prə-, -pərə-] *n* : temperamento *m* — **temperamental** [ˌtɛmpər'mentəl, -prə-, -pərə-] *adj* : temperamental — **temperate** ['tɛmpərət] *adj* **1** : moderado **2 ~ zone** : zona *f* templada
temperature ['tɛmpərˌtʃʊr, -prə-, -pərə-, -tʃər] *n* **1** : temperatura *f* **2 have a ~** : tener fiebre
tempest ['tɛmpəst] *n* : tempestad *f*
temple ['tɛmpəl] *n* **1** : templo *m* **2** : sien *f* (en anatomía)
tempo ['tɛmˌpo:] *n, pl* **-pi** [-ˌpi:] *or* **-pos 1** : tempo *m* **2** PACE : ritmo *m*
temporarily [ˌtɛmpə'rɛrəli] *adv* : temporalmente — **temporary** ['tɛmpəˌrɛri] *adj* : temporal
tempt ['tɛmpt] *vt* : tentar — **temptation** [tɛmp'teɪʃən] *n* : tentación *f*
ten ['tɛn] *adj* : diez — ~ *n* : diez *m*
tenacity [tə'næsəţi] *n* : tenacidad *f* — **tenacious** [tə'neɪʃəs] *adj* : tenaz
tenant ['tɛnənt] *n* : inquilino *m,* -na *f;* arrendatario *m,* -ria *f*
tend[1] ['tɛnd] *vt* MIND : cuidar
tend[2] *vi* **~ to** : tender a — **tendency** ['tɛndəntsi] *n, pl* **-cies** : tendencia *f*
tender[1] ['tɛndər] *adj* **1** : tierno **2** PAINFUL : dolorido
tender[2] *vt* : presentar — ~ *n* **1** : oferta *f* **2 legal ~** : moneda *f* de curso legal
tenderloin ['tɛndərˌlɔɪn] *n* : lomo *f* (de cerdo o vaca)
tenderness ['tɛndərnəs] *n* : ternura *f*
tendon ['tɛndən] *n* : tendón *m*
tenet ['tɛnət] *n* : principio *m*
tennis ['tɛnəs] *n* : tenis *m*
tenor ['tɛnər] *n* : tenor *m*
tense[1] ['tɛnts] *n* : tiempo *m* (de un verbo)
tense[2] *v* **tensed; tensing** *vt* : tensar — *vi* : tensarse — ~ *adj* **tenser; tensest** : tenso — **tension** ['tɛntʃən] *n* : tensión *f*
tent ['tɛnt] *n* : tienda *f* de campaña
tentacle ['tɛntɪkəl] *n* : tentáculo *m*
tentative ['tɛntəţɪv] *adj* **1** HESITANT : vacilante **2** PROVISIONAL : provisional
tenth ['tɛnθ] *adj* : décimo — ~ *n* **1** : décimo *m,* -ma *f* (en una serie) **2** : décimo *m* (en matemáticas)
tenuous ['tɛnjʊəs] *adj* : tenue, endeble
tepid ['tɛpɪd] *adj* : tibio
term ['tərm] *n* **1** WORD : término *m* **2** PERIOD : período *m* **3 be on good ~s** : tener buenas relaciones **4 in ~s of** : con respecto a — ~ *vt* : calificar de

terminal ['tərmənəl] *adj* : terminal — ~ *n* **1** : terminal *m* **2** *or* **bus** ~ : terminal *f*
terminate ['tərmə,neɪt] *v* **-nated; -nating** *vi* : terminar(se) — *vt* : poner fin a — **termination** [,tərmə'neɪʃən] *n* : terminación *f*
termite ['tər,maɪt] *n* : termita *f*
terrace ['tɛrəs] *n* : terraza *f*
terrain [tə'reɪn] *n* : terreno *m*
terrestrial [tə'restriəl] *adj* : terrestre
terrible ['tɛrəbəl] *adj* : espantoso, terrible — **terribly** ['tɛrəbli] *adv* : terriblemente
terrier ['tɛriər] *n* : terrier *mf*
terrific [tə'rɪfɪk] *adj* **1** HUGE : tremendo **2** EXCELLENT : estupendo
terrify ['tɛrə,faɪ] *vt* **-fied; -fying** : aterrar, aterrorizar — **terrifying** ['tɛrə,faɪɪŋ] *adj* : aterrador
territory ['tɛrə,tori] *n, pl* **-ries** : territorio *m* — **territorial** [,tɛrə'toriəl] *adj* : territorial
terror ['tɛrər] *n* : terror *m* — **terrorism** ['tɛrər,ɪzəm] *n* : terrorismo *m* — **terrorist** ['tɛrərɪst] *n* : terrorista *mf* — **terrorize** ['tɛrər,aɪz] *vt* **-ized; -izing** : aterrorizar
terse ['tərs] *adj* **terser; tersest** : seco, lacónico
test ['tɛst] *n* **1** TRIAL : prueba *f* **2** EXAM : examen *m*, prueba *f* **3** : análisis *m* (en medicina) — ~ *vt* **1** TRY : probar **2** QUIZ : examinar **3** : analizar (la sangre, etc.), examinar (los ojos, etc.)
testament ['tɛstəmənt] *n* **1** WILL : testamento *m* **2 the Old/New Testament** : el Antiguo/Nuevo Testamento
testicle ['tɛstɪkəl] *n* : testículo *m*
testify ['tɛstə,faɪ] *v* **-fied; -fying** : testificar
testimony ['tɛstə,mo:ni] *n, pl* **-nies** : testimonio *m*
test tube *n* : probeta *f*, tubo *m* de ensayo
tetanus ['tɛtənəs] *n* : tétano *m*
tether ['tɛðər] *vt* : atar
text ['tɛkst] *n* : texto *m* — **textbook** ['tɛkst,bʊk] *n* : libro *m* de texto
textile ['tɛk,staɪl, 'tɛkstəl] *n* : textil *m*
texture ['tɛkstʃər] *n* : textura *f*
than ['ðæn] *conj & prep* : que, de (con cantidades)
thank ['θæŋk] *vt* **1** : agradecer, dar (las) gracias a **2** ~ **you!** : ¡gracias! — **thankful** ['θæŋkfəl] *adj* : agradecido — **thankfully** ['θæŋkfəli] *adv* **1** : con agradecimiento **2** FORTUNATELY : gracias a Dios — **thanks** ['θæŋks] *npl* **1** : agradecimiento *m* **2** ~**!** : ¡gracias!
Thanksgiving [θæŋks'gɪvɪŋ, 'θæŋks,-] *n* : día *m* de Acción de Gracias
that ['ðæt] *pron, pl* **those** ['ðo:z] **1** : ése, ésa, eso **2** (*more distant*) : aquél, aquélla, aquello **3 is** ~ **you?** : ¿eres tú? **4 like** ~ : así **5** ~ **is...** : es decir... **6 those who...** : los que... — ~ *conj* : que — ~ *adj, pl* **those 1** : ese, esa **2** (*more distant*) : aquel, aquella **3** ~ **one** : ése, ésa — ~ *adv* : tan
thatched ['θætʃt] *adj* : con techo de paja
thaw ['θɔ] *vt* : descongelar (alimentos), derretir (hielo) — *vi* **1** : descongelarse **2** MELT : derretirse — ~ *n* : deshielo *m*
the [ðə, *before vowel sounds usu* ði:] *art* **1** : el, la, los, las **2** PER : por — ~ *adv* **1** ~ **sooner** ~ **better** : cuanto más pronto, mejor **2 I like this one** ~ **best** : éste es el que más me gusta
theater *or* **theatre** ['θi:əṭər] *n* : teatro *m* — **theatrical** [θi'ætrɪkəl] *adj* : teatral
theft ['θɛft] *n* : robo *m*, hurto *m*
their ['ðɛr] *adj* : su, sus, de ellos, de ellas — **theirs** ['ðɛrz] *pron* **1** : (el) suyo, (la) suya, (los) suyos, (las) suyas **2 some friends of** ~ : unos amigos suyos, unos amigos de ellos
them ['ðɛm] *pron* **1** (*used as direct object*) : los, las **2** (*used as indirect object*) : les, se **3** (*used as object of a preposition*) : ellos, ellas
theme ['θi:m] *n* **1** : tema *m* **2** ESSAY : trabajo *m* (escrito)
themselves [ðəm'sɛlvz, ðɛm-] *pron* **1** (*used reflexively*) : se **2** (*used emphatically*) : ellos mismos, ellas mismas **3** (*used after a preposition*) : sí (mismos), sí (mismas)
then ['ðɛn] *adv* **1** : entonces **2** NEXT : luego, después **3** BESIDES : además — ~ *adj* : entonces
thence ['ðɛnts, 'θɛnts] *adv* : de ahí (en adelante)
theology [θi'ɑlədʒi] *n, pl* **-gies** : teología *f* — **theological** [,θi:ə'lɑdʒɪkəl] *adj* : teológico
theorem ['θi:ərəm, 'θɪrəm] *n* : teorema *m* — **theoretical** [,θi:ə'rɛṭɪkəl] *adj* : teórico — **theory** ['θi:əri, 'θɪri] *n, pl* **-ries** : teoría *f*
therapeutic [,θɛrə'pju:ṭɪk] *adj* : terapéutico — **therapist** ['θɛrəpɪst] *n* : terapeuta *mf* — **therapy** ['θɛrəpi] *n, pl* **-pies** : terapia *f*
there ['ðær] *adv* **1** *or* **over** ~ : allí, allá **2** *or* **right** ~ : ahí **3 in** ~ : ahí (dentro) **4** ~**, it's done!** : ¡listo! **5 up/down** ~ : ahí arriba/abajo **6**

who's ~? : ¿quién es? — ~ *pron* **1** ~ **is/are** : hay **2** ~ **are three of us** : somos tres — **thereabouts** *or* **thereabout** [ˌðærəˈbauts, -ˈbaut; ˈðærə,-] *adv* **or** ~ : por ahí — **thereafter** [ðærˈæftər] *adv* : después — **thereby** [ðærˈbaɪ, ˈðærˌbaɪ] *adv* : así — **therefore** [ˈðærˌfor] *adv* : por lo tanto

thermal [ˈθərməl] *adj* : térmico

thermometer [θərˈmɑməṭər] *n* : termómetro *m*

thermos [ˈθərməs] *n* : termo *m*

thermostat [ˈθərməˌstæt] *n* : termostato *m*

thesaurus [θɪˈsɔrəs] *n, pl* **-sauri** [-ˈsɔrˌaɪ] *or* **-sauruses** [-ˈsɔrəsəz] : diccionario *m* de sinónimos

these → **this**

thesis [ˈθiːsɪs] *n, pl* **theses** [ˈθiːˌsiːz] : tesis *f*

they [ˈðeɪ] *pron* **1** : ellos, ellas **2** **where are** ~? : ¿dónde están? **3** **as** ~ **say** : como dicen — **they'd** [ˈðeɪd] (*contraction of* **they had** *or* **they would**) → **have, would** — **they'll** [ˈðeɪl, ˈðɛl] (*contraction of* **they shall** *or* **they will**) → **shall, will** — **they're** [ˈðɛr] (*contraction of* **they are**) → **be** — **they've** [ˈðeɪv] (*contraction of* **they have**) → **have**

thick [ˈθɪk] *adj* **1** : grueso **2** DENSE : espeso **3** **a** ~ **accent** : un acento marcado **4** **it's two inches** ~ : tiene dos pulgadas de grosor — ~ *n* **in the** ~ **of** : en medio de — **thicken** [ˈθɪkən] *vt* : espesar — *vi* : espesarse — **thicket** [ˈθɪkət] *n* : matorral *m* — **thickness** [ˈθɪknəs] *n* : grosor *m*, espesor *m*

thief [ˈθiːf] *n, pl* **thieves** [ˈθiːvz] : ladrón *m*, -drona *f*

thigh [ˈθaɪ] *n* : muslo *m*

thimble [ˈθɪmbəl] *n* : dedal *m*

thin [ˈθɪn] *adj* **thinner; -est** **1** : delgado **2** : ralo (dícese del pelo) **3** WATERY : claro, aguado **4** FINE : fino — ~ *v* **thinned; thinning** *vt* DILUTE : diluir — *vi* : ralear (dícese del pelo)

thing [ˈθɪŋ] *n* **1** : cosa *f* **2** **for one** ~ : en primer lugar **3** **how are** ~**s?** : ¿qué tal? **4** **it's a good** ~ **that...** : menos mal que... **5** **the important** ~ **is...** : lo importante es...

think [ˈθɪŋk] *v* **thought** [ˈθɔt]; **thinking** *vt* **1** : pensar **2** BELIEVE : creer **3** ~ **up** : idear — *vi* **1** : pensar **2** ~ **about** *or* ~ **of** CONSIDER : pensar en **3** ~ **of** REMEMBER : acordarse de **4** **what do you** ~ **of it?** : ¿qué te parece? — **thinker** [ˈθɪŋkər] *n* : pensador *m*, -dora *f*

third [ˈθərd] *adj* : tercero — ~ *or* **thirdly** [-li] *adv* : en tercer lugar — ~ *n* **1** : tercero *m*, -ra *f* (en una serie) **2** : tercero *m* (en matemáticas) — **Third World** *n* : Tercer Mundo *m*

thirst [ˈθərst] *n* : sed *f* — **thirsty** [ˈθərsti] *adj* **thirstier; -est** **1** : sediento **2** **be** ~ : tener sed

thirteen [ˌθərˈtiːn] *adj* : trece — ~ *n* : trece *m* — **thirteenth** [ˌθərˈtiːnθ] *adj* : décimo tercero — ~ *n* **1** : decimotercero *m*, -ra *f* (en una serie) **2** : treceavo *m* (en matemáticas)

thirty [ˈθərṭi] *adj* : treinta — ~ *n, pl* **thirties** : treinta *m* — **thirtieth** [ˈθərṭiəθ] *adj* : trigésimo — ~ *n* **1** : trigésimo *m*, -ma *f* (en una serie) **2** : treintavo *m* (en matemáticas)

this [ˈðɪs] *pron, pl* **these** [ˈðiːz] **1** : éste, ésta, esto **2** **like** ~ : así — ~ *adj, pl* **these** **1** : este, esta **2** ~ **one** : éste, ésta **3** ~ **way** : por aquí — ~ *adv* ~ **big** : así de grande

thistle [ˈθɪsəl] *n* : cardo *m*

thong [ˈθɔŋ] *n* **1** : correa *f* **2** SANDAL : chancla *f*

thorn [ˈθɔrn] *n* : espina *f* — **thorny** [ˈθɔrni] *adj* : espinoso

thorough [ˈθəroː] *adj* **1** : meticuloso **2** COMPLETE : completo — **thoroughly** *adv* **1** : a fondo **2** COMPLETELY : completamente — **thoroughbred** [ˈθəroˌbrɛd] *adj* : de pura sangre — **thoroughfare** [ˈθəroˌfær] *n* : vía *f* pública

those → **that**

though [ˈðoː] *conj* : aunque — ~ *adv* **1** : sin embargo **2** **as** ~ : como si

thought [ˈθɔt] → **think** — ~ *n* **1** : pensamiento *m* **2** IDEA : idea *f* — **thoughtful** [ˈθɔtfəl] *adj* **1** : pensativo **2** KIND : amable — **thoughtless** [ˈθɔtləs] *adj* **1** CARELESS : descuidado **2** RUDE : desconsiderado

thousand [ˈθauzənd] *adj* : mil — ~ *n, pl* **-sands** *or* **-sand** : mil *m* — **thousandth** [ˈθauzəntθ] *adj* : milésimo — ~ *n* **1** : milésimo *m*, -ma *f* (en una serie) **2** : milésimo *m* (en matemáticas)

thrash [ˈθræʃ] *vt* : dar una paliza a — *vi* *or* ~ **around** : agitarse, revolcarse

thread [ˈθrɛd] *n* **1** : hilo *m* **2** : rosca *f* (de un tornillo) — ~ *vt* : enhilar (una aguja), ensartar (cuentas) — **threadbare** [ˈθrɛdˈbær] *adj* : raído

threat [ˈθrɛt] *n* : amenaza *f* — **threaten** [ˈθrɛtən] *v* : amenazar — **threatening** [ˈθrɛtənɪŋ] *adj* : amenazador

three [ˈθriː] *adj* : tres — ~ *n* : tres *m* — **three hundred** *adj* : trescientos — ~ *n* : trescientos *m*

threshold [ˈθrɛʃˌhoːld, -ˌoːld] *n* : umbral *m*
threw → **throw**
thrift [ˈθrɪft] *n* : frugalidad *f* — **thrifty** [ˈθrɪfti] *adj* **thriftier; -est** : económico, frugal
thrill [ˈθrɪl] *vt* : emocionar — ~ *n* : emoción *f* — **thriller** [ˈθrɪlər] *n* : película *f* de suspense *Spain*, película *f* de suspenso *Lat* — **thrilling** [ˈθrɪlɪŋ] *adj* : emocionante
thrive [ˈθraɪv] *vi* **throve** [ˈθroːv] *or* **thrived; thriven** [ˈθrɪvən] **1** FLOURISH : florecer **2** PROSPER : prosperar
throat [ˈθroːt] *n* : garganta *f*
throb [ˈθrɑb] *vi* **throbbed; throbbing 1** PULSATE : palpitar **2** VIBRATE : vibrar **3** ~ **with pain** : tener un dolor punzante
throes [ˈθroːz] *npl* **1** PANGS : agonía *f* **2** **in the ~ of** : en medio de
throne [ˈθroːn] *n* : trono *m*
throng [ˈθrɔŋ] *n* : muchedumbre *f*, multitud *f*
throttle [ˈθrɑtəl] *vt* **-tled; -tling** : estrangular — ~ *n* : válvula *f* reguladora
through [ˈθruː] *prep* **1** : por, a través de **2** BETWEEN : entre **3** BECAUSE OF : a causa de **4** DURING : durante **5** → **throughout 6 Monday ~ Friday** : de lunes a viernes — ~ *adv* **1** : de un lado a otro (en el espacio), de principio a fin (en el tiempo) **2** COMPLETELY : completamente — ~ *adj* **1 be ~** : haber terminado **2 ~ traffic** : tráfico *m* de paso — **throughout** [θruːˈaut] *prep* : por todo (un lugar), a lo largo de (un período de tiempo)
throw [ˈθroː] *v* **threw** [ˈθruː]; **thrown** [ˈθroːn]; **throwing** *vt* **1** : tirar, lanzar **2** : proyectar (una sombra) **3** CONFUSE : desconcertar **4 ~ a party** : dar una fiesta **5 ~ away** *or* **~ out** : tirar, botar *Lat* — *vi* **~ up** VOMIT : vomitar — ~ *n* : tiro *m*, lanzamiento *m*
thrush [ˈθrʌʃ] *n* : tordo *m*, zorzal *m*
thrust [ˈθrʌst] *vt* **thrust; thrusting 1** : empujar (bruscamente) **2** PLUNGE : clavar **3 ~ upon** : imponer a — ~ *n* **1** : empujón *m* **2** : estocada *f* (en esgrima)
thud [ˈθʌd] *n* : ruido *m* sordo
thug [ˈθʌg] *n* : matón *m*
thumb [ˈθʌm] *n* : (dedo *m*) pulgar *m* — ~ *vt or* **~ through** : hojear — **thumbnail** [ˈθʌmˌneɪl] *n* : uña *f* del pulgar — **thumbtack** [ˈθʌmˌtæk] *n* : tachuela *f*, chinche *f Lat*
thump [ˈθʌmp] *vt* : golpear — *vi* : latir con fuerza (dícese del corazón) — ~ *n* : ruido *m* sordo
thunder [ˈθʌndər] *n* : truenos *mpl* — ~ *vi* : tronar — *vt* SHOUT : bramar — **thunderbolt** [ˈθʌndərˌboːlt] *n* : rayo *m* — **thunderous** [ˈθʌndərəs] *adj* : atronador — **thunderstorm** [ˈθʌndərˌstɔrm] *n* : tormenta *f* eléctrica
Thursday [ˈθərzˌdeɪ, -di] *n* : jueves *m*
thus [ˈðʌs] *adv* **1** : así **2** THEREFORE : por lo tanto
thwart [ˈθwɔrt] *vt* : frustrar
thyme [ˈtaɪm, ˈθaɪm] *n* : tomillo *m*
thyroid [ˈθaɪˌrɔɪd] *n* : tiroides *mf*
tiara [tiˈærə, -ˈɑr-] *n* : diadema *f*
tic [ˈtɪk] *n* : tic *m* (nervioso)
tick[1] [ˈtɪk] *n* : garrapata *f* (insecto)
tick[2] *n* **1** : tictac *m* (sonido) **2** CHECK : marca *f* — ~ *vi* : hacer tictac — *vt* **1** *or* **~ off** CHECK : marcar **2 ~ off** ANNOY : fastidiar
ticket [ˈtɪkət] *n* **1** : pasaje *m* (de avión), billete *m Spain* (de tren, avión, etc.), boleto *m Lat* (de tren o autobús) **2** : entrada *f* (al teatro, etc.) **3** FINE : multa *f*
tickle [ˈtɪkəl] *v* **-led; -ling** *vt* **1** : hacer cosquillas a **2** AMUSE : divertir — *vi* : picar — ~ *n* : cosquilleo *m* — **ticklish** [ˈtɪkəlɪʃ] *adj* **1** : cosquilloso **2** TRICKY : delicado
tidal wave [ˈtaɪdəl] *n* : maremoto *m*
tidbit [ˈtɪdˌbɪt] *n* MORSEL : golosina *f*
tide [ˈtaɪd] *n* : marea *f* — ~ *vt* **tided; tiding ~ over** : ayudar a superar un apuro
tidy [ˈtaɪdi] *adj* **-dier; -est** : ordenado, arreglado — ~ *vt* **-died; -dying** *or* **~ up** : ordenar, arreglar
tie [ˈtaɪ] *n* **1** : atadura *f*, cordón *m* **2** BOND : lazo *m* **3** : empate *m* (en deportes) **4** NECKTIE : corbata *f* — ~ *v* **tied; tying** *or* **tieing** *vt* **1** : atar, amarrar *Lat* **2 ~ a knot** : hacer un nudo — *vi* : empatar (en deportes)
tier [ˈtɪr] *n* : nivel *m*, piso (de un pastel), grada *f* (de un estadio)
tiger [ˈtaɪgər] *n* : tigre *m*
tight [ˈtaɪt] *adj* **1** : apretado **2** SNUG : ajustado, ceñido **3** TAUT : tirante **4** STINGY : agarrado **5** SCARCE : escaso **6 a ~ seal** : un cierre hermético **7 a ~ spot** : un aprieto — ~ *adv* **closed ~** : bien cerrado — **tighten** [ˈtaɪtən] *vt* **1** : apretar **2** TENSE : tensar **3** : hacer más estricto (reglas, etc.) — **tightly** [ˈtaɪtli] *adv* : bien, fuerte — **tightrope** [ˈtaɪtˌroːp] *n* : cuerda *f* floja — **tights** [ˈtaɪts] *npl* : leotardo *m*, mallas *fpl*
tile [ˈtaɪl] *n* **1** : azulejo *m*, baldosa *f* (de

piso) **2** *or* **roofing ~** : teja *f* — **~** *vt* **tiled; tiling 1** : revestir de azulejos, embaldosar (un piso) **2** : tejar (un techo)

till[1] ['tɪl] *prep & conj* → **until**

till[2] *vt* : cultivar

till[3] *n* : caja *f* (registradora)

tilt ['tɪlt] *n* **1** : inclinación *f* **2 at full ~** : a toda velocidad — **~** *vt* : inclinar — *vi* : inclinarse

timber ['tɪmbər] *n* **1** : madera *f* (para construcción) **2** BEAM : viga *f*

timbre ['tæmbər, 'tɪm-] *n* : timbre *m*

time ['taɪm] *n* **1** : tiempo *m* **2** AGE : época *f* **3** : compás *m* (en música) **4 at ~s** : a veces **5 at this ~** : en este momento **6 for the ~ being** : por el momento **7 from ~ to ~** : de vez en cuando **8 have a good ~** : pasarlo bien **9 many ~s** : muchas veces **10 on ~** : a tiempo **11 ~ after ~** : una y otra vez **12 what ~ is it?** : ¿qué hora es? — **~** *vt* **timed; timing** : tomar el tiempo a (algn), cronometrar (una carrera, etc.) — **timeless** ['taɪmləs] *adj* : eterno — **timely** ['taɪmli] *adj* **-lier; -est** : oportuno — **timer** ['taɪmər] *n* : temporizador *m*, avisador *m* (de cocina) — **times** ['taɪmz] *prep* **3 ~ 4 is 12** : 3 por 4 son 12 — **timetable** ['taɪm,teɪbəl] *n* : horario *m*

timid ['tɪmɪd] *adj* : tímido

tin ['tɪn] *n* **1** : estaño *m* **2** CAN : lata *f*, bote *m Spain* — **tinfoil** ['tɪn,fɔɪl] *n* : papel *m* (de) aluminio

tinge ['tɪndʒ] *vt* **tinged; tingeing** *or* **tinging** ['tɪndʒɪŋ] : matizar — **~** *n* **1** TINT : matiz *m* **2** TOUCH : dejo *m*

tingle ['tɪŋgəl] *vi* **-gled; -gling** : sentir (un) hormigueo — **~** *n* : hormigueo *m*

tinker ['tɪŋkər] *vi* **~ with** : intentar arreglar (con pequeños ajustes)

tinkle ['tɪŋkəl] *vi* **-kled; -kling** : tintinear — **~** *n* : tintineo *m*

tint ['tɪnt] *n* : tinte *m* — **~** *vt* : teñir

tiny ['taɪni] *adj* **-nier; -est** : diminuto, minúsculo

tip[1] ['tɪp] *v* **tipped; tipping** *vt* **1** TILT : inclinar **2** *or* **~ over** : volcar — *vi* : inclinarse

tip[2] *n* END : punta *f*

tip[3] *n* ADVICE : consejo *m* — **~** *vt* **~ off** : avisar

tip[4] *vt* : dar una propina a — **~** *n* GRATUITY : propina *f*

tipsy ['tɪpsi] *adj* **-sier; -est** : achispado

tiptoe ['tɪp,to:] *n* **on ~** : de puntillas — **~** *vi* **-toed; -toeing** : caminar de puntillas

tip–top ['tɪp'tɑp, -,tɑp] *adj* : excelente

tire[1] ['taɪr] *n* : neumático *m*, llanta *f Lat*

tire[2] *v* **tired; tiring** *vt* : cansar — *vi* : cansarse — **tired** ['taɪrd] *adj* **1 ~ of** : cansado de, harto de **2 ~ out** : agotado — **tireless** ['taɪrləs] *adj* : incansable — **tiresome** ['taɪrsəm] *adj* : pesado

tissue ['tɪ,ʃu:] *n* **1** : pañuelo *m* de papel **2** : tejido *m* (en biología)

title ['taɪtəl] *n* : título *m* — **~** *vt* **-tled; -tling** : titular

to ['tu:] *prep* **1** : a **2** TOWARD : hacia **3** IN ORDER TO : para **4** UP TO : hasta **5 a quarter ~ seven** : las siete menos cuarto **6 be nice ~ them** : trátalos bien **7 ten ~ the box** : diez por caja **8 the mate ~ this shoe** : el compañero de este zapato **9 two ~ four years old** : entre dos y cuatro años de edad **10 want ~ do** : querer hacer — **~** *adv* **1 come ~** : volver en sí **2 ~ and fro** : de un lado a otro

toad ['to:d] *n* : sapo *m*

toast ['to:st] *vt* **1** : tostar (pan, etc.) **2** : brindar por (una persona) — **~** *n* **1** : pan *m* tostado, tostadas *fpl* **2** DRINK : brindis *m* — **toaster** ['to:stər] *n* : tostador *m*

tobacco [tə'bæko:] *n, pl* **-cos** : tabaco *m*

toboggan [tə'bɑgən] *n* : tobogán *m*

today [tə'deɪ] *adv* : hoy — **~** *n* : hoy *m*

toddler ['tɑdələr] *n* : niño *m* pequeño, niña *f* pequeña (que comienza a caminar)

toe ['to:] *n* : dedo *m* (del pie) — **toenail** ['to:,neɪl] *n* : uña *f* (del pie)

together [tə'geðər] *adv* **1** : juntos **2 ~ with** : junto con

toil ['tɔɪl] *n* : trabajo *m* duro — **~** *vi* : trabajar duro

toilet ['tɔɪlət] *n* **1** BATHROOM : baño *m*, servicio *m* **2** : inodoro *m* (instalación) — **toilet paper** *n* : papel *m* higiénico — **toiletries** ['tɔɪlətriz] *npl* : artículos *mpl* de tocador

token ['to:kən] *n* **1** SIGN : muestra *f* **2** MEMENTO : recuerdo *m* **3** : ficha *f* (para un tren, etc.)

told → **tell**

tolerable ['tɑlərəbəl] *adj* : tolerable — **tolerance** ['tɑlərənts] *n* : tolerancia *f* — **tolerant** ['tɑlərənt] *adj* : tolerante — **tolerate** ['tɑlə,reɪt] *vt* **-ated; -ating** : tolerar

toll[1] ['to:l] *n* **1** : peaje *m* **2 death ~** : número *m* de muertos **3 take a ~ on** : afectar

toll[2] *vi* RING : tocar, doblar — **~** *n* : tañido *m*

tomato [tə'meɪt̬o, -'mɑ-] *n, pl* **-toes** : tomate *m*
tomb ['tu:m] *n* : tumba *f,* sepulcro *m* — **tombstone** ['tu:m,sto:n] *n* : lápida *f*
tome ['to:m] *n* : tomo *m*
tomorrow [tə'mɑro] *adv* : mañana — **~** *n* : mañana *m*
ton ['tən] *n* : tonelada *f*
tone ['to:n] *n* : tono *m* — **~** *vt* **toned; toning** *or* **~ down** : atenuar
tongs ['tɑŋz, 'tɔŋz] *npl* : tenazas *fpl*
tongue ['tʌŋ] *n* : lengua *f*
tonic ['tɑnɪk] *n* **1** : tónico *m* **2** *or* **~ water** : tónica *f*
tonight [tə'naɪt] *adv* : esta noche — **~** *n* : esta noche *f*
tonsil ['tɑntsəl] *n* : amígdala *f*
too ['tu:] *adv* **1** ALSO : también **2** EXCESSIVELY : demasiado
took → **take**
tool ['tu:l] *n* : herramienta *f* — **toolbox** ['tu:l,bɑks] *n* : caja *f* de herramientas
toot ['tu:t] *vt* : sonar (un claxon, etc.) — **~** *n* **1** WHISTLE : pitido *m* **2** HONK : bocinazo *m*
tooth ['tu:θ] *n, pl* **teeth** ['ti:θ] : diente *m* — **toothache** ['tu:θ,eɪk] *n* : dolor *m* de muelas — **toothbrush** ['tu:θ,brʌʃ] *n* : cepillo *m* de dientes — **toothpaste** ['tu:θ,peɪst] *n* : pasta *f* de dientes, pasta *f* dentífrica
top[1] ['tɑp] *n* **1** : parte *f* superior **2** SUMMIT : cima *f,* cumbre *f* **3** COVER : tapa *f,* cubierta *f* **4 on ~ of** : encima de — **~** *vt* **topped; topping 1** COVER : rematar (un edificio, etc.), bañar (un pastel, etc.) **2** SURPASS : superar **3 ~ off** : llenar — **~** *adj* **1** : de arriba, superior **2** BEST : mejor **3 a ~ executive** : un alto ejecutivo
top[2] *n* : trompo *m* (juguete)
topic ['tɑpɪk] *n* : tema *m* — **topical** ['tɑpɪkəl] *adj* : de interés actual
topmost ['tɑp,mo:st] *adj* : más alto
topple ['tɑpəl] *v* **-pled; -pling** *vi* : caerse — *vt* **1** OVERTURN : volcar **2** OVERTHROW : derrocar
torch ['tɔrtʃ] *n* : antorcha *f*
tore → **tear**[1]
torment ['tɔr,mɛnt] *n* : tormento *m* — **~** [tɔr'mɛnt, 'tɔr,-] *vt* : atormentar
torn → **tear**[1]
tornado [tɔr'neɪdo] *n, pl* **-does** *or* **-dos** : tornado *m*
torpedo [tɔr'pi:do] *n, pl* **-does** : torpedo *m* — **~** *vt* : torpedear
torrent ['tɔrənt] *n* : torrente *m*
torrid ['tɔrɪd] *adj* : tórrido
torso ['tɔr,so:] *n, pl* **-sos** *or* **-si** [-,si:] : torso *m*
tortilla [tɔr'ti:jə] *n* : tortilla *f*
tortoise ['tɔrt̬əs] *n* : tortuga *f* (terrestre) — **tortoiseshell** ['tɔrt̬əs,ʃɛl] *n* : carey *m,* concha *f*
tortuous ['tɔrtʃuəs] *adj* : tortuoso
torture ['tɔrtʃər] *n* : tortura *f* — **~** *vt* **-tured; -turing** : torturar
toss ['tɔs, 'tɑs] *vt* **1** : tirar, lanzar **2** : mezclar (una ensalada) — *vi* **~ and turn** : dar vueltas — **~** *n* : lanzamiento *m*
tot ['tɑt] *n* : pequeño *m,* -ña *f*
total ['to:təl] *adj* : total — **~** *n* : total *m* — **~** *vt* **-taled** *or* **-talled; -taling** *or* **-talling 1** : ascender a **2** *or* **~ up** : totalizar, sumar
totalitarian [to:,tælə'tɛriən] *adj* : totalitario
tote ['to:t] *vt* **toted; toting** : llevar
totter ['tɑtər] *vi* : tambalearse
touch ['tʌtʃ] *vt* **1** : tocar **2** MOVE : conmover **3** AFFECT : afectar **4 ~ up** : retocar — *vi* : tocarse — **~** *n* **1** : tacto *m* (sentido) **2** HINT : toque *m* **3** BIT : pizca *f* **4 keep in ~** : mantenerse en contacto **5 lose one's ~** : perder la habilidad — **touchdown** ['tʌtʃ,daun] *n* : touchdown *m* — **touchy** ['tʌtʃi] *adj* **touchier; -est 1** : delicado **2 be ~ about** : picarse a la mención de
tough ['tʌf] *adj* **1** : duro **2** STRONG : fuerte **3** STRICT : severo **4** DIFFICULT : difícil — **toughen** ['tʌfən] *vt or* **~ up** : endurecer — *vi* : endurecerse — **toughness** ['tʌfnəs] *n* : dureza *f*
tour ['tʊr] *n* **1** : viaje *m* (por un país, etc.), visita *f* (a un museo, etc.) **2** : gira *f* (de un equipo, etc.) — **~** *vi* **1** TRAVEL : viajar **2** : hacer una gira (dícese de equipos, etc.) — *vt* : viajar por, recorrer — **tourist** ['tʊrɪst, 'tər-] *n* : turista *mf*
tournament ['tərnəmənt, 'tʊr-] *n* : torneo *m*
tousle ['tauzəl] *vt* **-sled; -sling** : despeinar
tout ['taut] *vt* : promocionar
tow ['to:] *vt* : remolcar — **~** *n* : remolque *m*
toward ['tord, tə'wɔrd] *or* **towards** ['tordz, tə'wɔrdz] *prep* : hacia
towel ['tauəl] *n* : toalla *f*
tower ['tauər] *n* : torre *f* — **~** *vi* **~ over** : descollar sobre — **towering** ['tauərɪŋ] *adj* : altísimo
town ['taun] *n* **1** VILLAGE : pueblo *m* **2** CITY : ciudad *f* — **township** ['taun,ʃɪp] *n* : municipio *m*
tow truck ['to:,trʌk] *n* : grúa *f*
toxic ['tɑksɪk] *adj* : tóxico

toy ['tɔɪ] *n* : juguete *m* — ~ *vi* ~ **with** : juguetear con

trace ['treɪs] *n* **1** SIGN : rastro *m*, señal *f* **2** HINT : dejo *m* — ~ *vt* **traced; tracing 1** : calcar (un dibujo, etc.) **2** DRAW : trazar **3** FIND : localizar

track ['træk] *n* **1** : pista *f* **2** PATH : sendero *m* **3** *or* **railroad** ~ : vía *f* (férrea) **4 keep** ~ **of** : llevar la cuenta de — ~ *vt* TRAIL : seguir la pista de

tract[1] ['trækt] *n* **1** EXPANSE : extensión *f* **2** : tracto *m* (en anatomía)

tract[2] *n* PAMPHLET : folleto *m*

traction ['trækʃən] *n* : tracción *f*

tractor ['træktər] *n* **1** : tractor *m* **2** *or* ~ **-trailer** : camión *m* (con remolque)

trade ['treɪd] *n* **1** PROFESSION : oficio *m* **2** COMMERCE : comercio *m* **3** INDUSTRY : industria *f* **4** EXCHANGE : cambio *m* — ~ *v* **traded; trading** *vi* : comerciar — *vt* ~ **sth with s.o.** : cambiar algo a algn — **trademark** ['treɪd,mɑrk] *n* : marca *f* registrada

tradition [trə'dɪʃən] *n* : tradición *f* — **traditional** [trə'dɪʃənəl] *adj* : tradicional

traffic ['træfɪk] *n* : tráfico *m* — ~ *vi* **trafficked; trafficking** ~ **in** : traficar con — **traffic light** *n* : semáforo *m*

tragedy ['trædʒədi] *n, pl* **-dies** : tragedia *f* — **tragic** ['trædʒɪk] *adj* : trágico

trail ['treɪl] *vi* **1** DRAG : arrastrar **2** LAG : rezagarse **3** ~ **off** : apagarse — *vt* **1** DRAG : arrastrar **2** PURSUE : seguir la pista de — ~ *n* **1** : rastro *m*, huellas *fpl* **2** PATH : sendero *m* — **trailer** ['treɪlər] *n* **1** : remolque *m* **2** : caravana *f* (vivienda)

train ['treɪn] *n* **1** : tren *m* **2** : cola *f* (de un vestido) **3** SERIES : serie *f* **4** ~ **of thought** : hilo *m* (de las ideas) — ~ *vt* **1** : adiestrar, entrenar (atletas, etc.) **2** AIM : apuntar — *vi* : prepararse, entrenarse (en deportes, etc.) — **trainer** ['treɪnər] *n* : entrenador *m*, -dora *f*

trait ['treɪt] *n* : rasgo *m*

traitor ['treɪṭər] *n* : traidor *m*, -dora *f*

tramp ['træmp] *vi* : caminar (pesadamente) — ~ *n* VAGRANT : vagabundo *m*, -da *f*

trample ['træmpəl] *vt* **-pled; -pling** : pisotear

trampoline [,træmpə'li:n, 'træmpə,-] *n* : trampolín *m*

trance ['trænts] *n* : trance *m*

tranquillity *or* **tranquility** [træŋ'kwɪləṭi] *n* : tranquilidad *f* — **tranquil** ['træŋkwəl] *adj* : tranquilo — **tranquilize** ['træŋkwə,laɪz] *vt* **-ized; -izing** : tranquilizar — **tranquilizer** ['træŋkwə,laɪzər] *n* : tranquilizante *m*

transaction [træn'zækʃən] *n* : transacción *f*

transatlantic [,træntsət'læntɪk, ,trænz-] *adj* : transatlántico

transcend [træn'send] *vt* **1** : ir más allá de **2** OVERCOME : superar

transcribe [træn'skraɪb] *vt* **-scribed; -scribing** : transcribir — **transcript** ['træn,skrɪpt] *n* : transcripción *f*

transfer [trænts'fər, 'trænts,fər] *v* **-ferred; -ferring** *vt* **1** : transferir (fondos, etc.) **2** : trasladar (a un empleado, etc.) — *vi* **1** : cambiarse (de escuelas, etc.) **2** : hacer transbordo (entre trenes, etc.) — ~ ['trænts,fər] *n* **1** : transferencia *f* (de fondos, etc.), traslado *m* (de una persona) **2** : boleto *m* (para hacer transbordo) **3** DECAL : calcomanía *f*

transform [trænts'fɔrm] *vt* : transformar — **transformation** [,træntsfər'meɪʃən] *n* : transformación *f*

transfusion [trænts'fju:ʒən] *n* : transfusión *f*

transgression [trænts'grɛʃən, trænz-] *n* : transgresión *f* — **transgress** [trænts'grɛs, trænz-] *vt* : transgredir

transient ['træntʃənt, 'trænsiənt] *adj* : pasajero

transit ['træntsɪt, 'trænzɪt] *n* **1** : tránsito *m* **2** TRANSPORTATION : transporte *m* — **transition** [træn'sɪʃən, -'zɪʃ-] *n* : transición *f* — **transitive** ['træntsəṭɪv, 'trænzə-] *adj* : transitivo — **transitory** ['træntsə,tori, 'trænzə-] *adj* : transitorio

translate [trænts'leɪt, trænz-; 'trænts,-, 'træns,-] *vt* **-lated; -lating** : traducir — **translation** [trænts'leɪʃən, trænz-] *n* : traducción *f* — **translator** [trænts'leɪṭər, trænz-; 'trænts,-, 'træns,-] *n* : traductor *m*, -tora *f*

translucent [trænts'lu:sənt, trænz-] *adj* : translúcido

transmit [trænts'mɪt, trænz-] *vt* **-mitted; -mitting** : transmitir — **transmission** [trænts'mɪʃən, trænz-] *n* : transmisión *f* — **transmitter** [trænts'mɪṭər, trænz-; 'trænts,-, 'træns,-] *n* : transmisor *m*

transparent [trænts'pærənt] *adj* : transparente — **transparency** [trænts'pærəntsi] *n, pl* **-cies** : transparencia *f*

transpire [trænts'paɪr] *vi* **-spired; -spiring 1** TURN OUT : resultar **2** HAPPEN : suceder

transplant [trænts'plænt] *vt* : trasplantar — ~ ['trænts,plænt] *n* : trasplante *m*

transport [trænts'port, 'trænts,-] *vt* : transportar — ~ ['trænts,port] *n* : transporte *m* — **transportation** [,træntspər'teɪʃən] *n* : transporte *m*

transpose [trænts'po:z] *vt* **-posed;**

-posing 1 : trasponer **2** : transportar (en música)
trap ['træp] *n* : trampa *f* — ~ *vt* **trapped; trapping** : atrapar — **trapdoor** ['træp'dor] *n* : trampilla *f*
trapeze [træ'pi:z] *n* : trapecio *m*
trappings ['træpɪŋz] *npl* : adornos *mpl*, atavíos *mpl*
trash ['træʃ] *n* : basura *f*
trauma ['trɔmə, 'traʊ-] *n* : trauma *m* — **traumatic** [trə'mæṭɪk, trɔ-, traʊ-] *adj* : traumático
travel ['trævəl] *vi* **-eled** *or* **-elled; -eling** *or* **-elling 1** : viajar **2** MOVE : desplazarse — ~ *n* : viajes *mpl* — **traveler** *or* **traveller** ['trævələr] *n* : viajero *m*, -ra *f*
traverse [trə'vərs, træ'vərs, 'trævərs] *vt* **-versed; -versing** : atravesar
travesty ['trævəsti] *n, pl* **-ties** : parodia *f*
trawl ['trɔl] *vi* : pescar (con red de arrastre) — **trawler** ['trɔlər] *n* : barco *m* de pesca
tray ['treɪ] *n* : bandeja *f*
treachery ['trɛtʃəri] *n, pl* **-eries** : traición *f* — **treacherous** ['trɛtʃərəs] *adj* **1** : traidor **2** DANGEROUS : peligroso
tread ['trɛd] *v* **trod** ['trɑd]; **trodden** ['trɑdən] *or* **trod; treading** *vt* **1** *or* ~ **on** : pisar **2** ~ **water** : flotar — *vi* **1** STEP : pisar **2** WALK : caminar — ~ *n* **1** STEP : paso *m* **2** : banda *f* de rodadura (de un neumático) — **treadmill** ['trɛd,mɪl] *n* : rueda *f* de andar
treason ['tri:zən] *n* : traición *f* (a la patria)
treasure ['trɛʒər, 'treɪ-] *n* : tesoro *m* — ~ *vt* **-sured; -suring** : apreciar — **treasurer** ['trɛʒərər, 'treɪ-] *n* : tesorero *m*, -ra *f* — **treasury** ['trɛʒəri, 'treɪ-] *n, pl* **-suries** : erario *m*, tesoro *m*
treat ['tri:t] *vt* **1** : tratar **2** CONSIDER : considerar **3** ~ **s.o. to (dinner, etc.)** : invitar a algn (a cenar, etc.) — ~ *n* **1** : gusto *m*, placer *m* **2** **it's my** ~ : invito yo
treatise ['tri:ṭɪs] *n* : tratado *m*
treatment ['tri:tmənt] *n* : tratamiento *m*
treaty ['tri:ṭi] *n, pl* **-ties** : tratado *m*
treble ['trɛbəl] *adj* **1** TRIPLE : triple **2** : de tiple (en música) — ~ *vt* **-bled; -bling** : triplicar — **treble clef** : clave *f* de sol
tree ['tri:] *n* : árbol *m*
trek ['trɛk] *vi* **trekked; trekking** : viajar (con dificultad) — ~ *n* : viaje *m* difícil
trellis ['trɛlɪs] *n* : enrejado *m*
tremble ['trɛmbəl] *vi* **-bled; -bling** : temblar
tremendous [trɪ'mɛndəs] *adj* : tremendo
tremor ['trɛmər] *n* : temblor *m*
trench ['trɛntʃ] *n* **1** : zanja *f* **2** : trinchera *f* (militar)
trend ['trɛnd] *n* **1** : tendencia *f* **2** FASHION : moda *f* — **trendy** ['trɛndi] *adj* **trendier; -est** : de moda
trepidation [,trɛpə'deɪʃən] *n* : inquietud *f*
trespass ['trɛspəs, -,pæs] *vi* : entrar ilegalmente (en propiedad ajena)
trial ['traɪəl] *n* **1** : juicio *m*, proceso *m* **2** TEST : prueba *f* **3** ORDEAL : dura prueba *f* — ~ *adj* : de prueba
triangle ['traɪ,æŋgəl] *n* : triángulo *m* — **triangular** [traɪ'æŋgjələr] *adj* : triangular
tribe ['traɪb] *n* : tribu *f* — **tribal** ['traɪbəl] *adj* : tribal
tribulation [,trɪbjə'leɪʃən] *n* : tribulación *f*
tribunal [traɪ'bju:nəl, trɪ-] *n* : tribunal *m*
tribute ['trɪb,ju:t] *n* : tributo *m* — **tributary** ['trɪbjə,tɛri] *n, pl* **-taries** : afluente *m*
trick ['trɪk] *n* **1** : trampa *f* **2** PRANK : broma *f* **3** KNACK, FEAT : truco *m* **4** : baza *f* (en naipes) — ~ *vt* : engañar — **trickery** ['trɪkəri] *n* : engaño *m*
trickle ['trɪkəl] *vi* **-led; -ling** : gotear — ~ *n* : goteo *m*
tricky ['trɪki] *adj* **trickier; -est 1** SLY : astuto, taimado **2** DIFFICULT : difícil
tricycle ['traɪsəkəl, -,sɪkəl] *n* : triciclo *m*
trifle ['traɪfəl] *n* **1** TRIVIALITY : nimiedad *f* **2** **a** ~ : un poco — ~ *vi* **-fled; -fling** ~ **with** : jugar con — **trifling** ['traɪflɪŋ] *adj* : insignificante
trigger ['trɪgər] *n* : gatillo *m* — ~ *vt* : causar, provocar
trill ['trɪl] *n* : trino *m* — ~ *vi* : trinar
trillion ['trɪljən] *n* : billón *m*
trilogy ['trɪlədʒi] *n, pl* **-gies** : trilogía *f*
trim ['trɪm] *vt* **trimmed; trimming 1** : recortar **2** ADORN : adornar — ~ *adj* **trimmer; trimmest 1** SLIM : esbelto **2** NEAT : arreglado — ~ *n* **1** : recorte *m* **2** DECORATION : adornos *mpl* **3** **in** ~ : en buena forma — **trimming** ['trɪmɪŋ] *npl* **1** : adornos *mpl* **2** GARNISH : guarnición *f*
Trinity ['trɪnəṭi] *n* : Trinidad *f*
trinket ['trɪŋkət] *n* : chuchería *f*
trio ['tri:,o:] *n, pl* **trios** : trío *m*
trip ['trɪp] *v* **tripped; tripping** *vi* **1** : caminar (a paso ligero) **2** STUMBLE : tropezar **3** ~ **up** : equivocarse — *vt* **1** ACTIVATE : activar **2** ~ **s.o.** : hacer una zancadilla a algn **3** ~ **s.o. up** : hacer equivocar a algn — ~ *n* **1** : viaje *m* **2** STUMBLE : traspié *m*

tripe ['traɪp] *n* **1** : mondongo *m*, callos *mpl* **2** NONSENSE : tonterías *fpl*
triple ['trɪpəl] *vt* **-pled; -pling** : triplicar — ~ *n* : triple *m* — ~ *adj* : triple —
triplet ['trɪplət] *n* : trillizo *m*, -za *f* —
triplicate ['trɪplɪkət] *n* : triplicado *m*
tripod ['traɪˌpɑd] *n* : trípode *m*
trite ['traɪt] *adj* **triter; tritest** : trillado
triumph ['traɪəmpf] *n* : triunfo *m* — ~ *vi* : triunfar — **triumphal** [traɪ'ʌmpfəl] *adj* : triunfal — **triumphant** [traɪ'ʌmpfənt] *adj* : triunfante
trivial ['trɪviəl] *adj* : trivial — **trivia** ['trɪviə] *ns & pl* : trivialidades *fpl* — **triviality** [ˌtrɪvi'æləṭi] *n, pl* **-ties** : trivialidad *f*
trod, trodden → **tread**
trolley ['trɑli] *n, pl* **-leys** : tranvía *m*
trombone [trɑm'bo:n] *n* : trombón *m*
troop ['tru:p] *n* **1** : escuadrón *m* (de caballería), compañía *f* (de soldados) **2** ~**s** *npl* : tropas *fpl* — ~ *vi* ~ **in/out** : entrar/salir en tropel — **trooper** ['tru:pər] *n* **1** : soldado *m* **2** *or* **state** ~ : policía *mf* estatal
trophy ['tro:fi] *n, pl* **-phies** : trofeo *m*
tropic ['trɑpɪk] *n* **1** : trópico *m* **2 the** ~**s** : el trópico — ~ *or* **tropical** [-pɪkəl] *adj* : tropical
trot ['trɑt] *n* : trote *m* — ~ *vi* **trotted; trotting** : trotar
trouble ['trʌbəl] *v* **-bled; -bling** *vt* **1** WORRY : preocupar **2** BOTHER : molestar — *vi* : molestarse — ~ *n* **1** PROBLEMS : problemas *mpl* **2** EFFORT : molestia *f* **3 be in** ~ : estar en apuros **4 get in** ~ : meterse en problemas **5 I had** ~ **doing it** : me costó hacerlo — **troublemaker** ['trʌbəlˌmeɪkər] *n* : alborotador *m*, -dora *f* — **troublesome** ['trʌbəlsəm] *adj* : problemático
trough ['trɔf] *n, pl* **troughs** ['trɔfs, 'trɔvz] **1** : depresión *f* **2** *or* **feeding** ~ : comedero *m* **3** *or* **drinking** ~ : bebedero *m*
troupe ['tru:p] *n* : compañía *f* (de teatro)
trousers ['traʊzərz] *npl* : pantalón *m*, pantalones *mpl*
trout ['traʊt] *n, pl* **trout** : trucha *f*
trowel ['traʊəl] *n* : paleta *f* (de albañil), desplantador *m* (de jardinero)
truant ['tru:ənt] *n* : alumno *m*, -na *f* que falta a clase
truce ['tru:s] *n* : tregua *f*
truck ['trʌk] *vt* : transportar en camión — ~ *n* **1** : camión *m* **2** CART : carro *m* — **trucker** ['trʌkər] *n* : camionero *m*, -ra *f*
trudge ['trʌdʒ] *vi* **trudged; trudging** : caminar a paso pesado
true ['tru:] *adj* **truer; truest 1** : verdadero **2** LOYAL : fiel **3** GENUINE : auténtico **4 be** ~ : ser cierto, ser verdad
truffle ['trʌfəl] *n* : trufa *f*
truly ['tru:li] *adv* : verdaderamente
trump ['trʌmp] *n* : triunfo *m* (en naipes)
trumpet ['trʌmpət] *n* : trompeta *f*
trunk ['trʌŋk] *n* **1** STEM, TORSO : tronco *m* **2** : trompa *f* (de un elefante) **3** : baúl *m* (equipaje) **4** : maletero *m* (de un auto) **5** ~**s** *npl* : traje *m* de baño (de hombre)
truss ['trʌs] *n* **1** FRAMEWORK : armazón *m* **2** : braguero *m* (en medicina)
trust ['trʌst] *n* **1** CONFIDENCE : confianza *f* **2** HOPE : esperanza *f* **3** CREDIT : crédito *m* **4** : trust *m* (en finanzas) **5 in** ~ : en fideicomiso — ~ *vi* **1** : confiar **2** HOPE : esperar — *vt* **1** : confiar en, fiarse de (en frases negativas) **2** ~ **s.o. with sth** : confiar algo a algn — **trustee** [ˌtrʌs'ti:] *n* : fideicomisario *m*, -ria *f* — **trustworthy** ['trəstˌwərði] *adj* : digno de confianza
truth ['tru:θ] *n, pl* **truths** ['tru:ðz, 'tru:θs] : verdad *f* — **truthful** ['tru:θfəl] *adj* : sincero, veraz
try ['traɪ] *v* **tried; trying** *vt* **1** ATTEMPT : tratar (de), intentar **2** : juzgar (un caso, etc.) **3** TEST : poner a prueba **4** *or* ~ **out** : probar **5** ~ **on** : probarse (ropa) — *vi* : hacer un esfuerzo — ~ *n, pl* **tries** : intento *m* — **trying** *adj* **1** ANNOYING : irritante, pesado **2** DIFFICULT : duro — **tryout** ['traɪˌaʊt] *n* : prueba *f*
tsar ['zɑr, 'tsɑr, 'sɑr] → **czar**
T-shirt ['ti:ˌʃərt] *n* : camiseta *f*
tub ['tʌb] *n* **1** : cuba *f*, tina *f* **2** CONTAINER : envase *m* **3** BATHTUB : bañera *f*
tuba ['tu:bə, 'tju:-] *n* : tuba *f*
tube ['tu:b, 'tju:b] *n* **1** : tubo *m* **2** *or* **inner** ~ : cámara *f* **3 the** ~ : la tele
tuberculosis [tʊˌbərkjə'lo:sɪs, tjʊ-] *n, pl* **-loses** [-ˌsi:z] : tuberculosis *f*
tubing ['tu:bɪŋ, 'tju:-] *n* : tubería *f* — **tubular** ['tu:bjələr, 'tju:-] *adj* : tubular
tuck ['tʌk] *vt* **1** : meter **2** ~ **away** : guardar **3** ~ **in** : meter por dentro (una blusa, etc.) **4** ~ **s.o. in** : arropar a algn — ~ *n* : jareta *f*
Tuesday ['tu:zˌdeɪ, 'tju:z-, -di] *n* : martes *m*
tuft ['tʌft] *n* : mechón *m* (de pelo), penacho *m* (de plumas)
tug ['tʌg] *vt* **tugged; tugging** *or* ~ **at** : tirar de, jalar de — ~ *n* : tirón *m*, jalón *m* — **tugboat** ['tʌgˌbo:t] *n* : remolcador *m* — **tug-of-war** [ˌtʌgə'wɔr] *n, pl* **tugs-of-war** : tira y afloja *m*

tuition [tuˈɪʃən, tjuː-] *n* **1** : enseñanza *f* **2** *or* **~ fees** : matrícula *f*
tulip [ˈtuːlɪp, ˈtjuː-] *n* : tulipán *m*
tumble [ˈtʌmbəl] *vi* **-bled; -bling** : caerse — **~** *n* : caída *f* — **tumbler** [ˈtʌmblər] : vaso *m* (sin pie)
tummy [ˈtʌmi] *n, pl* **-mies** : barriga *f*, panza *f*
tumor [ˈtuːmər ˈtjuː-] *n* : tumor *m*
tumult [ˈtuːˌmʌlt ˈtjuː-] *n* : tumulto *m* — **tumultuous** [tʊˈmʌltʃʊəs, tjuː-] *adj* : tumultuoso
tuna [ˈtuːnə ˈtjuː-] *n, pl* **-na** *or* **-nas** : atún *m*
tune [ˈtuːn, ˈtjuːn] *n* **1** MELODY : melodía *f* **2** SONG : tonada *f* **3 in ~** : afinado **4 out of ~** : desafinado — **~** *v* **tuned; tuning** *vt* : afinar — *vi* **~ in** : sintonizar — **tuner** [ˈtuːnər, ˈtjuː-] *n* **1** : afinador *m*, -dora *f* (de pianos, etc.) **2** : sintonizador *m* (de un receptor)
tunic [ˈtuːnɪk, ˈtjuː-] *n* : túnica *f*
tunnel [ˈtʌnəl] *n* : túnel *m* — **~** *vi* **-neled** *or* **-nelled; -neling** *or* **-nelling** : hacer un túnel
turban [ˈtərbən] *n* : turbante *m*
turbine [ˈtərbən, -ˌbaɪn] *n* : turbina *f*
turbulent [ˈtərbjələnt] *adj* : turbulento — **turbulence** [ˈtərbjələnts] *n* : turbulencia *f*
turf [ˈtərf] *n* **1** GRASS : césped *m* **2** SOD : tepe *m*
turgid [ˈtərdʒɪd] *adj* : ampuloso (dícese de prosa, etc.)
turkey [ˈtərki] *n, pl* **-keys** : pavo *m*
turmoil [ˈtərˌmɔɪl] *n* : confusión *f*
turn [ˈtərn] *vt* **1** : hacer girar (una rueda, etc.), volver (la cabeza, una página, etc.) **2** : dar la vuelta a (una esquina) **3** SPRAIN : torcer **4 ~ down** REFUSE : rechazar **5 ~ down** LOWER : bajar **6 ~ in** : entregar **7 ~ off** : cerrar (una llave), apagar (la luz, etc.) **8 ~ on** : abrir (una llave), encender, prender *Lat* (la luz, etc.) **9 ~ out** EXPEL : echar **10 ~ out** PRODUCE : producir **11 ~ out** → **turn off 12** *or* **~ over** FLIP : dar la vuelta a, voltear *Lat* **13 ~ over** TRANSFER : entregar **14 ~ s.o.'s stomach** : revolver el estómago a algn **15 ~ sth into sth** : convertir algo en algo **16 ~ up** RAISE : subir — *vi* **1** ROTATE : girar, dar vueltas **2** BECOME : ponerse **3** SOUR : agriarse **4** RESORT : recurrir **5** *or* **~ around** : darse la vuelta, volverse **6 ~ into** : convertirse en **7 ~ left** : doblar a la izquierda **8 ~ out** COME : acudir **9 ~ out** RESULT : resultar **10 ~ up** APPEAR : aparecer — **~** *n* **1** : vuelta *f* **2** CHANGE : cambio *m* **3** CURVE : curva *f* **4 do a good ~** : hacer un favor **5 whose ~ is it?** : ¿a quién le toca?
turnip [ˈtərnəp] *n* : nabo *m*
turnout [ˈtərnˌaʊt] *n* : concurrencia *f* — **turnover** [ˈtərnˌoːvər] *n* **1** : tartaleta *f* (postre) **2** : volumen *m* (de ventas) **3** : movimiento *f* (de personal) — **turnpike** [ˈtərnˌpaɪk] *n* : carretera *f* de peaje — **turntable** [ˈtərnˌteɪbəl] *n* : plato *m* giratorio
turpentine [ˈtərpənˌtaɪn] *n* : trementina *f*
turquoise [ˈtərˌkɔɪz, -ˌkwɔɪz] *n* : turquesa *f*
turret [ˈtərət] *n* **1** : torrecilla *f* **2** : torreta *f* (de un tanque, etc.)
turtle [ˈtərtəl] *n* : tortuga *f* (marina) — **turtleneck** [ˈtərtəlˌnɛk] *n* : cuello *m* de tortuga
tusk [ˈtʌsk] *n* : colmillo *m*
tussle [ˈtʌsəl] *n* : pelea *f* — **~** *vi* **-sled; -sling** : pelearse
tutor [ˈtuːtər, ˈtjuː-] *n* : profesor *m*, -sora *f* particular — **~** *vt* : dar clases particulares a
tuxedo [ˌtəkˈsiːˌdoː] *n, pl* **-dos** *or* **-does** : esmoquin *m*, smoking *m*
TV [ˌtiːˈviː, ˈtiːˌviː] → **television**
twang [ˈtwæŋ] *n* **1** : tañido *m* **2** : acento *m* nasal (de la voz)
tweak [ˈtwiːk] *vt* : pellizcar — **~** *n* : pellizco *m*
tweed [ˈtwiːd] *n* : tweed *m*
tweet [ˈtwiːt] *n* : gorjeo *m*, pío *m* — **~** *vi* : piar
tweezers [ˈtwiːzərz] *npl* : pinzas *fpl*
twelve [ˈtwɛlv] *adj* : doce — **~** *n* : doce *m* — **twelfth** [ˈtwɛlfθ] *adj* : duodécimo — **~** *n* **1** : duodécimo *m*, -ma *f* (en una serie) **2** : doceavo *m* (en matemáticas)
twenty [ˈtwʌnti, ˈtwen-] *adj* : veinte — **~** *n, pl* **-ties** : veinte *m* — **twentieth** [ˈtwʌntiəθ, ˈtwɛn-] *adj* : vigésimo — **~** *n* **1** : vigésimo *m*, -ma *f* (en una serie) **2** : veinteavo *m* (en matemáticas)
twice [ˈtwaɪs] *adv* **1** : dos veces **2 ~ as much/many as** : el doble de (algo), el doble que (algn)
twig [ˈtwɪg] *n* : ramita *f*
twilight [ˈtwaɪˌlaɪt] *n* : crepúsculo *m*
twin [ˈtwɪn] *n* : gemelo *m*, -la *f*; mellizo *m*, -za *f* — **~** *adj* : gemelo, mellizo
twine [ˈtwaɪn] *n* : cordel *m*, bramante *m* *Spain*
twinge [ˈtwɪndʒ] *n* : punzada *f*
twinkle [ˈtwɪŋkəl] *vi* **-kled; -kling 1** : centellear **2** : brillar (dícese de los ojos) — **~** *n* : centelleo *m*, brillo *m* (de los ojos)

twirl ['twərl] *vt* : girar, dar vueltas a — *vi* : girar, dar vueltas — ~ *n* : giro *m*, vuelta *f*
twist ['twɪst] *vt* **1** : retorcer **2** TURN : girar **3** SPRAIN : torcerse **4** : tergiversar (palabras) — *vi* **1** : retorcerse **2** COIL : enrollarse **3** : serpentear (entre montañas, etc.) — ~ *n* **1** BEND : vuelta *f* **2** TURN : giro *m* **3** ~ **of lemon** : rodajita *f* de limón — **twister** ['twɪstər] → **tornado**
twitch ['twɪtʃ] *vi* : moverse (espasmódicamente) — ~ *n* **nervous** ~ : tic *m* nervioso
two ['tu:] *adj* : dos — ~ *n, pl* **twos** : dos *m* — **twofold** ['tu:,fo:ld] *adj* : doble — ~ ['tu:'fo:ld] *adv* : al doble — **two hundred** *adj* : doscientos — ~ *n* : doscientos *m*
tycoon [taɪ'ku:n] *n* : magnate *mf*
tying → **tie**
type ['taɪp] *n* : tipo *m* — ~ *v* **typed; typing** : escribir a máquina — **typewritten** ['taɪp,rɪtən] *adj* : escrito a máquina — **typewriter** ['taɪp,raɪt̬ər] *n* : máquina *f* de escribir
typhoon [taɪ'fu:n] *n* : tifón *m*
typical ['tɪpɪkəl] *adj* : típico, característico — **typify** ['tɪpə,faɪ] *vt* **-fied; -fying** : tipificar
typist ['taɪpɪst] *n* : mecanógrafo *m*, **-fa** *f*
typography [taɪ'pɑgrəfi] *n* : tipografía *f*
tyranny ['tɪrəni] *n, pl* **-nies** : tiranía *f* — **tyrant** ['taɪrənt] *n* : tirano *m*, **-na** *f*
tzar ['zɑr, 'tsɑr, 'sɑr] → **czar**

U

u ['ju:] *n, pl* **u's** *or* **us** ['ju:z] : u *f*, vigésima primera letra del alfabeto inglés
udder ['ʌdər] *n* : ubre *f*
UFO [,ju:,ɛf'o:, 'ju:,fo:] (*unidentified flying object*) *n, pl* **UFO's** *or* **UFOs** : ovni *m*, OVNI *m*
ugly ['ʌgli] *adj* **uglier; -est** : feo — **ugliness** ['ʌglinəs] *n* : fealdad *f*
ulcer ['ʌlsər] *n* : úlcera *f*
ulterior [,ʌl'tɪriər] *adj* ~ **motive** : segunda intención *f*
ultimate ['ʌltəmət] *adj* **1** FINAL : final, último **2** UTMOST : máximo **3** FUNDAMENTAL : fundamental — **ultimately** ['ʌltəmətli] *adv* **1** FINALLY : por último, finalmente **2** EVENTUALLY : a la larga
ultimatum [,ʌltə'meɪt̬əm, -'mɑ-] *n, pl* **-tums** *or* **-ta** [-t̬ə] : ultimátum *m*
ultraviolet [,ʌltrə'vaɪələt] *adj* : ultravioleta
umbilical cord [,ʌm'bɪlɪkəl] *n* : cordón *m* umbilical
umbrella [,ʌm'brɛlə] *n* : paraguas *m*
umpire ['ʌm,paɪr] *n* : árbitro *m*, **-tra** *f* — ~ *vt* **-pired; -piring** : arbitrar
umpteenth [,ʌmp'ti:nθ] *adj* : enésimo
unable [,ʌn'eɪbəl] *adj* **1** : incapaz **2 be** ~ **to** : no poder
unabridged [,ʌnə'brɪdʒd] *adj* : íntegro
unacceptable [,ʌnɪk'sɛptəbəl] *adj* : inaceptable
unaccountable [,ʌnə'kaʊntəd] *adj* : inexplicable
unaccustomed [,ʌnə'kʌstəmd] *adj* **be** ~ **to** : no estar acostumbrado a
unadulterated [,ʌnə'dʌltə,reɪt̬əd] *adj* : puro
unaffected [,ʌnə'fɛktəd] *adj* **1** : no afectado **2** NATURAL : sin afectación, natural
unafraid [,ʌnə'freɪd] *adj* : sin miedo
unaided [,ʌn'eɪdəd] *adj* : sin ayuda
unanimous [jʊ'nænəməs] *adj* : unánime
unannounced [,ʌnə'naʊnst] *adj* : sin dar aviso
unarmed [,ʌn'ɑrmd] *adj* : desarmado
unassuming [,ʌnə'su:mɪŋ] *adj* : modesto, sin pretensiones
unattached [,ʌnə'tætʃt] *adj* **1** : suelto **2** UNMARRIED : soltero
unattractive [,ʌnə'træktɪv] *adj* : poco atractivo
unauthorized [,ʌn'ɔθə,raɪzd] *adj* : no autorizado
unavailable [,ʌnə'veɪləbəl] *adj* : no disponible
unavoidable [,ʌnə'vɔɪdəbəl] *adj* : inevitable
unaware [,ʌnə'wær] *adj* **1** : inconsciente **2 be** ~ **of** : ignorar — **unawares** [,ʌnə'wærz] *adv* **catch s.o.** ~ : agarrar a algn desprevenido
unbalanced [,ʌn'bæləntst] *adj* : desequilibrado
unbearable [,ʌn'bærəbəl] *adj* : inaguantable, insoportable
unbelievable [,ʌnbə'li:vəbəl] *adj* : increíble
unbending [,ʌn'bɛndɪŋ] *adj* : inflexible
unbiased [,ʌn'baɪəst] *adj* : imparcial
unborn [,ʌn'bɔrn] *adj* : aún no nacido
unbreakable [,ʌn'breɪkəbəl] *adj* : irrompible

unbridled [ˌʌnˈbraɪdəld] *adj* : desenfrenado
unbroken [ˌʌnˈbroːkən] *adj* **1** INTACT : intacto **2** CONTINUOUS : continuo
unbutton [ˌʌnˈbʌtən] *vt* : desabrochar, desabotonar
uncalled–for [ˌʌnˈkɔldˌfɔr] *adj* : inapropiado, innecesario
uncanny [ənˈkæni] *adj* **-nier; -est** : extraño, misterioso
unceasing [ˌʌnˈsiːsɪŋ] *adj* : incesante
unceremonious [ˌʌnˌsɛrəˈmoːniəs] *adj* **1** INFORMAL : poco ceremonioso **2** ABRUPT : brusco
uncertain [ˌʌnˈsərtən] *adj* **1** : incierto **2** **in no ~ terms** : de forma vehemente — **uncertainty** [ˌʌnˈsərtənti] *n, pl* **-ties** : incertidumbre *f*
unchanged [ˌʌnˈtʃeɪndʒd] *adj* : igual, sin alterar — **unchanging** [ˌʌnˈtʃeɪdʒɪŋ] *adj* : inmutable
uncivilized [ˌʌnˈsɪvəˌlaɪzd] *adj* : incivilizado
uncle [ˈʌŋkəl] *n* : tío *m*
unclear [ˌʌnˈklɪr] *adj* : poco claro
uncomfortable [ˌʌnˈkʌmpfərṭəbəl] *adj* **1** : incómodo **2** DISCONCERTING : inquietante, desagradable
uncommon [ˌʌnˈkɑmən] *adj* : raro
uncompromising [ˌʌnˈkɑmprəˌmaɪzɪŋ] *adj* : intransigente
unconcerned [ˌʌnkənˈsərnd] *adj* : indiferente
unconditional [ˌʌnkənˈdɪʃənəl] *adj* : incondicional
unconscious [ˌʌnˈkɑntʃəs] *adj* : inconsciente
unconstitutional [ˌʌnˌkɑntstəˈtuːʃənəl, -ˈtjuː-] *adj* : inconstitucional
uncontrollable [ˌʌnkənˈtroːləbəl] *adj* : incontrolable
unconventional [ˌʌnkənˈvɛntʃənəl] *adj* : poco convencional
uncouth [ˌʌnˈkuːθ] *adj* : grosero
uncover [ˌʌnˈkʌvər] *vt* **1** : destapar **2** REVEAL : descubrir
undecided [ˌʌndiˈsaɪdəd] *adj* : indeciso
undeniable [ˌʌndiˈnaɪəbəl] *adj* : innegable
under [ˈʌndər] *adv* **1** : debajo **2** LESS : menos **3** *or* **~ anesthetic** : bajo los efectos de la anestesia — **~** *prep* **1** BELOW, BENEATH : debajo de, abajo de **2** **~ 20 minutes** : menos de 20 minutos **3** **~ the circumstances** : dadas las circunstancias
underage [ˌʌndərˈeɪdʒ] *adj* : menor de edad
underclothes [ˈʌndərˌkloːz, -ˌkloːðz] → **underwear**
undercover [ˌʌndərˈkʌvər] *adj* : secreto
undercurrent [ˈʌndərˌkərənt] *n* : tendencia *f* oculta
underdeveloped [ˌʌndərdɪˈvɛləpt] *adj* : subdesarrollado
underestimate [ˌʌndərˈɛstəˌmeɪt] *vt* **-mated; -mating** : subestimar
underfoot [ˌʌndərˈfʊt] *adv* : bajo los pies
undergo [ˌʌndərˈgoː] *vt* **-went** [-ˈwɛnt;]; **-gone** [-ˈgɔn]; **-going** : sufrir, experimentar
undergraduate [ˌʌndərˈgrædʒʊət] *n* : estudiante *m* universitario, estudiante *f* universitaria
underground [ˌʌndərˈgraʊnd] *adv* **1** : bajo tierra **2** **go ~** : pasar a la clandestinidad — **~** [ˈʌndərˌgraʊnd] *adj* **1** : subterráneo **2** SECRET : secreto, clandestino — **~** [ˈʌndərˌgraʊnd] *n* : movimiento *m* clandestino
undergrowth [ˈʌndərˈgroːθ] *n* : maleza *f*
underhanded [ˌʌndərˈhændəd] *adj* SLY : solapado
underline [ˈʌndərˌlaɪn] *vt* **-lined; -lining** : subrayar
underlying [ˌʌndərˈlaɪɪŋ] *adj* : subyacente
undermine [ˌʌndərˈmaɪn] *vt* **-mined; -mining** : socavar, minar
underneath [ˌʌndərˈniːθ] *adv* : debajo, abajo — **~** *prep* : debajo de, abajo de *Lat*
underpants [ˈʌndərˌpænts] *npl* : calzoncillos *mpl*, calzones *mpl Lat*
underpass [ˈʌndərˌpæs] *n* : paso *m* inferior
underprivileged [ˌʌndərˈprɪvlɪdʒd] *adj* : desfavorecido
underrate [ˌʌndərˈreɪt] *vt* **-rated; -rating** : subestimar
undershirt [ˈʌndərˌʃərt] *n* : camiseta *f*
understand [ˌʌndərˈstænd] *v* **-stood** [-ˈstʊd]; **-standing** : comprender, entender — **understandable** [ˌʌndərˈstændəbəl] *adj* : comprensible — **understanding** [ˌʌndərˈstændɪŋ] *adj* : comprensivo, compasivo — **~** *n* **1** : comprensión *f* **2** AGREEMENT : acuerdo *m*
understatement [ˌʌndərˈsteɪtmənt] *n* **that's an ~** : decir sólo eso es quedarse corto
understudy [ˈʌndərˌstʌdi] *n, pl* **-dies** : sobresaliente *mf* (en el teatro)
undertake [ˌʌndərˈteɪk] *vt* **-took** [-ˈtʊk]; **-taken** [-ˈteɪkən]; **-taking** : emprender (una tarea), encargarse de (una responsabilidad) — **undertaker** [ˈʌndərˌteɪkər] *n* : director *m*, -tora *f* de una funeraria — **undertaking** [ˈʌndərˌteɪkɪŋ, ˌʌndərˈ-] *n* : empresa *f*, tarea *f*

undertone [ˈʌndər͵to:n] *n* **1** : voz *f* baja **2** SUGGESTION : matiz *m*
undertow [ˈʌndər͵to:] *n* : resaca *f*
underwater [͵ʌndərˈwɔt̬ər, -ˈwɑ-] *adj* : submarino — **~** *adv* : debajo (del agua)
under way [͵ʌndərˈweɪ] *adv* **get ~** : ponerse en marcha
underwear [ˈʌndər͵wær] *n* : ropa *f* interior
underwent → **undergo**
underworld [ˈʌndər͵wərld] *n* **the ~** CRIMINALS : la hampa, los bajos fondos
underwriter [ˈʌndər͵raɪt̬ər, ͵ʌndərˈ-] *n* : asegurador *m*, -dora *f*
undesirable [͵ʌndiˈzaɪrəbəl] *adj* : indeseable
undeveloped [͵ʌndiˈvɛləpt] *adj* : sin desarrollar
undignified [͵ʌnˈdɪgnəfaɪd] *adj* : indecoroso
undisputed [͵ʌndɪˈspju:t̬əd] *adj* : indiscutible
undo [͵ʌnˈdu:] *vt* **-did** [-ˈdɪd]; **-done** [-ˈdʌn]; **-doing 1** UNFASTEN : deshacer, desatar **2** : reparar (daños, etc.)
undoubtedly [͵ʌnˈdaʊt̬ədli] *adv* : indudablemente
undress [͵ʌnˈdrɛs] *vt* : desnudar — *vi* : desnudarse
undue [͵ʌnˈdu:, -ˈdju:] *adj* : indebido, excesivo
undulate [ˈʌndʒə͵leɪt] *vi* **-lated; -lating** : ondular
unduly [͵ʌnˈdu:li, -ˈdju:-] *adv* : excesivamente
undying [͵ʌnˈdaɪɪŋ] *adj* : eterno
unearth [͵ʌnˈərθ] *vt* : desenterrar
unearthly [͵ʌnˈərθli] *adj* **-lier; -est** : sobrenatural, de otro mundo
uneasy [͵ʌnˈi:zi] *adj* **-easier; -est 1** AWKWARD : incómodo **2** WORRIED : inquieto **3** RESTLESS : agitado — **uneasily** [͵ʌnˈi:zəli] *adv* : inquietamente — **uneasiness** [͵ʌnˈi:zinəs] *n* : inquietud *f*
uneducated [͵ʌnˈɛdʒə͵keɪt̬əd] *adj* : inculto
unemployed [͵ʌnɪmˈplɔɪd] *adj* : desempleado — **unemployment** [͵ʌnɪmˈplɔɪmənt] *n* : desempleo *m*
unerring [͵ʌnˈɛrɪŋ, -ˈər-] *adj* : infalible
unethical [͵ʌnˈɛθɪkəl] *adj* : poco ético
uneven [͵ʌnˈi:vən] *adj* **1** : desigual **2** : impar (dícese de un número)
unexpected [͵ʌnɪkˈspɛktəd] *adj* : inesperado
unfailing [͵ʌnˈfeɪlɪŋ] *adj* **1** CONSTANT : constante **2** INEXHAUSTIBLE : inagotable
unfair [͵ʌnˈfær] *adj* : injusto — **unfairly** [͵ʌnˈfærli] *adv* : injustamente — **unfairness** [͵ʌnˈfærnəs] *n* : injusticia *f*
unfaithful [͵ʌnˈfeɪθfəl] *adj* : infiel — **unfaithfulness** [͵ʌnˈfeɪθfəlnəs] *n* : infidelidad *f*
unfamiliar [͵ʌnfəˈmɪljər] *adj* **1** : desconocido **2 be ~ with** : desconocer
unfasten [͵ʌnˈfæsən] *vt* **1** : desabrochar (ropa, etc.) **2** UNDO : desatar (una cuerda, etc.)
unfavorable [͵ʌnˈfeɪvərəbəl] *adj* : desfavorable
unfeeling [͵ʌnˈfi:lɪŋ] *adj* : insensible
unfinished [͵ʌnˈfɪnɪʃd] *adj* : sin terminar
unfit [͵ʌnˈfɪt] *adj* **1** UNSUITABLE : impropio **2** UNSUITED : no apto, incapaz
unfold [͵ʌnˈfo:ld] *vt* **1** : desplegar, desdoblar **2** REVEAL : revelar (un plan, etc.) — *vi* **1** : extenderse, desplegarse **2** DEVELOP : desarrollarse
unforeseen [͵ʌnforˈsi:] *adj* : imprevisto
unforgettable [͵ʌnfərˈgɛt̬əbəl] *adj* : inolvidable
unforgivable [͵ʌnfərˈgɪvəbəl] *adj* : imperdonable
unfortunate [͵ʌnˈfɔrtʃənət] *adj* **1** UNLUCKY : desgraciado, desafortunado **2** INAPPROPRIATE : inoportuno — **unfortunately** [͵ʌnˈfɔrtʃənətli] *adv* : desgraciadamente
unfounded [͵ʌnˈfaʊndəd] *adj* : infundado
unfriendly [͵ʌnˈfrɛndli] *adj* **-lier; -est** : poco amistoso
unfurl [͵ʌnˈfərl] *vt* : desplegar
unfurnished [͵ʌnˈfərnɪʃt] *adj* : desamueblado
ungainly [͵ʌnˈgeɪnli] *adj* : desgarbado
ungodly [͵ʌnˈgɔdli, -ˈgɑd-] *adj* **1** : impío **2 an ~ hour** : una hora intempestiva
ungrateful [͵ʌnˈgreɪtfəl] *adj* : desagradecido
unhappy [͵ʌnˈhæpi] *adj* **-pier; -est 1** SAD : infeliz, triste **2** UNFORTUNATE : desafortunado — **unhappily** [͵ʌnˈhæpəli] *adv* **1** SADLY : tristemente **2** UNFORTUNATELY : desgraciadamente — **unhappiness** [͵ʌnˈhæpinəs] *n* : tristeza *f*
unharmed [͵ʌnˈhɑrmd] *adj* : salvo, ileso
unhealthy [͵ʌnˈhɛlθi] *adj* **-thier; -est 1** : malsano **2** SICKLY : enfermizo
unheard–of [͵ʌnˈhərdəv] *adj* : sin precedente, insólito
unhook [͵ʌnˈhʊk] *vt* : desenganchar
unhurt [͵ʌnˈhərt] *adj* : ileso
unicorn [ˈju:nə͵kɔrn] *n* : unicornio *m*
unification [͵ju:nəfəˈkeɪʃən] *n* : unificación *f*
uniform [ˈju:nə͵fɔrm] *adj* : uniforme —

~ *n* : uniforme *m* — **uniformity** [ˌjuːnəˈfɔrməṭi] *n, pl* **-ties** : uniformidad *f*
unify [ˈjuːnəˌfaɪ] *vt* **-fied; -fying** : unificar
unilateral [ˌjuːnəˈlæṭərəl] *adj* : unilateral
unimaginable [ˌʌnɪˈmædʒənəbəl] *adj* : inconcebible
unimportant [ˌʌnɪmˈpɔrtənt] *adj* : insignificante
uninhabited [ˌʌnɪnˈhæbəṭəd] *adj* : deshabitado, despoblado
uninjured [ˌʌnˈindʒərd] *adj* : ileso
unintentional [ˌʌnɪnˈtɛntʃənəl] *adj* : involuntario
union [ˈjuːnjən] *n* **1** : unión *f* **2** *or* **labor ~** : sindicato *m*, gremio *m Lat*
unique [jʊˈniːk] *adj* : único — **uniquely** [jʊˈniːkli] *adv* EXCEPTIONALLY : excepcionalmente
unison [ˈjuːnəsən, -zən] *n* **in ~** : al unísono
unit [ˈjuːnɪt] *n* **1** : unidad *f* **2** : módulo *m* (de un mobiliario)
unite [jʊˈnaɪt] *v* **united; uniting** *vt* : unir — *vi* : unirse — **unity** [ˈjuːnəṭi] *n, pl* **-ties 1** : unidad *f* **2** HARMONY : acuerdo *m*
universe [ˈjuːnəˌvərs] *n* : universo *m* — **universal** [ˌjuːnəˈvərsəl] *adj* : universal
university [ˌjuːnəˈvərsəṭi] *n, pl* **-ties** : universidad *f*
unjust [ˌʌnˈdʒʌst] *adj* : injusto — **unjustified** [ˌʌnˈdʒʌstəˌfaɪd] *adj* : injustificado
unkempt [ˌʌnˈkɛmpt] *adj* **1** : descuidado, desaseado **2** : despeinado (dícese del pelo)
unkind [ˌʌnˈkaɪnd] *adj* : poco amable, cruel — **unkindness** [ˌʌnˈkaɪndnəs] *n* : falta *f* de amabilidad, crueldad *f*
unknown [ˌʌnˈnoːn] *adj* : desconocido
unlawful [ˌʌnˈlɔfəl] *adj* : ilegal
unless [ənˈlɛs] *conj* : a menos que, a no ser que
unlike [ˌʌnˈlaɪk] *adj* : diferente — ~ *prep* : a diferencia de — **unlikelihood** [ˌʌnˈlaɪkliˌhʊd] *n* : improbabilidad *f* — **unlikely** [ˌʌnˈlaɪkli] *adj* **-lier; -est** : improbable
unlimited [ˌʌnˈlɪməṭəd] *adj* : ilimitado
unload [ˌʌnˈloːd] *v* : descargar
unlock [ˌʌnˈlɑk] *vt* : abrir (con llave)
unlucky [ˌʌnˈlʌki] *adj* **-luckier; -est 1** UNFORTUNATE : desgraciado **2** : de mala suerte (dícese de un número, etc.)
unmarried [ˌʌnˈmærid] *adj* : soltero
unmask [ˌʌnˈmæsk] *vt* : desenmascarar
unmistakable [ˌʌnmɪˈsteɪkəbəl] *adj* : inconfundible
unnatural [ˌʌnˈnætʃərəl] *adj* **1** : anormal **2** AFFECTED : afectado, forzado
unnecessary [ˌʌnˈnɛsəˌsɛri] *adj* : innecesario — **unnecessarily** [-ˌnɛsəˈsɛrəli] *adv* : innecesariamente
unnerving [ˌʌnˈnərvɪŋ] *adj* : desconcertante
unnoticed [ˌʌnˈnoːṭəst] *adj* : inadvertido
unobtainable [ˌʌnəbˈteɪnəbəl] *adj* : inasequible
unobtrusive [ˌʌnəbˈstruːsɪv] *adj* : discreto
unofficial [ˌʌnəˈfɪʃəl] *adj* : no oficial
unorthodox [ˌʌnˈɔrθəˌdɑks] *adj* : poco ortodoxo
unpack [ˌʌnˈpæk] *vt* **1** : desempaquetar, desempacar *Lat* (un paquete, etc.) **2** : deshacer (una maleta) — *vi* : deshacer las maletas
unparalleled [ˌʌnˈpærəˌlɛld] *adj* : sin igual
unpleasant [ˌʌnˈplɛzənt] *adj* : desagradable
unplug [ˌʌnˈplʌg] *vt* **-plugged; -plugging** : desconectar, desenchufar
unpopular [ˌʌnˈpɑpjələr] *adj* : poco popular
unprecedented [ˌʌnˈprɛsəˌdɛntəd] *adj* : sin precedente
unpredictable [ˌʌnpriˈdɪktəbəl] *adj* : imprevisible
unprepared [ˌʌnpriˈpærd] *adj* **1** : no preparado **2** UNREADY : desprevenido
unqualified [ˌʌnˈkwɑləˌfaɪd] *adj* **1** : no calificado, sin título **2** COMPLETE : absoluto
unquestionable [ˌʌnˈkwɛstʃənəbəl] *adj* : indiscutible — **unquestioning** [ˌʌnˈkwɛstʃənɪŋ] *adj* : incondicional
unravel [ˌʌnˈrævəl] *v* **-eled** *or* **-elled; -eling** *or* **-elling** *vt* : desenmarañar — *vi* : deshacerse
unreal [ˌʌnˈriːl] *adj* : irreal — **unrealistic** [ˌʌnˌriːəˈlɪstɪk] *adj* : poco realista
unreasonable [ˌʌnˈriːzənəbəl] *adj* **1** : irrazonable **2** EXCESSIVE : excesivo
unrecognizable [ˌʌnˈrɛkəgˌnaɪzəbəl] *adj* : irreconocible
unrelated [ˌʌnriˈleɪṭəd] *adj* : no relacionado
unrelenting [ˌʌnriˈlɛntɪŋ] *adj* : implacable
unreliable [ˌʌnriˈlaɪəbəl] *adj* : que no es de fiar
unrepentant [ˌʌnriˈpɛntənt] *adj* : impenitente
unrest [ˌʌnˈrɛst] *n* **1** : inquietud *f*, malestar *m* **2** *or* **political ~** : disturbios *mpl*
unripe [ˌʌnˈraɪp] *adj* : verde, no maduro

unrivaled *or* **unrivalled** [ˌʌnˈraɪvəld] *adj* : incomparable, sin par

unroll [ˌʌnˈroːl] *vt* : desenrollar — *vi* : desenrollarse

unruly [ˌʌnˈruːli] *adj* : indisciplinado

unsafe [ˌʌnˈseɪf] *adj* : inseguro

unsaid [ˌʌnˈsɛd] *adj* : sin decir

unsanitary [ˌʌnˈsænəˌteri] *adj* : antihigiénico

unsatisfactory [ˌʌnˌsæt̬əsˈfæktəri] *adj* : insatisfactorio

unscathed [ˌʌnˈskeɪðd] *adj* : ileso

unscrew [ˌʌnˈskruː] *vt* : destornillar

unscrupulous [ˌʌnˈskruːpjələs] *adj* : sin escrúpulos

unseemly [ˌʌnˈsiːmli] *adj* **-lier; -est** : indecoroso

unseen [ˌʌnˈsiːn] *adj* **1** : no visto **2** UNNOTICED : inadvertido

unselfish [ˌʌnˈsɛlfɪʃ] *adj* : desinteresado

unsettle [ˌʌnˈsɛtəl] *vt* **-tled; -tling** DISTURB : perturbar — **unsettled** [ˌʌnˈsɛtəld] *adj* **1** CHANGEABLE : inestable **2** DISTURBED : agitado, inquieto **3** : variable (dícese del tiempo)

unsightly [ˌʌnˈsaɪtli] *adj* : feo

unskilled [ˌʌnˈskɪld] *adj* : no calificado — **unskillful** [ˌʌnˈskɪlfəl] *adj* : torpe, poco hábil

unsociable [ˌʌnˈsoːʃəbəl] *adj* : poco sociable

unsound [ˌʌnˈsaʊnd] *adj* **1** : defectuoso, erróneo **2 of ~ mind** : demente

unspeakable [ˌʌnˈspiːkəbəl] *adj* **1** : indecible **2** TERRIBLE : atroz

unstable [ˌʌnˈsteɪbəl] *adj* : inestable

unsteady [ˌʌnˈstɛdi] *adj* **1** : inestable **2** SHAKY : tembloroso

unsuccessful [ˌʌnsəkˈsɛsfəl] *adj* **1** : fracasado **2 be ~** : no tener éxito

unsuitable [ˌʌnˈsuːt̬əbəl] *adj* **1** : inadecuado **2** INCONVENIENT : inconveniente

unsure [ˌʌnˈʃʊr] *adj* : inseguro

unsuspecting [ˌʌnsəˈspɛktɪŋ] *adj* : confiado

unsympathetic [ˌʌnˌsɪmpəˈθɛt̬ɪk] *adj* : indiferente

unthinkable [ˌʌnˈθɪŋkəbəl] *adj* : inconcebible

untidy [ˌʌnˈtaɪdi] *adj* : desordenado (dícese de una sala, etc.), desaliñado (dícese de una persona)

untie [ˌʌnˈtaɪ] *vt* **-tied; -tying** *or* **-tieing** : desatar

until [ˌʌnˈtɪl] *prep* : hasta — **~** *conj* : hasta que

untimely [ˌʌnˈtaɪmli] *adj* **1** PREMATURE : prematuro **2** INOPPORTUNE : inoportuno

untold [ˌʌnˈtoːld] *adj* : incalculable

untoward [ˌʌnˈtɔrd, -ˈtoːərd, -təˈwɔrd] *adj* **1** ADVERSE : adverso **2** IMPROPER : indecoroso

untroubled [ˌʌnˈtrʌbəld] *adj* **1** : tranquilo **2 be ~ by** : no estar afectado por

untrue [ˌʌnˈtruː] *adj* : falso

unused [ˌʌnˈjuːzd, *in sense 2 usually* -ˈjuːst] *adj* **1** NEW : nuevo **2 be ~ to** : no estar acustumbrado a

unusual [ˌʌnˈjuːʒʊəl] *adj* : poco común, insólito — **unusually** [ˌʌnˈjuːʒʊəl, -ˈjuːʒəli] *adv* : excepcionalmente

unveil [ˌʌnˈveɪl] *vt* : descubrir, revelar

unwanted [ˌʌnˈwɑntəd] *adj* : superfluo (dícese de un objeto), no deseado (dícese de un niño, etc.)

unwarranted [ˌʌnˈwɔrəntəd] *adj* : injustificado

unwelcome [ˌʌnˈwɛlkəm] *adj* : inoportuno, molesto

unwell [ˌʌnˈwɛl] *adj* **be ~** : sentirse mal

unwieldy [ˌʌnˈwiːldi] *adj* : difícil de manejar

unwilling [ˌʌnˈwɪlɪŋ] *adj* : poco dispuesto — **unwillingly** [ˌʌnˈwɪlɪŋli] *adv* : de mala gana

unwind [ˌʌnˈwaɪnd] *v* **-wound** [-ˈwaʊnd]; **-winding** *vt* : desenrollar — *vi* **1** : desenrollarse **2** RELAX : relajarse

unwise [ˌʌnˈwaɪz] *adj* : imprudente

unworthy [ˌʌnˈwərði] *adj* **be ~ of** : no ser digno de

unwrap [ˌʌnˈræp] *vt* **-wrapped; -wrapping** : desenvolver

up [ˈʌp] *adv* **1** ABOVE : arriba **2** UPWARDS : hacia arriba **3 ten miles farther ~** : diez millas más adelante **4 ~ here/there** : aquí/allí arriba **5 ~ north** : en el norte **6 ~ until** : hasta — **~** *adj* **1** AWAKE : levantado **2** FINISHED : terminado **3 be ~ against** : enfrentarse con **4 be ~ on** : estar al corriente de **5 it's ~ to you** : depende de tí **6 prices are ~** : los precios han aumentado **7 the sun is ~** : ha salido el sol **8 what's ~?** : ¿qué pasa? — **~** *prep* **1 go ~ the river** : ir río arriba **2 go ~ the stairs** : subir la escalera **3 ~ the coast** : a lo largo de la costa — **~** *v* **upped** [ˈʌpt]; **upping; ups** *vt* : aumentar — *vi* **she ~ and left** : agarró y se fue

upbringing [ˈʌpˌbrɪŋɪŋ] *n* : educación *f*

upcoming [ˌʌpˈkʌmɪŋ] *adj* : próximo

update [ˌʌpˈdeɪt] *vt* **-dated; -dating** : poner al día, actualizar — **~** [ˈʌpˌdeɪt] *n* : puesta *f* al día

upgrade [ˈʌpˌgreɪd, ˌʌpˈ-] *vt* **-graded; -grading** : elevar la categoría de (un puesto, etc.), mejorar (una facilidad, etc.)

upheaval [ˌʌpˈhiːvəl] *n* : trastorno *m*
uphill [ˌʌpˈhɪl] *adv* : cuesta arriba — **~** [ˈʌpˌhɪl] *adj* **1** : en subida **2 be an ~ battle** : ser muy difícil
uphold [ˌʌpˈhoːld] *vt* **-held; -holding** : sostener, apoyar
upholstery [ˌʌpˈhoːlstəri] *n, pl* **-steries** : tapicería *f*
upkeep [ˈʌpˌkiːp] *n* : mantenimiento *m*
upon [əˈpɔn, əˈpɑn] *prep* **1** : en, sobre **2 ~ leaving** : al salir
upper [ˈʌpər] *adj* : superior — **~** *n* : parte *f* superior (del calzado, etc.)
uppercase [ˌʌpərˈkeɪs] *adj* : mayúsculo
upper class *n* : clase *f* alta
upper hand *n* : ventaja *f*, dominio *m*
uppermost [ˈʌpərˌmoːst] *adj* : más alto
upright [ˈʌpˌraɪt] *adj* **1** VERTICAL : vertical **2** ERECT : derecho **3** JUST : recto, honesto — **~** *n* : montante *m*, poste *m*
uprising [ˈʌpˌraɪzɪŋ] *n* : insurrección *f*, revuelta *f*
uproar [ˈʌpˌror] *n* COMMOTION : alboroto *m*
uproot [ˌʌpˈruːt, -ˈrʊt] *vt* : desarraigar
upset [ˌʌpˈsɛt] *vt* **-set; -setting 1** OVERTURN : volcar **2** DISTRESS : alterar, inquietar **3** DISRUPT : trastornar — **~** *adj* **1** DISTRESSED : alterado **2 have an ~ stomach** : estar mal del estómago — **~** [ˈʌpˌsɛt] *n* : trastorno *m*
upshot [ˈʌpˌʃɑt] *n* : resultado *m* final
upside down [ˌʌpˌsaɪdˈdaʊn] *adv* **1** : al revés **2 turn ~** : volver — **upside-down** [ˌʌpˌsaɪdˈdaʊn] *adj* : al revés
upstairs [ˌʌpˈstærz] *adv* : arriba — **~** [ˈʌpˌstærz, ˌʌpˈ-] *adj* : de arriba — **~** [ˈʌpˌstærz, ˌʌpˈ-] *ns & pl* : piso *m* de arriba
upstart [ˈʌpˌstɑrt] *n* : advenedizo *m*, -za *f*
upstream [ˈʌpˌstriːm] *adv* : río arriba
upswing [ˈʌpˌswɪŋ] *n* **be on the ~** : estar mejorándose
up–to–date [ˌʌptəˈdeɪt] *adj* **1** : corriente, al día **2** MODERN : moderno
uptown [ˈʌpˈtaʊn] *adv* : hacia la parte alta de la ciudad, hacia el distrito residencial
upturn [ˈʌpˌtərn] *n* : mejora *f*, auge *m* (económico)
upward [ˈʌpwərd] *or* **upwards** [-wərdz] *adv* : hacia arriba — **upward** *adj* : ascendente, hacia arriba
uranium [jʊˈreɪniəm] *n* : uranio *m*
urban [ˈərbən] *adj* : urbano
urbane [ˌərˈbeɪn] *adj* : urbano, cortés
urge [ˈərdʒ] *vt* **urged; urging 1** PRESS : instar, exhortar **2 ~ on** : animar — **~** *n* : impulso *m*, ganas *fpl* — **urgency** [ˈərdʒəntsi] *n, pl* **-cies** : urgencia *f* — **urgent** [ˈərdʒənt] *adj* **1** : urgente **2 be ~** : urgir
urine [ˈjʊrən] *n* : orina *f* — **urinate** [ˈjʊrəˌneɪt] *vi* **-nated; -nating** : orinar
urn [ˈərn] *n* : urna *f*
Uruguayan [ˌʊrəˈgwaɪən, ˌjʊr-, -ˈgweɪ-] *adj* : uruguayo
us [ˈʌs] *pron* **1** (*as direct or indirect object*) : nos **2** (*as object of a preposition*) : nosotros, nosotras **3 both of ~** : nosotros dos **4 it's ~!** : ¡somos nosotros!
usage [ˈjuːsɪdʒ, -zɪdʒ] *n* : uso *m*
use [ˈjuːz] *v* **used** [ˈjuːzd, *the phrase "used to" is usually* ˈjuːstuː]; **using** *vt* **1** : usar **2** CONSUME : consumir, tomar (drogas, etc.) **3 ~ up** : agotar, consumir — *vi* **1 she ~d to dance** : acostumbraba bailar **2 winters ~d to be colder** : los inviernos solían ser más fríos — **~** [ˈjuːs] *n* **1** : uso *m* **2 have no ~ for** : no necesitar **3 have the ~ of** : poder usar, tener acceso a **4 it's no ~!** : ¡es inútil! — **used** [ˈjuːzd, *in sense 2 usually* ˈjuːst] *adj* **1** SECONDHAND : usado **2 be ~ to** : estar acostumbrado a — **useful** [ˈjuːsfəl] *adj* : útil, práctico — **usefulness** [ˈjuːsfəlnəs] *n* : utilidad *f* — **useless** [ˈjuːsləs] *adj* : inútil — **user** [ˈjuːzər] *n* : usuario *m*, -ria *f*
usher [ˈʌʃər] *vt* **1** : acompañar, conducir **2 ~ in** : hacer entrar — **~** *n* : acomodador *m*, -dora *f*
usual [ˈjuːʒʊəl] *adj* **1** : habitual, usual **2 as ~** : como de costumbre — **usually** [ˈjuːʒʊəli, ˈjuːʒəli] *adv* : usualmente
usurp [jʊˈsərp, -ˈzərp] *vt* : usurpar
utensil [jʊˈtɛntsəl] *n* : utensilio *m*
uterus [ˈjuːt̬ərəs] *n, pl* **uteri** [-ˌraɪ] : útero *m*, matriz *f*
utility [juːˈtɪlət̬i] *n, pl* **-ties 1** : utilidad *f* **2** *or* **public ~** : empresa *f* de servicio público
utilize [ˈjuːt̬əlˌaɪz] *vt* **-lized; -lizing** : utilizar
utmost [ˈʌtˌmoːst] *adj* **1** FARTHEST : extremo **2 of the ~ importance** : de suma importancia — **~** *n* **do one's ~** : hacer todo lo posible
utopia [jʊˈtoːpiə] *n* : utopía *f* — **utopian** [jʊˈtoːpiən] *adj* : utópico
utter[1] [ˈʌt̬ər] *adj* : absoluto, completo
utter[2] *vt* : decir, pronunciar (palabras) — **utterance** [ˈʌt̬ərənts] *n* : declaración *f*, expresión *f*
utterly [ˈʌt̬ərli] *adv* : completamente, totalmente

V

v ['vi:] *n, pl* **v's** *or* **vs** ['vi:z] : v *f*, vigésima segunda letra del alfabeto inglés
vacant ['veɪkənt] *adj* **1** AVAILABLE : libre **2** UNOCCUPIED : desocupado **3** : vacante (dícese de un puesto) **4** : ausente (dícese de una mirada) — **vacancy** ['veɪkəntsi] *n, pl* **-cies 1** : (puesto *m*) vacante *f* **2** : habitación *f* libre (en un hotel, etc.)
vacate ['veɪ,keɪt] *vt* **-cated; -cating** : desalojar, desocupar
vacation [veɪ'keɪʃən, və-] *n* : vacaciones *fpl*
vaccination [,væksə'neɪʃən] *n* : vacunación *f* — **vaccinate** ['væksə,neɪt] *vt* **-nated; -nating** : vacunar — **vaccine** [væk'si:n, 'væk,-] *n* : vacuna *f*
vacuum ['væ,kju:m, -kjəm] *n, pl* **vacuums** *or* **vacua** : vacío *m* — ~ *vt* : pasar la aspiradora por — **vacuum cleaner** *n* : aspiradora *f*
vagina [və'dʒaɪnə] *n, pl* **-nae** [-,ni:, -,naɪ] *or* **-nas** : vagina *f*
vagrant ['veɪgrənt] *n* : vagabundo *m*, -da *f*
vague ['veɪg] *adj* **vaguer; -est** : vago, indistinto
vain ['veɪn] *adj* **1** CONCEITED : vanidoso **2 in** ~ : en vano
valentine ['vælən,taɪn] *n* : tarjeta *f* del día de San Valentín
valiant ['væljənt] *adj* : valiente, valeroso
valid ['væləd] *adj* : válido — **validate** ['vælə,deɪt] *vt* **-dated; -dating** : validar — **validity** [və'lɪdəṭi, væ-] *n* : validez *f*
valley ['væli] *n, pl* **-leys** : valle *m*
valor ['vælər] *n* : valor *m*, valentía *f*
value ['væl,ju:] *n* : valor *m* — ~ *vt* **-ued; -uing** : valorar — **valuable** ['væljuəbəl, 'væljəbəl] *adj* : valioso — **valuables** *npl* : objetos *mpl* de valor
valve ['vælv] *n* : válvula *f*
vampire ['væm,paɪr] *n* : vampiro *m*
van ['væn] *n* : furgoneta *f*, camioneta *f*
vandal ['vændəl] *n* : vándalo *m* — **vandalism** ['vændəl,ɪzəm] *n* : vandalismo *m* — **vandalize** ['vændəl,aɪz] *vt* : destrozar, destruir
vane ['veɪn] *n or* **weather** ~ : veleta *f*
vanguard ['væn,gɑrd] *n* : vanguardia *f*
vanilla [və'nɪlə, -'nɛ-] *n* : vainilla *f*
vanish ['vænɪʃ] *vi* : desaparecer
vanity ['vænəṭi] *n, pl* **-ties 1** : vanidad *f* **2** *or* ~ **table** : tocador *m*
vantage point ['væntɪdʒ] *n* : posición *f* ventajosa
vapor ['veɪpər] *n* : vapor *m*
variable ['vɛriəbəl] *adj* : variable — ~ *n* : variable *f* — **variance** ['vɛriənts] *n* **at** ~ **with** : en desacuerdo con — **variant** ['vɛriənt] *n* : variante *f* — **variation** [,vɛri'eɪʃən] *n* : variación *f* — **varied** ['vɛrid] *adj* : variado — **variegated** ['vɛriə,geɪṭɛd] *adj* : abigarrado, multicolor — **variety** [və'raɪəṭi] *n, pl* **-ties 1** : variedad *f* **2** ASSORTMENT : surtido *m* **3** SORT : clase *f* — **various** ['vɛriəs] *adj* : varios, diversos
varnish ['vɑrnɪʃ] *n* : barniz *f* — ~ *vt* : barnizar
vary ['vɛri] *v* **varied; varying** : variar
vase ['veɪs, 'veɪz, 'vɑz] *n* **1** : jarrón *m* **2** *or* **flower** ~ : florero *m*
vast ['væst] *adj* : vasto, enorme — **vastness** ['væstnəs] *n* : inmensidad *f*
vat ['væt] *n* : cuba *f*
vault[1] ['vɔlt] *vi* LEAP : saltar — ~ *n* : salto *m*
vault[2] *n* **1** DOME : bóveda *f* **2** *or* **bank** ~ : cámara *f* acorazada, bóveda *f* de seguridad *Lat* **3** CRYPT : cripta *f*
VCR [,vi:,si:'ɑr] (*videocassette recorder*) *n* : video *m*
veal ['vi:l] *n* : (carne *f* de) ternera *f*
veer ['vɪr] *vi* : virar
vegetable ['vɛdʒtəbəl, 'vɛdʒəṭə-] *adj* : vegetal — ~ *n* **1** : vegetal *m* (planta) **2** ~**s** *npl* : verduras *fpl* — **vegetarian** [,vɛdʒə'tɛriən] *n* : vegetariano *mf* — **vegetation** [,vɛdʒə'teɪʃən] *n* : vegetación *f*
vehemence ['vi:əmənts] *n* : vehemencia *f* — **vehement** ['vi:əmənt] *adj* : vehemente
vehicle ['vi:əkəl, 'vi:,hɪkəl] *n* : vehículo *m*
veil ['veɪl] *n* : velo *m* — ~ *vt* **1** : cubrir con un velo **2** CONCEAL : velar
vein ['veɪn] *n* **1** : vena *f* **2** : veta *f* (de un mineral, etc.)
velocity [və'lɑsəṭi] *n, pl* **-ties** : velocidad *f*
velvet ['vɛlvət] *n* : terciopelo *m* — **velvety** ['vɛlvəṭi] *adj* : aterciopelado
vending machine ['vɛndɪŋ-] *vt* : máquina *f* expendedora

vendor ['vɛndər] *n* : vendedor *m,* -dora *f*
veneer [və'nɪr] *n* **1** : chapa *f* **2** FACADE : apariencia *f*
venerable ['vɛnərəbəl] *adj* : venerable — **venerate** ['vɛnə,reɪt] *vt* **-ated; -ating** : venerar — **veneration** [,vɛnə'reɪʃən] *n* : veneración *f*
venereal [və'nɪriəl] *adj* : venéreo
venetian blind [və'ni:ʃən-] *n* : persiana *f* veneciana
Venezuelan [,vɛnə'zweɪlən, -zʊ'eɪ-] *adj* : venezolano
vengeance ['vɛndʒənts] *n* **1** : venganza *f* **2 take ~ on** : vengarse de — **vengeful** ['vɛndʒfəl] *adj* : vengativo
venison ['vɛnəsən, -zən] *n* : (carne *f* de) venado *m*
venom ['vɛnəm] *n* : veneno *m* — **venomous** ['vɛnəməs] *adj* : venenoso
vent ['vɛnt] *vt* : desahogar — **~** *n* **1** *or* **air ~** : rejilla *f* de ventilación **2** OUTLET : desahogo *m* — **ventilate** ['vɛntəl,eɪt] *vt* **-lated; -lating** : ventilar — **ventilation** [,vɛntəl'eɪʃən] *n* : ventilación *f* — **ventilator** ['vɛntəl,eɪţər] *n* : ventilador *m*
ventriloquist [vɛn'trɪlə,kwɪst] *n* : ventrílocuo *m,* -cua *f*
venture ['vɛntʃər] *v* **-tured; -turing** *vt* **1** RISK : arriesgar **2** : aventurar (una opinión, etc.) — *vi* : atreverse — **~** *n or* **business ~** : empresa *f*
venue ['vɛn,ju:] *n* : lugar *m*
Venus ['vi:nəs] *n* : Venus *m*
veranda *or* **verandah** [və'rændə] *n* : veranda *f*
verb ['vərb] *n* : verbo *m* — **verbal** ['vərbəl] *adj* : verbal — **verbatim** [vər'beɪţəm] *adv* : palabra por palabra — **~** *adj* : literal — **verbose** [vər'bo:s] *adj* : verboso
verdict ['vərdɪkt] *n* **1** : veredicto *m* **2** OPINION : opinión *f*
verge ['vərdʒ] *n* **1** : borde *m* **2 on the ~ of** : a punto de (hacer algo), al borde de (algo) — **~** *vi* **verged; verging ~ on** : rayar en
verify ['vɛrə,faɪ] *vt* **-fied; -fying** : verificar — **verification** [,vɛrəfə'keɪʃən] *n* : verificación *f*
vermin ['vərmən] *ns & pl* : alimañas *fpl*
vermouth [vər'mu:th] *n* : vermut *m*
versatile ['vərsəţəl] *adj* : versátil — **versatility** [,vərsə'tɪləţi] *n* : versatilidad *f*
verse ['vərs] *n* **1** LINE : verso *m* **2** POETRY : poesía *f* **3** : versículo *m* (en la Biblia) — **versed** ['vərst] *adj* **be well ~ in** : ser muy versado en
version ['vərʒən] *n* : versión *f*
versus ['vərsəs] *prep* : versus
vertebra ['vərtəbrə] *n, pl* **-brae** [-,breɪ, -,bri:] *or* **-bras** : vértebra *f*
vertical ['vərtɪkəl] *adj* : vertical — **~** *n* : vertical *f*
vertigo ['vərtɪ,go:] *n, pl* **-goes** *or* **-gos** : vértigo *m*
verve ['vərv] *n* : brío *m*
very ['vɛri] *adv* **1** : muy **2 at the ~ least** : por lo menos **3 the ~ same thing** : la misma cosa **4 ~ much** : mucho **5 ~ well** : muy bien — **~** *adj* **verier; -est 1** PRECISE, SAME : mismo **2** MERE : solo, mero **3 the ~ thing** : justo lo que hacía falta
vessel ['vɛsəl] *n* **1** CONTAINER : recipiente *m* **2** SHIP : nave *f,* buque *m* **3** *or* **blood ~** : vaso *m* sanguíneo
vest ['vɛst] *n* **1** : chaleco *m* **2** *Brit* UNDERSHIRT : camiseta *f*
vestibule ['vɛstə,bju:l] *n* : vestíbulo *m*
vestige ['vɛstɪdʒ] *n* : vestigio *m*
vet ['vɛt] *n* **1** → **veterinarian 2** → **veteran**
veteran ['vɛţərən, 'vɛtrən] *n* : veterano *m,* -na *f*
veterinarian [,vɛţərə'nɛriən, ,vɛţə'nɛr-] *n* : veterinario *m,* -ria *f* — **veterinary** ['vɛţərə,nɛri] *adj* : veterinario
veto ['vi:ţo] *n, pl* **-toes** : veto *m* — **~** *vt* : vetar
vex ['vɛks] *vt* ANNOY : irritar
via ['vaɪə, 'vi:ə] *prep* : por, vía
viable ['vaɪəbəl] *adj* : viable
viaduct ['vaɪə,dʌkt] *n* : viaducto *m*
vial ['vaɪəl] *n* : frasco *m*
vibrant ['vaɪbrənt] *adj* : vibrante — **vibrate** ['vaɪ,breɪt] *vi* **-brated; -brating** : vibrar — **vibration** [vaɪ'breɪʃən] *n* : vibración *f*
vicar ['vɪkər] *n* : vicario *m,* -ria *f*
vicarious [vaɪ'kæri:əs, vɪ-] *adj* : indirecto
vice ['vaɪs] *n* : vicio *m*
vice president *n* : vicepresidente *m,* -ta *f*
vice versa [,vaɪsɪ'vərsə, ,vaɪs'vər-] *adv* : viceversa
vicinity [və'sɪnəţi] *n, pl* **-ties 1** : inmediaciones *fpl* **2 in the ~ of** ABOUT : alrededor de
vicious ['vɪʃəs] *adj* **1** SAVAGE : feroz **2** MALICIOUS : malicioso
victim ['vɪktəm] *n* : víctima *f*
victor ['vɪktər] *n* : vencedor *m,* -dora *f*
victory ['vɪktəri] *n, pl* **-ries** : victoria *f* — **victorious** [vɪk'to:riəs] *adj* : victorioso
video ['vɪdi,o:] *n* : video *m,* vídeo *m Spain* — **~** *adj* : de video — **videocassette** [,vɪdiokə'sɛt] *n* : videocasete *m* — **videotape** ['vɪdio,teɪp] *n* : video-

cinta *f* — ~ *vt* **-taped; -taping** : videograbar

vie ['vaɪ] *vi* **vied; vying** ['vaɪɪŋ] : competir

Vietnamese [vi,ɛtnə'mi:z, -'mi:s] *adj* : vietnamita

view ['vju:] *n* **1** : vista *f* **2** OPINION : opinión *f* **3 come into ~** : aparecer **4 in ~ of** : en vista de (que) — ~ *vt* **1** : ver **2** CONSIDER : considerar — **viewer** ['vju:ər] *n or* **television ~** : televidente *mf* — **viewpoint** ['vju:,pɔɪnt] *n* : punto *m* de vista

vigil ['vɪdʒəl] *n* : vela *f* — **vigilance** ['vɪdʒələnts] *n* : vigilancia *f* — **vigilant** ['vɪdʒələnt] *adj* : vigilante

vigor *or Brit* **vigour** ['vɪgər] *n* : vigor *m* — **vigorous** ['vɪgərəs] *adj* **1** : enérgico **2** ROBUST : vigoroso

Viking ['vaɪkɪŋ] *n* : vikingo *m*, -ga *f*

vile ['vaɪl] *adj* **viler; vilest 1** : vil **2** REVOLTING : asqueroso **3** TERRIBLE : horrible

villa ['vɪlə] *n* : casa *f* de campo

village ['vɪlɪdʒ] *n* : pueblo *m* (grande), aldea *f* (pequeña) — **villager** ['vɪlɪdʒər] *n* : vecino *m*, -na *f* (de un pueblo); aldeano *m*, -na *f* (de una aldea)

villain ['vɪlən] *n* : villano *m*, -na *f*

vindicate ['vɪndə,keɪt] *vt* **-cated; -cating** **1** : vindicar **2** JUSTIFY : justificar

vindictive [vɪn'dɪktɪv] *adj* : vengativo

vine ['vaɪn] *n* **1** : enredadera *f* **2** GRAPEVINE : vid *f*

vinegar ['vɪnɪgər] *n* : vinagre *m*

vineyard ['vɪnjərd] *n* : viña *f*, viñedo *m*

vintage ['vɪntɪdʒ] *n* **1** : cosecha *f* (de vino) **2** ERA : época *f* — ~ *adj* **1** : añejo (dícese de un vino) **2** CLASSIC : de época

vinyl ['vaɪnəl] *n* : vinilo

viola [vi'o:lə] *n* : viola *f*

violate ['vaɪə,leɪt] *vt* **-lated; -lating** : violar — **violation** [,vaɪə'leɪʃən] *n* : violación *f*

violence ['vaɪlənts, 'vaɪə-] *n* : violencia *f* — **violent** ['vaɪlənt, 'vaɪə-] *adj* : violento

violet ['vaɪlət, 'vaɪə-] *n* : violeta *f* (flor), violeta *m* (color)

violin [,vaɪə'lɪn] *n* : violín *m* — **violinist** [,vaɪə'lɪnɪst] *n* : violinista *mf* — **violoncello** [,vaɪələn'tʃɛlo:, ,vi:-] → **cello**

VIP [,vi:,aɪ'pi:] *n, pl* **VIPs** [-'pi:z] : VIP *mf*

viper ['vaɪpər] *n* : víbora *f*

virgin ['vərdʒən] *n* : virgen *mf* — ~ *adj* **1** : virgen (dícese de la lana, etc.) **2** CHASTE : virginal — **virginity** [vər'dʒɪnəṭi] *n* : virginidad *f*

virile ['vɪrəl, -,aɪl] *adj* : viril — **virility** [və'rɪləṭi] *n* : virilidad *f*

virtual ['vərtʃʊəl] *adj* : virtual — **virtually** ['vərtʃʊəli, 'vərtʃəli] *adv* : prácticamente

virtue ['vər,tʃu:] *n* **1** : virtud *f* **2 by ~ of** : en virtud de

virtuoso [,vərtʃʊ'o:so:, -zo:] *n, pl* **-sos** *or* **-si** [-,si:, -,zi:] : virtuoso *m*, -sa *f*

virtuous ['vərtʃʊəs] *adj* : virtuoso

virulent ['vɪrələnt, 'vɪrjə-] *adj* : virulento

virus ['vaɪrəs] *n* : virus *m*

visa ['vi:zə, -sə] *n* : visado *m*, visa *f Lat*

vis-à-vis [,vi:zə'vi:, -sə-] *prep* : con respecto a

viscous ['vɪskəs] *adj* : viscoso

vise ['vaɪs] *n* : torno *m* de banco

visible ['vɪzəbəl] *adj* **1** : visible **2** NOTICEABLE : evidente — **visibility** [,vɪzə'bɪləṭi] *n, pl* **-ties** : visibilidad *f*

vision ['vɪʒən] *n* **1** : visión *f* **2 have ~s of** : imaginarse — **visionary** ['vɪʒə,nɛri] *adj* : visionario — ~ *n, pl* **-ries** : visionario *m*, -ria *f*

visit ['vɪzət] *vt* : visitar — *vi* **1** : hacer una visita **2 be ~ing** : estar de visita — ~ *n* : visita *f* — **visitor** ['vɪzəṭər] *n* **1** : visitante *mf* **2** GUEST : visita *f*

visor ['vaɪzər] *n* : visera *f*

vista ['vɪstə] *n* : vista *f*

visual ['vɪʒʊəl] *adj* : visual — **visualize** ['vɪʒʊə,laɪz] *vt* **-ized; -izing** : visualizar

vital ['vaɪṭəl] *adj* **1** : vital **2** CRUCIAL : esencial — **vitality** [vaɪ'tæləṭi] *n, pl* **-ties** : vitalidad *f*, energía *f*

vitamin ['vaɪṭəmən] *n* : vitamina *f*

vivacious [və'veɪʃəs, vaɪ-] *adj* : vivaz, animado

vivid ['vɪvəd] *adj* : vivo (dícese de colores), vívido (dícese de sueños, etc.)

vocabulary [vo:'kæbjə,lɛri] *n, pl* **-laries** : vocabulario *m*

vocal ['vo:kəl] *adj* **1** : vocal **2** OUTSPOKEN : vociferante — **vocal cords** *npl* : cuerdas *fpl* vocales — **vocalist** ['vo:kəlɪst] *n* : cantante *mf*, vocalista *mf*

vocation [vo'keɪʃən] *n* : vocación *f* — **vocational** [vo'keɪʃənəl] *adj* : profesional

vociferous [vo'sɪfərəs] *adj* : vociferante, ruidoso

vodka ['vɑdkə] *n* : vodka *m*

vogue ['vo:g] *n* **1** : moda *f*, boga *f* **2 be in ~** : estar de moda, estar en boga

voice ['vɔɪs] *n* : voz *f* — ~ *vt* **voiced; voicing** : expresar

void ['vɔɪd] *adj* **1** INVALID : nulo **2 ~ of** : falto de — ~ *n* : vacío *m* — ~ *vt* : anular

volatile [ˈvɑlət̬əl] *adj* : volátil — **volatility** [ˌvɑləˈtɪlət̬i] *n* : volatilidad *f*
volcano [vɑlˈkeɪˌno:] *n, pl* **-noes** *or* **-nos** : volcán *m* — **volcanic** [vɑlˈkænɪk] *adj* : volcánico
volition [voˈlɪʃən] *n* **of one's own ~** : por voluntad propia
volley [ˈvɑli] *n, pl* **-leys 1** : descarga *f* (de tiros) **2** : torrente *m* (de insultos, etc.) **3** : volea *f* (en deportes) — **volleyball** [ˈvɑliˌbɔl] *n* : voleibol *m*
volt [ˈvo:lt] *n* : voltio *m* — **voltage** [ˈvo:ltɪdʒ] *n* : voltaje *m*
voluble [ˈvɑljəbəl] *adj* : locuaz
volume [ˈvɑljəm, -ju:m] *n* : volumen *m* — **voluminous** [vəˈlu:mənəs] *adj* : voluminoso
voluntary [ˈvɑlənˌteri] *adj* : voluntario — **volunteer** [ˌvɑlənˈtɪr] *n* : voluntario *m*, -ria *f* — ~ *vt* : ofrecer — *vi* ~ **to** : ofrecerse a
voluptuous [vəˈlʌptʃuəs] *adj* : voluptuoso
vomit [ˈvɑmət] *n* : vómito *m* — ~ *v* : vomitar
voracious [vɔˈreɪʃəs, və-] *adj* : voraz
vote [ˈvo:t] *n* **1** : voto *m* **2** SUFFRAGE : derecho *m* al voto — ~ *vi* **voted; voting** : votar — **voter** [ˈvo:t̬ər] *n* : votante *mf* — **voting** [ˈvo:t̬ɪŋ] *n* : votación *f*
vouch [ˈvæʊtʃ] *vi* ~ **for** : responder de (algo), responder por (algn) — **voucher** [ˈvæʊtʃər] *n* : vale *m*
vow [væʊ] *n* : voto *m* — ~ *vt* : jurar
vowel [ˈvæʊəl] *n* : vocal *m*
voyage [ˈvɔɪɪdʒ] *n* : viaje *m*
vulgar [ˈvʌlgər] *adj* **1** COMMON : ordinario **2** CRUDE : grosero, vulgar — **vulgarity** [ˌvʌlˈgærət̬i] *n, pl* **-ties** : vulgaridad *f*
vulnerable [ˈvʌlnərəbəl] *adj* : vulnerable — **vulnerability** [ˌvʌlnərəˈbɪlət̬i] *n, pl* **-ties** : vulnerabilidad *f*
vulture [ˈvʌltʃər] *n* : buitre *m*
vying → **vie**

W

w [ˈdʌbəlju:] *n, pl* **w's** *or* **ws** [-ju:z] : w *f*, vigésima tercera letra del alfabeto inglés
wad [ˈwɑd] *n* : taco *m* (de papel, etc.), fajo *m* (de billetes)
waddle [ˈwɑdəl] *vi* **-dled; -dling** : andar como un pato
wade [ˈweɪd] *v* **waded; wading** *vi* : caminar por el agua — *vt or* ~ **across** : vadear
wafer [ˈweɪfər] *n* : barquillo *m*
waffle [ˈwɑfəl] *n* : gofre *m Spain*, wafle *m Lat*
waft [ˈwɑft, ˈwæft] *vt* : llevar por el aire — *vi* : flotar
wag [ˈwæg] *v* **wagged; wagging** *vt* : menear — *vi* : menearse
wage [ˈweɪdʒ] *n or* **wages** *npl* : salario *m* — ~ *vt* **waged; waging** ~ **war** : hacer la guerra
wager [ˈweɪdʒər] *n* : apuesta *f* — ~ *v* : apostar
wagon [ˈwægən] *n* **1** CART : carrito *m* **2** → **station wagon**
waif [ˈweɪf] *n* : niño *m* abandonado
wail [ˈweɪl] *vi* : lamentarse — ~ *n* : lamento *m*
waist [ˈweɪst] *n* : cintura *f* — **waistline** [ˈweɪstˌlaɪn] *n* : cintura *f*
wait [ˈweɪt] *vi* : esperar — *vt* **1** AWAIT : esperar **2** ~ **tables** : servir a la mesa — ~ *n* **1** : espera *f* **2 lie in** ~ : estar al acecho — **waiter** [ˈweɪt̬ər] *n* : camarero *m*, mozo *m Lat* — **waiting room** *n* : sala *f* de espera — **waitress** [ˈweɪtrəs] *n* : camarera *f*, moza *f Lat*
waive [ˈweɪv] *vt* **waived; waiving** : renunciar a — **waiver** [ˈweɪvər] *n* : renuncia *f*
wake[1] [ˈweɪk] *v* **woke** [ˈwo:k]; **woken** [ˈwo:kən] *or* **waked; waking** *vi or* ~ **up** : despertarse — *vt* : despertar — ~ *n* : velatorio *m* (de un difunto)
wake[2] *n* **1** : estela *f* (de un barco) **2 in the** ~ **of** : tras, como consecuencia de
waken [ˈweɪkən] *vt* : despertar — *vi* : despertarse
walk [ˈwɔk] *vi* **1** : caminar, andar **2** STROLL : pasear **3 too far to** ~ : demasiado lejos para ir a pie — *vt* **1** : caminar por **2** : sacar a pasear (a un perro) — ~ *n* **1** : paseo *m* **2** PATH : camino *m* **3** GAIT : andar *m* — **walker** [ˈwɔkər] *n* **1** : paseante *mf* **2** HIKER : excursionista *mf* — **walking stick** *n* : bastón *m* — **walkout** [ˈwɔkˌaʊt] *n* STRIKE : huelga *f* — **walk out** *vi* **1** STRIKE : declararse en huelga **2** LEAVE : salir, irse **3** ~ **on** : abandonar
wall [ˈwɔl] *n* : muro *m* (exterior), pared *f* (interior), muralla *f* (de una ciudad)

wallet ['wɑlət] *n* : billetera *f*, cartera *f*
wallflower ['wɔl͵flauər] *n* **be a ~** : comer pavo
wallop ['wɑləp] *vt* : pegar fuerte — **~** *n* : golpe *m* fuerte
wallow ['wɑ͵lo:] *vi* : revolcarse
wallpaper ['wɔl͵peɪpər] *n* : papel *m* pintado — **~** *vt* : empapelar
walnut ['wɔl͵nʌt] *n* : nuez *f*
walrus ['wɔlrəs, 'wɑl-] *n, pl* **-rus** *or* **-ruses** : morsa *f*
waltz ['wɔlts] *n* : vals *m* — **~** *vi* : valsar
wan ['wɑn] *adj* **wanner; -est** : pálido
wand ['wɑnd] *n* : varita *f* (mágica)
wander ['wɑndər] *vi* **1** : vagar, pasear **2** STRAY : divagar — *vt* : pasear por — **wanderer** ['wɑndərər] *n* : vagabundo *m*, -da *f* — **wanderlust** ['wɑndər͵lʌst] *n* : pasión *f* por viajar
wane ['weɪn] *vi* **waned; waning** : menguar — **~** *n* **be on the ~** : estar disminuyendo
want ['wɑnt, 'wɔnt] *vt* **1** DESIRE : querer **2** NEED : necesitar **3** LACK : carecer de — **~** *n* **1** NEED : necesidad *f* **2** LACK : falta *f* **3** DESIRE : deseo *m* — **wanting** ['wɑntɪŋ, 'wɔn-] *adj* **be ~** : carecer
wanton ['wɑntən, 'wɔn-] *adj* **1** LEWD : lascivo **2 ~ cruelty** : crueldad *f* despiadada
war ['wɔr] *n* : guerra *f*
ward ['wɔrd] *n* **1** : sala *f* (de un hospital, etc.) **2** : distrito *m* electoral **3** : pupilo *m*, -la *f* (de un tutor, etc.) — **~** *vt* **~ off** : protegerse contra — **warden** ['wɔrdən] *n* **1** : guardián *m*, -diana *f* **2** *or* **game ~** : guardabosque *mf* **3** *or* **prison ~** : alcaide *m*
wardrobe ['wɔrd͵ro:b] *n* **1** CLOSET : armario *m* **2** CLOTHES : vestuario *m*
warehouse ['wær͵haus] *n* : almacén *m*, bodega *f Lat* — **wares** ['wærz] *npl* : mercancías *fpl*
warfare ['wɔr͵fær] *n* : guerra *f*
warily ['wærəli] *adv* : cautelosamente
warlike ['wær͵laɪk] *adj* : belicoso
warm ['wɔrm] *adj* **1** : caliente **2** LUKEWARM : tibio **3** CARING : cariñoso **4 I feel ~** : tengo calor **5 ~ clothes** : ropa *f* de abrigo — **~** *vt or* **~ up** : calentar — *vi* **1** *or* **~ up** : calentarse **2 ~ to** : tomar simpatía a (algn), entusiasmarse con (algo) — **warm–blooded** ['wɔrm'blʌdəd] *adj* : de sangre caliente — **warmhearted** ['wɔrm'hɑrt̬əd] *adj* : cariñoso — **warmly** ['wɔrmli] *adv* **1** : calurosamente **2 dress ~** : abrigarse — **warmth** ['wɔrmpθ] *n* **1** : calor *m* **2** AFFECTION : cariño *m*, afecto *m*
warn ['wɔrn] *vt* : advertir, avisar— **warning** ['wɔrnɪŋ] *n* : advertencia *f*, aviso *m*
warp ['wɔrp] *vt* **1** : alabear (madera, etc.) **2** DISTORT : deformar — *vi* : alabearse
warrant ['wɔrənt] *n* **1** : autorización *f* **2 arrest ~** : orden *f* judicial — **~** *vt* : justificar — **warranty** ['wɔrənti, ͵wɔrən'ti:] *n, pl* **-ties** : garantía *f*
warrior ['wɔriər] *n* : guerrero *m*, -ra *f*
warship ['wɔr͵ʃɪp] *n* : buque *m* de guerra
wart ['wɔrt] *n* : verruga *f*
wartime ['wɔr͵taɪm] *n* : tiempo *m* de guerra
wary ['wæri] *adj* **warier; -est** : cauteloso
was → **be**
wash ['wɔʃ, 'wɑʃ] *vt* **1** : lavar(se) **2** CARRY : arrastrar **3 ~ away** : llevarse **4 ~ over** : bañar — *vi* : lavarse — **~** *n* **1** : lavado *m* **2** LAUNDRY : ropa *f* sucia — **washable** ['wɔʃəbəl, 'wɑ-] *adj* : lavable — **washcloth** ['wɔʃ͵klɔθ, 'wɑʃ-] *n* : toallita *f* (para lavarse) — **washed–out** ['wɔʃt'aut, 'wɑʃt-] *adj* **1** : desvaído (dícese de colores) **2** EXHAUSTED : agotado — **washer** ['wɔʃər, 'wɑ-] *n* **1** → **washing machine 2** : arandela *f* (de una llave, etc.) — **washing machine** *n* : máquina *f* de lavar, lavadora *f* — **washroom** ['wɔʃ͵ru:m, 'wɑʃ-, -͵rum] *n* : servicios *mpl* (públicos), baño *m*
wasn't ['wʌzənt] (*contraction of* **was not**) → **be**
wasp ['wɑsp] *n* : avispa *f*
waste ['weɪst] *v* **wasted; wasting** *vt* **1** : desperdiciar, derrochar, malgastar **2 ~ time** : perder tiempo — *vi or* **~ away** : consumirse — **~** *adj* : de desecho — **~** *n* **1** : derroche *m*, desperdicio *m* **2** RUBBISH : desechos *mpl* **3 a ~ of time** : una pérdida de tiempo — **wastebasket** ['weɪst͵bæskət] *n* : papelera *f* — **wasteful** ['weɪstfəl] *adj* : derrochador — **wasteland** ['weɪst͵lænd, -lənd] *n* : yermo *m*
watch ['wɑtʃ] *vi* **1** : mirar **2** *or* **keep ~** : velar **3 ~ out!** : ¡ten cuidado!, ¡ojo! — *vt* **1**: mirar **2** *or* **~ over** : vigilar, cuidar **3 ~ what you do** : ten cuidado con lo que haces — **~** *n* **1** reloj *m* **2** SURVEILLANCE : vigilancia *f* **3** LOOKOUT : guardia *mf* — **watchdog** ['wɑtʃ͵dɔg] *n* : perro *m* guardián — **watchful** ['wɑtʃfəl] *adj* : vigilante — **watchman** ['wɑtʃmən] *n, pl* **-men** [-mən, -͵mɛn] : vigilante *m*, guarda *m* — **watchword** ['wɑtʃ͵wərd] *n* : santo *m* y seña
water ['wɔt̬ər, 'wɑ-] *n* : agua *f* — **~** *vt* **1**

: regar (el jardín, etc.) **2 ~ down** DILUTE : diluir, aguar — *vi* **1** : lagrimar (dícese de los ojos) **2 my mouth is ~ing** : se me hace agua la boca — **watercolor** ['wɔt̬ər,kʌlər, 'wɑ-] *n* : acuarela *f* — **watercress** ['wɔt̬ər,krɛs, 'wɑ-] *n* : berro *m* — **waterfall** ['wɔt̬ər,fɔl, 'wɑ-] *n* : cascada *f*, salto *m* de agua — **water lily** *n* : nenúfar *m* — **waterlogged** ['wɔt̬ər,lɔgd, 'wɑt̬ər,lɑgd] *adj* : lleno de agua, empapado — **watermelon** ['wɔt̬ər,mɛlən, 'wɑ-] *n* : sandía *f* — **waterpower** ['wɔt̬ər,paʊər, 'wɑ-] *n* : energía *f* hidráulica — **waterproof** ['wɔt̬ər,pru:f, 'wɑ-] *adj* : impermeable — **watershed** ['wɔt̬ər,ʃɛd, 'wɑ-] *n* **1** : cuenca *f* (de un río) **2** : momento *m* crítico — **waterskiing** ['wɔt̬ər,ski:ɪŋ, 'wɑ-] *n* : esquí *m* acuático — **watertight** ['wɔt̬ər,taɪt, 'wɑ-] *adj* : hermético — **waterway** ['wɔt̬ər,weɪ, 'wɑ-] *n* : vía *f* navegable — **waterworks** ['wɔt̬ər,wərks, 'wɑ-] *npl* : central *f* de abastecimiento de agua — **watery** ['wɔt̬əri, 'wɑ-] *adj* **1** : acuoso **2** DILUTED : aguado, diluido **3** WASHED-OUT : desvaído (dícese de colores)

watt ['wɑt] *n* : vatio *m* — **wattage** ['wɑt̬ɪdʒ] *n* : vataje *m*

wave ['weɪv] *v* **waved; waving** *vi* **1** : saludar con la mano **2** : flotar (dícese de una bandera) — *vt* **1** SHAKE : agitar **2** CURL : ondular **3** SIGNAL : hacer señas a (con la mano) — **~** *n* **1** : ola *f* (de agua) **2** CURL : onda *f* **3** : onda *f* (en física) **4** : señal *f* (con la mano) **5** SURGE : oleada *f* — **wavelength** ['weɪv,lɛŋkθ] *n* : longitud *f* de onda

waver ['weɪvər] *vi* : vacilar

wax[1] ['wæks] *vi* : crecer (dícese de la luna)

wax[2] *n* : cera *f* (para pisos, etc.) — **~** *vt* : encerar — **waxy** ['wæksi] *adj* **waxier; -est** : ceroso

way ['weɪ] *n* **1** : camino *m* **2** MEANS : manera *f*, modo *m* **3 by the ~** : a propósito, por cierto **4 by ~ of** : vía, pasando por **5 come a long ~** : hacer grandes progresos **6 get in the ~** : meterse en el camino **7 get one's own ~** : salirse uno con la suya **8 mend one's ~s** : dejar las malas costumbres **9 out of the ~** REMOTE : remoto, recóndito **10 which ~ did he go?** : ¿por dónde fue?

we ['wi:] *pron* : nosotros, nosotras

weak ['wi:k] *adj* **1** : débil **2** DILUTED : aguado **3 a ~ excuse** : una excusa poco convincente — **weaken** ['wi:kən] *vt* : debilitar — *vi* : debilitarse — **weakling** ['wi:klɪŋ] *n* : debilucho *m*, -cha *f* — **weakly** ['wi:kli] *adv* : débilmente — **~** *adj* **weaklier; -est** : enfermizo — **weakness** ['wi:knəs] *n* **1** : debilidad *f* **2** FLAW : flaqueza *f*, punto *m* débil

wealth ['wɛlθ] *n* : riqueza *f* — **wealthy** ['wɛlθi] *adj* **wealthier; -est** : rico

wean ['wi:n] *vt* : destetar

weapon ['wɛpən] *n* : arma *f*

wear ['wær] *v* **wore** ['wor]; **worn** ['worn]; **wearing** *vt* **1** : llevar (ropa, etc.), calzar (zapatos) **2** *or* **~ away** : desgastar **3 ~ oneself out** : agotarse **4 ~ out** : gastar — *vi* **1** LAST : durar **2 ~ off** : desaparecer **3 ~ out** : gastarse — **~** *n* **1** USE : uso *m* **2** CLOTHING : ropa *f* **3 be the worse for ~** : estar deteriorado — **wear and tear** *n* : desgaste *m*

weary ['wɪri] *adj* **-rier; -est** : cansado — **~** *v* **-ried; -rying** *vt* : cansar — *vi* : cansarse — **weariness** ['wɪrinəs] *n* : cansancio *m* — **wearisome** ['wɪrisəm] *adj* : cansado

weasel ['wi:zəl] *n* : comadreja *f*

weather ['wɛðər] *n* : tiempo *m* — **~** *vt* **1** WEAR : erosionar, desgastar **2** ENDURE, OVERCOME : superar — **weather-beaten** ['wɛðər,bi:tən] *adj* : curtido — **weatherman** ['wɛðər,mæn] *n, pl* **-men** [-mən, -,mɛn] : meteorólogo *m*, -ga *f* — **weather vane** *n* : valeta *f*

weave ['wi:v] *v* **wove** ['wo:v] *or* **weaved; woven** ['wo:vən] *or* **weaved; weaving** *vt* **1** : tejer (tela) **2** INTERLACE : entretejer **3 ~ one's way** : abrirse camino — *vi* : tejer — **~** *n* : tejido *m* — **weaver** ['wi:vər] *n* : tejedor *m*, -dora *f*

web ['wɛb] *n* **1** : telaraña *f* (de araña) **2** : membrana *f* interdigital (de aves) **3** NETWORK : red *f*

wed ['wɛd] *v* **wedded; wedding** *vt* : casarse con — *vi* : casarse

we'd ['wi:d] (*contraction of* **we had, we should,** *or* **we would**) → **have, should, would**

wedding ['wɛdɪŋ] *n* : boda *f*, casamiento *m*

wedge ['wɛdʒ] *n* **1** : cuña *f* **2** PIECE : porción *f*, trozo *m* — **~** *vt* **wedged; wedging 1** : apretar (con una cuña) **2** CRAM : meter

Wednesday ['wɛnz,deɪ, -di] *n* : miércoles *m*

wee ['wi:] *adj* **1** : pequeñito **2 in the ~ hours** : a las altas horas

weed ['wi:d] *n* : mala hierba *f* — **~** *vt* **1** : desherbar **2 ~ out** : eliminar

week ['wi:k] *n* : semana *f* — **weekday** ['wi:k,deɪ] *n* : día *m* laborable — **weekend** ['wi:k,ɛnd] *n* : fin *m* de semana — **weekly** ['wi:kli] *adv* : semanalmente — ~ *adj* : semanal — ~ *n, pl* **-lies** : semanario *m*

weep ['wi:p] *v* **wept** ['wɛpt]; **weeping** : llorar — **weeping willow** *n* : sauce *m* llorón — **weepy** ['wi:pi] *adj* **weepier; -est** : lloroso

weigh ['weɪ] *vt* **1** : pesar **2** CONSIDER : sopesar **3** ~ **down** : sobrecargar (con una carga), abrumar (con preocupaciones, etc.) — *vi* : pesar

weight ['weɪt] *n* **1** : peso *m* **2 gain** ~ : engordar **3 lose** ~ : adelgazar — **weighty** ['weɪţi] *adj* **weightier; -est 1** HEAVY : pesado **2** IMPORTANT : importante, de peso

weird ['wɪrd] *adj* **1** : misterioso **2** STRANGE : extraño

welcome ['wɛlkəm] *vt* **-comed; -coming** : dar la bienvenida a, recibir — ~ *adj* **1** : bienvenido **2 you're** ~ : de nada — ~ *n* : bienvenida *f*, acojida *f*

weld ['wɛld] *v* : soldar

welfare ['wɛl,fær] *n* **1** WELL-BEING : bienestar *m* **2** AID : asistencia *f* social

well[1] ['wɛl] *adv* **better** ['bɛţər]; **best** ['bɛst] **1** : bien **2** CONSIDERABLY : bastante **3 as** ~ : también **4 as** ~ **as** : además de — ~ *adj* : bien — ~ *interj* **1** (*used to introduce a remark*) : bueno **2** (*used to express surprise*) : ¡vaya!

well[2] *n* : pozo *m* — ~ *vi or* ~ **up** : brotar, manar

we'll ['wi:l, wɪl] (*contraction of* **we shall** *or* **we will**) → **shall, will**

well-being ['wɛl'bi:ɪŋ] *n* : bienestar *m* — **well-bred** ['wɛl'brɛd] *adj* : fino, bien educado — **well-done** ['wɛl'dʌn] *adj* **1** : bien hecho **2** : bien cocido (dícese de la carne, etc.) — **well-known** ['wɛl'no:n] *adj* : famoso, bien conocido — **well-meaning** ['wɛl'mi:nɪŋ] *adj* : bienintencionado — **well-off** ['wɛl'ɔf] *adj* : acomodado — **well-rounded** ['wɛl'raʊndəd] *adj* : completo — **well-to-do** [,wɛltə'du:] *adj* : próspero, adinerado

Welsh ['wɛlʃ] *adj* : galés — ~ *n* **1** : galés *m* (idioma) **2 the** ~ : los galeses

went → **go**

wept → **weep**

were → **be**

we're ['wɪr, 'wər, 'wi:ər] (*contraction of* **we are**) → **be**

weren't ['wərənt, 'wərnt] (*contraction of* **were not**) → **be**

west ['wɛst] *adv* : al oeste — ~ *adj* : oeste, del oeste — ~ *n* **1** : oeste *m* **2 the West** : el Oeste, el Occidente — **westerly** ['wɛstərli] *adv* & *adj* : del oeste — **western** ['wɛstərn] *adj* **1** : del oeste **2 Western** : occidental — **Westerner** ['wɛstərnər] *n* : habitante *mf* del oeste — **westward** ['wɛstwərd] *adv* & *adj* : hacia el oeste

wet ['wɛt] *adj* **wetter; wettest 1** : mojado **2** RAINY : lluvioso **3** ~ **paint** : pintura *f* fresca — ~ *vt* **wet** *or* **wetted; wetting** : mojar, humedecer

we've ['wi:v] (*contraction of* **we have**) → **have**

whack ['hwæk] *vt* : golpear fuertemente — ~ *n* : golpe *m* fuerte

whale ['hweɪl] *n, pl* **whales** *or* **whale** : ballena *f*

wharf ['hwɔrf] *n, pl* **wharves** ['hwɔrvz] : muelle *m*, embarcadero *m*

what ['hwɑt, 'hwʌt] *adj* **1** (*used in questions and exclamations*) : qué **2** WHATEVER : cualquier — ~ *pron* **1** (*used in questions*) : qué **2** (*used in indirect statements*) : lo que, que **3** ~ **does it cost?** : ¿cuánto cuesta? **4** ~ **for?** : ¿por qué? **5** ~ **if** : y si — **whatever** [hwɑţ'ɛvər, 'hwʌţ-] *adj* **1** : cualquier **2 there's no chance** ~ : no hay ninguna posibilidad **3 nothing** ~ : nada en absoluto — ~ *pron* **1** ANYTHING : lo que **2** (*used in questions*) : qué **3** ~ **it may be** : sea lo que sea — **whatsoever** [,hwɑtso'ɛvər, 'hwʌţ-] *adj* & *pron* → **whatever**

wheat ['hwi:t] *n* : trigo *m*

wheedle ['hwi:dəl] *vt* **-dled; -dling** : engatusar

wheel ['hwi:l] *n* **1** : rueda *f* **2** *or* **steering** ~ : volante *m* (de automóviles, etc.), timón *m* (de barcos) — ~ *vt* : empujar (algo sobre ruedas) — *vi or* ~ **around** : darse la vuelta — **wheelbarrow** ['hwi:l,bær,o:] *n* : carretilla *f* — **wheelchair** ['hwi:l,tʃær] *n* : silla *f* de ruedas

wheeze ['hwi:z] *vi* **wheezed; wheezing** : resollar — ~ *n* : resuello *m*

when ['hwɛn] *adv* : cuándo — ~ *conj* **1** : cuando **2 the days** ~ **I clean the house** : los días (en) que limpio la casa — ~ *pron* : cuándo — **whenever** [hwɛn'ɛvər] *adv* : cuando sea — ~ *conj* **1** : cada vez que **2** ~ **you like** : cuando quieras

where ['hwɛr] *adv* **1** : dónde **2** ~ **are you going?** : ¿adónde vas? — ~ *conj*

& pron : donde — **whereabouts** [ˈhwɛrəˌbauts] *adv* : (por) dónde — ~ *ns & pl* : paradero *m* — **wherever** [hwɛrˈɛvər] *adv* **1** : en cualquier parte **2** WHERE : dónde, adónde — ~ *conj* : dondequiera que

whet [ˈhwɛt] *vt* **whetted; whetting 1** : afilar **2** ~ **the appetite** : estimular el apetito

whether [ˈhwɛðər] *conj* **1** : si **2 we doubt** ~ **he'll show up** : dudamos que aparezca **3** ~ **you like it or not** : tanto si quieras como si no

which [ˈhwɪtʃ] *adj* **1** : qué, cuál **2 in** ~ **case** : en cuyo caso — ~ *pron* **1** (*used in questions*) : cuál **2** (*used in relative clauses*) : que, el (la) cual — **whichever** [hwɪtʃˈɛvər] *adj* : cualquier — ~ *pron* : el (la) que, cualquiera que

whiff [ˈhwɪf] *n* **1** PUFF : soplo *m* **2** SMELL : olorcillo *m*

while [ˈhwaɪl] *n* **1** : rato *m* **2 be worth one's** ~ : valer la pena **3 in a** ~ : dentro de poco — ~ *conj* **1** : mientras **2** WHEREAS : mientras que **3** ALTHOUGH : aunque — ~ *vt* **whiled; whiling** ~ **away the time** : matar el tiempo

whim [ˈhwɪm] *n* : capricho *m*, antojo *m*

whimper [ˈhwɪmpər] *vi* : lloriquear— ~ *n* : quejido *m*

whimsical [ˈhwɪmzɪkəl] *adj* : caprichoso, fantasioso

whine [ˈhwaɪn] *vi* **whined; whining 1** : gimotear **2** COMPLAIN : quejarse — ~ *n* : quejido *m*, gemido *m*

whip [ˈhwɪp] *v* **whipped; whipping** *vt* **1** : azotar **2** BEAT : batir (huevos, crema, etc.) **3** ~ **up** AROUSE : avivar, despertar — *vi* FLAP : agitarse — ~ *n* : látigo *m*

whir [ˈhwər] *vi* **whirred; whirring** : zumbar — ~ *n* : zumbido *m*

whirl [ˈhwərl] *vi* **1** : dar vueltas, girar **2** *or* ~ **about** : arremolinarse — ~ *n* **1** : giro *m* **2** SWIRL : torbellino *m* — **whirlpool** [ˈhwərlˌpuːl] *n* : remolino *m* — **whirlwind** [ˈhwərlˌwɪnd] *n* : torbellino *m*

whisk [ˈhwɪsk] *vt* **1** : batir **2** ~ **away** : llevarse — ~ *n or* **egg** ~ : batidor *m* — **whisk broom** *n* : escobilla *f*

whisker [ˈhwɪskər] *n* **1** : pelo *m* (de la barba) **2** ~**s** *npl* : bigotes *mpl* (de animales)

whiskey *or* **whisky** [ˈhwɪski] *n, pl* **-keys** *or* **-kies** : whisky *m*

whisper [ˈhwɪspər] *vi* : cuchichear, susurrar — *vt* : susurrar — ~ *n* : susurro *m*

whistle [ˈhwɪsəl] *v* **-tled; -tling** *vi* **1** : silbar, chiflar *Lat* **2** : pitar (dícese de un tren, etc.) — *vt* : silbar — ~ *n* **1** : silbido *m*, chiflido *m* (sonido) **2** : silbato *m*, pito *m* (instrumento)

white [ˈhwaɪt] *adj* **whiter; -est** : blanco — ~ *n* **1** : blanco *m* (color) **2** : clara *f* (de huevos) **3** *or* ~ **person** : blanco *m*, -ca *f* — **white-collar** [ˈhwaɪtˈkɑlər] *adj* **1** : de oficina **2** ~ **worker** : oficinista *mf* — **whiten** [ˈhwaɪtən] *vt* : blanquear — **whiteness** [ˈhwaɪtnəs] *n* : blancura *f* — **whitewash** [ˈhwaɪtˌwɔʃ] *vt* **1** : enjalbegar **2** CONCEAL : encubrir (un escándalo, etc.) — ~ *n* **1** : jalbegue *m*, lechada *f* **2** COVER-UP : encubrimiento *m*

whittle [ˈhwɪtəl] *vt* **-tled; -tling 1** : tallar (madera) **2** *or* ~ **down** : reducir

whiz *or* **whizz** [ˈhwɪz] *vi* **whizzed; whizzing 1** BUZZ : zumbar **2** ~ **by** : pasar muy rápido — ~ *or* **whizz** *n, pl* **whizzes** : zumbido *m* — **whiz kid** *n* : joven *m* prometedor

who [ˈhuː] *pron* **1** (*used in direct and indirect questions*) : quién **2** (*used in relative clauses*) : que, quien — **whodunit** [huːˈdʌnɪt] *n* : novela *f* policíaca — **whoever** [huːˈɛvər] *pron* **1** : quienquiera que, quien **2** (*used in questions*) : quién

whole [ˈhoːl] *adj* **1** : entero **2** INTACT : intacto **3 a** ~ **lot** : muchísimo — ~ *n* **1** : todo *m* **2 as a** ~ : en conjunto **3 on the** ~ : en general — **wholehearted** [ˈhoːlˈhɑrtəd] *adj* : sincero — **wholesale** [ˈhoːlˌseɪl] *n* : venta *f* al por mayor — ~ *adj* **1** : al por mayor **2** ~ **slaughter** : matanza *f* sistématica — ~ *adv* : al por mayor — **wholesaler** [ˈhoːlˌseɪlər] *n* : mayorista *mf* — **wholesome** [ˈhoːlsəm] *adj* : sano — **whole wheat** *adj* : de trigo integral — **wholly** [ˈhoːli] *adv* : completamente

whom [ˈhuːm] *pron* **1** (*used in direct questions*) : a quién **2** (*used in indirect questions*) : de quién, con quién, en quién **3** (*used in relative clauses*) : que, a quien

whooping cough *n* : tos *f* ferina

whore [ˈhor] *n* : puta *f*

whose [ˈhuːz] *adj* **1** (*used in questions*) : de quién **2** (*used in relative clauses*) : cuyo — ~ *pron* : de quién

why [ˈhwaɪ] *adv* : por qué — ~ *n, pl* **whys** : porqué *m* — ~ *conj* : por qué — ~ *interj* (*used to express surprise*) : ¡vaya!, ¡mira!

wick [ˈwɪk] *n* : mecha *f*

wicked [ˈwɪkəd] *adj* **1** : malo, malvado **2**

MISCHIEVOUS : travieso **3** TERRIBLE : terrible, horrible — **wickedness** ['wɪkədnəs] *n* : maldad *f*

wicker ['wɪkər] *n* : mimbre *m* — ~ *adj* : de mimbre

wide ['waɪd] *adj* **wider; widest 1** : ancho **2** VAST : amplio, extenso **3** *or* **~ of the mark** : desviado — ~ *adv* **1 ~ apart** : muy separados **2 far and ~** : por todas partes **3 ~ open** : abierto de par en par — **wide–awake** ['waɪdə'weɪk] *adj* : (completamente) despierto — **widely** ['waɪdli] *adv* : extensivamente — **widespread** ['waɪd'sprɛd] *adj* : extendido

widow ['wɪˌdo:] *n* : viuda *f* — ~ *vt* : dejar viuda — **widower** ['wɪdowər] *n* : viudo *m*

width ['wɪdθ] *n* : ancho *m*, anchura *f*

wield ['wi:ld] *vt* **1** : usar, manejar **2** EXERT : ejercer

wiener ['wi:nər] → **frankfurter**

wife ['waɪf] *n, pl* **wives** ['waɪvz] : esposa *f*, mujer *f*

wig ['wɪg] *n* : peluca *f*

wiggle ['wɪgəl] *v* **-gled; -gling** *vt* : menear, contonear — *vi* : menearse — ~ *n* : meneo *m*

wigwam ['wɪgˌwɑm] *n* : wigwam *m*

wild ['waɪld] *adj* **1** : salvaje **2** DESOLATE : agreste **3** UNRULY : desenfrenado **4** RANDOM : al azar **5** FRANTIC : frenético **6** OUTRAGEOUS : extravagante — ~ *adv* **1** → **wildly 2 run ~** : volver al estado silvestre (dícese de las plantas), desmandarse (dícese de los niños) — **wildcat** ['waɪldˌkæt] *n* : gato *m* montés — **wilderness** ['wɪldərnəs] *n* : yermo *m*, desierto *m* — **wildfire** ['waɪldˌfaɪr] *n* **1** : fuego *m* descontrolado **2 spread like ~** : propagarse como un reguero de pólvora — **wildflower** ['waɪldˌflaʊər] *n* : flor *f* silvestre — **wildlife** ['waɪldˌlaɪf] *n* : fauna *f* — **wildly** ['waɪldli] *adv* **1** FRANTICALLY : frenéticamente **2** EXTREMELY : locamente

will[1] ['wɪl] *v past* **would** ['wʊd]; *pres sing & pl* **will** *vi* WISH : querer — *v aux* **1 tomorrow we ~ go shopping** : mañana iremos de compras **2 he ~ get angry over nothing** : se pone furioso por cualquier cosa **3 I ~ go despite them** : iré a pesar de ellos **4 I won't do it** : no lo haré **5 that ~ be the mailman** : eso ha de ser el cartero **6 the couch ~ hold three people** : en el sofá cabrán tres personas **7 accidents ~ happen** : los accidentes ocurrirán **8 you ~ do as I say** : harás lo que digo

will[2] *n* **1** : voluntad *f* **2** TESTAMENT : testamento *m* **3 free ~** : libre albedrío *m* — **willful** *or* **wilful** ['wɪlfəl] *adj* **1** OBSTINATE : terco **2** INTENTIONAL : intencionado — **willing** ['wɪlɪŋ] *adj* **1** : complaciente **2 be ~ to** : estar dispuesto a — **willingly** ['wɪlɪŋli] *adv* : con gusto — **willingness** ['wɪlɪŋnəs] *n* : buena voluntad *f*

willow ['wɪˌlo:] *n* : sauce *m*

willpower ['wɪlˌpaʊər] *n* : fuerza *f* de voluntad

wilt ['wɪlt] *vi* : marchitarse

wily ['waɪli] *adj* **wilier; -est** : artero, astuto

win ['wɪn] *v* **won** ['wʌn]; **winning** *vi* : ganar — *vt* **1** : ganar, conseguir **2 ~ over** : ganarse a — ~ *n* : triunfo *m*, victoria *f*

wince ['wɪnts] *vi* **winced; wincing** : hacer una mueca de dolor — ~ *n* : mueca *f* de dolor

winch ['wɪntʃ] *n* : torno *m*

wind[1] ['wɪnd] *n* **1** : viento *m* **2** BREATH : aliento *m* **3** FLATULENCE : flatulencia *f* **4 get ~ of** : enterarse de

wind[2] ['waɪnd] *v* **wound** ['waʊnd]; **winding** *vi* : serpentear — *vt* **1** COIL : enrollar **2 ~ a clock** : dar cuerda a un reloj

windfall ['wɪndˌfɔl] *n* : beneficio *m* imprevisto

winding ['waɪndɪŋ] *adj* : tortuoso

wind instrument *n* : instrumento *m* de viento

windmill ['wɪndˌmɪl] *n* : molino *m* de viento

window ['wɪnˌdo:] *n* : ventana *f* (de un edificio o una computadora), ventanilla *f* (de un vehículo), vitrina *f* (de una tienda) — **windowpane** ['wɪnˌdo:ˌpeɪn] *n* : vidrio *m* — **windowsill** ['wɪnˌdo:ˌsɪl] *n* : repisa *f* de la ventana

windpipe ['wɪndˌpaɪp] *n* : tráquea *f*

windshield ['wɪndˌʃi:ld] *n* **1** : parabrisas *m* **2 ~ wiper** : limpiaparabrisas *m*

window–shop ['wɪndoˌʃɑp] *vi* **-shopped; -shopping** : mirar las vitrinas

wind up ['waɪndˌʌp] *vt* : terminar, concluir — *vi* : terminar, acabar — **windup** *n* : conclusión *f*

windy ['wɪndi] *adj* **windier; -est 1** : ventoso **2 it's ~** : hace viento

wine ['waɪn] *n* : vino *m* — **wine cellar** *n* : bodega *f*

wing ['wɪŋ] *n* **1** : ala *f* **2 under s.o.'s ~** : bajo el cargo de algn — **winged** ['wɪŋd, 'wɪŋəd] *adj* : alado

wink ['wɪŋk] *vi* : guiñar — ~ *n* **1** : guiño *m* **2 not sleep a ~** : no pegar el ojo

winner ['wɪnər] *n* : ganador *m*, -dora *f* —

winning ['wɪnɪŋ] *adj* **1** : ganador **2** CHARMING : encantador — **winnings** ['wɪnɪŋz] *npl* : ganancias *fpl*

winter ['wɪntər] *n* : invierno *m* — ~ *adj* : invernal, de invierno — **wintergreen** ['wɪntər,griːn] *n* : gaulteria *f* — **wintertime** ['wɪntər,taɪm] *n* : invierno *m* — **wintry** ['wɪntri] *adj* **wintrier; -est** : invernal, de invierno

wipe ['waɪp] *vt* **wiped; wiping 1** : limpiar **2** ~ **away** : enjugar (lágrimas), borrar (una memoria) **3** ~ **out** : aniquilar, destruir — ~ *n* : pasada *f* (con un trapo, etc.)

wire ['waɪr] *n* **1** : alambre *m* **2** : cable *m* (eléctrico o telefónico) **3** TELEGRAM : telegrama *m* — ~ *vt* **-wired; wiring 1** : instalar el cableado en (una casa, etc.) **2** BIND : atar con alambre **3** TELEGRAPH : enviar un telegrama a — **wireless** ['waɪrləs] *adj* : inalámbrico — **wiring** ['waɪrɪŋ] *n* : cableado *m* — **wiry** ['waɪri] *adj* **wirier; -est 1** : hirsuto, tieso (dícese del pelo) **2** : esbelto y musculoso (dícese del cuerpo)

wisdom ['wɪzdəm] *n* : sabiduría *f* — **wisdom tooth** *n* : muela *f* de juicio

wise ['waɪz] *adj* **wiser; wisest 1** : sabio **2** SENSIBLE : prudente — **wisecrack** ['waɪz,kræk] *n* : broma *f*, chiste *m* — **wisely** ['waɪzli] *adv* : sabiamente

wish ['wɪʃ] *vt* **1** : desear **2** ~ **s.o. well** : desear lo mejor a algn — *vi* **1** : pedir (como deseo) **2 as you** ~ : como quieras — ~ *n* **1** : deseo *m* **2 best** ~**es** : muchos recuerdos — **wishbone** ['wɪʃ,boːn] *n* : espoleta *f* — **wishful** ['wɪʃfəl] *adj* **1** : deseoso **2** ~ **thinking** : ilusiones *fpl*

wishy–washy ['wɪʃi,wɔʃi, -,wɑʃi] *adj* : insípido, soso

wisp ['wɪsp] *n* **1** : mechón *m* (de pelo) **2** : voluta *f* (de humo)

wistful ['wɪstfəl] *adj* : melancólico

wit ['wɪt] *n* **1** CLEVERNESS : ingenio *m* **2** HUMOR : agudeza *f* **3 at one's** ~**'s end** : desesperado **4 scared out of one's** ~**s** : muerto de miedo

witch ['wɪtʃ] *n* : bruja *f* — **witchcraft** ['wɪtʃ,kræft] *n* : brujería *f*, hechicería *f*

with ['wɪð, 'wɪθ] *prep* **1** : con **2 I'm going** ~ **you** : voy contigo **3 it varies** ~ **the season** : varía según la estación **4 the girl** ~ **red hair** : la muchacha de pelo rojo **5** ~ **all his work, the business failed** : a pesar de su trabajo, el negocio fracasó

withdraw [wɪð'drɔ, wɪθ-] *v* **-drew** [-'druː]; **-drawn** [-'drɔn]; **-drawing** *vt* : retirar — *vi* : apartarse — **withdrawal** [wɪð'drɔəl, wɪθ-] *n* **1** : retirada *f* **2** : abandono (de drogas, etc.) — **withdrawn** [wɪð'drɔn, wɪθ-] *adj* : introvertido

wither ['wɪðər] *vi* : marchitarse

withhold [wɪθ'hoːld, wɪð-] *vt* **-held** [-'hɛld]; **-holding** : retener (fondos), negar (permiso, etc.)

within [wɪð'ɪn, wɪθ-] *adv* : dentro — ~ *prep* **1** : dentro de **2** (*in expressions of distance*) : a menos de **3** (*in expressions of time*) : dentro de, en menos de **4** ~ **reach** : al alcance de la mano

without [wɪð'aut, wɪθ-] *adv* **do** ~ : pasar sin algo — ~ *prep* : sin

withstand [wɪθ'stænd, wɪð-] *vt* **-stood** [-'stʊd]; **-standing 1** BEAR : aguantar **2** RESIST : resistir

witness ['wɪtnəs] *n* **1** : testigo *mf* **2** EVIDENCE : testimonio *m* **3 bear** ~ : atestiguar — ~ *vt* **1** SEE : ser testigo de **2** : atestiguar (una firma, etc.)

witticism ['wɪt̬ə,sɪzəm] *n* : agudeza *f*, ocurrencia *f*

witty ['wɪt̬i] *adj* **-tier; -est** : ingenioso, ocurrente

wives → **wife**

wizard ['wɪzərd] *n* **1** : mago *m*, brujo *m* **2 a math** ~ : un genio de matemáticas

wizened ['wɪzənd, 'wiː-] *adj* : arrugado

wobble ['wɑbəl] *vi* **-bled; -bling 1** : tambalearse **2** : temblar (dícese de la voz, etc.) — **wobbly** ['wɑbəli] *adj* : cojo

woe ['woː] *n* **1** : aflicción *f* **2** ~**s** *npl* TROUBLES : penas *fpl* — **woeful** ['woːfəl] *adj* : triste

woke, woken → **wake**

wolf ['wʊlf] *n, pl* **wolves** ['wʊlvz] : lobo *m*, -ba *f* — ~ *vt or* ~ **down** : engullir

woman ['wʊmən] *n, pl* **women** ['wɪmən] : mujer *f* — **womanly** ['wʊmənli] *adj* : femenino

womb ['wuːm] *n* : útero *m*, matriz *f*

won → **win**

wonder ['wʌndər] *n* **1** MARVEL : maravilla *f* **2** AMAZEMENT : asombro *m* — ~ *v* : preguntarse — **wonderful** ['wʌndərfəl] *adj* : maravilloso, estupendo

won't ['woːnt] (*contraction of* **will not**) → **will**

woo ['wuː] *vt* **1** COURT : cortejar **2** : buscar el apoyo de (clientes, votantes, etc.)

wood ['wʊd] *n* **1** : madera *f* (materia) **2** FIREWOOD : leña *f* **3** *or* ~**s** *npl* FOREST : bosque *m* — ~ *adj* : de madera — **woodchuck** ['wʊd,tʃʌk] *n* : marmota *f* de América — **wooded** ['wʊdəd] *adj* : arbolado, boscoso — **wooden**

['wʊdən] *adj* : de madera — **woodpecker** ['wʊd,pɛkər] *n* : pájaro *m* carpintero — **woodshed** ['wʊd,ʃɛd] *n* : leñera *f* — **woodwind** ['wʊd,wɪnd] *n* : instrumento *m* de viento de madera — **woodwork** ['wʊd,wərk] *n* : carpintería *f*

wool ['wʊl] *n* : lana *f* — **woolen** *or* **woollen** ['wʊlən] *adj* : de lana — ~ *n* **1** : lana *f* (tela) **2** ~**s** *npl* : prendas *fpl* de lana — **woolly** ['wʊli] *adj* **-lier; -est** : lanudo

word ['wərd] *n* **1** : palabra *f* **2** NEWS : noticias *fpl* **3** ~**s** *npl* : letra *f* (de una canción, etc.) **4 have** ~**s with** : reñir con **5 just say the** ~ : no tienes que decirlo **6 keep one's** ~ : cumplir su palabra — ~ *vt* : expresar — **word processing** *n* : procesamiento *m* de textos — **word processor** *n* : procesador *m* de textos — **wordy** ['wərdi] *adj* **wordier; -est** : prolijo

wore → **wear**

work ['wərk] *n* **1** LABOR : trabajo *m* **2** EMPLOYMENT : trabajo *m*, empleo *m* **3** : obra *f* (de arte, etc.) **4** ~**s** *npl* FACTORY : fábrica *f* **5** ~**s** *npl* MECHANISM : mecanismo *m* — ~ *v* **worked** ['wərkt] *or* **wrought** ['rɔt]; **working** *vt* **1** : hacer trabajar (a una persona) **2** : manejar, operar (una máquina, etc.) — *vi* **1** : trabajar **2** FUNCTION : funcionar **3** : surtir efecto (dícese de una droga), resultar (dícese de una idea, etc.) — **worked up** *adj* : nervioso — **worker** ['wərkər] *n* : trabajador *m*, -dora *f*; obrero *m*, -ra *f* — **working** ['wərkɪŋ] *adj* **1** : que trabaja (dícese de personas), de trabajo (dícese de la ropa, etc.) **2 be in** ~ **order** : funcionar bien — **working class** *n* : clase *f* obrera — **workingman** ['wərkɪŋ,mæn] *n, pl* **-men** [-mən, -,mɛn] : obrero *m* — **workman** ['wərkmən] *n, pl* **-men** [-mən, -,mɛn] **1** : obrero *m* **2** ARTISAN : artesano *m* — **workmanship** ['wərkmən,ʃɪp] *n* : artesanía *f*, destreza *f* — **workout** ['wərk,aʊt] *n* : ejercicios *mpl* (físicos) — **work out** *vt* **1** DEVELOP : elaborar **2** SOLVE : resolver — *vi* **1** TURN OUT : resultar **2** SUCCEED : lograr, salir bien **3** EXERCISE : hacer ejercicio — **workshop** ['wərk,ʃɑp] *n* : taller *m* — **work up** *vt* **1** EXCITE : ponerse como loco **2** GENERATE : desarrollar

world ['wərld] *n* : mundo *m* **2 think the** ~ **of s.o.** : tener a algn en alta estima — ~ *adj* : mundial, del mundo — **worldly** ['wərldli] *adj* : mundano — **worldwide** ['wərld'waɪd] *adv* : en todo el mundo — ~ *adj* : global, mundial

worm ['wərm] *n* **1** : gusano *m*, lombriz *f* **2** ~**s** *npl* : lombrices *fpl* (parásitos)

worn → **wear** — **worn–out** ['worn'aʊt] *adj* **1** USED : gastado **2** TIRED : agotado

worry ['wəri] *v* **-ried; -rying** *vt* : preocupar, inquietar — *vi* : preocuparse, inquietarse — ~ *n, pl* **-ries** : preocupación *f* — **worried** ['wərid] *adj* : preocupado — **worrisome** ['wərisəm] *adj* : inquietante

worse ['wərs] *adv* (*comparative of* **bad** *or of* **ill**) : peor — ~ *adj* (*comparative of* **bad** *or of* **ill**) **1** : peor **2 from bad to** ~ : de mal en peor **3 get** ~ : empeorar — ~ *n* **1 the** ~ : el (la) peor, lo peor **2 take a turn for the** ~ : ponerse peor — **worsen** ['wərsən] *v* : empeorar

worship ['wərʃəp] *v* **-shiped** *or* **-shipped; -shiping** *or* **-shipping** *vt* : adorar — *vi* : practicar una religión — ~ *n* : adoración *f*, culto *m* — **worshiper** *or* **worshipper** ['wərʃəpər] *n* : adorador *m*, -dora *f*

worst ['wərst] *adv* (*superlative of* **ill** *or of* **bad** *or* **badly**) : peor — ~ *adj* (*superlative of* **bad** *or of* **ill**) : peor — ~ *n* **the** ~ : lo peor, el (la) peor

worth ['wərθ] *n* **1** : valor *m* (monetario) **2** MERIT : mérito *m*, valía *f* **3 ten dollars'** ~ **of gas** : diez dólares de gasolina — ~ *prep* **1 it's** ~ **$ 10** : vale $ 10 **2 it's** ~ **doing** : vale la pena hacerlo — **worthless** ['wərθləs] *adj* **1** : sin valor **2** USELESS : inútil — **worthwhile** [wərθ'*h*waɪl] *adj* : que vale la pena — **worthy** ['wərði] *adj* **-thier; -est** : digno

would ['wʊd] *past of* **will 1 he** ~ **often take his children to the park** : solía llevar a sus hijos al parque **2 I** ~ **go if I had the money** : iría yo si tuviera el dinero **3 I** ~ **rather go alone** : preferiría ir sola **4 she** ~ **have won if she hadn't tripped** : habría ganado si no hubiera tropezado **5** ~ **you kindly help me with this?** : ¿tendría la bondad de ayudarme con esto? — **would–be** ['wʊd'bi:] *adj* **a** ~ **poet** : un aspirante a poeta — **wouldn't** ['wʊdənt] (*contraction of* **would not**) → **would**

wound[1] ['wu:nd] *n* : herida *f* — ~ *vt* : herir

wound[2] ['waʊnd] → **wind**

wove, woven → **weave**

wrangle ['ræŋgəl] *vi* **-gled; -gling** : reñir — ~ *n* : riña *f*, disputa *f*

wrap ['ræp] *vt* **wrapped; wrapping 1** : envolver **2 ~ up** FINISH : dar fin a — **~** *n* **1** : prenda *f* que envuelve (como un chal) **2** WRAPPER : envoltura *f* — **wrapper** ['ræpər] *n* : envoltura *f*, envoltorio *m* — **wrapping** ['ræpɪŋ] *n* : envoltura *f*, envoltorio *m*

wrath ['ræθ] *n* : ira *f*, cólera *f* — **wrathful** ['ræθfəl] *adj* : iracundo

wreath ['ri:θ] *n, pl* **wreaths** ['ri:ðz, 'ri:θs] : corona *f* (de flores, etc.)

wreck ['rɛk] *n* **1** WRECKAGE : restos *mpl* **2** RUIN : ruina *f*, desastre *m* **3 be a nervous ~** : tener los nervios destrozados — **~** *vt* : destrozar (un automóvil), naufragar (un barco) — **wreckage** ['rɛkɪdʒ] *n* : restos *mpl* (de un buque naufragado, etc.), ruinas *fpl* (de un edificio)

wren ['rɛn] *n* : chochín *m*

wrench ['rɛntʃ] *vt* **1** PULL : arrancar (de un tirón) **2** SPRAIN, TWIST : torcerse — **~** *n* **1** TUG : tirón *m*, jalón *m* **2** SPRAIN : torcedura *f* **3** *or* **monkey ~** : llave *f* inglesa

wrestle ['rɛsəl] *vi* **-tled; -tling** : luchar — **wrestler** ['rɛsələr] *n* : luchador *m*, -dora *f* — **wrestling** ['rɛsəlɪŋ] *n* : lucha *f*

wretch ['rɛtʃ] *n* : desgraciado *m*, -da *f* — **wretched** ['rɛtʃəd] *adj* **1** : miserable **2 ~ weather** : tiempo *m* espantoso

wriggle ['rɪgəl] *vi* **-gled; -gling** : retorcerse, menearse

wring ['rɪŋ] *vt* **wrung** ['rʌŋ]; **wringing 1** *or* **~ out** : escurrir (el lavado, etc.) **2** TWIST : retorcer **3** EXTRACT : arrancar (información, etc.)

wrinkle ['rɪŋkəl] *n* : arruga *f* — **~** *v* **-kled; -kling** *vt* : arrugar — *vi* : arrugarse

wrist ['rɪst] *n* : muñeca *f* — **wristwatch** ['rɪst,wɑtʃ] *n* : reloj *m* de pulsera

writ ['rɪt] *n* : orden *f* (judicial)

write ['raɪt] *v* **wrote** ['ro:t]; **written** ['rɪtən]; **writing** : escribir — **write down** *vt* : apuntar, anotar — **write off** *vt* CANCEL : cancelar — **writer** ['raɪt̬ər] *n* : escritor *m*, -tora *f*

writhe ['raɪð] *vi* **writhed; writhing** : retorcerse

writing ['raɪt̬ɪŋ] *n* : escritura *f*

wrong ['rɔŋ] *n* **1** INJUSTICE : injusticia *f*, mal *m* **2** : agravio *m* (en derecho) **3 be in the ~** : haber hecho mal — **~** *adj* **wronger** ['rɔŋər]; **wrongest** ['rɔŋəst] **1** : malo **2** UNSUITABLE : inadecuado, inapropiado **3** INCORRECT : incorrecto, equivocado **4 be ~** : no tener razón — **~** *adv* : mal, incorrectamente — **~** *vt* **wronged; wronging** : ofender, ser injusto con — **wrongful** ['rɔŋfəl] *adj* **1** UNJUST : injusto **2** UNLAWFUL : ilegal — **wrongly** ['rɔŋli] *adv* **1** UNJUSTLY : injustamente **2** INCORRECTLY : mal

wrote → **write**

wrought iron ['rɔt] *n* : hierro *m* forjado

wrung → **wring**

wry ['raɪ] *adj* **wrier** ['raɪər]; **wriest** ['raɪəst] : irónico, sardónico (dícese del humor)

XYZ

x *n, pl* **x's** *or* **xs** ['ɛksəz] : x *f*, vigésima cuarta letra del alfabeto inglés

xenophobia [,zɛnə'fo:biə, ,zi:-] *n* : xenofobia *f*

Xmas ['krɪsməs] *n* : Navidad *f*

X ray ['ɛks,reɪ] *n* **1** : rayo *m* X **2** *or* **~ photograph** : radiografía *f* — **x–ray** *vt* : radiografiar

xylophone ['zaɪlə,fo:n] *n* : xilófono *m*

y ['waɪ] *n, pl* **y's** *or* **ys** ['waɪz] : y *f*, vigésima quinta letra del alfabeto inglés

yacht ['jɑt] *n* : yate *m*

yam ['jæm] *n* **1** : ñame *m* **2** SWEET POTATO : batata *f*, boniato *m*

yank ['jæŋk] *vt* : tirar de, jalar *Lat* — **~** *n* : tirón *m*, jalón *m* *Lat*

Yankee ['jæŋki] *n* : yanqui *mf*

yap ['jæp] *vi* **yapped; yapping** : ladrar — **~** *n* : ladrido *m*

yard ['jɑrd] *n* **1** : yarda *f* (medida) **2** COURTYARD : patio *m* **3** : jardín *m* (de una casa) — **yardstick** ['jɑrd,stɪk] *n* **1** : vara *f* (de medir) **2** CRITERION : criterio *m*

yarn ['jɑrn] *n* **1** : hilado *m* **2** TALE : historia *f*, cuento *m*

yawn ['jɔn] *vi* : bostezar — **~** *n* : bostezo *m*

year ['jɪr] *n* **1** : año *m* **2 she's ten ~s old** : tiene diez años **3 I haven't seen them in ~s** : hace siglos que no los veo — **yearbook** ['jɪr,bʊk] *n* : anuario *m* — **yearling** ['jɪrlɪŋ, 'jərlən] *n* : animal *m* menor de dos años — **yearly** ['jɪrli] *adv* **1** : anualmente **2 three**

times ~ : tres veces al año — **~** *adj* : anual
yearn ['jərn] *vi* : anhelar — **yearning** ['jərnɪŋ] *n* : anhelo *m,* ansia *f*
yeast ['ji:st] *n* : levadura *f*
yell ['jɛl] *vi* : gritar, chillar — *vt* : gritar — **~** *n* : grito *m,* chillido *m*
yellow ['jɛlo] *adj* : amarillo — **~** *n* : amarillo *m* — **yellowish** ['jɛloɪʃ] *adj* : amarillento
yelp ['jɛlp] *n* : gañido *m* — **~** *vi* : dar un gañido
yes ['jɛs] *adv* **1** : sí **2 say ~** : decir que sí — **~** *n* : sí *m*
yesterday ['jɛstər,deɪ, -di] *adv* : ayer — **~** *n* **1** : ayer *m* **2 the day before ~** : anteayer
yet ['jɛt] *adv* **1** : aún, todavía **2 has he come ~?** : ¿ya ha venido? **3 not ~** : todavía no **4 ~ more problems** : más problemas aún **5** NEVERTHELESS : sin embargo — **~** *conj* : pero
yield ['ji:ld] *vt* **1** PRODUCE : producir **2 ~ the right of way** : ceder el paso — *vi* : ceder — **~** *n* : rendimiento *m,* rédito *m* (en finanzas)
yoga ['jo:gə] *n* : yoga *m*
yogurt ['jo:gərt] *n* : yogur *m,* yogurt *m*
yoke ['jo:k] *n* : yugo *m*
yolk ['jo:k] *n* : yema *f* (de un huevo)
you ['ju:] *pron* **1** (*used as subject—familiar*) : tú; vos (*in some Latin American countries*); ustedes *pl;* vosotros, vosotras *pl Spain* **2** (*used as subject—formal*) : usted, ustedes *pl* **3** (*used as indirect object—familiar*) : te, les *pl* (se *before lo, la, los, las*), os *pl Spain* **4** (*used as indirect object—formal*) : lo (*Spain sometimes* le), la; los (*Spain sometimes* les), las *pl* **5** (*used after a preposition—familiar*) : ti; vos (*in some Latin American countries*); ustedes *pl;* vosotros, vosotras *pl Spain* **6** (*used after a preposition—formal*) : usted, ustedes *pl* **7 with ~** (*familiar*) : contigo; con ustedes *pl;* con vosotros, con vosotras *pl Spain* **8 with ~** (*formal*) : con usted, con ustedes *pl* **9 ~ never know** : nunca se sabe — **you'd** ['ju:d, 'jʊd] (*contraction of* **you had** *or* **you would**) → **have, would** — **you'll** ['ju:l, 'jʊl] (*contraction of* **you shall** *or* **you will**) → **shall, will**
young ['jʌŋ] *adj* **younger** ['jʌŋgər]; **youngest** [-gəst] **1** : joven **2 my ~er brother** : mi hermano menor **3 she is the ~est** : es la más pequeña **4 the ~** : los jóvenes — **~** *npl* : jóvenes *mfpl* (de los humanos), crías *fpl* (de los animales) — **youngster** ['jʌŋkstər] *n* : chico *m,* -ca *f;* joven *mf*
your ['jʊr, 'jo:r, jər] *adj* **1** (*familiar singular*) : tu **2** (*familiar plural*) su, vuestro *Spain* **3** (*formal*) : su **4 on ~ left** : a la izquierda
you're ['jʊr, 'jo:r, 'jər, 'ju:ər] (*contraction of* **you are**) → **be**
yours ['jʊrz, 'jo:rz] *pron* **1** (*belonging to one person—familiar*) : (el) tuyo, (la) tuya, (los) tuyos, (las) tuyas **2** (*belonging to more than one person—familiar*) : (el) suyo, (la) suya, (los) suyos, (las) suyas; (el) vuestro, (la) vuestra, (los) vuestros, (las) vuestras *Spain* **3** (*formal*) : (el) suyo, (la) suya, (los) suyos, (las) suyas
yourself [jər'sɛlf] *pron, pl* **yourselves** [-'sɛlvz] **1** (*used reflexively—familiar*) : te, se *pl,* os *pl Spain* **2** (*used reflexively—formal*) : se **3** (*used for emphasis*) : tú mismo, tú misma; usted mismo, usted misma; ustedes mismos, ustedes mismas *pl;* vosotros mismos, vosotras mismas *pl Spain*
youth ['ju:θ] *n, pl* **youths** ['ju:ðz, 'ju:θs] **1** : juventud *f* **2** BOY : joven *m* **3 today's ~** : los jóvenes de hoy — **youthful** ['ju:θfəl] *adj* **1** : juvenil, de juventud **2** YOUNG : joven
you've ['ju:v] (*contraction of* **you have**) → **have**
yowl ['jaʊl] *vi* : aullar — **~** *n* : aullido *m*
yucca ['jʌkə] *n* : yuca *f*
Yugoslavian [ju:go'slɑviən] *adj* : yugoslavo
yule ['ju:l] *n* CHRISTMAS : Navidad *f* — **yuletide** ['ju:l,taɪd] *n* : Navidades *fpl*
z ['zi:] *n, pl* **z's** *or* **zs** : z *f,* vigésima sexta letra del alfabeto inglés
zany ['zeɪni] *adj* **-nier; -est** : alocado, disparatado
zeal ['zi:l] *n* : fervor *m,* celo *m* — **zealous** ['zɛləs] *adj* : entusiasta
zebra ['zi:brə] *n* : cebra *f*
zenith ['zi:nəθ] *n* **1** : cenit *m* (en astronomía) **2** PEAK : apogeo *m*
zero ['zi:ro, 'zɪro] *n, pl* **-ros** : cero *m*
zest ['zɛst] *n* **1** : gusto *m* **2** FLAVOR : sazón *f*
zigzag ['zɪg,zæg] *n* : zigzag *m* — **~** *vi* **-zagged; -zagging** : zigzaguear
zinc ['zɪŋk] *n* : cinc *m,* zinc *m*
zip ['zɪp] *v* **zipped; zipping** *vt or* **~ up** : cerrar la cremallera de, cerrar el cierre de *Lat* — *vi* SPEED : pasarse volando — **zip code** *n* : código *m* postal — **zipper** ['zɪpər] *n* : cremallera *f,* cierre *m Lat*

zodiac ['zo:di,æk] *n* : zodíaco *m*
zone ['zo:n] *n* : zona *f*
zoo ['zu:] *n, pl* **zoos** : zoológico *m,* zoo *m* — **zoology** [zo'ɑlədʒi, zu:-] *n* : zoología *f*
zoom ['zu:m] *vi* : zumbar, ir volando — ~ *n* **1** : zumbido *m* **2** *or* ~ **lens** : zoom *m*
zucchini [zu'ki:ni] *n, pl* **-ni** *or* **-nis** : calabacín *m,* calabacita *f Lat*

Common Spanish Abbreviations

SPANISH ABBREVIATION AND EXPANSION		ENGLISH EQUIVALENT	
abr.	abril	**Apr.**	April
A.C., a.C.	antes de Cristo	**BC**	before Christ
a. de J.C.	antes de Jesucristo	**BC**	before Christ
admon., admón.	administración	—	administration
a/f	a favor	—	in favor
ago.	agosto	**Aug.**	August
Apdo.	apartado (de correos)	—	P.O. box
aprox.	aproximadamente	**approx.**	approximately
Aptdo.	apartado (de correos)	—	P.O. box
Arq.	arquitecto	**arch.**	architect
A.T.	Antiguo Testamento	**O.T.**	Old Testament
atte.	atentamente	—	sincerely
atto., atta.	atento, atenta	—	kind, courteous
av., avda.	avenida	**ave.**	avenue
a/v.	a vista	—	on receipt
BID	Banco Interamericano de Desarrollo	**IDB**	Interamerican Development Bank
Bo	banco	—	bank
BM	Banco Mundial	—	World Bank
c/, C/	calle	**st.**	street
C	centígrado, Celsius	**C**	centigrade, Celsius
C.	compañía	**Co.**	company
CA	corriente alterna	**AC**	alternating current
cap.	capítulo	**ch., chap.**	chapter
c/c	cuenta corriente	—	current account, checking account
c.c.	centímetros cúbicos	**cu. cm**	cubic centimeters
CC	corriente continua	**DC**	direct current
c/d	con descuento	—	with discount
Cd.	ciudad	—	city
CE	Comunidad Europea	**EC**	European Community
CEE	Comunidad Económica Europea	**EEC**	European Economic Community
cf.	confróntese	**cf.**	compare
cg.	centígramo	**cg**	centigram
CGT	Confederación General de Trabajadores *o* del Trabajo	—	confederation of workers, workers' union
CI	coeficiente intelectual *o* de inteligencia	**IQ**	intelligence quotient
Cía.	compañía	**Co.**	company
cm.	centímetro	**cm**	centimeter
Cnel.	coronel	**Col.**	colonel
col.	columna	**col.**	column
Col. *Mex*	colonia	—	residential area
Com.	comandante	**Cmdr.**	commander
comp.	compárese	**comp.**	compare
Cor.	coronel	**Col.**	colonel
C.P.	código postal	—	zip code

SPANISH ABBREVIATION AND EXPANSION		ENGLISH EQUIVALENT	
CSF, c.s.f.	coste, seguro y flete	**c.i.f.**	cost, insurance, and freight
cta.	cuenta	**ac., acct.**	account
cte.	corriente	**cur.**	current
c/u	cada uno, cada una	**ea.**	each
CV	caballo de vapor	**hp**	horsepower
D.	Don	—	—
Da., D.ª	Doña	—	—
d.C.	después de Cristo	**AD**	anno Domini (in the year of our Lord)
dcha.	derecha	—	right
d. de J.C.	después de Jesucristo	**AD**	anno Domini (in the year of our lord)
dep.	departamento	**dept.**	department
DF, D.F.	Distrito Federal	—	Federal District
dic.	diciembre	**Dec.**	December
dir.	director, directora	**dir.**	director
dir.	dirección	—	address
Dña.	Doña	—	—
do.	domingo	**Sun.**	Sunday
dpto.	departamento	**dept.**	department
Dr.	doctor	**Dr.**	doctor
Dra.	doctora	**Dr.**	doctor
dto.	descuento	—	discount
E, E.	Este, este	**E**	East, east
Ed.	editorial	—	publishing house
Ed., ed.	edición	**ed.**	edition
edif.	edificio	**bldg.**	building
edo.	estado	**st.**	state
EEUU, EE.UU.	Estados Unidos	**US, U.S.**	United States
ej.	por ejemplo	**e.g.**	for example
E.M.	esclerosis multiple	**MS**	multiple sclerosis
ene.	enero	**Jan.**	January
etc.	etcétera	**etc.**	et cetera
ext.	extensión	**ext.**	extension
F	Fahrenheit	**F**	Fahrenheit
f.a.b.	franco a bordo	**f.o.b.**	free on board
FC	ferrocarril	**RR**	railroad
feb.	febrero	**Feb.**	February
FF AA, FF.AA.	Fuerzas Armadas	—	armed forces
FMI	Fondo Monetario Internacional	**IMF**	International Monetary Fund
g.	gramo	**g., gm, gr.**	gram
G.P.	giro postal	**M.O.**	money order
gr.	gramo	**g., gm, gr.**	gram
Gral.	general	**Gen.**	general
h.	hora	**hr.**	hour
Hnos.	hermanos	**Bros.**	brothers
I+D, I & D, I y D	investigación y desarrollo	**R & D**	research and development
i.e.	esto es, es decir	**i.e.**	that is
incl.	inclusive	**incl.**	inclusive, inclusively

SPANISH ABBREVIATION AND EXPANSION		ENGLISH EQUIVALENT	
Ing.	ingeniero, ingeniera	**eng.**	engineer
IPC	indice de precios al consumo	**CPI**	consumer price index
IVA	impuesto al valor agregado	**VAT**	value-added tax
izq.	izquierda	**l.**	left
juev.	jueves	**Thurs.**	Thursday
jul.	julio	**Jul.**	July
jun.	junio	**Jun.**	June
kg.	kilogramo	**kg**	kilogram
km.	kilómetro	**km**	kilometer
km/h	kilómetros por hora	**kph**	kilometers per hour
kv, kV	kilovatio	**kw, kW**	kilowatt
l.	litro	**l, lit.**	liter
Lic.	licenciado, licenciada	—	—
Ltda.	limitada	**Ltd.**	limited
lun.	lunes	**Mon.**	Monday
m	masculino	**m**	masculine
m	metro	**m**	meter
m	minuto	**m**	minute
mar.	marzo	**Mar.**	March
mart.	martes	**Tues.**	Tuesday
mg.	miligramo	**mg**	milligram
miérc.	miércoles	**Wed.**	Wednesday
min	minuto	**min.**	minute
mm.	milímetro	**mm**	millimeter
M-N, m/n	moneda nacional	—	national currency
Mons.	monseñor	**Msgr.**	monsignor
Mtra.	maestra	—	teacher
Mtro.	maestro	—	teacher
N, N.	Norte, norte	**N, no.**	North, north
n/o	nuestro	—	our
n.º	número	**no.**	number
N. de (la) R.	nota de (la) redacción	—	editor's note
NE	nordeste	**NE**	northeast
NN.UU.	Naciones Unidas	**UN**	United Nations
NO	noroeste	**NW**	northwest
nov.	noviembre	**Nov.**	November
N.T.	Nuevo Testamento	**N.T.**	New Testament
ntra., ntro.	nuestra, nuestro	—	our
NU	Naciones Unidas	**UN**	United Nations
núm.	número	**num.**	number
O, O.	Oeste, oeste	**W**	West, west
oct.	octubre	**Oct.**	October
OEA, O.E.A.	Organización de Estados Americanos	**OAS**	Organization of American States
OMS	Organización Mundial de la Salud	**WHO**	World Health Organization
ONG	organización no gubernamental	**NGO**	non-governmental organization
ONU	Organización de las Naciones Unidas	**UN**	United Nations
OTAN	Organización del Tratado del Atlántico Norte	**NATO**	North Atlantic Treaty Organization

SPANISH ABBREVIATION AND EXPANSION		ENGLISH EQUIVALENT	
p.	página	**p.**	page
P, P.	padre	**Fr.**	father
pág.	página	**pg.**	page
pat.	patente	**pat.**	patent
PCL	pantalla de cristal líquido	**LCD**	liquid crystal display
P.D.	post data	**P.S.**	postscript
p. ej.	por ejemplo	**e.g.**	for example
PNB	Producto Nacional Bruto	**GNP**	gross national product
p°	paseo	**Ave.**	avenue
p.p.	porte pagado	**ppd.**	postpaid
PP, p.p.	por poder, por poderes	**p.p.**	by proxy
prom.	promedio	**av., avg.**	average
ptas., pts.	pesetas	—	—
q.e.p.d.	que en paz descanse	**R.I.P.**	may he/she rest in peace
R, R/	remite	—	sender
RAE	Real Academia Española	—	—
ref., ref.ª	referencia	**ref.**	reference
rep.	república	**rep.**	republic
r.p.m.	revoluciones por minuto	**rpm.**	revolutions per minute
rte.	remite, remitente	—	sender
s.	siglo	**c., cent.**	century
s/	su, sus	—	his, her, your, their
S, S.	Sur, sur	**S, so.**	South, south
S.	san, santo	**St.**	saint
S.A.	sociedad anónima	**Inc.**	incorporated (company)
sáb.	sábado	**Sat.**	Saturday
s/c	su cuenta	—	your account
SE	sudeste, sureste	**SE**	southeast
seg.	segundo, segundos	**sec.**	second, seconds
sep., sept.	septiembre	**Sept.**	September
s.e.u.o.	salvo error u omisión	—	errors and omissions excepted
Sgto.	sargento	**Sgt.**	sergeant
S.L.	sociedad limitada	**Ltd.**	limited (corporation)
S.M.	Su Majestad	**HM**	His Majesty, Her Majesty
s/n	sin número	—	no (street) number
s.n.m.	sobre el nivel de mar	**a.s.l.**	above sea level
SO	sudoeste/suroeste	**SW**	southwest
S.R.C.	se ruega contestación	**R.S.V.P.**	please reply
ss.	siguientes	—	the following ones
SS, S.S.	Su Santidad	**H.H.**	His Holiness
Sta.	santa	**St.**	Saint
Sto.	santo	**St.**	saint
t, t.	tonelada	**t., tn**	ton
TAE	tasa anual efectiva	**APR**	annual percentage rate
tb.	también	—	also
tel., Tel.	teléfono	**tel.**	telephone
Tm.	tonelada métrica	**MT**	metric ton
Tn.	tonelada	**t., tn**	ton
trad.	traducido	**tr., trans., transl.**	translated
UE	Unión Europea	**EU**	European Union
Univ.	universidad	**Univ., U.**	university

SPANISH ABBREVIATION AND EXPANSION		ENGLISH EQUIVALENT	
UPC	unidad procesadora central	**CPU**	central processing unit
Urb.	urbanización	—	residential area
v	versus	**v., vs.**	versus
v	verso	**v., ver., vs.**	verse
v.	véase	**vid.**	see
Vda.	viuda	—	widow
v.g., v.gr.	verbigracia	**e.g.**	for example
vier., viern.	viernes	**Fri.**	Friday
V.M.	Vuestra Majestad	—	Your Majesty
VºBº, V.ºB.º	visto bueno	—	OK, approved
vol, vol.	volumen	**vol.**	volume
vra., vro.	vuestra, vuestro	—	your

Spanish Numbers

Cardinal Numbers

1	uno	28	veintiocho
2	dos	29	veintinueve
3	tres	30	treinta
4	cuatro	31	treinta y uno
5	cinco	40	cuarenta
6	seis	50	cincuenta
7	siete	60	sesenta
8	ocho	70	setenta
9	nueve	80	ochenta
10	diez	90	noventa
11	once	100	cien
12	doce	101	ciento uno
13	trece	200	doscientos
14	catorce	300	trescientos
15	quince	400	cuatrocientos
16	dieciséis	500	quinientos
17	diecisiete	600	seiscientos
18	dieciocho	700	setecientos
19	diecinueve	800	ochocientos
20	veinte	900	novecientos
21	veintiuno	1,000	mil
22	veintidós	1,001	mil uno
23	veintitrés	2,000	dos mil
24	veinticuatro	100,000	cien mil
25	veinticinco	1,000,000	un millón
26	veintiséis	1,000,000,000	mil millones
27	veintisiete	1,000,000,000,000	un billón

Ordinal Numbers

1st	primero, -ra	17th	decimoséptimo, -ma
2nd	segundo, -da	18th	decimoctavo, -va
3rd	tercero, -ra	19th	decimonoveno, -na; *or* decimonono, -na
4th	cuarto, -ta	20th	vigésimo, -ma
5th	quinto, -ta	21st	vigésimoprimero, vigésimaprimera
6th	sexto, -ta	30th	trigésimo, -ma
7th	séptimo, -ta	40th	cuadragésimo, -ma
8th	octavo, -ta	50th	quincuagésimo, -ma
9th	noveno, -na	60th	sexagésimo, -ma
10th	décimo, -ma	70th	septuagésimo, -ma
11th	undécimo, -ca	80th	octogésimo, -ma
12th	duodécimo, -ma	90th	nonagésimo, -ma
13th	decimotercero, -ra	100th	centésimo, -ma
14th	decimocuarto, -ta	1,000th	milésimo, -ma
15th	decimoquinto, -ta		
16th	decimosexto, -ta		

English Numbers

Cardinal Numbers

1	one	20	twenty
2	two	21	twenty-one
3	three	30	thirty
4	four	40	forty
5	five	50	fifty
6	six	60	sixty
7	seven	70	seventy
8	eight	80	eighty
9	nine	90	ninety
10	ten	100	one hundred
11	eleven	101	one hundred and one
12	twelve	200	two hundred
13	thirteen	1,000	one thousand
14	fourteen	1,001	one thousand and one
15	fifteen	2,000	two thousand
16	sixteen	100,000	one hundred thousand
17	seventeen	1,000,000	one million
18	eighteen	1,000,000,000	one billion
19	nineteen	1,000,000,000,000	one trillion

Ordinal Numbers

1st	first	16th	sixteenth
2nd	second	17th	seventeenth
3rd	third	18th	eighteenth
4th	fourth	19th	nineteenth
5th	fifth	20th	twentieth
6th	sixth	21st	twenty-first
7th	seventh	30th	thirtieth
8th	eighth	40th	fortieth
9th	ninth	50th	fiftieth
10th	tenth	60th	sixtieth
11th	eleventh	70th	seventieth
12th	twelfth	80th	eightieth
13th	thirteenth	90th	ninetieth
14th	fourteenth	100th	hundredth
15th	fifteenth	1,000th	thousandth